CU009 4538

Collins
Portuguese
Dictionary

HarperCollins Publishers
Westerhill Road
Bishopbriggs
Glasgow
G64 2QT
Great Britain

Third Edition 2000

Latest Reprint 2005

© William Collins Sons & Co.
Ltd. 1986
© HarperCollins Publishers
1993, 2000

ISBN 0-00-719592-3

Collins Gem® and Bank of
English® are registered
trademarks of HarperCollins
Publishers Limited

www.collins.co.uk

A catalogue record for this book
is available from the British
Library

Disal S.A.
Av. Marquês de São Vicente 182
Barra Funda
01139-000 São Paulo
Brazil

www.disal.com.br

ISBN 0-00-472407-0

Typeset by Wordcraft, Glasgow

Printed in Italy by Legoprint
S.P.A.

Acknowledgements
We would like to thank those
authors and publishers who
kindly gave permission for
copyright material to be used in
the Collins Word Web. We
would also like to thank Times
Newspapers Ltd for providing
valuable data.

CONTRIBUTORS/COLABORADORES
John Whitlam, Victoria Davies,
Mike Harland, Jane Horwood,
Lígia Xavier, Gerard Breslin,
Helen Newstead, Laura Neves

EDITORIAL STAFF/REDAÇÃO
Emma Aeppli, Jennifer Baird,
Marianne Davidson

COMPUTING/INFORMÁTICA
Jane Creevy

ÍNDICE

CONTENTS

Marcas Registradas

As palavras que acreditamos constituir marcas registradas foram assim denominadas. Todavia, não se deve supor que a presença ou a ausência dessa denominação possa afetar o status legal de qualquer marca.

Note on trademarks

Words which we have reason to believe constitute trademarks have been designated as such. However, neither the presence nor the absence of such designation should be regarded as affecting the legal status of any trademark.

INTRODUÇÃO

Ficamos felizes com a sua decisão de comprar o Dicionário Inglês-Português Collins Gem e esperamos que este lhe seja útil na escola, em casa, de férias ou no trabalho.

Esta introdução fornece algumas sugestões de como utilizar da melhor maneira possível o seu dicionário – não somente a partir da ampla lista de palavras mas também a partir das informações fornecidas em cada verbete. Este dicionário visa ajudá-lo a ler e a entender o inglês moderno assim como a exprimir-se corretamente.

No início do Dicionário Collins Gem aparecem as abreviaturas utilizadas, e a ilustração dos sons através de símbolos fonéticos. Você encontrará quadros de verbos irregulares ingleses na parte final do dicionário, seguidos por uma seção contendo números, expressões de tempo e um pequeno glossário de frases úteis.

COMO UTILIZAR O DICIONÁRIO COLLINS

Um grande número de informações pode ser encontrado neste dicionário. Vários tipos e tamanhos de letras, símbolos, abreviaturas e parênteses foram utilizados. As convenções e símbolos usados são explicados nas seções seguintes.

▶ Verbetes

As palavras que você procurou no dicionário – os verbetes – estão em ordem alfabética. Eles estão impressos **em negrito** para uma rápida identificação. Os dois verbetes que aparecem no topo de cada página indicam a primeira e a última palavras encontradas na página em questão.

Informações sobre a utilização ou forma de certos verbetes são dadas entre parênteses e, em geral, aparecem em forma abreviada e em itálico (p. ex.: (fam), (COM)).

Quando for apropriado, palavras derivadas aparecem agrupadas no mesmo verbete (**abade, abadia; produce, producer**) num formato ligeiramente menor do que o verbete.

As expressões comuns nas quais o verbete aparece estão impressas em um tamanho diferente de negrito romano. O símbolo '**~**' usado nas expressões representa o verbete principal no começo de cada parágrafo. Por exemplo, na entrada '**cold**', a expressão '**to be ~**' equivale a '**to be cold**'.

▶ **Significados**

A tradução para o verbete aparece em letra normal e quando há mais de um significado ou utilização, estes estão separados por um ponto e vírgula. Freqüentemente, você encontrará outras palavras em itálico e entre parênteses antes da tradução, sugerindo contextos nos quais o verbete pode aparecer (*p. ex.*: **rough** (*voice*) ou (*weather*) ou fornecer sinônimos (*p. ex.*: **rough** (*violent*)).

▶ **Palavras 'chaves'**

Atenção especial foi dada a certas palavras em inglês e em português consideradas palavras 'chaves' em cada língua. Elas podem, por exemplo, ser usadas com muita freqüência ou ter muitos tipos de utilização (*p. ex.*: **be, get**). Verbetes destacados com barras e números ajudam a distinguir as categorias gramaticais e diferentes significados. Informações complementares são fornecidas entre parênteses e em itálico na língua relevante para o usuário.

▶ **Informação gramatical**

As categorias gramaticais são dadas em itálico e abreviadas após a ortografia fonética do verbete (*p. ex.*: *vt, adj, vi*).

Os adjetivos aparecem em ambos os gêneros quando forem diferentes (**interno, -a**). Esta distinção também é feita quando os adjetivos têm uma forma irregular no feminino ou no plural (*p. ex.*: **ateu, atéia**). As formas irregulares de substantivos feminino ou plural também são indicadas (*p. ex.*: **child** (*pl* ~**ren**)).

v

INTRODUCTION

We are delighted you have decided to buy the Collins Portuguese Dictionary and hope you will enjoy and benefit from using it at school, at home, on holiday or at work.

This introduction gives you a few tips on how to get the most out of your dictionary – not simply from its comprehensive wordlist but also from the information provided in each entry. This will help you to read and understand modern Portuguese, as well as communicate and express yourself in the language.

The Collins Gem Portuguese Dictionary begins by listing the abbreviations used in the text and illustrating the sounds shown by the phonetic symbols. You will find Portuguese verb tables and English irregular verbs at the back, followed by a final section on numbers, time, dates, and useful phrases.

USING YOUR COLLINS DICTIONARY

A wealth of information is presented in the dictionary, using various typefaces, sizes of type, symbols, abbreviations and brackets. The conventions and symbols used are explained in the following sections.

▶ Headwords

The words you look up in the dictionary – 'headwords' – are listed alphabetically. They are printed in **bold type** for rapid identification. The two headwords appearing at the top of each page indicate the first and last word dealt with on the page in question.

Information about the usage or form of certain headwords is given in brackets after the phonetic spelling. This usually appears in abbreviated form and in italics. (*e.g.*: (*fam*), (*COMM*)).

Where appropriate, words related to headwords are grouped in the same entry (**abade, abadia; produce, producer**) in a slightly smaller bold type than the headword. Common expressions in which the headword appears are shown in a different size of bold roman type. The swung dash, **~**, represents the main headword at the start of each entry. For example, in the entry for '**caminho**', the phrase '**pôr-se a ~**' should be read '**pôr-se a caminho**'.

▶ Phonetic spellings

The phonetic spelling of each headword (indicating its pronunciation) is given in square brackets immediately after the headword (*eg.*: **grande** ['grãdʒi]. A list of these spellings is given on page xi.

▶ Meanings

Headword translations are given in ordinary type and, where more than one meaning or usage exists, they are separated by a semicolon. You will often find other words in italics in brackets before the translations. These offer suggested contexts in which the headword might appear (e.g. **intenso** (*emoção*)) or provide synonyms (e.g. **cândido** (*inocente*)).

▶ 'Key' Words

Special status is given to certain Portuguese and English words which are considered as 'key' words in each language. They may, for example, occur very frequently or have several types of usage (e.g. **bem**, **ficar**). A combination of lozenges and numbers helps you to distinguish different parts of speech and different meanings. Further helpful information is provided in brackets and in italics in the relevant language for the user.

▶ Grammatical information

Parts of speech are given in abbreviated form in italics after the phonetic spellings of headwords (e.g. *vt*, *adj*, *prep*).

Genders of Portuguese nouns are indicated as follows: *m* for a masculine and *f* for a feminine noun. Feminine and irregular plural forms of nouns are also shown next to the headword (**inglês, -esa**; **material** (*pl* **-ais**)). Adjectives are given in both masculine and feminine forms where these forms are different (**comilão, -lona**).

The gender of the Portuguese translation also appears in *italics* immediately following the key element of the translation, except where there is a regular masculine singular noun ending in 'o', or a regular feminine singular noun ending in 'a'.

ABREVIATURAS		ABBREVIATIONS
abreviatura	ab(b)r	abbreviation
adjetivo	adj	adjective
administração	ADMIN	administration
advérbio, locução adverbial	adv	adverb, adverbial phrase
aeronáutica	AER	flying, air travel
agricultura	AGR	agriculture
anatomia	ANAT	anatomy
arquitetura	ARQ, ARCH	architecture
artigo definido	art def	definite article
artigo indefinido	art indef	indefinite article
uso atributivo do substantivo	atr	compound element
automobilismo	AUT(O)	the motor car and motoring
auxiliar	aux	auxiliary
aeronáutica	AVIAT	flying, air travel
biologia	BIO	biology
botânica, flores	BOT	botany
português do Brasil	BR	Brazilian Portuguese
inglês britânico	BRIT	British English
química	CHEM	chemistry
linguagem coloquial (!chulo)	col(!)	colloquial (!offensive)
comércio, finanças, bancos	COM(M)	commerce, finance, banking
comparativo	compar	comparative
computação	COMPUT	computing
conjunção	conj	conjunction
construção	CONSTR	building
uso atributivo do substantivo	cpd	compound element
cozinha	CULIN	cookery
artigo definido	def art	definite article
economia	ECON	economics
educação, escola e universidade	EDUC	schooling, schools and universities
eletricidade, eletrônica	ELET, ELEC	electricity, electronics

ABREVIATURAS

ABBREVIATIONS

especialmente	**esp**	especially
exclamação	**excl**	exclamation
feminino	**f**	feminine
ferrovia	**FERRO**	railways
uso figurado	**fig**	figurative use
física	**FÍS**	physics
fotografia	**FOTO**	photography
(verbo inglês) do qual a partícula é inseparável	**fus**	(phrasal verb) where the particle is inseparable
geralmente	**gen**	generally
geografia, geologia	**GEO**	geography, geology
geralmente	**ger**	generally
impessoal	**impess, impers**	impersonal
artigo indefinido	**indef art**	indefinite article
linguagem coloquial (!chulo)	**inf(!)**	colloquial (!offensive)
infinitivo	**infin**	infinitive
invariável	**inv**	invariable
irregular	**irreg**	irregular
jurídico	**JUR**	law
gramática, lingüística	**LING**	grammar, linguistics
masculino	**m**	masculine
matemática	**MAT(H)**	mathematics
medicina	**MED**	medicine
ou masculino ou feminino, dependendo do sexo da pessoa	**m/f**	masculine/feminine
militar, exército	**MIL**	military matters
música	**MÚS, MUS**	music
substantivo	**n**	noun
navegação, náutica	**NÁUT, NAUT**	sailing, navigation
adjetivo ou substantivo numérico	**num**	numeral adjective or noun
	o.s.	oneself
pejorativo	**pej**	pejorative

ABREVIATURAS		ABBREVIATIONS
fotografia	**PHOT**	photography
física	**PHYS**	physics
fisiologia	**PHYSIO**	physiology
plural	**pl**	plural
política	**POL**	politics
particípio passado	**pp**	past participle
preposição	**prep**	preposition
pronome	**pron**	pronoun
português de Portugal	**PT**	European Portuguese
pretérito	**pt**	past tense
química	**QUÍM**	chemistry
religião e cultos	**REL**	religion, church services
	sb	somebody
educação, escola e universidade	**SCH**	schooling, schools and universities
singular	**sg**	singular
	sth	something
sujeito (gramatical)	**su(b)j**	(grammatical) subject
subjuntivo, conjuntivo	**sub(jun)**	subjunctive
superlativo	**superl**	superlative
também	**tb**	also
técnica, tecnologia	**TEC(H)**	technical term, technology
telecomunicações	**TEL**	telecommunications
tipografia, imprensa	**TIP**	typography, printing
televisão	**TV**	television
tipografia, imprensa	**TYP**	typography, printing
inglês americano	**US**	American English
ver	**V**	see
verbo	**vb**	verb
verbo intransitivo	**vi**	intransitive verb
verbo reflexivo	**vr**	reflexive verb
verbo transitivo	**vt**	transitive verb
zoologia	**ZOOL**	zoology
marca registrada	**®**	registered trademark
equivalente cultural	**≈**	cultural equivalent

PORTUGUESE PRONUNCIATION

The rules given below refer to Portuguese as spoken in the city and surrounding region of Rio de Janeiro, Brazil.

▶ Consonants

c	[k]	café	c before *a*, *o*, *u* is pronounced as in cat
ce, ci	[s]	cego	c before *e* or *i*, is pronounced as in receive
ç	[s]	raça	ç is pronounced as in receive
ch	[ʃ]	chave	ch is pronounced as in shock
d	[d]	data	as in English EXCEPT
de, di	[dʒ]	difícil cidade	d before an *i* sound or final unstressed *e* is pronounced as in judge
g	[g]	gado	g before *a*, *o*, *u* as in gap
ge, gi	[ʒ]	gíria	g before *e* or *i*, as in leisure
h		humano	h is always silent in Portuguese
j	[ʒ]	jogo	j is pronounced as s in leisure
l	[l]	limpo, janela	as in English EXCEPT
	[w]	falta, total	l after a vowel tends to become w
lh	[ʎ]	trabalho	lh is pronounced like the *lli* in million
m	[m]	animal, massa	as in English EXCEPT
	[ãw]	cantam	m at the end of a syllable preceded by a vowel nasalizes the preceding vowel
	[ĩ]	sim	
n	[n]	nadar, penal	as in English EXCEPT
	[ã]	cansar	n at the end of a syllable, preceded by a vowel and followed by a consonant, nasalizes the preceding vowel
	[ẽ]	alento	
nh	[ɲ]	tamanho	nh is pronounced like the *ni* in onion
q	[k]	queijo	qu before *i* or *e* is pronounced as in kick
q	[kw]	quanto cinqüenta	qu before *a* or *o*, or *qü* before *e* or *i*, is pronounced as in queen
-r-	[r]	compra	r preceded by a consonant (except *n*) and followed by a vowel is pronounced with a single trill
r-, -r-	[x]	rato, arpão	inital r, r followed by a consonant and rr pronounced similar to the Scottish ch in loch
rr	[x]	borracha	
-r	[*]	pintar, dizer	word-final r before a word beginning with a consonant or at the end of a sentence is pronounced [x]; before a word beginning with a vowel it is pronounced [r]. In colloquial speech this variable sound is often not pronounced at all.

s-	[s]	sol	as in English EXCEPT
-s-	[z]	mesa	intervocalic s is pronounced as in rose
-s-	[ʒ]	rasgar, desmaio	s before b, d, g, l, m, n, r, and v, as in leisure
-s-, -s	[ʃ]	escada, livros	s before c, f, p, qu, t and finally, as in sugar
-ss-	[s]	nosso	double s is always pronounced as in boss
t	[t]	todo	as in English EXCEPT
te, ti	[tʃ]	amante tipo	t followed by an i sound or final unstressed e is pronounced as ch in cheer
x-	[ʃ]	xarope explorar	initial x or x before a consonant (except c) is pronounced as in sugar
-xce-, -xci-	[s]	exceto excitar	x before ce or ci is unpronounced
ex-	[z]	exame	x in the prefix ex before a vowel is pronounced as z in squeeze
-x-	[ʃ]	relaxar	x in any other position may be pronounced
	[ks]	fixo	as in sugar, axe or sail
	[s]	auxiliar	
z-, -z-	[z]	zangar	as in English EXCEPT
-z	[ʒ]	cartaz	final z is pronounced as in leisure

b, f, k, p, v, w are pronounced as in English.

▶ Vowels

a, á, à, â	[a]	mata	a is normally pronounced as in father
ã	[ã]	irmã	ã is pronounced approximately as in sung
.e	[e]	vejo	unstressed (except final) e is pronounced like e in they, stressed e is pronounced either as in they or as in bet
-e	[i]	fome	final e is pronounced as in money
é	[ɛ]	miséria	é is pronounced as in bet
ê	[e]	pêlo	ê is pronounced as in they
i	[i]	vida	i is pronounced as in mean
o	[o]	locomotiva	unstressed (except final) o is pronounced as in local;
	[ɔ]	loja	stressed o is pronounced either as in local
	[o]	globo	or as in rock
-o	[u]	livro	final o is pronounced as in foot
ó	[ɔ]	óleo	ó is pronounced as in rock
ô	[o]	colônia	ô is pronounced as in local
u	[u]	luva	u is pronounced as in rule; it is silent in gue, gui, que and qui

xii

▶ **Diphthongs**

ãe	[ãj]	mãe	nasalized, approximately as in fly*ing*
ai	[aj]	vai	as is r*ide*
ao, au	[aw]	aos, auxílio	as is sh*out*
ão	[ãw]	vão	nasalized, approximately as in r*ound*
ei	[ej]	feira	as is th*ey*
eu	[ew]	deusa	both elements pronounced
oi	[oj]	boi	as is t*oy*
ou	[o]	cenoura	as is l*ocal*
õe	[õj]	aviões	nalized; approximately as in 'b*oing*!'

▶ **Stress**

The rules of stress in Portuguese are as follows:

(a) when a word ends in *a, e, o, m* (except *im, um* and their plural forms) or *s*, the second last syllable is stressed;
camar*a*da; camar*a*das
p*a*rte; p*a*rtem

(b) when a word ends in *i, u, im* (and plural), *um* (and plural), *n* or a consonant other than *m* or *s*, the stress falls on the last syllable:
ven*di*, al*gum*, al*guns*, fa*lar*

(c) when the rules set out in (a) and (b) are not applicable, an acute or circumflex accent appears over the stressed vowel:
*ó*tica, *â*nimo, in*glês*

In the phonetic transcription, the symbol ['] precedes the syllable on which the stress falls.

PRONÚNCIA INGLESA

▶ **Vogais**

	Exemplo Inglês	Explicação
[a:]	father	Entre o *a* de padre e o o de nó; como em fa*da*
[ʌ]	but, come	Aproximadamente como o primeiro *a* de ca*ma*
[æ]	man, cat	Som entre o *a* de lá e o *e* de pé
[ə]	father, ago	Som parecido com o *e* final pronunciado em Portugal
[ə:]	bird, heard	Entre o *e* aberto e o o fechado
[ɛ]	get, bed	Como em *pé*
[ɪ]	it, big	Mais breve do que em sí
[i:]	tea, see	Como em fíno
[ɔ]	hot, wash	Como em pó
[ɔ:]	saw, all	Como o o de porte
[u]	put, book	Som breve e mais fechado do que em burro
[u:]	too, you	Som aberto como em juro

▶ **Ditongos**

	Exemplo Inglês	Explicação
[aɪ]	fly, high	Como em baíle
[au]	how, house	Como em causa
[ɛə]	there, bear	Como o *e* de aeroporto
[eɪ]	day, obey	Como o *ei* de lei
[ɪə]	here, hear	Como ia de companhia
[əu]	go, note	[ə] seguido de um u breve
[ɔɪ]	boy, oil	Como em bóia
[uə]	poor, sure	Como ua em sua

▶ Consoantes

	Exemplo Inglês	Explicação
[d]	mended	Como em *dado*, an*dar*
[g]	get, big	Como em *grande*
[dʒ]	gin, judge	Como em i*dade*
[ŋ]	sing	Como em ci*nco*
[h]	house, he	*h* aspirado
[j]	young, yes	Como em *io*gurte
[k]	come, mock	Como em *cama*
[r]	red, tread	*r* como em *para*, mas pronunciado no céu da boca
[s]	sand, yes	Como em *sala*
[z]	rose, zebra	Como em *zebra*
[ʃ]	she, machine	Como em *cha*péu
[tʃ]	chin, rich	Como *t* em *timbre*
[w]	water, which	Como o *u* em ág*u*a
[ʒ]	vision	Como em *já*
[θ]	think, myth	Sem equivalente, aproximadamente como um *s* pronunciado entre os dentes
[ð]	this, the	Sem equivalente, aproximadamente como um *z* pronunciado entre os dentes

b, f, l, m, n, p, t, v pronunciam-se como em português.

O signo [*] indica que o r final escrito pronuncia-se apenas em inglês britânico, exceto quando a palavra seguinte começa por uma vogal. O signo ['] indica a sílaba acentuada.

EUROPEAN PORTUGUESE SPELLING

The spelling of European Portuguese differs significantly from that of Brazilian. The differences, which affect consonant groups and accents, follow general patterns but do not on the whole conform to fixed rules. Limited space makes it impossible to cover all European forms in the dictionary text, but major differences in spelling and vocabulary have been included. In addition, the following guide is intended as a broad outline of these differences.

The following changes in spelling are consistent:

- Brazilian *gü* and *qü* become European *gu* and *qu*, e.g. agüentar (BR), aguentar (PT); cinqüenta (BR), cinquenta (PT).
- Brazilian *-éia* becomes European *-eia*, e.g. idéia (BR), ideia (PT).
- European spelling links forms of the verb *haver de* with a hyphen, e.g. hei de (BR), hei-de (PT).
- The numbers dezesseis (BR), dezessete(BR), dezenove (BR) become dezasseis (PT), dezassete (PT), dezanove (PT).
- Adverbial forms of adjectives ending in *m* take double *m* in European spelling, single *m* in Brazilian, e.g. comumente (BR), comummente (PT).
- European spelling adds an acute accent to the final *a* in a first person plural preterite forms of irregular *-ar* verbs to distinguish them from the present tense, e.g. amamos (BR), amámos (PT).
- Brazilian conosco becomes European connosco.

The following changes may take place, but are not consistent:

▶ **Consonant changes**

- Brazilian *c* and *ç* double to *cc* and *cç*, acionista (BR), accionista (PT); seção (BR), secção (PT).
- Brazilian *t* becomes *ct*, e.g. elétrico (BR), eléctrico (PT).
- European spelling adds *b* to certain words, e.g. súdito (BR), súbdito (PT), sutilizar (BR), subtilizar (PT).
- European spelling changes *ç*, *t* to *pç*, *pt* , e.g. exceção (BR), excepção (PT), ótimo (BR), óptimo (PT).
- Brazilian *n*- becomes -*mn*-, e.g. anistia (BR), amnistia (PT).
- Brazilian *tr* becomes *t*, e.g. registro (BR), registo (PT).

▶ **Accentuation changes**

- Brazilian *ôo* loses circumflex accent, e.g. vôo (BR), voo (PT).
- European spelling changes circumflex accent on *e* and *o* to acute, e.g. tênis (BR), ténis (PT), abdômen (BR), abdómen (PT).

ENGLISH-PORTUGUESE
INGLÊS-PORTUGUÊS

A

A [eɪ] n (MUS) lá m

a [eɪ, ə] indef art (before vowel or silent h: an) 1 um(a); ~ **book/girl** um livro/uma menina; **an apple** uma maçã; **she's ~ doctor** ela é médica
2 (instead of the number "one") um(a); ~ **year ago** há um ano, um ano atrás; ~ **hundred/thousand** etc **pounds** cem/mil etc libras
3 (in expressing ratios, prices etc): **3 ~ day/week** 3 por dia/semana; **10 km an hour** 10 km por hora; **30p ~ kilo** 30p o quilo

AA n abbr (= Alcoholics Anonymous) AA m; (BRIT: = Automobile Association) ≈ TCB m (BR); ≈ ACP m (PT)

AAA n abbr (= American Automobile Association) ≈ TCB m (BR); ≈ ACP m (PT)

aback [ə'bæk] adv: **to be taken ~** ficar surpreendido, sobressaltar-se

abandon [ə'bændən] vt abandonar ♦ n: **with ~** com desenfreio

abbey ['æbɪ] n abadia, mosteiro

abbot ['æbət] n abade m

abbreviation [əbriːvɪ'eɪʃən] n abreviatura

abdicate ['æbdɪkeɪt] vt abdicar, renunciar a ♦ vi abdicar, renunciar ao trono

abdomen ['æbdəmən] n abdômen m

abduct [æb'dʌkt] vt seqüestrar

ability [ə'bɪlɪtɪ] n habilidade f, capacidade f; (talent) talento

ablaze [ə'bleɪz] adj em chamas

able ['eɪbl] adj capaz; (skilled) hábil,

competente; **to be ~ to do sth** poder fazer algo

abnormal [æb'nɔːməl] adj anormal

aboard [ə'bɔːd] adv a bordo ♦ prep a bordo de

abode [ə'bəud] n (LAW): **of no fixed ~** sem domicílio fixo

abolish [ə'bɔlɪʃ] vt abolir

aborigine [æbə'rɪdʒɪnɪ] n aborígene m/f

abort [ə'bɔːt] vt (MED) abortar; (plan) cancelar; **abortion** [ə'bɔːʃən] n aborto; **to have an abortion** fazer um aborto, abortar; **abortive** [ə'bɔːtɪv] adj fracassado

about [ə'baut] adv 1 (approximately) aproximadamente; **it takes ~ 10 hours** leva mais ou menos 10 horas; **it's just ~ finished** está quase terminado
2 (referring to place) por toda parte, por todo lado; **to run/walk** etc **~** correr/andar etc por todos os lados
3: **to be ~ to do sth** estar a ponto de fazer algo
♦ prep 1 (relating to) acerca de, sobre; **what is it ~?** do que se trata?, é sobre o quê?; **what** or **how ~ doing this?** que tal se fizermos isso?
2 (place) em redor de, por

above [ə'bʌv] adv em or sobre cima, acima; (greater) acima ♦ prep acima de, por cima de; (greater than: in rank) acima de; ~ **all** sobretudo; **aboveboard** adj legítimo, limpo

abrasive [əˈbreɪzɪv] adj abrasivo; (fig) cáustico, mordaz

abreast [əˈbrest] adv lado a lado; **to keep ~ of** (fig) estar a par de

abroad [əˈbrɔːd] adv (be) no estrangeiro; (go) ao estrangeiro

abrupt [əˈbrʌpt] adj (sudden) brusco; (curt) ríspido; **abruptly** adv bruscamente

abscess [ˈæbsɪs] n abscesso (BR), abcesso (PT)

absence [ˈæbsəns] n ausência

absent [ˈæbsənt] adj ausente; **absentee** [æbsənˈtiː] n ausente m/f; **absent-minded** adj distraído

absolute [ˈæbsəluːt] adj absoluto; **absolutely** [æbsəˈluːtlɪ] adv absolutamente

absorb [əbˈzɔːb] vt absorver; (business) incorporar; (changes) assimilar; (information) digerir; **absorbent cotton** (US) n algodão m hidrófilo

abstain [əbˈsteɪn] vi: **to ~ (from)** abster-se (de)

abstract [ˈæbstrækt] adj abstrato

absurd [əbˈsɜːd] adj absurdo

abuse [n əˈbjuːs, vb əˈbjuːz] n (insults) insultos mpl; (ill-treatment) maus-tratos mpl; (misuse) abuso ♦ vt insultar; maltratar; abusar de; **abusive** [əˈbjuːsɪv] adj ofensivo

abysmal [əˈbɪzməl] adj (ignorance) profundo; total; (failure) péssimo

abyss [əˈbɪs] n abismo

AC abbr (= alternating current) CA

academic [ækəˈdɛmɪk] adj acadêmico; (pej: issue) teórico ♦ n universitário(-a)

academy [əˈkædəmɪ] n (learned body) academia; **~ of music** conservatório

accelerate [ækˈsɛləreɪt] vt, vi acelerar; **accelerator** n acelerador m

accent [ˈæksənt] n (written) acento;

(pronunciation) sotaque m; (fig: emphasis) ênfase f

accept [əkˈsept] vt aceitar; (responsibility) assumir; **acceptable** adj (offer) bem-vindo; (risk) aceitável; **acceptance** n aceitação f

access [ˈækses] n acesso; **accessible** [ækˈsesəbl] adj acessível; (available) disponível

accessory [ækˈsesərɪ] n acessório; (LAW): **~ to** cúmplice m/f de

accident [ˈæksɪdənt] n acidente m; (chance) casualidade f; **by ~** (unintentionally) sem querer; (by coincidence) por acaso; **accidental** [æksɪˈdɛntl] adj acidental; **accidentally** [æksɪˈdɛntəlɪ] adv sem querer; **accident-prone** adj com tendência para sofrer ou causar acidentes, desastrado

acclaim [əˈkleɪm] n aclamação f

accommodate [əˈkɒmədeɪt] vt alojar; (subj: car, hotel, etc) acomodar; (oblige, help) comprazer a; **accommodation** [əkɒməˈdeɪʃən] n alojamento; **accommodations** (US) npl = accommodation

accompany [əˈkʌmpənɪ] vt acompanhar

accomplice [əˈkʌmplɪs] n cúmplice m/f

accomplish [əˈkʌmplɪʃ] vt (task) concluir; (goal) alcançar; **accomplishment** n realização f

accord [əˈkɔːd] n tratado ♦ vt conceder; **of his own ~** por sua iniciativa; **accordance** [əˈkɔːdəns] n: **in accordance with** de acordo com; **according**: **according to** prep segundo, conforme; **accordingly** adv por conseguinte; (appropriately) do modo devido

accordion [əˈkɔːdɪən] n acordeão m

account [əˈkaʊnt] n conta; (report)

relato; **~s** npl (books, department) contabilidade f; **of no ~** sem importância; **on ~** por conta; **on no ~** de modo nenhum; **on ~ of** por causa de; **to take into ~, take ~ of** levar em conta; **account for** vt fus (explain) explicar; (represent) representar; **accountancy** n contabilidade f; **accountant** n contador (a) m/f (BR), contabilista m/f (PT); **account number** n número de conta

accumulate [əˈkjuːmjuleɪt] vt acumular ♦ vi acumular-se

accuracy [ˈækjurəsɪ] n exatidão f, precisão f

accurate [ˈækjurɪt] adj (description) correto; (person, device) preciso; **accurately** adv com precisão

accusation [ækjuˈzeɪʃən] n (act) incriminação f; (instance) acusação f

accuse [əˈkjuːz] vt acusar; **accused** n: **the accused** o acusado (a acusada)

accustom [əˈkʌstəm] vt acostumar; **accustomed** adj: **accustomed to** acostumado a

ace [eɪs] n ás m

ache [eɪk] n dor ♦ vi (yearn): **to ~ to do sth** ansiar por fazer algo; **my head ~s** dói-me a cabeça

achieve [əˈtʃiːv] vt alcançar; (victory, success) obter; **achievement** n realização f; (success) proeza

acid [ˈæsɪd] adj ácido; (taste) azedo ♦ n ácido

acknowledge [əkˈnɔlɪdʒ] vt (fact) reconhecer; (also: **~ receipt of**) acusar o recebimento de (BR) or a recepção de (PT); **acknowledgement** n notificação f de recebimento

acne [ˈæknɪ] n acne f

acorn [ˈeɪkɔːn] n bolota

acoustic [əˈkuːstɪk] adj acústico; **acoustics** n, npl acústica

acquaint [əˈkweɪnt] vt: **to ~ sb with sth** pôr alguém ao corrente de algo; **to be ~ed with** conhecer; **acquaintance** n conhecimento m; (person) conhecido(-a)

acquire [əˈkwaɪəʳ] vt adquirir

acquit [əˈkwɪt] vt absolver; **to ~ o.s. well** desempenhar-se bem

acre [ˈeɪkəʳ] n acre m (= 4047m²)

acrobat [ˈækrəbæt] n acrobata m/f

across [əˈkrɔs] prep (on the other side of) no outro lado de; (crosswise) através de ♦ adv: **to go** (or **walk**) **~** atravessar; **the lake is 12km ~** o lago tem 12km de largura; **~ from** em frente de

acrylic [əˈkrɪlɪk] adj acrílico ♦ n acrílico

act [ækt] n ação f; (THEATRE) ato; (in show) número; (LAW) lei f ♦ vi tomar ação; (behave,. have effect, THEATRE) agir; (pretend) fingir ♦ vt (part) representar; **in the ~ of** no ato de; **to ~ as** servir de; **acting** adj interino ♦ n: **to do some acting** fazer teatro

action [ˈækʃən] n ação f; (MIL) batalha, combate m; (LAW) ação judicial; **out of ~** (person) fora de combate; (thing) com defeito; **to take ~** tomar atitude; **action replay** n (TV) replay m

activate [ˈæktɪveɪt] vt acionar

active [ˈæktɪv] adj ativo; (volcano) em atividade; **actively** adv ativamente; **activity** [ækˈtɪvɪtɪ] n atividade f

actor [ˈæktəʳ] n ator m

actress [ˈæktrɪs] n atriz f

actual [ˈæktjuəl] adj real; (emphatic use) em si; **actually** adv realmente; (in fact) na verdade; (even) mesmo

acute [əˈkjuːt] adj agudo; (person) perspicaz

ad [æd] n abbr = **advertisement**

A.D. adv abbr (= Anno Domini) d.C.

adamant ['ædəmənt] *adj* inflexível

adapt [ə'dæpt] *vt* adaptar ♦ *vi*: **to ~ (to)** adaptar-se (a); **adaptable** *adj* (*device*) ajustável; (*person*) adaptável; **adapter** *n* (ELEC) adaptador *m*; **adaptor** = **adapter**

add [æd] *vt* acrescentar; (*figures: also*: **~ up**) somar ♦ *vi*: **to ~ up** aumentar

addict ['ædɪkt] *n* viciado(-a); **drug ~** toxicômano(-a); **addicted** [ə'dɪktɪd] *adj*: **to be addicted to ~** viciado em; (*fig*) ser fanático por; **addiction** [ə'dɪkʃən] *n* dependência; **addictive** *adj* que causa dependência

addition [ə'dɪʃən] *n* adição *f*; (*thing added*) acréscimo; **in ~** além disso; **in ~ to** além de; **additional** *adj* adicional

additive ['ædɪtɪv] *n* aditivo

address [ə'drɛs] *n* endereço; (*speech*) discurso ♦ *vt* (*letter*) endereçar; (*speak to*) dirigir-se a, dirigir a palavra a; **to ~ (o.s. to)** enfocar

adept ['ædɛpt] *adj*: **~ at** hábil ou competente em

adequate ['ædɪkwɪt] *adj* (*enough*) suficiente; (*satisfactory*) satisfatório

adhere [əd'hɪːəʳ] *vi*: **to ~ to** aderir a; (*abide by*) ater-se a

adhesive [əd'hiːzɪv] *n* adesivo

adjective ['ædʒɛktɪv] *n* adjetivo

adjoining [ə'dʒɔɪnɪŋ] *adj* adjacente

adjourn [ə'dʒəːn] *vt* (*session*) suspender ♦ *vi* ser suspenso

adjust [ə'dʒʌst] *vt* (*change*) ajustar; (*clothes*) arrumar; (*machine*) regular ♦ *vi*: **to ~ (to)** adaptar-se (a); **adjustment** *n* ajuste *m*; (*of engine*) regulagem *f*; (*of prices, wages*) reajuste *m*; (*of person*) adaptação *f*

ad-lib [-lɪb] *vi* improvisar ♦ *adv*: **ad lib** à vontade

administer [əd'mɪnɪstəʳ] *vt* administrar; (*justice*) aplicar; (*drug*) minis-

trar; **administration** [ədmɪnɪs'treɪʃən] *n* administração *f*; (*management*) gerência; (*government*) governo; **administrative** [əd'mɪnɪstrətɪv] *adj* administrativo

admiral ['ædmərəl] *n* almirante *m*

admire [əd'maɪəʳ] *vt* (*respect*) respeitar; (*appreciate*) admirar

admission [əd'mɪʃən] *n* (*admittance*) entrada; (*fee*) ingresso; (*confession*) confissão *f*

admit [əd'mɪt] *vt* admitir; (*accept*) aceitar; (*confess*) confessar; **admit to** *vt fus* confessar; **admittance** *n* entrada; **admittedly** *adv* evidentemente

ado [ə'duː] *n*: **without (any) more ~** sem mais cerimônias

adolescent [ædəu'lɛsnt] *adj*, *n* adolescente *m/f*

adopt [ə'dɔpt] *vt* adotar; **adopted** *adj* adotivo; **adoption** *n* adoção *f*

adore [ə'dɔːʳ] *vt* adorar

Adriatic (Sea) [eɪdrɪ'ætɪk-] *n* (mar *m*) Adriático

adrift [ə'drɪft] *adv* à deriva

adult ['ædʌlt] *n* adulto(-a) ♦ *adj* adulto; (*literature, education*) para adultos

adultery [ə'dʌltərɪ] *n* adultério

advance [əd'vɑːns] *n* avanço; (*money*) adiantamento ♦ *adj* antecipado ♦ *vt* (*money*) adiantar ♦ *vi* (*move*) avançar; (*progress*) progredir; **in ~** com antecedência; **to make ~s to sb** fazer propostas a alguém; **advanced** *adj* adiantado

advantage [əd'vɑːntɪdʒ] *n* (*gen*, TENNIS) vantagem *f*; (*supremacy*) supremacia; **to take ~ of** aproveitar-se de, levar vantagem de

adventure [əd'vɛntʃəʳ] *n* façanha; (*excitement as thrill*) aventura

adverb ['ædvəːb] *n* advérbio

adverse ['ædvəːs] *adj* (*effect*) contrário; (*weather, publicity*) desfavorável

advert ['ædvə:t] *n abbr* = **advertisement**

advertise ['ædvətaɪz] *vi* anunciar ♦ *vt* (*event, job*) anunciar; (*product*) fazer a propaganda de; **to ~ for** (*staff*) procurar; **advertisement** [əd'və:tɪsmənt] *n* (*classified*) anúncio; (*display, tv*) propaganda, anúncio; **advertising** *n* publicidade *f*

advice [əd'vaɪs] *n* conselhos *mpl*; (*notification*) aviso; **piece of ~** conselho; **to take legal ~** consultar um advogado

advise [əd'vaɪz] *vt* aconselhar; (*inform*): **to ~ sb of sth** avisar alguém de algo; **to ~ sb against sth/doing sth** desaconselhar algo a alguém/aconselhar alguém a não fazer algo; **adviser** *or* **advisor** *n* conselheiro(-a); (*consultant*) consultor(a) *m/f*; **advisory** *adj* consultivo; **in an advisory capacity** na qualidade de assessor *or* consultor

advocate [*vb* 'ædvəkeɪt, *n* 'ædvəkɪt] *vt* defender; (*recommend*) advogar ♦ *n* advogado(-a); (*supporter*) defensor(a) *m/f*

Aegean [i:'dʒi:ən] *n*: **the ~ (Sea)** o (mar) Egeu

aerial ['ɛərɪəl] *n* antena ♦ *adj* aéreo

aerobics [ɛə'rəubɪks] *n* ginástica

aeroplane ['ɛərəplein] (*BRIT*) *n* avião *m*

aerosol ['ɛərəsɔl] *n* aerossol *m*

aesthetic [i:s'θɛtɪk] *adj* estético

afar [ə'fa:*] *adv*: **from ~** de longe

affair [ə'fɛə*] *n* (*matter*) assunto; (*business*) negócio; (*question*) questão *f*; (*also*: **love ~**) caso

affect [ə'fɛkt] *vt* afetar; (*move*) comover; **affected** *adj* afetado

affection [ə'fɛkʃən] *n* afeto, afeição *f*; **affectionate** *adj* afetuoso

afflict [ə'flɪkt] *vt* afligir

affluent ['æfluənt] *adj* rico; **the affluent society** a sociedade de abundância

afford [ə'fɔ:d] *vt* (*provide*) fornecer; (*goods etc*) ter dinheiro suficiente para; (*permit o.s.*): **I can't ~ the time/to** take that risk não tenho tempo/não posso correr esse risco

afloat [ə'fləut] *adj* flutuando

afoot [ə'fut] *adv*: **there is something ~** está acontecendo algo

afraid [ə'freɪd] *adj* assustado; **to be ~ of/to** ter medo de; **I am ~ that** lamento que; **I'm ~ so/not** receio que sim/não

Africa ['æfrɪkə] *n* África; **African** *adj, n* africano(-a)

after ['ɑ:ftə*] *prep* depois de ♦ *adv* depois ♦ *conj* depois que; **a quarter ~ two** (*US*) duas e quinze; **what/who are you ~?** o que você quer?/quem procura?; **~ having done** tendo feito; **he was named ~ his grandfather** ele recebeu o nome do avô; **to ask ~ sb** perguntar por alguém; **~ all** afinal (de contas); **~ you!** passe primeiro!; **aftermath** *n* consequências *fpl*; **afternoon** *n* tarde *f*; **afters** (*inf*) *n* sobremesa; **after-sales service** (*BRIT*) *n* serviço pós-vendas; **after-shave (lotion)** *n* loção *f* após-barba; **aftersun** *n* loção *f* pós-sol; **afterwards** *adv* depois

again [ə'gɛn] *adv* (*once more*) outra vez; (*repeatedly*) de novo; **to do sth ~** voltar a fazer algo; **not ... ~!** ... de novo!; **~ and ~** repetidas vezes

against [ə'gɛnst] *prep* contra; (*compared to*) em contraste com

age [eɪdʒ] *n* (*period*) época ♦ *vt, vi* envelhecer; **he's 20 years of ~** ele tem 20 anos de idade; **to come of ~** atingir a maioridade; **it's been ~s since I saw him** faz muito

agency · 6 · alcohol

[eɪdʒd] *adj:* **aged 10 de 10 anos de
idade; aged²** [ˈeɪdʒɪd] *adj* idoso
♦ *npl:* **the aged** os idosos; **age
group** *n* faixa etária; **age
limit** *n* idade *f* mínima/máxima

agency [ˈeɪdʒənsɪ] *n* agência;
(*government body*) órgão *m*

agenda [əˈdʒɛndə] *n* ordem *f* do dia

agent [ˈeɪdʒənt] *n* agente *m/f*

aggravate [ˈægrəveɪt] *vt* agravar;
(*annoy*) irritar

aggressive [əˈgrɛsɪv] *adj* agressivo

agitate [ˈædʒɪteɪt] *vt* agitar ♦ *vi:* **to ~
for** fazer agitação a favor de

AGM *n abbr* (= *annual general meeting*) AGO *f*

ago [əˈgəu] *adv:* **2 days ~** há 2 dias
(atrás); **not long ~** há pouco tempo;
how long ~? há quanto tempo?

agony [ˈægənɪ] *n* (*pain*) dor *f*; **to be
in ~** sofrer dores terríveis

agree [əˈgriː] *vt* combinar ♦ *vi*
(*correspond*) corresponder; **to ~
(with)** concordar (com); **to ~
sth/to do sth** consentir algo/aceitar
fazer algo; **to ~ that** concordar or
admitir que; **agreeable** *adj* agradável; (*willing*) disposto; **agreed** *adj*
combinado; **agreement** *n* acordo;
(*COMM*) contrato; **in agreement** de
acordo

agricultural [ægrɪˈkʌltʃərəl] *adj* (*of
crops*) agrícola; (*of cows and cattle*)
agropecuário

agriculture [ˈægrɪkʌltʃəʳ] *n* (*of
crops*) agricultura; (*of cows and cattle*) agropecuária

aground [əˈgraund] *adv:* **to run ~**
encalhar

ahead [əˈhɛd] *adv* adiante; **go right
or straight ~** siga em frente; **go ~!**
(*fig*) vá em frente!; **~ of** na frente de

aid [eɪd] *n* ajuda; (*device*) aparelho
♦ *vt* ajudar; **in ~ of** em benefício de;

to ~ and abet (*LAW*) ser cúmplice de

AIDS [eɪdz] *n abbr* (= *acquired immune deficiency syndrome*) AIDS *f*
(*BR*), SIDA *f* (*PT*)

aim [eɪm] *vt:* **to ~ sth (at)** apontar
algo (para); (*remark*) dirigir algo (a)
♦ *vi* (*also:* **take ~**) apontar ♦ *n* (*skill*)
pontaria; (*objective*) objetivo; **to ~ at**
mirar; **to ~ to do** pretender fazer

ain't [eɪnt] (*inf*) **= am not; aren't;
isn't**

air [ɛəʳ] *n* ar *m*; (*appearance*) aparência, aspeto; (*tune*) melodia ♦ *vt* arejar; (*grievances, ideas*) discutir ♦ *cpd*
aéreo; **to throw sth into the ~** jogar
algo para cima; **by ~** (*travel*) de
avião; **on the ~** (*RADIO, TV*) no ar; **air-
bed** (*BRIT*) *n* colchão *m* de ar; **air
conditioning** *n* ar condicionado;
aircraft *n inv* aeronave *f*; **airfield**
n campo de aviação; **Air Force** *n*
Força Aérea, Aeronáutica; **air
freshener** *n* perfumador *m* de ar;
airgun *n* espingarda de ar comprimido; **air hostess** (*BRIT*) *n* aeromoça *f* (*BR*), hospedeira *f* (*PT*); **air letter** (*BRIT*) *n* aerograma *m*; **airline** *n*
linha aérea; **airliner** *n* avião *m* de
passageiros; **airmail** *n:* **by airmail**
por via aérea; **air mile** *n* milha
aérea; **airplane** (*US*) *n* avião *m*; **airport** *n* aeroporto; **airsick** *adj:* **to
be airsick** enjoar (no avião); **air-
tight** *adj* hermético; **airy** *adj*
(*room*) arejado; (*manner*) leviano

aisle [aɪl] *n* (*of church*) nave *f*; (*of
theatre etc*) corredor *m*

ajar [əˈdʒɑːʳ] *adj* entreaberto

alarm [əˈlɑːm] *n* alarme *m*; (*anxiety*)
inquietação *f* ♦ *vt* alarmar; **alarm
clock** *n* despertador *m*

album [ˈælbəm] *n* (*for stamps etc*)
álbum *m*; (*record*) elepê *m*

alcohol [ˈælkəhɔl] *n* álcool *m*;
alcohol-free *adj* sem álcool; **alco-**

holic [ˈælkəˈhɔlɪk] *adj* alcoólico ♦ *n* alcoólatra *m/f*

ale [eɪl] *n* cerveja

alert [əˈlɜːt] *adj* atento; (*to danger, opportunity*) alerta ♦ *n* alerta ♦ *vt* alertar; **to be on the ~** estar alerta; (*MIL*) ficar de prontidão

Algarve [ælˈgɑːv] *m*: **the ~** o Algarve

algebra [ˈældʒɪbrə] *n* álgebra

Algeria [ælˈdʒɪərɪə] *n* Argélia

alias [ˈeɪlɪəs] *adv* também chamado ♦ *n* (*of criminal*) alcunha; (*of writer*) pseudónimo

alibi [ˈælɪbaɪ] *n* álibi *m*

alien [ˈeɪlɪən] *n* estrangeiro(-a); (*from space*) alienígena *m/f* ♦ *adj*: ~ **to** alheio a

alight [əˈlaɪt] *adj* em chamas; (*eyes*) aceso; (*expression*) intento ♦ *vi* (*passenger*) descer (de um veículo); (*bird*) pousar

alike [əˈlaɪk] *adj* semelhante ♦ *adv* similarmente, igualmente; **to look ~** parecer-se

alimony [ˈælɪmənɪ] *n* (*payment*) pensão *f* alimentícia

alive [əˈlaɪv] *adj* vivo; (*lively*) alegre

all [ɔːl] *adj* (*sg*) todo(-a); (*pl*) todos(-as); ~ **day/night** o dia inteiro/a noite inteira; ~ **five came** todos os cinco vieram; ~ **the books/food** todos os livros/toda a comida ♦ *pron* **1** tudo; ~ **of us/the boys went** todos nós fomos/todos os meninos foram; **is that ~?** é só isso?; (*in shop*) mais alguma coisa? **2** (*in phrases*): **above ~** sobretudo; **after ~** afinal (de contas); **at ~:** **not at ~** (*in answer to question*) em absoluto; absolutamente não; **I'm not at ~ tired** não estou nada cansado; **anything at ~ will do** qualquer

coisa serve; ~ **in** ao todo ♦ *adv* todo, completamente; ~ **alone** completamente só; **it's not as hard as** ~ **that** não é tão difícil assim; ~ **the more** ainda mais; ~ **the better** tanto melhor, melhor ainda; ~ **but** quase; **the score is 2** ~ o escore é 2 a 2

allege [əˈledʒ] *vt* alegar; **allegedly** [əˈledʒɪdlɪ] *adv* segundo dizem

allegiance [əˈliːdʒəns] *n* lealdade f

allergic [əˈlɜːdʒɪk] *adj*: ~ **(to)** alérgico (a)

allergy [ˈælədʒɪ] *n* alergia f

alleviate [əˈliːvɪeɪt] *vt* (*pain*) aliviar; (*difficulty*) minorar

alley [ˈælɪ] *n* viela

alliance [əˈlaɪəns] *n* aliança

all-in (*BRIT*) *adj*, *adv* (*charge*) tudo incluído

all-night *adj* (*café*) aberto toda a noite; (*party*) que dura toda a noite

allocate [ˈæləkeɪt] *vt* destinar

allot [əˈlɔt] *vt*: **to** ~ **to** designar para; **allotment** *n* partilha; (*garden*) lote *m*

all-out *adj* (*effort etc*) máximo ♦ *adv*: **all out** com toda a força

allow [əˈlau] *vt* permitir; (*claim, goal*) admitir; (*sum, time*) calcular; (*concede*): **to** ~ **that** reconhecer que; **to** ~ **sb to do** permitir a alguém fazer; **allow for** *vt fus* levar em conta; **allowance** [əˈlauəns] *n* ajuda de custo; (*welfare payment*) pensão *f*, auxílio; (*TAX*) abatimento; (*pocket money*) mesada; **to make allowances for** levar em consideração

all: **all right** *adv* (*well*) bem; (*correctly*) corretamente; (*as answer*) está bem!; **all-time** *adj* de todos os tempos

ally [*n* ˈælaɪ, *vb* əˈlaɪ] *n* aliado ♦ *vt*:

~ **o.s. with** aliar-se com
almighty [ɔːlˈmaɪtɪ] *adj* onipotente; (*row etc*) a maior
almond [ˈɑːmənd] *n* amêndoa
almost [ˈɔːlməust] *adv* quase
alone [əˈləun] *adj* só, sozinho; (*unaided*) sozinho ♦ *adv* só, somente, sozinho; **to leave sb ~** deixar alguém em paz; **to leave sth ~** não tocar em algo; **let ~ ...** sem falar em ...
along [əˈlɒŋ] *prep* por, ao longo de ♦ *adv*: **is he coming ~?** ele vem conosco?; **he was hopping/limping ~** ele ia pulando/coxeando; **with** junto com; **all ~** o tempo todo; **alongside** *prep* ao lado de ♦ *adv* encostado
aloof [əˈluːf] *adj* afastado, altivo ♦ *adv*: **to stand ~** afastar-se
aloud [əˈlaud] *adv* em voz alta
alphabet [ˈælfəbet] *n* alfabeto
Alps [ælps] *npl*: **the ~** os Alpes
already [ɔːlˈredɪ] *adv* já
alright [ˈɔːlˈraɪt] (*BRIT*) *adv* = **all right**
Alsatian [ælˈseɪʃən] (*BRIT*) *n* (*dog*) pastor *m* alemão
also [ˈɔːlsəu] *adv* também; (*moreover*) além disso
altar [ˈɔːltə*] *n* altar *m*
alter [ˈɔːltə*] *vt* alterar ♦ *vi* modificar-se
alternate [*adj* ɔlˈtəːnɪt, *vb* ˈɔːltəːneɪt] *adj* alternado; (*US*: *alternative*) alternativo ♦ *vi* alternar-se; **alternating** *adj*: **alternating current** corrente *f* alternada
alternative [ɔlˈtəːnətɪv] *adj* alternativo ♦ *n* alternativa; **alternatively** *adv*: **alternatively one could ...** por outro lado se podia ...
although [ɔːlˈðəu] *conj* embora; (*given that*) se bem que
altitude [ˈæltɪtjuːd] *n* altitude *f*
alto [ˈæltəu] *n* (*female*) contralto *f*; (*male*) alto

altogether [ɔːltəˈgeðə*] *adv* totalmente; (*on the whole*) no total
aluminium [ˈæljuˈmɪnɪəm] (*US* **aluminum**) *n* alumínio
always [ˈɔːlweɪz] *adv* sempre
Alzheimer's disease [ˈæltshaɪməz-] *n* doença de Alzheimer
am [æm] *vb see* **be**
a.m. *adv abbr* (= *ante meridiem*) da manhã
amateur [ˈæmətə*] *adj, n* amador(a) *m/f*
amaze [əˈmeɪz] *vt* pasmar; **to be ~d (at)** espantar-se (de *or* com); **amazement** *n* pasmo, espanto; **amazing** *adj* surpreendente; (*fantastic*) fantástico
Amazon [ˈæməzən] *n* Amazonas *m*
ambassador [æmˈbæsədə*] *n* embaixador (embaixatriz) *m/f*
amber [ˈæmbə*] *n* âmbar *m*; **at ~** (*BRIT*: *AUT*) em amarelo
ambiguous [æmˈbɪɡjuəs] *adj* ambíguo
ambition [æmˈbɪʃən] *n* ambição *f*; **ambitious** *adj* ambicioso
ambulance [ˈæmbjuləns] *n* ambulância
ambush [ˈæmbuʃ] *n* emboscada ♦ *vt* emboscar
amend [əˈmend] *vt* emendar; **to make ~s (for)** compensar
amenities [əˈmiːnɪtɪz] *npl* atrações *fpl*, comodidades *fpl*
America [əˈmerɪkə] *n* (*continent*) América; (*USA*) Estados Unidos *mpl*; **American** *adj* americano; norte-americano, estadunidense ♦ *n* americano(-a); norte-americano(-a)
amiable [ˈeɪmɪəbl] *adj* amável
amicable [ˈæmɪkəbl] *adj* amigável
amid(st) [əˈmɪd(st)] *prep* em meio a
amiss [əˈmɪs] *adj*: **to take sth ~** levar algo a mal; **there's something ~** aí tem coisa

ammunition [æmjuˈnɪʃən] n munição f

among(st) [əˈmʌŋ(st)] prep entre, no meio de

amount [əˈmaunt] n quantidade f; (of money etc) quantia ♦ vi: to ~ to (total) montar a; (be same as) equivaler a, significar

ampère(re) [ˈæmp(ɛə*)] n ampère m

ample [ˈæmpl] adj amplo; (abundant) abundante; (enough) suficiente

amplifier [ˈæmplɪfaɪə*] n amplificador m

amuse [əˈmjuːz] vt divertir; (distract) distrair; **amusement** n diversão f, (pleasure) divertimento m; (pastime) passatempo

an [æn, ən, n] indef art see **a**

anaemic [əˈniːmɪk] (US anemic) adj anêmico

anaesthetic [ænɪsˈθetɪk] (US anesthetic) n anestésico

analyse [ˈænəlaɪz] (US analyze) vt analisar; **analysis** [əˈnæləsɪs] (pl **analyses**) n análise f; **analyst** [ˈænəlɪst] n analista m/f; (psychoanalyst) psicanalista m/f

analyze [ˈænəlaɪz] (US) vt = **analyse**

anarchist [ˈænəkɪst] n anarquista m/f

anarchy [ˈænəkɪ] n anarquia f

anatomy [əˈnætəmɪ] n anatomia f

ancestor [ˈænsɪstə*] n antepassado m

anchor [ˈæŋkə*] n âncora ♦ vi (also: to drop ~) ancorar, fundear ♦ vt (also: to weigh ~) levantar âncoras

anchovy [ˈæntʃəvɪ] n enchova f

ancient [ˈeɪnʃənt] adj antigo; (person, car) velho

ancillary [ænˈsɪlərɪ] adj auxiliar

and [ænd] conj e; ~ so on e assim por diante; **try ~ come** tente vir; **he talked ~ talked** ele falou sem parar;

better ~ better cada vez melhor

Andes [ˈændiːz] npl: **the ~** os Andes

anemic [əˈniːmɪk] (US) n = **anaemic**

angel [ˈeɪndʒəl] n anjo

anger [ˈæŋgə*] n raiva

angina [ænˈdʒaɪnə] n angina (de peito)

angle [ˈæŋgl] n ângulo; (viewpoint): **from their ~** do ponto de vista deles

Anglican [ˈæŋglɪkən] adj, n anglicano(-a)

angling [ˈæŋglɪŋ] n pesca à vara (BR) or à linha (PT)

Angola [æŋˈgəulə] n Angola (no article)

angry [ˈæŋgrɪ] adj zangado; **to be ~ with sb/at sth** estar zangado com alguém/algo; **to get ~** zangar-se

anguish [ˈæŋgwɪʃ] n (physical) dor f, sofrimento; (mental) angústia

animal [ˈænɪməl] n animal m, bicho ♦ adj animal

animate [ˈænɪmɪt] adj animado; **animated** adj animado

aniseed [ˈænɪsiːd] n erva-doce f, anis f

ankle [ˈæŋkl] n tornozelo

annex [n ˈænɛks, vb əˈnɛks] n (also: BRIT: annexe: building) anexo ♦ vt anexar

anniversary [ænɪˈvɜːsərɪ] n aniversário

announce [əˈnauns] vt anunciar; **announcement** n anúncio; (official) comunicação f; (in letter etc) aviso; **announcer** n (RADIO, TV) locutor(a) m/f

annoy [əˈnɔɪ] vt aborrecer; **don't get ~ed!** não se aborreça!; **annoyance** n aborrecimento; **annoying** adj irritante

annual [ˈænjuəl] adj anual ♦ n (BOT) anual m; (book) anuário

annul [əˈnʌl] vt anular

anonymous   10   any

anonymous [ə'nɒnɪməs] *adj* anônimo

anorak ['ænəræk] *n* anoraque *m* (BR), anorak *m* (PT)

another [ə'nʌðə*] *adj*: ~ **book** (*one more*) outro livro, mais um livro; (*a different one*) um outro livro, um livro diferente ♦ *pron* outro; *see also* **one**

answer ['ɑːnsə*] *n* resposta; (*to problem*) solução *f* ♦ *vi* responder ♦ *vt* (*reply to*) responder a; (*problem*) resolver; **in ~ to your letter** em resposta a ou respondendo à sua carta; **to ~ the phone** atender o telefone; **to ~ the bell** *or* **the door** atender a porta; **answer back** *vt* replicar, retrucar; **answer for** *vt fus* responder por, responsabilizar-se por; **answer to** *vt fus* (*description*) corresponder a; **answering machine** *n* secretária eletrônica

ant [ænt] *n* formiga

antagonism [æn'tægənɪzəm] *n* antagonismo

antagonize [æn'tægənaɪz] *vt* contrariar, hostilizar

Antarctic [ænt'ɑːktɪk] *n*: **the ~** o Antártico

antenatal ['æntɪ'neɪtl] *adj* pré-natal

anthem ['ænθəm] *n*: **national ~** hino nacional

anti- ['æntɪ] *prefix* anti...; **anti-aircraft** *adj* antiaéreo; **antibiotic** ['æntɪbaɪ'ɒtɪk] *adj* antibiótico ♦ *n* antibiótico; **antibody** *n* anticorpo

anticipate [æn'tɪsɪpeɪt] *vt* prever; (*expect*) esperar; (*look forward to*) aguardar, esperar; **anticipation** *n* expectativa; (*eagerness*) entusiasmo

anticlimax [æntɪ'klaɪmæks] *n* desapontamento

anticlockwise [æntɪ'klɒkwaɪz] (BRIT) *adv* em sentido anti-horário

antics ['æntɪks] *npl* bobices *fpl*; (*of child*) travessuras *fpl*

antidepressant ['æntɪdɪ'presnt] *n* antidepressivo

antifreeze ['æntɪfriːz] *n* anticongelante *m*

antihistamine [æntɪ'hɪstəmiːn] *n* anti-histamínico

antiquated ['æntɪkweɪtɪd] *adj* antiquado

antique [æn'tiːk] *n* antiguidade *f* ♦ *adj* antigo; **antique shop** *n* loja de antiguidades

antiseptic [æntɪ'septɪk] *n* antiséptico

antisocial [æntɪ'səuʃəl] *adj* anti-social

antlers ['æntləz] *npl* esgalhos *mpl*, chifres *mpl*

anxiety [æŋ'zaɪətɪ] *n* (*worry*) inquietude *f*; (MED) ansiedade *f*; (*eagerness*): **~ to do** ânsia de fazer

anxious ['æŋkʃəs] *adj* (*worried*) preocupado; (*worrying*) angustiante; (*keen*): **~ to do** ansioso para fazer; **to be ~ that** desejar que

---

KEYWORD

any ['enɪ] *adj* **1** (*in questions etc*) algum(a); **have you ~ butter/children?** você tem manteiga/filhos?; **if there are ~ tickets left** se houver alguns bilhetes sobrando

2 (*with negative*) nenhum(a); **I haven't ~ money/books** não tenho dinheiro/livros

3 (*no matter which*) qualquer; **choose ~ book you like** escolha qualquer livro que quiser

4 (*in phrases*): **in ~ case** em todo o caso; **~ day now** qualquer dia desses; **at ~ moment** a qualquer momento; **at ~ rate** de qualquer modo; **~ time** a qualquer momento; (*whenever*) quando quer que seja ♦ *pron* **1** (*in questions etc*) algum(a)

have you got ~? tem algum?
2 (with negative) nenhum(a); **I haven't ~ (of them)** não tenho nenhum (deles)
3 (no matter which one(s)): **take ~ of those books (you like)** leve qualquer um desses livros (que você quiser)

♦ adv **1** (in questions etc) algo; **do you want ~ more soup/sandwiches?** quer mais sopa/sanduíches?; **are you feeling ~ better?** você está se sentindo melhor?
2 (with negative) nada; **I can't hear him ~ more** não consigo mais ouvi-lo

anybody ['ɛnɪbɔdɪ] pron = **anyone**
anyhow ['ɛnɪhau] adv (at any rate) de qualquer modo, de qualquer maneira; (haphazard) de qualquer jeito; **I shall go ~** eu irei de qualquer jeito; **do it ~ you like** faça do jeito que você quiser; **she leaves things just ~** ela deixa as coisas de qualquer maneira
anyone ['ɛnɪwʌn] pron (in questions etc) alguém; (with negative) ninguém; (no matter who) quem quer que seja; **can you see ~?** você pode ver alguém?; **if ~ should phone ...** se alguém telefonar ...; **~ could do it** qualquer um(a) poderia fazer isso
anything ['ɛnɪθɪŋ] pron (in questions etc) alguma coisa; (with negative) nada; (no matter what) qualquer coisa; **can you see ~?** você pode ver alguma coisa?
anyway ['ɛnɪweɪ] adv (at any rate) de qualquer modo; (besides) além disso; **I shall go ~** eu irei de qualquer jeito
anywhere ['ɛnɪwɛə*] adv (in questions etc) em algum lugar; (with

negative) em parte nenhuma; (no matter where) não importa onde, onde quer que seja; **can you see him ~?** você pode vê-lo em algum lugar?; **I can't see him ~** não o vejo em parte nenhuma; **~ in the world** em qualquer lugar do mundo
apart [ə'pɑːt] adv à parte, à distância; (separately) separado; (movement): **to move ~** distanciar-se; (aside): ... **~,** ... de lado, além de ...; **10 miles ~** separados por 10 milhas; **to take ~** desmontar; **~ from** com exceção de; (in addition to) além de
apartheid [ə'pɑːteɪt] n apartheid m
apartment [ə'pɑːtmənt] n (US) n apartamento
ape [eɪp] n macaco ♦ vt macaquear, imitar
aperitif [ə'pɛrɪtɪv] n aperitivo
aperture ['æpətʃjuə*] n orifício; (PHOT) abertura
APEX n abbr (= advance purchase excursion) tarifa aérea com desconto, adquirida com antecedência
apologetic [əpɔlə'dʒɛtɪk] adj cheio de desculpas
apologize [ə'pɔlədʒaɪz] vi: **to ~ (for sth to sb)** desculpar-se or pedir desculpas (por or de algo a alguém); **apology** n desculpas fpl
apostle [ə'pɔsl] n apóstolo
apostrophe [ə'pɔstrəfɪ] n apóstrofo
appalling [ə'pɔːlɪŋ] adj horrível; (ignorance) terrível
apparatus [æpə'reɪtəs] n aparelho; (in gym) aparelhos mpl; (organization) aparato
apparent [ə'pærənt] adj aparente; (obvious) claro, patente; **apparently** adv aparentemente, pelo(s) visto(s)
appeal [ə'piːl] vi (LAW) apelar, recorrer ♦ n (LAW) recurso, apelação f; (request) pedido; (plea) súplica;

(*charm*) atração *f*; **to ~ (to sb) for sth** (*request*) pedir algo (a alguém); (*plead*) suplicar algo (a alguém); **to ~ to** atrair; **appealing** *adj* atraente

appear [ə'pɪə*] *vi* aparecer; (*LAW*) apresentar-se, comparecer; (*publication*) ser publicado; (*seem*) parecer; **to ~ in "Hamlet"** trabalhar em "Hamlet"; **to ~ on TV** (*person, news item*) sair na televisão; (*programme*) passar na televisão; **appearance** *n* aparecimento; (*presence*) comparecimento; (*look*) aparência

appendicitis [əpendɪ'saɪtɪs] *n* apendicite *f*

appendix [ə'pendɪks] (*pl* **appendices**) *n* apêndice *m*

appetite ['æpɪtaɪt] *n* apetite *m*; (*fig*) desejo; **appetizer** *n* (*food*) tiragosto; (*drink*) aperitivo

applaud [ə'plɔːd] *vi* aplaudir ♦ *vt* aplaudir; (*praise*) admirar; **applause** *n* aplausos *mpl*

apple ['æpl] *n* maçã *f*; **apple tree** *n* macieira

appliance [ə'plaɪəns] *n* aparelho; **electrical** *or* **domestic ~s** eletrodomésticos *mpl*

applicant ['æplɪkənt] *n* (*for post*) candidato(-a); (*for benefit etc*) requerente *m/f*

application [æplɪ'keɪʃən] *n* aplicação *f*; (*for a job, a grant etc*) candidatura, requerimento; (*hard work*) esforço; **application form** *n* (formulário de) requerimento

apply [ə'plaɪ] *vt* (*paint etc*) usar; (*law etc*) pôr em prática ♦ *vi*: **to ~ to** (*be suitable for*) ser aplicável a; (*be relevant to*) valer para; (*ask*) pedir; **to ~ for** (*permit, grant*) solicitar, pedir; (*job*) candidatar-se a; **to ~ o.s. to** aplicar-se a, dedicar-se a

appoint [ə'pɔɪnt] *vt* (*to post*) nomear; **appointment** *n* (*engage-*

ment) encontro marcado, compromisso; (*at doctor's etc*) hora marcada; (*act*) nomeação *f*; (*post*) cargo; **to make an appointment (with sb)** marcar um encontro (com alguém)

appraisal [ə'preɪzl] *n* avaliação *f*

appreciate [ə'priːʃɪeɪt] *vt* (*like*) apreciar, estimar; (*be grateful for*) agradecer a; (*understand*) compreender ♦ *vi* (*COMM*) valorizar-se; **appreciation** *n* apreciação *f*, estima; (*understanding*) compreensão *f*; (*gratitude*) agradecimento; (*COMM*) valorização *f*; **appreciative** *adj* (*person*) agradecido; (*comment*) elogioso

apprehensive [æprɪ'hensɪv] *adj* apreensivo, receoso

apprentice [ə'prentɪs] *n* aprendiz *m/f*

approach [ə'prəʊtʃ] *vi* aproximar-se ♦ *vt* aproximar-se de; (*ask, apply to*) dirigir-se a; (*subject, passer-by*) abordar ♦ *n* aproximação *f*; (*access*) acesso *m*; (*to problem, situation*) enfoque *m*; **approachable** *adj* (*person*) tratável; (*place*) acessível

appropriate [adj ə'prəʊprɪɪt, vb ə'prəʊprɪeɪt] *adj* (*apt*) apropriado; (*relevant*) adequado ♦ *vt* apropriar-se de

approval [ə'pruːvəl] *n* aprovação *f*; **on ~** (*COMM*) a contento

approve [ə'pruːv] *vt* (*publication, product*) autorizar; (*motion, decision*) aprovar; **approve of** *vt fus* aprovar

approximate [ə'prɔksɪmɪt] *adj* aproximado; **approximately** *adv* aproximadamente

apricot ['eɪprɪkɔt] *n* damasco

April ['eɪprəl] *n* abril *m*

apron ['eɪprən] *n* avental *m*

apt [æpt] *adj* (*suitable*) adequado; (*appropriate*) apropriado; (*likely*): **~ to do** sujeito a fazer

Aquarius [əˈkwɛərɪəs] n Aquário

Arab [ˈærəb] adj, n árabe m/f

Arabian [əˈreɪbɪən] adj árabe

Arabic [ˈærəbɪk] adj árabe; (numerals) arábico ♦ n (LING) árabe m

arbitrary [ˈɑːbɪtrərɪ] adj arbitrário

arbitration [ɑːbɪˈtreɪʃən] n arbitragem f

arcade [ɑːˈkeɪd] n arcos mpl; (passage with shops) galeria

arch [ɑːtʃ] n arco; (of foot) curvatura ♦ vt arquear, curvar

archaeologist [ɑːkɪˈɔlədʒɪst] (US archeologist) n arqueólogo(-a)

archaeology [ɑːkɪˈɔlədʒɪ] (US archeology) n arqueologia

archbishop [ɑːtʃˈbɪʃəp] n arcebispo

archeology etc [ɑːkɪˈɔlədʒɪ] (US) = **archaeology** etc

archery [ˈɑːtʃərɪ] n tiro de arco

architect [ˈɑːkɪtɛkt] n arquiteto(-a)

architecture n arquitetura

archives [ˈɑːkaɪvz] npl arquivo

Arctic [ˈɑːktɪk] adj ártico ♦ n: **the ~** o Ártico

are [ɑː*] vb see **be**

area [ˈɛərɪə] n (zone) zona, região f; (part of place) região; (in room, of knowledge, experience) área; (MATH) superfície f, extensão f; **area code** (US) (TEL) código de discagem (BR), indicativo (PT)

aren't [ɑːnt] = **are not**

Argentina [ɑːdʒənˈtiːnə] n Argentina

arguably [ˈɑːgjʊəblɪ] adv possivelmente

argue [ˈɑːgjuː] vi (quarrel) discutir; (reason) argumentar; **to ~ that** sustentar que

argument [ˈɑːgjʊmənt] n (reasons) argumento; (quarrel) briga, discussão f; **argumentative** [ɑːgjuˈmɛntətɪv] adj briguento

Aries [ˈɛərɪz] n Áries m

arise [əˈraɪz] (pt **arose**, pp **arisen**) vi (emerge) surgir

aristocrat [ˈærɪstəkræt] n aristocrata m/f

arithmetic [əˈrɪθmətɪk] n aritmética

ark [ɑːk] n: **Noah's A~** arca de Noé

arm [ɑːm] n braço; (of clothing) manga; (of organization etc) divisão f ♦ vt armar; **~s** npl (weapons) armas fpl; (HERALDRY) brasão m; **~ in ~** de braços dados

armaments [ˈɑːməmənts] npl armamento

armchair [ˈɑːmtʃɛə*] n poltrona

armed [ɑːmd] adj armado

armour [ˈɑːmə*] (US **armor**) n armadura

armpit [ˈɑːmpɪt] n sovaco

armrest [ˈɑːmrɛst] n braço (de poltrona)

army [ˈɑːmɪ] n exército

aroma [əˈrəumə] n aroma; **aromatherapy** n aromaterapia

arose [əˈrəuz] pt of **arise**

around [əˈraund] adv em volta; (in the area) perto ♦ prep em volta de; (near) perto de; (fig: about) cerca de

arouse [əˈrauz] vt despertar; (anger) provocar

arrange [əˈreɪndʒ] vt (organize) organizar; (put in order) arrumar; **to ~ to do sth** combinar em or ficar de fazer algo; **arrangement** n (agreement) acordo; (order, layout) disposição f; **arrangements** npl (plans) planos mpl; (preparations) preparativos mpl; **home deliveries by arrangement** entregas a domicílio por convênio; **I'll make all the necessary arrangements** eu vou tomar todas as providências necessárias

array [əˈreɪ] n: **~ of** variedade f de

arrears [əˈrɪəz] npl atrasos mpl; **to be in ~ with one's rent** atrasar o aluguel

arrest [əˈrɛst] vt prender, deter; (sb's attention) chamar, prender ♦ n detenção f, prisão f; **under ~** preso

arrival [əˈraɪvl] n chegada; **new ~** recém-chegado; (baby) recém-nascido

arrive [əˈraɪv] vi chegar

arrogant [ˈærəɡənt] adj arrogante

arrow [ˈærəu] n flecha; (sign) seta

arse [ɑːs] (BRIT: inf!) n cu m (!)

arson [ˈɑːsn] n incêndio premeditado

art [ɑːt] n arte f; (skill) habilidade f, jeito; **A~s** (SCH) letras fpl

artery [ˈɑːtəri] n (MED) artéria; (fig) estrada principal

art gallery n museu m de belas artes; (small, private) galeria de arte

arthritis [ɑːˈθraɪtɪs] n artrite f

artichoke [ˈɑːtɪtʃəuk] n (also: **globe ~**) alcachofra; (also: **Jerusalem ~**) topinambo

article [ˈɑːtɪkl] n artigo; **~s** npl (BRIT: LAW: training) contrato de aprendizagem; **~s of clothing** peças fpl de vestuário

articulate [adj ɑːˈtɪkjulɪt, vb ɑːˈtɪkjuleɪt] adj (speech) bem articulado; (writing) bem escrito; (person) eloquente ♦ vt expressar; **articulated lorry** (BRIT) n caminhão m (BR) or camião m (PT) articulado, jamanta

artificial [ɑːtɪˈfɪʃl] adj artificial; (manner) afetado

artist [ˈɑːtɪst] n artista m/f; (MUS) intérprete m/f; **artistic** [ɑːˈtɪstɪk] adj artístico

art school n ≈ escola de artes

KEYWORD

as [æz, əz] conj **1** (time) quando; **the years went by** no decorrer dos anos; **he came in ~ I was leaving** ele chegou quando eu estava sain-

do; **~ from tomorrow** a partir de amanhã

2 (in comparisons) tão … (como), tanto(s) … (como); **~ big ~** tão grande como; **twice ~ big ~** duas vezes maior que; **~ much/many ~** tanto/tantos como; **~ much money/many books ~** tanto dinheiro quanto/tantos livros quanto; **~ soon ~** logo que, assim que

3 (since, because) como

4 (referring to manner, way) como; **do ~ you wish** faça como quiser

5 (concerning): **~ for** or **to that** quanto a isso

6: **~ if** or **though** como se; **he looked ~ if he was ill** ele parecia doente

♦ prep (in the capacity of): **he works ~ a driver** ele trabalha como motorista; **he gave it to me ~ a present** ele me deu isso de presente; see also **long; such; well**

a.s.a.p. abbr = **as soon as possible**

asbestos [æzˈbɛstəs] n asbesto, amianto

ascend [əˈsɛnd] vt subir; (throne) ascender

ascertain [æsəˈteɪn] vt averiguar, verificar

ash [æʃ] n cinza; (tree, wood) freixo

ashamed [əˈʃeɪmd] adj envergonhado; **to be ~ of** ter vergonha de

ashore [əˈʃɔːʳ] adv em terra; **to go ~** descer a terra, desembarcar

ashtray [ˈæʃtreɪ] n cinzeiro

Asia [ˈeɪʃə] n Ásia; **Asian** adj, n asiático(-a)

aside [əˈsaɪd] adv à parte, de lado ♦ n aparte m

ask [ɑːsk] vt perguntar; (invite) convidar; **to ~ sb sth/to do sth** perguntar algo a alguém/pedir para alguém fazer algo; **to ~ (sb) a ques-**

tion fazer uma pergunta (a alguém); **to ~ sb out to dinner** convidar alguém para jantar; **ask after** vt fus perguntar por; **ask for** vt fus pedir; **it's just ~ing for trouble** é procurar encrenca

asleep [əˈsliːp] adj dormindo; **to fall ~** dormir, adormecer

asparagus [əˈpærəgəs] n aspargo (BR), espargo (PT)

aspect [ˈæspekt] n aspecto; (direction in which a building etc faces) direção f

aspire [əsˈpaɪə*] vi: **to ~ to** aspirar a

aspirin [ˈæsprɪn] n aspirina

ass [æs] n jumento, burro; (inf) imbecil m/f; (US: inf!) cu m (!)

assailant [əˈseɪlənt] n assaltante m/f, atacante m/f

assassinate [əˈsæsɪneɪt] vt assassinar; **assassination** [əsæsɪˈneɪʃən] n assassinato, assassínio

assault [əˈsɔːlt] n assalto; (MIL, fig) ataque m ♦ vt assaltar, atacar; (sexually) agredir, violar

assemble [əˈsembl] vt (people) reunir; (objects) juntar; (TECH) montar ♦ vi reunir-se

assembly [əˈsemblɪ] n reunião f, (institution) assembléia f

assent [əˈsent] n aprovação f

assert [əˈsɜːt] vt afirmar

assess [əˈses] vt avaliar; (tax, damages) calcular; **assessment** n avaliação f, cálculo f

asset [ˈæset] n vantagem f, trunfo; **~s** npl (property, funds) bens mpl

assign [əˈsaɪn] vt (date) fixar; **to ~ (to)** (task) designar (a); (resources) destinar (a); **assignment** n tarefa

assist [əˈsɪst] vt ajudar; **assistance** n ajuda, auxílio; **assistant** n assistente m/f, auxiliar m/f; (BRIT: also: **shop assistant**) vendedor(a) m/f

associate [adj, n əˈsəuʃiɪt, vb]

əˈsəuʃieɪt] adj associado; (professor etc) adjunto ♦ n sócio(-a) ♦ vi: **to ~ with** associar-se com ♦ vt associar; **association** [əsəusiˈeɪʃən] n associação f; (link) ligação f

assorted [əˈsɔːtɪd] adj sortido

assortment [əˈsɔːtmənt] n (of shapes, colours) sortimento; (of books, people) variedade f

assume [əˈsjuːm] vt (suppose) supor, presumir; (responsibilities) assumir; (attitude, name) adotar, tomar; **assumption** [əˈsʌmpʃən] n suposição f, presunção f

assurance [əˈʃuərəns] n garantia; (confidence) confiança; (insurance) seguro

assure [əˈʃuə*] vt assegurar; (guarantee) garantir

asthma [ˈæsmə] n asma

astonish [əˈstɔnɪʃ] vt assombrar, espantar; **astonishment** n assombro, espanto

astound [əˈstaund] vt pasmar, estarrecer

astray [əˈstreɪ] adv: **to go ~** extraviar-se; **to lead ~** desencaminhar

astrology [əsˈtrɔlədʒɪ] n astrologia

astronaut [ˈæstrənɔːt] n astronauta m/f

astronomy [əsˈtrɔnəmɪ] n astronomia

asylum [əˈsaɪləm] n (refuge) asilo; (hospital) manicômio; **asylum seeker** n requerente m/f de asilo

┌─────────────────┐
│ KEYWORD │
└─────────────────┘

at [æt] prep **1** (referring to position) em; (referring to direction) a; **~ the top** em cima; **~ home** em casa; **to look ~ sth** olhar para algo
2 (referring to time): **~ 4 o'clock** às quatro horas; **~ night** à noite; **~ Christmas** no Natal; **~ times** às

vezes

3 (referring to rates, speed etc): ~ **£1 a kilo** a uma libra o quilo; **two ~ a time** de dois em dois
4 (referring to manner): ~ **a stroke** de um golpe; ~ **peace** em paz
5 (referring to activity): **to be ~ work** estar no trabalho; **to play ~ cowboys** brincar de mocinho
6 (referring to cause): **to be shocked/surprised/annoyed ~ sth** ficar chocado/surpreso/chateado com algo; **I went ~ his suggestion** eu fui por causa da sugestão dele

ate [eɪt] pt of **eat**
atheist ['eɪθɪɪst] n ateu (atéia) m/f
Athens ['æθɪnz] n Atenas
athlete ['æθliːt] n atleta m/f; **athletic** [æθ'lɛtɪk] adj atlético; **athletics** n atletismo
Atlantic [ət'læntɪk] adj atlântico ♦ n: **the ~ (Ocean)** o (oceano) Atlântico
atlas ['ætləs] n atlas m inv
ATM n abbr (= automated telling machine) caixa m automático
atmosphere ['ætməsfɪə²] n atmosfera; (of place) ambiente m
atom ['ætəm] n átomo; **atomic** [ə'tɒmɪk] adj atômico; **atomizer** n atomizador m, pulverizador m
atone [ə'təun] vi: **to ~ for** (sin) expiar; (mistake) reparar
atrocious [ə'trəuʃəs] adj péssimo
attach [ə'tætʃ] vt prender; (document) juntar, anexar; (importance etc) dar; **to be ~ed to sb/sth** (like) ter afeição por alguém/algo
attachment [ə'tætʃmənt] n (tool) acessório; (love): ~ **(to)** afeição f (por)
attack [ə'tæk] vt atacar; (subj: criminal) assaltar; (task etc) empreender ♦ n ataque m; (on sb's life) atentado;

heart ~ ataque cardíaco or de coração
attain [ə'teɪn] vt (also: ~ **to**: happiness, results) alcançar, atingir; (: knowledge) obter
attempt [ə'tɛmpt] n tentativa ♦ vt tentar; **to make an ~ on sb's life** atentar contra a vida de alguém; **attempted** adj: **attempted theft** tentativa de roubo
attend [ə'tɛnd] vt (lectures) assistir a; (school) cursar; (church) ir a; (course) fazer; (patient) tratar; **attend to** vt fus (matter) encarregar-se de; (needs, customer) atender a; (patient) tratar de; **attendance** n comparecimento; (people present) assistência; **attendant** n servidor(a) m/f ♦ adj concomitante
attention [ə'tɛnʃən] n atenção f; (care) cuidados mpl ♦ excl (MIL) sentido!; **for the ~ of ...** (ADMIN) atenção ...
attentive [ə'tɛntɪv] adj atento; (polite) cortês
attic ['ætɪk] n sótão m
attitude ['ætɪtjuːd] n atitude f
attorney [ə'təːnɪ] n (US: lawyer) advogado(-a)
attract [ə'trækt] vt atrair, chamar; **attraction** n atração f; **attractive** adj atraente; (idea, offer) interessante
attribute [n 'ætrɪbjuːt, vb ə'trɪbjuːt] n atributo ♦ vt: **to ~ sth to** atribuir algo a
aubergine ['əubəʒiːn] n berinjela
auction ['ɔːkʃən] n (also: **sale by ~**) leilão m ♦ vt leiloar
audience ['ɔːdɪəns] n audiência; (at concert, theatre) platéia; (public) público
audio-visual ['ɔːdɪəu-] adj audiovisual
audit ['ɔːdɪt] vt fazer a auditoria de

audition [ɔ:'dɪʃən] n audição f

August ['ɔ:gəst] n agosto

aunt [ɑ:nt] n tia; **auntie** n titia; **aunty** n titia

au pair ['əu'pɛə*] n (also: **~ girl**) au pair f

Australia [ɔs'treɪlɪə] n Austrália; **Australian** adj, n australiano(-a)

Austria ['ɔstrɪə] n Áustria; **Austrian** adj, n austríaco(-a)

authentic [ɔ:'θɛntɪk] adj autêntico

author ['ɔ:θə] n autor(a) m/f

authoritarian [ɔ:θɔrɪ'tɛərɪən] adj autoritário

authoritative [ɔ:'θɔrɪtətɪv] adj (account) autorizado; (manner) autoritário

authority [ɔ:'θɔrɪtɪ] n autoridade f; (government body) jurisdição f; (permission) autorização f; **the authorities** npl (ruling body) as autoridades

authorize [ɔ:'θəraɪz] vt autorizar

auto ['ɔ:təu] (US) n carro, automóvel m

autobiography [ɔ:təbaɪ'ɔgrəfɪ] n autobiografia

autograph ['ɔ:təgrɑ:f] n autógrafo ♦ vt (photo etc) autografar

automatic [ɔ:tə'mætɪk] adj automático ♦ n (gun) pistola automática; (washing machine) máquina de lavar roupa automática; (car) carro automático

automobile ['ɔ:təməbi:l] (US) n carro, automóvel m

autonomy [ɔ:'tɔnəmɪ] n autonomia

autumn ['ɔ:təm] n outono

auxiliary [ɔ:g'zɪlɪərɪ] adj, n auxiliar m/f

available [ə'veɪləbl] adj disponível; (time) livre

avalanche ['ævəlɑ:nʃ] n avalanche f

Ave. abbr (= avenue) Av., Avda.

avenge [ə'vɛndʒ] vt vingar

avenue ['ævənju:] n avenida; (drive) caminho; (means) solução f

average ['ævərɪdʒ] n média ♦ adj (mean) médio; (ordinary) regular ♦ vt alcançar uma média de; **on ~** em média; **average out** vi: **to ~ out at** dar uma média igual a

avert [ə'və:t] vt prevenir; (blow, one's eyes) desviar

avocado [ævə'kɑ:dəu] n (also: BRIT: **~ pear**) abacate m

avoid [ə'vɔɪd] vt evitar

await [ə'weɪt] vt esperar, aguardar

awake [ə'weɪk] (pt awoke or awoken, pp **~d**) adj acordado ♦ vt despertar, acordar; **~ to** atento a; **awakening** n despertar m

award [ə'wɔ:d] n prêmio, condecoração f; (LAW) indenização f ♦ vt outorgar, conceder; indenizar

aware [ə'wɛə*] adj: **~ of** (conscious) consciente de; (informed) informado de or sobre; **to become ~ of** reparar em, saber de; **awareness** n consciência

away [ə'weɪ] adv fora; (far~) muito longe; **two kilometres ~** a dois quilômetros de distância; **the holiday was two weeks ~** faltavam duas semanas para as férias; **he's ~ for a week** está ausente uma semana; **to take ~** levar; **to work** etc **~** trabalhar etc sem parar; **to fade ~** (colour) desbotar; (enthusiasm, sound) diminuir

awe [ɔ:] n temor m respeitoso; **awe-inspiring** ['ɔ:ɪnspaɪərɪŋ] adj imponente

awful ['ɔ:fəl] adj terrível, horrível; (quantity): **an ~ lot of** um monte de; **awfully** adv (very) muito

awkward ['ɔ:kwəd] adj (person, movement) desajeitado; (shape) incômodo; (problem) difícil; (situation) embaraçoso, delicado

awning 18 badly

awning ['ɔːnɪŋ] n toldo

awoke [ə'wəuk] pt of **awake**;
awoken [ə'wəukən] pp of **awake**

axe [æks] (US **ax**) n machado ♦ vt
(project etc) abandonar; (jobs) reduzir

axis ['æksɪs] (pl **axes**) n eixo

axle ['æksl] n (also: ~ **tree**: AUT) eixo

Azores [ə'zɔːz] npl: **the** ~ os Açores

B

B [biː] n (MUS) si m

BA n abbr = **Bachelor of Arts**

babble ['bæbl] vi balbuciar; (brook)
murmurinhar

baby ['beɪbɪ] n neném m/f, nenê
m/f, bebê m/f; (US: inf) querido(-a);
baby carriage (US) n carrinho de
bebê; **baby food** n comida de
bebê; **baby-sit** (irreg) vi tomar
conta da(s) criança(s); **baby-sitter**
n baby-sitter m/f

bachelor ['bætʃələ*] n solteiro; B~
of Arts/Science ≈ bacharel m em
Letras/Ciências

back [bæk] n (of person) costas fpl,
(of animal) lombo; (of hand) dorso;
(of car, train) parte f traseira; (of
house) fundos mpl; (of chair) encosto; (of page) verso; (of book) lomba-
da; (of crowd) fundo; (FOOTBALL)
zagueiro (BR), defesa m (PT) ♦ vt
(candidate: also: ~ **up**) apoiar;
(horse: at races) apostar em; (car)
recuar ♦ vi (car etc: also: ~ **up**) dar
marcha-ré (BR), fazer marcha atrás
(PT) ♦ cpd (payment) atrasado; (AUT:
seats, wheels) de trás ♦ adv (not for
ward) para trás; (returned): **he's** ~
ele voltou; (restitution): **throw the
ball** ~ devolva a bola; (again): **he
called** ~ chamou de novo; **he ran** ~
recuou correndo; **back down** vi

desistir; **back out** vi (of promise)
voltar atrás, recuar; **back up** vt
(support) apoiar; (COMPUT) tirar um
backup de; **backache** n dor f nas
costas; **backbone** n coluna vertebral; (fig) esteio; **backfire** vi (AUT)
engasgar; (plan) sair pela culatra;
background n fundo; (of events)
antecedentes mpl; (basic knowledge)
bases fpl; (experience) conhecimentos mpl, experiência; **family background** antecedentes mpl familia-
res; **backhand** n (TENNIS: also: backhand stroke) revés m; **backing** n
(fig) apoio; **backlog** n: **backlog of
work** atrasos mpl; **backpack** n
mochila; **back pay** n salário atrasado; **backside** (inf) n traseiro;
backstage adv nos bastidores;
backstroke n nado de costas;
backup adj (train, plane) reserva
inv; (COMPUT) de backup ♦ n (support) apoio; (COMPUT: also: **backup
file**) backup m; **backward** adj
(movement) para trás; (person,
country) atrasado; **backwards** adv
(move, go) para trás; (read a list) às
avessas; (fall) de costas; **back-
water** n (fig) lugar m atrasado;
backyard n quintal m

bacon ['beɪkən] n toucinho, bacon
m

bacteria [bæk'tɪərɪə] npl bactérias
fpl

bad [bæd] adj mau, ruim; (child)
levado; (mistake) grave; (food)
estragado; **his** ~ **leg** sua perna
machucada; **to go** ~ estragar-se

badge [bædʒ] n (of school etc)
emblema m; (policeman's) crachá m

badger ['bædʒə*] n texugo

badly ['bædlɪ] adv mal; ~ **wounded**
gravemente ferido; **he needs it** ~
faz-lhe grande falta; **to be** ~ **off** (for
money) estar com pouco dinheiro

badminton ['bædmɪntən] n badminton m

bad-tempered [-'temp] adj mal humorado; (temporary) de mau humor

baffle ['bæfl] vt (puzzle) deixar perplexo, desconcertar

bag [bæg] n saco, bolsa; (handbag) bolsa; (satchel) sacola; (case) mala; ~**s of ...** (inf: lots of) ... de sobra; **baggage** n bagagem f; **baggy** adj folgado, largo; **bagpipes** npl gaita de foles

bail [beɪl] n (payment) fiança; (release) liberdade f sob fiança ♦ vt (prisoner: gen: grant ~ to) libertar sob fiança; (boat: also: ~ out) baldear a água de; ~ **on** sob fiança; see also **bale**; **bail out** vt (prisoner) afiançar

bait [beɪt] n isca, engodo; (for criminal etc) atrativo, chamariz m ♦ vt iscar, cevar; (person) apoquentar

bake [beɪk] vt cozinhar ao forno; (TECH: clay etc) cozer ♦ vt assar; **baked beans** npl feijão m cozido com molho de tomate; **baked potato** n batata assada com a casca; **baker** n padeiro(-a); **bakery** n (for bread) padaria; (for cakes) confeitaria; **baking** n (act) cozimento; (batch) fornada ♦ adj (inf: hot) escaldante; **baking powder** n fermento em pó

balance ['bæləns] n equilíbrio; (scales) balança; (COMM) balanço; (remainder) resto, saldo ♦ vt equilibrar; (budget) nivelar; (account) fazer o balanço de; ~ **of trade/payments** balança comercial/balanço de pagamentos; **balanced** adj (report) objetivo; (personality, diet) equilibrado; **balance sheet** n balanço geral

balcony ['bælkənɪ] n varanda; (closed) galeria; (in theatre) balcão m

bald [bɔːld] adj calvo, careca; (tyre) careca

bale [beɪl] n (AGR) fardo; **bale out** vi (of a plane) atirar-se de pára-quedas

ball [bɔːl] n bola; (of wool, string) novelo; (dance) baile m; **to play ~ with sb** jogar bola com alguém; (fig) fazer o jogo de alguém

ballast ['bæləst] n lastro

ballerina [bælə'riːnə] n bailarina

ballet ['bæleɪ] n balé m; **ballet dancer** n bailarino(-a)

balloon [bə'luːn] n balão m

ballot ['bælət] n votação f

ballpoint (pen) ['bɔːlpɔɪnt-] n (caneta) esferográfica

balsamic vinegar [bɔl'sæmɪk-] n vinagre m balsâmico

ban [bæn] n proibição f, interdição f; (suspension) exclusão f ♦ vt proibir, interditar; excluir

banana [bə'nɑːnə] n banana

band [bænd] n (group) orquestra; (MIL) banda; (strip) faixa, cinta; **band together** vi juntar-se, associar-se

bandage ['bændɪdʒ] n atadura (BR), ligadura (PT) ♦ vt enfaixar

bandaid ['bændeɪd] ® (US) n esparadrapo

bang [bæŋ] n estalo; (of door) estrondo; (of gun, exhaust) explosão f; (blow) pancada ♦ excl bum!, bumba! ♦ vt (one's head etc) bater; (door) fechar com violência ♦ vi produzir estrondo; (door) bater; (fireworks) soltar

bangs [bæŋz] (US) npl (fringe) franja

banish ['bænɪʃ] vt banir

banister(s) ['bænɪstə(z)] n(pl) corrimão m

bank [bæŋk] n banco; (of river, lake) margem f; (of earth) rampa, ladeira ♦ vi (AVIAT) ladear-se; **bank on** vt fus contar com, apostar em; **bank**

account n conta bancária; **bank card** n cartão m de garantia de cheques; **banker** n banqueiro(-a); **banker's card** (BRIT) n = **bank card**; **Bank holiday** (BRIT) n feriado nacional; **banking** n transações fpl bancárias; **banknote** n nota (bancária); **bank rate** n taxa bancária

bankrupt ['bæŋkrʌpt] adj falido, quebrado; **to go ~** falir

bank statement n extrato bancário

banner ['bænə*] n faixa

baptism ['bæptizəm] n batismo

bar [bɑː*] n barra; (rod) vara; (of window: etc) grade f; (fig: hindrance) obstáculo; (prohibition) impedimento; (pub) bar m; (counter: in pub) balcão m ♦ vt (road) obstruir; (person) excluir; (activity) proibir ♦ prep: **~ none** sem exceção; **behind ~s** (prisoner) atrás das grades; **the B~** (LAW) a advocacia

barbaric [bɑːˈbærɪk] adj bárbaro

barbecue ['bɑːbɪkjuː] n churrasco

barbed wire ['bɑːbd-] n arame m farpado

barber ['bɑːbə*] n barbeiro, cabeleireiro

bar code n código de barras

bare [bɛə*] adj despido; (head) descoberto; (trees) sem vegetação; (minimum) básico ♦ vt mostrar; **barefoot** [adj, adv descalço; **barely** adv apenas, mal

bargain ['bɑːgɪn] n negócio; (agreement) acordo; (good buy) pechincha ♦ vi (haggle) regatear; (negotiate): **to ~ (with sb)** pechinchar (com alguém); **into the ~** ainda por cima; **bargain for** vt fus: **he got more than he ~ed for** ele conseguiu mais do que pediu

barge [bɑːdʒ] n barcaça; **barge in** vi irromper

bark [bɑːk] n (of tree) casca; (of dog) latido ♦ vi latir

barley ['bɑːlɪ] n cevada

barmaid ['bɑːmeɪd] n garçonete f (BR), empregada (de bar) (PT)

barman ['bɑːmən] (irreg) n garçom m (BR), empregado (de bar) (PT)

barn [bɑːn] n celeiro

barometer [bəˈrɒmɪtə*] n barômetro

baron ['bærən] n barão m; (of press, industry) magnata m; **baroness** ['bærənɪs] n baronesa

barracks ['bærəks] npl quartel m, caserna

barrage ['bærɑːʒ] n (MIL) fogo de barragem; (dam) barragem f; (fig): **a ~ of questions** uma saraivada de perguntas

barrel ['bærəl] n barril m; (of gun) cano

barren ['bærən] adj (land) árido

barricade [bærɪˈkeɪd] n barricada

barrier ['bærɪə*] n barreira; (fig: to progress etc) obstáculo

barrister ['bærɪstə*] (BRIT) n advogado(-a), causídico(-a)

barrow ['bærəʊ] n (wheel-)carrinho (de mão)

bartender ['bɑːtendə*] (US) n garçom m (BR), empregado (de bar) (PT)

barter ['bɑːtə*] vt: **to ~ sth for sth** trocar algo por algo

base [beɪs] n base f ♦ vt (opinion, belief): **to ~ sth on** basear or fundamentar algo em ♦ adj (thoughts) sujo; **baseball** n beisebol m

basement ['beɪsmənt] n porão m

bases¹ ['beɪsɪz] npl of **base**

bases² ['beɪsiːz] npl of **basis**

bash [bæʃ] (inf) vt (with fist) dar soco or murro em; (with object) bater em

bashful ['bæʃful] adj tímido,

envergonhado

basic ['beɪsɪk] adj básico; (facilities) mínimo; **basically** adv basicamente; (really) no fundo; **basics** npl: **the basics** o essencial

basin ['beɪsn] n (vessel, GEO) bacia; (also: **wash~**) pia

basis ['beɪsɪs] (pl **bases**) n base f; **on a part-time ~** num esquema de meio-expediente; **on a trial ~** em experiência

bask [bɑːsk] vi: **to ~ in the sun** tomar sol

basket ['bɑːskɪt] n cesto; (with handle) cesta; **basketball** n basquete(bol) m

bass [beɪs] n (MUS) baixo

bastard ['bɑːstəd] n bastardo(-a); (infl) filho-da-puta m (!)

bat [bæt] n (ZOOL) morcego; (for ball games) bastão m; (BRIT: for table tennis) raquete f ♦ vt: **he didn't ~ an eyelid** ele nem pestanejou

batch [bætʃ] n (of bread) fornada; (of papers) monte m

bath [bɑːθ] n banho; (bathtub) banheira ♦ vt banhar; **to have a ~** tomar banho (de banheira); see also **baths**

bathe [beɪð] vi banhar-se; (US: have a bath) tomar um banho ♦ vt (wound) lavar; **bathing** n banho; **bathing costume** (US **bathing suit**) n (woman's) maiô m (BR), fato de banho (PT)

bathrobe ['bɑːθrəʊb] n roupão m de banho

bathroom ['bɑːθrʊm] n banheiro (BR), casa de banho (PT)

baths [bɑːðz] npl banhos mpl públicos

baton ['bætən] n (MUS) batuta; (ATHLETICS) bastão m; (truncheon) cassete-te m

batter ['bætə*] vt espancar; (subj: wind, rain) castigar ♦ n massa (mole); **battered** ['bætəd] adj (hat, pan) amassado, surrado

battery ['bætərɪ] n bateria; (of torch) pilha

battle ['bætl] n batalha; (fig) luta ♦ vi lutar; **battlefield** n campo de batalha; **battleship** n navio de guerra (BR), couraçado (PT)

bawl [bɔːl] vi gritar; (child) berrar

bay [beɪ] n (GEO) baía; **to hold sb at ~** manter alguém à distância; **bay window** n janela saliente

bazaar [bə'zɑː*] n bázar m

B & B n abbr = **bed and breakfast**

BBC n abbr (= British Broadcasting Corporation) companhia britânica de rádio e televisão

B.C. adv abbr (= before Christ) a.C.

be [biː] (pt **was** or **were**, pp **been**) aux vb **1** (with present participle: forming continuous tense) estar; **what are you doing?** o que você está fazendo or a fazer (PT)?; **it is raining** está chovendo (BR) or a chover (PT); **I've been waiting for you for hours** há horas que eu espero por você

2 (with pp: forming passives): **to ~ killed** ser morto; **the box had been opened** a caixa tinha sido aberta; **the thief was nowhere to ~ seen** ninguém viu o ladrão

3 (in tag questions): **it was fun, wasn't it?** foi divertido, não foi?; **she's back again, is she?** ela voltou novamente, é?

4 (+ to + infin): **the house is to ~ sold** a casa está à venda; **you're to ~ congratulated for all your work** você devia ser cumprimentado pelo seu trabalho; **he's not to open it** ele não pode abrir isso

♦ vb + complement **1** (gen): **I'm English** sou inglês; **I'm tired** estou cansado; **2 and 2 are 4** dois e dois são quatro; ~ **careful!** tome cuidado!; ~ **quiet!** fique quieto!, fique calado!; ~ **good!** seja bonzinho!

2 (of health) estar; **how are you?** como está?

3 (of age): **how old are you?** quantos anos você tem?; **I'm twenty (years old)** tenho vinte anos

4 (cost) ser; **how much was the meal?** quanto foi a refeição?; **that'll** ~ **£5.75, please** são £5.75, por favor ♦ vi **1** (exist, occur etc) existir, haver; **the best singer that ever was** o maior cantor de todos os tempos; **is there a God?** Deus existe?; ~ **that as it may** ... de qualquer forma ...; **so** ~ **it** que seja assim

2 (referring to place) estar; **I won't** ~ **here tomorrow** eu não estarei aqui amanhã; **Edinburgh is in Scotland** Edimburgo é or fica na Escócia

3 (referring to movement) ir; **where have you been?** onde você foi?; **I've been in the garden** estava no quintal

♦ impers vb **1** (referring to time) ser; **it's 8 o'clock** são 8 horas; **it's the 28th of April** é 28 de abril

2 (referring to distance) ficar; **it's 10 km to the village** fica a 10 km do lugarejo

3 (referring to the weather) estar; **it's too hot/cold** está quente/frio demais

4 (emphatic): **it's only me** sou eu!; **it was Maria who paid the bill** foi Maria quem pagou a conta

beach [biːtʃ] n praia ♦ vt puxar para a terra or praia, encalhar

beacon ['biːkən] n (lighthouse) farol m; (marker) baliza

bead [biːd] n (of necklace) conta; (of sweat) gota

beak [biːk] n bico

beaker ['biːkə*] n copo com bico

beam [biːm] n (ARCH) viga; (of light) raio ♦ vi (smile) sorrir

bean [biːn] n feijão m; (of coffee) grão m; **runner/broad** ~ vagem f/fava

bear [bɛə*] (pt **bore**, pp **borne**) n urso ♦ vt (carry, support) arcar com; (tolerate) suportar ♦ vi: **to** ~ **right/left** virar à direita/à esquerda; **bear out** vt (theory, suspicion) confirmar, corroborar; **bear up** vi agüentar, resistir

beard [biəd] n barba; **bearded** adj barbado, barbudo

bearing ['bɛərɪŋ] n porte m, comportamento; (connection) relação f; ~**s** npl (also: **ball** ~**s**) rolimã m; **to take a** ~ fazer marcação

beast [biːst] n bicho; (inf) fera; **beastly** adj horrível

beat [biːt] (pt **beat**, pp **beaten**) n (of heart) batida; (MUS) ritmo, compasso; (of policeman) ronda ♦ vt (hit) bater em; (eggs) bater; (defeat) vencer, derrotar ♦ vi (heart) bater; **to** ~ **it** (inf) cair fora; **off the** ~**en track** fora de mão; **beat off** vt repelir; **beat up** vt (inf: person) espancar; (eggs) bater; **beating** n (thrashing) surra

beautiful ['bjuːtɪful] adj belo, lindo, formoso; **beautifully** adv admiravelmente

beauty ['bjuːtɪ] n beleza; (person) beldade f, beleza

beaver ['biːvə*] n castor m

because [bɪ'kɔz] conj porque; ~ **of** por causa de

beckon ['bɛkən] vt (also: ~ **to**) chamar com sinais, acenar para

become [bɪ'kʌm] (irreg: like **come**) vi (+ n) virar, fazer-se, tornar-se; (+

adj tornar-se, ficar

bed [bɛd] *n* cama; (*of flowers*) canteiro; (*of coal, clay*) camada, base *f*; (*of sea, lake*) fundo; (*of river*) leito; **to go to ~** ir dormir, deitar(-se); **bed and breakfast** *n* (*place*) pensão *f*; (*terms*) cama e café da manhã (*BR*) *or* pequeno almoço (*PT*); **bedclothes** *npl* roupa de cama; **bedding** *n* roupa de cama

bedraggled [bɪˈdrægld] *adj* molhado, ensopado

bed: bedridden *adj* acamado; **bedroom** *n* quarto, dormitório; **bedside** *n*: **at sb's bedside** à cabeceira de alguém; **bedsit** (*BRIT*) *n* conjugado; *ver quadro*

BEDSIT

Um *bedsit* é um quarto mobiliado cujo aluguel inclui uso de cozinha e banheiro comuns. Esse sistema de alojamento é muito comum na Grã-Bretanha entre estudantes, jovens profissionais liberais etc.

---

bedspread [ˈbɛdsprɛd] *n* colcha

bedtime [ˈbɛdtaɪm] *n* hora de ir para cama

bee [biː] *n* abelha

beech [biːtʃ] *n* faia

beef [biːf] *n* carne *f* de vaca; **roast ~** rosbife *m*; **beefburger** *n* hambúrguer *m*

beehive [ˈbiːhaɪv] *n* colméia

been [biːn] *pp of* **be**

beer [bɪə*] *n* cerveja

beetle [ˈbiːtl] *n* besouro

beetroot [ˈbiːtruːt] (*BRIT*) *n* beterraba

before [bɪˈfɔː*] *prep* (*of time*) antes de; (*of space*) diante de ♦ *conj* antes que ♦ *adv* antes, anteriormente; **~ going** antes de sair; **the week ~** a semana anterior; **I've never seen it ~** nunca vi

isso antes; **beforehand** *adv* antes

♦ *vt* (*also*: ~ **for**) mendigar; **to ~ sb to do sth** implorar a alguém para fazer algo; *see also* **pardon**

began [bɪˈgæn] *pt of* **begin**

beggar [ˈbɛgə*] *n* mendigo(-a)

begin [bɪˈgɪn] (*pt* **began**, *pp* **begun**) *vt, vi* começar, iniciar; **to ~ doing** *or* **to do sth** começar a fazer algo; **beginner** *n* principiante *m/f*; **beginning** *n* início, começo

behalf [bɪˈhɑːf] *n*: **on** *or* **in** (*US*) **~ of** (*as representative of*) em nome de; (*for benefit of*) no interesse de

behave [bɪˈheɪv] *vi* comportar-se; (*well: also:* **~ o.s.**) comportar-se (bem); **behaviour** (*US* **behavior**) *n* comportamento

behead [bɪˈhɛd] *vt* decapitar, degolar

behind [bɪˈhaɪnd] *prep* atrás de ♦ *adv* atrás; (*move*) para trás ♦ *n* traseiro; **to be ~ (schedule) with sth** estar atrasado *or* com atraso em algo; **~ the scenes** nos bastidores

beige [beɪʒ] *adj* bege

Beijing [beɪˈʒɪŋ] *m* Pequim

being [ˈbiːɪŋ] *n* (*state*) existência; (*entity*) ser *m*

belated [bɪˈleɪtɪd] *adj* atrasado

belch [bɛltʃ] *vi* arrotar ♦ *vt* (*also*: ~ **out**: *smoke etc*) vomitar

Belgian [ˈbɛldʒən] *adj, n* belga *m/f*

Belgium [ˈbɛldʒəm] *n* Bélgica

belief [bɪˈliːf] *n* (*opinion*) opinião *f*; (*trust, faith*) fé *f*

believe [bɪˈliːv] *vt*: **to ~ sth/sb** acreditar algo/em alguém ♦ *vi*: **to ~ in** (*God*) crer em; (*method, person*) acreditar em; **believer** *n* (*REL*) crente *m/f*, fiel *m/f*; (*in idea*) partidário(-a)

belittle [bɪˈlɪtl] *vt* diminuir, depreciar

bell [bɛl] *n* sino; (*small, door*-

campainha

belligerent [bɪ'lɪdʒərənt] adj agressivo

bellow ['beləu] vi mugir; (person) bramar

belly ['belɪ] n barriga, ventre m

belong [bɪ'lɒŋ] vi: to ~ to pertencer a; (club etc) ser sócio de; **the book ~s here** o livro fica guardado aqui; **belongings** npl pertences mpl

beloved [bɪ'lʌvɪd] adj querido, amado

below [bɪ'ləu] prep (beneath) embaixo de; (less than) abaixo de ♦ adv em baixo; **see ~** ver abaixo

belt [bɛlt] n cinto; (of land) faixa; (TECH) correia ♦ vt (thrash) surrar; **beltway** (US) n via circular

bemused [bɪ'mju:zd] adj bestificado, estupidificado

bench [bɛntʃ] n banco; (work ~) bancada (de carpinteiro); (BRIT: POL) assento num Parlamento; **the B~** (LAW: judge) o magistrado; (: judges) os magistrados, o corpo de magistrados

bend [bɛnd] (pt, pp **bent**) vt (leg, arm) dobrar; (pipe) curvar ♦ vi dobrar-se, inclinar-se ♦ n curva; (in pipe) curvatura; **bend down** vi abaixar-se, agachar-se; **bend over** vi debruçar-se

beneath [bɪ'ni:θ] prep abaixo de; (unworthy of) indigno de ♦ adv em baixo

benefactor ['bɛnɪfæktə*] n benfeitor(a) m/f

beneficial [bɛnɪ'fɪʃəl] adj: ~ (to) benéfico (a)

benefit ['bɛnɪfɪt] n benefício, vantagem f; (money) subsídio, auxílio ♦ vt beneficiar ♦ vi: to ~ from sth beneficiar-se de algo

benevolent [bɪ'nɛvələnt] adj benévolo

benign [bɪ'naɪn] adj (person, smile) afável, bondoso; (MED) benigno

bent [bɛnt] pt, pp of **bend** ♦ n inclinação f ♦ adj: **to be ~ on** estar empenhado em

bereaved [bɪ'ri:vd] npl: **the ~** os enlutados

beret ['bɛreɪ] n boina

Berlin [bə:'lɪn] n Berlim

berm [bə:m] (US) n acostamento (BR), berma (PT)

berry ['bɛrɪ] n baga

berserk [bə'sə:k] adj: **to go ~** perder as estribeiras

berth [bə:θ] n (bed) beliche m; (cabin) cabine f; (on train) leito m; (for ship) ancoradouro ♦ vi (in harbour) atracar, encostar-se; (at anchor) ancorar

beside [bɪ'saɪd] prep (next to) junto de, ao lado de, ao pé de; **to be ~ o.s. (with anger)** estar fora de si; **that's ~ the point** isso não tem nada a ver

besides [bɪ'saɪdz] adv além disso; (in any case) de qualquer jeito ♦ prep (as well as) além de

besiege [bɪ'si:dʒ] vt (town) sitiar, pôr cerco a; (fig) assediar

best [bɛst] adj melhor (o) melhor; **the ~ part of** (quantity) a maior parte de; **at ~** na melhor das hipóteses; **to make the ~ of sth** tirar o maior partido possível de algo; **to do one's ~** fazer o possível; **to the ~ of my knowledge** que eu saiba; **to the ~ of my ability** o melhor que eu puder; **best before date** n data f de validade; **best man** n padrinho de casamento

bet [bɛt] (pt, pp **bet** or **~ted**) n aposta ♦ vt, vi apostar

betray [bɪ'treɪ] vt trair; (denounce) delatar

better ['bɛtə*] adj, adv melhor ♦ vt

melhorar; (*go above*) superar ♦ *n*: **to get the ~ of** vencer; **you had ~ do it** é melhor você fazer isso; **he thought ~ of it** pensou melhor, mudou de opinião; **to get ~** melhorar; **better off** *adj* mais rico; (*fig*): **you'd be better off this way** seria melhor para você assim

betting ['bɛtɪŋ] *n* jogo; **betting shop** (*BRIT*) *n* agência de apostas

between [bɪ'twi:n] *prep* no meio de, entre ♦ *adv* no meio

beverage ['bɛvərɪdʒ] *n* bebida

beware [bɪ'wɛə*] *vi*: **to ~ (of)** precaver-se (de), ter cuidado (com); **"~ of the dog"** "cuidado com o cachorro"

bewildered [bɪ'wɪldəd] *adj* atordeado; (*confused*) confuso

beyond [bɪ'jɒnd] *prep* (*in space*) além de; (*exceeding*) acima de, fora de; (*date*) mais tarde que; (*above*) acima de ♦ *adv* além; (*in time*) mais longe, mais adiante; **~ doubt** fora de qualquer dúvida; **to be ~ repair** não ter conserto

bias ['baɪəs] *n* (*prejudice*) preconceito; **bias(s)ed** *adj* parcial

bib [bɪb] *n* babadouro, babador *m*

Bible ['baɪbl] *n* Bíblia

bicker ['bɪkə*] *vi* brigar

bicycle ['baɪsɪkl] *n* bicicleta

bid [bɪd] (*pt* **bade** *or* **bid**, *pp* **bidden** *or* **bid**) *n* oferta; (*at auction*) lance *m*; (*attempt*) tentativa ♦ *vi* fazer lance ♦ *vt* oferecer; **to ~ sb good day** dar bom dia a alguém

bide [baɪd] *vt*: **to ~ one's time** esperar o momento adequado

bifocals [baɪ'fəʊklz] *npl* óculos *mpl* bifocais

big [bɪg] *adj* grande; (*bulky*) volumoso; **~ brother/sister** irmão/irmã mais velho/a

bigheaded ['bɪg'hɛdɪd] *adj* convencido

bike [baɪk] *n* bicicleta

bikini [bɪ'ki:nɪ] *n* biquíni *m*

bilingual [baɪ'lɪŋgwəl] *adj* bilíngüe

bill [bɪl] *n* conta; (*invoice*) fatura; (*POL*) projeto de lei; (*US*: *banknote*) bilhete *m*, nota; (*in restaurant*) conta, notinha; (*of bird*) bico; (*THEATRE*) cartaz *m*; **to fit** *or* **fill the ~** (*fig*) servir; **billboard** *n* quadro para cartazes

billfold ['bɪlfəʊld] (*US*) *n* carteira

billiards ['bɪlɪədz] *n* bilhar *m*

billion ['bɪlɪən] *n* (*BRIT*) trilhão *m*; (*US*) bilhão *m*

bin [bɪn] *n* caixa; (*BRIT*: *for rubbish*) lata de lixo

bind [baɪnd] (*pt*, *pp* **bound**) *vt* atar, amarrar; (*oblige*) obrigar; (*book*) encadernar ♦ *n* (*inf*) saco; (*nuisance*) chatice *f*

binge [bɪndʒ] (*inf*) *n*: **to go on a ~** tomar uma bebedeira

bingo ['bɪngəʊ] *n* bingo *m*

binoculars [bɪ'nɔkjuləz] *npl* binóculo *m*

bio... [baɪəʊ] *prefix* bio...; **biochemistry** *n* bioquímica; **biography** *n* biografia; **biology** *n* biologia

birch [bə:tʃ] *n* bétula

bird [bə:d] *n* ave *f*, pássaro; (*BRIT*: *inf*: *girl*) gatinha

Biro ['baɪərəʊ] ® *n* (caneta) esferográfica

birth [bə:θ] *n* nascimento; **to give ~ to** dar à luz, parir; **birth certificate** *n* certidão *f* de nascimento; **birth control** *n* controle *m* de natalidade; (*methods*) métodos *mpl* anticoncepcionais; **birthday** *n* aniversário (*BR*), dia *m* de anos (*PT*) ♦ *cpd* de aniversário; *see also* **happy**

biscuit ['bɪskɪt] *n* (*BRIT*) bolacha, biscoito; (*US*) pão *m* doce

bishop ['bɪʃəp] *n* bispo; (*CHESS*) peça

bit 26 **blind**

de jogo de xadrez

bit [bɪt] *pt of* **bite** ♦ *n* pedaço, boca-do; (*of horse*) freio; (*COMPUT*) bit *m*; **a ~ of** (*a little*) um pouco de; **~ by ~** pouco a pouco

bitch [bɪtʃ] *n* (*dog*) cadela, cachorra; (*inf!*) cadela (*!*)

bite [baɪt] (*pt* **bit**, *pp* **bitten**) *vt, vi* morder; (*insect etc*) picar ♦ *n* (*insect ~*) picada; (*mouthful*) bocado; **to ~ one's nails** roer as unhas; **let's have a ~ (to eat)** (*inf*) vamos fazer uma boquinha

bitter ['bɪtə*] *adj* amargo; (*wind, criticism*) cortante, penetrante; (*weather*) horrível ♦ *n* (*BRIT: beer*) cer-veja amarga; **bitterness** *n* amargor *m*; (*anger*) rancor *m*

black [blæk] *adj* preto; (*humour*) negro ♦ *n* (*colour*) cor *f* preta; (*per-son*): **B~** negro(-a), preto(-a) ♦ *vt* (*BRIT: INDUSTRY*) boicotar; **to give sb a ~ eye** esmurrar alguém e deixá-lo de olho roxo; **~ and blue** contuso, contundido; **to be in the ~** (*in cred-it*) estar com saldo credor; **black-berry** *n* amora silvestre; **blackbird** *n* melro; **blackboard** *n* quadro(-negro); **black coffee** *n* café *m* preto, bica (*PT*); **blackcurrant** *n* groselha negra; **blackmail** *n* chan-tagem *f* ♦ *vt* fazer chantagem a; **black market** *n* mercado or câm-bio negro; **blackout** *n* blecaute *m*; (*fainting*) desmaio; (*of radio signal*) desvanecimento; **Black Sea** *n*: **the Black Sea** o mar Negro; **black-smith** *n* ferreiro

bladder ['blædə*] *n* bexiga

blade [bleɪd] *n* lâmina; (*of oar*) pá *f*; **a ~ of grass** uma folha de relva

blame [bleɪm] *n* culpa ♦ *vt*: **to ~ sb for sth** culpar alguém por algo; **to be to ~** ter a culpa

bland [blænd] *adj* (*taste*) brando

blank [blæŋk] *adj* em branco; (*look*) sem expressão ♦ *n* (*on form*) espaço em branco; (*cartridge*) bala de fes-tim; (*of memory*): **to go ~** dar um branco

blanket ['blæŋkɪt] *n* cobertor *m*

blare [bleə*] *vi* (*horn, radio*) clango-rar

blast [blɑːst] *n* (*of wind*) rajada; (*of explosive*) explosão *f* ♦ *vt* fazer voar; **blast-off** *n* (*SPACE*) lançamento

blatant ['bleɪtənt] *adj* descarado

blaze [bleɪz] *n* (*fire*) fogo; (*in building etc*) incêndio; (*fig: of colour*) esplen-dor *m*; (: *of glory, publicity*) explosão *f* ♦ *vi* (*fire*) arder; (*guns*) descarregar; (*eyes*) brilhar ♦ *vt*: **to ~ a trail** abrir (um) caminho

blazer ['bleɪzə*] *n* casaco esportivo, blazer *m*

bleach [bliːtʃ] *n* (*also*: **household ~**) água sanitária ♦ *vt* (*linen*) branquear

bleak [bliːk] *adj* (*countryside*) deso-lado; (*prospect*) desanimador(a), sombrio; (*weather*) ruim

bleed [bliːd] (*pt, pp* **bled**) *vi* sangrar

bleeper ['bliːpə*] *n* (*of doctor*) bip *m*

blemish ['blemɪʃ] *n* mancha; (*on reputation*) mácula

blend [blend] *n* mistura ♦ *vt* mistu-rar ♦ *vi* (*colours etc: also*: **~ in**) combinar-se, misturar-se; **blender** *n* liquidificador *m*

bless [bles] (*pt, pp* **~ed** *or* **blest**) *vt* abençoar; **~ you!** (*after sneeze*) saúde!; **blessing** *n* bênção *f*; (*god-send*) graça, dádiva; (*approval*) aprovação *f*

blew [bluː] *pt of* **blow**

blind [blaɪnd] *adj* cego ♦ *n* (*for win-dow*) persiana; (: *also*: **Venetian ~**) veneziana ♦ *vt* cegar; (*dazzle*) des-lumbrar; **the ~** *npl* (~ *people*) os cegos; **blind alley** *n* beco-sem-saída *m*; **blindfold** *n* venda ♦ *adj,* *adv* com os olhos vendados, às cegas ♦ *vt* vendar os olhos a; **blindness** *n* cegueira; **blind spot** *n* (AUT) local *m* pouco visível; (*fig*) ponto fraco

blink [blɪŋk] *vi* piscar

bliss [blɪs] *n* felicidade *f*

blister ['blɪstə*] *n* (on skin) bolha; (in paint, rubber) empola ♦ *vi* empolar-se

blizzard ['blɪzəd] *n* nevasca

bloated ['bləʊtɪd] *adj* (swollen) inchado; (full) empanturrado

blob [blɔb] *n* (drop) gota; (indistinct shape) ponto

block [blɔk] *n* (of wood) bloco; (of stone) laje *f*; (in pipes) entupimento; (of buildings) quarteirão *m* ♦ *vt* obstruir, bloquear; (progress) impedir; ~ **of flats** (BRIT) prédio *m* de apartamentos; **mental** ~ bloqueio; **blockade** [blɔ'keɪd] *n* bloqueio; **blockage** *n* obstrução *f*; **blockbuster** *n* grande sucesso

bloke [bləʊk] (BRIT: inf) *n* cara *m* (BR), gajo (PT)

blond(e) [blɔnd] *adj, n* louro(-a)

blood [blʌd] *n* sangue *m*; **blood donor** *n* doador(a) *m/f* de sangue; **blood group** *n* grupo sanguíneo; **bloodhound** *n* sabujo; **blood poisoning** *n* toxemia; **blood pressure** *n* pressão *f* arterial or sanguínea; **bloodshed** *n* matança, carnificina; **bloodshot** *adj* (eyes) injetado; **bloodstream** *n* corrente *f* sanguínea; **blood test** *n* exame *m* de sangue; **bloodthirsty** *adj* sangüinário; **blood vessel** *n* vaso sanguíneo; **bloody** *adj* sangrento; (nose) ensangüentado; (BRIT: inf!): **this bloody ...** essa droga de ..., esse maldito ...; **bloody strong/ good** forte/bom pra burro; **bloody-minded** (BRIT: inf) *adj* espírito de porco *inv*

bloom [bluːm] *n* flor *f* ♦ *vi* florescer

blossom ['blɔsəm] *n* flor *f* ♦ *vi* florescer; (fig): **to ~ into** (fig) tornar-se

blot [blɔt] *n* borrão *m*, (fig) mancha ♦ *vt* borrar; **blot out** *vt* (view) tapar; (memory) apagar

blotchy ['blɔtʃɪ] *adj* (complexion) cheio de manchas

blotting paper ['blɔtɪŋ-] *n* mata-borrão *m*

blouse [blauz] *n* blusa

blow [bləʊ] (pt **blew**, pp **blown**) *n* golpe *m*; (punch) soco ♦ *vi* soprar ♦ *vt* (subj: wind) soprar; (instrument) tocar; (fuse) queimar; **to ~ one's nose** assoar o nariz; **blow away** *vt* levar, arrancar ♦ *vi* ser levado pelo vento; **blow down** *vt* derrubar; **blow off** *vt* levar; **blow out** *vi* (candle) apagar; **blow over** *vi* (storm, crisis) passar; **blow up** *vi* explodir ♦ *vt* explodir; (tyre) encher; (PHOT) ampliar; **blow-dry** *n* escova; **blow-out** *n* (of tyre) furo

blue [bluː] *adj* azul; (depressed) deprimido; **~s** *n* (MUS): **the ~s** o blues; **~ film/joke** filme/anedota picante; **out of the ~** (fig) de estalo, inesperadamente; **bluebell** *n* campainha; **bluebottle** *n* varejeira azul

bluff [blʌf] *vi* blefar ♦ *n* blefe *m*; **to call sb's ~** pagar para ver alguém

blunder ['blʌndə*] *n* gafe *f* ♦ *vi* cometer or fazer uma gafe

blunt [blʌnt] *adj* (knife) cego; (pencil) rombudo; (person) franco, direto

blur [bləː*] *n* borrão *m* ♦ *vt* (vision) embaçar; (distinction) reduzir, diminuir

blush [blʌʃ] *vi* corar, ruborizar-se ♦ *n* rubor *m*, vermelhidão *f*

boar [bɔː*] *n* javali *m*

board [bɔːd] *n* tábua; (card~) quadro; (notice ~) quadro de avisos; (for chess etc) tabuleiro; (committee) junta, conselho; (in firm) diretoria, conselho administrativo; (NAUT, AVIAT): **on ~** a bordo ♦ vt embarcar em; **full ~** (BRIT) pensão f completa; **half ~** (BRIT) meia-pensão f; **~ and lodging** casa e comida; **to go by the ~** ficar abandonado, dançar (inf); **board up** vt entabuar; **boarder** n interno(-a); **boarding card** n = **boarding pass; boarding house** n pensão m; **boarding pass** (BRIT) n cartão m de embarque; **boarding school** n internato

boast [bəust] vi: **to ~** (about or of) gabar-se (de), jactar-se (de)

boat [bəut] n (small) bote m; (big) navio

bob [bɒb] vi balouçar-se; **bob up** vi aparecer, surgir

bobby ['bɒbɪ] (BRIT: inf) n policial m/f (BR), polícia m (PT)

bobsleigh ['bɒbsleɪ] n bob m, trenó m duplo

bodily ['bɒdɪlɪ] adj corporal; (needs) material ♦ adv (lift) em peso

body ['bɒdɪ] n corpo; (corpse) cadáver m; (of car) carroceria; (fig: group) grupo; (: organization) organização f; (quantity) conjunto; (of wine) corpo; **body-building** n musculação f; **bodyguard** n guarda-costas m inv; **bodywork** n lataria

bog [bɒg] n pântano, atoleiro ♦ vt: **to get ~ged down** (fig) atolar-se

bogus ['bəugəs] adj falso

boil [bɔɪl] vt ferver; (CULIN) cozer, cozinhar ♦ vi ferver ♦ n (MED) furúnculo; **to come to the** (BRIT) **or a** (US) **~** começar a ferver; **boil down to** vt fus (fig) reduzir-se a; **boil over** vi transbordar; **boiled egg** n ovo cozido; **boiled potatoes** npl batatas fpl cozidas; **boiler** n caldeira; (for central heating) boiler m; **boil-**

ing point n ponto de ebulição

boisterous ['bɔɪstərəs] adj (noisy) barulhento; (excitable) agitado; (crowd) turbulento

bold [bəuld] adj corajoso; (pej) atrevido, insolente; (outline, colour) forte

Bolivia [bə'lɪvɪə] n Bolívia

bollard ['bɒləd] (BRIT) n (AUT) poste m de sinalização

bolt [bəult] n (lock) trinco, ferrolho; (with nut) parafuso, cavilha ♦ adv: **~ upright** direito como um fuso ♦ vt (door) fechar a ferrolho, trancar; (food) engolir às pressas ♦ vi fugir; (horse) disparar

bomb [bɒm] n bomba ♦ vt bombardear

bombshell ['bɒmʃel] n (fig) bomba

bond [bɒnd] n (binding promise) compromisso; (link) vínculo, laço; (FINANCE) obrigação f; (COMM): **in ~** (goods) retido sob caução na alfândega

bone [bəun] n osso; (of fish) espinha ♦ vt desossar; tirar as espinhas de

bonfire ['bɒnfaɪə*] n fogueira

bonnet ['bɒnɪt] n toucado; (BRIT: of car) capô m

bonus ['bəunəs] n (payment) bônus m; (fig) gratificação f

bony ['bəunɪ] adj ossudo; (meat) cheio de ossos; (fish) cheio de espinhas

boo [bu:] vt vaiar ♦ excl ruuh!, bu!

booby trap ['bu:bɪ-] n armadilha explosiva

book [buk] n livro; (of stamps, tickets) talão m ♦ vt reservar; (driver) autuar; (football player) mostrar o cartão amarelo a; **~s** npl (COMM) contas fpl, contabilidade f; **bookcase** n estante f (para livros); **booking office** (BRIT) n (RAIL, THEATRE) bilheteria (BR), bilheteira (PT); **book-keeping** n escrituração f, contabilidade f; **booklet** n livrinho, brochura; **bookshop** n, **bookstore** n livraria

boom [bu:m] n (noise) barulho, estrondo; (in sales) aumento rápido ♦ vi retumbar; (business) tomar surto

boon [bu:n] n dádiva, benefício

boost [bu:st] n estímulo ♦ vt estimular

boot [bu:t] n bota; (for football) chuteira; (BRIT: of car) porta-malas m (BR), porta-bagagem m (PT) ♦ vt (COMPUT) dar carga em; **to ~** ... (in addition) ainda por cima ...

booth [bu:ð] n (at fair) barraca; (telephone ~, voting ~) cabine f

booze [bu:z] (inf) n bebida alcoólica

border ['bɔ:də*] n margem f; (for flowers) borda; (of a country) fronteira; (on cloth etc) debrum m, remate m ♦ vt (also: ~ on) fazer limite com; **border on** vt fus (fig) chegar às raias de; **borderline** n fronteira; **Borders** n: **the Borders** a região fronteiriça entre a Escócia e a Inglaterra

bore [bɔ:*] pt of **bear** ♦ vt (hole) abrir; (well) cavar; (person) aborrecer ♦ n (person) chato(-a), maçante m/f; (of gun) calibre m; **to be ~d** estar entediado; **boredom** n tédio, maçante; **boring** adj chato, maçante

born [bɔ:n] adj: **to be ~** nascer

borne [bɔ:n] pp of **bear**

borough ['bʌrə] n município

borrow ['bɔrəu] vt: **to ~ sth (from sb)** pedir algo emprestado (a alguém)

Bosnia (and) Herzegovina ['bɔznɪə(and)hɜːtsəgəu'vi:nə] n Bósnia e Herzegovina

bosom ['buzəm] n peito

boss [bɔs] n (employer) patrão(-troa) m/f ♦ vt (also: ~ about; ~ around) mandar em; **bossy** adj mandão(-dona)

botch [bɔtʃ] vt (also: ~ up) estropiar, atamancar

both [bəuθ] adj, pron ambos(-as), os dois (as duas) ♦ adv: **~ A and B** tanto A como B; **~ of us went, we ~ went** nós dois fomos, ambos fomos

bother ['bɔðə*] vt (worry) preocupar; (disturb) atrapalhar ♦ vi (also: ~ o.s.) preocupar-se ♦ n preocupação f; (nuisance) amolação f, inconveniente m

bottle ['bɔtl] n garrafa; (of perfume, medicine) frasco; (baby's) mamadeira (BR), biberão m (PT) ♦ vt engarrafar; **bottle up** vt conter, refrear; **bottle bank** n depósito de vidro para reciclagem, vidrão m (PT); **bottleneck** n (traffic) engarrafamento; (fig) obstáculo, problema m; **bottle-opener** n abridor m (de garrafas) (BR), abre-garrafas m inv (PT)

bottom ['bɔtəm] n fundo; (buttocks) traseiro; (of page, list) pé m; (of class) nível m mais baixo ♦ adj (low) inferior, mais baixo; (last) último

bough [bau] n ramo

bought [bɔ:t] pt, pp of **buy**

boulder ['bəuldə*] n pedregulho, matacão m

bounce [bauns] vi saltar, quicar; (cheque) ser devolvido ♦ vt fazer saltar ♦ n (rebound) salto; **bouncer** (inf) n leão-de-chácara m

bound [baund] pt, pp of **bind** ♦ n (leap) pulo, salto; (gen pl: limit) limite m ♦ vi (leap) pular, saltar ♦ vt (border) demarcar ♦ adj: **~ by** limitado por; **to be ~ to do sth** (obliged) ter a obrigação de fazer algo; (likely) na certa ir fazer algo; **~ for** com destino a

boundary ['baundrɪ] n limite m, fronteira

bout [baut] n (of malaria etc) ataque m; (of activity) explosão f; (BOXING *etc*) combate *m*

bow¹ [bau] *n* (*knot*) laço; (*weapon*, *MUS*) arco

bow² [bau] *n* (*of the body*) reverência; (*of the head*) inclinação *f*; (*NAUT*: *also*: ~s) proa ♦ *vi* curvar-se, fazer uma reverência; (*yield*): **to ~ to** *or* **before** ceder ante, submeter-se a

bowels ['bauəlz] *npl* intestinos *mpl*, tripas *fpl*; (*fig*) entranhas *fpl*

bowl [bəul] *n* tigela; (*ball*) bola ♦ *vi* (*CRICKET*) arremessar a bola

bowler ['bəulə*] *n* (*CRICKET*) lançador *m* (*da bola*); (*BRIT*: *also*: ~ **hat**) chapéu-coco *m*

bowling ['bəulɪŋ] *n* (*game*) boliche *m*; **bowling alley** *n* boliche *m*; **bowling green** *n* gramado (*BR*) *or* relvado (*PT*) para jogo de bolas

bowls [bəulz] *n* jogo de bolas

bow tie ['bəu-] *n* gravata-borboleta

box [bɔks] *n* caixa; (*THEATRE*) camarote *m* ♦ *vt* encaixotar; (*SPORT*) boxear contra ♦ *vi* (*SPORT*) boxear; **boxer** *n* (*person*) boxeador *m*, pugilista *m*; **boxer shorts** *npl* samba-canção *m* (*BR*), boxers *mpl* (*PT*); **boxing** *n* (*SPORT*) boxe *m*, pugilismo *m*; **Boxing Day** (*BRIT*) *n* Dia de Santo Estêvão (*26 de dezembro*); **box office** *n* bilheteria (*BR*), bilheteira (*PT*)

boy [bɔi] *n* (*young*) menino, garoto; (*older*) moço, rapaz *m*; (*son*) filho

boycott ['bɔikɔt] *n* boicote *m*, boicotagem *f* ♦ *vt* boicotar

boyfriend ['bɔifrend] *n* namorado

BR *abbr* = **British Rail**

bra [brɑ:] *n* sutiã *m* (*BR*), soutien *m* (*PT*)

brace [breis] *n* (*on teeth*) aparelho; (*tool*) arco de pua ♦ *vt* retesar; ~s *npl* (*BRIT*) suspensórios *mpl*; **to ~ o.s.** (*also fig*) preparar-se

bracelet ['breislɪt] *n* pulseira

bracing ['breisɪŋ] *adj* tonificante

bracket ['brækɪt] *n* (*TECH*) suporte *m*; (*group*) classe *f*, categoria; (*range*) faixa, parêntese *m* ♦ *vt* pôr entre parênteses; (*fig*) agrupar

brag [bræg] *vi* gabar-se, contar vantagem

braid [breid] *n* (*trimming*) galão *m*; (*of hair*) trança

brain [brein] *n* cérebro; ~s *npl* (*CULIN*) miolos *mpl*; (*intelligence*) inteligência, miolos; **brainwash** *vt* fazer uma lavagem cerebral em; **brainwave** *n* inspiração *f*, idéia luminosa *or* brilhante; **brainy** *adj* inteligente

braise [breiz] *vt* assar na panela

brake [breik] *n* freio (*BR*), travão *m* (*PT*) ♦ *vt*, *vi* frear (*BR*), travar (*PT*)

bran [bræn] *n* farelo

branch [brɑ:ntʃ] *n* ramo, galho; (*COMM*) sucursal *f*, filial *f*; **branch out** *vi* (*fig*) diversificar suas atividades; **to ~ out into** estender suas atividades a

brand [brænd] *n* marca; (*fig*: *type*) tipo ♦ *vt* (*cattle*) marcar com ferro quente

brand-new *adj* novo em folha, novinho

brandy ['brændi] *n* conhaque *m*

brash [bræʃ] *adj* descarado

Brasilia [brə'ziliə] *n* Brasília

brass [brɑ:s] *n* latão *m*; **the ~** (*MUS*) os metais *mpl*; **brass band** *n* banda de música

brat [bræt] (*pej*) *n* pirralho(-a), fedelho(-a), malcriado(-a)

brave [breiv] *adj* valente, corajoso ♦ *vt* (*face up to*) desafiar; **bravery** *n* coragem *f*, bravura

brazen ['breizn] *adj* descarado ♦ *vt*: **to ~ it out** defender-se descaradamente

Brazil [brə'zil] *n* Brasil *m*; **Brazilian** *adj*, *n* brasileiro(-a)

breach [briːtʃ] vt abrir brecha em
♦ n (gap) brecha; (breaking): ~ **of
contract** inadimplemento (BR), inadimplemento (PT); ~ **of the peace** perturbação f da ordem pública

bread [brɛd] n pão m; **bread and
butter** n pão m com manteiga; (fig)
ganha-pão m; **breadbin** (US **bread
box**) n caixa de pão; **breadcrumbs** npl migalhas fpl; (CULIN)
farinha de rosca

breadth [brɛtθ] n largura; (fig)
amplitude f

breadwinner ['brɛdwɪnə*] n arrimo de família

break [breɪk] (pt **broke**, pp **broken**)
vt quebrar (BR), partir (PT); (promise)
quebrar; (law) violar, transgredir;
(record) bater ♦ vi quebrar-se, partir-
se; (storm) começar subitamente;
(weather) mudar; (dawn) amanhecer; (story, news) revelar ♦ n (gap)
abertura; (fracture) fratura; (rest)
descanso; (interval) intervalo; (at
school) recreio; (chance) oportunidade f; **to ~ the news to sb** dar a
notícia a alguém; **to ~ even** sair sem
ganhar nem perder; **to ~ free** ou
loose soltar-se; **to ~ open** (door etc)
arrombar; **break down** vt (figures,
data) analisar ♦ vt (machine, AUT)
enguiçar, pifar (inf); (MED) sofrer
uma crise nervosa; (person: cry)
desatar a chorar; (talks) fracassar;
break in vt (horse etc) domar ♦ vi
(burglar) forçar uma entrada; (interrupt) interromper; **break into** vt fus
(house) arrombar; **break off** vi
(speaker) parar-se, deter-se; (branch)
partir; **break out** vi (war) estourar;
(prisoner) libertar-se; **to ~ out in
spots/a rash** aparecer cobeto de
manchas/brotoejas; **break up** vi
(ship) partir-se; (partnership) acabar;
(marriage) desmanchar-se ♦ vt

(rocks) partir; (biscuit etc) quebrar;
(journey) romper; (fight) intervir em;
breakage n quebradura; **breakdown** n (AUT) enguiço, avaria; (in
communications) interrupção f; (of
marriage) fracasso, término; (MED:
also: **nervous breakdown**) esgotamento nervoso; (of figures) discriminação f, desdobramento

breakfast ['brɛkfəst] n café m da
manhã (BR), pequeno almoço (PT)

break: **break-in** n roubo com
arrombamento; **breakthrough** n
(fig) avanço, novo progresso

breast [brɛst] n (of woman) peito,
seio; (chest, meat) peito; **breast-
feed** (irreg: like **feed**) vt, vi amamentar; **breast-stroke** n nado de
peito

breath [brɛθ] n fôlego, respiração f;
out of ~ ofegante, sem fôlego;
Breathalyser ['brɛθəlaɪzə*] ® n
bafômetro

breathe [briːð] vt, vi respirar;
breathe in vt, vi inspirar; **breathe
out** vt, vi expirar; **breathing** n respiração f

breathless ['brɛθlɪs] adj sem fôlego

breed [briːd] (pt, pp **bred**) vt (animals) criar; (plants) multiplicar ♦ vi
criar, reproduzir ♦ n raça

breeze [briːz] n brisa, aragem f;
breezy adj (person) despreocupado, animado; (weather) ventoso

brew [bruː] vt (tea) fazer; (beer) fermentar ♦ vi (storm, fig) armar-se;
brewery n cervejaria

bribe [braɪb] n suborno ♦ vt subornar; **bribery** n suborno

brick [brɪk] n tijolo; **bricklayer** n
pedreiro

bride [braɪd] n noiva; **bridegroom**
n noivo; **bridesmaid** n dama de
honra

bridge [brɪdʒ] n ponte f; (NAUT)

ponte de comando; (CARDS) bridge
m; (of nose) cavalete m ♦ vt transpor
bridle ['braɪdl] n cabeçada, freio
brief [bri:f] adj breve ♦ n (LAW) causa;
(task) tarefa ♦ vt (inform) informar;
~s npl (for men) cueca (BR), cuecas
fpl (PT); (for women) calcinha (BR),
cuecas fpl (PT); **briefcase** n pasta;
briefly adv (glance) rapidamente;
(say) em poucas palavras
bright [braɪt] adj claro, brilhante;
(weather) resplandecente; (person:
clever) inteligente; (: lively) alegre,
animado; (colour) vivo ♦ (future)
promissor(a), favorável; **brighten**
(also: **brighten up**) vt (room) tornar
mais alegre; (event) animar, alegrar
♦ vi (weather) clarear; (person) animar-se, alegrar-se; (face) iluminar-se; (prospects) tornar-se animado or
favorável
brilliance ['brɪljəns] n brilho, claridade f
brilliant ['brɪljənt] adj brilhante;
(inf: great) sensacional
brim [brɪm] n borda; (of hat) aba
brine [braɪn] n (CULIN) salmoura
bring [brɪŋ] (pt, pp brought) vt trazer; **bring about** vt ocasionar, produzir; **bring back** vt restabelecer;
(return) devolver; **bring down** vt
(price) abaixar; (government, plane)
derrubar; **bring forward** vt adiantar; **bring off** vt (plan) levar a
cabo; **bring out** vt (object) tirar;
(meaning) salientar; (book etc)
lançar; **bring round** vt fazer voltar
a si; **bring up** vt (person) educar,
criar; (carry up) subir; (question)
introduzir; (food) vomitar
brisk [brɪsk] adj vigoroso; (tone, person) enérgico; (trade) ativo
bristle ['brɪsl] n (of animal) pêlo rijo;
(of beard) pêlo de barba curta;
(of brush) cerda ♦ vi (in anger) encolerizar-se
Britain ['brɪtən] n (also: **Great ~**)
Grã-Bretanha
British ['brɪtɪʃ] adj britânico ♦ npl:
the ~ os britânicos; **British Isles**
npl: **the British Isles** as ilhas
Britânicas; **British Rail** n companhia ferroviária britânica
Briton ['brɪtən] n britânico(-a)
brittle ['brɪtl] adj quebradiço, frágil
broach [brəʊtʃ] vt abordar, tocar
em
broad [brɔ:d] adj (street, range)
amplo; (shoulders, smile) largo; (distinction) geral; (accent) carregado;
in ~ daylight em plena luz do dia;
broadcast (pt, pp ~cast) n transmissão f ♦ vt, vi transmitir; **broaden**
vt alargar ♦ vi alargar-se; **to broaden
one's mind** abrir os horizontes;
broadly adv em geral; **broad-
minded** adj tolerante, liberal
broccoli ['brɔkəli] n brócolis mpl
brochure ['brəʊʃjuə*] n folheto,
brochura
broke [brəʊk] pt of break ♦ adj (inf)
sem um vintém, duro; (: company):
to go ~ quebrar
broken ['brəʊkən] pp of break ♦ adj
quebrado; **in ~ English** num inglês
mascavado; **broken-hearted** adj
com o coração partido
broker ['brəʊkə*] n corretor(a) m/f
brolly ['brɔli] (BRIT: inf) n guarda-
chuva m
bronchitis [brɔŋ'kaɪtɪs] n bronquite f
bronze [brɔnz] n bronze m
brooch [brəʊtʃ] n broche m
brood [bru:d] n ninhada ♦ vi (person) cismar, remoer
broom [brum] n vassoura; (BOT)
giesta-das-vassouras
Bros. abbr (COMM: = brothers) Irmãos
broth [brɔθ] n caldo

brothel ['brɒθl] n bordel m

brother ['brʌðə*] n irmão m;
brother-in-law n cunhado

brought [brɔːt] pt, pp of **bring**

brow [brau] n (forehead) fronte f,
testa; (rare: gen: eye~) sobrancelha;
(of hill) cimo, cume m

brown [braun] adj marrom (BR),
castanho (PT); (hair) castanho; (tanned) bronzeado, moreno ♦ n
(colour) cor f marrom (BR) or castanha (PT) ♦ vt (CULIN) dourar; **brown
bread** n pão m integral; **Brownie**
n (also: **Brownie Guide**) fadinha de
bandeirante; **brownie** (US) n (cake)
docinho de chocolate com amêndoas;
brown paper n papel m pardo;
brown sugar n açúcar m mascavo

browse [brauz] vi (in shop) dar uma
olhada; **to ~ through a book** folhear
um livro; **browser** ['brauzə*] n
(COMPUT) browser m, navegador m

bruise [bruːz] n hematoma m, contusão f ♦ vt machucar

brunette [bruː'net] n morena

brunt [brʌnt] n: **the ~ of** (greater
part) a maior parte de

brush [brʌʃ] n escova; (for painting,
shaving) pincel m; (quarrel) bate-
boca m ♦ vt varrer; (groom) escovar;
(also: ~ **against**) tocar ao passar,
roçar; **brush aside** vt afastar, não
fazer caso de; **brush up** vt retocar,
revisar

Brussels ['brʌslz] n Bruxelas;
Brussels sprout n couve-de-
bruxelas f

brutal ['bruːtl] adj brutal

brute [bruːt] n bruto; (person) animal m ♦ adj: **by ~ force** por força
bruta

BSc n abbr = **Bachelor of Science**

BSE n abbr (= bovine spongiform
encephalopathy) BSE f

bubble ['bʌbl] n bolha (BR), borbu-

lha (PT) ♦ vi borbulhar; **bubble
bath** n banho de espuma; **bubble
gum** n chiclete m (de bola) (BR),
pastilha elástica (PT)

buck [bʌk] n (rabbit) macho; (deer)
cervo; (US: inf) dólar m ♦ vi corco-
vear; **to pass the ~** fazer o jogo de
empurra; **buck up** vi (cheer up)
animar-se, cobrar ânimo

bucket ['bʌkɪt] n balde m

buckle ['bʌkl] n fivela ♦ vt afivelar
♦ vi torcer-se, cambar-se

bud [bʌd] n broto; (of flower) botão
m ♦ vi brotar, desabrochar

Buddhism ['budɪzəm] n budismo

buddy ['bʌdɪ] (US) n camarada m,
companheiro

budge [bʌdʒ] vt mover ♦ vi mexer-se

budgerigar ['bʌdʒərɪgɑː*] n periquito

budget ['bʌdʒɪt] n orçamento ♦ vi:
to ~ for sth incluir algo no orçamento

budgie ['bʌdʒɪ] n = **budgerigar**

buff [bʌf] adj (colour) cor de
camurça ♦ n (inf: enthusiast) aficio-
nado(-a)

buffalo ['bʌfələu] (pl ~ or ~es) n
(BRIT) búfalo; (US: bison) bisão m

buffer ['bʌfə*] n pára-choque m;
(COMPUT) buffer m, memória inter-
mediária

buffet¹ ['bufeɪ] (BRIT) n (in station)
bar m; (food) bufê m; **buffet car**
(BRIT) n vagão-restaurante m

buffet² ['bʌfɪt] vt fustigar

bug [bʌg] n (esp US: insect) bicho;
(fig: germ) micróbio; (spy device)
microfone m oculto, escuta clandestina; (COMPUT: of program) erro ♦ vt
(inf: annoy) apoquentar, incomodar;
(room) colocar microfones em;
(phone) grampear

bugle ['bjuːgl] n trompa, corneta

build [bɪld] (pt, pp **built**) n (of person) talhe m, estatura ♦ vt construir, edificar; **build up** vt acumular; **builder** n construtor(-a) m/f, empreiteiro(-a); **building** n (trade) construção f; (house, structure) edifício, prédio; **building society** (BRIT) n sociedade f de crédito imobiliário, financiadora

built [bɪlt] pt, pp of **build** ♦ adj: ~-in embutido; **built-up area** ['bɪltʌp-] n zona urbanizada

bulb [bʌlb] n (BOT) bulbo; (ELEC) lâmpada

Bulgaria [bʌl'gɛərɪə] n Bulgária

bulge [bʌldʒ] n bojo, saliência ♦ vi inchar-se; (pocket etc) fazer bojo

bulk [bʌlk] n (of building, object) volume m; (of person) corpanzil m; **in ~** (COMM) a granel; **the ~ of** a maior parte de; **bulky** adj volumoso

bull [bul] n touro; **bulldog** n buldogue m

bulldozer ['buldəuzə*] n buldôzer m, escavadora

bullet ['bulɪt] n bala

bulletin ['bulɪtɪn] n noticiário; (journal) boletim m

bulletproof ['bulɪtpru:f] adj à prova de balas

bullfight ['bulfaɪt] n tourada; **bullfighter** n toureiro; **bullfighting** n tauromaquia

bullion ['buljən] n ouro (or prata) em barras

bullock ['bulək] n boi m, novilho

bullring ['bulrɪŋ] n praça de touros

bull's-eye n centro do alvo, mosca (do alvo) (BRIT)

bully ['bulɪ] n fanfarrão m, valentão m ♦ vt intimidar, tiranizar

bum [bʌm] n (inf: backside) bum-bum m; (esp US: tramp) vagabundo(-a), vadio(-a)

bumblebee ['bʌmblbi:] n maman-

gaba

bump [bʌmp] n (in car) batida; (jolt) sacudida; (on head) galo; (on road) elevação f ♦ vt bater contra, dar encontrão em ♦ vi dar sacudidas; **bump into** vt fus chocar-se com or contra, colidir com; (inf: person) dar com, topar com; **bumper** n (BRIT) pára-choque m ♦ adj: **bumper crop** supersafra; **bumper cars** npl carros mpl de trombada; **bumpy** ['bʌmpɪ] adj (road) acidentado, cheio de altos e baixos

bun [bʌn] n pão m doce (BR), pãozinho (PT); (in hair) coque m

bunch [bʌntʃ] n (of flowers) ramo; (of keys) molho; (of bananas) cacho; (of people) grupo; **~es** npl (in hair) cachos mpl

bundle ['bʌndl] n trouxa, embrulho; (of sticks) feixe m; (of papers) maço ♦ vt (also: ~ up) embrulhar, atar; (put): **to ~ sth/sb into** meter or enfiar algo/alguém correndo em

bungalow ['bʌŋɡələu] n bangalô m, chalé m

bungle ['bʌŋɡl] vt estropear, estragar

bunion ['bʌnjən] n joanete m

bunk [bʌŋk] n beliche m; **bunk beds** npl beliche m, cama-beliche f

bunker ['bʌŋkə*] n (coal store) carvoeira; (MIL) abrigo, casamata; (GOLF) bunker m

buoy [bɔɪ] n bóia; **buoy up** vt (fig) animar; **buoyant** adj flutuante; (person) alegre; (COMM: market) animado

burden ['bə:dn] n responsabilidade f, fardo; (load) carga ♦ vt sobrecarregar; (trouble): **to be a ~ to sb** ser um estorvo para alguém

bureau [bjuə'rəu] n (pl **~x**) (BRIT: desk) secretária, escrivaninha; (US:

chest of drawers) cômoda; *(office)* escritório, agência

bureaucracy [bjuə'rɔkrəsɪ] n burocracia

burglar ['bə:glə*] n ladrão m/f; **burglar alarm** n alarma de roubo; **burglary** n roubo

burial ['bɛrɪəl] n enterro

Burma ['bə:mə] n Birmânia

burn [bə:n] (pt, pp ~ed or burnt) vt queimar; *(house)* incendiar ♦ vi queimar-se, arder; *(sting)* arder, picar ♦ n queimadura; **burn down** vt incendiar; **burner** n *(on cooker, heater)* bico de gás, fogo; **burning** adj ardente; *(hot: sand etc)* abrasador(a); *(ambition)* grande

burrow ['bʌrəu] n toca, lura ♦ vi fazer uma toca, cavar; *(rummage)* esquadrinhar

bursary ['bə:sərɪ] (BRIT) n (SCH) bolsa

burst [bə:st] (pt, pp burst) vt arrebentar; *(banks)* romper ♦ vi estourar; *(tyre)* furar ♦ n rajada; to ~ **into flames** incendiar-se de repente; to ~ **into tears** desatar a chorar; to ~ **out laughing** cair na gargalhada; to be ~**ing** with *(subj: room, container)* estar abarrotado de; *(: person: emotion)* estar tomado de; **a ~ of energy** uma explosão de energia; **burst into** vt fus *(room etc)* irromper em

bury ['bɛrɪ] vt enterrar; *(at funeral)* sepultar; to ~ **one's head in one's hands** cobrir o rosto com as mãos; to ~ **one's head in the sand** *(fig)* bancar avestruz; to ~ **the hatchet** *(fig)* fazer as pazes

bus [bʌs] n ônibus m inv (BR), autocarro (PT)

bush [buʃ] n arbusto, mata; *(scrubland)* sertão m; to **beat about the ~** ser evasivo

bushy ['buʃɪ] adj *(thick)* espesso

business ['bɪznɪs] n negócio; *(trad-*

ing) comércio, negócios mpl; *(firm)* empresa; *(occupation)* profissão f; to **be away on ~** estar fora a negócios; **it's my ~ to ...** encarrego-me de ...; **it's none of my ~** eu não tenho nada com isto; **he means ~** fala a sério; **businesslike** adj eficiente, metódico; **businessman** *(irreg)* n homem m de negócios; **business trip** n viagem f de negócios; **businesswoman** *(irreg)* n mulher f de negócios

busker ['bʌskə*] (BRIT) n artista m/f de rua

bus: bus station n estação f rodoviária; **bus stop** n ponto de ônibus (BR), paragem f de autocarro (PT)

bust [bʌst] n (ANAT) busto ♦ adj *(inf: broken)* quebrado; to **go ~** falir

bustle ['bʌsl] n animação f, movimento ♦ vi apressar-se, andar azafamado; **bustling** adj *(town)* animado, movimentado

busy ['bɪzɪ] adj *(person)* ocupado, atarefado; *(place)* movimentado; *(US: TEL)* ocupado (BR), impedido (PT) ♦ vt: to ~ **o.s.** ocupar-se em ou de

<hr>

KEYWORD

but [bʌt] conj 1 *(yet)* mas, porém; **he's tired ~ Paul isn't** ele está cansado mas Paul não; **the trip was enjoyable ~ tiring** a viagem foi agradável porém cansativa

2 *(however)* mas; **I'd love to come, ~ I'm busy** eu adoraria vir, mas estou ocupado

3 *(showing disagreement, surprise etc)* mas; ~ **that's far too expensive!** mas isso é caro demais!

♦ prep *(apart from, except)* exceto, menos; **he was nothing ~ trouble** ele só deu problema; **no-one ~ him** só ele, ninguém a não ser ele; ~ **for**

sem, se não fosse; **(I'll do) anything ~ that** (eu faria) qualquer coisa menos isso
♦ *adv* (*just, only*) apenas; **had I ~ known** se eu soubesse; **I can ~ try** a única coisa que eu posso fazer é tentar; **all ~** quase

butcher ['butʃə*] *n* açougueiro (BR), homem *m* do talho (PT) ♦ *vt* (*prisoners etc*) chacinar, massacrar; (*cattle etc for meat*) abater e carnear; **butcher's (shop)** *n* açougue *m* (BR), talho (PT)

butler ['butlə*] *n* mordomo

butt [bʌt] *n* (*cask*) tonel *m*; (*of gun*) coronha; (*of cigarette*) toco (BR), ponta (PT); (BRIT: *fig: target*) alvo ♦ *vt* (*subj: goat*) marrar; (*: person*) dar uma cabeçada em; **butt in** *vi* (*interrupt*) interromper

butter ['bʌtə*] *n* manteiga ♦ *vt* untar com manteiga

butterfly ['bʌtəflai] *n* borboleta; (SWIMMING: *also:* **~ stroke**) nado borboleta

buttocks ['bʌtəks] *npl* nádegas *fpl*

button ['bʌtn] *n* botão *m*; (US: *badge*) emblema *m* ♦ *vt* (*also:* **~ up**) abotoar ♦ *vi* ter botões

buy [bai] (*pt, pp bought*) *vt* comprar ♦ *n* compra; **to ~ sb sth/sth from sb** comprar algo para alguém/algo a alguém; **to ~ sb a drink** pagar um drinque para alguém; **buyer** *n* comprador(a) *m/f*

buzz [bʌz] *n* zumbido; (*inf: phone call*) to give sb a ~ dar uma ligada para alguém ♦ *vi* zumbir; **buzzer** *n* cigarra, vibrador *m*; **buzz word** *n* modismo

┌─────────────┐
│ KEYWORD │
└─────────────┘

by [bai] *prep* 1 (*referring to cause, agent*) por, de; **killed ~ lightning** morto por um raio; **a painting ~ Picasso** um quadro de Picasso
2 (*referring to method, manner, means*) de, com; **~ bus/car/train** de ônibus/carro/trem; **to pay ~ cheque** pagar com cheque; **~ moonlight/candlelight** sob o luar/à luz de vela; **~ saving hard, he** ... economizando muito, ele ...
3 (*via, through*) por, via; **we came ~ Dover** viemos por *or* via Dover
4 (*close to*) perto de, ao pé de; **a holiday ~ the sea** férias à beira-mar; **she sat ~ his bed** ela sentou-se ao lado de seu leito
5 (*past*) por; **she rushed ~ me** ela passou por mim correndo
6 (*not later than*): **~ 4 o'clock** antes das quatro; **~ this time tomorrow** esta mesma hora amanhã; **~ the time I got here it was too late** quando eu cheguei aqui, já era tarde demais
7 (*during*): **~ daylight** durante o dia
8 (*amount*) por; **~ the kilometre** por quilômetro
9 (MATH, *measure*) por; **it's broader ~ a metre** tem um metro a mais de largura
10 (*according to*) segundo, de acordo com; **it's all right ~ me** por mim tudo bem
11: **(all) ~ oneself** *etc* (completamente) só, sozinho; **he did it (all) ~ himself** ele fêz tudo sozinho
12: **~ the way** a propósito
♦ *adv* 1 *see go*; **pass** *etc*
2: **~ and ~** logo, mais tarde; **~ and large** em geral

bye(-bye) ['bai('bai)] *excl* até logo (BR), tchau (BR), adeus (PT)

bypass ['baipɑ:s] *n* via secundária, desvio; (MED) ponte *f* de safena ♦ *vt*

evitar

bystander ['baɪstændə*] n circunstante m/f; (observer) espectador(a) m/f

byte [baɪt] n (COMPUT) byte m

C

C [si:] n (MUS) dó m

CA n abbr = **chartered accountant**

cab [kæb] n táxi m; (of truck etc) boléia; (of train) cabina de maquinista

cabaret ['kæbəreɪ] n cabaré m

cabbage ['kæbɪdʒ] n repolho (BR), couve f (PT)

cabin ['kæbɪn] n cabana; (on ship) camarote m; (on plane) cabina de passageiros; **cabin cruiser** n lancha a motor com cabine

cabinet ['kæbɪnɪt] n (POL) gabinete m; (furniture) armário m; (also: **display ~**) armário com vitrina

cable ['keɪbl] n cabo; (telegram) cabograma m ♦ vt enviar cabograma para; **cable-car** n bonde m (BR), teléférico (PT); **cable television** n televisão f a cabo

cache [kæʃ] n esconderijo; **a ~ of arms** etc um depósito secreto de armas etc

cactus ['kæktəs] (pl **cacti**) n cacto

cadge [kædʒ] (inf) vt filar

café ['kæfeɪ] n café m

cage [keɪdʒ] n (bird ~) gaiola; (for large animals) jaula; (of lift) cabina

cagey ['keɪdʒɪ] (inf) adj cuidadoso, reservado, desconfiado

cagoule [kə'gu:l] n casaco de náilon

Cairo ['kaɪərəu] n o Cairo

cake [keɪk] n (large) bolo; (small) doce m, bolinho; **~ of soap** sabonete m

calculate ['kælkjuleɪt] vt calcular;

(estimate) avaliar; **calculation** n cálculo; **calculator** n calculador m, calculadora

calendar ['kæləndə*] n calendário; **~ month/year** mês m/ano civil

calf [kɑ:f] (pl **calves**) n (of cow) bezerro, vitela; (of other animals) cria; (also: **~skin**) pele f ou couro de bezerro; (ANAT) barriga-da-perna

calibre ['kælɪbə*] (US **caliber**) n (of person) capacidade f, calibre m

call [kɔ:l] vt (name) chamar; (label) qualificar, descrever; (TEL) telefonar a, ligar para; (witness) citar; (meeting) convocar ♦ vi chamar; (shout) gritar; (TEL) telefonar; (visit: also: **~ in**; **~ round**) dar um pulo ♦ n (shout) chamada; (also: **telephone ~**) chamada, telefonema m; (of bird) canto; **to be ~ed** chamar-se; **on ~** de plantão; **call back** vi (return) voltar, passar de novo; (TEL) ligar de volta; **call for** vt fus (demand) requerer, exigir; (fetch) ir buscar; **call off** vt (cancel) cancelar; **call on** vt fus (visit) visitar; (appeal to work); **call out** vi gritar, bradar; **call up** vt (MIL) chamar às fileiras; (TEL) dar uma ligada; **callbox** (BRIT) n cabine f telefônica; **call centre** n (BRIT: TEL) central f de chamadas; **caller** n visitante m/f; (TEL) chamador(a) m/f; **call girl** n call girl f, prostituta; **calling card** (US) n cartão m de visita

callous ['kæləs] adj cruel, insensível

calm [kɑ:m] adj calmo; (peaceful) tranquilo; (weather) estável ♦ n calma ♦ vt acalmar; (fears, grief) abrandar; **calm down** vt acalmar, tranquilizar ♦ vi acalmar-se

Calor gas ['kælə*-] ® n butano

calorie ['kælərɪ] n caloria

calves [kɑ:vz] npl of **calf**

Cambodia [kæm'bəudjə] n Camboja

camcorder ['kæmkɔːdə*] n filmadora, máquina de filmar

came [keɪm] pt of **come**

camel ['kæməl] n camelo

camera ['kæmərə] n máquina fotográfica; (CINEMA, TV) câmera; **in ~** (LAW) em câmara

camouflage ['kæməflɑːʒ] n camuflagem f ♦ vt camuflar

camp [kæmp] n campo, acampamento; (MIL) acampamento; (for prisoners) campo; (faction) facção f ♦ vi acampar ♦ adj afeminado

campaign [kæm'peɪn] n (MIL, POL etc) campanha ♦ vi fazer campanha

camp bed (BRIT) n cama de campanha

camper ['kæmpə*] n campista m/f; (vehicle) reboque m

camping ['kæmpɪŋ] n camping (BR), campismo (PT); **to go ~** acampar

campsite ['kæmpsaɪt] n camping m (BR), parque m de campismo (PT)

campus ['kæmpəs] n campus m, cidade f universitária

can[1] [kæn] n lata ♦ vt enlatar

---KEYWORD---

can[2] [kæn] (negative **cannot** or **can't**, pt, conditional **could**) aux vb 1 (be able to) poder; **you ~ do it if you try** se você tentar, você consegue fazê-lo; **I'll help you all I ~** ajudarei você em tudo que eu puder; **she couldn't sleep that night** ela não conseguiu dormir aquela noite; **~ you hear me?** você está me ouvindo?
2 (know how to) saber; **I ~ swim** sei nadar; **~ you speak Portuguese?** você fala português?
3 (may) **could I have a word with you?** será que eu podia falar com você?
4 (expressing disbelief, puzzlement): **it CAN'T be true!** não pode ser ver-

dade!; **what CAN he want?** o que é que ele quer?
5 (expressing possibility, suggestion etc): **he could be in the library** ele talvez esteja na biblioteca; **they could have forgotten** eles podiam ter esquecido

Canada ['kænədə] n Canadá m; **Canadian** [kə'neɪdɪən] adj, n canadense m/f

canal [kə'næl] n canal m

canary [kə'nɛərɪ] n canário m

cancel ['kænsəl] vt cancelar; (contract) anular; (cross out) riscar, invalidar; **cancellation** [kænsə'leɪʃən] n cancelamento

cancer ['kænsə*] n câncer m (BR), cancro (PT); **C~** (ASTROLOGY) Câncer m

candid ['kændɪd] adj franco, sincero

candidate ['kændɪdeɪt] n candidato(-a)

candle ['kændl] n vela; (in church) círio; **candlelight** n: **by candlelight** à luz de vela; **candlestick** n (plain) castiçal m; (bigger, ornate) candelabro, lustre m

candour ['kændə*] (US **candor**) n franqueza

candy ['kændɪ] n (also: **sugar-~**) açúcar m cristalizado; (US) bala (BR), rebuçado (PT); **candy-floss** (BRIT) n algodão-doce m

cane [keɪn] n (BOT) cana; (stick) bengala ♦ vt (BRIT: SCH) castigar (com bengala)

canister ['kænɪstə*] n lata

cannabis ['kænəbɪs] n maconha

canned [kænd] adj (food) em lata, enlatado

cannon ['kænən] (pl inv or **~s**) n canhão m

cannot ['kænɔt] = **can not**

canoe [kə'nuː] n canoa

can opener n abridor m de latas

canopy 39 career

(BR), abre-latas m inv (PT)

canopy ['kænəpɪ] n dossel m

can't [kɑːnt] = can not

canteen [kæn'tiːn] n cantina; (BRIT: of cutlery) jogo (de talheres)

canter ['kæntə*] vi ir a meio galope

canvas ['kænvəs] n (material) lona; (for painting) tela; (NAUT) velas fpl

canvass ['kænvəs] vi (POL): **to ~ for** fazer campanha por ♦ vt sondar

canyon ['kænjən] n canhão m garganta, desfiladeiro

cap [kæp] n gorro; (of pen, bottle) tampa; (contraceptive: also: Dutch ~) diafragma m ♦ vt (outdo) superar; (put limit on) limitar

capable ['keɪpəbl] adj (of sth) capaz; (competent) competente, hábil

capacity [kə'pæsɪtɪ] n capacidade f; (of stadium etc) lotação f; (role) condição f, posição f

cape [keɪp] n capa; (GEO) cabo

caper ['keɪpə*] n (CULIN: gen: ~s) alcaparra; (prank) travessura

capital ['kæpɪtl] n (also: ~ city) capital f; (money) capital m; (also: ~ letter) maiúscula; **capitalism** n capitalismo; **capitalist** adj, n capitalista m/f; **capital punishment** n pena de morte

Capitol ['kæpɪtl] n: **the ~** o Capitólio; ver quadro

CAPITOL

O Capitólio (**Capitol**) é a sede do Congresso dos Estados Unidos, localizado no monte Capitólio (Capitol Hill), em Washington.

Capricorn ['kæprɪkɔːn] n Capricórnio

capsize [kæp'saɪz] vt, vi emborcar, virar

capsule ['kæpsjuːl] n cápsula

captain ['kæptɪn] n capitão m

caption ['kæpʃən] n legenda

captive ['kæptɪv] adj, n cativo(-a)

capture ['kæptʃə*] vt prender, aprisionar; (person) capturar; (place) tomar; (attention) atrair, chamar ♦ n captura; (of place) tomada

car [kɑː*] n carro, automóvel m; (RAIL) vagão m

caramel ['kærəməl] n (sweet) caramelo; (burnt sugar) caramelado

caravan ['kærəvæn] n reboque m (BR), trailer m (BR), rulote f (PT); (in desert) caravana

carbohydrate [kɑːbəʊ'haɪdreɪt] n hidrato de carbono; (food) carboidrato

carbon ['kɑːbən] n carbono; **carbon dioxide** [-daɪˈɒksaɪd] n dióxido de carbono; **carbon monoxide** [-mɒnˈɒksaɪd] n monóxido de carbono

carburettor ['kɑːbjuˈrɛtə*] (US **carburetor**) n carburador m

card [kɑːd] n (also: playing ~) carta; (visiting ~) cartão m; (thin cardboard) cartolina; **cardboard** n cartão m, papelão m

cardiac ['kɑːdɪæk] adj cardíaco

cardigan ['kɑːdɪgən] n casaco de lã, cardigã m

cardinal ['kɑːdɪnl] adj cardeal; (MATH) cardinal ♦ n (REL) cardeal m

care [kɛə*] n cuidado; (worry) preocupação f; (charge) encargo, custódia ♦ vi: **to ~ about** (person, animal) preocupar-se com; (thing, idea) ter interesse em; **~ of** (on letter) aos cuidados de; **in sb's ~** a cargo de alguém; **to take ~ (to do)** ter o cuidado (de fazer); **to take ~ of** (person) cuidar de; (situation) encarregar-se de; **I don't ~** não me importa; **I couldn't ~ less** não dou a mínima; **care for** vt fus cuidar de; (like) gostar de

career [kə'rɪə*] n carreira ♦ vi (also: ~

along) correr a toda velocidade

carefree ['kɛəfri:] *adj* despreocupado

careful ['kɛəful] *adj* (*thorough*) cuidadoso; (*cautious*) cauteloso; (**be**) **~!** tenha cuidado!; **carefully** *adv* cuidadosamente; cautelosamente

careless ['kɛəlɪs] *adj* descuidado; (*heedless*) desatento

caress [kə'rɛs] *n* carícia ♦ *vt* acariciar

caretaker ['kɛəteɪkə*] *n* zelador(a) *m/f*

car-ferry *n* barca para carros (BR), barco de passagem (PT)

cargo ['kɑ:gəu] (*pl* **-es**) *n* carga

car hire (BRIT) *n* aluguel *m* (BR) ou aluguer *m* (PT) de carros

Caribbean [kærɪ'bi:ən] *n*: **the ~ (Sea)** o Caribe

caring ['kɛərɪŋ] *adj* (*person*) bondoso; (*society*) humanitário

carnation [kɑ:'neɪʃən] *n* cravo

carnival ['kɑ:nɪvəl] *n* carnaval *m*; (*US: funfair*) parque *m* de diversões

carol ['kærəl] *n*: (**Christmas**) **~** cântico de Natal

carp [kɑ:p] *n inv* (*fish*) carpa; **carp at** *vt fus* criticar

car park (BRIT) *n* estacionamento

carpenter ['kɑ:pɪntə*] *n* carpinteiro

carpet ['kɑ:pɪt] *n* tapete *m* ♦ *vt* atapetar

car phone *n* telefone *m* de carro

carriage ['kærɪdʒ] *n* carruagem *f*; (BRIT: RAIL) vagão *m*; (*of goods*) transporte *m*; (: *cost*) porte *m*; **carriageway** (BRIT) *n* (*part of road*) pista

carrier ['kærɪə*] *n* transportador(a) *m/f*; (*company*) empresa de transportes, transportadora; (MED) portador(a) *m/f*; **carrier bag** (BRIT) *n* saco, sacola

carrot ['kærət] *n* cenoura

carry ['kærɪ] *vt* levar; (*transport*) transportar; (*involve: responsibilities*

etc) implicar ♦ *vi* (*sound*) projetar-se; **to get carried away** (*fig*) exagerar; **carry on** *vi* seguir, continuar ♦ *vt* prosseguir, continuar; **carry out** *vt* (*orders*) cumprir; (*investigation*) levar a cabo, realizar; **carrycot** (BRIT) *n* moisés *m inv*

cart [kɑ:t] *n* carroça, carreta ♦ *vt* transportar (em carroça)

carton ['kɑ:tən] *n* (*box*) caixa (de papelão); (*of yogurt*) pote *m*; (*of milk*) caixa; (*packet*) pacote *m*

cartoon [kɑ:'tu:n] *n* (*drawing*) desenho; (BRIT: *comic strip*) história em quadrinhos (BR), banda desenhada (PT); (*film*) desenho animado

cartridge ['kɑ:trɪdʒ] *n* cartucho; (*of record player*) cápsula

carve [kɑ:v] *vt* (*meat*) trinchar; (*wood, stone*) cinzelar, esculpir; (*initials, design*) gravar; **carve up** *vt* dividir, repartir; **carving** *n* (*object*) escultura; (*design*) talha, entalhe *m*; **carving knife** (*irreg*) *n* trinchante *m*, faca de trinchar

case [keɪs] *n* caso; (*for spectacles etc*) estojo; (LAW) causa; (MED: *also*: **suitcase**) mala; (*of wine etc*) caixa; **in ~ (of)** em caso (de); **in any ~** todo o caso; **just in ~** (*conj*) se por acaso ♦ *adv* por via das dúvidas

cash [kæʃ] *n* dinheiro (em espécie) ♦ *vt* descontar; **to pay (in) ~** pagar em dinheiro; **~ on delivery** pagamento contra entrega; **cash card** (BRIT) *n* cartão *m* de saque; **cash desk** (BRIT) *n* caixa; **cash dispenser** *n* caixa automática ou eletrônica

cashew [kæ'ʃu:] *n* (*also*: **~ nut**) castanha de caju

cashier [kæ'ʃɪə*] *n* caixa *m/f*

cash register *n* caixa registradora

casing ['keɪsɪŋ] *n* invólucro

casino [kə'si:nəu] *n* cassino

casket ['kɑːskɪt] n cofre m, porta-jóias m inv; (US: coffin) caixão m

casserole ['kæsərəʊl] n panela de ir ao forno; (food) ensopado (BR) no forno, guisado (PT) no forno

cassette [kæ'set] n fita-cassete f; **cassette player** n toca-fitas m inv; **cassette recorder** n gravador m

cast [kɑːst] (pt, pp **cast**) vt (throw) lançar, atirar; (THEATRE): **to ~ sb as Hamlet** dar a alguém o papel de Hamlet ♦ n (THEATRE) elenco; (also: plaster ~) gesso; **to ~ one's vote** votar; **cast off** vi (NAUT) soltar o cabo; (KNITTING) rematar os pontos; **cast on** vi montar os pontos

castaway ['kɑːstəweɪ] n náufrago(-a)

caster sugar ['kɑːstə*-] (BRIT) n açúcar m branco refinado

cast iron n ferro fundido

castle ['kɑːsl] n castelo; (CHESS) torre f

castor ['kɑːstə*] n (wheel) rodízio; **castor oil** n óleo de rícino

casual ['kæʒjuəl] adj (by chance) fortuito; (work) eventual; (unconcerned) despreocupado; (clothes) descontraído, informal; **casually** adv casualmente; (dress) informalmente

casualty ['kæʒjultɪ] n ferido(-a); (dead) morto(-a); (of situation) vítima; (department) pronto-socorro

cat [kæt] n gato

catalogue ['kætəlɔg] (US **catalog**) n catálogo ♦ vt catalogar

catalyst ['kætəlɪst] n catalisador m

catapult ['kætəpʌlt] (BRIT) n (sling) atiradeira

catarrh [kə'tɑː*] n catarro

catastrophe [kə'tæstrəfɪ] n catástrofe f

catch [kætʃ] (pt, pp **caught**) vt pegar (BR), apanhar (PT); (fish) pes-

car; (arrest) prender, deter; (person: by surprise) flagrar, surpreender; (attention) atrair; (hear) ouvir; (also: ~ up) alcançar ♦ vi (fire) pegar; (in branches etc) ficar preso, prender-se ♦ n (fish) pesca; (game) manha, armadilha; (of lock) trinco, lingüeta; **to ~ fire** pegar fogo; (building) incendiar-se; **to ~ sight of** avistar; **catch on** vi (understand) entender (BR), perceber (PT); (grow popular) pegar; **catch up** vi equiparar-se ♦ vt (also: ~ up with) alcançar; **catching** ['kætʃɪŋ] adj (MED) contagioso; **catch phrase** n clichê m, slogan m; **catchy** ['kætʃɪ] adj que pega fácil, que gruda no ouvido

category ['kætɪgərɪ] n categoria

cater ['keɪtə*] vi preparar comida; **cater for** vt fus (needs) atender a; (consumers) satisfazer; **catering** n serviço de bufê; (trade) abastecimento

caterpillar ['kætəpɪlə*] n lagarta

cathedral [kə'θiːdrəl] n catedral f

catholic ['kæθəlɪk] adj eclético; **Catholic** adj, n (REL) católico(-a)

cattle ['kætl] npl gado

catty ['kætɪ] adj malicioso

caught [kɔːt] pt, pp of **catch**

cauliflower ['kɔlɪflauə*] n couve-flor f

cause [kɔːz] n causa; (reason) motivo, razão f ♦ vt causar, provocar

caution ['kɔːʃən] n cautela, prudência; (warning) aviso ♦ vt acautelar, avisar

cautious ['kɔːʃəs] adj cauteloso, prudente, precavido

cavalry ['kævəlrɪ] n cavalaria

cave [keɪv] n caverna, gruta; **cave in** vi ceder; **caveman** ['keɪvmæn] (irreg) n troglodita m, homem m das cavernas

CB n abbr = Citizens' Band (Radio)

CBI n abbr (= Confederation of British Industry) federação de indústria

cc abbr (= cubic centimetre) cc; (on letter etc) = carbon copy

CD n abbr = compact disc; **compact disc player**; **CD-ROM** n abbr (= compact disc read-only memory) CD-ROM m

cease [si:s] vt, vi cessar; **ceasefire** n cessar-fogo m

cedar ['si:də*] n cedro

ceiling ['si:lɪŋ] n (also fig) teto

celebrate ['sɛlɪbreɪt] vt celebrar ♦ vi celebrar; (birthday, anniversary etc) festejar; (REL: mass) rezar; **celebrated** adj célebre; **celebration** [sɛlɪ'breɪʃən] n (party) festa

celery ['sɛlərɪ] n aipo

cell [sɛl] n cela; (BIO) célula; (ELEC) pilha, elemento

cellar ['sɛlə*] n porão m; (for wine) adega

cello ['tʃɛləu] n violoncelo

cellphone ['sɛlfəun] n telefone m celular

Celt [kɛlt, sɛlt] n celta m/f; **Celtic** adj celta

cement [sə'mɛnt] n cimento; **cement mixer** n betoneira

cemetery ['sɛmɪtrɪ] n cemitério

censor ['sɛnsə*] n censor(a) m/f ♦ vt censurar; **censorship** n censura

census ['sɛnsəs] n censo

cent [sɛnt] n cêntimo; see also **per**

centenary [sɛn'ti:nərɪ] n centenário

center ['sɛntə*] (US) = **centre**

centigrade ['sɛntɪgreɪd] adj centígrado

centimetre ['sɛntɪmi:tə*] (US **centimeter**) n centímetro

central ['sɛntrəl] adj central; **Central America** n América Central; **central heating** n aquecimento central

centre ['sɛntə*] (US **center**) n centro;

(of room, circle etc) meio ♦ vt centrar

century ['sɛntjurɪ] n século; **20th ~** século vinte

ceramic [sɪ'ræmɪk] adj cerâmico

cereal ['si:rɪəl] n cereal m

ceremony ['sɛrɪmənɪ] n cerimônia; (ritual) rito; **to stand on ~** fazer cerimônia

certain ['sə:tən] adj (sure) seguro; (person): **a ~ Mr Smith** um certo Sr. Smith; (particular): **~ days/places** certos dias/lugares; (some): **a ~ coldness/pleasure** uma certa frieza/um certo prazer; **for ~** com certeza; **certainly** adv certamente, com certeza; **certainty** n certeza

certificate [sə'tɪfɪkɪt] n certidão f

certified mail ['sə:tɪfaɪd-] (US) n correio registrado

certified public accountant ['sə:tɪfaɪd-] (US) n perito-contador m

certify ['sə:tɪfaɪ] vt certificar

cervical ['sə:vɪkl] adj: **~ cancer** câncer m (BR) or cancro (PT) do colo do útero

cf. abbr (= compare) cf.

CFC n abbr (= chlorofluorocarbon) CFC m

ch. abbr (= chapter) cap.

chafe [tʃeɪf] vt (rub) roçar

chain [tʃeɪn] n corrente f; (of islands) grupo; (of mountains) cordilheira; (of shops) cadeia; (of events) série f ♦ vt (also: **~ up**) acorrentar; **chain-smoke** vi fumar um (cigarro) atrás do outro; **chain store** n magazine m (BR), grande armazém f (PT)

chair [tʃeə*] n cadeira; (armchair) poltrona; (of university) cátedra; (of meeting) presidência, mesa ♦ vt (meeting) presidir; **chairlift** n teleférico; **chairman** (irreg) n presidente m

chalk [tʃɔ:k] n (GEO) greda; (for writing) giz m

challenge ['tʃælɪndʒ] n desafio ♦ vt

desafiar; *(right)* disputar, contestar; **challenging** *adj* desafiante; *(tone)* de desafio

chamber ['tʃeɪmbə*] *n* câmara; *(BRIT: LAW: gen pl)* sala de audiências; **~ of commerce** câmara de comércio; **chambermaid** *n* arrumadeira *(BR)*, empregada *(PT)*

champagne [ʃæm'peɪn] *n* champanhe *m* or *f*

champion ['tʃæmpɪən] *n* campeão(-peã) *m/f*; *(of cause)* defensor(a) *m/f*; **championship** *n* campeonato

chance [tʃɑːns] *n (opportunity)* oportunidade, ocasião *f; (likelihood)* chance *f; (risk)* risco ♦ *vt* arriscar ♦ *adj* fortuito, casual; **to take a ~** arriscar-se; **by ~** por acaso; **to ~ it** arriscar-se

chancellor ['tʃɑːnsələ*] *n* chanceler *m*; **C~ of the Exchequer** *(BRIT)* Ministro da Economia (Fazenda e Planejamento)

chandelier [ʃændə'lɪə*] *n* lustre *m*

change [tʃeɪndʒ] *vt (alter)* mudar; *(wheel, money)* trocar; *(replace)* substituir; *(clothes, house)* mudar de, trocar de; *(nappy)* mudar; *(transform)*: **to ~ sb into** transformar alguém *m* ♦ *vi* mudar(-se); *(change clothes)* trocar-se; *(trains)* fazer baldeação *(BR)*, mudar *(PT)*; *(be transformed)*: **to ~ into** transformar-se em ♦ *n* mudança; *(exchange)* troca; *(difference)* diferença *f; (of clothes)* muda; *(coins)* trocado; **to ~ gear** *(AUT)* trocar de marcha; **to ~ one's mind** mudar de idéia; **for a ~** para variar; **changeable** *adj* *(weather, mood)* instável; **change machine** *n* máquina que fornece trocado; **changeover** *n* mudança

changing ['tʃeɪndʒɪŋ] *adj* variável; **changing room** *(BRIT)* *n (in shop)*

cabine *f* de provas

channel ['tʃænl] *n* canal *m; (of river)* leito; *(groove)* ranhura; *(fig: medium)* meio, via ♦ *vt* canalizar; **the (English) C~** o Canal da Mancha

chant [tʃɑːnt] *n* canto; *(REL)* cântico ♦ *vt* cantar; *(slogan)* entoar

chaos ['keɪɔs] *n* caos *m*

chap [tʃæp] *n (BRIT: inf: man)* sujeito *(BR)*, tipo *(PT)*

chapel ['tʃæpəl] *n* capela

chaplain ['tʃæplɪn] *n* capelão *m*

chapped [tʃæpt] *adj* ressecado

chapter ['tʃæptə*] *n* capítulo

character ['kærɪktə*] *n* caráter *m; (in novel, film)* personagem *m/f; (letter)* letra; **characteristic** [kærɪktə'rɪstɪk] *adj* característico

charcoal ['tʃɑːkəul] *n* carvão *m* de lenha; *(ART)* carvão *m*

charge [tʃɑːdʒ] *n (LAW)* encargo, acusação *f; (fee)* preço, custo; *(responsibility)* encargo ♦ *vt (battery)* carregar; *(MIL)* atacar; *(customer)* cobrar dinheiro de; *(LAW)*: **to ~ sb (with)** acusar alguém (de) ♦ *vi* precipitar-se; **~ npl: bank ~s** taxas *fpl* cobradas pelo banco, to **reverse the ~s** *(BRIT: TEL)* ligar a cobrar; **how much do you ~?** quanto você cobra?; **to ~ an expense (up) to sb's account** pôr a despesa na conta de alguém; **to take ~ of** encarregar-se de, tomar conta de; **to be in ~ of** estar a cargo de or encarregado de; **charge card** *n* cartão *m* de crédito *(emitido por uma loja)*

charity ['tʃærɪtɪ] *n* caridade *f; (organization)* obra de caridade; *(kindness)* compaixão *f; (gifts)* donativo

charm [tʃɑːm] *n (quality)* charme *m; (talisman)* amuleto; *(on bracelet)* berloque *m* ♦ *vt* encantar, deliciar; **charming** *adj* encantador(a)

chart [tʃɑːt] *n (graph)* gráfico; *(dia-*

gram) diagrama m; (map) carta de navegação ♦ vt traçar; **~s** npl (MUS) paradas fpl (de sucesso)

charter ['tʃɑːtə*] vt fretar ♦ n (document) carta, alvará m; **chartered accountant** (BRIT) n perito-contador (perita-contadora) f; **charter flight** n vôo charter or fretado

chase [tʃeɪs] vt perseguir; (also: ~ away) enxotar ♦ n perseguição f, caça

chasm ['kæzəm] n abismo

chat [tʃæt] vi (also: **have a ~**) conversar, bater papo (BR), cavaquear (PT) ♦ n conversa, bate-papo m (BR), cavaqueira (PT); **chat show** (BRIT) n programa m de entrevistas

chatter ['tʃætə*] vi (person) tagarelar; (animal) emitir sons; (teeth) tiritar ♦ n tagarelice f; emissão f de sons; (of birds) chilro; **chatterbox** n tagarela m/f

chatty ['tʃætɪ] adj (style) informal; (person) conversador(a)

chauffeur ['ʃəufə*] n chofer m, motorista m

chauvinist ['ʃəuvɪnɪst] n chauvinista m/f; (also: **male ~**) machista m; (nationalist) chauvinista m/f

cheap [tʃiːp] adj barato; (poor quality) barato, de pouca qualidade; (behaviour) vulgar; (joke) de mau gosto ♦ adv barato; **cheaply** adv barato, por baixo preço

cheat [tʃiːt] vi trapacear; (at cards) roubar (BR), fazer batota (PT); (in exam) colar (BR), cabular (PT) ♦ vt to ~ **sb (out of sth)** passar o conto do vigário em alguém ♦ n fraude f; (person) trapaceiro(-a)

check [tʃɛk] vt (examine) verificar; (facts) verificar; (halt) conter, impedir; (restrain) parar, refrear ♦ n controle m, inspeção f; (curb) freio; (US:

bill) conta; (pattern: gen pl) xadrez m; (US) = **cheque** ♦ adj (pattern, cloth) xadrez inv; **check in** vi (in hotel) registrar-se; (in airport) apresentar-se ♦ vt (luggage) entregar; **check out** vi pagar a conta e sair; **check up** vi: to ~ **up on sth** verificar algo; to ~ **up on sb** investigar alguém; **checkers** n (jogo de) damas fpl; **check-in (desk)** n check-in m; **checking account** (US) n conta corrente; **checkout** n caixa; **checkpoint** n (ponto de controle m; **checkroom** (US) n depósito de bagagem; **checkup** n (MED) check-up m

cheek [tʃiːk] n bochecha; (impudence) folga, descaramento; **cheekbone** n maçã f do rosto; **cheeky** adj insolente, descarado

cheer [tʃɪə*] vt dar vivas a, aplaudir; (gladden) alegrar, animar ♦ vi gritar com entusiasmo ♦ n (gen pl) gritos mpl de entusiasmo; **~s** npl (of crowd) aplausos mpl; **~s!** saúde!; **cheer up** vi animar-se, alegrar-se ♦ vt alegrar, animar; **cheerful** adj alegre; **cheerio** (BRIT) excl tchau (BR), adeus (PT)

cheese [tʃiːz] n queijo; **cheeseboard** n (in restaurant) sortimento de queijos

cheetah ['tʃiːtə] n chitá m

chef [ʃɛf] n cozinheiro-chefe (cozinheira-chefe) f

chemical ['kɛmɪkl] adj químico ♦ n produto químico

chemist ['kɛmɪst] n (BRIT: pharmacist) farmacêutico(-a); (scientist) químico(-a); **chemistry** n química; **chemist's (shop)** (BRIT) n farmácia

cheque [tʃɛk] (BRIT) n cheque m; **chequebook** n talão m (BR) or livro (PT) de cheques; **cheque card** (BRIT) n cartão m (de garantia) de cheques

cherish ['tʃɛrɪʃ] vt (person) tratar com carinho; (memory) lembrar (com prazer)

cherry ['tʃɛrɪ] n cereja; (also: ~ tree) cerejeira

chess [tʃɛs] n xadrez m; **chessboard** n tabuleiro de xadrez

chest [tʃɛst] n (ANAT) peito; (box) caixa, cofre m; ~ **of drawers** cômoda

chestnut ['tʃɛsnʌt] n castanha

chew [tʃuː] vt mastigar; **chewing gum** n chiclete m (BR), pastilha elástica (PT)

chic [ʃiːk] adj elegante

chick [tʃɪk] n pinto; (inf: girl) broto

chicken ['tʃɪkɪn] n galinha; (food) galinha, frango; (inf: coward) covarde m/f, galinha; **chicken out** (inf) vi agalinhar-se; **chickenpox** n catapora (BR), varicela (PT)

chief [tʃiːf] n (of tribe) cacique m, morubixaba m; (of organization) chefe m/f ♦ adj principal; **chiefly** adv principalmente

chilblain ['tʃɪlbleɪn] n frieira

child [tʃaɪld] (pl ~ren) n criança; (offspring) filho(-a); **childbirth** n parto; **childhood** n infância; **childish** adj infantil; **child minder** (BRIT) n cuidadora de crianças; **children** ['tʃɪldrən] npl of **child**

Chile ['tʃɪlɪ] n Chile m

chill [tʃɪl] n frio, friagem f; (MED) resfriamento ♦ vt (CULIN) semi-congelar; (person) congelar

chilli ['tʃɪlɪ] (US **chili**) n pimentão m picante

chilly ['tʃɪlɪ] adj frio; (person) friorento

chime [tʃaɪm] n (of bell) repique m; (of clock) soar m ♦ vi repicar; soar

chimney ['tʃɪmnɪ] n chaminé f

chimpanzee [tʃɪmpæn'ziː] n chimpanzé m

chin [tʃɪn] n queixo

China ['tʃaɪnə] n China

china ['tʃaɪnə] n porcelana; (crockery) louça fina

Chinese [tʃaɪ'niːz] adj chinês(-esa) ♦ n inv chinês(-esa) m/f; (LING) chinês m

chip [tʃɪp] n (gen pl: CULIN) batata frita; (: US: also: **potato** ~) batatinha frita; (of wood) lasca; (of glass, stone) lasca, pedaço; (COMPUT: also: **micro**~) chip m ♦ vt (cup, plate) lascar; **chip in** (inf) vi interromper; (contribute) compartilhar as despesas

chiropodist [kɪ'rɔpədɪst] (BRIT) n pedicuro(-a)

chirp [tʃəːp] vi chilrar, piar

chisel ['tʃɪzl] n (for wood) formão m; (for stone) cinzel m

chit [tʃɪt] n talão m

chitchat ['tʃɪttʃæt] n conversa fiada

chivalry ['ʃɪvəlrɪ] n cavalheirismo

chives [tʃaɪvz] npl cebolinha

chocolate ['tʃɔklɪt] n chocolate m

choice [tʃɔɪs] n (selection) seleção f; (option) escolha; (preference) preferência ♦ adj seleto, escolhido

choir ['kwaɪə*] n coro

choke [tʃəuk] vi sufocar-se; (on food) engasgar ♦ vt estrangular; (block) obstruir ♦ n (AUT) afogador m (BR), ar m (PT)

cholesterol [kə'lɛstərɔl] n colesterol m

choose [tʃuːz] (pt **chose**, pp **chosen**) vt escolher; **to ~ to do** optar por fazer; **choosy** adj exigente

chop [tʃɔp] vt (wood) cortar, talhar; (CULIN: also: ~ **up**) cortar em pedaços; (meat) picar ♦ n golpe m; (CULIN) costeleta; **~s** npl (inf: jaws) beiços mpl

chopper ['tʃɔpə*] n helicóptero

choppy ['tʃɔpɪ] adj (sea) agitado

chopsticks ['tʃɒpstɪks] npl pauzinhos mpl, palitos mpl

chord [kɔːd] n (MUS) acorde m

chore [tʃɔː*] n tarefa; (routine task) trabalho de rotina

chorus ['kɔːrəs] n (group) coro; (song) coral m; (refrain) estribilho

chose [tʃəuz] pt of **choose**; **chosen** pp of **choose**

Christ [kraɪst] n Cristo

christen ['krɪsn] vt batizar; (nickname) apelidar

Christian ['krɪstɪən] adj, n cristão(-tã) m/f; **Christianity** [krɪstɪ-'ænɪtɪ] n cristianismo; **Christian name** n prenome m, nome m de batismo

Christmas ['krɪsməs] n Natal m; Happy or Merry ~! Feliz Natal!; **Christmas card** n cartão m de Natal; **Christmas cracker** n busca-pé-surpresa m; ver quadro

---

CHRISTMAS CRACKER

Um cilindro de papelão que ao ser aberto faz estourar uma bombinha. Contém um presente surpresa e um chapéu de papel que cada convidado coloca na cabeça durante a ceia de Natal.

Christmas: **Christmas Day** n dia m de Natal; **Christmas Eve** n véspera de Natal; **Christmas tree** n árvore f de Natal

chrome [krəum] n = **chromium**

chromium ['krəumɪəm] n cromo

chronic ['krɒnɪk] adj crônico

chubby ['tʃʌbɪ] adj roliço, gorducho

chuck [tʃʌk] vt jogar (BR), deitar (PT); (BRIT: also: ~ up, ~ in: job) largar; (: person) acabar com; **chuck out** vt (thing) jogar (BR) or deitar (PT) fora; (: person) expulsar

chuckle ['tʃʌkl] vi rir

chum [tʃʌm] n camarada m/f

chunk [tʃʌŋk] n pedaço, naco

church [tʃɜːtʃ] n igreja; **churchyard** n adro, cemitério

churn [tʃɜːn] n (for butter) batedeira; (also: milk ~) lata, vasilha; **churn out** vt produzir em série

chute [ʃuːt] n rampa; (also: rubbish ~) despejador m

CIA (US) n abbr (= Central Intelligence Agency) CIA f

CID (BRIT) n abbr = **Criminal Investigation Department**

cider ['saɪdə*] n sidra

cigar [sɪ'gɑː*] n charuto

cigarette [sɪgə'ret] n cigarro; **cigarette case** n cigarreira

Cinderella [sɪndə'relə] n Gata Borralheira

cine-camera ['sɪnɪ-] (BRIT) n câmera (cinematográfica)

cinema ['sɪnəmə] n cinema m

cinnamon ['sɪnəmən] n canela

circle ['sɜːkl] n círculo; (in cinema) balcão m ♦ vi dar voltas ♦ vt (surround) rodear, cercar; (move round) dar a volta de

circuit ['sɜːkɪt] n circuito; (lap) volta; (track) pista

circular ['sɜːkjulə*] adj circular ♦ n (carta) circular f

circulate ['sɜːkjuleɪt] vt, vi circular; **circulation** [sɜːkju'leɪʃən] n circulação f; (of newspaper, book etc) tiragem f

circumstances ['sɜːkəmstənsɪz] npl circunstâncias fpl; (conditions) condições fpl; (financial condition) situação f econômica

circus ['sɜːkəs] n circo

CIS n abbr (= Commonwealth of Independent States) CEI f

cistern ['sɪstən] n tanque m; (in toilet) caixa d'água

citizen ['sɪtɪzn] n (of country)

cidadão(-dã) m/f; (of town) habitante m/f; **citizenship** n cidadania
citrus fruit ['sɪtrəs-] n citrino
city ['sɪtɪ] n cidade f; **the C~** centro financeiro de Londres
civic ['sɪvɪk] adj cívico, municipal
civil ['sɪvɪl] adj civil; (polite) delicado, cortês; **civilian** [sɪ'vɪlɪən] adj, n civil m/f
civilized ['sɪvɪlaɪzd] adj civilizado
civil: civil servant n funcionário público (funcionária pública); **Civil Service** n administração f pública; **civil war** n guerra civil
claim [kleɪm] vt exigir, reclamar; (rights etc) reivindicar; (responsibility, credit) assumir; (assert): **to ~ that/to be** afirmar que/ser ♦ vi (for insurance) reclamar ♦ n reclamação f; (assertion) afirmação f; (wage ~ etc) reivindicação f
clam [klæm] n molusco
clammy ['klæmɪ] adj (hands, face) úmido e pegajoso
clamp [klæmp] n grampo ♦ vt (two things together) grampear; (put: one thing on another) prender; **clamp down on** vt fus suprimir, proibir
clan [klæn] n clã m
clap [klæp] vi bater palmas, aplaudir; **clapping** n aplausos mpl, palmas fpl
clarinet [klærɪ'nɛt] n clarinete m
clarity ['klærɪtɪ] n clareza
clash [klæʃ] n (fight) confronto; (disagreement) desavença; (of beliefs) divergência; (of colours, styles) choque m; (of dates) coincidência; (noise) estrondo ♦ vi (gangs, beliefs) chocar-se; (disagree) entrar em conflito, ter uma desavença; (colours) não combinar; (dates) coincidir; (weapons, cymbals etc) estrefifiar
clasp [klɑːsp] n fecho; (embrace) abraço ♦ vt prender; abraçar

class [klɑːs] n classe f; (lesson) aula f; (type) tipo ♦ vt classificar
classic ['klæsɪk] adj clássico ♦ n clássico; **classical** adj clássico
classified ['klæsɪfaɪd] adj secreto
classmate ['klɑːsmeɪt] n colega m/f de aula
classroom ['klɑːsrum] n sala de aula
clatter ['klætə*] n ruído, barulho; (of hooves) tropel m ♦ vi fazer barulho or ruído
clause [klɔːz] n cláusula; (LING) oração f
claw [klɔː] n (of animal) pata; (of bird of prey) garra; (of lobster) pinça; **claw at** vt fus arranhar; (tear) rasgar
clay [kleɪ] n argila
clean [kliːn] adj limpo; (story) inocente ♦ vt limpar; (hands etc) lavar; **clean out** vt limpar; **clean up** vt limpar, assear; **clean-cut** adj alinhado; **cleaner** n faxineiro(-a); (product) limpador m; **cleaner's** n (also: **dry cleaner's**) tinturaria; **cleaning** n limpeza; **cleanliness** ['klɛnlɪnɪs] n limpeza
cleanse [klɛnz] vt limpar; (purify) purificar; **cleanser** n (for face) creme m de limpeza
clean-shaven [-'ʃeɪvn] adj sem barba, de cara raspada
clear [klɪə*] adj claro; (footprint, photograph) nítido; (obvious) evidente; (glass, water) transparente; (road, way) limpo, livre; (conscience) tranqüilo; (skin) macio ♦ vt (space) abrir; (room) esvaziar; (LAW: suspect) absolver; (fence) saltar, transpor; (cheque) compensar ♦ vi (weather) abrir; (sky) clarear; (fog etc) dissipar-se ♦ adv: **~ of** a salvo de; **to ~ the table** tirar a mesa; **clear up** vt limpar; (mystery) resolver, esclarecer;

clearance n remoção f; (*permission*) permissão f; **clear-cut** *adj* bem definido, nítido; **clearing** n (*in wood*) clareira f; **clearly** *adv* distintamente; (*obviously*) claramente; (*coherently*) coerentemente; **clearway** (BRIT) n estrada onde não se pode estacionar

clef [klɛf] n (MUS) clave f

clementine ['klɛməntaɪn] n clementina

clench [klɛntʃ] vt apertar, cerrar; (*teeth*) trincar

clergy ['klɜːdʒɪ] n clero; **clergyman** (*irreg*) n clérigo, pastor m

clerical ['klɛrɪkəl] *adj* de escritório; (*REL*) clerical

clerk [klɑːk, (US) klɜːrk] n auxiliar m/f de escritório; (US: *sales person*) balconista m/f

clever ['klɛvə*] *adj* inteligente; (*deft*) hábil; (*arrangement*) engenhoso

click [klɪk] vt (*tongue*) estalar; (*heels*) bater; (*COMPUT*) clicar em ♦ vi (*make sound*) estalar; (*COMPUT*) clicar

client ['klaɪənt] n cliente m/f

cliff [klɪf] n penhasco

climate ['klaɪmɪt] n clima m

climax ['klaɪmæks] n clímax m, ponto culminante; (*sexual*) orgasmo

climb [klaɪm] vi subir; (*plant*) trepar; (*plane*) ganhar altitude; (*prices etc*) escalar ♦ vt (*stairs*) subir; (*tree*) trepar em; (*hill*) escalar ♦ n subida; (*of prices etc*) escalada; **climber** n alpinista m/f; (*plant*) trepadeira f; **climbing** n alpinismo

clinch [klɪntʃ] vt (*deal*) fechar; (*argument*) decidir, resolver

cling [klɪŋ] (*pt, pp* clung) vi: **to ~ to** pegar-se a, aderir a; (*support, idea*) agarrar-se a; (*clothes*) ajustar-se a

clinic ['klɪnɪk] n clínica; **clinical** *adj* clínico; (*fig*) frio, impessoal

clip [klɪp] n (*for hair*) grampo (BR),

gancho (PT); (*also*: **paper ~**) mola, clipe m; (TV, CINEMA) clipe ♦ vt (*cut*) aparar; (*fasten*) grampear; **clippers** npl (*for gardening*) podadeira; (*also*: **nail clippers**) alicate m de unhas; **clipping** n recorte m

cloak [kləuk] n capa, manto ♦ vt (*fig*) encobrir; **cloakroom** n vestiário; (BRIT: WC) sanitários mpl (BR), lavatórios mpl (PT)

clock [klɔk] n relógio; **clock in** or **on** (BRIT) vi assinar o ponto na entrada; **clock off** or **out** (BRIT) vi assinar o ponto na saída; **clockwise** *adv* em sentido horário; **clockwork** n mecanismo de relógio ♦ *adj* de corda

clog [klɔg] n tamanco ♦ vt entupir ♦ vi (*also*: **~ up**) entupir-se

cloister ['klɔɪstə*] n claustro

close¹ [kləus] *adj* (*near*): **~ (to)** próximo (a); (*friend*) íntimo; (*examination*) minucioso; (*watch*) atento; (*contest*) apertado; (*weather*) abafado ♦ *adv* perto; **~ to** perto de; **~ by**, **~ at hand** = by; **to have a ~ shave** (*fig*) livrar-se por um triz

close² [kləuz] vt fechar; (*end*) encerrar ♦ vi fechar; (*end*) concluir-se, terminar-se ♦ n (*end*) fim m, conclusão f, terminação f; **close down** vi fechar definitivamente; **closed** *adj* fechado

close-knit *adj* muito unido

closely ['kləuslɪ] *adv* (*watch*) de perto; (*connected, related*) intimamente; (*resemble*) muito

closet ['klɔzɪt] n (*cupboard*) armário

close-up ['kləus-] n close m, close-up m

closure ['kləuʒə*] n fechamento

clot [klɔt] n (*gen*: *blood* ~) coágulo; (*inf*: *idiot*) imbecil m/f ♦ vi coagular-se

cloth [klɔθ] n (*material*) tecido,

fazenda; (*rag*) pano
clothe [kləuð] *vt* vestir
clothes [kləuðz] *npl* roupa;
clothes brush *n* escova (para a
roupa); **clothes line** *n* corda (para
estender a roupa); **clothes peg** (*US*
clothes pin) *n* pregador *m*
clothing ['kləuðıŋ] *n* = **clothes**
cloud [klaud] *n* nuvem *f*; **cloudy**
adj nublado; (*liquid*) turvo
clout [klaut] *vt* dar uma bofetada em
clove [kləuv] *n* cravo; ~ **of garlic**
dente *m* de alho
clover ['kləuvə*] *n* trevo
clown [klaun] *n* palhaço ♦ *vi* (*also*: ~
about; ~ **around**) fazer palhaçadas
club [klʌb] *n* (*society*) clube *m*;
(*weapon*) cacete *m*; (*also*: **golf ~**) taco
♦ *vt* esbordoar ♦ *vi*: **to ~ together**
cotizar-se; ~**s** *npl* (*CARDS*) paus *mpl*
clue [klu:] *n* indício, pista; (*in crossword*) definição *f*; **I haven't a ~** não
faço idéia
clump [klʌmp] *n* (*of trees etc*) grupo
clumsy ['klʌmzı] *adj* (*person*) desajeitado; (*movement*) deselegante,
mal-feito; (*attempt*) inábil
clung [klʌŋ] *pt, pp of* **cling**
cluster ['klʌstə*] *n* grupo; (*of flowers*) ramo ♦ *vi* agrupar-se, apinhar-se
clutch [klʌtʃ] *n* (*grip, grasp*) garra;
(*AUT*) embreagem *f* (*BR*), embraia-
gem *f* (*PT*) ♦ *vt* empunhar, pegar em
clutter ['klʌtə*] *vt* (*also*: ~ **up**) abarrotar, encher desordenadamente
CND *n abbr* = **Campaign for
Nuclear Disarmament**
Co. *abbr* = **county**; (= *company*) Cia.
c/o *abbr* (= *care of*) a/c
coach [kəutʃ] *n* (*bus*) ônibus *m*
(*BR*), autocarro (*PT*); (*horse-drawn*)
carruagem *f*, coche *m*; (*of train*)
vagão *m*; (*SPORT*) treinador(a) *m/f*,
instrutor(a) *m/f*; (*tutor*) professor(a)
m/f particular ♦ *vt* (*SPORT*) treinar;

(*student*) preparar, ensinar; **coach
trip** *n* passeio de ônibus (*BR*) or
autocarro (*PT*)
coal [kəul] *n* carvão *m*
coalition [kəuə'lıʃən] *n* (*POL*) coalizão *f*
coalman (*irreg*) *n* carvoeiro
coalmine *n* mina de carvão
coarse [kɔ:s] *adj* grosso, áspero;
(*vulgar*) grosseiro, ordinário
coast [kəust] *n* costa, litoral *m* ♦ *vi*
(*AUT*) ir em ponto morto; **coastal**
adj costeiro; **coastguard** *n* (*person*) guarda *m* que policia a costa;
(*service*) guarda costeira; **coastline**
n litoral *m*
coat [kəut] *n* (*overcoat*) sobretudo;
(*of animal*) pelo; (*of paint*) demão *f*,
camada ♦ *vt* cobrir, revestir; **coat
hanger** *n* cabide *m*; **coating** *n*
camada
coax [kəuks] *vt* persuadir com mei-
guice
cobbles ['kɔblz] (*also*: ~ **cobble-
stones**) *npl* pedras *fpl* arredondadas
cobweb ['kɔbweb] *n* teia de aranha
cocaine [kə'keın] *n* cocaína
cock [kɔk] *n* (*rooster*) galo; (*male
bird*) macho ♦ *vt* (*gun*) engatilhar;
cockerel *n* frango, galo pequeno
cockle ['kɔkl] *n* berbigão *m*
cockney ['kɔknı] *n* londrino(-a)
(*nativo dos bairros populares do leste
de Londres*)
cockpit ['kɔkpıt] *n* (*in aircraft*) cabina; (*in car*) compartimento do piloto
cockroach ['kɔkrəutʃ] *n* barata
cocktail ['kɔkteıl] *n* coquetel *m* (*BR*),
cocktail *m* (*PT*); **cocktail party** *n*
coquetel (*BR*), cocktail (*BR*)
cocoa ['kəukəu] *n* cacau *m*; (*drink*)
chocolate *m*
coconut ['kəukənʌt] *n* coco
cocoon [kə'ku:n] *n* casulo
COD *abbr* = **cash** (*BRIT*) or **collect** (*US*)

on delivery

cod [kɔd] *n inv* bacalhau *m*

code [kəud] *n* cifra; (*dialling* ~, *post* ~) código; ~ **of practice** deontologia

coercion [kəu'ə:ʃən] *n* coerção *f*

coffee ['kɔfɪ] *n* café *m*; **coffee bar** (*BRIT*) *n* café *m*, lanchonete *f*; **coffee bean** *n* grão *m* de café; **coffeepot** *n* cafeteira; **coffee table** *n* mesinha de centro

coffin ['kɔfɪn] *n* caixão *m*

coil [kɔɪl] *n* rolo; (*ELEC*) bobina; (*contraceptive*) DIU *m* ♦ *vt* enrolar

coin [kɔɪn] *n* moeda *f* ♦ *vt* (*word*) cunhar, criar; **coin box** (*BRIT*) *n* telefone *m* público

coincide [kəuɪn'saɪd] *vi* coincidir; **coincidence** [kəu'ɪnsɪdəns] *n* coincidência

Coke [kəuk] ® *n* (*drink*) coca

coke [kəuk] *n* (*coal*) coque *m*

colander ['kɔləndə*] *n* coador *m*, passador *m*

cold [kəuld] *adj* frio ♦ *n* frio; (*MED*) resfriado (*BR*), constipação *f* (*PT*); **it's ~** está frio; **to be** *or* **feel ~** (*person*) estar com frio; (*object*) estar frio; **to catch ~** resfriar-se (*BR*), apanhar constipação (*PT*); **to catch a ~** apanhar um resfriado (*BR*) ou uma constipação (*PT*); **in ~ blood** a sangue frio; **cold sore** *n* herpes *m* labial

coleslaw ['kəulslɔː] *n* salada de repolho cru

collapse [kə'læps] *vi* cair, tombar; (*building*) desabar; (*resistance, government*) sucumbir; (*MED*) desmaiar ♦ *n* desabamento, desmoronamento; (*of government*) queda; (*MED*) colapso; **collapsible** *adj* dobrável

collar ['kɔlə*] *n* (*of shirt*) colarinho; (*of coat etc*) gola; (*for dog*) coleira; (*TECH*) aro, colar *m*; **collarbone** *n* clavícula

colleague ['kɔliːg] *n* colega *m/f*

collect [kə'lekt] *vt* (*as a hobby*) colecionar; (*gather*) recolher; (*wages, debts*) cobrar; (*donations, subscriptions*) colher; (*mail*) coletar; (*BRIT: call for*) (ir) buscar, vir apanhar ♦ *vi* (*people*) reunir-se ♦ *adv*: **to call ~** (*US: TEL*) ligar a cobrar; **collection** [kə'lekʃən] *n* coleção *f*; (*of people*) grupo; (*of donations*) arrecadação *f*; (*of post, for charity*) coleta; (*of writings*) coletânea; **collector** *n* colecionador(a) *m/f*; (*of taxes etc*) cobrador(a) *m/f*

college ['kɔlɪdʒ] *n* (*of university*) faculdade *f*; (*of technology, agriculture*) escola de nível superior; *ver quadro*

COLLEGE

Além de "universidade", **college** também se refere a um centro de educação superior para jovens que terminaram a educação obrigatória, *secondary school*. Alguns oferecem cursos de especialização em matérias técnicas, artísticas ou comerciais, outros oferecem disciplinas universitárias.

---

collide [kə'laɪd] *vi*: **to ~ (with)** colidir (com)

collision [kə'lɪʒən] *n* colisão *f*

Colombia [kə'lɔmbɪə] *n* Colômbia

colon ['kəulən] *n* (*sign*) dois pontos; (*MED*) cólon *m*

colonel ['kə:nl] *n* coronel *m*

colony ['kɔlənɪ] *n* colônia

colour ['kʌlə*] (*US* **color**) *n* cor *f* ♦ *vt* colorir; (*with crayons*) colorir, pintar; (*dye*) tingir; (*fig: account*) falsear ♦ *vi* (*blush*) corar; **~s** *npl* (*of party, club*) cores *fpl*; **in ~** (*photograph etc*) a cores; **colour in** *vt* (*drawing*) colorir; **colour-blind** *adj* daltônico;

coloured adj colorido; (person) de cor; **colour film** n filme m a cores;
colourful adj colorido; (account) vívido; (personality) vivo, animado;
colouring ['kʌlərɪŋ] n colorido; (complexion) tez f; (in food) colorante m; **colour television** n televisão f a cores

colt {kəult] n potro

column ['kɔləm] n coluna; (of smoke) faixa; (of people) fila

coma ['kəumə] n coma

comb [kəum] n pente m; (ornamental) crista ♦ vt pentear; (area) vasculhar

combat ['kɔmbæt] n combate m ♦ vt combater

combination [kɔmbɪ'neɪʃən] n combinação f; (of safe) segredo

combine [vb kəm'baɪn, n 'kɔmbaɪn] vt combinar; (qualities) reunir ♦ vi combinar-se ♦ n (ECON) associação f

---

KEYWORD

come [kʌm] (pt **came**, pp **come**) vi
1 (movement towards) vir; **~ with me** vem comigo; **to ~ running** vir correndo
2 (arrive) chegar; **she's ~ here to work** ela veio aqui para trabalhar; **to ~ home** chegar em casa
3 (reach): **to ~ to** chegar a; **the bill came to £40** a conta deu £40; **her hair came to her waist** o cabelo dela batia na cintura
4 (occur): **an idea came to me** uma idéia me ocorreu
5 (be, become) ficar; **to ~ loose/undone** soltar-se/desfazer-se; **I've ~ to like him** passei a gostar dele

come about vi suceder, acontecer
come across vt fus (person) topar com; (thing) encontrar
come away vi (leave) ir-se embora; (become detached) desprender-se, soltar-se

come back vi (return) voltar
come by vt fus (acquire) conseguir
come down vi (price) baixar; (tree) cair; (building) desmoronar-se
come forward vi apresentar-se
come from vt fus (subj: person) ser de; (: thing) originar-se de
come in vi entrar; (on deal) participar; (be involved) estar envolvido
come in for vt fus (criticism) merecer
come into vt fus (money) herdar; (fashion) ser; (be involved) estar envolvido em
come off vi (button) desprender-se, soltar-se; (attempt) dar certo
come on vi (pupil, work, project) avançar; (lights, electricity) ser ligado; **~ on!** vamos!, vai!
come out vi (fact) vir à tona; (book) ser publicado; (stain, sun) sair
come round vi voltar a si
come to vi voltar a si
come up vi (sun) nascer; (in conversation) surgir; (event) acontecer
come up against vt fus (resistance, difficulties) tropeçar com, esbarrar em
come up with vt fus (idea) propor, sugerir; (money) conseguir
come upon vt fus encontrar, achar

---

comedian [kə'miːdɪən] n cômico, humorista m

comedy ['kɔmɪdɪ] n comédia

comfort ['kʌmfət] n (well-being) bem-estar m; (relief) alívio ♦ vt consolar, confortar; **~s** npl (of home etc) conforto; **comfortable** adj confortável; (financially) tranqüilo; (walk, climb etc) fácil; **comfortably** adv confortavelmente; **comfort station** (US) n banheiro (BR), lavatórios mpl (PT)

comic ['kɔmɪk] adj (also: ~al) cômico ♦ n (person) humorista m/f; (BRIT: magazine) revista em quadrinhos (BR), revista de banda desenhada (PT), gibi m (BR: inf)

coming ['kʌmɪŋ] n vinda, chegada ♦ adj que vem, vindouro

comma ['kɔmə] n vírgula

command [kə'mɑːnd] n ordem f, mandado; (control) controle m; (MIL: authority) comando; (mastery) domínio ♦ vt mandar; **commander** n (MIL) comandante m/f

commemorate [kə'meməreɪt] vt (with monument) comemorar; (with celebration) celebrar

commence [kə'mens] vt, vi começar, iniciar

commend [kə'mend] vt elogiar, louvar; (recommend) recomendar

comment ['kɔment] n comentário ♦ vi: to ~ (on) comentar (sobre); "no ~" "sem comentário"; **commentary** ['kɔməntəri] n comentário; **commentator** ['kɔmenteɪtə*] n comentarista m/f

commerce ['kɔmə:s] n comércio

commercial [kə'mə:ʃəl] adj comercial ♦ n anúncio, comercial m

commiserate [kə'mɪzəreɪt] vi: to ~ with comiserar-se de, condoer-se de

commission [kə'mɪʃən] n comissão f; (order) empreitada, encomenda ♦ vt (work of art) encomendar; **out of** ~ com defeito; **commissioner** n comissário(-a)

commit [kə'mɪt] vt cometer; (resources) alocar; (to sb's care) entregar; **to** ~ **o.s. (to do)** comprometer-se (a fazer); **to** ~ **suicide** suicidar-se; **commitment** n compromisso; (political etc) engajamento; (undertaking) promessa

committee [kə'mɪti] n comitê m

commodity [kə'mɔdɪti] n mercadoria

common ['kɔmən] adj comum; (vulgar) vulgar ♦ n área verde aberta ao público; **C~s** npl (BRIT: POL): **the (House of) C~s** a Câmara dos Comuns; **in** ~ em comum; **commonly** adv geralmente; **Common Market** n Mercado Comum; **commonplace** adj vulgar; **common sense** n bom senso; **Commonwealth** n: **the Commonwealth** a Comunidade Britânica

commotion [kə'məuʃən] n tumulto, confusão f

communal ['kɔmju:nl] adj comum

commune [n 'kɔmju:n, vb kə-'mju:n] n (group) comuna ♦ vi: to ~ with comunicar-se com

communicate [kə'mju:nɪkeɪt] vt ♦ vi: to ~ (with) comunicar-se (com); **communication** [kəmju:nɪ'keɪʃən] n comunicação f; (letter, call) mensagem f; **communication cord** (BRIT) n sinal m de alarme

communion [kə'mju:nɪən] n (also: **Holy C~**) comunhão f

communism ['kɔmjunɪzəm] n comunismo; **communist** adj, n comunista m/f

community [kə'mju:nɪti] n comunidade f; **community centre** n centro social

commutation ticket [kɔmju-'teɪʃən-] (US) n passe m, bilhete m de assinatura

commute [kə'mju:t] vi viajar diariamente ♦ vt comutar; **commuter** n viajante m/f habitual

compact [adj kəm'pækt, n 'kɔmpækt] adj compacto ♦ n (also: **powder** ~) estojo; **compact disc** n disco laser, CD m; **compact disc player** n som cd m

companion [kəm'pænɪən] n companheiro(-a); **companionship** n companhia, companheirismo

company ['kʌmpənɪ] n companhia; (COMM) sociedade f, companhia; **to keep sb ~** fazer companhia a alguém

comparative [kəm'pærətɪv] adj (study) comparativo; (peace, safety) relativo; (stranger) meio; **comparatively** adv relativamente

compare [kəm'pɛə*] vt comparar ♦ vi: **to ~ with** comparar-se com; **comparison** [kəm'pærɪsn] n comparação f

compartment [kəm'pɑːtmənt] n compartimento f; (of wallet) divisão f

compass ['kʌmpəs] n bússola f; **~es** npl compasso

compassion [kəm'pæʃən] n compaixão f

compatible [kəm'pætɪbl] adj compatível

compel [kəm'pɛl] vt obrigar

compensate ['kɔmpənseɪt] vt indenizar ♦ vi: **to ~ for** compensar; **compensation** [kɔmpən'seɪʃən] n compensação f; (damages) indenização f

compete [kəm'piːt] vi (take part) competir; (vie): **to ~ (with)** competir (com), fazer competição (com)

competent ['kɔmpɪtənt] adj competente

competition [kɔmpɪ'tɪʃən] n (contest) concurso; (ECON) concorrência; (rivalry) competição f

competitive [kəm'petɪtɪv] adj competitivo; (person) competidor(a)

competitor [kəm'petɪtə*] n (rival) competidor(a) m/f; (participant, ECON) concorrente m/f

complain [kəm'pleɪn] vi queixar-se; **to ~ of** (pain) queixar-se de; **complaint** n (objection) objeção f; (criticism) queixa; (MED) achaque m, doença

complement ['kɔmplɪmənt] n complemento; (esp ship's crew) tripulação f ♦ vt complementar

complete [kəm'pliːt] adj completo; (finished) acabado ♦ vt (finish: building, task) acabar; (: set, group) completar; (a form) preencher; **completely** adv completamente; **completion** n conclusão f, término; (of contract etc) realização f

complex ['kɔmpleks] adj complexo ♦ n complexo; (of buildings) conjunto

complexion [kəm'plekʃən] n (of face) cor f, tez f

complicate ['kɔmplɪkeɪt] vt complicar; **complicated** adj complicado; **complication** [kɔmplɪ'keɪʃən] n problema m; (MED) complicação f

compliment [n 'kɔmplɪmənt, vb 'kɔmplɪment] n (praise) elogio f ♦ vt elogiar; **~s** npl (regards) cumprimentos mpl; **to pay sb a ~** elogiar alguém; **complimentary** [kɔmplɪ'mentərɪ] adj lisonjeiro; (free) gratuito

comply [kəm'plaɪ] vi: **to ~ with** cumprir com

component [kəm'pəunənt] adj componente ♦ n (part) peça

compose [kəm'pəuz] vt compor; **to be ~d of** compor-se de; **to ~ o.s.** tranqüilizar-se; **composed** adj calmo; **composer** n (MUS) compositor(a) m/f; **composition** [kɔmpə'zɪʃən] n composição f

compound ['kɔmpaund] n (CHEM, LING) composto; (enclosure) recinto ♦ adj composto

comprehend [kɔmprɪ'hend] vt compreender

comprehensive [kɔmprɪ'hensɪv]

adj abrangente; (*INSURANCE*) total; **comprehensive (school)** (*BRIT*) *n* escola secundária de amplo programa; *ver quadro*

COMPREHENSIVE SCHOOL

Criadas na década de 1960 pelo governo trabalhista da época, as **comprehensive schools** são estabelecimentos de ensino secundário polivalentes concebidos para acolher todos os alunos sem distinção e lhes oferecer oportunidades iguais, em oposição ao sistema seletivo das *grammar schools*. A maioria dos estudantes britânicos freqüenta atualmente uma **comprehensive school**, mas as *grammar schools* não desapareceram de todo.

---

compress [*vb* kəm'pres, *n* 'kɔmpres] *vt* comprimir; (*text, information etc*) reduzir ♦ *n* (*MED*) compressa

comprise [kəm'praɪz] *vt* (*also:* **be ~d of**) compreender, constar de; (*constitute*) constituir

compromise ['kɔmprəmaɪz] *n* meio-termo ♦ *vt* comprometer ♦ *vi* chegar a um meio-termo

compulsion [kəm'pʌlʃən] *n* compulsão *f*; (*force*) coação *f*, força

compulsive [kəm'pʌlsɪv] *adj* compulsivo

compulsory [kəm'pʌlsərɪ] *adj* obrigatório; (*retirement*) compulsório

computer [kəm'pju:tə*] *n* computador *m*; **computer game** *n* video game *m*; **computerize** *vt* informatizar, computadorizar; **computer progra(m)mer** *n* programador(a) *m/f*; **computer program(m)ing** *n* programação *f*; **computer science** *n* informática *f*; **computing** *n* computação *f*; (*science*)

informática

comrade ['kɔmrɪd] *n* camarada *m/f*

con [kɔn] *vt* enganar; (*cheat*) trapacear ♦ *n* vigarice *f*

conceal [kən'si:l] *vt* ocultar; (*information*) omitir

conceited [kən'si:tɪd] *adj* vaidoso

conceive [kən'si:v] *vt* conceber ♦ *vi* conceber, engravidar

concentrate ['kɔnsəntreɪt] *vi* concentrar-se ♦ *vt* concentrar; **concentration** *n* concentração *f*

concept ['kɔnsept] *n* conceito

concern [kən'sə:n] *n* (*COMM*) empresa; (*anxiety*) preocupação *f* ♦ *vt* preocupar; (*involve*) envolver; (*relate to*) dizer respeito a; **to be ~ed (about)** preocupar-se (com); **concerning** *prep* sobre, a respeito de, acerca de

concert ['kɔnsət] *n* concerto; **concerted** [kən'sə:tɪd] *adj* (*joint*) conjunto

concession [kən'seʃən] *n* concessão *f*; **tax ~** redução no imposto

conclude [kən'klu:d] *vt* (*finish*) acabar, concluir; (*treaty etc*) firmar; (*agreement*) chegar a; (*decide*) decidir; **conclusion** [kən'klu:ʒən] *n* conclusão *f*; **conclusive** [kən'klu:sɪv] *adj* conclusivo, decisivo

concoct [kən'kɔkt] *vt* (*excuse*) fabricar; (*plot*) tramar; (*meal*) preparar; **concoction** *n* (*mixture*) mistura

concrete ['kɔnkri:t] *n* concreto (*BR*), betão *m* (*PT*) ♦ *adj* concreto

concussion [kən'kʌʃən] *n* (*MED*) concussão *f* cerebral

condemn [kən'dem] *vt* denunciar; (*prisoner, building*) condenar

condensation [kɔnden'seɪʃən] *n* condensação *f*

condense [kən'dens] *vi* condensar-se ♦ *vt* condensar; **condensed milk** *n* leite *m* condensado

condition [kən'dıʃən] n condição f; (MED: illness) doença ♦ vt condicionar; ~s npl (circumstances) circunstâncias fpl; on ~ that com a condição (de) que; **conditioner** n (for hair) condicionador m; (for fabrics) amaciante m

condolences [kən'dəulənsız] npl pêsames mpl

condom ['kɔndəm] n preservativo, camisinha, camisa-de-Venus f

condominium [kɔndə'mınıəm] (US) n (building) edifício

condone [kən'dəun] vt admitir, aceitar

conducive [kən'dju:sıv] adj: ~ to conducente para or a

conduct [n 'kɔndʌkt, vb kən'dʌkt] n conduta f, comportamento ♦ vt (research etc) fazer; (heat, electricity) conduzir; (MUS) reger; to ~ o.s. comportar-se; **conducted tour** n viagem f organizada; **conductor** n (of orchestra) regente m/f; (on bus) cobrador(a) m/f; (US: RAIL) revisor(a) m/f; (ELEC) condutor m; **conductress** n cobradora

cone [kəun] n cone m; (BOT) pinha; (for ice-cream) casquinha; (on road) cone colorido para sinalizar obras

confectionery [kən'fekʃənrı] n (sweetmeats) doces mpl; (sweets) balas fpl

confer [kən'fə:*] vt: to ~ sth on conferir algo a; (advantage) conceder algo a ♦ vi conferenciar

conference ['kɔnfərns] n congresso

confess [kən'fes] vt confessar ♦ vi (admit) admitir; **confession** n admissão f; (REL) confissão f

confetti [kən'fetı] n confete m

confide [kən'faıd] vi: to ~ in confiar em, fiar-se em

confidence ['kɔnfıdns] n confiança f; (faith) fé f; (secret) confidên-

cia; **in** ~ em confidência; **confidence trick** n conto do vigário; **confident** adj confiante, convicto; (positive) seguro; **confidential** [kɔnfı'denʃəl] adj confidencial

confine [kən'faın] vt (shut up) encarcerar; (limit): **to** ~ (to) confinar (a); **confined** adj (space) reduzido; **confines** ['kɔnfaınz] npl confins mpl

confirm [kən'fə:m] vt confirmar; **confirmation** [kɔnfə'meıʃən] n confirmação f; (REL) crisma; **confirmed** adj inveterado

confiscate ['kɔnfıskeıt] vt confiscar

conflict [n 'kɔnflıkt, vb kən'flıkt] n (disagreement) discórdia; (of interests, loyalties etc) conflito; (fighting) combate m ♦ vi estar em conflito; (opinions) divergir; **conflicting** [kən'flıktıŋ] adj (reports) divergente; (interests) oposto

conform [kən'fə:m] vi conformar-se; to ~ to ajustar-se a, acomodar-se a

confound [kən'faund] vt confundir

confront [kən'frʌnt] vt (problems) enfrentar; (enemy, danger) defrontar-se com; **confrontation** [kɔnfrən'teıʃən] n confrontação f

confuse [kən'fju:z] vt (perplex) desconcertar; (mix up) confundir, misturar; (complicate) complicar; **confused** adj confuso; **confusing** adj confuso; **confusion** [kən'fju:ʒən] n (mix-up) mal-entendido; (perplexity) perplexidade f; (disorder) confusão f

congeal [kən'dʒi:l] vi coagular-se

congenial [kən'dʒi:nıəl] adj simpático, agradável

congestion [kən'dʒestʃən] n (MED) congestão f; (traffic) congestionamento

congratulate [kən'grætjuleıt] vt

parabenizar; **congratulations** [kəngrætjuˈleɪʃənz] npl parabéns mpl

congregate [ˈkɔŋgrɪgeɪt] vi reunir-se; **congregation** [kɔŋgrɪˈgeɪʃən] n (in church) fiéis mpl

congress [ˈkɔŋgres] n congresso; (US): **C~** Congresso; ver quadro

---

CONGRESS

O Congresso é o Parlamento dos Estados Unidos. Consiste na *House of Representatives* e no Senado *Senate*. Os representantes e senadores são eleitos por sufrágio universal direto. O Congresso se reúne no *Capitol*, em Washington.

---

congressman (US) (irreg) n deputado

conjunctivitis [kəndʒʌŋktɪˈvaɪtɪs] n conjuntivite f

conjure [ˈkʌndʒə*] vi fazer truques; **conjure up** vt (ghost, spirit) fazer aparecer, invocar; (memories) evocar; **conjurer** n mágico(-a), prestidigitador(a) m/f

con man (irreg) n vigarista m

connect [kəˈnekt] vt (ELEC, TEL) ligar; (fig: associate) associar; (join): to ~ sth (to) juntar or unir algo a ♦ vi: to ~ with (train) conectar com; to be ~ed with estar relacionado com; I'm trying to ~ you (TEL) estou tentando completar a ligação; **connection** n ligação f; (ELEC, RAIL, fig) conexão f; (TEL) ligação f

conquer [ˈkɔŋkə*] vt conquistar; (enemy) vencer; (feelings) superar; **conquest** [ˈkɔŋkwest] n conquista

conscience [ˈkɔnʃəns] n consciência

conscientious [kɔnʃɪˈenʃəs] adj consciencioso

conscious [ˈkɔnʃəs] adj consciente;

(deliberate) intencional; **consciousness** n consciência; (MED): **to lose/regain consciousness** perder/recuperar os sentidos

conscript [ˈkɔnskrɪpt] n recruta m/f

consent [kənˈsent] n consentimento ♦ vi: to ~ to consentir em

consequence [ˈkɔnsɪkwəns] n consequência; (significance): of ~ de importância; **consequently** adv por conseguinte

conservation [kɔnsəˈveɪʃən] n conservação f; (of the environment) preservação f

conservative [kənˈsɜːvətɪv] adj conservador(a); (cautious) moderado; (BRIT: POL): **C~** conservador(a) ♦ n (BRIT: POL) conservador(a) m/f

conservatory [kənˈsɜːvətrɪ] n (MUS) conservatório; (greenhouse) estufa

conserve [kənˈsɜːv] vt (preserve) preservar; (supplies, energy) poupar ♦ n conserva

consider [kənˈsɪdə*] vt considerar; (take into account) levar em consideração; (study) estudar, examinar; to ~ doing sth pensar em fazer algo

considerable [kənˈsɪdərəbl] adj considerável; (sum) importante

considerate [kənˈsɪdərɪt] adj atencioso; **consideration** [kənsɪdəˈreɪʃən] n consideração f; (deliberation) deliberação f; (factor) fator m

considering [kənˈsɪdərɪŋ] prep em vista de

consign [kənˈsaɪn] vt: to ~ to (place) relegar para; (care) confiar a; **consignment** n consignação f

consist [kənˈsɪst] vi: to ~ of (comprise) consistir em

consistency [kənˈsɪstənsɪ] n coerência; (thickness) consistência

consistent [kənˈsɪstənt] adj (person) coerente, estável; (idea) sólido

consolation 57 continent

consolation [kɔnsəˈleɪʃən] n conforto

console [vb kənˈsəul, n ˈkɔnsəul] vt confortar ♦ n consolo

consonant [ˈkɔnsənənt] n consoante f

conspicuous [kənˈspɪkjuəs] adj conspícuo

conspiracy [kənˈspɪrəsɪ] n conspiração f, trama

constable [ˈkʌnstəbl] (BRIT) n policial m/f (BR), polícia m/f (PT); **chief ~** chefe m/f de polícia

constant [ˈkɔnstənt] adj constante

constipated [ˈkɔnstɪpeɪtɪd] adj com prisão de ventre

constipation [kɔnstɪˈpeɪʃən] n prisão f de ventre

constituency [kənˈstɪtjuənsɪ] n (POL) distrito eleitoral; (people) eleitorado

constitution [kɔnstɪˈtjuːʃən] n constituição f; (health) compleição f

constraint [kənˈstreɪnt] n coação f, pressão f; (restriction) limitação f

construct [kənˈstrʌkt] vt construir; **construction** n construção f; (structure) estrutura

consul [ˈkɔnsl] n cônsul m/f; **consulate** [ˈkɔnsjulɪt] n consulado

consult [kənˈsʌlt] vt consultar; **consultant** n (MED) (médico-a) especialista m/f; (other specialist) assessor(a) m/f, consultor(a) m/f; **consulting room** (BRIT) n consultório

consume [kənˈsjuːm] vt (eat) comer; (drink) beber; (fire etc, COMM) consumir; **consumer** n consumidor(a) m/f

consumption [kənˈsʌmpʃən] n consumação f; (buying, amount) consumo

cont. abbr = continued

contact [ˈkɔntækt] n contato ♦ vt

entrar or pôr-se em contato com; **contact lenses** npl lentes fpl de contato

contagious [kənˈteɪdʒəs] adj contagioso; (fig: laughter etc) contagiante

contain [kənˈteɪn] vt conter; **to ~ o.s.** conter-se; **container** n recipiente m; (for shipping etc) container m, cofre m de carga

contaminate [kənˈtæmɪneɪt] vt contaminar

cont'd abbr = continued

contemplate [ˈkɔntəmpleɪt] vt (idea) considerar; (person etc) contemplar

contemporary [kənˈtempərərɪ] adj (account) contemporâneo; (design) moderno ♦ n contemporâneo(-a)

contempt [kənˈtempt] n desprezo; **~ of court** (LAW) desacato à autoridade do tribunal; **contemptuous** [kənˈtemptjuəs] adj desdenhoso

contend [kənˈtend] vt (assert): **to ~ that** afirmar que ♦ vi: **to ~ with** (struggle) lutar com; (difficulty) enfrentar; (compete): **to ~ for** competir por; **contender** n contendor(a) m/f

content [adj, vb kənˈtent, n ˈkɔntent] adj (happy) contente; (satisfied) satisfeito ♦ vt contentar, satisfazer ♦ n conteúdo; (fat ~, moisture ~) quantidade f; **~s** npl (of packet, book) conteúdo; **contented** adj contente, satisfeito

contest [n ˈkɔntest, vb kənˈtest] n contenda; (competition) concurso ♦ vt (legal case) defender; (POL) ser candidato a; (competition) disputar; (statement) contestar; **contestant** [kənˈtestənt] n competidor(a) m/f; (in fight) adversário(-a)

context [ˈkɔntekst] n contexto

continent [ˈkɔntɪnənt] n continen-

te m; **the C~** (BRIT) o continente
europeu; **continental** [kɔntɪ'nentl]
adj continental; **continental quilt**
(BRIT) n edredom m

contingency [kən'tɪndʒənsɪ] n
contingência

continual [kən'tɪnjuəl] adj contínuo

continuation [kəntɪnju'eɪʃən] n
prolongamento

continue [kən'tɪnju:] vi prosseguir,
continuar ♦ vt continuar; (start
again) recomeçar, retomar; **continuous** [kən'tɪnjuəs] adj contínuo;
continuous stationery (COMPUT) for-
mulários mpl contínuos

contour ['kɔntuə*] n contorno;
(also: ~ line) curva de nível

contraband ['kɔntrəbænd] n contrabando

contraceptive [kɔntrə'septɪv] adj
anticoncepcional ♦ n anticoncepcional f

contract [n 'kɔntrækt, vb kən'trækt]
n contrato ♦ vi (become smaller)
contrair-se, encolher-se; (COMM): **to
~ to do sth** comprometer-se por
contrato a fazer algo ♦ vt contrair;
contraction [kən'trækʃən] n con-
tração f

contradict [kɔntrə'dɪkt] vt contradizer, desmentir

contraption [kən'træpʃən] (pej) n
engenhoca, geringonça

contrary¹ ['kɔntrərɪ] adj contrário
♦ n contrário; **on the ~** muito pelo
contrário; **unless you hear to the** ~
salvo aviso contrário

contrary² [kən'trɛərɪ] adj teimoso

contrast [n 'kɔntrɑ:st, vb kən'trɑ:st]
n contraste m ♦ vt comparar; **in ~ to
or with** em contraste com, ao contrário de

contravene [kɔntrə'vi:n] vt infringir

contribute [kən'trɪbju:t] vt contri-

buir ♦ vi dar; **to ~ to** (charity) contribuir para; (newspaper) escrever
para; (discussion) participar de; **contribution** [kɔntrɪ'bju:ʃən] n (donation) doação f; (BRIT: for social
security) contribuição f; (to debate)
intervenção f; (to journal) colabo-
ração f; **contributor** [kən-
'trɪbjutə*] n (to appeal) contribuinte
m/f; (to newspaper) colaborador(a)
m/f

contrive [kən'traɪv] vi: **to ~ to do**
chegar a fazer

control [kən'trəul] vt controlar;
(machinery) regular; (temper) dominar ♦ n controle m; (of car) direção f
(BR), condução f (PT); (check) freio,
controle; **~s** npl (of vehicle) instrumentos mpl de controle; (on radio,
television etc) controle m; (govern-
mental) medidas fpl de controle; **to be
in ~ of** ter o controle de; (in charge
of) ser responsável por

controversial [kɔntrə'və:ʃl] adj
controvertido, polêmico

controversy ['kɔntrəvə:sɪ] n controvérsia, polêmica

convalesce [kɔnvə'les] vi convalescer

convector [kən'vektə*] n (heater)
aquecedor m de convecção

convenience [kən'vi:nɪəns] n
(easiness) facilidade f; (suitability)
conveniência; (advantage) vantagem f, conveniência; **at your ~**
quando lhe convier; **all modern ~s**
(also: BRIT: all mod cons) com todos
os confortos

convenient [kən'vi:nɪənt] adj conveniente

convent ['kɔnvənt] n convento

convention [kən'venʃən] n (custom) costume m; (agreement) convenção f; (meeting) assembléia;
conventional adj convencional

conversation [kɔnvə'seɪʃən] n conversação f, conversa

converse [n 'kɔnvə:s, vb kən'və:s] n inverso ♦ vi conversar; **conversely** [kɔn'və:slɪ] adv pelo contrário, inversamente

convert [vb kən'və:t, n 'kɔnvə:t] vt converter ♦ n convertido(-a); **convertible** [kən'və:təbl] n conversível m

convey [kən'veɪ] vt transportar, levar; (thanks) expressar; (information) exprimir; **conveyor belt** n correia transportadora

convict [vb kən'vɪkt, n 'kɔnvɪkt] vt condenar ♦ n presidiário(-a); **conviction** n condenação f; (belief) convicção f; (certainty) certeza

convince [kən'vɪns] vt (assure) assegurar; (persuade) convencer; **convincing** adj convincente

convulse [kən'vʌls] vt: **to be ~d with** (laughter, pain) morrer de

cook [kuk] vt cozinhar; (meal) preparar ♦ vi cozinhar ♦ n cozinheiro(-a); **cookbook** n livro de receitas; **cooker** n fogão m; **cookery** n culinária; **cookery book** (BRIT) n = **cookbook**; **cookie** (US) n bolacha, biscoito; **cooking** n cozinha

cool [ku:l] adj fresco; (calm) calmo; (unfriendly) frio ♦ vt resfriar ♦ vi esfriar

coop [ku:p] n (for poultry) galinheiro; (for rabbits) capoeira; **coop up** vt (fig) confinar

cooperate [kəu'ɔpəreɪt] vi colaborar; (assist) ajudar; **cooperative** [kəu'ɔpərətɪv] adj cooperativo ♦ n cooperativa

coordinate [vb kəu'ɔ:dɪneɪt, n kəu'ɔ:dɪnət] vt coordenar ♦ n (MATH) coordenada; **~s** npl (clothes) coordenados mpl

cop [kɔp] (inf) n polícia m/f (BR), poli-

cial m/f, tira m (inf)

cope [kəup] vi: **to ~ with** poder com, arcar com; (problem) estar à altura de

copper ['kɔpə*] n (metal) cobre m; (BRIT: inf: policeman/woman) polícia m/f, policial m/f (BR); **~s** npl (coins) moedas fpl de pouco valor

copy ['kɔpɪ] n duplicata; (of book etc) exemplar m ♦ vt copiar; (imitate) imitar; **copyright** n direitos mpl autorais, copirraite m

coral ['kɔrəl] n coral m

cord [kɔ:d] n corda; (ELEC) fio, cabo; (fabric) veludo cotelê

cordial ['kɔ:dɪəl] adj cordial ♦ n (BRIT) bebida à base de fruta

cordon ['kɔ:dn] n cordão m; **cordon off** vt isolar

corduroy ['kɔ:dərɔɪ] n veludo cotelê

core [kɔ:*] n centro; (of fruit) caroço; (of problem) âmago ♦ vt descaroçar

cork [kɔ:k] n rolha; (tree) cortiça; **corkscrew** n saca-rolhas m inv

corn [kɔ:n] n (BRIT) trigo; (US: maize) milho; (on foot) calo; **~ on the cob** (CULIN) espiga de milho

corned beef ['kɔ:nd-] n carne f de boi enlatada

corner ['kɔ:nə*] n (outside) esquina; (inside) canto; (in road) curva; (FOOTBALL, BOXING) córner m ♦ vt (trap) encurralar; (COMM) açambarcar, monopolizar ♦ vi fazer uma curva

cornet ['kɔ:nɪt] n (MUS) cornetim m; (BRIT: of ice-cream) casquinha

cornflakes ['kɔ:nfleɪks] npl flocos mpl de milho

cornflour ['kɔ:nflauə*] (BRIT) n farinha de milho, maisena ®

cornstarch ['kɔ:nstɑ:tʃ] (US) n = **cornflour**

Cornwall ['kɔ:nwəl] n Cornualha

corny ['kɔ:nɪ] (inf) adj (joke) gasto

coronary ['kɔrənərɪ] n: **~** (thrombosis) trombose f (coronária)

coronation [kɔrəˈneɪʃən] n coroação f

coroner [ˈkɔrənə*] n magistrado que investiga mortes suspeitas

corporal [ˈkɔːpərl] n cabo ♦ adj: ~ **punishment** castigo corporal

corporate [ˈkɔːpərɪt] adj coletivo; (finance) corporativo; (image) de empresa

corporation [kɔːpəˈreɪʃən] n (of town) município, junta; (COMM) sociedade f

corps [kɔː*, pl kɔːz] (pl **corps**) n (MIL) unidade f; (diplomatic) corpo; **the press** ~ a imprensa

corpse [kɔːps] n cadáver m

correct [kəˈrekt] adj exato; (proper) correto ♦ vt corrigir; **correction** n correção f

correspond [kɔrɪsˈpɔnd] vi (write): **to** ~ **(with)** corresponder-se (com); (be equal to): **to** ~ **to** corresponder a; (be in accordance): **to** ~ **(with)** corresponder a; **correspondence** n correspondência; **correspondent** n correspondente m/f

corridor [ˈkɔrɪdɔː*] n corredor m

corrode [kəˈrəʊd] vt corroer ♦ vi corroer-se

corrugated [ˈkɔrəgeɪtɪd] adj corrugado; **corrugated iron** n chapa ondulada or corrugada

corrupt [kəˈrʌpt] adj corrupto; (COMPUT) corrupto, danificado ♦ vt corromper; corromper, danificar; **corruption** n corrupção f; corrupção, danificação f

Corsica [ˈkɔːsɪkə] n Córsega

cosmetic [kɔzˈmetɪk] n cosmético ♦ adj (fig) simbólico, artificial

cost [kɔst] (pt, pp **cost**) n (price) preço ♦ vt custar; **~s** npl (COMM: overheads) custos mpl; (LAW) custas fpl; **at all ~s** custe o que custar

co-star [ˈkəʊ-] n co-estrela m/f

Costa Rica [ˈkɔstəˈriːkə] n Costa Rica

costly [ˈkɔstlɪ] adj caro

costume [ˈkɔstjuːm] n traje m; (BRIT: also: **swimming** ~: woman's) maiô m (BR), fato de banho (PT); (: man's) calção m (de banho) (BR), calções mpl de banho (PT); **costume jewellery** n bijuteria

cosy [ˈkəʊzɪ] (US **cozy**) adj aconchegante; (person) confortável

cot [kɔt] n (BRIT) cama (de criança), berço; (US) cama de lona

cottage [ˈkɔtɪdʒ] n casa de campo; **cottage cheese** n ricota (BR), queijo creme (PT)

cotton [ˈkɔtn] n algodão m; (thread) linha; **cotton on** (inf) vi: **to** ~ **on (to sth)** sacar (algo); **cotton candy** (US) n algodão m doce; **cotton wool** (BRIT) n algodão m (hidrófilo)

couch [kautʃ] n sofá m; (doctor's) cama; (psychiatrist's) divã m

couchette [kuːˈʃet] n leito

cough [kɔf] vi tossir ♦ n tosse f

could [kud] pt, conditional of **can²**

couldn't [ˈkudnt] = **could not**

council [ˈkaunsl] n conselho; **city** or **town** ~ câmara municipal; **council estate** (BRIT) n conjunto habitacional; **council house** (BRIT) n casa popular; **councillor** n vereador(a) m/f

counsellor [ˈkaunsələ*] (US **counselor**) n conselheiro(-a); (US: LAW) advogado(-a)

count [kaunt] vt contar; (include) incluir ♦ vi contar ♦ n (of votes etc) contagem f; (of pollen, alcohol) nível m; (nobleman) conde m; **count on** vt fus (expect) esperar; (depend on) contar com; **countdown** n contagem f regressiva

counter [ˈkauntə*] n (in shop)

balcão m; (in post office etc) guichê m; (in games) ficha ♦ vt contrariar ♦ adv: ~ to ao contrário de; **counteract** vt neutralizar

counterfeit ['kauntəfɪt] n falsificação f ♦ vt falsificar ♦ adj falso, falsificado

counterfoil ['kauntəfɔɪl] n canhoto (BR), talão m (PT)

counterpart ['kauntəpa:t] n (of person) homólogo(-a); (of company etc) equivalente m/f

countess ['kauntɪs] n condessa

countless ['kauntlɪs] adj inumerável

country ['kʌntrɪ] n país m; (nation) nação f; (native land) terra; (as opposed to town) campo; (region) região f, terra; **country dancing** (BRIT) n dança regional; **country house** n casa de campo; **countryman** n (national) compatriota m; (rural) camponês m; **countryside** n campo

county ['kauntɪ] n condado m

coup [ku:] n golpe m de mestre; (also: ~ d'état) golpe m (de estado)

couple ['kʌpl] n (of things, people) par m; (married ~) casal m; **a ~ of** um par de; (a few) alguns (algumas)

coupon ['ku:pɔn] n cupom m (BR), cupão m (PT); (voucher) vale m

courage ['kʌrɪdʒ] n coragem f

courier ['kurɪə*] n correio m; (for tourists) guia m/f, agente m/f de turismo

course [kɔ:s] n (direction) direção f; (process) desenvolvimento m; (of river, SCH) curso m; (of ship) rumo m; (GOLF) campo m; (part of meal) prato m; **~ of treatment** tratamento m; **of ~** naturalmente; (certainly) certamente m; **of ~!** claro!, lógico!

court [kɔ:t] n (royal) corte f; (LAW) tribunal m; (TENNIS etc) quadra ♦ vt

(woman) cortejar, namorar; **to take to ~** demandar, levar a julgamento

courteous ['kə:tɪəs] adj cortês(-esa)

courtesy ['kə:təsɪ] n cortesia f; **(by) ~ of** com permissão de

court-house (US) n palácio de justiça

court martial (pl **courts martial**) n conselho de guerra

courtroom ['kɔ:trum] n sala de tribunal

courtyard ['kɔ:tja:d] n pátio

cousin ['kʌzn] n primo m/f; **first ~** primo irmão (prima irmã)

cove [kəuv] n angra, enseada

cover ['kʌvə*] vt cobrir; (with lid) tapar; (chairs etc) revestir; (distance) percorrer; (include) abranger; (protect) abrigar; (issues) tratar ♦ n (lid) tampa; (for chair etc) capa; (for bed) cobertor m; (of book, magazine) capa; (shelter) abrigo; (INSURANCE: also: ~ of spy) cobertura; **to take ~** abrigar-se; **under ~** (indoors) abrigado; **under separate ~** (COMM) em separado; **cover up** vi: **to ~ up for sb** cobrir alguém; **coverage** n cobertura; **cover charge** n couvert m; **covering** n cobertura; (of snow, dust etc) camada; **covering letter** (US **cover letter**) n carta de cobertura; **cover note** n nota de cobertura

covert ['kʌvət] adj (threat) velado

cover-up n encobrimento (dos fatos)

covet ['kʌvɪt] vt cobiçar

cow [kau] n vaca f ♦ vt intimidar

coward ['kauəd] n covarde m/f; **cowardice** n covardia; **cowardly** adj covarde

cowboy ['kaubɔɪ] n vaqueiro m

coy [kɔɪ] adj tímido

cozy ['kəuzɪ] (US) adj = cosy

CPA (US) n abbr = **certified public accountant**

crab [kræb] n caranguejo m

crack [kræk] n rachadura; (gap) brecha; (noise) estalo; (drug) crack m ♦ vt quebrar; (nut) partir, descascar; (wall) rachar; (whip etc) estalar; (joke) soltar; (mystery) resolver; (code) decifrar ♦ adj (expert) de primeira classe; **crack down on** vi fus (crime) ser linha dura com; **crack up** vi (PSYCH) sofrer um colapso nervoso; **cracker** n (biscuit) biscoito, (Christmas ~) busca-pé-surpresa m

crackle ['krækl] vi crepitar

cradle ['kreɪdl] n berço

craft [krɑːft] n (skill) arte f; (trade) ofício; (boat: pl inv) barco; (plane: pl inv) avião; **craftsman** (irreg) n artífice m, artesão m; **craftsmanship** n qualidade f; **crafty** adj astuto, esperto

cram [kræm] vt (fill): **to ~ sth with** encher or abarrotar algo de; (put): **to ~ sth into** enfiar algo em ♦ vi (for exams) estudar na última hora

cramp [kræmp] n (MED) cãibra; **cramped** adj apertado, confinado

cranberry ['krænbərɪ] n oxicoco

crane [kreɪn] n (TECH) guindaste m; (bird) grou m

crank [kræŋk] n manivela; (person) excêntrico(-a)

crash [kræʃ] n (noise) estrondo; (of car) batida; (of plane) desastre m de avião; (COMM) falência, quebra; (STOCK EXCHANGE) craque m ♦ vt (car) colidir; (plane) espatifar ♦ vi bater; cair, espatifar-se; (cars) colidir, bater; (COMM) falir, quebrar; **crash course** n curso intensivo; **crash helmet** n capacete m; **crash landing** n aterrissagem f forçada (BR), aterragem f forçada (PT)

crate [kreɪt] n caixote m; (for bottles) engradado

crave [kreɪv] vt, vi: **to ~ for** ansiar por

crawl [krɔːl] vi arrastar-se; (child) engatinhar; (insect) andar; (vehicle) arrastar-se a passo de tartaruga ♦ n (SWIMMING) crawl m

crayfish ['kreɪfɪʃ] n inv (freshwater) camarão-d'água-doce m; (saltwater) lagostim m

crayon ['kreɪən] n lápis m de cera, crayon m

craze [kreɪz] n (fashion) moda

crazy ['kreɪzɪ] adj louco, maluco, doido

creak [kriːk] vi chiar, ranger

cream [kriːm] n (of milk) nata; (artificial ~, cosmetic) creme m; (élite): **the ~ of** a fina flor de ♦ adj (colour) creme inv; **cream cake** n bolo de creme; **cream cheese** n ricota (BR), queijo creme (PT); **creamy** adj (colour) creme inv; (taste) cremoso

crease [kriːs] n (fold) dobra, vinco; (in trousers) vinco; (wrinkle) ruga ♦ vt (wrinkle) amassar, amarrotar ♦ vi amassar-se, amarrotar-se

create [kriː'eɪt] vt criar; (produce) produzir

creature ['kriːtʃə*] n (animal) animal m, bicho; (living thing) criatura

credit ['krɛdɪt] n crédito; (merit) mérito ♦ vt (also: give ~ to) acreditar; (COMM) creditar; (FILM, TV) crédito; **to ~ sb with sth** (fig) atribuir algo a alguém; **to be in ~** ter fundos; **credit card** n cartão m de crédito; **creditor** n credor(a) m/f

creed [kriːd] n credo

creek [kriːk] n enseada; (US) riacho

creep [kriːp] (pt, pp **crept**) vi (animal) rastejar; (person) deslizar(-se); **creeper** n trepadeira; **creepy** adj horripilante

cremate [krɪ'meɪt] vt cremar; **crematorium** (pl **crematoria**) n crematório

crept [krɛpt] pt, pp of **creep**

crescent ['krɛsnt] n meia-lua; (street) rua semicircular

cress [krɛs] n agrião m

crest [krɛst] n (of bird) crista; (of hill) cimo, topo; (of coat of arms) timbre m; **crestfallen** adj abatido, cabisbaixo

Crete [kriːt] n Creta

crevice ['krɛvɪs] n fenda; (gap) greta

crew [kruː] n (of ship) tripulação f; (CINEMA) equipe f; **crew-cut** n corte m à escovinha

crib [krɪb] n manjedoura, presépio; (US: cot) berço ♦ vt (inf) colar

cricket ['krɪkɪt] n (insect) grilo; (game) criquete m, cricket m

crime [kraɪm] n (no pl: illegal activities) crime m; (offence) delito; (fig) pecado, maldade f; **criminal** ['krɪmɪnl] n criminoso ♦ adj criminal; (morally wrong) imoral

crimson ['krɪmzn] adj carmesim inv

cringe [krɪndʒ] vi encolher-se

cripple ['krɪpl] n aleijado(-a) ♦ vt aleijar

crisis ['kraɪsɪs] (pl **crises**) n crise f

crisp [krɪsp] adj fresco; (bacon etc) torrado; (manner) seco; **crisps** (BRIT) npl batatinhas fpl fritas

criss-cross ['krɪs-] adj (design) entrecruzado; (pattern) em xadrez; ~ **pattern** (padrão m em) xadrez m

criterion [kraɪ'tɪərɪən] (pl **criteria**) n critério

critic ['krɪtɪk] n crítico(-a); **critical** adj crítico; (illness) grave; **to be critical of sth/sb** criticar algo/alguém; **critically** adv (examine) criteriosamente; (speak) criticamente; (ill) gravemente; **criticism** ['krɪtɪsɪzm] n crítica; **criticize** ['krɪtɪsaɪz] vt criticar

croak [krəuk] vi (frog) coaxar; (bird) crocitar; (person) estar rouco

Croatia [krəu'eɪʃə] n Croácia

crochet ['krəuʃeɪ] n crochê m

crockery ['krɔkərɪ] n louça

crocodile ['krɔkədaɪl] n crocodilo

crocus ['krəukəs] n açafrão-da-primavera m

croft [krɔft] (BRIT) n pequena chácara

crook [kruk] n (inf: criminal) vigarista m/f; (of shepherd) cajado; **crooked** ['krukɪd] adj torto; (dishonest) desonesto

crop [krɔp] n (produce) colheita; (amount produced) safra; (riding ~) chicotinho ♦ vt cortar; **crop up** vi surgir

cross [krɔs] n cruz f; (hybrid) cruzamento ♦ vt cruzar; (street etc) atravessar; (thwart) contrariar ♦ adj zangado, mal-humorado; **cross out** vt riscar; **cross over** vi atravessar; **crossbar** n barra transversal; **cross-examine** vt (LAW) reperguntar; **cross-eyed** adj vesgo; **crossing** n (sea passage) travessia; (also: **pedestrian crossing**) faixa (para pedestres) (BR), passadeira (PT); **cross-reference** n referência remissiva; **crossroads** n cruzamento; **cross section** n (of object) corte m transversal; (of population) grupo representativo; **crosswalk** (US) n faixa (para pedestres) (BR), passadeira (PT); **crossword** n palavras fpl cruzadas

crouch [krautʃ] vi agachar-se

crow [krəu] n (bird) corvo; (of cock) canto, cocoricó m ♦ vi (cock) cantar, cocoricar

crowbar ['krəubɑː*] n pé-de-cabra m

crowd [kraud] n multidão f ♦ vt (fill) apinhar ♦ vi (gather): **to ~ round** reunir-se; (cram): **to ~ in** apinhar-se em; **crowded** adj (full) lotado;

(densely populated) superlotado

crown [kraun] n coroa; *(of head, hill)* topo ♦ vt coroar; *(fig)* rematar; **crown jewels** npl jóias fpl reais

crucial ['kru:ʃl] adj *(decision)* vital; *(vote)* decisivo

crucifix ['kru:sɪfɪks] n crucifixo

crude [kru:d] adj *(materials)* bruto; *(fig: basic)* tosco; *(: vulgar)* grosseiro

cruel ['kruəl] adj cruel

cruise [kru:z] n cruzeiro ♦ vi *(ship)* fazer um cruzeiro; *(car)*: **to ~ at ... km/h** ir a ... km por hora; **cruiser** n *(motorboat)* barco a motor; *(warship)* cruzador m

crumb [krʌm] n *(of bread)* migalha; *(of cake)* farelo

crumble ['krʌmbl] vt esfarelar ♦ vi *(building)* desmoronar-se; *(plaster, earth)* esfacelar-se; *(fig)* desintegrar-se

crumpet ['krʌmpɪt] n bolo leve

crumple ['krʌmpl] vt *(paper)* amassar; *(material)* amarrotar

crunch [krʌntʃ] vt *(food etc)* mastigar; *(underfoot)* esmagar ♦ n *(fig)*: **the ~** o momento decisivo; **crunchy** adj crocante

crusade [kru:'seɪd] n *(campaign)* campanha

crush [krʌʃ] n *(crowd)* aglomeração f; *(love)*: **to have a ~ on sb** ter um rabicho por alguém; *(drink)*: **lemon ~** limonada ♦ vt *(press)* esmagar; *(squeeze)* espremer; *(paper)* amassar; *(cloth)* enrugar; *(army, opposition)* aniquilar; *(hopes)* destruir; *(person)* arrasar

crust [krʌst] n *(of bread)* casca; *(of snow)* crosta; *(of earth)* camada

crutch [krʌtʃ] n muleta

crux [krʌks] n ponto crucial

cry [kraɪ] vi chorar; *(shout: also: ~ out)* gritar ♦ n grito; *(of bird)* pio; *(of animal)* voz f; **cry off** vi desistir

cryptic ['krɪptɪk] adj enigmático

crystal ['krɪstl] n cristal m; **crystal-clear** adj cristalino, claro

cub [kʌb] n filhote m; *(also: ~ scout)* lobinho

Cuba ['kju:bə] n Cuba

cube [kju:b] n cubo ♦ vt *(MATH)* elevar ao cubo; **cubic** adj cúbico

cubicle ['kju:bɪkl] n cubículo

cuckoo ['kuku:] n cuco; **cuckoo clock** n relógio de cuco

cucumber ['kju:kʌmbə*] n pepino

cuddle ['kʌdl] vt abraçar ♦ vi abraçar-se

cue [kju:] n *(SNOOKER)* taco; *(THEATRE etc)* deixa

cuff [kʌf] n *(of shirt, coat etc)* punho; *(US: on trousers)* bainha; *(blow)* bofetada; **off the ~** de improviso; **cuff links** npl abotoaduras fpl

cul-de-sac ['kʌldəsæk] n beco sem saída

cull [kʌl] vt *(story, idea)* escolher, selecionar ♦ n matança seletiva

culminate ['kʌlmɪneɪt] vi: **to ~ in** terminar em

culprit ['kʌlprɪt] n culpado(-a)

cult [kʌlt] n culto

cultivate ['kʌltɪveɪt] vt cultivar; **cultivation** [kʌltɪ'veɪʃən] n cultivo

cultural ['kʌltʃərəl] adj cultural

culture ['kʌltʃə*] n cultura; **cultured** adj culto

cumbersome ['kʌmbəsəm] adj pesado, desajeitado; *(person)* lente, ineficiente

cunning ['kʌnɪŋ] n astúcia ♦ adj astuto, malandro; *(device, idea)* engenhoso

cup [kʌp] n xícara *(BR)*, chávena *(PT)*; *(prize, of bra)* taça

cupboard ['kʌbəd] n armário

curator [kjuə'reɪtə*] n diretor(a) m/f

curb [kə:b] vt refrear ♦ n freio; *(US:*

kerb) meio-fio (*BR*), borda do passeio (*PT*)

curdle ['kə:dl] *vi* coalhar

cure [kjuə*] *vt* curar ♦ *n* (*MED*) tratamento, cura; (*solution*) remédio

curfew ['kə:fju:] *n* toque *m* de recolher

curious ['kjuərɪəs] *adj* curioso; (*nosy*) abelhudo; (*unusual*) estranho

curl [kə:l] *n* (*of hair*) cacho ♦ *vt* (*loosely*) frisar; (: *tightly*) encrespar ♦ *vi* (*hair*) encaracolar; **curl up** *vi* encaracolar-se; **curler** *n* rolo, bobe *m*; **curly** *adj* cacheado, crespo

currant ['kʌrnt] *n* passa de corinto; (*black~, red~*) groselha

currency ['kʌrnsɪ] *n* moeda; **to gain ~** (*fig*) consagrar-se

current ['kʌrnt] *n* corrente *f* ♦ *adj* corrente; (*present*) atual; **current account** (*BRIT*) *n* conta corrente; **current affairs** *npl* atualidades *fpl*; **currently** *adv* atualmente

curriculum [kə'rɪkjuləm] (*pl ~s* or **curricula**) *n* programa *m* de estudos; **curriculum vitae** *n* curriculum vitae *m*, currículo

curry ['kʌrɪ] *n* caril *m* ♦ *vt*: **to ~ favour with** captar simpatia de

curse [kə:s] *vi* xingar (*BR*), praguejar (*PT*) ♦ *vt* (*swear at*) xingar (*BR*); (*bemoan*) amaldiçoar ♦ *n* maldição *f*; (*swearword*) palavrão *m* (*BR*), baixo calão *m* (*PT*); (*problem*) castigo

cursor ['kə:sə*] *n* (*COMPUT*) cursor *m*

curt [kə:t] *adj* seco, brusco

curtail [kə:'teɪl] *vt* (*freedom, rights*) restringir; (*visit etc*) abreviar, encurtar; (*expenses etc*) reduzir

curtain ['kə:tn] *n* cortina; (*THEATRE*) pano

curts(e)y ['kə:tsɪ] *vi* fazer reverência

curve [kə:v] *n* curva ♦ *vi* encurvar-se, torcer-se; (*road*) fazer (uma) curva

cushion ['kuʃən] *n* almofada; (*of air*) colchão *m* ♦ *vt* amortecer

custard ['kʌstəd] *n* nata, creme *m*

custody ['kʌstədɪ] *n* custódia; **to take into ~** deter

custom ['kʌstəm] *n* (*tradition*) tradição *f*; (*convention*) costume *m*; (*habit*) hábito; (*COMM*) clientela; **customary** *adj* costumeiro; **customer** *n* cliente *m/f*; **customized** *adj* (*car etc*) feito sob encomenda

customs ['kʌstəmz] *npl* alfândega; **customs officer** *n* inspetor(a) *m/f* da alfândega, aduaneiro(-a)

cut [kʌt] (*pt, pp* **cut**) *vt* cortar; (*reduce*) reduzir ♦ *vi* cortar ♦ *n* corte *m*; (*in spending*) redução *f*; (*of garment*) talho; **cut down** *vt* (*tree*) derrubar; (*consumption*) reduzir; **cut off** *vt* (*piece, TEL*) cortar; (*person, village*) isolar; (*supply*) suspender; **cut out** *vt* (*shape*) recortar; (*activity etc*) suprimir; (*remove*) remover; **cut up** *vt* cortar em pedaços

cute [kju:t] *adj* bonitinho, gracinha

cutlery ['kʌtlərɪ] *n* talheres *mpl*

cutlet ['kʌtlɪt] *n* costeleta; (*vegetable ~, nut ~*) medalhão *m*

cut: **cut-price** (*US* **cut-rate**) *adj* a preço reduzido; **cutting** *adj* cortante ♦ *n* (*BRIT: from newspaper*) recorte *m*; (*from plant*) muda

CV *n abbr* = **curriculum vitae**

cwt *abbr* = **hundredweight**

cyanide ['saɪənaɪd] *n* cianeto

cybercafé ['saɪbəkæfeɪ] *n* cibercafé *m*

cyberspace ['saɪbəspeɪs] *n* ciberespaço

cycle ['saɪkl] *n* ciclo; (*bicycle*) bicicleta ♦ *vi* andar de bicicleta; **cycle lane** or **path** *n* ciclovia *f*

cycling ['saɪklɪŋ] *n* ciclismo

cyclist ['saɪklɪst] *n* ciclista *m/f*

cylinder ['sɪlɪndə*] *n* cilindro; (*of*

gas) bujão *m*

cymbals ['sɪmblz] *npl* pratos *mpl*

cynic ['sɪnɪk] *n* cínico(-a); **cynical** *adj* cínico

Cyprus ['saɪprəs] *n* Chipre *f*

cyst [sɪst] *n* cisto; **cystitis** *n* cistite *f*

czar [zɑː*] *n* czar *m*

Czech [tʃek] *adj* tcheco ♦ *n* tcheco(-a); *(LING)* tcheco; **Czech Republic** *n:* **the Czech Republic** a República Tcheca

D

D [diː] *n (MUS)* ré *m*

dab [dæb] *vt (eyes, wound)* tocar (de leve); *(paint, cream)* aplicar de leve

dabble ['dæbl] *vi:* **to ~ in** interessar-se por

dad [dæd] *(inf) n* papai *m*

daddy ['dædɪ] *n* = **dad**

daffodil ['dæfədɪl] *n* narciso-dos-prados *m*

daft [dɑːft] *adj* bobo, besta

dagger ['dægə*] *n* punhal *m*, adaga

daily ['deɪlɪ] *adj* diário ♦ *n (paper)* jornal *m*, diário ♦ *adv* diariamente

dainty ['deɪntɪ] *adj* delicado

dairy ['dɛərɪ] *n* leiteria; **dairy products** *npl* laticínios *mpl*; **dairy store** *(US) n* leiteria

daisy ['deɪzɪ] *n* margarida

dam [dæm] *n* represa, barragem *f* ♦ *vt* represar

damage ['dæmɪdʒ] *n (harm)* prejuízo; *(dents etc)* avaria ♦ *vt* danificar; *(harm)* prejudicar; **~s** *npl (LAW)* indenização *f* por perdas e danos

damn [dæm] *vt* condenar; *(curse)* maldizer ♦ *n (inf):* **I don't give a ~** não dou a mínima, estou me lixando ♦ *adj (inf: also:* **~ed**) danado, maldito; **~ (it)!** (que) droga!; **damning** *adj (evidence)* prejudicial

damp [dæmp] *adj* úmido ♦ *n* umidade *f* ♦ *vt (also:* **~en**: *cloth, rag)* umedecer; *(: enthusiasm etc)* jogar água fria em

damson ['dæmzən] *n* ameixa pequena

dance [dɑːns] *n* dança; *(party etc)* baile *m* ♦ *vi* dançar; **dance hall** *n* salão *m* de baile; **dancer** *n* dançarino(-a); *(professional)* bailarino(-a); **dancing** *n* dança

dandelion ['dændɪlaɪən] *n* dente-de-leão *m*

dandruff ['dændrəf] *n* caspa

Dane [deɪn] *n* dinamarquês(-esa) *m/f*

danger ['deɪndʒə*] *n* perigo; *(risk)* risco; **"~!"** *(on sign)* "perigo!"; **to be in ~ of** correr o risco de; **in ~** em perigo; **dangerous** *adj* perigoso

dangle ['dæŋgl] *vt* balançar ♦ *vi* pender balançando

Danish ['deɪnɪʃ] *adj* dinamarquês(-esa) ♦ *n (LING)* dinamarquês *m*

dare [dɛə*] *vt:* **to ~ sb to do sth** desafiar alguém a fazer algo ♦ *vi:* **to ~ (to) do sth** atrever-se a fazer algo, ousar fazer algo; **I ~ say** *(I suppose)* acho provável que; **daring** *adj* audacioso; *(bold)* ousado ♦ *n* coragem *f*, destemor *m*

dark [dɑːk] *adj* escuro; *(complexion)* moreno ♦ *n:* **in the ~** estar no escuro sobre; **to be in the ~ about** *(fig)* estar no escuro sobre; **after ~** depois de escurecer; **darken** *vt* escurecer; *(colour)* fazer mais escuro ♦ *vi* escurecer-se; **dark glasses** *npl* óculos *mpl* escuros; **darkness** *n* escuridão *f*; **darkroom** *n* câmara escura

darling ['dɑːlɪŋ] *adj, n* querido(-a)

darn [dɑːn] *vt* cerzir

dart [dɑːt] *n* dardo; *(in sewing)* alinhavo ♦ *vi* precipitar-se, correr para; **to ~ away/along** ir-se/seguir precipitadamente; **darts** *n (game)* jogo de dardos

dash [dæʃ] n (sign) hífen m; (: long) travessão m; (quantity) pontinha ♦ vt arremessar; (hopes) frustrar ♦ vi correr para, ir depressa; **dash away** vi sair apressado; **dash off** = **dash away**

dashboard ['dæʃbɔːd] n painel m de instrumentos

data ['deɪtə] npl dados mpl; **database** n banco de dados; **data processing** n processamento de dados

date [deɪt] n data; (with friend) encontro; (fruit) tâmara ♦ vt datar; (person) namorar ♦ to ~ até agora; **out of** ~ fora de moda; (expired) desatualizado; **up to** ~ moderno; **dated** ['deɪtɪd] adj antiquado; **date rape** n estupro cometido pelo acompanhante da vítima, geralmente após encontro romântico

daub [dɔːb] vt borrar

daughter ['dɔːtə*] n filha; **daughter-in-law** (pl ~s-in-law) n nora

daunting ['dɔːntɪŋ] adj desanimador(a)

dawdle ['dɔːdl] vi (go slow) vadiar

dawn [dɔːn] n alvorada, amanhecer m; (of period, situation) surgimento, início ♦ vi (day) amanhecer; (fig): it ~ed on him that ... começou a perceber que ...

day [deɪ] n dia m; (working ~) jornada, dia útil; (heyday) apogeu m; **the** ~ **before** a véspera; **the** ~ **before yesterday** anteontem; **the** ~ **after tomorrow** depois de amanhã; **by** ~ de dia; **daybreak** n amanhecer m; **daydream** vi devanear; **daylight** n luz f (do dia); **day return** (BRIT) n bilhete m de ida e volta no mesmo dia; **daytime** n dia m; **day-to-day** adj cotidiano

daze [deɪz] vt (stun) aturdir ♦ n: **in a**

~ aturdido

dazzle ['dæzl] vt (bewitch) deslumbrar; (blind) ofuscar

DC abbr (ELEC) = **direct current**

dead [dɛd] adj morto; (numb) dormente; (telephone) cortado; (ELEC) sem corrente ♦ adv completamente; (exactly) absolutamente ♦ npl: **the** ~ os mortos; **to shoot sb** ~ matar alguém a tiro; **to stop** ~ estacar; **to** ~ **tired** morto de cansado; **deaden** vt (blow, sound) amortecer; (pain) anestesiar; **dead end** n beco sem saída; **deadline** n prazo final; **deadlock** n impasse m; **dead loss** (inf) n: **to be a dead loss** não ser de nada; **deadly** adj mortal, fatal; (accuracy, insult) devastador(a); (weapon) mortífero; **deadpan** adj sem expressão

deaf [dɛf] adj surdo; **deafen** vt ensurdecer; **deafness** n surdez f

deal [diːl] (pt, pp **dealt**) n (agreement) acordo ♦ vt (cards, blows) dar; **a good** or **great** ~ (of) bastante, muito; **deal in** vt fus (COMM) negociar em or com; **deal with** vt fus (people) tratar com; (problem) ocupar-se de; (subject) tratar de; **dealer** n negociante m/f; **dealings** npl transações fpl

dean [diːn] n (REL) decano; (SCH: BRIT) reitor(a) m/f; (: US) orientador(a) m/f de estudos

dear [dɪə*] adj querido, caro; (expensive) caro ♦ n: **my** ~ meu querido (minha querida) ♦ excl: ~ **me!** ai, meu Deus!; **D~ Sir/Madam** (in letter) Ilmo. Senhor (Exma. Senhora) (BR), Exmo. Senhor (Exma. Senhora) (PT); **D~ Mr/Mrs X** Caro Sr. X/Cara Sra. X; **dearly** adv (love) ternamente; (pay) caro

death [dɛθ] n morte f; (ADMIN) óbito; **death certificate** n certidão f de óbito; **deathly** adj (colour) pálido; (silence) profundo; **death penalty** n pena de morte

debatable [dɪ'beɪtəbl] adj discutível

debate [dɪ'beɪt] n debate m ♦ vt debater

debit ['debɪt] n débito ♦ vt: **to ~ a sum to sb** or **to sb's account** lançar uma quantia ao débito de alguém or à conta de alguém

debt [det] n dívida; (state) endividamento; **to be in ~** ter dívidas, estar endividado; **debtor** n devedor(a) m/f

decade ['dekeɪd] n década

decaff ['diː'kæf] (inf) n descafeinado m

decaffeinated [dɪ'kæfɪneɪtd] adj descafeinado

decanter [dɪ'kæntə*] n garrafa ornamental

decay [dɪ'keɪ] n ruína; (also: **tooth ~**) cárie ♦ vi (rot) apodrecer-se

deceased [dɪ'siːst] n falecido(-a)

deceit [dɪ'siːt] n engano; (duplicity) fraude f; **deceitful** adj enganador(a)

deceive [dɪ'siːv] vt enganar

December [dɪ'sembə*] n dezembro

decent ['diːsənt] adj (proper) decente; (kind, honest) honesto, amável

deception [dɪ'sepʃən] n engano; (deceitful act) fraude f; **deceptive** adj enganador(a)

decide [dɪ'saɪd] vt (person) convencer; (question) resolver ♦ vi decidir; **to ~ on sth** decidir-se por algo; **decided** adj (definite) claro, definido; **decidedly** adv claramente; (emphatically) decididamente

decimal ['desɪml] adj decimal ♦ n decimal m

decision [dɪ'sɪʒən] n (choice) escolha; (act of choosing) decisão f; (de-

cisiveness) resolução f

decisive [dɪ'saɪsɪv] adj (action) decisivo; (person) decidido

deck [dek] n (NAUT) convés m; (of bus): **top ~** andar m de cima; (of cards) baralho; **record ~** toca-discos m inv; **deckchair** n cadeira de lona, espreguiçadeira

declare [dɪ'kleə*] vt (intention) revelar; (result) divulgar; (income, at customs) declarar

decline [dɪ'klaɪn] n declínio; (lessening) diminuição f, baixa ♦ vt recusar ♦ vi diminuir

decorate ['dekəreɪt] vt (adorn) adornar; (paint) pintar; (paper) decorar com papel; **decoration** [dekə'reɪʃən] n enfeite m; (act) decoração f; (medal) condecoração f; **decorator** n (painter) pintor(a) m/f

decoy ['diːkɔɪ] n (person) armadilha; (object) engodo, chamariz m

decrease [n 'diːkriːs, vb diː'kriːs] n: **~ (in)** diminuição f (de) ♦ vt reduzir ♦ vi diminuir

decree [dɪ'kriː] n decreto

dedicate ['dedɪkeɪt] vt dedicar; **dedication** [dedɪ'keɪʃən] n dedicação f; (in book) dedicatória; (on radio) mensagem f

deduce [dɪ'djuːs] vt deduzir

deduct [dɪ'dʌkt] vt deduzir; **deduction** n (deducting) redução f; (amount) subtração f; (deducing) dedução f

deed [diːd] n feito, ato; (LAW) escritura, título

deep [diːp] adj profundo; (voice) baixo, grave; (breath) fundo; (colour) forte, carregado ♦ adv: **the spectators stood 20 ~** os espectadores formaram-se em 20 fileiras; **to be 4 metres ~** ter 4 metros de profundidade; **deepen** vt aprofundar

♦ vi aumentar; **deepfreeze** n congelador m, freezer m (BR); **deep-fry** vt fritar em recipiente fundo; **deeply** adv fundo; (moved) profundamente; **deep-seated** adj arraigado

deer [dɪə*] n inv veado, cervo

deface [dɪ'feɪs] vt desfigurar

default [dɪ'fɔːlt] n (COMPUT: also: ~ value) valor m de default; **by ~** (win) por desistência

defeat [dɪ'fiːt] n derrota; (failure) malogro ♦ vt derrotar, vencer

defect [n 'diːfɛkt, vb dɪ'fɛkt] n defeito ♦ vi: **to ~ to the enemy** desertar para se juntar ao inimigo; **defective** [dɪ'fɛktɪv] adj defeituoso

defence [dɪ'fɛns] (US **defense**) n defesa, justificação f; **defenceless** adj indefeso

defend [dɪ'fɛnd] vt defender; (LAW) contestar; **defendant** n acusado(-a); (in civil case) réu (ré) m/f; **defender** n defensor(a) m/f; (SPORT) defesa

defer [dɪ'fɔː*] vt (postpone) adiar

defiance [dɪ'faɪəns] n desafio, rebeldia; **in ~ of** a despeito de

defiant [dɪ'faɪənt] adj desafiador(a)

deficiency [dɪ'fɪʃənsɪ] n (lack) deficiência, falta; (defect) defeito

deficit ['dɛfɪsɪt] n déficit m

define [dɪ'faɪn] vt definir

definite ['dɛfɪnɪt] adj (fixed) definitivo; (clear, obvious) claro, categórico; (certain) certo; **he was ~ about it** ele foi categórico; **definitely** adv sem dúvida

deflate [diː'fleɪt] vt esvaziar

deflect [dɪ'flɛkt] vt desviar

defraud [dɪ'frɔːd] vt: **to ~ sb (of sth)** trapacear alguém (por causa de algo)

defrost [diː'frɔst] vt descongelar

defuse [diː'fjuːz] vt tirar o estopim

or a espoleta de; (situation) neutralizar

defy [dɪ'faɪ] vt desafiar; (resist) opor-se a

degenerate [vb dɪ'dʒɛnəreɪt, adj dɪ'dʒɛnərɪt] vi degenerar ♦ adj degenerado

degree [dɪ'griː] n grau m; (SCH) diploma m, título; **in maths** formatura em matemática; **by ~s** (gradually) pouco a pouco; **to some ~, to a certain ~** até certo ponto

dehydrated [diːhaɪ'dreɪtɪd] adj desidratado; (eggs, milk) em pó

de-ice vt (windscreen) descongelar

deign [deɪn] vi: **to ~ to do** dignar-se a fazer

dejected [dɪ'dʒɛktɪd] adj deprimido

delay [dɪ'leɪ] vt (postpone) retardar, atrasar; (train) atrasar ♦ vi hesitar ♦ n demora; (postponement) adiamento; **to be ~ed** estar atrasado; **without ~** sem demora or atraso

delegate [n 'dɛlɪgɪt, vb 'dɛlɪgeɪt] n delegado(-a) ♦ vt (person) autorizar; (task) delegar

delete [dɪ'liːt] vt eliminar, riscar; (COMPUT) deletar

deliberate [adj dɪ'lɪbərɪt, vb dɪ'lɪbəreɪt] adj (intentional) intencional; (slow) pausado, lento ♦ vi considerar; **deliberately** [dɪ'lɪbərɪtlɪ] adv (on purpose) de propósito

delicacy ['dɛlɪkəsɪ] n delicadeza; (of problem) dificuldade f; (food) iguaria

delicate ['dɛlɪkɪt] adj delicado; (health) frágil

delicatessen [dɛlɪkə'tɛsn] n delicatessen m

delicious [dɪ'lɪʃəs] adj delicioso; (food) saboroso

delight [dɪ'laɪt] n prazer m, deleite m; (person) encanto; (experience) delícia ♦ vt encantar, deleitar; **to**

take (a) ~ in deleitar-se com; **delighted** adj: **delighted** (at or with) encantado (com); **delightful** adj encantado/a, delicioso

delinquent [dɪ'lɪŋkwənt] adj, n delinquente m/f

delirious [dɪ'lɪrɪəs] adj delirante; **to be ~** delirar

deliver [dɪ'lɪvə*] vt (distribute) distribuir; (hand over) entregar; (message) comunicar; (speech) proferir; (MED) partejar; **delivery** n distribuição f; (of speaker) enunciação f; (MED) parto; **to take delivery of** receber

delude [dɪ'lu:d] vt iludir, enganar

delusion [dɪ'lu:ʒən] n ilusão f

demand [dɪ'ma:nd] vt exigir; (rights) reivindicar, reclamar ♦ n exigência; (claim) reivindicação f; (ECON) procura; **to be in ~** estar em demanda; **on ~** à vista; **demanding** adj (boss) exigente; (work) absorvente

demeanour [dɪ'mi:nə*] (US **demeanor**) n conduta, comportamento

demented [dɪ'mentɪd] adj demente, doido

demise [dɪ'maɪz] n falecimento

demo ['deməu] (inf) n abbr (= demonstration) passeata

democracy [dɪ'mɔkrəsɪ] n democracia; **democrat** ['deməkræt] n democrata m/f; **democratic** [demə'krætɪk] adj democrático

demolish [dɪ'mɔlɪʃ] vt demolir, derrubar; (argument) refutar, contestar

demonstrate ['demənstreɪt] vt demonstrar ♦ vi: **to ~ (for/against)** manifestar-se (a favor de/contra); **demonstration** [demən'streɪʃən] n (POL) manifestação f; (: march) passeata; (proof) demonstração f; (exhibition) exibição f; **demonstra-**

tor n manifestante m/f

demote [dɪ'məut] vt rebaixar de posto

den [den] n (of animal) covil m; (of thieves) antro, esconderijo; (room) aposento privado, cantinho

denial [dɪ'naɪəl] n refutação f; (refusal) negativa

denim ['denɪm] n brim m, zuarte m; **~s** npl jeans m (BR), jeans mpl (PT)

Denmark ['denmɑ:k] n Dinamarca

denomination [dɪnɔmɪ'neɪʃən] n valor m, denominação f; (REL) confissão f, seita

denounce [dɪ'nauns] vt denunciar

dense [dens] adj denso, espesso; (inf: stupid) estúpido, bronco; **densely** adv: **densely populated** com grande densidade de população

density ['densɪtɪ] n densidade f; **single/double ~ disk** (COMPUT) disco de densidade simples/dupla

dent [dent] n amolgadura, depressão f ♦ vt amolgar, dentar

dental ['dentl] adj (treatment) dentário; (hygiene) dental

dentist ['dentɪst] n dentista m/f

dentures ['dentʃəz] npl dentadura

deny [dɪ'naɪ] vt negar; (refuse) recusar

deodorant [di:'əudərənt] n desodorante m (BR), desodorizante m (PT)

depart [dɪ'pɑ:t] vi ir-se, partir; (train etc) sair; **to ~ from** (fig: differ from) afastar-se de

department [dɪ'pɑ:tmənt] n (SCH) departamento; (COMM) seção f; (POL) repartição f; **department store** n magazine m (BR), grande armazém m (PT)

departure [dɪ'pɑ:tʃə*] n partida, ida; (of train etc) saída; (of employee) saída; **a new ~** uma nova orientação; **departure lounge** n sala de embarque

depend [dɪˈpɛnd] vi: **to ~ (up)on**
depender de; (rely on) contar com;
it ~s depende; **~ing on the result ...**
dependendo do resultado ...;
dependable adj (person) de confiança, seguro; (car) confiável;
dependant n dependente m/f;
dependent adj: **to be dependent
(on)** depender (de), ser dependente
(de) ♦ n = **dependant**

depict [dɪˈpɪkt] vt (in picture) retratar, representar; (describe) descrever

deport [dɪˈpɔːt] vt deportar

deposit [dɪˈpɔzɪt] n (COMM, GEO)
depósito; (CHEM) sedimento; (of ore,
oil) jazida; (down payment) sinal m
♦ vt depositar; (luggage) guardar;
deposit account n conta de
depósito a prazo

depot [ˈdɛpəʊ] n (storehouse) depósito, armazém m; (for vehicles) garagem f, parque m; (US) estação f

depress [dɪˈprɛs] vt deprimir;
(wages) reduzir; (press down) apertar; **depressed** adj deprimido;
(area) em depressão; **depressing**
adj deprimente; **depression** n
depressão f; (hollow) achatamento

deprivation [dɛprɪˈveɪʃən] n privação f

deprive [dɪˈpraɪv] vt: **to ~ sb of** privar alguém de; **deprived** adj carente

depth [dɛpθ] n profundidade f; (of
feeling) intensidade f; **in the ~s of
despair** no auge do desespero; **to
be out of one's ~** (BRIT: swimmer)
estar sem pé; (fig) estar voando

deputy [ˈdɛpjʊtɪ] adj: **~ chairman**
vice-presidente(-a) ♦ n (in assistant) adjunto(-a); (POL: MP) deputa-
do(-a); **~ head** (BRIT: SCH) diretor
adjunto (diretora adjunta) m/f

derail [dɪˈreɪl] vt: **to be ~ed**

descarrilhar

deranged [dɪˈreɪndʒd] adj (person)
louco, transtornado

derby [ˈdɑːbɪ] (US) n chapéu-coco

derelict [ˈdɛrɪlɪkt] adj abandonado

derive [dɪˈraɪv] vt: **to ~ (from)** obter
or tirar de ♦ vi: **to ~ from** derivar-
se de

derogatory [dɪˈrɔgətəri] adj depreciativo

descend [dɪˈsɛnd] vt, vi descer; **to ~
from** descer de; **to ~ to** descambar
em; **descent** n descida; (origin)
descendência

describe [dɪsˈkraɪb] vt descrever;
description [dɪsˈkrɪpʃən] n descrição f; (sort) classe f, espécie f

desert [n ˈdɛzət, vb dɪˈzɜːt] n deserto ♦ vt (place) desertar; (partner,
family) abandonar ♦ vi (MIL) desertar; **deserter** [dɪˈzɜːtə*] n desertor
m; **desert island** n ilha deserta;
deserts npl: **to get one's just
deserts** receber o que merece

deserve [dɪˈzɜːv] vt merecer;
deserving adj (person) merece-
dor(a), digno; (action, cause) meri-
tório

design [dɪˈzaɪn] n (sketch) desenho,
esboço; (layout, shape) plano, projeto; (pattern) desenho, padrão m;
(art) design m; (intention) propósito,
intenção f ♦ vt (plan) projetar

designer [dɪˈzaɪnə*] n (ART) artista
m/f gráfico(-a); (TECH) desenhista
m/f, projetista m/f; (fashion ~) estilista m/f

desire [dɪˈzaɪə*] n anseio; (sexual)
desejo ♦ vt querer, desejar, cobiçar

desk [dɛsk] n (in office) mesa, secretária; (for pupil) carteira f; (at airport) balcão m; (in hotel) recepção
f; (BRIT: shop, restaurant) caixa;
desktop publishing n editoração
f eletrônica

desolate ['dɛsəlɪt] adj (place) deserto; (person) desolado

despair [dɪs'pɛə*] n desesperança ♦ vi: **to ~ of** desesperar-se de

despatch [dɪs'pætʃ] n, vt = **dispatch**

desperate ['dɛsprɪt] adj desesperado; (situation) desesperador(a); (fugitive) violento; **to be ~ for sth/to do** estar louco por algo/para fazer; **desperately** adv desesperadamente; (very: unhappy) terrivelmente; (: ill) gravemente; **desperation** [dɛspə'reɪʃən] n desespero, desesperança; **in (sheer) desperation** desesperado

despise [dɪs'paɪz] vt desprezar

despite [dɪs'paɪt] prep apesar de, a despeito de

despondent [dɪs'pɔndənt] adj abatido, desanimado

dessert [dɪ'zə:t] n sobremesa

destination [dɛstɪ'neɪʃən] n destino

destined ['dɛstɪnd] adj: **to be ~ to do sth** estar destinado a fazer algo; **~ for** com destino a

destiny ['dɛstɪnɪ] n destino

destitute ['dɛstɪtjuːt] adj indigente, necessitado

destroy [dɪs'trɔɪ] vt destruir; (animal) sacrificar; **destruction** n destruição f

detach [dɪ'tætʃ] vt separar; (unstick) desprender; **detached** adj (attitude) imparcial, objetivo; (house) independente, isolado

detail [dɪ'teɪl] n detalhe m; (trifle) bobagem f ♦ vt detalhar; **in ~** pormenorizado, em detalhe

detain [dɪ'teɪn] vt deter; (in captivity) prender; (in hospital) hospitalizar

detect [dɪ'tɛkt] vt perceber; (MED, POLICE) identificar; (MIL, RADAR, TECH)

detectar; **detection** n descoberta;

detective n detetive m/f; **detective story** n romance m policial

detention [dɪ'tɛnʃən] n detenção f, prisão f; (SCH) castigo

deter [dɪ'tə:*] vt (discourage) desanimar; (dissuade) dissuadir

detergent [dɪ'tə:dʒənt] n detergente m

deteriorate [dɪ'tɪərɪəreɪt] vi deteriorar-se

determine [dɪ'tə:mɪn] vt descobrir; (limits) demarcar; **determined** adj (person) resoluto; **determined to do** decidido a fazer

detour ['di:tuə*] n desvio

detract [dɪ'trækt] vi: **to ~ from** diminuir

detrimental [dɛtrɪ'mɛntl] adj: **~ (to)** prejudicial (a)

devastate ['dɛvəsteɪt] vt devastar; (fig): **to be ~d by** estar arrasado com

develop [dɪ'vɛləp] vt desenvolver; (PHOT) revelar; (disease) contrair; (resources) explotar ♦ vi (advance) progredir; (evolve) evoluir; (appear) aparecer; **developer** [dɪ'vɛləpə*] n empresário(-a) de imóveis; **developing country** país m em desenvolvimento; **development** [dɪ'vɛləpmənt] n desenvolvimento; (advance) progresso; (of land) urbanização f

device [dɪ'vaɪs] n aparelho, dispositivo

devil ['dɛvl] n diabo

devious ['di:vɪəs] adj (person) malandro, esperto

devise [dɪ'vaɪz] vt (plan) criar; (machine) inventar

devoid [dɪ'vɔɪd] adj: **~ of** destituído de

devote [dɪ'vəut] vt: **to ~ sth to** dedicar algo a; **devoted** [dɪ'vəutɪd] adj (friendship) leal; (partner) fiel; **to be**

devoted to estar devotado a; **the book is devoted to politics** o livro trata de política; **devotee** [devəˈtiː] n adepto(-a), entusiasta m/f; (REL) devoto(-a); **devotion** n devoção f; (to duty) dedicação f

devour [dɪˈvaʊə*] vt devorar

devout [dɪˈvaʊt] adj devoto

dew [djuː] n orvalho

diabetes [daɪəˈbiːtiːz] n diabete f

diabolical [daɪəˈbɒlɪkl] (inf) adj (dreadful) horrível

diagnosis [daɪəgˈnəʊsɪs] (pl diagnoses) n diagnóstico

diagonal [daɪˈægənl] adj diagonal ♦ n diagonal f

diagram [ˈdaɪəgræm] n diagrama m, esquema m

dial [ˈdaɪəl] n disco ♦ vt (number) discar (BR), marcar (PT)

dialect [ˈdaɪəlɛkt] n dialeto

dialling code [ˈdaɪəlɪŋ-] (US **dial code**) n código de discagem

dialling tone [ˈdaɪəlɪŋ-] (US **dial tone**) n sinal de discagem (BR) or de marcar (PT)

dialogue [ˈdaɪəlɒg] (US **dialog**) n diálogo; (conversation) conversa

diameter [daɪˈæmɪtə*] n diâmetro

diamond [ˈdaɪəmənd] n diamante m; (shape) losango, rombo; **~s** npl (CARDS) ouros mpl

diaper [ˈdaɪəpə*] (US) n fralda

diaphragm [ˈdaɪəfræm] n diafragma m

diarrhoea [daɪəˈriːə] (US **diarrhea**) n diarréia

diary [ˈdaɪərɪ] n (daily account) diário; (engagements book) agenda

dice [daɪs] n inv dado ♦ vt (CULIN) cortar em cubos

dictate [dɪkˈteɪt] vt ditar; **dictation** n (of letter) ditado; (of orders) ordem f

dictator [dɪkˈteɪtə*] n ditador(a) m/f; **dictatorship** n ditadura

dictionary [ˈdɪkʃənrɪ] n dicionário

did [dɪd] pt of **do**

didn't [ˈdɪdnt] = **did not**

die [daɪ] vi morrer; (fig: fade) murchar; **to be dying for sth/to do sth** estar louco por algo/para fazer algo; **die away** vi (sound, light) extinguir-se lentamente; **die down** vi (fire) apagar-se; (wind) abrandar; (excitement) diminuir; **die out** vi desaparecer

diesel [ˈdiːzl] n diesel m; (also: ~ **oil**) óleo diesel

diet [ˈdaɪət] n dieta; (restricted food) regime m ♦ vi (also: **be on a** ~) estar de dieta, fazer regime

differ [ˈdɪfə*] vi (be different): **to** ~ **from sth** ser diferente de algo, diferenciar-se de algo; (disagree): **to** ~ **(about)** discordar (sobre); **difference** n diferença; (disagreement) divergência; **different** adj diferente; **differentiate** [dɪfəˈrenʃɪeɪt] vi: **to differentiate (between)** distinguir (entre)

difficult [ˈdɪfɪkəlt] adj difícil; **difficulty** n dificuldade f

dig [dɪg] (pt, pp **dug**) vt cavar ♦ n (prod) pontada; (archaeological) escavação f; (remark) alfinetada; **to** ~ **one's nails into sth** cravar as unhas em algo; **dig into** vt fus (savings) gastar; **dig up** vt (plant) arrancar; (information) trazer à tona

digest [vb daɪˈdʒɛst, n ˈdaɪdʒɛst] vt (food) digerir; (facts) assimilar ♦ n sumário; **digestion** n (dɪˈdʒɛstʃən) n digestão f

digit [ˈdɪdʒɪt] n (MATH) dígito; (finger) dedo; **digital** adj digital; **digital camera** n câmara digital; **digital TV** n televisão f digital

dignified [ˈdɪgnɪfaɪd] adj digno

dignity [ˈdɪgnɪtɪ] n dignidade f

digress [daɪˈgres] vi: **to** ~ **from**

afastar-se de

digs [dɪgz] (BRIT: inf) npl pensão f, alojamento

dilapidated [dɪ'læpɪdeɪtɪd] adj arruinado

dilemma [daɪ'lemə] n dilema m

diligent ['dɪlɪdʒənt] adj (worker) diligente; (research) cuidadoso

dilute [daɪ'luːt] vt diluir

dim [dɪm] adj fraco; (outline) indistinto; (room) escuro; (inf: person) burro ♦ vt diminuir; (US: AUT) baixar

dime [daɪm] (US) n dez centavos

dimension [dɪ'menʃən] n dimensão f; (measurement) medida; (also: ~s: scale, size) tamanho

diminish [dɪ'mɪnɪʃ] vi diminuir

diminutive [dɪ'mɪnjutɪv] adj diminuto ♦ n (LING) diminutivo

dimple ['dɪmpl] n covinha

din [dɪn] n zoeira

dine [daɪn] vi jantar; **diner** n comensal m/f; (US: eating place) lanchonete f

dinghy ['dɪŋgɪ] n dingue m; (also: rubber ~) bote m; (: also: sailing ~) bote de borracha

dingy ['dɪndʒɪ] adj (room) sombrio, lúgubre; (clothes, curtains etc) sujo

dining car ['daɪnɪŋ-] (BRIT) n (RAIL) vagão-restaurante m

dining room ['daɪnɪŋ-] n sala de jantar

dinner ['dɪnə*] n (evening meal) jantar m; (lunch) almoço; (banquet) banquete m; **dinner jacket** n smoking m; **dinner party** n jantar m; **dinner time** n (midday) hora do almoçar; (evening) hora de jantar

dip [dɪp] n (slope) inclinação f; (in sea) mergulho; (CULIN) pasta para servir com salgadinhos ♦ vt (in water) mergulhar; (ladle) meter; (BRIT: AUT: lights) baixar ♦ vi descer subitamente

diploma [dɪ'pləumə] n diploma m

diplomat ['dɪpləmæt] n diplomata m/f

dipstick ['dɪpstɪk] n (AUT) vareta medidora

dire [daɪə*] adj terrível

direct [daɪ'rekt] adj direto; (route) reto; (manner) franco, sincero ♦ vt dirigir; (order): **to ~ sb to do sth** ordenar alguém para fazer algo ♦ adv direto; **can you ~ me to ...?** pode me indicar o caminho a ...?; **direction** n (way) indicação f; (TV, RADIO, CINEMA) direção f; **directions** (instructions) instruções fpl; **directions for use** modo de usar; **directly** adv diretamente; (at once) imediatamente; **director** n diretor(a) m/f

directory [dɪ'rektərɪ] n (TEL) lista (telefônica); (also: COMM) anuário comercial; (COMPUT) diretório; **directory enquiries** (US **directory assistance**) n informações fpl

dirt [dəːt] n sujeira (BR), sujidade (PT); **dirty** adj sujo; (joke) indecente ♦ vt sujar; **dirty trick** n golpe m baixo, sujeira

disability [dɪsə'bɪlɪtɪ] n incapacidade f

disabled [dɪs'eɪbld] adj deficiente ♦ npl: **the ~** os deficientes

disadvantage [dɪsəd'vɑːntɪdʒ] n desvantagem f; (prejudice) inconveniente m

disagree [dɪsə'griː] vi (differ) diferir; (be against, think otherwise): **to ~ (with)** não concordar (com), discordar (de); **disagreeable** adj desagradável; **disagreement** n desacordo; (quarrel) desavença

disallow ['dɪsə'lau] vt (LAW) vetar, proibir

disappear [dɪsə'pɪə*] vi desaparecer, sumir; (custom etc) acabar; **disappearance** n desaparecimento, desaparição f

disappoint [dɪsə'pɔɪnt] *vt* decepcionar; **disappointed** *adj* desiludido; **disappointment** *n* decepção f; (*cause*) desapontamento

disapproval [dɪsə'pru:vəl] *n* desaprovação f

disapprove [dɪsə'pru:v] *vi*: to ~ of desaprovar

disarmament [dɪs'ɑ:məmənt] *n* desarmamento

disaster [dɪ'zɑ:stə*] *n* (*accident*) desastre *m*; (*natural*) catástrofe f

disbelief [dɪsbə'li:f] *n* incredulidade f

disc [dɪsk] *n* disco; (*COMPUT*) = **disk**

discard [dɪs'kɑ:d] *vt* (*old things*) desfazer-se de; (*fig*) descartar

discern [dɪ'sə:n] *vt* perceber; (*identify*) identificar; **discerning** *adj* perspicaz

discharge [*vb* dɪs'tʃɑ:dʒ, *n* 'dɪstʃɑ:dʒ] *vt* (*duties*) cumprir, desempenhar; (*patient*) dar alta; (*employee*) despedir; (*soldier*) dar baixa em, dispensar; (*defendant*) pôr em liberdade; (*waste etc*) descarregar, despejar ♦ *n* (*ELEC, CHEM*) descarga; (*dismissal*) despedida; (*of duty*) desempenho; (*of debt*) quitação f; (*from hospital*) alta; (*from army*) baixa; (*LAW*) absolvição f; (*MED*) secreção f

discipline ['dɪsɪplɪn] *n* disciplina ♦ *vt* disciplinar; (*punish*) punir

disc jockey *n* (*on radio*) radialista *m/f*; (*in disco*) discotecário(-a)

disclose [dɪs'kləʊz] *vt* revelar; **disclosure** *n* revelação f

disco ['dɪskəʊ] *n abbr* discoteca

discomfort [dɪs'kʌmfət] *n* (*unease*) inquietação f; (*physical*) desconforto *m*

disconcert [dɪskən'sə:t] *vt* desconcertar

disconnect [dɪskə'nɛkt] *vt* desligar;

(*pipe, tap*) desmembrar

discontent [dɪskən'tɛnt] *n* descontentamento; **discontented** *adj* descontente

discontinue [dɪskən'tɪnju:] *vt* interromper; (*payments*) suspender; "~d" (*COMM*) "fora de linha"

discount [*n* 'dɪskaunt, *vb* dɪs'kaunt] *n* desconto ♦ *vt* descontar; (*idea*) ignorar

discourage [dɪs'kʌrɪdʒ] *vt* (*dishearten*) desanimar; (*advise against*) to ~ sth/sb from doing desaconselhar algo/alguém a fazer

discover [dɪs'kʌvə*] *vt* descobrir; (*missing person*) encontrar; (*mistake*) achar; **discovery** *n* descoberta

discredit [dɪs'krɛdɪt] *vt* desacreditar; (*claim*) desmerecer

discreet [dɪ'skri:t] *adj* discreto; (*careful*) cauteloso

discrepancy [dɪ'skrɛpənsɪ] *n* diferença

discretion [dɪ'skrɛʃən] *n* discrição f; at the ~ of ao arbítrio de

discriminate [dɪ'skrɪmɪneɪt] *vi*: to ~ between fazer distinção entre; to ~ against discriminar contra; **discriminating** *adj* criterioso; **discrimination** [dɪskrɪmɪ'neɪʃən] *n* (*discernment*) discernimento; (*bias*) discriminação f

discuss [dɪ'skʌs] *vt* discutir; (*analyse*) analisar; **discussion** *n* discussão f; (*debate*) debate *m*

disdain [dɪs'deɪn] *n* desdém *m*

disease [dɪ'zi:z] *n* doença

disembark [dɪsɪm'bɑ:k] *vt*, *vi* desembarcar

disentangle [dɪsɪn'tæŋgl] *vt* desvencilhar; (*wool, wire*) desembaraçar

disfigure [dɪs'fɪgə*] *vt* (*person*) desfigurar; (*object*) estragar, enfear

disgrace [dɪs'greɪs] *n* ignomínia; (*shame*) desonra ♦ *vt* (*family*) enver-

gonhar; (*name, country*) desonrar;
disgraceful [dɪs'greɪful] *adj* vergonhoso;
(*behaviour*) escandaloso
disgruntled [dɪs'grʌntld] *adj* descontente
disguise [dɪs'gaɪz] *n* disfarce *m* ♦ *vt*:
to ~ (as) disfarçar (de); **in ~** disfarçado
disgust [dɪs'gʌst] *n* repugnância
♦ *vt* repugnar a, dar nojo em; **disgusting** *adj* repugnante; (*unacceptable*) inaceitável
dish [dɪʃ] *n* prato; (*serving ~*) travessa; **to do** *or* **wash the ~es** lavar os
pratos *or* a louça; **dish out** *vt* repartir; **dish up** *vt* servir; **dishcloth** *n*
pano de prato *or* de louça
dishearten [dɪs'hɑːtn] *vt* desanimar
dishevelled [dɪ'ʃevəld] (*US* disheveled) *adj* (*hair*) despenteado;
(*clothes*) desalinhado
dishonest [dɪs'ɔnɪst] *adj* (*person*)
desonesto; (*means*) fraudulento
dishonour [dɪs'ɔnə*] (*US* dishonor)
n desonra
dishtowel [dɪʃtauəl] (*US*) *n* pano de
prato
dishwasher [dɪʃwɔʃə*] *n* máquina
de lavar louça *or* pratos
disillusion [dɪsɪ'luːʒən] *vt* desiludir
disinfectant [dɪsɪn'fektənt] *n*
desinfetante *m*
disintegrate [dɪs'ɪntɪgreɪt] *vi*
desintegrar-se
disjointed [dɪs'dʒɔɪntɪd] *adj* desconexo
disk [dɪsk] *n* (*COMPUT*) disco; **single-/
double-sided ~** disquete de face
simples/dupla; **disk drive** *n* unidade *f* de disco; **diskette** [dɪs'ket] (*US*)
n = **disk**
dislike [dɪs'laɪk] *n* (*feeling*) desagrado; (*gen pl*: *object of ~*) antipatia,
aversão *f* ♦ *vt* antipatizar com, não

gostar de
dislocate [dɪsləkeɪt] *vt* deslocar
dislodge [dɪs'lɔdʒ] *vt* mover, deslocar
disloyal [dɪs'lɔɪəl] *adj* desleal
dismal [dɪzml] *adj* (*depressing*)
deprimente; (*very bad*) horrível
dismantle [dɪs'mæntl] *vt* desmontar, desmantelar
dismay [dɪs'meɪ] *n* consternação *f*
♦ *vt* consternar
dismiss [dɪs'mɪs] *vt* (*worker*) despedir; (*pupils*) dispensar; (*soldiers*) dar
baixa a; (*LAW, possibility*) rejeitar;
dismissal *n* demissão *f*
dismount [dɪs'maunt] *vi* (*from
horse*) desmontar; (*from bicycle*) descer
disobedient *adj* desobediente
disobey [dɪsə'beɪ] *vt* desobedecer a;
(*rules*) transgredir
disorder [dɪs'ɔːdə*] *n* desordem *f*;
(*rioting*) distúrbios *mpl*, tumulto;
(*MED*) distúrbio; **disorderly** *adj*
(*untidy*) desarrumado; (*meeting*) tumultuado; (*behaviour*) escandaloso
disown [dɪs'əun] *vt* repudiar;
(*child*) rejeitar
disparaging [dɪs'pærɪdʒɪŋ] *adj*
depreciativo
dispatch [dɪs'pætʃ] *vt* (*send: parcel
etc*) expedir; (: *messenger*) enviar ♦ *n*
(*sending*) remessa, urgência; (*PRESS*)
comunicado; (*MIL*) parte *f*
dispel [dɪs'pɛl] *vt* dissipar
dispense [dɪs'pɛns] *vt* (*medicine*)
preparar (e vender); **dispense
with** *vt fus* prescindir de; **dispenser** *n* (*device*) distribuidor *m* automático
disperse [dɪs'pəːs] *vt* espalhar;
(*crowd*) dispersar ♦ *vi* dispersar-se
displace [dɪs'pleɪs] *vt* (*shift*) deslocar
display [dɪs'pleɪ] *n* (*in shop*) mostra;

(exhibition) exposição f; *(COMPUT, TECH: information)* apresentação f visual; *(: device)* display m; *(of feeling)* manifestação f ♦ vt mostrar; *(ostentatiously)* ostentar

displease [dɪs'pliːz] vt *(offend)* ofender; *(annoy)* aborrecer; **displeased** adj: **displeased with** descontente com; *(disappointed)* aborrecido com; **displeasure** [dɪs'plɛʒə*] n desgosto

disposable [dɪs'pəuzəbl] adj descartável; *(income)* disponível

disposal [dɪs'pəuzl] n *(of rubbish)* destruição f; *(of property etc)* venda, traspasse m; **at sb's ~** à disposição de alguém

disposed [dɪs'pəuzd] adj: **to be ~ to do sth** estar disposto a fazer algo; **to be well ~ towards sb** estar predisposto a favor de alguém

dispose of [dɪs'pəuz-] vt fus *(unwanted goods)* desfazer-se de; *(problem, task)* lidar; **disposition** [dɪspə'zɪʃən] n disposição f; *(temperament)* índole f

disprove [dɪs'pruːv] vt refutar

dispute [dɪs'pjuːt] n *(domestic)* briga; *(also: industrial ~)* conflito, disputa ♦ vt *(fact, statement)* questionar; *(ownership)* contestar

disqualify [dɪs'kwɔlɪfaɪ] vt *(SPORT)* desclassificar; **to ~ sb for sth/from doing sth** desqualificar alguém para algo/de fazer algo

disregard [dɪsrɪ'gɑːd] vt ignorar

disreputable [dɪs'rɛpjutəbl] adj *(person)* de má fama; *(behaviour)* vergonhoso

disrupt [dɪs'rʌpt] vt *(plans)* desfazer; *(conversation)* perturbar, interromper

dissect [dɪ'sɛkt] vt dissecar

dissent [dɪ'sɛnt] n dissensão f

dissertation [dɪsə'teɪʃən] n *(also:*

SCH) dissertação f, tese f

dissolve [dɪ'zɔlv] vt dissolver ♦ vi dissolver-se; **to ~ in(to) tears** debulhar-se em lágrimas

distance ['dɪstns] n distância; **in the ~** ao longe

distant ['dɪstnt] adj distante; *(manner)* afastado, reservado

distaste [dɪs'teɪst] n repugnância; **distasteful** adj repugnante

distil [dɪs'tɪl] *(US* **distill)** vt destilar; **distillery** n destilaria

distinct [dɪs'tɪŋkt] adj distinto; *(clear)* claro; *(unmistakable)* nítido; **as ~ from** em oposição a; **distinction** n diferença; *(honour)* honra; *(in exam)* distinção f

distinguish [dɪs'tɪŋgwɪʃ] vt *(differentiate)* diferenciar; *(identify)* identificar; **to ~ o.s.** distinguir-se; **distinguished** adj *(eminent)* eminente; *(in appearance)* nítido; **distinguishing** adj *(feature)* distintivo

distort [dɪs'tɔːt] vt distorcer

distract [dɪs'trækt] vt distrair; *(attention)* desviar; **distracted** adj distraído; *(anxious)* aturdido; **distraction** n distração f; *(confusion)* aturdimento, perplexidade f; *(amusement)* divertimento

distraught [dɪs'trɔːt] adj desesperado

distress [dɪs'trɛs] n angústia ♦ vt afligir; **distressing** adj angustiante

distribute [dɪs'trɪbjuːt] vt distribuir; *(share out)* repartir, dividir; **distribution** [dɪstrɪ'bjuːʃən] n distribuição f; *(of profits)* repartição f; **distributor** n *(AUT)* distribuidor m; *(COMM)* distribuidor(a) m/f

district ['dɪstrɪkt] n *(of country)* região f; *(of town)* zona; *(ADMIN)* distrito; **district attorney** *(US)* n promotor público *(promotora pública)* m/f

distrust [dɪs'trʌst] n desconfiança
♦ vt desconfiar de

disturb [dɪs'tə:b] vt (disorganize)
perturbar; (upset) incomodar; (interrupt) atrapalhar; **disturbance** n
(upheaval) convulsão f; (political,
violent) distúrbio m; (of mind) transtorno; **disturbed** adj perturbado;
(childhood) infeliz; **to be emotionally disturbed** ter problemas emocionais; **disturbing** adj perturbador(a)

ditch [dɪtʃ] n fosso; (irrigation ~)
rego ♦ vt (inf: partner) abandonar;
(: car, plan etc) desfazer-se de

dither ['dɪðə*] vi vacilar

ditto ['dɪtəu] adv idem

dive [daɪv] n (from board) salto;
(underwater) mergulho ♦ vi mergulhar; **to** ~ **into** (bag, drawer) enfiar a
mão em; (shop, car) enfiar-se em;
diver n mergulhador m/f

diversion [daɪ'və:ʃən] n (BRIT: AUT)
desvio; (distraction) diversão f; (of
funds) desvio

divert [daɪ'və:t] vt desviar

divide [dɪ'vaɪd] vt (MATH) dividir;
(separate) separar; (share out) repartir ♦ vi dividir-se; (road) bifurcar-se;
divided highway (US) n pista dupla

dividend ['dɪvɪdɛnd] n (dividendo;
(fig): **to pay** ~**s** valer a pena

divine [dɪ'vaɪn] adj divino

diving ['daɪvɪŋ] n salto; (underwater)
mergulho; **diving board** n trampolim m

divinity [dɪ'vɪnɪtɪ] n divindade f;
(SCH) teologia

division [dɪ'vɪʒən] n divisão f; (sharing out) repartição f; (disagreement)
discórdia; (FOOTBALL) grupo

divorce [dɪ'vɔ:s] n divórcio ♦ vt
divorciar-se de; (dissociate) dissociar;
divorced adj divorciado; **divorcee** n divorciado(-a)

DIY n abbr = **do-it-yourself**

dizzy ['dɪzɪ] adj tonto

DJ n abbr = **disc jockey**

┌─── KEYWORD ───┐

do [du:] (pt did, pp done) vb aux
1 (in negative constructions): **I don't
understand** eu não compreendo
2 (to form questions): **don't you
know?** você não sabia?; **what ~ you
think?** o que você acha?
3 (for emphasis, in polite expressions)
she does seem rather late ela está
muito atrasada; ~ **sit down/help
yourself** sente-se/sirva-se; ~ **take
care!** tome cuidado!
4 (used to avoid repeating vb): **she
swims better than I** ~ ela nada melhor que eu; ~ **you agree? – yes, I ~/
no, I don't** você concorda? – sim,
concordo/não, não concordo; **she
lives in Glasgow – so ~ I** ela mora
em Glasgow – eu também; **who
broke it? – I did** quem quebrou
isso? – (fui) eu
5 (in question tags): **you like him,
don't you?** você gosta dele, não é?;
he laughed, didn't he? ele riu, não
foi?
♦ vt **1** (gen: carry out, perform etc)
fazer; **what are you ~ing tonight?** o
que você vai fazer hoje à noite?; **to**
~ **the washing-up/cooking** lavar a
louça/cozinhar; **to** ~ **one's teeth/
nails** escovar os dentes/fazer as
unhas; **to** ~ **one's hair** (comb)
pentear-se; (style) fazer um penteado; **we're** ~**ing Othello at school**
(studying) nós estamos estudando
Otelo na escola; (performing) nós
vamos encenar Otelo na escola
2 (AUT etc): **the car was** ~**ing 100** o
carro estava a 100 por hora; **we've
done 200 km already** nós já fizemos
200 km; **he can** ~ **100 in that car** ele
consegue dar 100 nesse carro

♦ vi 1 (act, behave) fazer; ~ as I ~ faça como eu faço

2 (get on, fare) ir; how ~ you ~? como você está indo?

3 (suit) servir; will it ~? serve?

4 (be sufficient) bastar; will £10 ~? £10 dá?; that'll ~ é suficiente; that'll ~! (in annoyance) basta!, chega!; to make ~ (with) contentar-se (com)

♦ n (inf: party etc) festa; it was rather a ~ foi uma festança

do away with vt fus (kill) matar; (law etc) abolir; (withdraw) retirar

do up vt (laces) atar; (zip) fechar; (dress, skirt) abotoar; (renovate: room, house) arrumar, renovar

do with vt fus (need): I could ~ with a drink/some help eu bem que gostaria de tomar alguma coisa/eu bem que precisaria de uma ajuda; (be connected) ter a ver com; what has it got to ~ with you? o que é que isso tem a ver com você?

do without vi: if you're late for tea then you'll ~ without se você chegar atrasado ficará sem almoço

♦ vt fus passar sem

dock [dɔk] n (NAUT) doca; (LAW) banco (dos réus) ♦ vi (NAUT: enter ~) entrar no estaleiro; (SPACE) unir-se no espaço; ~s npl docas fpl; **docker** n portuário, estivador m; **dockyard** n estaleiro

doctor ['dɔktə*] n médico(-a); (PhD etc) doutor(a) m/f ♦ vt (drink etc) falsificar

document ['dɔkjumənt] n documento; **documentary** [dɔkju'mentəri] adj documental ♦ n documentário

dodge [dɔdʒ] n (trick) trapaça ♦ vt esquivar-se de, evitar; (tax) sonegar; (blow) furtar-se a

Dodgems ['dɔdʒəmz] ® (BRIT) npl

carros mpl de choque

does [dʌz] vb see do; **doesn't** = does not

dog [dɔg] n (zool) cachorro, cão m ♦ vt (subj: person) seguir; (: bad luck) perseguir; **dog-eared** adj surrado

dogged ['dɔgɪd] adj tenaz, persistente

dogsbody ['dɔgzbɔdi] (BRIT: inf) n faz-tudo m/f

doings ['duɪŋz] npl atividades fpl

do-it-yourself n sistema m faça-você-mesmo

dole [dəul] (BRIT) n (payment) subsídio de desemprego; **on the ~** desempregado; **dole out** vt distribuir

doll [dɔl] n boneca; (US: inf: woman) mulher f jovem e bonita

dollar ['dɔlə*] n dólar m

dolphin ['dɔlfɪn] n golfinho

dome [dəum] n (ARCH) cúpula

domestic [də'mestɪk] adj doméstico; (national) nacional; **domesticated** adj domesticado; (home-loving) prendado

dominate ['dɔmɪneɪt] vt dominar

domineering [dɔmɪ'nɪərɪŋ] adj dominante, mandão(-dona)

domino ['dɔmɪnəu] (pl ~es) n peça de dominó; ~s n (game) dominó m

donate [də'neɪt] vt: to ~ (to) doar (para)

done [dʌn] pp of do

donkey ['dɔŋkɪ] n burro

donor ['dəunə*] n doador(a) m/f; **donor card** n cartão m de doador

don't [dəunt] = do not

doodle ['du:dl] vi rabiscar

doom [du:m] n (fate) destino ♦ vt: to be ~ed to failure estar destinado or fadado ao fracasso

door [dɔ:*] n porta; **doorbell** n campainha; **doorman** (irreg) n porteiro; **doormat** n capacho; **door-**

step n degrau m da porta, soleira;
doorway n vão m da porta, entrada
dope [dəup] n (inf: person) imbecil
m/f; (: drug) maconha ♦ vt (horse
etc) dopar
dormitory ['dɔ:mɪtrɪ] n dormitório;
(US) residência universitária
dormouse ['dɔ:maus] (pl dormice)
n rato de (campo)
dose [dəus] n dose f
dot [dɔt] n ponto; (speck) marca
pequena ♦ vt: **~ted with** salpicado
de; **on the ~** em ponto
dote [dəut]: **to ~ on** vt fus adorar,
idolatrar
dotted line ['dɔtɪd-] n linha ponti-
lhada
double ['dʌbl] adj duplo ♦ adv
(twice): **to cost ~ (sth)** custar o
dobro (de algo) ♦ n (person) du-
plo(-a) ♦ vt dobrar ♦ vi dobrar; **at the
~** (BRIT), **on the ~** em passo acelerado; **double bass** n contrabaixo;
double bed n cama de casal;
double-click vi (COMPUT) dar um
clique duplo; **doublecross** vt
(trick) enganar; (betray) atraiçoar;
doubledecker n ônibus m (BR) or
autocarro (PT) de dois andares;
double room n quarto de casal
doubt [daut] n dúvida ♦ vt duvidar;
(suspect) desconfiar de; **to ~ if** or
whether duvidar que; **doubtful** adj
duvidoso; **doubtless** adv sem dúvida
dough [dəu] n massa; **doughnut**
(US **donut**) n sonho (BR), bola de
Berlim (PT)
dove [dʌv] n pomba
dowdy ['daudɪ] adj (clothes) desalinhado; (person) deselegante, pouco
elegante
down [daun] n (feathers) penugem f
♦ adv (~wards) para baixo; (on the
ground) por terra ♦ prep (towards

lower level) embaixo de; (movement
along) ao longo de ♦ vt (drink)
tomar de um gole só; **~ with
X!** abaixo X!; **down-and-out** n
(tramp) vagabundo(-a); **down-at-
heel** adj descuidado, desmazelado;
(appearance) deselegante; **downcast** adj abatido; **downfall** n
queda, ruína; **downhearted** adj
desanimado; **downhill** adv: **to go
downhill** descer, ir morro abaixo;
(fig: business) degringolar

Downing Street ['daunɪŋ-] (BRIT)
n ver quadro

DOWNING STREET

Downing Street é a rua de
Westminster (Londres) onde estão
localizadas as residências oficiais
do Primeiro-ministro (número 10)
e do Ministro da Fazenda (número 11). O termo Downing Street
é freqüentemente utilizado para
designar o governo britânico.

---

down: download [daun'ləud] vt
(COMPUT) fazer o download de,
baixar; **downpour** n aguaceiro;
downright adj (lie) patente; (refusal) categórico; **downstairs** adv
(below): (lá) em baixo; (downwards)
para baixo; **downstream** adv água
or rio abaixo; **down-to-earth** adj
prático, realista; **downtown** adv
no centro da cidade; **down under**
adv na Austrália (or Nova Zelândia);
downward adj, adv para baixo;
downwards adv = **downward**
doz. abbr (= dozen) dz.
doze [dəuz] vi dormitar; **doze off** vi
cochilar
dozen ['dʌzn] n dúzia; **a ~ books**
uma dúzia de livros; **~s of** milhares
de
Dr abbr (= doctor) Dr(a) m/f

drab
81
drift

drab [dræb] *adj* sombrio

draft [drɑːft] *n* (*first copy*) rascunho; (*POL: of bill*) projeto de lei; (*bank* ~) saque *m*, letra; (*US: call-up*) recrutamento ♦ *vt* (*plan*) esboçar; (*speech, letter*) rascunhar; *see also* **draught**

drag [dræg] *vt* arrastar; (*river*) dragar ♦ *vi* arrastar-se ♦ *n* (*inf*) chatice *f* (*BR*), maçada (*PT*); (*women's clothing*): in ~ em travesti; **drag on** *vi* arrastar-se

dragon ['drægən] *n* dragão *m*

dragonfly ['drægənflaɪ] *n* libélula

drain [dreɪn] *n* bueiro; (*source of loss*) sorvedouro ♦ *vt* (*glass*) esvaziar; (*land, marshes*) drenar; (*vegetables*) coar ♦ *vi* (*water*) escorrer, escoar-se

drainage *n* (*act*) drenagem *f*; (*system*) esgoto; **drainpipe** *n* cano de esgoto

drama ['drɑːmə] *n* (*art*) teatro; (*play*) drama *m*; **dramatic** [drə-'mætɪk] *adj* dramático; (*theatrical*) teatral

drank [dræŋk] *pt of* **drink**

drape [dreɪp] *vt* ornar, cobrir; **drapes** (*US*) *npl* cortinas *fpl*

drastic ['dræstɪk] *adj* drástico

draught [drɑːft] (*US* **draft**) *n* (*of air*) corrente *f*; (*NAUT*) calado; (*beer*) chope *m*; **on** ~ (*beer*) de barril; **draughts** (*BRIT*) *n* (*jogo de*) damas *fpl*

draw [drɔː] (*pt* **drew**, *pp* **drawn**) *vt* desenhar; (*cart*) puxar; (*curtain*) fechar; (*gun*) sacar; (*attract*) atrair; (*money*) tirar; (: *from bank*) sacar ♦ *vi* empatar ♦ *n* empate *m*; (*lottery*) sorteio; **to** ~ **near** aproximar-se; **draw out** *vi* (*money*) sacar; **draw up** *vi* (*stop*) parar(-se) ♦ *vt* (*chair etc*) puxar; (*document*) redigir; **drawback** *n* inconveniente *m*, desvantagem *f*; **drawbridge** *n* ponte *f* leva-

diça; **drawer** *n* gaveta; **drawing** *n* desenho; **drawing pin** (*BRIT*) *n* tachinha (*BR*), pionés *m* (*PT*); **drawing room** *n* sala de visitas

drawl [drɔːl] *n* fala arrastada

drawn [drɔːn] *pp of* **draw**

dread [drɛd] *n* medo, pavor *m* ♦ *vt* temer, recear, ter medo de; **dreadful** *adj* terrível

dream [driːm] *n* (*pt, pp* ~**ed** *or* ~**t**) *n* sonho ♦ *vt, vi* sonhar; **dreamy** *adj* sonhador(a), distraído; (*music*) sentimental

dreary ['drɪərɪ] *adj* (*talk, time*) monótono; (*weather*) sombrio

dregs [drɛgz] *npl* lia; (*of humanity*) escória, ralé *f*

drench [drɛntʃ] *vt* encharcar

dress [drɛs] *n* vestido; *no pl*: (*clothing*) traje *m* ♦ *vt* vestir; (*wound*) fazer curativo em ♦ *vi* vestir-se; **to get** ~**ed** vestir-se; **dress up** *vi* vestir-se com elegância; (*in fancy dress*) fantasiar-se; **dress circle** (*BRIT*) *n* balcão *m* nobre; **dresser** *n* (*BRIT: cupboard*) aparador *m*; (*US: chest of drawers*) cômoda de espelho; **dressing** *n* (*MED*) curativo; (*CULIN*) molho; **dressing gown** (*BRIT*) *n* roupão *m*; (*woman's*) peignoir *m*; **dressing room** *n* (*THEATRE*) camarim *m*; (*SPORT*) vestiário; **dressing table** *n* penteadeira (*BR*), toucador *m* (*PT*); **dressmaker** *n* costureiro(-a); **dress rehearsal** *n* ensaio geral

drew [druː] *pt of* **draw**

dribble ['drɪbl] *vi* (*baby*) babar ♦ *vt* (*ball*) driblar

dried [draɪd] *adj* (*fruit, beans*) seco; (*eggs, milk*) em pó

drier ['draɪə*] *n* = **dryer**

drift [drɪft] *n* (*of current etc*) força; (*of snow*) monte *m*; (*meaning*) sentido ♦ *vi* (*boat*) derivar; (*sand, snow*) amontoar-se

drill [drɪl] n furadeira; (of dentist) broca; (for mining etc) broca, furadeira; (MIL) exercícios mpl militares ♦ vt furar, brocar; (MIL) exercitar ♦ vi (for oil) perfurar

drink [drɪŋk] (pt **drank**, pp **drunk**) n bebida; (sip) gole m ♦ vt, vi beber; a ~ **of water** um copo d'água; **drinker** n bebedor(a) m/f; **drinking water** n água potável

drip [drɪp] n gotejar m; (one ~) gota, pingo; (MED) gota a gota m ♦ vi gotejar; (tap) pingar; **drip-dry** adj de lavar e vestir; **dripping** n gordura

drive [draɪv] (pt **drove**, pp **driven**) n passeio (de automóvel); (journey) trajeto, percurso; (also: ~**way**) entrada; (energy) energia, vigor m; (campaign) campanha; (COMPUT: also: **disk** ~) unidade f de disco ♦ vt (car) dirigir (BR), guiar (PT); (push) empurrar; (TECH: motor) acionar; (nail etc) cravar ♦ vi (AUT: at controls) dirigir (BR), guiar (PT); (: travel) ir de carro; **left-/right-hand** ~ carro à esquerda/direita; **to** ~ **sb mad** deixar alguém louco

drivel ['drɪvl] (inf) n bobagem f, besteira

driver ['draɪvə*] n motorista m/f; (RAIL) maquinista m; **driver's license** (US) n carteira de motorista (BR), carta de condução (PT)

driveway ['draɪvweɪ] n entrada

driving ['draɪvɪŋ] n direção f (BR), condução f (PT); **driving instructor** n instrutor(a) m/f de auto-escola (BR) ou de condução (PT); **driving licence** (BRIT) n carteira de motorista (BR), carta de condução (PT); **driving school** n auto-escola f; **driving test** n exame m de motorista

drizzle ['drɪzl] n chuvisco

drool [dru:l] vi babar-se

droop [dru:p] vi pender

drop [drɔp] n (of water) gota; (lessening) diminuição f; (fall: distance) declive m ♦ vt (allow to fall) deixar cair; (voice, eyes, price) baixar; (set down from car) deixar (saltar/descer); (omit) omitir ♦ vi cair; (wind) parar; ~**s** npl (MED) gotas fpl; **drop off** vi (sleep) cochilar ♦ vt (passenger) deixar (saltar/descer); **drop out** vi (withdraw) retirar-se; **dropout** n pessoa que abandona o trabalho, os estudos etc

drought [draut] n seca

drove [drəuv] pt of **drive**

drown [draun] vt afogar; (also: ~ **out**: sound) encobrir ♦ vi afogar-se

drowsy ['drauzɪ] adj sonolento

drug [drʌg] n remédio, medicamento; (narcotic) droga ♦ vt drogar; **to be on** ~**s** estar viciado em drogas; (MED) estar sob medicação; **drug addict** n toxicômano(-a); **druggist** (US) n farmacêutico(-a); **drugstore** (US) n drogaria

drum [drʌm] n tambor m; (for oil, petrol) tambor, barril m; ~**s** npl (kit) bateria; **drummer** n baterista m/f

drunk [drʌŋk] pp of **drink** ♦ adj bêbado ♦ n (also: ~**ard**) bêbado(-a); **drunken** adj (laughter) de bêbado; (party) cheio de bêbado; (person) bêbado

dry [draɪ] adj seco; (day) sem chuva; (humour) irônico ♦ vt secar, enxugar; (tears) limpar ♦ vi secar; **dry up** vi secar completamente; **dry-cleaner's** n tinturaria; **dryer** n secador m; (US: spin-dryer) secadora

DSS (BRIT) n abbr (= Department of Social Security) = INAMPS m

DTP n abbr (= desktop publishing) DTP m, editoração f eletrônica

dual

83

dyslexia

dual ['djuəl] *adj* dual, duplo; **dual carriageway** (BRIT) *n* pista dupla; **dual-purpose** *adj* de duplo uso

dubbed [dʌbd] *adj* (CINEMA) dublado

dubious ['dju:bɪəs] *adj* duvidoso; (*reputation, company*) suspeitoso

duchess ['dʌtʃɪs] *n* duquesa

duck [dʌk] *n* pato ♦ *vi* abaixar-se repentinamente; **duckling** ['dʌklɪŋ] *n* patinho

due [dju:] *adj* (*proper*) devido; (*expected*) esperado ♦ *n*: **to give sb his** (*or* **her**) ~ ser justo com alguém ♦ *adv*: ~ **north** exatamente ao norte; ~s *npl* (*for club, union*) quota; (*in harbour*) direitos *mpl*; **in ~ course** no devido tempo; (*eventually*) no final; ~ **to** devido a

duet [dju:'ɛt] *n* dueto

dug [dʌg] *pt, pp* de **dig**

duke [dju:k] *n* duque *m*

dull [dʌl] *adj* (*light*) sombrio; (*wit*) lento; (*boring*) enfadonho; (*sound, pain*) surdo; (*weather*) nublado, carregado ♦ *vt* (*pain*) aliviar; (*mind, senses*) entorpecer

duly ['dju:lɪ] *adv* devidamente; (*on time*) no devido tempo

dumb [dʌm] *adj* mudo; (*pej: stupid*) estúpido; **dumbfounded** *adj* pasmado

dummy ['dʌmɪ] *n* (*tailor's model*) manequim *m*; (*mock-up*) modelo; (BRIT: *for baby*) chupeta ♦ *adj* falso

dump [dʌmp] *n* (*also: rubbish ~*) depósito de lixo; (*inf: place*) chiqueiro ♦ *vt* (*put down*) depositar, descarregar; (*get rid of*) desfazer-se de; (COMPUT) tirar um dump de

dumpling ['dʌmplɪŋ] *n* bolinho cozido

dunce [dʌns] *n* burro, ignorante *m/f*

dung [dʌŋ] *n* estrume *m*

dungarees [dʌŋgə'ri:z] *npl* ma-

cacão *m* (BR), fato macaco (PT)

dungeon ['dʌndʒən] *n* calabouço

duplex ['dju:plɛks] (US) *n* casa geminada; (*also:* ~ **apartment**) duplex *m*

duplicate [*n* 'dju:plɪkət, *vb* 'dju:plɪkeɪt] *n* (*of document*) duplicata; (*of key*) cópia ♦ *vt* duplicar; (*photocopy*) multigrafar; (*repeat*) reproduzir

durable ['djuərəbl] *adj* durável; (*clothes, metal*) resistente

during ['djuərɪŋ] *prep* durante

dusk [dʌsk] *n* crepúsculo, anoitecer *m*

dust [dʌst] *n* pó *m*, poeira ♦ *vt* (*furniture*) tirar o pó de; (*cake etc*): **to ~ with** polvilhar com; **dustbin** *n* (BRIT) lata de lixo; **duster** *n* pano de pó; **dustman** (BRIT) (*irreg*) *n* lixeiro, gari *m* (BR: *inf*); **dusty** *adj* empoeirado

Dutch [dʌtʃ] *adj* holandês(-esa) ♦ *n* (LING) holandês *m* ♦ *adv*: **let's go** ~ (*inf*) cada um paga o seu, vamos rachar; **the** ~ *npl* (*people*) os holandeses; **Dutchman** (*irreg*) *n* holandês *m*; **Dutchwoman** (*irreg*) *n* holandesa

duty ['dju:tɪ] *n* dever *m*; (*tax*) taxa; **on** ~ de serviço; **off** ~ de folga; **duty-free** *adj* livre de impostos

duvet ['du:veɪ] (BRIT) *n* edredom *m* (BR), edredão *m* (PT)

DVD *n abbr* (= *digital versatile or video disc*) DVD *m*

dwarf [dwɔ:f] (*pl* **dwarves**) *n* anão (anã) *m/f* ♦ *vt* ananicar

dwindle ['dwɪndl] *vi* diminuir

dye [daɪ] *n* tintura, tinta ♦ *vt* tingir

dynamite ['daɪnəmaɪt] *n* dinamite *f*

dyslexia [dɪs'lɛksɪə] *n* dislexia

E

E [i:] n (MUS) mi m

each [i:tʃ] adj cada inv ♦ pron cada um(a); ~ **other** um ao outro; **they hate ~ other** (eles) se odeiam

eager ['i:gə*] adj ávido; **to be ~ for/ to do sth** ansiar por/fazer algo

eagle ['i:gl] n águia

ear [ɪə*] n (external) orelha; (inner, fig) ouvido; (of corn) espiga; **earache** n dor f de ouvidos; **eardrum** n tímpano

earl [ə:l] (BRIT) n conde m

earlier ['ə:lɪə*] adj mais adiantado; (edition) anterior ♦ adv mais cedo

early ['ə:lɪ] adv cedo; (before time) com antecedência ♦ adj cedo; (sooner than expected) prematuro; (reply) pronto; (Christians, settlers) primeiro; (man) primitivo; (life, work) juvenil; **in the ~ or ~ in the spring/19th century** no princípio da primavera/do século dezenove

earmark ['ɪəmɑ:k] vt: **to ~ sth for** reservar ou destinar algo para

earn [ə:n] vt ganhar; (COMM: interest) render; (praise) merecer

earnest ['ə:nɪst] adj (wish) intenso; (manner) sério; **in ~** a sério

earnings ['ə:nɪŋz] npl (personal) vencimentos mpl salário, ordenado; (of company) lucro

ear: earphones npl fones mpl de ouvido; **earring** n brinco; **earshot** n: **within earshot** ao alcance do ouvido ou da voz

earth [ə:θ] n terra; (BRIT: ELEC) fio terra ♦ vt (BRIT: ELEC) ligar à terra; **earthenware** n louça de barro ♦ adj de barro; **earthquake** n terremoto (BR), terramoto (PT)

ease [i:z] n facilidade f; (relaxed state) sossego; (comfort) conforto ♦ vt facilitar; (pain, tension) aliviar;

(help pass): **to ~ sth in/out** meter/ tirar algo com cuidado; **at ~!** (MIL) descansar!; **ease off** vi acalmar-se; (wind) baixar; (rain) moderar-se; **ease up** vi = ease off

easel ['i:zl] n cavalete m

easily ['i:zɪlɪ] adv facilmente, fácil (inf)

east [i:st] n leste m ♦ adj (region) leste; (wind) do leste ♦ adv para o leste; **the E~** o Oriente; (POL) o leste

Easter ['i:stə*] n Páscoa; **Easter egg** n ovo de Páscoa

easterly ['i:stəlɪ] adj (to the east) para o leste; (from the east) do leste

eastern ['i:stən] adj do leste, oriental

eastward(s) ['i:stwəd(z)] adv ao leste

easy ['i:zɪ] adj fácil; (comfortable) folgado, cômodo; (relaxed) natural, complacente; (victim, prey) desprotegido ♦ adv: **to take it** ou **things ~** (not worry) levar as coisas com calma; (go slowly) ir devagar; (rest) descansar; **easy chair** n poltrona; **easy-going** adj pacato, fácil

eat [i:t] (pt ate, pp eaten) vt, vi comer; **eat away** vt corroer; **eat away at** vt fus corroer; **eat into** vt fus = eat away at

eavesdrop ['i:vzdrɔp] vi: **to ~ (on)** escutar às escondidas

ebb [eb] n refluxo ♦ vi baixar; (fig: also: ~ **away**) declinar

ebony ['ebənɪ] n ébano

EC n abbr (= European Community) CE f

ECB n abbr (= European Central Bank) BCE m, Banco Central Europeu

eccentric [ɪk'sɛntrɪk] adj, n excêntrico(-a)

echo ['ɛkəu] (pl ~es) n eco ♦ vt ecoar, repetir ♦ vi ressoar, repetir

eclipse [ɪ'klɪps] n eclipse m

ecology [ɪˈkɔlədʒɪ] n ecologia
e-commerce n abbr (= electronic commerce) comércio eletrônico
economic [i:kəˈnɔmɪk] adj econômico; (business etc) rentável; **economical** adj econômico; **economics** n economia ♦ npl aspectos mpl econômicos
economize [ɪˈkɔnəmaɪz] vi economizar, fazer economias
economy [ɪˈkɔnəmɪ] n economia; **economy class** n (AVIAT) classe f econômica
ecstasy [ˈɛkstəsɪ] n êxtase m; **ecstatic** [ɛksˈtætɪk] adj extasiado
ECU [eɪkju:] n abbr (= European Currency Unit) ECU m
eczema [ˈɛksɪmə] n eczema m
edge [ɛdʒ] n (of knife etc) fio; (of table, chair etc) borda; (of lake etc) margem f ♦ vt (trim) embainhar; on ~ (fig) = edgy; to ~ away from afastar-se pouco a pouco de; **edgy** adj nervoso, inquieto
edible [ˈɛdɪbl] adj comestível
Edinburgh [ˈɛdɪnbərə] n Edimburgo
edit [ˈɛdɪt] vt editar; (be the editor of) dirigir; (cut) cortar, redigir; (COMPUT, TV) editar; (CINEMA) montar; **edition** [ɪˈdɪʃən] n edição f; **editor** n redator(a) m/f; (of newspaper) diretor(a) m/f; (of column) editor(a) m/f; (of book) organizador(a) m/f; **editorial** [ɛdɪˈtɔːrɪəl] adj editorial
educate [ˈɛdjukeɪt] vt educar
education [ɛdjuˈkeɪʃən] n educação f; (schooling) ensino; (teaching) pedagogia; **educational** adj (policy, experience) educacional; (toy etc) educativo
eel [i:l] n enguia
eerie [ˈɪərɪ] adj (strange) estranho; (mysterious) misterioso
effect [ɪˈfɛkt] n efeito ♦ vt (repairs)

fazer; (savings) efetuar; **to take ~** (law) entrar em vigor; (drug) fazer efeito; **in ~** na realidade; **effective** [ɪˈfɛktɪv] adj eficaz; (actual) efetivo; **effectiveness** n eficácia
efficiency [ɪˈfɪʃənsɪ] n eficiência
efficient [ɪˈfɪʃənt] adj eficiente; (machine) rentável
effort [ˈɛfət] n esforço; **effortless** adj fácil
e.g. adv abbr (= exempli gratia) p. ex.
egg [ɛg] n ovo; **hard-boiled/soft-boiled** ~ ovo duro/mole; **egg on** vt incitar; **eggcup** n oveiro; **eggplant** (esp US) n beringela; **eggshell** n casca de ovo
ego [ˈiːgəu] n ego; **egotism** n egotismo m
Egypt [ˈiːdʒɪpt] n Egito; **Egyptian** [ɪˈdʒɪpʃən] adj, n egípcio(-a)
eiderdown [ˈaɪdədaun] n edredom m (BR), edredão m (PT)
eight [eɪt] num oito; **eighteen** [eɪˈtiːn] num dezoito; **eighth** [eɪtθ] num oitavo; **eighty** [ˈeɪtɪ] num oitenta
Eire [ˈɛərə] n (República da) Irlanda
either [ˈaɪðə*] adj (one or other) um ou outro; (each) cada; (both) ambos ♦ pron: ~ (of them) qualquer (dos dois) ♦ adv: no, I don't ~ eu também não ♦ conj: ~ yes or no eu sim ou não
eject [ɪˈdʒɛkt] vt expulsar
elaborate [adj ɪˈlæbərɪt, vb ɪˈlæbəreɪt] adj complicado ♦ vt (expand) expandir; (refine) aperfeiçoar ♦ vi: to ~ on acrescentar detalhes a
elastic [ɪˈlæstɪk] adj elástico; (adaptable) flexível, adaptável ♦ n elástico; **elastic band** (BRIT) n elástico
elated [ɪˈleɪtɪd] adj: to be ~ rejubilar-se
elbow [ˈɛlbəu] n cotovelo

elder [ˈɛldə*] adj mais velho ♦ n
(tree) sabugueiro; (person) o mais
velho (a mais velha); **elderly** adj
idoso, de idade ♦ npl: **the elderly** as
pessoas de idade, os idosos

eldest [ˈɛldɪst] adj mais velho ♦ n o
mais velho (a mais velha)

elect [ɪˈlɛkt] vt eleger ♦ adj: **the
president ~** o presidente eleito; **to ~
to do** (choose) optar por fazer; **election** n (voting) votação f; (installation) eleição f; **electioneering**
[ɪlɛkʃəˈnɪərɪŋ] n campanha or propaganda eleitoral; **electorate** n eleitorado

electric [ɪˈlɛktrɪk] adj elétrico; **electrical** adj elétrico; **electric fire**
lareira elétrica

electrician [ɪlɛkˈtrɪʃən] n eletricista
m/f

electricity [ɪlɛkˈtrɪsɪtɪ] n eletricidade f

electrify [ɪˈlɛktrɪfaɪ] vt (fence, RAIL)
eletrificar; (audience) eletrizar

electronic [ɪlɛkˈtrɔnɪk] adj eletrônico; **electronic mail** n correio
eletrônico; **electronics** n eletrônica

elegant [ˈɛlɪɡənt] adj (person, building) elegante; (idea) refinado

element [ˈɛlɪmənt] n elemento;
elementary [ɛlɪˈmɛntərɪ] adj (gen)
elementar; (primitive) rudimentar;
elementary school (US) n escola
primária; ver quadro

ELEMENTARY SCHOOL

Nos Estados Unidos e no Canadá,
uma **elementary school** (também chamada de grade school ou
grammar school nos Estados
Unidos) é uma escola pública
onde os alunos passam de seis a
oito dos primeiros anos escolares.

---

elephant [ˈɛlɪfənt] n elefante(-a)
m/f

elevator [ˈɛlɪveɪtə*] n (US) n elevador
m

eleven [ɪˈlɛvn] num onze; **eleventh**
num décimo-primeiro

elicit [ɪˈlɪsɪt] vt: **to ~ (from)** (information) extrair (de); (response, reaction)
provocar (de)

eligible [ˈɛlɪdʒəbl] adj elegível,
apto; **to be ~ for sth** (job etc) ter
qualificações para algo

elm [ɛlm] n olmo

elongated [ˈiːlɔŋɡeɪtɪd] adj alongado

elope [ɪˈləʊp] vi fugir

eloquent [ˈɛləkwənt] adj eloqüente

El Salvador [ɛlˈsælvədɔː*] n El
Salvador

else [ɛls] adv outro, mais; **something ~** outra coisa; **nobody ~**
spoke ninguém mais falou; **elsewhere** adv (be) em outro lugar (BR),
noutro sítio (PT); (go) para outro
lugar (BR), a outro sítio (PT)

elusive [ɪˈluːsɪv] adj esquivo; (quality) indescritível

e-mail [ˈiːmeɪl] n e-mail m, correio
eletrônico ♦ vt (person) enviar um
e-mail a

emancipate [ɪˈmænsɪpeɪt] vt libertar; (women) emancipar

embankment [ɪmˈbæŋkmənt] n
aterro; (of river) dique m

embark [ɪmˈbɑːk] vi embarcar ♦ vt
embarcar; **to ~ on** (fig) empreender,
começar

embarrass [ɪmˈbærəs] vt constran-
ger; (politician) embaraçar; **embarrassed** adj descomfortável;
embarrassing adj embaraçoso,
constrangedor(a); **embarrassment**
n embaraço, constrangimento

embassy [ˈɛmbəsɪ] n embaixada

embellish [ɪmˈbelɪʃ] vt embelezar; (story) florear

embers [ˈembəz] npl brasa, borralho, cinzas fpl

embezzle [ɪmˈbezl] vt desviar

embitter [ɪmˈbɪtə*] vt (person) amargurar; (relations) azedar

embody [ɪmˈbɒdɪ] vt (features) incorporar; (ideas) expressar

embrace [ɪmˈbreɪs] vt abraçar, dar um abraço em; (include) abarcar, abranger ♦ vi abraçar-se ♦ n abraço

embroider [ɪmˈbrɔɪdə*] vt bordar; **embroidery** n bordado

emerald [ˈemərəld] n esmeralda

emerge [ɪˈmɜːdʒ] vi sair; (from sleep) acordar; (fact, idea) emergir

emergency [ɪˈmɜːdʒənsɪ] n emergência; **in an ~** em caso de urgência; **emergency cord** (US) n sinal m de alarme; **emergency exit** n saída de emergência; **emergency landing** n aterrissagem f forçada (BR), aterragem f forçosa (PT)

emigrate [ˈemɪɡreɪt] vi emigrar

eminent [ˈemɪnənt] adj eminente

emit [ɪˈmɪt] vt (smoke) soltar; (smell) exalar; (sound) produzir

emotion [ɪˈməuʃən] n emoção f; **emotional** adj (needs) emocional; (person) sentimental, emotivo; (scene) comovente; (tone) emocionante

emperor [ˈempərə*] n imperador m

emphasis [ˈemfəsɪs] (pl emphases) n ênfase f

emphasize [ˈemfəsaɪz] vt (word, point) enfatizar, acentuar; (feature) salientar

emphatic [emˈfætɪk] adj (statement) vigoroso, expressivo; (person) convincente; (manner) enfático

empire [ˈempaɪə*] n império

employ [ɪmˈplɔɪ] vt empregar; (tool) utilizar; **employee** n empre-

gado(-a); **employer** n empregador(a) m/f, patrão(-troa) m/f; **employment** n (gen) emprego; (work) trabalho

empress [ˈempris] n imperatriz f

emptiness [ˈemptɪnɪs] n vazio, vácuo

empty [ˈemptɪ] adj vazio; (place) deserto; (house) desocupado; (threat) vão(vã) ♦ vt esvaziar; (place) evacuar ♦ vi esvaziar-se; (place) ficar deserto; **empty-handed** adj de mãos vazias

EMU n abbr (= economic and monetary union) UEM f, União Econômica e Monetária

emulate [ˈemjuleɪt] vt emular com

emulsion [ɪˈmʌlʃən] n emulsão f; (also: ~ paint) tinta plástica

enable [ɪˈneɪbl] vt: **to ~ sb to do sth** (allow) permitir que alguém faça algo; (make possible) tornar possível que alguém faça algo

enamel [ɪˈnæməl] n esmalte m

enchant [ɪnˈtʃɑːnt] vt encantar; **enchanting** adj encantador(a)

enc(l). abbr (in letters etc) = **enclosed; enclosure**

enclose [ɪnˈkləuz] vt (land) cercar; (with letter) anexar (BR), enviar junto (PT); **please find ~d** segue junto

enclosure [ɪnˈkləuʒə*] n cercado

encompass [ɪnˈkʌmpəs] vt abranger, encerrar

encore [ɔŋˈkɔː*] excl bis!, outra! ♦ n bis m

encounter [ɪnˈkauntə*] n encontro ♦ vt encontrar, topar com; (difficulty) enfrentar

encourage [ɪnˈkʌrɪdʒ] vt (activity) encorajar; (growth) estimular; (person): **to ~ sb to do sth** animar alguém a fazer algo; **encouragement** n estímulo

encroach [ɪnˈkrəutʃ] vi: **to ~ (up)on**

invadir; (*time*) ocupar

encyclop(a)edia [ɪnsaɪkləʊ'piːdɪə] n enciclopédia

end [end] n fim m; (of table, rope etc) ponta; (of street, town) final m ♦ vt acabar, terminar; (also: **bring to an ~, put an ~ to**) acabar com, pôr fim a ♦ vi terminar, acabar; **in the ~** ao fim, por fim, finalmente; **on ~** na ponta; **to stand on ~** (*hair*) arrepiar-se; **for hours on ~** por horas a fio; **end up** vi: **to ~ up in** terminar em; (*place*) ir parar em

endanger [ɪn'deɪndʒə*] vt pôr em risco

endearing [ɪn'dɪərɪŋ] adj simpático, atrativo

endeavour [ɪn'devə*] (US **endeavor**) n esforço; (*attempt*) tentativa ♦ vi: **to ~ to do** esforçar-se para fazer; (*try*) tentar fazer

ending ['endɪŋ] n fim m, conclusão f; (of book) desenlace m; (LING) terminação f

endless ['endlɪs] adj interminável; (*possibilities*) infinito

endorse [ɪn'dɔːs] vt (*cheque*) endossar; (*approve*) aprovar; **endorsement** n (BRIT: on driving licence) descrição f das multas; (*approval*) aval m

endure [ɪn'djuə*] vt (*bear*) agüentar, suportar ♦ vi (*last*) durar

enemy ['enəmɪ] adj, n inimigo/a

energy ['enədʒɪ] n energia

enforce [ɪn'fɔːs] vt (LAW) fazer cumprir

engage [ɪn'geɪdʒ] vt (*attention*) chamar; (*interest*) atrair; (*lawyer*) contratar; (*clutch*) engrenar ♦ vi engrenar; **to ~ in** dedicar-se a, ocupar-se com; **to ~ sb in conversation** travar conversa com alguém; **engaged** adj (BRIT: phone) ocupado (PT), impedido (PT); (: *toilet*) ocupado;

(*betrothed*) noivo; **to get engaged** ficar noivo; **engaged tone** (BRIT) n (TEL) sinal m de ocupado (BR) or de impedido (PT); **engagement** n encontro; (*booking*) contrato; (*to marry*) noivado; **engagement ring** n aliança de noivado

engaging [ɪn'geɪdʒɪŋ] adj atraente, simpático

engine ['endʒɪn] n (AUT) motor m; (RAIL) locomotiva

engineer [endʒɪ'nɪə*] n engenheiro(-a); (US: RAIL) maquinista m/f; (BRIT: for repairs) técnico(-a); (on ship) engenheiro(-a) naval; **engineering** n engenharia

England ['ɪŋglənd] n Inglaterra

English ['ɪŋglɪʃ] adj inglês (inglesa) ♦ n (LING) inglês m; **the ~** npl (*people*) os ingleses; **English Channel** n: **the English Channel** o Canal da Mancha; **Englishman/woman** (*irreg*) n inglês (inglesa) m/f

engraving [ɪn'greɪvɪŋ] n gravura

engrossed [ɪn'grəust] adj: ~ **in** absorto em

engulf [ɪn'gʌlf] vt (*subj: fire, water*) engolfar, tragar; (: *panic, fear*) tomar conta de

enhance [ɪn'hɑːns] vt (*gen*) ressaltar, salientar; (*enjoyment*) aumentar; (*beauty*) realçar; (*reputation*) melhorar; (*add to*) aumentar

enjoy [ɪn'dʒɔɪ] vt gostar de; (*health, privilege*) desfrutar de; **to ~ o.s.** divertir-se; **enjoyable** adj agradável; **enjoyment** n prazer m

enlarge [ɪn'lɑːdʒ] vt aumentar; (PHOT) ampliar ♦ vi: **to ~ on** (*subject*) desenvolver, estender-se sobre

enlighten [ɪn'laɪtn] vt (*inform*) informar, instruir; **enlightened** adj sábio; (*cultured*) culto; (*knowledgeable*) bem informado; (*tolerant*) compreensivo; **enlightenment** n esclarecimento; (*HISTORY*): **the Enlightenment** o Século das Luzes

enlist [ɪnˈlɪst] *vt* alistar; (*support*) conseguir, aliciar ♦ *vi* alistar-se

enmity [ˈɛnmɪtɪ] *n* inimizade *f*

enormous [ɪˈnɔːməs] *adj* enorme

enough [ɪˈnʌf] *adj*: ~ **time/books** tempo suficiente/livros suficientes ♦ *pron*: **have you got** ~? você tem o suficiente? ♦ *adv*: **big** ~ suficientemente grande; ~! basta!, chega!; **that's** ~, **thanks** chega, obrigado; **I've had** ~ **of him** estou farto dele; **which, funnily** *or* **oddly** ~ ... o que, por estranho que pareça ...

enquire [ɪnˈkwaɪə*] *vt*, *vi* = **inquire**

enrage [ɪnˈreɪdʒ] *vt* enfurecer, enraivecer

enrol [ɪnˈrəul] (*US* **enroll**) *vt* inscrever; (*SCH*) matricular ♦ *vi* inscrever-se; matricular-se; **enrolment** *n* inscrição *f*; (*SCH*) matrícula

ensure [ɪnˈʃuə*] *vt* assegurar

entail [ɪnˈteɪl] *vt* implicar

enter [ˈɛntə*] *vt* entrar em; (*club*) ficar *or* fazer-se sócio de; (*army*) alistar-se em; (*competition*) inscrever-se em; (*sb for a competition*) inscrever; (*write down*) registar; (*COMPUT*) entrar em ♦ *vi* entrar; **enter for** *vt fus* inscrever-se em; **enter into** *vt fus* estabelecer; (*plans*) fazer parte de; (*debate*) entrar em; (*agreement*) chegar a, firmar

enterprise [ˈɛntəpraɪz] *n* empresa; (*undertaking*) empreendimento; (*initiative*) iniciativa; **enterprising** *adj* empreendedor(a)

entertain [ɛntəˈteɪn] *vt* divertir, entreter; (*guest*) receber (em casa); (*idea*) estudar; **entertainer** *n* artista *m/f*; **entertaining** *adj* divertido; **entertainment** *n* (*amusement*) entretenimento, diversão *f*; (*show*)

espetáculo

enthusiasm [ɪnˈθuːzɪæzəm] *n* entusiasmo

enthusiast [ɪnˈθuːzɪæst] *n* entusiasta *m/f*; **enthusiastic** [ɪnθuːzɪˈæstɪk] *adj* entusiasmado; **to be enthusiastic about** entusiasmar-se por

entire [ɪnˈtaɪə*] *adj* inteiro; **entirely** *adv* totalmente, completamente; **entirety** [ɪnˈtaɪərɪtɪ] *n*: **in its entirety** na sua totalidade

entitle [ɪnˈtaɪtl] *vt*: **to** ~ **sb to sth** dar a alguém direito a algo; **entitled** [ɪnˈtaɪtld] *adj* (*book etc*) intitulado; **to be entitled to do** ter direito de fazer

entrance [*n* ˈɛntrns, *vb* ɪnˈtrɑːns] *n* entrada; (*arrival*) chegada ♦ *vt* encantar, fascinar; **to gain** ~ **to** (*university etc*) ser admitido em; **entrance examination** *n* exame *m* de admissão; **entrance fee** *n* jóia

entrant [ˈɛntrənt] *n* participante *m/f*; (*BRIT: in exam*) candidato(-a)

entrepreneur [ɔntrəprəˈnəː*] *n* empresário(-a)

entrust [ɪnˈtrʌst] *vt*: **to** ~ **sth to sb** confiar algo a alguém

entry [ˈɛntrɪ] *n* entrada; (*in competition*) participante *m/f*; (*in register*) registro, assentamento; (*in account*) lançamento; (*in dictionary*) verbete *m*; (*arrival*) chegada; **"no** ~**"** "entrada proibida"; (*AUT*) "contramão (*BR*), "entrada proibida" (*PT*); **entry phone** (*BRIT*) *n* interfone *m* (*em apartamento*)

envelope [ˈɛnvələup] *n* envelope *m*

envious [ˈɛnvɪəs] *adj* invejoso; (*look*) de inveja

environment [ɪnˈvaɪərnmənt] *n* meio ambiente *m*; **environmental** [ɪnvaɪərnˈmɛntl] *adj* ambiental; **environmentally friendly** (*products, industry*) não agressivo ao meio ambiente

envisage [ɪnˈvɪzɪdʒ] vt prever

envoy [ˈɛnvɔɪ] n enviado(-a)

envy [ˈɛnvɪ] n inveja ♦ vt ter inveja de; **to ~ sb sth** invejar alguém por algo, cobiçar algo de alguém

epic [ˈɛpɪk] n epopéia ♦ adj épico

epidemic [ɛpɪˈdɛmɪk] n epidemia

epilepsy [ˈɛpɪlɛpsɪ] n epilepsia

episode [ˈɛpɪsəud] n episódio

epitomize [ɪˈpɪtəmaɪz] vt epitomar, resumir

equal [ˈiːkwl] adj igual; (treatment) equitativo, equivalente ♦ n igual m/f ♦ vt ser igual a; **to be ~ to** (task) estar à altura de; **equality** [iːˈkwɔlɪtɪ] n igualdade f; **equalize** vi igualar; (SPORT) empatar; **equally** adv igualmente; (share etc) igual

equate [ɪˈkweɪt] vt: **to ~ sth with** equiparar algo com

equator [ɪˈkweɪtə*] n equador m

equilibrium [iːkwɪˈlɪbrɪəm] n equilíbrio

equip [ɪˈkwɪp] vt equipar; (person) prover, munir; **to be well ~ped** estar bem preparado or equipado; **equipment** n equipamento; (machines) equipamentos mpl, aparelhagem f

equivalent [ɪˈkwɪvəlnt] adj: **~ (to)** equivalente (a) ♦ n equivalente m

era [ˈɪərə] n era, época

erase [ɪˈreɪz] vt apagar; **eraser** n borracha (de apagar)

erect [ɪˈrɛkt] adj (posture) ereto; (tail, ears) levantado ♦ vt erigir, levantar; (assemble) montar; **erection** n construção f; (of tent, PHYSIO) ereção f; (assembly) montagem f

ERM n abbr (= Exchange Rate Mechanism) SME m

erode [ɪˈrəud] vt (GEO) causar erosão em; (confidence) minar

erotic [ɪˈrɔtɪk] adj erótico

errand [ˈɛrnd] n recado, mensagem f

erratic [ɪˈrætɪk] adj imprevisível

error [ˈɛrə*] n erro

erupt [ɪˈrʌpt] vi entrar em erupção; (fig) explodir, estourar; **eruption** n erupção f; explosão f

escalate [ˈɛskəleɪt] vi intensificar-se

escalator [ˈɛskəleɪtə*] n escada rolante

escapade [ɛskəˈpeɪd] n peripécia

escape [ɪˈskeɪp] n fuga; (of gas) escapatória ♦ vi escapar; (flee) fugir, evadir-se; (leak) vazar, escapar ♦ vt fugir de; (elude): **his name ~s me** o nome dele me foge da memória; **to ~ from** (place) escapar de; (person) escapulir de

escort [n ˈɛskɔːt, vb ɪsˈkɔːt] n acompanhante m/f; (MIL) escolta ♦ vt acompanhar

Eskimo [ˈɛskɪməu] n esquimó m/f

especially [ɪˈspɛʃlɪ] adv (above all) sobretudo; (particularly) em particular

espionage [ˈɛspɪənɑːʒ] n espionagem f

Esquire [ɪˈskwaɪə*] n (abbr Esq.): **J. Brown, ~** Sr. J. Brown

essay [ˈɛseɪ] n ensaio

essence [ˈɛsns] n essência

essential [ɪˈsɛnʃl] adj (necessary) indispensável; (basic) essencial ♦ n elemento essencial

establish [ɪˈstæblɪʃ] vt estabelecer; (facts) verificar; (proof) demonstrar; (reputation) firmar; **established** adj consagrado; (business) estabelecido; **establishment** n estabelecimento; **the Establishment** a classe dirigente

estate [ɪˈsteɪt] n (land) fazenda (BR), propriedade f (PT); (LAW) herança; (POL) estado; (BRIT: also: **housing ~**) conjunto habitacional; **estate agent** (BRIT) n corretor(a) m/f de

imóveis (BR), agente m/f imobiliá-
rio(-a) (PT); **estate car** (BRIT) n
perua (BR), canadiana (PT)
esteem [ɪˈstiːm] n: **to hold sb in
high ~** estimar muito alguém
esthetic [ɪsˈθetɪk] (US) adj = aesthetic
estimate [n ˈestɪmət, vb ˈestɪmeɪt] n
(assessment) avaliação f; (calculation) cálculo m; (COMM) orçamento ♦ vt
estimar, avaliar, calcular; **estima-
tion** [estɪˈmeɪʃən] n opinião f; cálculo
etc. abbr (= et cetera) etc.
eternal [ɪˈtəːnl] adj eterno
eternity [ɪˈtəːnɪtɪ] n eternidade f
ethical [ˈeθɪkl] adj ético
ethics [ˈeθɪks] n ética ♦ npl moral f
Ethiopia [iːθɪˈəupɪə] n Etiópia
ethnic [ˈeθnɪk] adj étnico; (culture)
folclórico
etiquette [ˈetɪket] n etiqueta f
EU n abbr (= European Union) UE f
euro [ˈjuərəu] n (currency) euro m
Eurocheque [ˈjuərəutʃek] n eurocheque m
Europe [ˈjuərəp] n Europa; **European** [juərəˈpiːən] adj, n europeu
(-péia); **European Union** n: **the
European Union** a União Européia
evacuate [ɪˈvækjueɪt] vt evacuar
evade [ɪˈveɪd] vt (person) evitar; (question, duties) evadir; (tax) sonegar
evaporate [ɪˈvæpəreɪt] vi evaporar-se
evasion [ɪˈveɪʒən] n fuga f; (of tax)
sonegação f
eve [iːv] n: **on the ~ of** na véspera de
even [ˈiːvn] adj (level) plano;
(smooth) liso; (equal) igual; (number) par ♦ adv até, mesmo; (showing
surprise) até (mesmo); (introducing a
comparison) ainda; **~ if** mesmo que;
~ though mesmo que, embora; **~
more** ainda mais; **~ so** mesmo
assim; **not ~** nem; **to get ~ with sb**

ficar quite com alguém; **even out**
vi nivelar-se
evening [ˈiːvnɪŋ] n (early) tarde f;
(late) noite f; (event) noitada f; **in the
~** à noite; **evening class** n aula
noturna; **evening dress** n (man's)
traje m de rigor (BR) or de cerimônia
(PT); (woman's) vestido de noite
event [ɪˈvent] n acontecimento;
(SPORT) prova; **in the ~ of** no caso de;
eventful adj movimentado, cheio
de acontecimentos; (game etc)
cheio de emoção, agitado
eventual [ɪˈventʃuəl] adj final;
eventually adv finalmente; (in
time) por fim
ever [ˈevə*] adv (always) sempre; (at
any time) em qualquer momento; (in
question) why ~ not? por que
não?; **the best ~** o melhor que já se
viu; **have you ~ seen it?** você alguma vez já viu isto?; **better than ~**
melhor que nunca; **~ since** ♦ adv
desde então ♦ conj depois que;
evergreen n sempre-verde f;
everlasting adj eterno, perpétuo

every [ˈevrɪ] adj 1 (each) cada; **~ one
of them** cada um deles; **~ shop in
the town was closed** todas as lojas
da cidade estavam fechadas
2 (all possible) todo(-a); **I have ~
confidence in her** tenho absoluta
confiança nela; **we wish you ~ success** desejamo-lhe o maior sucesso;
he's ~ bit as clever as his brother
ele é tão inteligente quanto o irmão
3 (showing recurrence) todo(-a); **~
other car had been broken into** em
cada dois carros foram arrombados;
she visits me ~ other/third day ele
me visita cada dois/três dias; **~ now
and then** de vez em quando

everybody ['ɛvrɪbɔdɪ] *pron* todos, todo mundo (*BR*), toda a gente (*PT*)

everyday ['ɛvrɪdeɪ] *adj* (*daily*) diário; (*usual*) corrente; (*common*) comum

everyone ['ɛvrɪwʌn] *pron* = **everybody**

everything ['ɛvrɪθɪŋ] *pron* tudo

everywhere ['ɛvrɪwɛə*] *adv* (*be*) em todo lugar (*BR*), em toda a parte (*PT*); (*go*) a todo lugar (*BR*), a toda a parte (*PT*); (*wherever*) ~ **you go you meet** ... aonde quer que se vá, encontra-se ...

evict [ɪ'vɪkt] *vt* despejar

evidence ['ɛvɪdəns] *n* (*proof*) prova(s) *f* (*pl*); (*of witness*) testemunho, depoimento; (*indication*) sinal *m*; **to give ~** testemunhar, prestar depoimento

evident ['ɛvɪdənt] *adj* evidente; **evidently** *adv* evidentemente; (*apparently*) aparentemente

evil ['iːvl] *adj* mau (má) ♦ *n* mal *m*, maldade *f*

evoke [ɪ'vəuk] *vt* evocar

evolution [iːvə'luːʃən] *n* evolução *f*; (*development*) desenvolvimento

evolve [ɪ'vɔlv] *vt* desenvolver ♦ *vi* desenvolver-se

ex- [ɛks] *prefix* ex-

exact [ɪg'zækt] *adj* exato; (*person*) meticuloso ♦ *vt*: **to ~ sth (from)** exigir algo (de); **exacting** *adj* exigente; (*conditions*) difícil; **exactly** *adv* exatamente; (*indicating agreement*) isso mesmo

exaggerate [ɪg'zædʒəreɪt] *vt*, *vi* exagerar; **exaggeration** [ɪgzædʒə'reɪʃən] *n* exagero

exam [ɪg'zæm] *n abbr* = **examination**

examination [ɪgzæmɪ'neɪʃən] *n* exame *m*; (*inquiry*) investigação *f*

examine [ɪg'zæmɪn] *vt* examinar; (*inspect*) inspecionar; **examiner** *n* examinador(a) *m/f*

example [ɪg'zɑːmpl] *n* exemplo; **for ~** por exemplo

exasperate [ɪg'zɑːspəreɪt] *vt* exasperar, irritar

excavate ['ɛkskəveɪt] *vt* escavar

exceed [ɪk'siːd] *vt* exceder; (*number*) ser superior a; (*speed limit*) ultrapassar; (*limits*) ir além de; (*powers*) exceder-se em; (*hopes*) superar; **exceedingly** *adv* extremamente

excellent ['ɛksələnt] *adj* excelente

except [ɪk'sɛpt] *prep* (*also:* ~ **for**, ~ **ing**) exceto, a não ser ♦ *vt* excluir; ~ **if/when** a menos que, a não ser que; **exception** *n* exceção *f*; **to take exception to** ressentir-se de

excerpt ['ɛksəːpt] *n* trecho

excess [ɪk'sɛs] *n* excesso; **excess baggage** *n* excesso de bagagem; **excess fare** (*BRIT*) *n* (*RAIL*) sobretaxa de excesso; **excessive** *adj* excessivo

exchange [ɪks'tʃeɪndʒ] *n* troca; (*of teachers, students*) intercâmbio; (*also:* **telephone ~**) estação *f* telefônica (*BR*), central *f* telefónica (*PT*) ♦ *vt*: **to ~ (for)** trocar (por); **exchange rate** *n* (taxa de) câmbio

Exchequer [ɪks'tʃɛkə*] (*BRIT*) *n*: **the ~** ≈ o Tesouro Nacional

excite [ɪk'saɪt] *vt* excitar; **to get ~d** entusiasmar-se; **excitement** *n* emoções *fpl*; (*agitation*) agitação *f*; **exciting** *adj* emocionante, empolgante

exclaim [ɪk'skleɪm] *vi* exclamar; **exclamation** [ɛksklə'meɪʃən] *n* exclamação *f*; **exclamation mark** *n* ponto de exclamação (*BR*) or de admiração (*PT*)

exclude [ɪkˈskluːd] vt excluir

exclusive [ɪksˈs|uːsɪv] adj exclusivo; ~ **of tax** sem incluir os impostos

excruciating [ɪksˈkruːʃieɪtɪŋ] adj doloroso, martirizante

excursion [ɪksˈkəːʃən] n excursão f

excuse [n ɪksˈkjuːs, vb ɪksˈkjuːz] n desculpa ♦ vt desculpar, perdoar; **to ~ sb from doing sth** dispensar alguém de fazer algo; ~ **me!** desculpe!; **if you will ~ me** ... com a sua licença ...

ex-directory (BRIT) adj: ~ **(phone) number** número que não figura na lista telefônica

execute ['ɛksɪkjuːt] vt (plan) realizar; (order) cumprir; (person, movement) executar; **execution** n realização f; (killing) execução f

executive [ɪgˈzɛkjutɪv] adj, n executivo(-a)

exempt [ɪgˈzɛmpt] adj isento ♦ vt: **to ~ sb from** dispensar or isentar alguém de

exercise ['ɛksəsaɪz] n exercício ♦ vt exercer; (right) valer-se de; (dog) levar para passear; (mind) ocupar ♦ vi (also: **to take ~**) fazer exercício; **exercise book** n caderno

exert [ɪgˈzəːt] vt exercer; **to ~ o.s.** esforçar-se, empenhar-se; **exertion** n esforço

exhale [ɛksˈheɪl] vt expirar; (air) exalar; (smoke) emitir ♦ vi expirar

exhaust [ɪgˈzɔːst] n (AUTO: also: ~ **pipe**) escape m, exaustor m; (fumes) escapamento (de gás) ♦ vt esgotar; **exhaustion** n exaustão f

exhibit [ɪgˈzɪbɪt] n (ART) obra exposta; (LAW) objeto exposto ♦ vt (courage) manifestar, mostrar; (quality, emotion) demonstrar; (paintings) expor; **exhibition** [ɛksɪˈbɪʃən] n exposição f; (of talent etc) mostra

exhilarating [ɪgˈzɪləreɪtɪŋ] adj esti-

mulante, tônico

exile ['ɛksaɪl] n exílio f; (person) exilado(-a) ♦ vt desterrar, exilar

exist [ɪgˈzɪst] vi existir; (live) viver; **existence** n existência; vida; **existing** adj atual

exit ['ɛksɪt] n saída ♦ vi (COMPUT, THEATRE) sair

exonerate [ɪgˈzɔnəreɪt] vt: **to ~ from** desobrigar de; (guilt) isentar de

exotic [ɪgˈzɔtɪk] adj exótico

expand [ɪkˈspænd] vt aumentar ♦ vi aumentar; (gas etc) expandir-se; (metal) dilatar-se

expanse [ɪkˈspæns] n extensão f

expansion [ɪkˈspænʃən] n (of town) desenvolvimento; (of trade) expansão f; (of population) aumento

expect [ɪkˈspɛkt] vt esperar; (suppose) supor; (require) exigir ♦ vi: **to be ~ing** estar grávida; **expectant mother** n gestante f; **expectation** [ɛkspɛkˈteɪʃən] n esperança; (belief) expectativa

expedient [ɛkˈspiːdɪənt] adj conveniente, oportuno ♦ n expediente m, recurso

expedition [ɛkspəˈdɪʃən] n expedição f

expel [ɪkˈspɛl] vt expelir; (from place, school) expulsar

expend [ɪkˈspɛnd] vt gastar; **expenditure** [ɪkˈspɛndɪtʃə*] n gastos mpl; (of energy) consumo

expense [ɪkˈspɛns] n gasto, despesa; (expenditure) despesas fpl; ~**s** npl (costs) despesas fpl; **at the ~ of** à custa de; **expense account** n relatório de despesas

expensive [ɪkˈspɛnsɪv] adj caro

experience [ɪkˈspɪərɪəns] n experiência ♦ vt (situation) enfrentar; (feeling) sentir; **experienced** adj experiente

experiment [ɪkˈspɛrɪmənt] n experimento, experiência ♦ vi: **to ~ (with/on)** fazer experiências (com/em)

expert [ˈɛkspəːt] adj hábil, perito ♦ n especialista m/f; **expertise** [ɛkspəːˈtiːz] n perícia

expire [ɪkˈspaɪə*] vi expirar; (run out) vencer; **expiry** n expiração f, vencimento

explain [ɪkˈspleɪn] vt explicar; (clarify) esclarecer; **explanatory** [ɪksˈplænətrɪ] adj explicativo

explicit [ɪkˈsplɪsɪt] adj explícito

explode [ɪkˈspləud] vi estourar, explodir

exploit [n ˈɛksplɔɪt, vb ɪksˈplɔɪt] n façanha ♦ vt explorar; **exploitation** [ɛksplɔɪˈteɪʃən] n exploração f

explore [ɪkˈsplɔː*] vt explorar; (fig) examinar, pesquisar; **explorer** n explorador(a) m/f

explosion [ɪkˈspləuʒən] n explosão f

explosive [ɪkˈspləusɪv] adj explosivo ♦ n explosivo

export [vb ɛksˈpɔːt, n ˈɛkspɔːt] vt exportar ♦ n exportação f ♦ cpd de exportação; **exporter** n exportador(a) m/f

expose [ɪkˈspəuz] vt expor; (unmask) desmascarar; **exposed** adj (house etc) desabrigado

exposure [ɪkˈspəuʒə*] n exposição f; (publicity) publicidade f; (PHOT) revelação f; **to die from ~** (MED) morrer de frio

express [ɪkˈsprɛs] adj expresso, explícito; (BRIT: letter etc) urgente ♦ n rápido ♦ vt exprimir, expressar; (quantity) representar; **expression** n expressão f; **expressly** adv expressamente; **expressway** (US) n rodovia (BR), auto-estrada (PT)

exquisite [ɛkˈskwɪzɪt] adj requintado

extend [ɪkˈstɛnd] vt (visit, street) prolongar; (building) aumentar; (offer) fazer; (hand) estender

extension [ɪkˈstɛnʃən] n (ELEC) extensão f; (building) acréscimo, expansão f; (of time) prorrogação f; (of rights) ampliação f; (TEL) ramal m (BR), extensão f (PT); (of deadline) prolongamento, prorrogação f

extensive [ɪkˈstɛnsɪv] adj extenso; (damage) considerável; (coverage) amplo; (broad) vasto, amplo; **extensively** adv: **he's travelled extensively** ele já viajou bastante

extent [ɪkˈstɛnt] n (breadth) extensão f; (of damage etc) dimensão f; (scope) alcance m; **to some ~** até certo ponto

exterior [ɛkˈstɪərɪə*] adj externo ♦ n exterior m; (appearance) aspecto

external [ɛkˈstəːnl] adj externo

extinct [ɪkˈstɪŋkt] adj extinto

extinguish [ɪkˈstɪŋgwɪʃ] vt extinguir

extort [ɪkˈstɔːt] vt extorquir; **extortionate** adj extorsivo, excessivo

extra [ˈɛkstrə] adj adicional ♦ adv adicionalmente ♦ n (luxury) luxo; (surcharge) extra m, suplemento; (CINEMA, THEATRE) figurante m/f

extract [vb ɪksˈtrækt, n ˈɛkstrækt] vt tirar, extrair; (tooth) arrancar; (mineral) extrair; (money) extorquir; (promise) conseguir, obter ♦ n extrato

extradite [ˈɛkstrədaɪt] vt (from country) extraditar; (to country) obter a extradição de

extraordinary [ɪkˈstrɔːdnrɪ] adj extraordinário; (odd) estranho

extravagance [ɪkˈstrævəgəns] n extravagância; (no pl: spending) esbanjamento

extravagant [ɪkˈstrævəgənt] adj

(*lavish*) extravagante; (*wasteful*) gastador(a), esbanjador(a)
extreme [ɪkˈstriːm] *adj* extremo ♦ *n* extremo; **extremely** *adv* muito, extremamente
extrovert [ˈɛkstrəvəːt] *n* extroverti-do(-a)
eye [aɪ] *n* olho; (*of needle*) buraco ♦ *vt* olhar, observar; **to keep an ~ on** vigiar, ficar de olho em; **eyebrow** *n* sobrancelha; **eyedrops** *npl* gotas *fpl* para os olhos; **eyelash** *n* cílio; **eyelid** *n* pálpebra; **eyeliner** *n* delineador *m*; **eye-opener** *n* revelação *f*, grande surpresa; **eyeshadow** *n* sombra de olhos; **eyesight** *n* vista, visão *f*; **eyesore** *n* monstruosidade *f*; **eye witness** *n* testemunha *m/f* ocular

F

F [ɛf] *n* (*MUS*) fá *m* ♦ *abbr* = **Fahrenheit**
fable [ˈfeɪbl] *n* fábula
fabric [ˈfæbrɪk] *n* tecido, pano
face [feɪs] *n* cara, rosto; (*grimace*) careta; (*of clock*) mostrador *m*; (*side*) superfície *f*; (*of building*) frente *f*, fachada ♦ *vt* (*facts*) enfrentar; (*direction*) dar para; **~ down** de bruços; (*card*) virado para baixo; **to lose ~** perder o prestígio; **to save ~** salvar as aparências; **to make** *or* **pull a ~** fazer careta; **in the ~ of** diante de, à vista de; **on the ~ of it** a julgar pelas aparências, à primeira vista; **face up to** *vt fus* enfrentar; **face cloth** (*BRIT*) *n* toalhinha de rosto; **face cream** *n* creme *m* facial; **face lift** *n* (operação *f*) plástica; (*of façade*) remodelamento; **face powder** *n* pó *m* de arroz; **face value** *n* (*of coin*, *stamp*) valor *m* nominal; **to take sth at face value** (*fig*) tomar

algo em sentido literal
facilities [fəˈsɪlɪtɪz] *npl* facilidades *fpl*, instalações *fpl*; **credit ~** crediário
facing [ˈfeɪsɪŋ] *prep* de frente para
facsimile [fækˈsɪmɪlɪ] *n* fac-símile *m*
fact [fækt] *n* fato; **in ~** realmente, na verdade
factor [ˈfæktə*] *n* fator *m*
factory [ˈfæktərɪ] *n* fábrica
factual [ˈfæktjuəl] *adj* real, fatual
faculty [ˈfækəltɪ] *n* faculdade *f*; (*US*) corpo docente
fad [fæd] (*inf*) *n* mania, modismo
fade [feɪd] *vi* desbotar; (*sound*, *hope*) desvanecer-se; (*light*) apagar-se; (*flower*) murchar
fag [fæg] (*BRIT*: *inf*) *n* cigarro
fail [feɪl] *vt* (*candidate*) reprovar; (*exam*) não passar em, ser reprovado em; (*subj*: *leader*) fracassar; (: *courage*): **his courage ~ed him** faltou-lhe a coragem; (: *memory*) falhar ♦ *vi* fracassar; (*brakes*) falhar; (*health*) deteriorar; (*light*) desaparecer; **to ~ to do sth** deixar de fazer algo; (*be unable*) não conseguir fazer algo; **without ~** sem falta; **failing** *n* defeito ♦ *prep* na *or* à falta de; **failing that** senão, caso contrário; **failure** *n* fracasso; (*mechanical*) falha
faint [feɪnt] *adj* fraco; (*recollection*) vago; (*mark*) indistinto; (*smell*) leve ♦ *n* desmaio ♦ *vi* desmaiar; **to feel ~** sentir tonteira
fair [fɛə*] *adj* justo; (*hair*) louro; (*complexion*) branco; (*weather*) bom; (*good enough*) razoável; (*sizeable*) considerável ♦ *adv*: **to play ~** fazer jogo limpo ♦ *n* (*also*: **trade ~**) feira; (*BRIT*: *funfair*) parque *m* de diversões; **fairly** *adv* (*justly*) com justiça; (*quite*) bastante; **fairness** *n* justiça; (*impartiality*) imparcialidade *f*
fairy [ˈfɛərɪ] *n* fada
faith [feɪθ] *n* fé *f*; (*trust*) confiança;

(denomination) seita; **faithful** adj fiel; *(account)* exato; **faithfully** adv fielmente; **yours faithfully** *(BRIT: in letters)* atenciosamente

fake [feɪk] n *(painting etc)* falsificação f; *(person)* impostor(a) m/f ♦ adj falso ♦ vt fingir; *(painting etc)* falsificar

falcon ['fɔːlkən] n falcão m

fall [fɔːl] *(pt fell, pp fallen)* n queda; *(us: autumn)* outono ♦ vi cair; *(price)* baixar; *(country)* render-se; ~**s** npl *(waterfall)* cascata, queda d'água; **to ~ flat** cair de cara no chão; *(plan)* falhar; *(joke)* não agradar; **fall back** vi retroceder; **fall back on** vt fus recorrer a; **fall behind** vi ficar para trás; **fall down** vi *(person)* cair; *(building)* desabar; **fall for** vt fus *(trick)* cair em; *(person)* enamorar-se de; **fall in** vi ruir; *(MIL)* alinhar-se; **fall off** vi cair; *(diminish)* declinar, diminuir; **fall out** vi cair; *(friends etc)* brigar; **fall through** vi falhar

fallacy ['fæləsɪ] n erro; *(misconception)* falácia

fallout ['fɔːlaut] n chuva radioativa

false [fɔːls] adj falso; **under ~ pretences** por meios fraudulentos; **false teeth** *(BRIT)* npl dentadura postiça

falter ['fɔːltə*] vi *(engine)* falhar; *(person)* vacilar

fame [feɪm] n fama

familiar [fə'mɪlɪə*] adj *(well-known)* conhecido; *(tone)* familiar, íntimo; **to be ~ with** *(subject)* estar familiarizado com

family ['fæmɪlɪ] n família

famine ['fæmɪn] n fome f

famished ['fæmɪʃt] adj faminto

famous ['feɪməs] adj famoso, célebre

fan [fæn] n *(hand-held)* leque m; *(ELEC)* ventilador m; *(person)* fã m/f *(BR)*, fan m/f *(PT)* ♦ vt abanar; *(fire, quarrel)* atiçar; **fan out** vi espalhar-se

fanatic [fə'nætɪk] n fanático(-a)

fan belt n correia do ventilador *(BR)* or da ventoinha *(PT)*

fancy ['fænsɪ] n capricho; *(imagination)* imaginação f; *(fantasy)* fantasia ♦ adj ornamental; *(clothes)* extravagante; *(food)* elaborado, luxuoso ♦ vt desejar, querer; *(imagine)* imaginar; *(think)* acreditar, achar; **to take a ~** tomar gosto por; **he fancies her** *(inf)* ele está a fim dela; **fancy dress** n fantasia

fang [fæŋ] n presa

fantastic [fæn'tæstɪk] adj fantástico

fantasy ['fæntəsɪ] n *(dream)* sonho; *(unreality)* fantasia; *(imagination)* imaginação f

far [fɑː*] adj *(distant)* distante ♦ adv muito; *(also: ~ away, ~ off)* longe; **at the ~ side/end** do lado/extremo mais afastado; **~ better** muito melhor; **~ from** longe de; **by ~** de longe; **go as ~ as the farm** vá até a *(BR)* or à *(PT)* fazenda; **as ~ as I know** que eu saiba; **how ~?** até onde?; *(fig)* até que ponto?; **faraway** ['fɑːrəweɪ] adj remoto, distante

farce [fɑːs] n farsa

fare [feə*] n *(on trains, buses)* preço *(da passagem)*; *(in taxi: cost)* tarifa; *(food)* comida; **half/full ~** meia/inteira passagem

Far East n: **the ~** o Extremo Oriente

farewell [feə'wel] excl adeus ♦ n despedida

farm [fɑːm] n fazenda *(BR)*, quinta *(PT)* ♦ vt cultivar; **farmer** n fazendeiro(-a), agricultor m; **farmhand** n lavrador(a) m/f, trabalhador(a) m/f; **farmhouse** n casa da fazenda *(BR)* or da quinta *(PT)*; **farming** n agricultura; *(tilling)* cultura; *(of ani-*

mals) criação f; **farmland** n terra de cultivo; **farmyard** n curral m

far-reaching [-'ri:tʃɪŋ] adj de grande alcance, abrangente

fart [fɑːt] (inf!) vi soltar um peido (!), peidar (!)

farther ['fɑːðə*] adv mais longe ♦ adj mais distante, mais afastado

farthest ['fɑːðɪst] superl adj far

fascinate ['fæsɪneɪt] vt fascinar

fascism ['fæʃɪzəm] n fascismo

fashion ['fæʃən] n moda; (~ industry) indústria da moda; (manner) maneira ♦ vt modelar, dar feitio a; **in ~** na moda; **fashionable** adj da moda, elegante; **fashion show** n desfile m de modas

fast [fɑːst] adj rápido; (dye, colour) firme, permanente; (clock): **to be ~** estar adiantado ♦ adv rápido, rapidamente; (stuck, held) firmemente ♦ n jejum m ♦ vi jejuar; **~ asleep** dormindo profundamente

fasten ['fɑːsn] vt fixar, prender; (coat) fechar; (belt) apertar ♦ vi prender-se, fixar-se; **fastener** n presilha, fecho; **fastening** n = **fastener**

fast food n fast food f

fat [fæt] adj gordo; (book) grosso; (wallet) recheado; (profit) grande ♦ n gordura; (lard) banha, gordura

fatal [feɪtl] adj fatal; (injury) mortal

fate [feɪt] n destino; (of person) sorte f; **fateful** adj fatídico

father ['fɑːðə*] n pai m; **father-in-law** n sogro; **fatherly** adj paternal

fathom ['fæðəm] n braça ♦ vt compreender

fatigue [fə'tiːg] n fadiga, cansaço

fatten ['fætn] vt, vi engordar

fatty ['fæti] adj (food) gorduroso ♦ n (inf) gorducho(-a)

faucet ['fɔːsɪt] (US) n torneira

fault [fɔːlt] n (blame) culpa; (defect)

defeito; (GEO) falha; (TENNIS) falta, bola fora ♦ vt criticar; **to find ~ with** criticar, queixar-se de; **at ~** culpado; **faulty** adj defeituoso

favour ['feɪvə*] (US **favor**) n favor m ♦ vt favorecer; (assist) auxiliar; **to do sb a ~** fazer favor a alguém; **to find ~ with** cair nas boas graças de; **in ~ of** em favor de; **favourite** ['feɪvrɪt] adj predileto ♦ n favorito(-a)

fawn [fɔːn] n cervo novo, cervato ♦ adj (also: **~-coloured**) castanho-claro inv ♦ vi: **to ~ (up)on** bajular

fax [fæks] n fax m, fac-símile m ♦ vt enviar por fax m, fac-símile

FBI n abbr (= Federal Bureau of Investigation) FBI m

fear [fɪə*] n medo ♦ vt ter medo de, temer; **for ~ of** com medo de; **fearful** adj medonho, temível; (cowardly) medroso; (awful) terrível

feasible ['fiːzəbl] adj viável

feast [fiːst] n banquete m; (REL: also: **~ day**) festa ♦ vi banquetear-se

feat [fiːt] n façanha, feito

feather ['feðə*] n pena, pluma

feature ['fiːtʃə*] n característica; (article) reportagem f ♦ vt (subj: film) apresentar ♦ vi: **to ~ in** figurar em; **~s** npl (of face) feições fpl; **feature film** n longa-metragem m

February ['februəri] n fevereiro

fed [fed] pt, pp of **feed**

federal ['fedərəl] adj federal

fed up adj: **to be ~** estar (de saco) cheio (BR), estar farto (PT)

fee [fiː] n taxa (BR), propina (PT); (of school) matrícula; (of doctor, lawyer) honorários mpl

feeble ['fiːbl] adj fraco; (attempt) ineficaz

feed [fiːd] n (of baby) alimento infantil; (of animal) ração f; (on printer) mecanismo alimentador ♦ vt alimentar; (baby) amamen-

tar; (*animal*) dar de comer a; (*data*):
to ~ into introduzir em; **feed on** vt
fus alimentar-se de; **feedback** m
reação f

feel [fi:l] (*pt, pp* **felt**) n sensação f;
(*sense*) tato; (*impression*) impressão f
♦ vt tocar, apalpar; (*anger, pain etc*)
sentir; (*think*) achar, acreditar; **to ~
hungry/cold** estar com fome/frio
(*BR*), ter fome/frio (*PT*); **to ~ lonely/
better** sentir-se só/ melhor; **I don't ~
well** não estou me sentindo bem; **it
~s soft** é macio; **to ~ like** querer; **to
~ about** or **around** tatear; **feeling** n
sensação f; (*emotion*) sentimento m;
(*impression*) impressão f

feet [fi:t] *npl of* **foot**

feign [feɪn] vt fingir

fell [fel] *pt of* **fall** ♦ vt (*tree*) lançar por
terra, derrubar

fellow ['feləʊ] n camarada m/f; (*inf:
man*) cara m (*BR*), tipo (*PT*); (*of
learned society*) membro ♦ cpd: **~
students** colegas m/fpl de curso;
fellowship n amizade f; (*grant*)
bolsa de estudo; (*society*) associação
f

felony ['feIənI] n crime m

felt [felt] *pt, pp of* **feel** ♦ n feltro; **felt-
tip pen** n caneta pilot ® (*BR*) or de
feltro (*PT*)

female ['fi:meɪl] n (*ZOOL*) fêmea;
(*pej: woman*) mulher f ♦ adj fê-
meo(-a); (*sex, character*) feminino;
(*vote*) das mulheres; (*child*) do sexo
feminino

feminine ['femɪnɪn] adj feminino

feminist ['femɪnɪst] n feminista m/f

fence [fens] n cerca ♦ vt (*also:* **~ in**)
cercar ♦ vi esgrimir; **fencing** n
(*sport*) esgrima

fend [fend] vi: **to ~ for o.s.** defender-
se, virar-se; **fend off** vt defender-se
de

fender ['fendə*] n (*of fireplace*)

guarda-fogo m; (*on boat*) defesa de
embarcação; (*US: AUT*) pára-lama m

ferment [vb fə'ment, n 'fɜ:ment] vi
fermentar ♦ n (*fig*) agitação f

fern [fɜ:n] n samambaia (*BR*), feto
(*PT*)

ferocious [fə'rəʊʃəs] adj feroz

ferret ['ferɪt] n furão m; **ferret out**
vt (*information*) desenterrar, descobrir

ferry ['ferɪ] n (*small*) barco (de travessia); (*large: also:* **~boat**) balsa ♦ vt
transportar

fertile ['fɜːtaɪl] adj fértil; (*BIO*) fecun-
do; **fertilizer** ['fɜːtɪlaɪzə*] n adubo,
fertilizante m

fester ['festə*] vi inflamar-se

festival ['festɪvəl] n (*REL*) festa; (*ART,
MUS*) festival m

festive ['festɪv] adj festivo; **the ~
season** (*BRIT: Christmas*) a época do
Natal

festivities [fes'tɪvɪtɪz] npl festas fpl,
festividades fpl

fetch [fetʃ] vt ir buscar, trazer; (*sell
for*) alcançar

fête [feɪt] n festa

feud [fju:d] n disputa, rixa

fever ['fi:və*] n febre f; **feverish** adj
febril

few [fju:] adj, pron poucos(-as); **a ~
...** alguns (algumas) ...; **fewer**
['fju:ə*] adj menos; **fewest** ['fju:ɪst]
adj o menor número de

fiancé(e) [fɪ'ɑ: nseɪ] n noivo(-a)

fib [fɪb] n lorota

fibre ['faɪbə*] (*US* fiber) n fibra;
fibreglass ['faɪbəglɑːs] n fibra de
vidro

fickle ['fɪkl] adj inconstante; (*weather*) instável

fiction ['fɪkʃən] n ficção f; **fictional**
adj de ficção; **fictitious** adj fictício

fiddle ['fɪdl] n (*MUS*) violino; (*swindle*) trapaça ♦ vt (*BRIT: accounts*) falsi-

ficar; **fiddle with** vt fus brincar
com

fidget ['fidʒit] vi estar irrequieto,
mexer-se

field [fi:ld] n campo; (fig) área, esfera, especialidade f; **fieldwork** n
trabalho de campo

fiend [fi:nd] n demônio

fierce [fiəs] adj feroz; (wind) violento; (heat) intenso

fiery ['faiəri] adj ardente; (temperament) fogoso

fifteen [fif'ti:n] num quinze

fifth [fifθ] num quinto

fifty ['fifti] num cinqüenta; **fifty-
fifty** adv: **to ~ share** or **go fifty-fifty
with sb** dividir meio a meio com
alguém, rachar com alguém ♦ adj:
to have a fifty-fifty chance ter 50%
de chance

fig [fig] n figo

fight [fait] n briga; (MIL) combate m;
(struggle: against illness etc) luta ♦ vt
lutar contra; (cancer, alcoholism)
combater; (election) competir ♦ vi
lutar, brigar, bater-se; **fighter** n
combatente m/f; (plane) caça m;
fighting n batalha; (brawl) briga

figment ['figmənt] n: **a ~ of the
imagination** um produto da imaginação

figurative ['figjurətiv] adj (expression) figurado; (style) figurativo

figure ['figə*] n (DRAWING, MATH) figura, desenho; (number) número,
cifra; (outline) forma; (person) personagem m ♦ vt (esp us) imaginar
♦ vi figurar; **figure out** vt compreender

file [fail] n (tool) lixa; (dossier) dossiê
m, pasta; (folder) pasta; (COMPUT)
arquivo; (row) fila, coluna ♦ vt (wood,
nails) lixar; (papers) arquivar; (LAW:
claim) apresentar, dar entrada em

♦ vi: **to ~ in/out** entrar/sair em fila

filing cabinet n fichário, arquivo

fill [fil] vt: **to ~ with** encher com;
(vacancy) preencher; (need) satisfazer ♦ n: **to eat one's ~** encher-se or
fartar-se de comer; **fill in** vt (form)
preencher; (hole) tapar; (time)
encher; **fill up** vt encher ♦ vi (AUT)
abastecer o carro

fillet ['filit] n filete m, filé m; **fillet
steak** n filé m

filling ['filiŋ] n (CULIN) recheio; (for
tooth) obturação f (BR), chumbo
(PT); **filling station** n posto de
gasolina

film [film] n filme m; (of liquid)
camada, veu m ♦ vt rodar, filmar ♦ vi
filmar; **film star** n astro/estrela do
cinema

filter ['filtə*] n filtro ♦ vt filtrar;
filter-tipped adj filtrado

filth [filθ] n sujeira (BR), sujidade f
(PT); **filthy** ['filθi] adj sujo; (language)
indecente, obsceno

fin [fin] n barbatana

final ['fainl] adj final, último; (ultimate) maior; (definitive) definitivo
♦ n (SPORT) final f; **~s** npl (SCH) exames mpl finais; **finale** [fi'nɑ:li] n
final m; **finalize** vt concluir, completar; **finally** adv finalmente, por
fim

finance [fai'næns] n fundos mpl;
(money management) finanças fpl
♦ vt financiar; **~s** npl (personal ~s)
finanças fpl; **financial** [fai'nænʃəl] adj
financeiro

find [faind] (pt, pp **found**) vt encontrar, achar; (discover) descobrir ♦ n
achado, descoberta; **to ~ sb guilty**
(LAW) declarar alguém culpado; **find
out** vt descobrir; (person) desmascarar ♦ vi: **to ~ out about** (by
chance) saber de; **findings** npl
(LAW) veredito, decisão f; (of report)

constatações fpl

fine [faɪn] adj fino; (excellent) excelente; (subtle) sutil ♦ adv muito bem ♦ n (LAW) multa ♦ vt (LAW) multar; **to be ~** (person) estar bem; (weather) estar bem; **fine arts** npl belas artes fpl

finger ['fɪŋgə*] n dedo ♦ vt manusear; **fingernail** n unha; **fingerprint** n impressão f digital; **fingertip** n ponta do dedo

finish ['fɪnɪʃ] n fim m; (SPORT) chegada; (on wood etc) acabamento ♦ vt, vi terminar, acabar; **to ~ doing sth** terminar de fazer algo; **to ~ third** chegar no terceiro lugar; **finish off** vt terminar; (kill) liquidar; **finish up** vt acabar ♦ vi parar; **finishing line** n linha de chegada, meta

Finland ['fɪnlənd] n Finlândia

Finn [fɪn] n finlandês(-esa) m/f; **Finnish** adj finlandês(-esa) ♦ n (LING) finlandês m

fir [fə:*] n abeto

fire ['faɪə*] n fogo; (accidental) incêndio; (gas ~, electric ~) aquecedor m ♦ vt (gun) disparar; (arrow) atirar; (interest) estimular; (dismiss) despedir ♦ vi disparar; **on ~** em chamas; **fire alarm** n alarme m de incêndio; **firearm** n arma de fogo; **fire brigade** (US **fire department**) n (corpo de) bombeiros mpl; **fire engine** n carro de bombeiro; **fire escape** n escada de incêndio; **fire extinguisher** n extintor m de incêndio; **fireman** (irreg) n bombeiro; **fireplace** n lareira; **fire station** n posto de bombeiros; **firewood** n lenha; **fireworks** npl fogos mpl de artifício

firing squad n pelotão m de fuzilamento

firm [fə:m] adj firme ♦ n firma

first [fə:st] adj primeiro ♦ adv (before others) primeiro; (listing reasons) em primeiro lugar ♦ n (in race) primeiro(-a); (AUT) primeira; (BRIT: SCH) menção f honrosa; **at ~** no início; **~ of all** antes de tudo, antes de mais nada; **first aid** n primeiros socorros mpl; **first-aid kit** n estojo de primeiros socorros; **first-class** adj de primeira classe; **first-hand** adj de primeira mão; **first lady** (US) n primeira dama; **firstly** adv primeiramente, em primeiro lugar; **first name** n primeiro nome m; **first-rate** adj de primeira categoria

fish [fɪʃ] n inv peixe m ♦ vt, vi pescar; **to go ~ing** ir pescar; **fisherman** (irreg) n pescador m; **fish fingers** (BRIT) npl filezinhos mpl de peixe; **fishing boat** n barco de pesca; **fishing line** n linha de pesca; **fishing rod** n vara (de pesca); **fishmonger's (shop)** n peixaria; **fish sticks** (US) npl = fish fingers; **fishy** (inf) adj (tale) suspeito

fist [fɪst] n punho

fit [fɪt] adj em (boa) forma; (suitable) adequado, apropriado ♦ vt (subj: clothes) caber em; (put in) colocar; (equip) equipar; (suit) assentar a ♦ vi (clothes) servir; (parts) ajustar-se; (in space) caber ♦ n (MED) ataque m; (of anger) acesso; **to ~ to** bom para; **~ for** adequado para; **by fits and starts** espasmodicamente; **fit in** vi encaixar-se; (person) dar-se bem (com todos); **fitment** n móvel m; **fitness** n (MED) saúde f, boa forma; **fitting** adj apropriado ♦ n (of dress) prova; **fittings** npl (in building) instalações fpl, acessórios mpl

five [faɪv] num cinco; **fiver** (inf) n (BRIT) nota de cinco libras; (US) nota de cinco dólares

fix [fɪks] vt (secure) fixar, colocar; (arrange) arranjar; (mend) consertar; (*meal, drink*) preparar ♦ *n*: to be in a ~ estar em apuros; **fix up** vt (*meeting*) marcar; **to ~ sb up with sth** arranjar algo para alguém; **fixation** [fɪk'seɪʃən] *n* fixação *f*; **fixed** *adj* (*prices, smile*) fixo; **fixture** *n* (*furniture*) móvel *m* fixo; (*SPORT*) desafio, encontro

fizzy ['fɪzɪ] *adj* com gás, gasoso

flabbergasted [ˈflæbəgɑːstɪd] *adj* pasmado

flabby ['flæbɪ] *adj* flácido

flag [flæg] *n* bandeira, (*for signalling*) bandeirola; (~*stone*) laje *f* ♦ *vi* acabar-se, descair; **flag down** vt: **to ~ sb down** fazer sinais a alguém para que pare

flagpole ['flægpəul] *n* mastro de bandeira

flagship ['flægʃɪp] *n* nau *f* capitânia; (*fig*) carro-chefe *m*

flair [flɛə*] *n* (*talent*) talento; (*style*) habilidade *f*

flake [fleɪk] *n* (*of rust, paint*) lasca; (*of snow, soap powder*) floco ♦ *vi* (*also*: ~ **off**) lascar, descamar-se

flamboyant [flæm'bɔɪənt] *adj* (*dress*) espalhafatoso; (*person*) extravagante

flame [fleɪm] *n* chama

flammable ['flæməbl] *adj* inflamável

flan [flæn] *n* (*BRIT*) torta

flannel ['flænl] *n* (*BRIT*: *also*: **face~**) toalhinha de rosto; (*fabric*) flanela; ~**s** *npl* calça (*BR*) or calças *fpl* (*PT*) de flanela

flap [flæp] *n* (*of pocket*) aba; (*of envelope*) dobra ♦ *vt* (*arms*) oscilar; (*wings*) bater ♦ *vi* (*sail, flag*) ondular; (*inf*: *also*: **be in a** ~) estar atarantado

flare [flɛə*] *n* fogacho, chama; (*MIL*) artifício de sinalização; (*in skirt etc*) folga; **flare up** *vi* chamejar; (*fig*: *person*) encolerizar-se; (*: violence*) irromper

flash [flæʃ] *n* (*of lightning*) clarão *m*; (*also*: **news~**) notícias *fpl* de última hora; (*PHOT*) flash *m* ♦ *vt* piscar; (*news, message*) transmitir; (*look, smile*) brilhar ♦ *vi* brilhar; (*light on ambulance, eyes etc*) piscar; **in a** ~ num instante; **to ~ by** or **past** passar como um raio; **flashlight** *n* lanterna de bolso

flashy ['flæʃɪ] (*pej*) *adj* espalhafatoso

flask [flɑːsk] *n* frasco; (*also*: **vacuum** ~) garrafa térmica (*BR*), termo (*PT*)

flat [flæt] *adj* (*battery*) descarregado; (*tyre*) vazio; (*beer*) choco; (*denial*) categórico; (*MUS*) abemolado; (: *voice*) desafinado; (*rate*) único; (*fee*) fixo ♦ *n* (*BRIT*: *apartment*) apartamento; (*MUS*) bemol *m*; (*AUT*) pneu *m* furado; ~ **out** (*work*) a toque de caixa; **flatly** *adv* terminantemente; **flatten** vt (*also*: **flatten out**) aplanar; (*demolish*) arrasar

flatter ['flætə*] *vt* lisonjear; **flattering** *adj* lisonjeiro; (*clothes etc*) favorecedor(a); **flattery** *n* bajulação *f*

flaunt [flɔːnt] *vt* ostentar, pavonear

flavour ['fleɪvə*] (*US* **flavor**) *n* sabor *m* ♦ *vt* condimentar, aromatizar; **strawberry-~ed** com sabor de morango; **flavouring** *n* condimento; (*synthetic*) aromatizante *m*

flaw [flɔː] *n* defeito; (*in character*) falha; **flawless** *adj* impecável

flax [flæks] *n* linho

flea [fliː] *n* pulga

fleck [flɛk] *n* mancha, sinal *m*

flee [fliː] (*pt, pp* **fled**) *vt* fugir de ♦ *vi* fugir

fleece [fliːs] *n* tosão *m*; (*wool*) lã *f*; (*coat*) velo ♦ *vt* (*inf*) espoliar

fleet [fliːt] *n* (*of lorries etc*) frota; (*of ships*) esquadra

fleeting ['fliːtɪŋ] *adj* (*glimpse, happiness*) fugaz; (*visit*) passageiro

Flemish ['flɛmɪʃ] *adj* flamengo

flesh [fleʃ] n carne f; (of fruit) polpa
flew [fluː] pt of **fly**
flex [fleks] n fio ♦ vt (muscles) flexionar; **flexible** adj flexível
flick [flɪk] n pancada leve; (with finger) peteleco, piparote m; (with whip) chicotada ♦ vt dar um peteleco; (towel) dar uma lambada; (whip) dar uma chicotada; (switch) apertar; **flick through** vt fus folhear
flicker ['flɪkə*] vi tremular; (eyelids) tremer
flight [flaɪt] n vôo m; (escape) fuga; (of steps) lance m; **flight attendant** (US) n comissário(-a) m de bordo; **flight deck** n (AVIAT) cabine f do piloto; (NAUT) pista de aterrissagem (BR) or aterragem (PT)
flimsy ['flɪmzɪ] adj (thin) delgado, franzino; (shoes) ordinário; (clothes) de tecido fino; (building) barato; (weak) débil; (excuse) fraco
flinch [flɪntʃ] vi encolher-se; **to ~ from sth/from doing sth** vacilar diante de algo/em fazer algo
fling [flɪŋ] (pt, pp flung) vt lançar
flint [flɪnt] n pederneira; (in lighter) pedra
flippant ['flɪpənt] adj petulante, irreverente
flipper ['flɪpə*] n (of animal) nadadeira; (for swimmer) pé-de-pato, nadadeira
flirt [fləːt] vi flertar ♦ n namorador(a) m/f, paquerador(a) m/f
float [fləut] n bóia; (in procession) carro alegórico; (sum of money) caixa ♦ vi flutuar; (swimmer) boiar
flock [flɔk] n rebanho; (of birds) bando ♦ vi: **to ~ to** afluir a
flog [flɔg] vt açoitar
flood [flʌd] n enchente f, inundação f; (of letters, imports etc) enxurrada ♦ vt inundar, alagar ♦ vi (place) alagar; (people, goods): **to ~ into** inun-

dar; **flooding** n inundação f; **floodlight** n refletor m, holofote m
floor [flɔː*] n chão m; (storey) andar m; (of sea) fundo ♦ vt (fig: confuse) confundir, pasmar; (subj: blow) derrubar; (: question, remark) aturdir; **ground ~** (BRIT) or **first ~** (US) andar térreo (BR), rés-do-chão (PT); **first ~** (BRIT) or **second ~** (US) primeiro andar; **floorboard** n tábua de assoalho; **floor show** n show m
flop [flɔp] n fracasso ♦ vi fracassar; (into chair) cair pesadamente
floppy ['flɔpɪ] adj frouxo, mole; **floppy (disk)** n disquete m
florist ['flɔrɪst] n florista m/f; **florist's (shop)** n floricultura
flounder ['flaundə*] (pl ~ or ~s) n (ZOOL) linguado ♦ vi (swimmer) debater-se; (fig: speaker) atrapalharse; (: economy) flutuar
flour ['flauə*] n farinha
flourish ['flʌrɪʃ] vi florescer ♦ vt brandir, menear ♦ n gesto floreado
flow [fləu] n fluxo; (of river, ELEC) corrente f; (of blood) circulação f ♦ vi correr; (traffic) fluir; (blood, ELEC) circular; (clothes, hair) ondular; **flow chart** n fluxograma m
flower ['flauə*] n flor f ♦ vi florescer, florir; **flower bed** n canteiro; **flowerpot** n vaso; **flowery** adj (perfume) a base de flor; (pattern) florido; (speech) floreado
flown [fləun] pp of **fly**
flu [fluː] n gripe f
fluctuate ['flʌktjueɪt] vi flutuar; (temperature) variar
fluent ['fluːənt] adj fluente; **he speaks ~ French, he's ~ in French** ele fala francês fluentemente
fluff [flʌf] n felpa, penugem f; **fluffy** adj macio, fofo; (toy) de pelúcia
fluid ['fluːɪd] adj fluido ♦ n fluido

fluke [fluːk] (*inf*) *n* sorte *f*

flung [flʌŋ] *pt, pp of* **fling**

fluoride ['fluəraid] *n* fluoreto *m*

flurry ['flʌrɪ] *n* (*of snow*) lufada; **~ of activity** muita atividade

flush [flʌʃ] *n* (*on face*) rubor *m*; (*fig*) resplendor *m* ♦ *vt* lavar com água ♦ *vi* ruborizar-se ♦ *adj*: **~ with** rente com; **to ~ the toilet** dar descarga; **flush out** *vt* levantar; **flushed** *adj* ruborizado, corado

flustered ['flʌstəd] *adj* atrapalhado

flute [fluːt] *n* flauta

flutter ['flʌtə*] *n* agitação *f*; (*of wings*) bater *m* ♦ *vi* esvoaçar

flux [flʌks] *n*: **in a state of ~** mudando continuamente

fly [flai] (*pt* **flew**, *pp* **flown**) *n* mosca; (*on trousers: also:* **flies**) braguilha ♦ *vt* (*plane*) pilotar; (*passengers, cargo*) transportar (de avião); (*distances*) percorrer ♦ *vi* voar; (*passengers*) ir de avião; (*escape*) fugir; (*flag*) hastear-se; **fly away** *or* **off** *vi* voar; **flying** *n* aviação *f* ♦ *adj*: **flying visit** visita de médico; **with flying colours** brilhantemente; **flying saucer** *n* disco voador; **flyover** (*BRIT*) *n* viaduto *m*; **flysheet** *n* duplo teto

foal [fəul] *n* potro

foam [fəum] *n* espuma; (*also:* **~ rubber**) espuma de borracha ♦ *vi* espumar

focal point ['fəukl-] *n* foco

focus ['fəukəs] (*pl* **~es**) *n* foco ♦ *vt* enfocar ♦ *vi*: **to ~ on** enfocar, focalizar; **in/out of ~** em foco/fora de foco

foe [fəu] *n* inimigo

fog [fɔg] *n* nevoeiro; **foggy** *adj*: **it's foggy** está nevoento

foil [fɔil] *vt* frustrar ♦ *n* folha metálica; (*also:* **kitchen ~**) folha *or* papel *m* de alumínio; (*complement*) contraste

m, complemento; (*FENCING*) florete *m*

fold [fəuld] *n* dobra, vinco, prega; (*of skin*) ruga; (*AGR*) redil *m*, curral *m* ♦ *vt* dobrar; (*arms*) cruzar; **fold up** *vi* dobrar; (*business*) abrir falência ♦ *vt* dobrar; **folder** *n* pasta; **folding** *adj* dobrável

folk [fəuk] *npl* gente *f* ♦ *cpd* popular, folclórico; **~s** *npl* (*family*) família, parentes *mpl*; (*parents*) pais *mpl*; **folklore** ['fəuklɔː*] *n* folclore *m*

follow ['fɔləu] *vt* seguir; (*event, story*) acompanhar ♦ *vi* seguir; (*person, period of time*) acompanhar; (*result*) resultar; **to ~ suit** fazer o mesmo; **follow up** *vt* (*letter*) responder a; (*offer*) levar adiante; (*case*) acompanhar; **follower** *n* seguidor(a) *m/f*; **following** *adj* seguinte ♦ *n* adeptos *mpl*

folly ['fɔlɪ] *n* loucura

fond [fɔnd] *adj* carinhoso; (*hopes*) absurdo, descabido; **to be ~ of** gostar de

fondle ['fɔndl] *vt* acariciar

font [fɔnt] *n* (*REL*) pia batismal; (*TYP*) fonte *f*, família

food [fuːd] *n* comida; **food mixer** *n* batedeira; **food poisoning** *n* intoxicação *f* alimentar; **food processor** *n* multiprocessador *m* de cozinha; **foodstuffs** *npl* gêneros *mpl* alimentícios

fool [fuːl] *n* tolo(-a); (*CULIN*) purê *m* de frutas com creme ♦ *vt* enganar ♦ *vi* (*gen: ~ around*) brincar; **foolhardy** *adj* temerário; **foolish** *adj* burro; (*careless*) imprudente; **foolproof** *adj* infalível

foot [fut] (*pl* **feet**) *n* pé *m*; (*of animal*) pata; (*measure*) pé (304 *mm*; 12 *inches*) ♦ *vt* (*bill*) pagar; **on ~ a** pé; **footage** *n* (*CINEMA: length*) = metragem *f*; (*material*) sequências *fpl*; **football** *n* bola; (*game: BRIT*) futebol m; (: US) futebol norte-americano; **football player** n (BRIT: also: **footballer**) jogador de futebol; **footbrake** n freio (BR) or travão m (PT) de pé; **footbridge** n passarela; **foothills** npl contraforte m; **foothold** n apoio para o pé; **footing** n (fig) posição f; **to lose one's footing** escorregar; **footnote** n nota ao pé da página, nota de rodapé; **footpath** n caminho, atalho; **footprint** n pegada, pisada; **footstep** n passo; **footwear** n calçados mpl

---

KEYWORD

for [fɔ:*] prep **1** (indicating destination, direction) para; he went ~ the paper foi pegar o jornal; is this ~ me? é para mim?; it's time ~ lunch é hora de almoçar

2 (indicating purpose) para, what is it ~? para quê serve?; to pray ~ peace orar pela paz

3 (on behalf of, representing) por; he works ~ the government/a local firm ele trabalha para o governo/uma firma local; G ~ George G de George

4 (because of) por; ~ this reason por esta razão; ~ fear of being criticised com medo de ser criticado

5 (with regard to) para; it's cold ~ July está frio para julho

6 (in exchange for) por; it was sold ~ £5 foi vendido por £5

7 (in favour of) a favor de; are you ~ or against us? você está a favor de ou contra nós?; I'm all ~ it concordo plenamente, tem todo o meu apoio; vote ~ X vote em X

8 (referring to distance): there are roadworks ~ 5 km há obras na estrada por 5 quilômetros; we walked ~ miles andamos quilômetros

9 (referring to time) she will be away ~ a month ela ficará fora um mês; I have known her ~ years eu a conheço há anos; can you do it ~ tomorrow? você pode fazer isso para amanhã?

10 (with infinite clause): it is not ~ me to decide não cabe a mim decidir; it would be best ~ you to leave seria melhor que você fosse embora; there is still time ~ you to do it ainda há tempo para você fazer isso; ~ this to be possible ... para que isso seja possível ...

11 (in spite of) apesar de
♦ conj (since, as: rather formal) pois, porque

forbid [fəˈbɪd] (pt forbad(e), pp forbidden) vt proibir; to ~ sb to do sth proibir alguém de fazer algo; **forbidding** adj (prospect) sombrio, (look) severo

force [fɔ:s] n força ♦ vt forçar; the F~s npl (BRIT) as Forças Armadas; in ~ em vigor; **forceful** adj enérgico, vigoroso

forcibly [ˈfɔ:səblɪ] adv à força

ford [fɔ:d] n vau m

fore [fɔ:*] n: to come to the ~ salientar-se

forearm [ˈfɔ:rɑ:m] n antebraço

foreboding [fɔ:ˈbəʊdɪŋ] n mau presságio

forecast [ˈfɔ:kɑ:st] (irreg: like cast) n previsão f; (also: weather ~) previsão do tempo ♦ vt prognosticar, prever

forefinger [ˈfɔ:fɪŋgə*] n (dedo) indicador m

foregone [ˈfɔ:gɒn] pp of forego ♦ adj: it's a ~ conclusion é uma conclusão inevitável

foreground [ˈfɔ:graʊnd] n primeiro plano

forehead [ˈfɒrɪd] n testa

foreign ['fɔrɪn] adj estrangeiro; (trade) exterior; (object, matter) estranho; **foreigner** n estrangeiro(-a); **foreign exchange** n câmbio; **Foreign Office** n (BRIT) Ministério das Relações Exteriores

foreman ['fɔːmən] (irreg) n capataz m; (in construction) contramestre m

foremost ['fɔːməʊst] adj principal ♦ adv: **first and ~** antes de mais nada

forensic [fə'rensɪk] adj forense; **~ medicine** medicina legal

forerunner ['fɔːrʌnə*] n precursor(a) m/f

foresee [fɔː'siː] (irreg: like see) vt prever; **foreseeable** adj previsível

foresight ['fɔːsaɪt] n previdência

forest ['fɔrɪst] n floresta

forestry ['fɔrɪstrɪ] n silvicultura

foretaste ['fɔːteɪst] n amostra

foretell [fɔː'tel] (irreg: like tell) vt predizer, profetizar

forever [fə'revə*] adv para sempre

foreword ['fɔːwɜːd] n prefácio

forfeit ['fɔːfɪt] vt perder (direito a)

forgave [fə'ɡeɪv] pt of **forgive**

forge [fɔːdʒ] n ferraria ♦ vt falsificar; (metal) forjar; **forge ahead** vi avançar constantemente; **forger** n falsificador(a) m/f; **forgery** n falsificação f

forget [fə'ɡet] (pt forgot, pp forgotten) vt, vi esquecer; **forgetful** adj esquecido; **forget-me-not** n miosótis m

forgive [fə'ɡɪv] (pt forgave, pp ~n) vt perdoar; **to ~ sb for sth** perdoar algo a alguém, perdoar alguém de algo; **forgiveness** n perdão m

fork [fɔːk] n (for eating) garfo; (for gardening) forquilha; (of roads etc) bifurcação f ♦ vi bifurcar-se; **fork out** (inf) vt (pay) desembolsar;

morrer em

forlorn [fə'lɔːn] adj desolado; (attempt) desesperado; (hope) último

form [fɔːm] n forma; (type) tipo; (SCH) série f; (questionnaire) formulário ♦ vt formar; (organization) criar; **to ~ a queue** (BRIT) fazer fila; **in top ~** em plena forma

formal ['fɔːməl] adj (offer) oficial; (person) cerimonioso; (occasion, education) formal; (dress) a rigor (BR), de cerimónia (PT); (garden) simétrico; **formally** adv formalmente

format ['fɔːmæt] n formato ♦ vt (COMPUT) formatar

former ['fɔːmə*] adj anterior; (earlier) antigo; **the ~ ... the latter ...** aquele ... este ...; **formerly** adv anteriormente

formidable ['fɔːmɪdəbl] adj terrível, temível

formula ['fɔːmjʊlə] (pl ~s or ~e) n fórmula

forsake [fə'seɪk] (pt forsook, pp forsaken) vt abandonar

fort [fɔːt] n forte m

forth [fɔːθ] adv para adiante; **back and ~** de cá para lá; **and so ~** e assim por diante; **forthcoming** adj próximo, que está para aparecer; (help) disponível; (person) comunicativo; **forthright** adj franco

fortify ['fɔːtɪfaɪ] vt (city) fortificar; (person) fortalecer

fortnight ['fɔːtnaɪt] (BRIT) n quinzena, quinze dias mpl; **fortnightly** adj quinzenal ♦ adv quinzenalmente

fortunate ['fɔːtʃənɪt] adj (event) feliz; (person): **to be ~** ter sorte; **it is ~ that ...** é uma sorte que ...; **fortunately** adv felizmente

fortune ['fɔːtʃən] n sorte f; (wealth)

fortuna; **fortune-teller** n adivinho(-a)

forty ['fɔːtɪ] num quarenta

forward ['fɔːwəd] adj (movement) para a frente; (position) avançado; (in time) futuro; (not shy) imodesto, presunçoso ♦ n (SPORT) atacante m ♦ vt (letter) remeter; (goods, parcel) expedir; (career) promover; (plans) ativar; **to move ~** avançar; **forward(s)** adv para a frente

fossil ['fɔsl] n fóssil m

foster ['fɔstə*] vt adotar (por um tempo limitado); (activity) promover; **foster child** (irreg) n filho adotivo (por um tempo limitado)

fought [fɔːt] pt, pp of **fight**

foul [faul] adj horrível; (language) obsceno ♦ n (SPORT) falta ♦ vt sujar; **foul play** n (LAW) crime m

found [faund] pt, pp of **find** ♦ vt (establish) fundar; **foundation** [faun'deɪʃən] n (act, organization) fundação f; (base) base f; (also: **foundation cream**) creme m base; **foundations** npl (of building) alicerces mpl

founder ['faundə*] n fundador(a) m/f ♦ vi naufragar

fountain ['fauntɪn] n chafariz m; **fountain pen** n caneta-tinteiro f

four [fɔː*] num quatro; **on all ~s** de quatro; **fourteen** num catorze; **fourth** num quarto

fowl [faul] n ave f (doméstica)

fox [fɔks] n raposa ♦ vt deixar perplexo

foyer ['fɔɪeɪ] n saguão m

fraction ['frækʃən] n fração f

fracture ['fræktʃə*] n fratura ♦ vt fraturar

fragile ['frædʒaɪl] adj frágil

fragment ['frægmənt] n fragmento

fragrant ['freɪɡrənt] adj fragrante, perfumado

frail [freɪl] adj (person) fraco; (structure) frágil

frame [freɪm] n (of building) estrutura; (body) corpo; (of picture, door) moldura; (of spectacles: also: **~s**) armação f, aro ♦ vt (picture) emoldurar; **frame of mind** n estado de espírito; **framework** n armação f

France [frɑːns] n França

frank [fræŋk] adj franco ♦ vt (letter) franquear; **frankly** adv francamente; (candidly) abertamente

frantic ['fræntɪk] adj frenético; (person) fora de si

fraternity [frə'tɜːnɪtɪ] n (feeling) fraternidade f; (club) confraria

fraud [frɔːd] n fraude f; (person) impostor(a) m/f

fraught [frɔːt] adj tenso; **~ with** repleto de

fray [freɪ] n guerra ♦ vi esfiapar-se; **tempers were ~ed** estavam com os nervos em frangalhos

freak [friːk] n (person) anormal m/f; (event) anomalia

freckle ['frɛkl] n sarda

free [friː] adj livre; (seat) desocupado; (costing nothing) grátis, gratuito ♦ vt (do en liberdade; (jammed object) soltar; **~ (of charge)** grátis, de graça; **freedom** n liberdade f; **Freefone** ® n número de discagem gratuita; **free gift** n brinde m; **freelance** adj autônomo; **freely** adv livremente; **free-range** (egg) caseiro; **freeway** (US) n autoestrada; **free will** n livre arbítrio; **of one's own free will** por sua própria vontade

freeze [friːz] (pt **froze**, pp **frozen**) vi gelar-se, congelar-se ♦ vt congelar ♦ n geada; (on arms, wages) congelamento; **freezer** n congelador m, freezer m (BR); **freezing** adj: **freezing (cold)** (weather) glacial; (water) gelado; **3 degrees below freezing** 3 graus abaixo de zero; **freezing point** n ponto de congelamento

freight [freɪt] n (goods) carga; (money charged) frete m; **freight train** (US) n trem m de carga

French [frɛntʃ] adj francês(-esa) ♦ n (LING) francês m; **the** ~ npl (people) os franceses; **French bean** (BRIT) n feijão m comum; **French fried potatoes** (US French fries) npl batatas fpl fritas; **Frenchman** (irreg) n francês m; **Frenchwoman** (irreg) n francesa

frenzy ['frɛnzɪ] n frenesi m

frequent [adj 'friːkwənt, vt frɪ'kwɛnt] adj freqüente ♦ vt freqüentar; **frequently** adv freqüentemente, a miúdo

fresh [frɛʃ] adj fresco; (new) novo; (cheeky) atrevido; **freshen** vi (wind, air) tornar-se mais forte; **freshen up** vi (person) lavar-se, refrescar-se; **freshly** adv recentemente, há pouco; **freshness** n frescor m; **freshwater** adj de água doce

fret [frɛt] vi afligir-se

friar ['fraɪə*] n frade m

friction ['frɪkʃən] n fricção f, (between people) atrito

Friday ['fraɪdɪ] n sexta-feira f

fridge [frɪdʒ] (BRIT) n geladeira (BR), frigorífico (PT)

fried [fraɪd] adj frito; ~ **egg** ovo estrelado or frito

friend [frɛnd] n amigo(-a); **friendly** adj simpático; (match) amistoso; **friendship** n amizade f

fright [fraɪt] n terror m; (scare) pavor m; **to take** ~ assustar-se; **frighten** vt assustar; **frightened** adj: **to be frightened of** ter medo de; **frightening** adj assustador(a); **frightful** adj terrível, horrível

frigid ['frɪdʒɪd] adj frígido, frio

frill [frɪl] n babado

fringe [frɪndʒ] n franja; (on shawl etc) beira, orla; (edge: of forest etc) margem f

Frisbee ® ['frɪzbɪ] n Frisbee ® m

frisk [frɪsk] vt revistar

fritter ['frɪtə*] n bolinho frito; **fritter away** vt desperdiçar

frivolous ['frɪvələs] adj frívolo; (activity) fútil

frizzy ['frɪzɪ] adj frisado

fro [frəu] adj see **to**

frock [frɔk] n vestido

frog [frɔg] n rã f; **frogman** (irreg) n homem-rã m

KEYWORD

from [frɔm] prep 1 (indicating starting place) de; **where do you come** ~? de onde você é?; ~ **London to Glasgow** de Londres para Glasgow; **to escape** ~ **sth/sb** escapar de algo/ alguém

2 (indicating origin etc): **a letter/ telephone call** ~ **my sister** uma carta/um telefonema da minha irmã; **tell him** ~ **me that** ... diga a ele que da minha parte ...; **to drink** ~ **the bottle** beber na garrafa

3 (indicating time): ~ **one o'clock to** or **until** or **till two** da uma hora até às duas; ~ **May** (on) a partir de maio

4 (indicating distance): **we're still a long way** ~ **home** ainda estamos muito longe de casa

5 (indicating price, number etc) de; **prices range** ~ **£10 to £50** os preços vão de £10 a £50

6 (indicating difference) de; **he can't tell red** ~ **green** ele não pode diferenciar vermelho do verde

7 (because of/on the basis of): ~ **what he says** pelo que ele diz; **to act** ~ **conviction** agir por convicção; **weak** ~ **hunger** fraco de fome

front [frʌnt] n frente f; (of vehicle) parte f dianteira; (of house, fig) fachada; (also: **sea ~**) orla marítima ♦ adj da frente; **in ~ (of)** em frente (de); **front door** n porta principal; **frontier** ['frʌntɪə*] n fronteira; **front page** n primeira página; **front room** n (BRIT) salão m, sala de estar; **front-wheel drive** n tração f dianteira

frost [frɔst] n geada; (also: **hoar~**) gelo; **frostbite** n ulceração f produzida pelo frio; **frosty** adj (window) coberto de geada; (welcome) glacial

froth [frɔθ] n espuma

frown [fraun] vi franzir as sobrancelhas, amarrar a cara

froze [frəuz] pt of **freeze**

frozen ['frəuzn] pp of **freeze**

fruit [fru:t] n inv fruta; (fig: pl ~s) fruto; **fruitful** adj proveitoso; **fruit juice** n suco (BR) or sumo (PT) de frutas; **fruit machine** (BRIT) n caça-níqueis m inv (BR), máquina de jogo (PT); **fruit salad** n salada de frutas

frustrate [frʌs'treɪt] vt frustrar

fry [fraɪ] (pt, pp **fried**) vt fritar; **frying pan** n frigideira

ft. abbr = **foot**; **feet**

fudge [fʌdʒ] n (CULIN) ≈ doce m de leite

fuel [fjuəl] n (for heating) combustível m; (for propelling) carburante m; **fuel oil** n óleo combustível; **fuel tank** n depósito de combustível

fugitive ['fju:dʒɪtɪv] n fugitivo(-a)

fulfil [ful'fɪl] (US **fulfill**) vt (function) cumprir; (condition) satisfazer; (wish, desire) realizar

full [ful] adj cheio; (use, volume) máximo; (complete) completo; (information) detalhado; (price) integral; (skirt) folgado ♦ adv: **~ well** perfeitamente; **I'm ~ (up)** estou

satisfeito; **~ employment** pleno emprego; **a ~ two hours** duas horas completas; **at ~ speed** a toda a velocidade; **in ~** integralmente; **full stop** n ponto (final); **full-time** adj, adv (work) de tempo completo or integral; **fully** adv completamente; (at least) pelo menos; **fully-fledged** adj (teacher etc) diplomado

fumble ['fʌmbl] vi: **to ~ with** ♦ vt fus atrapalhar-se

fume [fju:m] vi fumegar; (be angry) estar com raiva; **fumes** npl gases mpl

fun [fʌn] n divertimento; **to have ~** divertir-se; **for ~** de brincadeira; **to make ~ of** fazer troça de, zombar de

function ['fʌŋkʃən] n função f; (reception, dinner) recepção f ♦ vi funcionar; **functional** adj funcional; (practical) prático

fund [fʌnd] n fundo; (source, store) fonte f; **~s** npl (money) fundos mpl

fundamental [fʌndə'mɛntl] adj fundamental

funeral ['fju:nərəl] n (burial) enterro

funfair ['fʌnfɛə*] (BRIT) n parque m de diversões

fungus ['fʌŋgəs] (pl **fungi**) n fungo; (mould) bolor m, mofo

funnel ['fʌnl] n funil m; (of ship) chaminé m

funny ['fʌnɪ] adj engraçado, divertido; (strange) esquisito, estranho

fur [fə:*] n pele f; (BRIT: in kettle etc) depósito, crosta

furious ['fjuərɪəs] adj furioso; (effort) incrível

furnace ['fə:nɪs] n forno

furnish ['fə:nɪʃ] vt mobiliar (BR), mobilar (PT); (supply): **to ~ sb with sth** fornecer algo a alguém; **furnishings** npl mobília

furniture ['fə:nɪtʃə*] n mobília, móveis mpl; **piece of ~** móvel m

furry ['fɜːrɪ] *adj* peludo

further ['fɜːðə*] *adj* novo, adicional ♦ *adv* mais longe; (*more*) mais; (*moreover*) além disso ♦ *vt* promover; **further education** (*BRIT*) n educação f superior; **furthermore** *adv* além disso

furthest ['fɜːðɪst] *superl of* **far**

fury ['fjʊərɪ] *n* fúria

fuse [fjuːz] *n* fusível *m*; (*for bomb etc*) espoleta, mecha ♦ *vt* fundir; (*fig*) unir ♦ *vi* (*metal*) fundir-se; unir-se; **to ~ the lights** (*BRIT: ELEC*) queimar as luzes; **fuse box** *n* caixa de fusíveis

fuss [fʌs] *n* estardalhaço; (*complaining*) escândalo; **to make a ~** criar caso; **to make a ~ of sb** paparicar alguém; **fussy** *adj* (*person*) exigente; (*dress, style*) espalhafatoso

future ['fjuːtʃə*] *adj* futuro ♦ *n* futuro; in ~ no futuro

fuze [fjuːz] (*US*) = **fuse**

fuzzy ['fʌzɪ] *adj* (*PHOT*) indistinto; (*hair*) frisado, encrespado

G

G [dʒiː] *n* (*MUS*) sol *m*

G7 *n abbr* (= *Group of 7*) G7

gable ['geɪbl] *n* cumeeira

gadget ['gædʒɪt] *n* aparelho, engenhoca

Gaelic ['geɪlɪk] *adj* gaélico(-a) ♦ *n* (*LING*) gaélico

gag [gæg] *n* (*on mouth*) mordaça; (*joke*) piada ♦ *vt* amordaçar

gain [geɪn] *n* ganho; (*profit*) lucro ♦ *vt* ganhar ♦ *vi* (*watch*) adiantar-se; (*benefit*): **to ~ from sth** tirar proveito de algo; **to ~ on sb** aproximar-se de alguém; **to ~ 3lbs (in weight)** engordar 3 libras

gal. *abbr* = **gallon**

Galapagos (Islands) [gə'læpəgəs-]

npl: **the ~** as ilhas Galápagos

gale [geɪl] *n* ventania; **~ force 10** vento de força 10

gallant ['gælənt] *adj* valente; (*polite*) galante

gallery ['gælərɪ] *n* (*in theatre etc*) galeria; (*also:* **art ~:** *public*) museu *m*; (*: private*) galeria (de arte)

gallon ['gælən] *n* galão *m* (= *8 pints*; *BRIT* = *4.5l; US* = *3.8l*)

gallop ['gæləp] *n* galope *m* ♦ *vi* galopar

gallows ['gæləuz] *n* forca

gallstone ['gɔːlstəun] *n* cálculo biliar

galore [gə'lɔː*] *adv* à beça

gamble ['gæmbl] *n* risco ♦ *vt* apostar ♦ *vi* jogar, arriscar; **gambler** *n* jogador(a) *m/f*; **gambling** *n* jogo

game [geɪm] *n* jogo; (*match*) partida; (*esp TENNIS*) jogada; (*strategy*) plano, esquema *m*; (*HUNTING*) caça ♦ *adj* (*willing*): **to be ~ for anything** topar qualquer parada; **big ~** caça grossa; **gamekeeper** *n* guarda-caça *m*

gammon ['gæmən] *n* (*bacon*) toucinho (defumado); (*ham*) presunto

gang [gæŋ] *n* bando, grupo; (*of criminals*) gangue *f*; (*of workmen*) turma ♦ *vi*: **to ~ up on sb** conspirar contra alguém

gangster ['gæŋstə*] *n* gângster *m*, bandido

gaol [dʒeɪl] (*BRIT*) *n, vt* = **jail**

gap [gæp] *n* brecha, fenda; (*in trees, traffic*) abertura; (*in time*) intervalo; (*difference*) diferença

gape [geɪp] *vi* (*person*) estar *or* ficar boquiaberto; (*hole*) abrir-se; **gaping** (*hole*) muito aberto

garage ['gærɑːʒ] *n* garagem *f*; (*for car repairs*) oficina (mecânica)

garbage ['gɑːbɪdʒ] *n* (*US*) lixo; (*inf: nonsense*) disparates *mpl*; **garbage can** (*US*) *n* lata de lixo

garbled ['gɑːbld] *adj* deturpado,

destorcido

garden ['gɑ:dn] n jardim m; ~s npl (public park) jardim público, parque m; **gardener** ['gɑ:dnə*] n jardineiro(-a); **gardening** n jardinagem f

gargle ['gɑ:gl] vi gargarejar

garish ['gɛərɪʃ] adj (colour) berrante; (light) brilhante

garland ['gɑ:lənd] n guirlanda

garlic ['gɑ:lɪk] n alho

garment ['gɑ:mənt] n peça de roupa

garrison ['gærɪsn] n guarnição f

garter ['gɑ:tə*] n liga

gas [gæs] n gás m; (US: gasoline) gasolina ♦ vt asfixiar com gás; **gas cooker** (BRIT) n fogão m a gás; **gas cylinder** n bujão m de gás; **gas fire** (BRIT) n aquecedor m a gás

gash [gæʃ] n talho m; (tear) corte m ♦ vt talhar; cortar

gasket ['gæskɪt] n (AUT) junta, gaxeta

gasoline ['gæsəli:n] (US) n gasolina

gasp [gɑ:sp] n arfada f ♦ vi arfar; **gasp out** vt dizer com voz entrecortada

gas station (US) n posto de gasolina

gate [geɪt] n portão m; **gatecrash** (BRIT) vt entrar de penetra em; **gateway** n portão m, passagem f

gather ['gæðə*] vt colher; (assemble) reunir; (SEWING) franzir; (understand) compreender ♦ vi reunir-se; **to ~ speed** acelerar-se; **gathering** n reunião f, assembléia

gauge [geɪdʒ] n (instrument) medidor m ♦ vt (fig: character) avaliar

gaunt [gɔ:nt] adj descarnado; (bare, stark) desolado

gauze [gɔ:z] n gaze f

gave [geɪv] pt of **give**

gay [geɪ] adj (homosexual) gay; (oldfashioned: cheerful) alegre; (colour) vistoso; (music) vivo

gaze [geɪz] n olhar m fixo ♦ vi: **to ~ at sth** fitar algo

GB abbr = **Great Britain**

GCE (BRIT) n abbr = **General Certificate of Education**

GCSE (BRIT) n abbr = **General Certificate of Secondary Education**

gear [gɪə*] n equipamento; (TECH) engrenagem f; (AUT) velocidade f, marcha (BR), mudança (PT) ♦ vt (fig: adapt): **to ~ sth to** preparar algo para; **top** (BRIT) or **high** (US)/**low** ~ quarta/primeira (marcha); **in** ~ engrenado; **gearbox** n caixa de mudanças (BR) or de velocidades (PT)

geese [gi:s] npl of **goose**

gel [dʒɛl] n gel m

gem [dʒɛm] n jóia, gema

Gemini ['dʒɛmɪnaɪ] n Gêminis m, Gêmeos mpl

gender ['dʒɛndə*] n gênero

general ['dʒɛnərl] n general m ♦ adj geral; **in** ~ em geral; **general anaesthetic** n anestesia geral; **generally** adv geralmente; **general practitioner** n clínico(-a) geral

generate ['dʒɛnəreɪt] vt gerar; **generator** n gerador m

generous ['dʒɛnərəs] adj generoso; (measure etc) abundante

genetic engineering [dʒɪ'nɛtɪk-] n engenharia genética

Geneva [dʒɪ'ni:və] n Genebra

genial ['dʒi:nɪəl] adj cordial, simpático

genitals ['dʒɛnɪtlz] npl órgãos mpl genitais

genius ['dʒi:nɪəs] n gênio

gentle ['dʒɛntl] adj (touch) leve, suave; (landscape) suave; (animal) manso

gentleman ['dʒɛntlmən] (irreg) n senhor m; (social position) fidalgo; (well-bred man) cavalheiro

gently ['dʒɛntlɪ] adv suavemente

gentry ['dʒɛntrɪ] n pequena nobreza

gents [dʒɛnts] n banheiro de

homens (*BR*), casa de banho dos homens (*PT*)

genuine ['dʒɛnjuɪn] *adj* autêntico; (*person*) sincero

geography [dʒɪ'ɔgrəfi] *n* geografia

geology [dʒɪ'ɔlədʒɪ] *n* geologia

geometry [dʒɪ'ɔmɪtrɪ] *n* geometria

geranium [dʒɪ'reɪnjəm] *n* gerânio

geriatric [dʒɛrɪ'ætrɪk] *adj* geriátrico

germ [dʒəːm] *n* micróbio, bacilo

German ['dʒəːmən] *adj* ale-mão(-mã) ♦ *n* alemão(-mã) *m/f*; (*LING*) alemão *m*; **German measles** *n* rubéola

Germany ['dʒəːmənɪ] *n* Alemanha

gesture ['dʒɛstɪə*] *n* gesto

get [gɛt] (*pt, pp* **got**) (*US: pp* **gotten**) *vi* **1** (*become, be*) ficar, tornar-se; **to ~ old/tired/cold** envelhecer/cansar-se/resfriar-se; **to ~ annoyed/bored** aborrecer-se/amuar-se; **to ~ drunk** embebedar-se; **to ~ dirty** sujar-se; **to ~ killed/married** ser morto/casar-se; **when do I ~ paid?** quando eu recebo?, quando eu vou ser pago?; **it's ~ting late** está ficando tarde

2 (*go*): **to ~ to/from** ir para/de; **to ~ home** chegar em casa

3 (*begin*) começar a; **to ~ to know sb** começar a conhecer alguém; **let's ~ going** *or* **started** vamos lá!

♦ *modal aux vb*: **you've got to do it** você tem que fazê-lo

♦ *vt* **1**: **to ~ sth done** (*do*) fazer algo; (*have done*) mandar fazer algo; **to ~ one's hair cut** cortar o cabelo; **to ~ the car going** *or* **to go** fazer o carro andar; **to ~ sb to do sth** convencer alguém a fazer algo; **to ~ sth/sb ready** preparar algo/arrumar alguém

2 (*obtain*) ter; (*find*) achar; (*fetch*)

buscar; **to ~ sth for sb** arranjar algo para alguém; (*fetch*) ir buscar algo para alguém; **~ me Mr Jones, please** (*TEL*) pode chamar o Sr Jones por favor; **can I ~ you a drink?** você está servido?

3 (*receive: present, letter*) receber; (*acquire: reputation, prize*) ganhar

4 (*catch*) agarrar; (*hit: target etc*) pegar; **to ~ sb by the arm/throat** agarrar alguém pelo braço/pela garganta; **~ him!** pega ele!

5 (*take, move*) levar; **to ~ sth to sb** levar algo para alguém; **I can't ~ it in/out/through** não consigo enfiá-lo/tirá-lo/passá-lo; **do you think we'll ~ it through the door?** você acha que conseguiremos passar isto na porta?

6 (*plane, bus etc*) pegar, tomar

7 (*understand*) entender; (*hear*) ouvir; **I've got it** entendi; **I don't ~ your meaning** não entendo o que você quer dizer

8 (*have, possess*): **to have got** ter

get about *vi* espalhar-se

get along *vi* (*agree*) entender-se; (*depart*) ir embora; (*manage*) = **get by**

get around = **get round**

get at *vt fus* (*attack, criticize*) atacar; (*reach*) alcançar; **what are you ~ting at?** o que você está querendo dizer?

get away *vi* (*leave*) partir; (*escape*) escapar

get away with *vt fus* conseguir fazer impunemente

get back *vi* (*return*) regressar, voltar ♦ *vt* receber de volta, recobrar

get by *vi* (*pass*) passar; (*manage*) virar-se

get down *vi* descer ♦ *vt fus* abaixar ♦ *vt* (*object*) abaixar, descer; (*depress: person*) deprimir

get down to vt fus (work) pôr-se a (fazer)

get in vi entrar; (train) chegar; (arrive home) voltar para casa

get into vt fus entrar em; (vehicle) subir em; (clothes) pôr, vestir, enfiar; **to ~ into bed/a rage** meter-se na cama/ficar com raiva

get off vi (from train etc) saltar (BR), descer (PT); (depart) sair; (escape) escapar ♦ vt (remove: clothes, stain) tirar; (send off) mandar ♦ vt fus (train, bus) saltar de (BR), sair de (PT)

get on vi (at exam etc): **how are you ~ting on?** como vai?; (agree): **to ~ on (with)** entender-se (com) ♦ vt fus (train etc) subir em (BR), subir para (PT); (horse) montar em

get out vi (of place, vehicle) sair ♦ vt (take out) tirar

get out of vt fus (duty etc) escapar de

get over vt fus (illness) restabelecer-se de

get round vt fus rodear; (fig: person) convencer

get through vi (TEL) completar a ligação

get through to vt fus (TEL) comunicar-se com

get together vi (people) reunir-se ♦ vt reunir

get up vi levantar-se ♦ vt fus levantar

get up to vt fus (reach) chegar a; (BRIT: prank etc) fazer

getaway ['gɛtəweɪ] n fuga, escape m

ghastly ['gɑːstlɪ] adj horrível; (building) medonho; (appearance) horripilante; (pale) pálido

gherkin ['gəːkɪn] n pepino em vinagre

ghost [gəust] n fantasma m

giant ['dʒaɪənt] n gigante m ♦ adj gigantesco, gigante

gibberish ['dʒɪbərɪʃ] n algaravia

giblets ['dʒɪblɪts] npl miúdos mpl

Gibraltar [dʒɪ'brɔːltə*] n Gibraltar m (no article)

giddy ['gɪdɪ] adj (dizzy): **to be** or **feel ~** estar com vertigem

gift [gɪft] n presente m, dádiva; (ability) dom m, talento; **gifted** adj bem-dotado

gigantic [dʒaɪ'gæntɪk] adj gigantesco

giggle ['gɪgl] vi dar risadinha boba

gill [dʒɪl] n (measure) = 0.25 pints (BRIT = 0.148l, US = 0.118l)

gills [gɪlz] npl (of fish) guelras fpl, brânquias fpl

gilt [gɪlt] adj dourado ♦ n dourado

gimmick ['gɪmɪk] n truque m or macete m (publicitário)

gin [dʒɪn] n gim m, genebra

ginger ['dʒɪndʒə*] n gengibre m; **gingerbread** n (cake) pão m de gengibre; (biscuit) biscoito de gengibre

gipsy ['dʒɪpsɪ] n cigano

giraffe [dʒɪ'rɑːf] n girafa

girl [gəːl] n (small) menina (BR), rapariga (PT); (young woman) jovem f, moça; (daughter) filha; **girlfriend** n (of girl) amiga; (of boy) namorada

gist [dʒɪst] n essencial m

KEYWORD

---

give [gɪv] (pt **gave**, pp **given**) vt
1 (hand over) dar; **to ~ sb sth**, **~ sth to sb** dar algo a alguém
2 (used with n to replace a vb): **to ~ a cry/sigh/push** etc dar um grito/suspiro/empurrão etc; **to ~ a speech/a lecture** fazer um discurso/uma palestra
3 (tell, deliver: news, advice, message etc) dar; **to ~ the right/wrong ans-**

glacier

glacier 113 **glossary**

wer dar a resposta certa/errada
4 (supply, provide: opportunity, job etc) dar; (bestow: title, right) conceder; **the sun ~s warmth and light** o sol fornece calor e luz
5 (dedicate: time, one's life) dedicar; **she gave it all her attention** ela dedicou toda sua atenção a isto
6 (organize): **to ~ a party/dinner** etc dar uma festa/jantar etc
♦ vi **1** (also: ~ **way**: break, collapse) dar folga; **his legs gave beneath him** suas pernas bambearam; **the roof/floor gave as I stepped on it** o telhado/chão desabou quando eu pisei nele
2 (stretch: fabric) dar de si
give away vt (money, opportunity) dar; (secret, information) revelar
give back vt devolver
give in vi (yield) ceder ♦ vt (essay etc) entregar
give off vt (heat, smoke) soltar
give out vt (distribute) distribuir; (make known) divulgar
give up vi (surrender) desistir, darse por vencido ♦ vt (job, boyfriend, habit) renunciar a; (idea, hope) abandonar; **to ~ up smoking** deixar de fumar; **to ~ o.s. up** entregar-se
give way vi (yield) ceder; (break, collapse: rope) arrebentar; (: ladder) quebrar; (BRIT: AUT) dar a preferência (BR), dar prioridade (PT)

glacier ['glæsɪə*] n glaciar m, geleira
glad [glæd] adj contente
gladly ['glædlɪ] adv com muito prazer
glamorous ['glæmərəs] adj encantador(a), glamouroso
glamour ['glæmə*] n encanto, glamour m
glance [glɑːns] n relance m, vista de

olhos ♦ vi: **to ~ at** olhar (de relance)
glance off vt fus (bullet) ricochetear de; **glancing** adj (blow) oblíquo
gland [glænd] n glândula
glare [glɛə*] n (of anger) olhar m furioso; (of light) luminosidade f; (of publicity) foco ♦ vi brilhar; **to ~ at** olhar furiosamente para; **glaring** adj (mistake) notório
glass [glɑːs] n vidro, cristal m; (for drinking) copo; **~es** npl (spectacles) óculos mpl; **glassware** n objetos mpl de cristal
glaze [gleɪz] vt (door) envidraçar; (pottery) vitrificar ♦ n verniz m
gleam [gliːm] vi brilhar
glean [gliːn] vt (information) colher
glib [glɪb] adj (answer) pronto; (person) lábioso
glide [glaɪd] vi deslizar; (AVIAT, birds) planar; **glider** n (AVIAT) planador m; **gliding** n (AVIAT) vôo sem motor
glimmer ['glɪmə*] n luz f trêmula; (of interest, hope) lampejo
glimpse [glɪmps] n vista rápida, vislumbre m ♦ vt vislumbrar, ver de relance
glint [glɪnt] vi cintilar
glisten ['glɪsn] vi brilhar
glitter ['glɪtə*] vi reluzir, brilhar
gloat [gləʊt] vi: **to ~ (over)** exultar (com)
global ['gləʊbl] adj mundial
globe [gləʊb] n globo, esfera
gloom [gluːm] n escuridão f; (sadness) tristeza; **gloomy** adj escuro; triste
glorious ['glɔːrɪəs] adj (weather) magnífico; (future) glorioso
glory ['glɔːrɪ] n glória
gloss [glɒs] n (shine) brilho m; (also: ~ paint) pintura brilhante, esmalte m; **gloss over** vt fus encobrir
glossary ['glɒsərɪ] n glossário

glossy ['glɔsɪ] adj lustroso

glove [glʌv] n luva

glow [gləu] vi (shine) brilhar; (fire) arder

glower ['glauə*] vi: **to ~ at** (sb) olhar (alguém) de modo ameaçador

glucose ['glu:kəus] n glicose f

glue [glu:] n cola ♦ vt colar

glum [glʌm] adj (mood) abatido; (person, tone) triste

glut [glʌt] n abundância, fartura

glutton ['glʌtn] n glutão(-ona) m/f; **a ~ for work** um(a) trabalhador(a) incansável

GM adj abbr (= genetically modified) geneticamente modificado

gnat [næt] n mosquito

gnaw [nɔ:] vt roer

KEYWORD

go [gəu] (pt went, pp gone, pl ~es) vi **1** (travel, move) viajar; **a car went by** um carro passou; **he has gone to Aberdeen** ele foi para Aberdeen

2 (depart) partir, ir-se

3 (attend) ir; **she went to university in Rio** ela fez universidade no Rio; **he ~es to the local church** ele freqüenta a igreja local

4 (take part in an activity) ir; **to ~ for a walk** ir passear

5 (work) funcionar; **the bell went just then** a campainha acabou de tocar

6 (become): **to ~ pale/mouldy** ficar pálido/mofado

7 (be sold): **to ~ for £10** ser vendido por £10

8 (fit, suit): **to ~ with** acompanhar, combinar com

9 (be about to, intend to): **he's ~ing to do it** ele vai fazê-lo; **are you ~ing to come?** você vem?

10 (time) passar

11 (event, activity) ser; **how did it ~?** como foi?

12 (be given): **the job is to ~ to someone else** o emprego vai ser dado para outra pessoa

13 (break) romper-se; **the fuse went** o fusível queimou; **the leg of the chair went** a perna da cadeira quebrou

14 (be placed): **where does this cup ~?** onde é que põe esta xícara?; **the milk ~es in the fridge** pode guardar o leite na geladeira

♦ n **1** (try): **to have a ~ (at)** tentar a sorte (com)

2 (turn) vez f

3 (move): **to be on the ~** ter muito para fazer; **go about** vi (also: ~ around): rumour: espalhar-se

♦ vt fus: **how do I ~ about this?** como é que eu faço isto?

go ahead vi (make progress) progredir; (get going) ir em frente

go along vi ir ♦ vt fus ladear; **to ~ along with** concordar com

go away vi (leave) ir-se, ir embora

go back vi (return) voltar; (go again) ir de novo

go back on vt fus (promise) faltar com

go by vi (years, time) passar ♦ vt fus (book, rule) guiar-se por

go down vi (descend) descer, baixar; (ship) afundar; (sun) pôr-se ♦ vt fus (stairs, ladder) descer

go for vt fus (fetch) ir buscar; (like) gostar de; (attack) atacar

go in vi (enter) entrar

go in for vt fus (competition) inscrever-se em; (like) gostar de

go into vt fus (enter) entrar em; (investigate) investigar; (embark on) embarcar em

go off vi (leave) ir-se; (food) estragar, apodrecer; (bomb, gun) explo-

dir; (*event*) realizar-se ♦ vt fus (*person, food etc*) deixar de gostar de
go on vi (*continue*) seguir, continuar; (*happen*) acontecer, ocorrer
go out vi sair; (*for entertainment*): **are you ~ing out tonight?** você vai sair hoje à noite?; (*couple*): **they went out for 3 years** eles namoraram 3 anos; (*fire, light*) apagar-se
go over vi (*ship*) soçobrar ♦ vt fus (*check*) revisar
go round vi (*news, rumour*) circular
go through vt fus (*town etc*) atravessar; (*search through*) vascular; (*examine*) percorrer de cabo a rabo
go up vi subir; (*price*) aumentar
go without vt fus passar sem

goad [gəud] vt aguilhoar
go-ahead adj empreendedor(a) ♦ n luz f verde
goal [gəul] n meta, alvo; (*SPORT*) gol m (*BR*), golo (*PT*); **goalkeeper** n goleiro(-a) (*BR*), guarda-redes m/f inv (*PT*)
goat [gəut] n cabra
gobble ['gɔbl] vt (*also: ~ down, ~ up*) engolir rapidamente, devorar
god [gɔd] n deus m; **G~** Deus; **godchild** n afilhado(-a); **goddess** n deusa; **godfather** n padrinho; **godmother** n madrinha; **godsend** n dádiva do céu
goggles ['gɔglz] npl óculos mpl de proteção
going ['gəuɪŋ] n (*conditions*) estado do terreno ♦ adj: **the ~ rate** tarifa corrente or em vigor
gold [gəuld] n ouro ♦ adj (*made of gold*) de ouro; **golden** adj (*made of gold*) de ouro; (*gold in colour*) dourado; **goldfish** n inv peixe-dourado m; **gold-plated** adj plaquê inv; **goldsmith** n ourives m/f inv
golf [gɔlf] n golfe m; **golf ball** n

bola de golfe; (*on typewriter*) esfera; **golf club** n clube m de golfe; (*stick*) taco; **golf course** n campo de golfe; **golfer** n jogador(a) m/f, golfista m/f
gone [gɔn] pp of go
gong [gɔŋ] n gongo
good [gud] adj bom (boa); (*kind*) bom, bondoso; (*well-behaved*) educado ♦ n bem m; **~s** npl (*COMM*) mercadorias fpl; **~!** bom!; **to be ~ at** ser bom em; **to be ~ for** servir para; **it's ~ for you** faz-lhe bem; **a ~ deal (of)** muito; **a ~ many** muitos; **to make ~** reparar; **it's no ~ complaining** não adianta se queixar; **for ~** para sempre, definitivamente; **~ morning/afternoon/evening!** bom dia/boa tarde/boa noite!; **~ night!** boa noite!; **goodbye** excl até logo (*BR*), adeus (*PT*); **to say goodbye** despedir-se; **Good Friday** n Sexta-Feira Santa; **good-looking** adj bonito; **good-natured** adj (*person*) de bom gênio; (*pet*) de boa índole; **goodwill** n boa vontade f
goose [gu:s] n (*pl geese*) n ganso
gooseberry ['guzbərɪ] n groselha; **to play ~** (*BRIT*) ficar de vela
gooseflesh ['gu:sfleʃ], **goose pimples** npl pele f arrepiada
gore [gɔ:*] vt escornar ♦ n sangue m
gorge [gɔ:dʒ] n desfiladeiro ♦ vt: **to ~ o.s. (on)** empanturrar-se (de)
gorgeous ['gɔ:dʒəs] adj magnífico, maravilhoso; (*person*) lindo
gorilla [gə'rɪlə] n gorila m
gorse [gɔ:s] n tojo
gory ['gɔ:rɪ] adj sangrento
gospel ['gɔspl] n evangelho
gossip ['gɔsɪp] n (*scandal*) fofocas fpl, mexericos mpl (*PT*); (*chat*) conversa; (*scandalmonger*) fofoqueiro(-a) (*BR*), mexeriqueiro(-a) (*PT*) ♦ vi (*chat*) bater (um) papo (*BR*), cava-

quear (PT)

got [gɔt] pt, pp of **get**

gotten ['gɔtn] (US) pp of **get**

gout [gaut] n gota

govern ['gʌvən] vt governar; (event) controlar

governess ['gʌvənɪs] n governanta

government ['gʌvnmənt] n governo

governor ['gʌvənə*] n governador(a) m/f; (of school, hospital, jail) diretor(a) m/f

gown [gaun] n vestido; (of teacher, judge) toga

GP n abbr (MED) = **general practitioner**

grab [græb] vt agarrar ♦ vi: **to ~ at** tentar agarrar

grace [greis] n (REL) graça; (gracefulness) elegância, fineza ♦ vt (honour) honrar; (adorn) adornar; **5 days' ~** um prazo de 5 dias; **graceful** adj elegante, gracioso; **gracious** ['greiʃəs] adj gracioso, afável

grade [greid] n (quality) classe f, qualidade f; (degree) grau m; (US: SCH) série f, classe ♦ vt classificar; **grade crossing** (US) n passagem f de nível; **grade school** (US) n escola primária

gradient ['greidiənt] n declive m

gradual ['grædjuəl] adj gradual, gradativo; **gradually** adv gradualmente, pouco a pouco

graduate [n 'grædjuit, vb 'grædjueit] n graduado, (US) n diplomado do colégio ♦ vi formar-se, licenciar-se; **graduation** [grædju'eiʃən] n formatura

graffiti [grə'fi:ti] n, npl pichações fpl

graft [gra:ft] n (AGR, MED) enxerto; (BRIT: inf) trabalho pesado; (bribery) suborno ♦ vt enxertar

grain [grein] n grão m; (no pl: cereals) cereais mpl; (in wood) veio, fibra

gram [græm] n grama m

grammar ['græmə*] n gramática; **grammar school** n (BRIT) = liceo; **grammatical** [grə'mætikl] adj gramatical

gramme [græm] n = **gram**

grand [grænd] adj esplêndido; (inf: wonderful) ótimo, formidável; **granddad** n vovô m; **granddaughter** n neta; **grandfather** n avô m; **grandma** n avó f, vovó f; **grandmother** n avó f; **grandpa** n = **grandad**; **grandparents** npl avós mpl; **grand piano** n piano de cauda; **grandson** n neto

granite ['grænit] n granito

granny ['græni] (inf) n avó f, vovó f

grant [gra:nt] vt (concede) conceder; (a request etc) anuir a; (admit) admitir ♦ n (SCH) bolsa; (ADMIN) subvenção f, subsídio; **to take sth for ~ed** dar algo por certo

grape [greip] n uva

grapefruit ['greipfru:t] (pl inv or ~s) n toranja, grapefruit m (BR)

graph [gra:f] n gráfico; **graphic** ['græfik] adj gráfico; **graphics** n (art) artes fpl gráficas ♦ npl (drawings) desenhos mpl

grasp [gra:sp] vt agarrar, segurar; (understand) compreender, entender ♦ n (grip) aperto de mão; (understanding) compreensão f; **grasping** adj avaro

grass [gra:s] n grama (BR), relva (PT); **grasshopper** n gafanhoto

grate [greit] n (fireplace) lareira ♦ vi ranger ♦ vt (CULIN) ralar

grateful ['greitful] adj agradecido, grato

grater ['greitə*] n ralador m

gratitude ['grætitju:d] n agradeci-

mento
gratuity [grəˈtjuːɪtɪ] n gratificação f, gorjeta
grave [greɪv] n cova, sepultura ♦ adj sério; (mistake) grave
gravel [ˈɡrævl] n cascalho
gravestone [ˈɡreɪvstəun] n lápide f
graveyard [ˈɡreɪvjɑːd] n cemitério
gravity [ˈɡrævɪtɪ] n (PHYS) gravidade f; (seriousness) seriedade f, gravidade
gravy [ˈɡreɪvɪ] n molho (de carne)
gray [ɡreɪ] (US) adj = **grey**
graze [ɡreɪz] vi pastar ♦ vt (touch lightly) roçar; (scrape) raspar ♦ n (MED) esfoladura, arranhadura
grease [ɡriːs] n (fat) gordura; (lubricant) graxa, lubrificante m ♦ vt untar, lubrificar, engraxar; **greasy** adj gordurento, gorduroso; (skin, hair) oleoso
great [ɡreɪt] adj grande; (inf) genial; (pain, heat) forte; (important) importante; **Great Britain** n Grã-Bretanha; ver quadro

---

GREAT BRITAIN

A Grã-Bretanha, **Great Britain** ou **Britain** em inglês, designa a maior das ilhas britânicas e, portanto, engloba a Escócia e o País de Gales. Junto com a Irlanda, a ilha de Man e as ilhas Anglo-normandas, a Grã-Bretanha forma as ilhas Britânicas, ou **British Isles**. Reino Unido, em inglês **United Kingdom** ou **UK**, é o nome oficial da entidade política que compreende a Grã-Bretanha e a Irlanda do Norte.

---

great: **great-grandfather** n bisavô m; **great-grandmother** n bisavó f; **greatly** adv imensamente, muito

Greece [ɡriːs] n Grécia
greed [ɡriːd] n (also: ~iness) avidez f, cobiça; **greedy** adj avarento; (for food) guloso
Greek [ɡriːk] adj grego ♦ n grego(-a); (LING) grego
green [ɡriːn] adj verde; (inexperienced) inexperiente, ingênuo ♦ n verde m; (stretch of grass) gramado (BR), relvado (PT); (on golf course) green m; ~s npl (vegetables) verduras fpl; **greenery** n verdura; **greengrocer** (BRIT) n verdureiro(-a); **greenhouse** n estufa; **greenhouse effect** n efeito estufa; **greenhouse gas** n gás provocado pelo efeito estufa
Greenland [ˈɡriːnlənd] n Groenlândia
greet [ɡriːt] vt acolher; (news) receber; **greeting** n acolhimento; **greeting(s) card** n cartão m comemorativo
grenade [ɡrəˈneɪd] n granada
grew [ɡruː] pt of **grow**
grey [ɡreɪ] (US **gray**) adj cinzento; (dismal) sombrio; **grey-haired** adj grisalho; **greyhound** n galgo
grid [ɡrɪd] n grade f; (ELEC) rede f
grief [ɡriːf] n dor f, pesar m
grievance [ˈɡriːvəns] n motivo de queixa, agravo
grieve [ɡriːv] vi sofrer ♦ vt dar pena a, afligir; **to ~ for** chorar por
grill [ɡrɪl] n (on cooker) grelha; (also: mixed ~) prato de grelhados ♦ vt (BRIT) grelhar; (inf: question) interrogar cerradamente
grille [ɡrɪl] n grade f; (AUT) grelha
grim [ɡrɪm] adj desagradável; (unattractive) feio; (stern) severo
grimace [ɡrɪˈmeɪs] n careta ♦ vi fazer caretas
grime [ɡraɪm] n sujeira (BR),

sujidade f (PT)

grin [grɪn] n sorriso largo ♦ vi: **to ~ (at)** dar um sorriso largo (para)

grind [graɪnd] (pt, pp **ground**) vt triturar; (coffee etc) moer; (make sharp) afiar; (US: meat) picar ♦ n (work) trabalho (repetitivo e maçante)

grip [grɪp] n (of person) aperto de mão; (of animal) força; (handle) punho; (of tyre, shoe) aderência; (holdall) valise f ♦ vt agarrar; (attention) prender; **to come to ~s with** arcar com

gripping ['grɪpɪŋ] adj absorvente, emocionante

grisly ['grɪzlɪ] adj horrendo, medonho

gristle ['grɪsl] n (on meat) nervo

grit [grɪt] n areia, grão m de areia; (courage) coragem f ♦ vt (road) pôr areia em; **to ~ one's teeth** cerrar os dentes

groan [grəun] n gemido ♦ vi gemer

grocer ['grəusə*] n dono(-a) de mercearia; **groceries** npl comestíveis mpl; **grocer's (shop)** n mercearia

groin [grɔɪn] n virilha

groom [gruːm] n cavalariço; (also: **bride~**) noivo ♦ vt (horse) tratar; (fig): **to ~ sb for sth** preparar alguém para algo; **well-~ed** bem posto

groove [gruːv] n ranhura, entalhe m

grope [grəup] vi: **to ~ for** procurar às cegas

gross [grəus] adj (flagrant) grave; (vulgar) vulgar; (: building) de maugosto; (COMM) bruto

grotto ['grɔtəu] n gruta

grotty ['grɔtɪ] (BRIT: inf) adj vagabundo

ground [graund] pt, pp of **grind** ♦ n terra, chão m; (SPORT) campo; (land) terreno; (reason: gen pl) motivo, razão f; (US: also: **~wire**) (ligação f à) terra, fio-terra m ♦ vt (plane) manter em terra; (US: ELEC) ligar à terra; **~s** npl (of coffee etc) borra; (gardens etc) jardins mpl, parque m; **on the ~** no chão; **to the ~** por terra; **ground cloth** (US) n = **groundsheet**; **groundless** adj infundado; **groundsheet** (BRIT) n capa impermeável; **groundwork** n base f, preparação f

group [gruːp] n grupo; (also: **pop ~**) conjunto ♦ vt (also: **~ together**) agrupar ♦ vi (also: **~ together**) agrupar-se

grouse [graus] n inv (bird) tetraz m, galo-silvestre m ♦ vi (complain) queixar-se, resmungar

grove [grəuv] n arvoredo

grovel ['grɔvl] vi (fig): **to ~ (before)** abaixar-se (diante de)

grow [grəu] (pt grew, pp grown) vi crescer; (increase) aumentar; (develop): **to ~ (out of/from)** originar-se; (become): **to ~ rich/weak** enriquecer(-se)/enfraquecer-se ♦ vt plantar, cultivar; (beard) deixar crescer; **grow up** vi crescer, fazer-se homem/mulher; **grower** n cultivador(a) m/f, produtor(a) m/f; **growing** adj crescente

growl [graul] vi rosnar

grown [grəun] pp of **grow**

grown-up n adulto(-a), pessoa mais velha

growth [grəuθ] n crescimento; (increase) aumento; (MED) abscesso, tumor m

grub [grʌb] n larva, lagarta; (inf: food) comida, rango (BR)

grubby ['grʌbɪ] adj encardido

grudge [grʌdʒ] n motivo de rancor

♦ vt: **to ~ sb sth** dar algo a alguém de má vontade, invejar algo a alguém; **to bear sb a ~ for sth** guardar rancor de alguém por algo

gruelling ['gruəlıŋ] (US **grueling**) adj duro, árduo

gruesome ['gru:səm] adj horrível

gruff [grʌf] adj (voice) rouco; (manner) brusco

grumble ['grʌmbl] vi resmungar, bufar

grumpy ['grʌmpı] adj rabugento

grunt [grʌnt] vi grunhir

G-string n tapa-sexo m

guarantee [gærən'ti:] n garantia ♦ vt garantir

guard [gɑ:d] n guarda; (one person) guarda m; (BRIT: RAIL) guarda-freio; (on machine) dispositivo de segurança; (also: **fire~**) guarda-fogo ♦ vt (protect): **to ~ (against)** proteger (contra); (prisoner) vigiar; **to be on one's ~** estar prevenido; **guard against** vt fus prevenir-se contra; **guarded** adj (statement) cauteloso; **guardian** n protetor(a) m/f; (of minor) tutor(a) m/f

Guatemala [gwɔtə'mɑ:lə] n Guatemala

guerrilla [gə'rılə] n guerrilheiro(-a)

guess [ges] vt, vi (estimate) avaliar, conjeturar; (answer) adivinhar; (US) achar, supor ♦ n suposição f, conjetura; **to take** or **have a ~** adivinhar, chutar (inf)

guest [gest] n convidado(-a); (in hotel) hóspede m/f; **guest-house** n pensão f; **guest room** n quarto de hóspedes

guffaw [gʌ'fɔ:] vi dar gargalhadas

guidance ['gaidəns] n conselhos mpl

guide [gaid] n (person) guia m/f; (book, fig) guia m; (BRIT: also: **girl ~**) escoteira ♦ vt guiar; **guidebook** n guia m; **guide dog** n cão m de guia; **guidelines** npl (advice) orientação f

guillotine ['gɪlətiːn] n guilhotina

guilt [gɪlt] n culpa; **guilty** adj culpado

guinea pig ['gɪnɪ-] n porquinho-da-Índia m, cobaia; (fig) cobaia

guitar [gɪ'tɑː*] n violão m

gulf [gʌlf] n golfo; (abyss: also fig) abismo

gull [gʌl] n gaivota

gullible ['gʌlɪbl] adj crédulo

gully ['gʌlɪ] n barranco

gulp [gʌlp] vi engolir em seco ♦ vt (also: ~ **down**) engolir

gum [gʌm] n (ANAT) gengiva; (glue) goma; (also: ~ **drop**) bala de goma; (also: **chewing-~**) chiclete m (BR), pastilha elástica (PT) ♦ vt colar; **gumboots** (BRIT) npl botas fpl de borracha, galochas fpl

gun [gʌn] n (gen) arma (de fogo); (revolver) revólver m; (small) pistola; (rifle) espingarda; (cannon) canhão m; **gunfire** n tiroteio; **gunman** (irreg) n pistoleiro; **gunpoint** n: **at gunpoint** sob a ameaça de uma arma; **gunpowder** n pólvora; **gunshot** n tiro (de arma de fogo)

gurgle ['gə:gl] vi (baby) balbuciar; (water) gorgolejar

gust [gʌst] n (of wind) rajada

gusto ['gʌstəu] n: **with ~** com garra

gut [gʌt] n intestino, tripa; **~s** npl (ANAT) entranhas fpl; (inf: courage) coragem f, raça (inf)

gutter ['gʌtə*] n (of roof) calha; (in street) sarjeta

guy [gaı] n (also: ~**rope**) corda; (inf: man) cara m (BR), tipo (PT); **Guy Fawkes' Night** n ver quadro

GUY FAWKES' NIGHT

A **Guy Fawkes' Night**, também chamada de *bonfire night*, é a ocasião em que se comemora o fracasso da conspiração (a *Gunpowder Plot*) contra James I e o Parlamento, em 5 de novembro de 1605. Um dos conspiradores, Guy Fawkes, foi surpreendido no porão do Parlamento quando estava prestes a atear fogo a explosivos. Todo ano, no dia 5 de novembro, as crianças preparam antecipadamente um boneco de Guy Fawkes e pedem às pessoas que passam na rua a *penny for the Guy* (uma moedinha para o Guy), com o qual compram fogos de artifício.

gym [dʒɪm] n (*also*: **gymnasium**) ginásio; (*also*: **gymnastics**) ginástica
gymnast ['dʒɪmnæst] n ginasta m/f
gymnastics [dʒɪm'næstɪks] n ginástica
gynaecologist [gaɪnɪ'kɔlədʒɪst] (US **gynecologist**) n ginecologista m/f
gypsy ['dʒɪpsɪ] n = gipsy

H

haberdashery ['hæbə'dæʃərɪ] (BRIT) n armarinho
habit ['hæbɪt] n hábito, costume m; (*addiction*) vício; (REL) hábito
habitual [hə'bɪtjuəl] adj habitual, costumeiro; (*drinker, liar*) inveterado
hack [hæk] vt (*cut*) cortar; (*chop*) talhar ♦ n (*pej*: writer) escrevinhador(a) m/f; **hacker** n (COMPUT) pirata m (de dados de computador)
had [hæd] pt, pp of **have**

haddock ['hædək] (*pl inv or* **~s**) n hadoque m (BR), eglefim m (PT)
hadn't ['hædnt] = **had not**
haemorrhage ['hɛmərɪdʒ] (US **hemorrhage**) n hemorragia
haemorrhoids ['hɛmərɔɪdz] (US **hemorrhoids**) npl hemorróidas fpl
haggle ['hægl] vi pechinchar, regatear
Hague [heɪg] n: **The ~** Haia
hail [heɪl] n granizo; (*of objects*) chuva; (*of criticism*) torrente f ♦ vt (*greet*) cumprimentar; (*taxi*) chamar; (*person, event*) saudar ♦ vi chover granizo; **hailstone** n pedra de granizo
hair [hɛə*] n (*of human*) cabelo; (*of animal*) pêlo; **to do one's ~** pentear-se; **hairbrush** n escova de cabelo; **haircut** n corte m de cabelo; **hairdo** n penteado; **hairdresser** n cabeleireiro(-a); **hairdresser's** n cabeleireiro; **hair dryer** n secador m de cabelo; **hair gel** n gel m para o cabelo; **hairgrip** n grampo (BRIT), gancho (PT); **hairnet** n rede f de cabelo; **hairpin** n grampo (BRIT), gancho (PT); **hairpin bend** (US **hairpin curve**) n curva muito fechada; **hair-raising** adj horripilante, de arrepiar os cabelos; **hair remover** n (creme m) depilatório; **hair spray** n laquê m (BR), laca (PT); **hairstyle** n penteado; **hairy** adj cabeludo, peludo; (*inf*: *situation*) perigoso
hake [heɪk] (*pl inv or* **~s**) n abrótea
half [hɑːf] (*pl* **halves**) n metade f; (RAIL, bus, of beer etc) meia ♦ adj meio ♦ adv meio, pela metade; **a pound** meia libra; **two and a ~** dois e meio; **~ a dozen** meia-dúzia; **to cut sth in ~** cortar algo ao meio; **~ asleep/empty/closed** meio adormecido/vazio/fechado; **half-caste** ['hɑːkɑːst] n mestiço(-a); **half-**

hearted adj irresoluto, indiferente; **half-hour** n meia hora; **half-price** adj, adv pela metade do preço; **half term** (BRIT) n (SCH) dias de folga no meio do semestre; **half-time** n meio tempo; **halfway** adv a meio caminho; (in time) no meio

hall [hɔ:l] n (for concerts) sala; (entrance way) hall m, entrada

hallmark ['hɔ:lmɑ:k] n (also fig) marca

hallo [hə'ləu] excl = **hello**

hall of residence (BRIT) (pl **halls of residence**) n residência universitária

Hallowe'en ['hæləu'i:n] n Dia m das Bruxas (31 de outubro); ver quadro

---

HALLOWE'EN

Segundo a tradição, **Hallowe'en** é a noite dos fantasmas e dos bruxos. Na Escócia e nos Estados Unidos, sobretudo (bem menos na Inglaterra), as crianças, para festejar o **Hallowe'en**, se fantasiam e batem de porta em porta pedindo prendas (chocolates, maçãs etc).

---

hallway ['hɔ:lweɪ] n hall m, entrada

halo ['heɪləu] n (of saint etc) auréola

halt [hɔ:lt] n parada (BR), paragem f (PT) ♦ vi parar ♦ vt deter; (process) interromper

halve [hɑ:v] vt (divide) dividir ao meio; (reduce by half) reduzir à metade

halves [hɑ:vz] npl of **half**

ham [hæm] n presunto, fiambre m (PT)

hamburger ['hæmbə:gə*] n hambúrguer m

hammer ['hæmə*] n martelo ♦ vt martelar ♦ vi (on door) bater insistentemente

hammock ['hæmək] n rede f

hamper ['hæmpə*] vt dificultar, atrapalhar ♦ n cesto

hamster ['hæmstə*] n hamster m

hand [hænd] n mão f; (of clock) ponteiro; (writing) letra; (of cards) cartas fpl; (worker) trabalhador m ♦ vt dar, passar; **to give** or **lend sb a ~** dar uma mãozinha a alguém, dar uma ajuda a alguém; **at ~** à mão, disponível; **in ~** livre; (situation) sob controle; **to be on ~** (person) estar disponível; (emergency services) estar num estado de prontidão; **on the one ~ ...**, **on the other ~ ...** por um lado ..., por outro (lado) ...; **hand in** vt entregar; **hand out** vt distribuir; **hand over** vt entregar; (responsibility) transferir; **handbag** n bolsa; **handbook** n manual m; **handbrake** n freio (BR) or travão m (PT) de mão; **handcuffs** npl algemas fpl; **handful** n punhado; (of people) grupo

handicap ['hændɪkæp] n (MED) incapacidade f; (disadvantage) desvantagem f; (SPORT) handicap m ♦ vt prejudicar; **mentally/physically ~ped** deficiente menta/físico

handicraft ['hændɪkrɑ:ft] n artesanato, trabalho manual

handiwork ['hændɪwɔ:k] n obra

handkerchief ['hæŋkətʃɪf] n lenço

handle ['hændl] n (of door etc) maçaneta; (of cup etc) asa; (of knife etc) cabo; (for winding) manivela ♦ vt manusear; (deal with) tratar de; (treat: people) lidar com; **"~ with care"** "cuidado - frágil"; **to fly off the ~** perder as estribeiras; **handlebar(s)** n(pl) guidom m (BR), guidão m (PT)

hand-luggage n bagagem f de mão; **handmade** adj feito a mão; **handout** n (money, food) doação f; (leaflet) folheto; (at lec-

ture) apostila; **handrail** n corrimão m; **handshake** n aperto de mão
handsome ['hænsəm] *adj* bonito, elegante; (*profit*) considerável
handwriting ['hændraɪtɪŋ] n letra, caligrafia
handy ['hændɪ] *adj* (*close at hand*) à mão; (*useful*) útil; (*skilful*) habilidoso, hábil
hang [hæŋ] (*pt, pp* hung) *vt* pendurar; (*criminal: pt, pp* –ed) enforcar ♦ *vi* estar pendurado; (*hair, drapery*) cair ♦ n (*inf*): **to get the ~ of sth** pegar o jeito de algo; **hang about** *or* **around** *vi* vadiar, vagabundear; **hang on** *vi* (*wait*) esperar; **hang up** *vt* (*coat*) pendurar ♦ *vi* (*TEL*) desligar; **to ~ up on sb** bater o telefone na cara de alguém
hanger ['hæŋə*] n cabide m
hang-gliding n vôo livre
hangover ['hæŋəʊvə*] n ressaca
hanker ['hæŋkə*] *vi*: **to ~ after** (*long for*) ansiar por
hankie ['hæŋkɪ] n *abbr* = handkerchief
hanky ['hæŋkɪ] n *abbr* = handkerchief
haphazard [hæp'hæzəd] *adj* desorganizado
happen ['hæpən] *vi* acontecer; **to ~ to do sth** fazer algo por acaso; **as it ~s ...** acontece que ...; **happening** n acontecimento, ocorrência
happily ['hæpɪlɪ] *adv* (*luckily*) felizmente; (*cheerfully*) alegremente
happiness ['hæpɪnɪs] n felicidade f
happy ['hæpɪ] *adj* feliz; (*cheerful*) contente; **to be ~ (with)** estar contente (com); **to be ~ to do** (*willing*) estar disposto a fazer; **~ birthday!** feliz aniversário; **happy-go-lucky** *adj* despreocupado
harass ['hærəs] *vt* importunar;

harassment n perseguição f
harbour ['hɑ:bə*] (*us* harbor) n porto ♦ *vt* (*hope etc*) abrigar; (*hide*) esconder
hard [hɑ:d] *adj* duro; (*difficult*) difícil; (*work*) árduo; (*person*) severo, cruel; (*facts*) verdadeiro ♦ *adv* (*work*) muito, diligentemente; (*think, try*) seriamente; **to look ~ at** olhar firme *or* fixamente para; **no ~ feelings!** sem ressentimentos!; **to be ~ of hearing** ser surdo; **to be ~ done by** ser tratado injustamente; **hardback** n livro de capa dura; **hard disk** n (*comput*) disco rígido; **harden** *vt* endurecer; (*steel*) temperar; (*fig*) tornar insensível ♦ *vi* endurecer-se
hardly ['hɑ:dlɪ] *adv* (*scarcely*) apenas; (*no sooner*) mal; **~ ever/anywhere** quase nunca/em lugar nenhum
hardship ['hɑ:dʃɪp] n privação f
hard shoulder n acostamento m
hard up (*inf*) *adj* duro (*BR*), liso (*PT*)
hardware ['hɑ:dwɛə*] n ferragens fpl; (*comput*) hardware m
hard-working *adj* trabalhador(a); (*student*) aplicado
hardy ['hɑ:dɪ] *adj* forte; (*plant*) resistente
hare [hɛə*] n lebre f
harm [hɑ:m] n mal m; (*damage*) dano ♦ *vt* (*person*) fazer mal a, prejudicar; (*thing*) danificar; **out of ~'s way** a salvo; **harmful** *adj* prejudicial, nocivo; **harmless** *adj* inofensivo
harmony ['hɑ:mənɪ] n harmonia
harness ['hɑ:nɪs] n (*for horse*) arreios *mpl*; (*for child*) correia; (*safety ~*) correia de segurança ♦ *vt* (*horse*) arrear, pôr arreios em; (*resources*) aproveitar
harp [hɑ:p] n harpa ♦ *vi*: **to ~ on**

about bater sempre na mesma tecla sobre

harrowing ['hærəʊɪŋ] adj doloroso, pungente

harsh [hɑːʃ] adj (life) duro; (sound) desarmonioso; (light) forte

harvest ['hɑːvɪst] n colheita ♦ vt colher

has [hæz] vb see **have**

hash [hæʃ] n (CULIN) picadinho; (fig: mess) confusão f

hasn't ['hæznt] = has not

hassle ['hæsl] (inf) n complicação f

haste [heɪst] n pressa; **hasten** ['heɪsn] vt acelerar ♦ vi: **to hasten to do sth** apressar-se em fazer algo; **hastily** adv depressa; **hasty** adj apressado; (rash) precipitado

hat [hæt] n chapéu m

hatch [hætʃ] n (NAUT: also: ~way) escotilha; (also: **service** ~) comunicação f entre a cozinha e a sala de jantar ♦ vi sair do ovo, chocar

hatchet ['hætʃɪt] n machadinha

hate [heɪt] vt odiar, detestar ♦ n ódio; **hateful** adj odioso; **hatred** ['heɪtrɪd] n ódio

haughty ['hɔːtɪ] adj soberbo, arrogante

haul [hɔːl] vt puxar ♦ n (of fish) redada; (of stolen goods etc) pilhagem f, presa; **haulage** ['hɔːlɪdʒ] n transporte m (rodoviário); (costs) gasto m com transporte; **haulier** ['hɔːlɪə*] (BRIT) n (firm) transportadora; (person) transportador(a) m/f

haunt [hɔːnt] vt (subj: ghost) assombrar; (: problem, memory) perseguir ♦ n reduto; (~ed house) casa malassombrada

KEYWORD

have [hæv] (pt, pp **had**) aux vb
1 (gen) ter; **to ~ gone/eaten** ter ido/comido; **he has been kind/pro-**moted ele foi bondoso/promovido; **having finished** or **when he had finished, he left** quando ele terminou, foi embora

2 (in tag questions): **you've done it, ~n't you?** você fez isto, não foi?; **he hasn't done it, has he?** ele não fez isto, fez?

3 (in short questions and answers): **you've made a mistake – no I ~n't/ so I ~** você fez um erro – não, eu não fiz/sim, eu fiz; **I've been there before, ~ you?** eu já estive lá, e você?

♦ modal aux vb (be obliged): **to ~ (got) to do sth** ter que fazer algo; **I ~n't got** or **I don't ~ to wear glasses** eu não preciso usar óculos

♦ vt 1 (possess) ter; **he has (got) blue eyes/dark hair** ele tem olhos azuis/cabelo escuro

2 (referring to meals etc): **to ~ break-fast** tomar café (BR), tomar o pequeno almoço (PT); **to ~ lunch/dinner** almoçar/jantar; **to ~ a drink/a ciga-rette** tomar um drinque/fumar um cigarro

3 (receive, obtain etc): **may I ~ your address?** pode me dar seu endereço?; **you can ~ it for 5 pounds** você pode levá-lo por 5 libras; **to ~ a baby** dar à luz (BR), ter um nenê or bebê (PT)

4 (maintain, allow): **he will ~ it that he is right** ele vai insistir que ele está certo; **I won't ~ it/this nonsense!** não vou agüentar isso/este absurdo!; **we can't ~ that** não podemos permitir isto

5: **to ~ sth done** mandar fazer algo; **to ~ one's hair cut** ir cortar o cabelo; **to ~ sb do sth** mandar alguém fazer algo

6 (experience, suffer): **to ~ a cold** estar resfriado (BR) or constipado

(PT); **to ~ flu** estar com gripe; **she had her bag stolen** ela teve sua bolsa roubada; **to ~ an operation** fazer uma operação

7 (+ n: take, hold etc): **to ~ a swim/walk/bath/rest** ir nadar/passear/tomar um banho/descansar; **let's ~ a look** vamos dar uma olhada; **to ~ a party** fazer uma festa

8 (inf: dupe): **he's been had** ele comprou gato por lebre

have out vt: **to ~ it out with sb** (settle a problem) explicar-se com alguém

haven ['heɪvn] n porto; (fig) abrigo, refúgio

haven't ['hævnt] = have not

havoc ['hævək] n destruição f; **to play ~ with** (fig) estragar

hawk [hɔ:k] n falcão m

hay [heɪ] n feno; **hay fever** n febre f do feno; **haystack** n palheiro

haywire ['heɪwaɪə*] (inf) adj: **to go ~** desorganizar-se, degringolar

hazard ['hæzəd] n perigo, risco ♦ vt aventurar, arriscar; **hazard warning lights** npl (AUT) pisca-alerta m

haze [heɪz] n névoa

hazelnut ['heɪzlnʌt] n avelã f

hazy ['heɪzɪ] adj nublado; (idea) confuso

he [hi:] pron ele; **~ who ...** quem ..., aquele que ...

head [hed] n cabeça; (of table) cabeceira; (of queue) frente f; (of organization) chefe m/f; (of school) diretor(a) m/f ♦ vt (list) encabeçar; (group) liderar; (ball) cabecear; **~s or tails** cara ou coroa; **~ first** de cabeça; **~ over heels** de pernas para o ar; **~ over heels in love** estar apaixonadíssimo; **head for** vt fus dirigir-se a; (disaster) estar procurando; **headache** n dor f de cabeça; **heading** n

título, cabeçalho; **headlamp** (BRIT) n = **headlight**; **headland** n promontório; **headlight** n farol m; **headline** n manchete f; **headlong** adv (fall) de cabeça; (rush) precipitadamente; **headmaster** n diretor m (de escola); **headmistress** n diretora (de escola); **head office** n matriz f; **head-on** adj (collision) de frente; (confrontation) direto; **headphones** npl fones mpl de ouvido; **headquarters** npl sede f; (MIL) quartel m general; **headrest** n apoio para a cabeça; **headroom** n (in car) espaço (para a cabeça); (under bridge) vão m livre; **head-scarf** (irreg) n lenço de cabeça; **headstrong** adj voluntarioso, teimoso; **headway** n: **to make headway** avançar; **headwind** n vento contrário; **heady** adj emocionante; (intoxicating) estonteante

heal [hi:l] vt curar ♦ vi cicatrizar

health [helθ] n saúde f; **good ~!** saúde!; **health food(s)** n(pl) alimentos mpl naturais; **healthy** adj (person) saudável; (air, walk) sadio; (economy) próspero, forte

heap [hi:p] n pilha, montão m ♦ vt: **to ~ sth** with encher algo de; **~s (of)** (inf) um monte (de); **to ~ sth** on empilhar algo em

hear [hɪə*] (pt, pp **~d** [hɑ:d]) vt ouvir; (listen to) escutar; (news) saber; **to ~ about** ouvir falar de; **to ~ from sb** ter notícias de alguém; **hearing** n (sense) audição f; (LAW) audiência; **hearing aid** n aparelho para a surdez

hearse [hɑ:s] n carro fúnebre

heart [hɑ:t] n coração m; (of problem, city) centro; **~s** npl (CARDS) copas fpl; **to lose/take ~** perder o ânimo/criar coragem; **at ~** no fundo; **by ~** (learn, know) saber

heart attack n ataque m de coração; **heartbeat** n batida do coração; **heartbreaking** adj desolador(a); **heartbroken** adj: to be heartbroken estar inconsolável; **heartburn** n azia; **heart failure** n parada cardíaca; **heartfelt** adj sincero

hearth [hɑːθ] n lareira

hearty ['hɑːtɪ] adj (person) energético; (laugh) animado; (appetite) bom (boa); (welcome) sincero; (dislike) absoluto

heat [hiːt] n calor m; (excitement) ardor m; (SPORT: also: qualifying ~) (prova) eliminatória ♦ vt esquentar; (room, house) aquecer; **heat up** vi aquecer-se, esquentar ♦ vt aquecer, esquentar; **heated** adj aquecido; (fig) acalorado; **heater** n aquecedor m

heath [hiːθ] (BRIT) n charneca

heather ['hɛðə*] n urze f

heating ['hiːtɪŋ] n aquecimento, calefação f

heatstroke ['hiːtstrəuk] n insolação f

heave [hiːv] vt (pull) puxar; (push) empurrar (com esforço); (lift) levantar (com esforço) ♦ vi (chest) palpitar; (retch) ter ânsias de vômito ♦ n puxão m; empurrão m; **to ~ a sigh** soltar um suspiro

heaven ['hɛvn] n céu m, paraíso; **heavenly** adj celestial; (REL) divino

heavily ['hɛvɪlɪ] adv pesadamente; (drink, smoke) excessivamente; (sleep, depend) profundamente

heavy ['hɛvɪ] adj pesado; (work) duro; (responsibility) grande; (rain, meal) forte; (drinker, smoker) inveterado; (weather) carregado; **heavy goods vehicle** (BRIT) n caminhão m de carga pesada; **heavyweight** n (SPORT) peso-pesado

Hebrew ['hiːbruː] adj hebreu

(hebréia) ♦ n (LING) hebraico

Hebrides ['hɛbrɪdiːz] npl: the ~ as (ilhas) Hébridas

hectic ['hɛktɪk] adj agitado

he'd [hiːd] = he would; he had

hedge [hɛdʒ] n cerca viva, sebe f ♦ vi dar evasivas ♦ vt: to ~ one's bets (fig) resguardar-se

hedgehog ['hɛdʒhɒg] n ouriço

heed [hiːd] vt (also: take ~ of) prestar atenção a

heel [hiːl] n (of shoe) salto; (of foot) calcanhar m ♦ vt (shoe) pôr salto em

hefty ['hɛftɪ] adj (person) robusto; (parcel) pesado; (profit) alto

height [haɪt] n (of person) estatura; (of building, tree) altura; (altitude) altitude f; (high ground) monte m; (fig: of power) auge m; (: of luxury) máximo; (: of stupidity) cúmulo; **heighten** vt elevar; (fig) aumentar

heir [ɛə*] n herdeiro; **heiress** n herdeira; **heirloom** n relíquia de família

held [hɛld] pt, pp of **hold**

helicopter ['hɛlɪkɒptə*] n helicóptero

hell [hɛl] n inferno; ~! (inf) droga!

he'll [hiːl] = he will; he shall

hello [hə'ləu] excl oi! (BR), olá! (PT); (surprise) ora essa!

helm [hɛlm] n (NAUT) timão m, leme m

helmet ['hɛlmɪt] n capacete m

help [hɛlp] n ajuda; (charwoman) faxineira ♦ vt ajudar; ~! socorro!; ~ yourself sirva-se; he can't ~ it não tem culpa; **helper** n ajudante m/f; **helpful** adj prestativo; (advice) útil; **helping** n porção f; **helpless** adj (incapable) incapaz; (defenceless) indefeso

hem [hɛm] n bainha ♦ vt embainhar; **hem in** vt cercar, encurralar

hemorrhage ['hɛmərɪdʒ] (US) n = **haemorrhage**

hemorrhoids ['hɛmərɔɪdz] (US) npl

= haemorrhoids

hen [hɛn] n galinha; (female bird) fêmea

hence [hɛns] adv daí, portanto; **2 years ~** daqui a 2 anos; **henceforth** adv de agora em diante, doravante

her [hɜːʳ] pron (direct) a; (indirect) lhe; (stressed, after prep) ela ♦ adj seu (sua), dela; see also **me; my**

heraldry ['hɛrəldrı] n heráldica

herb [hɜːb] n erva

herd [hɜːd] n rebanho

here [hɪəʳ] adv aqui; (at this point) nesse ponto; **~!** (present) presente!; **~ is/are** aqui está/estão; **~ she is!** aqui está ela!; **hereafter** adv daqui por diante

heresy ['hɛrəsı] n heresia

heritage ['hɛrıtıdʒ] n patrimônio

hermit ['hɜːmıt] n eremita m/f

hernia ['hɜːnıə] n hérnia

hero ['hɪərəu] (pl **~es**) n herói m; (of book, film) protagonista m

heroin ['hɛrəuın] n heroína

heroine ['hɛrəuın] n heroína; (of book, film) protagonista m

heron ['hɛrən] n garça

herring ['hɛrıŋ] (pl inv or **~s**) n arenque m

hers [hɜːz] pron o seu (a sua), o(a) dela; see also **mine¹**

herself [hɜː'sɛlf] pron (reflexive) se; (emphatic) ela mesma; (after prep) si (mesma); see also **oneself**

he's [hiːz] = he is; he has

hesitant ['hɛzıtənt] adj hesitante, indeciso

hesitate ['hɛzıteıt] vi hesitar; **hesitation** [hɛzı'teıʃən] n hesitação f, indecisão f

heterosexual ['hɛtərəu'sɛksjuəl] adj heterossexual

heyday ['heıdeı] n: **the ~ of** o auge or apogeu de

HGV (BRIT) n abbr = **heavy goods vehicle**

hi [haı] excl oi!

hibernate ['haıbəneıt] vi hibernar

hiccough ['hıkʌp] vi soluçar ♦ npl: **~s: to have (the) ~s** estar com soluço

hiccup ['hıkʌp] = **hiccough**

hide [haıd] (pt **hid**, pp **hidden**) n (skin) pele f ♦ vt esconder, ocultar; (view) obscurecer ♦ vi: **to ~ (from sb)** esconder-se or ocultar-se (de alguém)

hideous ['hıdıəs] adj horrível

hiding ['haıdıŋ] n (beating) surra; **to be in ~** (concealed) estar escondido

hierarchy ['haıəraːkı] n hierarquia

hi-fi ['haıfaı] n alta-fidelidade f; (system) som m ♦ adj de alta-fidelidade

high [haı] adj alto; (number) grande; (price) alto, elevado; (wind) forte; (voice) agudo; (opinion) ótimo; (principles) nobre ♦ adv alto, a grande altura; **it is 20 m ~** tem 20 m de altura; **~ in the air** nas alturas; **highbrow** adj intelectual, erudito; **highchair** n cadeira alta (para criança); **higher education** n ensino superior; **high-handed** adj despótico; **high-heeled** adj de salto alto; **high jump** n (SPORT) salto em altura; **the Highlands** npl a Alta Escócia; **highlight** n (fig) ponto alto; (in hair) mecha ♦ vt realçar, ressaltar; **highly** adv: **highly paid** muito bem pago; (a lot): **to speak/ think highly of** falar elogiosamente de/pensar muito bem de; **high-pitched** adj agudo; **high-rise** adj alto; **high school** n (BRIT) escola secundária; (US) científico; ver quadro

---

HIGH SCHOOL

Uma **high school** é um estabelecimento de ensino secundário. Nos Estados Unidos, existem a *Junior High School*, que equivale aproximadamente aos dois últimos anos do primeiro grau, e a *Senior High School*, que corresponde ao segundo grau. Na Grã-Bretanha, esse termo às vezes é utilizado para as escolas secundárias.

---

high street (*BRIT*) *n* rua principal

highway ['haɪweɪ] (*US*) *n* estrada; (*main road*) rodovia

hijack ['haɪdʒæk] *vt* seqüestrar; **hijacker** *n* seqüestrador(a) *m/f* (de avião)

hike [haɪk] *vi* caminhar ♦ *n* caminhada, excursão *f* a pé; **hiker** *n* caminhante *m/f*, andarilho(-a)

hilarious [hɪ'lɛərɪəs] *adj* hilariante

hill [hɪl] *n* colina; (*high*) montanha; (*slope*) ladeira, rampa; **hillside** *n* vertente *f*; **hill-walking** *n* caminhada em montanha; **to go hill-walking** fazer trilha; **hilly** *adj* montanhoso

him [hɪm] *pron* (*direct*) o; (*indirect*) lhe; (*stressed, after prep*) ele; *see also* **me**; **himself** *pron* (*reflexive*) se; (*emphatic*) ele mesmo; (*after prep*) si (mesmo); *see also* **oneself**

hinder ['hɪndə*] *vt* retardar

hindsight ['haɪndsaɪt] *n*: **with ~** em retrospecto

Hindu ['hɪnduː] *adj* hindu

hinge [hɪndʒ] *n* dobradiça *f* ♦ *vi* (*fig*): **to ~ on** depender de

hint [hɪnt] *n* (*suggestion*) insinuação *f*; (*advice*) palpite *m*, dica; (*sign*) sinal *m* ♦ *vt*: **to ~ that** insinuar que ♦ *vi*: **to ~ at** fazer alusão a

hip [hɪp] *n* quadril *m*

hippopotamus [hɪpə'pɔtəməs] (*pl* **~es** *or* **hippopotami**) *n* hipopótamo

hire ['haɪə*] *vt* (*BRIT: car, equipment*) alugar; (*worker*) contratar ♦ *n* aluguel *m* (*BR*), aluguer *m* (*PT*); **for ~** aluga-se; (*taxi*) livre; **hire purchase** (*BRIT*) *n* compra a prazo

his [hɪz] *pron* o seu (a sua), o(a) dele ♦ *adj* seu (sua), dele; *see also* **my**; **mine**[1]

hiss [hɪs] *vi* (*snake, fat*) assoviar; (*gas*) silvar; (*boo*) vaiar

historic(al) [hɪ'stɔrɪk(l)] *adj* histórico

history ['hɪstərɪ] *n* história

hit [hɪt] (*pt, pp* **hit**) *vt* bater em; (*target*) acertar, alcançar; (*car*) bater em, colidir com; (*fig: affect*) atingir ♦ *n* golpe *m*; (*success*) sucesso; **to ~ it off with sb** dar-se bem com alguém; **hit-and-run driver** *n* motorista que atropela alguém e foge da cena do acidente

hitch [hɪtʃ] *vt* (*fasten*) atar, amarrar; (*also: ~ up*) levantar ♦ *n* (*difficulty*) dificuldade *f*; **to ~ a lift** pegar carona (*BR*), arranjar uma boleia (*PT*)

hitch-hike *vi* pegar carona (*BR*), andar à boleia (*PT*); **hitch-hiker** *n* pessoa que pega carona (*BR*) or anda à boleia (*PT*)

hi-tech *adj* tecnologicamente avançado ♦ *n* alta tecnologia

HIV *abbr*: **~-negative/-positive** ♦ *adj* HIV negativo/positivo

hive [haɪv] *n* colméia; **hive off** (*inf*) *vt* transferir

HMS (*BRIT*) *abbr* = **His** (*or* **Her**) **Majesty's Ship**

hoard [hɔːd] *n* provisão *f*; (*of money*) tesouro ♦ *vt* acumular; **hoarding** (*BRIT*) *n* tapume *m*, outdoor *m*

hoarse [hɔːs] *adj* rouco

hoax [həʊks] *n* trote *m*

hob [hɔb] *n* parte de cima do fogão

hobble ['hɔbl] vi mancar

hobby ['hɔbɪ] n hobby m, passatempo predileto

hobo ['həubəu] (US) n vagabundo

hockey ['hɔkɪ] n hóquei m

hog [hɔg] n porco m; (*col*) monopolizar; **to go the whole ~** ir até o fim

hoist [hɔɪst] vt içar

hold [həuld] (*pt, pp* **held**) vt segurar; (*contain*) conter; (*have*) ter; (*record etc: meeting*) realizar; (*detain*) deter; (*consider*): **to ~ sb responsible (for sth)** responsabilizar alguém (por algo); (*keep in certain position*): **to ~ one's head up** manter a cabeça erigida ♦ vi (*withstand pressure*) resistir; (*be valid*) ser válido ♦ n (*grasp*) pressão f; (:*fig*) influência, domínio; (*of ship*) porão m (*of plane*) compartimento para cargo; (*control*) controle m; **to ~ the line!** (*TEL*) não desligue!; **to ~ one's own** (*fig*) virar-se, sair-se bem; **to catch** *or* **get (a) ~ of** agarrar, pegar; **hold back** vt reter; (*secret*) manter, guardar; **hold down** vt (*person*) segurar; (*job*) manter; **hold off** vt (*enemy*) afastar, repelir; **hold on** vi agarrar-se; (*wait*) esperar; **~ on!** espera aí!; (*TEL*) não desligue!; **hold on to** vt fus agarrar-se a; (*keep*) guardar, ficar com; **hold out** vt (*hand*) estender; (*hope*) ter ♦ vi (*resist*) resistir; **hold up** vt (*raise*) levantar; (*support*) apoiar; (*delay*) atrasar; (*rob*) assaltar; **holdall** (*BRIT*) n bolsa de viagem; **holder** n (*container*) recipiente m; (*of ticket*) portador(a) m/f; (*of record*) detentor(a) m/f; (*of office, title*) titular m/f; **hold-up** n (*robbery*) assalto; (*delay*) demora; (*BRIT: in traffic*) engarrafamento

hole [həul] n buraco; (*small: in sock etc*) furo ♦ vt esburacar

holiday ['hɔlədɪ] n (*BRIT: vacation*) férias *fpl*; (*day off*) dia m de folga; (*public ~*) feriado; **on ~** de férias; **holiday camp** (*BRIT*) n colônia de férias; **holiday-maker** (*BRIT*) n pessoa (que está) de férias; **holiday resort** n local m de férias

Holland ['hɔlənd] n Holanda

hollow ['hɔləu] adj oco, vazio; (*cheeks*) côncavo; (*eyes*) fundo; (*sound*) surdo; (*laugh, claim*) falso ♦ n (*in ground*) cavidade f, depressão f ♦ vt: **to ~ out** escavar

holly ['hɔlɪ] n azevinho

holster ['həulstə*] n coldre m

holy ['həulɪ] adj sagrado; (*person*) santo, bento

homage ['hɔmɪdʒ] n homenagem f; **to pay ~ to** prestar homenagem a, homenagear

home [həum] n casa, lar m; (*country*) pátria; (*institution*) asilo ♦ *cpd* caseiro, doméstico; (*ECON, POL*) nacional, interno; (*SPORT: team*) de casa; (:*game*) no próprio campo ♦ adv (*direction*) para casa; (*right in: nail etc*) até o fundo; **at ~** em casa; **make yourself at ~** fique à vontade; **home address** n endereço residencial; **homeland** n terra (natal); **homeless** adj sem casa, desabrigado; **homely** adj (*simple*) simples inv; **home-made** adj caseiro; **Home Office** (*BRIT*) n Ministério do Interior; **home page** n (*COMPUT*) home page f, página inicial; **Home Secretary** (*BRIT*) n Ministro(-a) do Interior; **homesick** adj: **to be homesick** estar com saudades (do lar); **home town** n cidade f natal; **homework** n dever m de casa

homoeopathic [həumɪəu'pæθɪk] (*US* **homeopathic**) adj homeopático

homosexual [hɔməu'sɛksjuəl] adj, n homossexual m/f

Honduras [hɔn'djuərəs] n Honduras f (no article)

honest ['ɔnɪst] adj (truthful) franco; (trustworthy) honesto; (sincere) sincero; **honestly** adv honestamente; **honesty** n honestidade f, sinceridade f

honey ['hʌnɪ] n mel m; **honeycomb** n favo de mel; **honeymoon** n lua-de-mel f; (trip) viagem f de lua-de-mel

honk [hɔŋk] vi buzinar

honorary ['ɔnərərɪ] adj (unpaid) não remunerado; (duty, title) honorário

honour ['ɔnə*] (US honor) vt honrar ♦ n honra; **honourable** adj honrado

hood [hud] n capuz m; (of cooker) tampa; (BRIT: AUT) capota; (US: AUT) capô m

hoof [hu:f] (pl hooves) n casco, pata

hook [huk] n gancho; (on dress) gancho, colchete m; (for fishing) anzol m ♦ vt prender com gancho (or colchete); (fish) fisgar

hooligan ['hu:lɪgən] n desordeiro(-a), bagunceiro(-a)

hoop [hu:p] n arco

hooray [hu:'reɪ] excl = **hurrah**

hoot [hu:t] vi (AUT) buzinar; (siren) tocar; (owl) piar

hoover ['hu:və*] ® (BRIT) n aspirador m (de pó) ♦ vt passar o aspirador em

hooves [hu:vz] npl of **hoof**

hop [hɔp] vi saltar, pular; (on one foot) pular num pé só

hope [həup] vt, vi esperar ♦ n esperança; **I ~ so/not** espero que sim/não; **hopeful** adj (person) otimista, esperançoso; (situation) promissor(a); **hopefully** adv esperançosamente; **hopefully, they'll come back** é de esperar or esperamos que

voltem; **hopeless** adj desesperado, irremediável; (useless) inútil

hops [hɔps] npl lúpulo

horizon [hə'raɪzn] n horizonte m; **horizontal** [hɔrɪ'zɔntl] adj horizontal

horn [hɔ:n] n corno, chifre m; (material) chifre; (MUS) trompa; (AUT) buzina

hornet ['hɔ:nɪt] n vespão m

horoscope ['hɔrəskəup] n horóscopo

horrendous [hə'rendəs] adj horrendo

horrible ['hɔrɪbl] adj horrível; (terrifying) terrível

horrid ['hɔrɪd] adj horrível

horrify ['hɔrɪfaɪ] vt horrorizar

horror ['hɔrə*] n horror m; **horror film** n filme m de terror

horse [hɔ:s] n cavalo; **horseback**: **on horseback** adj, adv a cavalo; **horse chestnut** n castanha-da-índia; **horsepower** n cavalo-vapor m; **horse-racing** n corridas fpl de cavalo, turfe m; **horseshoe** n ferradura

hose [həuz] n (also: **~pipe**) mangueira

hospitable ['hɔspɪtəbl] adj hospitaleiro

hospital ['hɔspɪtl] n hospital m

hospitality [hɔspɪ'tælɪtɪ] n hospitalidade f

host [həust] n anfitrião m; (TV, RADIO) apresentador(a) m/f; (REL) hóstia; (large number): **a ~ of** uma multidão de

hostage ['hɔstɪdʒ] n refém m/f

hostel ['hɔstl] n albergue m, abrigo; (also: **youth ~**) albergue da juventude

hostess ['həustɪs] n anfitriã f; (BRIT: air ~) aeromoça (BR), hospedeira de bordo (PT); (TV, RADIO) apresentadora

hostile ['hɔstaɪl] adj hostil

hostility [hɔ'stɪlɪtɪ] n hostilidade f

hot [hɔt] adj quente; (as opposed to only warm) muito quente; (spicy) picante; (fierce) ardente; **to be ~** (person) estar com calor; (thing, weather) estar quente; **hot dog** n cachorro-quente m

hotel [həu'tɛl] n hotel m

hot: hothouse n estufa; **hotplate** n (on cooker) chapa elétrica; **hot-water bottle** n bolsa de água quente

hound [haund] vt acossar, perseguir ♦ n cão m de caça, sabujo

hour ['auə*] n hora; **hourly** adj de hora em hora; (rate) por hora

house [n haus, vb hauz] n casa; (POL) câmara; (THEATRE) assistência, lotação f ♦ vt (person) alojar; (collection) abrigar; **on the ~** (fig) por conta da casa; **houseboat** n casa flutuante; **household** n família; (house) casa; **housekeeper** n governanta; **housekeeping** n (work) trabalhos mpl domésticos; (money) economia doméstica; **house-warming (party)** n festa de inauguração de uma casa; **housewife** (irreg) n dona de casa; **housework** n trabalhos mpl domésticos; **housing** n (provision) alojamento; (houses) residências fpl; **housing development** (BRIT housing estate) n conjunto residencial

hovel ['hɔvl] n casebre m

hover ['hɔvə*] vi pairar; **hovercraft** n aerobarco

KEYWORD

how [hau] adv 1 (in what way) como; **~ was the film?** que tal o filme?; **~ are you?** como vai? 2 (to what degree) quanto; **~ much milk/many people?** quanto de

leite/quantas pessoas?; **~ long have you been here?** quanto tempo você está aqui?; **~ old are you?** quantos anos você tem?; **~ tall is he?** qual é a altura dele?; **~ lovely/awful!** que ótimo/terrível!

however [hau'evə*] adv de qualquer modo; (+ adj) por mais ... que; (in questions) como ♦ conj no entanto, contudo

howl [haul] vi uivar

H.P. (BRIT) n abbr = hire purchase

h.p. abbr (AUT: = horsepower) CV

HQ n abbr (= headquarters) QG m

HTML n abbr (= Hypertext Mark-up Language) HTML f

hub [hʌb] n cubo; (fig) centro

huddle ['hʌdl] vi: **to ~ together** aconchegar-se

hue [hju:] n cor f, matiz m

huff [hʌf] n: **in a ~** com raiva

hug [hʌg] vt abraçar; (thing) agarrar, prender

huge [hju:dʒ] adj enorme, imenso

hulk [hʌlk] n (wreck) navio velho, carcaça; (person) brutamontes m inv; (building) trambolho

hull [hʌl] n (of ship) casco

hullo [hə'ləu] excl = hello

hum [hʌm] vt cantarolar ♦ vi cantarolar; (insect, machine etc) zumbir

human ['hju:mən] adj humano ♦ n (also: ~ being) ser m humano

humane [hju:'meɪn] adj humano

humanitarian [hju:mænɪ'teərɪən] adj humanitário

humanity [hju:'mænɪtɪ] n humanidade f

humble ['hʌmbl] adj humilde ♦ vt humilhar

humid ['hju:mɪd] adj úmido

humiliate [hju:'mɪlɪeɪt] vt humilhar

humorous ['hju:mərəs] adj humorístico; (person) engraçado

humour ['hju:mə*] (US **humor**) n humorismo, senso de humor; (mood) humor m ♦ vt fazer a vontade de

hump [hʌmp] n (in ground) elevação f; (camel's) corcova, giba; (deformity) corcunda

hunch [hʌntʃ] n (premonition) pressentimento, palpite m; **hunchback** n corcunda m/f; **hunched** adj recurcunda

hundred ['hʌndrəd] num cem; (before lower numbers) cento; **~s of people** centenas de pessoas; **hundredweight** n (BRIT) = 50.8 kg; 112 lb; (US) = 45.3 kg; 100 lb

hung [hʌŋ] pt, pp of **hang**

Hungary ['hʌŋgəri] n Hungria

hunger ['hʌŋgə*] n fome f ♦ vi: **to ~ for** (desire) desejar ardentemente

hungry ['hʌŋgri] adj faminto, esfomeado; (keen): **~ for** (fig) ávido de, ansioso por; **to be ~** estar com fome

hunt [hʌnt] vt buscar; (criminal, fugitive) perseguir; (SPORT, for food) caçar ♦ vi caçar; (search) **to ~ (for)** procurar (por) ♦ n caça, caçada; **hunter** n caçador(a) m/f; **hunting** n caça

hurdle ['hə:dl] n (SPORT) barreira, (fig) obstáculo

hurl [hə:l] vt arremessar, lançar; (abuse) gritar

hurrah [hu'rɑ:] excl oba!, viva!

hurray [hu'rei] excl = **hurrah**

hurricane ['hʌrikən] n furacão m

hurried ['hʌrid] adj apressado; (rushed) feito às pressas; **hurriedly** adv depressa, apressadamente

hurry ['hʌri] n pressa ♦ vi (also: **~ up**) apressar-se ♦ vt (also: **~ up**: person) apressar; (: work) acelerar; **to be in a ~** estar com pressa

hurt [hə:t] (pt, pp **hurt**) vt machucar; (injure) ferir; (fig) magoar ♦ vi doer; **hurtful** adj (remark) que magoa, ofensivo

husband ['hʌzbənd] n marido, esposo

hush [hʌʃ] n silêncio, quietude f ♦ vt silenciar, fazer calar; **~!** silêncio!, psiu!; **hush up** vt abafar, encobrir

husk [hʌsk] n (of wheat) casca; (of maize) palha

husky ['hʌski] adj rouco ♦ n cão m esquimó

hut [hʌt] n cabana, choupana; (shed) alpendre m

hutch [hʌtʃ] n coelheira

hyacinth ['haiəsinθ] n jacinto

hydrant ['haidrənt] n (also: **fire ~**) hidrante m

hydroelectric [haidrəu'lɛktrik] adj hidroelétrico

hydrofoil ['haidrəfɔil] n hidrofoil m, aliscafo

hydrogen ['haidrədʒən] n hidrogênio

hyena [hai'i:nə] n hiena

hygiene ['haidʒi:n] n higiene f

hymn [him] n hino

hype [haip] (inf) n tititi m, falatório

hypermarket ['haipəma:kit] (BRIT) n hipermercado

hyphen ['haifn] n hífen m

hypnotize ['hipnətaiz] vt hipnotizar

hypocrite ['hipəkrit] n hipócrita m/f; **hypocritical** adj hipócrita

hysterical [hi'stɛrikl] adj histérico; (funny) hilariante; **hysterics** npl: **to be in** or **have hysterics** (anger, panic) ter uma crise histérica; (laughter) ter um ataque de riso

I

I [ai] pron eu

ice [ais] n gelo; (~ cream) sorvete m ♦ vt (cake) cobrir com glacê ♦ vi (also: **~ over**, **~ up**) gelar; **iceberg** n iceberg m; **icebox** n (US) geladeira,

(BRIT: in fridge) congelador m; (insulated box) geladeira portátil; **ice cream** n sorvete m (BR), gelado (PT); **ice cube** n pedra de gelo; **iced** adj (drink) gelado; (cake) glaçado; **ice hockey** n hóquei m sobre o gelo

Iceland ['aɪslənd] n Islândia

ice: ice lolly (BRIT) n picolé m; **ice rink** n pista de gelo, rinque m; **ice-skating** n patinação f no gelo

icicle ['aɪsɪkl] n pingente m de gelo

icing ['aɪsɪŋ] n (CULIN) glacê m; **icing sugar** (BRIT) n açúcar m glacê

icon ['aɪkɔn] n (gen, COMPUT) ícone m

icy ['aɪsɪ] adj gelado

I'd [aɪd] = I would; I had

idea [aɪ'dɪə] n idéia

ideal [aɪ'dɪəl] n ideal m ♦ adj ideal

identical [aɪ'dɛntɪkl] adj idêntico

identification [aɪdɛntɪfɪ'keɪʃən] n identificação f; **means of ~** documentos pessoais

identify [aɪ'dɛntɪfaɪ] vt identificar

identity [aɪ'dɛntɪtɪ] n identidade f; **identity card** n carteira de identidade

idiom ['ɪdɪəm] n expressão f idiomática; (style) idioma m, linguagem f

idiosyncrasy [ɪdɪəʊ'sɪŋkrəsɪ] n idiossincrasia

idiot ['ɪdɪət] n idiota m/f; **idiotic** [ɪdɪ'ɔtɪk] adj idiota

idle ['aɪdl] adj ocioso; (lazy) preguiçoso; (unemployed) desempregado; (question, conversation) fútil; (pleasure) descontraído ♦ vi (machine) funcionar com a transmissão desligada; **idle away** vt: **to ~ away the time** perder ou desperdiçar tempo

idol ['aɪdl] n ídolo m; **idolize** vt idolatrar

i.e. abbr (= id est: that is) i.e., isto é

KEYWORD

if [ɪf] conj 1 (conditional use) se; **~ necessary** se necessário; **~ I were you** se eu fosse você
2 (whenever) quando
3 (although): **(even) ~** mesmo que
4 (whether) se
5: **~ so/not** sendo assim/do contrário; **~ only** se pelo menos; see also **as**

ignition [ɪg'nɪʃən] n (AUT) ignição f; **to switch on/off the ~** ligar/desligar o motor; **ignition key** n (AUT) chave f de ignição

ignorant ['ɪgnərənt] adj ignorante; **to be ~ of** ignorar

ignore [ɪg'nɔ:*] vt (person) não fazer caso de; (fact) não levar em consideração, ignorar

I'll [aɪl] = I will; I shall

ill [ɪl] adj doente; (harmful: effects) nocivo ♦ n mal m ♦ adv: **to speak/ think ~ of sb** falar/pensar mal de alguém; **to be taken ~** ficar doente; **ill-at-ease** adj constrangido, pouco à vontade

illegal [ɪ'li:gl] adj ilegal

illegible [ɪ'lɛdʒɪbl] adj ilegível

illegitimate [ɪlɪ'dʒɪtɪmət] adj ilegítimo

ill-fated adj malfadado

ill feeling n má vontade f, rancor m

illiterate [ɪ'lɪtərət] adj analfabeto

ill-mannered [-'mænəd] adj maleducado, grosseiro

illness ['ɪlnɪs] n doença

ill-treat vt maltratar

illuminate [ɪ'lu:mɪneɪt] vt iluminar, clarear; **illumination** [ɪlu:mɪ'neɪʃən] n iluminação f; **illuminations** npl (decorative lights) luminárias fpl

illusion [ɪˈluːʒən] n ilusão f

illustrate [ˈɪləstreɪt] vt ilustrar; (point) exemplificar; **illustration** [ɪləˈstreɪʃən] n ilustração f; (example) exemplo; (explanation) esclarecimento

ill will n animosidade f

I'm [aɪm] = I am

image [ˈɪmɪdʒ] n imagem f; **imagery** n imagens fpl

imaginary [ɪˈmædʒɪnərɪ] adj imaginário

imagination [ɪmædʒɪˈneɪʃən] n imaginação f; (inventiveness) inventividade f

imagine [ɪˈmædʒɪn] vt imaginar

imbalance [ɪmˈbæləns] n desigualdade f

imitate [ˈɪmɪteɪt] vt imitar; **imitation** [ɪmɪˈteɪʃən] n imitação f; (copy) cópia; (mimicry) mímica

immaculate [ɪˈmækjulət] adj impecável; (REL) imaculado

immaterial [ɪməˈtɪərɪəl] adj irrelevante

immature [ɪməˈtjuə*] adj imaturo; (fruit) verde; (cheese) fresco

immediate [ɪˈmiːdɪət] adj imediato; (pressing) urgente, premente; (neighbourhood, family) próximo; **immediately** adv imediatamente; (directly) diretamente; **immediately next to** bem junto a

immense [ɪˈmens] adj imenso; (importance) enorme

immerse [ɪˈməːs] vt submergir; **to be ~d in** (fig) estar absorto em

immersion heater [ɪˈməːʃn-] (BRIT) n aquecedor m de imersão

immigrant [ˈɪmɪɡrənt] n imigrante m/f

immigration [ɪmɪˈɡreɪʃən] n imigração f

imminent [ˈɪmɪnənt] adj iminente

immoral [ɪˈmɒrl] adj imoral

immortal [ɪˈmɔːtl] adj imortal

immune [ɪˈmjuːn] adj: **~ to** imune a, imunizado contra

impact [ˈɪmpækt] n impacto (BR), impacte m (PT)

impair [ɪmˈpeə*] vt prejudicar

impartial [ɪmˈpɑːʃl] adj imparcial

impassable [ɪmˈpɑːsəbl] adj (river) intransponível; (road) intransitável

impatience [ɪmˈpeɪʃəns] n impaciência

impatient [ɪmˈpeɪʃənt] adj impaciente; **to get** or **grow ~** impacientar-se

impeccable [ɪmˈpekəbl] adj impecável

impediment [ɪmˈpedɪmənt] n obstáculo; (also: **speech ~**) defeito (de fala)

impending [ɪmˈpendɪŋ] adj iminente, próximo

imperative [ɪmˈperətɪv] adj (tone) imperioso, obrigatório; (need) vital; (necessary) indispensável ♦ n (LING) imperativo

imperfect [ɪmˈpəːfɪkt] adj imperfeito; (goods etc) defeituoso ♦ n (LING: also: **~ tense**) imperfeito

imperial [ɪmˈpɪərɪəl] adj imperial

impersonal [ɪmˈpəːsənl] adj impessoal

impersonate [ɪmˈpəːsəneɪt] vt fazer-se passar por, personificar; (THEATRE) imitar

impertinent [ɪmˈpəːtɪnənt] adj impertinente, insolente

impervious [ɪmˈpəːvɪəs] adj (fig): **~ to** insensível a

impetuous [ɪmˈpetjuəs] adj impetuoso, precipitado

implement [n ˈɪmplɪmənt, vb ˈɪmplɪment] n instrumento, ferramenta; (for cooking) utensílio ♦ vt efetivar

implicit [ɪmˈplɪsɪt] adj implícito

(complete) absoluto

imply [ɪmˈplaɪ] vt *(mean)* significar; *(hint)* dar a entender que

impolite [ɪmpəˈlaɪt] adj indelicado, mal-educado

import [vb ɪmˈpɔːt, n ˈɪmpɔːt] vt importar ♦ n importação f; *(article)* mercadoria importada

importance [ɪmˈpɔːtəns] n importância

important [ɪmˈpɔːtənt] adj importante; **it's not ~** não tem importância, não importa

impose [ɪmˈpəʊz] vt impor ♦ vi: **to ~ on sb** abusar de alguém; **imposing** adj imponente; **imposition** [ɪmpəˈzɪʃən] n *(of tax etc)* imposição f; **to be an imposition on sb** *(person)* abusar de alguém

impossible [ɪmˈpɒsɪbl] adj impossível; *(situation)* inviável; *(person)* insuportável

impotent [ˈɪmpətənt] adj impotente

impound [ɪmˈpaʊnd] vt confiscar

impoverished [ɪmˈpɒvərɪʃt] adj empobrecido; *(land)* esgotado

impractical [ɪmˈpræktɪkl] adj pouco prático

impress [ɪmˈpres] vt impressionar; *(mark)* imprimir; **to ~ sth on sb** inculcar algo em alguém

impression [ɪmˈpreʃən] n impressão f; *(imitation)* caricatura; **to be under the ~ that** estar com a impressão de que; **impressionist** n *(ART)* impressionista m/f; *(entertainer)* caricaturista m/f

impressive [ɪmˈpresɪv] adj impressionante

imprint [ˈɪmprɪnt] n impressão f, marca; *(PUBLISHING)* nome m *(da coleção)*

imprison [ɪmˈprɪzn] vt encarcerar

improbable [ɪmˈprɒbəbl] adj im-

provável; *(story)* inverossímil *(BR)*, inverosímil *(PT)*

improper [ɪmˈprɒpə*] adj *(unsuitable)* impróprio; *(dishonest)* desonesto

improve [ɪmˈpruːv] vt melhorar ♦ vi melhorar; *(pupils)* progredir; **improvement** n melhora; progresso

improvise [ˈɪmprəvaɪz] vt, vi improvisar

impudent [ˈɪmpjudnt] adj insolente, impudente

impulse [ˈɪmpʌls] n impulso; **on ~** sem pensar, num impulso

---

KEYWORD

in [ɪn] prep 1 *(indicating place, position)* em; **~ the house/garden** na casa/no jardim; **I have it ~ my hand** eu estou assegurando isto; **~ here/ there** aqui dentro/lá dentro
2 *(with place names: of town, country, region)* em; **~ London/Rio** em Londres/no Rio; **~ England/ Japan/the United States** na Inglaterra/no Japão/nos Estados Unidos
3 *(indicating time: during)* em; **~ spring/autumn** na primavera/no outono; **~ 1988** em 1988; **~ May** em maio; **I'll see you ~ July** até julho; **~ the morning** de manhã; **at 4 o'clock ~ the afternoon** às 4 da tarde
4 *(indicating time: in the space of)* em; **I did it ~ 3 hours/days** fiz isto em 3 horas/dias; **~ 2 weeks** or **~ 2 weeks' time** daqui a 2 semanas
5 *(indicating manner etc)*: **~ a loud/ soft voice** em voz alta/numa voz suave; **written ~ pencil/ink** escrito a lápis/à caneta; **~ English/ Portuguese** em inglês/português; **the boy ~ the blue shirt** o menino de camisa azul

6 (*indicating circumstances*): ~ **the sun** ao or sob o sol; ~ **the rain** na chuva; **a rise** ~ **prices** um aumento nos preços
7 (*indicating mood, state*): ~ **tears** aos prantos; ~ **anger/despair** com raiva/desesperado; ~ **good condition** em boas condições
8 (*with ratios, numbers*): **1** ~ **10** 1 em 10, 1 em cada 10; **20 pence** ~ **the pound** vinte pênis numa libra; **they lined up** ~ **twos** eles se alinharam dois a dois
9 (*referring to people, works*) em
10 (*indicating profession etc*): **to be** ~ **teaching/publishing** ser professor/ trabalhar numa editora
11 (*after superl*): **the best pupil** ~ **the class** o melhor aluno da classe; **the biggest/smallest** ~ **Europe** o maior/menor na Europa
12 (*with present participle*): ~ **saying this** ao dizer isto
♦ *adv*: **to be** ~ (*person: at home*) estar em casa; (: *at work*) estar no trabalho; (*fashion*) estar na moda; (*ship, plane, train*): **it's** ~ chegou; **is he** ~? ele está?; **to ask sb** ~ convidar alguém para entrar; **to run/limp** *etc* ~ entrar correndo/mancando *etc*
♦ *n*: **the** ~**s and outs** (*of proposal, situation etc*) os cantos e recantos, os pormenores

---

in. *abbr* = **inch(es)**
inability [ɪnəˈbɪlɪtɪ] *n*: ~ **(to do)** incapacidade *f* (de fazer)
inaccurate [ɪnˈækjurət] *adj* inexato, impreciso
inadequate [ɪnˈædɪkwət] *adj* insuficiente; (*person*) impróprio
inadvertently [ɪnədˈvɜːtntlɪ] *adv* inadvertidamente, sem querer
inadvisable [ɪnədˈvaɪzəbl] *adj* desaconselhável, inoportuno

inane [ɪˈneɪn] *adj* tolo
inanimate [ɪnˈænɪmət] *adj* inanimado
inappropriate [ɪnəˈprəuprɪət] *adj* inadequado; (*word, expression*) impróprio
inarticulate [ɪnɑːˈtɪkjulət] *adj* (*person*) incapaz de expressar-se (bem); (*speech*) inarticulado
inasmuch as [ɪnəzˈmʌtʃ-] *adv* na medida em que
inauguration [ɪˈnɔːgjureɪʃən] *n* inauguração *f*; (*of president, official*) posse *f*
inborn [ɪnˈbɔːn] *adj* inato
inbred [ɪnˈbred] *adj* inato; (*family*) de procriação consangüínea
Inc. (*us*) *abbr* = **incorporated**
incapable [ɪnˈkeɪpəbl] *adj* incapaz
incapacitate [ɪnkəˈpæsɪteɪt] *vt* incapacitar
incense [*n* ˈɪnsens, *vb* ɪnˈsens] *n* incenso ♦ *vt* (*anger*) exasperar, enraivecer
incentive [ɪnˈsentɪv] *n* incentivo
incessant [ɪnˈsesnt] *adj* incessante, contínuo; **incessantly** *adv* constantemente
inch [ɪntʃ] *n* polegada (= 25 mm; 12 *in a foot*); **to be within an** ~ **of** estar a um passo de; **he didn't give an** ~ ele não cedeu nem um milímetro; **inch forward** *vi* avançar palmo a palmo
incident [ˈɪnsɪdnt] *n* incidente *m*, evento
incidental [ɪnsɪˈdentl] *adj* adicional; ~ **to** relacionado com; **incidentally** *adv* (*by the way*) a propósito
inclination [ɪnklɪˈneɪʃən] *n* (*tendency*) tendência; (*disposition*) inclinação *f*
incline [*n* ˈɪnklaɪn, *vb* ɪnˈklaɪn] *n* inclinação *f*, ladeira ♦ *vt* curvar, inclinar ♦ *vi* inclinar-se; **to be** ~**d to** ten-

der a, ser propenso a

include [ɪnˈkluːd] vt incluir

including [ɪnˈkluːdɪŋ] prep inclusive

inclusive [ɪnˈkluːsɪv] adj incluído, incluso; ~ **of** incluindo

income [ˈɪnkʌm] n (earnings) renda, rendimentos mpl; (unearned) renda; **income tax** n imposto de renda (BR), imposto complementar (PT)

incoming [ˈɪnkʌmɪŋ] adj (flight) de chegada; (mail) de entrada; (government) novo; (tide) enchente

incompetent [ɪnˈkɔmpɪtənt] adj incompetente

incomplete [ɪnkəmˈpliːt] adj incompleto; (unfinished) por terminar

inconsiderate [ɪnkənˈsɪdərət] adj sem consideração

inconsistent [ɪnkənˈsɪstnt] adj inconsistente; ~ **with** incompatível com

inconspicuous [ɪnkənˈspɪkjuəs] adj modesto, discreto

inconvenience [ɪnkənˈviːnjəns] n (quality) inconveniência; (problem) inconveniente m ♦ vt incomodar

inconvenient [ɪnkənˈviːnjənt] adj inconveniente, incômodo; (time, place) inoportuno

incorporate [ɪnˈkɔːpəreɪt] vt incorporar; (contain) compreender

incorrect [ɪnkəˈrekt] adj incorreto

increase [n ˈɪnkriːs, vb ɪnˈkriːs] n aumento ♦ vi, vt aumentar; **increasing** adj crescente, em aumento; **increasingly** adv (more intensely) progressivamente; (more often) cada vez mais

incredible [ɪnˈkrɛdɪbl] adj inacreditável; (enormous) incrível

incubator [ˈɪnkjubeɪtə*] n incubadora

incur [ɪnˈkəː*] vt incorrer em; (expenses) contrair

indebted [ɪnˈdɛtɪd] adj: **to be ~ to**

sb estar em dívida com alguém, dever obrigação a alguém

indecent [ɪnˈdiːsnt] adj indecente

indecisive [ɪndɪˈsaɪsɪv] adj indeciso

indeed [ɪnˈdiːd] adv de fato; (certainly) certamente; (furthermore) aliás; **yes ~!** claro que sim!

indefinitely [ɪnˈdɛfɪnɪtlɪ] adv indefinidamente

independence [ɪndɪˈpɛndns] n independência; **Independence Day** n Dia m da Independência; ver quadro

---

INDEPENDENCE DAY

Independence Day é a festa nacional dos Estados Unidos. Todo dia 4 de julho os americanos comemoram a adoção, em 1776, da declaração de Independência escrita por Thomas Jefferson que proclamava a separação das 13 colônias americanas da Grã-Bretanha.

---

independent [ɪndɪˈpɛndnt] adj independente; (inquiry) imparcial

index [ˈɪndeks] n (pl ~es) (in book) índice m; (in library etc) catálogo; (pl: indices: ratio, sign) índice m, expoente m; **index finger** n dedo indicador; **index-linked** (US **indexed**) adj vinculado ao índice (do custo de vida)

India [ˈɪndɪə] n Índia; **Indian** adj, n (from India) indiano(-a); (American, Brazilian) índio(-a); **Red Indian** índio (-a) pele vermelha; **Indian Ocean** n: **the Indian Ocean** o oceano Índico

indicate [ˈɪndɪkeɪt] vt (show) sugerir; (point to, mention) indicar; **indication** [ɪndɪˈkeɪʃən] n indício, sinal m; **indicative** [ɪnˈdɪkətɪv] adj: **indicative of** sintomático de ♦ n (LING) indicativo; **indicator** n indicador m; (AUT) pisca-pisca m

indices ['ɪndɪsiːz] npl of **index**

indifferent [ɪn'dɪfrənt] adj indiferente; (quality) mediocre

indigenous [ɪn'dɪdʒɪnəs] adj indígena, nativo

indigestion [ɪndɪ'dʒestʃən] n indigestão f

indignant [ɪn'dɪgnənt] adj: to be ~ about sth/with sb estar indignado com algo/alguém, indignar-se de algo/alguém

indignity [ɪn'dɪgnɪtɪ] n indignidade f

indirect [ɪndɪ'rekt] adj indireto

indiscreet [ɪndɪ'skriːt] adj indiscreto

indiscriminate [ɪndɪ'skrɪmɪnət] adj indiscriminado

indisputable [ɪndɪ'spjuːtəbl] adj incontestável

individual [ɪndɪ'vɪdjuəl] n indivíduo ♦ adj individual; (personal) pessoal; (characteristic) particular

Indonesia [ɪndə'niːzɪə] n Indonésia

indoor ['ɪndɔː*] adj (inner) interno, interior; (inside) dentro de casa; (plant) para dentro de casa; (swimming pool) coberto; (games, sport) de salão; **indoors** adv em lugar fechado

induce [ɪn'djuːs] vt (MED) induzir; (bring about) causar, produzir

indulge [ɪn'dʌldʒ] vt (desire) satisfazer; (whim) condescender com; (person) comprazer; (child) fazer a vontade de ♦ vi: to ~ in entregar-se a, satisfazer-se com; **indulgence** n (of desire) satisfação f; (leniency) indulgência, tolerância f; **indulgent** adj indulgente

industrial [ɪn'dʌstrɪəl] adj industrial; **industrial action** n greve f

industrious [ɪn'dʌstrɪəs] adj trabalhador(a); (student) aplicado

industry ['ɪndəstrɪ] n indústria; (diligence) aplicação f, diligência

inebriated [ɪ'niːbrɪeɪtɪd] adj embriagado, bêbado

inedible [ɪn'edɪbl] adj não-comestível

ineffective [ɪnɪ'fektɪv] adj ineficaz

ineffectual [ɪnɪ'fektʃuəl] adj = **ineffective**

inefficient [ɪnɪ'fɪʃnt] adj ineficiente

inequality [ɪnɪ'kwɔlɪtɪ] n desigualdade f

inescapable [ɪnɪ'skeɪpəbl] adj inevitável

inevitable [ɪn'evɪtəbl] adj inevitável; **inevitably** adv inevitavelmente

inexpensive [ɪnɪk'spensɪv] adj barato, econômico

inexperienced [ɪnɪk'spɪərɪənst] adj inexperiente

infallible [ɪn'fælɪbl] adj infalível

infamous ['ɪnfəməs] adj infame, abominável

infancy ['ɪnfənsɪ] n infância

infant ['ɪnfənt] n (baby) bebê m; (young child) criança

infant school (BRIT) n pré-escola

infatuated [ɪn'fætjueɪtɪd] adj: ~ with apaixonado por

infatuation [ɪnfætju'eɪʃən] n gamação f, paixão f louca

infect [ɪn'fekt] vt (person) contagiar; (food) contaminar; **infection** n infecção f; **infectious** adj contagioso; (fig) infeccioso

infer [ɪn'fəː*] vt deduzir, inferir

inferior [ɪn'fɪərɪə*] adj inferior; (goods) de qualidade inferior ♦ n inferior m/f; (in rank) subalterno(-a); **inferiority** [ɪnfɪərɪ'ɔrɪtɪ] n inferioridade f

infertile [ɪn'fəːtaɪl] adj infértil; (person, animal) estéril

infinite ['ɪnfɪnɪt] adj infinito

infinitive [ɪnˈfɪnɪtɪv] n infinitivo

infinity [ɪnˈfɪnɪtɪ] n (also MATH) infinito; (an ~) infinidade f

infirmary [ɪnˈfəːmərɪ] n enfermaria, hospital m

inflamed [ɪnˈfleɪmd] adj inflamado

inflammable [ɪnˈflæməbl] adj inflamável

inflammation [ɪnfləˈmeɪʃən] n inflamação f

inflatable [ɪnˈfleɪtəbl] adj inflável

inflate [ɪnˈfleɪt] vt (tyre, balloon) inflar, encher; (price) inflar; **inflation** [ECON] inflação f

inflict [ɪnˈflɪkt] vt: **to ~ on** infligir em

influence [ˈɪnfluəns] n influência ♦ vt influir em, influenciar; **under the ~ of alcohol** sob o efeito do álcool; **influential** [ɪnfluˈɛnʃl] adj influente

influenza [ɪnfluˈɛnzə] n gripe f

infomercial [ˈɪnfəuməːʃl] (US) n (for product) infomercial m

inform [ɪnˈfɔːm] vt informar ♦ vi: **to ~ on sb** delatar alguém

informal [ɪnˈfɔːml] adj informal; (visit, discussion) extra-oficial; **informality** [ɪnfɔːˈmælɪtɪ] n informalidade f

information [ɪnfəˈmeɪʃən] n informação f, informações fpl; (knowledge) conhecimento; **a piece of ~** uma informação; **information desk** n balcão m de informações

informative [ɪnˈfɔːmətɪv] adj informativo

informer [ɪnˈfɔːmə*] n informante m/f

infringe [ɪnˈfrɪndʒ] vt infringir, transgredir ♦ vi: **to ~ on** violar

infuriating [ɪnˈfjuərɪeɪtɪŋ] adj de dar raiva, enfurecedor(a)

ingenious [ɪnˈdʒiːnjəs] adj engenhoso; **ingenuity** [ɪndʒɪˈnjuːɪtɪ] n engenho, habilidade f

ingot [ˈɪŋgət] n lingote m

ingratiate [ɪnˈgreɪʃɪeɪt] vt: **to ~ o.s. with** cair nas (boas) graças de

ingredient [ɪnˈgriːdɪənt] n ingrediente m; (of situation) fator m

inhabit [ɪnˈhæbɪt] vt habitar; **inhabitant** n habitante m/f

inhale [ɪnˈheɪl] vt inalar ♦ vi (in smoking) tragar

inherent [ɪnˈhɪərənt] adj: **~ in** or **to** inerente a

inherit [ɪnˈhɛrɪt] vt herdar; **inheritance** n herança

inhibit [ɪnˈhɪbɪt] vt inibir; **inhibition** [ɪnhɪˈbɪʃən] n inibição f

inhuman [ɪnˈhjuːmən] adj inumano, desumano

initial [ɪˈnɪʃl] adj inicial ♦ n inicial f ♦ vt marcar com iniciais; **~s** npl (of name) iniciais fpl; **initially** adv inicialmente, no início

initiate [ɪˈnɪʃɪeɪt] vt (start) iniciar, começar; (person) iniciar; **to ~ sb into a secret** revelar um segredo a alguém

initiative [ɪˈnɪʃətɪv] n iniciativa

inject [ɪnˈdʒɛkt] vt (liquid, also: money) injetar; (person) dar uma injeção em; **injection** n injeção f

injure [ˈɪndʒə*] vt ferir; (reputation etc) prejudicar; (feelings) ofender; **injured** adj ferido; (feelings) ofendido, magoado; **injury** n ferida

injustice [ɪnˈdʒʌstɪs] n injustiça

ink [ɪŋk] n tinta

inkling [ˈɪŋklɪŋ] n vaga idéia

inlaid [ˈɪnleɪd] adj (with gems) incrustado; (table etc) marchetado

inland [adj ˈɪnlənd, adv ɪnˈlænd] adj interior, interno ♦ adv para o interior; **Inland Revenue** [BRIT] n ≈ fisco, receita federal (BR)

inmate [ˈɪnmeɪt] n (in prison) presidiário(-a); (in asylum) internado(-a)

inn [ɪn] n hospedaria, taberna

innate [ɪ'neɪt] adj inato

inner ['ɪnə*] adj (place) interno; (feeling) interior; **inner city** n aglomeração f urbana, metrópole f

innings ['ɪnɪŋz] n (SPORT) turno

innocent ['ɪnəsnt] adj inocente

innocuous [ɪ'nɒkjuəs] adj inócuo

innuendo [ɪnju'ɛndəu] (pl **~es**) n insinuação f, indireta

innumerable [ɪ'nju:mrəbl] adj incontável

in-patient n paciente m/f interno(-a)

input ['ɪnput] n entrada; (resources) investimento

inquest ['ɪnkwɛst] n inquérito judicial

inquire [ɪn'kwaɪə*] vi pedir informação ♦ vt perguntar; **inquire about** vt fus pedir informações sobre; **inquire into** vt fus investigar, indagar; **inquiry** n pergunta; (LAW) investigação f, inquérito

inquisitive [ɪn'kwɪzɪtɪv] adj curioso, perguntador(a)

ins. abbr = **inches**

insane [ɪn'seɪn] adj louco, doido; (MED) demente, insano; **insanity** [ɪn'sænɪtɪ] n loucura; insanidade f, demência

inscription [ɪn'skrɪpʃən] n inscrição f; (in book) dedicatória

inscrutable [ɪn'skru:təbl] adj inescrutável, impenetrável

insect ['ɪnsɛkt] n inseto; **insecticide** [ɪn'sɛktɪsaɪd] n inseticida m

insecure [ɪnsɪ'kjuə*] adj inseguro

insensitive [ɪn'sɛnsɪtɪv] adj insensível

insert [ɪn'sə:t] vt (between things) intercalar; (into sth) introduzir, inserir

inshore [ɪn'ʃɔ:*] adj perto da costa, costeiro ♦ adv (be) perto da costa; (move) em direção à costa

inside ['ɪn'saɪd] n interior m ♦ adj interior, interno, interno ♦ adv (be) dentro; (go) para dentro ♦ prep dentro de; (of time): **~ 10 minutes** em menos de 10 minutos; **~s** npl (inf) entranhas fpl; **inside out** adv às avessas; (know) muito bem; **to turn sth inside out** virar algo pelo avesso

insight ['ɪnsaɪt] n insight m

insignificant [ɪnsɪg'nɪfɪknt] adj insignificante

insincere [ɪnsɪn'sɪə*] adj insincero

insinuate [ɪn'sɪnjuɛt] vt insinuar

insist [ɪn'sɪst] vi insistir; **to ~ on doing** insistir em fazer; **to ~ that** insistir que; (claim) cismar que; **insistent** adj insistente, pertinaz; (continual) persistente

insomnia [ɪn'sɒmnɪə] n insônia f

inspect [ɪn'spɛkt] vt inspecionar; (building) vistoriar; (BRIT: tickets) fiscalizar; (troops) passar revista em; **inspection** n inspeção f; vistoria, fiscalização f; **inspector** n inspetor(a) m/f; (BRIT: on buses, trains) fiscal m

inspire [ɪn'spaɪə*] vt inspirar

install [ɪn'stɔ:l] vt instalar; (official) nomear; **installation** [ɪnstə'leɪʃən] n instalação f

installment [ɪn'stɔ:lmənt] (US **installment**) n (of money) prestação f; (of story) fascículo; (of TV serial etc) capítulo; **in ~s** (pay) a prestações; (receive) em várias vezes

instance ['ɪnstəns] n exemplo; **for ~** por exemplo; **in the first ~** em primeiro lugar

instant ['ɪnstənt] n instante m, momento ♦ adj imediato; (coffee) instantâneo; **instantly** adv imediatamente

instead [ɪn'stɛd] adv em vez disso; **~ of** em vez de, em lugar de

instigate ['ɪnstɪgeɪt] vt fomentar

instil [ɪn'stɪl] vt: to ~ sth (into) infundir or incutir algo (em)

instinct ['ɪnstɪŋkt] n instinto

institute ['ɪnstɪtjuːt] n instituto; (professional body) associação f ♦ vt (inquiry) começar, iniciar; (proceedings) instituir, estabelecer

institution [ɪnstɪ'tjuːʃən] n instituição f; (organization) instituto; (MED: home) asilo; (asylum) manicômio; (custom) costume m

instruct [ɪn'strʌkt] vt: to ~ sb in sth instruir alguém em or sobre algo; to ~ sb to do sth dar instruções a alguém para fazer algo; **instruction** n (teaching) instrução f; **instructions** npl (orders) ordens fpl; **instructions** (for use) modo de usar; **instructor** n instrutor (a) m/f

instrument ['ɪnstrumənt] n instrumento

insufficient [ɪnsə'fɪʃənt] adj insuficiente

insular ['ɪnsjulə*] adj (outlook) estreito; (person) de mente limitada

insulate ['ɪnsjuleɪt] vt isolar; (protect) segregar; **insulation** [ɪnsju'leɪʃən] n isolamento

insulin ['ɪnsjulɪn] n insulina

insult [n 'ɪnsʌlt, vb ɪn'sʌlt] n ofensa ♦ vt insultar, ofender

insurance [ɪn'ʃuərəns] n seguro; **fire/life** ~ seguro contra incêndio/ de vida

insure [ɪn'ʃuə*] vt segurar

intact [ɪn'tækt] adj intacto, íntegro; (unharmed) ileso, são e salvo

intake ['ɪnteɪk] n (of food) quantidade f ingerida; (BRIT: SCH): **an ~ of 200 a year** 200 matriculados por ano

integral ['ɪntɪɡrəl] adj (part) integrante, essencial

integrate ['ɪntɪɡreɪt] vt integrar ♦ vi integrar-se

intellect ['ɪntəlekt] n intelecto;

intellectual [ɪntə'lektjuəl] adj, n intelectual m/f

intelligence [ɪn'telɪdʒəns] n inteligência; (MIL etc) informações fpl

intelligent [ɪn'telɪdʒənt] adj inteligente

intend [ɪn'tend] vt (gift etc): to ~ sth for destinar algo a; to ~ to do sth tencionar or pretender fazer algo; (plan) planejar fazer algo

intense [ɪn'tens] adj intenso; (person) muito emotivo

intensive [ɪn'tensɪv] adj intensivo; **intensive care unit** n unidade f de tratamento intensivo

intent [ɪn'tent] n intenção f ♦ adj: to be ~ on doing sth estar resolvido a fazer algo; to all ~s and purposes para todos os efeitos

intention [ɪn'tenʃən] n intenção f, propósito; **intentional** adj intencional, proposital; **intentionally** adv de propósito

intently [ɪn'tentlɪ] adv atentamente

interact [ɪntər'ækt] vi interagir; **interactive** adj interactivo

interchange ['ɪntətʃeɪndʒ] n intercâmbio; (exchange) troca, permuta; (on motorway) trevo; **interchangeable** adj permutável

intercom ['ɪntəkɔm] n interfone m

intercourse ['ɪntəkɔːs] n: **sexual ~** relações fpl sexuais

interest ['ɪntrɪst] n interesse m; (COMM: sum) juros mpl; (: in company) participação f ♦ vt interessar; **to be ~ed in** interessar-se por, estar interessado em; **interesting** adj interessante

interface ['ɪntəfeɪs] n (COMPUT) interface f

interfere [ɪntə'fɪə*] vi: to ~ in interferir or intrometer-se em; to ~ with (objects) mexer em; (hinder) impedir; (plans) interferir em

interference [ɪntəˈfɪərəns] *n* intromissão *f*; (RADIO, TV) interferência

interior [ɪnˈtɪərɪə*] *n* interior *m* ♦ *adj* interno; (*ministry*) do interior

interjection [ɪntəˈdʒɛkʃən] *n* interrupção *f*; (LING) interjeição *f*, exclamação *f*

interlude [ˈɪntəluːd] *n* interlúdio; (*rest*) descanso; (THEATRE) intervalo

intermediate [ɪntəˈmiːdɪət] *adj* intermediário

intermission [ɪntəˈmɪʃən] *n* intervalo

intern [*vb* ɪnˈtəːn, *n* ˈɪntəːn] *vt* internar ♦ *n* (US) médico-interno (médica-interna)

internal [ɪnˈtəːnl] *adj* interno; **internally** *adv*: "not to be taken internally" "uso externo"; **Internal Revenue Service** (US) *n* Receita Federal (BR), Direcção *f* Geral das Contribuições e Impostos (PT)

international [ɪntəˈnæʃnl] *adj* internacional ♦ *n* (BRIT: SPORT: *game*) jogo internacional

Internet [ˈɪntənɛt] *n*: **the ~** a Internet; **Internet café** *n* cibercafé *m*; **Internet Service Provider** *n* provedor *m* de acesso à Internet

interpret [ɪnˈtəːprɪt] *vt* interpretar; (*translate*) traduzir ♦ *vi* interpretar; **interpreter** *n* intérprete *m/f*

interrelated [ɪntərɪˈleɪtɪd] *adj* inter-relacionado

interrogate [ɪnˈtɛrəugeɪt] *vt* interrogar; **interrogation** [ɪntɛrəuˈgeɪʃən] *n* interrogatório

interrupt [ɪntəˈrʌpt] *vt, vi* interromper; **interruption** *n* interrupção *f*

intersect [ɪntəˈsɛkt] *vi* (*roads*) cruzar-se; **intersection** *n* cruzamento

interval [ˈɪntəvl] *n* intervalo

intervene [ɪntəˈviːn] *vi* intervir; (*event*) ocorrer; (*time*) decorrer;

intervention *n* intervenção *f*

interview [ˈɪntəvjuː] *n* entrevista ♦ *vt* entrevistar; **interviewer** *n* entrevistador(a) *m/f*

intestine [ɪnˈtɛstɪn] *n* intestino

intimacy [ˈɪntɪməsɪ] *n* intimidade *f*

intimate [*adj* ˈɪntɪmət, *vb* ˈɪntɪmeɪt] *adj* íntimo; (*knowledge*) profundo ♦ *vt* insinuar, sugerir

into [ˈɪntu] *prep* em; **she burst ~ tears** ela desatou a chorar; **come ~ the house** venha para dentro; **research ~ cancer** pesquisa sobre o câncer; **he worked late ~ the night** ele trabalhou até altas horas; **he was shocked ~ silence** ele ficou mudo de choque; **~ 3 pieces/French** em 3 pedaços/para o francês

intolerant [ɪnˈtɔlərnt] *adj*: **~ (of)** intolerante (com ou para com)

intoxicated [ɪnˈtɔksɪkeɪtɪd] *adj* embriagado

intranet [ˈɪntrənɛt] *n* intranet *f*

intricate [ˈɪntrɪkət] *adj* complexo, complicado

intrigue [ɪnˈtriːg] *n* intriga ♦ *vt* intrigar; (*fascinate*) fascinar; **intriguing** *adj* curioso

introduce [ɪntrəˈdjuːs] *vt* introduzir; **to ~ sb (to sb)** apresentar alguém (a alguém); **to ~ sb to** (*pastime, technique*) iniciar alguém em; **introduction** *n* introdução *f*; (*of person*) apresentação *f*; **introductory** *adj* introdutório

intrude [ɪnˈtruːd] *vi*: **to ~ (on)** intrometer-se (em); **intruder** *n* intruso(-a)

inundate [ˈɪnʌndeɪt] *vt*: **to ~ with** inundar de

invade [ɪnˈveɪd] *vt* invadir

invalid [*n* ˈɪnvəlɪd, *adj* ɪnˈvælɪd] *n* inválido(-a) ♦ *adj* inválido, nulo

invaluable [ɪnˈvæljuəbl] *adj* valioso, inestimável

invariably [ɪn'vɛərɪəblɪ] adv invariavelmente

invent [ɪn'vɛnt] vt inventar; **invention** n invenção f; (inventiveness) engenho; (lie) ficção f, mentira; **inventor** n inventor(a) m/f

inventory ['ɪnvəntrɪ] n inventário, relação f

invert [ɪn'vəːt] vt inverter; **inverted commas** (BRIT) npl aspas fpl

invest [ɪn'vɛst] vt investir ♦ vi: **to ~** in investir em; (acquire) comprar

investigate [ɪn'vɛstɪgeɪt] vt investigar; **investigation** [ɪnvɛstɪ'geɪʃən] n investigação f

investment [ɪn'vɛstmənt] n investimento

invigorating [ɪn'vɪɡəreɪtɪŋ] adj revigorante

invisible [ɪn'vɪzɪbl] adj invisível

invitation [ɪnvɪ'teɪʃən] n convite m

invite [ɪn'vaɪt] vt convidar; (opinions etc) incitar; **inviting** adj convidativo

invoice ['ɪnvɔɪs] n fatura ♦ vt faturar

involuntary [ɪn'vɔləntrɪ] adj involuntário

involve [ɪn'vɔlv] vt (entail) implicar; (require) exigir; (concern) envolver; **to ~ sb (in)** envolver alguém (em); **involved** adj (complex) complexo; **to be involved in** estar envolvido em; **involvement** n envolvimento

inward ['ɪnwəd] adj (movement) interior, interno; (thought, feeling) íntimo; **inward(s)** adv para dentro

iodine ['aɪəudiːn] n iodo

iota [aɪ'əutə] n (fig) pouquinho, tiquinho

IOU n abbr (= I owe you) vale m

IQ n abbr (= intelligence quotient) QI m

IRA n abbr (= Irish Republican Army) IRA m

Iran [ɪ'rɑːn] n Irã m (BR), Irão m (PT)

Iraq [ɪ'rɑːk] n Iraque m

irate [aɪ'reɪt] adj irado, enfurecido

Ireland ['aɪələnd] n Irlanda

iris ['aɪrɪs] (pl **~es**) n íris f

Irish ['aɪrɪʃ] adj irlandês(-esa) ♦ npl: **the ~** os irlandeses; **Irishman** (irreg) n irlandês m; **Irish Sea** n: **the Irish Sea** o mar da Irlanda; **Irishwoman** (irreg) n irlandesa

iron ['aɪən] n ferro; (for clothes) ferro de passar roupa ♦ adj de ferro ♦ vt (clothes) passar; **iron out** vt (problem) resolver

ironic(al) [aɪ'rɔnɪk(l)] adj irônico

ironing ['aɪənɪŋ] n (activity) passar m roupa; (clothes) roupa passada; **ironing board** n tábua de passar roupa

irony ['aɪrənɪ] n ironia

irrational [ɪ'ræʃənl] adj irracional

irregular [ɪ'rɛgjulə*] adj irregular; (surface) desigual

irrelevant [ɪ'rɛləvənt] adj irrelevante

irresistible [ɪrɪ'zɪstɪbl] adj irresistível

irrespective [ɪrɪ'spɛktɪv]: **~ of** prep independente de, sem considerar

irresponsible [ɪrɪ'spɔnsɪbl] adj irresponsável

irrigation [ɪrɪ'geɪʃən] n irrigação f

irritate ['ɪrɪteɪt] vt irritar; **irritating** adj irritante; **irritation** [ɪrɪ'teɪʃən] n irritação f

IRS (US) n abbr = **Internal Revenue Service**

is [ɪz] vb see **be**

ISDN n abbr (= Integrated Services Digital Network) RDSI f, ISDN f

Islam ['ɪzlɑːm] n islamismo

island ['aɪlənd] n ilha; **islander** n ilhéu (ilhoa) m/f

isle [aɪl] n ilhota, ilha

isn't ['ɪznt] = **is not**

isolate ['aɪsəleɪt] vt isolar; **isolated**

adj isolado; **isolation** [aɪsə'leɪʃən] *n* isolamento

ISP *n abbr* = **Internet Service Provider**

Israel ['ɪzreɪl] *n* Israel *m* (*no article*); **Israeli** [ɪz'reɪlɪ] *adj, n* israelense *m/f*

issue ['ɪʃjuː] *n* questão *f*, tema *m*; (*of book*) edição *f*; (*of stamps*) emissão *f* ♦ *vt* (*statement*) fazer; (*rations, equipment*) distribuir; (*orders*) dar; **at ~ em** debate; **to take ~ with sb (over sth)** discordar de alguém (sobre algo); **to make an ~ of sth** criar caso com algo

---

KEYWORD

---

it [ɪt] *pron* **1** (*specific: subject*) ele (ela); (*: direct object*) o (a); (*: indirect object*) lhe; **~'s on the table** está em cima da mesa; **I can't find ~** não consigo achá-lo; **give ~ to me** dê-mo; **about/from ~** sobre/de isto; **did you go to ~?** (*party, concert etc*) você foi?

2 (*impers*) isto, isso; (*after prep*) ele, ela; **~'s raining** está chovendo (*BR*) or a chover (*PT*); **~'s six o'clock/the 10th of August** são seis horas/hoje é (dia) 10 de agosto; **who is ~? – ~'s me** quem é? – sou eu

Italian [ɪ'tæljən] *adj* italiano ♦ *n* italiano(-a); (*LING*) italiano

italics [ɪ'tælɪks] *npl* itálico

Italy ['ɪtəlɪ] *n* Itália

itch [ɪtʃ] *n* comichão *f*, coceira ♦ *vi* (*person*) estar com or sentir comichão or coceira; (*part of body*) comichar, coçar; **I'm itching to do sth** estou louco para fazer algo; **itchy** *adj* que coça; **to be itchy =** to **itch**

it'd ['ɪtd] = **it would**; **it had**

item ['aɪtəm] *n* item *m*; (*on agenda*) assunto; (*in programme*) número;

(*also:* **news ~**) notícia; **itemize** *vt* detalhar, especificar

itinerary [aɪ'tɪnərərɪ] *n* itinerário

it'll ['ɪtl] = **it will**; **it shall**

its [ɪts] *adj* seu (sua), dele (dela) ♦ *pron* o seu (a sua), o dele (a dela)

it's [ɪts] = **it is**; **it has**

itself [ɪt'sɛlf] *pron* (*reflexive*) si mesmo(-a); (*emphatic*) ele mesmo (ela mesma)

ITV (*BRIT*) *n abbr* (= *Independent Television*) canal de televisão comercial

IUD *n abbr* (= *intra-uterine device*) DIU *m*

I've [aɪv] = **I have**

ivory ['aɪvərɪ] *n* marfim *m*

ivy ['aɪvɪ] *n* hera

J

jab [dʒæb] *vt* cutucar ♦ *n* cotovelada, murro; (*inf*) injeção *f*; **to ~ sth into sth** cravar algo em algo

jack [dʒæk] *n* (*AUT*) macaco; (*CARDS*) valete *m*; **jack up** *vt* (*AUT*) levantar com macaco

jackal ['dʒækl] *n* chacal *m*

jacket ['dʒækɪt] *n* jaqueta, casaco curto, forro; (*of book*) sobrecapa; **jacket potato** *n* batata assada com a casca

jack-knife *vi*: **the lorry ~d** o reboque do caminhão deu uma guinada

jackpot ['dʒækpɔt] *n* bolada, sorte *f* grande

jaded ['dʒeɪdɪd] *adj* (*tired*) cansado; (*fed-up*) aborrecido, amolado

jagged ['dʒægɪd] *adj* dentado, denteado

jail [dʒeɪl] *n* prisão *f*, cadeia ♦ *vt* encarcerar

jam [dʒæm] *n* geléia; (*also:* **traffic ~**) engarrafamento; (*inf*) apuro ♦ *vt* obstruir, atravancar; (*mechanism*) emperrar; (RADIO) bloquear, interferir ♦ vi (mechanism, drawer etc) emperrar; **to ~ sth into sth** forçar algo dentro de algo

Jamaica [dʒəˈmeɪkə] n Jamaica f

janitor [ˈdʒænɪtə*] n zelador m

January [ˈdʒænjuərɪ] n janeiro

Japan [dʒəˈpæn] n Japão m; **Japanese** [dʒæpəˈniːz] adj japonês(-esa) ♦ n inv japonês(-esa) m/f; (LING) japonês m

jar [dʒɑː*] n jarro ♦ vi (sound) ranger, chiar; (colours) destoar

jargon [ˈdʒɑːgən] n jargão m

jaundice [ˈdʒɔːndɪs] n icterícia f

javelin [ˈdʒævlɪn] n dardo de arremesso

jaw [dʒɔː] n mandíbula, maxilar m

jaywalker [ˈdʒeɪwɔːkə*] n pedestre m/f imprudente (BR), peão m imprudente (PT)

jazz [dʒæz] n jazz m; **jazz up** vt animar, avivar

jealous [ˈdʒeləs] adj ciumento; **jealousy** n ciúmes mpl

jeans [dʒiːnz] npl jeans m(pl PT)

jeer [dʒɪə*] vi: **to ~ (at)** zombar (de)

jelly [ˈdʒelɪ] n gelatina; (jam) geléia; **jellyfish** [ˈdʒelɪfɪʃ] n inv água-viva

jeopardy [ˈdʒepədɪ] n: **to be in ~** estar em perigo, estar correndo risco

jerk [dʒɜːk] n solavanco, sacudida; (wrench) puxão m; (inf: idiot) babaca m ♦ vt sacudir ♦ vi dar um solavanco

jersey [ˈdʒɜːzɪ] n suéter m or f (BR), camisola (PT); (fabric) jérsei m, malha

Jesus [ˈdʒiːzəs] n Jesus m

jet [dʒet] n (of gas, liquid) jato; (AVIAT) avião m a jato; (stone) azeviche m; **jet engine** n motor m a jato; **jet lag** n cansaço devido à diferença de fuso horário

jettison [ˈdʒetɪsn] vt alijar

jetty [ˈdʒetɪ] n quebra-mar m, cais m

Jew [dʒuː] n judeu(-dia) m/f

jewel [ˈdʒuːəl] n jóia; **jeweller** (US **jeweler**) n joalheiro(-a); **jeweller's (shop)** n joalheria; **jewellery** (US **jewelry**) n jóias fpl

Jewess [ˈdʒuːɪs] n (offensive) judia

Jewish [ˈdʒuːɪʃ] adj judeu (judia)

jiffy [ˈdʒɪfɪ] (inf) n: **in a ~** num instante

jigsaw [ˈdʒɪgsɔː] n (also: ~ **puzzle**) quebra-cabeça m

jilt [dʒɪlt] vt dar o fora em

jingle [ˈdʒɪŋgl] n (for advert) música de propaganda ♦ vi tilintar, retinir

jinx [dʒɪŋks] (inf) n caipora, pé m frio

job [dʒɔb] n trabalho; (task) tarefa; (duty) dever m; (post) emprego; **it's not my ~** não faz parte das minhas funções; **it's a good ~ that ...** ainda bem que ...; **just the ~!** justo o que queria!; **jobless** adj desempregado

jockey [ˈdʒɔkɪ] n jóquei m ♦ vi: **to ~ for position** manobrar para conseguir uma posição

jog [dʒɔg] vt empurrar, sacudir ♦ vi fazer jogging ou cooper; **jog along** vi ir levando; **jogging** n jogging m

join [dʒɔɪn] vt (things) juntar, unir; (queue) entrar em; (become member of) associar-se a; (meet) encontrar-se com; (accompany) juntar-se a ♦ vi (roads, rivers) confluir ♦ n junção f; **join in** vi participar ♦ vt fus participar em; **join up** vi unir-se; (MIL) alistar-se

joint [dʒɔɪnt] n (TECH) junta, união f; (wood) encaixe m; (ANAT) articulação f; (BRIT: CULIN) quarto; (inf: place) espelunca; (: of marijuana) baseado ♦ adj comum; (combined) conjunto; (committee) misto

joke [dʒəuk] n piada; (also: practical ~) brincadeira, peça ♦ vi brincar; **to play a ~ on** pregar uma peça em; **joker** n (CARDS) curingão m

jolly ['dʒɔlɪ] adj (merry) alegre; (enjoyable) divertido ♦ adv (BRIT: inf) muito, extremamente

jolt [dʒəult] n (shake) sacudida, solavanco; (shock) susto ♦ vt sacudir; (emotionally) abalar

Jordan ['dʒɔːdən] n Jordânia; (river) Jordão m

jostle ['dʒɔsl] vt acotovelar, empurrar

jot [dʒɔt] n: **not one ~** nem um pouquinho; **jot down** vt anotar; **jotter** (BRIT) n bloco de anotações

journal ['dʒəːnl] n jornal m; (magazine) revista; (diary) diário; **journalism** n jornalismo; **journalist** n jornalista m/f

journey ['dʒəːnɪ] n viagem f; (distance covered) trajeto

joy [dʒɔɪ] n alegria; **joyful** adj alegre; **joystick** n (AVIAT) manche m, alavanca de controle; (COMPUT) joystick m

Jr abbr = **junior**

judge [dʒʌdʒ] n juiz (juíza m/f); (in competition) árbitro; (fig: expert) especialista m/f, conhecedor(a) m/f ♦ vt julgar; (competition) arbitrar; (estimate) avaliar; (consider) considerar; **judg(e)ment** n juízo; (opinion) opinião f; (discernment) discernimento

judo ['dʒuːdəu] n judô m

jug [dʒʌg] n jarro

juggernaut ['dʒʌgənɔːt] (BRIT) n (huge truck) jamanta

juggle ['dʒʌgl] vi fazer malabarismos; **juggler** n malabarista m/f

juice [dʒuːs] n suco (BR), sumo (PT); **juicy** adj suculento

jukebox ['dʒuːkbɔks] n juke-box m

July [dʒuːˈlaɪ] n julho

jumble ['dʒʌmbl] n confusão f, mixórdia ♦ vt (also: ~ up: mix up) misturar; **jumble sale** n (BRIT) bazar m; ver quadro

---

JUMBLE SALE

As **jumble sales** têm lugar dentro de igrejas, salões de festa e escolas, onde são vendidos diversos tipos de mercadorias, em geral baratas e sobretudo de segunda mão, a fim de coletar dinheiro para uma obra de caridade, uma escola ou uma igreja.

---

jumbo (jet) ['dʒʌmbəu-] n avião m jumbo

jump [dʒʌmp] vi saltar, pular; (start) sobressaltar-se; (increase) disparar ♦ vt pular, saltar ♦ n pulo, salto; (increase) alta; (fence) obstáculo; **to ~ the queue** (BRIT) furar a fila (BR), pôr-se à frente (PT)

jumper ['dʒʌmpə*] n (BRIT: pullover) suéter m (BR), camisola (PT); (US: pinafore dress) avental m; **jumper cables** (US) npl = **jump leads**

jump leads (BRIT) npl cabos mpl para ligar a bateria

jumpy ['dʒʌmpɪ] adj nervoso

Jun. abbr = **junior**

junction ['dʒʌŋkʃən] (BRIT) n (of roads) cruzamento; (RAIL) entroncamento

June [dʒuːn] n junho

jungle ['dʒʌŋgl] n selva, mato

junior ['dʒuːnɪə*] adj (in age) mais novo or moço; (position) subalterno ♦ n jovem m/f

junk [dʒʌŋk] n (cheap goods) tranqueira, velharias fpl; (rubbish) lixo; **junk food** n comida pronta de baixo valor nutritivo; **junk mail** n correspondência não-solicitada; **junk shop** n loja de objetos usados

Junr abbr = **junior**

jury ['dʒuəri] n júri m
just [dʒʌst] adj justo ♦ adv (exactly) justamente, exatamente; (only) apenas, somente; **he's ~ done it/left** ele acabou (BR) or acaba (PT) de fazê-lo/ir; **~ right** perfeito; **~ two o'clock** duas (horas) em ponto; **she's ~ as clever as you** ela é tão inteligente como você; **it's ~ as well that ...** ainda bem que ...; **~ as he was leaving** no momento em que ele saía; **~ before/enough** justo antes/o suficiente; **~ here** bem aqui; **he ~ missed** falhou por pouco; **~ listen!** escute aqui!
justice ['dʒʌstɪs] n justiça; (US: judge) juiz (juíza) m/f; **to do ~ to** (fig) apreciar devidamente
justify ['dʒʌstɪfaɪ] vt justificar
jut [dʒʌt] vi (also: **~ out**) sobressair
juvenile ['dʒuːvənaɪl] adj juvenil; (court) de menores; (books) para adolescentes; (humour, mentality) infantil ♦ n menor m/f de idade

K

K abbr (= kilobyte) K ♦ n abbr (= one thousand) mil
kangaroo [kæŋgə'ruː] n canguru m
karate [kə'rɑːtɪ] n karatê m
kebab [kə'bæb] n churrasquinho, espetinho
keen [kiːn] adj (interest, desire) grande, vivo; (eye, intelligence) penetrante; (competition) acirrado, intenso; (edge) afiado; (eager) entusiasmado; **to be ~ to do** or **on doing sth** sentir muita vontade de fazer algo; **to be ~ on sth/sb** gostar de algo/alguém
keep [kiːp] (pt, pp **kept**) vt guardar, ficar com; (house etc) cuidar, (detain) deter; (shop etc) tomar conta de; (preserve) conservar; (accounts, family) manter; (promise) cumprir; (chickens, bees etc) criar; (prevent): **to ~ sb from doing sth** impedir alguém de fazer algo ♦ vi (food) conservar-se; (remain) ficar ♦ n (of castle) torre f de menagem; (food etc): **to earn one's ~** ganhar a vida; (inf): **for ~s** para sempre; **to ~ doing sth** continuar fazendo algo; **to ~ sb happy** manter alguém satisfeito; **to ~ a place tidy** manter um lugar limpo; **keep on** vi: **to ~ on doing** continuar fazendo; **to ~ on (about sth)** falar sem parar sobre algo; **keep out** vt impedir de entrar; **"~ out"** "entrada proibida"; **keep up** vt manter ♦ vi não atrasar-se, acompanhar; **to ~ up with** (pace) acompanhar; (level) manter-se ao nível de; **keep fit** n ginástica
kennel ['kɛnl] n casa de cachorro; **~s** n (establishment) canil m
kerb [kəːb] (BRIT) n meio-fio (BR), borda do passeio (PT)
kernel ['kəːnl] n amêndoa; (fig) cerne m
kettle ['kɛtl] n chaleira
key [kiː] n chave f; (MUS) clave f; (of piano, typewriter) tecla ♦ cpd (issue etc) chave ♦ vt (also: **~ in**) colocar; **keyboard** n teclado; **keyhole** n buraco da fechadura; **keyring** n chaveiro
khaki ['kɑːkɪ] adj cáqui
kick [kɪk] vt dar um pontapé em; (ball) chutar; (inf: habit) conseguir superar ♦ vi (horse) dar coices ♦ n (from person) pontapé m; (from animal) coice m, patada; (to ball) chute m; (inf: thrill): **he does it for ~s** faz isso para curtir; **kick off** vi (SPORT) dar o chute inicial
kid [kɪd] n (inf: child) criança; (ani-

mal) cabrito; (*leather*) pelica ♦ *vi*
(*inf*) brincar

kidnap ['kɪdnæp] *vt* seqüestrar; **kid-napper** *n* seqüestrador(a) *m/f*; **kid-napping** *n* seqüestro

kidney ['kɪdnɪ] *n* rim *m*

kill [kɪl] *vt* matar; (*murder*) assassinar ♦ *n* ato de matar; **killer** *n* assassino(-a); **killing** *n* assassinato *m*; **to make a killing** (*inf*) faturar uma boa nota; **killjoy** *n* desmancha-prazeres *m inv*

kiln [kɪln] *n* forno

kilo ['ki:ləu] *n* quilo; **kilobyte** *n* quilobyte *m*; **kilogram(me)** *n* quilograma *m*; **kilometre** (*US* **kilometer**) *n* quilômetro; **kilowatt** *n* quilowatt *m*

kilt [kɪlt] *n* saiote *m* escocês

kin [kɪn] *n* see **next**

kind [kaɪnd] *adj* (*friendly*) gentil; (*generous*) generoso; (*good*) bom (boa) bondoso, amável; (*voice*) suave ♦ *n* espécie f, classe f; (*species*) gênero; **in ~** (*COMM*) em espécie

kindergarten ['kɪndəgɑːtn] *n* jardim *m* de infância

kind-hearted *adj* de bom coração, bondoso

kindly ['kaɪndlɪ] *adj* bom (boa) bondoso; (*gentle*) gentil, carinhoso ♦ *adv* bondosamente, amavelmente; **will you ~ ...** você pode fazer o favor de ...

kindness ['kaɪndnɪs] *n* bondade f, gentileza

king [kɪŋ] *n* rei *m*; **kingdom** *n* reino; **kingfisher** *n* martim-pescador *m*; **king-size(d)** *adj* tamanho grande

kiosk ['ki:ɔsk] *n* banca (*BR*), quiosque *m* (*PT*); (*BRIT: TEL*) cabine f

kipper ['kɪpə*] *n* arenque defumado

kiss [kɪs] *n* beijo ♦ *vt* beijar; **to ~ (each other)** beijar-se; **kiss of life**

(*BRIT*) *n* respiração f artificial

kit [kɪt] *n* (*for sport etc*) kit *m*; (*equipment*) equipamento; (*tools*) caixa de ferramentas; (*for assembly*) kit *m* para montar

kitchen ['kɪtʃɪn] *n* cozinha; **kitchen sink** *n* pia (de cozinha)

kite [kaɪt] *n* (*toy*) papagaio, pipa

kitten ['kɪtn] *n* gatinho

kitty ['kɪtɪ] *n* fundo comum, vaquinha

km *abbr* (= *kilometre*) km

knack [næk] *n* jeito

knapsack ['næpsæk] *n* mochila

knead [niːd] *vt* amassar

knee [niː] *n* joelho; **kneecap** *n* rótula

kneel [niːl] (*pt, pp* **knelt**) *vi* (*also: ~ down*) ajoelhar-se

knew [njuː] *pt of* **know**

knickers ['nɪkəz] (*BRIT*) *npl* calcinha (*BR*), cuecas *fpl* (*PT*)

knife [naɪf] (*pl* **knives**) *n* faca ♦ *vt* esfaquear

knight [naɪt] *n* cavaleiro; (*CHESS*) cavalo; **knighthood** (*BRIT*) *n* (*title*): **to get a knighthood** receber o título de Sir

knit [nɪt] *vt* tricotar; (*brows*) franzir ♦ *vi* tricotar (*PT*), fazer malha (*PT*); (*bones*) consolidar-se; **knitting** *n* tricô *m*; **knitting needle** *n* agulha de tricô (*BR*) or de malha (*PT*); **knitwear** *n* roupa de malha

knives [naɪvz] *npl of* **knife**

knob [nɔb] *n* (*of door*) maçaneta; (*of stick*) castão *m*; (*on TV etc*) botão *m*

knock [nɔk] *vt* bater em; (*bump into*) colidir com; (*inf*) criticar, malhar ♦ *n* pancada, golpe *m*; (*on door*) batida ♦ *vi*: **to ~ at** or **on the door** bater à porta; **knock down** *vt* derrubar; (*pedestrian*) atropelar; **knock off** *vi* (*inf: finish*) terminar ♦ *vt* (*inf: steal*) abafar; (*from price*):

to ~ off £10 fazer um desconto de £10; **knock out** vt pôr nocaute, nocautear; (*defeat*) eliminar; **knock over** vt derrubar; (*pedestrian*) atropelar; **knocker** n aldrava

knot [nɔt] n nó m ♦ vt dar nó em

know [nəu] (*pt* **knew**, *pp* **known**) vt saber; (*person, author, place*) conhecer; to ~ **how to swim** saber nadar; to ~ **about** *or* **of sth** saber de algo; **know-how** n know-how m, experiência; **knowingly** adv de propósito; (*spitefully*) maliciosamente

knowledge ['nɔlɪdʒ] n conhecimento; (*learning*) saber m, conhecimentos mpl; **knowledgeable** adj entendido, versado

knuckle ['nʌkl] n nó m

Koran [kɔ'rɑːn] n: the ~ o Alcorão

Korea [kə'rɪə] n Coréia

kosher ['kəuʃə*] adj kosher inv

Kosovo ['kɔsəvəu] n Kosovo m

L

L (*BRIT*) abbr (*AUT*) of **learner**

lab [læb] n abbr = **laboratory**

label ['leɪbl] n etiqueta, rótulo ♦ vt etiquetar, rotular

labor etc ['leɪbə*] (*US*) = **labour** etc

laboratory [lə'bɔrətərɪ] n laboratório

labour ['leɪbə*] (*US* **labor**) n trabalho; (*workforce*) mão-de-obra f; (*MED*): to be in ~ estar em trabalho de parto ♦ vi trabalhar ♦ vt insistir em; **the Labour Party** (*BRIT*) o Partido Trabalhista; **labourer** n operário; **farm labourer** trabalhador m rural, peão m

lace [leɪs] n renda; (*of shoe etc*) cadarço ♦ vt (*shoe*) amarrar

lack [læk] n falta ♦ vt (*money, confidence*) faltar; (*intelligence*) carecer

de; **through** *or* **for ~ of** por falta de; **to be ~ing** faltar; **to be ~ing in** carecer de

lacquer ['lækə*] n laca; (*hair ~*) fixador m

lad [læd] n menino, rapaz m, moço

ladder ['lædə*] n escada f de mão; (*BRIT: in tights*) defeito (em forma de escada)

laden ['leɪdn] adj: ~ **(with)** carregado(de)

ladle ['leɪdl] n concha (de sopa)

lady ['leɪdɪ] n senhora; (*distinguished, noble*) dama; (*in address*): **ladies and gentlemen** ... senhores e senhores ...; **young** ~ senhorita; **"ladies' (toilets)"** "senhoras"; **ladybird** (*US* **ladybug**) n joaninha; **ladylike** adj elegante, refinado

lag [læg] n atraso, retardamento ♦ vi (*also:* ~ **behind**) ficar para trás ♦ vt (*pipes*) revestir com isolante térmico

lager ['lɑːgə*] n cerveja leve e clara

lagoon [lə'guːn] n lagoa

laid [leɪd] pt, pp of **lay**; **laid-back** (*inf*) adj descontraído; **laid up** adj: **to be laid up with flu** ficar de cama com gripe

lain [leɪn] pp of **lie**

lake [leɪk] n lago

lamb [læm] n cordeiro

lame [leɪm] adj coxo, manco; (*excuse, argument*) pouco convincente, fraco

lament [lə'mɛnt] n lamento, queixa ♦ vt lamentar-se de

laminated ['læmɪneɪtɪd] adj laminado

lamp [læmp] n lâmpada; **lamppost** (*BRIT*) n poste m; **lampshade** n abajur m, quebra-luz m

lance [lɑːns] n lança ♦ vt (*MED*) lancetar

land [lænd] n terra; (*country*) país m; (*piece of ~*) terreno; (*estate*) terras *fpl*, propriedades *fpl* ♦ *vi* (*from ship*) desembarcar; (AVIAT) pousar, aterrissar (BR), aterrar (PT); (*fig: arrive*) cair, terminar ♦ *vt* desembarcar; **to ~ sb with sth** (*inf*) sobrecarregar alguém com algo; **land up** *vi* ir parar; **landing** *n* (AVIAT) pouso, aterrissagem *f* (BR), aterragem *f* (PT); (*of staircase*) patamar *m*; **landing strip** *n* pista de aterrissagem (BR) *or* de aterragem (PT); **landlady** *n* senhoria; (*of pub*) dona, proprietária; **landlord** *n* senhorio, locador *m*; (*of pub*) dono, proprietário; **landmark** *n* lugar *m* conhecido; (*fig*) marco; **landowner** *n* latifundiário(-a)

landscape ['lændskeıp] *n* paisagem *f*

landslide ['lændslaıd] *n* (GEO) desmoronamento, desabamento *f*; (*fig:* POL) vitória esmagadora

lane [leın] *n* caminho, estrada estreita; (AUT) pista; (*in race*) raia

language ['læŋgwıdʒ] *n* língua; (*way one speaks*) linguagem *f*; **bad ~** palavrões *mpl*; **language laboratory** *n* laboratório de línguas

lank [læŋk] *adj* (*hair*) liso

lanky ['læŋkı] *adj* magricela

lantern ['læntn] *n* lanterna

lap [læp] *n* (*of track*) volta; (*of person*) colo ♦ *vt* (*also:* **~ up**) lamber ♦ *vi* (*waves*) marulhar; **lap up** *vt* (*fig*) receber com sofreguidão

lapel [lə'pɛl] *n* lapela

Lapland ['læplænd] *n* Lapônia

lapse [læps] *n* lapso; (*bad behaviour*) deslize *m* ♦ *vi* (*law*) prescrever; **to ~ into bad habits** adquirir maus hábitos

laptop (computer) ['læptɔp-] *n* laptop *m*

lard [lɑːd] *n* banha de porco

larder ['lɑːdə*] *n* despensa

large [lɑːdʒ] *adj* grande; **at ~** (*free*)

em liberdade; (*generally*) em geral; **largely** *adv* em grande parte; (*introducing reason*) principalmente; **large-scale** *adj* (*map*) em grande escala; (*fig*) importante, de grande alcance

lark [lɑːk] *n* (*bird*) cotovia; (*joke*) brincadeira, peça; **lark about** *vi* divertir-se, brincar

laryngitis [lærın'dʒaıtıs] *n* laringite *f*

laser ['leızə*] *n* laser *m*; **laser printer** *n* impressora a laser

lash [læʃ] *n* (*blow*) chicotada; (*also:* eye~) pestana, cílio ♦ *vt* chicotear, açoitar; (*subj: rain, wind*) castigar; (*tie*) atar; **lash out** *vi*: **to ~ out at sb** atacar alguém violentamente; (*criticize*) atacar alguém verbalmente

lass [læs] (BRIT) *n* moça

lasso [læ'suː] *n* laço

last [lɑːst] *adj* último; (*final*) derradeiro ♦ *adv* em último lugar ♦ *vi* durar; (*continue*) continuar; **~ night/week** ontem à noite/na semana passada; **at ~** finalmente; **~ but one** penúltimo; **lasting** *adj* duradouro; **lastly** *adv* por fim, por último; (*finally*) finalmente; **last-minute** *adj* de última hora

latch [lætʃ] *n* trinco, fecho, tranca

late [leıt] *adj* (*not on time*) atrasado; (*far on in day etc*) tardio; (*former*) antigo, ex-, anterior; (*dead*) falecido ♦ *adv* tarde; (*behind time, schedule*) atrasado; **of ~** recentemente; **in ~** May no final de maio; **latecomer** *n* retardatário(-a); **lately** *adv* ultimamente

later ['leıtə*] *adj* (*date etc*) posterior; (*version etc*) mais recente ♦ *adv* mais tarde, depois; **~ on** mais tarde

latest ['leıtıst] *adj* último; **at the ~** no mais tardar

lathe [leıð] *n* torno

lather ['lɑːðə*] n espuma (de sabão)
♦ vt ensaboar

Latin ['lætɪn] n (LING) latim m ♦ adj
latino; **Latin America** n América
Latina; **Latin American** adj, n
latino-americano(-a)

latitude ['lætɪtjuːd] n latitude f

latter ['lætə*] adj último; (of two)
segundo ♦ n: the ~ o último, este

laugh [lɑːf] n riso, risada ♦ vi rir, dar
risada (or gargalhada); **(to do sth)
for a ~** (fazer algo) só de curtição;
laugh at vt fus rir de; **laugh off** vt
disfarçar sorrindo; **laughable** adj
ridículo, absurdo; **laughter** n riso,
risada

launch [lɔːntʃ] n (boat) lancha; (COMM,
of rocket etc) lançamento ♦ vt
lançar; **launch into** vt fus lançar-se a

launderette [lɔːndəˈrɛt] (BRIT) n
lavanderia automática

Laundromat ['lɔːndrəmæt] ® (US)
n = launderette

laundry [lɔːndrɪ] n lavanderia;
(clothes) roupa para lavar

laurel ['lɒrl] n loureiro

lava ['lɑːvə] n lava

lavatory ['lævətərɪ] n privada (BR),
casa de banho (PT)

lavender ['lævəndə*] n lavanda

lavish ['lævɪʃ] adj (amount) generoso; (person): ~ with pródigo em,
generoso com ♦ vt: to ~ sth on sb
encher or cobrir alguém de algo

law [lɔː] n lei f; (rule) regra; (SCH)
direito; **law-abiding** adj obediente
à lei; **law and order** n a ordem
pública; **law court** n tribunal m de
justiça; **lawful** adj legal, lícito

lawn [lɔːn] n gramado (BR), relvado
(PT); **lawnmower** n cortador m de
grama (BR) or de relva (PT); **lawn
tennis** n tênis m de gramado (BR) or
de relvado (PT)

law school (US) n faculdade f de

direito

lawsuit ['lɔːsuːt] n ação f judicial,
processo

lawyer ['lɔːjə*] n advogado(-a); (for
sales, wills etc) notário(-a), tabe-
lião(-liã) m/f

lax [læks] adj (discipline) relaxado;
(person) negligente

laxative ['læksətɪv] n laxante m

lay [leɪ] (pt, pp laid) pt of lie ♦ adj
leigo ♦ vt colocar; (eggs, table) pôr;
lay aside or **by** vt pôr de lado; **lay
down** vt depositar; (rules etc)
impor, estabelecer; **to ~ down the
law** (pej) impor regras; **to ~ down
one's life** sacrificar voluntariamente
a vida; **lay off** vt (workers) demitir;
lay on vt (meal etc) prover; **lay out**
vt (spread out) dispor em ordem;
layabout (inf) n vadio(-a), pre-
guiçoso(-a); **lay-by** (BRIT) n acostamento

layer ['leɪə*] n camada

layman ['leɪmən] (irreg) n leigo

layout ['leɪaʊt] n (of garden, building) desenho; (of writing) leiaute m

laze [leɪz] vi (also: ~ about) vadiar

lazy ['leɪzɪ] adj preguiçoso; (movement) lento

lb. abbr = pound (weight)

lead¹ [liːd] (pt, pp led) n (front position) dianteira; (SPORT) liderança; (fig)
vantagem f; (clue) pista; (ELEC) fio;
(for dog) correia; (in play, film) papel
m principal ♦ vt levar; (be the leader of)
chefiar; (start, guide: activity) encabeçar ♦ vi encabeçar; **to be in the ~**
(SPORT: in race) estar na frente; (: in
match) estar ganhando; **to ~ the
way** assumir a direção; **lead away**
vt levar; **lead back** vt levar de
volta; **lead on** vt (tease) provocar;
lead to vt fus levar a, conduzir a;
lead up to vt fus conduzir a

lead² [led] n chumbo; (in pencil)

grafite f
leader ['li:də*] n líder m/f; **leadership** n liderança; (quality) poder m de liderança
lead-free [lɛd-] adj sem chumbo
leading ['li:dɪŋ] adj principal; (role) de destaque; (first, front) primeiro, dianteiro
lead singer [li:d-] n cantor(a) m/f
leaf [li:f] (pl **leaves**) n folha ♦ vi: **to ~ through** (book) folhear; **to turn over a new ~** mudar de vida, partir para outra (inf)
leaflet ['li:flɪt] n folheto
league [li:g] n liga; **to be in ~ with** estar de comum acordo com
leak [li:k] n (of liquid, gas) escape m, vazamento; (hole) buraco, rombo; (in roof) goteira; (fig: of information) vazamento ♦ vi (ship) fazer água; (shoe) deixar entrar água; (roof) gotejar; (pipe, container, liquid) vazar; (gas) escapar ♦ vt (news) vazar
lean [li:n] (pt, pp ~ed or ~t) adj magro ♦ vt: **to ~ sth on** encostar or apoiar algo em ♦ vi inclinar-se; **to ~ against** encostar-se or apoiar-se contra; **to ~ on** encostar-se or apoiar-se em; **lean forward/back** vi inclinar-se para frente/para trás; **lean out** vi inclinar-se; **lean over** vi debruçar-se ♦ vt fus debruçar-se sobre
leap [li:p] (pt, pp ~ed or ~t) n salto, pulo ♦ vi saltar; **leap year** n ano bissexto
learn [lə:n] (pt, pp ~ed or ~t) vt aprender; (by heart) decorar ♦ vi aprender; **to ~ about sth** (SCH: hear, read) saber de algo; **learned** ['lə:nɪd] adj erudito; **learner** n principiante m/f; (BRIT: also: **learner driver**) aprendiz m/f de motorista
lease [li:s] n arrendamento ♦ vt arrendar

leash [li:ʃ] n correia
least [li:st] adj: **the ~ +** n o(a) menor; (smallest amount of) a menor quantidade de ♦ adv: **the ~ +** adj o(a) menos; **at ~** pelo menos; **not in the ~** de maneira nenhuma
leather ['lɛðə*] n couro
leave [li:v] (pt, pp **left**) vt deixar; (go away from) abandonar ♦ vi ir-se, sair; (train) sair ♦ n licença; **to ~ sth to sb** deixar algo para alguém; **to be left** sobrar; **leave behind** vt deixar para trás; (forget) esquecer; **leave out** vt omitir
leaves [li:vz] npl of **leaf**
Lebanon ['lɛbənən] n Líbano
lecherous ['lɛtʃərəs] (pej) adj lascivo
lecture ['lɛktʃə*] n conferência, palestra; (SCH) aula ♦ vi dar aulas, lecionar ♦ vt (scold) passar um sermão em; **lecturer** (BRIT) n (at university) professor(a) m/f
led [lɛd] pt, pp of **lead¹**
ledge [lɛdʒ] n (of window) peitoril m; (of mountain) saliência, proeminência
ledger ['lɛdʒə*] n livro-razão m, razão m
leech [li:tʃ] n sanguessuga
leek [li:k] n alho-poró m
leeway ['li:weɪ] n (fig): **to have some ~** ter certa liberdade de ação
left [lɛft] pt, pp of **leave** ♦ adj esquerdo ♦ n esquerda ♦ adv à esquerda; **on the ~** à esquerda; **to the ~** para a esquerda; **the Left** (POL) a Esquerda; **left-handed** adj canhoto; **left-hand side** n lado esquerdo; **left-luggage (office)** (BRIT) n depósito de bagagem; **leftovers** npl sobras fpl; **left-wing** adj (POL) de esquerda, esquerdista
leg [lɛg] n perna; (of animal) pata; (CULIN: of meat) perna; (of journey)

etapa; **lst/2nd ~** (SPORT) primeiro/
segundo turno

legacy ['lɛgəsɪ] n legado; (fig)
herança

legal ['liːgl] adj legal

legend ['lɛdʒənd] n lenda; (person)
mito

leggings ['lɛgɪŋz] npl legging f

legislation [lɛdʒɪs'leɪʃən] n legislação f

legislature ['lɛdʒɪslətʃə*] n legisla-
tura

legitimate [lɪ'dʒɪtɪmət] adj legítimo

leg-room n espaço para as pernas

leisure ['lɛʒə*] n lazer m; **at ~** desocupado, livre

lemon ['lɛmən] n limão(-galego) m;
lemonade [lɛmə'neɪd] n limonada;
lemon tea n chá m de limão

lend [lɛnd] (pt, pp lent) vt emprestar

length [lɛŋθ] n comprimento,
extensão f; (amount of time)
duração f; **at ~** (at last) finalmente,
afinal; (lengthily) por extenso;
lengthen vt encompridar, alongar
♦ vi encompridar-se; **lengthways**
adv longitudinalmente, ao comprido; **lengthy** adj comprido, longo;
(meeting) prolongado

lenient ['liːnɪənt] adj indulgente

lens [lɛnz] n (of spectacles) lente f;
(of camera) objetiva

Lent [lɛnt] n Quaresma

lent [lɛnt] pt, pp of **lend**

lentil ['lɛntl] n lentilha

Leo ['liːəʊ] n Leão m

leotard ['liːətɑːd] n collant m

leprosy ['lɛprəsɪ] n lepra

lesbian ['lɛzbɪən] n lésbica

less [lɛs] adj, pron, adv menos
♦ prep: **~ tax/10% discount** menos
imposto/10% de desconto; **~ than
ever** menos do que nunca; **~ and ~**
cada vez menos; **the ~ he works ...**
quanto menos trabalha ...

lessen ['lɛsn] vi diminuir, minguar
♦ vt diminuir, reduzir

lesser ['lɛsə*] adj menor; **to a ~
extent** nem tanto

lesson ['lɛsn] n aula; (example,
warning) lição f; **to teach sb a ~** (fig)
dar uma lição em alguém

let [lɛt] (pt, pp let) vt (allow) deixar;
(BRIT: lease) alugar; **to ~ sb know sth**
avisar alguém de algo; **~'s go!**
vamos!; **"to ~" "aluga-se"**; **let
down** vt (tyre) esvaziar; (disappoint)
desapontar; **let go** vt, vi soltar; **let
in** vt deixar entrar; (visitor etc) fazer
entrar; **let off** vt (culprit) perdoar;
(firework etc) soltar; **let on** vi revelar; **let out** vt deixar sair; (scream)
soltar; **let up** vi cessar, afrouxar

lethal ['liːθl] adj letal

letter ['lɛtə*] n (of alphabet) letra;
(correspondence) carta; **letter
bomb** n carta-bomba; **letterbox**
(BRIT) n caixa do correio; **lettering** n
letras fpl

lettuce ['lɛtɪs] n alface f

leukaemia [luːˈkiːmɪə] (US leukemia) n leucemia

level ['lɛvl] adj (flat) plano ♦ adv: **to
draw ~ with** alcançar ♦ n nível m;
(height) altura ♦ vt aplanar; **to be ~
with** estar no mesmo nível que; **on
the ~** em nível; (fig: honest) sincero;
"A" levels (BRIT) npl = vestibular
m; **"O" levels** npl exames optativos
feitos após o término do 10 Grau;
level off or **out** vi (prices etc) estabilizar-se; **level crossing** (BRIT) n
passagem f de nível; **level-headed**
adj sensato

lever ['liːvə*] n alavanca; (fig) estratagema m; **leverage** n força de
uma alavanca; (fig: influence)
influência

lewd [luːd] adj obsceno, lascivo

liability [laɪə'bɪlətɪ] n responsabili-

dade f; (handicap) desvantagem f;
liabilities npl (COMM) exigibilidades
fpl, obrigações fpl

liable ['laɪəbl] adj (subject): ~ to
sujeito a; (responsible): ~ for responsável por; (likely): ~ to do capaz de
fazer

liaise [li:'eɪz] vi: to ~ (with) cooperar
(com)

liaison [li:'eɪzɒn] n (coordination)
ligação f; (affair) relação f amorosa

liar ['laɪə*] n mentiroso(-a)

libel ['laɪbl] n difamação f ♦ vt caluniar, difamar

liberal ['lɪbərl] adj liberal; (generous)
generoso

liberation [lɪbə'reɪʃən] n liberação f,
libertação f

liberty ['lɪbətɪ] n liberdade f; (criminal): to be at ~ estar livre; to be at
~ to do ser livre de fazer

Libra ['li:brə] n Libra, Balança

librarian [laɪ'brɛərɪən] n bibliotecário(-a)

library ['laɪbrərɪ] n biblioteca

Libya ['lɪbɪə] n Líbia

lice [laɪs] npl of louse

licence ['laɪsns] (US **license**) n
(gen, COMM) licença; (AUT) carta de
motorista (BR), carta de condução
(PT)

license ['laɪsns] n (US) = **licence** ♦ vt
autorizar, dar licença a; **licensed**
adj (car) autorizado oficialmente;
(for alcohol) autorizado para vender
bebidas alcoólicas; **license plate**
(US) n (AUT) placa de (identificação)
(do carro)

lick [lɪk] vt lamber; (inf: defeat) arrasar, surrar; to ~ one's lips (also fig)
lamber os beiços

lid [lɪd] n tampa; (eye~) pálpebra

lie [laɪ] (pt lay, pp lain) vi (act) deitar-se; (state) estar deitado; (object: be
situated) estar, encontrar-se; (fig:

problem, cause) residir; (in race,
league) ocupar; (tell ~s: pt, pp ~d)
mentir ♦ n mentira; to ~ **low** (fig)
esconder-se; **lie about** or **around**
vi (things) estar espalhado; (people)
vadiar; **lie-in** (BRIT) n: **to have a lie-
in** dormir até tarde

lieutenant [lef'tɛnənt, (US) lu:-
'tɛnənt] n (MIL) tenente m

life [laɪf] (pl **lives**) n vida; **to come to
~** animar-se; **lifebelt** (BRIT) n cinto
salva-vidas; **lifeboat** n barco salva-
vidas; **lifeguard** n (guarda m/f)
salva-vidas m/f inv; **life jacket** n
colete m salva-vidas; **lifeless** adj
sem vida; **lifelike** adj natural; (realistic) realista; **lifelong** adj que dura
toda a vida; **life preserver** (US) n =
lifebelt; **life jacket**; **life sentence**
n pena de prisão perpétua; **life-
size(d)** adj de tamanho natural; **life-
span** n vida, duração f; **life style** n
estilo de vida; **lifetime** n vida

lift [lɪft] vt levantar ♦ vi (fog)
dispersar-se, dissipar-se ♦ n (BRIT: elevator) elevador m; **to give sb a ~**
(BRIT) dar uma carona para alguém
(BR), dar uma boleia a alguém (PT);
lift-off n decolagem f

light [laɪt] (pt, pp lit) n luz f; (AUT:
headlight) farol m; (: rear ~) luz traseira; (for cigarette etc): **have you
got a ~?** tem fogo? ♦ vt acender;
(room) iluminar ♦ adj (colour, room)
claro; (not heavy, fig) leve; (rain, traffic) fraco; (movement) delicado; **~s**
npl (AUT) sinal m de trânsito; **to
come to ~** vir à tona; **in the ~ of** à
luz de; **light up** vi iluminar-se ♦ vt
iluminar; **light bulb** n lâmpada;
lighten vt tornar mais leve; **lighter**
n (also: cigarette lighter) isqueiro,
acendedor m; **light-hearted** adj
alegre, despreocupado; **lighthouse** n farol m; **lighting** n ilumi-

nação f; **lightly** adv ligeiramente;
to get off lightly conseguir se safar,
livrar a cara (inf)

lightning ['laɪtnɪŋ] n relâmpago,
raio

light pen n caneta leitora

lightweight ['laɪtweɪt] adj (suit)
leve; (BOXING) peso-leve

like [laɪk] vt gostar de ♦ prep como;
(such as) tal qual ♦ adj parecido,
semelhante ♦ n: **the ~** coisas fpl
parecidas; **his ~s and dislikes** seus
gostos e aversões; **I would ~, I'd ~**
(eu) gostaria de; **to be** or **look ~ sb/**
sth parecer-se com alguém/algo,
parecer alguém/algo; **do it ~ this**
faça isso assim; **it is nothing ~ ...**
não se parece nada com ...; **like-**
able adj simpático, agradável

likelihood ['laɪklɪhʊd] n probabilidade f

likely ['laɪklɪ] adj provável; **he's ~ to**
leave é provável que ele se vá; **not**
~! (inf) nem morto!

likeness ['laɪknɪs] n semelhança;
that's a good ~ tem uma grande
semelhança

likewise ['laɪkwaɪz] adv igualmente; **to do ~** fazer o mesmo

liking ['laɪkɪŋ] n afeição f, simpatia;
to be to sb's ~ ser ao gosto de
alguém

lilac ['laɪlək] n lilás m

lily ['lɪlɪ] n lírio, açucena

limb [lɪm] n membro

limbo ['lɪmbəʊ] n: **to be in ~** (fig)
viver na expectativa

lime [laɪm] n (tree) limeira; (fruit)
limão m; (also: **~ juice**) suco (BR) or
sumo (PT) de limão; (GEO) cal f

limelight ['laɪmlaɪt] n: **to be in the**
~ ser o centro das atenções

limerick ['lɪmərɪk] n quintilha
humorística

limestone ['laɪmstəʊn] n pedra

calcária

limit ['lɪmɪt] n limite m ♦ vt limitar;
limited adj limitado; **to be limited**
to limitar-se a

limp [lɪmp] n: **to have a ~** mancar,
ser coxo ♦ vi mancar ♦ adj frouxo

limpet ['lɪmpɪt] n lapa

line [laɪn] n linha; (rope) corda;
(wire) fio; (row) fila, fileira; (on face)
ruga ♦ vt (road, room) encarreirar;
(container, clothing) forrar; **to ~ the**
streets ladear as ruas; **in ~ with** de
acordo com; **line up** vi enfileirar-se
♦ vt enfileirar; (set up, have ready)
preparar, arranjar

lined [laɪnd] adj (face) enrugado;
(paper) pautado

linen ['lɪnɪn] n artigos m de cama e
mesa; (cloth) linho

liner ['laɪnə*] n navio de linha regular; (also: **bin ~**) saco para lata de lixo

linesman ['laɪnzmən] (irreg) n
(SPORT) juiz m de linha

linger ['lɪŋgə*] vi demorar-se,
retardar-se; (smell, tradition) persistir

linguistics ['lɪŋgwɪstɪks] n linguís-
tica

lining ['laɪnɪŋ] n forro; (ANAT) parede f

link [lɪŋk] n (of a chain) elo; (connection) conexão f ♦ vt vincular, unir;
(associate): **to ~ with** or **to** unir a; **~s**
npl (GOLF) campo de golfe; **link up**
vt acoplar ♦ vi unir-se

lion ['laɪən] n leão m; **lioness** n leoa

lip [lɪp] n lábio; **lipread** (irreg) vi ler
os lábios; **lip salve** n pomada para
os lábios; **lipstick** n batom m

liqueur [lɪ'kjʊə*] n licor m

liquid ['lɪkwɪd] adj líquido ♦ n líquido

liquidize ['lɪkwɪdaɪz] (BRIT) vt (CULIN)
liquidificar, passar no liquidificador;
liquidizer (BRIT) n liquidificador m

liquor ['lɪkə*] n licor m, bebida alcoólica

liquor store (US) n loja que vende bebidas alcoólicas

Lisbon ['lɪzbən] n Lisboa

lisp [lɪsp] n ceceio ♦ vi cecear, falar com a língua presa

list [lɪst] n lista ♦ vt (write down) fazer uma lista ou relação de; (enumerate) enumerar

listen ['lɪsn] vi escutar, ouvir; **to ~ to** escutar; **listener** n ouvinte m/f

lit [lɪt] pt, pp of **light**

liter ['liːtə*] (US) n = **litre**

literacy ['lɪtərəsɪ] n capacidade f de ler e escrever, alfabetização f

literal ['lɪtərl] adj literal

literary ['lɪtərərɪ] adj literário

literate ['lɪtərət] adj alfabetizado, instruído; (educated) culto, letrado

literature ['lɪtərɪtʃə*] n literatura; (brochures etc) folhetos mpl

litre ['liːtə*] (US **liter**) n litro

litter ['lɪtə*] n (rubbish) lixo; (young animals) ninhada; **litter bin** (BRIT) n lata de lixo

little ['lɪtl] adj (small) pequeno; (not much) pouco ♦ often translated by suffix: eg: ~ house casinha ♦ adv pouco; **a ~** um pouco (de); **for a ~ while** por um instante; **as ~ as possible** o menos possível; **~ by ~** pouco a pouco

live [vb lɪv, adj laɪv] vi viver; (reside) morar ♦ adj vivo; (wire) eletrizado; (broadcast) ao vivo; (shell) carregado; ~ **ammunition** munição de guerra; **live down** vt redimir; **live on** vt fus viver de, alimentar-se de; **to ~ on £50 a week** viver com £50 por semana; **live together** vi viver juntos; **live up to** vt fus (fulfil) cumprir

livelihood ['laɪvlɪhud] n meio de vida, subsistência

lively ['laɪvlɪ] adj vivo

liven up vt animar ♦ vi animar-se

liver ['lɪvə*] n fígado

lives [laɪvz] npl of **life**

livestock ['laɪvstɔk] n gado

livid ['lɪvɪd] adj lívido, (inf: furious) furioso

living ['lɪvɪŋ] adj vivo ♦ n: **to earn or make a ~** ganhar a vida; **living room** n sala de estar

lizard ['lɪzəd] n lagarto

load [ləud] n carga; (weight) peso ♦ vt (gen, COMPUT) carregar; **a ~ of**, **~s of** (fig) um monte de, uma porção de; **loaded** adj (vehicle): **to be loaded with** estar carregado de; (question) intencionado; (inf: rich) cheio da nota

loaf [ləuf] (pl **loaves**) n pão-de-forma m

loan [ləun] n empréstimo ♦ vt emprestar; **on ~** emprestado

loath [ləuθ] adj: **to be ~ to do sth** estar pouco inclinado a fazer algo, relutar em fazer algo

loathe [ləuð] vt detestar, odiar

loaves [ləuvz] npl of **loaf**

lobby ['lɔbɪ] n vestíbulo, saguão m; (POL: pressure group) grupo de pressão, lobby m ♦ vt pressionar

lobster ['lɔbstə*] n lagostim m; (large) lagosta

local ['ləukl] adj local ♦ n (pub) bar m (local); **the ~s** npl (~ inhabitants) os moradores locais; **local anaesthetic** n anestesia local

locate [ləu'keɪt] vt (find) localizar, situar; (situate) situate; **to be ~d in** estar localizado em

location [ləu'keɪʃən] n local m, posição f; **on ~** (CINEMA) em externas

loch [lɔx] n lago

lock [lɔk] n (of door, box) fechadura; (of canal) eclusa; (of hair) anel m, mecha ♦ vt (with key) trancar ♦ vi (door etc) fechar-se à chave; (wheels) travar-se; **lock in** vt trancar dentro; **lock out** vt trancar do lado de fora; **lock up** vt (criminal, mental patient) prender; (house) trancar ♦ vi fechar tudo

locker ['lɔkə*] n compartimento com chave

locket ['lɔkɪt] n medalhão m

locksmith ['lɔksmɪθ] n serralheiro(-a)

lodge [lɔdʒ] n casa da guarda, guarita; (hunting ~) pavilhão m de caça ♦ vi (person): **to ~ (with)** alojar-se (na casa de) ♦ vt (complaint) apresentar; **lodger** n inquilino(-a), hóspede m/f

lodgings ['lɔdʒɪŋz] npl quarto (mobiliado)

loft [lɔft] n sótão m

lofty ['lɔftɪ] adj (haughty) altivo, arrogante; (sentiments, aims) nobre

log [lɔg] n (of wood) tora; (book) = **logbook** ♦ vt registrar

logbook ['lɔgbʊk] n (NAUT) diário de bordo; (AVIAT) diário de vôo; (of car) documentação f (do carro)

logic ['lɔdʒɪk] n lógica; **logical** adj lógico

loin [lɔɪn] n (CULIN) (carne f de) lombo

loiter ['lɔɪtə*] vi perder tempo

lollipop ['lɔlɪpɔp] n pirulito (BR), chupa-chupa m (PT); **lollipop lady/man** n (BRIT var quadro

---

LOLLIPOP LADY/MAN

Lollipop ladies/men são as pessoas que ajudam as crianças a atravessar a rua nas proximidades das escolas na hora da entrada e da saída. São facilmente localizados graças a suas longas capas brancas e à placa redonda com a qual pedem aos motoristas que parem. São chamados assim por causa da forma circular da placa, que lembra um pirulito (lollipop).

London ['lʌndən] n Londres; **Londoner** n londrino(-a)

lone [ləun] adj (person) solitário; (thing) único

loneliness ['ləunlɪnɪs] n solidão f, isolamento

lonely ['ləunlɪ] adj (person) só; (place) solitário, isolado

long [lɔŋ] adj longo; (road, hair, table) comprido ♦ adv muito tempo ♦ vi: **to ~ for sth** ansiar or suspirar por algo; **how ~ is the street?** qual é a extensão da rua?; **how ~ is the lesson?** quanto dura a lição?; **all night ~** a noite inteira; **he no ~ comes** ele não vem mais; **~ before/after** muito antes/depois; **before ~** (+ future) dentro de pouco; (+ past) pouco tempo depois; **at ~ last** por fim, no final; **so or as ~ as** contanto que; **long-distance** adj (travel) de longa distância; (call) interurbano; **longhand** n escrita usual; **longing** n desejo, anseio

longitude ['lɔŋgɪtjuːd] n longitude f

long: **long jump** n salto em distância; **long-range** adj de longo alcance; (forecast) a longo prazo; **long-sighted** adj presbita; **long-standing** adj de muito tempo; **long-suffering** adj paciente, resignado; **long-term** adj a longo prazo; **long wave** n (RADIO) onda longa; **long-winded** adj prolixo, cansativo

loo [luː] n (BRIT: inf) banheiro (BR), casa de banho (PT)

look [luk] vi olhar; (seem) parecer; (building etc): **to ~ south/(out) onto the sea** dar para o sul/o mar ♦ n olhar m; (glance) olhada, vista de olhos; (appearance) aparência, aspecto; **~s** npl (good ~s) físico, aparência; **~ (here)!** (annoyance) escuta aqui!; **~!** (surprise) olha!;

look after vt fus cuidar de; (deal with) lidar com; **look at** vt fus olhar (para); (read quickly) ler rapidamente; (consider) considerar; **look back** vi: **to ~ back on** (remember) recordar, rever; **look down on** vt fus (fig) desdenhar, desprezar; **look for** vt fus procurar; **look forward to** vt fus aguardar com prazer, ansiar por; (in letter): **we ~ forward to hearing from you** no aguardo de suas notícias; **look into** vt fus investigar; **look on** vi assistir; **look out** vi (beware): **to ~ out (for)** tomar cuidado (com); **look out for** vt fus (await) esperar; **look round** vi virar a cabeça, voltar-se; **look through** vt fus (papers, book) examinar; **look to** vt fus (rely on) contar com; **look up** vi levantar os olhos; (improve) melhorar ♦ vt (word) procurar

loop [lu:p] n laço ♦ vt: **to ~ sth round sth** prender algo em torno de algo

loose [lu:s] adj solto; (not tight) frouxo ♦ n: **to be on the ~** estar solto; **loose change** n trocado; **loosely** adv frouxamente, folgadamente; **loosen** vt (free) soltar; (slacken) afrouxar

loot [lu:t] n saque m, despojo ♦ vt saquear, pilhar

lopsided [lɔp'saidid] adj torto

lord [lɔ:d] n senhor m; **L~ Smith** Lord Smith; **the ~** (REL) o Senhor; **good L~!** Deus meu!; **the (House of) L~s** a Câmara dos Lordes

lorry ['lɔri] (BRIT) n caminhão m (BR), camião m (PT); **lorry driver** (BRIT) n caminhoneiro (BR), camionista m/f (PT)

lose [lu:z] (pt, pp **lost**) vt, vi perder; **to ~ (time)** (clock) atrasar-se; **loser** n perdedor(a) m/f; (inf: failure) derrotado(-a), fracassado(-a)

loss [lɔs] n perda; (COMM): **to make**

a **~** sair com prejuízo; **heavy ~es** (MIL) grandes perdas; **to be at a ~** estar perplexo

lost [lɔst] pt, pp of **lose** ♦ adj perdido; **~ and found** (US) (seção f de) perdidos e achados mpl; **lost property** (BRIT) n (objetos mpl) perdidos e achados mpl

lot [lɔt] n (set of things) porção f; (at auctions) lote m; **the ~** tudo, todos(-as); **a ~** muito, bastante; **a ~ of**, **~s of** muito(s); **I read a ~** leio bastante; **to draw ~s** tirar à sorte

lotion ['ləuʃən] n loção f

lottery ['lɔtəri] n loteria

loud [laud] adj (voice) alto; (shout) forte; (noise) barulhento; (support, condemnation) veemente; (gaudy) berrante ♦ adv alto; **out ~** em voz alta; **loudly** adv ruidosamente; (aloud) em voz alta; **loudspeaker** n alto-falante m

lounge [laundʒ] n sala f de estar; (of airport) salão m; (BRIT: also: ~ **bar**) bar m social ♦ vi recostar-se, espreguiçar-se; **lounge about** vi ficar à-toa; **lounge around** vi = **lounge about**; **lounge suit** (BRIT) n terno (BR), fato (PT)

louse [laus] (pl **lice**) n piolho

lousy ['lauzi] (inf) adj ruim, péssimo; (ill): **to feel ~** sentir-se mal

lout [laut] n rústico, grosseiro

lovable ['lʌvəbl] adj adorável, simpático

love [lʌv] n amor m ♦ vt amar; (care for) gostar; (activity): **to do** (or gostar (muito)); **~ (from) Anne** (on letter) um abraço or um beijo, Anne; **I ~ coffee** adoro o café; **"15 ~"** (TENNIS) "15 a zero"; **to be in ~ with** estar apaixonado por; **to fall in ~ with** apaixonar-se por; **to make ~** fazer amor; **love affair** n aventura (amorosa), caso (de amor); **love**

life n vida sentimental

lovely ['lʌvlɪ] adj encantador(a), delicioso; (beautiful) lindo, belo; (holiday) muito agradável, maravilhoso

lover ['lʌvə*] n amante m/f

loving ['lʌvɪŋ] adj carinhoso, afetuoso; (actions) dedicado

low [ləu] adj baixo; (depressed) deprimido; (ill) doente ♦ adv baixo ♦ n (METEOROLOGY) área de baixa pressão; **to be ~ on** (supplies) ter pouco; **to reach a new** or **an alltime ~** cair para o seu nível mais baixo; **low-alcohol** adj com baixo teor alcoólico; **low-calorie** adj de baixas calorias; **low-cut** adj (dress) decotado; **lower** adj mais baixo; (less important) inferior ♦ vt abaixar; (reduce) reduzir, diminuir; **low-fat** adj magro; **lowlands** npl planície f; **lowly** adj humilde

loyal ['lɔɪəl] adj leal; **loyalty** n lealdade f; **loyalty card** n (BRIT) cartão m de fidelidade

lozenge ['lɔzɪndʒ] n (MED) pastilha

LP n abbr (= long-playing record) elepê m (BR), LP m (PT)

L-plates ['ɛlpleɪts] (BRIT) npl placas fpl de aprendiz de motorista; ver quadro

---

L-PLATES

As **L-plates** são placas quadradas com um "L" vermelho que são colocadas na parte de trás do carro para mostrar que a pessoa ao volante ainda não tem carteira de motorista. Até à obtenção da carteira, o motorista aprendiz possui uma permissão provisória e não tem direito de dirigir sem um motorista qualificado ao lado. Os motoristas aprendizes não podem dirigir em rodovias mesmo que estejam acompanhados.

Ltd (BRIT) abbr (= limited (liability) company) SA

lubricate ['lu:brɪkeɪt] vt lubrificar

luck [lʌk] n sorte f; **bad ~** azar m; **good ~!** boa sorte!; **bad** or **hard** or **tough ~!** que azar!; **luckily** adv por sorte, felizmente; **lucky** adj (person) sortudo; (situation) afortunado; (object) de sorte

ludicrous ['lu:dɪkrəs] adj ridículo

lug [lʌg] (inf) vt arrastar

luggage ['lʌgɪdʒ] n bagagem f; **luggage rack** n porta-bagagem m, bagageiro

lukewarm ['lu:kwɔ:m] adj morno, tépido; (fig) indiferente

lull [lʌl] n pausa, interrupção f ♦ vt: **to ~ sb to sleep** acalentar alguém; **to be ~ed into a false sense of security** ser acalmado com uma falsa sensação de segurança

lullaby ['lʌləbaɪ] n canção f de ninar

lumber ['lʌmbə*] n (junk) trastes mpl velhos; (wood) madeira serrada, tábua ♦ vt: **to ~ sb with sth/sb** empurrar algo/alguém para cima de alguém; **lumberjack** n madeireiro, lenhador m

luminous ['lu:mɪnəs] adj luminoso

lump [lʌmp] n torrão m; (fragment) pedaço; (on body) galo, caroço; (also: sugar ~) cubo de açúcar ♦ vt: **to ~ together** amontoar; **a ~ sum** uma quantia global; **lumpy** adj encaroçado

lunatic ['lu:nətɪk] adj louco(-a)

lunch [lʌntʃ] n almoço

luncheon ['lʌntʃən] n almoço formal; **luncheon meat** n bolo de carne

lung [lʌŋ] n pulmão m

lunge [lʌndʒ] vi (also: ~ forward) dar estocada or bote; **to ~ at** arremeter-se contra

lurch [lə:tʃ] vi balançar ♦ n solavanco; **to leave sb in the ~** deixar alguém em apuros, deixar alguém na mão (inf)

lure [luə*] n isca ♦ vt atrair, seduzir

lurid ['luərɪd] adj horrível

lurk [lə:k] vi (hide) esconder-se; (wait) estar à espreita

luscious ['lʌʃəs] adj (person, thing) atraente; (food) delicioso

lush [lʌʃ] adj exuberante

lust [lʌst] n (sex) luxúria; (greed) cobiça; **lust after** or **for** vt fus cobiçar

Luxembourg [ˈlʌɡˈzjuːəriəs] n Luxemburgo

luxurious [lʌɡˈzjuəriəs] adj luxuoso

luxury ['lʌkʃəri] n luxo ♦ cpd de luxo

lying ['laɪɪŋ] n mentira(s) f(pl) ♦ adj mentiroso, falso

lyrical ['lɪrɪkəl] adj lírico

lyrics ['lɪrɪks] npl (of song) letra

M

m abbr (= metre) m; (= mile) mil.; = million

M.A. abbr (SCH) = Master of Arts

mac [mæk] (BRIT) n capa impermeável

Macao [məˈkau] n Macau

macaroni [mækəˈrəʊnɪ] n macarrão m

machine [məˈʃiːn] n máquina ♦ vt (dress etc) costurar à máquina; (TECH) usinar; **machine gun** n metralhadora; **machinery** n maquinaria; (fig) máquina

mackerel ['mækrl] n inv cavala

mackintosh ['mækɪntɒʃ] (BRIT) n capa impermeável

mad [mæd] adj louco; (foolish) tolo; (angry) furioso, brabo; (keen): **to be ~ about** ser louco por

madam ['mædəm] n senhora, madame f

madden ['mædn] vt exasperar

made [meɪd] pt, pp of **make**

Madeira [məˈdɪərə] n (GEO) Madeira; (wine) (vinho) Madeira m

made-to-measure (BRIT) adj feito sob medida

madly ['mædlɪ] adv loucamente; **~ in love** louco de amor

madman ['mædmən] (irreg) n louco

madness ['mædnɪs] n loucura; (foolishness) tolice f

magazine [mægəˈziːn] n (PRESS) revista; (RADIO, TV) programa m de atualidades

maggot ['mægət] n larva de inseto

magic ['mædʒɪk] n magia, mágica ♦ adj mágico; **magical** adj mágico; **magician** [məˈdʒɪʃən] n mago(-a); (entertainer) mágico(-a)

magistrate ['mædʒɪstreɪt] n magistrado(-a), juiz (juíza) m/f

magnet ['mægnɪt] n ímã m; **magnetic** [mægˈnetɪk] adj magnético

magnificent [mægˈnɪfɪsnt] adj magnífico

magnify ['mægnɪfaɪ] vt aumentar; **magnifying glass** n lupa, lente f de aumento

magnitude ['mægnɪtjuːd] n magnitude f

magpie ['mægpaɪ] n pega

mahogany [məˈhɒɡənɪ] n mogno, acaju m

maid [meɪd] n empregada; **old ~** (pej) solteirona

maiden name n nome m de solteira

mail [meɪl] n correio; (letters) cartas fpl ♦ vt pôr no correio; **mailbox** (US) n caixa do correio; **mailing list** n lista de clientes, mailing list m; **mail order** n pedido por reembolso postal

maim [meɪm] vt mutilar, aleijar

main [meɪn] adj principal ♦ n (pipe)

cano *or* esgoto principal; **the ~s** *npl* (ELEC, *gas*, *water*) a rede; **in the ~** na maior parte; **mainframe** *n* (COMPUT) mainframe *m*; **mainland** *n*: **the mainland** o continente; **mainly** *adv* principalmente; **main road** *n* estrada principal; **mainstay** *n* (*fig*) esteio; **mainstream** *n* corrente *f* principal

maintain [meɪnˈteɪn] *vt* manter; (*keep up*) conservar (em bom estado); (*affirm*) sustentar, afirmar; **maintenance** [ˈmeɪntənəns] *n* manutenção *f*; (*alimony*) alimentos *mpl*, pensão *f* alimentícia

maize [meɪz] *n* milho

majestic [məˈdʒestɪk] *adj* majestoso

majesty [ˈmædʒɪstɪ] *n* majestade *f*

major [ˈmeɪdʒə*] *n* (MIL) major *m* ♦ *adj* (*main*) principal; (*considerable*) importante; (MUS) maior

Majorca [məˈjɔːkə] *n* Maiorca

majority [məˈdʒɒrɪtɪ] *n* maioria

make [meɪk] (*pt, pp* made) *vt* fazer; (*manufacture*) fabricar, produzir; (*cause to be*): **to ~ sb sad** entristecer alguém, fazer alguém ficar triste; (*force*): **to ~ sb do sth** fazer com que alguém faça algo; (*equal*): **2 and 2 ~ 4** dois e dois são quatro ♦ *n* marca; **to ~ a profit/loss** ter um lucro/uma perda; **to ~ it** (*arrive*) chegar; (*succeed*) ter sucesso; **what time do you ~ it?** que horas você tem?; **to ~ do with** contentar-se com; **make for** *vt fus* (*place*) dirigir-se a; **make out** *vt* (*decipher*) decifrar; (*understand*) compreender; (*see*) divisar, avistar; (*cheque*) preencher; **make up** *vt* (*constitute*) constituir; (*invent*) inventar; (*parcel*) embrulhar ♦ *vi* reconciliar-se; (*with cosmetics*) maquilar-se (BR), maquilhar-se (PT); **make up for** *vt fus* compensar; **make-believe** *n*: **a world of make-**

believe um mundo de faz-de-conta; **maker** *n* (*of film etc*) criador *m*; (*manufacturer*) fabricante *m/f*; **makeshift** *adj* provisório; **make-up** *n* maquilagem *f* (BR), maquilhagem *f* (PT)

malaria [məˈlɛərɪə] *n* malária

Malaysia [məˈleɪzɪə] *n* Malaísia (BR), Malásia (PT)

male [meɪl] *n* macho ♦ *adj* masculino; (*child etc*) do sexo masculino

malevolent [məˈlevələnt] *adj* malévolo

malfunction [mælˈfʌŋkʃən] *n* funcionamento defeituoso

malice [ˈmælɪs] *n* (*ill will*) malícia; (*rancour*) rancor *m*; **malicious** [məˈlɪʃəs] *adj* malevolente

malignant [məˈlɪgnənt] *adj* (MED) maligno

mall [mɔːl] *n* (*also*: **shopping ~**) shopping *m*

mallet [ˈmælɪt] *n* maço, marreta

malt [mɔːlt] *n* malte *m*

Malta [ˈmɔːltə] *n* Malta

mammal [ˈmæml] *n* mamífero

mammoth [ˈmæməθ] *n* mamute *m* ♦ *adj* gigantesco, imenso

man [mæn] (*pl* **men**) *n* homem *m* ♦ *vt* (NAUT) tripular; (MIL) guarnecer; (*machine*) operar; **an old ~** um velho; **~ and wife** marido e mulher

manage [ˈmænɪdʒ] *vi* arranjar-se, virar-se ♦ *vt* (*be in charge of*) dirigir, administrar; (*business*) gerenciar; (*ship, person*) controlar; **manageable** *adj* manejável; (*task etc*) viável; **management** *n* administração *f*, direção *f*, gerência; **manager** *n* gerente *m/f*; (SPORT) técnico(-a); **manageress** [mænɪdʒəˈres] *n* gerente *f*; **managerial** [mænɪˈdʒɪərɪəl] *adj* administrativo, gerencial; **managing director** *n* diretor(a) *m/f* geral, diretor-gerente (diretora-gerente) m/f

mandarin ['mændərɪn] n (fruit) tangerina; (person) mandarim m

mandatory ['mændətərɪ] adj obrigatório

mane [meɪn] n (of horse) crina; (of lion) juba

maneuver [mə'nu:və*] (US) = **manoeuvre**

mangle ['mæŋgl] vt mutilar, estropiar

mango ['mæŋgəʊ] (pl ~es) n manga

mangy ['meɪndʒɪ] adj sarnento, esfarrapado

manhandle ['mænhændl] vt maltratar

manhole ['mænhəʊl] n poço de inspeção

manhood ['mænhʊd] n (age) idade f adulta; (masculinity) virilidade f

man-hour n hora-homem f

manhunt ['mænhʌnt] n caça ao homem

mania ['meɪnɪə] n mania; **maniac** ['meɪnɪæk] n maníaco(-a); (fig) louco(-a)

manic ['mænɪk] adj maníaco

manicure ['mænɪkjʊə*] n manicure f (BR), manicura (PT)

manifest ['mænɪfest] vt manifestar, mostrar ♦ adj manifesto, evidente

manipulate [mə'nɪpjʊleɪt] vt manipular

mankind [mæn'kaɪnd] n humanidade f, raça humana

man-made adj sintético, artificial

manner ['mænə*] n modo, maneira; (behaviour) conduta, comportamento; (type): **all ~ of things** todos os tipos de coisa; **~s** npl (conduct) boas maneiras fpl, educação f; **bad ~s** falta de educação; **all ~ of** todo tipo de; **mannerism** n maneirismo, hábito

manoeuvre [mə'nu:və*] (US **maneuver**) vt manobrar; (manipulate) manipular ♦ vi manobrar ♦ n manobra

manor ['mænə*] n (also: ~ **house**) casa senhorial, solar m

manpower ['mænpaʊə*] n potencial m humano, mão-de-obra f

mansion ['mænʃən] n mansão f, palacete m

manslaughter ['mænslɔ:tə*] n homicídio involuntário

mantelpiece ['mæntlpi:s] n consolo da lareira

manual ['mænjʊəl] adj manual ♦ n manual m

manufacture [mænju'fæktʃə*] vt manufaturar, fabricar ♦ n fabricação f; **manufacturer** n fabricante m/f

manure [mə'njʊə*] n estrume m, adubo

manuscript ['mænjʊskrɪpt] n manuscrito

many ['menɪ] adj, pron muitos(-as); **a great ~** muitíssimos; **~ a time** muitas vezes

map [mæp] n mapa m; **map out** vt traçar

maple ['meɪpl] n bordo

mar [mɑ:*] vt estragar

marathon ['mærəθən] n maratona

marble ['mɑ:bl] n mármore m; (toy) bola de gude

March [mɑ:tʃ] n março

march [mɑ:tʃ] vi marchar; (demonstrators) desfilar ♦ n marcha; passeata

mare [mɛə*] n égua

margarine [mɑ:dʒə'ri:n] n margarina

margin ['mɑ:dʒɪn] n margem f; **marginal** adj marginal; **marginal seat** (POL) cadeira ganha por pequena maioria

marigold ['mærɪgəʊld] n malmequer m

marijuana [mærɪ'wɑːnə] n maconha

marine [mə'riːn] adj marinho; (engineer) naval ♦ n fuzileiro naval

marital ['mærɪtl] adj matrimonial, marital; ~ **status** estado civil

marjoram ['mɑːdʒərəm] n manjerona

mark [mɑːk] n marca, sinal m; (imprint) impressão f; (stain) mancha; (BRIT: SCH) nota; (currency) marco ♦ vt marcar; (stain) manchar; (indicate) indicar; (commemorate) comemorar; (BRIT: SCH) dar nota em; (: correct) corrigir; **to ~ time** marcar passo; **marker** n (sign) marcador m, marca; (bookmark) marcador

market ['mɑːkɪt] n mercado ♦ vt (COMM) comercializar; **market garden** (BRIT) n horta; **marketing** n marketing m; **marketplace** n mercado; **market research** n pesquisa de mercado

marksman ['mɑːksmən] (irreg) n bom atirador m

marmalade ['mɑːməleɪd] n geléia de laranja

maroon [mə'ruːn] vt: **to be ~ed** ficar abandonado (numa ilha) ♦ adj de cor castanho-avermelhado, vinho inv

marquee [mɑː'kiː] n toldo, tenda

marriage ['mærɪdʒ] n casamento

married ['mærɪd] adj casado; (life, love) conjugal

marrow ['mærəu] n medula; (vegetable) abóbora

marry ['mærɪ] vt casar(-se) com; (subj: father, priest etc) casar, unir ♦ vi (also: **get married**) casar(-se)

Mars [mɑːz] n Marte m

marsh [mɑːʃ] n pântano; (salt ~) marisma

marshal ['mɑːʃl] n (MIL: also: **field ~**) marechal m; (at sports meeting etc)

oficial m ♦ vt (thoughts, support) organizar; (soldiers) formar

martyr ['mɑːtə*] n mártir m/f

marvel ['mɑːvl] n maravilha ♦ vi: **to ~ (at)** maravilhar-se (de ou com); **marvellous** (US **marvelous**) adj maravilhoso

Marxist ['mɑːksɪst] adj, n marxista m/f

marzipan ['mɑːzɪpæn] n maçapão m

mascara [mæs'kɑːrə] n rímel ® m

masculine ['mæskjulɪn] adj masculino

mash [mæʃ] vt (CULIN) fazer um purê de; (crush) amassar; **mashed potatoes** n purê m de batatas

mask [mɑːsk] n máscara ♦ vt (face) encobrir; (feelings) esconder, ocultar

mason ['meɪsn] n (also: **stone ~**) pedreiro(-a) (also: **free~**) maçom m; **masonry** n alvenaria

mass [mæs] n quantidade f; (people) multidão f; (PHYS) massa; (REL) missa; (great quantity) montão m ♦ cpd de massa ♦ vi reunir-se; (MIL) concentrar-se; **the ~es** npl (ordinary people) as massas; **~es of** (inf) montes de

massacre ['mæsəkə*] n massacre m, carnificina

massage ['mæsɑːʒ] n massagem f

massive ['mæsɪv] adj (large) enorme; (support) massivo

mass media npl meios mpl de comunicação de massa, mídia

mass production n produção f em massa, fabricação f em série

mast [mɑːst] n (NAUT) mastro m; (RADIO etc) antena

master ['mɑːstə*] n mestre m; (fig: of situation) dono; (in secondary school) professor m; (title for boys): **M~ X** o menino X ♦ vt controlar; (learn) conhecer a fundo; **masterly**

mat 163 **mean**

adj magistral; **mastermind** *n* (*fig*) cabeça ♦ *vt* dirigir, planejar; **Master of Arts/Science** *n* (*degree*) mestrado; **masterpiece** *n* obra-prima

mat [mæt] *n* esteira; (*also*: **door~**) capacho; (*also*: **table~**) descanso

match [mætʃ] *n* fósforo; (*game*) jogo, partida; (*equal*) igual *m/f* ♦ *vt* (*also*: ~ **up**) casar, emparelhar; (*go well with*) combinar com; (*equal*) igualar; (*correspond to*) corresponder a ♦ *vi* combinar; (*couple*) formar um bom casal; **matchbox** *n* caixa de fósforos; **matching** *adj* que combina (com)

mate [meɪt] *n* (*inf*) colega *m/f*; (*assistant*) ajudante *m/f*; (*animal*) macho/fêmea; (*in merchant navy*) imediato ♦ *vi* acasalar-se

material [mə'tɪərɪəl] *n* (*substance*) matéria; (*equipment*) material *m*; (*cloth*) pano, tecido; (*data*) dados *mpl* ♦ *adj* material; **~s** *npl* (*equipment*) material

maternal [mə'təːnl] *adj* maternal

maternity [mə'təːnɪtɪ] *n* maternidade *f*

mathematical [mæθə'mætɪkl] *adj* matemático

mathematics [mæθə'mætɪks] *n* matemática

maths [mæθs] (*US* **math**) *n* matemática

matrimony ['mætrɪmənɪ] *n* matrimônio, casamento

matron ['meɪtrən] *n* (*in hospital*) enfermeira-chefe *f*; (*in school*) inspetora

matted ['mætɪd] *adj* embaraçado

matter ['mætə*] *n* questão *f*, assunto; (*PHYS*) matéria; (*substance*) substância; (*reading* ~ *etc*) material *m*; (*MED*: *pus*) pus *m* ♦ *vi* importar; **~s** *npl* (*affairs*) questões *fpl*; **it doesn't ~**

não importa; (*I don't mind*) tanto faz; **what's the ~?** o que (é que) há?, qual é o problema?; **no ~ what** aconteça o que acontecer; **as a ~ of course** por rotina; **as a ~ of fact** na realidade, de fato; **matter-of-fact** *adj* prosaico, prático

mattress ['mætrɪs] *n* colchão *m*

mature [mə'tjuə*] *adj* maduro; (*cheese, wine*) amadurecido ♦ *vi* amadurecer

maul [mɔːl] *vt* machucar, maltratar

mauve [məuv] *adj* cor de malva *inv*

maximum ['mæksɪməm] (*pl* **maxima** *or* **~s**) *adj* máximo ♦ *n* máximo

May [meɪ] *n* maio

may [meɪ] (*pt, conditional* **might**) *aux vb* (*indicating possibility*): **he ~ come** pode ser que ele venha, é capaz de vir; (*be allowed to*): **~ I smoke?** posso fumar?; (*wishes*): **~ God bless you!** que Deus lhe abençoe

maybe ['meɪbɪ] *adv* talvez; **~ not** talvez não

mayhem ['meɪhem] *n* caos *m*

mayonnaise [meɪə'neɪz] *n* maionese *f*

mayor [mɛə*] *n* prefeito (*BR*), presidente *m* do município (*PT*); **mayoress** *n* prefeita (*BR*), presidenta do município (*PT*)

maze [meɪz] *n* labirinto

me [miː] *pron* me; (*stressed, after prep*) mim; **he heard ~** ele me ouviu; **it's ~** sou eu; **he gave ~ the money** ele me deu o dinheiro para mim; **give it to ~** dê-mo; **with ~** comigo; **without ~** sem mim

meadow ['mɛdəu] *n* prado, campina

meagre ['miːgə*] (*US* **meager**) *adj* escasso

meal [miːl] *n* refeição *f*; (*flour*) farinha; **mealtime** *n* hora da refeição

mean [miːn] (*pt, pp* **~t**) *adj* (*with*

money) sovina, avarento, pão-duro _inv_ (_BR_); (_unkind_) mesquinho; (_shabby_) malcuidado, dilapidado; (_average_) médio ♦ vt (_signify_) significar, querer dizer; (_refer to_): **I thought you ~t her** eu pensei que você estivesse se referindo a ela; (_intend_): **to ~ to do sth** pretender ou tencionar fazer algo ♦ n meio, meio termo; **~s** npl (_way, money_) meio; **by ~s of** por meio de, mediante; **by all ~s!** claro que sim!, pois não; **do you ~ it?** você está falando sério?

meaning ['mi:nɪŋ] n sentido, significado; **meaningful** adj significativo; (_relationship_) sério; **meaningless** adj sem sentido

meant [mɛnt] pt, pp of **mean**

meantime ['mi:ntaɪm] adv (also: **in the ~**) entretanto, enquanto isso

meanwhile ['mi:nwaɪl] adv = **meantime**

measles ['mi:zlz] n sarampo

measure ['mɛʒə*] vt, vi medir ♦ n medida; (_ruler: also:_ **tape ~**) fita métrica; **measurements** npl (_size_) medidas fpl

meat [mi:t] n carne f; **cold ~s** (_BRIT_) frios; **meatball** n almôndega

Mecca ['mɛkə] n Meca; (_fig_): **a ~ (for)** a meca (de)

mechanic [mɪ'kænɪk] n mecânico; **mechanical** adj mecânico; **mechanism** ['mɛkənɪzəm] n mecanismo

medal ['mɛdl] n medalha; **medallion** [mɪ'dælɪən] n medalhão m; **medallist** (_US_ **medalist**) n (_SPORT_) ganhador(a) m/f

meddle ['mɛdl] vi: **to ~ in** meter-se em, intrometer-se em; **to ~ with sth** mexer em algo

media ['mi:dɪə] npl meios mpl de comunicação, mídia

mediaeval [mɛdɪ'i:vl] adj = **medieval**

mediate ['mi:dɪeɪt] vi mediar

Medicaid ['mɛdɪkeɪd] (_US_) n programa de ajuda médica

medical ['mɛdɪkl] adj médico ♦ n (_examination_) exame m médico

Medicare ['mɛdɪkeə*] (_US_) n sistema federal de seguro saúde

medication [mɛdɪ'keɪʃən] n medicação f

medicine ['mɛdsɪn] n medicina; (_drug_) remédio, medicamento

medieval [mɛdɪ'i:vl] adj medieval

mediocre [mi:dɪ'əʊkə*] adj medíocre

meditate ['mɛdɪteɪt] vi meditar

Mediterranean [mɛdɪtə'reɪnɪən] adj mediterrâneo; **the ~ (Sea)** o (mar) Mediterrâneo

medium ['mi:dɪəm] (_pl_ **media** or **~s**) adj médio ♦ n (_means_) meio; (_pl_ **~s: person**) médium m/f

medley ['mɛdlɪ] n mistura; (_MUS_) pot-pourri m

meek [mi:k] adj manso, dócil

meet [mi:t] (_pt, pp_ **met**) vt encontrar; (_accidentally_) topar com, dar de cara com; (_by arrangement_) encontrar-se com, ir ao encontro de; (_for the first time_) conhecer; (_go and fetch_) ir buscar; (_opponent, problem_) enfrentar; (_obligations_) cumprir; (_need_) satisfazer ♦ vi encontrar-se; (_for talks_) reunir-se; (_join_) unir-se; (_get to know_) conhecer-se; **meet with** vt fus reunir-se com; (_difficulty_) encontrar; **meeting** n encontro; (_session: of club etc_) reunião f; (_assembly_) assembléia; (_SPORT_) corrida

megabyte ['mɛgəbaɪt] n (_COMPUT_) megabyte m

megaphone ['mɛgəfəʊn] n megafone m

melancholy ['mɛlənkəlɪ] n melancolia ♦ adj melancólico

melody ['mɛlədɪ] n melodia
melon ['mɛlən] n melão m
melt [mɛlt] vi (metal) fundir-se; (snow) derreter ♦ vt derreter; **melt down** vt fundir; **meltdown** n fusão f
member ['mɛmbə*] n membro(-a); (of club) sócio(-a); (ANAT) membro; **M~ of Parliament** (BRIT) deputado(-a); **membership** n (state) adesão f; (members) número de sócios; **membership card** n carteira de sócio
memento [mə'mɛntəu] n lembrança
memo ['mɛməu] n memorando, nota
memoirs ['mɛmwɑːz] npl memórias fpl
memorandum [mɛmə'rændəm] (pl **memoranda**) n memorando
memorial [mɪ'mɔːrɪəl] n monumento comemorativo ♦ adj comemorativo; **Memorial Day** (US) n ver quadro

---

MEMORIAL DAY

Memorial Day é um feriado nos Estados Unidos, a última segunda-feira de maio na maior parte dos estados, em memória aos soldados americanos mortos em combate.

---

memorize ['mɛməraɪz] vt decorar, aprender de cor
memory ['mɛmərɪ] n memória; (recollection) lembrança
men [mɛn] npl de **man**
menace ['mɛnəs] n ameaça; (nuisance) droga ♦ vt ameaçar
mend [mɛnd] vt consertar, reparar; (darn) remendar ♦ n: **to be on the ~** estar melhorando
menial ['miːnɪəl] adj (often pej) humilde, subalterno

meningitis [mɛnɪn'dʒaɪtɪs] n meningite f
menopause ['mɛnəupɔːz] n menopausa
menstruation [mɛnstru'eɪʃən] n menstruação f
mental ['mɛntl] adj mental; **mentality** [mɛn'tælɪtɪ] n mentalidade f
mention ['mɛnʃən] n menção f (speak of) falar de; **don't ~ it!** não tem de quê!, de nada!
menu ['mɛnjuː] n (set ~, COMPUT) menu m; (printed) cardápio (BR), ementa (PT)
MEP n abbr = **Member of the European Parliament**
mercenary ['mɜːsɪnərɪ] adj mercenário ♦ n mercenário
merchandise ['mɜːtʃəndaɪz] n mercadorias fpl
merchant ['mɜːtʃənt] n comerciante m/f
merciful ['mɜːsɪful] adj (person) misericordioso, humano; (release) afortunado
merciless ['mɜːsɪlɪs] adj desumano, inclemente
mercury ['mɜːkjurɪ] n mercúrio
mercy ['mɜːsɪ] n piedade f; (REL) misericórdia; **at the ~ of** à mercê de
mere [mɪə*] adj mero, simples inv; **merely** adv simplesmente, somente, apenas
merge [mɜːdʒ] vt unir ♦ vi unir-se; (COMM) fundir-se; **merger** n fusão f
meringue [mə'ræŋ] n suspiro, merengue m
merit ['mɛrɪt] n mérito; (advantage) vantagem f ♦ vt merecer
mermaid ['mɜːmeɪd] n sereia
merry ['mɛrɪ] adj alegre; **M~ Christmas!** Feliz Natal!; **merry-go-round** n carrossel m
mesh [mɛʃ] n malha

mesmerize [ˈmɛzməraɪz] vt hipnotizar

mess [mɛs] n confusão f; (in room) bagunça; (MIL) rancho; **to be in a** ~ ser uma bagunça, estar numa bagunça; **mess down** (inf) vi perder tempo; (pass the time) vadiar; **mess about with** (inf) fus mexer com; **mess around** (inf) vi = mess about; **mess around with** (inf) vt fus = mess about with; **mess up** vt (spoil) estragar; (dirty) sujar

message [ˈmɛsɪdʒ] n recado, mensagem f

messenger [ˈmɛsɪndʒə*] n mensageiro(-a)

Messrs [ˈmɛsəz] abbr (on letters: = messieurs) Srs

messy [ˈmɛsɪ] adj (dirty) sujo; (untidy) desarrumado

met [mɛt] pt, pp of meet

metal [ˈmɛtl] n metal m

meteorology [miːtɪəˈrɒlədʒɪ] n meteorologia

meter [ˈmiːtə*] n (instrument) medidor m; (also: parking ~) parcômetro; (US: unit) = metre

method [ˈmɛθəd] n método; **methodical** [mɪˈθɒdɪkl] adj metódico

metre [ˈmiːtə*] (US meter) n metro

metric [ˈmɛtrɪk] adj métrico

metropolitan [mɛtrəˈpɒlɪtən] adj metropolitano

México [ˈmɛksɪkəu] n México

miaow [miːˈau] vi miar

mice [maɪs] npl of mouse

micro... [ˈmaɪkrəu] prefix micro...; **microchip** n microchip m; **microphone** n microfone m; **microscope** n microscópio; **microwave** n (also: microwave oven) forno microondas

mid [mɪd] adj: ~ May/afternoon meados de maio (meio da tarde);

in ~ air em pleno ar; **midday** n meio-dia m

middle [ˈmɪdl] n meio; (waist) cintura ♦ adj meio; (quantity, size) médio, mediano; **middle-aged** adj de meia-idade; **Middle Ages** npl: **the Middle Ages** a Idade Média; **middle class** n: **the middle class(es)** a classe média ♦ adj (also: middle-class) de classe média; **Middle East** n: **the Middle East** o Oriente Médio; **middleman** n intermediário; **middle name** n segundo nome m

midge [mɪdʒ] n mosquito

midget [ˈmɪdʒɪt] n anão (anã) m/f

Midlands [ˈmɪdləndz] npl região central da Inglaterra

midnight [ˈmɪdnaɪt] n meia-noite f

midriff [ˈmɪdrɪf] n barriga

midst [mɪdst] n: **in the ~ of** no meio de, entre

midsummer [mɪdˈsʌmə*] n: **a ~ day** um dia em pleno verão

midway [mɪdˈweɪ] adj, adv: ~ (between) no meio do caminho (entre)

midweek [mɪdˈwiːk] adv no meio da semana

midwife [ˈmɪdwaɪf] (pl midwives) n parteira

might [maɪt] see may ♦ n poder m, força; **mighty** adj poderoso, forte

migraine [ˈmiːɡreɪn] n enxaqueca

migrant [ˈmaɪɡrənt] adj migratório; (worker) emigrante

migrate [maɪˈɡreɪt] vi emigrar; (birds) arribar

mike [maɪk] n abbr = microphone

mild [maɪld] adj (character) pacífico; (climate) temperado; (taste) suave; (illness) leve, benigno; (interest) pequeno

mile [maɪl] n milha (1609 m); **mileage** n número de milhas; (AUT?) quilometragem f

milestone [ˈmaɪlstəun] n marco

miliário

militant ['mɪlɪtnt] adj, n militante m/f

military ['mɪlɪtəɪɪ] adj militar

milk [mɪlk] n leite m ♦ vt (cow) ordenhar; (fig) explorar, chupar; **milk chocolate** n chocolate m de leite; **milkman** (irreg) n leiteiro; **milk shake** n milk-shake m, leite m batido com sorvete; **milky** adj leitoso; **Milky Way** n Via Láctea

mill [mɪl] n (wind– etc) moinho; (coffee –) moedor m de café; (factory) moinho, engenho ♦ vt moer ♦ vi (also: ~ **about**) aglomerar-se, remoinhar

millimetre (US **millimeter**) n milímetro

million ['mɪljən] n milhão m; **a ~ times** um milhão de vezes; **millionaire** n milionário(-a)

mime [maɪm] n mímo; (actor) mímico(-a), comediante m/f ♦ vt imitar ♦ vi fazer mímica

mimic ['mɪmɪk] n mímico(-a), imitador(a) m/f ♦ vt imitar, parodiar

min. abbr (= minute, minimum) min.

mince [mɪns] vt moer ♦ vi (in walking) andar com afetação ♦ n (BRIT: CULIN) carne f moída; **mincemeat** n recheio de sebo e frutas picadas; (US: meat) carne f moída; **mince pie** n pastel com recheio de sebo e frutas picadas

mind [maɪnd] n mente f; (intellect) intelecto; (opinion): **to my ~** a meu ver; (sanity): **to be out of one's ~** estar fora de si ♦ vt (attend to, look after) tomar conta de, cuidar de; (be careful of) ter cuidado com; (object to): **I don't ~ the noise** o barulho não me incomoda; **it is on my ~** não me sai da cabeça; **to keep** or **bear sth in ~** levar algo em consideração, não esquecer-se de algo; **to**

make up one's ~ decidir-se; **I don't ~ (it doesn't worry me)** eu nem ligo; (it's all the same to me) para mim tanto faz; **~ you, ...** ... se bem que ...; **never ~!** não faz mal!, não importa!; (don't worry) não se preocupe!; **"~ the step"** "cuidado com o degrau"; **mindless** adj (violence) insensato; (job) monótono

mine¹ [maɪn] pron (o) meu m, (a) minha f; **a friend of ~** um amigo meu

mine² [maɪn] n mina ♦ vt (coal) extrair, explorar; (ship, beach) minar

miner ['maɪnə*] n mineiro

mineral ['mɪnərəl] adj mineral ♦ n mineral m; **~s** npl (BRIT: soft drinks) refrigerantes mpl; **mineral water** n água mineral

mingle ['mɪŋgl] vi: **to ~ with** misturar-se com

miniature ['mɪnətʃə*] adj em miniatura ♦ n miniatura

minibus ['mɪnɪbʌs] n microônibus m

MiniDisc ['mɪnɪdɪsk] ® n MiniDisc ® m

minimal ['mɪnɪml] adj mínimo

minimum ['mɪnɪməm] (pl **minima**) adj mínimo ♦ n mínimo

mining ['maɪnɪŋ] n exploração f de minas

miniskirt ['mɪnɪskəːt] n minissaia

minister ['mɪnɪstə*] n (BRIT: POL) ministro(-a); (REL) pastor m ♦ vi: **to ~ to sb** prestar assistência a alguém; **to ~ to sb's needs** atender às necessidades de alguém

ministry ['mɪnɪstrɪ] n (BRIT: POL) ministério; (REL): **to go into the ~** ingressar no sacerdócio

mink [mɪŋk] n marta

minor ['maɪnə*] adj menor; (unimportant) de pouca importância; (MUS) menor ♦ n (LAW) menor m/f de idade

minority [mar'nɒrɪtɪ] n minoria

mint [mɪnt] n (plant) hortelã f; (sweet) bala de hortelã ♦ vt (coins) cunhar; **the (Royal) M~** (BRIT) or **the (US) M~** (US) ≈ a Casa da Moeda; **in ~ condition** em perfeito estado

minus ['maɪnəs] n (also: **~ sign**) sinal m de subtração ♦ prep menos

minute[1] ['mɪnjuːt] adj miúdo, diminuto; (search) minucioso

minute[2] ['mɪnɪt] n minuto; **~s** npl (of meeting) atas fpl; **at the last ~** no último momento

miracle ['mɪrəkl] n milagre m

mirage ['mɪrɑːʒ] n miragem f

mirror ['mɪrə*] n espelho; (in car) retrovisor m

mirth [mɜːθ] n risada

misadventure [mɪsəd'ventʃə*] n desgraça, infortúnio

misappropriate [mɪsə'prəuprɪeɪt] vt desviar

misbehave [mɪsbɪ'heɪv] vi comportar-se mal

miscarriage ['mɪskærɪdʒ] n (MED) aborto (espontâneo); (failure): **~ of justice** erro judicial

miscellaneous [mɪsɪ'leɪnɪəs] adj (items, expenses) diverso; (selection) variado

mischief ['mɪstʃɪf] n (naughtiness) travessura; (fun) diabrura; (maliciousness) malícia; **mischievous** ['mɪstʃɪvəs] adj (naughty) travesso; (playful) traquino

misconception [mɪskən'sepʃən] n concepção f errada, conceito errado

misconduct [mɪs'kɒndʌkt] n comportamento impróprio; **professional ~** má conduta profissional

misdemeanour [mɪsdɪ'miːnə*] (US **misdemeanor**) n má ação f, contravenção f

miser ['maɪzə*] n avaro(-a), sovina m/f

miserable ['mɪzərəbl] adj triste; (wretched) miserável; (weather, person) deprimente; (contemptible: offer) desprezível; (: failure) humilhante

miserly ['maɪzəlɪ] adj avarento, mesquinho

misery ['mɪzərɪ] n (unhappiness) tristeza; (wretchedness) miséria

misfire [mɪs'faɪə*] vi falhar

misfit ['mɪsfɪt] n inadaptado(-a), deslocado(-a)

misfortune [mɪs'fɔːtʃən] n desgraça, infortúnio

misgiving(s) [mɪs'gɪvɪŋ(z)] n(pl) mau pressentimento; **to have ~s about sth** ter desconfianças em relação a algo

misguided [mɪs'gaɪdɪd] adj enganado

mishandle [mɪs'hændl] vt manejar mal

mishap ['mɪshæp] n desgraça, contratempo

misinform [mɪsɪn'fɔːm] vt informar mal

misinterpret [mɪsɪn'tɜːprɪt] vt interpretar mal

misjudge [mɪs'dʒʌdʒ] vt fazer um juízo errado de, julgar mal

mislay [mɪs'leɪ] (irreg) vt extraviar, perder

mislead [mɪs'liːd] (irreg) vt induzir em erro, enganar; **misleading** adj enganoso, errôneo

mismanage [mɪs'mænɪdʒ] vt administrar mal; (situation) tratar de modo ineficiente

misplace [mɪs'pleɪs] vt extraviar, perder

misprint ['mɪsprɪnt] n erro tipográfico

Miss [mɪs] n Senhorita (BR), a

menina (PT)

miss [mɪs] vt (train, class, opportunity) perder; (fail to hit) errar, não acertar em; (fail to see): **you can't ~ it** é impossível não ver; (regret the absence of): **I ~ him** sinto a falta dele ♦ vi falhar ♦ n (shot) tiro perdido or errado; **miss out** (BRIT) vt omitir

misshapen [mɪs'ʃeɪpən] adj disforme

missile ['mɪsaɪl] n míssil m; (object thrown) projétil m

missing ['mɪsɪŋ] adj (pupil) ausente; (thing) perdido; (removed) que está faltando; (MIL) desaparecido; **to be ~** estar desaparecido; **to go ~** desaparecer

mission ['mɪʃən] n missão f; (official representatives) delegação f

mist [mɪst] n (light) neblina; (heavy) névoa; (at sea) bruma ♦ vi (eyes: also: **~ over, ~ up**: windows) embaçar

mistake [mɪs'teɪk] (irreg) n erro, engano ♦ vt entender or interpretar mal; **by ~** por engano; **to make a ~** fazer um erro; **to ~ A for B** confundir A com B; **mistaken** pp of **mistake** ♦ adj errado; **to be mistaken** enganar-se, equivocar-se

mister ['mɪstə*] (inf) n senhor m; see **Mr**

mistletoe ['mɪsltəu] n visco

mistook [mɪs'tuk] pt of **mistake**

mistress ['mɪstrɪs] n (lover) amante f; (of house) dona (da casa); (BRIT: in school) professora, mestra; (of situation) dona; see **Mrs**

mistrust [mɪs'trʌst] vt desconfiar de

misty ['mɪstɪ] adj (day) nublado; (glasses etc) embaçado

misunderstand [mɪsʌndə'stænd] (irreg) vt, vi entender or interpretar mal; **misunderstanding** n mal-entendido; (disagreement) desentendimento

misuse [n mɪs'ju:s, vb mɪs'ju:z] n uso impróprio; (of power) abuso; (of funds) desvio ♦ vt abusar de; desviar

mitigate ['mɪtɪɡeɪt] vt mitigar, atenuar

mix [mɪks] vt misturar; (combine) combinar ♦ vi (people) entrosar-se ♦ n mistura; (combination) combinação f; **mix up** vt (confuse: things) misturar; (: people) confundir; **mixed** adj misto; **mixed-up** adj confuso; **mixer** n (for food) batedeira; (person) pessoa sociável; **mixture** n mistura; (MED) preparado; **mix-up** n trapalhada, confusão f

mm abbr (= millimetre) mm

moan [məun] n gemido ♦ vi gemer; (inf: complain): **to ~ (about)** queixar-se (de), bufar (sobre) (inf)

moat [məut] n fosso

mob [mɔb] n multidão f ♦ vt cercar

mobile ['məubaɪl] adj móvel ♦ n móvel m; **mobile phone** n telefone m celular

mock [mɔk] vt ridicularizar; (laugh at) zombar de, gozar de ♦ adj falso, fingido; (exam etc) simulado; **mockery** n zombaria; **to make a mockery of** ridicularizar

mode [məud] n modo; (of transport) meio

model ['mɔdl] n modelo; (ARCH) maqueta f; (person: for fashion, ART) modelo m/f ♦ adj exemplar ♦ vt modelar ♦ vi servir de modelo; (in fashion) trabalhar como modelo; **to ~ o.s. on** mirar-se em

modem ['məudem] n modem m

moderate [adj 'mɔdərət, vb 'mɔdəreɪt] adj moderado ♦ vi moderar-se, acalmar-se ♦ vt moderar

modern ['mɔdən] adj moderno; **modernize** vt modernizar, atualizar

modest ['mɔdɪst] *adj* modesto;
  modesty *n* modéstia
modify ['mɔdɪfaɪ] *vt* modificar
moist [mɔɪst] *adj* úmido (*BR*), húmido (*PT*), molhado; **moisten** *vt*
umedecer (*BR*), humedecer (*PT*);
  moisture *n* umidade *f* (*BR*), humidade *f* (*PT*); **moisturizer** *n* creme *m*
hidratante
molar ['məulə*] *n* molar *m*
mold [məuld] *n* (*US*), *vt* = **mould**
mole [məul] *n* (*animal*) toupeira;
(*spot*) sinal *m*, lunar *m*; (*spy*) es-
pião(-piã) *m/f*
molest [məu'lest] *vt* molestar;
(*attack sexually*) atacar sexualmente
mollycoddle ['mɔlɪkɔdl] *vt* mimar
molt [məult] (*US*) *vi* = **moult**
molten ['məultən] *adj* fundido;
(*lava*) liquefeito
mom [mɔm] (*US*) *n* = **mum**
moment ['məumənt] *n* momento; **at the ~** neste momento;
  momentary *adj* momentâneo;
  momentous [məu'mentəs] *adj*
importantíssimo
momentum [məu'mentəm] *n* momento; (*fig*) ímpeto; **to gather ~**
ganhar ímpeto
mommy ['mɔmɪ] (*US*) *n* = **mummy**
Monaco ['mɔnəkəu] *n* Mônaco (*no*
article)
monarch ['mɔnək] *n* monarca *m/f*;
  monarchy *n* monarquia
monastery ['mɔnəstərɪ] *n* mosteiro, convento
Monday ['mʌndɪ] *n* segunda-feira
monetary ['mʌnɪtərɪ] *adj* monetário
money ['mʌnɪ] *n* dinheiro; (*currency*) moeda; **to make ~** ganhar
dinheiro; **money order** *n* vale *m*
(*postal*)
mongrel ['mʌŋgrəl] *n* (*dog*) vira-
lata *m*

monitor ['mɔnɪtə*] *n* (*TV*, *COMPUT*)
terminal *m* (de vídeo) ♦ *vt* (*heartbeat*, *pulse*) controlar; (*broadcasts*,
progress) monitorar
monk [mʌŋk] *n* monge *m*
monkey ['mʌŋkɪ] *n* macaco
monopoly [mə'nɔpəlɪ] *n* monopólio
monotonous [mə'nɔtənəs] *adj* monótono
monsoon [mɔn'su:n] *n* monção *f*
monster ['mɔnstə*] *n* monstro
monstrous ['mɔnstrəs] *adj* (*huge*)
descomunal; (*atrocious*) monstruoso
month [mʌnθ] *n* mês *m*; **monthly**
adj mensal ♦ *adv* mensalmente
monument ['mɔnjumənt] *n* monumento
mood [mu:d] *n* humor *m*; (*of crowd*)
atmosfera; **to be in a good/bad ~**
estar de bom/mau humor; **moody**
adj (*variable*) caprichoso, de veneta;
(*sullen*) rabugento
moon [mu:n] *n* lua; **moonlight** *n*
luar *m* ♦ *vi* ter dois empregos, ter
um bico; **moonlit** *adj*: **a moonlit
night** uma noite de lua
moor [muə*] *n* charneca ♦ *vt* (*ship*)
amarrar ♦ *vi* fundear, atracar
moorland ['muələnd] *n* charneca
moose [mu:s] *n inv* alce *m*
mop [mɔp] *n* esfregão *m*; (*for dishes*)
esponja com cabeça; (*of hair*)
grenha ♦ *vt* esfregar; **mop up** *vt*
limpar
mope [məup] *vi* estar *or* andar deprimido *or* desanimado
moped ['məuped] *n* moto *f* pequena
(*BR*), motorizada *f* (*PT*)
moral ['mɔrl] *adj* moral ♦ *n* moral *f*;
  ~s *npl* (*principles*) moralidade *f*,
costumes *mpl*
morale [mɔ'rɑ:l] *n* moral *f*, estado
de espírito
morality [mə'rælɪtɪ] *n* moralidade *f*;

(correctness) retidão f, probidade f

more [mɔ:*] adj **1** *(greater in number etc)* mais; **~ people/work/letters than we expected** mais pessoas/trabalho/cartas do que esperávamos
2 *(additional)* mais; **do you want (some) ~ tea?** você quer mais chá?; **I have no** or **I don't have any ~ money** não tenho mais dinheiro
♦ pron **1** *(greater amount)* mais; **~ than 10** mais de 10; **it cost ~ than we expected** custou mais do que esperávamos
2 *(further or additional amount)* mais; **is there any ~?** tem ainda mais?; **there's no ~** não tem mais
♦ adv mais; **~ dangerous/difficult** etc than mais perigoso/difícil etc do que; **~ easily (than)** mais fácil (do que); **~ and ~** cada vez mais; **~ or less** mais ou menos; **~ than ever** mais do que nunca

moreover [mɔ:ˈrəuvə*] adv além do mais, além disso
morning [ˈmɔ:nɪŋ] n manhã f; *(early ~)* madrugada ♦ cpd da manhã; **in the ~** de manhã; **7 o'clock in the ~** (as) 7 da manhã; **morning sickness** n náusea matinal
Morocco [məˈrɒkəu] n Marrocos m
moron [ˈmɔ:rɒn] *(inf)* n débil mental m/f, idiota m/f
Morse [mɔ:s] n *(also:* **~ code)** código Morse
morsel [ˈmɔ:sl] n *(of food)* bocado
mortar [ˈmɔ:tə*] n *(cannon)* morteiro; *(CONSTR)* argamassa; *(dish)* pilão m, almofariz m
mortgage [ˈmɔ:gɪdʒ] n hipoteca ♦ vt hipotecar
mortuary [ˈmɔ:tjuərɪ] n necrotério

mosaic [məuˈzeɪɪk] n mosaico
Moscow [ˈmɒskəu] n Moscou (BR), Moscovo (PT)
Moslem [ˈmɒzləm] adj, n = **Muslim**
mosque [mɒsk] n mesquita
mosquito [mɒsˈki:təu] *(pl* **~es)** n mosquito
moss [mɒs] n musgo

most [məust] adj **1** *(almost all: people, things etc)* a maior parte de, a maioria de; **~ people** a maioria das pessoas
2 *(largest, greatest: interest)* máximo; *(money)*: **who has (the) ~ money?** quem é que tem mais dinheiro?; **he derived the ~ pleasure from her visit** ele teve o maior prazer em recebê-la
♦ pron *(greatest quantity, number)* a maior parte, a maioria; **~ of it/them** a maioria deles/delas; **~ of the money** a maior parte do dinheiro; **do the ~ you can** faça o máximo que você puder; **I saw the ~** vi mais; **to make the ~ of** aproveitar algo ao máximo; **at the (very) ~** quando muito, no máximo
♦ adv *(+ vb)* mais; *(+ adj)*: **the ~ intelligent/expensive** etc o mais inteligente/caro etc; *(+ adv: carefully, easily etc)* o mais; *(very: polite, interesting etc)* muito; **a ~ interesting book** um livro interessantíssimo

mostly [ˈməustlɪ] adv principalmente, na maior parte
MOT *(BRIT)* n abbr *(= Ministry of Transport)*: **the ~ (test)** vistoria anual dos veículos automotores
motel [məuˈtel] n motel m
moth [mɒθ] n mariposa; *(clothes ~)* traça
mother [ˈmʌðə*] n mãe f ♦ adj

materno ♦ vt (care for) cuidar de (como uma mãe); **motherhood** n maternidade f; **mother-in-law** n sogra; **motherly** adj maternal; **mother-of-pearl** n madrepérola; **mother-to-be** n futura mamãe f; **mother tongue** n língua materna

motion ['məʊʃən] n movimento; (gesture) gesto, sinal m; (at meeting) moção f ♦ vt, vi: **to ~ (to) sb to do sth** fazer sinal a alguém para que faça algo; **motionless** adj imóvel; **motion picture** n filme m (cinematográfico)

motivated ['məʊtɪveɪtɪd] adj: ~ (by) motivado (por)

motive ['məʊtɪv] n motivo

motor ['məʊtə*] n motor m; (BRIT: inf: vehicle) carro, automóvel m ♦ cpd (industry) de automóvel; **motorbike** n moto(cicleta) f, motoca (inf); **motorboat** n barco a motor; **motorcar** (BRIT) n carro, automóvel m; **motorcycle** n motocicleta; **motorist** n motorista m/f; **motor racing** (BRIT) n corrida de carros, automobilismo; **motorway** (BRIT) n rodovia (BR), autoestrada (PT)

mottled ['mɔtld] adj mosqueado, em furta-cores

motto ['mɔtəʊ] (pl ~es) n lema m

mould [məʊld] (US **mold**) n molde m; (mildew) mofo, bolor m ♦ vt moldar; (fig) moldar; **mouldy** adj mofado

moult [məʊlt] (US **molt**) vi mudar (de penas etc)

mound [maʊnd] n (of earth) monte m; (of blankets, leaves etc) pilha, montanha

mount [maʊnt] n monte m ♦ vt (horse etc) montar em, subir a; (stairs) subir; (exhibition) montar; (picture) emoldurar ♦ vi (increase) aumentar; **mount up** vi aumentar

mountain ['maʊntɪn] n montanha ♦ cpd de montanha; **mountain bike** n mountain bike f; **mountaineer** [maʊntɪ'nɪə*] n alpinista m/f, montanhista m/f; **mountaineering** n alpinismo; **mountainous** adj montanhoso; **mountainside** n lado da montanha

mourn [mɔːn] vt chorar, lamentar ♦ vi: **to ~ for** chorar o lamentar a morte de; **mourning** n luto; **in mourning** de luto

mouse [maʊs] (pl **mice**) n camundongo (BR), rato (PT); (COMPUT) mouse m; **mouse mat** or **pad** n (COMPUT) mouse pad m; **mousetrap** n ratoeira

mousse [muːs] n musse f; (for hair) musse f

moustache [məs'tɑːʃ] (US **mustache**) n bigode m

mousy ['maʊsɪ] adj pardacento

mouth [maʊθ] n boca; (of cave, hole) entrada; (of river) desembocadura; **mouthful** n bocado; **mouth organ** n gaita; **mouthwash** n colutório; **mouth-watering** adj de dar água na boca

movable ['muːvəbl] adj móvel

move [muːv] n movimento; (in game) lance m, jogada; (: turn to play) turno, vez f; (of house, job) mudança ♦ vt (change position of) mudar; (: in game) jogar; (emotionally) comover; (POL: resolution etc) propor ♦ vi mexer-se, mover-se; (traffic) circular; (also: ~ house) mudar-se; (develop: situation) desenvolver; **to ~ sb to do sth** convencer alguém a fazer algo; **to get a ~ on** apressar-se; **move about** or **around** vi (fidget) mexer-se; (travel) deslocar-se; **move along** vi avançar; **move away** vi afastar-se

move back vi voltar; **move forward** vi avançar; **move in** vi (to a house) instalar-se (numa casa); **move on** vi ir andando; **move out** vi sair (de uma casa); **move over** vi afastar-se; **move up** vi ser promovido

movement ['mu:vmənt] n movimento; (gesture) gesto; (of goods) transporte m; (in attitude) mudança

movie ['mu:vɪ] n filme m; **to go to the ~s** ir ao cinema

moving ['mu:vɪŋ] adj (emotional) comovente; (that moves) móvel

mow [məu] (pt **~ed**, pp **~ed** or **~n**) vt (grass) cortar; (corn) ceifar; **mow down** vt (massacre) chacinar; **mower** n ceifeira m; (also: **lawnmower**) cortador m de grama (BR) or de relva (PT)

Mozambique [məuzəm'bi:k] n Moçambique m (no article)

MP n abbr = Member of Parliament

mph abbr = miles per hour (60 mph = 96 km/h)

Mr ['mɪstə*] n: **~ Smith** (o) Sr. Smith

Mrs ['mɪsɪz] n: **~ Smith** (a) Sra. Smith

Ms [mɪz] n (= Miss or Mrs) ver quadro

Ms

Ms é um título utilizado em lugar de Mrs (senhora) ou de Miss (senhorita) para evitar a distinção tradicional entre mulheres casadas e solteiras. É aceito, portanto, como o equivalente de Mr (senhor) para os homens. Muitas vezes reprovado por ter surgido como manifestação de um feminismo exacerbado, é uma forma de tratamento muito comum hoje em dia.

MSc n abbr = Master of Science

much [mʌtʃ] adj muito; **how ~ money/time do you need?** quanto dinheiro/tempo você precisa?; **he's done so ~ work for the charity** ele trabalhou muito para a obra de caridade; **as ~ as** tanto como

♦ pron muito; **~ has been gained from our discussions** nossas discussões foram muito proveitosas; **how ~ does it cost? – too ~** quanto custa isso? – caro demais

♦ adv 1 (greatly) muito; **thank you very ~** muito obrigado(-a); **we are very ~ looking forward to your visit** estamos aguardando a sua visita com muito ansiedade; **he is very ~ the gentleman/politician** ele é muito cavalheiro/político; **as ~ as** tanto como; **as ~ as you** tanto quanto você

2 (by far) de longe; **I'm ~ better now** estou bem melhor agora

3 (almost) quase; **how are you feeling? – ~ the same** como você está (se sentindo)? – do mesmo jeito

muck [mʌk] n (dirt) sujeira (BR), sujidade f (PT); **muck about** or **around** (inf) vi fazer besteiras; **muck up** (inf) vt estragar

mud [mʌd] n lama

muddle ['mʌdl] n confusão f, bagunça; (mix-up) trapalhada ♦ vt (also: **~ up**: person, story) confundir; (: things) misturar; **muddle through** vi virar-se

muddy ['mʌdɪ] adj (road) lamacento

mudguard ['mʌdgɑ:d] n pára-lama m

muesli ['mju:zlɪ] n muesli m

muffin ['mʌfɪn] n bolinho redondo e

chato

muffle ['mʌfl] *vt* (*sound*) abafar; (*against cold*) agasalhar; **muffled** *adj* abafado, surdo; **muffler** (*US*) *n* (*AUT*) silencioso (*BR*), panela de escape (*PT*)

mug [mʌg] *n* (*cup*) caneca; (*: for beer*) caneco, canecão; (*inf: face*) careta; (*: fool*) bobo(-a) ♦ *vt* (*assault*) assaltar; **mugging** *n* assalto

muggy [ˈmʌgɪ] *adj* abafado

mule [mjuːl] *n* mula

multimedia [mʌltɪˈmiːdɪə] *adj* multimídia

multiple [ˈmʌltɪpl] *adj* múltiplo ♦ *n* múltiplo; **multiple sclerosis** [-sklɪˈrəʊsɪs] *n* esclerose *f* múltipla

multiply [ˈmʌltɪplaɪ] *vt* multiplicar ♦ *vi* multiplicar-se

multistorey [mʌltɪˈstɔːrɪ] (*BRIT*) *adj* de vários andares

mum [mʌm] *n* (*BRIT: inf*) mamãe *f* ♦ *adj*: **to keep ~** ficar calado

mumble [ˈmʌmbl] *vt, vi* resmungar, murmurar

mummy [ˈmʌmɪ] *n* (*BRIT: mother*) mamãe *f*; (*embalmed*) múmia

mumps [mʌmps] *n* caxumba

mundane [mʌnˈdeɪn] *adj* banal, mundano

municipal [mjuːˈnɪsɪpl] *adj* municipal

murder [ˈmɜːdə*] *n* assassinato ♦ *vt* assassinar; **murderer** *n* assassino

murky [ˈmɜːkɪ] *adj* escuro; (*water*) turvo

murmur [ˈmɜːmə*] *n* murmúrio ♦ *vt, vi* murmurar

muscle [ˈmʌsl] *n* músculo; (*fig: strength*) força (muscular); **muscle in** *vi* imiscuir-se, impor-se; **muscular** *adj* muscular; (*person*) musculoso

museum [mjuːˈzɪəm] *n* museu *m*

mushroom [ˈmʌʃrʊm] *n* cogumelo

♦ *vi* crescer da noite para o dia, pipocar

music [ˈmjuːzɪk] *n* música; **musical** *adj* musical; (*harmonious*) melodioso ♦ *n* musical *m*; **musician** [mjuːˈzɪʃən] *n* músico(-a)

Muslim [ˈmʌzlɪm] *adj, n* muçulmano(-a)

mussel [ˈmʌsl] *n* mexilhão *m*

must [mʌst] *aux vb* (*obligation*): **I ~ do it** tenho que or devo fazer isso; (*probability*): **he ~ be there by now** ele já deve estar lá; (*suggestion, invitation*): **you ~ come and see me soon** você tem que vir me ver em breve; (*indicating sth unwelcome*): **why ~ he behave so badly?** por que ele tem que se comportar tão mal? ♦ *n* necessidade *f*; **it's a ~** é imprescindível

mustache [ˈmʌstæʃ] (*US*) *n* = **moustache**

mustard [ˈmʌstəd] *n* mostarda

muster [ˈmʌstə*] *vt* (*support*) reunir; (*energy*) juntar; (*MIL*) formar

mustn't [ˈmʌsnt] = **must not**

mute [mjuːt] *adj* mudo

mutiny [ˈmjuːtɪnɪ] *n* motim *m*, rebelião *f*

mutter [ˈmʌtə*] *vt, vi* resmungar, murmurar

mutton [ˈmʌtn] *n* carne *f* de carneiro

mutual [ˈmjuːtʃʊəl] *adj* mútuo; (*shared*) comum

muzzle [ˈmʌzl] *n* (*of animal*) focinho; (*guard: for dog*) focinheira; (*of gun*) boca ♦ *vt* pôr focinheira em

my [maɪ] *adj* meu (minha); **this is ~ house/car/brother** esta é a minha casa/meu carro/meu irmão; **I've washed ~ hair/cut ~ finger** lavei meu cabelo/cortei meu dedo

myself [maɪˈself] *pron* (*reflexive*) me;

(*emphatic*) eu mesmo; (*after prep*) mim mesmo; *see also* **oneself**

mysterious [mɪsˈtɪərɪəs] *adj* misterioso

mystery [ˈmɪstərɪ] *n* mistério

mystify [ˈmɪstɪfaɪ] *vt* mistificar

myth [mɪθ], *n* mito; **mythology** [mɪˈθɔlədʒɪ] *n* mitologia

N

n/a *abbr* = **not applicable**

nag [næg] *vt* ralhar, apoquentar; **nagging** *adj* (*doubt*) persistente; (*pain*) contínuo

nail [neɪl] *n* (*human*) unha; (*metal*) prego ♦ *vt* pregar; **to ~ sb down to a date/price** conseguir que alguém se defina sobre a data/o preço; **nail-brush** *n* escova de unhas; **nailfile** *n* lixa de unhas; **nail polish** *n* esmalte *m* (*BR*) or verniz *m* (*PT*) de unhas; **nail polish remover** *n* removedor *m* de esmalte (*BR*) or verniz (*PT*); **nail scissors** *npl* tesourinha de unhas; **nail varnish** (*BRIT*) *n* = **nail polish**

naïve [naɪˈiːv] *adj* ingênuo

naked [ˈneɪkɪd] *adj* nu (nua)

name [neɪm] *n* nome *m*; (*surname*) sobrenome *m*; (*reputation*) reputação *f*, fama ♦ *vt* (*child*) pôr nome em; (*criminal*) apontar; (*price*) fixar; (*date*) marcar; **what's your ~?** qual é o seu nome?, como (você) se chama?; **by ~** de nome; **in the ~ of** em nome de; **namely** *adv* a saber, isto é; **namesake** *n* xará *m/f* (*BR*), homónimo(-a) (*PT*)

nanny [ˈnænɪ] *n* babá *f*

nap [næp] *n* (*sleep*) soneca ♦ *vi*: **to be caught ~ping** ser pego de surpresa

nape [neɪp] *n*: **~ of the neck** nuca

napkin [ˈnæpkɪn] *n* (*also*: **table ~**)

guardanapo

nappy [ˈnæpɪ] (*BRIT*) *n* fralda; **nappy rash** *n* assadura

narcotic [nɑːˈkɔtɪk] *adj* narcótico ♦ *n* narcótico

narrative [ˈnærətɪv] *n* narrativa

narrow [ˈnærəu] *adj* estreito; (*fig: majority*) pequeno; (*: ideas*) tacanho ♦ *vi* (*road*) estreitar-se; (*difference*) diminuir; **to have a ~ escape** escapar por um triz; **to ~ sth down to** restringir o reduzir algo a; **narrowly** *adv* (*miss*) por pouco; **narrow-minded** *adj* de visão limitada

nasty [ˈnɑːstɪ] *adj* (*remark*) desagradável; (*: person*) mau, ruim; (*malicious*) maldoso; (*rude*) grosseiro, obsceno; (*taste*, *smell*) repugnante, asqueroso; (*wound etc*) grave, sério

nation [ˈneɪʃən] *n* nação *f*

national [ˈnæʃənl] *adj*, *n* nacional *m/f*; **national anthem** *n* hino nacional; **National Health Service** (*BRIT*) *n* ≈ Instituto Nacional de Assistência Médica e Previdência Social, ≈ INAMPS *m*; **nationality** [næʃəˈnælɪtɪ] *n* nacionalidade *f*; **nationalize** *vt* nacionalizar; **nationally** *adv* (*nationwide*) de âmbito nacional; (*as a nation*) nacionalmente, como nação; **national park** *n* parque *m* nacional; **National Trust** (*BRIT*) *n* ver quadro

---

NATIONAL TRUST

O **National Trust** é uma instituição independente, sem fins lucrativos, cuja missão é proteger e valorizar os monumentos e a paisagem da Grã-Bretanha devido ao seu interesse histórico ou beleza natural.

---

nationwide [ˈneɪʃənwaɪd] *adj* de âmbito or a nível nacional ♦ *adv* em todo o país

native ['neɪtɪv] n natural m/f, nativo(-a); (in colonies) indígena m/f, nativo(-a) ♦ adj (indigenous) indígena; (of one's birth) natal; (language) materno; (innate) inato, natural; **a ~ speaker of Portuguese** uma pessoa de língua (materna) portuguesa

NATO ['neɪtəʊ] n abbr (= North Atlantic Treaty Organization) OTAN f

natural ['nætʃrəl] adj natural; **naturally** adv naturalmente; (of course) claro, evidentemente

nature ['neɪtʃə*] n natureza; (character) caráter m, índole f

naught [nɔ:t] n = nought

naughty ['nɔ:tɪ] adj travesso, levado

nausea ['nɔ:sɪə] n náusea

naval ['neɪvl] adj naval

nave [neɪv] n nave f

navel ['neɪvl] n umbigo

navigate ['nævɪgeɪt] vi navegar; (AUT) ler o mapa; **navigation** [nævɪ'geɪʃən] n (action) navegação f; (science) náutica

navvy ['nævɪ] (BRIT) n trabalhador m braçal, cavouqueiro

navy ['neɪvɪ] n marinha (de guerra); **navy(-blue)** adj azul-marinho inv

Nazi ['nɑ:tsɪ] n nazista m/f e (BR), nazi m/f (PT)

NB abbr (= nota bene) NB

near [nɪə*] adj (place) vizinho; (time) próximo; (relation) íntimo ♦ adv perto ♦ prep (also: **~ to**: space) perto de; (: time) perto de, quase ♦ vt aproximar-se de; **nearby** [nɪə'baɪ] adj próximo, vizinho ♦ adv à mão, perto; **nearly** adv quase; **I nearly fell** quase que caí; **nearside** n (AUT: right-hand drive) lado esquerdo; (: left-hand drive) lado direito ♦ adj esquerdo, direito; **near-sighted** adj míope

neat [ni:t] adj (place) arrumado, em

ordem; (person) asseado, arrumado; (work) organizado; (plan) engenhoso, bem bolado; (spirits) puro; **neatly** adv caprichosamente, com capricho; (skilfully) habilmente

necessarily ['nesɪsrɪlɪ] adv necessariamente

necessary ['nesɪsrɪ] adj necessário

necessity [nɪ'sesɪtɪ] n (thing needed) necessidade f, requisito; (compelling circumstances) necessidade; **necessities** npl (essentials) artigos mpl de primeira necessidade

neck [nek] n (ANAT) pescoço; (of garment) gola; (of bottle) gargalo ♦ vi (inf) ficar de agarramento; **~ and ~** emparelhados

necklace ['neklɪs] n colar m

neckline ['neklaɪn] n decote m

necktie ['nektaɪ] (esp US) n gravata

need [ni:d] n (lack) falta, carência; (necessity) necessidade f; (thing) requisito, necessidade ♦ vt precisar de; **I ~ to do it** preciso fazê-lo

needle ['ni:dl] n agulha ♦ vt (inf) provocar, alfinetar

needless ['ni:dlɪs] adj inútil, desnecessário; **~ to say** ... desnecessário dizer que ...

needlework ['ni:dlwə:k] n (item(s)) trabalho de agulha; (activity) costura

needn't ['ni:dnt] = **need not**

needy ['ni:dɪ] adj necessitado, carente

negative ['negətɪv] adj negativo ♦ n (PHOT) negativo; (LING) negativa

neglect [nɪ'glekt] vt (one's duty) negligenciar, não cumprir com; (child) descuidar, esquecer-se de ♦ n (of child) descuido, desatenção f; (of house etc) abandono; (of duty) negligência

negotiate [nɪ'gəʊʃɪeɪt] vi: **to ~ (with)** negociar (com) ♦ vt (treaty, transaction) negociar; (obstacle) contornar; (*bend in road*) fazer; **negotiation** [nɪgəʊʃˈeɪʃən] n negociação f

neigh [neɪ] vi relinchar

neighbour ['neɪbə*] (US **neighbor**) n vizinho(-a); **neighbourhood** n (*place*) vizinhança, bairro; (*people*) vizinhos mpl; **neighbouring** adj vizinho; **neighbourly** adj amistoso, prestativo

neither ['naɪðə*] conj: I didn't even and ~ did he não me movi nem ele ♦ adj, pron nenhum (dos dois), nem um nem outro ♦ adv: ~ good nor bad nem bom nem mau; ~ story is true nenhuma das estórias é verdade

neon ['niːɔn] n neônio, néon m; **neon light** n luz f de neônio

nephew ['nevjuː] n sobrinho

nerve [nəːv] n (ANAT) nervo m; (*courage*) coragem f; (*impudence*) descaramento, atrevimento; **to have a fit of ~s** ter uma crise nervosa; **nerve-racking** adj angustiante

nervous ['nəːvəs] adj (ANAT) nervoso; (*anxious*) apreensivo; (*timid*) tímido, acanhado; **nervous breakdown** n crise f nervosa

nest [nest] vi aninhar-se ♦ n (*of bird*) ninho; (*of wasp*) vespeiro

net [nɛt] n rede f; (*fabric*) filó m; (*fig*) sistema m ♦ adj (COMM) líquido ♦ vt pegar na rede; (*money*: subj: *person*) faturar; (: *deal, sale*) render; **the N~** (*the Internet*) a Rede; **netball** n espécie de basquetebol

Netherlands ['nɛðələndz] npl: **the ~ os Países Baixos**

nett [nɛt] adj = **net**

nettle ['nɛtl] n urtiga

network ['nɛtwɜːk] n rede f

neurotic [njuəˈrɔtɪk] adj, n neurótico(-a)

neuter ['njuːtə*] adj neutro ♦ vt (*cat etc*) castrar, capar

neutral ['njuːtrəl] adj neutro ♦ n (AUT) ponto morto

never ['nɛvə*] adv nunca; *see also* **mind**; **never-ending** adj sem fim, interminável; **nevertheless** adv todavia, contudo

new [njuː] adj novo; **newborn** adj recém-nascido; **newcomer** n recém-chegado(-a), novato(-a); **new-found** adj (*friend*) novo; (*enthusiasm*) recente; **newly** adv recém, novamente; **newly-weds** npl recém-casados mpl

news [njuːz] n notícias fpl; (RADIO, TV) noticiário; **a piece of ~** uma notícia, **newsagent** (BRIT) n jornaleiro(-a); **newscaster** n locutor(a) m/f; **news flash** n notícia de última hora; **newsletter** n boletim m informativo; **newspaper** n jornal m; **newsreader** n = **newscaster**; **newsreel** n jornal m cinematográfico, atualidades fpl

newt [njuːt] n tritão m

New Year n ano novo; **New Year's Day** n dia m de ano novo; **New Year's Eve** n véspera de ano novo

New Zealand [-ˈziːlənd] n Nova Zelândia; **New Zealander** n neozelandês(-esa) m/f

next [nɛkst] adj (*in space*) próximo, vizinho; (*in time*) seguinte, próximo ♦ adv depois; depois, logo; ~ **time** na próxima vez; ~ **year** o ano que vem; ~ **to** ao lado de; ~ **to nothing** quase nada; **next door** adv na casa do lado ♦ adj vizinho; **next-of-kin** n parentes mpl mais próximos

NHS n abbr = **National Health Service**

nib [nɪb] n ponta or bico da pena

nibble ['nɪbl] vt mordiscar, beliscar

Nicaragua [ˌnɪkəˈræɡjuə] n Nicarágua

nice [naɪs] adj (likeable) simpático; (kind) amável, atencioso; (pleasant) agradável; (attractive) bonito; **nicely** adv agradavelmente, bem

nick [nɪk] n (wound) corte m; (cut, indentation) entalhe m, incisão f ♦ vt (inf: steal) furtar, arranchar; **in the ~ of time** na hora N, no momento exato

nickel ['nɪkl] n níquel m; (US) moeda de 5 centavos

nickname ['nɪkneɪm] n apelido (BR), alcunha (PT) ♦ vt apelidar de (BR), alcunhar de (PT)

niece [niːs] n sobrinha

Nigeria [naɪ'dʒɪərɪə] n Nigéria

niggling ['nɪɡlɪŋ] adj (trifling) insignificante, mesquinho; (annoying) irritante

night [naɪt] n noite f; **at** or **by ~** à or de noite; **the ~ before last** anteontem à noite; **nightcap** n bebida tomada antes de dormir; **nightclub** n boate f; **nightdress** n camisola (BR), camisa de noite (PT); **nightfall** n anoitecer m; **nightgown** n = **nightdress**; **nightie** ['naɪtɪ] n = **nightdress**

nightingale ['naɪtɪŋɡeɪl] n rouxinol m

nightlife ['naɪtlaɪf] n vida noturna

nightly ['naɪtlɪ] adj noturno, de noite ♦ adv todas as noites, cada noite

nightmare ['naɪtmɛə*] n pesadelo

night-time n noite f

nil [nɪl] n nada; (BRIT: SPORT) zero

Nile [naɪl] n: **the ~** o Nilo

nimble ['nɪmbl] adj (agile) ágil, ligeiro; (skilful) hábil, esperto

nine [naɪn] num nove; **nineteen** ['naɪn'tiːn] num dezenove (BR), dezanove (PT); **ninety** ['naɪntɪ] num noventa; **ninth** [naɪnθ] num nono

nip [nɪp] vt (pinch) beliscar; (bite) morder

nipple ['nɪpl] n (ANAT) bico do seio, mamilo

nitrogen ['naɪtrədʒən] n nitrogênio

KEYWORD

no [nəu] (pl ~es) adv (opposite of "yes") não; **are you coming? - -** (I'm not) você vem? – não (eu não) ♦ adj (not any) nenhum(a), não … algum(a); **I have ~ more money/time/books** não tenho mais dinheiro/tempo/livros; **"~ entry"** "entrada proibida"; **"~ smoking"** "é proibido fumar"
♦ n não m, negativa

nobility [nəu'bɪlɪtɪ] n nobreza

noble ['nəubl] adj (person) nobre; (title) de nobreza

nobody ['nəubədɪ] pron ninguém

nod [nɔd] vi (greeting) cumprimentar com a cabeça; (in agreement) acenar (que sim) com a cabeça; (doze) cochilar, dormitar ♦ vt: **to ~ one's head** inclinar a cabeça ♦ n inclinação f da cabeça; **nod off** vi cochilar

noise [nɔɪz] n barulho; **noisy** adj barulhento

nominate ['nɔmɪneɪt] vt (propose) propor; (appoint) nomear; **nominee** [nɔmɪ'niː] n pessoa nomeada, candidato(-a)

non-alcoholic [nɔn-] adj sem álcool

nondescript ['nɔndɪskrɪpt] adj qualquer; (pej) medíocre

none [nʌn] pron (person) ninguém; (thing) nenhum(a), nada; **~ of you** nenhum de vocês; **I've ~ left** não tenho mais

nonentity [nɔ'nentɪtɪ] n nulidade f, zero à esquerda m

nonetheless [nʌnðə'les] adv no entanto, apesar disso, contudo

non-existent [nɔnɪɡ'zɪstənt] adj

inexistente

non-fiction [nɔn-] n literatura de não-ficção

nonplussed [nɔn'plʌst] adj perplexo, pasmado

nonsense ['nɔnsəns] n disparate m, besteira, absurdo; ~! bobagem!, que nada!

non [nɔn-]: **non-smoker** n não-fumante m/f; **non-stick** adj tefal ®, não-aderente; **non-stop** adj ininterrupto; (RAIL) direto; (AVIAT) sem escala ♦ adv sem parar

noodles ['nuːdlz] npl talharim m

noon [nuːn] n meio-dia m

no-one pron = **nobody**

noose [nuːs] n laço corrediço; (hangman's) corda da forca

nor [nɔː*] conj = **neither** ♦ adv see **neither**

norm [nɔːm] n (convention) norma; (requirement) regra

normal ['nɔːml] adj normal

north [nɔːθ] n norte m ♦ adj do norte, setentrional ♦ adv ao or para o norte; **North America** n América do Norte; **north-east** n nordeste m; **northerly** ['nɔːðəlɪ] adj norte; **northern** ['nɔːðən] adj do norte, setentrional; **Northern Ireland** n Irlanda do Norte; **North Pole** n: the North Pole o Pólo Norte; **North Sea** n: the North Sea o Mar do Norte; **northward(s)** adv em direção norte; **north-west** n noroeste m

Norway ['nɔːweɪ] n Noruega; **Norwegian** [nɔː'wiːdʒən] adj norueguês(-esa) ♦ n norueguês(-esa) m/f; (LING) norueguês m

nose [nəuz] n (ANAT) nariz m; (ZOOL) focinho; (sense of smell: of person) olfato; (: of animal) faro; **nose about** vi bisbilhotar; **nose around** vi = **nose about**; **nosebleed** n

hemorragia nasal; **nose-dive** n (deliberate) vôo picado; (involuntary) parafuso; **nosey** (inf) adj = **nosy**

nostalgia [nɔs'tældʒɪə] n nostalgia

nostril ['nɔstrɪl] n narina

nosy ['nəuzɪ] (inf) adj intrometido, abelhudo

not [nɔt] adv não; **he is ~** or **isn't here** ele não está aqui; **it's too late, isn't it?** é muito tarde, não?; **he asked me ~ to do it** ele me pediu para não fazer isto; **~ yet/now** ainda/agora não; see also **all**; **only**

notably ['nəutəblɪ] adv (particularly) particularmente; (markedly) notavelmente

notch [nɔtʃ] n (in wood) entalhe m; (in blade) corte m

note [nəut] n (MUS, bank~) nota; (letter) nota, bilhete m; (record) nota, anotação f; (tone) tom m ♦ vt (observe) observar, reparar em; (also: ~ down) anotar, tomar nota de; **notebook** n caderno; **notepad** n bloco de anotações; **notepaper** n papel m de carta

nothing ['nʌθɪŋ] n nada m; (zero) zero; **he does ~** ele não faz nada; **~ new/much** nada de novo/quase nada; **for ~** de graça, grátis; (in vain) em vão, por nada

notice ['nəutɪs] n (sign) aviso, anúncio; (warning) aviso; (dismissal) demissão f; (of leaving) aviso prévio; (period of time) prazo ♦ vt reparar em, notar; **at short ~** de repente, em cima da hora; **until further ~** até nova ordem; **to hand in one's ~** demitir, pedir a demissão; **to take ~ of** prestar atenção a, fazer caso de; **to bring sth to sb's ~** levar algo ao conhecimento de alguém; **noticeable** adj evidente, visível; **notice board** (BRIT) n quadro de avisos

notify ['nəutɪfaɪ] vt: **to ~ sb of sth**

avisar alguém de algo

notion ['nəʊʃən] n noção f, idéia

nought [nɔ:t] n zero

noun [naʊn] n substantivo

nourish ['nʌrɪʃ] vt nutrir, alimentar; (fig) fomentar, alentar; **nourishing** adj nutritivo, alimentício; **nourishment** n alimento, nutrimento

novel ['nɒvl] n romance m ♦ adj novo, recente; **novelist** n romancista m/f; **novelty** n novidade f

November [nəʊ'vembə*] n novembro

now [naʊ] adv agora; (these days) atualmente, hoje em dia ♦ conj: ~ (that) agora que; **right** ~ agora mesmo; **by** ~ já; **just** ~ atualmente; ~ **and then**, ~ **and again** de vez em quando; **from** ~ **on** de agora em diante; **nowadays** adv hoje em dia

nowhere ['nəʊweə*] adv (go) a lugar nenhum; (be) em nenhum lugar

nozzle ['nɒzl] n bocal m

nuclear ['nju:klɪə*] adj nuclear

nucleus ['nju:klɪəs] (pl **nuclei**) n núcleo

nude [nju:d] adj nu (nua) ♦ n (ART) nu m; **in the** ~ nu, pelado

nudge [nʌdʒ] vt acotovelar, cutucar (BR)

nudist ['nju:dɪst] n nudista m/f

nuisance ['nju:sns] n amolação f, aborrecimento; (person) chato; **what a** ~! que saco! (BR), que chatice! (PT)

numb [nʌm] adj: ~ **with cold** duro de frio; ~ **with fear** paralisado de medo

number ['nʌmbə*] n número; (numeral) algarismo ♦ vt (pages etc) numerar; (amount to) montar a; **a** ~ **of** vários, muitos; **to be ~ed among** figurar entre; **they were ten in** ~ eram em número de dez; **number**

plate (BRIT) n placa (do carro)

numeral ['nju:mərəl] n algarismo

numerical [nju:'merɪkl] adj numérico

numerous ['nju:mərəs] adj numeroso

nun [nʌn] n freira

nurse [nə:s] n enfermeiro(-a) (also: ~**maid**) ama-seca, babá f ♦ vt (patient) cuidar de, tratar de

nursery ['nə:sərɪ] n (institution) creche f; (room) quarto das crianças; (for plants) viveiro; **nursery rhyme** n poesia infantil; **nursery school** n escola maternal

nursing ['nə:sɪŋ] n (profession) enfermagem f; (care) cuidado, assistência; **nursing home** n sanatório, clínica de repouso

nut [nʌt] n (TECH) porca; (BOT) noz f; **nutcrackers** npl quebra-nozes m inv

nutmeg ['nʌtmeg] n noz-moscada

nutritious [nju:'trɪʃəs] adj nutritivo

nuts [nʌts] (inf) adj: **he's** ~ ele é doido

nutshell ['nʌtʃel] n casca de noz; **in a** ~ (fig) em poucas palavras

nylon ['naɪlɒn] n náilon m (BR), nylon m (PT) ♦ adj de náilon

O

oak [əʊk] n carvalho ♦ adj de carvalho

OAP (BRIT) n abbr = **old-age pensioner**

oar [ɔ:*] n remo

oasis [əʊ'eɪsɪs] (pl **oases**) n oásis m inv

oath [əʊθ] n juramento; (swear word) palavrão m

oatmeal ['əʊtmi:l] n farinha or mingau m de aveia

oats [əuts] n aveia

obedient [ə'bi:dɪənt] adj obediente

obey [ə'beɪ] vt obedecer a; (instructions, regulations) cumprir

obituary [ə'bɪtjuərɪ] n necrológio

object [n 'ɒbdʒɪkt, vb əb'dʒekt] n objeto; (purpose) objetivo ♦ vi: to ~ to (attitude) desaprovar, objetar a; (proposal) opor-se a; **I ~! protesto!**; **he ~ed that ...** ele objetou que ...; **expense is no ~** o preço não é problema; **objection** [əb'dʒekʃən] n objeção f; **I have no objection to ...** não tenho nada contra ...; **objectionable** adj desagradável; (conduct) censurável; **objective** n objetivo

obligation [ɒblɪ'geɪʃən] n obrigação f; **without ~** sem compromisso

obligatory [ə'blɪgətərɪ] adj obrigatório

oblige [ə'blaɪdʒ] vt (do a favour for) obsequiar, fazer um favor a; (force) obrigar, forçar; **to be ~d to sb for doing sth** ter que agradecido por alguém fazer algo; **obliging** adj prestativo

oblique [ə'bli:k] adj oblíquo; (allusion) indireto

oblivion [ə'blɪvɪən] n esquecimento; **oblivious** adj: **oblivious of** inconsciente de, esquecido de

oblong ['ɒblɒŋ] adj oblongo, retangular ♦ n retângulo

obnoxious [əb'nɒkʃəs] adj odioso, detestável; (smell) enjoativo

oboe ['əubəu] n oboé m

obscene [əb'si:n] adj obsceno

obscure [əb'skjuə*] adj obscuro, desconhecido; (difficult to understand) pouco claro ♦ vt ocultar, escurecer; (hide: sun etc) esconder

observant [əb'zɜ:vnt] adj observador(a)

observation [ɒbzə'veɪʃən] n observação f; (MED) exame m

observatory [əb'zɜ:vətrɪ] n observatório

observe [əb'zɜ:v] vt observar; (rule) cumprir; **observer** n observador(a) m/f

obsess [əb'ses] vt obsedar, obcecar

obsolete ['ɒbsəli:t] adj obsoleto

obstacle ['ɒbstəkl] n obstáculo; (hindrance) estorvo, impedimento

obstinate ['ɒbstɪnɪt] adj obstinado

obstruct [əb'strʌkt] vt obstruir; (block: hinder) estorvar

obtain [əb'teɪn] vt obter; (achieve) conseguir

obvious ['ɒbvɪəs] adj óbvio; **obviously** adv evidentemente; **obviously not!** (é) claro que não!

occasion [ə'keɪʒən] n ocasião f; (event) acontecimento; **occasional** adj de vez em quando; **occasionally** adv de vez em quando

occupation [ɒkju'peɪʃən] n ocupação f; (job) profissão f

occupier ['ɒkjupaɪə*] n inquilino(-a)

occupy ['ɒkjupaɪ] vt ocupar; (house) morar em; **to ~ o.s. in doing** ocupar-se de fazer

occur [ə'kɜ:*] vi ocorrer; (phenomenon) acontecer; **to ~ to sb** ocorrer a alguém; **occurrence** n ocorrência, acontecimento; (existence) existência

ocean ['əuʃən] n oceano

o'clock [ə'klɒk] adv: **it is 5 ~** são cinco horas

OCR n abbr = **optical character reader; optical character recognition**

October [ɒk'təubə*] n outubro

octopus ['ɒktəpəs] n polvo

odd [ɒd] adj (strange) estranho, esquisito; (number) ímpar; (sock etc) desemparelhado; **60~** 60 e tantos; **at ~ times** às vezes, de vez em

quando; **to be the ~ one out** ficar
sobrando, ser a exceção; **odd jobs**
npl biscates mpl, bicos mpl; **oddly**
adv curiosamente; see also **enough**;
odds npl (in betting) pontos mpl de
vantagem; **it makes no odds** dá no
mesmo; **at odds** brigados(-as), de mal

odour ['əʊdə*] (US **odor**) n odor m,
cheiro; (unpleasant) fedor m

KEYWORD

of [ɔv, əv] prep 1 (gen) de; **a friend ~
ours** um amigo nosso; **a boy ~ 10**
um menino de 10 anos; **that was
very kind ~ you** foi muito gentil da
sua parte

2 (expressing quantity, amount, dates
etc) de; **how much ~ this do you
need?** de quanto você precisa?; **3 ~
them** 3 deles; **3 ~ us went** 3 de nós
foram; **the 5th ~ July** dia 5 de julho
3 (from, out of) de; **made ~ wood**
feito de madeira

KEYWORD

off [ɔf] adv 1 (distance, time): **it's a
long way ~** fica bem longe; **the
game is 3 days ~** o jogo é daqui a 3
dias

2 (departure): **I'm ~** estou de partida; **to go ~ to Paris/Italy** ir para
Paris/a Itália; **I must be ~** devo ir-me
3 (removal): **to take ~ one's hat/
coat/clothes** tirar o chapéu/o casa-
co/a roupa; **the button came ~** o
botão caiu; **10% ~** (COMM) 10% de
abatimento ou desconto

4 (not at work): **to have a day ~** tirar
um dia de folga; (: sick): **to be ~ sick**
estar ausente por motivo de saúde
♦ adj 1 (not turned on: machine,
water, gas) desligado; (: light) apagado; (: tap) fechado

2 (cancelled) cancelado

3 (BRIT: not fresh: food) passado; (:
milk) talhado, anulado

4: **on the ~ chance** (just in case) ao
acaso; **today I had an ~ day** (not as
good as usual) hoje não foi o meu
dia

♦ prep 1 (indicating motion, removal
etc) de; **the button came ~ my coat**
o botão do meu casaco caiu

2 (distant from): **5 km ~ (the
road)** a 5 km (da estrada); **~ the
coast** em frente à costa

3: **to be ~ meat** (no longer eat it)
não comer mais carne; (no longer
like it) enjoar de carne

offal ['ɔfl] n (CULIN) sobras fpl, restos
mpl

off-colour (BRIT) adj (ill) indisposto
offence [ə'fɛns] (US **offense**) n
(crime) delito; **to take ~ at** ofender-
se com, melindrar-se com

offend [ə'fɛnd] vt ofender; **offender** n delinquente m/f

offensive [ə'fɛnsɪv] adj (weapon,
remark) ofensivo; (smell etc) repugnante ♦ n (MIL) ofensiva

offer ['ɔfə*] n oferta; (proposal) proposta ♦ vt oferecer; (opportunity)
proporcionar; **"on ~"** (COMM) "em
oferta"

off-hand [ɔf'hænd] adj informal
♦ adv de improviso

office ['ɔfɪs] n (place) escritório;
(room) gabinete m; (position) cargo,
função f; **to take ~** tomar posse;
doctor's ~ (US) consultório; **office
block** (US **office building**) n conjunto de escritórios

officer ['ɔfɪsə*] n (MIL etc) oficial
m/f; (of organization) diretor(a) m/f;
(also: **police ~**) agente m/f policial
 or de polícia

office worker n empregado(-a) ou
funcionário(-a) de escritório

official [ə'fɪʃl] adj oficial ♦ n oficial m/f; (civil servant) funcionário público (funcionária pública)

officious [ə'fɪʃəs] adj intrometido

off-licence (BRIT) n ver quadro

OFF-LICENCE

Uma loja **off-licence** vende bebidas alcoólicas (para viagem) nos horários em que os pubs estão fechados. Nesses estabelecimentos também se pode comprar bebidas não-alcoólicas, cigarros, batatas fritas, balas, chocolates etc.

---

off: off-line adj, adv (COMPUT) fora de linha; **off-peak** adj (heating etc) de período de pouco consumo; (ticket, train) de período de pouco movimento; **off-putting** (BRIT) adj desconcertante; **off-season** adj, adv fora de estação or temporada

offset ['ɒfsɛt] (irreg) vt compensar, contrabalançar

offshore [ɒf'ʃɔː*] adj (breeze) de terra; (fishing) costeiro; ~ **oilfield** campo petrolífero ao largo

offside [ɒf'saɪd] adj (SPORT) impedido; (AUT) do lado do motorista

offspring ['ɒfsprɪŋ] n descendência, prole f

offstage [ɒf'steɪdʒ] adv nos bastidores

often ['ɒfn] adv muitas vezes, freqüentemente; **how ~ do you go?** quantas vezes você vai?

oil [ɔɪl] n (CULIN) azeite m; (petroleum) petróleo; (for heating) óleo ♦ vt (machine) lubrificar; **oil painting** n pintura a óleo; **oil rig** n torre f de perfuração; **oil slick** n mancha negra; **oil tanker** n (ship) petroleiro; (truck) carro-tanque m de petróleo; **oil well** n poço petrolífero; **oily** adj oleoso; (food) gorduroso

ointment ['ɔɪntmənt] n pomada

O.K. ['əu'keɪ] excl está bem, está bom, tá (bem or bom) (inf) ♦ adj bom; (correct) certo ♦ vt aprovar

okay ['əu'keɪ] = O.K.

old [əuld] adj velho; (former) antigo, anterior; **how ~ are you?** quantos anos você tem?; **he's 10 years ~** ele tem 10 anos; **~er brother** irmão mais velho; **old age** n velhice f; **old-age pensioner** (BRIT) n aposentado(-a) (BR), reformado(-a) (PT); **old-fashioned** adj fora de moda; (person) antiquado; (values) absoleto, retrógrado

olive ['ɒlɪv] n (fruit) azeitona; (tree) oliveira ♦ adj (also: ~-green) verde-oliva inv; **olive oil** n azeite m de oliva

Olympic [əu'lɪmpɪk] adj olímpico

omelet(te) ['ɒmlɪt] n omelete f (BR), omeleta (PT)

omen ['əumən] n presságio, agouro

ominous ['ɒmɪnəs] adj preocupante

omit [əu'mɪt] vt omitir

KEYWORD

---

on [ɒn] prep **1** (indicating position) sobre, em (cima de); ~ **the wall** na parede; ~ **the left** à esquerda

2 (indicating means, method, condition etc): ~ **foot** a pé; ~ **the train/plane** no trem/avião; ~ **the telephone/radio** no telefone/rádio; ~ **television** na televisão; **to be ~ drugs** (addicted) ser viciado em drogas; (MED) estar sob medicação; **to be ~ holiday** estar de férias

3 (referring to time): ~ **Friday** na sexta-feira; **a week** ~ **Friday** sem ser esta sexta-feira, a outra; ~ **arrival** ao chegar; ~ **seeing this** ao ver isto

4 (about, concerning) sobre

♦ adv **1** (referring to dress, covering): **to have one's coat ~** estar de casaco; **what's she got ~?** o que ela está usando?; **she put her boots ~** ela calçou as botas; **he put his gloves/hat ~** ele colocou as luvas/o chapéu; **screw the lid ~ tightly** atarraxar bem a tampa

2 (*further, continuously*): **to walk/drive ~** continuar andando/dirigindo; **to go ~** continuar (em frente); **to read ~** continuar a ler

♦ *adj* **1** (*functioning, in operation: machine*) em funcionamento; (*light*) aceso; (*radio*) ligado; (*tap*) aberto; (*brakes: of car etc*): **to be ~** estar freado; (*meeting*): **is the meeting still ~?** (*in progress*) a reunião ainda está sendo realizada?; (*not cancelled*) ainda vai haver reunião?; **there's a good film ~ at the cinema** tem um bom filme passando no cinema

2: **that's not ~!** (*inf: of behaviour*) isso não se faz!

once [wʌns] *adv* uma vez; (*formerly*) outrora ♦ *conj* depois que; **~ he had left/it was done** depois que ele saiu/foi feito; **at ~** imediatamente; (*simultaneously*) de uma vez, ao mesmo tempo; **~ more** mais uma vez; **~ and for all** uma vez por todas; **~ upon a time** era uma vez

oncoming [ˈɔnkʌmɪŋ] *adj* (*traffic*) que vem de frente

one [wʌn] *num* um(a); **~ hundred and fifty** cento e cinqüenta; **~ by ~** um por um

♦ *adj* **1** (*sole*) único; **the ~ book which ...** o único livro que ...

2 (*same*) mesmo; **they came in the ~ car** eles vieram no mesmo carro

♦ *pron* **1** (*gen*): **this ~** este (esta); **that ~** esse (essa), aquele (aquela); **I've already got ~/a red ~** eu já

tenho um/um vermelho

2: **~ another** um ao outro; **do you two ever see ~ another?** vocês dois se vêem de vez em quando?

3 (*impers*): **~ never knows** nunca se sabe; **to cut ~'s finger** cortar o dedo; **~ needs to eat** é preciso comer

oneself [wʌnˈself] *pron* (*reflexive*) se; (*after prep, emphatic*) si (mesmo(-a)); **by ~** sozinho(-a); **to hurt ~** ferir-se; **to keep sth for ~** guardar algo para si mesmo; **to talk to ~** falar consigo mesmo

one: **one-sided** *adj* (*argument*) parcial; **one-way** *adj* (*street, traffic*) de mão única (*BR*), de sentido único (*PT*)

ongoing [ˈɔngəuɪŋ] *adj* (*project*) em andamento; (*situation*) existente

onion [ˈʌnjən] *n* cebola

on line *adj* (*COMPUT*) on-line, em linha ♦ *adv* em linha

onlooker [ˈɔnlukə*] *n* espectador(a) m/f

only [ˈəunlɪ] *adv* somente, apenas ♦ *adj* único, só ♦ *conj* só que, porém; **an ~ child** um filho único; **not ~ ... but also ...** não só ... mas também ...

onset [ˈɔnsɛt] *n* começo

onshore [ˈɔnʃɔː*] *adj* (*wind*) do mar

onslaught [ˈɔnslɔːt] *n* investida, arremetida

onto [ˈɔntu] *prep* = **on to**

onward(s) [ˈɔnwəd(z)] *adv* (*move*) para diante, para a frente; **from this time ~** de (ag)ora em diante

ooze [uːz] *vi* ressumar, filtrar-se

opaque [əuˈpeɪk] *adj* opaco, fosco

OPEC [ˈəupɛk] *n abbr* (= *Organization of Petroleum-Exporting Countries*) OPEP f

open [ˈəupn] *adj* aberto; (*car*) descoberto; (*road*) livre; (*fig: frank*) aberto, franco; (*meeting*) aberto, sem restrições ♦ *vt* abrir ♦ *vi* abrir(-se); (*book etc*) começar; **in the ~ (air)** ao ar livre; **open on to** *vt fus* (*subj: room, door*) dar para; **open up** *vt* abrir; (*blocked road*) desobstruir ♦ *vi* (*COMM*) abrir; **opening** *adj* de abertura ♦ *n* abertura; (*start*) início; (*opportunity*) oportunidade *f*; **openly** *adv* abertamente; **open-minded** *adj* aberto, imparcial; **open-necked** *adj* aberto no colo; **open-plan** *adj* sem paredes divisórias; **Open University** (*BRIT*) *n* ver quadro

OPEN UNIVERSITY

Fundada em 1969, a **Open University** oferece um tipo de ensino que compreende cursos (alguns blocos da programação da TV e do rádio são reservados para esse fim), deveres que são enviados pelo aluno ao diretor ou diretora de estudos e uma estada obrigatória em uma universidade de verão. É preciso cumprir um certo número de unidades ao longo de um período determinado e obter a média em um certo número delas para receber o diploma almejado.

opera [ˈɔpərə] *n* ópera
operate [ˈɔpəreɪt] *vt* fazer funcionar, pôr em funcionamento ♦ *vi* funcionar; (*MED*): **to ~ on sb** operar alguém
operation [ɔpəˈreɪʃən] *n* operação *f*; (*of machine*) funcionamento; **to be in ~** (*system*) estar em vigor
operator [ˈɔpəreɪtə*] *n* (*of machine*) operador(a) *m/f*, manipulador(a) *m/f*; (*TEL*) telefonista *m/f*
opinion [əˈpɪnɪən] *n* opinião *f*; **in my ~** na minha opinião, a meu ver;

opinionated *adj* opinioso
opponent [əˈpəunənt] *n* oponente *m/f*; (*MIL, SPORT*) adversário(-a)
opportunity [ɔpəˈtjuːnɪtɪ] *n* oportunidade *f*; **to take the ~ of doing** aproveitar a oportunidade para fazer
oppose [əˈpəuz] *vt* opor-se a; **to be ~d to sth** opor-se a algo, estar contra algo; **as ~d to** em oposição a
opposing [əˈpəuzɪŋ] *adj* oposto, contrário
opposite [ˈɔpəzɪt] *adj* oposto; (*house etc*) em frente ♦ *adv* (lá) em frente ♦ *prep* em frente de, defronte de ♦ *n* oposto, contrário
opposition [ɔpəˈzɪʃən] *n* oposição *f*
opt [ɔpt] *vi*: **to ~ for** optar por; **to ~ to do** optar por fazer; **opt out**: **to ~ out of doing sth** optar por não fazer algo
optician [ɔpˈtɪʃən] *n* oculista *m/f*
optimist [ˈɔptɪmɪst] *n* otimista *m/f*; **optimistic** [ɔptɪˈmɪstɪk] *adj* otimista
option [ˈɔpʃən] *n* opção *f*; **optional** *adj* opcional, facultativo
or [ɔː*] *conj* ou; (*with negative*): **he hasn't seen ~ heard anything** ele não viu nem ouviu nada; **~ else** senão
oral [ˈɔːrəl] *adj* oral ♦ *n* (*exame m*) oral *f*
orange [ˈɔrɪndʒ] *n* (*fruit*) laranja ♦ *adj* cor de laranja *inv*, alaranjado
orbit [ˈɔːbɪt] *n* órbita ♦ *vt* orbitar
orchard [ˈɔːtʃəd] *n* pomar *m*
orchestra [ˈɔːkɪstrə] *n* orquestra *f*; (*US: seating*) platéia *f*
orchid [ˈɔːkɪd] *n* orquídea *f*
ordeal [ɔːˈdiːl] *n* experiência penosa, provação *f*
order [ˈɔːdə*] *n* ordem *f*; (*COMM*) encomenda; (*good ~*) bom estado ♦ *vt* (*also: put in ~*) pôr em ordem,

arrumar; (*in restaurant*) pedir; (COMM) encomendar; (*command*) mandar, ordenar; **in ~ (working)** ~ em bom estado; **in ~ to/that** para fazer/que (+ sub); **on ~** (COMM) encomendado; **out of ~** com defeito, enguiçado; **order form** n impresso para encomendas; **orderly** n (MIL) ordenança m; (MED) servente m/f ♦ adj (room) arrumado, ordenado; (person) metódico

ordinary [ˈɔːdnrɪ] adj comum, usual; (pej) ordinário, medíocre; **out of the ~** fora do comum, extraordinário

ore [ɔː*] n minério

organ [ˈɔːɡən] n órgão m; **organic** [ɔːˈɡænɪk] adj orgânico

organization [ɔːɡənaɪˈzeɪʃən] n organização f

organize [ˈɔːɡənaɪz] vt organizar

orgasm [ˈɔːɡæzəm] n orgasmo

Orient [ˈɔːrɪənt] n: **the ~** o Oriente; **oriental** [ɔːrɪˈɛntl] adj, n oriental m/f

origin [ˈɔrɪdʒɪn] n origem f

original [əˈrɪdʒɪnl] adj original ♦ n original m

originate [əˈrɪdʒɪneɪt] vi: **to ~ from** originar-se de, surgir de; **to ~ in** ter origem em

Orkneys [ˈɔːknɪz] npl: **the ~** (also: **the Orkney Islands**) as ilhas Órcadas

ornament [ˈɔːnəmənt] n ornamento; (on dress) enfeite m; **ornamental** [ɔːnəˈmɛntl] adj decorativo, ornamental

ornate [ɔːˈneɪt] adj enfeitado, requintado

orphan [ˈɔːfn] n órfão (órfã) m/f

orthopaedic [ɔːθəˈpiːdɪk] (US **orthopedic**) adj ortopédico

ostentatious [ɔstɛnˈteɪʃəs] adj pomposo, espalhafatoso; (person) ostentoso

ostrich [ˈɔstrɪtʃ] n avestruz m/f

other [ˈʌðə*] adj outro ♦ pron: **the ~ (one)** o outro (a outra) ♦ adv (usually in negatives): **~ than** (apart from) a não ser; (anything but) exceto; **~s** (~ people) outros; **otherwise** adv (in a different way) de outra maneira; (apart from that) do contrário, caso contrário ♦ conj (if not) senão

otter [ˈɔtə*] n lontra

ouch [autʃ] excl ai!

ought [ɔːt] (pt ought) aux vb: **I ~ to do it** eu deveria fazê-lo; **he ~ to win** (probability) ele deve ganhar

ounce [auns] n onça (= 28.35g; 16 in a pound)

our [ˈauə*] adj nosso; see also **my**; **ours** pron (o) nosso ((a) nossa) etc; see also **mine¹**; **ourselves** [auəˈsɛlvz] pron pl (reflexive, after prep) nós; (emphatic) nós mesmos(-as); see also **oneself**

oust [aust] vt expulsar

┌─────────────────────────────┐
│ KEYWORD   │
└─────────────────────────────┘

out [aut] adv **1** (not in) fora; **(to stand) ~ in the rain/snow** (estar em pé) na chuva/neve; **~ loud** em voz alta
2 (not at home, absent) fora (de casa); **Mr Green is ~ at the moment** Sr. Green não está no momento; **to have a day/night ~** passar o dia fora/sair à noite
3 (indicating distance): **the boat was 10 km ~** o barco estava a 10 km da costa
4 (SPORT): **the ball is/has gone ~** a bola caiu fora; **~!** (TENNIS etc) fora!
♦ adj **1**: **to be ~** (unconscious) estar inconsciente; (~ of game) estar fora; (~ of fashion) estar fora de moda
2 (have appeared): news, secret) do conhecimento público; (~ flowers): **the flowers are ~** as flores desabrocham

3 (*extinguished: light, fire*) apagado;
before the week was ~ (*finished*)
antes da semana acabar
4: **to be ~ to do sth** (*intend*) pretender fazer algo; **to be ~ in one's calculations** (*wrong*) enganar-se nos cálculos
♦ *prep*: **~ of 1** (*outside, beyond*): **~ of fora de**; **to go ~ of the house** sair da casa; **to look ~ of the window** olhar pela janela
2 (*cause, motive*) por
3 (*origin*): **to drink sth ~ of a cup** beber algo na xícara
4 (*from among*): **1 ~ of every 3** 1 entre 3
5 (*without*) sem; **to be ~ of milk/sugar/petrol** *etc* não ter leite/açúcar/gasolina *etc*

out-and-out *adj* (*liar etc*) completo, rematado
outback ['autbæk] *n* (*in Australia*): **the ~** o interior
outbreak ['autbreık] *n* (*of war*) deflagração *f*; (*of disease*) surto; (*of violence etc*) explosão *f*
outburst ['autbə:st] *n* explosão *f*
outcast ['autkɑ:st] *n* pária *m/f*
outcome ['autkʌm] *n* resultado
outcry ['autkraı] *n* clamor *m* (de protesto)
outdated [aut'deıtıd] *adj* antiquado, fora de moda
outdo [aut'du:] (*irreg*) *vt* ultrapassar, exceder
outdoor [aut'dɔ:*] *adj* ao ar livre; (*clothes*) de sair; **outdoors** *adv* ao ar livre
outer ['autə*] *adj* exterior, externo; **outer space** *n* espaço (exterior)
outfit ['autfıt] *n* roupa, traje *m*
outgoing ['autgəuıŋ] *adj* de saída; (*character*) extrovertido, sociável; **outgoings** (*BRIT*) *npl* despesas *fpl*

outgrow [aut'grəu] (*irreg*) *vt*: **he has ~n his clothes** a roupa ficou pequena para ele
outing ['autıŋ] *n* excursão *f*
outlaw ['autlɔ:] *n* fora-da-lei *m/f* ♦ *vt* (*person*) declarar fora da lei; (*practice*) declarar ilegal
outlay ['autleı] *n* despesas *fpl*
outlet ['autlet] *n* saída, escape *m*; (*of pipe*) desagüe *m*, escoadouro; (*US: ELEC*) tomada; (*also:* **retail ~**) posto de venda
outline ['autlaın] *n* (*shape*) contorno, perfil *m*; (*of plan*) traçado; (*sketch*) esboço, linhas *fpl* gerais ♦ *vt* (*theory, plan*) traçar, delinear
outlive [aut'lıv] *vt* sobreviver a
outlook ['autluk] *n* (*attitude*) ponto de vista; (*fig: prospects*) perspectiva; (*: for weather*) previsão *f*
outnumber [aut'nʌmbə*] *vt* exceder em número
out-of-date *adj* (*passport, ticket*) sem validade; (*clothes*) fora de moda
out-of-the-way *adj* remoto, afastado
outpatient ['autpeı∫ənt] *n* paciente *m/f* externo(-a) or de ambulatório
outpost ['autpəust] *n* posto avançado
output ['autput] *n* (volume *m* de) produção *f*; (*COMPUT*) saída ♦ *vt* (*COMPUT*) liberar
outrage ['autreıdʒ] *n* escândalo; (*atrocity*) atrocidade *f* ♦ *vt* ultrajar; **outrageous** [aut'reıdʒəs] *adj* ultrajante, escandaloso
outright [*adv* aut'raıt, *adj* 'autraıt] *adv* (*kill, win*) completamente; (*ask, refuse*) abertamente ♦ *adj* completo; franco
outset ['autset] *n* início, princípio
outside [aut'saıd] *n* exterior *m* ♦ *adj* exterior, externo ♦ *adv* (lá) fora

♦ prep fora de; (beyond) além (dos limites) de; **at the ~** (fig) no máximo; **outsider** n (stranger) estranho(-a), forasteiro(-a)

outsize ['autsaɪz] adj (clothes) de tamanho extra-grande or especial

outskirts ['autskɜːts] npl arredores mpl, subúrbios mpl

outspoken [aut'spəukən] adj franco, sem rodeios

outstanding [aut'stændɪŋ] adj excepcional; (work, debt) pendente

outstay [aut'steɪ] vt: **to ~ one's welcome** abusar da hospitalidade (demorando mais tempo)

outstretched [aut'stretʃt] adj (hand) estendido

outstrip [aut'strɪp] vt ultrapassar

outward ['autwəd] adj externo; (journey) de ida

outweigh [aut'weɪ] vt ter mais valor do que

outwit [aut'wɪt] vt passar a perna em

oval ['əuvl] adj ovalado ♦ n oval m; **Oval Office** n ver quadro

---

OVAL OFFICE

O Salão Oval (**Oval Office**) é o escritório particular do presidente dos Estados Unidos na Casa Branca, assim chamado devido a sua forma oval. Por extensão, o termo se refere à presidência em si.

---

ovary ['əuvərɪ] n ovário

oven ['ʌvn] n forno

KEYWORD

---

over ['əuvə*] adv **1** (across: walk, jump, fly etc) por cima; **to cross ~ to the other side of the road** atravessar para o outro lado da rua; **~ here** por aqui, cá; **~ there** por ali, lá; **to ask sb ~** (to one's home) convidar alguém

2: **to fall ~** cair; **to knock ~** derrubar; **to turn ~** virar; **to bend ~** curvar-se, debruçar-se

3 (finished): **to be ~** estar acabado

4 (excessively: clever, rich, fat etc) muito, demais; **she's not ~ intelligent** ela não é superdotada

5 (remaining: money, food etc): **there are 3 ~** tem 3 sobrando/sobraram 3

6: **all ~** (everywhere) por todos os lados; **~ and ~** (again) repetidamente

♦ prep **1** (on top of) sobre; (above) acima de

2 (on the other side of) no outro lado de; **he jumped ~ the wall** ele pulou o muro

3 (more than) mais de; **~ and above** além de

4 (during) durante

overall [adj, n 'əuvərɔːl, adv əuvər'ɔːl] adj (length) total; (study) global ♦ adv (view) globalmente; (measure, paint) totalmente ♦ n (also: **~s**) macacão m (BR), (fato) macaco (PT)

overawe ['əuvər'ɔː] vt intimidar

overboard ['əuvəbɔːd] adv (NAUT) ao mar

overcast ['əuvəkɑːst] adj nublado, fechado

overcharge [əuvə'tʃɑːdʒ] vt: **to ~ sb** cobrar em excesso a alguém

overcoat ['əuvəkəut] n sobretudo

overcome [əuvə'kʌm] (irreg) vt vencer, dominar; (difficulty) superar

overcrowded [əuvə'kraudɪd] adj superlotado

overdo [əuvə'duː] (irreg) vt exagerar; (overcook) cozinhar demais; **to ~ it** (work too hard) exceder-se

overdose ['əuvədəus] n overdose f, dose f excessiva

overdraft ['əuvədrɑːft] n saldo negativo

overdrawn [əuvə'drɔːn] adj (account) sem fundos, a descoberto

overdue [əuvə'djuː] adj atrasado; (change) tardio

overestimate [əuvər'estimeit] vt sobrestimar

overflow [vb əuvə'fləu, n 'əuvəfləu] vi transbordar ♦ n (also: ~ pipe) tubo de descarga, ladrão m

overgrown [əuvə'grəun] adj (garden) coberto de vegetação

overhaul [vb əuvə'hɔːl, n 'əuvəhɔːl] vt revisar ♦ n revisão f

overhead [adv əuvə'hed, adj, n 'əuvəhed] adv por cima, em cima; (in the sky) no céu ♦ adj (lighting) suspenso; (railway) suspenso ♦ n (us) = **~s**; **~s** npl (expenses) despesas fpl gerais

overhear [əuvə'hiə*] (irreg) vt ouvir por acaso

overheat [əuvə'hiːt] vi (engine) aquecer demais

overjoyed [əuvə'dʒɔɪd] adj: **to be ~ (at)** estar muito alegre (com)

overland ['əuvəlænd] adj, adv por terra

overlap [əuvə'læp] vi (edges) sobrepor-se em parte; (fig) coincidir

overleaf [əuvə'liːf] adv no verso

overload [əuvə'ləud] vt sobrecarregar

overlook [əuvə'luk] vt (have view on) dar para; (miss) omitir; (forgive) fazer vista grossa a

overnight [adv əuvə'nait, adj 'əuvənait] adv durante a noite; (fig) da noite para o dia ♦ adj de uma (or de) noite; **to stay ~** passar a noite, pernoitar

overpass ['əuvəpɑːs] (esp US) n viaduto

overpower [əuvə'pauə*] vt domi-

nar, subjugar; (fig) assolar

overrate [əuvə'reit] vt sobrestimar, supervalorizar

override [əuvə'raid] (irreg) vt (order, objection) não fazer caso de, ignorar

overrule [əuvə'ruːl] vt (decision) anular; (claim) indeferir

overrun [əuvə'rʌn] (irreg) vt (country etc) invadir; (time limit) ultrapassar, exceder

overseas [əuvə'siːz] adv (abroad) no estrangeiro, no exterior ♦ adj (trade) exterior; (visitor) estrangeiro

overshadow [əuvə'ʃædəu] vt ofuscar

oversight ['əuvəsait] n descuido

oversleep [əuvə'sliːp] (irreg) vi dormir além da hora

overt [əu'vəːt] adj aberto, indissimulado

overtake [əuvə'teik] (irreg) vt ultrapassar

overthrow [əuvə'θrəu] (irreg) vt (government) derrubar

overtime ['əuvətaim] n horas fpl extras

overtone ['əuvətəun] n (fig: also: ~s) implicação f, tom m

overture ['əuvətʃuə*] n (MUS) abertura; (fig) proposta, oferta

overturn [əuvə'təːn] vt virar; (system) derrubar; (decision) anular ♦ vi (car etc) capotar

overweight [əuvə'weit] adj gordo demais, com excesso de peso

overwhelm [əuvə'welm] vt esmagar, assolar; **overwhelming** adj (victory, defeat) esmagador(a); (heat) sufocante; (desire) irresistível

overwrought [əuvə'rɔːt] adj extenuado, superexcitado

owe [əu] vt: **to ~ sb sth, to ~ sth to sb** dever algo a alguém; **owing to** prep devido a, por causa de

owl [aul] n coruja

own [əun] *adj* próprio ♦ *vt* possuir, ter; **a room of my ~** meu próprio quarto; **to get one's ~ back** ir à forra; **on one's ~** sozinho; **own up** *vi*: **to ~ up to sth** confessar algo; **owner** *n* dono(-a), proprietário(-a); **ownership** *n* posse f

ox [ɔks] (*pl* **~en**) *n* boi *m*

oxtail ['ɔksteɪl] *n*: **~ soup** sopa de rabada

oxygen ['ɔksɪdʒən] *n* oxigênio

oyster ['ɔɪstə*] *n* ostra

oz. *abbr* = **ounce(s)**

ozone ['əuzəun] *n* ozônio; **ozone-friendly** *adj* (*products*) que não destrói a camada de ozônio; **ozone layer** *n* camada de ozônio

P

p [piː] *abbr* (= *page*) p; (*BRIT*) = **penny**; **pence**

PA *n abbr* = **personal assistant**; **public address system**

p.a. *abbr* (= *per annum*) p.a.

pace [peɪs] *n* passo *m*; (*speed*) velocidade f ♦ *vi*: **to ~ up and down** andar de um lado para o outro; **to keep ~ with** acompanhar o passo de; **pacemaker** *n* (*MED*) marcapasso *m*

Pacific [pə'sɪfɪk] *n*: **the ~ (Ocean)** (Oceano) Pacífico

pack [pæk] *n* pacote *m*, embrulho; (*US*: *of cigarettes*) maço *m*; (*of hounds*) matilha; (*of thieves*) bando, quadrilha; (*of cards*) baralho; (*back-*) mochila ♦ *vt* encher; (*in suitcase*) arrumar (na mala); (*cram*): **to ~** into entupir de, entulhar com; **to ~ (one's bags)** fazer as malas; **to ~ sb off** despedir alguém; **~ it in!** pára com isso!

package ['pækɪdʒ] *n* pacote *m*; (*bulky*) embrulho, fardo; (*also:* ~

deal) acordo global, pacote; **package tour** (*BRIT*) *n* excursão f organizada

packed lunch [pækt-] (*BRIT*) *n* merenda

packet ['pækɪt] *n* pacote *m*; (*of cigarettes*) maço m; (*of washing powder etc*) caixa

packing ['pækɪŋ] *n* embalagem f; (*act*) empacotamento

pad [pæd] *n* (*of paper*) bloco; (*to prevent friction*) acolchoado; (*inf*: *home*) casa ♦ *vt* acolchoar, enchumaçar

paddle ['pædl] *n* remo curto; (*US*: *for table tennis*) raquete f ♦ *vt* remar ♦ *vi* patinhar; **paddling pool** (*BRIT*) *n* lago de recreação

paddock ['pædək] *n* cercado; (*at race course*) paddock *m*

padlock ['pædlɔk] *n* cadeado

pagan ['peɪgən] *adj*, *n* pagão (pagã) *m/f*

page [peɪdʒ] *n* página; (*also:* ~ **boy**) mensageiro ♦ *vt* mandar chamar

pager ['peɪdʒə*], **paging device** ['peɪdʒɪŋ-] *n* bip *m*

paid [peɪd] *pt*, *pp* *of* **pay** ♦ *adj* (*work*) remunerado; (*holiday*) pago; (*official*) assalariado; **to put ~ to** (*BRIT*) acabar com

pail [peɪl] *n* balde *m*

pain [peɪn] *n* dor f; **to be in ~** sofrer *or* sentir dor; **to take ~s to do sth** dar-se ao trabalho de fazer algo; **painful** *adj* doloroso; (*laborious*) penoso; (*unpleasant*) desagradável; **painfully** *adv* (*fig*) terrivelmente; **painkiller** *n* analgésico; **painless** *adj* sem dor, indolor; **painstaking** ['peɪnzteɪkɪŋ] *adj* (*work*) esmerado; (*person*) meticuloso

paint [peɪnt] *n* pintura ♦ *vt* pintar; **paintbrush** *n* (*artist's*) pincel *m*; (*decorator's*) broxa; **painter** *n* (*artist*) pintor(a) *m/f*; (*decorator*

pintor(a) de paredes; **painting** n
pintura; (*picture*) tela, quadro;
paintwork n pintura
pair [pɛə*] n par m; **a ~ of scissors**
uma tesoura; **a ~ of trousers** uma
calça (BR), umas calças (PT)
pajamas [prˈdʒɑːməz] (US) npl pijama m
Pakistan [pɑːkɪˈstɑːn] n Paquistão
m; **Pakistani** adj, n paquista-
nês(-esa) m/f
pal [pæl] (inf) n camarada m/f, colega m/f
palace [ˈpæləs] n palácio
pale [peɪl] adj pálido; (*colour*) claro;
(*light*) fraco ♦ vi empalidecer ♦ n:
to be beyond the ~ passar dos limites
Palestine [ˈpælɪstaɪn] n Palestina;
Palestinian [pælɪsˈtɪnɪən] adj, n
palestino(-a)
palm [pɑːm] n (of hand) palma;
(*also*: **~ tree**) palmeira ♦ vt: **to ~ sth
off on sb** (inf) impingir algo a
alguém
pamper [ˈpæmpə*] vt paparicar,
mimar
pamphlet [ˈpæmflət] n panfleto
pan [pæn] n (also: **sauce~**) panela
(BR), caçarola (PT); (also: **frying ~**) frigideira
Panama [ˈpænəmɑː] n Panamá
m
pancake [ˈpænkeɪk] n panqueca
panda [ˈpændə] n panda m/f
pane [peɪn] n vidraça, vidro
panel [ˈpænl] n (of wood, RADIO, TV)
painel m; **panelling** (US **paneling**) n
painéis mpl
pang [pæŋ] n: **a ~ of regret** uma
sensação de pesar; **~s of hunger**
fome aguda
panic [ˈpænɪk] n pânico ♦ vi entrar
em pânico; **panicky** adj (person)
assustadiço, apavorado; **panic-**

stricken adj tomado de pânico
pansy [ˈpænzɪ] n (BOT) amor-perfeito;
(inf: pej) bicha (BR), maricas m (PT)
pant [pænt] vi arquejar, ofegar
panther [ˈpænθə*] n pantera
panties [ˈpæntɪz] npl calcinha (BR),
cuecas fpl (PT)
pantihose [ˈpæntɪhəʊz] (US) n
meia-calça (BR), collants mpl (PT)
pantomime [ˈpæntəmaɪm] (BRIT) n
pantomima; *ver quadro*

PANTOMIME

Uma **pantomime**, também chamada simplesmente de *panto*, é
um gênero de comédia em que o
personagem principal em geral é
um rapaz e na qual há sempre
uma *dame*, isto é, uma mulher
idosa representada por um homem, e um vilão. Na maior parte
das vezes, a história é baseada em
um conto de fadas, como "A gata
borralheira" ou "O gato de botas",
e a platéia é encorajada a participar prevenindo os heróis dos peri-
gos que estão por vir. Esse tipo de
espetáculo, voltado sobretudo
para as crianças, visa também ao
público adulto por meio de diver-
sas brincadeiras que fazem alusão
aos fatos atuais.

---

pantry [ˈpæntrɪ] n despensa
pants [pænts] npl (BRIT: underwear:
woman's) calcinha (BR), cuecas fpl
(PT); (: man's) cueca (BR), cuecas
fpl (PT); (US: trousers) calça (BR), calças
fpl (PT)
paper [ˈpeɪpə*] n (also: **news~**) jornal m; (also: **wall~**) papel
de parede; (study, article) artigo, dis-
sertação f; (exam) exame m, prova
♦ adj de papel ♦ vt (room) revestir
(com papel de parede); **~s** npl (also:

identity ~s) documentos mpl;
paperback n livro de capa mole;
paper bag n saco de papel; **paper
clip** n clipe m; **paper hankie** n
lenço de papel; **paperweight** n
pesa-papéis m inv; **paperwork** n
trabalho burocrático; (pej) papelada
par [pɑː*] n paridade f, igualdade f,
(GOLF) média f; **on a ~ with** em pé
de igualdade com
parachute ['pærəʃuːt] n pára-
quedas m inv
parade [pə'reɪd] n desfile m ♦ vt
(show off) exibir ♦ vi (MIL) passar
revista
paradise ['pærədaɪs] n paraíso
paraffin ['pærəfɪn] (BRIT) n: ~ (oil)
querosene m
paragraph ['pærəgrɑːf] n parágrafo
Paraguay ['pærəgwaɪ] n Paraguai m
parallel ['pærəlɛl] adj (lines etc)
paralelo; (fig) correspondente ♦ n
paralela; correspondência
paralyse ['pærəlaɪz] (BRIT) vt paralisar
paralysis [pə'rælɪsɪs] (pl paralyses)
n paralisia
paralyze ['pærəlaɪz] (US) vt = paralyse
paranoid ['pærənɔɪd] adj paranóico
parasol ['pærəsɔl] n guarda-sol m,
sombrinha
paratrooper ['pærətruːpə*] n pára-
quedista m/f
parcel ['pɑːsl] n pacote m vt (also:
~ up) embrulhar, empacotar
pardon ['pɑːdn] n (LAW) indulto ♦ vt
perdoar; ~ me!, I beg your ~
(apologizing) desculpe(-me); (I beg
your) ~? (BRIT), ~ me? (US) (not hearing) como?, como disse?
parent ['pɛərənt] n (father) pai m;
(mother) mãe f; ~s npl (mother and
father) pais mpl
Paris ['pærɪs] n Paris

parish ['pærɪʃ] n paróquia, freguesia
park [pɑːk] n parque m ♦ vt, vi estacionar
parking ['pɑːkɪŋ] n estacionamento; "no ~" "estacionamento proibido"; **parking lot** (US) n (parque
m de) estacionamento; **parking
meter** n parquímetro; **parking
ticket** n multa por estacionamento
proibido
parliament ['pɑːləmənt] (BRIT) n
parlamento
parlour ['pɑːlə*] (US parlor) n sala
de visitas, salão m, saleta
parochial [pə'rəukɪəl] (pej) adj provinciano
parole [pə'rəul] n: **on ~** em liberdade condicional, sob promessa
parrot ['pærət] n papagaio
parsley ['pɑːslɪ] n salsa
parsnip ['pɑːsnɪp] n cherivia, pasti-
naga
parson ['pɑːsn] n padre m, clérigo;
(in Church of England) pastor m
part [pɑːt] n parte f; (of machine)
peça; (THEATRE etc) papel m; (of serial)
capítulo; (US: in hair) risca, repartido
♦ adv = **partly** n vt dividir; (hair)
repartir ♦ vi (people) separar-se;
(crowd) dispersar-se; **to take ~ in**
participar de, tomar parte em; **to
take sb's ~** defender alguém; **for
my ~** pela minha parte; **for the
most** na maior parte; **to take sth
in good** não se ofender com algo;
part with vt fus ceder, entregar;
(money) pagar; **part exchange**
(BRIT) n: **in part exchange** como
parte do pagamento
partial ['pɑːʃl] adj parcial; **to be ~ to**
gostar de, ser apreciador(a) de
participate [pɑː'tɪsɪpeɪt] vi: **to
~ in** participar de; **participation**
[pɑːtɪsɪ'peɪʃən] n participação f
particle ['pɑːtɪkl] n partícula; (of

dust) grão *m*

particular [pə'tıkjulə*] *adj (special)* especial; *(specific)* específico; *(fussy)* exigente, minucioso; **in ~** em particular; **particularly** *adv* em particular, especialmente; **particulars** *npl* detalhes *mpl*; *(personal details)* dados *mpl* pessoais

parting ['pɑ:tıŋ] *n (act)* separação *f*; *(farewell)* despedida, *(BRIT: in hair)* risca, repartido ♦ *adj* de despedida

partition [pɑ:'tıʃən] *n (POL)* divisão *f*; *(wall)* tabique *m*, divisória

partly ['pɑ:tlı] *adv* em parte

partner ['pɑ:tnə*] *n (COMM)* sócio(-a); *(SPORT)* parceiro(-a); *(at dance)* par *m*; *(spouse)* cônjuge *m/f*; **partnership** *n* associação *f*, parceria; *(COMM)* sociedade *f*

partridge ['pɑ:trıdʒ] *n* perdiz *f*

part-time *adj, adv* de meio expediente

party ['pɑ:tı] *n (POL)* partido; *(celebration)* festa; *(group)* grupo; *(LAW)* parte *f* interessada, litigante *m/f* ♦ *cpd (POL)* do partido, partidário

pass [pɑ:s] *vt (exam)* passar em; *(place)* passar por; *(overtake)* ultrapassar; *(approve)* aprovar ♦ *vi* passar; *(SCH)* ser aprovado, passar ♦ *n (permit)* passe *m*; *(membership card)* carteira; *(in mountains)* desfiladeiro; *(SPORT)* passe *m*; *(SCH):* **to get a ~** ser aprovado em; **to make a ~ at sb** tomar liberdade com alguém; **pass away** *vi* falecer; **pass by** *vi* passar ♦ *vt* passar por cima de; **pass for** *vt fus* passar por; **pass on** *vt (news, illness)* transmitir; *(object)* passar para, passar; **pass out** *vi* desmaiar; **pass up** *vt* deixar passar; **passable** *adj (road)* transitável; *(work)* aceitável

passage ['pæsıdʒ] *n (also: ~way: indoors)* corredor *m*; (: *outdoors*)

passagem *f*; *(ANAT)* via; *(act of passing)* trânsito; *(in book)* passagem, trecho; *(by boat)* travessia

passenger ['pæsındʒə*] *n* passageiro(-a)

passer-by ['pɑ:sə*-] *(pl* **passers-by)** *n* transeunte *m/f*

passing ['pɑ:sıŋ] *adj (fleeting)* passageiro, fugaz; **in ~** de passagem

passion ['pæʃən] *n* paixão *f*; **passionate** *adj* apaixonado

passive ['pæsıv] *adj* passivo

passport ['pɑ:spɔ:t] *n* passaporte *m*

password ['pɑ:swə:d] *n* senha, contra-senha

past [pɑ:st] *prep (in front of)* por; *(beyond)* mais além de; *(later than)* depois de ♦ *adj* passado; *(president etc)* ex-, anterior ♦ *n* passado; **he's ~ forty** ele tem mais de quarenta anos; **ten/quarter ~ four** quatro e dez/quinze; **for the ~ few/3 days** nos últimos/3 dias

pasta ['pæstə] *n* massa

paste [peıst] *n* pasta; *(glue)* grude *m*, cola ♦ *vt* grudar; **tomato ~** massa de tomate

pasteurized ['pæstəraızd] *adj* pasteurizado

pastille ['pæstıl] *n* pastilha

pastime ['pɑ:staım] *n* passatempo

pastry ['peıstrı] *n* massa; *(cake)* bolo

pasture ['pɑ:stʃə*] *n* pasto

pasty [*n* 'pæstı, *adj* 'peıstı] *n* empadão *m* de carne ♦ *adj (complexion)* pálido

pat [pæt] *vt* dar palmadinhas em; *(dog etc)* fazer festa em

patch [pætʃ] *n* retalho *m*; *(eye ~)* tapa-olho *m*, tampão *m*; *(area)* área pequena; *(mend)* remendo ♦ *vt* remendar; **(to go through) a bad ~** (passar por) um mau pedaço; **patch up** *vt* consertar provisoriamente; *(quarrel)* resolver; **patchy**

adj (*colour*) desigual; (*information*) incompleto

pâté ['pæteɪ] *n* patê *m*

patent ['peɪtnt] *n* patente *f* ♦ *vt* patentear ♦ *adj* patente, evidente; **patent leather** *n* verniz *m*

paternal [pə'tɜːnl] *adj* paternal; (*relation*) paterno

path [pɑːθ] *n* caminho *m* (*trail*, *track*) trilha, senda; (*trajectory*) trajetória

pathetic [pə'θetɪk] *adj* (*pitiful*) patético, digno de pena; (*very bad*) péssimo

pathway ['pɑːθweɪ] *n* caminho, trilha

patience ['peɪʃns] *n* paciência

patient ['peɪʃnt] *adj*, *n* paciente *m/f*

patio ['pætɪəʊ] *n* pátio

patrol [pə'trəʊl] *n* patrulha ♦ *vt* patrulhar; **patrol car** *n* carro de patrulha; **patrolman** (*US*: *irreg*) *n* guarda *m*, policial *m* (*BR*), polícia *m* (*PT*)

patron ['peɪtrən] *n* (*customer*) cliente *m/f*, freguês(-esa) *m/f*; (*of charity*) benfeitor(a) *m/f*; **~ of the arts** mecenas *m*; **patronize** ['pætrənaɪz] *vt* (*pej*) tratar com ar de superioridade; (*shop*) ser cliente de; (*business*, *artist*) patrocinar

patter ['pætə*] *n* (*of rain*) tamborilada; (*of feet*) passos miúdos *mpl*; (*sales talk*) jargão *m* profissional ♦ *vi* correr dando passinhos; (*rain*) tamborilar

pattern ['pætən] *n* (*SEWING*) molde *m*; (*design*) desenho

pauper ['pɔːpə*] *n* pobre *m/f*

pause [pɔːz] *n* pausa ♦ *vi* fazer uma pausa

pave [peɪv] *vt* pavimentar; **to ~ the way for** preparar o terreno para

pavement ['peɪvmənt] (*BRIT*) *n* calçada (*BR*), passeio (*PT*)

pavilion [pə'vɪlɪən] *n* (*SPORT*) barraca

paving ['peɪvɪŋ] *n* pavimento, calçamento; **paving stone** *n* laje *f*, paralelepípedo

paw [pɔː] *n* pata; (*of cat*) garra

pawn [pɔːn] *n* (*CHESS*) peão *m*; (*fig*) títere *m* ♦ *vt* empenhar; **pawnbroker** *n* agiota *m/f*

pay [peɪ] (*pt*, *pp* **paid**) *n* salário; (*of manual worker*) paga ♦ *vt* pagar; (*debt*) liquidar, saldar; (*visit*) fazer ♦ *vi* valer a pena, render; **to ~ attention (to)** prestar atenção (a); **to ~ one's respects to sb** fazer uma visita de cortesia a alguém; **pay back** *vt* (*money*) devolver; (*person*) pagar; **pay for** *vt fus* pagar a; (*fig*) recompensar; **pay in** *vt* depositar; **pay off** *vt* (*debts*) saldar, liquidar; (*creditor*) pagar, reembolsar ♦ *vi* (*plan*) valer a pena; **pay up** *vi* pagar; **payable** *adj* pagável; (*cheque*): **payable to** nominal em favor de; **payee** [peɪ'iː] *n* beneficiário(-a); **payment** *n* pagamento; **monthly payment** *n* pagamento mensal; **pay packet** (*BRIT*) *n* envelope *m* de pagamento; **pay phone** *n* telefone *m* público; **payroll** *n* folha de pagamento; **pay television** *n* televisão *f* por assinatura

PC *n abbr* (= *personal computer*) PC *m*

pc *abbr* = **per cent**

pea [piː] *n* ervilha

peace [piːs] *n* paz *f*; (*calm*) tranqüilidade *f*, quietude *f*; **peaceful** *adj* (*person*) tranqüilo, pacífico; (*place*, *time*) tranqüilo, sossegado

peach [piːtʃ] *n* pêssego

peacock ['piːkɔk] *n* pavão *m*

peak [piːk] *n* (*of mountain*: *top*) cume *m*; (*of cap*) pala, viseira; (*fig*) apogeu *m*

peanut ['piːnʌt] *n* amendoim *m*; **peanut butter** *n* manteiga de amendoim

pear [pɛə*] *n* pêra

pearl [pɜːl] *n* pérola

peasant ['pɛznt] *n* camponês(-esa) *m/f*

peat [piːt] *n* turfa

pebble ['pɛbl] *n* seixo, calhau *m*

peck [pɛk] *vt* (*also*: ~ **at**) bicar, dar bicadas em ♦ *n* bicada; (*kiss*) beijoca; **peckish** (*BRIT: inf*) *adj*: **I feel peckish** estou a fim de comer alguma coisa

peculiar [pɪˈkjuːlɪə*] *adj* (*strange*) estranho, esquisito; (*belonging to*): ~ **to** próprio de

pedal ['pɛdl] *n* pedal *m* ♦ *vi* pedalar

pedestrian [pɪˈdɛstrɪən] *n* pedestre *m/f* (*BR*), peão *m* (*PT*) ♦ *adj* (*fig*) prosaico; **pedestrian crossing** *n* passagem *f* para pedestres (*BR*), passadeira (*PT*)

pedigree ['pɛdɪgriː] *n* raça; (*fig*) genealogia ♦ *cpd* (*animal*) de raça

pee [piː] (*inf*) *vi* fazer xixi, mijar

peek [piːk] *vi*: **to** ~ **at** espiar, espreitar

peel [piːl] *n* casca ♦ *vt* descascar ♦ *vi* (*paint, skin*) descascar; (*wallpaper*) desprender-se

peep [piːp] *n* (*BRIT: look*) espiadela; (*sound*) pio ♦ *vi* espreitar; **peep out** (*BRIT*) *vi* mostrar-se, surgir; **peephole** *n* vigia, olho mágico

peer [pɪə*] *vi*: **to** ~ **at** perscrutar, fitar ♦ *n* (*noble*) par *m/f*; (*equal*) igual *m/f*; (*contemporary*) contemporâneo(-a)

peg [pɛg] *n* (*for coat etc*) cabide *m*; (*BRIT: also: clothes* ~) pregador *m*

pelican ['pɛlɪkən] *n* pelicano

pellet ['pɛlɪt] *n* bolinha; (*for shotgun*) pelota de chumbo

pelt [pɛlt] *vt*: **to** ~ **sb with sth** atirar algo em alguém ♦ *vi* (*rain: also*: ~ **down**) chover a cântaros; (*inf: run*)

pelvis ['pɛlvɪs] *n* pelvis *f*, bacia

pen [pɛn] *n* caneta; (*for sheep etc*) redil *m*, cercado

penal ['piːnl] *adj* penal; **penalize** ['piːnəlaɪz] *vt* impor penalidade a; (*SPORT*) penalizar

penalty ['pɛnltɪ] *n* pena, penalidade *f*; (*fine*) multa; (*SPORT*) punição *f*

pence [pɛns] (*BRIT*) *npl of* **penny**

pencil ['pɛnsl] *n* lápis *m*; **pencil case** *n* lapiseira, porta-lápis *m inv*; **pencil sharpener** *n* apontador *m* (de lápis) (*BR*), apara-lápis *m inv* (*PT*)

pendant ['pɛndnt] *n* pingente *m*

pending ['pɛndɪŋ] *prep, adj* pendente

penetrate ['pɛnɪtreɪt] *vt* penetrar

penfriend ['pɛnfrɛnd] (*BRIT*) *n* amigo(-a) por correspondência, correspondente *m/f*

penguin ['pɛŋgwɪn] *n* pingüim *m*

peninsula [pəˈnɪnsjulə] *n* península

penis ['piːnɪs] *n* pênis *m*

penitentiary [pɛnɪˈtɛnʃərɪ] (*US*) *n* penitenciária, presídio

penknife ['pɛnnaɪf] (*irreg*) *n* canivete *m*

penniless ['pɛnɪlɪs] *adj* sem dinheiro, sem um tostão

penny ['pɛnɪ] *n* (*pl pennies or* (*BRIT*) **pence**) *n* pêni *m*; (*US*) cêntimo

penpal ['pɛnpæl] *n* amigo(-a) por correspondência, correspondente *m/f*

pension ['pɛnʃən] *n* pensão *f*; (*old-age* ~) aposentadoria, pensão do governo; **pensioner** (*BRIT*) *n* aposentado(-a) (*BR*), reformado(-a) (*PT*)

Pentagon ['pɛntəgən] *n*: **the** ~ o Pentágono; *ver quadro*

penthouse ['penthaus] n cobertura

pent-up [pent-] adj reprimido

people ['pi:pl] npl gente f, pessoas fpl; (inhabitants) habitantes m/fpl; (citizens) povo; (POL): **the ~** o povo ♦ n povo; **several ~ came** vieram várias pessoas; **~ say that** ... dizem que ...

pepper ['pepə*] n pimenta; (vegetable) pimentão m ♦ vt apimentar; (fig): **to ~ with** salpicar de; **peppermint** n (sweet) bala de hortelã

peptalk ['peptɔ:k] (inf) n conversa para levantar o espírito

per [pə:*] prep por

perceive [pə'si:v] vt perceber; (notice) notar; (realize) compreender

per cent n por cento

percentage [pə'sentɪdʒ] n porcentagem f, percentagem f

perceptive [pə'septɪv] adj perceptivo

perch [pə:tʃ] (pl ~es or ~ fish) n (for bird) poleiro; (pl: inv or ~es: fish) perca ♦ vi: **to ~ (on)** (bird) empoleirar-se (em); (person) encarapitar-se (em)

percolator ['pə:kəleɪtə*] n (also: **coffee ~**) cafeteira de filtro

perfect [adj, n 'pə:fɪkt, vb pə'fekt] adj perfeito; (utter) completo ♦ n (also: **~ tense**) perfeito ♦ vt aperfeiçoar; **perfectly** adv perfeitamente

perform [pə'fɔ:m] vt (carry out) realizar, fazer; (piece of music) interpretar ♦ vi (well, badly) interpretar; **performance** n desempenho; (of play, by artist) atuação f; (of car) performance f; **performer** n (actor) artista m/f, ator (atriz) m/f; (MUS) intérprete m/f

perfume ['pə:fju:m] n perfume m

perhaps [pə'hæps] adv talvez

peril ['perɪl] n perigo, risco

perimeter [pə'rɪmɪtə*] n perímetro

period ['pɪərɪəd] n período; (SCH) aula; (full stop) ponto final; (MED) menstruação f, regra ♦ adj (costume, furniture) da época; **periodic(al)** [pɪərɪ'ɔdɪk(l)] adj periódico; **periodical** [pɪərɪ'ɔdɪkl] n periódico

peripheral [pə'rɪfərəl] adj periférico ♦ n (COMPUT) periférico

perish ['perɪʃ] vi perecer; (decay) deteriorar-se

perjury ['pə:dʒərɪ] n (LAW) perjúrio, falso testemunho

perk [pə:k] (inf) n mordomia, regalia; **perk up** vi (cheer up) animar-se

perm [pə:m] n permanente f

permanent ['pə:mənənt] adj permanente

permission [pə'mɪʃən] n permissão f; (authorization) autorização f

permit [n 'pə:mɪt, vb pə'mɪt] n licença; (to enter) passe m ♦ vt permitir; (authorize) autorizar

perplex [pə'pleks] vt deixar perplexo

persecute ['pə:sɪkju:t] vt importunar

persevere [pə:sɪ'vɪə*] vi perseverar

Persian ['pə:ʃən] adj persa ♦ n (LING) persa m; **the (~) Gulf** o golfo Pérsico

persist [pə'sɪst] vi: **to ~ (in)** persistir (em); **persistent** [pə'sɪstənt] adj persistente; (determined) teimoso

person ['pə:sn] n pessoa; **in ~** em

pessoa; **personal** adj pessoal; (private) particular; (visit) em pessoa, pessoal; **personal assistant** n secretário(-a) particular; **personal computer** n computador m pessoal; **personality** [pə:sə'næliti] n personalidade f; **personal organizer** n agenda; **personal stereo** n Walkman ® m

personnel [pə:sə'nel] n pessoal m

perspective [pə'spɛktiv] n perspectiva

Perspex ['pə:spɛks] ® (BRIT) n Blindex ® m

perspiration [pə:spi'reiʃən] n transpiração f

persuade [pə'sweid] vt: to ~ sb to do sth persuadir alguém a fazer algo

Peru [pə'ru:] n Peru m

pervert [n pə:və:t] n pervertido(-a) ♦ vt perverter, corromper; (truth) distorcer

pessimist ['pɛsimist] n pessimista m/f; **pessimistic** [pɛsi'mistik] adj pessimista

pest [pɛst] n (insect) inseto nocivo; (fig) peste f

pester ['pɛstə*] vt incomodar

pet [pɛt] n animal m de estimação ♦ cpd predileto ♦ vt acariciar ♦ vi acariciar-se; **teacher's ~** (favourite) preferido(-a) do professor

petal ['pɛtl] n pétala

peter out ['pi:tə*-] vi (conversation) esgotar-se; (road etc) acabar-se

petite [pə'ti:t] adj delicado, mignon

petition [pə'tiʃən] n petição f; (list of signatures) abaixo-assinado

petrified ['pɛtrifaid] adj (fig) petrificado, paralisado

petrol ['pɛtrəl] (BRIT) n gasolina; **two-/four-star ~** gasolina de duas/ quatro estrelas

petroleum [pə'trəuliəm] n petróleo

petrol: **petrol pump** (BRIT) n bomba de gasolina; **petrol station** (BRIT) n posto (BR) ou bomba (PT) de gasolina; **petrol tank** (BRIT) n tanque m de gasolina

petticoat ['pɛtikəut] n anágua

petty ['pɛti] adj (mean) mesquinho; (unimportant) insignificante; **petty cash** n fundo para despesas miúdas, caixa pequena, fundo de caixa

pew [pju:] n banco (de igreja)

pewter ['pju:tə*] n peltre m

phantom ['fæntəm] n fantasma m

pharmacy ['fɑ:məsi] n farmácia

phase [feiz] n fase f ♦ vt: to ~ in/out introduzir/retirar por etapas

PhD n abbr = Doctor of Philosophy

pheasant ['fɛznt] n faisão m

phenomenon [fə'nɔminən] (pl phenomena) n fenômeno

philosophical [filə'sɔfikl] adj filosófico; (fig) calmo, sereno

philosophy [fi'lɔsəfi] n filosofia

phobia ['fəubjə] n fobia

phone [fəun] n telefone m ♦ vt telefonar para, ligar para; **to be on the ~** ter telefone; (be calling) estar no telefone; **phone back** vt, vi ligar de volta; **phone up** vt telefonar para ♦ vi telefonar; **phone book** n lista telefônica; **phone box** (BRIT) n cabine f telefônica; **phone call** n telefonema m, ligada; **phone card** n cartão para uso em telefone público; **phone-in** (BRIT) n (RADIO) programa com participação dos ouvintes; (TV) programa com participação dos espectadores; **phone number** n (número de) telefone m

phonetics [fə'nɛtiks] n fonética

phoney ['fəuni] adj falso; (person) fingido

photo ['fəutəu] n foto f

photo... ['fəutəu] prefix foto...; **photocopier** n fotocopiadora f;

photocopy n fotocópia, xerox ®
m ♦ vt fotocopiar, xerocar

photograph ['fəʊtəgra:f] n fotografia ♦ vt fotografar; **photographer** [fə'tɒgrəfə*] n fotógrafo(-a); **photography** [fə'tɒgrəfɪ] n fotografia

phrase [freɪz] n frase f ♦ vt expressar; **phrase book** n livro de expressões idiomáticas (para turistas)

physical ['fɪzɪkl] adj físico

physician [fɪ'zɪʃən] n médico(-a)

physics ['fɪzɪks] n física

physiotherapy [fɪzɪəʊ'θerəpɪ] n fisioterapia

physique [fɪ'zi:k] n físico

pianist ['pɪənɪst] n pianista m/f

piano [pɪ'ænəʊ] n piano

pick [pɪk] n (tool: also: ~axe) picareta ♦ vt (select) escolher, selecionar; (gather) colher; (remove) tirar; (lock) forçar; **take your** ~ escolha o que quiser; **the** ~ **of** o melhor de; **to** ~ **one's nose** colocar o dedo no nariz; **to** ~ **one's teeth** palitar os dentes; **to** ~ **a quarrel with sb** comprar uma briga com alguém; **pick at** vt fus (food) beliscar; **pick on** vt fus (person: criticize) criticar; (: treat badly) azucrinar, aporrinhar; **pick out** vt escolher; (distinguish) distinguir; **pick up** vi (improve) melhorar ♦ vt (from floor, AUT) apanhar; (collect) buscar; (for sexual encounter) paquerar; (learn) aprender; (RADIO) pegar; **to** ~ **up speed** acelerar; **to** ~ **o.s. up** levantar-se

picket ['pɪkɪt] n (in strike) piquete m ♦ vt formar piquete em frente de

pickle ['pɪkl] n (also: ~s: as condiment) picles mpl; (fig: mess) apuro ♦ vt (in vinegar) conservar em vinagre; (in salt) conservar em sal e água

pickpocket ['pɪkpɒkɪt] n batedor(a) m/f de carteira (BR),

carteirista m/f (PT)

picnic ['pɪknɪk] n piquenique m

picture ['pɪktʃə*] n quadro; (painting) pintura; (drawing) desenho; (etching) água-forte f; (photograph) foto(grafia) f; (TV) imagem f; (film) filme m; (fig: description) descrição f; (: situation) conjuntura ♦ vt imaginar-se; **the** ~**s** npl (BRIT: inf) o cinema; **picture book** n livro de figuras

pie [paɪ] n (vegetable) pastelão m; (fruit) torta; (meat) empadão m

piece [pi:s] n pedaço; (portion) fatia; (item): **a** ~ **of clothing/furniture/advice** uma roupa/um móvel/um conselho ♦ vt: **to** ~ **together** juntar; **to take to** ~**s** desmontar; **piecemeal** adv pouco a pouco; **piecework** n trabalho por empreitada ou peça

pie chart n gráfico de setores

pier [pɪə*] n cais m; (jetty) embarcadouro, molhe m

pierce [pɪəs] n furar, perfurar

pig [pɪg] n porco; (fig) porcalhão(-lhona) m/f; (pej: unkind person) grosseiro(-a); (: greedy person) ganancioso(-a)

pigeon ['pɪdʒən] n pombo; **pigeonhole** n escaninho

piggy bank ['pɪgɪ-] n cofre em forma de porquinho

pigskin ['pɪgskɪn] n couro de porco

pigsty ['pɪgstaɪ] n chiqueiro

pigtail ['pɪgteɪl] n rabo-de-cavalo, trança

pike [paɪk] n (pl inv or ~s) (fish) lúcio

pilchard ['pɪltʃəd] n sardinha

pile [paɪl] n (heap) monte m; (of carpet) pêlo; (of cloth) lado felpudo ♦ vt (also: ~ up) empilhar ♦ vi (also: ~ up: objects) empilhar-se; (: problems, work) acumular-se; **pile into** vt fus (car) apinhar-se

piles [paɪlz] *npl* hemorróidas *fpl*

pile-up *n* (AUT) engavetamento

pilgrim ['pɪlgrɪm] *n* peregrino(-a)

pill [pɪl] *n* pílula; **the ~** a pílula

pillar ['pɪlə*] *n* pilar *m*; **pillar box** (BRIT) *n* caixa coletora (do correio) (BR), marco do correio (PT)

pillion ['pɪljən] *n*: **to ride ~** andar na garupa

pillow ['pɪləʊ] *n* travesseiro (BR), almofada (PT); **pillowcase** *n* fronha

pilot ['paɪlət] *n* piloto(-a) ♦ *cpd* (scheme etc) piloto *inv* ♦ *vt* pilotar; **pilot light** *n* piloto

pimp [pɪmp] *n* cafetão *m* (BR), cáften *m* (PT)

pimple ['pɪmpl] *n* espinha

PIN [pɪn] *n abbr* (= *personal identification number*) número de identificação pessoal, senha

pin [pɪn] *n* alfinete *m* ♦ *vt* alfinetar; **~s and needles** comichão *f*, sensação *f* de formigamento; **to ~ sth on sb** (fig) culpar alguém de algo; **pin down** *vt* (fig): **to ~ sb down** conseguir que alguém se defina or tome atitude

pinafore ['pɪnəfɔ:*] *n* (also: **~ dress**) avental *m*

pincers ['pɪnsəz] *npl* pinça, tenaz *f*

pinch [pɪntʃ] *n* (of salt etc) pitada ♦ *vt* beliscar; (inf: steal) afanar; **at a ~** em último caso

pincushion ['pɪnkʊʃən] *n* alfineteira

pine [paɪn] *n* pinho ♦ *vi*: **to ~ for** ansiar por; **pine away** *vi* consumir-se, definhar

pineapple ['paɪnæpl] *n* abacaxi *m* (BR), ananás *m* (PT)

ping-pong ['pɪŋpɔŋ] ® *n* pingue-pongue *m*

pink [pɪŋk] *adj* cor de rosa *inv* ♦ *n* (colour) cor *f* de rosa; (BOT) cravo, cravina

PIN number ['pɪn-] *n* = PIN

pinpoint ['pɪnpɔɪnt] *vt* (discover) descobrir; (explain) identificar; (locate) localizar com precisão

pint [paɪnt] *n* quartilho (BRIT: = 568cc; US: = 473cc)

pioneer [paɪə'nɪə*] *n* pioneiro(-a)

pious ['paɪəs] *adj* pio, devoto

pip [pɪp] *n* (seed) caroço, semente *f*; **the ~s** *npl* (BRIT: time signal on radio) = o toque de seis segundos

pipe [paɪp] *n* cano; (for smoking) cachimbo ♦ *vt* canalizar, encanar; **~s** *npl* (also: **bagpipes**) gaita de foles; **pipe down** (inf) *vi* calar o bico, meter a viola no saco; **pipeline** *n* (for oil) oleoduto; (for gas) gaseoduto

piping ['paɪpɪŋ] *adv*: **~ hot** chiando de quente

pirate ['paɪərət] *n* pirata *m* ♦ *vt* piratear

Pisces ['paɪsi:z] *n* Pisces *m*, Peixes *mpl*

piss [pɪs] (inf!) *vi* mijar; **pissed** (inf!) *adj* (drunk) bêbado, de porre

pistol ['pɪstl] *n* pistola

piston ['pɪstən] *n* pistão *m*, êmbolo

pit [pɪt] *n* cova, fossa; (quarry, hole in surface of sth) buraco; (also: **coal ~**) mina de carvão ♦ *vt*: **to ~ one's wits against sb** competir em conhecimento or inteligência contra alguém; **~s** *npl* (AUT) box *m*

pitch [pɪtʃ] *n* (MUS) tom *m*; (fig: degree) intensidade *f*; (BRIT: SPORT) campo; (tar) piche *m*, breu *m* ♦ *vt* (throw) arremessar, lançar; (tent) armar ♦ *vi* (fall forwards) cair (para frente); **pitch-black** *adj* escuro como o breu

pitfall ['pɪtfɔ:l] *n* perigo (imprevisto), armadilha

pitiful ['pɪtɪful] *adj* comovente, tocante

pittance ['pɪtns] n ninharia, miséria

pity ['pɪtɪ] n compaixão f, piedade f
♦ vt ter pena de, compadecer-se de

pizza ['pi:tsə] n pizza

placard ['plækɑ:d] n placar m; (in march etc) cartaz m

placate [plə'keɪt] vt apaziguar, aplacar

place [pleɪs] n lugar m; (position) posição f; (post) posto; (role) papel m; (home): **at/to his ~** na/para a casa dele ♦ vt por, colocar; (identify) identificar, situar; **to take ~** realizar-se; (occur) ocorrer; **out of ~** (not suitable) fora de lugar, deslocado; **in the first ~** em primeiro lugar; **to change ~s with sb** trocar de lugar com alguém; **to be ~d** (in race, exam) classificar-se

plague [pleɪg] n (MED) peste f; (fig) praga ♦ vt atormentar, importunar

plaice [pleɪs] n inv solha

plain [pleɪn] adj (unpatterned) liso; (clear) claro, evidente; (simple) simples inv, despretensioso; (not handsome) sem atrativos ♦ adv claramente, com franqueza ♦ n planície f, campina; **plain chocolate** n chocolate m amargo; **plain-clothes** adj (police officer) à paisana; **plainly** adv claramente, obviamente; (hear, see) facilmente; (state) francamente

plaintiff ['pleɪntɪf] n querelante m/f, queixoso(-a)

plait [plæt] n trança, dobra

plan [plæn] n plano; (scheme) projeto; (schedule) programa m ♦ vt planejar (BR), planear (PT) ♦ vi fazer planos; **to ~ to do** pretender fazer

plane [pleɪn] n (AVIAT) avião m; (also: **~ tree**) plátano; (fig) nível m; (tool) plaina; (MATH) plano

planet ['plænɪt] n planeta m

plank [plæŋk] n tábua

planning ['plænɪŋ] n planejamento

(BR), planeamento (PT); **family ~** planejamento or planeamento familiar

plant [plɑ:nt] n planta; (machinery) maquinaria; (factory) usina, fábrica ♦ vt plantar; (field) semear; (bomb) colocar, pôr

plaster ['plɑ:stə*] n (for walls) reboco; (also: **~ of Paris**) gesso; (BRIT: also: **sticking ~**) esparadrapo, band-aid m ♦ vt rebocar; (cover): **to ~ with** encher or cobrir de; **plastered** (inf) adj bêbado, de porre

plastic ['plæstɪk] n plástico ♦ adj de plástico; **plastic bag** n sacola de plástico

plastic surgery n cirurgia plástica

plate [pleɪt] n prato, chapa; (dental) chapa; (in book) gravura; **gold/silver ~** n placa de ouro/prata

plateau ['plætəu] (pl **~s** or **~x**) n planalto

platform ['plætfɔ:m] n (RAIL) plataforma (BR), cais m (PT); (at meeting) tribuna; (raised structure: for landing etc) plataforma; (BRIT: of bus) plataforma; (POL) programa m partidário

platinum ['plætɪnəm] n platina

plausible ['plɔ:zɪbl] adj plausível; (person) convincente

play [pleɪ] n (THEATRE) obra, peça ♦ vt jogar; (team) jogar contra; (music) tocar; (role) fazer o papel de ♦ vi (music) tocar; (frolic) brincar; **to ~ safe** não se arriscar, não correr riscos; **play down** vt minimizar; **play up** vi (person) dar trabalho; (TV, car) estar com defeito; **playboy** n playboy m; **player** n jogador(a) m/f; (THEATRE) ator (atriz) m/f; (MUS) músico(-a); **playful** adj brincalhão(-lhona); **playground** n (in park) playground m; (in school) pátio de recreio; **playgroup** n espécie de jardim de infância; **playing card** n carta de baralho; **playing**

field n campo de esportes (BR) or jogos (PT); **playmate** n colega m/f, camarada m/f; **playpen** n cercado para crianças; **plaything** n brinquedo; (fig) joguete m; **playtime** n (SCH) recreio; **playwright** n dramaturgo(-a)

plc abbr = public limited company

plea [pli:] n (request) apelo, petição f; (LAW) defesa

plead [pli:d] vt (LAW) advogar; (give as excuse) alegar ♦ vi (LAW) declarar-se; (beg): **to ~ with sb** suplicar or rogar a alguém

pleasant ['plɛznt] adj agradável; (person) simpático

please [pli:z] excl por favor ♦ vt agradar a, dar prazer a ♦ vi agradar, dar prazer; (think fit): **do as you ~** faça o que or como quiser; **~ yourself!** (inf) como você quiser!, você que sabe!; **pleased** adj (happy): **pleased (with)** satisfeito (com); **pleased to meet you** prazer (em conhecê-lo); **pleasing** adj agradável

pleasure ['plɛʒə*] n prazer m; "it's a ~" "não tem de quê"

pleat [pli:t] n prega

pledge [plɛdʒ] n (promise) promessa ♦ vt prometer; **to ~ support for sb** empenhar-se a apoiar alguém

plentiful ['plɛntɪful] adj abundante

plenty ['plɛntɪ] n: **~ of** (of food, money) bastante; (jobs, people) muitos(-as)

pliable ['plaɪəbl] adj flexível; (fig: person) adaptável, moldável

pliers ['plaɪəz] npl alicate m

plimsolls ['plɪmsəlz] (BRIT) npl tênis mpl

plod [plɔd] vi caminhar pesadamente; (fig) trabalhar laboriosamente

plonk [plɔŋk] (inf) n (BRIT: wine) zurrapa ♦ vt: **to ~ sth down** deixar cair algo (pesadamente)

plot [plɔt] n (scheme) conspiração f,

complô m; (of story, play) enredo, trama; (of land) lote m ♦ vt (conspire) tramar, planejar (BR), planear (PT); (AVIAT, NAUT, MATH) plotar ♦ vi conspirar; **a vegetable ~** (BRIT) uma horta

plough [plau] (US **plow**) n arado m, arar; **to ~ money into** investir dinheiro em; **plough through** vt fus abrir caminho por; **ploughman's lunch** (BRIT) n lanche de pão, queijo e picles

ploy [plɔɪ] n estratagema m

pluck [plʌk] vt (fruit) colher; (musical instrument) dedilhar; (bird) depenar ♦ n coragem f, puxão m; **to ~ one's eyebrows** fazer as sobrancelhas; **to ~ up courage** criar coragem

plug [plʌg] n (ELEC) tomada (BR), ficha (PT); (in sink) tampa; (AUT: also: **spark(ing) ~**) vela (de ignição) f; (hole) tapar; (inf: advertise) fazer propaganda de; **plug in** vt (ELEC) ligar

plum [plʌm] n (fruit) ameixa ♦ cpd (inf): **a ~ job** um emprego jóia

plumber ['plʌmə*] n bombeiro(-a) (BR), encanador(a) m/f (BR), canalizador(a) m/f (PT)

plumbing ['plʌmɪŋ] n (trade) ofício de encanador; (piping) encanamento

plummet ['plʌmɪt] vi: **to ~ (down)** (bird, aircraft) cair rapidamente; (price) baixar rapidamente

plump [plʌmp] adj roliço, rechonchudo ♦ vi: **to ~ for** (inf: choose) escolher, optar por; **plump up** vt (cushion) afofar

plunder ['plʌndə*] n pilhagem f; (loot) despojo ♦ vt pilhar, espoliar

plunge [plʌndʒ] n (dive) salto; (fig) queda ♦ vt (hand, knife) enfiar, meter ♦ vi (fall, fig) cair; (dive) mergulhar; **to take the ~** topar a parada

plural ['pluərl] *adj* plural ♦ *n* plural *m*

plus [plʌs] *n* (*also*: **~ sign**) sinal *m* de adição ♦ *prep* mais; **ten/twenty ~** dez/vinte e tantos

plush [plʌʃ] *adj* suntuoso

ply [plaɪ] *n* (*of wool*) fio ♦ *vt* (*a trade*) exercer ♦ *vi* (*ship*) ir e vir; **to ~ sb with drink/questions** bombardear alguém com bebidas/perguntas

plywood *n* madeira compensada

PM (*BRIT*) *n abbr* = **Prime Minister**

p.m. *adv abbr* (= *post meridiem*) da tarde, da noite

PMT *n abbr* (= *premenstrual tension*) TPM *f*, tensão *f* pré-menstrual

pneumatic drill [nju:'mætɪk-] *n* perfuratriz *f*

poach [pəʊtʃ] *vt* (*COOK: fish*) escaldar; (: *eggs*) fazer pochê (*BR*), escalfar (*PT*); (*steal*) furtar ♦ *vi* caçar (or pescar) em propriedade alheia

PO Box *n abbr* (= *Post Office Box*) caixa postal

pocket ['pɒkɪt] *n* bolso; (*fig: small area*) pedaço ♦ *vt* meter no bolso; (*steal*) embolsar; **to be out of ~** (*BRIT*) perder, ter prejuízo; **pocket-book** (*US*) *n* carteira; **pocket knife** (*irreg*) *n* canivete *m*; **pocket money** *n* dinheiro para despesas miúdas; (*for child*) mesada

pod [pɒd] *n* vagem *f*

podgy ['pɒdʒɪ] (*inf*) *adj* gorducho, rechonchudo

podiatrist [pɔ'di:ətrɪst] (*US*) *n* pedicuro(-a)

poem ['pəʊɪm] *n* poema *m*

poet ['pəʊɪt] *n* poeta (poetisa) *m/f*; **poetic** [pəʊ'etɪk] *adj* poético; **poetry** ['pəʊɪtrɪ] *n* poesia

point [pɔɪnt] *n* ponto; (*of needle etc*) ponta; (*purpose*) finalidade *f*; (*significant part*) ponto principal; (*position*) lugar *m*, posição *f*; (*moment*)

momento; (*stage*) estágio; (*ELEC: also*: **power ~**) tomada; (*ELEC: decimal ~*): **2 ~ 3 (2.3)** dois vírgula três ♦ *vt* mostrar; (*gun etc*): **to ~ sth at sb** apontar algo para alguém ♦ *vi*: **to ~ at** apontar para; **~s** *npl* (*AUT*) platinado, contato; (*RAIL*) agulhas *fpl*; **to be on the ~ of doing sth** estar prestes a *or* a ponto de fazer algo; **to make a ~ of** fazer questão de, insistir em; **to get the ~** perceber; **to miss the ~** compreender mal; **to come to the ~** ir ao assunto; **there's no ~ (in doing)** não há razão (para fazer); **point out** *vt* (*in debate etc*) ressaltar; **point to** *vt fus* (*fig*) indicar; **point-blank** *adv* categoricamente; (*also*: **at point-blank range**) à queima-roupa; **pointed** *adj* (*stick etc*) pontudo; (*remark*) mordaz; **pointer** *n* (*on chart*) indicador *m*; (*on machine*) ponteiro; (*fig*) dica; **pointless** *adj* (*useless*) inútil; (*senseless*) sem sentido; **point of view** *n* ponto de vista

poise [pɔɪz] *n* (*composure*) elegância; (*calmness*) serenidade *f*

poison ['pɔɪzn] *n* veneno ♦ *vt* envenenar; **poisonous** *adj* venenoso; (*fumes etc*) tóxico

poke [pəʊk] *vt* cutucar; (*put*): **to ~ sth in(to)** enfiar *or* meter algo em; **poke about** *vi* escarafunchar

poker ['pəʊkə*] *n* atiçador *m* (de brasas); (*CARDS*) pôquer *m*

Poland ['pəʊlənd] *n* Polônia

polar ['pəʊlə*] *adj* polar; **polar bear** *n* urso polar

Pole [pəʊl] *n* polonês(-esa) *m/f*

pole [pəʊl] *n* vara; (*GEO*) pólo; (*telegraph ~*) poste *m*; (*flag~*) mastro; **pole bean** (*US*) *n* feijão-trepador *m*; **pole vault** *n* salto com vara

police [pə'li:s] *n* polícia ♦ *vt* policiar; **police car** *n* rádio-patrulha *f*

policeman (*irreg*) n policial m (*BR*), polícia m (*PT*); **police station** n delegacia (de polícia) (*BR*), esquadra (*PT*); **policewoman** (*irreg*) n policial f (feminina) (*BR*), mulher f polícia (*PT*)

policy ['pɔlɪsɪ] n política; (*also*: **insurance ~**) apólice f

polio ['pəʊlɪəʊ] n polio(mielite) f

Polish ['pəʊlɪʃ] adj polonês(-esa) ♦ n (*LING*) polonês m

polish ['pɔlɪʃ] n (for shoes) graxa; (for floor) cera (para encerar); (shine) brilho; (fig) refinamento, requinte m ♦ vt (shoes) engraxar; (make shiny) lustrar, dar brilho a; **polish off** vt (work) dar os arremates a; (food) raspar

polite [pə'laɪt] adj educado; **politeness** n gentileza, cortesia

political [pə'lɪtɪkl] adj político

politician [pɔlɪ'tɪʃən] n político(-a)

politics ['pɔlɪtɪks] n, npl política f

poll [pəʊl] n (in votes) votação f; (also: **opinion ~**) pesquisa, sondagem f ♦ vt (votes) receber, obter

pollen ['pɔlən] n pólen m

polling day ['pəʊlɪŋ-] (*BRIT*) n dia m de eleição

pollute [pə'luːt] vt poluir; **pollution** n poluição f

polo-necked ['pəʊləʊnɛkt] adj de gola rulê

polyester [pɔlɪ'ɛstə*] n poliéster m

polystyrene [pɔlɪ'staɪriːn] n isopor ® m

polythene ['pɔlɪθiːn] n politeno

pomegranate ['pɔmɪɡrænɪt] n romã f

pond [pɔnd] n (natural) lago pequeno; (artificial) tanque m

ponder ['pɔndə*] vt, vi ponderar, meditar (sobre)

pony ['pəʊnɪ] n pônei m; **ponytail** n rabo-de-cavalo; **pony trekking**

(*BRIT*) n excursão f em pônei

poodle ['puːdl] n cão-d'água m

pool [puːl] n (puddle) poça, charco; (pond) lago; (also: **swimming ~**) piscina; (fig: of light) feixe m; (: of liquid) poça; (*SPORT*) sinuca ♦ vt juntar; **~s** npl (football ~s) loteria esportiva (*BR*), totobola (*PT*); **typing** (*BRIT*) or **secretary** (*US*) **~** seção f de datilografia

poor [pʊə*] adj pobre; (bad) inferior, mau ♦ npl: **the ~s** os pobres; **~ in** (resources etc) deficiente em; **poorly** adj adoentado, indisposto ♦ adv mal

pop [pɔp] n (sound) estalo, estouro; (*MUS*) pop m; (*US*: inf: father) papai m; (inf: fizzy drink) bebida gasosa ♦ vt: **to ~ sth into/onto** etc (put) pôr em/sobre etc ♦ vi estourar; (cork) saltar; **pop in** vi dar um pulo; **pop out** vi dar uma saída; **pop up** vi surgir, aparecer inesperadamente; **popcorn** n pipoca

pope [pəʊp] n papa m

poplar ['pɔplə*] n álamo, choupo

poppy ['pɔpɪ] n papoula

popsicle ['pɔpsɪkl] ® (*US*) n picolé m

popular ['pɔpjʊlə*] adj popular; (person) querido

population [pɔpjʊ'leɪʃən] n população f

porcelain ['pɔːslɪn] n porcelana

porch [pɔːtʃ] n pórtico; (*US*: verandah) varanda

porcupine ['pɔːkjʊpaɪn] n porcoespinho

pore [pɔː*] n poro ♦ vi: **to ~ over** examinar minuciosamente

pork [pɔːk] n carne f de porco

pornography [pɔː'nɔɡrəfɪ] n pornografia

porpoise ['pɔːpəs] n golfinho, boto

porridge ['pɔrɪdʒ] n mingau m (de aveia)

port [pɔːt] n (harbour) porto; (NAUT: left side) bombordo; (wine) vinho do Porto; ~ **of call** porto de escala

portable ['pɔːtəbl] adj portátil

porter ['pɔːtə*] n (for luggage) carregador m; (doorkeeper) porteiro

portfolio [pɔːt'fəuliəu] n (case) pasta; (POL) pasta ministerial; (FINANCE) carteira de ações ou títulos; (of artist) pasta, portfólio

porthole ['pɔːthəul] n vigia

portion ['pɔːʃən] n porção f, quinhão m; (of food) ração f

portrait ['pɔːtreit] n retrato

portray [pɔː'trei] vt retratar; (act) interpretar

Portugal ['pɔːtjugl] n Portugal m (no article)

Portuguese [pɔːtju'giːz] adj português(-esa) ♦ n inv português(-esa) m/f; (LING) português m

pose [pəuz] n postura, pose f ♦ vi (pretend): **to ~ as** fazer-se passar por ♦ vt (question) fazer; (problem) causar; **to ~ for** (painting) posar para

posh [pɔʃ] (inf) adj fino, chique; (upper-class) de classe alta

position [pə'zɪʃən] n posição f; (job) cargo; (situation) situação f ♦ vt colocar, situar

positive ['pɔzɪtɪv] adj positivo; (certain) certo; (definite) definitivo

possess [pə'zes] vt possuir; **possession** n posse f, possessão f; **possessions** npl (belongings) pertences mpl; **to take possession of sth** tomar posse de algo

possibility [pɔsɪ'bɪlɪtɪ] n possibilidade f; (of sth happening) probabilidade f

possible ['pɔsɪbl] adj possível; **possibly** adv pode ser, talvez; (surprise): **what could they possibly want with me?** o que eles podem querer comigo?; (emphasizing

effort): **they did everything they possibly could** fizeram tudo o que podiam; **I cannot possibly come** estou impossibilitado de vir

post [pəust] n (BRIT: mail) correio; (job) cargo, posto; (pole) poste m; (MIL) nomeação f ♦ vt (BRIT: send by ~) pôr no correio; (: appoint): **to ~ to** destinar a; **postage** n porte m, franquia; **postal order** n vale m postal; **postbox** (BRIT) n caixa de correio; **postcard** n cartão m postal; **postcode** (BRIT) n código postal, ≈ CEP m (BR)

poster ['pəustə*] n cartaz m; (as decoration) pôster m

postman ['pəustmən] (irreg) n carteiro

postmark ['pəustmɑːk] n carimbo do correio

postmortem [pəust'mɔːtəm] n autópsia

post office n (building) agência do correio, correio; (organization) ≈ Empresa Nacional dos Correios e Telégrafos (BR), ≈ Correios, Telégrafos e Telefones (PT)

postpone [pəs'pəun] vt adiar

posture ['pɔstʃə*] n postura; (fig) atitude f

postwar [pəust'wɔː*] adj de após-guerra

pot [pɔt] n (for cooking) panela; (for flowers) vaso; (container, tea~, coffee~) pote m; (inf: marijuana) maconha ♦ vt (plant) plantar em vaso; **to go to ~** (inf) arruinar-se, degringolar

potato [pə'teitəu] (pl ~es) n batata; **potato peeler** n descascador m de batatas

potent ['pəutnt] adj poderoso; (drink) forte; (man) potente

potential [pə'tenʃl] adj potencial ♦ n potencial m

pothole ['pɒthəul] n (in road) buraco; (BRIT: underground) caldeirão m, cova; **potholing** (BRIT) n: **to go potholing** dedicar-se à espeleologia

potluck [pɒt'lʌk] n: **to take ~** contentar-se com o que houver

potter ['pɒtə*] n (artistic) ceramista m/f; (artisan) oleiro(-a) ♦ vi (BRIT): **to ~ around, ~ about** ocupar-se com pequenos trabalhos; **pottery** n cerâmica; (factory) olaria

potty ['pɒtɪ] adj (inf: mad) maluco, doido ♦ n penico

pouch [pautʃ] n (ZOOL) bolsa; (for tobacco) tabaqueira

poultry ['pəultrɪ] n aves fpl domésticas; (meat) carne f de aves domésticas

pounce [pauns] vi: **to ~ on** lançar-se sobre; (person) agarrar em; (fig: mistake etc) apontar

pound [paund] n libra (weight = 453g, 16 ounces; money = 100 pence) ♦ vt (beat) socar, esmurrar; (crush) triturar ♦ vi (heart) bater

pour [pɔ:*] vt despejar; (drink) servir ♦ vi correr, jorrar; **pour away** vt esvaziar, decantar; **pour in** vi (people) entrar numa enxurrada; (information) chegar numa enxurrada; **pour off** vt esvaziar, decantar; **pour out** vi (people) sair aos borbotões ♦ vt (drink) servir; (fig) extravasar; **pouring** ['pɔ:rɪŋ] adj: **pouring rain** chuva torrencial

pout [paut] vi fazer beicinho or biquinho

poverty ['pɒvətɪ] n pobreza, miséria

powder ['paudə*] n pó m; (face ~) pó-de-arroz m ♦ vt (face) empoar, passar pó em; **powdered milk** n leite m em pó; **powder room** n toucador m, banheiro de senhoras

power ['pauə*] n poder m; (of explosion, engine) força, potência; (abil-ity) poder, poderio; (electricity) força; **to be in ~** estar no poder; **power cut** (BRIT) n corte m de energia, blecaute m (BR); **powerful** adj poderoso; (engine) potente; (body) vigoroso; (blow) violento; (argument) convincente; (emotion) intenso; **powerless** adj impotente; **power point** (BRIT) n tomada; **power station** n central f elétrica

pp abbr (= per procurationem) p.p.; = **pages**

PR n abbr = **public relations**

practical ['præktɪkl] adj prático; **practical joke** n brincadeira, peça

practice ['præktɪs] n (habit, REL) costume m, hábito; (exercise) prática; (of profession) exercício m; (training) treinamento; (MED) consultório; (LAW) escritório ♦ vt, vi (US) = **practise; in ~** na prática; **out of ~** destreinado

practise ['præktɪs] (US **practice**) vt praticar; (profession) exercer; (sport) treinar ♦ vi (doctor) ter consultório; (lawyer) ter escritório; (train) treinar, praticar

practitioner [præk'tɪʃənə*] n (MED) médico(-a)

prairie ['prɛərɪ] n campina, pradaria

praise [preɪz] n louvor m; (admiration) elogio ♦ vt elogiar, louvar; **praiseworthy** adj louvável, digno de elogio

pram [præm] (BRIT) n carrinho de bebê

prance [prɑ:ns] vi: **to ~ about/up and down** etc (horse) curvetear, fazer cabriolas; (person) andar espalhafatosamente

prank [præŋk] n travessura, peça

prawn [prɔ:n] n pitu m; (small) camarão m

pray [preɪ] vi: **to ~ for/that** rezar por/para que; **prayer** [prɛə*] n (*activity*) reza; (*words*) oração f, prece f

preach [priːtʃ] *vt* pregar ♦ *vi* pregar; (*pej*) catequizar

precede [prɪˈsiːd] *vt* preceder

precedent [ˈpresɪdənt] *n* precedente *m*

preceding [prɪˈsiːdɪŋ] *adj* anterior

precinct [ˈpriːsɪŋkt] *n* (*us: district*) distrito policial; ~s *npl* (*of large building*) arredores *mpl*; **pedestrian ~** (*BRIT*) zona para pedestres (*BR*) or peões (*PT*); **shopping ~** (*BRIT*) zona comercial

precious [ˈpreʃəs] *adj* precioso

precipitate [prɪˈsɪpɪteɪt] *vt* precipitar, acelerar

precise [prɪˈsaɪs] *adj* exato, preciso; (*plans*) detalhado

precocious [prɪˈkəuʃəs] *adj* precoce

predecessor [ˈpriːdɪsesə*] *n* predecessor(a) *m/f*, antepassado(-a)

predicament [prɪˈdɪkəmənt] *n* situação f difícil, apuro

predict [prɪˈdɪkt] *vt* prever, predizer, prognosticar; **predictable** *adj* previsível

predominantly [prɪˈdɒmɪnəntlɪ] *adv* predominantemente, na maioria

preen [priːn] *vt*: **to ~ itself** (*bird*) limpar e alisar as penas (com o bico); **to ~ o.s.** enfeitar-se, envaidecer-se

prefab [ˈpriːfæb] *n* casa pré-fabricada

preface [ˈprefəs] *n* prefácio

prefect [ˈpriːfekt] *n* (*BRIT: SCH*) monitor(a) *m/f*, tutor(a) *m/f*; (*in Brazil*) prefeito(-a)

prefer [prɪˈfəː*] *vt* preferir; **preferably** [ˈprefrəblɪ] *adv* de preferência; **preferential** [prefəˈrenʃəl] *adj*; **preferential treatment** preferência

prefix [ˈpriːfɪks] *n* prefixo

pregnancy [ˈpregnənsɪ] *n* gravidez

f; (*animal*) prenhez f

pregnant [ˈpregnənt] *adj* grávida; (*animal*) prenha

prehistoric [priːhɪsˈtɔrɪk] *adj* pré-histórico

prejudice [ˈpredʒudɪs] *n* preconceito; **prejudiced** *adj* cheio de preconceitos; **to be prejudiced against sb/sth** estar com prevenção contra alguém/algo

premarital [priːˈmærɪtl] *adj* pré-nupcial

premature [ˈpremətjuə*] *adj* prematuro

première [ˈpremɪeə*] *n* estréia

premise [ˈpremɪs] *n* premissa; ~s *npl* (*of business, institution*) local *m*

premium [ˈpriːmɪəm] *n* prêmio; **to be at a ~** ser caro

premonition [preməˈnɪʃən] *n* presságio, pressentimento

preoccupied [priːˈɔkjupaɪd] *adj* preocupado

prepaid [priːˈpeɪd] *adj* com porte pago

preparation [prepəˈreɪʃən] *n* preparação f; ~s *npl* (*arrangements*) preparativos *mpl*

preparatory [prɪˈpærətərɪ] *adj* preparatório

prepare [prɪˈpeə*] *vt* preparar ♦ *vi*: **to ~ for** preparar-se or aprontar-se para; **~d to** disposto a; **~d for** pronto para

preposition [prepəˈzɪʃən] *n* preposição f

preposterous [prɪˈpɔstərəs] *adj* absurdo, disparatado

prerequisite [priːˈrekwɪzɪt] *n* pré-requisito, condição f prévia

prescribe [prɪˈskraɪb] *vt* prescrever; (*MED*) receitar

prescription [prɪˈskrɪpʃən] *n* receita

presence [ˈprezns] *n* presença; (*spirit*) espectro

present [*adj, n* 'prɛznt, *vb* prɪ'zɛnt] *adj* presente; (*current*) atual ♦ *n* presente *m*; (*actuality*): **the ~** o presente ♦ *vt* (*give*): **to ~ sth to sb, to ~ sb with sth** entregar algo a alguém; (*information, programme, threat*) apresentar; (*describe*) descrever; **at ~** no momento, agora; **to give sb a ~** presentear alguém; **presentation** [prɛznˈteɪʃən] *n* apresentação *f*; (*ceremony*) entrega; (*of plan etc*) exposição *f*; **present-day** *adj* atual, de hoje; **presenter** *n* apresentador(a) *m/f*; **presently** *adv* (*after*) logo após; (*soon*) logo, em breve; (*now*) atualmente

preservative [prɪˈzəːvətɪv] *n* conservante *m*

preserve [prɪˈzəːv] *vt* (*situation*) conservar, manter; (*building, manuscript*) preservar; (*food*) pôr em conserva ♦ *n* (*often pl*: *jam*) geléia; (: *fruit*) compota, conserva

president ['prɛzɪdənt] *n* presidente(-a) *m/f*; **presidential** [prɛzɪˈdɛnʃl] *adj* presidencial

press [prɛs] *n* (*printer's*) imprensa, prelo; (*newspapers*) ·imprensa; (*of switch*) pressão *f* ♦ *vt* apertar; (*clothes: iron*) passar; (*put pressure on: person*) assediar; (*insist*): **to ~ sth on sb** insistir para que alguém aceite algo ♦ *vi* (*squeeze*) apertar; (*pressurize*): **to ~** pressionar por; **we are ~ed for time/money** estamos com pouco tempo/dinheiro; **press on** *vi* continuar; **pressing** *adj* urgente; **press stud** (*BRIT*) *n* botão *m* de pressão; **press-up** (*BRIT*) *n* flexão *f*

pressure ['prɛʃə*] *n* pressão *f*; **to put ~ on sb** (*to do sth*) pressionar alguém (a fazer algo); **pressure cooker** *n* panela de pressão

prestige [prɛsˈtiːʒ] *n* prestígio

presume [prɪˈzjuːm] *vt* supor

pretence [prɪˈtɛns] (*US* **pretense**) *n* pretensão *f*; **under false ~s** por meios fraudulentos

pretend [prɪˈtɛnd] *vt, vi* fingir

pretense [prɪˈtɛns] (*US*) *n* = **pretence**

pretty ['prɪtɪ] *adj* bonito ♦ *adv* (*quite*) bastante

prevail [prɪˈveɪl] *vi* triunfar; (*be current*) imperar

prevalent ['prɛvələnt] *adj* (*common*) predominante

prevent [prɪˈvɛnt] *vt* impedir

preview ['priːvjuː] *n* pré-estréia

previous ['priːvɪəs] *adj* (*earlier*) anterior; **previously** *adv* (*before*) previamente; (*in the past*) anteriormente

prewar [priːˈwɔː*] *adj* anterior à guerra

prey [preɪ] *n* presa ♦ *vi*: **to ~ on** (*feed on*) alimentar-se de; **it was ~ing on his mind** preocupava-o, atormentava-o

price [praɪs] *n* preço ♦ *vt* fixar o preço de; **priceless** *adj* inestimável; (*inf: amusing*) impagável

prick [prɪk] *n* picada ♦ *vt* picar; (*make hole in*) furar; **to ~ up one's ears** aguçar os ouvidos

prickle ['prɪkl] *n* (*sensation*) comichão *f*, ardência; (*BOT*) espinho; **prickly** *adj* espinhoso; **prickly heat** *n* brotoeja

pride [praɪd] *n* orgulho; (*pej*) soberba ♦ *vt*: **to ~ o.s. on** orgulhar-se de

priest [priːst] *n* (*Christian*) padre *m*; (*non-Christian*) sacerdote *m*

prim [prɪm] (*pej*) *adj* (*formal*) empertigado; (*affected*) afetado; (*easily shocked*) pudico

primarily ['praɪmərɪlɪ] *adv* principalmente

primary ['praɪmərɪ] *adj* primário;

(first in importance) principal ♦ n *(us: election)* eleição f primária; **primary school** *(BRIT)* n escola primária; *ver* quadro

---

PRIMARY SCHOOL

As **primary schools** da Grã-Bretanha acolhem crianças de 5 a 11 anos. Assinalam o início do ciclo escolar obrigatório e são compostas de duas partes: a pré-escola *(infant school)* e o primário *(junior school)*.

---

prime [praɪm] *adj* primeiro, principal; *(excellent)* de primeira ♦ vt *(wood)* imprimar; *(fig)* aprontar, preparar ♦ n: **in the ~ of life** na primavera da vida; ~ **example** exemplo típico; **prime minister** n primeiro-ministro (primeira-ministra)
primeval [praɪˈmiːvl] *adj* primitivo
primitive [ˈprɪmɪtɪv] *adj* primitivo; *(crude)* rudimentar
primrose [ˈprɪmrəuz] n prímula, primavera
prince [prɪns] n príncipe m
princess [prɪnˈses] n princesa
principal [ˈprɪnsɪpl] *adj* principal ♦ n *(of school, college)* diretor(a) m/f
principle [ˈprɪnsɪpl] n princípio; **in ~** em princípio; **on ~** por princípio
print [prɪnt] n *(letters)* letra de forma; *(fabric)* estampado; *(ART)* estampa, gravura; *(PHOT)* cópia; *(foot~)* pegada; *(finger~)* impressão f digital ♦ vt imprimir; *(write in capitals)* escrever em letra de imprensa; **out of ~** esgotado; **printed matter** n impressos mpl; **printer** n *(person)* impressor(a) m/f; *(firm)* gráfica; *(machine)* impressora; **printing** n *(art)* imprensa; *(act)* impressão f; **printout** n *(COMPUT)* cópia impressa
prior [ˈpraɪə*] *adj* anterior, prévio;

(more important) prioritário; ~ **to doing** antes de fazer
priority [praɪˈɔrɪtɪ] n prioridade f
prise [praɪz] vt: **to ~ open** arrombar
prison [ˈprɪzn] n prisão f ♦ cpd carcerário; **prisoner** n *(in prison)* preso(-a); *(under arrest)* detido(-a)
privacy [ˈprɪvəsɪ] n isolamento, solidão f, privacidade f
private [ˈpraɪvɪt] *adj* privado; *(personal)* particular; *(confidential)* confidencial, reservado; *(personal: belongings)* pessoal; (: *thoughts, plans)* secreto, íntimo; *(place)* isolado; *(quiet: person)* reservado; *(intimate)* íntimo ♦ n soldado raso; "~" *(on envelope)* "confidencial"; *(on door)* "privativo"; **in ~** em particular;
privatize vt privatizar
privet [ˈprɪvɪt] n alfena
privilege [ˈprɪvɪlɪdʒ] n privilégio
privy [ˈprɪvɪ] *adj*: **to be ~ to** estar inteirado de
prize [praɪz] n prêmio ♦ *adj* de primeira classe ♦ vt valorizar; **prize-winner** n premiado(-a)
pro [prəu] n *(SPORT)* profissional m/f ♦ *prep* a favor de; **the ~s and cons** os prós e os contras
probability [prɔbəˈbɪlɪtɪ] n probabilidade f
probable [ˈprɔbəbl] *adj* provável; *(plausible)* verossímil
probation [prəˈbeɪʃn] n: **on ~** *(employee)* em estágio probatório; *(LAW)* em liberdade condicional
probe [prəub] n *(MED, SPACE)* sonda; *(enquiry)* pesquisa ♦ vt investigar, esquadrinhar
problem [ˈprɔbləm] n problema m
procedure [prəˈsiːdʒə*] n procedimento; *(method)* método, processo
proceed [prəˈsiːd] vi *(do afterwards)*: **to ~ to do sth** passar a fazer algo; *(continue)*: **to ~ (with)** continuar or

prosseguir (com); (*activity*) continuar; (*go*) ir em direção a, dirigir-se a; **proceedings** *npl* evento, acontecimento; (*LAW*) processo; **proceeds** ['prəusi:dz] *npl* produto, proventos *mpl*

process ['prəuses] *n* processo ♦ *vt* processar; **procession** [prə'sɛʃən] *n* desfile *m*, procissão *f*; **funeral procession** cortejo fúnebre

proclaim [prə'kleɪm] *vt* anunciar

procure [prə'kjuə*] *vt* obter

prod [prɔd] *vt* empurrar; (*with finger, stick*) cutucar ♦ *n* empurrão *m*; cotovelada; espetada

prodigal ['prɔdɪgl] *adj* pródigo

prodigy ['prɔdɪdʒɪ] *n* prodígio

produce [*n* 'prɔdju:s, *vb* prə'dju:s] *n* (*AGR*) produtos *mpl* agrícolas ♦ *vt* produzir; (*cause*) provocar; (*evidence, argument*) apresentar, mostrar; (*show*) apresentar, exibir; (*THEATRE*) pôr em cena or em cartaz; **producer** *n* (*THEATRE*) diretor(a) *m/f*; (*AGR, CINEMA, of record*) produtor(a) *m/f*; (*country*) produtor *m*

product ['prɔdʌkt] *n* produto

production [prə'dʌkʃən] *n* produção *f*; (*of electricity*) geração *f*; (*THEATRE*) encenação *f*; **production line** *n* linha de produção or de montagem

profession [prə'fɛʃən] *n* profissão *f*; (*people*) classe *f*; **professional** *n* profissional *m/f* ♦ *adj* profissional; (*work*) de profissional

professor [prə'fɛsə*] *n* (*BRIT*) catedrático(-a); (*US, CANADA*) professor(a) *m/f*

profile ['prəufaɪl] *n* perfil *m*

profit ['prɔfɪt] *n* (*COMM*) lucro ♦ *vi*: **to ~ by** or **from** (*benefit*) aproveitar-se de, tirar proveito de; **profitable** *adj* lucrativo, rendoso

profound [prə'faund] *adj* profundo

programme ['prəugræm] (*US* pro-

gram) *n* programa *m* ♦ *vt* programar; **programming** (*US* programing) *n* (*COMPUT*) programação *f*

progress [*n* 'prəugres, *vi* prə'gres] *n* progresso ♦ *vi* progredir, avançar; **in ~** em andamento; **progressive** [prə'gresɪv] *adj* progressivo; (*person*) progressista

prohibit [prə'hɪbɪt] *vt* proibir

project [*n* 'prɔdʒekt, *vb* prə'dʒekt] *n* projeto; (*SCH: research*) pesquisa ♦ *vt* projetar; (*figure*) estimar ♦ *vi* (*stick out*) ressaltar, sobressair

projection [prə'dʒekʃən] *n* projeção *f*; (*overhang*) saliência

projector [prə'dʒektə*] *n* projetor *m*

prolong [prə'lɔŋ] *vt* prolongar

prom [prɔm] *n abbr* = **promenade**; **promenade concert**

promenade [prɔmə'nɑ:d] *n* (*by sea*) passeio (à orla marítima); (*US: ball*) baile *m* de estudantes; **promenade concert** (*BRIT*) *n* concerto (de música clássica); *ver quadro*

PROMENADE CONCERT

Na Grã-Bretanha, um **promenade concert** (ou **prom**) é um concerto de música clássica, assim chamado porque originalmente o público não ficava sentado, mas de pé ou caminhando. Hoje em dia, uma parte do público permanece de pé, mas há também lugares sentados (mais caros). Os **Proms** mais conhecidos são os londrinos. A última sessão (*the Last Night of the Proms*) é um acontecimento carregado de emoção, quando são executadas árias tradicionais e patrióticas. Nos Estados Unidos e no Canadá, o **prom**, ou **promenade**, é um baile organizado pelas escolas secundárias.

prominent ['prɒmɪnənt] adj (standing out) proeminente; (important) eminente, notório

promise ['prɒmɪs] n promessa; (hope) esperança ♦ vt, vi prometer; **promising** adj promissor(a), prometedor(a)

promote [prə'məut] vt promover; (product) promover, fazer propaganda de; **promoter** n (of sporting event) patrocinador(a) m/f; (of cause etc) partidário(-a); **promotion** n promoção f

prompt [prɒmpt] adj pronto, rápido ♦ adv (exactly) em ponto, pontualmente ♦ n (COMPUT) sinal m de orientação, prompt m ♦ vt (urge) incitar, impelir; (cause) provocar, ocasionar; **to ~ sb to do sth** induzir alguém a fazer algo; **promptly** adv imediatamente; (exactly) pontualmente

prone [prəun] adj (lying) de bruços; **~ to** propenso a, predisposto a

pronoun ['prəunaun] n pronome m

pronounce [prə'nauns] vt pronunciar; (verdict, opinion) declarar

pronunciation [prənʌnsɪ'eɪʃən] n pronúncia

proof [pru:f] n prova ♦ adj: **~ against** à prova de

prop [prɒp] n suporte m, escora; (fig) amparo, apoio ♦ vt (also: **~ up**) apoiar, escorar; (lean): **to ~ sth against** apoiar algo contra

propaganda [prɒpə'gændə] n propaganda

propel [prə'pɛl] vt propelir, propulsionar; (fig) impelir; **propeller** n hélice f

proper ['prɒpə*] adj (correct) correto; (socially acceptable) respeitável, digno; (authentic) genuíno, autêntico; (referring to place): **the village ~** a cidadezinha propriamente dita; **properly** adv (eat, study) bem;

(behave) decentemente

property ['prɒpətɪ] n propriedade f; (goods) posses fpl, bens mpl; (buildings) imóveis mpl

prophesy ['prɒfɪsaɪ] vt profetizar

prophet ['prɒfɪt] n profeta m/f

proportion [prə'pɔ:ʃən] n proporção f; **proportional** adj proporcional; **proportionate** adj proporcionado

proposal [prə'pəuzl] n proposta; (of marriage) pedido

propose [prə'pəuz] vt propor; (toast) erguer ♦ vi propor casamento; **to ~ to do** propor-se fazer

proposition [prɒpə'zɪʃən] n proposta, proposição f; (offer) oferta

proprietor [prə'praɪətə*] n proprietário(-a), dono(-a)

prose [prəuz] n prosa

prosecute ['prɒsɪkju:t] vt processar; **prosecution** [prɒsɪ'kju:ʃən] n acusação f; (accusing side) autor m da demanda

prospect [n 'prɒspɛkt, vb prə'spɛkt] n (chance) probabilidade f; (outlook) perspectiva ♦ vi: **to ~ (for)** prospectar (por); **~s** npl (for work etc) perspectivas fpl

prospectus [prə'spɛktəs] n prospecto, programa m

prostitute ['prɒstɪtju:t] n prostituta; **male ~** prostituto

protect [prə'tɛkt] vt proteger; **protection** n proteção f; **protective** adj protetor(a)

protein ['prəuti:n] n proteína

protest [n 'prəutɛst, vb prə'tɛst] n protesto ♦ vi protestar ♦ vt insistir

Protestant ['prɒtɪstənt] adj, n protestante m/f

protester [prə'tɛstə*] n manifestante m/f

protrude [prə'tru:d] vi projetar-se

proud [praud] adj orgulhoso; (pej)

vaidoso, soberbo

prove [pruːv] vt comprovar ♦ vi: **to ~ (to be) correct** etc vir a ser correto etc; **to ~ o.s.** pôr-se à prova

proverb ['prɔvəːb] n provérbio

provide [prə'vaɪd] vt fornecer, proporcionar; **to ~ sb with sth** fornecer algo a alguém ou algo de algo, fornecer algo a alguém; **provide for** vt fus (person) prover à subsistência de; **provided (that)** conj contanto que (+ sub), sob condição de (que) (+ sub)

providing [prə'vaɪdɪŋ] conj: **~ (that)** contanto que (+ sub)

province ['prɔvɪns] n província; (fig) esfera; **provincial** [prə'vɪnʃəl] adj provincial; (pej) provinciano

provision [prə'vɪʒən] n (supplying) abastecimento; (in contract) cláusula, condição f; **~s** npl (food) mantimentos mpl; **provisional** adj provisório, interino; (agreement, licence) provisório

proviso [prə'vaɪzəu] n condição f

provocative [prə'vɔkətɪv] adj provocante; (sexually) excitante

provoke [prə'vəuk] vt provocar; (cause) causar

prowl [praul] vi (also: **~ about, ~ around**) rondar, andar à espreita ♦ n: **on the ~** de ronda, rondando; **prowler** n tarado(-a)

proxy ['prɔksɪ] n: **by ~** por procuração

prudent ['pruːdənt] adj prudente

prune [pruːn] n ameixa seca ♦ vt podar

pry [praɪ] vi: **to ~ (into)** intrometer-se (em)

PS n abbr (= postscript) PS m

pseudonym ['sjuːdənɪm] n pseudônimo

psychiatrist [saɪ'kaɪətrɪst] n psiquiatra m/f

psychic ['saɪkɪk] adj psíquico; (also:

~al: person) sensível a forças psíquicas

psychoanalyst [saɪkəu'ænəlɪst] n psicanalista m/f

psychologist [saɪ'kɔlədʒɪst] n psicólogo(-a)

psychology [saɪ'kɔlədʒɪ] n psicologia

PTO abbr (= please turn over) v.v., vire

pub [pʌb] n abbr (= public house) pub m, bar m, botequim m; ver quadro

---

PUB

Um **pub** geralmente consiste em duas salas: uma (the lounge) é bastante confortável, com poltronas e bancos estofados, enquanto a outra (the public bar) é simplesmente um bar onde a consumação é em geral mais barata. O public bar é muitas vezes também um salão de jogos, dos quais os mais comuns são: os dardos, dominó e bilhar. Atualmente muitos pubs servem refeições, sobretudo na hora do almoço, e essa é a única hora em que a entrada de crianças é permitida, desde que estejam acompanhadas por adultos. Em geral os pubs funcionam das 11 às 23 horas, mas isso pode variar de acordo com sua permissão de funcionamento; alguns pubs fecham à tarde.

---

public ['pʌblɪk] adj público ♦ n público; **in ~** em público; **to make ~** tornar público; **public address system** n sistema m (de reforço) de som

publican ['pʌblɪkən] n dono(-a) de pub

public: public convenience (BRIT) n banheiro público; **public holiday** n feriado; **public house** (BRIT) n pub m, bar m, taberna

publicity [pʌb'lisiti] n publicidade f

publicize ['pʌblisaiz] vt divulgar

public: public relations relações fpl públicas; **public school** n (BRIT) escola particular; (US) escola pública; **public transport** (US **public transportation**) n transporte m coletivo

publish ['pʌbliʃ] vt publicar; **publisher** n editor(a) m/f; (company) editora; **publishing** n a indústria editorial

pudding ['pudiŋ] n (BRIT: dessert) sobremesa; (cake) pudim m, doce m; **black** (BRIT) **or blood** (US) ~ morcela

puddle ['pʌdl] n poça

puff [pʌf] n sopro; (of cigarette) baforada; (of air, smoke) lufada ♦ vt: **to ~ one's pipe** tirar baforadas do cachimbo ♦ vi (pant) arquejar; **puff out** vt (cheeks) encher; **puff pastry** (US **puff paste**) n massa folhada; **puffy** adj inchado

pull [pul] n (tug): **to give sth a ~** dar um puxão em algo ♦ vt puxar; (trigger) apertar; (curtain, blind) fechar ♦ vi puxar, dar um puxão; **to ~ to pieces** picar em pedacinhos; **to ~ one's punches** não usar toda a força; **to ~ one's weight** fazer a sua parte; **to ~ o.s. together** recompor-se; **to ~ sb's leg** (fig) brincar com alguém, sacanear alguém (inf); **pull apart** vt (break) romper; **pull down** vt (building) demolir, derrubar; **pull in** vi (AUT: at the kerb) encostar; (RAIL) chegar (na plataforma); **pull off** vt tirar; (fig: deal etc) acertar; **pull out** vi (AUT: from kerb) sair; (RAIL) partir ♦ vt tirar, arrancar; **pull over** vi (AUT) encostar; **pull through** vi (MED) sobreviver; **pull up** vi (stop) deter-se, parar ♦ vt levantar; (uproot) desarraigar, arrancar

pulley ['puli] n roldana

pullover ['puləuvə*] n pulôver m

pulp [pʌlp] n (of fruit) polpa

pulsate [pʌl'seit] vi pulsar, palpitar

pulse [pʌls] n (ANAT) pulso; (of music, engine) cadência; (BOT) legume m

pump [pʌmp] n bomba; (shoe) sapatilha (de dança) ♦ vt bombear; **pump up** vt encher

pumpkin ['pʌmpkin] n abóbora

pun [pʌn] n jogo de palavras, trocadilho

punch [pʌntʃ] n (blow) soco, murro; (tool) punção m; (drink) ponche m ♦ vt (hit): **to ~ sb/sth** esmurrar ou socar alguém/algo; **punchline** n remate m

punctual ['pʌŋktjuəl] adj pontual

puncture ['pʌŋktʃə*] n furo ♦ vt furar

pungent ['pʌndʒənt] adj acre

punish ['pʌniʃ] vt punir, castigar; **punishment** n castigo, punição f

punk [pʌŋk] n (also: ~ **rocker**) punk m/f; (also: ~ **rock**) punk m; (US: inf: hoodlum) pinta-brava m

punt [pʌnt] n (boat) chalana

puny ['pju:ni] adj débil, fraco

pupil ['pju:pl] n aluno(-a); (of eye) pupila

puppet ['pʌpit] n marionete f, títere m; (fig) fantoche m

puppy ['pʌpi] n cachorro, cachorrinho (BR)

purchase ['pə:tʃis] n compra ♦ vt comprar

pure [pjuə*] adj puro

purge [pə:dʒ] n (POL) expurgo

purple ['pə:pl] adj roxo, purpúreo

purpose ['pə:pəs] n propósito, objetivo; **on ~** de propósito; **purposeful** adj decidido, resoluto

purr [pə:*] vi ronronar

purse [pə:s] n (BRIT) carteira; (US) bolsa ♦ vt enrugar, franzir

purser ['pə:sə*] n (NAUT) comissário

pursue 213 **qualified**

de bordo

pursue [pə'sju:] vt perseguir; (fig: activity) exercer; (: interest, plan) dedicar-se a; (: result) lutar por

pursuit [pə'sju:t] n caça; (fig) busca; (pastime) passatempo

push [puʃ] n empurrão m; (of button) aperto ♦ vt empurrar; (button) apertar; (promote) promover ♦ vi empurrar; (press) apertar; (fig): **to ~ for** reivindicar; **push aside** vt afastar com a mão; **push off** (inf) vi dar o fora; **push on** vi prosseguir; **push through** vi abrir caminho ♦ vt (measure) forçar a aceitação de; **push up** vt forçar a alta de; **push-chair** (BRIT) n carrinho; **pusher** n (also: **drug pusher**) traficante m/f or passador(a) m/f de drogas; **push-up** (US) n flexão f; **pushy** (pej) adj intrometido, agressivo

pussy(cat) ['pusi(kæt)] (inf) n gatinho

put [put] (pt, pp put) vt pôr, colocar; (~ into) meter; (person: in institution etc) internar; (say) dizer, expressar; (case) expor; (question) fazer; (estimate) avaliar, calcular; (write, type etc) colocar; **put about** vt (rumour) espalhar; **put across** vt (ideas) comunicar; **put away** vt guardar; **put back** vt (replace) repor; (postpone) adiar; (delay) atrasar; **put by** vt (money etc) poupar, pôr de lado; **put down** vt pôr em; (animal) sacrificar; (in writing) anotar, inscrever; (revolt etc) sufocar; (attribute: case, view) **to ~ sth down to** atribuir algo a; **put forward** vt apresentar, propor; **put in** vt (application, complaint) apresentar; (time, effort) investir, gastar; **put off** vt adiar, protelar; (discourage) desencorajar; **put on** vt (clothes, make-up, dinner) pôr; (light) acender; (play)

encenar; (weight) ganhar; (brake) aplicar; (record, video, kettle) ligar; (accent, manner) assumir; **put out** vt (take out) colocar fora; (fire, cigarette, light) apagar; (one's hand) estender; (inf: person): **to be ~ out** estar aborrecido; **put through** vt (call) transferir; (plan) ser aprovado; **put up** vt (raise) levantar, erguer; (hang) prender; (build) construir, edificar; (tent) armar; (increase) aumentar; (accommodate) hospedar; **put up with** vt fus suportar, agüentar

putty ['pʌti] n massa de vidraceiro, betume m

puzzle ['pʌzl] n (jigsaw) quebra-cabeça m; (also: **crossword ~**) palavras cruzadas fpl; (mystery) mistério ♦ vt desconcertar, confundir ♦ vi: **to ~ over sth** tentar entender algo; **puzzling** adj intrigante, confuso

pyjamas [pɪ'dʒɑːməz] (us **pajamas**) npl pijama m or f

pylon ['paɪlən] n pilono, poste m

pyramid ['pɪrəmɪd] n pirâmide f

Pyrenees [pɪrə'niːz] npl: **the ~** os Pirineus

Q

quack [kwæk] n grasnido; (pej: doctor) curandeiro(-a), charlatão(-tã) m/f

quadrangle ['kwɔdræŋgl] n pátio quadrangular

quaint [kweɪnt] adj (ideas) curioso, esquisito; (village etc) pitoresco

quake [kweɪk] vi (with fear) tremer ♦ n abbr = **earthquake**

qualification [kwɔlɪfɪ'keɪʃən] n (skill, quality) qualificação f; (reservation) restrição f, ressalva; (modification) modificação f; (often pl: degree, training) título, qualificação

qualified ['kwɔlɪfaɪd] adj (trained) habilitado, qualificado; (profession-

qualify 214 quiet

ally) diplomado; (*fit*): ~ **to** apto para, capaz de; (*limited*) limitado

qualify ['kwɔlɪfaɪ] vt (*modify*) modificar ♦ vi: **to ~ (as)** (*pass examination(s)*) formar-se or diplomar-se (em); **to ~ (for)** reunir os requisitos (para)

quality ['kwɔlɪtɪ] n qualidade f; **quality (news)papers** npl ver quadro

---

QUALITY (NEWS)PAPERS

Os **quality (news)papers** (ou *quality press*) englobam os jornais "sérios", diários ou semanais, em oposição aos jornais populares (*tabloid press*). Esses jornais visam a um público que procura informações detalhadas sobre uma grande variedade de assuntos e que está disposto a dedicar um bom tempo à leitura. Geralmente os **quality newspapers** são publicados em formato grande.

---

quantity ['kwɔntɪtɪ] n quantidade f
quarantine ['kwɔrəntiːn] n quarentena
quarrel ['kwɔrl] n (*argument*) discussão f ♦ vi: **to ~ (with)** brigar (com)
quarry ['kwɔrɪ] n (*for stone*) pedreira; (*animal*) presa, caça
quart [kwɔːt] n quarto de galão (1.136 l)
quarter ['kwɔːtə*] n quarto, quarta parte f; (*of year*) trimestre m; (*district*) bairro; (*US: 25 cents*) (moeda de) 25 centavos mpl de dólar ♦ vt dividir em quatro; (*MIL: lodge*) aquartelar; **~s** npl (*MIL*) quartel m; (*living ~s*) alojamento; **a ~ of an hour** um quarto de hora; **quarter final** n quarta de final; **quarterly** adj trimestral ♦ adv trimestralmente
quaver ['kweɪvə*] n (*BRIT: MUS*) col-

cheia ♦ vi tremer
quay [kiː] n (*also:* **~side**) cais m
queasy ['kwiːzɪ] adj (*sickly*) enjoado
queen [kwiːn] n rainha; (*also:* ~ **bee**) abelha-mestra, rainha; (*CARDS etc*) dama; **queen mother** n rainha-mãe f
queer [kwɪə*] adj (*odd*) esquisito, estranho ♦ n (*inf: homosexual*) bicha m (*BR*), maricas m inv (*PT*)
quench [kwɛntʃ] vt: **to ~ one's thirst** matar a sede
query ['kwɪərɪ] n pergunta ♦ vt questionar
quest [kwɛst] n busca
question ['kwɛstʃən] n pergunta; (*doubt*) dúvida; (*issue*) questão f; (*in text*) problema m ♦ vt (*doubt*) duvidar; (*interrogate*) interrogar, inquirir; **beyond ~** sem dúvida; **out of the ~** fora de cogitação, impossível; **questionable** adj discutível; (*doubtful*) duvidoso; **question mark** n ponto de interrogação; **questionnaire** [kwɛstʃə'nɛə*] n questionário
queue [kjuː] (*BRIT*) n fila (*BR*), bicha (*PT*) ♦ vi (*also:* ~ **up**) fazer fila (*BR*) or bicha (*PT*)
quibble ['kwɪbl] vi: **to ~ about** or **over/with** tergiversar sobre/com
quick [kwɪk] adj rápido; (*agile*) ágil; (*mind*) sagaz, despachado ♦ n: **to cut sb to the ~** ferir alguém; **be ~!** ande depressa!, vai rápido!; **quicken** vt apressar ♦ vi apressar-se; **quickly** adv rapidamente, depressa; **quicksand** n areia movediça; **quick-witted** adj perspicaz, vivo
quid [kwɪd] (*BRIT: inf*) n inv libra
quiet ['kwaɪət] adj (*voice, music*) baixo; (*peaceful: place*) tranquilo; (*person: calm*) calmo; (*not noisy: place*) silencioso; (: *person*) calado; (*silent*) silencioso; (*ceremony*) discreto ♦ n (*peacefulness*) sossego; (*si-

lence) quietude f ♦ vt, vi (us) = ~**en**;

quieten (also: **quieten down**) vt (grow calm) acalmar-se; (grow silent) calar-se ♦ vt tranqüilizar; fazer calar; (talk) baixo

quilt [kwɪlt] n acolchoado, colcha; (**continental**) ~ (BRIT) edredom m (BR), edredão m (PT)

quip [kwɪp] n escárnio, dito espirituoso

quirk [kwə:k] n peculiaridade f

quit [kwɪt] (pt, pp quit or ~**ted**) vt (smoking etc) parar; (job) deixar; (premises) desocupar ♦ vi desistir; (resign) demitir-se, deixar o emprego

quite [kwaɪt] adv (rather) bastante; (entirely) completamente, totalmente; **that's not** ~ **big enough** não é suficientemente grande; ~ **a few of them** um bom número deles; ~ (**so**)! exatamente!, isso mesmo!

quiver [ˈkwɪvə*] vi estremecer

quiz [kwɪz] n concurso (de cultura geral) ♦ vt interrogar; **quizzical** adj zombeteiro

quota [ˈkwəʊtə] n cota, quota

quotation [kwəʊˈteɪʃən] n citação f; (estimate) orçamento; **quotation marks** npl aspas fpl

quote [kwəʊt] n citação f; (estimate) orçamento ♦ vt citar; (price) propor; (figure, example) citar; ~**s** npl aspas fpl

R

rabbi [ˈræbaɪ] n rabino

rabbit [ˈræbɪt] n coelho

rabble [ˈræbl] (pej) n povinho, ralé f

rabies [ˈreɪbi:z] n raiva

RAC (BRIT) n abbr (= Royal Automobile Club) ≈ TCB m (BR), ≈ ACP m (PT)

raccoon [rəˈku:n] n mão-pelada m, guaxinim m

race [reɪs] n corrida; (species) raça ♦ vt (horse) fazer correr ♦ vi (compete) competir; (run) correr; (pulse) bater rapidamente; **race car** (us) n = **racing car**; **racecourse** n hipódromo; **racehorse** n cavalo de corridas; **racetrack** n pista de corridas; (for cars) autódromo

racing [ˈreɪsɪŋ] n corrida; **racing car** (BRIT) n carro de corrida; **racing driver** (BRIT) n piloto(-a) de corrida

racism [ˈreɪsɪzəm] n racismo; **racist** (pej) adj, n racista m/f

rack [ræk] n (also: **luggage** ~) bagageiro; (shelf) estante f; (also: **roof** ~) xalmas fpl, porta-bagagem m; (dish ~) secador m de prato ♦ vt: ~**ed by** (pain, anxiety) tomado por; **to** ~ **one's brains** quebrar a cabeça

racket [ˈrækɪt] n (for tennis) raquete f (BR), raqueta (PT); (noise) barulheira, zoeira; (swindle) negócio ilegal, fraude f

racquet [ˈrækɪt] n raquete f (BR), raqueta (PT)

racy [ˈreɪsɪ] adj ousado, picante

radiant [ˈreɪdɪənt] adj radiante, brilhante

radiate [ˈreɪdɪeɪt] vt irradiar ♦ vi difundir-se, estender-se

radiation [reɪdɪˈeɪʃən] n radiação f

radiator [ˈreɪdɪeɪtə*] n radiador m

radical [ˈrædɪkl] adj radical

radii [ˈreɪdɪaɪ] npl of **radius**

radio [ˈreɪdɪəʊ] n rádio ♦ vt: **to** ~ **sb** comunicar-se por rádio com alguém

radio... [reɪdɪəʊ] prefix radio...;
radioactive [reɪdɪəʊˈæktɪv] adj radioativo; **radio station** n emissora, estação f de rádio

radish [ˈrædɪʃ] n rabanete m

radius ['reɪdɪəs] (pl **radii**) n raio

RAF (BRIT) n abbr = **Royal Air Force**

raffle ['ræfl] n rifa

raft [rɑːft] n balsa

rafter ['rɑːftə*] n viga, caibro

rag [ræg] n trapo; (torn cloth) farrapo; (pej: newspaper) jornaleco; (UNIVERSITY) atividades estudantis beneficentes; **~s** npl (torn clothes) trapos mpl, farrapos mpl; **rag doll** n boneca de trapo

rage [reɪdʒ] n (fury) raiva, furor m ♦ vi (person) estar furioso; (storm) assolar; (debate) continuar calorosamente; **it's all the ~** é a última moda

ragged ['rægɪd] adj (edge) irregular, desigual; (clothes) puído, gasto; (appearance) esfarrapado, andrajoso

raid [reɪd] n (MIL) incursão f; (criminal) assalto; (attack) ataque m; (by police) batida ♦ vt invadir, atacar; assaltar; atacar; fazer uma batida em

rail [reɪl] n (on stair) corrimão m; (on bridge) parapeito, antepara; (of ship) amurada; **~s** npl (for train) trilhos mpl; **by ~** de trem (BR), por caminho de ferro (PT); **railing(s)** n(pl) grade f; **railroad** (US) n = **railway**; **railway** n estrada ou caminho (PT) de ferro; **railway line** (BRIT) n linha de trem (BR) ou de comboio (PT); **railway station** (BRIT) n estação f ferroviária (BR) ou de caminho de ferro (PT)

rain [reɪn] n chuva ♦ vi chover; **it's ~ing** está chovendo (BR), está a chover (PT); **rainbow** n arco-íris m inv; **raincoat** n impermeável m, capa de chuva; **raindrop** n gota de chuva; **rainfall** n chuva; (measurement) pluviosidade f; **rainforest** n floresta tropical; **rainy** adj chuvoso; **a rainy day** um dia de chuva

raise [reɪz] n aumento ♦ vt (lift) levantar; (salary, production)

aumentar; (morale, standards) melhorar; (doubts) suscitar, despertar; (cattle, family) criar; (crop) cultivar, plantar; (army) recrutar, alistar; (funds) angariar; (loan) levantar, obter; **to ~ one's voice** levantar a voz

raisin ['reɪzn] n passa, uva seca

rake [reɪk] n ancinho ♦ vt (garden) revolver ou limpar com o ancinho; (with machine gun) varrer

rally ['rælɪ] n (POL etc) comício; (AUT) rally m, rali m; (TENNIS) rebatida ♦ vt reunir ♦ vi reorganizar-se; (sick person, Stock Exchange) recuperar-se; **rally round** vt fus dar apoio a

RAM [ræm] n abbr (COMPUT) (= random access memory) RAM f

ram [ræm] n carneiro ♦ vt (push) cravar; (crash into) colidir com

ramble ['ræmbl] n caminhada, excursão f a pé ♦ vi caminhar; (talk: also: **~ on**) divagar; **rambler** n caminhante m/f; (BOT) roseira trepadeira; **rambling** adj (speech) desconexo, incoerente; (house) cheio de recantos; (plant) rastejante

ramp [ræmp] n (incline) rampa; **on/off ~** (US: AUT) entrada (para a rodovia)/saída da rodovia

rampage [ræm'peɪdʒ] n: **to be on the ~** alvoroçar-se

rampant ['ræmpənt] adj caindo aos pedaços

ran [ræn] pt of **run**

ranch [rɑːntʃ] n rancho, fazenda, estância; **rancher** n rancheiro(-a), fazendeiro(-a)

rancid ['rænsɪd] adj rançoso, râncio

rancour ['ræŋkə*] (US **rancor**) n rancor m

random ['rændəm] adj ao acaso, casual, fortuito; (COMPUT, MATH) aleatório ♦ n: **at ~** a esmo, aleatoriamente

randy ['rændɪ] (BRIT: inf) adj de fogo

rang [ræŋ] pt of **ring**

range [reɪndʒ] n (of mountains) cadeia, cordilheira; (of missile) alcance m; (of voice) extensão f; (series) série f; (of products) gama, sortimento; (MIL: also: **shooting ~**) estande m; (also: **kitchen ~**) fogão m ♦ vt (place) colocar; (arrange) arrumar, ordenar ♦ vi: **to ~ over** (extend) estender-se por; **to ~ from ... to ...** variar de ... a ..., oscilar entre ... e ...

rank [ræŋk] n (row) fila, fileira; (MIL) posto; (status) categoria, posição f; (BRIT: also) ~ ponto de táxi ♦ vi: **to ~ among** figurar entre ♦ adj fétido, malcheiroso; **the ~ and file** (fig) a gente comum

ransack ['rænsæk] vt (search) revistar; (plunder) saquear, pilhar

ransom ['rænsəm] n resgate m; **to hold sb to ~** (fig) encostar alguém contra a parede

rant [rænt] vi arengar

rap [ræp] vt bater de leve ♦ n: ~ **(music)** rap m

rape [reɪp] n estupro m; (BOT) colza f ♦ vt violentar, estuprar

rapid ['ræpɪd] adj rápido; **rapids** npl (GEO) cachoeira f

rapist ['reɪpɪst] n estuprador m

rapport [ræ'pɔ:*] n harmonia, afinidade f

rare [rɛə*] adj raro; (CULIN: steak) mal passado

rascal ['rɑ:skl] n maroto, malandro

rash [ræʃ] adj impetuoso, precipitado ♦ n (MED) exantema m, erupção f cutânea; (of events) série f, torrente f

rasher ['ræʃə*] n fatia fina

raspberry ['rɑ:zbərɪ] n framboesa f

rat [ræt] n rato (PT), ratazana (PT)

rate [reɪt] n (ratio) razão f; (price) preço, taxa; (: of hotel) diária; (of

interest, change) taxa; (speed) velocidade f ♦ vt (value) taxar; (estimate) avaliar; ~**s** npl (BRIT) imposto predial e territorial; (fees) pagamento; **to rate sb/sth as** considerar alguém/algo como

rather ['rɑ:ðə*] adv (somewhat) um tanto, meio; (to some extent) até certo ponto; (more accurately) ou melhor, ou; **it's ~ expensive** (quite) é meio caro; (too) é caro demais; **there's ~ a lot** há bastante or muito; **I would ~ go** preferiria or preferia ir

ratio ['reɪʃɪəu] n razão f, proporção f

ration ['ræʃən] n ração f ♦ vt racionar; ~**s** npl (MIL) mantimentos mpl, víveres mpl

rational ['ræʃənl] adj lógico; (person) sensato, razoável; **rationale** [ræʃə'nɑ:l] n razão f fundamental

rat race n: **the ~** a competição acirrada na vida moderna

rattle ['rætl] n (of door) batida; (of train etc) chocalhada; (of coins) chocalhar m; (object: for baby) chocalho ♦ vi (small objects) tamborilar; (vehicle): **to ~ along** mover-se ruidosamente ♦ vt sacudir, fazer bater; (unnerve) perturbar; **rattlesnake** n cascavel f

raucous ['rɔ:kəs] adj espalhafatoso, banelhento

rave [reɪv] vi (in anger) encolerizar-se; (MED) delirar; (with enthusiasm): **to ~ about** vibrar com

raven ['reɪvən] n corvo

ravenous ['rævənəs] adj morto de fome, esfomeado

ravine [rə'vi:n] n ravina, barranco

raving ['reɪvɪŋ] adj: ~ **lunatic** doido(-a) varrido(-a)

ravishing ['rævɪʃɪŋ] adj encantador(-a)

raw [rɔ:] adj (uncooked) cru(a); (not processed) bruto; (sore) vivo; (inex-

perienced) inexperiente, novato; (*weather*) muito frio; **raw material** n matéria-prima

ray [reɪ] n raio; ~ **of hope** fio de esperança

razor ['reɪzə*] n (*open*) navalha; (*safety* ~) aparelho de barbear; (*electric*) aparelho de barbear elétrico; **razor blade** n gilete f (BR), lâmina de barbear (PT)

Rd abbr = **road**

re [ri:] prep referente a

reach [ri:tʃ] n alcance m; (*of river etc*) extensão f ♦ vt alcançar; (*arrive at*: *place*) chegar em; (: *agreement*) chegar a; (*by telephone*) conseguir falar com ♦ vi (*stretch out*) esticar-se; **within** ~ ao alcance (da mão); **out of** ~ fora de alcance; **reach out** vt (*hand*) esticar ♦ vi: **to** ~ **out for sth** estender ou esticar ã mão para pegar (em) algo

react [ri:'ækt] vi reagir; **reaction** n reação f; **~ions** npl (*reflexes*) reflexos mpl

reactor [ri:'æktə*] n (*also*: **nuclear** ~) reator m nuclear

read [ri:d, pt, pp read] (pt, pp **read**) vi ler ♦ vt ler; (*understand*) compreender; (*study*) estudar; **read out** vt ler em voz alta; **reader** n leitor(a) m/f; (*book*) livro de leituras; (BRIT: *at university*) professor(a) m/f adjunto(-a)

readily ['redɪlɪ] adv (*willingly*) de boa vontade; (*easily*) facilmente; (*quickly*) sem demora, prontamente

reading ['ri:dɪŋ] n leitura f; (*on instrument*) indicação f, registro (BR), registo (PT)

ready ['redɪ] adj pronto, preparado; (*willing*) disposto; (*available*) disponível ♦ n: **at the** ~ (MIL) pronto para atirar; **to get** ~ vi preparar-se ♦ vt preparar; **ready-made** adj (já) feito; (*clothes*) pronto; **ready-to-**

wear adj pronto, prêt à porter inv

real [rɪəl] adj real; (*genuine*) verdadeiro, autêntico; **in** ~ **terms** em termos reais; **real estate** n bens mpl imobiliários or de raiz; **realistic** [rɪə'lɪstɪk] adj realista

reality [ri:'ælɪtɪ] n realidade f

realization [rɪəlaɪ'zeɪʃən] n (*fulfilment*) realização f; (*understanding*) compreensão f; (COMM) conversão f em dinheiro, realização

realize ['rɪəlaɪz] vt (*understand*) perceber; (*fulfil*, COMM) realizar

really ['rɪəlɪ] adv (*for emphasis*): **what** ~ **happened?** o que aconteceu na verdade?; ~? (*interest*) é mesmo?; (*surprise*) verdade!; ~! (*annoyance*) realmente!

realm [relm] n reino; (*fig*) esfera, domínio

realtor ['rɪəltə*] n (US) corretor(a) m/f de imóveis (BR), agente m/f imobiliário(-a) (PT)

reap [ri:p] vt segar, ceifar; (*fig*) colher

reappear [ri:ə'pɪə*] vi reaparecer

rear [rɪə*] adj traseiro, de trás ♦ n traseira f ♦ vt criar ♦ vi (*also*: ~ **up**) empinar-se

reason ['ri:zn] n (*cause*) razão f; (*ability*) raciocínio; (*sense*) bom-senso ♦ vi: **to** ~ **with sb** argumentar com alguém, persuadir alguém; **it stands to** ~ **that** é razoável ou lógico que; **reasonable** adj (*fair*) razoável; (*sensible*) sensato; **reasonably** adv razoavelmente; sensatamente; **reasoning** n raciocínio

reassurance [ri:ə'ʃuərəns] n garantia

reassure [ri:ə'ʃuə*] vt tranquilizar; **to** ~ **sb** reafirmar a confiança de alguém acerca de

rebate ['ri:beɪt] n devolução f

rebel [n 'rɛbl, vb rɪ'bɛl] n rebelde m/f ♦ vi rebelar-se; **rebellious** [rɪ'bɛljəs] adj insurreto; (behaviour) rebelde

rebound [vb rɪ'baund, n 'ri:baund] vi (ball) ressaltar ♦ n: **on the ~** res-salto; (person): **she married him on the ~** ela casou com ele logo após o rompimento do casamento (or relacionamento) anterior

rebuff [rɪ'bʌf] n repulsa, recusa

rebuke [rɪ'bju:k] vt repreender

recall [vb rɪ'kɔ:l, n 'ri:kɔ:l] vt recordar, lembrar; (parliament) reunir de volta; (ambassador) chamar de volta ♦ n (memory) recordação f, lembrança; (of ambassador) chamada (de volta)

recap ['ri:kæp] vt sintetizar ♦ vi recapitular

recd. abbr = **received**

recede [rɪ'si:d] vi recuar

receding [rɪ'si:dɪŋ] adj (chin) meti-do or puxado para dentro; (hair) que está escasseando nas têmporas

receipt [rɪ'si:t] n recibo, (act) rece-bimento (BR), recepção f (PT); **~s** npl (COMM) receitas fpl

receive [rɪ'si:v] vt receber; (guest) acolher; (wound, criticism) sofrer; **receiver** n (TEL) fone m (BR), auscul-tador m (PT); (RADIO, TV) receptor m; (of stolen goods) receptador m/f; (COMM) curador(a) m/f síndico(-a) de massa falida

recent ['ri:snt] adj recente; **re-cently** adv recentemente; (in recent times) ultimamente

reception [rɪ'sɛpʃən] n recepção f; (welcome) acolhida; **reception desk** n (mesa de) recepção f; **receptionist** n recepcionista m/f

recess [rɪ'sɛs] n (in room) recesso, vão m; (secret place) esconderijo; (POL etc: holiday) férias fpl

recession [rɪ'sɛʃən] n recessão f

recipe ['rɛsɪpɪ] n receita

recipient [rɪ'sɪpɪənt] n recipiente m/f, recebedor(a) m/f; (of letter) destinatário(-a)

recite [rɪ'saɪt] vt recitar

reckless ['rɛkləs] adj (driver) impru-dente; (speed) imprudente, excessi-vo; (spending) irresponsável

reckon ['rɛkən] vt (calculate) calcu-lar, contar; (think): **I ~ that ...** acho que ...; **reckon on** vt fus contar com

reclaim [rɪ'kleɪm] vt (demand back) reivindicar; (land: from sea) aterrar; (waste materials) reaproveitar

recline [rɪ'klaɪn] vi reclinar-se; **reclining** adj (seat) reclinável

recognition [rɛkəg'nɪʃən] n reco-nhecimento

recognize ['rɛkəgnaɪz] vt reconhe-cer

recoil [vb rɪ'kɔɪl, n 'ri:kɔɪl] vi (per-son): **to ~ from doing sth** recusar-se a fazer algo ♦ n (of gun) coice m

recollect [rɛkə'lɛkt] vt lembrar, recordar; **recollection** n (memory) recordação f; (remembering) lem-brança

recommend [rɛkə'mɛnd] vt reco-mendar

reconcile ['rɛkənsaɪl] vt reconciliar; (facts) conciliar, harmonizar; **to ~ o.s. to sth** resignar-se a or conformar-se com algo

reconsider [ri:kən'sɪdə*] vt consi-derar

reconstruct [ri:kən'strʌkt] vt re-construir; (event) reconstituir

record [n, adj 'rɛkɔ:d, vb rɪ'kɔ:d] n (MUS) disco; (of meeting etc) ata, minuta; (COMPUT, of attendance) registro (BR), registo (PT); (written) história; (also: **criminal ~**) antece-dentes mpl; (SPORT) recorde m ♦ vt (write down) anotar; (temperature,

speed) registrar (BR), registar (PT);
(MUS: song etc) gravar ♦ adj: **in ~
time** num tempo recorde; **off the ~**
♦ adj confidencial ♦ adv confidencialmente; **recorder** n (MUS) flauta;
recording n (MUS) gravação f;
record player n toca-discos m inv
(BR), gira-discos m inv (PT)
re-count [ri:kaunt] n (POL: of votes)
nova contagem f, recontagem f
recoup [rɪ'ku:p] vt: **to ~ one's
losses** recuperar os seus prejuízos
recover [rɪ'kʌvə*] vt recuperar ♦ vi
(from illness) recuperar-se; (from
shock) refazer-se; **recovery** n recuperação f; (MED) recuperação, melhora
recreation [rɛkrɪ'eɪʃən] n recreio;
recreational adj recreativo
recruit [rɪ'kru:t] n recruta m/f; (in
company) novato(-a) ♦ vt recrutar
rectangle ['rɛktæŋgl] n retângulo
rector ['rɛktə*] n (REL) pároco
recuperate [rɪ'ku:pəreɪt] vi
recuperar-se
recur [rɪ'kə:*] vi repetir-se, ocorrer
outra vez; (symptoms) reaparecer;
recurrent adj repetido, periódico
recycle [ri:'saɪkl] vt reciclar; **recycling** n reciclagem f
red [rɛd] n vermelho; (POL: pej) vermelho(-a) ♦ adj vermelho; (hair)
ruivo; (wine) tinto; **to be in the ~**
não ter fundos; **Red Cross** n Cruz f
Vermelha; **redden** vt avermelhar
♦ vi corar, ruborizar-se
redeem [rɪ'di:m] vt (REL) redimir;
(sth in pawn) tirar do prego; (loan,
fig: situation) salvar; **redeeming**
adj: **redeeming feature** lado bom ou
que salva
red: **red-haired** adj ruivo; **redhanded** adj: **to be caught redhanded** ser apanhado em flagrante,
ser flagrado; **redhead** n ruivo(-a);

red herring n (fig) pista falsa; **red-
hot** adj incandescente
redirect [ri:daɪ'rɛkt] vt (mail) endereçar de novo
red-light district n zona (de
meretrício)
redo [ri:'du:] (irreg) vt refazer
redress [rɪ'drɛs] n compensação f
♦ vt retificar
Red Sea n: **the ~** o mar Vermelho
redskin ['rɛdskɪn] n pele-vermelha
m/f
red tape n (fig) papelada, burocracia
reduce [rɪ'dju:s] vt reduzir; (lower)
rebaixar; **"~ speed now"** (AUT)
"diminua a velocidade"; **to ~ sb to**
(silence, begging) levar alguém a;
(tears) reduzir alguém a; **reduction**
[rɪ'dʌkʃən] n redução f; (of price)
abatimento
redundancy [rɪ'dʌndənsɪ] (BRIT) n
(dismissal) demissão f; (unemployment) desemprego
redundant [rɪ'dʌndnt] adj (BRIT:
worker) desempregado; (detail, object) redundante, supérfluo; **to be
made ~** ficar desempregado ou sem
trabalho
reed [ri:d] n (BOT) junco; (MUS: of
clarinet etc) palheta
reef [ri:f] n (at sea) recife m
reek [ri:k] vi: **to ~ (of)** cheirar (a),
feder (a)
reel [ri:l] n carretel m, bobina; (of
film) rolo, filme m; (on fishing-rod)
carretilha; (dance) dança típica da
Escócia ♦ vi (sway) cambalear, oscilar; **reel in** vt puxar enrolando a
linha
ref [rɛf] (inf) n abbr = referee
refectory [rɪ'fɛktərɪ] n refeitório
refer [rɪ'fə:*] vt (matter, problem): **to
~ sth to** submeter algo à apreciação
de; (person, patient): **to ~ sb to**
encaminhar alguém a ♦ vi: **to ~ to**

referir-se or aludir a; (consult) recorrer a

referee [refə'ri:] n árbitro(-a), (BRIT: for job application) referência ♦ vt apitar

reference ['refrəns] n referência; (mention) menção f; **with ~ to** com relação a; (COMM: in letter) com referência a; **reference book** n livro de consulta

refill [vb ri:'fil, n 'ri:fil] vt reencher; (lighter etc) reabastecer ♦ n (for pen) carga nova

refine [ri'fain] vt refinar; **refined** adj refinado, culto

reflect [ri'flekt] vt refletir ♦ vi (think) refletir, meditar; **it ~s badly/well on him** isso repercute mal/bem para ele; **reflection** n reflexo; (thought, act) reflexão f; (criticism): **reflection on** crítica de; **on reflection** pensando bem

reflex ['ri:fleks] adj reflexo ♦ n reflexo; **reflexive** [ri'fleksiv] adj (LING) reflexivo

reform [ri'fɔ:m] n reforma ♦ vt reformar; **reformatory** [ri'fɔ:mətəri] (US) n reformatório

refrain [ri'frein] vi: **to ~ from doing** abster-se de fazer ♦ n estribilho, refrão m

refresh [ri'frɛʃ] vt refrescar; **refresher course** (BRIT) n curso de reciclagem; **refreshing** adj refrescante; (sleep) repousante; **refreshments** npl bebidas fpl (não-alcoólicas) e guloseimas

refrigerator [ri'fridʒəreitə*] n refrigerador m, geladeira (BRIT), frigorífico (PT)

refuel [ri:'fjuəl] vi reabastecer

refuge ['refju:dʒ] n refúgio; **to take ~ in** refugiar-se em

refugee [refju'dʒi:] n refugiado(-a)

refund [n 'ri:fʌnd, vb ri'fʌnd] n

reembolso ♦ vt devolver, reembolsar

refurbish [ri:'fə:biʃ] vt renovar

refusal [ri'fju:zəl] n recusa, negativa; **first ~** primeira opção

refuse¹ [ri'fju:z] vt recusar; (order) recusar-se a ♦ vi recusar-se, negar-se; (horse) recusar-se a pular a cerca

refuse² ['refju:s] n refugo, lixo

regain [ri'gein] vt recuperar, recobrar

regal ['ri:gl] adj real, régio

regard [ri'gɑ:d] n (gaze) olhar m firme; (attention) atenção f; (esteem) estima, consideração f ♦ vt (consider) considerar; **to give one's ~s to** lembranças a; **"with kindest ~s"** "cordialmente"; **as ~s, with ~ to** com relação a, com respeito a, quanto a; **regarding** prep com relação a; **regardless** adv apesar de tudo; **regardless of** apesar de

régime [rei'ʒi:m] n regime m

regiment ['redʒimənt] n regimento

region ['ri:dʒən] n região f; **in the ~ of** (fig) por volta de, ao redor de; **regional** adj regional

register ['redʒistə*] n registro (BR), registo (PT); (SCH) chamada ♦ vt registrar (BR), registar (PT); (subj: instrument) marcar, indicar ♦ vi (at hotel) registrar-se (BR), registar-se (PT); (for work) candidatar-se; (as student) inscrever-se; (make impression) causar impressão; **registered** adj (letter, parcel) registrado (BR), registado (PT)

registrar ['redʒistrɑ:*] n oficial m/f de registro (BR) or registo (PT), escrivão(-vã) m/f; (in college) funcionário(-a) administrativo(-a) sênior; (in hospital) médico(-a) sênior

registration [redʒis'treiʃən] n (act) registro (BR), registo (PT); (AUT: also: ~ number) número da placa

registry ['redʒistri] n registro (BR),

registo (_PT_), cartório; **registry office** (_BRIT_) n registro (_BR_) or registo (_PT_) civil, cartório; **to get married in a ~ office** casar-se no civil

regret [rɪ'grɛt] n desgosto, pesar m ♦ vt lamentar; (_repent of_) arrepender-se de; **regretfully** adv com pesar, pesarosamente

regular ['rɛgjulə*] adj regular; (_frequent_) freqüente; (_usual_) habitual; (_soldier_) de linha ♦ n habitual m/f; **regularly** adv regularmente; (_shaped_) simetricamente; (_often_) freqüentemente

regulate ['rɛgjuleɪt] vt (_speed_) regular; (_spending_) controlar; (_TECH_) regular, ajustar; **regulation** [rɛgju'leɪʃən] n (_rule_) regra, regulamento; (_adjustment_) ajuste m

rehearsal [rɪ'həːsəl] n ensaio

rehearse [rɪ'həːs] vt ensaiar

reign [reɪn] n reinado; (_fig_) domínio ♦ vi reinar; imperar

reimburse [riːɪm'bəːs] vt reembolsar

rein [reɪn] n (_for horse_) rédea

reindeer ['reɪndɪə*] n inv rena

reinforce [riːɪn'fɔːs] vt reforçar; **reinforcements** npl (_MIL_) reforços mpl

reinstate [riːɪn'steɪt] vt (_worker_) readmitir; (_tax, law_) reintroduzir

reject [n 'riːdʒɛkt, vb rɪ'dʒɛkt] n (_COMM_) artigo defeituoso ♦ vt rejeitar; (_offer of help_) recusar; (_goods_) refugar; **rejection** n rejeição f; recusa

rejoice [rɪ'dʒɔɪs] vi: **to ~ at** or **over** regozijar-se or alegrar-se de

relapse [rɪ'læps] n (_MED_) recaída

relate [rɪ'leɪt] vt (_tell_) contar, relatar; (_connect_) relacionar; **to ~ sth to** relacionar algo com ♦ vi: **to ~ to** relacionar-se com; **~d to** ligado a, relacionado a; **relating: relating to** prep relativo a, acerca de

relation [rɪ'leɪʃən] n (_person_) parente m/f; (_link_) relação f; **~s** npl (_dealings_) relações fpl; (_relatives_) parentes mpl; **relationship** n relacionamento; (_between two things_) relação f; (_also:_ **family relationship**) parentesco

relative ['rɛlətɪv] n parente m/f ♦ adj relativo; **relatively** adv relativamente

relax [rɪ'læks] vi (_unwind_) descontrair-se; (_muscle_) relaxar-se ♦ vt (_grip_) afrouxar; (_control_) relaxar; (_mind, person_) descansar; **relaxation** [riːlæk'seɪʃən] n (_rest_) descanso; (_of muscle, control_) relaxamento; (_of grip_) afrouxamento; (_recreation_) lazer m; **relaxed** adj relaxado; (_tranquil_) descontraído

relay [n 'riːleɪ, vb rɪ'leɪ] n (_race_) (corrida de) revezamento ♦ vt (_message_) retransmitir

release [rɪ'liːs] n (_from prison_) libertação f; (_from obligation_) liberação f; (_of gas_) escape m; (_of water_) despejo; (_of film, book etc_) lançamento ♦ vt (_prisoner_) pôr em liberdade; (_book, film_) lançar; (_report, news_) publicar; (_gas etc_) soltar; (_free: from wreckage etc_) soltar; (_TECH: catch, spring etc_) desengatar, desapertar

relegate ['rɛləgeɪt] vt relegar; (_SPORT_): **to be ~d** ser rebaixado

relent [rɪ'lɛnt] vi (_yield_) ceder; **relentless** adj (_unceasing_) contínuo; (_determined_) implacável

relevant ['rɛləvənt] adj pertinente; **~ to** relacionado com

reliable [rɪ'laɪəbl] adj (_person, firm:_) digno) de confiança, confiável, sério; (_method, machine_) seguro; (_news_) fidedigno; **reliably** adv: **to be reliably informed that ...** saber através de fonte segura que ...

relic ['rɛlɪk] n (_REL_) relíquia; (_of the_

past) vestígio

relief [rɪ'liːf] *n* alívio; (*help, supplies*) ajuda, socorro; (ART, GEO) relevo

relieve [rɪ'liːv] *vt* (*pain, fear*) aliviar; (*bring help to*) ajudar, socorrer; (*take over from: gen*) substituir, revezar; (: *guard*) render; **to ~ sb of sth** (*load*) tirar algo de alguém; (*duties*) destituir alguém de algo; **to ~ o.s.** fazer as necessidades

religion [rɪ'lɪdʒən] *n* religião *f*; **religious** *adj* religioso

relinquish [rɪ'lɪŋkwɪʃ] *vt* abandonar; (*plan, habit*) renunciar a

relish ['relɪʃ] *n* (CULIN) condimento, tempero; (*enjoyment*) entusiasmo ♦ *vt* (*food etc*) saborear; (*thought*) ver com satisfação

reluctant [rɪ'lʌktənt] *adj* relutante; **reluctantly** *adv* relutantemente, de má vontade

rely on [rɪ'laɪ-] *vt fus* confiar em, contar com; (*be dependent on*) depender de

remain [rɪ'meɪn] *vi* (*survive*) sobreviver; (*stay*) ficar, permanecer; (*be left*) sobrar; (*continue*) continuar; **remainder** *n* resto, restante *m*; **remaining** *adj* restante; **remains** *npl* (*of body*) restos *mpl*; (*of meal*) sobras *fpl*; (*of building*) ruínas *fpl*

remand [rɪ'mɑːnd] *n*: **on ~** sob prisão preventiva ♦ *vt*: **to be ~ed in custody** continuar sob prisão preventiva, manter sob custódia

remark [rɪ'mɑːk] *n* observação *f*, comentário ♦ *vt* comentar; **remarkable** *adj* (*outstanding*) extraordinário

remarry [rɪ'mærɪ] *vi* casar-se de novo

remedial [rɪ'miːdɪəl] *adj* de reforço; (*exercise*) terapêutico

remedy ['remədɪ] *n*: **~ (for)** remédio (contra or a) ♦ *vt* remediar

remember [rɪ'membə*] *vt* lembrar-se de, lembrar; (*bear in mind*) ter

em mente; (*send greetings*): **~ me to her** dê lembranças a ela

remembrance [rɪ'membrəns] *n* (*memory*) memória; (*souvenir*) lembrança, recordação *f*; **Remembrance Day** or **Sunday** *n* Dia *m* do Armistício; *ver quadro*

REMEMBRANCE DAY

Remembrance Day ou Remembrance Sunday é o domingo mais próximo do dia 11 de novembro, dia em que a Primeira Guerra Mundial terminou oficialmente e no qual se homenageia as vítimas das duas guerras mundiais. Nessa ocasião são observados dois minutos de silêncio às 11 horas, horário da assinatura do armistício com a Alemanha em 1918. Nos dias anteriores, papoulas de papel são vendidas por associações de caridade e a renda é revertida aos ex-combatentes e suas famílias.

---

remind [rɪ'maɪnd] *vt*: **to ~ sb to do sth** lembrar a alguém que tem de fazer algo; **to ~ sb of sth** lembrar algo a alguém, lembrar alguém de algo; **reminder** *n* lembrança; (*letter*) carta de advertência

reminisce [remɪ'nɪs] *vi* relembrar velhas histórias; **reminiscent** *adj*: **to be reminiscent of sth** lembrar algo

remit [rɪ'mɪt] *vt* remeter, enviar, mandar; **remittance** *n* remessa

remnant ['remnənt] *n* resto; (*of cloth*) retalho; **~s** *npl* (COMM) retalhos *mpl*

remorse [rɪ'mɔːs] *n* remorso; **remorseful** *adj* arrependido

remote [rɪ'məut] *adj* remoto; (*person*) reservado, afastado; **remote**

control n controle m remoto;
remotely adv remotamente; (slightly) levemente

removal [rɪ'muːvəl] n (taking away)
remoção f; (BRIT: from house)
mudança; (from office: sacking) afastamento, demissão f; (MED)
extração f; **removal van** (BRIT)
n caminhão m (BR) or camião m (PT)
de mudanças

remove [rɪ'muːv] vt tirar, retirar;
(clothing) tirar; (stain) remover;
(employee) afastar, demitir; (name
from list; obstacle) eliminar, remover;
(doubt, abuse) afastar; (MED) extrair

render ['rɛndə*] vt (thanks) trazer;
(service) prestar; (make) fazer, tornar

rendezvous ['rɔndɪvuː] n encontro; (place) ponto de encontro

renew [rɪ'njuː] vt retomar, recomeçar;
(loan etc) prorrogar; (negotiations)
reatar; **renewal** n (of contract)
renovação f; (resumption) retomada

renounce [rɪ'nauns] vt renunciar a

renovate ['rɛnəveɪt] vt renovar;
(house) reformar

renown [rɪ'naun] n renome m;
renowned adj renomado, famoso

rent [rɛnt] n aluguel m (BR), aluguer
m (PT) ♦ vt (also: ~ out) alugar;
rental n (for television, car) aluguel
m (BR), aluguer m (PT)

rep [rɛp] n abbr (COMM) = **representative**

repair [rɪ'pɛə*] n reparação f, conserto ♦ vt consertar; **in good/bad**
em bom/mau estado; **repair kit** n
caixa de ferramentas

repay [riː'peɪ] (irreg) vt (money)
reembolsar, restituir; (person) pagar
de volta; (debt) saldar, liquidar; (sb's
efforts) corresponder, retribuir; (favour) retribuir; **repayment** n reembolso; (of debt) pagamento

repeal [rɪ'piːl] n (of law) revogação f

♦ vt revogar

repeat [rɪ'piːt] n (RADIO, TV) repetição
f ♦ vt repetir; (COMM: order) renovar
♦ vi repetir-se

repel [rɪ'pɛl] vt repelir; (disgust)
repugnar; **repellent** adj repugnante ♦ n: **insect repellent** repelente m
de insetos

repent [rɪ'pɛnt] vi arrepender-se;
repentance n arrependimento

repetitive [rɪ'pɛtɪtɪv] adj repetitivo

replace [rɪ'pleɪs] vt (put back)
repor, devolver; (take the place of)
substituir; **replacement** n (substitution) substituição f; (substitute)
substituto(-a)

replay ['riː'pleɪ] n (of match) partida
decisiva; (TV: also: **action ~**) replay m

replenish [rɪ'plɛnɪʃ] vt (glass) encher; (stock etc) completar, prover

replica ['rɛplɪkə] n réplica, cópia,
reprodução f

reply [rɪ'plaɪ] n resposta ♦ vi responder

report [rɪ'pɔːt] n relatório; (PRESS etc)
reportagem f; (BRIT: also: **school ~**)
boletim m escolar; (of gun) estampido, detonação f ♦ vt informar sobre;
(PRESS etc) fazer uma reportagem
sobre; (bring to notice) comunicar,
anunciar ♦ vi (make a report): **to
~ (on)** apresentar um relatório
(sobre); (present o.s.): **to ~ (to sb)**
apresentar-se (a alguém); (be responsible to): **to ~ to sb** obedecer
às ordens de alguém; **report card**
(US, SCOTTISH) n boletim m escolar;
reportedly adv: **she is reportedly
living in Spain** dizem que ela mora
na Espanha; **reporter** n repórter
m/f

represent [rɛprɪ'zɛnt] vt representar; (constitute) constituir; (COMM)
ser representante de; **representation** [rɛprɪzɛn'teɪʃən] n represen-

tação f; (picture, statue) representação, retrato; (petition) petição f;
~ations npl (protest) reclamação f,
protesto; **representative** [rɛprɪ-
'zɛntətɪv] n representante m/f; (us:
POL) deputado(-a) ♦ adj: **representative (of)** representativo (de)

repress [rɪ'prɛs] vt reprimir; **repression** n repressão f

reprisal [rɪ'praɪzl] n represália

reproach [rɪ'prəʊtʃ] n reprovação f,
censura ♦ vt: **to ~ sb for sth**
reprender alguém por algo; **re-
proachful** adj repreensivo, acu-
satório

reproduce [riːprə'djuːs] vt reproduzir ♦ vi reproduzir-se

reproof [rɪ'pruːf] n reprovação f,
repressão f

reptile ['rɛptaɪl] n réptil m

republic [rɪ'pʌblɪk] n república;
republican adj, n republicano(-a);
(us: POL): **Republican** membro(-a)
do Partido Republicano

reputable ['rɛpjutəbl] adj (make
etc) bem conceituado, de confiança;
(person) honrado, respeitável

reputation [rɛpju'teɪʃən] n reputação f

reputedly [rɪ'pjuːtɪdlɪ] adv segundo
se diz, supostamente

request [rɪ'kwɛst] n pedido; (formal) petição f ♦ vt: **to ~ sth of or
from sb** pedir algo a alguém; (formally) solicitar algo a alguém;
request stop (BRIT) n (for bus)
parada não obrigatória

require [rɪ'kwaɪə*] vt (need: subj:
person) precisar de, necessitar; (:
thing, situation) exigir, requerer;
(want) pedir; (order): **to ~ sb to do
sth/sth of sb** exigir que alguém
faça algo/algo de alguém; **requirement** n (need) necessidade f;
(want) pedido

rescue ['rɛskjuː] n salvamento, resgate m ♦ vt: **to ~ (from)** resgatar
(de); (save, fig) salvar (de); **rescue
party** n grupo or expedição f de
resgate

research [rɪ'səːtʃ] n pesquisa ♦ vt
pesquisar

resemblance [rɪ'zɛmbləns] n semelhança

resemble [rɪ'zɛmbl] vt parecer-se
com

resent [rɪ'zɛnt] vt (attitude) ressentir-se
de; (person) estar ressentido com;
resentful adj ressentido

reservation [rɛzə'veɪʃən] n reserva

reserve [rɪ'zəːv] n reserva; (SPORT)
suplente m/f, reserva m/f (BR) ♦ vt
reservar; ~s npl (MIL) (tropas fpl da)
reserva; (COMM) reserva; **in ~** de
reserva; **reserved** adj reservado

residence ['rɛzɪdəns] n residência;
(formal: home) domicílio; **residence permit** (BRIT) n autorização f
de residência

resident ['rɛzɪdənt] n (of country,
town) habitante m/f; (in hotel) hóspede m/f ♦ adj (population) permanente; (doctor) interno, residente;
residential [rɛzɪ'dɛnʃəl] adj residencial

residue ['rɛzɪdjuː] n resto

resign [rɪ'zaɪn] vt renunciar a,
demitir-se de ♦ vi: **to ~ (from)** demitir-se (de); **to ~ o.s. to** resignar-se a;
resignation [rɛzɪg'neɪʃən] n
demissão f; (state of mind) resignação f; **resigned** adj resignado

resilient [rɪ'zɪlɪənt] adj (person)
forte; (material) resistente

resist [rɪ'zɪst] vt resistir a

resolution [rɛzə'luːʃən] n resolução
f; (of problem) solução f

resolve [rɪ'zɔlv] n resolução f ♦ vt
resolver ♦ vi: **to ~ to do** resolver-se a
fazer

resort [rɪ'zɔːt] n local m turístico, estação f de veraneio; (recourse) recurso ♦ vi: **to ~ to** recorrer a; **in the last ~** em último caso, em última instância

resounding [rɪ'zaundɪŋ] adj retumbante

resource [rɪ'sɔːs] n (raw material) recurso natural; **~s** npl (coal, money, energy) recursos mpl; **resourceful** adj engenhoso, habilidoso

respect [rɪs'pɛkt] n respeito ♦ vt respeitar; **~s** npl (greetings) cumprimentos mpl; **respectable** adj respeitável; (large) considerável; (result, player) razoável; **respectful** adj respeitoso

respond [rɪs'pɔnd] vi (answer) responder; (react) reagir; (to treatment) responder; **response** [rɪs'pɔns] n resposta; reação f

responsibility [rɪspɔnsɪ'bɪlɪtɪ] n responsabilidade f; (duty) dever m

responsible [rɪs'pɔnsɪbl] adj sério, responsável; (job) de responsabilidade; (liable): **~ (for)** responsável (por)

responsive [rɪs'pɔnsɪv] adj receptivo

rest [rɛst] n descanso, repouso; (pause) pausa, intervalo; (support) apoio; (remainder) resto; (MUS) pausa ♦ vi descansar; (stop) parar; (be supported): **to ~ on** apoiar-se em ♦ vt descansar; (lean): **to rest sth on/against** apoiar algo em or sobre/ contra; **the ~ of them** os outros; **it ~s with him to do it** cabe a ele fazê-lo

restaurant ['rɛstərɒŋ] n restaurante m; **restaurant car** (BRIT) n vagão-restaurante m

restful ['rɛstful] adj tranqüilo, repousante

restive ['rɛstɪv] adj inquieto, impaciente; (horse) rebelão(-ona), teimoso

restless ['rɛstlɪs] adj desassossegado, irrequieto

restore [rɪ'stɔː*] vt (building, order) restaurar; (sth stolen) restituir; (health) restabelecer

restrain [rɪs'treɪn] vt (feeling) reprimir; (person) refrear; (person): **to ~ (from doing)** impedir (de fazer); **restrained** adj (style) moderado, comedido; (person) comedido; **restraint** n (restriction) restrição f; (moderation) moderação f, comedimento f; (of style) sobriedade f

restrict [rɪs'trɪkt] vt restringir, limitar; (people, animals) confinar; (activities) limitar; **restriction** n restrição f, limitação f

rest room (US) n banheiro (BR), lavabo (PT)

result [rɪ'zʌlt] n resultado ♦ vi: **to ~ in** resultar em; **as a ~ of** como resultado or conseqüência de

resume [rɪ'zjuːm] vt (work, journey) retomar, recomeçar ♦ vi recomeçar

résumé ['reɪzjuːmeɪ] n (summary) resumo; (US: curriculum vitae) curriculum vitae m, currículo f

resurrection [rɛzə'rɛkʃən] n ressurreição f

resuscitate [rɪ'sʌsɪteɪt] vt (MED) ressuscitar, reanimar

retail ['riːteɪl] adj a varejo (BR), a retalho (PT) ♦ adv a varejo (BR), a retalho (PT); **retailer** n varejista m/f (BR), retalhista m/f (PT)

retain [rɪ'teɪn] vt (keep) reter, conservar; **retainer** n (fee) adiantamento

retaliate [rɪ'tælɪeɪt] vi: **to ~ (against)** revidar (contra); **retaliation** [rɪtælɪ'eɪʃən] n represálias fpl, vingança

retch [rɛtʃ] vi fazer esforço para vomitar

retire [rɪˈtaɪə*] vi aposentar-se;
(withdraw) retirar-se; (go to bed)
deitar-se; **retired** adj aposentado
(BR), reformado (PT); **retirement** n
aposentadoria (BR), reforma (PT);
retiring adj de saída; (shy) acanhado, retraído

retort [rɪˈtɔːt] vi replicar, retrucar

retrace [riːˈtreɪs] vt: to ~ one's
steps voltar sobre (os) seus passos,
refazer o mesmo caminho

retract [rɪˈtrækt] vt (statement) retirar, retratar; (claws) encolher;
(undercarriage, aerial) recolher

retrain [riːˈtreɪn] vt reciclar

retreat [rɪˈtriːt] n (place) retiro; (act)
retirada ♦ vi retirar-se

retrieval [rɪˈtriːvəl] n recuperação f

retrieve [rɪˈtriːv] vt (sth lost) reaver,
recuperar; (situation, honour) salvar;
(error, loss) reparar

retrospect [ˈretrəspekt] n: in ~
retrospectivamente, em retrospecto; **retrospective** [retrəˈspektɪv]
adj retrospectivo; (law) retroativo

return [rɪˈtɜːn] n regresso, volta; (of
sth stolen etc) devolução f; (FINANCE:
from land, shares) rendimento ♦ cpd
(journey) de volta; (BRIT: ticket) de
ida e volta; (match) de revanche ♦ vi
voltar, regressar; (symptoms) voltar;
(regain): to ~ to (consciousness)
recobrar; (power) retornar a ♦ vt
devolver; (favour etc) retribuir; (verdict) proferir, anunciar; (POL: candidate) eleger; ~s npl (COMM) receita;
in ~ (for) em troca (de); many
happy ~s (of the day)! parabéns!;
by ~ (of post) por volta do correio

reunion [riːˈjuːnɪən] n (family) reunião f; (two people, class) reencontro

reunite [riːjuːˈnaɪt] vt reunir; (reconcile) reconciliar

rev [rev] n abbr (AUT: = revolution)
revolução f ♦ vt (also: ~ up) aumen-

tar a velocidade de

revamp [ˈriːˈvæmp] vt dar um jeito
em

reveal [rɪˈviːl] vt revelar; (make visible) mostrar; **revealing** adj revela-
dor(a)

revel [ˈrevl] vi: to ~ in sth/in doing
sth deleitar-se com algo/em fazer
algo

revenge [rɪˈvendʒ] n vingança, desforra; **to take ~ on** vingar-se de

revenue [ˈrevənjuː] n receita, renda

reverberate [rɪˈvɜːbəret] vi (sound)
ressoar, repercutir, ecoar; (fig) repercutir

reversal [rɪˈvɜːsl] n (of order)
reversão f; (of direction) mudança
em sentido contrário; (of decision)
revogação f; (of roles) inversão f

reverse [rɪˈvɜːs] n (opposite) contrário; (of cloth) avesso; (of coin) reverso; (of paper) dorso; (AUT: also: ~
gear) marcha à ré (BR), marcha atrás
(PT); (setback) revés m, derrota ♦ adj
(order) inverso, oposto; (direction)
contrário; (process) inverso ♦ vt
inverter; (position) mudar; (process,
decision) revogar; (car) dar marcha-
a-ré em ♦ vi (BRIT: AUT) dar (marcha à)
ré (BR), fazer marcha atrás (PT);
reverse-charge call (BRIT) n (TEL)
ligação f a cobrar

revert [rɪˈvɜːt] vi: to ~ to voltar a;
(LAW) reverter a

review [rɪˈvjuː] n (magazine, MIL)
revista; (of book, film) crítica, resenha; (examination) recapitulação f,
exame m ♦ vt rever, examinar; (MIL)
passar em revista; (book, film) fazer a
crítica or resenha de

revise [rɪˈvaɪz] vt (manuscript) corrigir; (opinion, procedure) alterar;
(price) revisar; **revision** [rɪˈvɪʒən] n
correção f; (for exam) revisão f

revival [rɪˈvaɪvəl] n (recovery) restabelecimento; (of interest) renascença, renascimento; (THEATRE) reestréia; (of faith) despertar m

revive [rɪ'vaɪv] vt (person) reanimar, ressuscitar; (economy) recuperar; (custom) restabelecer, restaurar; (hope, courage) despertar ; (play) reapresentar ♦ vi (person: from faint) voltar a si, recuperar os sentidos; (: from ill-health) recuperar-se; (activity, economy) reativar; (hope, interest) renascer

revolt [rɪ'vəult] n revolta, rebelião f, insurreição f ♦ vi revoltar-se ♦ vt causar aversão a, repugnar; **revolting** adj revoltante, repulsivo

revolution [revə'luːʃən] n revolução f; (of wheel, earth) rotação f

revolve [rɪ'vɔlv] vi girar

revolver [rɪ'vɔlvə*] n revólver m

revolving [rɪ'vɔlvɪŋ] adj giratório

revulsion [rɪ'vʌlʃən] n aversão f, repugnância

reward [rɪ'wɔːd] n recompensa ♦ vt: **to ~ (for)** recompensar or premiar (por); **rewarding** adj (fig) gratificante, compensador(a)

rewind [riː'waɪnd] (irreg) vt (tape) voltar para trás

rewire [riː'waɪə*] vt (house) renovar a instalação elétrica de

rheumatism ['ruːmətɪzəm] n reumatismo

rhinoceros [raɪ'nɔsərəs] n rinoceronte m

rhubarb ['ruːbɑːb] n ruibarbo

rhyme [raɪm] n rima; (verse) verso(s) m(pl) rimado(s), poesia

rhythm ['rɪðm] n ritmo

rib [rɪb] n (ANAT) costela ♦ vt (mock) zombar de, encarnar em

ribbon ['rɪbən] n fita; **in ~s** (torn) em tirinhas, esfarrapado

rice [raɪs] n arroz m; **rice pudding** n arroz m doce

rich [rɪtʃ] adj rico; (clothes) valioso; (soil) fértil; (food) suculento, forte; (colour) intenso; (voice) suave, cheio ♦ npl: **the ~** os ricos; **~es** npl (wealth) riquezas fpl

rickets ['rɪkɪts] n raquitismo

rid [rɪd] (pt, pp rid) vt: **to ~ sb of sth** livrar alguém de algo; **to get ~ of** livrar-se de; (sth no longer required) desfazer-se de

riddle ['rɪdl] n (conundrum) adivinhação f; (mystery) enigma m, charada ♦ vt: **to be ~d with** estar cheio de

ride [raɪd] (pt rode, pp ridden) n (gen) passeio; (on horse) passeio a cavalo; (distance covered) percurso, trajeto ♦ vi (as sport) montar; (go somewhere: on horse, bicycle) ir (a cavalo, de bicicleta); (journey: on bicycle, motorcycle, bus) viajar ♦ vt (a horse) montar a; (bicycle, motorcycle) andar de; (distance) percorrer; **to ~ at anchor** (NAUT) estar ancorado; **to take sb for a ~** (fig) enganar alguém; **rider** n (on horse: male) cavaleiro; (: female) amazona; (on bicycle) ciclista m/f; (on motorcycle) motociclista m/f

ridge [rɪdʒ] n (of hill) cume m, topo; (of roof) cumeeira; (wrinkle) ruga

ridicule ['rɪdɪkjuːl] n escárnio, zombaria, mofa ♦ vt ridicularizar, zombar de; **ridiculous** adj ridículo

riding ['raɪdɪŋ] n equitação f

rife [raɪf] adj: **to be ~** ser comum; **to be ~ with** estar repleto de, abundar em

rifle ['raɪfl] n rifle m, fuzil m ♦ vt saquear; **rifle through** vt fus vasculhar

rift [rɪft] n fenda, fratura; (in clouds) brecha; (fig: between friends) desentendimento; (: in party) rompimento, divergência

rig [rɪg] n (also: **oil ~**) torre f de perfuração ♦ vt adulterar or falsificar os resultados de; **rig out** (BRIT) vt: **to ~ out as/in** ataviar or vestir como/com; **rig up** vt instalar, montar, improvisar

right [raɪt] adj certo, correto; (suitable) adequado, conveniente; (: decision) certo; (just) justo; (morally good) bom; (not left) direito ♦ n direito; (not left) direita ♦ adv bem, corretamente; (fairly) adequadamente, justamente; (not on the left) à direita; (exactly): **~ now** agora mesmo ♦ vt colocar em pé; (correct) corrigir, indireitar ♦ excl bom!; **to be ~** (person) ter razão; (answer, clock) estar certo; **by ~s** por direito; **on the ~** à direita; **to be in the ~** ter razão; **~ away** imediatamente, logo, já; **in the middle** bem no meio; **righteous** ['raɪtʃəs] adj justo, honrado; (anger) justificado; **rightful** adj (heir) legítimo; (place) justo; legítimo; **right-handed** adj destro; **right-hand man** n braço direito; **right-hand side** n lado direito; **rightly** adv (with reason) com razão; **right of way** n prioridade f de passagem; (AUT) preferência f; **right-wing** adj de direita

rigid ['rɪdʒɪd] adj rígido; (principle) inflexível

rim [rɪm] n borda, beira; (of spectacles, wheel) aro

rind [raɪnd] n (of bacon) pele f; (of lemon etc) casca; (of cheese) crosta, casca

ring [rɪŋ] (pt **rang**, pp **rung**) n (of metal) aro; (on finger) anel m; (of people, objects) círculo, grupo; (for boxing) ringue m; (of circus) pista, picadeiro; (bull~) picadeiro, arena; (of light, smoke) círculo; (of small bell) toque m; (of large bell) badalada, repique m ♦ vi (on telephone)

telefonar; (bell) tocar; (also: ~ out) soar; (ears) zumbir ♦ vt (BRIT: TEL) telefonar a, ligar para; (bell etc) badalar; (doorbell) tocar; **to give sb a ~** (BRIT: TEL) dar uma ligada or ligar para alguém; **ring back** (BRIT) vi (TEL) telefonar or ligar de volta ♦ vt telefonar or ligar de volta para; **ring off** (BRIT) vi (TEL) desligar; **ring up** (BRIT) vt (TEL) telefonar a, ligar para; **ringing** ['rɪŋɪŋ] n (of telephone) toque m; (of bell) repicar m; (in ears) zumbido; **ringing tone** (BRIT) n (TEL) sinal m de chamada; **ringleader** n cabeça m/f, cérebro

ringlets ['rɪŋlɪts] npl caracóis mpl, anéis mpl

ring road (BRIT) n estrada periférica or perimetral

rink [rɪŋk] n (also: ice ~) pista de patinação, rinque m

rinse [rɪns] n enxaguada ♦ vt enxaguar; (also: ~ out: mouth) bochechar

riot ['raɪət] n distúrbio, motim m, desordem f; (of colour) festival m, profusão f ♦ vi provocar distúrbios, amotinar-se; **to run** ~ desenfrear-se; **riotous** adj (crowd) desordeiro; (behaviour) turbulento; (party) tumultuado, puxadíssimo

rip [rɪp] n rasgão m ♦ vt rasgar ♦ vi rasgar-se

ripe [raɪp] adj maduro; **ripen** vt, vi amadurecer

ripple ['rɪpl] n ondulação f, encrespação f; (of laughter etc) onda ♦ vi encrespar-se

rise [raɪz] (pt **rose**, pp **risen**) n elevação f, ladeira; (hill) colina, rampa; (in wages: BRIT) aumento; (in prices, temperature) subida; (to power etc) ascensão f ♦ vi levantar-se, erguer-se; (prices, waters) subir; (sun) nascer; (from bed etc) levantar(-se);

(*sound*) aumentar, erguer-se; (*also:* ~ **up**: *building*) erguer-se; (: *rebel*) sublevar-se; (*in rank*) ascender, subir; **to give** ~ **to** ocasionar, dar origem a; **to** ~ **to the occasion** mostrar-se à altura da situação; **rising** *adj* (*prices*) em alta; (*number*) crescente, cada vez maior; (*tide*) montante; (*sun, moon*) nascente

risk [rɪsk] *n* risco, perigo; (INSURANCE) risco ♦ *vt* pôr em risco; (*chance*) arriscar, aventurar; **to take** ~ **or run the** ~ **of doing** correr o risco de fazer; **at** ~ em perigo; **at one's own** ~ por sua própria conta e risco; **risky** *adj* perigoso

rite [raɪt] *n* rito; **last** ~**s** últimos sacramentos

ritual [ˈrɪtjuəl] *adj* ritual ♦ *n* ritual *m*; (*of initiation*) rito

rival [ˈraɪvl] *adj, n* rival *m/f*; (*in business*) concorrente *m/f* ♦ *vt* competir com; **rivalry** *n* rivalidade *f*

river [ˈrɪvə*] *n* rio ♦ *cpd* (*port, traffic*) fluvial; **up/down** ~ rio acima/abaixo; **riverbank** *n* margem *f* (do rio); **riverbed** *n* leito do rio

rivet [ˈrɪvɪt] *n* rebite *m*, cravo ♦ *vt* (*fig*) fixar

road [rəud] *n* via; (*motorway etc*) estrada (de rodagem); (*in town*) rua ♦ *cpd* rodoviário; **roadblock** *n* barricada; **roadhog** *n* dono da estrada; **road map** *n* mapa *m* rodoviário; **road rage** *n* conduta agressiva dos motoristas no trânsito; **roadside** *n* beira da estrada; **road-sign** *n* placa de sinalização; **roadway** *n* pista, estrada; **road works** *npl* obras *fpl* (na estrada); **road-worthy** *adj* em bom estado de conservação e segurança

roam [rəum] *vi* vagar, perambular, errar

roar [rɔ:*] *n* (*of animal*) rugido, urro; (*of crowd*) bramido; (*of vehicle, storm*) estrondo; (*of laughter*) barulho ♦ *vi* (*animal, engine*) rugir; (*person, crowd*) bradar; **to** ~ **with laughter** dar gargalhadas

roast [rəust] *n* carne *f* assada, assado ♦ *vt* assar; (*coffee*) torrar; **roast beef** *n* rosbife *m*

rob [rɔb] *vt* roubar; (*bank*) assaltar; **to** ~ **sb of sth** roubar algo de alguém; (*fig: deprive*) despojar alguém de algo; **robber** *n* ladrão (ladra) *m/f*; **robbery** *n* roubo

robe [rəub] *n* toga, beca; (*also:* bath ~) roupão *m* (de banho)

robin [ˈrɔbɪn] *n* pisco-de-peito-ruivo (BR), pintarroxo (PT)

robot [ˈrəubɔt] *n* robô *m*

robust [rəuˈbʌst] *adj* robusto, forte; (*appetite*) sadio; (*economy*) forte

rock [rɔk] *n* rocha; (*boulder*) penhasco, rochedo; (US: *small stone*) cascalho; (BRIT: *sweet*) pirulito ♦ *vt* (*swing gently*: *cradle*) balançar, oscilar; (: *child*) embalar, acalentar; (*shake*) sacudir ♦ *vi* (*object*) balançar-se; (*person*) embalar-se; **on the** ~**s** (*drink*) com gelo; (*marriage etc*) arruinado, em dificuldades; **rock and roll** *n* rock-and-roll *m*; **rock-bottom** *adj* (*fig*) mínimo, ínfimo; **rockery** *n* jardim de plantas rasteiras entre pedras

rocket [ˈrɔkɪt] *n* foguete *m*

rocky [ˈrɔkɪ] *adj* rochoso, bambo, instável; (*marriage*) instável

rod [rɔd] *n* vara, varinha; (*also: fishing* ~) vara de pescar

rode [rəud] *pt of* **ride**

rodent [ˈrəudnt] *n* roedor *m*

rodeo [ˈrəudɪəu] (US) *n* rodeio *m*

roe [rəu] *n* (*also:* ~ **deer**) corça, cerva; (*of fish*): **hard/soft** ~ ova/ esperma *m* de peixe

rogue [rəug] n velhaco, maroto

role [rəul] n papel m

roll [rəul] n rolo; (of banknotes) maço; (also: **bread ~**) pãozinho; (register) rol m, lista; (of drums etc) rufar m ♦ vt rolar; (also: **~ up**: string) enrolar; (: sleeves) arregaçar; (cigarette) enrolar; (eyes) virar; (also: **~ out**: pastry) esticar; (lawn, road etc) aplanar ♦ vi rolar; (drum) rufar; (vehicle: also: **~ along**) rodar; (ship) balançar, jogar; **roll about** or **around** vi ficar rolando; **roll by** (time) passar; **roll in** vi (mail, cash) chegar em grande quantidade; **roll over** vi dar uma volta; **roll up** vi (inf) pintar, chegar, aparecer ♦ vt enrolar; **roll call** n chamada, toque m de chamada; **roller** n (in machine) rolo, cilindro; (wheel) roda, roldana; (for lawn, road) rolo compressor; (for hair) rolo; **Rollerblades** ® ['rəuləbleidz] n patins mpl em linha; **roller coaster** n montanha-russa; **roller skates** npl patins mpl de roda

rolling pin ['rəulɪŋ-] n rolo de pastel

ROM [rɔm] n abbr (COMPUT: = read-only memory) ROM m

Roman ['rəumən] adj, n romano(-a); **Roman Catholic** adj, n católico(-a) (romano(-a))

romance [rə'mæns] n aventura amorosa, romance m; (book) história de amor; (charm) romantismo

Romania [ru:'meɪnɪə] n Romênia; **Romanian** adj romeno ♦ n romeno(-a); (LING) romeno

romantic [rə'mæntɪk] adj romântico

Rome [rəum] n Roma

romp [rɔmp] n brincadeira, travessura ♦ vi (also: **~ about**) brincar ruidosamente

rompers ['rɔmpəz] npl macacão m de bebê

roof [ru:f] n (of house) telhado; (of car) capota, teto ♦ vt telhar, cobrir com telhas; **the ~ of the mouth** o céu da boca; **roof rack** n (AUT) bagageiro

rook [ruk] n (bird) gralha; (CHESS) torre f

room [ru:m] n (in house) quarto, aposento; (also: **bed~**) quarto, dormitório; (in school etc) sala; (space) espaço, lugar m; (scope: for improvement etc) espaço; **~s** npl (lodging) alojamento; **"~s to let"** (BRIT), **"~s for rent"** (US) "alugam-se quartos or apartamentos"; **roommate** n companheiro(-a) de quarto; **room service** n serviço de quarto; **roomy** adj espaçoso; (garment) folgado

rooster ['ru:stə*] n galo

root [ru:t] n raiz f; (fig) origem f ♦ vi enraizar, arraigar; **~s** npl (family origins) raízes fpl; **root about** vi (fig): **to ~ about in** (drawer) vasculhar; (house) esquadrinhar; **root for** vt fus torcer por; **root out** vt extirpar

rope [rəup] n corda; (NAUT) cabo ♦ vt (tie) amarrar; (climbers: also: **~ together**) amarrar or atar com uma corda; (area: also: **~ off**) isolar; **to know the ~s** (fig) estar por dentro (do assunto); **rope in** vt (fig): **to ~ sb in** persuadir alguém a tomar parte

rosary ['rəuzərɪ] n rosário

rose [rəuz] pt of **rise** ♦ n rosa; (also: **~bush**) roseira; (on watering can) crivo

rosé ['rəuzeɪ] n rosado, rosé m

rosemary ['rəuzmərɪ] n alecrim m

rosy ['rəuzɪ] adj rosado, rosáceo; (cheeks) rosado; (situation) cor-de-rosa inv; **a ~ future** um futuro promissor

rot [rɔt] n (decay) putrefação f, podridão f; (fig: pej) besteira ♦ vt, vi apodrecer

rota ['rəutə] n lista de tarefas, escala de serviço

rotate [rəu'teɪt] vt fazer girar, dar voltas em; (jobs) alternar, revezar ♦ vi girar, dar voltas; **rotating** adj rotativo

rotten ['rɔtn] adj podre; (wood) carcomido; (fig) corrupto; (inf: bad) péssimo; **to feel ~** (ill) sentir-se podre

rough [rʌf] adj (skin, surface) áspero; (terrain) acidentado; (road) desigual; (voice) áspero, rouco; (person, manner: violent) violento; (: brusque) ríspido; (weather) tempestuoso; (treatment) brutal, mau (má); (sea) agitado; (district) violento; (plan) preliminar; (work) grosseiro; (guess) aproximado ♦ n (GOLF): **in the ~** na grama crescida; **to sleep ~** (BRIT) dormir na rua; **roughage** n fibras fpl; **rough copy** n rascunho; **rough draft** n rascunho; **roughly** adv bruscamente; (make) toscamente; (approximately) aproximadamente

roulette [ruː'lɛt] n roleta

Romania etc [ruː'meɪnɪə] n = **Rumania** etc

round [raund] adj redondo ♦ n (BRIT: of toast) rodela; (of policeman) ronda; (of milkman) trajeto; (of doctor) visitas fpl; (game: of cards etc) partida; (of ammunition) cartucho; (BOXING) rounde m, assalto; (of talks) ciclo ♦ vt virar, dobrar ♦ prep (surrounding): **~ his neck/the table** em volta da seu pescoço/ao redor da mesa; (in a circular movement): **to move ~ the room/~ the world** mover-se pelo quarto/dar a volta

ao mundo; (in various directions) por; (approximately): **about** ♦ adv: **all ~** por todos os lados; **the long way ~** o caminho mais comprido; **all the year ~** durante todo o ano; **it's just ~ the corner** (fig) está pertinho; **~ the clock** ininterrupto; **to go ~ the back** passar por detrás; **to go ~ a house** visitar uma casa; **enough to go ~** suficiente para todos; **a ~ of applause** uma salva de palmas; **a ~ of drinks** uma rodada de bebidas; **~ of sandwiches** sanduíche m (BR), sandes f inv (PT); **round off** vt terminar, completar; **round up** vt (cattle) encurralar; (people) reunir; (price, figure) arredondar; **roundabout** n (BRIT: AUT) rotatória; (: at fair) carrossel m ♦ adj indireto; **round trip** n viagem f de ida e volta

rouse [rauz] vt (wake up) despertar, acordar; (stir up) suscitar; **rousing** adj emocionante, vibrante

route [ruːt] n caminho, rota; (of bus) trajeto; (of shipping) rumo, rota; (of procession) rota

routine [ruː'tiːn] adj (work) rotineiro; (procedure) de rotina ♦ n (THEATRE) número

row¹ [rəu] n (line) fila, fileira; (in theatre, boat) fileira; (KNITTING) carreira, fileira ♦ vi, vt remar; **in a ~** (fig) a fio, seguido

row² [rau] n barulho, balbúrdia; (dispute) discussão f, briga; (scolding) repreensão f ♦ vi brigar

rowboat ['rəubəut] (US) n barco a remo

rowdy ['raudɪ] adj (person: noisy) barulhento; (occasion) tumultuado

rowing ['rəuɪŋ] n remo; **rowing boat** (BRIT) n barco a remo

royal [ˈrɔɪəl] adj real

Royal Academy (of Arts) (BRIT) n ver quadro

ROYAL ACADEMY

A Royal Academy, ou Royal Academy of Arts, fundada em 1768 por George III para desenvolver a pintura, a escultura e a arquitetura, situa-se em Burlington House, Piccadilly, em Londres. A cada verão há uma exposição de obras de artistas contemporâneos. A Royal Academy também oferece cursos de pintura, escultura e arquitetura.

Royal Air Force (BRIT) n força aérea britânica

royalty n família real, realeza; (payment: to author) direitos mpl autorais

rpm abbr (= revolutions per minute) rpm

RSVP abbr (= répondez s'il vous plaît) ER

Rt Hon. (BRIT) abbr (= Right Honourable) título honorífico de conselheiro do estado ou juiz

rub [rʌb] n friccionar; (part of body) esfregar ♦ n: **to give sth a ~** dar uma esfregada em algo; **to ~ sb up** (BRIT) or **~ sb** (US) **the wrong way** irritar alguém; **rub off** vi sair esfregando; **rub off on** vt fus transmitir-se para, influir sobre; **rub out** vt apagar

rubber [ˈrʌbə*] n borracha; (BRIT: eraser) borracha; **rubber band** n elástico, tira elástica

rubbish [ˈrʌbɪʃ] n (waste) refugo; (from household, in street) lixo; (junk) coisas fpl sem valor; (fig: pej: nonsense) disparates mpl, asneiras fpl; **rubbish bin** (BRIT) n lata de lixo; **rubbish dump** n (in town) depósito (de lixo)

rubble [ˈrʌbl] n (debris) entulho; (CONSTR) escombros mpl

ruby [ˈruːbɪ] n rubi m

rucksack [ˈrʌksæk] n mochila

rudder [ˈrʌdə*] n leme m; (of plane) leme de direção

rude [ruːd] adj (person) grosso, mal-educado; (word, manners) grosseiro; (shocking) obsceno, chocante

rug [rʌg] n tapete m; (BRIT: for knees) manta (de viagem)

rugby [ˈrʌgbɪ] n (also: ~ **football**) rúgbi m (BR), râguebi m (PT)

rugged [ˈrʌgɪd] adj (landscape) acidentado, irregular; (features) marcado; (character) severo, austero

ruin [ˈruːɪn] n ruína; (of plans) destruição f; (downfall) queda; (bankruptcy) bancarrota ♦ vt destruir; (future, person) arruinar; (spoil) estragar; **~s** npl (of building) ruínas fpl

rule [ruːl] n (norm) regra; (regulation) regulamento; (government) governo, domínio; (ruler) régua ♦ vt governar ♦ vi governar; (monarch) reger; (LAW): **to ~ in favour of/against** decidir oficialmente a favor de/contra; **as a ~** por via de regra, geralmente; **rule out** vt excluir; **ruler** n (sovereign) soberano(-a); (for measuring) régua; **ruling** adj (party) dominante; (class) dirigente ♦ n (LAW) parecer m, decisão f

rum [rʌm] n rum m

Rumania etc [ruːˈmeɪnɪə] n = **Romania** etc

rumble [ˈrʌmbl] n ruído surdo, barulho; (of thunder) estrondo, ribombo ♦ vi ribombar, ressoar; (stomach) roncar; (pipe) fazer barulho; (thunder) ribombar

rummage [ˈrʌmɪdʒ] vi revolver

rumour [ˈruːmə*] (US **rumor**) n rumor m, boato ♦ vt: **it is ~ed that ...** corre o boato de que ...

rump steak [rʌmp-] n alcatra
rumpus ['rʌmpəs] n barulho, confusão f, zorra
run [rʌn] (pt ran, pp run) n corrida; (in car) passeio (de carro); (distance travelled) trajeto, percurso; (journey) viagem f; (series) série f; (THEATRE) temporada; (SKI) pista; (in stockings) fio puxado ♦ vt (race) correr; (operate: business) dirigir; (: competition, course) organizar; (: hotel, house) administrar; (water) deixar correr; (bath) encher; (PRESS: feature) publicar; (COMPUT) rodar; (hand, finger) passar ♦ vi correr; (work: machine) funcionar; (bus, train: operate) circular; (: travel) ir; (continue: play) continuar em cartaz; (: contract) ser válido; (river, bath) fluir, correr; (colours) desbotar; (in election) candidatar-se; (nose) escorrer; **there was a ~** n houve muita procura; **in the long ~** no final das contas, mais cedo ou mais tarde; **on the ~** em fuga, foragido; **run about** or **around** vi correr por todos os lados; **run across** vt fus encontrar por acaso, topar com, dar com; **run away** vi fugir; **run down** vt (AUT) atropelar; (production) reduzir; (criticize) criticar; **to be ~ down** estar enfraquecido or exausto; **run in** (BRIT) vt (car) rodar; **run into** vt fus (meet: person) dar com, topar com; (: trouble) esbarrar em; (collide with) bater em; **run off** vi fugir; **run out** vi (person) sair correndo; (liquid) escorrer, esgotar-se; (lease, passport) caducar, vencer; (money) acabar; **run out of** vt fus ficar sem; **run over** vt (AUT) atropelar ♦ vt fus (revise) recapitular; **run through** vt fus (instructions, play) recapitular; **run up** vt (debt) acumular ♦ vi: **to ~ up against** esbarrar em; **runaway** adj (horse)

desembestado; (truck) desgovernado; (person) fugitivo
rung [rʌŋ] pp of **ring** ♦ n (of ladder) degrau m
runner ['rʌnə*] n (in race) corredor(a) m/f; (horse) corredor m; (on sledge) patim m, lâmina; (for drawer) corrediça; **runner bean** (BRIT) n (BOT) vagem f (BR), feijão m verde (PT); **runner-up** n segundo(-a) colocado(-a)
running ['rʌnɪŋ] n (sport) corrida; (of business) direção f ♦ adj (water) corrente; (commentary) contínuo, seguido; **6 days** ~ 6 dias seguidos or consecutivos; **to be in/out of the** ~ **for sth** disputar algo/estar fora da disputa por algo
runny ['rʌnɪ] adj aguado; (egg) mole; **to have a ~ nose** estar com coriza, estar com o nariz escorrendo
runt [rʌnt] n (animal) nanico; (pej: person) anão (anã) m/f
run-up n: ~ **to sth** (election etc) período que antecede algo
runway ['rʌnweɪ] n (AVIAT) pista (de decolagem or de pouso)
rupture ['rʌptʃə*] n (MED) hérnia
rural ['ruərl] adj rural
rush [rʌʃ] n (hurry) pressa; (COMM) grande procura or demanda; (BOT) junco; (current) torrente f; (of emotion) ímpeto ♦ vt apressar ♦ vi apressar-se, precipitar-se; **rush hour** n rush m (BR), hora de ponta (PT)
rusk [rʌsk] n rosca
Russia ['rʌʃə] n Rússia; **Russian** adj russo ♦ n russo(-a); (LING) russo
rust [rʌst] n ferrugem f ♦ vi enferrujar
rustle ['rʌsl] vi sussurrar ♦ vt (paper) farfalhar; (US: cattle) roubar, afanar

rustproof ['rʌstpruːf] adj inoxidável, à prova de ferrugem

rusty ['rʌstɪ] adj enferrujado

rut [rʌt] n sulco; (ZOOL) cio; **to be in a ~** ser escravo da rotina

ruthless ['ruːθlɪs] adj implacável, sem piedade

rye [raɪ] n centeio

S

Sabbath ['sæbəθ] n (Christian) domingo; (Jewish) sábado

sabotage ['sæbətɑːʒ] n sabotagem f ♦ vt sabotar

saccharin(e) ['sækərɪn] n sacarina

sachet ['sæʃeɪ] n sachê m

sack [sæk] n (bag) saco, saca ♦ vt (dismiss) despedir; (plunder) saquear; **to get the ~** ser demitido; **sacking** n (dismissal) demissão f; (material) aniagem f

sacred ['seɪkrɪd] adj sagrado

sacrifice ['sækrɪfaɪs] n sacrifício ♦ vt sacrificar

sad [sæd] adj triste; (deplorable) deplorável, triste

saddle ['sædl] n sela; (of cycle) selim m ♦ vt selar; **to ~ sb with sth** (inf: task, bill) pôr algo nas costas de alguém; (: responsibility) sobrecarregar alguém com algo; **saddlebag** n alforje m

sadistic [sə'dɪstɪk] adj sádico

sadly ['sædlɪ] adv tristemente; (regrettably) infelizmente; (mistaken, neglected) gravemente; **~ lacking (in)** muito carente (de)

sadness ['sædnɪs] n tristeza

sae abbr = **stamped addressed envelope**

safe [seɪf] adj seguro; (out of danger) fora de perigo; (unharmed) ileso, incólume ♦ n cofre m, caixa-forte f;

~ from protegido de; **~ and sound** são e salvo; **(just) to be on the ~ side** por via das dúvidas; **safeguard** n salvaguarda, proteção f ♦ vt proteger, defender; **safekeeping** n custódia, proteção f; **safely** adv com segurança, a salvo; (without mishap) sem perigo

safety ['seɪftɪ] n segurança; **safety belt** n cinto de segurança; **safety pin** n alfinete m de segurança

sag [sæg] vi (breasts) cair; (roof) afundar; (hem) desmanchar

sage [seɪdʒ] n salva; (man) sábio

Sagittarius [sædʒɪ'tɛərɪəs] n Sagitário

Sahara [sə'hɑːrə] n: **the ~ (Desert)** o Saara

said [sed] pt, pp of **say**

sail [seɪl] n (on boat) vela; (trip): **to go for a ~** dar um passeio de barco a vela ♦ vt (boat) governar ♦ vi (travel: ship) navegar, velejar; (: passenger) ir de barco; (SPORT) velejar; (set off) zarpar; **they ~ed into Rio de Janeiro** entraram no porto do Rio de Janeiro; **sail through** vt fus (fig) fazer com facilidade; **sailboat** (US) n barco a vela; **sailing** n (SPORT) navegação f a vela, vela; **to go sailing** ir velejar; **sailing boat** n barco a vela; **sailing ship** n veleiro

sailor ['seɪlə*] n marinheiro, marujo

saint [seɪnt] n santo(-a)

sake [seɪk] n: **for the ~ of** (causa de), em consideração a; **for sb's/ sth's ~** pelo bem de alguém/algo

salad ['sæləd] n salada; **salad cream** (BRIT) n maionese f; **salad dressing** n tempero or molho da salada

salami [sə'lɑːmɪ] n salame m

salary ['sælərɪ] n salário

sale [seɪl] n venda; (at reduced prices) liquidação f, saldo; (auction) leilão *m;* ~s *npl* (*total amount sold*) vendas *fpl;* **"for ~"** "vende-se"; on ~ à venda; **on ~ or return** em consignação; **sales assistant** (*US* **sales clerk**) *n* vendedor(a) *m/f;* **salesman/woman** (*irreg*) *n* vendedor(a) *m/f;* (*representative*) vendedor(a) *m/f* viajante

salmon ['sæmən] *n inv* salmão *m*

salon ['sælɔn] *n* (*hairdressing ~*) salão *m* (de cabeleireiro); (*beauty ~*) salão (de beleza)

saloon [sə'lu:n] *n* (*US*) bar *m,* botequim *m;* (*BRIT: AUT*) sedã *m;* (*ship's lounge*) salão *m*

salt [sɔːlt] *n* sal *m* ♦ *vt* salgar; **salt cellar** *n* saleiro *m;* **saltwater** *adj* de água salgada; **salty** *adj* salgado

salute [sə'lu:t] *n* (*greeting*) saudação *f;* (*of guns*) salva; (*MIL*) continência ♦ *vt* saudar; (*MIL*) fazer continência a

salvage ['sælvɪdʒ] *n* (*saving*) salvamento, recuperação *f;* (*things saved*) salvados *mpl* ♦ *vt* salvar

salvation [sæl'veɪʃən] *n* salvação *f*

same [seɪm] *adj* mesmo ♦ *pron:* **the ~** o mesmo (a mesma); **the ~ book as** o mesmo livro que; **all** *or* **just the ~** apesar de tudo, mesmo assim; **the ~ to you!** igualmente!

sample ['sɑːmpl] *n* amostra ♦ *vt* (*food, wine*) provar, experimentar

sanction ['sæŋkʃən] *n* sanção *f* ♦ *vt* sancionar

sanctity ['sæŋktɪtɪ] *n* santidade *f*

sanctuary ['sæŋktjuərɪ] *n* (*holy place*) santuário *n;* (*refuge*) refúgio, asilo; (*for animals*) reserva

sand [sænd] *n* areia, (*beach: also:* ~s) praia *f* (*also:* ~ **down**) lixar

sandal ['sændl] *n* sandália *f*

sand: sandbox (*US*) *n* caixa de areia; **sandcastle** *n* castelo de areia; **sandpaper** *n* lixa; **sandpit** *n* (*for children*) caixa de areia; **sand-**

stone *n* arenito, grés *m*

sandwich ['sændwɪtʃ] *n* sanduíche *m* (*BR*), sandes *f inv* (*PT*) ♦ *vt:* ~ed between encaixado entre

sandy ['sændɪ] *adj* arenoso; (*colour*) vermelho amarelado

sane [seɪn] *adj* são (sã) do juízo; (*sensible*) ajuizado, sensato

sang [sæŋ] *pt of* **sing**

sanitary ['sænɪtərɪ] *adj* (*system, arrangements*) sanitário; (*clean*) higiênico; **sanitary towel** (*US* **sanitary napkin**) *n* toalha higiênica or absorvente

sanitation [sænɪ'teɪʃən] *n* (*in house*) instalações *fpl* sanitárias; (*in town*) saneamento; **sanitation department** (*US*) *n* comissão *f* de limpeza urbana

sanity ['sænɪtɪ] *n* sanidade *f,* equilíbrio mental; (*common sense*) juízo, sensatez *f*

sank [sæŋk] *pt of* **sink**

Santa Claus [sæntə'klɔːz] *n* Papai Noel *m*

sap [sæp] *n* (*of plants*) seiva ♦ *vt* (*strength*) esgotar, minar

sapling ['sæplɪŋ] *n* árvore *f* nova

sapphire ['sæfaɪə*] *n* safira

sarcasm ['sɑːkæzm] *n* sarcasmo

sardine [sɑː'diːn] *n* sardinha

Sardinia [sɑː'dɪnɪə] *n* Sardenha *f*

sash [sæʃ] *n* faixa, banda

sat [sæt] *pt, pp of* **sit**

satchel ['sætʃl] *n* sacola

satellite ['sætəlaɪt] *n* satélite *m;* **satellite dish** *n* antena parabólica; **satellite television** *n* televisão *f* via satélite

satin ['sætɪn] *n* cetim *m* ♦ *adj* acetinado

satire ['sætaɪə*] *n* sátira

satisfaction [sætɪs'fækʃən] *n* satisfação *f;* (*refund, apology etc*) compensação *f;* **satisfactory**

satisfatório

satisfy ['sætɪsfaɪ] vt satisfazer; (convince) convencer, persuadir; **satisfying** adj satisfatório

Saturday ['sætədɪ] n sábado

sauce [sɔːs] n molho; (sweet) calda; **saucepan** n panela (BR), caçarola (PT)

saucer ['sɔːsə*] n pires m inv

Saudi ['saʊdɪ]: ~ **Arabia** n Arábia Saudita; **Saudi (Arabian)** adj saudita

sauna ['sɔːnə] n sauna

saunter ['sɔːntə*] vi: **to ~ over/along** andar devagar para/por; **to ~ into** entrar devagar em

sausage ['sɔsɪdʒ] n salsicha, linguiça; (cold meat) frios mpl; **sausage roll** n folheado de salsicha

savage ['sævɪdʒ] adj (cruel, fierce) cruel, feroz; (primitive) selvagem ♦ n selvagem m/f

save [seɪv] vt (rescue, COMPUT) salvar; (money) poupar, economizar; (time) ganhar; (SPORT) impedir; (avoid: trouble) evitar; (keep: seat) guardar ♦ vi (also: ~ **up**) poupar ♦ n (SPORT) salvamento ♦ prep salvo, exceto

saving ['seɪvɪŋ] n (on price etc) economia ♦ adj: **the ~ grace of** o único mérito de; **~s** fpl (money) economias fpl; **savings account** n (caderneta de) poupança

saviour ['seɪvjə*] (US **savior**) n salvador(a) m/f

savour ['seɪvə*] (US **savor**) vt saborear; (experience) apreciar; **savoury** adj (dish: not sweet) salgado

saw [sɔː] (pt **~ed**, pp **~ed** or **~n**) pt of **see** ♦ n (tool) serra ♦ vt serrar; **sawdust** n serragem f, pó m de serra; **sawn-off shotgun** (BRIT) n espingarda de cano serrado

saxophone ['sæksəfəun] n saxofone m

say [seɪ] (pt, pp **said**) n: **to have one's ~** exprimir sua opinião, ven-

der seu peixe (inf) ♦ vt dizer, falar; **to have a** or **some ~ in sth** opinar sobre algo, ter que ver com algo; **could you ~ that again?** poderia repetir?; **that is to ~** ou seja; **saying** n ditado, provérbio

scab [skæb] n casca, crosta (de ferida); (pej) fura-greve m/f inv

scaffold ['skæfəʊld] n (for execution) cadafalso, patíbulo; **scaffolding** n andaime m

scald [skɔːld] n escaldadura ♦ vt escaldar, queimar

scale [skeɪl] n escala; (of fish) escama; (of salaries, fees etc) tabela ♦ vt (mountain) escalar; **~s** npl (for weighing) balança; **~ of charges** tarifa, lista de preços; **scale down** vt reduzir

scallop ['skɔləp] n (ZOOL) vieira, venera; (SEWING) barra, arremate m

scalp [skælp] n couro cabeludo ♦ vt escalpar

scampi ['skæmpɪ] npl camarões mpl fritos

scan [skæn] vt (examine) esquadrinhar, perscrutar; (glance at quickly) passar uma vista de olhos por; (TV, RADAR) explorar ♦ n (MED) exame m

scandal ['skændl] n escândalo; (gossip) fofocas fpl; (fig: disgrace) vergonha

Scandinavian [skændɪ'neɪvɪən] adj escandinavo

scanner ['skænə*] n (MED, COMPUT) scanner m

scant [skænt] adj escasso, insuficiente; **scanty** ['skæntɪ] adj (meal) insuficiente, pobre; (underwear) sumário

scapegoat ['skeɪpgəʊt] n bode m expiatório

scar [skɑː*] n cicatriz f ♦ vt marcar (com uma cicatriz)

scarce [skɛəs] adj escasso, raro; **to make o.s. ~** (inf) dar o fora, cair fora; **scarcely** adv mal, quase não; (barely) apenas

scare [skɛə*] n susto; (panic) pânico ♦ vt assustar; **to ~ sb stiff** deixar alguém morrendo de medo; **bomb ~** alarme de bomba; **scare away** vt espantar; **scare off** vt = **scare away**; **scarecrow** n espantalho; **scared** adj: **to be scared** estar assustado or com medo

scarf [skɑːf] (pl ~s or **scarves**) n cachecol m; (square) lenço (de cabeça)

scarlet ['skɑːlɪt] adj escarlate; **scarlet fever** n escarlatina

scary ['skɛərɪ] (inf) adj assustador(a)

scathing ['skeɪðɪŋ] adj mordaz

scatter ['skætə*] vt espalhar; (put to flight) dispersar ♦ vi espalhar-se; **scatterbrained** (inf) adj esquecido

scene [siːn] n (THEATRE, fig) cena; (of crime, accident) cenário; (sight) vista, panorama m; (fuss) escândalo; **scenery** ['siːnərɪ] n (THEATRE) cenário; (landscape) paisagem f; **scenic** adj pitoresco

scent [sɛnt] n perfume m; (smell) aroma; (track, fig) pista, rasto

schedule ['ʃɛdjuːl, (us) 'skɛdjuːl] n (of trains) horário; (of events) programa m; (list) lista ♦ vt (timetable) planejar; (visit) marcar (a hora de); **on ~** na hora, sem atraso; **to be ahead of/behind ~** estar adiantado/ atrasado

scheme [skiːm] n (plan) maquinação f; (pension ~) projeto; (arrangement) arranjo ♦ vi conspirar

scholar ['skɔlə*] n aluno(-a), estudante m/f; (learned person) sábio(-a), erudito(-a); **scholarship** n erudição f; (grant) bolsa de estudos

school [skuːl] n escola; (secondary ~) colégio; (us: university) universidade f ♦ cpd escolar; **schoolboy** n aluno;

schoolchildren npl alunos mpl; **schoolgirl** n aluna; **schooling** n educação f, ensino; **schoolmaster** n professor m; **schoolmistress** n professora; **schoolteacher** n professor(a) m/f

science ['saɪəns] n ciência; **science fiction** n ficção f científica; **scientific** [saɪən'tɪfɪk] adj científico; **scientist** n cientista m/f

scissors ['sɪzəz] npl tesoura; **a pair of ~** uma tesoura

scoff [skɔf] vt (BRIT: inf: eat) engolir ♦ vi: **to ~ (at)** (mock) zombar (de)

scold [skəuld] vt ralhar

scone [skɔn] n bolinho de trigo

scoop [skuːp] n colherona; (for flour etc) pá f; (PRESS) furo (jornalístico); **scoop out** vt escavar; **scoop up** vt recolher

scooter ['skuːtə*] n (also: **motor ~**) lambreta; (toy) patinete m

scope [skəup] n liberdade f de ação; (of undertaking) âmbito; (of person) competência; (opportunity) oportunidade f

scorch [skɔːtʃ] vt (clothes) chamuscar; (earth, grass) secar, queimar

score [skɔː*] n (points etc) escore m, contagem f; (MUS) partitura; (twenty) vintena ♦ vt (goal, point) fazer; (mark) marcar, entalhar; (success) alcançar ♦ vi (in game) marcar; (FOOTBALL) marcar or fazer um gol; (keep score) marcar o escore; **on that ~** a esse respeito, por esse motivo; **~s of** (fig) um monte de; **to ~ 6 out of 10** conseguir um escore de 6 num total de 10; **score out** vt riscar; **scoreboard** n marcador m, placar m

scorn [skɔːn] n desprezo ♦ vt desprezar, rejeitar

Scorpio ['skɔːpɪəu] n Escorpião m

Scot [skɔt] n escocês(-esa) m/f

Scotch [skɔtʃ] n uísque m (BR) or whisky m (PT) escocês

Scotland ['skɔtlənd] n Escócia; **Scots** adj escocês(-esa); **Scotsman** (irreg) n escocês m; **Scotswoman** (irreg) n escocesa; **Scottish** adj escocês(-esa)

scoundrel ['skaundrəl] n canalha m/f, patife m

scour ['skauə*] vt (search) esquadrinhar, procurar em

scout [skaut] n (MIL) explorador m, batedor m; (also: **boy** ~) escoteiro; **girl** ~ (US) escoteira; **scout around** vi explorar

scowl [skaul] vi franzir a testa; to ~ **at sb** olhar de cara feia para alguém

scrabble ['skræbl] vi (climb) escalada (difícil); (struggle) luta ♦ vi: to ~ **out/through** conseguir sair com dificuldade; to ~ **for** lutar por; **scrambled eggs** npl ovos mpl mexidos

scram [skræm] (inf) vi dar o fora, safar-se

scramble ['skræmbl] n (climb) escalada (difícil); (struggle) luta ♦ vi: to ~ **around/about** mexe-mexe m; to ~ **(around) for sth** (search) tatear procurando algo

scrap [skræp] n (of paper) pedacinho; (of material) fragmento; (fig: of truth) mínimo; (fight) rixa, luta; (also: ~ **iron**) ferro velho, sucata ♦ vt sucatar, jogar no ferro velho; (fig) descartar, abolir ♦ vi brigar; ~**s** npl (leftovers) sobras fpl, restos mpl; **scrapbook** n álbum m de recortes

scrape [skreɪp] n (fig): to get into a ~ meter-se numa enrascada ♦ vt raspar; (~ against: hand, car) arranhar, roçar ♦ vi: to ~ **through** (in exam) passar raspando; **scrape together** vt (money) juntar com dificuldade

scrap: **scrapheap** n (fig): on the **scrapheap** rejeitado, jogado fora;

scrap paper n papel m de rascunho

scratch [skrætʃ] n arranhão m; (from claw) arranhadura ♦ cpd: ~ **team** time m improvisado; escrete m ♦ vt (rub) coçar; (with claw, nail) arranhar, unhar; (damage) arranhar ♦ vi coçar(-se); **to start from** ~ partir do zero; **to be up to** ~ estar à altura (das circunstâncias)

scrawl [skrɔːl] n garrancho; garatuja ♦ vi garatujar, rabiscar

scream [skriːm] n grito ♦ vi gritar

screech [skriːtʃ] vi guinchar

screen [skriːn] n (CINEMA, TV, COMPUT) tela (BR), écran m (PT); (movable) biombo; (fig) cortina ♦ vt (conceal) esconder, tapar; (from the wind etc) proteger; (film) projetar; (candidates etc) examinar; **screenplay** n roteiro; **screensaver** n protetor m de tela

screw [skruː] n parafuso ♦ vt aparafusar; (also: ~ **in**) apertar, atarraxar; **to ~ up one's eyes** franzir os olhos; **screw up** vt (paper etc) amassar; **screwdriver** n chave f de fenda or de parafuso

scribble ['skrɪbl] n garrancho ♦ vt escrevinhar ♦ vi rabiscar

script [skrɪpt] n (CINEMA etc) roteiro, script m; (writing) escrita, caligrafia

Scripture(s) ['skrɪptʃə(z)] n(pl) Sagrada Escritura

scroll [skrəul] n rolo de pergaminho

scrounge [skraundʒ] (inf) vt filar ♦ vi: **to be on the** ~ viver às custas de alguém (or dos outros etc)

scrub [skrʌb] n mato, cerrado ♦ vt esfregar; (inf) cancelar, eliminar

scruff [skrʌf] n: **by the** ~ **of the neck** pelo cangote

scruffy ['skrʌfɪ] adj desmazelado

scruple ['skruːpl] n escrúpulo

scrutiny ['skruːtɪnɪ] n escrutínio, exame m cuidadoso

scuff [skʌf] vt desgastar

scuffle ['skʌfl] n tumulto

sculptor ['skʌlptə*] n escultor(a) m/f

sculpture ['skʌlptʃə*] n escultura

scum [skʌm] n (on liquid) espuma; (pej: people) ralé f, gentinha

scurry ['skʌrɪ] vi sair correndo; **scurry off** vi sair correndo, dar no pé

scythe [saɪð] n segadeira, foice f grande

SDP (BRIT) n abbr = Social Democratic Party

sea [si:] n mar m ♦ cpd do mar, marino; **on the ~** (boat) no mar; (town) junto ao mar; **to go by ~** viajar por mar; **out to** or **at ~** em alto mar; **to be all at ~** (fig) estar confuso or desorientado; **seafood** n mariscos mpl; **seafront** n orla marítima; **seagoing** adj (ship) de longo curso; **seagull** n gaivota

seal [si:l] n (animal) foca; (stamp) selo ♦ vt fechar; **seal off** vt fechar

sea level n nível m do mar

sea lion n leão-marinho m

seam [si:m] n costura; (where edges meet) junta; (of coal) veio, filão m

seaman ['si:mən] (irreg) n marinheiro

search [sə:tʃ] n busca, procura; (COMPUT) procura; (inspection) exame m, investigação f ♦ vt (look in) procurar em; (examine) examinar; (person) revistar ♦ vi: **to ~** for procurar; **in ~** of à procura de; **search through** vt fus dar busca em; **search engine** n (on Internet) ferramenta f de busca; **searching** adj penetrante, perscrutador(a); **searchlight** n holofote m; **search party** n equipe f de salvamento

sea: **seashore** n praia, beira-mar f, litoral m; **seasick** adj: **to be seasick** enjoar; **seaside** n praia; **seaside resort** n balneário

season ['si:zn] n (of year) estação f; (sporting etc) temporada; (of films etc) série f ♦ vt (food) temperar; **to be in/out of ~** (fruit) estar na época/fora de época; **seasoned** adj (fig: traveller) experiente; **season ticket** n bilhete m de temporada

seat [si:t] n (in bus, train: place) assento; (chair) cadeira; (POL) lugar m, cadeira; (buttocks) traseiro, nádegas fpl; (of trousers) fundilhos mpl ♦ vt sentar; (have room for) ter capacidade para; **to be ~ed** estar sentado; **seat belt** n cinto de segurança

sea: **sea water** n água do mar; **seaweed** n alga marinha; **seaworthy** adj em condições de navegar, resistente

sec. abbr (= second) seg

secluded [sɪ'klu:dɪd] adj (place) afastado; (life) solitário

second ['sɛkənd] (BRIT) vt (employee) transferir temporariamente

second² ['sɛkənd] adj segundo ♦ adv (in race etc) em segundo lugar ♦ n segundo; (AUT: also: ~ **gear**) segunda; (COMM) artigo defeituoso; (BRIT: SCH: degree) qualificação boa mas sem distinção ♦ vt (motion) apoiar, secundar; **secondary** adj secundário; **secondary school** n escola secundária, colégio; ver quadro

---

SECONDARY SCHOOL

Uma **secondary school** é um estabelecimento de ensino para alunos de 11 a 18 anos, alguns dos quais interrompem os estudos aos 16 anos. A maior parte dessas escolas é formada por comprehensive schools, mas algumas secondary schools ainda têm sistemas rigorosos de seleção.

second

241

self...

second ['sɛkənd]: **second-class** adv em segunda classe; **secondhand** adj de (BR) or em (PT) segunda mão, usado; **second hand** n (on clock) ponteiro de segundos; **secondly** adv em segundo lugar; **second-rate** adj de segunda categoria; **second thoughts** (US **second thought**) npl: **to have second thoughts (about doing sth)** pensar duas vezes (antes de fazer algo); **on second thoughts** pensando bem

secrecy ['si:krəsɪ] n sigilo

secret ['si:krɪt] adj secreto ♦ n segredo

secretary ['sɛkrətərɪ] n secretário(-a); (BRIT: POL): **S~ of State** Ministro(-a) de Estado

secretive ['si:krətɪv] adj sigiloso, reservado

section ['sɛkʃən] n seção f; (part) parte f, porção f; (of document) parágrafo, artigo; (of opinion) setor m; **cross-~** corte m transversal

sector ['sɛktə*] n setor m

secular ['sɛkjulə*] adj (priest) secular; (music, society) leigo

secure [sɪ'kjuə*] adj (safe) seguro; (firmly fixed) firme, rígido ♦ vt (fix) prender; (get) conseguir, obter; **security** n segurança; (for loan) fiança, garantia; **security guard** n guarda m

sedate [sɪ'deɪt] adj calmo ♦ vt sedar, tratar com calmantes; **sedative** n calmante m, sedativo

seduce [sɪ'dju:s] vt seduzir; **seductive** adj sedutor(a)

see [si:] (pt saw, pp ~n) vt ver; (understand) entender; (accompany): **to ~ sb to the door** acompanhar or levar alguém até a porta ♦ vi ver; (find out) achar ♦ n sé f, sede f; **to ~ that** (ensure) assegurar que; **~ you soon!** até logo!; **see about**

vt fus tratar de; **see off** vt despedir-se de; **see through** vt fus enxergar através de ♦ vt levar a cabo; **see to** vt fus providenciar

seed [si:d] n semente f; (sperm) esperma m; (fig: gen pl) germe m; (TENNIS) pré-selecionado(-a); **to go to ~** produzir sementes; (fig) deteriorar-se; **seedling** n planta brotada da semente, muda; **seedy** adj (shabby: place) mal-cuidado; (: person) maltrapilho

seeing ['si:ɪŋ] conj: **~ (that)** visto (que), considerando (que)

seek [si:k] (pt, pp sought) vt procurar; (post) solicitar

seem [si:m] vi parecer; **there ~s to be ...** parece que há ...

seen [si:n] pp of see

seep [si:p] vi filtrar-se, penetrar

seesaw ['si:sɔ:] n gangorra, balanço

seethe [si:ð] vi ferver; **to ~ with anger** estar danado (da vida)

see-through adj transparente

segment ['sɛgmənt] n segmento; (of orange) gomo

seize [si:z] vt agarrar, pegar; (power, hostage) apoderar-se de, confiscar; (territory) tomar posse de; (opportunity) aproveitar; **seize up** vi (TECH) gripar; **seize (up)on** vt fus valer-se de; **seizure** n (MED) ataque m, acesso; (LAW, of power) confisco, embargo

seldom ['sɛldəm] adv raramente

select [sɪ'lɛkt] adj seleto, fino ♦ vt escolher, selecionar; (SPORT) selecionar, escalar; **selection** n seleção f, escolha; (COMM) sortimento

self [sɛlf] (pl **selves**) pron see herself; himself; itself; myself; oneself; ourselves; themselves; yourself ♦ n: **the ~** o eu ou

self... [sɛlf] prefix: **self-assured** adj seguro de si; **self-catering**

(BRIT) adj (flat) com cozinha; (holiday) em casa alugada; **self-centred** (US **self-centered**) adj egocêntrico; **self-confidence** n autoconfiança, confiança em si; **self-conscious** adj inibido, constrangido; **self-control** n autocontrole m, autodomínio; **self-defence** (US **self-defense**) n legítima defesa, autodefesa; **in self-defence** em legítima defesa; **self-discipline** n autodisciplina; **self-employed** adj autônomo; **self-evident** adj patente; **self-interest** n egoísmo; **selfish** adj egoísta; **selfless** adj desinteressado; **self-pity** n pena de si mesmo; **self-respect** n amor m próprio; **self-righteous** adj farisaico, santarrão(-rona); **self-sacrifice** n abnegação f, altruísmo; **self-satisfied** adj satisfeito consigo mesmo; **self-service** adj de auto-serviço; **self-sufficient** adj auto-suficiente; **self-tanning** adj autobronzeador; **self-taught** adj autodidata

sell [sɛl] (pt, pp **sold**) vt vender; (fig): **to ~ sb an idea** convencer alguém de uma idéia ♦ vi vender-se; **to ~ at** or **for £10** vender a or por £10; **sell off** vt liquidar; **sell out** vi vender todo o estoque ♦ vt: **the tickets are all sold out** todos os ingressos já foram vendidos; **sell-by date** n vencimento; **seller** n vendedor(a) m/f; **selling price** n preço de venda

sellotape ['sɛləteɪp] ® (BRIT) n fita adesiva, durex ® m (BR)

selves [sɛlvz] pl of **self**

semi... [sɛmɪ] prefix semi..., meio...; **semicircle** n semicírculo; **semicolon** n ponto e vírgula; **semi-detached (house)** (BRIT) n (casa) geminada; **semifinal** n semifinal f

seminar ['sɛmɪnɑ:*] n seminário
semiskilled [sɛmɪ'skɪld] adj (work, worker) semi-especializado
semi-skimmed milk [sɛmɪ'skɪmd-] n leite m semidesnatado
senate ['sɛnɪt] n senado; **senator** n senador(a) m/f
send [sɛnd] (pt, pp **sent**) vt mandar, enviar; (dispatch) expedir, remeter; (transmit) transmitir; **send away** vt (letter, goods) expedir, mandar; (unwelcome visitor) mandar embora; **send away for** vt fus encomendar, pedir pelo correio; **send back** vt devolver, mandar de volta; **send for** vt fus mandar buscar; (by post) encomendar, pedir pelo correio; **send off** vt (goods) despachar, expedir; (BRIT: SPORT: player) expulsar; **send out** vt (invitation) distribuir; (signal) emitir; **send up** vt (person, price) fazer subir; (BRIT: parody) parodiar; **sender** n remetente m/f; **send-off** n: **a good send-off** uma boa despedida
senior ['si:nɪə*] adj (older) mais velho or idoso; (on staff) mais antigo; (of higher rank) superior; **senior citizen** n idoso(-a); **seniority** [si:nɪ'ɔrɪtɪ] n (in service) status m
sensation [sɛn'seɪʃən] n sensação f; **sensational** adj sensacional; (headlines, result) sensacionalista
sense [sɛns] n sentido; (feeling) sensação f; (good ~) bom senso ♦ vt sentir, perceber; **it makes ~** faz sentido; **senseless** adj insensato, estúpido; (unconscious) sem sentidos, inconsciente; **sensible** adj sensato, de bom senso; (reasonable: price) razoável; (: advice, decision) sensato
sensitive ['sɛnsɪtɪv] adj sensível; (fig: touchy) suscetível
sensual ['sɛnsjuəl] adj sensual

sensuous ['sɛnsjuəs] adj sensual

sent [sɛnt] pt, pp of **send**

sentence ['sɛntəns] n (LING) frase f, oração f; (LAW) sentença ♦ vt: **to ~ sb to death/to 5 years** condenar alguém à morte/a 5 anos de prisão

sentiment ['sɛntɪmənt] n sentimento; (opinion: also pl) opinião f; **sentimental** [sɛntɪ'mɛntl] adj sentimental

separate [adj 'sɛprɪt, vb 'sɛpəreɪt] adj separado; (distinct) diferente ♦ vt separar; (part) dividir ♦ vi separar-se; **separately** adv separadamente

September [sɛp'tɛmbə*] n setembro

septic ['sɛptɪk] adj séptico; (wound) infeccionado

sequel ['si:kwl] n consequência, resultado; (of film, story) continuação f

sequence ['si:kwəns] n série f, seqüência; (CINEMA) série

sequin ['si:kwɪn] n lantejoula, paetê m

serene [sɪ'ri:n] adj sereno, tranqüilo

sergeant ['sɑ:dʒənt] n sargento

serial ['sɪərɪəl] n seriado; **serial number** n número de série

series ['sɪəri:z] n inv série f

serious ['sɪərɪəs] adj sério; (matter) importante; (illness) grave; **seriously** adv a sério, com seriedade; (hurt) gravemente

sermon ['sə:mən] n sermão m

serrated [sɪ'reɪtɪd] adj serrado, dentado

servant ['sə:vənt] n empregado(-a); (fig) servidor(a) m/f

serve [sə:v] vt servir; (customer) atender; (subj: train) passar por; (apprenticeship) fazer; (prison term) cumprir ♦ vi (at table) servir-se; (TENNIS) sacar; (be useful): **to ~ as/for/to do** servir como/para/para fazer ♦ n

(TENNIS) saque m; **it ~s him right** é bem feito para ele; **serve out** vt (food) servir; **serve up** vt = **serve out**

service ['sə:vɪs] n serviço; (REL) culto; (AUT) revisão f; (TENNIS) saque m; (also: **dinner ~**) aparelho de jantar ♦ vt (car, washing machine) fazer a revisão de, revisar; **the S~s** npl (army, navy etc) as Forças Armadas; **to be of ~ to sb** ser útil a alguém; **service area** n (on motorway) posto de gasolina com bar, restaurante etc; **service charge** (BRIT) n serviço; **serviceman** (irreg) n militar m; **service station** n posto de gasolina (BR), estação f de serviço (PT)

serviette [sə:vɪ'ɛt] n (BRIT) guardanapo

session ['sɛʃən] n sessão f; **to be in ~** estar reunido em sessão

set [sɛt] (pt, pp **set**) n (of things) jogo; (radio ~, TV ~) aparelho; (of utensils) bateria de cozinha; (of cutlery) talher m; (of books) coleção f; (of people) grupo; (TENNIS) set m; (THEATRE, CINEMA) cenário; (HAIRDRESSING) penteado; (MATH) conjunto ♦ adj fixo; (ready) pronto ♦ vt pôr, colocar; (table) pôr; (price) fixar; (rules etc) estabelecer, decidir; (record) estabelecer; (time) marcar; (adjust) ajustar; (task, exam) passar ♦ vi (sun) pôr-se; (jam, jelly, concrete) endurecer, solidificar-se; **to be ~ on doing sth** estar decidido a fazer algo; **to ~ music** musicar, pôr música em; **to ~ on fire** botar fogo em, incendiar; **to ~ free** libertar; **to ~ sth going** pôr algo em movimento; **set about** vt fus começar com; **set aside** vt deixar de lado; **set back** vt (cost): **it ~ me back £5** me deu um prejuízo de £5; (in time): **to**

~ **sb back (by)** atrasar alguém (em);
set off *vi* partir, ir indo ♦ *vt* (*bomb*)
fazer explodir; (*alarm*) disparar;
(*chain of events*) iniciar; (*show up
well*) ressaltar; **set out** *vi* partir ♦ *vt*
(*arrange*) colocar, dispor; (*state*)
expor, explicar; **to ~ out to do sth**
pretender fazer algo; **set up** *vt* fundar, estabelecer; **setback** *n* revés
m, contratempo; **set menu** *n*
refeição *f* a preço fixo

settee [sɛ'tiː] *n* sofá *m*

setting ['sɛtɪŋ] *n* (*background*)
cenário; (*position*) posição *f*; (*of
sun*) pôr(-do-sol) *m*; (*of jewel*)
engaste *m*

settle ['sɛtl] *vt* (*argument, matter*)
resolver, esclarecer; (*accounts*) ajustar, liquidar; (MED: *calm down*)
tranquilizar ♦ *vi* (*dust etc*) assentar; (*calm down: children*) acalmar-se; (*also: ~ **down**) instalar-se,
estabilizar-se; **to ~ for sth** concordar em aceitar algo; **to ~ on sth**
optar por algo; **settle in** *vi* instalar-se; **settle up** *vi*: **to ~ up with sb**
ajustar as contas com alguém; **settlement** *n* (*payment*) liquidação *f*;
(*agreement*) acordo, convênio;
(*village etc*) povoado, povoação
f; **settler** *n* colono(-a), colonizador(a) *m/f*

setup ['sɛtʌp] *n* (*organization*) organização *f*; (*situation*) situação *f*

seven ['sɛvn] *num* sete; **seventeen**
num dezessete; **seventh** *num* sétimo; **seventy** *num* setenta

sever ['sɛvə*] *vt* cortar; (*relations*)
romper

several ['sɛvərl] *adj*, *pron* vários(-as); ~ **of us** vários de nós

severe [sɪ'vɪə*] *adj* severo; (*serious*)
grave; (*hard*) duro; (*pain*) intenso;
(*dress*) austero

sew [səu] (*pt* **~ed**, *pp* **sewn**) *vt*

coser, costurar; **sew up** *vt* coser,
costurar

sewage ['suːɪdʒ] *n* detritos *mpl*

sewer ['suːə*] *n* (*cano de*) esgoto,
bueiro

sewing ['səuɪŋ] *n* costura; **sewing
machine** *n* máquina de costura

sewn [səun] *pp* of **sew**

sex [sɛks] *n* sexo; **sexist** *adj* sexista

sexual ['sɛksjuəl] *adj* sexual

sexy ['sɛksɪ] *adj* sexy

shabby ['ʃæbɪ] *adj* (*person*) esfarrapado, maltrapilho; (*clothes*) usado,
surrado; (*behaviour*) indigno

shack [ʃæk] *n* choupana, barraca

shade [ʃeɪd] *n* sombra; (*for lamp*)
quebra-luz *m*; (*of colour*) tom *m*,
tonalidade *f*; (*small quantity*): **a ~
(more/too large)** um pouquinho
(mais/grande) ♦ *vt* dar sombra a;
(*eyes*) sombrear; **in the ~** à sombra

shadow ['ʃædəu] *n* sombra ♦ *vt*
(*follow*) seguir de perto (sem ser
visto)

shady ['ʃeɪdɪ] *adj* à sombra; (*fig: dishonest: person*) suspeito, duvidoso;
(: *deal*) desonesto

shaft [ʃɑːft] *n* (*of arrow, spear*) haste
f; (AUT, TECH) eixo, manivela; (*of
mine, of lift*) poço; (*of light*) raio

shaggy ['ʃægɪ] *adj* desgrenhado

shake [ʃeɪk] (*pt* **shook**, *pp* **shaken**)
vt sacudir; (*building, confidence*)
abalar; (*surprise*) surpreender ♦ *vi*
tremer; **to ~ hands with sb** apertar
a mão de alguém; **to ~ one's head**
(*in refusal etc*) dizer não com a
cabeça; (*in dismay*) sacudir a
cabeça; **shake off** *vt* sacudir; (*fig*)
livrar-se de; **shake up** *vt* sacudir;
(*fig*) reorganizar; **shaky** *adj* (*hand,
voice*) trêmulo; (*table*) instável;
(*building*) abalado

shall [ʃæl] *aux vb*: **I ~ go** irei; ~ **I
open the door?** posso abrir a

porta?; **I'll get some, ~ I?** eu vou pegar algum, está bem?

shallow ['ʃæləu] *adj* raso; (*breathing*) fraco; (*fig*) superficial

sham [ʃæm] *n* fraude *f*, fingimento ♦ *vt* fingir, simular

shambles ['ʃæmblz] *n* confusão *f*

shame [ʃeɪm] *n* vergonha ♦ *vt* envergonhar; **it is a ~ (that/to do)** é (uma) pena (que/fazer); **what a ~!** que pena!; **shameful** *adj* vergonhoso; **shameless** *adj* sem vergonha, descarado

shampoo [ʃæm'puː] *n* xampu *m* (*BR*), champô *m* (*PT*) ♦ *vt* lavar o cabelo (com xampu or champô)

shandy ['ʃændɪ] *n* mistura de cerveja com refresco gaseificado

shan't [ʃɑːnt] = **shall not**

shanty town ['ʃæntɪ-] *n* favela

shape [ʃeɪp] *n* forma ♦ *vt* (*form*) moldar; (*sb's ideas*) formar; (*sb's life*) definir, determinar; **to take ~** tomar forma; **shape up** *vi* (*events*) desenrolar-se; (*person*) tomar jeito; **shapeless** *adj* informe, sem forma definida; **shapely** *adj* escultural

share [ʃɛə*] *n* parte *f*; (*contribution*) cota; (*COMM*) ação *f* ♦ *vt* dividir; (*have in common*) compartilhar; **share out** *vt* distribuir; **shareholder** *n* acionista *m/f*

shark [ʃɑːk] *n* tubarão *m*

sharp [ʃɑːp] *adj* (*razor, knife*) afiado; (*point, features*) pontiagudo; (*outline*) definido, bem marcado; (*pain, voice*) agudo; (*taste*) acre (*MUS*) desafinado; (*contrast*) marcado; (*quick-witted*) perspicaz; (*dishonest*) desonesto ♦ *n* (*MUS*) sustenido ♦ *adv*: **at 2 o'clock ~** às 2 (horas) em ponto; **sharpen** *vt* afiar; (*pencil*) apontar, fazer a ponta de; (*fig*) aguçar; **sharpener** *n* (*also*: **pencil sharpener**) apontador *m* (*BR*),

apara-lápis *m inv* (*PT*); **sharply** *adv* (*abruptly*) bruscamente; (*clearly*) claramente; (*harshly*) severamente

shatter ['ʃætə*] *vt* despedaçar, estilhaçar; (*fig: ruin*) destruir, acabar com; (: *upset*) arrasar ♦ *vi* despedaçar-se, estilhaçar-se

shave [ʃeɪv] *vt* barbear, fazer a barba de ♦ *vi* fazer a barba, barbear-se ♦ *n*: **to have a ~** fazer a barba; **shaver** *n* (*also*: **electric shaver**) barbeador *m* elétrico; **shaving** *n* (*action*) barbeação *f*; **shavings** *npl* (*of wood*) aparas *fpl*; **shaving brush** *n* pincel *m* de barba; **shaving cream** *n* creme *m* de barbear; **shaving foam** *n* espuma de barbear

shawl [ʃɔːl] *n* xale *m*

she [ʃiː] *pron* ela ♦ *prefix*: **~-elephant** *etc* elefante *etc* fêmea

sheaf [ʃiːf] (*pl* **sheaves**) *n* (*of corn*) gavela (*of papers*) maço

shear [ʃɪə*] (*pt* **~ed**, *pp* **shorn**) *vt* (*sheep*) tosquiar, tosar; **shear off** *vi* cisalhar; **shears** *npl* (*for hedge*) tesoura de jardim

sheath [ʃiːθ] *n* bainha; (*contraceptive*) camisa-de-vênus *f*, camisinha

shed [ʃɛd] (*pt, pp* **shed**) *n* alpendre *m*, galpão *m* ♦ *vt* (*skin*) mudar; (*load*) perder; (*tears, blood*) derramar; (*workers*) despedir

she'd [ʃiːd] = **she had; she would**

sheen [ʃiːn] *n* brilho

sheep [ʃiːp] *n inv* ovelha; **sheepdog** *n* cão *m* pastor; **sheepskin** *n* pele *f* de carneiro, pelego

sheer [ʃɪə*] *adj* (*utter*) puro, completo; (*steep*) íngreme, empinado; (*almost transparent*) fino, translúcido ♦ *adv* a pique

sheet [ʃiːt] *n* (*on bed*) lençol *m*; (*of paper*) folha; (*of glass, metal*) lâmina, chapa; (*of ice*) camada

sheik(h) [ʃeɪk] *n* xeque *m*

shelf

shoot

shelf [ʃɛlf] (*pl* **shelves**) *n* prateleira

shell [ʃɛl] *n* (*on beach*) concha; (*of egg, nut etc*) casca; (*explosive*) obus *m*; (*of building*) armação *f*, esqueleto *m* ♦ *vt* (*peas*) descascar; (MIL) bombardear

she'll [ʃiːl] = **she will**; **she shall**

shellfish [ˈʃɛlfɪʃ] *n inv* crustáceo; (*pl: as food*) frutos *mpl* do mar, mariscos *mpl*

shell suit *n* conjunto de náilon para jogging

shelter [ˈʃɛltə*] *n* (*building*) abrigo; (*protection*) refúgio ♦ *vt* (*protect*) proteger; (*give lodging to*) abrigar ♦ *vi* abrigar-se, refugiar-se

shelve [ʃɛlv] *vt* (*also: fig*) pôr de lado, engavetar; **shelves** *npl of* **shelf**

shepherd [ˈʃɛpəd] *n* pastor *m* ♦ *vt* guiar, conduzir; **shepherd's pie** (BRIT) *n* empadão *m* de carne e batata

sheriff [ˈʃɛrɪf] (US) *n* xerife *m*

sherry [ˈʃɛrɪ] *n* (vinho do) Xerez *m*

she's [ʃiːz] = **she is**; **she has**

Shetland [ˈʃɛtlənd] *n* (*also:* the **~s**, the **~ Isles**) as ilhas Shetland

shield [ʃiːld] *n* escudo; (SPORT) escudo, brasão *m*; (*protection*) proteção *f* ♦ *vt*: **to ~ (from)** proteger (contra)

shift [ʃɪft] *n* mudança; (*of work*) turno; (*of workers*) turma ♦ *vt* transferir; (*remove*) tirar ♦ *vi* mudar; **shifty** *adj* esperto, trapaceiro; (*eyes*) velhaco, maroto

shimmer [ˈʃɪmə*] *vi* cintilar, tremeluzir

shin [ʃɪn] *n* canela (da perna)

shine [ʃaɪn] (*pt, pp* **shone**) *n* brilho, lustre *m* ♦ *vi* brilhar ♦ *vt* (*glasses*) polir; (*shoes; pt, pp ~d*) lustrar; **to ~ a torch on sth** apontar uma lanterna para algo

shingles [ˈʃɪŋglz] *n* (MED) herpes-zoster *m*

shiny [ˈʃaɪnɪ] *adj* brilhante, lustroso

ship [ʃɪp] *n* barco ♦ *vt* (*goods*) embarcar; (*send*) transportar or mandar (por via marítima); **shipment** *n* carregamento; **shipping** *n* (*ships*) navios *mpl*; (*cargo*) transporte *m* de mercadorias (por via marítima); (*traffic*) navegação *f*; **shipwreck** *n* (*event*) malogro; (*ship*) naufrágio ♦ *vt*: **to be shipwrecked** naufragar; **shipyard** *n* estaleiro

shirt [ʃəːt] *n* (*man's*) camisa; (*woman's*) blusa; **in ~ sleeves** em manga de camisa

shit [ʃɪt] (*inf!*) *excl* merda (!)

shiver [ˈʃɪvə*] *n* tremor *m*, arrepio ♦ *vi* tremer, estremecer, tiritar

shoal [ʃəul] *n* (*of fish*) cardume *m*; (*fig: also: ~s*) bando, multidão *f*

shock [ʃɔk] *n* (*impact*) choque *m*; (ELEC) descarga; (*emotional*) comoção *f*, abalo; (*start*) susto, sobressalto; (MED) trauma *m* ♦ *vt* dar um susto a, chocar; (*offend*) escandalizar; **shock absorber** *n* amortecedor *m*; **shocking** *adj* chocante, lamentável; (*outrageous*) revoltante, chocante

shoddy [ˈʃɔdɪ] *adj* de má qualidade

shoe [ʃuː] (*pt, pp* **shod**) *n* sapato; (*for horse*) ferradura ♦ *vt* (*horse*) ferrar; **shoelace** *n* cadarço, cordão *m* (de sapato); **shoe polish** *n* graxa de sapato; **shoeshop** *n* sapataria

shone [ʃɔn] *pt, pp of* **shine**

shook [ʃuk] *pt of* **shake**

shoot [ʃuːt] (*pt, pp* **shot**) *n* (*on branch, seedling*) broto ♦ *vt* disparar; (*kill*) matar à bala, balear; (*wound*) ferir à bala, balear; (*execute*) fuzilar; (*film*) filmar, rodar ♦ *vi*: **to ~ (at)** atirar (em); (FOOTBALL) chutar; **shoot down** *vt* (*plane*) derrubar, abater; **shoot in/out** *vi* entrar/sair correndo; **shoot up** vi (fig) subir vertiginosamente; **shooting star** n estrela cadente

shop [ʃɔp] n loja; (workshop) oficina ♦ vi (also: **go ~ping**) ir fazer compras; **shop assistant** (BRIT) n vendedor(a) m/f; **shopkeeper** n lojista m/f; **shoplifting** n furto (em lojas); **shopper** n comprador(a) m/f; **shopping** n (goods) compras fpl; **shopping bag** n bolsa (de compras); **shopping centre** (US **shopping center**) n shopping (center) m; **shop window** n vitrine f (BR), montra (PT)

shore [ʃɔː*] n (of sea) costa, praia; (of lake) margem f ♦ vt: **to ~ (up)** reforçar, escorar; **on ~** em terra

shorn [ʃɔːn] pp of **shear**

short [ʃɔːt] adj curto; (in time) breve, de curta duração; (person) baixo; (curt) seco, brusco; (insufficient) insuficiente, em falta; **to be ~ of sth** estar em falta de algo; **in ~** em resumo; **~ of doing ...** a não ser fazer ...; **everything ~ of ...** tudo a não ser ...; **it is ~ for** é a abreviatura de; **to cut ~** (speech, visit) encurtar; **to fall ~ of** não se à altura de; **to run ~ of sth** ficar sem algo; **to stop ~** parar de repente; **to stop ~ of** chegar quase a; **shortage** n escassez f, falta; **shortbread** n biscoito amanteigado; **short circuit** n curto-circuito ♦ vt provocar um curto-circuito ♦ vi entrar em curto-circuito; **shortcoming** n defeito, imperfeição f, falha; **short(crust) pastry** (BRIT) n massa amanteigada; **shortcut** n atalho; **shorten** vt encurtar; (visit) abreviar; **shorthand** (BRIT) n estenografia f; **short list** (BRIT) n lista dos candidatos escolhidos; **shortly** adv em breve, dentro em pouco; **shorts** npl: **(a pair of) shorts** um

calção (BR), um short (BR), uns calções (PT); **short-sighted** (BRIT) adj míope; (fig) imprevidente; **short-staffed** adj com falta de pessoal; **short story** n conto; **short-tempered** adj irritadiço; **short-term** adj a curto prazo; **short wave** n (RADIO) onda curta

shot [ʃɔt] pt, pp of **shoot** ♦ n (of gun) tiro; (pellets) chumbo; (try, FOOTBALL) tentativa; (injection) injeção f; (PHOT) fotografia; **to be a good/bad ~** (person) ter boa/má pontaria; **like a ~** como um relâmpago, de repente; **shotgun** n espingarda

should [ʃud] aux vb: **I ~ go now** devo ir embora agora; **he ~ be there now** ele já deve ter chegado; **I ~ go if I were you** se eu fosse você eu iria; **I ~ like to** eu gostaria de

shoulder ['ʃəuldə*] n ombro ♦ vt (fig) arcar com; **shoulder blade** n omoplata m

shouldn't ['ʃudnt] = **should not**

shout [ʃaut] n grito ♦ vt gritar ♦ vi (also: **~ out**) gritar, berrar; **shout down** vt fazer calar com gritos; **shouting** n gritaria, berreiro

shove [ʃʌv] vt empurrar; (inf: put): **to ~ sth in** botar algo em; **shove off** vi (inf) vi dar o fora

shovel ['ʃʌvl] n pá f; (mechanical) escavadeira ♦ vt cavar com pá

show [ʃəu] (pt **~ed**, pp **~n**) n (of emotion) demonstração f; (semblance) aparência; (exhibition) exibição f; (THEATRE) espetáculo, representação f; (CINEMA) sessão f ♦ vt mostrar; (courage etc) demonstrar, dar prova de; (exhibit) exibir, expor; (depict) ilustrar; (film) exibir ♦ vi mostrar-se; (appear) aparecer; **to be on ~** estar em exposição; **show in** vt mandar entrar; **show off** vi (pej) mostrar-se, exibir-se ♦ vt (*display*) exibir, mostrar; **show out** vt levar até a porta; **show up** vi (*stand out*) destacar-se de; (*inf: turn up*) aparecer, pintar ♦ vt descobrir; **show business** n o mundo do espetáculo; **showdown** n confrontação f

shower ['ʃauə*] n (*rain*) pancada de chuva; (*of stones etc*) chuva, enxurrada; (*also: ~ bath*) chuveiro ♦ vt: **to ~ sb with** (*gifts etc*) cumular alguém de; **to have** *or* **take a ~** tomar banho (de chuveiro)

showing ['ʃəuŋ] n (*of film*) projeção f, exibição f

show jumping ['-'dʒʌmpɪŋ] n hipismo

shown [ʃəun] pp of **show**

show: **show-off** (*inf*) n (*person*) exibicionista m/f, faroleiro(-a); **showpiece** n (*of exhibition etc*) obra mais importante; **showroom** n sala de exposição

shrank [ʃræŋk] pt of **shrink**

shred [ʃred] n (*gen pl*) tira, pedaço ♦ vt rasgar em tiras, retalhar; (*CULIN*) desfiar, picar

shrewd [ʃruːd] adj perspicaz

shriek [ʃriːk] n grito ♦ vi gritar, berrar

shrill [ʃrɪl] adj agudo, estridente

shrimp [ʃrɪmp] n camarão m

shrine [ʃraɪn] n santuário

shrink [ʃrɪŋk] (*pt* **shrank**, *pp* **shrunk**) vi encolher; (*be reduced*) reduzir-se; (*also: ~ away*) encolher-se ♦ vt (*cloth*) fazer encolher ♦ n (*inf, pej*) psicanalista m/f; **to ~ from doing sth** não se atrever a fazer algo

shrivel ['ʃrɪvl] vt (*also: ~ up: dry*) secar; (: *crease*) enrugar ♦ vi secar-se, enrugar-se, murchar

Shrove Tuesday [ʃrəuv-] n terça-

feira gorda

shrub [ʃrʌb] n arbusto; **shrubbery** n arbustos mpl

shrug [ʃrʌg] n encolhimento dos ombros ♦ vt, vi: **to ~ (one's shoulders)** encolher os ombros, dar de ombros (*BR*); **shrug off** vt negar a importância de

shrunk [ʃrʌŋk] pp of **shrink**

shudder ['ʃʌdə*] n estremecimento, tremor m ♦ vi estremecer, tremer de medo

shuffle ['ʃʌfl] vt (*cards*) embaralhar ♦ vi: **to ~ (one's feet)** arrastar os pés

shun [ʃʌn] vt evitar, afastar-se de

shut [ʃʌt] (*pt*, *pp* **shut**) vt fechar ♦ vi fechar(-se); **shut down** vt, vi fechar; **shut off** vt cortar, interromper; **shut up** vi (*inf: keep quiet*) calar-se, calar a boca ♦ vt (*close*) fechar; (*silence*) calar; **shutter** n veneziana; (*PHOT*) obturador m

shuttle ['ʃʌtl] n (*in plane: also: ~ service*) ponte f aérea; (*space ~*) ônibus m espacial

shuttlecock ['ʃʌtlkɔk] n peteca

shy [ʃaɪ] adj tímido; (*reserved*) reservado

sick [sɪk] adj (*ill*) doente; (*nauseated*) enjoado; (*humour*) negro; (*vomiting*): **to be ~** vomitar; **to feel ~** estar enjoado; **to be ~ of** (*fig*) estar cheio *or* farto de; **sicken** vt (*disgust*) enojar, repugnar; **sickening** adj (*fig*) repugnante

sickle ['sɪkl] n foice f

sick: **sick leave** n licença por doença; **sickly** adj doentio; (*causing nausea*) nauseante; **sickness** n doença, indisposição f; (*vomiting*) náusea, enjôo

side [saɪd] n lado; (*of body*) flanco; (*of lake*) margem f; (*aspect*) aspecto; (*team*) time m (*BR*), equipa (*PT*);

siege   249   sincere

(of hill) declive m ♦ cpd (door, entrance) lateral ♦ vi: to ~ with sb tomar o partido de alguém; by the ~ of ao lado de; ~ by ~ lado a lado, juntos; from ~ to ~ para lá e para cá; to take ~s with pôr-se ao lado de; **sideboard** n aparador m; **sideboards** npl (BRIT) = sideburns; **sideburns** npl suíças fpl, costeletas fpl; **side effect** n efeito colateral; **sidelight** n (AUT) luz f lateral; **sideshow** n (stall) barraca; **sidestep** n evitar; **sidetrack** vt (fig) desviar (do seu propósito); **sidewalk** (US) n calçada; **sideways** adv de lado

siege [si:dʒ] n sítio, assédio

sieve [sɪv] n peneira ♦ vt peneirar

sift [sɪft] vt peneirar; (fig) esquadrinhar, analisar minuciosamente

sigh [saɪ] n suspiro ♦ vi suspirar

sight [saɪt] n (faculty) visão, visão f; (spectacle) espetáculo ♦ vt avistar; in ~ à vista; on ~ (shoot) no local; out of ~ longe dos olhos; **sightseeing** n turismo; to go sightseeing fazer turismo, passear

sign [saɪn] n (with hand) sinal m, aceno; (indication) indício; (notice) letreiro, tabuleta; (written) signo m ♦ vt assinar; to ~ sth over to sb assinar a transferência de algo para alguém; **sign on** vi (MIL) alistar-se; (BRIT: as unemployed) cadastrar-se para receber auxílio-desemprego; (for course) inscrever-se ♦ vt (MIL) alistar; (employee) efetivar; **sign up** vi (MIL) alistar-se; (for course) inscrever-se ♦ vt recrutar

signal ['sɪgnl] n sinal m, aviso ♦ vi (also: ~) sinalizar, dar sinal ♦ vt (person) fazer sinais para; (message) transmitir

signature ['sɪgnətʃə*] n assinatura; **signature tune** n tema m (de

abertura)

significance [sɪg'nɪfɪkəns] n importância; **significant** adj significativo; (important) importante

sign language n mímica, linguagem f através de sinais

silence ['saɪlns] n silêncio ♦ vt silenciar, impor silêncio a; **silencer** n (on gun) silenciador m; (BRIT: AUT) silencioso

silent ['saɪlənt] adj silencioso; (not speaking) calado; (film) mudo; to remain ~ manter-se em silêncio

silhouette [sɪlu:'et] n silhueta

silicon chip ['sɪlɪkən-] n placa ou chip m de silício

silk [sɪlk] n seda ♦ adj de seda; **silky** adj sedoso

silly ['sɪlɪ] adj (person) bobo, idiota, imbecil; (idea) absurdo, ridículo

silt [sɪlt] n sedimento, aluvião m

silver ['sɪlvə*] n prata; (money) moedas fpl; (also: ~ware) prataria ♦ adj de prata; **silver-plated** adj prateado, banhado a prata; **silvery** adj prateado

similar ['sɪmɪlə*] adj: ~ to parecido com, semelhante a

simmer ['sɪmə*] vi cozer em fogo lento, ferver lentamente

simple ['sɪmpl] adj simples inv; (foolish) ingênuo; **simply** adv de maneira simples; (merely) simplesmente

simultaneous [sɪməl'teɪnɪəs] adj simultâneo

sin [sɪn] n pecado ♦ vi pecar

since [sɪns] adv desde então, depois ♦ prep desde ♦ conj (time) desde que; (because) porque, visto que, já que; ~ then desde então; (ever) ~ desde que

sincere [sɪn'sɪə*] adj sincero; **sincerely** adv: yours sincerely (at end of letter) atenciosamente; **sincerity**

[sɪnˈseriti] n sinceridade f

sing [sɪŋ] (pt **sang**, pp **sung**) vt, vi cantar

Singapore [sɪŋgəˈpɔ:*] n Cingapura (no article)

singe [sɪndʒ] vt chamuscar

singer [ˈsɪŋə*] n cantor(a) m/f

singing [ˈsɪŋɪŋ] n canto; (songs) canções fpl

single [ˈsɪŋgl] adj único, só; (unmarried) solteiro; (not double) simples inv ♦ n (BRIT: also: ~ **ticket**) passagem f de ida; (record) compacto, single; **single out** vt (choose) escolher; (distinguish) distinguir; **single file** n: **in single file** em fila indiana; **single-handed** adv sem ajuda, sozinho; **single-minded** adj determinado; **single room** n quarto individual; **singly** adv separadamente

singular [ˈsɪŋgjulə*] adj (odd) esquisito; (outstanding) extraordinário, excepcional; (LING) singular ♦ n (LING) singular m

sinister [ˈsɪnɪstə*] adj sinistro

sink [sɪŋk] (pt **sank**, pp **sunk**) n pia ♦ vt (ship) afundar; (foundations) escavar ♦ vi afundar-se; (heart) partir; (spirits) ficar deprimido; (also: ~ **back**, ~ **down**) cair ou mergulhar gradativamente; **to ~ sth into** enterrar algo em; **sink in** vi (fig) penetrar

sinner [ˈsɪnə*] n pecador(a) m/f

sinus [ˈsaɪnəs] n (ANAT) seio paranasal

sip [sɪp] n gole m ♦ vt sorver, bebericar

siphon [ˈsaɪfən] n sifão m; **siphon off** vt extrair com sifão; (funds) desviar

sir [sə*] n senhor m; **S~ John Smith** Sir John Smith; **yes, ~** sim, senhor

siren [ˈsaɪərn] n sirena

sirloin [ˈsə:lɔɪn] n lombo de vaca

sissy [ˈsɪsɪ] (inf) n fresco

sister [ˈsɪstə*] n irmã f; (BRIT: nurse) enfermeira-chefe f; (nun) freira; **sister-in-law** n cunhada

sit [sɪt] (pt, pp sat) vi sentar-se; (be sitting) estar sentado; (assembly) reunir-se; (for painter) posar ♦ vt (exam) prestar; **sit down** vi sentar-se; **sit in on** vt fus assistir a; **sit up** vi (after lying) levantar-se; (straight) endireitar-se; (not go to bed) aguardar acordado, velar

sitcom [ˈsɪtkɔm] n abbr (= situation comedy) comédia de costumes

site [saɪt] n local m, sítio; (also: building ~) lote m (de terreno) ♦ vt situar, localizar

sit-in n (demonstration) ocupação de um local como forma de protesto, manifestação f pacífica

sitting [ˈsɪtɪŋ] n (in canteen) turno; **sitting room** n sala de estar

situation [sɪtjuˈeɪʃən] n situação f; (job) posição f; (location) local m; "**~s vacant**" (BRIT) "empregos oferecem-se"

six [sɪks] num seis; **sixteen** num dezesseis; **sixth** num sexto; **sixty** num sessenta

size [saɪz] n tamanho; (extent) extensão f; (of clothing) tamanho, medida; (of shoes) número; **size up** vt avaliar, formar uma opinião sobre; **sizeable** adj considerável, importante

sizzle [ˈsɪzl] vi chiar

skate [skeɪt] n patim m; (fish: pl inv) arraia ♦ vi patinar; **skateboard** n skate m, patim-tábua m; **skating** n patinação f; **skating rink** n rinque m de patinação

skeleton [ˈskelɪtn] n esqueleto; (TECH) armação f; (outline) esquema m, esboço

sketch [sketʃ] n (drawing) desenho;

' (outline) esboço, croqui m; (THEATRE) quadro, esquete m ♦ vt desenhar, esboçar; (ideas: also: ~ out) esboçar; **sketchbook** n caderno de rascunho; **sketchy** adj incompleto, superficial

skewer ['skjuːə*] n espetinho

ski [skiː] n esqui m ♦ vi esquiar; **ski boot** n bota de esquiar

skid [skɪd] n derrapagem f ♦ vi deslizar; (AUT) derrapar

ski: **skier** n esquiador(a) m/f; **skiing** n esqui m

skilful ['skɪlful] (US **skillful**) adj habilidoso, jeitoso

ski lift n ski lift m

skill [skɪl] n habilidade f, perícia; (for work) técnica; **skilled** adj hábil, perito; (worker) especializado, qualificado; **skillful** (US) adj = **skilful**

skim [skɪm] vt (milk) desnatar; (glide over) roçar ♦ vi: to ~ through (book) folhear; **skimmed milk** n leite m desnatado

skimpy ['skɪmpɪ] adj (meagre) escasso, insuficiente; (skirt) sumário

skin [skɪn] n pele f; (of fruit, vegetable) casca ♦ vt (fruit etc) descascar; (animal) tirar a pele de; **skin-deep** adj superficial; **skin diving** n caça-submarina; **skinny** adj magro, descarnado; **skintight** adj justo, grudado (no corpo)

skip [skɪp] n salto, pulo; (BRIT: container) balde m ♦ vi saltar; (with rope) pular corda ♦ vt (pass over) omitir, saltar; (miss) deixar de

skipper ['skɪpə*] n capitão m

skipping rope ['skɪpɪŋ-] (BRIT) n corda (de pular)

skirt [skəːt] n saia ♦ vt orlar, circundar; **skirting board** (BRIT) n rodapé m

ski suit n traje m de esqui

skittle ['skɪtl] n pau m; **~s** n (game)

(jogo de) boliche m (BR), jogo da bola (PT)

skive [skaɪv] (BRIT: inf) vi evitar trabalhar

skull [skʌl] n caveira; (ANAT) crânio

skunk [skʌŋk] n gambá m

sky [skaɪ] n céu m; **skylight** n claraboia, escotilha; **skyscraper** n arranha-céu m

slab [slæb] n (stone) bloco; (flat) laje f; (of cake) fatia grossa

slack [slæk] adj (loose) frouxo; (slow) lerdo; (careless) descuidoso, desmazelado; **slacks** npl (trousers) calça (BR), calças fpl (PT)

slam [slæm] vt (door) bater or fechar (com violência); (throw) atirar violentamente; (criticize) malhar, criticar ♦ vi fechar-se (com violência)

slander ['slɑːndə*] n calúnia, difamação f

slang [slæŋ] n gíria; (jargon) jargão m

slant [slɑːnt] n declive m, inclinação f; (fig) ponto de vista; **slanted**, **slanting** adj inclinado; (eyes) puxado

slap [slæp] n tapa m or f ♦ vt dar um(a) tapa em; (paint etc): to ~ sth on sth passar algo em algo descuidadamente ♦ adv diretamente, exatamente; **slapstick** n (comédia-)pastelão m

slash [slæʃ] vt cortar, talhar; (fig: prices) cortar

slate [sleɪt] n ardósia ♦ vt (fig: criticize) criticar duramente, arrasar

slaughter ['slɔːtə*] n (of animals) matança; (of people) carnificina ♦ vt abater; matar, massacrar; **slaughterhouse** n matadouro

slave [sleɪv] n escravo(-a) ♦ vi (also: ~ away) trabalhar como escravo; **slavery** n escravidão f

slay [sleɪ] (pt **slew**, pp **slain**) vt (literary) matar

sleazy ['sli:zɪ] adj sórdido

sledge [slɛdʒ] n trenó m; **sledge-
hammer** n marreta, malho

sleek [sli:k] adj (hair, fur) macio, lustroso; (car, boat) aerodinâmico

sleep [sli:p] (pt, pp **slept**) n sono
♦ vi dormir; **to go to ~** dormir, adormecer; **sleep around** vi ser promíscuo sexualmente; **sleep in** vi
(oversleep) dormir demais; **sleeper** n (RAIL: train) vagão-leitos m
(BR), carruagem-camas f (PT);
sleeping bag n saco de dormir;
sleeping car n vagão-leitos m (BR),
carruagem-camas f (PT); **sleeping
partner** (BRIT) n (COMM) sócio
comanditário; **sleeping pill** n pílula para dormir; **sleepless** adj: a
sleepless night uma noite em
claro; **sleepy** adj sonolento; (fig)
morto

sleet [sli:t] n chuva com neve e
granizo

sleeve [sli:v] n manga; (of record)
capa

sleigh [sleɪ] n trenó m

slender ['slɛndə*] adj esbelto, delgado; (means) escasso, insuficiente

slept [slɛpt] pt, pp of **sleep**

slice [slaɪs] n (of meat, bread) fatia;
(of lemon) rodela; (utensil) pá f or
espátula de bolo ♦ vt cortar em
fatias

slick [slɪk] adj (skilful) jeitoso, ágil,
engenhoso; (clever) esperto, astuto
♦ n (also: **oil ~**) mancha de óleo

slide [slaɪd] (pt, pp **slid**) n desliza-
mento, escorregão m; (in play-
ground) escorregador m; (PHOT)
slide m; (BRIT: also: **hair ~**) passador
m ♦ vt deslizar ♦ vi escorregar; **slid-
ing** adj (door) corrediço

slight [slaɪt] adj (slim) fraco, franzino; (frail) delicado; (small) pequeno; (trivial) insignificante ♦ n

desfeita, desconsideração f; **not in
the ~est** em absoluto, de maneira
alguma; **slightly** adv ligeiramente,
um pouco

slim [slɪm] adj esbelto, delgado;
(chance) pequeno ♦ vi emagrecer

slime [slaɪm] n lodo, limo, lama

slimming ['slɪmɪŋ] n emagrecimento

sling [slɪŋ] (pt, pp **slung**) n (MED)
tipóia; (for baby) bebêbag m;
(weapon) estilingue m, funda ♦ vt
atirar, arremessar, lançar

slip [slɪp] n (fall) escorregão m; (mistake) erro, lapso; (underskirt) combinação f; (of paper) tira ♦ vt deslizar
♦ vi (slide) deslizar (on ease); (lose balance)
escorregar; (decline) decair; (move
smoothly): **to ~ into/out of** entrar
furtivamente em/sair furtivamente
de; **to ~ sth on/off** enfiar/tirar algo;
to give sb the ~ esquerdar-se de
alguém; **a ~ of the tongue** um
lapso da língua; **slip away** vi escapulir; **slip in** vt meter ♦ vi (errors)
surgir; **slip out** vi (go out) sair (um
momento); **slip up** vi cometer um
erro

slipper ['slɪpə*] n chinelo

slippery ['slɪpərɪ] adj escorregadio

slip-up n equívoco, mancada

slit [slɪt] (pt, pp **slit**) n fenda; (cut)
corte m ♦ vt (cut) rachar, cortar;
(open) abrir

slither ['slɪðə*] vi escorregar, deslizar

sliver ['slɪvə*] n (of glass, wood)
lasca; (of cheese etc) fatia fina

slob [slɔb] (inf) n (in manners) por-
co(-a); (in appearance) maltrapi-
lho(-a)

slog [slɔg] (BRIT) vi mourejar ♦ n: **it
was a ~** deu um trabalho louco

slogan ['sləugən] n lema m, slogan
m

slope [sləup] n ladeira; (side of

sloppy *mountain*) encosta, vertente f; (*ski* ~) pista; (*slant*) inclinação f, declive m ♦ vi: **to ~ down** estar em declive; **to ~ up** inclinar-se; **sloping** adj inclinado, em declive; (*handwriting*) torto

sloppy ['slɔpɪ] adj (*work*) descuidado; (*appearance*) relaxado

slot [slɔt] n (*in machine*) fenda ♦ vt: **to ~ into** encaixar em

slouch [slautʃ] vi ter má postura

slovenly ['slʌvənlɪ] adj (*dirty*) desalinhado, sujo; (*careless*) desmazelado

slow [sləu] adj lento; (*not clever*) bronco, de raciocínio lento; (*watch*): **to be ~** atrasar ♦ adv lentamente, devagar ♦ vt, vi ir (mais) devagar; **"~"** (*road sign*) "devagar"; **slowly** adv lentamente, devagar; **slow motion** n: **in slow motion** em câmara lenta

sludge [slʌdʒ] n lama, lodo

slug [slʌg] n lesma; **sluggish** adj vagaroso; (*business*) lento

sluice [slu:s] n (*gate*) comporta, eclusa; (*channel*) canal m

slum [slʌm] n (*area*) favela; (*house*) cortiço, barraco

slump [slʌmp] n (*economic*) depressão f; (*comm*) baixa, queda ♦ vi (*person*) cair; (*prices*) baixar repentinamente

slung [slʌŋ] pt, pp of **sling**

slur [slə:*] n calúnia ♦ vt pronunciar indistintamente

slush [slʌʃ] n neve f meio derretida

slut [slʌt] n (*pej*) mulher f desmazelada

sly [slaɪ] adj (*person*) astuto; (*smile, remark*) malicioso, velhaco

smack [smæk] n palmada ♦ vt bater; (*child*) dar uma palmada em; (*on face*) dar um tabefe em ♦ vi: **to ~ of** cheirar a, saber a

small [smɔ:l] adj pequeno; **small change** n trocado; **small hours** npl: **in the small hours** na madrugada, lá pelas tantas (*inf*); **smallpox** n varíola; **small talk** n conversa fiada

smart [smɑ:t] adj elegante; (*clever*) inteligente, astuto; (*quick*) vivo, esperto ♦ vi sofrer; **smart card** n smart card m, cartão m inteligente; **smarten up** vi arrumar-se ♦ vt arrumar

smash [smæʃ] n (*also*: **~-up**) colisão f, choque m; (~ *hit*) sucesso de bilheteira ♦ vt (*break*) espatalhar, despedaçar; (*car etc*) bater com; (*sport*: *record*) quebrar ♦ vi despedaçar-se; (*against wall etc*) espatifar-se; **smashing** (*inf*) adj excelente

smattering ['smætərɪŋ] n: **a ~ of** um conhecimento superficial de

smear [smɪə*] n mancha, nódoa; (*med*) esfregaço ♦ vt untar; (*to make dirty*) lambuzar

smell [smɛl] (*pt, pp* **smelt** or **~ed**) n cheiro; (*sense*) olfato ♦ vt cheirar ♦ vi (*food etc*) cheirar; (*pej*) cheirar mal; **to ~ of** cheirar a; **smelly** (*pej*) adj fedorento, malcheiroso

smile [smaɪl] n sorriso ♦ vi sorrir

smirk [smə:k] (*pej*) n sorriso falso or afetado

smock [smɔk] n guarda-pó m; (*children's*) avental m

smog [smɔg] n nevoeiro com fumaça (*br*) or fumo (*pt*)

smoke [sməuk] n fumaça (*br*), fumo (*pt*) ♦ vi fumar; (*chimney*) fumegar ♦ vt (*cigarettes*) fumar; **smoked** adj (*bacon*) defumado; (*glass*) fumée; **smoker** n (*person*) fumante m/f; (*rail*) vagão m para fumantes; **smokescreen** n cortina de fumaça; **smoking** n: "no smok-

ing" *(sign)* "proibido fumar";
smoky *adj* enfumaçado; *(taste)*
defumado
smolder ['sməuldə*] *(US) vi* =
smoulder
smooth [smu:ð] *adj* liso, macio;
(sauce) cremoso; *(sea)* tranqüilo,
calmo; *(flavour, movement)* suave;
(person: pej) meloso ♦ *vt (also: ~
out)* alisar; *(: difficulties)* aplainar
smother ['smʌðə*] *vt (fire)* abafar;
(person) sufocar; *(emotions)* reprimir
smoulder ['sməuldə*] *(US* smolder*)
vi* arder sem chamas; *(fig)* estar
latente
smudge [smʌdʒ] *n* mancha ♦ *vt*
manchar, sujar
smug [smʌg] *(pej) adj* convencido
smuggle ['smʌgl] *vt* contrabandear; **smuggler** *n* contrabandista
m/f; **smuggling** *n* contrabando
smutty ['smʌtɪ] *adj (fig)* obsceno,
indecente
snack [snæk] *n* lanche *m (BR)*,
merenda *(PT);* **snack bar** *n* lanchonete *f (BR)*, snackbar *m (PT)*
snag [snæg] *n* dificuldade *f*, obstáculo
snail [sneɪl] *n* caracol *m*
snake [sneɪk] *n* cobra
snap [snæp] *n (sound)* estalo;
(photograph) foto *f* ♦ *adj* repentino
♦ *vt* quebrar; *(fingers)* estalar ♦ *vi*
quebrar; *(fig)* retrucar aspe-
ramente; **to ~ shut** fechar com um
estalo; **snap at** *vt fus (subj: dog)*
tentar morder; **snap off** *vt (break)*
partir; **snap up** *vt* arrebatar, comprar rapidamente; **snappy** *(inf) adj*
rápido; *(slogan)* vigoroso; **make it
snappy!** faça rápido!; **snapshot** *n*
foto *f* (instantânea)
snare [snɛə*] *n* armadilha, laço
snarl [snɑ:l] *vi* grunhir
snatch [snætʃ] *n (small piece)* tre-

cho ♦ *vt* agarrar; *(fig: look)* roubar
sneak [sni:k] *(pt* ~ed *or (US)* snuck*)
vi:* **to ~ in/out** entrar/sair furtivamente ♦ *n (inf)* dedo-duro; **to ~ up
on sb** chegar de mausinho perto de
alguém; **sneakers** *npl* tênis *m (BR)*,
sapatos *mpl* de treino *(PT)*
sneer [snɪə*] *vi* rir-se com desdém;
(mock): **to ~ at** zombar de, desprezar
sneeze [sni:z] *n* espirro ♦ *vi* espirrar
sniff [snɪf] *n* fungada; *(of dog)* fare-
jada; *(of person)* fungadela ♦ *vi* fungar ♦ *vt* fungar, farejar; *(glue, drug)*
cheirar
snigger ['snɪgə*] *vi* rir-se com dissi-
mulação
snip [snɪp] *n* tesourada; *(BRIT: inf)*
pechincha ♦ *vt* cortar com tesoura
sniper ['snaɪpə*] *n* franco-
atirador(a) *m/f*
snob [snɔb] *n* esnobe *m/f;* **snobbish** *adj* esnobe
snooker ['snu:kə*] *n* sinuca
snoop [snu:p] *vi:* **to ~ about** bisbilhotar
snooze [snu:z] *n* soneca ♦ *vi* tirar
uma soneca, dormitar
snore [snɔ:*] *vi* roncar ♦ *n* ronco
snorkel ['snɔ:kl] *n* tubo snorkel
snort [snɔ:t] *n* bufo, bufido ♦ *vi*
bufar
snout [snaut] *n* focinho
snow [snəu] *n* neve *f* ♦ *vi* nevar;
snowball *n* bola de neve ♦ *vi (fig)*
aumentar *(como bola de neve)*;
snowbound *adj* bloqueado pela
neve; **snowdrift** *n* monte *m* de
neve *(formado pelo vento)*; **snow-
drop** *n* campainha branca; **snow-
fall** *n* nevada; **snowflake** *n* floco
de neve; **snowman** *(irreg)* *n* boneco de neve; **snowplough** *(US*
snowplow*) n* máquina limpa-neve,
removedor *m* de neve; **snow-**

storm n nevasca, tempestade f de neve

snub [snʌb] vt desdenhar, menosprezar ♦ n repulsa

snug [snʌg] adj (sheltered) abrigado, protegido; (fitted) justo, cômodo

snuggle ['snʌgl] vi: **to ~ up to sb** aconchegar-se or aninhar-se a alguém

KEYWORD

so [səu] adv **1** (thus, likewise) assim, deste modo; **~ saying he walked away** falou isto e foi embora; **if ~** se for assim, se assim é; **I didn't do it – you did** – não fiz isso – você fez!; **~ do I, ~ am I** etc eu também; **~ it is!** é verdade!; **I hope/think ~** espero/acho que sim; **~ far** até aqui
2 (in comparisons etc: to such a degree) tão; **~ big/quickly (that)** tão grande/rápido (que)
3: **~ much** ♦ adj, adv tanto; **I've got ~ much work** tenho tanto trabalho; **~ many** tantos(-as); **there are ~ many people to see** tem tanta gente para ver
4 (phrases): **10 or ~** 10 mais ou menos; **~ long!** (inf: goodbye) tchau!
♦ conj **1** (expressing purpose): **~ as to** do para fazer; **we hurried ~ as not to be late** nós apressamos para não chegarmos atrasados, **~ (that)** para que, a fim de que
2 (result) de modo que; **he didn't arrive, ~ I left** como ele não chegou, eu fui embora; **~ I was right after all** então eu estava certo no final das contas

soak [səuk] vt embeber, ensopar; (put in water) pôr de molho ♦ vi estar de molho, impregnar-se;

soak in vi infiltrar; **soak up** vt absorver

soap [səup] n sabão m; **soap opera** n novela; **soap powder** n sabão m em pó; **soapy** adj ensaboado

soar [sɔ:*] vi (on wings) elevar-se em vôo; (rocket, temperature) subir; (building etc) levantar-se; (price, production) disparar

sob [sɔb] n soluço ♦ vi soluçar

sober ['səubə*] adj (serious) sério; (not drunk) sóbrio; (colour, style) discreto; **sober up** vi ficar sóbrio

so-called [-kɔ:ld] adj chamado

soccer ['sɔkə*] n futebol m

social ['səuʃl] adj social ♦ n reunião f social; **socialism** n socialismo; **socialist** adj, n socialista m/f; **socialize** vi: **to socialize (with)** socializar (com); **social security** (BRIT) n previdência social; **social work** n assistência social, serviço social; **social worker** n assistente m/f social

society [sə'saɪətɪ] n sociedade f; (club) associação f; (also: **high ~**) alta sociedade

sociology [səusɪ'ɔlədʒɪ] n sociologia

sock [sɔk] n meia (BR), peúga (PT)

socket ['sɔkɪt] n bocal m, encaixe m; (BRIT: ELEC) tomada

soda ['səudə] n (CHEM) soda; (also: **~ water**) água com gás; (US: also: **~ pop**) soda

sofa ['səufə] n sofá m

soft [sɔft] adj mole; (voice, music, light) suave; (kind) meigo, bondoso; **soft drink** n refrigerante m; **soften** vt amolecer, amaciar; (effect) abrandar; (expression) suavizar ♦ vi amolecer-se; (voice, expression) suavizar-se; **softly** adv suavemente; (gently) delicadamente; **softness** n maciez f; (gentleness) suavidade f; **software** n (COMPUT) software m

soggy ['sɔgɪ] adj ensopado, encharcado

soil [sɔɪl] n terra, solo; (territory) território ♦ vt sujar, manchar

solar ['səʊlə*] adj solar

sold [səʊld] pt, pp of **sell** ♦ adj: **~ out** (COMM) esgotado

solder ['səʊldə*] vt soldar ♦ n solda

soldier ['səʊldʒə*] n soldado; (army man) militar m

sole [səʊl] n (of foot, shoe) sola; (fish: pl inv) solha, linguado ♦ adj único

solemn ['sɔləm] adj solene

solicitor [sə'lɪsɪtə*] n (BRIT) (for wills etc) tabelião(-lioa) m/f; (in court) = advogado(-a)

solid ['sɔlɪd] adj sólido; (gold etc) maciço; (person) sério ♦ n sólido; **~s** npl (food) comida sólida

solitary ['sɔlɪtərɪ] adj solitário, só; (walk) só; (isolated) isolado, retirado; (single) único

solo ['səʊləʊ] n, adv solo; **soloist** n solista m/f

solution [sə'luːʃən] n solução f

solve [sɔlv] vt resolver, solucionar

solvent ['sɔlvənt] adj (COMM) solvente ♦ n (CHEM) solvente m

KEYWORD

some [sʌm] adj 1 (a certain number or amount): **~ tea/water/biscuits** um pouco de chá/água/uns biscoitos; **~ children came** algumas crianças vieram

2 (certain: in contrasts) algum(a); **~ people say that ...** algumas pessoas dizem que ...

3 (unspecified) um pouco de; **~ woman was asking for you** uma mulher estava perguntando por você; **~ day** um dia

♦ pron 1 (a certain number) alguns

(algumas); **I've got ~** (books etc) tenho alguns; **~ went for a taxi and ~ walked** alguns foram pegar um táxi e outros foram andando

2 (a certain amount) um pouco; **I've got ~** (milk etc) tenho um pouco ♦ adv: **~ 10 people** umas 10 pessoas

some: **somebody** ['sʌmbədɪ] pron = someone; **somehow** ['sʌmhaʊ] adv de alguma maneira; (for some reason) por uma razão ou outra; **someone** ['sʌmwʌn] pron alguém; **someplace** ['sʌmpleɪs] (US) adv = somewhere

somersault ['sʌməsɔːlt] n (deliberate) salto-mortal; (accidental) cambalhota ♦ vi dar um salto-mortal (or uma cambalhota)

something ['sʌmθɪŋ] pron alguma coisa, algo (BR)

sometime ['sʌmtaɪm] adv (in future) algum dia, em outra oportunidade; (in past): **~ last month** durante o mês passado

sometimes ['sʌmtaɪmz] adv às vezes, de vez em quando

somewhat ['sʌmwɔt] adv um tanto

somewhere ['sʌmwɛə*] adv (be) em algum lugar; (go) para algum lugar; **~ else** em outro lugar; para outro lugar

son [sʌn] n filho

song [sɔŋ] n canção f; (of bird) canto

son-in-law ['sʌnɪnlɔː] n genro

soon [suːn] adv logo, brevemente; (a short time after) logo após; (early) cedo; **~ afterwards** pouco depois; see also **as**; **sooner** adv antes, mais cedo; (preference): **I would sooner do that** preferia fazer isso; **sooner or later** mais cedo ou mais tarde

soot [sut] n fuligem f

soothe [suːð] *vt* acalmar, sossegar; (*pain*) aliviar, suavizar

sophomore [ˈsɔfəmɔː*] (*us*) *n* segundanista *m/f*

sopping [ˈsɔpɪŋ] *adj*: ~ (**wet**) encharcado

soppy [ˈsɔpɪ] (*pej*) *adj* piegas *inv*

soprano [səˈprɑːnəu] *n* soprano *m/f*

sorcerer [ˈsɔːsərə*] *n* feiticeiro

sore [sɔː*] *adj* dolorido ♦ *n* chaga, ferida; **sorely** [ˈsɔːlɪ] *adv*: **I am sorely tempted (to)** estou muito tentado (a)

sorrow [ˈsɔrəu] *n* tristeza, mágoa, dor *f*; **~s** *npl* (*causes of grief*) tristezas *fpl*

sorry [ˈsɔrɪ] *adj* (*regretful*) arrependido; (*condition*, *excuse*) lamentável; ~**!** desculpe!, perdão!, sinto muito!; **to feel ~ for sb** sentir pena de alguém

sort [sɔːt] *n* tipo ♦ *vt* (*also*: ~ **out**: *papers*) classificar; (: *problems*) solucionar, resolver

SOS *n abbr* (= *save our souls*) S.O.S. *m*

so-so *adv* mais ou menos, regular

sought [sɔːt] *pt*, *pp* of **seek**

soul [səul] *n* alma; (*person*) criatura, *m/f*; **soulful** [ˈsəulful] *adj* emocional, sentimental

sound [saund] *adj* (*healthy*) saudável, sadio; (*safe*, *not damaged*) válido, completo; (*secure*) seguro; (*reliable*) confiável; (*sensible*) sensato ♦ *adv*: ~ **asleep** dormindo profundamente ♦ *n* (*noise*) som *m*, ruído, barulho; (*volume*: *on TV etc*) volume *m*; (GEO) estreito, braço (de mar) ♦ *vt* (*alarm*) soar ♦ *vi* soar, tocar; (*fig*: *seem*) parecer; **to ~ like** parecer; **sound out** *vi* sondar; **sound barrier** *n* barreira do som; **sound effects** *npl* efeitos *mpl*

sonoros; **soundly** *adv* (*sleep*) profundamente; (*beat*) completamente; **soundproof** *adj* à prova de som; **soundtrack** *n* trilha sonora

soup [suːp] *n* sopa; **in the** ~ (*fig*) numa encrenca; **soupspoon** *n* colher *f* de sopa

sour [ˈsauə*] *adj* azedo, ácido; (*milk*) talhado; (*fig*) mal-humorado, rabugento; **it's ~ grapes!** (*fig*) é despeito!

source [sɔːs] *n* fonte *f*

south [sauθ] *n* sul *m* ♦ *adj* do sul, meridional ♦ *adv* ao or para o sul; **South Africa** *n* África do Sul; **South African** *adj*, *n* sul-african(a-); **South America** *n* América do Sul; **South American** *adj*, *n* sul-americano(-a); **south-east** *n* sudeste *m*; **southerly** [ˈsʌðəlɪ] *adj* para o sul; (*from the south*) do sul; **southern** [ˈsʌðən] *adj* (*to the south*) para o sul, em direção do sul; (*from the south*) do sul, sulista; **the southern hemisphere** o Hemisfério Sul; **South Pole** *n* Pólo Sul; **southward(s)** *adv* para o sul; **south-west** *n* sudoeste *m*

souvenir [suːvəˈnɪə*] *n* lembrança

sovereign [ˈsɔvrɪn] *n* soberano(-a)

soviet [ˈsəuvɪət] *adj* soviético; **the S~ Union** a União Soviética

sow[1] [sau] *n* porca

sow[2] [səu] (*pt* ~**ed**, *pp* ~**n**) *vt* semear; (*fig*: *spread*) disseminar, espalhar

soya [ˈsɔɪə] (*us* **soy**) *n*: ~ **bean** semente *f* de soja; ~ **sauce** molho de soja

spa [spɑː] *n* (*town*) estância hidromineral; (*us*: *also*: **health** ~) estância balnear

space [speɪs] *n* (*gen*) espaço; (*room*) lugar *m*; (*cpd*) espacial ♦ *vt* (*also*: ~ **out**) espaçar; **spacecraft** *n* nave *f* espacial; **spaceman** (*irreg*) *n* astronauta *m*, cosmonauta *m*; **spaceship** *n* = **spacecraft**; **spacious** ['speɪʃəs] *adj* espaçoso

spade [speɪd] *n* pá *f*; **~s** *npl* (CARDS) espadas *fpl*

Spain [speɪn] *n* Espanha

span [spæn] *n* (*also*: **wing~**) envergadura; (*of arch*) vão *m*; (*in time*) lapso, espaço ♦ *vt* estender-se sobre, atravessar; (*fig*) abarcar

Spaniard ['spænjəd] *n* espanhol(a) *m/f*

Spanish ['spænɪʃ] *adj* espanhol(a) ♦ *n* (LING) espanhol *m*, castelhano; **the ~** *npl* os espanhóis

spank [spæŋk] *vt* bater, dar palmadas em

spanner ['spænə*] (BRIT) *n* chave *f* inglesa

spare [spɛə*] *adj* vago, desocupado; (*surplus*) de sobra, a mais ♦ *n* = **part** ♦ *vt* dispensar, passar sem; (*make available*) dispor de; (*refrain from hurting*) perdoar, poupar; **to ~** de sobra; **spare part** *n* peça sobressalente; **spare time** *n* tempo livre; **spare wheel** *n* estepe *m*; **sparingly** *adv* frugalmente, com moderação

spark [spɑːk] *n* chispa, faísca; (*fig*) centelha

sparkle ['spɑːkl] *n* cintilação *f*, brilho ♦ *vi* (*shine*) brilhar, faiscar; **sparkling** *adj* (*mineral water*) gasoso; (*wine*) espumante; (*conversation*) animado; (*performance*) brilhante

sparrow ['spærəu] *n* pardal *m*

sparse [spɑːs] *adj* escasso; (*hair*) ralo

spasm ['spæzəm] *n* (MED) espasmo

spastic ['spæstɪk] *n* espástico(-a)

spat [spæt] *pt*, *pp of* **spit**

speak [spiːk] (*pt* **spoke**, *pp* **spoken**) *vt* (*language*) falar; (*truth*) dizer ♦ *vi* falar; (*make a speech*) discursar; **~**

up! fale alto!; **speaker** *n* (*in public*) orador(a) *m/f*; (*also*: **loudspeaker**) alto-falante *m*; (POL): **the Speaker** o Presidente da Câmara

spear [spɪə*] *n* lança ♦ *vt* lancear, arpoar

spec [spɛk] (*inf*) *n*: **on ~** por acaso

special ['spɛʃl] *adj* especial; (*edition etc*) extra; (*delivery*) rápido; **specialist** *n* especialista *m/f*; **speciality** [spɛʃɪ'ælɪtɪ] *n* especialidade *f*; **specialize** *vi*: **to specialize (in)** especializar-se (em); **specially** *adv* especialmente; **specialty** ['spɛʃəltɪ] (*esp US*) *n* = **speciality**

species ['spiːʃɪːz] *n inv* espécie *f*

specific [spə'sɪfɪk] *adj* específico; **specification** [spɛsɪfɪ'keɪʃən] *n* especificação *f*; (*requirement*) requinto; **~ations** *npl* (TECH) ficha técnica

specimen ['spɛsɪmən] *n* espécime *m*, amostra; (*for testing*, MED) espécime

speck [spɛk] *n* mancha, pinta

speckled ['spɛkld] *adj* pintado

specs [spɛks] (*inf*) *npl* óculos *mpl*

spectacle ['spɛktəkl] *n* espetáculo; **~s** *npl* (*glasses*) óculos *mpl*; **spectacular** [spɛk'tækjulə*] *adj* espetacular ♦ *n* (CINEMA *etc*) superprodução *f*

spectator [spɛk'teɪtə*] *n* espectador(a) *m/f*

spectrum ['spɛktrəm] (*pl* **spectra**) *n* espectro

speech [spiːtʃ] *n* (*faculty*, THEATRE) fala; (*formal talk*) discurso; **speechless** *adj* estupefato, emudecido

speed [spiːd] *n* velocidade *f*; (*rate*) rapidez *f*; (*haste*) pressa; (*promptness*) prontidão *f*; **at full** *or* **top ~** a toda a velocidade; **speed up** (*pt*, *pp* **speeded up**) *vt*, *vi* acelerar; **speedboat** *n* lancha; **speedily**

adv depressa, rapidamente; **speed-ing** *n* (AUT) excesso de velocidade; **speed limit** *n* limite *m* de velocidade, velocidade *f* máxima; **speedometer** [spiːˈdɔmitəʳ] *n* velocímetro; **speedway** *n* (SPORT: *also*: **speedway racing**) corrida de motocicleta; **speedy** *adj* veloz, rápido; (*prompt*) pronto, imediato

spell [spɛl] (*pt*, *pp* **~ed**, (BRIT) **spelt**) *n* (*also*: **magic ~**) encanto, feitiço; (*period of time*) período, temporada ♦ *vt* (*also*: **~ out**) soletrar; (*fig*) pressagiar, ser sinal de; **to cast a ~ on sb** enfeitiçar alguém; **he can't ~** não sabe escrever bem, comete erros de ortografia; **spellbound** *adj* enfeitiçado, fascinado; **spelling** *n* ortografia

spend [spɛnd] (*pt*, *pp* **spent**) *vt* (*money*) gastar; (*time*) passar

sperm [spəːm] *n* esperma

sphere [sfiəʳ] *n* esfera

spice [spaɪs] *n* especiaria ♦ *vt* condimentar

spicy [ˈspaɪsɪ] *adj* condimentado

spider [ˈspaɪdəʳ] *n* aranha

spike [spaɪk] *n* (*point*) ponta, espigão *m*; (BOT) espiga

spill [spɪl] (*pt*, *pp* **spilt** *or* **~ed**) *vt* entornar, derramar ♦ *vi* derramar-se; **spill over** *vi* transbordar

spin [spɪn] (*pt* **spun** *or* **span**, *pp* **spun**) *n* (AVIAT) parafuso; (*trip in car*) volta *or* passeio de carro; (*ball*): **to put ~ on** fazer girar ♦ *vt* (*wool etc*) fiar, tecer ♦ *vi* girar, rodar; (*make thread*) tecer; **spin out** *vt* prolongar; (*money*) fazer render

spinach [ˈspɪnɪtʃ] *n* espinafre *m*

spinal cord [ˈspaɪnl-] *n* espinha dorsal

spin-dryer (BRIT) *n* secadora

spine [spaɪn] *n* espinha dorsal; (*thorn*) espinho; **spineless** *adj* (*fig*) fraco, covarde

spinster [ˈspɪnstəʳ] *n* solteira

spiral [ˈspaɪərl] *n* espiral *f* ♦ *vi* (*prices*) disparar; **spiral staircase** *n* escada em caracol

spire [ˈspaɪəʳ] *n* flecha, agulha

spirit [ˈspɪrɪt] *n* (*soul*) alma; (*ghost*) fantasma *m*; (*courage*) coragem *f*, ânimo; (*frame of mind*) estado de espírito; (*sense*) sentido; **~s** *npl* (*drink*) álcool *m*; **in good ~s** alegre, de bom humor; **spirited** *adj* animado, espirituoso; **spiritual** *adj* espiritual ♦ *n* (*also*: **Negro spiritual**) canto religioso dos negros

spit [spɪt] (*pt*, *pp* **spat**) *n* (*for roasting*) espeto; (*saliva*) saliva ♦ *vi* cuspir; (*sound*) escarrar; (*rain*) chuviscar

spite [spaɪt] *n* rancor *m*, ressentimento ♦ *vt* contrariar; **in ~ of** apesar de, a despeito de; **spiteful** *adj* maldoso, malévolo

splash [splæʃ] *n* (*sound*) borrifo, respingo; (*of colour*) mancha ♦ *vt*: **to ~ (with)** salpicar (de) ♦ *vi* (*also*: **~ about**) borrifar, respingar

spleen [spliːn] *n* (ANAT) baço

splendid [ˈsplɛndɪd] *adj* esplêndido; (*impressive*) impressionante

splint [splɪnt] *n* tala

splinter [ˈsplɪntəʳ] *n* (*of wood, glass*) lasca; (*in finger*) farpa ♦ *vi* lascar-se, estilhaçar-se, despedaçar-se

split [splɪt] (*pt*, *pp* **split**) *n* fenda, brecha; (*fig: division*) rompimento; (: *difference*) diferença; (POL) divisão *f* ♦ *vt* partir, fender; (*party, work*) dividir; (*profits*) repartir ♦ *vi* (*divide*) dividir-se, repartir-se; **split up** *vi* (*couple*) separar-se, acabar; (*meeting*) terminar

spoil [spɔɪl] (*pt*, *pp* **~t** *or* **~ed**) *vt* (*damage*) danificar; (*mar*) estragar, arruinar; (child) mimar; **spoils** npl desojo, saque m; **spoilsport** (pej) n desmancha-prazeres m/f inv

spoke [spəuk] n de speak ♦ n raio

spoken ['spəukn] pp de **speak**

spokesman ['spəuksmən] (irreg) n porta-voz m

spokeswoman ['spəukswumən] (irreg) n porta-voz f

sponge [spʌndʒ] n esponja; (cake) pão-de-ló m ♦ vt lavar com esponja ♦ vi: **to ~ on sb** viver às custas de alguém; **sponge bag** (BRIT) n bolsa de toalete

sponsor ['sponsə*] n patrocinador(a) m/f ♦ vt patrocinar; apadrinhar; fiar; (applicant, proposal) apoiar, defender; **sponsorship** n patrocínio

spontaneous [spon'teiniəs] adj espontâneo

spooky ['spu:ki] (inf) adj arrepiante

spoon [spu:n] n colher f; **spoon-feed** (irreg) vt dar de comer com colher; (fig) dar tudo mastigado a; **spoonful** n colherada

sport [spɔ:t] n esporte m (BR), desporto (PT); (person) bom perdedor (boa perdedora) m/f ♦ vt (wear) exibir; **sporting** adj esportivo (BR), desportivo (PT); (generous) nobre; **to give sb a sporting chance** dar uma grande chance a alguém; **sport jacket** (US) n = **sports jacket**; **sports car** n carro esporte (BR), carro de sport (PT); **sports jacket** (BRIT) n casaco esportivo (BR) or desportivo (PT); **sportsman** (irreg) n esportista m (BR), desportista m (PT); **sportsmanship** n espírito esportivo (BR) or desportivo (PT); **sportswear** n roupa esportiva (BR) or desportiva (PT) or esporte; **sportswoman** (irreg) n esportista (BR), desportista (PT); **sporty** adj

esportivo (BR), desportivo (PT)

spot [spot] n (mark) marca; (place) lugar m, local m; (dot: on pattern) mancha, ponto; (on skin) espinha; (RADIO, TV) hora; (small amount): **a ~ of** um pouquinho de ♦ vt notar; **on the ~** na hora; (there) ali mesmo; (in difficulty) em apuros; **spot check** n fiscalização f de surpresa; **spotless** adj sem mancha, imaculado; **spotlight** n holofote m, refletor m; **spotted** adj com bolinhas; **spotty** adj cheio de espinhas

spouse [spauz] n cônjuge m/f

spout [spaut] n (of jug) bico; (of pipe) cano ♦ vi jorrar

sprain [sprein] n distensão f, torcedura ♦ vt torcer

sprang [spræŋ] pt of **spring**

sprawl [sprɔ:l] vi esparramar-se

spray [sprei] n borrifo; (container) spray m, atomizador m; (garden ~) vaporizador m; (of flowers) ramalhete m ♦ vt pulverizar; (crops) borrifar, regar

spread [spred] (pt, pp **spread**) n extensão f; (distribution) expansão f, difusão f; (CULIN) pasta; (inf: food) banquete m ♦ vt espalhar; (butter) untar, passar; (wings, sails) abrir, desdobrar; (workload, wealth) distribuir; (scatter) disseminar ♦ vi (news, stain) espalhar-se; (disease) alastrar-se; **spread out** vi espalhar-se; **spread-eagled** adj estirado; **spreadsheet** n (COMPUT) planilha

spree [spri:] n: **to go on a ~** cair na farra

sprightly ['spraitli] adj ativo, ágil

spring [spriŋ] (pt **sprang**, pp **sprung**) n salto, pulo; (coiled metal) mola; (season) primavera; (of water) fonte f; **spring up** vi aparecer de repente; **springboard** n trampolim m; **spring-cleaning** n limpeza total, faxina (geral); **springtime** n primavera

sprinkle ['sprɪŋkl] vt (liquid) salpicar; (salt, sugar) borrifar; **to ~ water on, ~ with water** salpicar de água

sprint [sprɪnt] n corrida de pequena distância ♦ vi correr a toda velocidade; **sprinter** n corredor(a) m/f

sprout [spraut] vi brotar, germinar; **sprouts** npl (also: **Brussels ~s**) couves-de-Bruxelas fpl

sprung [sprʌŋ] pp of **spring**

spun [spʌn] pt, pp of **spin**

spur [spə:*] n espora; (fig) estímulo ♦ vt (also: **~ on**) incitar, estimular; **on the ~ of the moment** de improviso, de repente

spurn [spə:n] vt desdenhar, desprezar

spurt [spə:t] n (of energy) acesso; (of blood etc) jorro ♦ vi jorrar

spy [spaɪ] n espião (espiã) m/f ♦ vi: **to ~ on** espiar, espionar ♦ vt enxergar, avistar; **spying** n espionagem f

sq. abbr (MATH etc) = **square**

squabble ['skwɔbl] vi brigar, discutir

squad [skwɔd] n (MIL, POLICE) pelotão m, esquadra; (FOOTBALL) seleção f

squadron ['skwɔdrən] n (MIL) esquadrão m; (AVIAT) esquadrilha; (NAUT) esquadra

squalid ['skwɔlɪd] adj (conditions) esquálido; (story etc) sórdido

squall [skwɔ:l] n (storm) tempestade f; (wind) pé m (de vento), rajada

squalor ['skwɔlə*] n sordidez f

squander ['skwɔndə*] vt esbanjar, dissipar; (chances) desperdiçar

square [skwɛə*] n quadrado; (in town) praça; (inf: person) quadrado(-a), careta m/f ♦ adj quadrado; (inf: ideas, tastes) careta, antiquado ♦ vt (arrange) ajustar, acertar; (MATH) elevar ao quadrado; (reconcile) con-

ciliar; **all ~** igual, quite; **a ~ meal** uma refeição substancial; **2 metres ~** um quadrado de 2 metros de lado; **2 ~ metres** 2 metros quadrados; **squarely** adv diretamente; (fully) em cheio

squash [skwɔʃ] n (BRIT: drink): **lemon/orange ~** limonada/laranjada concentrada; (SPORT) squash m; (US: vegetable) abóbora ♦ vt esmagar

squat [skwɔt] adj atarracado ♦ vi (also: **~ down**) agachar-se, acocorar-se; **squatter** n posseiro(-a)

squeak [skwi:k] vi (door) ranger; (mouse) guinchar

squeal [skwi:l] vi guinchar, gritar agudamente

squeamish ['skwi:mɪʃ] adj melindroso, delicado

squeeze [skwi:z] n (gen, of hand) aperto; (ECON) arrocho ♦ vt comprimir, socar; (hand, arm) apertar; **squeeze out** vt espremer; (fig) extorquir

squelch [skwɛltʃ] vi fazer ruído de passos na lama

squid [skwɪd] n (pl inv or **~s**) n lula

squiggle ['skwɪgl] n garatuja

squint [skwɪnt] vi olhar or ser vesgo ♦ n (MED) estrabismo

squirm [skwə:m] vi retorcer-se

squirrel ['skwɪrəl] n esquilo

squirt [skwə:t] vi, vt jorrar, esguichar

Sr abbr = **senior**

St abbr (= saint) S.; = **street**

stab [stæb] n (with knife etc) punhalada; (of pain) pontada; (inf: try): **to have a ~ at (doing) sth** tentar (fazer) algo ♦ vt apunhalar

stable ['steɪbl] adj estável ♦ n estábulo, cavalariça

stack [stæk] n montão m, pilha ♦ vt amontoar, empilhar

stadium ['steɪdɪəm] n (pl **stadia** or

~s) n estádio

staff [stɑ:f] n (work force) pessoal m, quadro; (BRIT: SCH: also: **teaching** ~) corpo docente ♦ vt prover de pessoal

stag [stæg] n veado, cervo

stage [steɪdʒ] n palco, cena; (point) etapa, fase f; (platform) plataforma, estrado; (profession): **the** ~ o palco, o teatro ♦ vt pôr em cena, representar; (demonstration) montar, organizar; in ~s por etapas; **stagecoach** n diligência

stagger [ˈstægə*] vi cambalear ♦ vt (amaze) surpreender, chocar; (hours, holidays) escalonar; **staggering** adj (amazing) surpreendente, chocante

stag party n despedida de solteiro

staid [steɪd] adj sério, sóbrio

stain [steɪn] n mancha; (colouring) tinta, tintura ♦ vt manchar; (wood) tingir; **stained glass window** n janela com vitral; **stain remover** n tira-manchas m

stair [steə*] n (step) degrau m; ~s npl (flight of steps) escada; **staircase** n escadaria, escada; **stairway** n = staircase

stake [steɪk] n estaca, poste m; (COMM: interest) interesse m, participação f; (BETTING: gen pl) aposta ♦ vt apostar; (claim) reivindicar; **to be at** ~ estar em jogo

stale [steɪl] adj (bread) dormido; (food) estragado; (air) viciado; (smell) mofado; (beer) velho

stalk [stɔ:k] n talo, haste f ♦ vt caçar de tocaia; ~ **in/out** entrar/sair silenciosamente; **to** ~ **off** andar com arrogância

stall [stɔ:l] n (BRIT: in market) barraca; (in stable) baia ♦ vt (AUT) fazer morrer; (fig: delay) impedir, atrasar ♦ vi morrer; esquivar-se, ganhar

tempo; ~s npl (BRIT: in cinema, theatre) platéia

stallion [ˈstæljən] n garanhão m

stamina [ˈstæmɪnə] n resistência

stammer [ˈstæmə*] n gagueira ♦ vi gaguejar, balbuciar

stamp [stæmp] n selo; (rubber ~) carimbo, timbre m; (mark, also fig) marca, impressão f ♦ vi (also: ~ **one's foot**) bater com o pé ♦ vt (letter) selar; (mark) marcar; (with rubber ~) carimbar; **stamp collecting** n filatelia

stampede [stæmˈpiːd] n debandada, estouro (da boiada)

stance [stæns] n postura, posição f

stand [stænd] n (pt, pp **stood**) n posição f, postura; (for taxis) ponto; (also: **hall** ~) pedestal m; (also: **music** ~) estante f; (SPORT) tribuna, palanque m; (stall) barraca ♦ vi (be) estar, encontrar-se; (be on foot) estar em pé; (rise) levantar-se; (remain: decision, offer) estar de pé; (in election) candidatar-se ♦ vt (place) pôr, colocar; (tolerate) agüentar, suportar; (cost) pagar; **to make a** ~ resistir; (fig) ater-se a um princípio; **to** ~ **for parliament** (BRIT) apresentar-se como candidato ao parlamento; **stand by** vi estar a postos ♦ vt fus (opinion) aferrar-se a; (person) ficar ao lado de; **stand down** vi retirar-se; **stand for** vt fus (signify) significar; (represent) representar; (tolerate) tolerar, permitir; **stand in for** vt fus substituir; **stand out** vi (be prominent) destacar-se; **stand up** vi levantar-se; **stand up for** vt fus defender; **stand up to** vt fus enfrentar

standard [ˈstændəd] n o padrão m, critério; (flag) estandarte m; (level) nível m ♦ adj padronizado, regular,

normal; **~s** npl (morals) valores mpl
morais; **standard lamp** (BRIT) n
abajur m de pé; **standard of
living** n padrão m de vida (BR),
nível m de vida (PT)

stand-by adj de reserva ♦ n: **to be
on ~** estar de sobreaviso or de prontidão; **stand-by ticket** n bilhete m
de stand-by

stand-in n suplente m/f

standing ['stændɪŋ] adj (on foot)
em pé; (permanent) permanente ♦ n
posição f, reputação f; **of many
years' ~** de muitos anos; **standing
joke** n piada conhecida; **standing
order** (BRIT) n instrução f permanente

standpoint ['stændpɔɪnt] n ponto
de vista

standstill ['stændstɪl] n: **at a ~**
paralisado, parado; **to come to a ~**
(car) parar; (factory, traffic) ficar
paralisado

stank [stæŋk] pt of stink

staple ['steɪpl] n (for papers) grampo ♦ adj (food etc) básico ♦ vt grampear; **stapler** n grampeador m

star [stɑː*] n estrela; (celebrity) astro/
estrela ♦ vi: **to ~** ser a estrela em,
estrelar ♦ vt (CINEMA) ser estrelado
por; **the ~s** npl (horoscope) o horóscopo

starboard ['stɑːbəd] n estibordo

starch [stɑːtʃ] n (in food) amido,
fécula; (for clothes) goma

stardom ['stɑːdəm] n estrelato

stare [steə*] n olhar m fixo ♦ vi: **to ~
at** olhar fixamente, fitar

starfish ['stɑːfɪʃ] n inv estrela-do-
mar f

stark [stɑːk] adj severo, áspero
♦ adv: **~ naked** completamente nu,
em pêlo

starling ['stɑːlɪŋ] n estorninho

starry ['stɑːrɪ] adj estrelado; **starry-**

eyed adj (innocent) deslumbrado

start [stɑːt] n princípio, começo;
(departure) partida f; (sudden movement) sobressalto, susto; (advantage) vantagem f ♦ vt começar,
iniciar; (cause) causar; (found) fundar; (engine) ligar ♦ vi começar, iniciar; (with fright) sobressaltar-se,
assustar-se; (train etc) sair; **start
off** vi começar, principiar; (leave)
sair, pôr-se a caminho; **start up** vi
começar; (car) começar, pôr-se em
marcha ♦ vt começar; (car) ligar;
starter n (AUT) arranque m; (SPORT:
official) juiz (juíza) m/f da partida;
(BRIT: CULIN) entrada; **starting
point** n ponto de partida

startle ['stɑːtl] vt assustar, aterrar;
startling adj surpreendente

starvation [stɑː'veɪʃən] n fome f

starve [stɑːv] vi passar fome; (to
death) morrer de fome ♦ vt fazer
passar fome; (fig) privar

state [steɪt] n estado; (pomp) pompa
♦ vt afirmar, declarar; **the S~s** npl
(GEO) os Estados Unidos; **to be in a ~**
estar agitado; **stately** adj majestoso,
imponente; **statement** n declaração f; **statesman** (irreg) n estadista m

static ['stætɪk] n (RADIO, TV) interferência ♦ adj estático

station ['steɪʃən] n estação f; (PO-
LICE) delegacia, (RADIO) emissora ♦ vt
colocar

stationary ['steɪʃnərɪ] adj estacionário

stationer ['steɪʃənə*] n dono de
papelaria; **stationer's (shop)** n
papelaria; **stationery** n artigos mpl
de papelaria

station wagon (US) n perua (BR),
canadiana (PT)

statistic [stə'tɪstɪk] n estatística;
statistics [stə'tɪstɪks] n (science)

estatística

statue ['stætju:] n estátua

status ['steɪtəs] n posição f; (classification) categoria; (importance) status m

statute ['stætju:t] n estatuto, lei f

staunch [stɔ:ntʃ] adj leal

stay [steɪ] n estadia, estada ♦ vi ficar; (as guest) hospedar-se; (spend some time) demorar-se; **to ~ put** não se mexer; **to ~ the night** pernoitar; **stay behind** vi ficar atrás; **stay in** vi ficar em casa; **stay on** vi ficar; **stay out** vi ficar fora de casa; **stay up** vi (at night) velar, ficar acordado

steadfast ['stɛdfɑ:st] adj firme, estável, resoluto

steadily ['stɛdɪlɪ] adv (firmly) firmemente; (unceasingly) sem parar, constantemente; (walk) regularmente

steady ['stɛdɪ] adj (job, boyfriend) constante; (speed) fixo; (regular) regular; (person, character) sensato; (calm) calmo, sereno ♦ vt (stabilize) estabilizar; (nerves) acalmar

steak [steɪk] n filé m; (beef) bife m

steal [sti:l] (pt **stole**, pp **stolen**) vt roubar ♦ vi mover-se furtivamente

steam [sti:m] n vapor m ♦ vt (CULIN) cozinhar no vapor ♦ vi fumegar; **steam engine** n máquina a vapor; **steamer** n vapor m, navio (a vapor); **steamy** adj vaporoso; (room) cheio de vapor, úmido (BR), húmido (PT); (heat, atmosphere) vaporoso

steel [sti:l] n aço ♦ adj de aço

steep [sti:p] adj íngreme; (increase) acentuado; (price) exorbitante ♦ vt (food) colocar de molho; (cloth) ensopar, encharcar

steeple ['sti:pl] n campanário, torre f

steer [stɪə*] vt (person) guiar; (vehicle) dirigir ♦ vi conduzir; **steering** n

(AUT) direção f; **steering wheel** n volante m

stem [stɛm] n (of plant) caule m, haste f; (of glass) pé m ♦ vt deter, reter; (blood) estancar; **stem from** vt fus originar-se de

stench [stɛntʃ] (pej) n fedor m

stencil ['stɛnsl] n (pattern, design) estêncil m; (lettering) gabarito de letra ♦ vt imprimir com estêncil

stenographer [stɛ'nɔgrəfə*] (US) n estenógrafo(-a)

step [stɛp] n passo m; (stair) degrau m ♦ vi: **to ~** forward dar um passo a frente/atrás; **~s** npl (BRIT) = **~ladder**; **to be in ~ (with)** (fig) manter a paridade (com); **to be out of ~ (with)** (fig) estar em disparidade (com); **step down** vi (fig) renunciar; **step on** vt fus pisar; **step up** vt aumentar; **stepbrother** n meio-irmão m; **stepdaughter** n enteada; **stepfather** n padrasto; **stepladder** (BRIT) n escada portátil or de abrir; **stepmother** n madrasta; **stepsister** n meia-irmã f; **stepson** n enteado

stereo ['stɛrɪəu] n estéreo m; (record player) (aparelho de) som m ♦ adj (also: **~phonic**) estereofônico

sterile ['stɛraɪl] adj esterelizado; (barren) estéril; **sterilize** ['stɛrɪlaɪz] vt esterilizar

sterling ['stə:lɪŋ] adj esterlino; (silver) de lei ♦ n (currency) libra esterlina; **one pound ~** uma libra esterlina

stern [stə:n] adj severo, austero ♦ n (NAUT) popa, ré f

stew [stju:] n guisado, ensopado ♦ vt guisar, ensopar; (fruit) cozinhar

steward ['stju:əd] (n (AVIAT) comissário de bordo; **stewardess** n aeromoça (BR), hospedeira de bordo (PT)

stick [stɪk] (pt, pp **stuck**) n pau m; (as weapon) cacete m; (walking ~)

bengala, cajado ♦ vt (glue) colar; (thrust): to ~ sth into cravar or enfiar algo em; (inf: put) meter; (: tolerate) agüentar, suportar ♦ vi (become attached) colar-se; (be unmoveable) emperrar; (in mind etc) gravar-se; **stick out** vi estar saliente, projetar-se; **stick up** vi estar saliente, projetar-se; **stick up for** vt fus defender; **sticker** n adesivo; **sticking plaster** n esparadrapo

sticky ['stɪkɪ] adj pegajoso, (label) adesivo; (fig) delicado

stiff [stɪf] adj (strong) forte; (hard) duro; (difficult) difícil; (moving with difficulty: person) teso; (: door, zip) empenado; (formal) formal ♦ adv (bored, worried) extremamente; **stiffen** vi enrijecer-se; (grow stronger) fortalecer-se

stifle ['staɪfl] vt sufocar, abafar; (opposition) sufocar

stigma ['stɪgmə] n estigma m

stiletto [stɪ'letəu] (BRIT) n (also: ~ heel) salto alto e fino

still [stɪl] adj parado ♦ adv (up to this time) ainda; (even, yet) ainda; (nonetheless) entretanto, contudo, todavia ♦ n (CINEMA) foto f; **stillborn** adj nascido morto, natimorto; **still life** n natureza morta

stilted ['stɪltɪd] adj afetado

stimulate ['stɪmjuleɪt] vt estimular

stimulus ['stɪmjuləs] (pl **stimuli**) n estímulo, incentivo

sting [stɪŋ] (pt, pp **stung**) n (wound) picada; (pain) ardência; (of insect) ferrão m ♦ vt aguilhar ♦ vi (insect, animal) picar; (eyes, ointment) queimar

stingy ['stɪndʒɪ] (pej) adj pão-duro, sovina

stink [stɪŋk] (pt **stank**, pp **stunk**) n fedor m, catinga ♦ vi feder, cheirar mal; **stinking** (inf) adj (fig) maldito

stint [stɪnt] n tarefa, parte f ♦ vi: **to ~ on** ser parco com

stir [stə:*] n (fig) comoção f, rebuliço ♦ vt mexer; (fig) comover ♦ vi mover-se, remexer-se; **stir up** vt excitar; (trouble) provocar

stirrup ['stɪrəp] n estribo

stitch [stɪtʃ] n (SEWING, KNITTING, MED) ponto; (pain) pontada ♦ vt costurar; (MED) dar pontos em, suturar

stoat [stəut] n arminho

stock [stɔk] n suprimento, (COMM: reserves) estoque m, provisão f; (: selection) sortimento; (AGR) gado; (CULIN) caldo; (lineage) estirpe f, linhagem f; (FINANCE) valores mpl, títulos mpl ♦ adj (reply etc) de sempre, costumeiro ♦ vt ter em estoque, estocar; **in/out of ~** em estoque/esgotado; **to take ~ of** (fig) fazer um balanço de; **~s and shares** valores e títulos mobiliários; **stock up** vi: **to ~ up (with)** abastecer-se (de); **stockbroker** n corretor(a) m/f de valores or da Bolsa; **stock cube** (BRIT) n cubo de caldo; **stock exchange** n Bolsa de Valores

stocking ['stɔkɪŋ] n meia

stock: stock market (BRIT) n Bolsa, mercado de valores; **stockpile** n reservas fpl, estocagem f ♦ vt acumular reservas de, estocar; **stocktaking** (BRIT) n (COMM) inventário

stocky ['stɔkɪ] adj (strong) robusto; (short) atarracado

stodgy ['stɔdʒɪ] adj pesado

stoke [stəuk] vt atiçar, alimentar

stole [stəul] pt of **steal** ♦ n estola

stolen ['stəuln] pp of **steal**

stomach ['stʌmək] n (ANAT) estômago; (belly) barriga, ventre m ♦ vt suportar, tolerar; **stomach-ache** n dor f de estômago

stone [stəun] n pedra; (pebble)

pedrinha; (in fruit) caroço; (MED) pedra, cálculo; (BRIT: weight) = 6.348kg; 14 pounds ♦ adj de pedra ♦ vt apedrejar; (fruit) tirar o(s) caroço(s) de; **stone-cold** adj gelado; **stone-deaf** adj surdo como uma porta; **stonework** n cantaria

stood [stud] pt, pp of **stand**

stool [stu:l] n tamborete m, banco

stoop [stu:p] vi (also: **have a ~**) ser corcunda; (also: **~ down**) debruçar-se, curvar-se

stop [stɔp] n parada, interrupção f; (for bus etc) parada (BR), paragem f (PT) (also: **full ~**) ponto ♦ vt parar, deter; (break off) interromper; (cheque) sustar, suspender; (also: **put a ~ to**) impedir ♦ vi parar, deter-se; (end) terminar, acabar; **to ~ doing sth** deixar de fazer algo; **stop dead** vi parar de repente; **stop off** vi dar uma parada; **stop up** vt tapar; **stopover** n parada rápida; (AVIAT) escala; **stopper** n tampa, rolha; **stopwatch** n cronômetro

storage ['stɔ:rɪdʒ] n armazenagem f

store [stɔ:*] n (stock) suprimento; (depot) armazém m; (reserve) estoque m; (BRIT: large shop) loja de departamentos; (US) loja ♦ vt armazenar; **~s** npl (provisions) víveres mpl, provisões fpl; **who knows what is in ~ for us?** quem sabe o que nos espera?; **store up** vt acumular; **storeroom** n depósito, almoxarifado

storey ['stɔ:rɪ] (US **story**) n andar m

stork [stɔ:k] n cegonha

storm [stɔ:m] n tempestade f; (fig) tumulto ♦ vi enfurecer-se ♦ vt tomar de assalto, assaltar; **stormy** adj tempestuoso

story ['stɔ:rɪ] n história, estória; (lie) mentira; (US) = **storey**; **storybook** n livro de contos

stout [staut] adj sólido, forte; (fat) gordo, corpulento; (resolute) decidido, resoluto ♦ n cerveja preta

stove [stəuv] n (for cooking) fogão m; (for heating) estufa, fogareiro

stow [stəu] vt guardar; **stowaway** n passageiro(-a) clandestino(-a)

straddle ['strædl] vt cavalgar

straggle ['strægl] vi (houses) espalhar-se desordenadamente; (people) vagar, perambular

straight [streɪt] adj reto; (back) esticado; (hair) liso; (honest) honesto; (simple) simples inv ♦ adv reto; (drink) puro; **to put** or **get sth ~** esclarecer algo; **~ away**, **~ off** imediatamente; **straighten** vt arrumar; **straighten out** vt endireitar; (fig) esclarecer; **to straighten things up** arrumar as coisas; **straightforward** adj (simple) simples inv, direto; (honest) honesto, franco

strain [streɪn] n tensão f; (TECH) esforço; (MED: back ~) distensão f; (: tension) luxação f; (breed) raça, estirpe f ♦ vt forçar, torcer, distender; (stretch) puxar, estirar; (CULIN) coar; **~s** npl (MUS) acordes mpl; **strained** adj distendido; (laugh) forçado; (relations) tenso; **strainer** n coador m; (sieve) peneira

strait [streɪt] n estreito; **~s** npl (fig): **to be in dire ~s** estar em apuros; **straitjacket** n camisa-de-força

strand [strænd] n (of thread, hair) fio; (of rope) tira; **stranded** adj preso

strange [streɪndʒ] adj (not known) desconhecido; (odd) estranho, esquisito; **strangely** adv estranhamente; **stranger** n desconhecido(-a); (from another area) forasteiro(-a)

strangle ['stræŋgl] vt estrangular;

(fig) sufocar

strap [stræp] *n* correia; *(of slip, dress)* alça

strategic [strə'ti:dʒɪk] *adj* estratégico

strategy ['strætɪdʒɪ] *n* estratégia

straw [strɔ:] *n* palha; *(drinking ~)* canudo; **that's the last ~!** essa foi a última gota!

strawberry ['strɔ:bərɪ] *n* morango

stray [streɪ] *adj (animal)* extraviado; *(bullet)* perdido; *(scattered)* espalhado ♦ *vi* perder-se

streak [stri:k] *n* listra, traço; *(in hair)* mecha ♦ *vt* listrar ♦ *vi*: **to ~ past** passar como um raio

stream [stri:m] *n* riacho, córrego; *(of people, vehicles)* fluxo; *(of smoke)* rastro; *(of questions etc)* torrente f ♦ *vt (SCH)* classificar ♦ *vi* correr, fluir; **to ~ in/out** entrar/sair em massa

streamer ['stri:mə*] *n* serpentina; *(pennant)* flâmula

streamlined ['stri:mlaɪnd] *adj* aerodinâmico

street [stri:t] *n* rua; **streetcar** *(US)* *n* bonde *m (BR)*, eléctrico *(PT)*; **street lamp** *n* poste *m* de iluminação; **street plan** *n* mapa *m*; **streetwise** *(inf)* *adj* malandro

strength [strenθ] *n* força; *(of girder etc)* firmeza, resistência; *(fig)* poder *m*; **strengthen** *vt* fortificar; *(fig)* fortalecer

strenuous ['strenjuəs] *adj* enérgico; *(determined)* tenaz

stress [stres] *n* pressão f; *(mental strain)* tensão f, stress *m*; *(emphasis)* ênfase f; *(TECH)* tensão ♦ *vt* realçar, dar ênfase a; *(syllable)* acentuar

stretch [stretʃ] *n (of sand etc)* trecho, extensão f ♦ *vi* espreguiçar-se; *(extend)*: **to ~ to** or **as far as** estender-se até ♦ *vt* estirar, esticar; *(fig: subj: job, task)* exigir o máximo

de; **stretch out** *vi* esticar-se ♦ *vt (arm etc)* esticar; *(spread)* estirar

stretcher ['stretʃə*] *n* maca, padiola

strewn [stru:n] *adj*: **~ with** coberto or cheio de

stricken ['strɪkən] *adj (wounded)* ferido; *(devastated)* arrasado; *(ill)* acometido; **~ with** tomado por

strict [strɪkt] *adj (person)* severo, rigoroso; *(meaning)* exato, estrito

stride [straɪd] *(pt* **strode**, *pp* **stridden** [strɪdən]) *n* passo largo ♦ *vi* andar a passos largos

strife [straɪf] *n* conflito

strike [straɪk] *(pt, pp* **struck**) *n* greve f; *(of oil etc)* descoberta; *(attack)* ataque *m* ♦ *vt* bater em; *(fig)*: **the thought** or **it ~s me that ...** me ocorre que ...; *(oil etc)* descobrir; *(deal)* fechar, acertar ♦ *vi* estar em greve; *(attack: soldiers, illness)* atacar; (: *disaster)* assolar; *(clock)* bater; **on ~** em greve; **to ~ a match** acender um fósforo; **strike down** *vt* derrubar; **strike up** *vt (MUS)* começar a tocar; *(conversation, friendship)* travar; **striker** *n* grevista *m/f*; *(SPORT)* atacante *m/f*; **striking** *adj* impressionante

string [strɪŋ] *(pt, pp* **strung**) *n (cord)* barbante or *(BR)*, cordel m *(PT)*; *(of beads)* cordão m; *(of onions)* réstia; *(MUS)* corda ♦ *vt*: **to ~ out** esticar; **the ~s** *npl (MUS)* os instrumentos de corda; **to ~ together** *(words)* unir; *(ideas)* concatenar; **to get a job by pulling ~s** *(fig)* usar pistolão; **string(ed) instrument** *n (MUS)* instrumento de corda

stringent ['strɪndʒənt] *adj* rigoroso

strip [strɪp] *n* tira; *(of land)* faixa; *(of metal)* lâmina, tira ♦ *vt* despir; *(also:* **~ down**: *machine)* desmontar ♦ *vi* despir-se; **strip cartoon** *n* história

em quadrinhos (BR), banda desenhada (PT)

stripe [straɪp] n listra; (MIL) galão m;
striped adj listrado, com listras

strive [straɪv] (pt strove, pp ~n
[strɪvən]) vi: **to ~ for sth/to do sth**
esforçar-se por or batalhar para
algo/para fazer algo

strode [strəud] pt of **stride**

stroke [strəuk] n (blow) golpe m;
(MED) derrame m cerebral; (of paintbrush) pincelada; (SWIMMING: style)
nado ♦ vt acariciar, afagar; **at a ~** de
repente, de golpe

stroll [strəul] n volta, passeio ♦ vi
passear, dar uma volta; **stroller**
(US) n carrinho (de criança)

strong [strɔŋ] adj forte; (imagination) fértil; (personality) forte, dominante; (nerves) de aço; **they are 50
~** são 50; **stronghold** n fortaleza;
(fig) baluarte m; **strongly** adv forte-
mente; (defend) vigorosamente;
(believe) profundamente

strove [strəuv] pt of **strive**

struck [strʌk] pt, pp of **strike**

structure [ˈstrʌktʃə*] n estrutura;
(building) construção f

struggle [ˈstrʌgl] n luta, contenda
♦ vi (fight) lutar; (try hard) batalhar

strum [strʌm] vt (guitar) dedilhar

strung [strʌŋ] pt, pp of **string**

strut [strʌt] n escora, suporte m ♦ vi
pavonear-se, empertigar-se

stub [stʌb] n (of ticket etc) canhoto;
(of cigarette) toco, ponta; **to ~ one's
toe** dar uma topada; **stub out** vt
apagar

stubble [ˈstʌbl] n restolho m; (on chin)
barba por fazer

stubborn [ˈstʌbən] adj teimoso,
cabeçudo, obstinado

stuck [stʌk] pt, pp of **stick** ♦ adj
(jammed) emperrado; **stuck-up**
adj convencido, metido, esnobe

stud [stʌd] n (shirt ~) botão m;
(earring) tarraxa, rosca; (of boot)
cravo; (also: ~ farm) fazenda de
cavalos; (also: ~ horse) garanhão m
♦ vt (fig): **~ded with** salpicado de

student [ˈstjuːdənt] n estudante
m/f ♦ adj estudantil; **student driver** (US) n aprendiz m/f

studio [ˈstjuːdɪəu] n estúdio; (sculptor's) ateliê m

studious [ˈstjuːdɪəs] adj estudioso,
aplicado; (careful) cuidadoso; **stu-
diously** adv (carefully) com esmero

study [ˈstʌdɪ] n estudo; (room) sala
de leitura or estudo ♦ vt estudar;
(examine) examinar, investigar ♦ vi
estudar; **studies** npl (subjects) estudos mpl, matérias fpl

stuff [stʌf] n (substance) troço;
(things) troços mpl, coisas fpl ♦ vt
(CULIN) rechear; (animals) empalhar;
(inf: push) enfiar; **~ed toy** brinquedo de pelúcia; **stuffing** n recheio;
stuffy adj (room) abafado, mal
ventilado; (person) rabugento, melindroso

stumble [ˈstʌmbl] vi tropeçar; **to ~
across** or on (fig) topar com; **stum-
bling block** n pedra no caminho

stump [stʌmp] n (of tree) toco; (of
limb) coto ♦ vt: **to be ~ed** ficar perplexo

stun [stʌn] vt (subj: blow) aturdir;
(: news) pasmar

stung [stʌŋ] pt, pp of **sting**

stunk [stʌŋk] pp of **stink**

stunning [ˈstʌnɪŋ] adj (news) ator-
doante; (appearance) maravilhoso

stunt [stʌnt] n façanha sensacional;
(publicity ~) truque m publicitário;
stuntman [ˈstʌntmæn] (irreg) n
dublê m

stupendous [stjuːˈpɛndəs] adj
monumental

stupid [ˈstjuːpɪd] adj estúpido, idiota

sturdy ['stɜːdɪ] adj (person) robusto, firme; (thing) sólido

stutter ['stʌtə*] n gagueira, gaguez f ♦ vi gaguejar

sty [staɪ] n (for pigs) chiqueiro

stye [staɪ] n (MED) terçol m

style [staɪl] n estilo; (elegance) elegância; **stylish** adj elegante, chique

suave [swɑːv] adj suave, melífluo

subconscious [sʌb'kɒnʃəs] adj do subconsciente

subdue [səb'djuː] vt subjugar; (passions) dominar; **subdued** adj (light) tênue; (person) desanimado

subject [n 'sʌbdʒɪkt, vb səb'dʒɛkt] n (of king) súdito(-a); (theme) assunto; (SCH) matéria; (LING) sujeito ♦ vt: to ~ sb to sth submeter alguém a algo; to be ~ to estar sujeito a; **subjective** [səb'dʒɛktɪv] adj subjetivo; **subject matter** n assunto; (content) conteúdo

sublet [sʌb'lɛt] vt sublocar, subalugar

submarine ['sʌbməriːn] n submarino

submerge [səb'mɜːdʒ] vt submergir ♦ vi submergir-se

submission [səb'mɪʃən] n submissão f; (to committee) petição f; (of plan) apresentação f, exposição f

submit [səb'mɪt] vt submeter ♦ vi submeter-se

subnormal [sʌb'nɔːməl] adj (temperature) abaixo do normal

subordinate [sə'bɔːdɪnət] adj, n subordinado(-a)

subscribe [səb'skraɪb] vi subscrever; to ~ to (opinion) concordar com; (fund) contribuir para; (newspaper) assinar; **subscription** [səb'skrɪpʃən] n assinatura

subsequent ['sʌbsɪkwənt] adj

subseqüente, posterior; **subsequently** adv posteriormente, depois

subside [səb'saɪd] vi (feeling, wind) acalmar-se; (flood) baixar; **subsidence** [səb'saɪdns] n (in road etc) afundamento da superfície

subsidiary [səb'sɪdɪərɪ] adj secundário ♦ n (also: ~ company) subsidiária

subsidize ['sʌbsɪdaɪz] vt subsidiar

subsidy ['sʌbsɪdɪ] n subsídio

substance ['sʌbstəns] n substância

substantial [səb'stænʃl] adj (solid) sólido; (reward, meal) substancial; **substantially** adv consideravelmente; (in essence) substancialmente

substitute ['sʌbstɪtjuːt] n substituto(-a); (person) suplente m/f ♦ vt: to ~ A for B substituir B por A

subterranean [sʌbtə'reɪnɪən] adj subterrâneo

subtitle ['sʌbtaɪtl] n (CINEMA) legenda

subtle ['sʌtl] adj sutil

subtotal [sʌb'təʊtl] n total m parcial, subtotal m

subtract [səb'trækt] vt subtrair, deduzir

suburb ['sʌbɜːb] n subúrbio; **suburban** [sə'bɜːbən] adj suburbano; (train etc) de subúrbio; **suburbia** [sə'bɜːbɪə] n os subúrbios

subway ['sʌbweɪ] n (BRIT) passagem f subterrânea; (US) metrô m (BR), metro(-politano) (PT)

succeed [sək'siːd] vi (person) ser bem sucedido, ter êxito; (plan) sair bem ♦ vt suceder a; to ~ in doing conseguir fazer; **succeeding** adj sucessivo, posterior

success [sək'sɛs] n êxito; (hit, person) sucesso; **successful** adj (venture) bem sucedido; (writer) de sucesso, bem sucedido; **to be successful (in doing)** conseguir (fazer); **successfully** adv com sucesso, com êxito

succession [sək'seʃən] n sucessão f, série f; (to throne) sucessão

such [sʌtʃ] adj tal, semelhante; (of that kind: sg): ~ **a book** um livro parecido, tal livro; (: pl): ~ **books** tais livros; (so much): ~ **courage** tanta coragem ♦ adv tão; ~ **a long trip** uma viagem tão longa; ~ **a lot of** tanto; ~ **as** tal como; as ~ como tal; **such-and-such** adj tal e qual

suck [sʌk] vt chupar; (breast) mamar; **sucker** n (ZOOL) ventosa; (inf) trouxa m/f, otário/-a f

sudden ['sʌdn] adj (rapid) repentino, súbito; (unexpected) imprevisto; **all of a** ~ inesperadamente; **suddenly** adv inesperadamente

sue [su:] vt processar

suede [sweɪd] n camurça

suet ['suɪt] n sebo

suffer ['sʌfə*] vt sofrer; (bear) agüentar, suportar ♦ vi sofrer, padecer; **to** ~ **from** sofrer de, estar com; **sufferer** n: **a** ~**er from** (MED) uma pessoa que sofre de; **suffering** n sofrimento

sufficient [sə'fɪʃənt] adj suficiente, bastante; **sufficiently** adv suficientemente

suffocate ['sʌfəkeɪt] vi sufocar(-se), asfixiar(-se)

sugar ['ʃugə*] n açúcar m ♦ vt pôr açúcar em, açucarar; **sugar cane** n cana-de-açúcar f

suggest [sə'dʒɛst] vt sugerir; (indicate) indicar; **suggestion** n sugestão f; indicação f

suicide ['suɪsaɪd] n suicídio; (person) suicida m/f; see also **commit**

suit [su:t] n (man's) terno (BR), fato (PT); (woman's) conjunto; (LAW) pro-

cesso; (CARDS) naipe m ♦ vt convir a; (clothes) ficar bem a; (adapt): **to** ~ **sth to** adaptar or acomodar algo a; **they are well** ~**ed** fazem um bom par; **suitable** adj conveniente, (appropriate) apropriado; **suitably** adv (dressed) apropriadamente; (impressed) bem

suitcase ['su:tkeɪs] n mala

suite [swi:t] n (of rooms) conjunto de salas; (MUS) suite f; (furniture) conjunto

suitor ['su:tə*] n pretendente m

sulfur ['sʌlfə*] (US) n = **sulphur**

sulk [sʌlk] vi ficar emburrado, fazer beicinho or biquinho (inf); **sulky** adj emburrado

sullen ['sʌlən] adj rabugento; (silence) pesado

sulphur ['sʌlfə*] (US **sulfur**) n enxofre m

sultana [sʌl'tɑːnə] n passa branca

sultry ['sʌltrɪ] adj abafado

sum [sʌm] n (total), (calculation) cálculo; **sum up** vt, vi resumir

summarize ['sʌməraɪz] vt resumir

summary ['sʌmərɪ] n resumo

summer ['sʌmə*] n verão m ♦ adj de verão; **in** ~ no verão; **summertime** n (season) verão m

summit ['sʌmɪt] n topo, cume m; (also: ~ **conference**) (conferência de) cúpula

summon ['sʌmən] vt (person) mandar chamar; (meeting) convocar; (LAW: witness) convocar; **summon up** vt concentrar

sun [sʌn] n sol m; **sunbathe** vi tomar sol; **sunblock** n bloqueador m solar; **sunburn** n queimadura do sol; **sunburned** adj = **sunburnt**; **sunburnt** adj bronzeado; (painfully) queimado

Sunday ['sʌndɪ] n domingo; **Sunday school** n escola dominical

sundial ['sʌndaɪəl] n relógio de sol

sundown ['sʌndaun] n pôr m do sol

sundries ['sʌndrɪz] npl gêneros mpl diversos

sundry ['sʌndrɪ] adj vários, diversos; **all and ~** todos

sunflower ['sʌnflauə*] n girassol m

sung [sʌŋ] pp of **sing**

sunglasses ['sʌnglɑːsɪz] npl óculos mpl de sol

sunk [sʌŋk] pp of **sink**

sun: sunlight n (luz f do) sol m; **sunlit** adj ensolarado, iluminado pelo sol; **sunny** adj cheio de sol; (day) ensolarado, de sol; **sunrise** n nascer m do sol; **sun roof** n (AUT) teto solar; **sunscreen** n protetor m solar; **sunset** n pôr m do sol; **sunshade** n pára-sol m; **sunshine** n (luz f do) sol m; **sunstroke** n insolação f; **suntan** n bronzeado; **suntan lotion** n loção f de bronzear

super ['suːpə*] (inf) adj bacana (BR), muito giro (PT)

superannuation [suːpərænjuˈeɪʃən] n pensão f de aposentadoria

superb [suːˈpəːb] adj excelente

supercilious [suːpəˈsɪlɪəs] adj arrogante, desdenhoso; (haughty) altivo

superintendent [suːpərɪnˈtendənt] n superintendente m/f; (POLICE) chefe m/f de polícia

superior [suˈpɪərɪə*] adj superior; (smug) desdenhoso ♦ n superior m

supermarket ['suːpəmɑːkɪt] n supermercado

supernatural [suːpəˈnætʃərəl] adj sobrenatural ♦ n: **the ~** o sobrenatural

superpower ['suːpəpauə*] n (POL) superpotência

superstitious [suːpəˈstɪʃəs] adj supersticioso

supervise ['suːpəvaɪz] vt supervisar,

supervisionar; **supervision** [suːpəˈvɪʒən] n supervisão f; **supervisor** n supervisor(a) m/f; (academic) orientador(a) m/f

supper ['sʌpə*] n jantar m; (late evening) ceia

supple ['sʌpl] adj flexível

supplement [n 'sʌplɪmənt, vb sʌplɪˈment] n suplemento ♦ vt suprir, completar; **supplementary** [sʌplɪˈmentərɪ] adj suplementar

supplier [səˈplaɪə*] n abastecedor(a) m/f, fornecedor(a) m/f

supply [səˈplaɪ] vt (provide): **to ~ sth (to sb)** fornecer algo (para alguém); (equip): **to ~ (with)** suprir (de) ♦ n fornecimento, provisão f; (stock) estoque m; (supplying) abastecimento; **supplies** npl (food) víveres mpl; (MIL) apetrechos mpl

support [səˈpɔːt] n (moral, financial etc) apoio; (TECH) suporte m ♦ vt apoiar; (financially) manter; (TECH: hold up) sustentar; (theory etc) defender; **supporter** n (POL etc) partidário(-a); (SPORT) torcedor(a) m/f

suppose [səˈpəuz] vt supor; (imagine) imaginar; (duty): **to be ~d to do sth** dever fazer algo; **supposedly** [səˈpəuzɪdlɪ] adv supostamente, pretensamente; **supposing** conj caso, supondo-se que

suppress [səˈpres] vt (information) suprimir; (feelings, revolt) reprimir; (yawn) conter

supreme [suˈpriːm] adj supremo

surcharge ['səːtʃɑːdʒ] n sobretaxa

sure [ʃuə*] adj seguro; (definite) certo; (aim) certeiro; **to make ~ of sth/that** assegurar-se de algo/que; **~!** claro que sim!; **~ enough** efetivamente; **surely** adv (certainly: US: also: **sure**) certamente

surf [sə:f] n (waves) ondas fpl, arrebentação f

surface ['sə:fɪs] n superfície f ♦ vt (road) revestir ♦ vi vir à superfície or à tona; (fig: news, feeling) vir à tona; **surface mail** n correio comum

surfboard ['sə:fbɔ:d] n prancha de surfe

surfing ['sə:fɪŋ] n surfe m

surge [sə:dʒ] n onda ♦ vi (sea) encapelar-se; (people, vehicles) precipitar-se; (feeling) aumentar repentinamente

surgeon ['sə:dʒən] n cirurgião(-giã) m/f

surgery ['sə:dʒərɪ] n cirurgia; (BRIT: room) consultório; (: also: ~ hours) horas fpl de consulta

surgical ['sə:dʒɪkl] adj cirúrgico; **surgical spirit** (BRIT) n álcool m

surname ['sə:neɪm] n sobrenome m (BR), apelido (PT)

surplus ['sə:pləs] n excedente m; (COMM) superávit m ♦ adj excedente, de sobra

surprise [sə'praɪz] n surpresa ♦ vt surpreender; **surprising** adj surpreendente

surrender [sə'rɛndə*] n rendição f, entrega f ♦ vi render-se, entregar-se

surrogate ['sʌrəgɪt] n (BRIT) substituto(-a)

surround [sə'raund] vt circundar, rodear; (MIL etc) cercar; **surrounding** adj circundante, adjacente; **surroundings** npl arredores mpl, cercanias fpl

surveillance [sə:'veɪləns] n vigilância

survey [n 'sə:veɪ, vb sə:'veɪ] n inspeção f; (of habits etc) pesquisa; (of land) levantamento; (of house) inspeção f ♦ vt observar, contemplar; (land) fazer um levantamento de;

surveyor n (of land) agrimensor(a) m/f; (of building) inspetor(a) m/f

survival [sə'vaɪvl] n sobrevivência; (relic) remanescente m

survive [sə'vaɪv] vi sobreviver; (custom etc) perdurar ♦ vt sobreviver a; **survivor** n sobrevivente m/f

susceptible [sə'sɛptɪbl] adj: ~ (to) (injury) suscetível or sensível (a); (flattery, pressure) vulnerável (a)

suspect [adj, n 'sʌspɛkt, vb sə-'pɛkt] adj, n suspeito(-a) ♦ vt suspeitar, desconfiar

suspend [səs'pɛnd] vt suspender; **suspenders** npl (BRIT) ligas fpl; (US) suspensórios mpl

suspense [səs'pɛns] n incerteza, ansiedade f; (in film etc) suspense m; **to keep sb in ~** manter alguém em suspense or na expectativa

suspension [səs'pɛnʃən] n suspensão f; (of driving licence) cassação f

suspicion [səs'pɪʃən] n suspeita; **suspicious** adj (suspecting) suspeitoso; (causing suspicion) suspeito

sustain [səs'teɪn] vt sustentar; (suffer) sofrer; **sustained** adj (effort) contínuo; **sustenance** ['sʌstɪnəns] n sustento

swab [swɔb] n (MED) mecha de algodão

swagger ['swægə*] vi andar com ar de superioridade

swallow ['swɔləu] n (bird) andorinha ♦ vt engolir, tragar; (fig: story) engolir; (pride) pôr de lado; (one's words) retirar; **swallow up** vt (savings etc) consumir

swam [swæm] pt of **swim**

swamp [swɔmp] n pântano, brejo ♦ vt atolar, inundar; (fig) assoberar

swan [swɔn] n cisne m

swap [swɔp] n troca, permuta ♦ vt:

swarm   273   switch

to ~ (for) trocar (por); (*replace with*) substituir (por)
swarm [swɔːm] n (of bees) enxame m; (of people) multidão f ♦ vi enxamear; aglomerar-se; (*place*): **to be ~ing with** estar apinhado de
swastika ['swɒstɪkə] n suástica
swat [swɔt] vt esmagar
sway [sweɪ] vi balançar-se, oscilar ♦ vt (*influence*) influenciar
swear [sweə*] (pt swore, pp sworn) vi (curse) xingar ♦ vt (promise) jurar; **swearword** n palavrão m
sweat [swet] n suor m ♦ vi suar; **sweater** n suéter m or f (BR), camisola (PT); **sweaty** adj suado
Swede [swiːd] n sueco(-a)
swede [swiːd] n tipo de nabo
Sweden ['swiːdən] n Suécia; **Swedish** adj sueco ♦ n (LING) sueco
sweep [swiːp] (pt, pp swept) n (act) varredura; (*also: chimney ~*) limpador m de chaminés ♦ vt varrer; (with arm) empurrar; (: subj: current) arrastar; (: fashion, craze) espalhar-se por ♦ vi varrer; **sweep away** vt varrer; **sweep past** vi passar rapidamente; **sweep up** vi varrer; **sweeping** adj (gesture) dramático; (statement) generalizado
sweet [swiːt] n (candy) bala (BR), rebuçado (PT); (BRIT: pudding) sobremesa f ♦ adj doce; (fig: air) fresco; (: water, smell) doce; (: sound) suave; (: kind) meigo; (baby, kitten) bonitinho; **sweetcorn** n milho; **sweeten** vt pôr açúcar em; (temper) abrandar; **sweetheart** n namorado(-a); **sweet pea** n ervilha-de-cheiro f
swell [swel] (pt ~ed, pp swollen or ~ed) n (of sea) vaga, onda ♦ adj (US: inf: excellent) bacana ♦ vi (increase) aumentar; (get stronger) intensificar-se; (*also: ~ up*) inchar-

se; **swelling** n (MED) inchação f
sweltering ['sweltərɪŋ] adj (heat) sufocante; (day) mormacento
swept [swept] pt, pp of sweep
swerve [swəːv] vi desviar-se
swift [swɪft] n (bird) andorinhão m ♦ adj rápido
swim [swɪm] (pt swam, pp swum) n: **to go for a ~** ir nadar ♦ vi nadar; (head, room) rodar ♦ vt atravessar a nado; (distance) percorrer (a nado); **swimmer** n nadador(a) m/f; **swimming** n natação f; **swimming cap** n touca de natação; **swimming costume** (BRIT) n (woman's) maiô m (BR), fato de banho (PT); (man's) calção m de banho (BR), calções mpl de banho (PT); **swimming pool** n piscina; **swimming trunks** npl sunga (BR), calções mpl de banho (PT); **swimsuit** n maiô m (BR), fato de banho (PT)
swindle ['swɪndl] n fraude f ♦ vt defraudar
swine [swaɪn] (inf!) n canalha m, calhorda m
swing [swɪŋ] (pt, pp swung) n (in playground) balanço; (movement) balanceio, oscilação f; (in opinion) mudança, virada; (MUS) ritmo ♦ vt balançar; (*also: ~ round*) girar, rodar ♦ vi oscilar; (on swing) balançar; (*also: ~ round*) voltar-se bruscamente; **to be in full ~** estar a todo vapor; **swing door** (US swinging door) n porta de vaivém
swipe [swaɪp] (inf) vt (steal) afanar, roubar
swirl [swəːl] vi redemoinhar
Swiss [swɪs] adj, n inv suíço(-a)
switch [swɪtʃ] n (for light, radio etc) interruptor m; (change) mudança ♦ vt (change) trocar; **switch off** vt apagar; (engine) desligar; **switch**

on vt acender; ligar; **switchboard** n (TEL) mesa telefônica

Switzerland ['switsələnd] n Suíça

swivel ['swivl] vi (also: ~ **round**) girar (sobre um eixo), fazer pião

swollen ['swəulən] pp of **swell**

swoop [swu:p] n (by police etc) batida ♦ vi (also: ~ **down**) precipitar-se, cair

swop [swɔp] n, vt = **swap**

sword [sɔ:d] n espada

swore [swɔ:*] pt of **swear**

sworn [swɔ:n] pp of **swear** ♦ adj (statement) sob juramento; (enemy) declarado

swum [swʌm] pp of **swim**

swung [swʌŋ] pt, pp of **swing**

syllable ['sɪləbl] n sílaba

syllabus ['sɪləbəs] n programa m de estudos

symbol ['sɪmbl] n símbolo

symmetry ['sɪmɪtrɪ] n simetria

sympathetic [sɪmpə'θetɪk] adj (understanding) compreensivo; (likeable) agradável; (supportive): ~ **to (wards)** solidário com

sympathize ['sɪmpəθaɪz] vi: to ~ **with** (person) compadecer-se de; (sb's feelings) compreender; (cause) simpatizar com; **sympathizer** n (POL) simpatizante m/f

sympathy ['sɪmpəθɪ] n compaixão f; **sympathies** npl (tendencies) simpatia; **in ~** em acordo; (strike) em solidariedade; **with our deepest ~** com nossos mais profundos pêsames

symphony ['sɪmfənɪ] n sinfonia

symptom ['sɪmptəm] n sintoma m; (sign) indício

syndicate ['sɪndɪkɪt] n sindicato; (of newspapers) cadeia

synthetic [sɪn'θetɪk] adj sintético

syphon ['saɪfən] n = **siphon**

Syria ['sɪrɪə] n Síria

syringe [sɪ'rɪndʒ] n seringa

syrup ['sɪrəp] n xarope m; (also: **golden ~**) melaço

system ['sɪstəm] n sistema m; (method) método; (ANAT) organismo; **systematic** [sɪstə'mætɪk] adj sistemático; **system disk** n (COMPUT) disco do sistema; **systems analyst** n analista m/f de sistemas

T

tab [tæb] n lingüeta, aba; (label) etiqueta; **to keep ~s on** (fig) vigiar

tabby ['tæbɪ] n (also: ~ **cat**) gato malhado or listrado

table ['teɪbl] n mesa ♦ vt (motion etc) apresentar; **to lay** or **set the ~** pôr a mesa; ~ **of contents** índice m, sumário; **tablecloth** n toalha de mesa; **tablemat** n descanso; **tablespoon** n colher f de sopa; (also: **tablespoonful:** as measurement) colherada

tablet ['tæblɪt] n (MED) comprimido; (of stone) lápide f

table tennis n pingue-pongue m, tênis m de mesa

table wine n vinho de mesa

tabloid ['tæblɔɪd] n tablóide m; **tabloid press** n ver quadro

---

TABLOID PRESS

O termo **tabloid press** refere-se aos jornais populares de formato meio jornal que apresentam muitas fotografias e adotam um estilo bastante conciso. O público-alvo desses jornais é composto por leitores que se interessam pelos fatos do dia que contenham um certo toque de escândalo; veja **quality (news)papers**.

---

tack [tæk] n (nail) tachinha, percevejo ♦ vt prender com tachinha; (stitch) alinhavar ♦ vi virar de bordo

tackle ['tækl] n (gear) equipamento; (also: fishing ~) apetrechos mpl; (for lifting) guincho; (FOOTBALL) ato de tirar a bola de adversário ♦ vt (difficulty) atacar; (challenge: person) desafiar; (grapple with) atracar-se com; (FOOTBALL) tirar a bola de

tacky ['tæki] adj pegajoso, grudento; (inf: tasteless) cafona

tact [tækt] n tato, diplomacia; **tactful** adj diplomático

tactics ['tæktiks] n, npl tática

tactless ['tæktlis] adj sem diplomacia

tadpole ['tædpəul] n girino

tag [tæg] n (label) etiqueta; **tag along** vi seguir

tail [teil] n rabo; (of comet, plane) cauda; (of shirt, coat) aba ♦ vt (follow) seguir bem de perto; **tail away** or **off** vi diminuir gradualmente

tailor ['teilə*] n alfaiate m; **tailor-made** adj feito sob medida; (fig) especial

tailwind ['teilwind] n vento de popa or de cauda

tainted ['teintid] adj (food) estragado, passado; (water, air) poluído; (fig) manchado

take [teik] (pt took, pp taken) vt tomar; (photo, holiday) tirar; (grab) pegar (em); (prize) ganhar; (effort, courage) requerer, exigir; (tolerate) agüentar; (accompany, bring: person) acompanhar, trazer; (: thing) trazer, carregar; (exam) fazer; (passengers etc): **it ~s 50 people** cabem 50 pessoas; **to ~ sth from** (drawer etc) tirar algo de; (person) pegar algo de; **I ~ it that** ... suponho que ...; **take after** vt fus parecer-se com; **take apart** vt desmontar;

take away vt (extract) tirar; (carry off) levar; (subtract) subtrair; **take back** vt (return) devolver; (one's words) retirar; **take down** vt (building) demolir; (dismantle) desmontar; (letter etc) tomar por escrito; **take in** vt (deceive) enganar; (understand) compreender; (include) abranger; (lodger) receber; **take off** vi (AVIAT) decolar; (go away) ir-se ♦ vt (remove) tirar; **take on** vt (work) empreender; (employee) empregar; (opponent) desafiar; **take out** vt tirar; (extract) extrair; (invite) acompanhar; **take over** vt (business) assumir; (country) tomar posse de ♦ vi: **to ~ over from sb** suceder a alguém; **take to** vt fus (person) simpatizar com; (activity) afeiçoar-se a; **to ~ to doing sth** criar o hábito de fazer algo; **take up** vt (dress) encurtar; (time, space) ocupar; (hobby etc) dedicar-se a; (offer) aceitar; **to ~ sb up on a suggestion/offer** aceitar a oferta/sugestão de alguém sobre algo; **takeaway** (BRIT) adj (food) para levar; **takeoff** n (AVIAT) decolagem f; **takeover** n (COMM) aquisição f de controle; **takings** npl (COMM) receita, renda

talc [tælk] n (also: **~um powder**) talco

tale [teil] n (story) conto; (account) narrativa; **to tell ~s** (fig: lie) dizer mentiras

talent ['tælənt] n talento; **talented** adj talentoso

talk [tɔːk] n conversa, fala; (gossip) mexerico, fofocas fpl; (conversation) conversa, conversação f ♦ vi falar; ~s npl (POL etc) negociações fpl; **to ~ about** falar sobre; **to ~ sb into/out of doing sth** convencer alguém a fazer algo/dissuadir alguém de fazer algo; **to ~ shop** falar sobre negócios/questões profissionais; **talk over** vt discutir; **talkative** adj loquaz, tagarela; **talk show** n programa m de entrevistas

tall [tɔ:l] adj alto; **to be 6 feet** ≈ medir 1,80 m

tally ['tælɪ] n conta ♦ vi: **to ~ (with)** conferir (com)

talon ['tælən] n garra

tame [teɪm] adj domesticado; (fig: story, style) sem graça, insípido

tamper ['tæmpə*] vi: **to ~ with** mexer em

tampon ['tæmpɔn] n tampão m

tan [tæn] n (also: **sun~**) bronzeado ♦ vi bronzear-se ♦ adj (colour) bronzeado, marrom claro

tangent ['tændʒənt] n (MATH) tangente f; **to go off at a ~** (fig) sair pela tangente

tangerine [tændʒə'ri:n] n tangerina, mexerica

tangle ['tæŋgl] n emaranhado; **to get in(to) a ~** meter-se num rolo

tank [tæŋk] n depósito, tanque m; (for fish) aquário; (MIL) tanque m

tanker ['tæŋkə*] n (ship) navio-tanque m; (truck) caminhão-tanque m

tantalizing ['tæntəlaɪzɪŋ] adj tentador(a)

tantamount ['tæntəmaunt] adj: **~ to** equivalente a

tantrum ['tæntrəm] n chilique m, acesso (de raiva)

tap [tæp] n (on sink etc) torneira; (gentle blow) palmadinha; (gas ~) chave f ♦ vt dar palmadinha em, bater de leve; (resources) utilizar, explorar; (telephone) grampear; **on ~** disponível; **tap-dancing** n sapateado

tape [teɪp] n fita; (also: **magnetic ~**) fita magnética; (sticky ~) fita adesiva ♦ vt (record) gravar (em fita); (stick

with tape) colar; **tape deck** n gravador m, toca-fitas m inv; **tape measure** n fita métrica, trena

taper ['teɪpə*] n círio ♦ vi afilar-se, estreitar-se

tape recorder n gravador m

tapestry ['tæpɪstrɪ] n (object) tapete m de parede; (art) tapeçaria

tar [tɑ:*] n alcatrão m

target ['tɑ:gɪt] n alvo

tariff ['tærɪf] n tarifa

tarmac ['tɑ:mæk] n (BRIT: on road) macadame m; (AVIAT) pista

tarnish ['tɑ:nɪʃ] vt empanar o brilho de

tarpaulin [tɑ:'pɔ:lɪn] n lona alcatroada

tart [tɑ:t] n (CULIN) torta; (BRIT: inf: pej: woman) piranha ♦ adj (flavour) ácido, azedo; **tart up** (inf) vt arrumar, dar um jeito em; **to ~ o.s. up** arrumar-se; (pej) empetecar-se

tartan ['tɑ:tn] n tartan (pano escocês axadrezado) ♦ adj axadrezado

tartar ['tɑ:tə*] n (on teeth) tártaro; **tartar(e) sauce** n molho tártaro

task [tɑ:sk] n tarefa; **to take to ~** repreender

tassel ['tæsl] n borla, pendão m

taste [teɪst] n gosto; (also: **after~**) gosto residual; (sample, fig) amostra, idéia ♦ vt provar; (test) experimentar ♦ vi: **to ~ of** or **like** ter gosto or sabor de; **you can ~ the garlic (in it)** sente-se o gosto de alho; **in good/bad ~** de bom/mau gosto; **tasteful** adj de bom gosto; **tasteless** adj insípido, insosso; (remark) de mau gosto; **tasty** adj saboroso, delicioso

tatters ['tætəz] npl: **in ~** (clothes) em farrapos; (papers etc) em pedaços

tattoo [tə'tu:] n tatuagem f; (spec-

tacle) espetáculo militar ♦ vt tatuar
tatty ['tætɪ] (BRIT: inf) adj (clothes) surrado; (shop, area) mal-cuidado
taught [tɔːt] pt, pp of **teach**
taunt [tɔːnt] n zombaria, escárnio ♦ vt zombar de, mofar de
Taurus ['tɔːrəs] n Touro
taut [tɔːt] adj esticado
tax [tæks] n imposto ♦ vt tributar; (fig: test) sobrecarregar; (: patience) esgotar; **taxation** [tæk'seɪʃən] n (system) tributação f; (money paid) imposto; **tax-free** adj isento de impostos
taxi ['tæksɪ] n táxi m ♦ vi (AVIAT) taxiar; **taxi driver** n motorista m/f de táxi; **taxi rank** (BRIT) n ponto de táxi; **taxi stand** n = taxi rank
tax payer n contribuinte m/f
tax return n declaração f de rendimentos
TB abbr of **tuberculosis**
tea [tiː] n chá m; (BRIT: meal) refeição f à noite; **high ~** adj ajantarado; **tea bag** n saquinho (BR) or carteira (PT) de chá; **tea break** (BRIT) n pausa f para o chá
teach [tiːtʃ] (pt, pp **taught**) vt: to ~ sb sth, ~ sth to sb ensinar algo a alguém; (in school) lecionar ♦ vi ensinar; (be a teacher) lecionar; **teacher** n professor(a) m/f; **teaching** n ensino; (as profession) magistério
tea cosy n coberta do bule, abafador m
teacup ['tiːkʌp] n xícara (BR) or chávena (PT) de chá
teak [tiːk] n madeira de teca
tea leaves npl folhas fpl de chá
team [tiːm] n (SPORT) time m (BR), equipa f (PT); (group) equipe f (BR), equipa (PT); (of animals) parelha; **teamwork** n trabalho de equipe
teapot ['tiːpɔt] n bule m de chá
tear¹ [tɛə*] n (pt **tore**, pp **torn**) n

rasgão m ♦ vt rasgar ♦ vi rasgar-se; **tear along** vi (rush) precipitar-se; **tear up** vt rasgar
tear² [tɪə*] n lágrima; **in ~s** chorando, em lágrimas; **tearful** adj choroso; **tear gas** n gás m lacrimogênio
tearoom ['tiːruːm] n salão m de chá
tease [tiːz] vt implicar com
tea set n aparelho de chá
teaspoon ['tiːspuːn] n colher f de chá; (also: **~ful**: as measurement) (conteúdo de) colher de chá
teat [tiːt] n bico (de mamadeira)
teatime ['tiːtaɪm] n hora do chá
tea towel (BRIT) n pano de prato
technical ['tɛknɪkl] adj técnico; **technicality** [tɛknɪ'kælɪtɪ] n detalhe m técnico; (point of law) particularidade f
technician [tɛk'nɪʃn] n técnico(-a)
technique [tɛk'niːk] n técnica
technology [tɛk'nɔlədʒɪ] n tecnologia
teddy (bear) ['tɛdɪ-] n ursinho de pelúcia
tedious ['tiːdɪəs] adj maçante, chato
teem [tiːm] vi abundar, pulular; **to ~ with** abundar em; **it is ~ing (with rain)** está chovendo a cântaros
teenage ['tiːneɪdʒ] adj (fashions etc) de or para adolescentes; **teenager** n adolescente m/f, jovem m/f
teens [tiːnz] npl: **to be in one's ~** estar entre os 13 e 19 anos, estar na adolescência
tee-shirt n = T-shirt
teeth [tiːθ] npl of **tooth**; **teethe** vi começar a ter dentes; **teething troubles** npl (fig) dificuldades fpl iniciais
teetotal ['tiː'təutl] adj abstêmio
teleconferencing [tɛlɪ'kɔnfərənsɪŋ] n teleconferência f

telegram ['telɪɡræm] n telegrama m

telegraph ['telɪɡrɑːf] n telégrafo

telephone ['telɪfəun] n telefone m ♦ vt (person) telefonar para; (message) telefonar; **to be on the ~** (BRIT), **to have a ~** (subscriber) ter telefone; **to be on the ~** (be speaking) estar falando no telefone; **telephone booth** n, **telephone box** n cabine f telefónica; **telephone call** n telefonema m; **telephone directory** n lista telefónica, catálogo (BR); **telephone number** n (número de) telefone m; **telephonist** [tə'lefənɪst] (BRIT) n telefonista m/f

telesales ['telɪseɪlz] npl televendas fpl

telescope ['telɪskəup] n telescópio

television ['telɪvɪʒən] n televisão f; **on ~** na televisão; **television set** n (aparelho de) televisão f, televisor m

teleworking ['telɪwəːkɪŋ] n teletrabalho m

telex ['teleks] n telex m ♦ vt (message) enviar por telex, telexar; (person) mandar um telex para

tell [tel] (pt, pp **told**) vt dizer; (relate: story) contar; (distinguish): **to ~ sth from** distinguir algo de ♦ vi (have effect) ter efeito; (talk): **to ~ (of)** falar (de or em); **to ~ sb to do sth** dizer a alguém para fazer algo; **tell off** vt repreender; **telltale** adj (sign) revelador(a)

telly ['telɪ] (BRIT: inf) n abbr = **television**

temp [temp] (BRIT: inf) abbr (= temporary) ♦ n temporário(-a) ♦ vi trabalhar como temporário(-a)

temper ['tempə*] n (nature) temperamento; (mood) humor m; (fit of anger) cólera f ♦ vt (moderate) moderar; **to be in a ~** estar de mau

humor; **to lose one's ~** perder a paciência or a calma, ficar zangado

temperament ['tempərəmənt] n temperamento; **temperamental** [temprə'mentl] adj temperamental

temperate ['temprət] adj moderado; (climate) temperado

temperature ['temprətʃə*] n temperatura; **to have** or **run a ~** ter febre

temple ['templ] n (building) templo; (ANAT) têmpora

temporary ['tempərərɪ] adj temporário; (passing) transitório

tempt [tempt] vt tentar; **tempting** adj tentador(a)

ten [ten] num dez

tenancy ['tenənsɪ] n aluguel m

tenant ['tenənt] n inquilino(-a), locatário(-a)

tend [tend] vt (sick etc) cuidar de ♦ vi: **to ~ to do sth** tender a fazer algo

tendency ['tendənsɪ] n tendência

tender ['tendə*] adj terno; (age) tenro; (sore) sensível, dolorido; (meat) macio ♦ n (COMM: offer) oferta, proposta; (money): **legal ~** moeda corrente or legal ♦ vt oferecer; **to ~ one's resignation** pedir demissão

tenement ['tenəmənt] n conjunto habitacional

tennis ['tenɪs] n tênis m; **tennis ball** n bola de tênis; **tennis court** n quadra de tênis; **tennis player** n jogador(a) m/f de tênis; **tennis racket** n raquete f de tênis

tenor ['tenə*] n (MUS) tenor m

tenpin bowling ['tenpɪn-] (BRIT) n boliche m com 10 paus

tense [tens] adj tenso; (muscle) rígido, teso ♦ n (LING) tempo

tension ['tenʃən] n tensão f

tent [tɛnt] n tenda, barraca

tentative ['tɛntətɪv] adj provisório, tentativo; (person) hesitante, indeciso

tenth [tɛnθ] num décimo

tent peg n estaca

tent pole n pau m

tenure ['tɛnjuə*] n (of property) posse f; (of job) estabilidade f

tepid ['tɛpɪd] adj tépido, morno

term [tə:m] n (expression) termo, expressão f; (period) período; (SCH) trimestre m ♦ vt denominar; ~s npl (conditions) condições fpl; (COMM) cláusulas fpl, termos mpl; **in the short/long** ~ a curto/longo prazo; **to be on good** ~**s** with sb dar-se bem com alguém; **to come to** ~**s with** aceitar

terminal ['tə:mɪnl] adj incurável ♦ n (ELEC) borne m; (COMPUT: also: **air** ~) terminal m; (also COMPUT) terminal m; (BRIT: also: **coach** ~) estação f rodoviária

terminate ['tə:mɪneɪt] vt terminar; **to** ~ **a pregnancy** fazer um aborto

terminus ['tə:mɪnəs] (pl **termini**) n terminal m

terrace ['tɛrəs] n terraço m; (BRIT: houses) lance m de casas; **the** ~**s** npl (BRIT: SPORT) a arquibancada (BR), a geral (PT); **terraced** adj (house) ladeado por outras casas; (garden) em dois níveis

terrain [tɛˈreɪn] n terreno

terrible ['tɛrɪbl] adj terrível, horroroso; (conditions) precário; (inf: awful) terrível; **terribly** adv terrivelmente; (very badly) pessimamente

terrific [təˈrɪfɪk] adj terrível, magnífico; (wonderful) maravilhoso, sensacional

terrify ['tɛrɪfaɪ] vt apavorar

territory ['tɛrɪtərɪ] n território

terror ['tɛrə*] n terror m; **terrorist** n terrorista m/f

test [tɛst] n (trial, check) prova, ensaio; (of courage etc, CHEM) prova; (MED) exame m; (exam) teste m, prova; (also: **driving** ~) exame de motorista ♦ vt testar, pôr à prova

testament ['tɛstəmənt] n testamento; **the Old/New T~** o Velho/Novo Testamento

testicle ['tɛstɪkl] n testículo

testify ['tɛstɪfaɪ] vi (LAW) depor, testemunhar; **to** ~ **to sth** atestar algo, testemunhar algo

testimony ['tɛstɪmənɪ] n (LAW) testemunho, depoimento; **to be (a)** ~ to ser uma prova de

test: **test match** n (CRICKET, RUGBY) jogo internacional; **test tube** n proveta, tubo de ensaio

tetanus ['tɛtənəs] n tétano

text [tɛkst] n texto; **textbook** n livro didático; (SCH) livro escolar

texture ['tɛkstʃə*] n textura

Thailand ['taɪlænd] n Tailândia

Thames [tɛmz] n: **the** ~ o Tâmisa (BR), o Tamisa (PT)

than [ðæn, ðən] conj (in comparisons) do que; **more** ~ **10** mais de 10; **I have more/less** ~ **you** tenho mais/menos do que você; **she has more apples** ~ **pears** ela tem mais maçãs do que peras; **she is older** ~ **you think** ela é mais velha do que você pensa

thank [θæŋk] vt agradecer; ~ **you (very much)** muito obrigado(-a); **thankful** adj: **thankful (for)** agradecido (por); **thankful that** aliviado que; **thankless** adj ingrato; **thanks** npl agradecimentos mpl ♦ excl obrigado(-a)!; **Thanksgiving (Day)** n Dia m de Ação de Graças; ver quadro

---

THANKSGIVING DAY

O feriado de Ação de graças **Thanksgiving Day** nos Estados Unidos, quarta quinta-feira do mês de novembro, é o dia em que se comemora a boa colheita feita pelos peregrinos originários da Grã-Bretanha em 1621; tradicionalmente, é um dia em que se agradece a Deus e se organiza um grande banquete. Uma festa semelhante é celebrada no Canadá na segunda segunda-feira de outubro.

KEYWORD

that [ðæt, ðət] (pl **those**) adj (demonstrative) esse (essa); (more remote) aquele (aquela); ~ **man/ woman/book** aquele homem/ aquela mulher/aquele livro; ~ **one** esse (essa)

♦ pron **1** (demonstrative) esse (essa), aquele (aquela); (neuter) isso, aquilo; **who's/what's ~?** quem é?/o que é isso?; **is ~ you?** é você?; **I prefer this to ~** eu prefiro isto a aquilo; **~'s what he said** foi isso o que ele disse; **~ is (to say)** isto é, quer dizer **2** (relative: direct: thing, person) que; (: person) quem; (relative: indirect: thing, person) o qual (a qual) sg, os quais (as quais) pl; (: person) quem; **the book** (~) **I read** o livro que eu li; **the box** (~) **I put it in** a caixa na qual eu botei-o; **the man** (~) **I spoke to** o homem com quem or o qual falei **3** (relative: of time): **on the day ~ he came** no dia em que ele veio

♦ conj que; **she suggested ~ I phone you** ela sugeriu que eu telefonasse para você

♦ adv (demonstrative): **I can't work ~ much** não posso trabalhar tanto; **I didn't realize it was ~ bad** não pensei que fosse tão ruim; **~ high** dessa altura, até essa altura

thatched [θætʃt] adj (roof) de sapê; **~ cottage** chalé m com telhado de sapê or de colmo

thaw [θɔː] n degelo ♦ vi (ice) derreter-se; (food) descongelar-se ♦ vt (food) descongelar

---

KEYWORD

the [ðiː, ðə] def art **1** (gen: sg) o (a); (: pl) os (as); **~ books/children** os livros/as crianças; **she put it on ~ table** ela colocou-o na mesa; **he took it from ~ drawer** ele tirou isto da gaveta; **to play ~ piano/violin** tocar piano/violino; **I'm going to ~ cinema** vou ao cinema **2** (+ adj to form n): **~ rich and ~ poor** os ricos e os pobres; **to attempt ~ impossible** tentar o impossível **3** (in titles): **Richard ~ Second** Ricardo II; **Peter ~ Great** Pedro o Grande **4** (in comparisons: + adv): **~ more he works, ~ more he earns** quanto mais ele trabalha, mais ele ganha

theatre ['θɪətə*] (US **theater**) n teatro; (MED: also: **operating ~**) sala de operação; **theatrical** [θɪ'ætrɪkl] adj teatral

theft [θeft] n roubo

their [ðeə*] adj seu (sua), deles (delas); **theirs** pron (o) seu ((a) sua); see also **mine²**

them [ðem, ðəm] pron (direct) os (as); (indirect) lhes; (stressed, after prep) a eles (a elas)

theme [θiːm] n tema m; **theme**

park n parque de diversões em torno de um único tema

themselves [ðəm'selvz] pron eles mesmos (elas mesmas), se; (after prep) si (mesmos(-as))

then [ðɛn] adv (at that time) então; (next) em seguida; (later) logo, depois; (and also) além disso ♦ conj (therefore) então, nesse caso, portanto ♦ adj: **the ~ president** o então presidente; **by ~** (past) até então; (future) até lá; **from ~ on** a partir de então

theology [θɪ'ɔlədʒɪ] n teologia

theoretical [θɪə'rɛtɪkl] adj teórico

theory ['θɪərɪ] n teoria; **in ~** em teoria, teoricamente

therapy ['θɛrəpɪ] n terapia

---KEYWORD---

there [ðɛə*] adv **1 ~ is, ~ are** há, tem; **~ are 3 of them** há 3 deles; **~ is no-one here/no bread left** não tem ninguém aqui/não tem mais pão; **~ has been an accident** houve um acidente

2 (referring to place) aí, ali, lá; **put it in/on/up/down ~** põe isto lá dentro/cima/em cima/embaixo; **I want that book ~** quero aquele livro ali; **he is!** lá está ele!

3: **~, ~!** (esp to child) calma!

---

thereabouts ['ðɛərəbauts] adv por aí; (amount) aproximadamente

thereafter [ðɛər'ɑ:ftə*] adv depois disso

thereby ['ðɛəbaɪ] adv assim, deste modo

therefore ['ðɛəfɔ:] adv portanto

there's [ðɛəz] = **there is**; **there has**

thermal ['θə:ml] adj térmico

thermometer [θə'mɔmɪtə*] n termômetro

Thermos ['θə:məs] ® n (also: ~

flask) garrafa térmica (BR), termo (PT)

thermostat ['θə:məustæt] n termostato

thesaurus [θɪ'sɔ:rəs] n tesouro, dicionário de sinônimos

these [ði:z] adj, pron estes (estas)

thesis ['θi:sɪs] (pl **theses**) n tese f

they [ðeɪ] pl pron eles (elas); **~ say that ...** (it is said that) diz-se que ..., dizem que ...; **they'd** = **they had**; **they would**; **they'll** = **they shall**; **they will**; **they've** = **they have**

thick [θɪk] adj espesso; (mud, fog, forest) denso; (sauce) grosso; (stupid) burro ♦ n: **in the ~ of the battle** em plena batalha; **it's 20 cm ~** tem 20 cm de espessura; **thicken** vi (fog) adensar-se; (plot etc) complicar-se ♦ vt engrossar; **thickness** n espessura, grossura; **thickset** adj troncudo

thief [θi:f] (pl **thieves**) n ladrão (ladra) m/f

thigh [θaɪ] n coxa

thimble ['θɪmbl] n dedal m

thin [θɪn] adj magro; (slice) fino; (light) leve; (hair) ralo; (crowd) pequeno; (soup, sauce) aguado ♦ vt (also: ~ **down**) diluir

thing [θɪŋ] n coisa; (object) negócio; (matter) assunto, negócio; (mania) mania; **~s** npl (belongings) pertences mpl; **to have a ~ about sb/sth** ser vidrado em alguém/algo; **the best ~ would be to ...** o melhor seria ...; **how are ~s?** como vai?, tudo bem?; **she's got a ~ about ...** ela detesta ...; **poor ~!** coitadinho(-a)!

think [θɪŋk] (pt, pp **thought**) vi pensar; (believe) achar ♦ vt pensar, achar; (imagine) imaginar; **what did you ~ of them?** o que você achou deles?; **to ~ about sb/sth** pensar em alguém/algo; **I'll ~ about it** vou pensar sobre isso; **to ~ of doing sth** pensar em fazer algo; **I ~ so/not** acho que sim/não; **to ~ well of sb** fazer bom juízo de alguém; **think over** vt refletir sobre, meditar sobre; **think up** vt inventar, bolar

thinly ['θɪnlɪ] adv (cut) em fatias finas; (spread) numa camada fina

third [θəːd] adj terceiro ♦ n terceiro(-a); (fraction) terço; (AUT) terceira; (SCH: degree) terceira categoria; **thirdly** adv em terceiro lugar; **third party insurance** n seguro contra terceiros; **third-rate** adj medíocre; **Third World** n: **the Third World** o Terceiro Mundo

thirst [θəːst] n sede f; **thirsty** adj (person) sedento, com sede; (work) que dá sede; **to be thirsty** estar com sede

thirteen ['θəː'tiːn] num treze
thirty ['θəːtɪ] num trinta

this [ðɪs] (pl **these**) adj (demonstrative) este (esta); **~ man/woman/book** este homem/esta mulher/este livro; **these people/children/records** estas pessoas/crianças/estes discos; **~ one** este aqui ♦ pron (demonstrative) este (esta); (neuter) isto; **who/what is ~?** quem é esse?/o que é isso?; **~ is where I live** é aqui que eu moro; **~ is Mr Brown** este é o Sr Brown; (on phone) aqui é o Sr Brown ♦ adv (demonstrative): **~ high/long** desta altura/deste comprimento; **we can't stop now we've gone ~ far** não podemos parar agora que fomos tão longe

thistle ['θɪsl] n cardo
thorn [θɔːn] n espinho

thorough ['θʌrə] adj (search) minucioso; (knowledge, research, person) metódico, profundo; **thorough-bred** adj (horse) de puro sangue; **thoroughfare** n via, passagem f; **"no thoroughfare"** "passagem proibida"; **thoroughly** adv minuciosamente; (search) profundamente; (wash) completamente; (very) muito

those [ðəuz] pl pron, adj esses (essas)

though [ðəu] conj embora, se bem que ♦ adv no entanto

thought [θɔːt] pt, pp of **think** ♦ n pensamento; (idea) idéia; (opinion) opinião f; (reflection) reflexão f; **thoughtful** adj pensativo; (serious) sério; (considerate) atencioso; **thoughtless** adj desatencioso; (words) inconseqüente

thousand ['θauzənd] num mil; **two ~** dois mil; **~s (of)** milhares mpl (de); **thousandth** num milésimo

thrash [θræʃ] vt surrar, malhar; (defeat) derrotar; **thrash about** vi debater-se; **thrash out** vt discutir exaustivamente

thread [θrɛd] n fio, linha; (of screw) rosca ♦ vt (needle) enfiar

threat [θrɛt] n ameaça; **threaten** vi ameaçar ♦ vt: **to threaten sb with sth/to do** ameaçar alguém com algo/de fazer

three [θriː] num três; **three-dimensional** adj tridimensional, em três dimensões; **three-piece suit** n terno (3 peças) (BR), fato de 3 peças (PT); **three-piece suite** n conjunto de sofá e duas poltronas

threshold ['θrɛʃhəuld] n limiar m
threw [θruː] pt of **throw**

thrifty ['θrɪftɪ] adj econômico, frugal

thrill [θrɪl] n emoção f; (shudder) estremecimento ♦ vt emocionar, vibrar; **to be ~ed** (with gift etc) estar emocionado; **thriller** n romance m (or filme m) de suspense; **thrilling** adj emocionante

thrive [θraɪv] (pt ~d or **throve**, pp ~d or **thriven**) vi (grow) vicejar; (do well) **to ~ on sth** realizar-se ao fazer algo; **thriving** adj próspero

throat [θrəʊt] n garganta; **to have a sore ~** estar com dor de garganta

throb [θrɔb] n (of heart) batida; (of engine) vibração f; (of pain) latejo ♦ vi (heart) bater, palpitar; (pain) dar pontadas; (engine) vibrar

throne [θrəʊn] n trono

throng [θrɔŋ] n multidão f ♦ vt apinhar, apinhar-se em

throttle [ˈθrɔtl] n (AUT) acelerador m ♦ vt estrangular

through [θruː] prep por, através de; (time) durante; (by means of) por meio de, por intermédio de; (owing to) devido a ♦ adj (ticket, train) direto ♦ adv através; **to put sb ~ to** (TEL) ligar alguém com alguém; **to be ~** (TEL) estar na linha; (have finished) acabar; **"no ~ road"** "rua sem saída"; **I'm halfway ~ the book** estou na metade do livro; **throughout** prep (place) por todo(-a) o (a); (time) durante todo(-a) o (a) ♦ adv por or em todas as partes

throw [θrəʊ] (pt **threw**, pp **thrown**) n arremesso, tiro; (SPORT) lançamento ♦ vt jogar, atirar; lançar; (rider) derrubar; (fig) desconcertar; **to ~ a party** dar uma festa; **throw away** vt (dispose of) jogar fora; (waste) desperdiçar; **throw off** vt desfazer-se de; (habit, cold) livrar-se; **throw out** vt expulsar; (rubbish) jogar fora; (idea) rejeitar; **throw up** vi vomitar, botar para fora; **throwaway** adj descartável; (remark) gratuito;

throw-in n (SPORT) lance m

thru [θruː] (US) prep, adj, adv = **through**

thrush [θrʌʃ] n (ZOOL) tordo

thrust [θrʌst] (pt, pp **thrust**) n impulso; (TECH) empuxo ♦ vt empurrar

thud [θʌd] n baque m, som m surdo

thug [θʌg] n facínora m/f

thumb [θʌm] n (ANAT) polegar m; **to ~ a lift** pegar carona (BR); arranjar uma boléia (PT); **thumb through** vt fus folhear; **thumbtack** (US) n percevejo, tachinha

thump [θʌmp] n murro, pancada; (sound) baque m ♦ vt dar um murro em ♦ vi bater

thunder [ˈθʌndə*] n trovão m ♦ vi trovejar; (train etc): **to ~ past** passar como um raio; **thunderbolt** n raio; **thunderclap** n estampido do trovão; **thunderstorm** n tempestade f com trovoada, temporal m

Thursday [ˈθɜːzdɪ] n quinta-feira

thus [ðʌs] adv assim, desta maneira; (consequently) conseqüentemente

thwart [θwɔːt] vt frustrar

thyme [taɪm] n tomilho

tiara [tɪˈɑːrə] n tiara, diadema m

tick [tɪk] n (of clock) tique-taque m; (mark) toque m, marca; (ZOOL) carrapato; (BRIT: inf): **in a ~** num instante ♦ vi fazer tique-taque ♦ vt marcar, ticar; **tick off** vt assinalar, ticar; (person) dar uma bronca em; **tick over** (BRIT) vi (engine) funcionar em marcha lenta; (fig) ir indo

ticket [ˈtɪkɪt] n (for bus, plane) passagem f; (for theatre, raffle) bilhete m; (for cinema) entrada; (in shop: on goods) etiqueta; (parking ~: fine) multa; (for library) cartão n; **to get a (parking) ~** (AUT) ganhar uma multa (por estacionamento ilegal); **ticket collector** n revisor(a) m/f;

ticket office n bilheteria (BR), bilheteira (PT)

tickle ['tɪkl] vt fazer cócegas em ♦ vi fazer cócegas; **ticklish** adj coceguento; (problem) delicado

tidal ['taɪdl] adj de maré; **tidal wave** n macaréu m, onda gigantesca

tidbit ['tɪdbɪt] (esp US) n = **titbit**

tide [taɪd] n maré f; (fig) curso; **high/low** ~ maré alta/baixa; **the ~ of public opinion** a corrente da opinião pública; **tide over** vt ajudar num período difícil

tidy ['taɪdɪ] adj (room) arrumado; (dress, work) limpo; (person) bem arrumado ♦ vt (also: ~ **up**) pôr em ordem, arrumar

tie [taɪ] n (string etc) fita, corda; (BRIT: also: **neck**~) gravata; (fig: link) vínculo, laço; (SPORT: draw) empate m ♦ vt amarrar ♦ vi (SPORT) empatar; **to** ~ **in a bow** dar um laço em; **to** ~ **a knot in sth** dar um nó em algo; **tie down** vt amarrar; (fig: restrict) limitar, restringir; (to date, price etc) obrigar; **tie up** vt embrulhar; (dog) prender; (boat, prisoner) amarrar; (arrangements) concluir; **to be ~d up** estar ocupado

tier [tɪə*] n fileira; (of cake) camada

tiger ['taɪgə*] n tigre m

tight [taɪt] adj (rope) esticado, firme; (money) escasso; (clothes, shoes) justo; (bend) fechado; (budget, programme) rigoroso; (inf: drunk) bêbado ♦ adv (squeeze) bem forte; (shut) hermeticamente; **tighten** vt (rope) esticar; (screw, grip) apertar; (security) aumentar ♦ vi esticar-se; apertar-se; **tight-fisted** adj pãoduro; **tightly** adv firmemente; **tight-rope** n corda (bamba)

tights [taɪts] (BRIT) npl collant m

tile [taɪl] n (on roof) telha; (on floor) ladrilho; (on wall) azulejo, ladrilho; **tiled** adj ladrilhado; (roof) de telhas

till [tɪl] n caixa (registradora) ♦ vt (land) cultivar ♦ prep, conj = **until**

tiller ['tɪlə*] n (NAUT) cana do leme

tilt [tɪlt] vt inclinar ♦ vi inclinar-se

timber ['tɪmbə*] n (material) madeira; (trees) mata, floresta

time [taɪm] n tempo; (epoch: often pl) época; (by clock) hora; (moment) momento; (occasion) vez f; (MUS) compasso ♦ vt calcular ou medir o tempo de; (visit etc) escolher o momento para; **a long** ~ muito tempo; **4 at a** ~ quatro de uma vez; **for the** ~ **being** por enquanto; **from** ~ **to** ~ de vez em quando; **at** ~**s** às vezes; **in** ~ (soon enough) a tempo; (after some time) com o tempo; (MUS) no compasso; **in a week's** ~ dentro de uma semana; **in no** ~ num abrir e fechar de olhos; **any** ~ a qualquer hora; **on** ~ na hora; **5** ~**s 5 is 25** 5 vezes 5 são 25; **what** ~ **is it?** que horas são?; **to have a good** ~ divertir-se; **time bomb** n bomba-relógio f; **timeless** adj eterno; **timely** adj oportuno; **time switch** (BRIT) n interruptor m horário; **timetable** n horário; **time zone** n fuso horário

timid ['tɪmɪd] adj tímido

timing ['taɪmɪŋ] n escolha do momento; (SPORT) cronometragem f; **the** ~ **of his resignation** o momento que escolheu para se demitir

tin [tɪn] n estanho; (also: ~ **plate**) folha-de-flandres f; (BRIT: can) lata; **tin foil** n papel m de estanho

tingle ['tɪŋgl] vi formigar

tinned [tɪnd] (BRIT) adj (food) em lata, em conserva

tin opener (BRIT) n abridor m de latas (BR), abre-latas m inv (PT)

tinsel ['tɪnsl] n ouropel m

tint [tɪnt] n matiz m; (for hair) tintura, tinta; **tinted** adj pintado; (spectacles, glass) fumê inv

tiny ['taɪnɪ] adj pequeninito, minúsculo

tip [tɪp] n ponta; (gratuity) gorjeta; (BRIT: for rubbish) depósito; (advice) dica ♦ vt dar uma gorjeta a; (tilt) inclinar; (overturn: also: ~ over) virar, emborcar; (empty: also: ~ out) esvaziar, entornar; **tipped** (BRIT) adj (cigarette) com filtro

tipsy ['tɪpsɪ] adj embriagado, tocado

tiptoe ['tɪptəu] n: **on ~** na ponta dos pés

tire ['taɪə*] n (US) = tyre ♦ vt cansar ♦ vi cansar-se; (become bored) chatear-se; **tired** adj cansado; **to be tired of sth** estar farto or cheio de algo; **tireless** adj incansável; **tiresome** adj enfadonho, chato; **tiring** adj cansativo

tissue ['tɪʃuː] n tecido; (paper handkerchief) lenço de papel; **tissue paper** n papel m de seda

tit [tɪt] n (bird) passarinho; **to give ~ for tat** pagar na mesma moeda

titbit ['tɪtbɪt] n (in food) guloseima; (news) boato, rumor m

title ['taɪtl] n título

TM n abbr = **trademark**

━━━━━━━━━━━━━━
KEYWORD
━━━━━━━━━━━━━━

to [tuː, tə] prep **1** (direction) a, para; (towards) para; **to go ~ France/London/school/the station** ir à França/a Londres/ao colégio/à estação; **to go ~ Lígia's/the doctor's** ir à casa de Lígia/ao médico; **the road ~ Edinburgh** a estrada para Edimburgo; **~ the left/right** à esquerda/direita

2 (as far as) até; **to count ~ 10** con-

tar até 10; **from 40 ~ 50 people** de 40 a 50 pessoas

3 (with expressions of time): **a quarter ~ 5** quinze para as 5 (BR), 5 menos um quarto (PT)

4 (for, of) de, para; **the key ~ the front door** a chave da porta da frente; **a letter ~ his wife** uma carta para a sua mulher

5 (expressing indirect object): **to give sth ~ sb** dar algo a alguém; **to talk ~ sb** falar com alguém; **I sold it ~ a friend** vendi isto para um amigo; **to cause damage ~ sth** causar danos em algo

6 (in relation to) para; **3 goals ~ 2** 3 a 2; **8 apples ~ the kilo** 8 maçãs por quilo

7 (purpose, result) para; **to come ~ sb's aid** prestar ajuda a alguém; **to sentence sb ~ death** condenar alguém à morte; **~ my surprise** para minha surpresa

♦ with vb **1** (simple infin): **~ go/eat** ir/comer

2 (following another vb): **~ want/try ~ do** querer/tentar fazer; **~ start ~ do** começar a fazer

3 (with vb omitted): **I don't want ~** eu não quero; **you ought ~** você deve

4 (purpose, result) para

5 (equivalent to relative clause) para, a; **I have things ~ do** eu tenho coisas para fazer; **the main thing is ~ try** o principal é tentar

6 (after adj etc) para; **ready ~ go** pronto para ir; **too old/young ~ ...** muito velho/jovem para ...

♦ adv: **pull/push the door ~** puxar/empurrar a porta

toad [təud] n sapo

toadstool ['təudstuːl] n chapéu-decobra m, cogumelo venenoso

toast [təust] n (CULIN) torradas fpl;

(drink, speech) brinde m ♦ vt torrar;
brindar; **toaster** n torradeira

tobacco [tə'bækəu] n tabaco, fumo
(BR); **tobacconist** n vendedor(a)
m/f de tabaco

toboggan [tə'bɔgən] n tobogã
m

today [tə'deɪ] adv, n hoje m

toddler ['tɔdlə*] n criança que
começa a andar

toe [təu] n dedo do pé; (of shoe)
bico ♦ vt: **to ~ the line** (fig)
conformar-se, cumprir as obrigações

toffee ['tɔfɪ] n puxa-puxa m (BR),
caramelo (PT); **toffee apple** (BRIT)
n maçã f do amor

together [tə'geðə*] adv juntos; (at
same time) ao mesmo tempo; **~
with** junto com

toil [tɔɪl] n faina, labuta ♦ vi labutar,
trabalhar arduamente

toilet ['tɔɪlət] n privada, vaso sanitário; (BRIT: lavatory) banheiro (BR),
casa de banho (PT) ♦ cpd de toalete;
toilet paper n papel m higiênico;
toiletries npl artigos mpl de toalete; **toilet roll** n rolo de papel higiênico

token ['təukən] n (sign) sinal m,
símbolo, prova; (souvenir) lembrança; (substitute coin) ficha ♦ adj
simbólico; **book/record ~** (BRIT) vale
para comprar livros/discos

told [təuld] pt, pp of **tell**

tolerable ['tɔlərəbl] adj (bearable)
suportável; (fairly good) passável

tolerant ['tɔlərənt] adj: **~ of** tolerante com

tolerate ['tɔləreɪt] vt suportar; (MED,
TECH) tolerar

toll [təul] n (of casualties) número de
baixas; (charge) pedágio m (BR), portagem f (PT) ♦ vi dobrar, tanger

tomato [tə'mɑːtəu] (pl ~es) n

tomate m

tomb [tuːm] n tumba

tomboy ['tɔmbɔɪ] n menina moleque

tombstone ['tuːmstəun] n lápide
f

tomcat ['tɔmkæt] n gato

tomorrow [tə'mɔrəu] adv, n amanhã m; **the day after ~** depois de
amanhã; **~ morning** amanhã de
manhã

ton [tʌn] n tonelada (BRIT = 1016kg;
US = 907kg); **~s of** (inf) um monte
de

tone [təun] n tom m ♦ vi harmonizar; **tone down** vt (colour, criticism)
suavizar; (sound) baixar; (muscles) entoar; **tone up** vt (muscles) tonificar;
tone-deaf adj que não tem ouvido

tongs [tɔŋz] npl (for coal) tenaz f;
(for hair) ferros mpl de frisar cabelo

tongue [tʌŋ] n língua; **~ in cheek**
ironicamente; **tongue-tied** adj
(fig) calado; **tongue-twister** n
trava-língua m

tonic ['tɔnɪk] n (MED) tônico; (also:
~ water) (água) tônica

tonight [tə'naɪt] adv, n esta noite,
hoje à noite

tonsil ['tɔnsl] n amígdala; **tonsillitis** [tɔnsɪ'laɪtɪs] n amigdalite f

too [tuː] adv (excessively) demais,
muito; (also) também; **~ much**
(adv) demais; (adj) demasiado; **~
many** demasiados(-as)

took [tuk] pt of **take**

tool [tuːl] n ferramenta

toot [tuːt] n (of horn) buzinada; (of
whistle) apito ♦ vi buzinar

tooth [tuːθ] (pl **teeth**) n (ANAT, TECH)
dente m; (molar) molar m; **toothache** n dor f de dente; **to have
toothache** estar com dor de dente;
toothbrush n escova de dentes;
toothpaste n pasta de dentes;

creme *m* dental; **toothpick** *n* palito

top [tɔp] *n* (*of mountain*) cume *m*, cimo; (*of tree*) topo; (*of head*) cocuruto; (*of cupboard, table*) superfície *f*, topo; (*of box, jar, bottle*) tampa; (*of ladder, page*) topo; (*toy*) pião *m*; (*blouse etc*) top *m*, blusa ♦ *adj* (*shelf, step*) mais alto; (*marks*) máximo; (*in rank*) principal, superior ♦ *vt* exceder; (*be first in*) estar à cabeça de; **on ~ of** sobre, em cima de; (*in addition to*) além de; **from ~ to toe** (*BRIT*) da cabeça aos pés; **from ~ to bottom** de cima abaixo; **top up** (*US* **top off**) *vt* completar; **top floor** *n* último andar *m*; **top hat** *n* cartola; **top-heavy** *adj* desequilibrado

topic ['tɔpɪk] *n* tópico, assunto; **topical** *adj* atual

topless *adj* (*bather etc*) topless *inv*, sem a parte superior do biquíni

topmost *adj* o mais alto

topple ['tɔpl] *vt* derrubar ♦ *vi* cair para frente

top-secret *adj* ultra-secreto, supersecreto

topsy-turvy ['tɔpsɪ'təːvɪ] *adj, adv* de pernas para o ar, confuso, às avessas

torch [tɔːtʃ] *n* (*BRIT: electric*) lanterna

tore [tɔː*] *pt of* **tear**

torment [*n* 'tɔːmɛnt, *vb* tɔː'mɛnt] *n* tormento, suplício ♦ *vt* atormentar; (*fig: annoy*) chatear, aborrecer

torn [tɔːn] *pp of* **tear**

tornado [tɔː'neɪdəu] (*pl* **~es**) *n* tornado

torrent ['tɔrənt] *n* torrente *f*

tortoise ['tɔːtəs] *n* tartaruga

torture ['tɔːtʃə*] *n* tortura ♦ *vt* torturar; (*fig*) atormentar

Tory ['tɔːrɪ] (*BRIT*) *adj, n* (*POL*) conservador(a) *m/f*

toss [tɔs] *vt* atirar, arremessar; (*head*) lançar para trás ♦ *vi*: **to ~ and**

turn in bed virar de um lado para o outro na cama; **to ~ a coin** tirar cara ou coroa; **to ~ up for sth** (*BRIT*) jogar cara ou coroa por algo

tot [tɔt] *n* (*BRIT: drink*) copinho, golinho; (*child*) criancinha

total ['təutl] *adj* total *n* total *m*, soma ♦ *vt* (*add up*) somar; (*amount to*) montar a

totter ['tɔtə*] *vi* cambalear

touch [tʌtʃ] *n* (*sense*) toque *m*; (*contact*) contato ♦ *vt* tocar (em); (*tamper with*) mexer com; (*make contact with*) fazer contato com; (*emotionally*) comover; **a ~ of** (*fig*) um traço de; **to get in ~ with sb** entrar em contato com alguém; **to lose ~** perder o contato; **touch on** *vt fus* (*topic*) tocar em, fazer menção de; **touch up** *vt* (*paint*) retocar; **touchdown** *n* aterrissagem *f* (*BR*), aterragem *f* (*PT*); (*on sea*) amerissagem *f* (*BR*), amaragem *f* (*PT*); (*US: FOOTBALL*) touchdown *m*; **touching** *adj* comovedor(a); **touchy** *adj* suscetível, sensível

tough [tʌf] *adj* duro; (*difficult*) difícil; (*resistant*) resistente; (*person: physically*) forte; (: *mentally*) tenaz; (*firm*) firme, inflexível

tour [tuə*] *n* viagem *f*, excursão *f*; (*also: package ~*) excursão organizada; (*of town, museum*) visita; (*by artist*) turnê *f* ♦ *vt* (*country, city*) excursionar por; (*factory*) visitar

tourism ['tuərɪzm] *n* turismo

tourist ['tuərɪst] *n* turista *m/f* ♦ *cpd* turístico; **tourist office** *n* (*in country*) escritório de turismo; (*in embassy etc*) departamento de turismo

tournament ['tuənəmənt] *n* torneio

tow [təu] *vt* rebocar; **"on ~"** (*BRIT*), **"in ~"** (*US*) (*AUT*) "rebocado"

toward(s) [tə'wɔːd(z)] *prep* em direção a; (*of attitude*) para com; (*of purpose*) para; ◆ **noon/the end of the year** perto do meio-dia/do fim do ano

towel ['tauəl] *n* toalha; **towelling** *n* (*fabric*) tecido para toalhas

tower ['tauə*] *n* torre *f*; **tower block** (*BRIT*) *n* prédio alto, espigão *m*, cortiço (*BR*); **towering** *adj* elevado; (*figure*) eminente

town [taun] *n* cidade *f*; **to go to ~** ir à cidade; (*fig*) fazer com entusiasmo, mandar brasa (*BR*); **town centre** *n* centro (da cidade); **town hall** *n* prefeitura (*BR*), concelho (*PT*)

towrope ['təurəup] *n* cabo de reboque

tow truck (*US*) *n* reboque *m* (*BR*), pronto socorro (*PT*)

toy [tɔɪ] *n* brinquedo; **toy with** *vt fus* brincar com; (*idea*) contemplar

trace [treɪs] *n* (*sign*) sinal *m*; (*small amount*) traço ◆ *vt* (*draw*) traçar, esboçar; (*follow*) seguir a pista de; (*locate*) encontrar

track [træk] *n* (*mark*) pegada, vestígio; (*path: gen*) caminho, vereda; (*: of bullet etc*) trajetória; (*: of suspect, animal*) pista, rasto; (*RAIL*) trilhos (*BR*), carris *mpl* (*PT*); (*SPORT*) trilha; (*on record*) faixa ◆ *vt* seguir a pista de; **to keep ~ of** não perder de vista; (*fig*) manter-se informado sobre; **track down** *vt* (*prey*) seguir a pista de; (*lost item*) procurar e encontrar; **track suit** *n* roupa de jogging

tractor ['træktə*] *n* trator *m*

trade [treɪd] *n* comércio; (*skill, job*) ofício ◆ *vi* negociar, comerciar ◆ *vt*: **to ~ sth (for sth)** trocar algo (por algo); **trade in** *vt* dar como parte do pagamento; **trademark** *n* marca registrada; **trade name** *n*

marca *or* nome comercial de um produto; (*of company*) razão *f* social; **trader** *n* comerciante *m/f*; **tradesman** (*irreg*) *n* lojista *m*; **trade union** *n* sindicato

tradition [trə'dɪʃən] *n* tradição *f*; **traditional** *adj* tradicional

traffic ['træfɪk] *n* trânsito; (*air ~ etc*) tráfego; (*illegal*) tráfico ◆ *vi*: **to ~ in** (*pej: liquor, drugs*) traficar com, fazer tráfico com; **traffic circle** (*US*) *n* rotatória; **traffic jam** *n* engarrafamento, congestionamento; **traffic lights** *npl* sinal *m* luminoso; **traffic warden** *n* guarda *m/f* de trânsito

tragedy ['trædʒədɪ] *n* tragédia

tragic ['trædʒɪk] *adj* trágico

trail [treɪl] *n* (*tracks*) rasto, pista; (*path*) caminho, trilha; (*of smoke, dust*) rasto ◆ *vt* (*drag*) arrastar; (*follow*) seguir a pista de ◆ *vi* arrastar-se; (*hang loosely*) pender; (*in game, contest*) ficar para trás; **trail behind** *vi* atrasar-se; **trailer** *n* (*AUT*) reboque *m*; (*US: caravan*) trailer *m* (*BR*), rulote *f* (*PT*); (*CINEMA*) trailer; **trailer truck** (*US*) *n* caminhão-reboque *m*

train [treɪn] *n* trem *m* (*BR*), comboio *m* (*PT*); (*of dress*) cauda ◆ *vt* formar; (*teach skills to*) instruir; (*SPORT*) treinar; (*dog*) adestrar, amestrar; (*point: gun etc*): **to ~ on** apontar para ◆ *vi* (*learn a skill*) instruir; (*SPORT*) treinar; (*be educated*) ser treinado; **to lose one's ~ of thought** perder o fio; **trained** *adj* especializado; (*teacher*) formado; (*animal*) adestrado; **trainee** [treɪ'niː] *n* estagiário(-a); **trainer** *n* (*SPORT*) treinador(a) *m/f*; (*of animals*) adestrador(a) *m/f*; **trainers** *npl* (*shoes*) tênis *m*; **training** *n* instrução *f*; (*SPORT, for occupation*) treinamento; (*professional*) formação f; **training college** n (for teachers) ≈ escola normal

trait [treɪt] n traço

traitor ['treɪtə*] n traidor(a) m/f

tram [træm] (BRIT) n (also: **~car**) bonde m (BR), eléctrico (PT)

tramp [træmp] n (person) vagabundo(-a); (inf: pej: woman) piranha ♦ vi caminhar pesadamente

trample ['træmpl] vt: **to ~ (underfoot)** calcar aos pés

trampoline ['træmpəli:n] n trampolim m

tranquil ['træŋkwɪl] adj tranqüilo; **tranquillizer** n (MED) tranqüilizante m

transact [træn'zækt] vt (business) negociar; **transaction** n transação f, negócio

transfer [n 'trænsfə:*, vb træns'fə:*] n transferência; (picture, design) decalcomania ♦ vt transferir; **to ~ the charges** (BRIT: TEL) ligar a cobrar

transform [træns'fɔ:m] vt transformar

transfusion [træns'fju:ʒən] n (also: **blood ~**) transfusão f (de sangue)

transistor [træn'zɪstə*] n (ELEC: also: **~ radio**) transistor m

transit ['trænzɪt] n: **in ~** em trânsito, de passagem

translate [trænz'leɪt] vt traduzir; **translation** n tradução f; **translator** n tradutor(a) m/f

transmission [trænz'mɪʃən] n transmissão f

transmit [trænz'mɪt] vt transmitir

transparency [træns'pɛərnsɪ] n transparência; (BRIT: PHOT) diapositivo

transparent [træns'pærnt] adj transparente

transplant [vb træns'plɑ:nt, n 'trænsplɑ:nt] vt transplantar ♦ n (MED) transplante m

transport [n 'trænspɔ:t, vb træns'pɔ:t] n transporte m ♦ vt transportar; (carry) acarretar; **transportation** ['trænspɔ:'teɪʃən] n transporte m

trap [træp] n (snare) armadilha, cilada; (trick) cilada; (carriage) aranha, charrete ♦ vt pegar na armadilha; (person: trick) armar; (: in bad marriage) prender; (: in fire): **to be ~ped** ficar preso; (immobilize) bloquear; **trap door** n alçapão m

trapeze [trə'pi:z] n trapézio

trappings ['træpɪŋz] npl adornos mpl, enfeites mpl

trash [træʃ] n (pej: nonsense) besteiras fpl; (US: rubbish) lixo; **trash can** (US) n lata de lixo

trauma ['trɔ:mə] n trauma m

travel ['trævl] n viagem f ♦ vi viajar; (sound) propagar-se; (news) levar; (wine): **this wine ~s well** este vinho não sofre alteração ao ser transportado ♦ vt percorrer; **~s** npl (journeys) viagens fpl; **travel agent** n agente m/f de viagens; **traveller** (US **traveler**) n viajante m/f; (COMM) caixeiro (-a) viajante; **traveller's cheque** (US **traveler's check**) n cheque m de viagem; **travelling** (US **traveling**) n as viagens, viajar m ♦ adj (circus, exhibition) itinerante; (salesman) viajante ♦ cpd de viagem; **travel sickness** n enjôo

trawler ['trɔ:lə*] n traineira

tray [treɪ] n bandeja; (on desk) cesta

treacherous ['trɛtʃərəs] adj traiçoeiro; (ground, tide) perigoso

treacle ['tri:kl] n melado

tread [trɛd] (pt **trod**, pp **trodden**) n (step) passo, pisada; (sound) passada; (of stair) piso; (of tyre) banda de rodagem ♦ vi pisar; **tread on** vt fus pisar (em)

treason ['tri:zn] *n* traição *f*

treasure ['treʒə*] *n* tesouro; (*person*) jóia ♦ *vt* (*value*) apreciar, estimar; **~s** *npl* (*art* ~s *etc*) preciosidades *fpl*

treasurer ['treʒərə*] *n* tesoureiro(-a)

treasury ['treʒərɪ] *n* tesouraria

treat [tri:t] *n* regalo, deleite *m* ♦ *vt* tratar; **to** ~ **sb to sth** convidar alguém para algo

treatment ['tri:tmənt] *n* tratamento

treaty ['tri:tɪ] *n* tratado, acordo

treble ['trɛbl] *adj* tríplice ♦ *vt* triplicar ♦ *vi* triplicar(-se)

tree [tri:] *n* árvore *f*

trek [trɛk] *n* (*long journey*) jornada; (*walk*) caminhada

tremble ['trɛmbl] *vi* tremer

tremendous [trɪ'mɛndəs] *adj* tremendo; (*enormous*) enorme; (*excellent*) sensacional, fantástico

tremor ['trɛmə*] *n* tremor *m*; (*also*: **earth** ~) tremor de terra

trench [trɛntʃ] *n* trincheira

trend [trɛnd] *n* (*tendency*) tendência; (*of events*) curso; (*fashion*) modismo, tendência; **trendy** *adj* (*idea*) de acordo com a tendência atual; (*clothes*) da última moda

trespass ['trɛspəs] *vi*: **to** ~ **on** invadir; **"no ~ing"** "entrada proibida"

trial ['traɪəl] *n* (*LAW*) processo; (*test: of machine etc*) prova, teste *m*; ~s *npl* (*unpleasant experiences*) dissabores *mpl*; **by** ~ **and error** por tentativas; **to be on** ~ ser julgado; **trial period** *n* período de experiência

triangle ['traɪæŋgl] *n* (*MATH, MUS*) triângulo

tribe [traɪb] *n* tribo *f*

tribunal [traɪ'bju:nl] *n* tribunal *m*

tributary ['trɪbjutərɪ] *n* afluente *m*

tribute ['trɪbju:t] *n* homenagem *f*;

to pay ~ **to** prestar homenagem a, homenagear

trick [trɪk] *n* truque *m*; (*joke*) peça, brincadeira; (*skill, knack*) habilidade *f*; (*CARDS*) vaza *f* ♦ *vt* enganar; **to play a** ~ **on sb** pregar uma peça em alguém; **that should do the** ~ (*inf*) isso deveria dar resultado; **trickery** *n* trapaça, astúcia

trickle ['trɪkl] *n* (*of water etc*) fio (de água) ♦ *vi* gotejar, pingar

tricky ['trɪkɪ] *adj* difícil, complicado

tricycle ['traɪsɪkl] *n* triciclo

trifle ['traɪfl] *n* bobagem *f*, besteira; (*CULIN*) tipo de bolo com fruta e creme ♦ *adv*: **a** ~ **long** um pouquinho longo; **trifling** *adj* insignificante

trigger ['trɪgə*] *n* (*of gun*) gatilho; **trigger off** *vt* desencadear

trim [trɪm] *adj* (*figure*) elegante; (*house*) arrumado; (*garden*) bem cuidado *m*; (*haircut*) aparada; (*on car*) estofamento ♦ *vt* aparar, cortar; (*decorate*): **to** ~ (**with**) enfeitar (com); (*NAUT: sail*) ajustar; **trimmings** *npl* decoração *f*; (*CULIN*) acompanhamentos *mpl*

trinket ['trɪŋkɪt] *n* bugiganga; (*piece of jewellery*) berloque *m*, bijuteria

trip [trɪp] *n* viagem *f*; (*outing*) excursão *f*; (*stumble*) tropeção *m* ♦ *vi* tropeçar; (*go lightly*) andar com passos ligeiros; **on a** ~ de viagem; **trip up** *vi* tropeçar ♦ *vt* passar uma rasteira em

tripe [traɪp] *n* (*CULIN*) bucho, tripa; (*pej: rubbish*) bobagem *f*

triple ['trɪpl] *adj* triplo, tríplice; **triplets** *npl* trigêmeos(-as) *m/fpl*

tripod ['traɪpɔd] *n* tripé *m*

trite [traɪt] *adj* gasto, banal

triumph ['traɪʌmf] *n* (*satisfaction*) satisfação *f*; (*great achievement*) triunfo ♦ *vi*: **to** ~ (**over**) triunfar

(sobre)

trivia ['trɪvɪə] npl trivialidades fpl

trivial ['trɪvɪəl] adj insignificante; (commonplace) trivial

trod [trɒd] pt of tread; **trodden** pp of tread

trolley ['trɒlɪ] n carrinho; (table on wheels) mesa volante

trombone [trɒm'bəʊn] n trombone m

troop [tru:p] n bando, grupo ♦ vi: to ~ in/out entrar/sair em bando; ~s npl (MIL) tropas fpl; **~ing the colour** (BRIT) saudação da bandeira

trophy ['trəʊfɪ] n troféu m

tropic ['trɒpɪk] n trópico; **tropical** adj tropical

trot [trɒt] n trote m; (fast pace) passo rápido ♦ vi trotar; (person) andar rapidamente; **on the ~** (fig: inf) a fio

trouble ['trʌbl] n problema(s) m(pl), dificuldade(s) f(pl); (worry) preocupação f; (effort) incômodo, trabalho; (POL) distúrbios mpl; (MED): **stomach etc ~** problemas mpl gástricos etc ♦ vt perturbar; (worry) preocupar, incomodar ♦ vi: **to ~ to do sth** incomodar-se or preocupar-se de fazer algo; **~s** npl (POL etc) distúrbios mpl; **to be in ~** estar num aperto; (ship, climber etc) estar em dificuldade; **what's the ~?** qual é o problema?; **troubled** adj preocupado; (epoch, life) agitado; **troublemaker** n criador(a)-de-casos m/f; (child) encrenqueiro(-a); **troublesome** adj importuno; (child, cough) incômodo

trough [trɒf] n (also: drinking ~) bebedouro, cocho; (also: feeding ~) gamela; (depression) depressão f

trousers ['traʊzəz] npl calça sg, calças fpl (PT)

trout [traʊt] n inv truta

truant ['truənt] (BRIT) n: **to play ~**

matar aula (BR), fazer gazeta (PT)

truce [tru:s] n trégua, armistício

truck [trʌk] n caminhão m (BR), camião m (PT); (RAIL) vagão m; **truck driver** n caminhoneiro(-a) (BR), camionista m/f (PT); **truck farm** (US) n horta

true [tru:] adj verdadeiro; (accurate) exato; (genuine) autêntico; (faithful) fiel, leal; **to come ~** realizar-se, tornar-se realidade

truffle ['trʌfl] n trufa; (sweet) docinho de chocolate or rum

truly ['tru:lɪ] adv realmente; (truthfully) verdadeiramente; (faithfully) fielmente; **yours ~** (in letter) atenciosamente

trump [trʌmp] n trunfo

trumpet ['trʌmpɪt] n trombeta

truncheon ['trʌntʃən] n cassetete m

trunk [trʌŋk] n tronco; (of elephant) tromba; (case) baú m; (US: AUT) mala (BR), porta-bagagens m (PT); ~s npl (also: swimming ~s) sunga (BR), calções mpl de banho (PT)

trust [trʌst] n confiança; (responsibility) responsabilidade f; (LAW) fideicomisso ♦ vt (rely on) confiar em; (entrust): **to ~ sth to sb** confiar algo a alguém; (hope): **to ~ (that)** esperar que; **to take sth on ~** aceitar algo sem verificação prévia; **trusted** adj de confiança; **trustful** adj confiante; **trustworthy** adj digno de confiança

truth [tru:θ] n verdade f; **truthful** adj (person) sincero, honesto

try [traɪ] n tentativa; (RUGBY) ensaio ♦ vt (LAW) julgar; (test: sth new) provar, pôr à prova; (strain) cansar ♦ vi tentar; **to have a ~** fazer uma tentativa; **to ~ to do sth** tentar fazer algo; **try on** vt (clothes) experimentar, provar; **trying** adj exasperante

T-shirt n camiseta (BR), T-shirt f (PT)

tub [tʌb] n tina; (bath) banheira

tubby [ˈtʌbɪ] adj gorducho

tube [tjuːb] n tubo; (pipe) cano; (BRIT: underground) metrô m (BR), metro(-politano) (PT); (for tyre) câmara-de-ar f

tuberculosis [tjubəːkjuˈləusɪs] n tuberculose f

TUC n abbr (= Trades Union Congress) ≈ CUT f

tuck [tʌk] vt (put) enfiar, meter; **tuck away** vt esconder; **to be ~ed away** estar escondido; **tuck in** vi enfiar para dentro; (child) aconchegar ♦ vi (eat) comer com apetite; **tuck up** vt (child) aconchegar

Tuesday [ˈtjuːzdɪ] n terça-feira

tuft [tʌft] n penacho; (of grass etc) tufo

tug [tʌg] n (ship) rebocador m ♦ vt puxar; **tug-of-war** n cabo-de-guerra m; (fig) disputa

tuition [tjuˈɪʃən] n ensino; (private ~) aulas fpl particulares; (US: fees) taxas fpl escolares

tulip [ˈtjuːlɪp] n tulipa

tumble [ˈtʌmbl] n (fall) queda ♦ vi cair, tombar; **to ~ to sth** (inf) sacar algo; **tumbledown** adj em ruínas; **tumble dryer** (BRIT) n máquina de secar roupa

tumbler [ˈtʌmblə*] n copo

tummy [ˈtʌmɪ] (inf) n (belly) barriga; (stomach) estômago

tumour [ˈtjuːmə*] (US **tumor**) n tumor m

tuna [ˈtjuːnə] n inv (also: ~ **fish**) atum m

tune [tjuːn] n melodia ♦ vt (MUS) afinar; (RADIO, TV) sintonizar; (AUT) regular; **to be in/out of ~** (instrument) estar afinado/desafinado; (singer) cantar afinado/desafinar; **to be in/out of ~ with** (fig) harmonizar-se

com/destoar de; **tune in** vi (RADIO, TV): **to ~ in (to)** sintonizar (com); **tune up** vi (musician) afinar (seu instrumento); **tuneful** adj melodioso; **tuner** n: **piano tuner** afinador(a) m/f de pianos

tunic [ˈtjuːnɪk] n túnica

Tunisia [tjuˈnɪzɪə] n Tunísia

tunnel [ˈtʌnl] n túnel m; (in mine) galeria ♦ vi abrir um túnel (or uma galeria)

turbulence [ˈtəːbjuləns] n (AVIAT) turbulência

tureen [təˈriːn] n terrina

turf [təːf] n torrão m ♦ vt relvar, gramar; **turf out** (inf) vt (person) pôr no olho da rua

Turk [təːk] n turco(-a)

Turkey [ˈtəːkɪ] n Turquia

turkey [ˈtəːkɪ] n peru(a) m/f

Turkish [ˈtəːkɪʃ] adj turco(-a) ♦ n (LING) turco

turmoil [ˈtəːmɔɪl] n tumulto, distúrbio, agitação f; **in ~** agitado, tumultuado

turn [təːn] n volta, turno; (in road) curva; (of mind, events) propensão f, tendência; (THEATRE) número; (MED) choque m ♦ vt dar volta a, fazer girar; (collar) virar; (change): **to ~ sth into** converter algo em ♦ vi virar; (person: look back) voltar-se; (reverse direction) mudar de direção; (milk) azedar; (become) tornar-se, virar; **to ~ nasty** engrossar; **to ~ forty** fazer quarenta anos; **a good ~** um favor; **it gave me quite a ~** me deu um susto enorme; **"no left ~"** (AUT) "proibido virar à esquerda"; **it's your ~** é a sua vez; **in ~** por sua vez; **to take ~s (at)** revezar (em); **turn away** vi virar a cabeça ♦ vt recusar; **turn back** vi voltar atrás ♦ vt voltar para trás; (clock) atrasar; **turn down** vt (refuse) recusar;

(reduce) baixar; (fold) dobrar, virar para baixo; **turn in** vi (inf: go to bed) ir dormir ♦ vt (fold) dobrar para dentro; **turn off** vi (from road) virar, sair do caminho ♦ vt (light, radio etc) apagar; (engine) desligar; **turn on** vt (light) acender; (engine, radio) ligar; (tap) abrir; **turn out** vt (light, gas) apagar; (produce) produzir ♦ vi (troops) ser mobilizado; **to ~ out to be ...** revelar-se (ser) ..., resultar (ser) ..., vir a ser ...; **turn over** vi (person) virar-se ♦ vt (object) virar; **turn round** vi voltar-se, virar-se; **turn up** vi (person) aparecer, pintar; (lost object) aparecer ♦ vt (collar) subir; (radio etc) aumentar; **turning** n (in road) via lateral

turnip ['tɑːnɪp] n nabo

turnout ['tɑːnaut] n assistência; (in election) comparecimento às urnas

turnover ['tɑːnəuvə*] n (COMM: amount of money) volume m de negócios; (: of goods) movimento; (of staff) rotatividade f

turnpike ['tɑːnpaɪk] (US) n estrada or rodovia com pedágio (BR) or portagem (PT)

turnstile ['tɑːnstaɪl] n borboleta (BR), torniquete m (PT)

turntable ['tɑːnteɪbl] n (on record player) prato

turn-up (BRIT) n (on trousers) volta, dobra

turpentine ['tɑːpəntaɪn] n (also: turps) aguarrás f

turquoise ['tɑːkwɔːz] n (stone) turquesa ♦ adj azul-turquesa inv

turret ['tʌrɪt] n torrinha

turtle ['tɑːtl] n tartaruga, cágado

tusk [tʌsk] n defesa (de elefante)

tutor ['tjuːtə*] n professor(a) m/f; (private ~) professor(a) m/f particular; **tutorial** [tjuː'tɔːrɪəl] n (SCH)

seminário

tuxedo [tʌk'siːdəu] (US) n smoking m

TV n abbr (= television) TV f

twang [twæŋ] n (of instrument) dedilhado; (of voice) timbre m nasal

tweed [twiːd] n tweed m, pano grosso de lã

tweezers ['twiːzəz] npl pinça (pequena)

twelfth [twelfθ] num décimo segundo

twelve [twelv] num doze; **at ~ (o'clock)** (midday) ao meio-dia; (midnight) à meia-noite

twentieth ['twentɪɪθ] num vigésimo

twenty ['twentɪ] num vinte

twice [twaɪs] adv duas vezes; **~ as much** duas vezes mais

twig [twɪg] n graveto, varinha ♦ vi (inf) sacar

twilight ['twaɪlaɪt] n crepúsculo, meia-luz f

twin [twɪn] adj gêmeo; (beds) separado ♦ n gêmeo ♦ vt irmanar; **twin (-bedded) room** n quarto com duas camas

twine [twaɪn] n barbante m (BR), cordel m (PT) ♦ vi enroscar-se, enrolar-se

twinge [twɪndʒ] n (of pain) pontada; (of conscience) remorso

twinkle ['twɪŋkl] n cintilar, vi cintilar; (eyes) pestanejar

twirl [twɑːl] vt fazer girar ♦ vi girar rapidamente

twist [twɪst] n torção f; (in road, coil) curva; (in flex) virada; (in story) mudança imprevista ♦ vt torcer, retorcer; (ankle) torcer; (weave) entrelaçar; (roll around) enrolar; (fig) deturpar ♦ vi serpentear

twit [twɪt] (inf) n idiota m/f, bobo(-a)

twitch [twitʃ] n puxão m; (nervous) tique m nervoso ♦ vi contrair-se

two [tu:] num dois; **to put ~ and ~ together** (fig) tirar conclusões; **two-faced** (pej) adj (person) falso; **two-way** adj: **two-way traffic** trânsito em mão dupla

tycoon [taɪˈkuːn] n: (business) ~ magnata m

type [taɪp] n (category) tipo, espécie f; (model) modelo; (TYP) tipo, letra ♦ vt (letter etc) datilografar, bater (à máquina); **typescript** n texto datilografado; **typewriter** n máquina de escrever

typhoid [ˈtaɪfɔɪd] n febre f tifóide

typical [ˈtɪpɪkl] adj típico

typing [ˈtaɪpɪŋ] n datilografia

typist [ˈtaɪpɪst] n datilógrafo(-a) m/f

tyrant [ˈtaɪərənt] n tirano(-a)

tyre [ˈtaɪə*] (US tire) n pneu m

U

ubiquitous [juːˈbɪkwɪtəs] adj ubíquo, onipresente

udder [ˈʌdə*] n ubre f

UFO [ˈjuːfəu] n abbr (= unidentified flying object) óvni m

Uganda [juːˈgændə] n Uganda (no article)

ugly [ˈʌglɪ] adj feio; (dangerous) perigoso

UK n abbr = **United Kingdom**

ulcer [ˈʌlsə*] n úlcera; **mouth ~** afta

Ulster [ˈʌlstə*] n Ulster m

ulterior [ʌlˈtɪərɪə*] adj: ~ **motive** segundas intenções fpl

ultimate [ˈʌltɪmət] adj último, final; (authority) máximo; **ultimately** adv (in the end) no final, por último; (fundamentally) essencialmente

ultrasound [ˈʌltrəsaund] n (MED) ultra-som m

umbilical cord [ʌmbɪˈlaɪkl-] n cordão m umbilical

umbrella [ʌmˈbrɛlə] n guarda-chuva m; (for sun) guarda-sol m, barraca de praia

umpire [ˈʌmpaɪə*] n árbitro ♦ vt arbitrar

umpteen [ʌmpˈtiːn] adj inúmeros(-as)

UN n abbr (= United Nations) ONU f

unable [ʌnˈeɪbl] adj: **to be ~ to do sth** não poder fazer algo

unaccompanied [ʌnəˈkʌmpənɪd] adj desacompanhado; (singing, song) sem acompanhamento

unanimous [juːˈnænɪməs] adj unânime

unarmed [ʌnˈɑːmd] adj (without a weapon) desarmado; (defenceless) indefeso

unattached [ʌnəˈtætʃt] adj (person) livre; (part etc) solto, separado

unattended [ʌnəˈtɛndɪd] adj (car, luggage) abandonado

unattractive [ʌnəˈtræktɪv] adj sem atrativos; (building, appearance, idea) pouco atraente

unauthorized [ʌnˈɔːθəraɪzd] adj não autorizado, sem autorização

unavoidable [ʌnəˈvɔɪdəbl] adj inevitável

unaware [ʌnəˈwɛə*] adj: **to be ~ of** ignorar, não perceber

unawares [ʌnəˈwɛəz] adv improvisadamente, de surpresa

unbalanced [ʌnˈbælənst] adj desequilibrado

unbearable [ʌnˈbɛərəbl] adj insuportável

unbeatable [ʌnˈbiːtəbl] adj (team) invencível; (price) sem igual

unbelievable [ʌnbɪˈliːvəbl] adj inacreditável; (amazing) incrível

unborn [ʌnˈbɔːn] adj por nascer

unbroken [ʌnˈbrəukən] adj (seal)

intacto; (*line*) contínuo; (*silence, series*) ininterrupto; (*record*) mantido; (*spirit*) indômito

unbutton [ʌn'bʌtn] vt desabotoar

uncalled-for [ʌn'kɔːld-] adj desnecessário, gratuito

uncanny [ʌn'kænɪ] adj estranho; (*knack*) excepcional

uncertain [ʌn'sɜːtn] adj incerto; (*character*) indeciso; (*unsure*): ~ **about** inseguro sobre; **in no ~ terms** em termos precisos; **uncertainty** n incerteza; (*also: doubts*) dúvidas fpl

uncivilized [ʌn'sɪvəlaɪzd] adj (*country, people*) primitivo; (*fig: behaviour*) incivilizado; (: *hour*) de manhã bem cedo

uncle ['ʌŋkl] n tio

uncomfortable [ʌn'kʌmfətəbl] adj incômodo; (*uneasy*) pouco à vontade; (*situation*) desagradável

uncommon [ʌn'kɔmən] adj raro, incomum, excepcional

uncompromising [ʌn'kɔmprə-maɪzɪŋ] adj intransigente, inflexível

unconcerned [ʌnkən'sɜːnd] adj indiferente, despreocupado

unconditional [ʌnkən'dɪʃənl] adj incondicional

unconscious [ʌn'kɔnʃəs] adj sem sentidos, desacordado; (*unaware*): ~ **of** inconsciente de ♦ n: **the** ~ o inconsciente

uncontrollable [ʌnkən'trəʊləbl] adj (*temper*) ingovernável; (*child, animal, laughter*) incontrolável

unconventional [ʌnkən'venʃənl] adj inconvencional

uncouth [ʌn'kuːθ] adj rude, grosseiro

uncover [ʌn'kʌvə*] vt descobrir; (*take lid off*) destapar, destampar

undecided [ʌndɪ'saɪdɪd] adj indeci-

so; (*question*) não respondido, pendente

under ['ʌndə*] prep embaixo de (BR), debaixo de (PT); (*fig*) sob; (*less than*) menos de; (*according to*) segundo, de acordo com ♦ adv embaixo; (*movement*) por baixo; **there** ali embaixo; ~ **repair** em conserto

under... [ʌndə*] prefix: **under-age** adj menor de idade; **undercarriage** (BRIT) n (AVIAT) trem m de aterrissagem; **undercharge** vt não cobrar o suficiente; **underclothes** npl roupa de baixo, roupa íntima; **undercover** adj secreto, clandestino; **undercurrent** n (fig) tendência; **undercut** (irreg) vt (*person*) prejudicar; (*prices*) vender por menos que; **underdog** n o mais fraco; **underdone** adj (CULIN) mal passado; **underestimate** vt subestimar; **underexposed** adj (PHOT) sem exposição suficiente; **underfed** adj subnutrido; **underfoot** adv sob os pés; **undergo** (irreg) vt sofrer; (*test*) passar por; (*operation, treatment*) ser submetido a; **undergraduate** n universitário(-a); **underground** n (BRIT) metrô m (BR), metro(-politano) (PT); (POL) organização f clandestina ♦ adj subterrâneo; (fig) clandestino ♦ adv (*work*) embaixo da terra; (fig) na clandestinidade; **undergrowth** n vegetação f rasteira; **underhand(ed)** adj (fig) secreto e desonesto; **underlie** (irreg) vt (fig) ser a base de; **underline** vt sublinhar; **undermine** vt minar, solapar; **underneath** adv embaixo, debaixo, por baixo ♦ prep embaixo de (BR), debaixo de (PT); **underpaid** adj mal pago; **underpants** (BRIT) npl cueca(s) f (pl) (BR), cuecas fpl (PT);

underpass (BRIT) n passagem f inferior; **underprivileged** adj menos favorecido; **underrate** vt depreciar, subestimar; **undershirt** (US) n camiseta; **undershorts** (US) npl cueca (BR), cuecas fpl (PT); **underside** n parte f inferior; **underskirt** (BRIT) n anágua

understand [ʌndə'stænd] (irreg) vt entender, compreender ♦ vi: **to ~ that** acreditar que; **understandable** adj compreensível; **understanding** adj compreensivo ♦ n compreensão f; (knowledge) entendimento; (agreement) acordo

understatement [ʌndə'steɪtmənt] n (quality) subestimação f; (euphemism) eufemismo; **it's an ~ to say that** ... é uma subestimação dizer que ...

understood [ʌndə'stud] pt, pp of **understand** ♦ adj entendido; (implied) subentendido, implícito

understudy [ʌndəstʌdɪ] n ator m substituto (atriz f substituta)

undertake [ʌndə'teɪk] (irreg: like take) vt incumbir-se de, encarregar-se de; **to ~ to do sth** comprometer-se a fazer algo

undertaker [ˈʌndəteɪkə*] n agente m/f funerário(-a)

undertaking [ˈʌndəteɪkɪŋ] n empreendimento; (promise) promessa

underwater [ʌndə'wɔːtə*] adv sob a água ♦ adj subaquático

underwear [ˈʌndəwɛə*] n roupa de baixo, roupa íntima

underworld [ˈʌndəwəːld] n (of crime) submundo

undies [ˈʌndɪz] (inf) npl roupa de baixo, roupa íntima

undo [ʌn'duː] (irreg: like do) vt (unfasten) desatar; (spoil) desmanchar

undoing [ʌn'duːɪŋ] n ruína, desgraça

undoubted [ʌn'dautɪd] adj indubitável

undress [ʌn'drɛs] vi despir-se, tirar a roupa

undue [ʌn'djuː] adj excessivo

unduly [ʌn'djuːlɪ] adv excessivamente

unearth [ʌn'əːθ] vt desenterrar; (fig) revelar

uneasy [ʌn'iːzɪ] adj (person) preocupado; (feeling) incômodo; (peace, truce) desconfortável

uneconomic(al) [ʌniːkə'nɔmɪk(l)] adj antieconômico

uneducated [ʌn'ɛdjukeɪtɪd] adj inculto, sem instrução, não escolarizado

unemployed [ʌnɪm'plɔɪd] adj desempregado ♦ npl: **the ~** os desempregados

unemployment [ʌnɪm'plɔɪmənt] n desemprego

unending [ʌn'ɛndɪŋ] adj interminável

unerring [ʌn'əːrɪŋ] adj infalível

uneven [ʌn'iːvn] adj desigual; (road etc) irregular, acidentado

unexpected [ʌnɪk'spɛktɪd] adj inesperado; **unexpectedly** [ʌnɪks-'pɛktdlɪ] adv inesperadamente

unfair [ʌn'fɛə*] adj: **~ (to)** injusto (com)

unfaithful [ʌn'feɪθful] adj infiel

unfamiliar [ʌnfə'mɪlɪə*] adj pouco familiar, desconhecido; **to be ~ with sth** não estar familiarizado com algo

unfashionable [ʌn'fæʃnəbl] adj fora da moda

unfasten [ʌn'fɑːsn] vt desatar; (open) abrir

unfavourable [ʌn'feɪvərəbl] (US **unfavorable**) adj desfavorável

unfeeling [ʌnˈfiːlɪŋ] *adj* insensível
unfinished [ʌnˈfɪnɪʃt] *adj* incompleto, inacabado
unfit [ʌnˈfɪt] *adj* sem preparo físico; *(incompetent)*: ~ **(for)** incompetente (para), incapaz (de); ~ **for work** inapto para trabalhar
unfold [ʌnˈfəʊld] *vt* desdobrar ♦ *vi (situation)* desdobrar-se
unforeseen [ʌnfɔːˈsiːn] *adj* imprevisto
unfortunate [ʌnˈfɔːtʃənət] *adj* infeliz; *(event, remark)* inoportuno
unfounded [ʌnˈfaʊndɪd] *adj* infundado
unfriendly [ʌnˈfrɛndlɪ] *adj* antipático
ungainly [ʌnˈgeɪnlɪ] *adj* desalinhado
ungrateful [ʌnˈgreɪtful] *adj* mal agradecido, ingrato
unhappiness [ʌnˈhæpɪnɪs] *n* infelicidade *f*
unhappy [ʌnˈhæpɪ] *adj* triste; *(unfortunate)* desventurado; *(childhood)* infeliz; *(dissatisfied)*: ~ **with** descontente com, insatisfeito com
unharmed [ʌnˈhɑːmd] *adj* ileso
unhealthy [ʌnˈhɛlθɪ] *adj* insalubre; *(person)* doentio; *(fig)* anormal
unheard-of [ʌnˈhɜːd-] *adj* insólito
unhurt [ʌnˈhɜːt] *adj* ileso
uniform [ˈjuːnɪfɔːm] *n* uniforme *m* ♦ *adj* uniforme
uninhabited [ʌnɪnˈhæbɪtɪd] *adj* inabitado
unintentional [ʌnɪnˈtɛnʃənəl] *adj* involuntário, não intencional
union [ˈjuːnjən] *n* união *f*; *(also: trade* ~*)* sindicato (de trabalhadores) ♦ *cpd* sindical; **Union Jack** *n* bandeira britânica
unique [juːˈniːk] *adj* único, sem igual
unison [ˈjuːnɪsn] *n*: **in** ~ em harmo-

nia, em uníssono
unit [ˈjuːnɪt] *n* unidade *f*; *(of furniture etc)* seção *f*; *(team, squad)* equipe *f*; **kitchen** ~ armário de cozinha
unite [juːˈnaɪt] *vt* unir ♦ *vi* unir-se;
united *adj* unido; *(effort)* conjunto; **United Kingdom** *n* Reino Unido; **United Nations (Organization)** *n* (Organização *f* das) Nações *fpl* Unidas; **United States (of America)** *n* Estados Unidos *mpl* (da América)
universal [juːnɪˈvəːsl] *adj* universal
universe [ˈjuːnɪvəːs] *n* universo
university [juːnɪˈvəːsɪtɪ] *n* universidade *f*
unjust [ʌnˈdʒʌst] *adj* injusto
unkempt [ʌnˈkɛmpt] *adj* desleixado, descuidado; *(hair)* despenteado; *(beard)* mal tratado
unkind [ʌnˈkaɪnd] *adj* maldoso; *(comment etc)* cruel
unknown [ʌnˈnəʊn] *adj* desconhecido
unlawful [ʌnˈlɔːful] *adj* ilegal
unleaded [ʌnˈlɛdɪd] *adj* *(petrol, fuel)* sem chumbo
unleash [ʌnˈliːʃ] *vt* *(fig)* desencadear
unless [ʌnˈlɛs] *conj* a menos que, a não ser que; ~ **he comes** a menos que ele venha
unlike [ʌnˈlaɪk] *adj* diferente ♦ *prep* diferentemente de, ao contrário de
unlikely [ʌnˈlaɪklɪ] *adj* *(not likely)* improvável; *(unexpected)* inesperado
unlisted [ʌnˈlɪstɪd] *(US) adj (TEL)* que não consta na lista telefônica
unload [ʌnˈləʊd] *vt* descarregar
unlock [ʌnˈlɔk] *vt* destrancar
unlucky [ʌnˈlʌkɪ] *adj* infeliz; *(object, number)* de mau agouro; **to be** ~ azarado, ter azar

unmarried [ʌnˈmærɪd] adj solteiro

unmistak(e)able [ʌnmɪsˈteɪkəbl] adj inconfundível

unnatural [ʌnˈnætʃrəl] adj antinatural, artificial; (manner) afetado; (habit) depravado

unnecessary [ʌnˈnɛsəsərɪ] adj desnecessário, inútil

unnoticed [ʌnˈnəʊtɪst] adj: (to go or pass) ~ (passar) despercebido

UNO [ˈjuːnəʊ] n abbr (= United Nations Organization) ONU f

unobtainable [ʌnəbˈteɪnəbl] adj inacessível; (TEL) ocupado

unofficial [ʌnəˈfɪʃl] adj não-oficial, informal; (strike) desautorizado

unpack [ʌnˈpæk] vi desembrulhar
♦ vt desfazer

unpalatable [ʌnˈpælətəbl] adj desagradável

unparalleled [ʌnˈpærəleld] adj sem paralelo

unpleasant [ʌnˈplɛznt] adj desagradável; (person, manner) antipático

unplug [ʌnˈplʌg] vt desligar

unpopular [ʌnˈpɒpjulə*] adj impopular

unprecedented [ʌnˈprɛsɪdəntɪd] adj sem precedentes

unpredictable [ʌnprɪˈdɪktəbl] adj imprevisível

unprofessional [ʌnprəˈfɛʃənl] adj (conduct) pouco profissional

unravel [ʌnˈrævl] vt desemaranhar; (mystery) desvendar

unreal [ʌnˈrɪəl] adj irreal, ilusório; (extraordinary) extraordinário

unrealistic [ʌnrɪəˈlɪstɪk] adj pouco realista

unreasonable [ʌnˈriːznəbl] adj insensato; (demand) absurdo

unrelated [ʌnrɪˈleɪtɪd] adj sem relação, (family) sem parentesco

unreliable [ʌnrɪˈlaɪəbl] adj (person)

indigno de confiança; (machine) incerto, perigoso

unrest [ʌnˈrɛst] n inquietação f, desassossego; (POL) distúrbios mpl

unroll [ʌnˈrəʊl] vt desenrolar

unruly [ʌnˈruːlɪ] adj indisciplinado; (hair) desalinhado

unsafe [ʌnˈseɪf] adj perigoso

unsatisfactory [ʌnsætɪsˈfæktərɪ] adj insatisfatório

unsavoury [ʌnˈseɪvərɪ] (US unsavory) adj (fig) repugnante, vil

unscrew [ʌnˈskruː] vt desparafusar

unscrupulous [ʌnˈskruːpjuləs] adj inescrupuloso, imoral

unsettled [ʌnˈsetld] adj (weather) instável; (person) inquieto

unshaven [ʌnˈʃeɪvn] adj com a barba por fazer

unsightly [ʌnˈsaɪtlɪ] adj feio, disforme

unskilled [ʌnˈskɪld] adj não-especializado

unspeakable [ʌnˈspiːkəbl] adj indescritível; (awful) inqualificável

unstable [ʌnˈsteɪbl] adj em falso; (mentally) instável

unsteady [ʌnˈstedɪ] adj trêmulo; (ladder) em falso

unstuck [ʌnˈstʌk] adj: to come ~ despregar-se; (fig) fracassar

unsuccessful [ʌnsəkˈsesful] adj (attempt) frustrado, vão (vã); (writer, proposal) sem êxito; to be ~ (in attempting sth) ser mal sucedido, não conseguir; (application) ser recusado

unsuitable [ʌnˈsuːtəbl] adj inadequado; (time) inconveniente

unsure [ʌnˈʃuə*] adj inseguro, incerto; to be ~ of o.s. não ser seguro de si

unsympathetic [ʌnsɪmpəˈθetɪk] adj insensível; (unlikeable) antipático

unthinkable [ʌnˈθɪŋkəbl] adj impensável, inconcebível, incalculável

untidy [ʌnˈtaɪdɪ] adj (room) desarrumado, desleixado; (appearance) desmazelado, desalinhado

untie [ʌnˈtaɪ] vt desatar, desfazer; (dog, prisoner) soltar

until [ənˈtɪl] prep até ♦ conj até que; ~ he comes até que ele venha; ~ now até agora; ~ then até então

unused [ʌnˈjuːzd] adj novo, sem uso

unusual [ʌnˈjuːʒuəl] adj (strange) estranho; (rare) incomum; (exceptional) extraordinário

unveil [ʌnˈveɪl] vt desvelar, descobrir

unwanted [ʌnˈwɔntɪd] adj não desejado, indesejável

unwelcome [ʌnˈwɛlkəm] adj (guest) inoportuno; (news) desagradável

unwell [ʌnˈwɛl] adj: to be ~ estar doente; to feel ~ estar indisposto

unwilling [ʌnˈwɪlɪŋ] adj: to be ~ to do sth relutar em fazer algo, não querer fazer algo; **unwillingly** adv de má vontade

unwind [ʌnˈwaɪnd] (irreg) vt desenrolar ♦ vi (relax) relaxar-se

unwise [ʌnˈwaɪz] adj imprudente

unworthy [ʌnˈwəːðɪ] adj indigno

unwrap [ʌnˈræp] vt desembrulhar

unwritten [ʌnˈrɪtən] adj (agreement) tácito

KEYWORD

up [ʌp] prep: to go/be ~ sth subir algo/estar em cima de algo; we climbed/walked ~ the hill nós subimos/andamos até em cima da colina; they live further ~ the street eles moram mais adiante nesta rua ♦ adv 1 (upwards, higher) em cima, para cima; ~ in the sky/the mountains lá no céu/nas montanhas; ~ there lá em cima; ~ above em cima 2: to be ~ (out of bed) estar de pé; (prices, level) estar elevado; (building, tent) estar erguido

3: ~ to (as far as) até; ~ to now até agora

4: to be ~ (depending on): it is ~ to you você é quem sabe, você decide

5: to be ~ (equal to) estar à altura; he's not ~ to it (job, task etc) ele não é capaz de fazê-lo; his work is not ~ to the required standard seu trabalho não atende aos padrões exigidos

6: to be ~ to (inf: be doing) estar fazendo (BR) or a fazer (PT); what is he ~ to? o que ele está querendo?, o que ele está tramando?

♦ n: ~s and downs altos mpl e baixos mpl

upbringing [ˈʌpbrɪŋɪŋ] n educação f, criação f

update [ʌpˈdeɪt] vt atualizar, pôr em dia

upgrade [ʌpˈgreɪd] vt (person) promover; (job) melhorar; (house) reformar

upheaval [ʌpˈhiːvl] n transtorno; (unrest) convulsão f

uphill [ʌpˈhɪl] adj ladeira acima; (fig: task) trabalhoso, árduo ♦ adv: to go ~ ir morro acima; (face, look) para cima

uphold [ʌpˈhəʊld] (irreg: like hold) vt defender, preservar

upholstery [ʌpˈhəʊlstərɪ] n estofamento

upkeep [ˈʌpkiːp] n manutenção f

upon [əˈpɔn] prep sobre

upper [ˈʌpə*] adj superior, de cima ♦ n (of shoe) gáspea, parte f superior; **upper-class** adj de classe alta; **upper hand** n: to have the upper hand ter controle or domínio; **uppermost** adj mais elevado; what was uppermost in my mind o que me preocupava mais

upright ['ʌpraɪt] adj vertical; (straight) reto; (fig) honesto

uprising ['ʌpraɪzɪŋ] n revolta, rebelião f, sublevação f

uproar ['ʌprɔ:*] n tumulto, algazarra f

uproot [ʌp'ru:t] vt (tree) arrancar; (fig) desarraigar

upset [n 'ʌpset, vb, adj ʌp'set (irreg: like set) n (to plan etc) revés m, reviravolta; (stomach ~) indisposição f ♦ vt (glass etc) virar; (plan) perturbar; (person: annoy) aborrecer ♦ adj aflito; (stomach) indisposto

upshot ['ʌpʃɔt] n resultado, conclusão f

upside down ['ʌpsaɪd-] adv de cabeça para baixo; **to turn a place ~** (fig) deixar um lugar de cabeça para baixo

upstairs [ʌp'stɛəz] adv (be) em cima; (go) lá em cima ♦ adj (room) de cima ♦ n andar de cima

upstart ['ʌpstɑ:t] (pej) n novo-rico, pessoa sem classe

upstream [ʌp'stri:m] adv rio acima

uptight [ʌp'taɪt] (inf) adj nervoso

up-to-date adj (person) moderno, atualizado; (information) atualizado

upward ['ʌpwəd] adj ascendente, para cima; **upward(s)** adv para cima; (more than): **upward(s) of** para cima de

urban ['ə:bən] adj urbano, da cidade

urge [ə:dʒ] n desejo ♦ vt: **to ~ sb to do sth** incitar alguém a fazer algo

urgent ['ə:dʒənt] adj urgente; (tone, plea) insistente

urinal ['juərɪnl] (BRIT) n (vessel) urinol m; (building) mictório

urine ['juərɪn] n urina

urn [ə:n] n urna; (also: **tea ~**) samovar m

Uruguay ['juərəgwaɪ] n Uruguai m

us [ʌs] pron nos; (after prep) nós; see also **me**

US(A) n abbr (= United States (of America)) EUA mpl

use [n ju:s, vb ju:z] n uso, emprego, (usefulness) utilidade f ♦ vt usar, utilizar; (phrase) empregar; **in ~** em uso; **out of ~** fora de uso; **to be of ~** ser útil; **it's no ~** (pointless) é inútil; (not useful) não serve; **to be ~d to** estar acostumado a; **she ~d to do it** ela costumava fazê-lo; **use up** vt esgotar, consumir; (money) gastar; **used** [ju:zd] adj usado; **useful** ['ju:sful] adj útil; **usefulness** n utilidade f; **useless** ['ju:slɪs] adj inútil; (person) incapaz; **user** ['ju:zə*] n usuário(-a) (BR), utente m/f (PT); **user-friendly** adj de fácil utilização

usher ['ʌʃə*] n (at wedding) oficial m de justiça; **usherette** [ʌʃə'ret] n (in cinema) lanterninha (BR), arrumadora (PT)

usual ['ju:ʒuəl] adj usual, habitual; **as ~** como de hábito, como sempre; **usually** ['ju:ʒuəlɪ] adv normalmente

utensil [ju:'tensl] n utensílio

utmost ['ʌtməust] adj maior ♦ n: **to do one's ~** fazer todo o possível

utter ['ʌtə*] adj total ♦ vt (sounds) emitir; (words) proferir, pronunciar; **utterly** adv completamente, totalmente

U-turn n retorno

V

v abbr = **verse**; (= vide: see) vide; (= versus) x; (= volt) v

vacancy ['veɪkənsɪ] n (BRIT: job) vaga; (room) quarto livre

vacant ['veɪkənt] adj desocupado, livre; (expression) distraído

vacate [və'keɪt] vt (house) desocupar; (job) deixar

vacation [vəˈkeɪʃən] n (esp US) férias fpl

vaccinate [ˈvæksɪneɪt] vt vacinar

vacuum [ˈvækjum] n vácuo m; **vacuum cleaner** n aspirador m de pó

vagina [vəˈdʒaɪnə] n vagina

vagrant [ˈveɪgrənt] n vagabundo(-a), vadio(-a)

vague [veɪg] adj vago; (blurred: memory) fraco; **vaguely** adv vagamente

vain [veɪn] adj vaidoso; (useless) vão (vã) inútil; **in ~** em vão

valentine [ˈvæləntaɪn] n (also: ~ card) cartão m do Dia dos Namorados; (person) namorado

valiant [ˈvæliənt] adj corajoso

valid [ˈvælɪd] adj válido

valley [ˈvælɪ] n vale m

valuable [ˈvæljuəbl] adj (jewel) de valor; (time) valioso; (help) precioso; **valuables** npl objetos mpl de valor

valuation [væljuˈeɪʃən] n avaliação f; (of quality) apreciação f

value [ˈvæljuː] n valor m; (importance) importância ♦ vt (fix price of) avaliar; (appreciate) valorizar, estimar; **~s** npl (principles) valores mpl; **valued** adj (appreciated) valorizado

valve [vælv] n válvula

van [væn] n (AUT) camionete f (BR), camioneta (PT)

vandal [ˈvændl] n vândalo(-a); **vandalize** vt destruir, depredar

vanilla [vəˈnɪlə] n baunilha

vanish [ˈvænɪʃ] vi desaparecer, sumir

vanity [ˈvænɪtɪ] n vaidade f

vapour [ˈveɪpə*] (US **vapor**) n vapor m

variety [vəˈraɪətɪ] n variedade f, diversidade f; (type, quantity) variedade

various [ˈvɛərɪəs] adj vários(-as), diversos(-as); (several) vários(-as)

varnish [ˈvɑːnɪʃ] n verniz m; (nail ~) esmalte m ♦ vt envernizar, pintar (com esmalte)

vary [ˈvɛərɪ] vt mudar ♦ vi variar; (become different): **to ~ with** variar de acordo com

vase [vɑːz] n vaso

vaseline [ˈvæsɪliːn] ® n vaselina ®

vast [vɑːst] adj enorme

VAT [væt] (BRIT) n abbr (= value added tax) ≈ ICM m (BR), IVA m (PT)

vat [væt] n tina, cuba

vault [vɔːlt] n (of roof) abóbada; (tomb) sepulcro; (in bank) caixaforte f ♦ vt (also: ~ over) saltar (por cima de)

VCR n abbr = video cassette recorder

VDU n abbr = visual display unit

veal [viːl] n carne f de vitela

veer [vɪə*] vi virar

vegan [ˈviːgən] n vegetalista m/f

vegetable [ˈvedʒtəbl] n (BOT) vegetal m; (edible plant) legume m, hortaliça ♦ adj vegetal

vegetarian [vedʒɪˈtɛərɪən] adj, n vegetariano(-a)

vehement [ˈviːɪmənt] adj veemente; (attack) violento

vehicle [ˈviːɪkl] n veículo

veil [veɪl] n véu m ♦ vt velar

vein [veɪn] n veia; (of ore etc) filão m; (on leaf) nervura

velvet [ˈvelvɪt] n veludo ♦ adj aveludado

vending machine [ˈvendɪŋ-] n vendedor m automático

veneer [vəˈnɪə*] n (in wood) compensado; (fig) aparência

venereal [vɪˈnɪərɪəl] adj: **~ disease** doença venérea

Venetian blind [vɪˈniːʃən-] n persiana

Venezuela [venɛˈzweɪlə] n Venezuela

vengeance [ˈvɛndʒəns] n vingança; **with a ~** (fig) para valer

venison [ˈvɛnɪsn] n carne f de veado

venom [ˈvɛnəm] n veneno; (bitterness) malevolência

vent [vɛnt] n (in jacket) abertura; (also: **air ~**) respiradouro ♦ vt (fig: feelings) desabafar, descarregar

ventriloquist [vɛnˈtrɪləkwɪst] n ventríloquo

venture [ˈvɛntʃə*] n empreendimento ♦ vt (opinion) arriscar ♦ vi arriscar-se; **business ~** empreendimento comercial

venue [ˈvɛnjuː] n local m

verb [vəːb] n verbo

verbatim [vəːˈbeɪtɪm] adj, adv palavra por palavra

verdict [ˈvəːdɪkt] n veredicto, decisão f; (fig) opinião f, parecer m

verge [vəːdʒ] n beira, margem f; (on road) acostamento (BR), berma (PT); **"soft ~s"** (BRIT: AUT) "acostamento mole"; **to be on the ~ of doing sth** estar a ponto or à beira de fazer algo; **verge on** vt fus beirar em

vermin [ˈvəːmɪn] npl (animals) bichos mpl; (insects) insetos mpl nocivos

vermouth [ˈvəːməθ] n vermute m

versatile [ˈvəːsətaɪl] adj (person) versátil; (machine, tool etc) polivalente

verse [vəːs] n verso, poesia; (stanza) estrofe f; (in bible) versículo

version [ˈvəːʃən] n versão f

versus [ˈvəːsəs] prep contra, versus

vertical [ˈvəːtɪkl] adj vertical

vertigo [ˈvəːtɪgəu] n vertigem f

verve [vəːv] n garra, pique m

very [ˈvɛrɪ] adv muito ♦ adj: **the ~ book which** o mesmo livro que; **the ~ last** o último (de todos), bem o último; **at the ~ least** no mínimo; **~ much** muitíssimo

vessel [ˈvɛsl] n (NAUT) navio, barco; (container) vaso, vasilha

vest [vɛst] n (BRIT) camiseta (BR), camisola interior (PT); (US: waistcoat) colete m

vet [vɛt] n abbr (= veterinary surgeon) veterinário(-a) ♦ vt examinar

veteran [ˈvɛtərn] n (also: **war ~**) veterano de guerra

veto [ˈviːtəu] (pl **~es**) n veto ♦ vt vetar

vex [vɛks] vt irritar, apoquentar; **vexed** adj (question) controvertido, discutido

via [ˈvaɪə] prep por, via

vibrate [vaɪˈbreɪt] vi vibrar

vicar [ˈvɪkə*] n vigário; **vicarage** n vicariato

vice [vaɪs] n (evil) vício; (TECH) torno mecânico

vice- [vaɪs] prefix vice-

vice versa [ˈvaɪsɪˈvəːsə] adv vice-versa

vicinity [vɪˈsɪnɪtɪ] n: **in the ~ of** nas proximidades de

vicious [ˈvɪʃəs] adj violento; (cruel) cruel; **vicious circle** n círculo vicioso

victim [ˈvɪktɪm] n vítima f

victor [ˈvɪktə*] n vencedor(a) m/f

Victorian [vɪkˈtɔːrɪən] adj vitoriano

victory [ˈvɪktərɪ] n vitória

video [ˈvɪdɪəu] n (~ film) vídeo; (also: **~ cassette**) videocassete m; (also: **~ cassette recorder**) videocassete m

Vienna [vɪˈɛnə] n Viena

Vietnam ['vjet'næm] n Vietnã m;
Vietnamese [vjetnə'mi:z] adj vietnamita ♦ n inv vietnamita m/f; (LING)
vietnamita m

view [vju:] n vista; (outlook) perspectiva; (opinion) opinião f, parecer
m ♦ vt olhar; in full ~ (of) à plena
vista (de); in my ~ na minha opinião; in ~ of the weather/the fact
that em vista do tempo/do fato de
que; **viewer** n telespectador/a
m/f; **viewfinder** n visor m; **viewpoint** n ponto de vista; (place)
lugar m

vigorous ['vɪgərəs] adj vigoroso;
(plant) vigoso

vile [vaɪl] adj vil, infame; (smell)
repugnante, repulsivo; (temper) violento

villa ['vɪlə] n (country house) casa de
campo; (suburban house) vila, quinta

village ['vɪlɪdʒ] n aldeia, povoado;
villager n aldeão (aldeã) m/f

villain ['vɪlən] n (scoundrel) patife
m; (in novel etc) vilão m; (BRIT: criminal) marginal m/f

vindicate ['vɪndɪkeɪt] vt vingar;
(justify) justificar

vindictive [vɪn'dɪktɪv] adj vingativo

vine [vaɪn] n planta trepadeira

vinegar ['vɪnɪgə*] n vinagre m

vineyard ['vɪnjɑ:d] n vinha, vinhe-
do

vintage ['vɪntɪdʒ] n vindima; (year)
safra, colheita ♦ cpd (comedy) de
época; (performance) clássico; the
1970 ~ a safra de 1970; **vintage
car** n carro antigo; **vintage wine**
n vinho velho

viola [vɪ'əʊlə] n viola

violate ['vaɪəleɪt] vt violar

violence ['vaɪələns] n violência;
(strength) força

violent ['vaɪələnt] adj violento;
(intense) intenso

violet ['vaɪələt] adj violeta ♦ n violeta

violin [vaɪə'lɪn] n violino; **violinist**
[vaɪə'lɪnɪst] n violinista m/f

VIP n abbr (= very important person)
VIP m/f

virgin ['vɜːdʒɪn] n virgem m/f ♦ adj
virgem

Virgo ['vɜːgəʊ] n Virgem f

virtually ['vɜːtjʊəlɪ] adv pratica-
mente

virtue ['vɜːtju:] n virtude f; (advantage) vantagem f; **by ~ of** em virtude de

virtuous ['vɜːtjʊəs] adj virtuoso

virus ['vaɪərəs] n vírus m

visa ['viːzə] n visto

visible ['vɪzəbl] adj visível

vision ['vɪʒən] n (sight) vista, visão
f; (foresight, in dream) visão f

visit ['vɪzɪt] n visita ♦ vt (person: us:
also: ~ with) visitar, fazer uma visita
a; (place) ir a, ir conhecer; **visiting
hours** npl horário de visita; **visitor**
n visitante m/f; (to one's house) visita; (tourist) turista m/f

visor ['vaɪzə*] n viseira

visual ['vɪzjʊəl] adj visual; **visual
display unit** n terminal m de
vídeo; **visualize** vt visualizar

vital ['vaɪtl] adj essencial, indispensável; (important) de importância
vital; (crucial) crucial; (person) vivo;
(of life) vital; **vitally** adv: **~ly
important** de importância vital

vitamin ['vɪtəmɪn] n vitamina

vivacious [vɪ'veɪʃəs] adj vivaz, animado

vivid ['vɪvɪd] adj (account) vívido;
(light) claro, brilhante; (imagination,
colour) vivo; **vividly** adv vividamen-
te; (remember) distintamente

V-neck n: **~ jumper, ~ pullover** suéter f com decote em V

vocabulary [vəuˈkæbjulərɪ] n vocabulário

vocal [ˈvəukl] adj vocal; (noisy) clamoroso; (articulate) claro, eloqüente; **vocal cords** npl cordas fpl vocais

vocation [vəuˈkeɪʃən] n vocação f

vociferous [vəˈsɪfərəs] adj vociferante

vodka [ˈvɒdkə] n vodca

vogue [vəug] n voga, moda; **to be in** ~ estar na moda

voice [vɔɪs] n voz f ♦ vt expressar; **voice mail** n (TEL) correio m de voz

void [vɔɪd] n vazio; (hole) oco ♦ adj nulo; (empty): ~ **of** destituído de

volatile [ˈvɒlətaɪl] adj volátil; (situation, person) imprevisível

volcano [vɒlˈkeɪnəu] n (pl ~es) n vulcão m

volley [ˈvɒlɪ] n (of gunfire) descarga, salva; (of stones etc) chuva; (of questions etc) enxurrada, chuva; (TENNIS etc) voleio; **volleyball** n voleibol m, vôlei m (BR)

volt [vəult] n volt m

volume [ˈvɒljuːm] n volume m; (of tank) capacidade f

voluntarily [ˈvɒləntrɪlɪ] adv livremente, voluntariamente

voluntary [ˈvɒləntərɪ] adj voluntário; (unpaid) a título gratuito

volunteer [vɒlənˈtɪə*] n voluntário(-a) ♦ vt oferecer voluntariamente ♦ vi (MIL) alistar-se voluntariamente; **to ~ to do** oferecer-se voluntariamente para fazer

vomit [ˈvɒmɪt] n vômito ♦ vt, vi vomitar

vote [vəut] n voto; (votes cast) votação f; (right to ~) direito de votar ♦ vt ♦ vi: **to be ~d chairman** etc ser eleito presidente etc; (propose): **to ~ that** propor que; (in election) votar

♦ vi votar; **voter** n votante m/f, eleitor(a) m/f

voucher [ˈvautʃə*] n (also: lunch-eon ~) vale-refeição m; (with petrol etc) vale m; (gift ~) vale m para presente

vouch for [vautʃ-] vt fus garantir, responder por

vow [vau] n voto ♦ vt: **to ~ to do/ that** prometer solenemente fazer/ que

vowel [ˈvauəl] n vogal f

voyage [ˈvɔɪdʒ] n viagem f

vulgar [ˈvʌlgə*] adj grosseiro, ordinário; (in bad taste) vulgar, baixo

vulture [ˈvʌltʃə*] n abutre m, urubu m

W

wad [wɒd] n (of cotton wool) chumaço; (of paper) bola; (of banknotes etc) maço

wade [weɪd] vi: **to ~ through** andar em; (fig: a book) ler com dificuldade

wafer [ˈweɪfə*] n (biscuit) bolacha

waffle [ˈwɒfl] n (CULIN) waffle m; (empty talk) lengalenga ♦ vi encher lingüiça

waft [wɒft] vt levar ♦ vi flutuar

wag [wæg] vt (tail) sacudir; (finger) menear ♦ vi abanar

wage [weɪdʒ] n (also: ~s) salário, ordenado ♦ vt: **to ~ war** empreender or fazer guerra; **wage earner** n assalariado(-a)

wager [ˈweɪdʒə*] n aposta, parada

wag(g)on [ˈwægən] n (horse-drawn) carroça; (BRIT: RAIL) vagão m

wail [weɪl] n lamento, gemido ♦ vi lamentar-se, gemer; (siren) soar

waist [weɪst] n cintura; **waistcoat** n colete m; **waistline** n cintura

wait [weɪt] n espera ♦ vi esperar;

can't ~ to (fig) estou morrendo de vontade de; **to ~ for sb/sth** esperar por alguém/algo; **wait behind** vi ficar para trás; **wait on** vt fus servir; **waiter** n garçom m (BR), empregado (PT); **waiting list** n lista de espera; **waiting room** n sala de espera; **waitress** n garçonete f (BR), empregada (PT)

waive [weɪv] vt abrir mão de

wake [weɪk] (pt **woke** or **~d**, pp **woken** or **~d**) vt (also: **~ up**) acordar ♦ vi acordar ♦ n (for dead person) velório; (NAUT) esteira

Wales [weɪlz] n País m de Gales

walk [wɔːk] n passeio m; (hike) excursão f a pé, caminhada; (gait) passo, modo de andar; (path etc) alameda, passeio ♦ vi andar; (for pleasure, exercise) passear ♦ vt (distance) percorrer a pé, andar; (dog) levar para passear; **it's 10 minutes' ~ from here** daqui são 10 minutos a pé; **people from all ~s of life** pessoas de todos os níveis; **walk out** vi sair; (audience) retirar-se (em protesto); (strike) entrar em greve; **walk out on** vt fus abandonar; **walkie-talkie** n transmissor-receptor m portátil, walkie-talkie m; **walking** n o andar; **walking shoes** npl sapatos mpl para caminhar; **walking stick** n bengala; **Walkman** ® n Walkman ® m; **walkover** (inf) n barbada; **walkway** n passeio, passadiço

wall [wɔːl] n parede f; (exterior) muro; (city ~ etc) muralha; **walled** adj (city) cercado por muralhas; (garden) murado, cercado

wallet ['wɔlɪt] n carteira

wallow ['wɔləʊ] vi (in mud) chafurdar; (in water) rolar; (person: in guilt) regalar-se

wallpaper ['wɔːlpeɪpə*] n papel m

de parede ♦ vt colocar papel de parede em

walnut ['wɔːlnʌt] n noz f; (tree, wood) nogueira

walrus ['wɔːlrəs] (pl inv or **~es**) n morsa, vaca marinha

waltz [wɔːls] n valsa ♦ vi valsar

wand [wɔnd] n (also: **magic ~**) varinha de condão

wander ['wɔndə*] vi (person) vagar, perambular; (thoughts) divagar ♦ vt perambular

wane [weɪn] vi diminuir; (moon) minguar

want [wɔnt] vt querer; (demand) exigir; (need) precisar de, necessitar; **to ~ sb to do sth** querer que alguém faça algo; **wanted** adj (criminal) procurado (pela polícia); **"cook wanted"** (in advertisement) "precisa-se cozinheiro"

war [wɔː*] n guerra; **to make ~ (on)** fazer guerra (contra)

ward [wɔːd] n (in hospital) ala; (POL) distrito eleitoral; (LAW: child) tutelado(-a), pupilo(-a); **ward off** vt desviar, aparar; (attack) repelir

warden ['wɔːdn] n (BRIT: of institution) diretor(a) m/f; (of park, youth hostel) administrador(a) m/f; (BRIT: also: **traffic ~**) guarda m/f

warder ['wɔːdə*] (BRIT) n carcereiro(-a)

wardrobe ['wɔːdrəʊb] n guarda-roupa m; (CINEMA, THEATRE) figurinos mpl

warehouse ['wɛəhaʊs] n armazém m, depósito

warfare ['wɔːfɛə*] n guerra, combate m

warhead ['wɔːhɛd] n ogiva

warm [wɔːm] adj quente; (thanks, welcome) caloroso; **it's ~** está quente; **I'm ~** estou com calor; **warm up** vt, vi esquentar; **warm-**

hearted *adj* afetuoso; **warmly** *adv* (*applaud*, *welcome*) calorosamente; (*dress*): **to dress warmly** vestir-se com roupas de inverno; **warmth** *n* calor *m*; (*friendliness*) calor humano

warn [wɔ:n] *vt* prevenir, avisar; **to sb that/of/(not) to do** prevenir alguém de que/de/para (não) fazer

warning ['wɔ:nɪŋ] *n* advertência; (*in writing*) aviso; (*signal*) sinal *m*

warp [wɔ:p] *vt* deformar ♦ *vi* empenar, deformar-se

warrant ['wɔrnt] *n* (*voucher*) comprovante *m*; (LAW: *to arrest*) mandado de prisão; (: *to search*) mandado de busca; **warranty** *n* garantia

warrior ['wɔrɪə*] *n* guerreiro(-a)

Warsaw ['wɔ:sɔ:] *n* Varsóvia

warship ['wɔ:ʃɪp] *n* navio de guerra

wart [wɔ:t] *n* verruga

wartime ['wɔ:taɪm] *n*: **in ~** em tempo de guerra

wary ['wɛərɪ] *adj* cauteloso, precavido

was [wɔz] *pt of* **be**

wash [wɔʃ] *vt* lavar ♦ *vi* lavar-se; (*subj*: ~*ing machine*) lavar; (*sea etc*): **to ~ over/against sth** bater contra/chocar-se contra algo; (*clothes*): **this shirt ~es well** esta camisa resiste bem à lavagem ♦ *n* (*clothes etc*) lavagem *f*; (~*ing programme*) programa *m* de lavagem; (*of ship*) esteira; **to have a ~** lavar-se; **wash away** *vt* (*stain*) tirar ao lavar; (*subj*: *river etc*) levar, arrastar; **wash off** *vt* tirar lavando ♦ *vi* sair ao lavar; **wash up** *vi* (BRIT) lavar a louça; (US) lavar-se; **washbasin** *n* pia (BR), lavatório (PT); **washcloth** (US) *n* toalhinha para lavar o rosto; **washing** *n* (*dirty*) roupa suja; (*clean*) roupa lavada; **washing machine** *n* máquina de lavar roupa, lavadora; **washing powder** (BRIT) *n* sabão *m*

em pó; **washing-up** *n*: **to do the washing-up** lavar a louça; **washing-up liquid** *n* detergente *m*; **wash-out** (*inf*) *n* fracasso, fiasco; **washroom** (US) *n* banheiro (BR), casa de banho (PT)

wasn't ['wɔznt] = **was not**

wasp [wɔsp] *n* vespa

wastage ['weɪstɪdʒ] *n* desgaste *m*, desperdício; (*loss*) perda

waste [weɪst] *n* desperdício, esbanjamento; (*of time*) perda; (*also*: **household ~**) detritos *mpl* domésticos; (*rubbish*) lixo ♦ *adj* (*material*) de refugo; (*left over*) de sobra; (*land*) baldio ♦ *vt* (*squander*) esbanjar, desperdiçar; (*time*, *opportunity*) perder; ~**s** *npl* (*land*) ermos *mpl*; **to lay ~** devastar; **waste away** *vi* definhar; **wasteful** *adj* esbanjador(a); (*process*) anti-econômico; **wastepaper basket** *n* cesta de papéis

watch [wɔtʃ] *n* (*clock*) relógio; (*also*: **wrist~**) relógio de pulso; (*act of* ~*ing*) vigia; (*guard*: MIL) sentinela; (NAUT: *spell of duty*) quarto ♦ *vt* (*look at*) observar, olhar; (*programme*, *match*) assistir a; (*television*) ver; (*spy on*, *guard*) vigiar; (*be careful of*) tomar cuidado com ♦ *vi* ver, olhar; (*keep guard*) montar guarda; **watch out** *vi* ter cuidado; **watchdog** *n* cão *m* de guarda; (*fig*) vigia *m/f*; **watchful** *adj* vigilante, atento; **watchmaker** *n* relojoeiro(-a); **watchman** (*irreg*) *n* see **night**; **watchstrap** *n* pulseira de relógio

water ['wɔ:tə*] *n* água ♦ *vt* (*plant*) regar ♦ *vi* (*eyes*) lacrimejar; (*mouth*) salivar; **in British ~s** nas águas territoriais britânicas; **water down** *vt* (*milk*) aguar; (*fig*) diluir; **watercolour** (US **watercolor**) *n* aquarela; **waterfall** *n* cascata, cachoeira;

watering can n regador m; **water lily** n nenúfar m; **waterline** n (NAUT) linha d'água; **waterlogged** adj alagado; **watermelon** n melancia; **waterproof** adj impermeável; **watershed** n (GEO) linha divisória das águas; (fig) momento crítico; **water-skiing** n esqui m aquático; **watertight** adj hermético, à prova d'água; **waterworks** npl usina hidráulica; **watery** adj (eyes) húmido

watt [wɔt] n watt m

wave [weɪv] n onda; (of hand) aceno, sinal m; (in hair) onda, ondulação ♦ vi acenar com a mão; (flag, grass) tremular ♦ vt (hand) acenar; (handkerchief) acenar com; (weapon) brandir; **wavelength** n comprimento de onda; **to be on the same wavelength as** ter os mesmos gostos e atitudes que

waver ['weɪvə*] vi vacilar; (voice, eyes, love) hesitar

wavy ['weɪvɪ] adj (hair) ondulado; (line) ondulante

wax [wæks] n cera ♦ vt encerar; (car) polir ♦ vi (moon) crescer; **waxworks** n museu m de cera ♦ npl (models) figuras fpl de cera

way [weɪ] n caminho; (distance) percurso; (direction) direção f, sentido; (manner) maneira, modo; (habit) costume m; **which ~? - this ~** por onde? - por aqui; **on the ~ (to)** a caminho (de); **to be on one's ~** estar a caminho; **to be in the ~** atrapalhar; **to go out of one's ~ to do sth** dar-se ao trabalho de fazer algo; **to lose one's ~** perder-se; **to be under ~** estar em andamento; **in a ~** de certo modo, até certo ponto; **in some ~s** a certos respeitos; **by the ~** a propósito; **"~ in"** (BRIT) "entrada"; **"~ out"** (BRIT) "saída";

the ~ back o caminho de volta; **"give ~"** (BRIT: AUT) "dê a preferência"; **no ~!** (inf) de jeito nenhum!; **waylay** vt armar uma cilada para; **wayward** adj caprichoso, voluntarioso

WC ['dʌblju:'si:] n abbr (= water closet) privada

we [wi:] pl pron nós

weak [wi:k] adj fraco, débil; (morally, currency) fraco; (excuse) pouco convincente; (tea) aguado, ralo; **weaken** vi enfraquecer(-se); (give way) ceder; (influence, power) diminuir ♦ vt enfraquecer; **weakling** n pessoa fraca ou delicada; (morally) pessoa de personalidade fraca; **weakness** n fraqueza; (fault) ponto fraco; **to have a weakness for** ter uma queda por

wealth [wεlθ] n riqueza; (of details) abundância; **wealthy** adj rico, abastado; (country) rico

wean [wi:n] vt desmamar

weapon ['wεpən] n arma

wear [wεə*] (pt wore, pp worn) n (use) uso; (deterioration) desgaste m; (clothing): **baby/sports ~** roupa infantil/de esporte ♦ vt (clothes) usar; (shoes) usar, calçar; (put on) vestir; (damage: through use) desgastar ♦ vi (last) durar; (rub through etc) gastar-se; **town/evening ~** traje m de passeio/de noite; **wear away** vt gastar ♦ vi desgastar-se; **wear down** vt gastar; (strength) esgotar; **wear off** vi (pain etc) passar; **wear out** vt desgastar; (person, strength) esgotar; **wear and tear** n desgaste m

weary ['wɪərɪ] adj cansado; (dispirited) deprimido ♦ vi: **to ~ of** cansar-se de

weasel ['wi:zl] n (ZOOL) doninha

weather ['wεðə*] n tempo ♦ vt

(*storm, crisis*) resistir a; **under the ~** (*fig: ill*) doente; **weather-beaten** *adj* curtido; (*building, stone*) castigado, erodido; **weather forecast** *n* previsão *f* do tempo; **weatherman** (*irreg: inf*) *n* meteorologista *m*

weave [wiːv] (*pt* **wove**, *pp* **woven**) *vt* tecer

web [web] *n* (*of spider*) teia; (*on foot*) membrana; (*network*) rede *f*; **the (World Wide) W~** a (World Wide) Web; **website** ['websaɪt] *n* site *m*, website *m*

wed [wed] (*pt, pp* **~ded**) *vt* casar *vi* casar-se

we'd [wiːd] = **we had**; **we would**

wedding ['wedɪŋ] *n* casamento, núpcias *fpl*; **silver/golden ~** (*anniversary*) bodas *fpl* de prata/de ouro; **wedding dress** *n* vestido de noiva; **wedding ring** *n* anel *m* or aliança de casamento

wedge [wedʒ] *n* (*of wood etc*) cunha, calço; (*of cake*) fatia *vt* (*pack tightly*) apinhar; (*door*) pôr calço em

Wednesday ['wednzdɪ] *n* quarta-feira

wee [wiː] (*SCOTTISH*) *adj* pequeno, pequenino

weed [wiːd] *n* erva daninha *vt* capinar; **weedkiller** *n* herbicida *m*; **weedy** *adj* (*man*) fraquinho

week [wiːk] *n* semana; **a ~ today** daqui a uma semana; **a ~ on Tuesday** sem ser essa terça-feira, a próxima; **weekday** *n* dia *m* de semana; (*COMM*) dia útil; **weekend** *n* fim *m* de semana; **weekly** *adv* semanalmente *adj* semanal *n* semanário

weep [wiːp] (*pt, pp* **wept**) *vi* (*person*) chorar; **weeping willow** *n* salgueiro chorão

weigh [weɪ] *vt, vi* pesar; **to ~ anchor**

levantar ferro; **weigh down** *vt* sobrecarregar; (*fig: with worry*) deprimir, acabrunhar; **weigh up** *vt* ponderar, avaliar

weight [weɪt] *n* peso; **to lose/put on ~** emagrecer/engordar; **weight-lifter** *n* levantador *m* de pesos; **weighty** *adj* pesado; (*matters*) importante

weir [wɪə*] *n* represa, açude *m*

weird [wɪəd] *adj* esquisito, estranho

welcome ['welkəm] *adj* bem-vindo *n* boas-vindas, recepção *f* *vt* dar as boas-vindas a; (*be glad of*) saudar; **you're ~** (*after thanks*) de nada

weld [weld] *n* solda *vt* soldar, unir

welfare ['welfeə*] *n* bem-estar *m*; (*social aid*) assistência social; **welfare state** *n* país auto-financiador da sua assistência social

well [wel] *n* poço *adv* bem *adj*: **to be ~** estar bem (de saúde) *excl* bem!, então!; **as ~ também**; **as ~ as** assim como; **~ done!** muito bem!; **get ~ soon!** melhoras!; **to do ~** ir or sair-se bem; (*business*) ir bem; **well up** *vi* brotar

we'll [wiːl] = **we will**; **we shall**

well: well-behaved *adj* bem comportado; **well-being** *n* bem-estar *m*; **well-built** *adj* robusto; **well-deserved** *adj* bem merecido; **well-dressed** *adj* bem vestido

wellingtons ['welɪŋtənz] *n* (*also:* **wellington boots**) botas *de* borracha até os joelhos

well: well-known *adj* conhecido; **well-meaning** *adj* bem intencionado; **well-off** *adj* próspero, rico; **well-read** *adj* lido, versado; **well-to-do** *adj* abastado

Welsh [welʃ] *adj* galês (galesa) *n* (*LING*) galês *m*; **the ~** *npl* (*people*) os galeses; **Welshman** (*irreg*) *n* galês *m*; **Welshwoman** (*irreg*) *n* galesa

went [wɛnt] *pt of* **go**
wept [wɛpt] *pt, pp of* **weep**
were [wɜ:*] *pt of* **be**
we're [wɪə*] = **we are**
weren't [wɜ:nt] = **were not**
west [wɛst] *n* oeste *m* ♦ *adj* ocidental, do oeste ♦ *adv* para o oeste *or* ao oeste; **the W~** (*POL*) o Oeste, o Ocidente; **West Country** (*BRIT*) *n*: **the West Country** o sudoeste da Inglaterra; **westerly** *adj* (*situation*) ocidental; (*wind*) oeste; **western** *adj* ocidental ♦ *n* (*CINEMA*) western *m*, bangue-bangue (*BR: INF*); **West Indian** *adj, n* antilhano(-a); **West Indies** *npl* Antilhas *fpl*; **westward(s)** *adv* para o oeste
wet [wɛt] *adj* molhado; (*damp*) úmido; (~ *through*) encharcado; (*rainy*) chuvoso ♦ *n* (*BRIT: POL*) político de tendência moderada; **to get** ~ molhar-se; "~ **paint**" "tinta fresca"; **wetsuit** *n* roupa de mergulho
we've [wi:v] = **we have**
whale [weɪl] *n* (*ZOOL*) baleia
wharf [wɔ:f] (*pl* **wharves**) *n* cais *m inv*

KEYWORD

what [wɔt] *adj* **1** (*in direct/indirect questions*) que, qual; ~ **size is it?** que tamanho é este?; ~ **colour/shape is it?** qual é a cor/o formato?; **he asked me** ~ **books I needed** ele me perguntou de quais os livros eu precisava
2 (*in exclamations*) quê!, como!; ~ **a mess!** que bagunça!
♦ *pron* **1** (*interrogative*) que, o que; ~ **are you doing?** o que é que você está fazendo?; ~ **is it called?** como se chama?; ~ **about me?** e eu?; ~ **about doing ...?** que tal fazer ...?
2 (*relative*) o que; **I saw** ~ **you did/was on the table** eu vi o que você

fez/estava na mesa; **he asked me** ~ **she had said** ele me perguntou o que ela tinha dito
♦ *excl* (*disbelieving*): ~, **no coffee!** o que, não tem café!

whatever [wɔt'ɛvə*] *adj*: ~ **book** qualquer livro ♦ *pron*: **do** ~ **is necessary/you want** faça tudo o que for preciso/o que você quiser; ~ **happens** aconteça o que acontecer; **no reason** ~ *or* **whatsoever** nenhuma razão seja qual for *or* em absoluto; **nothing** ~ nada em absoluto
whatsoever [wɔtsəu'ɛvə*] *adj* = **whatever**
wheat [wi:t] *n* trigo
wheel [wi:l] *n* roda; (*also*: **steering** ~) volante *m*; (*NAUT*) roda do leme ♦ *vt* (*pram etc*) empurrar ♦ *vi* (*birds*) dar voltas; (*also*: ~ **round**) girar, dar voltas, virar-se; **wheelbarrow** *n* carrinho de mão; **wheelchair** *n* cadeira de rodas; **wheel clamp** *n* (*AUT*) grampo com que se imobiliza carros estacionados ilegalmente
wheeze [wi:z] *vi* respirar ruidosamente

KEYWORD

when [wɛn] *adv* quando
♦ *conj* **1** (*at, during, after the time that*) quando; ~ **you've read it, tell me what you think** depois que você tiver lido isto, diga-me o que acha; **that was** ~ **I needed you** foi quando eu precisei de você
2 (*on, at which*) quando, em que; **on the day** ~ **I met him** no dia em que o conheci; **one day** ~ **it was raining** um dia quando estava chovendo
3 (*whereas*) ao passo que; **you said I was wrong** ~ **in fact I was right**

você disse que eu estava errado quando, na verdade, eu estava certo

whenever [wen'evə*] *conj* quando, quando quer que; *(every time that)* sempre que ♦ *adv* quando você quiser

where [weə*] *adv* onde ♦ *conj* onde, aonde; **this is ~** ... aqui é onde ...; **whereabouts** [weərə'bauts] *adv* (por) onde ♦ *n*: **nobody knows his whereabouts** ninguém sabe o seu paradeiro; **whereas** [weər'æz] *conj* uma vez que, ao passo que; **whereby** *adv (formal)* pelo qual *(or* pela qual *etc)*; **wherever** [weər'evə*] *conj* onde quer que ♦ *adv (interrogative)* onde?

whether ['weðə*] *conj* se; **I don't know ~ to accept or not** não sei se aceito ou não; **~ you go or not** quer você vá quer não; **it's doubtful ~** ... não é certo que ...

KEYWORD

which [wɪtʃ] *adj* **1** *(interrogative: direct, indirect)* que, qual; **~ picture do you want?** que quadro você quer?; **~ books are yours?** quais são os seus livros?; **~ one?** qual?
2: in ~ case em cujo caso; **by ~ time** momento em que
♦ *pron* **1** *(interrogative)* qual; **~ (of these) are yours?** quais (destes) são seus?
2 *(relative)* que, o que, o qual *etc*; **the apple ~ you ate** a maçã que você comeu; **the chair on ~ you are sitting** a cadeira na qual você está sentado; **he said he knew, ~ is true** ele disse que sabia, o que é verdade; **after ~** depois do que

whichever [wɪtʃ'evə*] *adj*: **take ~**

book you prefer pegue o livro que preferir; **~ book you take** qualquer livro que você pegue

while [waɪl] *n* tempo, momento ♦ *conj* enquanto, ao mesmo tempo que; *(as long as)* contanto que; *(although)* embora; **for a ~** durante algum tempo; **while away** *vt (time)* encher

whim [wɪm] *n* capricho, veneta

whimper ['wɪmpə*] *n (moan)* lamúria ♦ *vi* choramingar, soluçar

whimsical ['wɪmzɪkl] *adj (person)* caprichoso, de veneta; *(look)* excêntrico

whine [waɪn] *n (of pain)* gemido; *(of engine, siren)* zunido ♦ *vi* gemer; zunir; *(fig)* lamuriar-se

whip [wɪp] *n* açoite m; *(for riding)* chicote m; *(POL)* líder m/f da bancada ♦ *vt* chicotear; *(snatch)* apanhar de repente; *(cream, eggs)* bater; *(move quickly)*: **to ~ sth out/off/away** tirar/arrancar algo; **whipped cream** *n* (creme *m*) chantilly m; **whip-round** *n (BRIT)* coleta, vaquinha

whirl [wə:l] *vt* fazer girar ♦ *vi (dancers)* rodopiar; *(leaves, water etc)* redemoinhar; **whirlpool** *n* remoinho; **whirlwind** *n* furacão m, remoinho

whirr [wə:*] *vi* zumbir

whisk [wɪsk] *n (CULIN)* batedeira ♦ *vt* bater; **to ~ sb away** *or* **off** levar alguém rapidamente

whiskers ['wɪskəz] *npl (of animal)* bigodes *mpl*; *(of man)* suíças *fpl*

whisky ['wɪskɪ] *(US, IRELAND* **whiskey)** *n* uísque m *(BR)*, whisky m *(PT)*

whisper ['wɪspə*] *n* sussurro, murmúrio ♦ *vt, vi* sussurrar

whistle ['wɪsl] *n (sound)* assobio; *(object)* apito ♦ *vt, vi* assobiar

white [waɪt] *adj* branco; *(pale)* pálido ♦ *n* branco; (*of egg*) clara; **white coffee** *n* café *m* com leite; **White House** *n*: the W~ House a Casa Branca; *ver quadro*

WHITE HOUSE

A White House é um grande edifício branco situado em Washington D.C. onde reside o presidente dos Estados Unidos. Por extensão, o termo se refere também ao poder executivo americano.

---

white lie *n* mentira inofensiva *or* social

whitewash *n* (*paint*) cal f ♦ *vt* caiar; (*fig*) encobrir

whiting ['waɪtɪŋ] *n inv* pescada

Whitsun ['wɪtsn] *n* Pentecostes *m*

whizz [wɪz] *vi*: to ~ **past** *or* **by** passar a toda velocidade; **whizz kid** (*inf*) *n* prodígio

KEYWORD

who [hu:] *pron* **1** (*interrogative*) quem?; ~ **is it?** quem é?
2 (*relative*) que, o qual *etc*, quem; **my cousin**, ~ **lives in New York** meu primo que mora em Nova Iorque; **the man** ~ **spoke to me** o homem que falou comigo

whole [həʊl] *adj* (*complete*) todo, inteiro; (*not broken*) intacto ♦ *n* (*all*): **the** ~ **of the time** o tempo todo; (*entire amount*) conjunto; **on the** ~**, as a** ~ como um todo, no conjunto; **wholefoods** *n* comida integral; **wholehearted** *adj* total; **wholemeal** (*BRIT*) *adj* integral; **wholesale** *n* venda por atacado ♦ *adj* por atacado; (*destruction*) em grande escala ♦ *adv* por atacado; **wholesaler** *n* atacadista *m/f*; **wholesome** *adj*

saudável, sadio; **wholewheat** *adj* = **wholemeal**; **wholly** ['həʊlɪ] *adv* totalmente, completamente

KEYWORD

whom [hu:m] *pron* **1** (*interrogative*) quem?; **to** ~ **did you give it?** para quem você deu isto?
2 (*relative*) que, quem; **the man** ~ **I saw/to** ~ **I spoke** o homem que eu vi/com quem eu falei

whooping cough ['hu:pɪŋ-] *n* coqueluche f

whore [hɔ:*] (*inf: pej*) *n* puta

KEYWORD

whose [hu:z] *adj* **1** (*possessive: interrogative*): ~ **book is this?**, ~ **is this book?** de quem é este livro?
2 (*possessive: relative*): **the man** ~ **son you rescued** o homem cujo filho você salvou; **the woman** ~ **car was stolen** a mulher de quem o carro foi roubado
♦ *pron* de quem; **I don't know** ~ **it is** eu não sei de quem é isto

KEYWORD

why [waɪ] *adv* por que (*BR*), porque (*PT*); (*at end of sentence*) por quê (*BR*), porquê (*PT*)
♦ *conj* por que; **that's not** ~ **I'm here** não é por isso que estou aqui; **the reason** ~ a razão por que
♦ *excl* (*expressing surprise, shock, annoyance*) ora essa!; (*explaining*) bem!; ~, **it's you!** ora, é você!

wicked ['wɪkɪd] *adj* perverso; (*smile*) malicioso

wicket ['wɪkɪt] *n* (*CRICKET*) arco

wide [waɪd] *adj* largo; (*area, publicity, knowledge*) amplo ♦ *adv*: to open ~ abrir totalmente; **to shoot ~** atirar longe do alvo; **wide-awake** *adj* bem acordado; **widely** *adv* extremamente; (*travelled*) muito; (*believed*, *known*) amplamente; **widen** *vt* alargar; (*one's experience*) aumentar ♦ *vi* alargar-se; **wide open** *adj* (*eyes*) arregalado; (*door*) escancarado; **widespread** *adj* (*belief etc*) difundido, comum

widow ['wɪdəu] *n* viúva; **widowed** *adj* viúvo; **widower** *n* viúvo

width [wɪdθ] *n* largura

wield [wi:ld] *vt* (*sword*) brandir, empunhar; (*pl*) exercer

wife [waɪf] (*pl* **wives**) *n* mulher f, esposa

wig [wɪg] *n* peruca

wiggle ['wɪgl] *vt* menear, agitar

wild [waɪld] *adj* (*animal*) selvagem; (*plant*) silvestre; (*rough*) violento, furioso; (*idea*) disparatado, extravagante; (*person*) insensato; **wilderness** ['wɪldənɪs] *n* ermo; **wildlife** *n* animais *mpl* selvagens; **wildly** *adv* (*behave*) freneticamente; (*hit*, *guess*) irrefletidamente; (*happy*) extremamente

wilful ['wɪlful] (*US* **willful**) *adj* (*person*) teimoso, voluntarioso; (*action*) deliberado, intencional

---KEYWORD---

will [wɪl] (*vt*) (*pt*, *pp* **~ed**) *aux vb*
1 (*forming future tense*): **I ~ finish it tomorrow** vou acabar isto amanhã; **I ~ have finished it by tomorrow** até amanhã eu terei terminado isto; **~ you do it? - yes I ~/no I won't** você vai fazer isto? – sim, vou/não eu não vou

2 (*in conjectures*, *predictions*): **he ~ come** ele virá; **he ~ or he'll be there by now** nesta altura ele está lá; **that ~ be the postman** deve ser o cartei-

ro; **this medicine ~/won't help you** este remédio vai/não vai fazer efeito em você

3 (*in commands*, *requests*, *offers*): **~ you be quiet!** fique quieto, por favor!; **~ you come?** você vem?; **~ you help me?** você pode me ajudar?; **~ you have a cup of tea?** você vai querer uma xícara de chá or um chá?; **I won't put up with it** eu não vou tolerar isto

♦ *vt*: **to ~ sb to do sth** desejar que alguém faça algo; **he ~ed himself to go on** reuniu grande força de vontade para continuar

♦ *n* (*volition*) vontade f; (*testament*) testamento

---

willful ['wɪlful] (*US*) *adj* = **wilful**

willing ['wɪlɪŋ] *adj* disposto, pronto; (*enthusiastic*) entusiasmado; **willingly** *adv* de bom grado, de boa vontade; **willingness** *n* boa vontade f, disposição f

willow ['wɪləu] *n* salgueiro

willpower ['wɪlpauə*] *n* força de vontade

wilt [wɪlt] *vi* (*flower*) murchar; (*plant*) morrer

win [wɪn] (*pt*, *pp* **won**) *n* vitória ♦ *vt* ganhar, vencer; (*obtain*) conseguir, obter; (*support*) alcançar ♦ *vi* ganhar; **win over** *vt* conquistar; **win round** (*BRIT*) *vt* = **win over**

wince [wɪns] *vi* encolher-se, estremecer

winch [wɪntʃ] *n* guincho

wind¹ [wɪnd] *n* vento; (*MED*) gases *mpl*, flatulência; (*breath*) fôlego ♦ *vt* (*take breath away from*) deixar sem fôlego

wind² [waɪnd] (*pt*, *pp* **wound**) *vt* enrolar, bobinar; (*wrap*) envolver; (*clock*, *toy*) dar corda a ♦ *vi* (*road*, *river*) serpentear; **wind up** (*clock*) dar corda em; (*debate*) rematar, concluir

windfall ['wɪndfɔːl] *n* golpe *m* de sorte

winding ['waɪndɪŋ] *adj* (*road*) sinuoso, tortuoso; (*staircase*) de caracol, em espiral

wind instrument *n* (MUS) instrumento de sopro

windmill ['wɪndmɪl] *n* moinho de vento

window ['wɪndəu] *n* janela; (*in shop etc*) vitrine *f* (BR), montra (PT); **window box** *n* jardineira (no peitoril da janela); **window cleaner** *n* limpador(a) *m/f* de janelas; **window ledge** *n* peitoril *m* da janela; **window pane** *n* vidraça, vidro; **window-shopping** *n*: **to go window-shopping** ir ver vitrines; **windowsill** ['wɪndəusɪl] *n* (*inside*) peitoril *m*; (*outside*) soleira

windpipe ['wɪndpaɪp] *n* traquéia

wind power *n* energia eólica

windscreen ['wɪndskriːn] (BRIT) *n* pára-brisa *m*; **windscreen wiper** (BRIT) *n* limpador *m* de pára-brisa

windshield *etc* ['wɪndʃiːld] (US) *n* = **windscreen** *etc*

windswept ['wɪndswept] *adj* varrido pelo vento

windy ['wɪndɪ] *adj* com muito vento, batido pelo vento; **it's ~** está ventando (BR), faz vento (PT)

wine [waɪn] *n* vinho; **wine bar** *n* bar *m* (para degustação de vinhos); **wine cellar** *n* adega; **wine glass** *n* cálice *m* (de vinho); **wine list** *n* lista de vinhos; **wine waiter** *n* garção *m* dos vinhos

wing [wɪŋ] *n* asa; (*of building*) ala; (AUT) aleta, pára-lamas *m inv*; (THEATRE) **~s** *npl* bastidores *mpl*

wink [wɪŋk] *n* piscadela ♦ *vi* piscar o olho; (*light etc*) piscar

winner ['wɪnə*] *n* vencedor(a) *m/f*

winning ['wɪnɪŋ] *adj* (*team*) vencedor(a); (*goal*) decisivo; (*smile*) sedutor(a); **winnings** *npl* ganhos *mpl*

winter ['wɪntə*] *n* inverno; **winter sports** *npl* esportes *mpl* (BR) or desportos *mpl* (PT) de inverno

wipe [waɪp] *n*: **to give sth a ~** limpar algo com um pano ♦ *vt* limpar; (*rub*) esfregar; (*erase: tape*) apagar; **wipe off** *vt* remover esfregando; **wipe out** *vt* (*debt*) liquidar; (*memory*) apagar; (*destroy*) exterminar; **wipe up** *vt* limpar

wire ['waɪə*] *n* arame *m*; (ELEC) fio (elétrico); (*telegram*) telegrama *m* ♦ *vt* (*house*) instalar a rede elétrica em; (*also: ~ up*) conectar; (*telegram*) telegrafar para

wiring ['waɪərɪŋ] *n* instalação *f* elétrica

wiry ['waɪərɪ] *adj* nervoso; (*hair*) grosso

wisdom ['wɪzdəm] *n* prudência; (*of action, remark*) bom-senso, sabedoria; **wisdom tooth** (*irreg*) *n* dente *m* do siso

wise [waɪz] *adj* prudente; (*action, remark*) sensato

wish [wɪʃ] *n* desejo ♦ *vt* (*want*) querer; **best ~es** (*on birthday etc*) parabéns *mpl*, felicidades *fpl*; **with best ~es** (*in letter*) cumprimentos; **to ~ sb goodbye** despedir-se de alguém; **he ~ed me well** me desejou boa sorte; **to ~ to do/sb to do sth** querer fazer/que alguém faça algo; **to ~ for** desejar; **wishful thinking** *n*: **it's wishful thinking** é doce ilusão

wistful ['wɪstful] *adj* melancólico

wit [wɪt] *n* (*wittiness*) presença de espírito, engenho; (*intelligence: also:* **~s**) entendimento; (*person*) espirituoso(-a)

witch [wɪtʃ] *n* bruxa

with [wɪð, wɪθ] prep **1** (accompanying, in the company of) com; **I was ~ him** eu estava com ele; **to stay overnight ~ friends** dormir na casa de amigos; **we'll take the children ~ us** vamos levar as crianças conosco; **I'll be ~ you in a minute** vou vê-lo num minuto; **I'm ~ you** (I understand) compreendo; **to be ~ it** (inf) estar por dentro; (aware) estar a par da situação; (: up-to-date) estar atualizado com **2** (descriptive) com, de; **a room ~ a view** um quarto com vista; **the man ~ the grey hat/blue eyes** o homem do chapéu cinza/de olhos azuis **3** (indicating manner, means, cause) com, de; **~ tears in her eyes** com os olhos cheios de lágrimas; **to fill sth ~ water** encher algo de água

withdraw [wɪðˈdrɔː] (irreg) vt tirar, remover; (offer) retirar ♦ vi retirar-se; **to ~ money (from the bank)** retirar dinheiro (do banco); **withdrawal** n retirada; **withdrawal symptoms** npl síndrome f de abstinência; **withdrawn** adj (person) reservado, introvertido

wither [ˈwɪðə*] vi murchar

withhold [wɪðˈhəuld] (irreg: like hold) vt (money) reter; (permission) negar; (information) ocultar

within [wɪðˈɪn] prep dentro de ♦ adv dentro; **~ reach (of)** ao alcance (de); **~ sight (of)** à vista (de); **~ the week** antes do fim da semana; **~ a mile of** a uma milha de

without [wɪðˈaut] prep sem; **~ anybody knowing** sem ninguém saber; **to go ~ sth** passar sem algo

withstand [wɪðˈstænd] (irreg: like stand) vt resistir a

witness [ˈwɪtnɪs] n testemunha ♦ vt testemunhar, presenciar; (document) legalizar; **to bear ~ to sth** (fig) testemunhar algo; **witness box** (us **~ stand**) n banco das testemunhas

witty [ˈwɪtɪ] adj espirituoso

wives [waɪvz] npl of **wife**

wizard [ˈwɪzəd] n feiticeiro, mago

wk abbr = **week**

wobble [ˈwɔbl] vi oscilar; (chair) balançar

woe [wəu] n dor f, mágoa

woke [wəuk] pt of **wake**; **woken** pp of **wake**

wolf [wulf] (pl **wolves**) n lobo

woman [ˈwumən] (pl **women**) n mulher f; **~ doctor** médica

womb [wuːm] n (ANAT) matriz f, útero

women [ˈwɪmɪn] npl of **woman**

won [wʌn] pt, pp of **win**

wonder [ˈwʌndə*] n maravilha, prodígio; (feeling) espanto ♦ vi perguntar-se a si mesmo; **to ~ at** admirar-se de; **to ~ about** pensar sobre or em; **it's no ~ that** não é de admirar que; **wonderful** adj maravilhoso; (miraculous) impressionante

won't [wəunt] = will not

wood [wud] n (timber) madeira; (forest) floresta, bosque m; **wood carving** n (act) escultura em madeira; (object) entalhe m; **wooded** adj arborizado, de madeira; (fig) inexpressivo; **woodpecker** n pica-pau m; **woodwind** n (MUS) instrumentos mpl de sopro de madeira; **woodwork** n carpintaria; **woodworm** n carcoma, caruncho

wool [wul] n lã f; **to pull the ~ over sb's eyes** (fig) enganar alguém, vender a alguém gato por lebre; **woollen** adj de lã; **woolly** (us

wooly adj de lã; (fig) confuso
word [wə:d] n palavra; (news) notícia ♦ vt redigir; **in other ~s** em outras palavras, ou seja; **to break/ keep one's ~** faltar à palavra/cumprir a promessa; **to have ~s with sb** discutir com alguém; **wording** n fraseado; **word processing** n processamento de textos; **word processor** n processador m de textos
wore [wɔː*] pt of **wear**
work [wə:k] n trabalho; (job) emprego, trabalho; (ART, LITERATURE) obra ♦ vi trabalhar; (mechanism) funcionar; (medicine etc) surtir efeito, ser eficaz ♦ vt (clay) moldar; (wood) talhar; (mine etc) explorar; (machine) fazer trabalhar, manejar; (effect, miracle) causar; **to ~ loose** (part) soltar-se; (knot) afrouxar-se; **work on** vt fus trabalhar em, dedicar-se a; (person: influence) tentar convencer; (problem) resolver; (plan) elaborar, formular; **it ~s out at £100** monta or soma a £100; **workaholic** [wə:kə'hɔlɪk] n burro de carga; **worker** n trabalhador(a) m/f, operário(-a); **working class** n proletariado, classe f operária ♦ adj: **working-class** do proletariado, da classe operária; **working order** n: **in working order** em perfeito estado; **workman** (irreg) n operário, trabalhador m; **workmanship** n (skill) habilidade f; **workshop** n oficina; (practical session) aula prática; **work station** n estação f de trabalho
world [wə:ld] n mundo ♦ cpd mundial; **to think the ~ of sb** (fig) ter alguém em alto conceito; **worldly** adj mundano; (knowledgeable) experiente; **worldwide** adj

dial, universal
worm [wə:m] n (also: **earth~**) minhoca, lombriga
worn [wɔːn] pp of **wear** ♦ adj gasto; **worn-out** adj (object) gasto; (person) esgotado, exausto
worry [ˈwʌrɪ] n preocupação f ♦ vt preocupar, inquietar ♦ vi preocupar-se, afligir-se
worse [wə:s] adj, adv pior ♦ n o pior; **a change for the ~** uma mudança para pior, uma piora; **worsen** vt, vi piorar; **worse off** adj com menos dinheiro; (fig): **you'll be worse off this way** assim você ficará pior que nunca
worship [ˈwə:ʃɪp] n adoração f ♦ vt adorar, venerar; (person, thing) adorar; **Your W~** (BRIT: to mayor) vossa Excelência; (: to judge) senhor Juiz
worst [wə:st] adj (o (a)) pior ♦ adv pior ♦ n o pior; **at ~** na pior das hipóteses
worth [wə:θ] n valor m, mérito f ♦ adj: **to be ~** valer; **it's ~ it** vale a pena; **to be ~ one's while** (to do) valer a pena (fazer); **worthless** adj (person) imprestável; (thing) inútil; **worthwhile** adj (activity) que vale a pena; (cause) de mérito, louvável
worthy [ˈwə:ðɪ] adj (person) merecedor(a), respeitável; (motive) justo; **~ of** digno de

─────── KEYWORD ───────

would [wud] aux vb **1** (conditional tense): **if you asked him, he ~ do it** se você pedisse, ele faria isto; **if you had asked him, he ~ have done it** se você tivesse pedido, ele teria feito isto
2 (in offers, invitations, requests): **~ you like a biscuit?** você quer um biscoito?; **~ you ask him to come in?** pode pedir a ele para entrar?;

you close the door, please? quer
fechar a porta, por favor?
3 (in indirect speech): **I said I ~ do it**
eu disse que eu faria isto
4 (emphatic) **you WOULD say that,
~n't you?** é lógico que você vai
dizer isso
5 (insistence): **she ~n't behave** não
houve feito dela se comportar
6 (conjecture): **it ~ have been midnight** devia ser meia-noite; **it ~
seem so** parece que sim
7 (indicating habit): **he ~ go on Mon-
days** costumava ir às segundas-
feiras

wouldn't ['wudnt] = **would not**
wound¹ [waund] pt, pp of **wind²**
wound² [wu:nd] n ferida ♦ vt ferir
wove [wəuv] pt of **weave**; **woven**
pp of **weave**
wrap [ræp] n (stole) xale m; (cape)
capa ♦ vt (cover) envolver; (also: ~
up) embrulhar; (wind: tape etc)
amarrar; **wrapper** n invólucro;
(BRIT: of book) capa; **wrapping
paper** n papel m de embrulho;
(fancy) papel de presente
wreak [ri:k] vt: **to ~ havoc (on)** causar estragos (em); **to ~ vengeance
on** vingar-se em, tirar vingança de
wreath [ri:θ] n coroa
wreck [rek] n (vehicle) destroços
mpl; (ship) restos mpl do naufrágio;
(pej: person) ruína, caco ♦ vt destruir, danificar; (fig) arruinar, arrasar;
wreckage n (of car, plane) destroços mpl; (of ship) restos mpl; (of
building) escombros mpl
wren [ren] n (ZOOL) carriça
wrench [rentʃ] n (TECH) chave f
inglesa; (tug) puxão m; (fig) separação f penosa ♦ vt torcer com força;
to ~ sth from sb arrancar algo de
alguém

wrestle ['resl] vi: **to ~ (with sb)**
lutar (com or contra alguém);
wrestler n lutador m; **wrestling** n
luta (livre)
wretched ['retʃid] adj desventurado, infeliz; (inf) maldito
wriggle ['rɪgl] vi (also: ~ about)
retorcer-se, contorcer-se
wring [rɪŋ] (pt, pp **wrung**) vt
(clothes, neck) torcer; (hands) apertar; (fig): **to ~ sth out of sb** arrancar
algo de alguém
wrinkle ['rɪŋkl] n (on skin) ruga; (on
paper) prega ♦ vt franzir ♦ vi
enrugar-se
wrist [rɪst] n pulso; **wristwatch** n
relógio m de pulso
write [raɪt] (pt **wrote**, pp **written**) vt
escrever; (cheque, prescription) pas-
sar ♦ vi escrever; **to ~ to sb** escrever
para alguém; **write down** vt (note)
anotar; (put on paper) pôr no papel;
write off vt cancelar; **write out** vt
escrever por extenso; (cheque etc)
passar; **write up** vt redigir; **write-
off** n perda total; **writer** n escri-
tor(a) m/f
writing ['raɪtɪŋ] n escrita; (hand~)
caligrafia, letra; (of author) obra; **in
~** por escrito
wrong [rɒŋ] adj (bad) errado,
mau; (unfair) injusto; (incorrect)
errado, equivocado; (inappropriate) impróprio ♦ adv mal, errado
♦ n injustiça ♦ vt ser injusto com;
you are ~ to do it você se engana
ao fazê-lo; **you are ~ about that,
you've got it ~** você está enganado sobre isso; **to be in the ~** não
ter razão; **what's ~?** o que é que
há?; **to go ~** (person) desencami-
nhar-se; (plan) dar errado;
(machine) sofrer uma avaria;
wrongful ['rɒŋful] adj injusto;
wrongly ['rɒŋlɪ] adv errado

wrote [rəut] *pt of* **write**

wrung [rʌŋ] *pt, pp of* **wring**

wt. *abbr* = **weight**

WWW *n abbr* (= *World Wide Web*): **the ~** a WWW

X

Xmas ['eksməs] *n abbr* = **Christmas**

X-ray [eks'reɪ] *n* radiografia ♦ *vt* radiografar, tirar uma chapa de

Y

yacht [jɔt] *n* iate *m*; **yachting** *n* iatismo

Yank [jæŋk] *n (pej)* ianque *m/f*

yap [jæp] *vi (dog)* ganir

yard [jɑːd] *n* pátio, quintal *m*; *(measure)* jarda (914 mm; 3 feet)

yarn [jɑːn] *n* fio; *(tale)* história inverossímil

yawn [jɔːn] *n* bocejo ♦ *vi* bocejar

yd *abbr* = **yard(s)**

yeah [jeə] *(inf) adv* é

year [jɪə*] *n* ano; **to be 8 ~s old** ter 8 anos; **an eight-~-old child** uma criança de oito anos (de idade); **yearly** *adj* anual ♦ *adv* anualmente

yearn [jəːn] *vi:* **to ~ to do/for sth** ansiar fazer/por algo

yeast [jiːst] *n* levedura, fermento

yell [jel] *n* grito, berro ♦ *vi* gritar, berrar

yellow ['jeləu] *adj* amarelo

yes [jes] *adv, n* sim *m*

yesterday ['jestədɪ] *adv, n* ontem *m*

yet [jet] *adv* ainda ♦ *conj* porém, no entanto; **the best ~** o melhor até agora; **as ~** até agora, ainda

yew [juː] *n* teixo

yield [jiːld] *n* (AGR) colheita; (COMM) rendimento ♦ *vt* produzir; *(profit)*

render; *(surrender)* ceder ♦ *vi* render-se, ceder; *(US: AUT)* ceder

YMCA *n abbr* (= *Young Men's Christian Association*) = ACM *f*

yog(h)ourt ['jəugət] *n* iogurte *m*

yoke [jəuk] *n (of oxen)* junta; *(fig)* jugo

yolk [jəuk] *n* gema (do ovo)

KEYWORD

you [juː] *pron* **1** *(subj: sg)* tu, você; (: *pl*) vós, vocês; **~ French enjoy your food** vocês franceses gostam de comer; **~ and I will go** nós iremos **2** *(direct object: sg)* te, o (a); (: *pl*) vos, os (as); *(indirect object: sg)* te, lhe; (: *pl*) vos, lhes; **I know ~** eu lhe conheço; **I gave it to ~** dei isto para você

3 *(stressed)* você; **I told YOU to do it** eu disse para você fazer isto

4 *(after prep, in comparisons: sg)* ti, você; (: *pl*) vós, vocês; *(polite form: sg)* o senhor (a senhora); (: *pl*) os senhores (as senhoras); **it's for ~** é para você; **with ~** contigo, com você; convosco, com vocês; com o senhor *etc*

5 *(impers: one):* **~ never know** nunca se sabe; **apples do ~ good** as maçãs fazem bem à saúde

you'd [juːd] = **you had**; **you would**

you'll [juːl] = **you will**; **you shall**

young [jʌŋ] *adj* jovem ♦ *npl (of animal)* filhotes *mpl*, crias *fpl*; *(people)*: **the ~** a juventude, os jovens; **younger** [ˈjʌŋɡə*] *adj* mais novo; **youngster** *n* jovem *m/f*, moço(-a)

your [jɔː*] *adj* teu (tua), seu (sua); *(pl)* vosso, seu (sua); *(formal)* do senhor (da senhora); *see also* **my**

you're [juə*] = **you are**

yours [jɔːz] *pron* teu (tua), seu (sua); *(pl)* vosso, seu (sua); do senhor (da senhora); **~ sincerely** or **faithfully** atenciosamente; *see also* **mine**¹

yourself [jɔːˈsɛlf] *pron* (*emphatic*) tu mesmo, você mesmo; (*object, reflexive*) te, se; (*after prep*) ti mesmo, si mesmo; (*formal*) o senhor mesmo (a senhora mesma); **yourselves** *pl*, *pron* vós mesmos, vocês mesmos; vos, se; vós mesmos, vocês mesmos; os senhores mesmos (as senhoras mesmas); *see also* **oneself**

youth [juːθ] *n* mocidade *f*, juventude *f*; (*young man*) jovem *m*; **youth club** *n* associação *f* de juventude; **youthful** *adj* juvenil; **youth hostel** *n* albergue *m* da juventude

you've [juːv] = **you have**

YTS (*BRIT*) *n abbr* (= *Youth Training Scheme*) *programa de ensino profissionalizante*

Yugoslav [ˈjuːgəuslɑːv] *adj*, *n* iugoslavo(-a)

Yugoslavia [juːgəuˈslɑːvɪə] *n* Iugoslávia

yuppie [ˈjʌpɪ] (*inf*) *adj*, *n* yuppie *m/f*

YWCA *n abbr* (= *Young Women's Christian Association*) ≈ ACM *f*

Z

zany [ˈzeɪnɪ] *adj* tolo, bobo

zap [zæp] *vt* (*COMPUT*) apagar

zebra [ˈziːbrə] *n* zebra; **zebra crossing** (*BRIT*) *n* faixa (para pedestres) (*BR*), passadeira (*PT*)

zero [ˈzɪərəu] *n* zero

zest [zɛst] *n* vivacidade *f*, entusiasmo *f*; (*of lemon etc*) zesto

zigzag [ˈzɪgzæg] *n* ziguezague *n* ♦ *vi* ziguezaguear

Zimbabwe [zɪmˈbɑːbwɪ] *n* Zimbábue *m*

zinc [zɪŋk] *n* zinco

zip [zɪp] *n* (*also*: **~ fastener**) fecho ecler (*BR*) or éclair (*PT*) ♦ *vt* (*also*: **~ up**) fechar o fecho ecler de, subir o fecho ecler de; **zip code** (*US*) *n* código postal; **zipper** (*US*) *n* = **zip**

zodiac [ˈzəudɪæk] *n* zodíaco

zone [zəun] *n* zona

zoo [zuː] *n* (jardim *m*) zoológico

zoom [zuːm] *vi*: **to ~ past** passar zunindo; **zoom lens** *n* zoom *m*, zum *m*

zucchini [zuːˈkiːnɪ] (*US*) *n(pl)* abobrinha

PORTUGUÊS-INGLÊS
PORTUGUESE-ENGLISH

A

PALAVRA CHAVE
---

a [a] (*a* + *o(s)* = ao(s); *a* + *a(s)* = à(s); *a* + *aquele/a(s)* = àquele/a(s)) *art def* the; *V tb* **o**

♦ *pron* (*ela*) her; (*você*) you; (*coisa*) it; *V tb* **o**

♦ *prep* **1** (*direção*) to; **à direita/esquerda** to *ou* on the right/left

2 (*distância*): **está ~ 15 km daqui** it's 15 km from here

3 (*posição*): **ao lado de** beside, at the side of

4 (*tempo*) at; **~ que horas?** at what time?; **às 5 horas** at 5 o'clock; **à noite** at night; **aos 15 anos** at 15 years of age

5 (*maneira*): **à francesa** in the French way; **~ cavalo/pé** on horseback/foot

6 (*meio, instrumento*): **à força** by force; **~ mão** by hand; **~ lápis** in pencil; **fogão ~ gás** gas stove

7 (*razão*): **~ R$1 o quilo** at R$1 a kilo; **~ mais de 100 km/h** at over 100 km/h

8 (*depois de certos verbos*): **começou ~ nevar** it started snowing *ou* to snow; **passar ~ fazer** to become

9 (+ *infin*): **ao vê-lo, o reconheci imediatamente** when I saw him, I recognized him immediately; **ele ficou muito nervoso ao falar com o professor** he became very nervous while he was talking to the teacher

10 (*PT*: + *infin*: *gerúndio*): **~ correr** running; **estou ~ trabalhar** I'm working

---

à [a] = **a** + **a**

(a) *abr* (= **assinado**) signed

aba ['aba] *f* (*de chapéu*) brim; (*de casaco*) tail; (*de montanha*) foot

abacate [aba'katʃi] *m* avocado (pear)

abacaxi [abaka'ʃi] (*BR*) *m* pineapple

abade, ssa [a'badʒi, aba'dεsa] *m/f* abbot/abbess; **abadia** [aba'dʒia] *f* abbey

abafado, -a [aba'fadu, a] *adj* (*ar*) stuffy; (*tempo*) humid, close; (*ocupado*) (extremely) busy; (*angustiado*) anxious

abafar [aba'fa*] *vt* to suffocate; (*ocultar*) to suppress; (*col*) to pinch

abagunçar [abagũ'sa*] *vt* to mess up

abaixar [abaj'ʃa*] *vt* to lower; (*luz, som*) to turn down; **abaixar-se** *vr* to stoop

abaixo [a'bajʃu] *adv* down ♦ *prep*: **~ de** below; **~ o governo!** down with the government!; **morro ~** downhill; **rio ~** downstream; **mais ~** further down; **~ e acima** up and down; **~ assinado** undersigned; **abaixo-assinado** [-asi'nadu] (*pl* **abaixo-assinados**) *m* petition

abalado, -a [aba'ladu, a] *adj* (*objeto*) unstable, unsteady; (*fig: pessoa*) shaken

abalar [aba'la*] *vt* to shake; (*fig: comover*) to affect ♦ *vi* to shake; **abalar-se** *vr* to be moved

abalo [a'balu] *m* (*comoção*) shock; (*ação*) shaking; **~ sísmico** earth tremor

abanar [aba'na*] *vt* to shake; (*rabo*) to wag; (*com leque*) to fan

abandonar [abãdo'na*] *vt* to leave;

(*idéia*) to reject; (*esperança*) to
give up; (*descuidar*) to neglect;
abandonar-se *vr*: ~-se a to abandon o.s. to; **abandono** [abã'donu]
m (*ato*) desertion; (*estado*) neglect
abarcar [abax'ka*] *vt* (*abranger*:
assunto, país) to cover; (: *suj*: *vista*)
to take in
abarrotado, -a [abaxo'tadu, a] *adj*
(*gaveta*) crammed full; (*lugar*) packed
abastado, -a [abaʃ'tadu, a] *adj*
wealthy
abastecer [abaʃte'se*] *vt* to supply;
(*motor*) to fuel; (AUTO) to fill up; (AER)
to refuel; **abastecer-se** *vr*: ~-se de
to stock up with
abastecimento [abaʃtesi'mẽtu] *m*
supply; (*comestíveis*) provisions *pl*;
(*ato*) supplying; ~s *mpl* (*suprimen-
tos*) supplies
abater [aba'te*] *vt* (*gado*) to slaughter; (*preço*) to reduce; (*desalentar*)
to upset; **abatido, -a** [aba'tʃidu, a]
adj depressed, downcast; **abatimento** [abatʃi'mẽtu] *m* (*fraqueza*)
weakness; (*de preço*) reduction;
(*prostração*) depression; **fazer um
abatimento em** to give a discount on
abdicar [abdʒi'ka*] *vi, vt* to abdicate
abdômen [ab'domẽ] *m* abdomen
á-bê-cê [abe'se] *m* alphabet
abecedário [abese'darju] *m* alphabet, ABC
abelha [a'beʎa] *f* bee
abelhudo, -a [abe'ʎudu, a] *adj* nosy
abençoar [abẽ'swa*] *vt* to bless
aberto, -a [a'bextu, a] *pp de* **abrir**
♦ *adj* open; (*céu*) clear; (*sinal*)
green; (*torneira*) running; **a torneira
estava aberta** the tap was on
abertura [abex'tura] *f* opening;
(FOTO) aperture; (*ranhura*) gap,
crevice; (POL) liberalization
abestalhado, -a [abeʃta'ʎadu, a]
adj stupid

abismado, -a [abiʒ'madu, a] *adj*
astonished
abismo [a'biʒmu] *m* abyss, chasm;
(*fig*) depths *pl*
abjeção [abʒe'sãw] (PT **-çç-**) *f* base-
ness
abjeto, -a [ab'ʒetu, a] (PT **-ct-**) *adj*
abject, contemptible
ABL *abr f* = **Academia Brasileira de
Letras**
abnegação [abnega'sãw] *f* self-denial
abnegado, -a [abne'gadu, a] *adj*
self-sacrificing
abnegar [abne'ga*] *vt* to renounce
abóbada [a'bɔbada] *f* vault; (*telhado*) arched roof
abobalhado, -a [aboba'ʎadu, a]
adj (*criança*) simple
abóbora [a'bɔbora] *f* pumpkin
abobrinha [abo'briɲa] *f* courgette
(BRIT), zucchini (US)
abolir [abo'li*] *vt* to abolish
abonar [abo'na*] *vt* to guarantee
abono [a'bonu] *m* guarantee; (JUR)
bail; (*louvor*) praise; **~ de família**
child benefit
abordar [abox'da*] *vt* (NÁUT) to
board; (*pessoa*) to approach;
(*assunto*) to broach, tackle
aborrecer [aboxe'se*] *vt* (*chatear*)
to annoy; (*maçar*) to bore;
aborrecer-se *vr* to get upset; to
get bored; **aborrecido, -a** [aboxe-
'sidu, a] *adj* annoyed; boring; **aborrecimento** [aboxesi'mẽtu] *m*
annoyance; boredom
abortar [abox'ta*] *vi* (MED) to have a
miscarriage; (: *de propósito*) to have
an abortion; **aborto** [a'boxtu] *m*
miscarriage; abortion; **fazer/ter um
aborto** to have an abortion/a miscarriage
abotoadura [abotwa'dura] *f* cufflink
abotoar [abo'twa*] *vt* to button up
♦ *vi* (BOT) to bud

abraçar [abra'sa*] vt to hug; (causa) to embrace; **abraçar-se** vr to embrace; **ele abraçou-se a mim** he embraced me; **abraço** [a'brasu] m embrace, hug; **com um abraço** (em carta) with best wishes

abrandar [abrã'da*] vt to reduce; (suavizar) to soften ♦ vi to diminish; (acalmar) to calm down

abranger [abrã'ʒe*] vt (assunto) to cover; (alcançar) to reach

abre-garrafas ['abri-] (PT) m inv bottle opener

abre-latas ['abri-] (PT) m inv tin (BRIT) ou can opener

abreviar [abre'vja*] vt to abbreviate; (texto) to abridge; **abreviatura** [abrevja'tura] f abbreviation

abridor [abri'do*] (BR) m: ~ (de lata) tin (BRIT) ou can opener; ~ de garrafa bottle opener

abrigar [abri'ga*] vt to shelter; (proteger) to protect; **abrigar-se** vr to take shelter

abrigo [a'brigu] m shelter, cover; ~ anti-aéreo air-raid shelter; ~ anti-nuclear fall-out shelter

abril [a'briw] (PT A-) m April; **25 de Abril** (PT) see boxed note

abrir [a'bri*] vt to open; (fechadura) to unlock; (vestuário) to unfasten; (torneira) to turn on; (exceção) to make ♦ vi to open; (sinal) to turn green; **abrir-se** vr: ~-se com alguém to confide in sb

abrupto, -a [a'bruptu, a] adj abrupt; (repentino) sudden

absolutamente [absoluta'mẽtʃi] adv absolutely; (em resposta) absolutely not, not at all

absoluto, -a [abso'lutu, a] adj absolute; **em ~** absolutely not, not at all

absolver [absow've*] vt to absolve; (JUR) to acquit; **absolvição** [absowvi'sãw] (pl -ões) f absolution; acquittal

absorto, -a [ab'soxtu, a] pp de absorver ♦ adj absorbed, engrossed

absorvente [absox'vẽtʃi] adj (papel etc) absorbent; (livro etc) absorbing

absorver [absox've*] vt to absorb; **absorver-se** vr: ~-se em to concentrate on

abstêmio, -a [abʃ'temju, a] adj abstemious; (álcool) teetotal ♦ m/f abstainer; teetotaller (BRIT), teetotaler (US)

abster-se [abʃ'texsi] (irreg: como ter) vr: ~ de to abstain ou refrain from

abstinência [abʃtʃi'nẽsja] f abstinence; (jejum) fasting

abstracto, -a [abʃ'tratu, a] (PT) adj = abstrato

abstrair [abʃtra'i*] vt to abstract; (omitir) to omit; (separar) to separate

abstrato, -a [abʃ'tratu, a] adj abstract

absurdo, -a [abi'suxdu, a] adj absurd ♦ m nonsense

abundante [abũ'dãtʃi] adj abundant; **abundar** [abū'da*] *vi* to abound

abusar [abu'za*] *vi* to go too far; ~ **de** to abuse

abuso [a'buzu] *m* abuse; (*JUR*) indecent assault

a.C. *abr* (= *antes de Cristo*) B.C.

a/c *abr* (= *aos cuidados de*) c/o

acabado, -a [aka'badu, a] *adj* finished; (*esgotado*) worn out

acabamento [akaba'mētu] *m* finish

acabar [aka'ba*] *vt* to finish, complete; (*consumir*) to use up; (*rematar*) to finish off ♦ *vi* to finish, end; **acabar-se** *vr* to be over; (*prazo*) to expire; (*esgotar-se*) to run out; ~ **com** to put an end to; ~ **de chegar** to have just arrived; ~ **por fazer** to end up (by) doing; **acabou-se!** it's all over!; (*basta!*) that's enough!

academia [akade'mia] *f* academy; **A~ Brasileira de Letras** *see boxed note*

ACADEMIA BRASILEIRA DE LETRAS

Founded in 1896 in Rio de Janeiro, on the initiative of the author Machado de Assis, the **Academia Brasileira de Letras**, or ABL, aims to preserve and develop the Portuguese language and Brazilian literature. Machado de Assis was its president until 1908. It is made up of forty life members known as the *imortais*. The Academia's activities include the publication of reference books, promotion of literary prizes, and running a library, museum and archive.

---

acadêmico, -a [aka'demiku, a] *adj, m/f* academic

açafrão [asa'frãw] *m* saffron

acalmar [akaw'ma*] *vt* to calm ♦ *vi* (*vento etc*) to abate; **acalmar-se** *vr* to calm down

acamado, -a [aka'madu, a] *adj* bedridden

acampamento [akãpa'mētu] *m* camping; (*MIL*) camp, encampment

acampar [akã'pa*] *vi* to camp

acanhado, -a [aka'ɲadu, a] *adj* shy

acanhamento [akaɲa'mētu] *m* shyness

acanhar-se [aka'ɲaxsi] *vr* to be shy

ação [a'sãw] (*pl* -ões) *f* action; (*ato*) act, deed; (*MIL*) battle; (*enredo*) plot; (*JUR*) lawsuit; (*COM*) share; ~ **ordinária/preferencial** (*COM*) ordinary/preference share

acarajé [akara'ʒɛ] *m* (*CULIN*) beans fried in palm oil

acariciar [akari'sja*] *vt* to caress; (*fig*) to cherish

acarretar [akaxe'ta*] *vt* to result in, bring about

acaso [a'kazu] *m* chance; **ao** ~ at random; **por** ~ by chance

acatar [aka'ta*] *vt* to respect; (*lei*) to obey

acção [a'sãw] (*PT*) *f* = **ação**

accionar *etc* [asjo'na*] (*PT*) = **acionar** *etc*

aceitação [asejta'sãw] *f* acceptance; (*aprovação*) approval

aceitar [asej'ta*] *vt* to accept; (*aprovar*) to approve; **aceitável** [asej'tavew] (*pl* -eis) *adj* acceptable; **aceito, -a** [a'sejtu, a] *pp de* **aceitar**

acelerado, -a [asele'radu, a] *adj* (*rápido*) quick; (*apressado*) hasty

acelerador [aselera'do*] *m* accelerator

acelerar [asele'ra*] *vt* to accelerate; ~ **o carro** to accelerate; (*ritmo, negociações*) to speed up ♦ *vi* to accelerate; ~ **o passo** to go faster

acenar [ase'na*] *vi* (*com a mão*) to

wave; (*com a cabeça: afirmativo*) to
nod; (*: negativo*) to shake one's
head

acender [asẽ'de*] *vt* (*cigarro, fogo*)
to light; (*luz*) to switch on; (*fig*) to
excite, inflame

aceno [a'senu] *m* sign, gesture;
(*com a mão*) wave; (*com a cabeça:
afirmativo*) nod; (*: negativo*) shake

acento [a'sẽtu] *m* accent; (*de intensidade*) stress; **acentuar** [asẽ'twa*]
vt to accent; (*salientar*) to stress,
emphasize

acepção [asep'sãw] (*pl* -**ões**) *f* (*de
uma palavra*) sense

acerca [a'sexka]: ~ **de** *prep* about,
concerning

acertado, -a [asex'tadu, a] *adj*
right, correct; (*sensato*) sensible

acertar [asex'ta*] *vt* (*ajustar*) to put
right; (*relógio*) to set; (*alvo*) to hit;
(*acordo*) to reach; (*pergunta*) to get
right ♦ *vi* to get it right, be right; ~
o caminho to find the right way; ~
com to hit upon

aceso, -a [a'sezu, a] *pp de* **acender**
♦ *adj*: **a luz estava acesa/o fogo
estava** ~ the light was on/the fire
was alight; (*excitado*) excited;
(*furioso*) furious

acessar [ase'sa*] *vt* (*COMPUT*) to
access

acessível [ase'sivew] (*pl* -**eis**) *adj*
accessible; (*pessoa*) approachable

acesso [a'sesu] *m* access; (*MED*) fit,
attack

acessório, -a [ase'sɔrju, a] *adj*
(*máquina, equipamento*) backup;
(*EDUC*): **matéria acessória** subsidiary
subject ♦ *m* accessory

achado, -a [a'ʃadu, a] *m* find, discovery; (*pechincha*) bargain; (*sorte*)
godsend

achar [a'ʃa*] *vt* (*descobrir*) to find;
(*pensar*) to think; **achar-se** *vr* to

think (that) one is; (*encontrar-se*) to
be; ~ **de fazer** (*resolver*) to decide to
do; **o que é que você acha disso?**
what do you think of that?; **acho
que sim** I think so

achatar [aʃa'ta*] *vt* to squash, flatten

acidentado, -a [asidẽ'tadu, a] *adj*
(*terreno*) rough; (*estrada*) bumpy;
(*viagem*) eventful; (*vida*) difficult
♦ *m/f* injured person

acidental [asidẽ'taw] (*pl* -**ais**) *adj*
accidental

acidente [asi'dẽtʃi] *m* accident; **por**
~ by accident

acidez [asi'deʒ] *f* acidity

ácido, -a ['asidu, a] *adj* acid;
(*azedo*) sour ♦ *m* acid

acima [a'sima] *adv* above; (*para
cima*) up ♦ *prep*: ~ **de** above; (*além
de*) beyond; **mais** ~ higher up; **rio** ~
up river; **passar rua** ~ to go up the
street; ~ **de 1000** more than 1000

acionado, -a [asjo'nadu, a] *m/f*
(*JUR*) defendant

acionar [asjo'na*] *vt* to set in
motion; (*máquina*) to operate; (*JUR*)
to sue

acionista [asjo'niʃta] *m/f* shareholder

acirrado, -a [asi'xadu, a] *adj* (*luta,
competição*) tough

acirrar [asi'xa*] *vt* to incite, stir up

aclamação [aklama'sãw] *f* accla-
mation; (*ovação*) applause

aclamar [akla'ma*] *vt* to acclaim;
(*aplaudir*) to applaud

aço ['asu] *m* steel

acocorar-se [akoko'raxsi] *vr* to
squat, crouch

acode *etc* [a'kɔdʒi] *vb V* **acudir**

ações [a'sõjʃ] *fpl de* **ação**

açoitar [asoj'ta*] *vt* to whip, lash;
açoite [a'sojtʃi] *m* whip, lash

acolá [ako'la] *adv* over there

acolchoado [akowˈʃwadu] m quilt

acolhedor, a [akoʎeˈdo*, a] adj welcoming; (*hospitaleiro*) hospitable

acolher [akoˈʎe*] vt to welcome; (*abrigar*) to shelter; (*aceitar*) to accept; **acolher-se** vr to shelter; **acolhida** [akoˈʎida] f (*recepção*) reception, welcome; (*refúgio*) refuge; **acolhimento** [akoʎiˈmẽtu] m = **acolhida**

acomodação [akomodaˈsãw] (*pl -ões*) f accommodation; (*arranjo*) arrangement; (*adaptação*) adaptation

acomodar [akomoˈda*] vt to accommodate; (*arrumar*) to arrange; (*adaptar*) to adapt

acompanhamento [akõpaɲaˈmẽtu] m attendance; (*cortejo*) procession; (*MÚS*) accompaniment; (*CULIN*) side dish

acompanhante [akõpaˈɲãtʃi] m/f companion; (*MÚS*) accompanist

acompanhar [akõpaˈɲa*] vt to accompany

aconchegante [akõʃeˈgãtʃi] adj cosy (*BRIT*), cozy (*US*)

aconchego [akõˈʃegu] m cuddle

aconselhar [akõseˈʎa*] vt to advise; **aconselhar-se** vr: ~-se com to consult

acontecer [akõteˈse*] vi to happen; **acontecimento** [akõtesiˈmẽtu] m event

acordar [akoxˈda*] vt to wake (up); (*concordar*) to agree (on) ♦ vi to wake up

acorde [aˈkɔrdʒi] m chord

acordeão [akoxˈdʒjãw] (*pl -ões*) m accordion

acordo [aˈkoxdu] m agreement; **"de ~!"** "agreed!"; **de ~ com** (*pessoa*) in agreement with; (*conforme*) in accordance with; **estar de ~** to agree

Açores [aˈsoriʃ] mpl: **os ~** the Azores; **açoriano, -a** [asoˈrjanu, a] adj, m/f Azorean

acossar [akoˈsa*] vt (*perseguir*) to pursue; (*atormentar*) to harass

acostamento [akoʃtaˈmẽtu] m hard shoulder (*BRIT*), berm (*US*)

acostumado, -a [akoʃtuˈmadu, a] adj usual, customary; **estar ~ a algo** to be used to sth

acostumar [akoʃtuˈma*] vt to accustom; **acostumar-se** vr: ~-se a to get used to

açougue [aˈsogi] m butcher's (shop); **açougueiro** [asoˈgejru] m butcher

acovardar-se [akovaxˈdaxsi] vr (*desanimar*) to lose courage; (*amedrontar-se*) to flinch, cower

acre [ˈakri] adj (*gosto*) bitter; (*cheiro*) acrid; (*fig*) harsh

acreditado, -a [akredʒiˈtadu, a] adj accredited

acreditar [akredʒiˈta*] vt to believe; (*COM*) to credit; (*afiançar*) to guarantee ♦ vi: ~ **em** to believe in

acre-doce adj (*CULIN*) sweet and sour

acrescentar [akresẽˈta*] vt to add

acrescer [akreˈse*] vt to increase; (*juntar*) to add ♦ vi to increase; **acréscimo** [aˈkresimu] m increase; addition; (*elevação*) rise

activo, -a etc [aˈtivu, a] (*PT*) = **ativo** etc

acto [ˈatu] (*PT*) m = **ato**

actor [aˈto*] (*PT*) m = **ator**

actriz [aˈtriʒ] (*PT*) f = **atriz**

actual etc [aˈtwaw] (*PT*) = **atual** etc

actuar etc [aˈtwa*] (*PT*) = **atuar** etc

açúcar [aˈsuka*] m sugar; **açucareiro** [asukaˈrejru] m sugar bowl

açude [aˈsudʒi] m dam

acudir [akuˈdʒi*] vt (*ir em socorro*) to help, assist ♦ vi (*responder*) to reply, respond; **~ a** to come to the aid of

acumular [akumu'la*] vt to accumulate; (reunir) to collect; (funções) to combine

acusação [akuza'sãw] (pl **-ões**) f accusation, charge; (JUR) prosecution

acusar [aku'za*] vt to accuse; (revelar) to reveal; (culpar) to blame; **~ o recebimento de** to acknowledge receipt of

acústica [a'kuʃtʃika] f (ciência) acoustics sg; (de uma sala) acoustics pl

acústico, -a [a'kuʃtʃiku, a] adj acoustic

adaptar [adap'ta*] vt to adapt; (acomodar) to fit; **adaptar-se** vr: **~-se a** to adapt to

adega [a'dɛga] f cellar

ademais [adʒi'majʃ] adv besides, moreover

adentro [a'dẽtru] adv inside, in; **mata ~** into the woods

adepto, -a [a'deptu, a] m/f follower; (de time) supporter

adequado, -a [ade'kwadu, a] adj appropriate

adereço [ade'resu] m adornment; **adereços** mpl (TEATRO) stage props

aderente [ade'rẽtʃi] adj adhesive, sticky ♦ m/f supporter

aderir [ade'ri*] vi to adhere

adesão [ade'zãw] f adhesion; (patrocínio) support

adesivo, -a [ade'zivu, a] adj adhesive, sticky ♦ m adhesive tape; (MED) sticking plaster

adestrar [adeʃ'tra*] vt to train; (cavalo) to break in

adeus [a'dewʃ] excl goodbye!

adiamento [adʒia'mẽtu] m postponement; (de uma sessão) adjournment

adiantado, -a [adʒjã'tadu, a] adj advanced; (relógio) fast; **chegar ~** to arrive ahead of time; **pagar ~** to pay in advance

adiantamento [adʒjãta'mẽtu] m progress; (dinheiro) advance (payment)

adiantar [adʒjã'ta*] vt (dinheiro, trabalho) to advance; (relógio) to put forward; **não adianta reclamar** there's no point on it's no use complaining

adiante [a'dʒjãtʃi] adv (na frente) in front; (para a frente) forward; **mais ~** further on; (no futuro) later on

adiar [a'dʒja*] vt to postpone, put off; (sessão) to adjourn

adição [adʒi'sãw] f (pl **-ões**) f addition; (MAT) sum; **adicionar** [adʒi-sjo'na*] vt to add

adido, -a [a'dʒidu, a] m/f attaché

adiro etc [a'diru] vb V **aderir**

adivinhação [adʒivina'sãw] f (destino) fortune-telling; (conjectura) guessing, guesswork

adivinhar [adʒivi'na*] vt to guess; (ler a sorte) to foretell ♦ vi to guess; **~ o pensamento de alguém** to read sb's mind; **adivinho, -a** [adʒi'vinu, a] m/f fortune-teller

adjetivo [adʒe'tʃivu] m adjective

adjudicar [adʒudʒi'ka*] vt to award, grant

administração [adʒiminiʃtra'sãw] (pl **-ões**) f administration; (direção) management; (comissão) board

administrador, a [adʒiminiʃtra'do*, a] m/f administrator; (diretor) director; (gerente) manager

administrar [adʒiminiʃ'tra*] vt to administer, manage; (governar) to govern

admiração [adʒimira'sãw] f wonder; (estima) admiration; **ponto de ~** (PT) exclamation mark

admirado, -a [adʒimi'radu, a] *adj*
astonished, surprised

admirar [adʒimi'ra*] *vt* to admire;
admirar-se *vr*: **~-se de** to be surprised at; **admirável** [adʒimi'ravew] (*pl* -**eis**) *adj* amazing

admissão [adʒimi'sãw] (*pl* -**ões**) *f*
admission; (*consentimento para entrar*) admittance; (*de escola*) intake

admitir [adʒimi'tʃi*] *vt* to admit;
(*permitir*) to allow; (*funcionário*) to take on

adoção [ado'sãw] *f* adoption

adoçar [ado'sa*] *vt* to sweeten

adoecer [adoe'se*] *vi*: **~** (**de** *ou* **com**) to fall ill (with) ♦ *vt* to make ill

adoidado, -a [adoj'dadu, a] *adj*
crazy

adolescente [adole'sẽtʃi] *adj, m/f*
adolescent

adoptar *etc* [ado'ta*] (*PT*) = **adotar**
etc

adorar [ado'ra*] *vt* to adore; (*venerar*) to worship

adormecer [adoxme'se*] *vi* to fall
asleep; (*entorpecer-se*) to go numb;
adormecido, -a [adoxme'sidu, a]
adj sleeping ♦ *m/f* sleeper

adorno [a'doxnu] *m* adornment

adotar [ado'ta*] *vt* to adopt; **adotivo, -a** [ado'tʃivu, a] *adj* (*filho*)
adopted

adquirir [adʒiki'ri*] *vt* to acquire

Adriático, -a [a'drjatʃiku, a] *adj*: **o
(mar) ~** the Adriatic

adro ['adru] *m* (church) forecourt;
(*em volta da igreja*) churchyard

adulação [adula'sãw] *f* flattery

adulterar [aduwte'ra*] *vt* to adulterate; (*contas*) to falsify ♦ *vi* to commit adultery

adultério [aduw'terju] *m* adultery

adulto, -a [a'duwtu, a] *adj, m/f*
adult

advento [ad'vẽtu] *m* advent; **o A~**
Advent

advérbio [ad'vexbju] *m* adverb

adverso, -a [adʒi'vexsu, a] *adj*
adverse; (*oposto*): **~ a** opposed to

advertência [adʒivex'tẽʒa] *f* warning

advertir [adʒivex'tʃi*] *vt* to warn;
(*repreender*) to reprimand; (*chamar
a atenção a*) to draw attention to

advogado, -a [adʒivo'gadu, a] *m/f*
lawyer

advogar [adʒivo'ga*] *vt* to advocate; (*JUR*) to plead ♦ *vi* to practise
(*BRIT*) *ou* practice (*US*) law

aéreo, -a [a'erju, a] *adj* air *atr*

aerobarco [aero'baxku] *m* hovercraft

aeromoço, -a [aero'mosu, a] (*BR*)
m/f steward/air hostess

aeronáutica [aero'nawtʃika] *f* air
force; (*ciência*) aeronautics *sg*

aeronave [aero'navi] *f* aircraft

aeroporto [aero'poxtu] *m* airport

aerossol [aero'sɔw] (*pl* -**óis**) *m*
aerosol

afã [a'fã] *m* (*entusiasmo*) enthusiasm;
(*diligência*) diligence; (*ânsia*) eagerness; (*esforço*) effort

afagar [afa'ga*] *vt* to caress; (*cabelo*)
to stroke

afanar [afa'na*] (*col*) *vt* to nick,
pinch

afastado, -a [afaʃ'tadu, a] *adj* (*distante*) remote; (*isolado*) secluded;
manter-se ~ to keep to o.s.

afastamento [afaʃta'mẽtu] *m*
removal; (*distância*) distance; (*de
pessoal*) lay off

afastar [afaʃ'ta*] *vt* to remove; (*separar*) to separate; (*idéia*) to put out
of one's mind; (*pessoal*) to lay off;
afastar-se *vr* to move away

afável [a'favew] (*pl* -**eis**) *adj*
friendly

afazeres [afaˈzeriʃ] *mpl* business *sg*; (*dever*) duties, tasks; **~ domésticos** household chores

afectar *etc* [afekˈta*] (*PT*) = **afetar** *etc*

afeição [afejˈsɐ̃w] *f* affection, fondness; (*dedicação*) devotion; **afeiçoado, -a** [afejˈswadu, a] *adj*: **afeiçoado a** (*amoroso*) fond of; (*devotado*) devoted to; **afeiçoar-se** [afejˈswaxsi] *vr*: **afeiçoar-se a** to take a liking to

afeito, -a [aˈfejtu, a] *adj*: **~ a** accustomed to, used to

aferrado, -a [afeˈxadu, a] *adj* obstinate, stubborn

afetado, -a [afeˈtadu, a] *adj* affected

afetar [afeˈta*] *vt* to affect; (*fingir*) to feign

afetivo, -a [afeˈtʃivu, a] *adj* affectionate; (*problema*) emotional

afeto [aˈfetu] *m* affection; **afetuoso, -a** [afeˈtwozu, ɔza] *adj* affectionate

afiado, -a [aˈfjadu, a] *adj* sharp; (*pessoa*) well-trained

afiar [aˈfja*] *vt* to sharpen

aficionado, -a [afisjoˈnadu, a] *m/f* enthusiast

afilhado, -a [afiˈʎadu, a] *m/f* godson/goddaughter

afim [aˈfĩ] (*pl* **-ns**) *adj* (*semelhante*) similar; (*consangüíneo*) related ♦ *m/f* relative, relation

afinado, -a [afiˈnadu, a] *adj* in tune

afinal [afiˈnaw] *adv* at last, finally; **~ (de contas)** after all

afinar [afiˈna*] *vt* (*MÚS*) to tune

afinco [aˈfĩku] *m* tenacity, persistence

afins [aˈfĩʃ] *pl de* **afim**

afirmação [afixmaˈsɐ̃w] (*pl* **-ões**) *f* affirmation; (*declaração*) statement

afirmar [afixˈma*] *vt*, *vi* to affirm,

assert; (*declarar*) to declare

afirmativo, -a [afixmaˈtʃivu, a] *adj* affirmative

afixar [afikˈsa*] *vt* (*cartazes*) to stick, post

aflição [afliˈsɐ̃w] *f* affliction; (*ansiedade*) anxiety; (*angústia*) anguish

afligir [afliˈʒi*] *vt* to distress; (*atormentar*) to torment; (*inquietar*) to worry; **afligir-se** *vr*: **~-se com** to worry about; **aflito, -a** [aˈflitu, a] *pp de* **afligir** ♦ *adj* distressed, anxious

afluência [aˈflwēsja] *f* affluence; (*corrente copiosa*) flow; (*de pessoas*) stream; **afluente** [aˈflwētʃi] *adj* copious; (*rico*) affluent ♦ *m* tributary

afobação [afobaˈsɐ̃w] *f* fluster; (*ansiedade*) panic

afobado, -a [afoˈbadu, a] *adj* flustered; (*ansioso*) panicky, nervous

afobar [afoˈba*] *vt* to fluster; (*deixar ansioso*) to make nervous ou panicky ♦ *vi* to get flustered, to panic, get nervous; **afobar-se** *vr* to get flustered

afogar [afoˈga*] *vt* to drown ♦ *vi* (*AUTO*) to flood; **afogar-se** *vr* to drown

afoito, -a [aˈfojtu, a] *adj* bold, daring

afortunado, -a [afoxtuˈnadu, a] *adj* fortunate, lucky

África [ˈafrika] *f*: **a ~** Africa; **a ~ do Sul** South Africa; **africano, -a** [afriˈkanu, a] *adj*, *m/f* African

afro-brasileiro, -a [ˈafru-] (*pl* **~s**) *adj* Afro-Brazilian

afronta [aˈfrõta] *f* insult, affront; **afrontar** [afrõˈta*] *vt* to insult; (*ofender*) to offend

afrouxar [afroˈʃa*] *vt* (*desapertar*) to slacken; (*soltar*) to loosen ♦ *vi* to come loose

afta [ˈafta] *f* (mouth) ulcer

afugentar [afuʒẽ'ta*] *vt* to drive away, put to flight

afundar [afũ'da*] *vt* to sink; (*cavidade*) to deepen; **afundar-se** *vr* to sink

agachar-se [aga'faxsi] *vr* (*acaçapar-se*) to crouch, squat; (*curvar-se*) to stoop

agarrar [aga'xa*] *vt* to seize, grasp; **agarrar-se** *vr*: **~-se a** to cling to, hold on to

agasalhar [agaza'ʎa*] *vt* to dress warmly, wrap up; **agasalhar-se** *vr* to wrap o.s. up

agasalho [aga'zaʎu] *m* (*casaco*) coat; (*suéter*) sweater

ágeis ['aʒejʃ] *pl de* **ágil**

agência [a'ʒẽsja] *f* agency; (*escritório*) office; **~ de correio** (*BR*) post office; **~ de viagens** travel agency

agenda [a'ʒẽda] *f* diary

agente [a'ʒẽtʃi] *m/f* agent; (*de polícia*) policeman/woman

ágil ['aʒiw] (*pl* **-eis**) *adj* agile

agir [a'ʒi*] *vi* to act

agitação [aʒita'sãw] (*pl* **-ões**) *f* agitation; (*perturbação*) disturbance; (*inquietação*) restlessness

agitado, -a [aʒi'tadu, a] *adj* agitated, disturbed; (*inquieto*) restless

agitar [aʒi'ta*] *vt* to agitate, disturb; (*sacudir*) to shake; (*cauda*) to wag; (*mexer*) to stir; **agitar-se** *vr* to get upset; (*mar*) to get rough

aglomeração [aglomera'sãw] (*pl* **-ões**) *f* gathering; (*multidão*) crowd

aglomerado [aglome'radu] *m*: **~ urbano** city

aglomerar [aglome'ra*] *vt* to heap up, pile up; **aglomerar-se** *vr* (*multidão*) to crowd together

agonia [ago'nia] *f* agony, anguish; (*ânsia da morte*) death throes *pl*; **agonizante** [agoni'zãtʃi] *adj* dying

♦ *m/f* dying person; **agonizar** [agoni'za*] *vi* to be dying; (*afligir-se*) to agonize

agora [a'gɔra] *adv* now; **~ mesmo** right now; (*há pouco*) a moment ago; **até ~** so far, up to now; **por ~** for now

agosto [a'goʃtu] (*PT* **A~**) *m* August

agouro [a'goru] *m* omen

agraciar [agra'sja*] *vt* to decorate

agradar [agra'da*] *vt* to please; (*fazer agrados a*) to be nice to ♦ *vi* to be pleasing; (*satisfazer*) to go down well

agradável [agra'davew] (*pl* **-eis**) *adj* pleasant

agradecer [agrade'se*] *vt*: **~ algo a alguém**, **~ a alguém por algo** to thank sb for sth; **agradecido, -a** [agrade'sidu, a] *adj* grateful; **mal agradecido** ungrateful; **agradecimento** [agradesi'mẽtu] *m* gratitude; **agradecimentos** *mpl* (*gratidão*) thanks

agrado [a'gradu] *m*: **fazer um ~ a alguém** (*afagar*) to be affectionate with sb; (*ser agradável*) to be nice to sb

agrário, -a [a'grarju, a] *adj* agrarian; **reforma agrária** land reform

agravante [agra'vãtʃi] *adj* aggravating ♦ *f* aggravating circumstance

agravar [agra'va*] *vt* to aggravate, make worse; **agravar-se** *vr* (*piorar*) to get worse

agravo [a'gravu] *m* (*JUR*) appeal

agredir [agre'dʒi*] *vt* to attack; (*insultar*) to insult

agregar [agre'ga*] *vt* (*juntar*) to collect; (*acrescentar*) to add

agressão [agre'sãw] (*pl* **-ões**) *f* aggression; (*ataque*) attack; (*assalto*) assault

agressivo, -a [agre'sivu, a] *adj* aggressive

agressões [agre'sõjʃ] *fpl de* **agressão**

agreste [a'grɛʃtʃi] *adj* rural, rustic; (*terreno*) wild

agrião [a'grjãw] *m* watercress

agrícola [a'grikola] *adj* agricultural

agricultor [agrikuw'to*] *m* farmer

agricultura [agrikuw'tura] *f* agriculture, farming

agrido *etc* [a'gridu] *vb V* **agredir**

agridoce [agri'dosi] *adj* bittersweet

agronomia [agrono'mia] *f* agronomy

agropecuária [agrope'kwarja] *f* farming, agriculture

agrupar [agru'pa*] *vt* to group; **agrupar-se** *vr* to group together

agrura [a'grura] *f* bitterness

água ['agwa] *f* water; ~ **spl** (*mar*) waters; (*chuvas*) rain *sg*; (*maré*) tides; ~ **abaixo/acima** downstream/upstream; **dar** ~ **na boca** (*comida*) to be mouthwatering; **estar na** ~ (*bêbado*) to be drunk; **fazer** ~ (*NÁUT*) to leak; ~ **benta/corrente/doce** holy/running/fresh water; ~ **dura/leve** hard/soft water; ~ **mineral** mineral water; ~ **oxigenada** peroxide; ~ **salgada** salt water; ~ **sanitária** household bleach

aguaceiro [agwa'sejru] *m* (*chuva*) (heavy) shower, downpour

água-de-coco *f* coconut milk

água-de-colônia (*pl* **águas-de-colônia**) *f* eau-de-cologne

aguado, -a [a'gwadu, a] *adj* watery

aguardar [agwax'da*] *vt* to await; (*contar com*) to expect ♦ *vi* to wait

aguardente [agwax'dẽtʃi] *m* kind of brandy

aguarrás [agwa'xajʃ] *f* turpentine

aguçado, -a [agu'sadu, a] *adj* pointed; (*espírito, sentidos*) acute

agudo, -a [a'gudu, a] *adj* sharp, shrill; (*intenso*) acute

agüentar [agwẽ'ta*] *vt* (*muro etc*) to hold up; (*dor, injustiças*) to stand, put up with; (*peso*) to withstand ♦ *vi* to last; **agüentar-se** *vr* to remain, hold on; ~ **fazer algo** to manage to do sth; **não** ~ **de** not to be able to stand

águia ['agja] *f* eagle; (*fig*) genius

agulha [a'guʎa] *f* (*de coser, tricô*) needle; (*NÁUT*) compass; (*FERRO*) points *pl* (*BRIT*), switch (*US*); **trabalho de** ~ needlework

ai [aj] *excl* (*suspiro*) ow!; (*de dor*) ouch! ♦ *m* (*suspiro*) sigh; (*gemido*) groan; ~ **de mim** poor me!

aí [a'i] *adv* there; (*então*) then; **por** ~ (*em lugar indeterminado*) somewhere over there, thereabouts; **espera** ~! wait!, hang on a minute!; **está** ~! (*col*) right!; **e** ~? and then what?

AIDS ['ajdʒs] *abr f* AIDS

ainda [a'ĩda] *adv* still; (*mesmo*) even; ~ **agora** just now; ~ **assim** even so, nevertheless; ~ **bem** just as well; ~ **por cima** on top of all that, in addition; ~ **não** not yet; ~ **que** even if; **maior** ~ even bigger

aipo ['ajpu] *m* celery

ajeitar [aʒej'ta*] *vt* (*roupa, cabelo*) to adjust; (*emprego*) to arrange; **ajeitar-se** *vr* to adapt

ajo *etc* ['aʒu] *vb V* **agir**

ajoelhar [aʒwe'ʎa*] *vi* to kneel (down); **ajoelhar-se** *vr* to kneel down

ajuda [a'ʒuda] *f* help; (*subsídio*) grant, subsidy; **dar** ~ **a alguém** to lend ou give sb a hand; ~ **de custo** allowance; **ajudante** *m/f* assistant, helper; (*MIL*) adjutant

ajudar [aʒu'da*] *vt* to help

ajuizado, -a [aʒwi'zadu, a] *adj* (*sensato*) sensible; (*sábio*) wise; (*prudente*) discreet

ajuntamento [aʒũta'mẽtu] *m*
gathering

ajuntar [aʒũ'ta*] *vt* (*unir*) to join;
(*documentos*) to attach; (*reunir*) to
gather

ajustagem [aʒuʃ'taʒẽ] (*BR*) (*pl* **-ns**) *f*
(*TEC*) adjustment

ajustamento [aʒuʃta'mẽtu] *m*
adjustment; (*de contas*) settlement

ajustar [aʒuʃ'ta*] *vt* to adjust;
(*conta, disputa*) to settle; (*acomodar*) to fit; (*roupa*) to take in;
(*preço*) to agree on; **ajustar-se** *vr*:
~-se a to conform to; (*adaptar-se*)
to adapt to

ajuste [a'ʒuʃtʃi] *m* (*acordo*) agreement; (*de contas*) settlement;
(*adaptação*) adaptation

ala ['ala] *f* wing; (*fileira*) row; (*passagem*) aisle

alagar [ala'ga*] *vt, vi* to flood

alameda [ala'meda] *f* (*avenida*)
avenue; (*arvoredo*) grove

alarde [a'laxdʒi] *m* ostentation; (*jac-
tância*) boasting; **fazer ~ de** to
boast about; **alardear** [alax'dʒja*]
vt to show off; (*gabar-se de*) to
boast of ♦ *vi* to show off; to boast;
alardear-se *vr* to boast

alargar [alax'ga*] *vt* to extend;
(*fazer mais largo*) to widen, broad-
en; (*afrouxar*) to loosen, slacken

alarma [a'laxma] *f* alarm; (*susto*)
panic; (*tumulto*) tumult; (*vozearia*)
outcry; **dar o sinal de ~** to raise the
alarm; **~ de roubo** burglar alarm;
alarmante [alax'mãtʃi] *adj* alarm-
ing; **alarmar** [alax'ma*] *vt* to
alarm; **alarmar-se** *vr* to be
alarmed

alarme [a'laxmi] *m* = **alarma**

alastrar [alaʃ'tra*] *vt* to scatter; (*disseminar*) to spread; **alastrar-se** *vr*
(*epidemia, rumor*) to spread

alavanca [ala'vãka] *f* lever; (*pé-de-*

cabra) crowbar; **~ de mudanças**
gear lever

albergue [aw'bexgi] *m* (*estalagem*)
inn; (*refúgio*) hospice, shelter; **~
noturno** hotel; **~ para jovens** youth
hostel

albufeira [awbu'fejra] *f* lagoon

álbum ['awbũ] (*pl* **-ns**) *m* album; **~
de recortes** scrapbook

alça ['awsa] *f* strap; (*asa*) handle; (*de
fusil*) sight

alcachofra [awka'ʃofra] *f* artichoke

alcançar [awkã'sa*] *vt* to reach;
(*estender*) to hand, pass; (*obter*) to
obtain, get; (*atingir*) to attain;
(*compreender*) to understand;
(*desfalcar*): **~ uma firma em $1 mi-
lhão** to embezzle $1 million from a
firm

alcance [aw'kãsi] *m* reach; (*competência*) power; (*compreensão*)
understanding, grasp; (*de tiro, visão*)
range; **ao ~** within reach *ou*
range of; **ao ~ da voz** within
earshot; **de grande ~** far-reaching;
fora do ~ da mão out of reach; **fora
do ~ de alguém** beyond sb's grasp

alcaparra [awka'paxa] *f* caper

alçar [aw'sa*] *vt* to lift (up); (*voz*) to
raise

alcatrão [awka'trãw] *m* tar

álcool ['awkow] *m* alcohol; **alcoólatra** [aw'kɔlatra] *m/f* alcoholic;
alcoólico, -a [aw'kɔliku, a] *adj*,
m/f alcoholic

Alcorão [awko'rãw] *m* Koran

alcova [aw'kova] *f* bedroom

alcunha [aw'kuɲa] *f* nickname

aldeão, -eã [aw'dʒjãw, jã] (*pl* **-ões**,
~s) *m/f* villager

aldeia [aw'deja] *f* village

aldeões [aw'dʒjõjʃ] *mpl de* **aldeão**

alecrim [ale'krĩ] *m* rosemary

alegar [ale'ga*] *vt* to allege; (*JUR*) to
plead

alegoria [alego'ria] f allegory

alegórico, -a [ale'gɔriku, a] adj allegorical; **carro alegórico** float

alegrar [ale'gra*] vt to cheer (up), gladden; (ambiente) to brighten up; (animar) to liven (up); **alegrar-se** vr to cheer up

alegre [a'lɛgri] adj cheerful; (contente) happy, glad; (cores) bright; (embriagado) merry, tight; **alegria** [ale'gria] f joy, happiness

aleijado, -a [alej'ʒadu, a] adj crippled ♦ m/f cripple

aleijar [alej'ʒa*] vt to maim

além [a'lɛj] adv (lá ao longe) over there; (mais adiante) further on ♦ m: **o ~** the hereafter ♦ prep: **~ de** beyond; (no outro lado de) on the other side of; (para mais de) over; (ademais de) apart from, besides; **~ disso** moreover; **mais ~** further

alemã [ale'mã] f de alemão

alemães [ale'mãjʃ] mpl de alemão

Alemanha [ale'mãɲa] f: **a ~** Germany

alemão, -mã [ale'mãw, 'mã] (pl **-ães**) ♦ adj, m/f German ♦ m (LING) German

alentador, a [alẽta'do*, a] adj encouraging

alento [a'lẽtu] m (fôlego) breath; (ânimo) courage; **dar ~** to encourage; **tomar ~** to draw breath

alergia [alex'ʒia] f: **~ a** (a) allergy (to); (fig) aversion (to); **alérgico, -a** [a'lɛxʒiku, a] adj: **alérgico (a)** allergic (to); **ele é alérgico a João/política** he can't stand João/politics

alerta [a'lɛxta] adj alert ♦ adv on the alert ♦ m alert

alfabetizar [awfabetʃi'za*] vt to teach to read and write; **alfabetizar-se** vr to learn to read and write

alfabeto [awfa'bɛtu] m alphabet

alface [aw'fasi] f lettuce

alfaiate [awfa'jatʃi] m tailor

alfândega [aw'fãdʒiga] f customs pl, customs house; **alfandegário, -a** [awfãde'garju, a] m/f customs officer

alfazema [awfa'zema] f lavender

alfinete [awfi'netʃi] m pin; **~ de segurança** safety pin

alga ['awga] f seaweed

algarismo [awga'riʒmu] m numeral, digit

Algarve [aw'gaxvi] m: **o ~** the Algarve

algazarra [awga'zaxa] f uproar, racket

álgebra ['awʒebra] f algebra

algemas [aw'ʒemaʃ] fpl handcuffs

algo ['awgu] adv somewhat, rather ♦ pron something; (qualquer coisa) anything

algodão [awgo'dãw] m cotton; **~ (hidrófilo)** cotton wool (BRIT), absorbent cotton (US)

alguém [aw'gẽj] pron someone, somebody; (em frases interrogativas ou negativas) anyone, anybody

algum, -ma [aw'gũ, 'guma] (pl **-ns, ~s**) adj some; (em frases interrogativas ou negativas) any ♦ pron one; (no plural) some; (negativa): **de modo ~** in no way; **coisa ~a** nothing; **~ dia** one day; **~ tempo** for a while; **~a coisa** something; **~a vez** sometime

algures [aw'guriʃ] adv somewhere

alheio, -a [a'ʎeju, a] adj (de outrem) someone else's; (estranho) alien; (estrangeiro) foreign; (impróprio) irrelevant

alho ['aʎu] m garlic

ali [a'li] adv there; **até ~** up to there; **por ~** around there; (direção) that way; **~ por** (tempo) round about; **de ~ por diante** from then on;

~ **dentro** in there
aliado, -a [a'ljadu, a] *adj* allied
♦ *m/f* ally
aliança [a'ljãsa] *f* alliance; (*anel*) wedding ring
aliar [a'lja*] *vt* to ally; **aliar-se** *vr* to form an alliance
aliás [a'ljajʃ] *adv* (*a propósito*) as a matter of fact; (*ou seja*) rather, that is; (*contudo*) nevertheless; (*diga-se de passagem*) incidentally
álibi ['alibi] *m* alibi
alicate [ali'katʃi] *m* pliers *pl*; ~ **de unhas** nail clippers *pl*
alienação [aljena'sãw] *f* alienation; (*de bens*) transfer (of property); ~ **mental** insanity
alienado, -a [alje'nadu, a] *adj* alienated; (*demente*) insane; (*bens*) transferred ♦ *m/f* lunatic
alienar [alje'na*] *vt* (*afastar*) to alienate; (*bens*) to transfer
alimentação [alimẽta'sãw] *f* (*alimentos*) food; (*ação*) feeding; (*nutrição*) nourishment; (*ELET*) supply
alimentar [alimẽ'ta*] *vt* to feed; (*fig*) to nurture ♦ *adj* (*produto*) food *atr*; (*hábitos*) eating *atr* **alimentar-se** *vr*: ~-**se de** to feed on
alimento [ali'mẽtu] *m* food; (*nutrição*) nourishment
alinhado, -a [ali'nadu, a] *adj* (*elegante*) elegant; (*texto*): ~ **à esquerda/direita** ranged left/right
alinhar [ali'na*] *vt* to align; **alinhar-se** *vr* to form a line
alinho [a'liɲu] *m* (*alinhamento*) alignment; (*elegância*) neatness
alisar [ali'za*] *vt* to smooth; (*cabelo*) to straighten; (*acariciar*) to stroke
aliviar [ali'vja*] *vt* to relieve
alívio [a'livju] *m* relief
alma ['awma] *f* soul; (*entusiasmo*) enthusiasm; (*caráter*) character
almejar [awme'ʒa*] *vt* to long for,

yearn for
almirante [awmi'rãtʃi] *m* admiral
almoçar [awmo'sa*] *vi* to have lunch ♦ *vt*: ~ **peixe** to have fish for lunch
almoço [aw'mosu] *m* lunch; **pequeno** ~ (*PT*) breakfast
almofada [awmo'fada] *f* cushion; (*PT: travesseiro*) pillow
almoxarifado [awmoʃari'fadu] *m* storeroom
alô [a'lo] (*BR*) *excl* (*TEL*) hullo
alocar [alo'ka*] *vt* to allocate
alojamento [aloʒa'mẽtu] *m* accommodation (*BRIT*), accommodations *pl* (*US*); (*habitação*) housing
alojar [alo'ʒa*] *vt* (*hóspede: numa pensão*) to accommodate; (: *numa casa*) to put up; (*sem teto, refugiado*) to house; (*MIL*) to billet; **alojar-se** *vr* to stay
alongar [alõ'ga*] *vt* to lengthen; (*braço*) to stretch out; (*prazo, contrato*) to extend; (*reunião, sofrimento*) to prolong; **alongar-se** *vr* (*sobre um assunto*) to dwell
aloprado, -a [alo'pradu, a] (*col*) *adj* nutty
alpendre [aw'pẽdri] *m* (*telheiro*) shed; (*pórtico*) porch
Alpes ['awpiʃ] *mpl*: **os** ~ the Alps
alpinismo [awpi'niʒmu] *m* mountaineering, climbing; **alpinista** [awpi'niʃta] *m/f* mountaineer, climber
alta ['awta] *f* (*de preços*) rise; (*de hospital*) discharge
altar [aw'ta*] *m* altar
alteração [awtera'sãw] (*pl* -**ões**) *f* alteration; (*desordem*) disturbance; (*falsificação*) falsification
alterado, -a [awte'radu, a] *adj* bad-tempered, irritated
alterar [awte'ra*] *vt* to alter; (*falsificar*) to falsify; **alterar-se** *vr*

change; (*enfurecer-se*) to get angry, lose one's temper

alternar [awtex'na*] vt, vi to alternate; **alternar-se** vr to alternate; (*por turnos*) to take turns

alternativa [awtexna'tʃiva] f alternative

alternativo, -a [awtexna'tʃivu, a] adj alternative; (*ELET*) alternating

alteza [aw'teza] f highness

altitude [awtʃi'tudʒi] f altitude

altivez [awtʃi'veʒ] f (*arrogância*) haughtiness; (*nobreza*) loftiness; **altivo, -a** [aw'tʃivu, a] adj haughty; lofty

alto, -a ['awtu, a] adj high; (*pessoa*) tall; (*som*) high, sharp; (*voz*) loud; (*GEO*) upper ♦ adv (*falar*) loudly, loud; (*voar*) high ♦ excl halt! ♦ m top, summit; **do** ~ from above; **por** ~ superficially; **alta fidelidade** high fidelity, hi-fi; **na alta noite** at dead of night

alto-falante (*pl* ~s) m loudspeaker

altura [aw'tura] f height; (*momento*) point, juncture; (*altitude*) altitude; (*de um som*) pitch; **em que** ~ **do Rio Branco fica a livraria?** whereabouts in Rio Branco is the bookshop?; **nesta** ~ at this juncture; **estar à** ~ **de** (*ser capaz de*) to be up to; **ter 1.80 metros de** ~ to be 1.80 metres (*BRIT*) ou meters (*US*) tall

alucinado, -a [alusi'nadu, a] adj crazy

alucinante [alusi'nãtʃi] adj crazy

alugar [alu'ga*] vt (*tomar de aluguel*) to rent, hire; (*dar de aluguel*) to let, rent out; **alugar-se** vr to let; **aluguel** [alu'gew] (*pl* -**éis**) (*BR*) m rent; (*ação*) renting; **aluguel de carro** car hire (*BRIT*) ou rental (*US*); **aluguer** [alu'ge*] (*PT*) m = **aluguel**

alumiar [alu'mja*] vt to light (up) ♦ vi to give light

alumínio [alu'minju] m aluminium (*BRIT*), aluminum (*US*)

aluno, -a [a'lunu, a] m/f pupil, student

alvejar [awve'ʒa*] vt (*tomar como alvo*) to aim at; (*branquear*) to bleach

alvenaria [awvena'ria] f masonry; **de** ~ brick atr, brick-built

alvéolo [aw'vɛolu] m cavity

alvo, -a ['awvu, a] adj white ♦ m target

alvorada [awvo'rada] f dawn

alvorecer [awvore'se*] vi to dawn

alvoroço [awvo'rosu] m commotion; (*entusiasmo*) enthusiasm

amabilidade [amabili'dadʒi] f kindness; (*simpatia*) friendliness

amaciante [ama'sjãtʃi] m: ~ (**de roupa**) fabric conditioner

amaciar [ama'sja*] vt (*tornar macio*) to soften; (*carro*) to run in

amado, -a [a'madu, a] m/f beloved, sweetheart

amador, a [ama'do*, a] adj, m/f amateur

amadurecer [amadure'se*] vt, vi (*frutos*) to ripen; (*fig*) to mature

âmago ['amagu] m (*centro*) heart, core; (*medula*) pith; (*essência*) essence

amaldiçoar [amawdʒi'swa*] vt to curse, swear at

amalgamar [amawga'ma*] vt to amalgamate; (*combinar*) to fuse (*BRIT*), fuze (*US*), blend

amalucado, -a [amalu'kadu, a] adj crazy, whacky

amamentar [amamẽ'ta*] vt, vi to breast-feed

amanhã [ama'ɲã] adv, m tomorrow

amanhecer [amaɲe'se*] vi (*alvorecer*) to dawn; (*encontrar-se pela manhã*): **amanhecemos em Paris** we were in Paris at daybreak ♦ m dawn; **ao ~ at** daybreak

amansar [amã'sa*] vt (animais) to
tame; (cavalos) to break in; (aplacar) to placate

amante [a'mãtʃi] m/f lover

amar [a'ma*] vt to love

amarelo, -a [ama'rɛlu, a] adj yellow
♦ m yellow

amargar [amax'ga*] vt to make bitter; (fig) to embitter

amargo, -a [a'maxgu, a] adj bitter;
amargura [amax'gura] f bitterness

amarrar [ama'xa*] vt to tie (up);
(NÁUT) to moor; **~ a cara** to frown,
scowl

amarrotar [amaxo'ta*] vt to crease

amassar [ama'sa*] vt (pão) to
knead; (misturar) to mix; (papel) to
screw up; (roupa) to crease; (carro)
to dent

amável [a'mavew] (pl -eis) adj kind

Amazonas [ama'zonaʃ] m: **o ~ the**
Amazon

Amazônia [ama'zonja] f: **a ~ the**
Amazon region; see boxed note

AMAZÔNIA

Amazônia is the region formed
by the basin of the river Amazon
(the river with the largest volume
of water in the world) and its
tributaries. With a total area of almost 7 million square kilometres,
it stretches from the Atlantic to
the Andes. Most of Amazônia is
in Brazilian territory, although it
also extends into Peru, Colombia,
Venezuela and Bolivia. It contains
the richest biodiversity and largest
area of tropical rainforest in the
world.

ambição [ambi'sãw] (pl -ões) f
ambition; **ambicionar** [ãbisjo'na*]
vt to aspire to; **ambicioso, -a**

[ãbi'sjozu, ɔza] adj ambitious

ambidestro, -a [ãbi'deʃtru, a] adj
ambidextrous

ambientar [ãbjẽ'ta*] vt (filme etc) to
set; (adaptar): **~ alguém a algo** to
get sb used to sth; **ambientar-se**
vr to fit in

ambiente [ã'bjẽtʃi] m atmosphere;
(meio, COMPUT) environment; **meio ~**
environment; **temperatura ~** room
temperature

ambíguo, -a [ã'bigwu, a] adj
ambiguous

âmbito ['ãbitu] m extent; (campo de
ação) scope, range

ambos, -as ['ãbuʃ, aʃ] adj pl both

ambulância [ãbu'lãsja] f ambulance

ambulante [ãbu'lãtʃi] adj walking;
(errante) wandering; (biblioteca)
mobile

ambulatório [ãbula'tɔrju] m outpatient department

ameaça [ame'asa] f threat; **ameaçar** [amea'sa*] vt to threaten

amedrontar [amedrõ'ta*] vt to
scare, intimidate; **amedrontar-se**
vr to be frightened

ameixa [a'mejʃa] f plum; (passa)
prune

amém [a'mẽj] excl amen

amêndoa [a'mẽdwa] f almond;
amendoeira [amẽ'dwejra] f almond tree

amendoim [amẽdo'ĩ] (pl -ns) m
peanut

amenidade [ameni'dadʒi] f well-
being; **~s** fpl (assuntos superficiais)
small talk sg

amenizar [ameni'za*] vt (abrandar)
to soften; (tornar agradável) to
make pleasant; (facilitar) to ease

ameno, -a [a'mɛnu, a] adj pleasant;
(clima) mild

América [a'mɛrika] f: **a ~** America;

a ~ do Norte/do Sul North/South America; **a ~ Central/Latina** Central/Latin America; **americano, -a** [ameri'kanu, a] adj, m/f American

amestrar [ameʃ'tra*] vt to train

amianto [a'mjãtu] m asbestos

amido [a'midu] m starch

amigável [ami'gavew] (pl -eis) adj amicable, friendly

amígdala [a'migdala] f tonsil; **amigdalite** [amigda'litʃi] f tonsillitis

amigo, -a [a'migu, a] adj friendly ♦ m/f friend; **ser ~ de** to be friends with

amistoso, -a [amiʃ'tozu, ɔza] adj friendly, cordial ♦ m (jogo) friendly

amiúde [a'mjudʒi] adv often, frequently

amizade [ami'zadʒi] f (relação) friendship; (simpatia) friendliness

amnistia [amniʃ'tia] (PT) f = **anistia**

amolação [amola'sãw] (pl -ões) f bother, annoyance

amolar [amo'la*] vt to sharpen; (aborrecer) to annoy, bother ♦ vi to be annoying

amolecer [amole'se*] vt to soften ♦ vi to soften; (abrandar-se) to relent

amônia [a'monja] f ammonia

amoníaco [amo'niaku] m ammonia

amontoar [amõ'twa*] vt to pile up, accumulate; **~ riquezas** to amass a fortune

amor [a'mo*] m love; **por ~ de** for the sake of; **fazer ~** to make love

amora [a'mɔra] f: **~ silvestre** blackberry

amordaçar [amoxda'sa*] vt to gag

amoroso, -a [amo'rozu, ɔza] adj loving, affectionate

amor-perfeito (pl **amores-perfeitos**) m pansy

amortecedor [amoxtese'do*] m shock absorber

amortização [amoxtʃiza'sãw] f payment in instalments (BRIT) ou installments (US)

amortizar [amoxtʃi'za*] vt to pay in instalments (BRIT) ou installments (US)

amostra [a'mɔʃtra] f sample

amparar [ãpa'ra*] vt to support; (ajudar) to help, assist; **ampararse** vr: **~-se em** to lean on

amparo [ã'paru] m support; help, assistance

ampliação [amplia'sãw] (pl -ões) f enlargement; (extensão) extension

ampliar [ã'plja*] vt to enlarge; (conhecimento) to broaden

amplificador [ãplifika'do*] m amplifier

amplificar [ãplifi'ka*] vt to amplify

amplitude [ãpli'tudʒi] f (espaço) spaciousness; (fig: extensão) extent

amplo, -a [ã'plu, a] adj (sala) spacious; (conhecimento, sentido) broad; (possibilidade) ample

amputar [ãpu'ta*] vt to amputate

Amsterdã [amiʃtex'dã] (BR) n Amsterdam

Amsterdão [amiʃtex'dãw] (PT) n = **Amsterdã**

amuado, -a [a'mwadu, a] adj sulky

aná [a'nã] f de **anão**

anais [a'najʃ] mpl annals

analfabeto, -a [anawfa'betu, a] adj, m/f illiterate

analgésico [anaw'ʒeziku] m painkiller, analgesic

analisar [anali'za*] vt to analyse; **análise** [a'nalizi] f analysis; **analista** [ana'liʃta] m/f analyst

ananás [ana'naʃ] (pl **ananases**) m (BR) variety of pineapple (PT) pineapple

anão, -anã [a'nãw, a'nã] (pl -ões,

~s) m/f dwarf

anarquia [anax'kia] f anarchy;
anarquista [anax'kiʃta] m/f anarchist

anatomia [anato'mia] f anatomy

anca ['ãka] f (de pessoa) hip; (de animal) rump

ancião, -anciã [ã'sjãw, ã'sjã] (pl
-ões, ~s) adj old ♦ m/f old man/
woman; (de uma tribo) elder

anciões [a'sjõjʃ] mpl de ancião

âncora ['ãkora] f anchor; **ancorar**
[ãko'ra*] vt, vi to anchor

andaime [ã'dajmi] m (ARQ) scaffolding

andamento [ãda'mẽtu] m (progresso) progress; (rumo) course; (MÚS)
tempo; **em ~** in progress

andar [ã'da*] vi to walk; (máquina)
to work; (progredir) to progress; (estar): **ela anda triste** she's been
sad lately ♦ m gait; (pavimento)
floor, storey (BRIT), story (US); **anda!**
hurry up!; **~ a cavalo** to ride; **~ de
trem/avião/bicicleta** to travel by
train/fly/ride a bike

Andes ['ãdʒiʃ] mpl: **os ~** the Andes

andorinha [ãdo'riɲa] f (pássaro)
swallow

anedota [ane'dɔta] f anecdote

anel [a'new] (pl -éis) m ring; (elo)
link; (de cabelo) curl; **~ de casamento** wedding ring

anemia [ane'mia] f anaemia (BRIT),
anemia (US)

anestesia [aneʃte'zia] f anaesthesia
(BRIT), anesthesia (US); (anestésico)
anaesthetic (BRIT), anesthetic (US)

anexar [anek'sa*] vt to annex; (juntar) to attach; (documento) to
enclose; **anexo, -a** [a'neksu, a]
adj attached ♦ m annexe; (em carta)
enclosure; **segue em anexo** please
find enclosed

anfitrião, -triã [ãfi'trjãw, 'trjã] (pl

-ões, ~s) m/f host/hostess

angina [ã'ʒina] f: **~ do peito** angina
(pectoris)

Angola [ã'gɔla] f Angola

angu [ã'gu] m corn-meal purée

ângulo ['ãgulu] m angle; (canto)
corner

angústia [ã'guʃtʃa] f anguish, distress; **angustiante** [ãguʃ'tʃjãtʃi]
adj distressing; (momentos) anxious,
nerve-racking

animação [anima'sãw] f (vivacidade) liveliness; (movimento) bustle;
(entusiasmo) enthusiasm

animado, -a [ani'madu, a] adj lively; (alegre) cheerful; **~ com** enthusiastic about

animador, a [anima'do*, a] adj
encouraging ♦ m/f (BR: TV) presenter

animal [ani'maw] (pl -ais) adj, m
animal; **~ de estimação** pet (animal)

animar [ani'ma*] vt to liven up;
(encorajar) to encourage; **animarse** vr to cheer up; (festa etc) to liven
up; **~-se a** to bring o.s. to

ânimo ['animu] m (coragem)
courage; **~!** cheer up!; **perder o ~**
to lose heart, **reobrar o ~** to pluck
up courage; (alegrar) to cheer up

aninhar [ani'ɲa*] vt to nestle;
aninhar-se vr to nestle

anis [a'niʃ] m aniseed

anistia [aniʃ'tʃia] f amnesty

aniversário [anivex'sarju] m
anniversary; (de nascimento) birthday; (: festa) birthday party

anjo ['ãʒu] m angel; **~ da guarda**
guardian angel

ano ['anu] m year; **Feliz A~ Novo!**
Happy New Year!; **o ~ que vem**
next year; **por per annum**; **fazer ~s**
to have a birthday; **ter dez ~s** to be
ten (years old); **dia de ~s** (PT) birthday; **~ letivo** academic year; (da

escola) school year

anões [a'nõjʃ] *mpl de* **anão**·

anoitecer [anojte'se*] *vi* to grow dark ♦ *m* nightfall

anomalia [anoma'lia] *f* anomaly

anônimo, -a [a'nonimu, a] *adj* anonymous

anoraque [ano'raki] *m* anorak

anormal [anox'maw] (*pl* **-ais**) *adj* abnormal; (*excepcional*) handicapped; **anormalidade** [anoxmali'dadʒi] *f* abnormality

anotação [anota'sãw] (*pl* **-ões**) *f* annotation; (*nota*) note

anotar [ano'ta*] *vt* to annotate; (*tomar nota*) to note down

anseio *etc* [ã'seju] *vb V* **ansiar**

ânsia ['ãsja] *f* anxiety; (*desejo*): **~ (de)** longing (for); **ter ~s (de vômito)** to feel sick

ansiar [ã'sja*] *vi*: **~ por** (*desejar*) to yearn for; **~ por fazer** to long to do

ansiedade [ãsje'dadʒi] *f* anxiety; (*desejo*) eagerness

ansioso, -a [ã'sjozu, ɔza] *adj* anxious; (*desejoso*) eager

Antártico [ã'taxtʃiku] *m*: **o ~** the Antarctic

ante ['ãtʃi] *prep* (*na presença de*) before; (*em vista de*) in view of, faced with

antecedência [ãtese'dẽsja] *f*: **com ~** in advance; **3 dias de ~** three days' notice

antecedente [ãtese'dẽtʃi] *adj* preceding ♦ *m* antecedent; **~s** *mpl* (*registro*) record *sg*; (*passado*) background *sg*

anteceder [ãtese'de*] *vt* to precede

antecipação [ãtesipa'sãw] *f* anticipation; **com um mês de ~** a month in advance; **~ de pagamento** advance (payment)

antecipadamente [ãtesipada-'mẽtʃi] *adv* in advance, beforehand

antecipado, -a [ãtesi'padu, a] *adj* (*pagamento*) (in) advance

antecipar [ãtesi'pa*] *vt* to anticipate, forestall; (*adiantar*) to bring forward

antemão [ãte'mãw]: **de ~** *adv* beforehand

antena [ã'tena] *f* (*BIO*) antenna, feeler; (*RÁDIO*, *TV*) aerial

anteontem [ãtʃi'õtẽ] *adv* the day before yesterday

antepassado [ãtʃipa'sadu] *m* ancestor

anterior [ãte'rjo*] *adj* previous; (*antigo*) former; (*de posição*) front

antes ['ãtʃiʃ] *adv* before; (*antigamente*) formerly; (*ao contrário*) rather ♦ *prep*: **~ de** before; **o quanto ~ as** soon as possible; **~ de partir** before leaving; **~ de tudo** above all; **~ que** before

anti- [ãtʃi] *prefixo* anti-

antiácido, -a [ã'tʃjasidu, a] *adj* antacid ♦ *m* antacid

antibiótico, -a [ãtʃi'bjɔtʃiku, a] *adj* antibiotic ♦ *m* antibiotic

anticaspa [ãtʃi'kaʃpa] *adj inv*: **xampu ~** dandruff shampoo

anticlímax [ãtʃi'klimakʃ] *m* anticlimax

anticoncepcional [ãtʃikõsepsjo-'naw] (*pl* **-ais**) *adj, m* contraceptive

anticongelante [ãtʃikõʒe'lãtʃi] *m* antifreeze

antidepressivo [ãtʃidepre'sivu] *m* antidepressant

antigamente [ãtʃiga'mẽtʃi] *adv* formerly; (*no passado*) in the past

antigo, -a [ã'tʃigu, a] *adj* old; (*histórico*) ancient; (*de estilo*) antique; (*chefe etc*) former

antiguidade [ãtʃigi'dadʒi] *f* antiquity, ancient times *pl*; (*de emprego*) seniority; **~s** *fpl* (*monumentos*) ancient monuments; (*artigos*) antiques

anti-horário, -a adj anticlockwise

antilhano, -a [ãtʃiˈʎanu, a] adj, m/f West Indian

Antilhas [ãˈtʃiʎaʃ] fpl: **as ~** the West Indies

antipatia [ãtʃipaˈtʃia] f dislike; **antipático, -a** [ãtʃiˈpatʃiku, a] adj unpleasant, unfriendly

antipatizar [ãtʃipatʃiˈza*] vi: **~ com** alguém to dislike sb

antiquado, -a [ãtʃiˈkwadu, a] adj antiquated; (fora de moda) out of date, old-fashioned

antiquário, -a [ãtʃiˈkwarju, a] m/f antique dealer ♦ m (loja) antique shop

anti-semita adj m anti-Semitic

anti-séptico, -a adj antiseptic ♦ m antiseptic

anti-social (pl **-ais**) adj antisocial

antologia [ãtoloˈʒia] f anthology

anual [aˈnwaw] (pl **-ais**) adj annual, yearly

anulação [anulaˈsãw] (pl **-ões**) f cancellation; (de contrato, casamento) annulment

anular [anuˈla*] vt to cancel; (contrato, casamento) to annul; (efeito) to cancel out ♦ m ring finger

anunciante [anũˈsjãtʃi] m (COM) advertiser

anunciar [anũˈsja*] vt to announce; (COM) to advertise

anúncio [aˈnũsju] m announcement; (COM) advertisement; (cartaz) notice; **~s classificados** small ou classified ads

ânus [ˈanuʃ] m inv anus

anzol [ãˈzɔw] (pl **-óis**) m fish-hook

ao [aw] = a + o

aonde [aˈõdʒi] adv where; **~ quer que** wherever

aos [awʃ] = a + os

Ap. abr = apartamento

apagado, -a [apaˈgadu, a] adj: **o fogo estava ~/a luz estava apagada** the fire was out/the light was off

apagar [apaˈga*] vt (luz elétrica) to switch off; (vela) to blow out; (com borracha) to rub out, erase; **apagar-se** vr to go out

apaixonado, -a [apajʃoˈnadu, a] adj (discurso) impassioned; (pessoa): **ele está ~ por ela** he is in love with her; **ele é ~ por tênis** he's mad about tennis

apaixonar-se [apajʃoˈnaxsi] vr: **~ por** to fall in love with

apalpar [apawˈpa*] vt to touch, feel; (MED) to examine

apanhado [apaˈɲadu] m (de flores) bunch; (resumo) summary

apanhar [apaˈɲa*] vt to catch; (algo à mão, do chão) to pick up; (surra, táxi) to get; (flores, frutas) to pick; (agarrar) to grab ♦ vi to get a beating; **~ sol/chuva** to sunbathe/get soaked

aparador [aparaˈdo*] m sideboard

apara-lápis [aparaˈlapiʃ] (PT) m inv pencil sharpener

aparar [apaˈra*] vt (cabelo) to trim; (lápis) to sharpen; (algo arremessado) to catch

aparato [apaˈratu] m pomp; (coleção) array

aparecer [apareˈse*] vi to appear; (apresentar-se) to turn up; (ser publicado) to be published; **~ em casa de alguém** to call on sb; **aparecimento** [aparesiˈmẽtu] m appearance; (publicação) publication

aparelhado, -a [apareˈʎadu, a] adj ready, prepared

aparelho [apaˈreʎu] m apparatus; (equipamento) equipment; (PESCA) tackle; (máquina) machine; (BR: fone) telephone; **~ de barbear** electric shaver; **~ de chá** tea set; **~ de rádio/TV** radio/TV set; **~ doméstico** domestic appliance

aparência [apaˈrẽsja] f appearance; **na ~** apparently; **sob a ~ de** under the guise of; **ter ~ de** to look like, seem

aparentar [aparẽˈta*] vt (fingir) to feign; (parecer) to look; **não aparenta a sua idade** he doesn't look his age

aparente [apaˈrẽtʃi] adj apparent

aparição [apariˈsãw] (pl -ões) f (visão) apparition; (fantasma) ghost

apartamento [apaxtaˈmẽtu] m apartment, flat (BRIT)

apartar [apaxˈta*] vt to separate; **apartar-se** vr to separate

apartheid [apaxˈtajdʒi] m apartheid

apatia [apaˈtʃia] f apathy

apático, -a [aˈpatʃiku, a] adj apathetic

apavorado, -a [apavoˈradu, a] adj terrified

apavorante [apavoˈrãtʃi] adj terrifying

apavorar [apavoˈra*] vt to terrify ♦ vi to be terrifying; **apavorar-se** vr to be terrified

apear-se [aˈpjaxsi] vr: **~ de** (cavalo) to dismount from

apegado, -a [apeˈgadu, a] adj: **~ a** (gostar de) to be attached to

apegar-se [apeˈgaxsi] vr: **~ a** (afeiçoar-se) to become attached to

apego [aˈpegu] m (afeição) attachment

apelação [apelaˈsãw] (pl -ões) f appeal

apelar [apeˈla*] vi to appeal; **~ da sentença** (JUR) to appeal against the sentence; **~ para** to appeal to; **~ para a ignorância/violência** to resort to abuse/violence

apelido [apeˈlidu] m (BR: alcunha) nickname; (PT: nome de família) surname

apelo [aˈpelu] m appeal

apenas [aˈpenaʃ] adv only

apendicite [apẽdʒiˈsitʃi] f appendicitis

aperfeiçoamento [apexfejswaˈmẽtu] m (perfeição) perfection; (melhoramento) improvement

aperfeiçoar [apexfejˈswa*] vt to perfect; (melhorar) to improve; **aperfeiçoar-se** vr to improve o.s.

apertado, -a [apexˈtadu, a] adj tight; (estreito) narrow; (sem dinheiro) hard-up; (vida) hard

apertar [apexˈta*] vt (agarrar) to hold tight; (roupa) to take in; (esponja) to squeeze; (botão) to press; (despesas) to limit; (vigilância) to step up; (coração) to break; (fig: pessoa) to put pressure on ♦ vi (sapatos) to pinch; (chuva, frio) to get worse; (estrada) to narrow; **~ em** (insistir) to insist on; **~ a mão de alguém** to shake hands with sb

aperto [aˈpextu] m pressure; (situação difícil) spot of bother, jam; **um ~ de mãos** a handshake

apesar [apeˈza*]: **~ de** prep in spite of, despite; **~ disso** nevertheless; **~ de que** even though

apetecer [apeteˈse*] vi (comida) to be appetizing

apetite [apeˈtʃitʃi] m appetite; **bom ~!** enjoy your meal!

apetrechos [apeˈtreʃuʃ] mpl gear sg; (PESCA) tackle sg

ápice [ˈapisi] m (cume) summit, top; (vértice) apex

apiedar-se [apjeˈdaxsi] vr: **~ de** to pity; (compadecer-se) to take pity on

apinhado, -a [apiˈɲadu, a] adj crowded

apinhar [apiˈɲa*] vt to crowd, pack;
apinhar-se vr to crowd together;
~-se de (gente) to be filled ou
packed with

apitar [apiˈta*] vi to whistle; **apito**
[aˈpitu] m whistle

aplacar [aplaˈka*] vt to placate ♦ vi
to calm down; **aplacar-se** vr to
calm down

aplaudir [aplawˈdʒi*] vt to applaud

aplauso [aˈplawzu] m applause;
(apoio) support; (elogio) praise;
(aprovação) approval; **~s** applause
sg

aplicação [aplikaˈsãw] (pl -ões) f
application; (esforço) effort; (da lei)
enforcement; (de dinheiro) investment

aplicado, -a [apliˈkadu, a] adj
hard-working

aplicar [apliˈka*] vt to apply; (lei)
to enforce; (dinheiro) to invest;
aplicar-se vr: **~-se a** to devote o.s.
to

apoderar-se [apodeˈraxsi] vr: **~ de**
to seize, take possession of

apodrecer [apodreˈse*] vt to rot;
(dente) to decay ♦ vi to rot; to decay

apogeu [apoˈʒew] m (fig) height,
peak

apoiar [apoˈja*] vt to support; (basear) to base; (moção) to second;
apoiar-se vr: **~-se em** to rest on

apoio [aˈpoju] m support; (financeiro) backing

apólice [aˈpɔlisi] f (certificado) policy, certificate; (ação) share, bond; **~**
de seguro insurance policy

apontamento [apõtaˈmẽtu] m
(nota) note

apontar [apõˈta*] vt (fusil) to aim;
(erro) to point out; (com o dedo) to
point at ou to; (razão) to put forward ♦ vi to begin to appear; (brotar) to sprout; (com o dedo) to

point; **~ para** to point to; (com
arma) to aim at

após [aˈpɔjʃ] prep after

aposentado, -a [apozẽˈtadu, a] adj
retired ♦ m/f retired person, pensioner; **ser ~** to be retired; **aposentadoria** [apozẽtadoˈria] f retirement; (dinheiro) pension

aposentar [apozẽˈta*] vt to retire;
aposentar-se vr to retire

aposento [apoˈzẽtu] m room

apossar-se [apoˈsaxsi] vr: **~ de** to
take possession of, seize

aposta [aˈpɔʃta] f bet

apostar [apoʃˈta*] vt to bet ♦ vi: **~
em** to bet on

apóstolo [aˈpɔʃtolu] m apostle

apóstrofo [aˈpɔʃtrofu] m apostrophe

aprazível [apraˈzivew] (pl -eis) adj
pleasant

apreciação [apresjaˈsãw] f appreciation

apreciar [apreˈsja*] vt to appreciate; (gostar de) to enjoy

apreço [aˈpresu] m esteem, regard;
(consideração) consideration; **em ~**
in question

apreender [aprjẽˈde*] vt to appre-
hend; (tomar) to seize; (entender) to
grasp

apreensão [aprjẽˈsãw] (pl -ões) f
(percepção) perception; (tomada)
seizure; (receio) apprehension

apreensivo, -a [aprjẽˈsivu, a] adj
apprehensive

apreensões [aprjẽˈsõjʃ] fpl of
apreensão

apregoar [apreˈgwa*] vt to proclaim, announce; (mercadorias) to
cry

aprender [aprẽˈde*] vt, vi to learn; **~
a ler** to learn to read; **~ de cor** to
learn by heart

aprendizagem [aprẽdʒiˈzaʒẽ] f

(*num ofício*) apprenticeship; (*numa profissão*) training; (*escolar*) learning

apresentação [aprezēta'sāw] (*pl -ōes*) f presentation; (*de peça, filme*) performance; (*de pessoas*) introduction; (*de porte pessoal*) appearance

apresentador, a [aprezēta'do*, a] m/f presenter

apresentar [aprezē'ta*] vt to present; (*pessoas*) to introduce; **apresentar-se** vr to introduce o.s.; (*problema*) to present itself; (*à polícia etc*) to report; **quero apresentar-lhe** may I introduce you to

apressado, -a [apre'sadu, a] adj hurried, hasty; **estar ~** to be in a hurry

apressar [apre'sa*] vt to hurry; **apressar-se** vr to hurry (up)

aprisionar [aprizjo'na*] vt (*cativar*) to capture; (*encarcerar*) to imprison

aprontar [aprõ'ta*] vt to get ready, prepare; **aprontar-se** vr to get ready

apropriação [aproprja'sāw] (*pl -ōes*) f appropriation; (*tomada*) seizure

apropriado, -a [apro'prjadu, a] adj appropriate, suitable

apropriar [apro'prja*] vt to appropriate; **apropriar-se** vr: **~-se de** to seize, take possession of

aprovação [aprova'sāw] f approval; (*louvor*) praise; (*num exame*) pass

aprovado, -a [apro'vadu, a] adj approved; **ser ~ num exame** to pass an exam

aprovar [apro'va*] vt to approve of; (*exame*) to pass ♦ vi to make the grade

aproveitador, a [aprovejta'do*, a] m/f opportunist

aproveitamento [aprovejta'mētu] m use, utilization; (*nos estudos*) progress

aproveitar [aprovej'ta*] vt to take advantage of; (*utilizar*) to use; (*oportunidade*) to take ♦ vi to make the most of it; (*PT*) to be of use; **aproveite!** enjoy yourself!

aproximação [aprosima'sāw] (*pl -ōes*) f approximation; (*chegada*) approach; (*proximidade*) nearness

aproximar [aprosi'ma*] vt to bring near; (*aliar*) to bring together; **aproximar-se** vr: **~-se de** to approach

aptidão [aptʃi'dāw] f aptitude; (*jeito*) knack; **~ física** physical fitness

apto, -a ['aptu, a] adj apt; (*capaz*) capable

apto. abr = **apartamento**

apunhalar [apuɲa'la*] vt to stab

apurado, -a [apu'radu, a] adj refined

apurar [apu'ra*] vt to perfect; (*averiguar*) to investigate; (*dinheiro*) to raise, get; (*votos*) to count; **apurar-se** vr to dress up

aquarela [akwa'rɛla] f watercolour (BRIT), watercolor (US)

aquário [a'kwarju] m aquarium; **A~** (ASTROLOGIA) Aquarius

aquático, -a [a'kwatʃiku, a] adj aquatic, water atr

aquecer [ake'se*] vt to heat ♦ vi to heat up; **aquecer-se** vr to heat up; **aquecido, -a** [a'kesidu, a] adj heated; **aquecimento** [akesi'mētu] m heating; **aquecimento central** central heating

aquele, -ela [a'keli, ɛla] adj (sg) that; (pl) those ♦ pron (sg) that one; (pl) those

àquele, -ela [a'keli, ɛla] = **a + aquele/ela**

aquém [a'kēj] adv on this side; **~ de** on this side of

aqui [a'ki] adv here; **eis ~** here is/are; **~ mesmo** right here; **até ~** up to here; **por ~** hereabouts; (*nesta direção*) this way

aquilo [a'kilu] *pron* that; **~ que** what

àquilo [a'kilu] = **a + aquilo**

aquisição [akizi'sāw] (*pl* **-ões**) *f* acquisition

ar [a*] *m* air; (*aspecto*) look; (*brisa*) breeze; (*PT: AUTO*) choke; **~es** *mpl* (*atitude*) airs; (*clima*) climate *sg*; **ao ~ livre** in the open air; **no ~** (*TV, RÁDIO*) on air; (*fig: planos*) up in the air; **dar-se ~es** to put on airs; **~ condicionado** (*aparelho*) air conditioner; (*sistema*) air conditioning

árabe ['arabi] *adj*, *m/f* Arab ♦ *m* (*LING*) Arabic

Arábia [a'rabja] *f*: **a ~ Saudita** Saudi Arabia

arame [a'rami] *m* wire

aranha [a'raɲa] *f* spider

arara [a'rara] *f* macaw

arbitragem [axbi'traʒē] *f* arbitration

arbitrar [axbi'tra*] *vt* to arbitrate; (*ESPORTE*) to referee

arbitrário, -a [axbi'trarju, a] *adj* arbitrary

arbítrio [ax'bitrju] *m* decision; **ao ~ de** at the discretion of

árbitro ['axbitru] *m* (*juiz*) arbiter; (*JUR*) arbitrator; (*FUTEBOL*) referee; (*TÉNIS etc*) umpire

arbusto [ax'buʃtu] *m* shrub, bush

arca ['axka] *f* chest, trunk; **~ de Noé** Noah's Ark

arcar [ax'ka*] *vt*: **~ com** (*responsabilidades*) to shoulder; (*despesas*) to handle; (*consequências*) to take

arcebispo [arse'biʃpu] *m* archbishop

arco ['axku] *m* (*ARQ*) arch; (*MIL, MÚS*) bow; (*ELET, MAT*) arc

arco-íris *m inv* rainbow

ardente [ax'dētʃi] *adj* burning;

(*intenso*) fervent; (*apaixonado*) ardent

arder [ax'de*] *vi* to burn; (*pele, olhos*) to sting; **~ de raiva** to seethe (with rage)

ardiloso, -a [axdʒi'lozu, ɔza] *adj* cunning

ardor [ax'do*] *m* ardour (*BRIT*), ardor (*US*); **ardoroso, -a** [axdo'rozu, ɔza] *adj* ardent

árduo, -a ['axdwu, a] *adj* arduous; (*difícil*) hard, difficult

área ['arja] *f* area; (*ESPORTE*) penalty area; (*fig*) field; **~ (de serviço)** balcony (*for hanging washing etc*)

areia [a'reja] *f* sand; **~ movediça** quicksand

arejar [are'ʒa*] *vt* to air ♦ *vi* to get some air; (*descansar*) to have a breather; **arejar-se** *vr* to get some air; to have a break

arena [a'rena] *f* arena; (*de circo*) ring

Argélia [ax'ʒɛlja] *f*: **a ~ Algeria**

Argentina [axʒē'tʃina] *f*: **a ~ Argentina**

argila [ax'ʒila] *f* clay

argola [ax'gɔla] *f* ring; **~s** *fpl* (*brincos*) hooped earrings; **~ (de porta)** door-knocker

argumentação [axgumēta'sāw] *f* line of argument

argumentar [axgumē'ta*] *vt*, *vi* to argue

argumento [axgu'mētu] *m* argument; (*de obra*) theme

aridez [ari'deʒ] *f* dryness; (*esterilidade*) barrenness; (*falta de interesse*) dullness

árido, -a ['aridu, a] *adj* arid, dry; (*estéril*) barren; (*maçante*) dull

Áries ['ariʃ] *f* Aries

aristocrata [ariʃto'krata] *m/f* aristocrat

aritmética [aritʃ'mɛtʃika] *f* arithmetic

arma ['axma] f weapon; **~s** fpl (nucleares etc) arms; (brasão) coat sg of arms; **passar pelas ~s** to shoot, execute; **~ convencional/nuclear** conventional/nuclear weapon; **~ de fogo** firearm

armação [axma'sãw] (pl **-ões**) f (armadura) frame; (PESCA) tackle; (NÁUT) rigging; (de óculos) frames pl

armadilha [axma'dʒiʎa] f trap

armado, -a [ax'madu, a] adj armed

armamento [axma'mẽtu] m (armas) armaments pl, weapons pl; (NÁUT) equipment; (ato) arming

armar [ax'ma*] vt to arm; (montar) to assemble; (barraca) to pitch; (um aparelho) to set up; (armadilha) to set; (NÁUT) to fit out; **armar-se** vr to arm o.s.; **~ uma briga com** to pick a quarrel with

armarinho [axma'riɲu] m haberdashery (BRIT), notions pl (US)

armário [ax'marju] m cupboard; (de roupa) wardrobe

armazém [axma'zẽj] (pl **-ns**) m (depósito) warehouse; (loja) grocery store; **armazenar** [axmaze'na*] vt to store; (provisões) to stock

aro ['aru] m (argola) ring; (de óculos, roda) rim; (de porta) frame

aroma [a'rɔma] m aroma; **aromático, -a** [aro'matʃiku, a] adj (comida) aromatic; (perfume) fragrant

arpão [ax'pãw] (pl **-ões**) m harpoon

arqueiro, -a [ax'kejru, a] m/f archer; (goleiro) goalkeeper

arqueologia [axkjolo'ʒia] f archaeology (BRIT), archeology (US); **arqueólogo, -a** [ax'kjɔlogu, a] m/f archaeologist (BRIT), archeologist (US)

arquiteto, -a [axki'tetu, a] (PT -ect-) m/f architect; **arquitetônico, -a** [axkite'toniku, a] (PT -ectó-) adj architectural; **arquitetura**

[axkite'tura] (PT -ect-) f architecture

arquivar [axki'va*] vt to file; (projeto) to shelve

arquivo [ax'kivu] m (ger, COMPUT) file; (lugar) archive; (de empresa) files pl; (móvel) filing cabinet

arraial [axa'jaw] (pl **-ais**) (PT) m (festa) fair

arraigado, -a [axaj'gadu, a] adj deep-rooted; (fig) ingrained

arraigar [axaj'ga*] vi to root; **arraigar-se** vr to take root; (estabelecer-se) to settle

arrancada [axã'kada] f (movimento, puxão) jerk; **dar uma ~ em** (puxar) to jerk; **dar uma ~** (em carro) to pull away (suddenly)

arrancar [axã'ka*] vt to pull out; (botão etc) to pull off; (arrebatar) to snatch (away); (fig: confissão) to extract ♦ vi to start (off); **arrancar-se** vr to leave; (fugir) to run off

arranha-céu [a'xaɲa-] (pl **~s**) m skyscraper

arranhão [axa'ɲãw] (pl **-ões**) m scratch

arranhar [axa'ɲa*] vt to scratch

arranjar [axã'ʒa*] vt to arrange; (emprego, namorado) to get, find; (doença) to get, catch; (questão) to settle; **arranjar-se** vr to manage; (conseguir emprego) to get a job; **~-se sem** to do without

arranjo [a'xãʒu] m arrangement

arranque [a'xãki] m: **motor de ~** starter (motor)

arrasar [axa'za*] vt to devastate; (demolir) to demolish; (estragar) to ruin; **arrasar-se** vr to be devastated; (destruir-se) to destroy o.s.; (arruinar-se) to lose everything

arrastão [axaʃ'tãw] (pl **-ões**) m tug; (rede) dragnet

arrastar [axaʃ'ta*] vt to drag; (atrair) to draw ♦ vi to trail; **arrastar-se** vr crawl; (*tempo, processo*) to drag (on)

arrebatado, -a [axeba'tadu, a] *adj* rash, impetuous

arrebatar [axeba'ta*] *vt* to snatch (away); (*levar*) to carry off; (*enlevar*) to entrance; (*enfurecer*) to enrage; **arrebatar-se** *vr* to be entranced

arrebentado, -a [axebē'tadu, a] *adj* broken; (*estafado*) worn out

arrebentar [axebē'ta*] *vt* (*to*) to break; (*porta*) to break down; (*corda*) to snap ♦ *vi* to break; (*corda*) to snap; (*guerra*) to break out

arrebitado, -a [axebi'tadu, a] *adj* turned-up; (*nariz*) snub

arrecadar [axeka'da*] *vt* (*impostos etc*) to collect

arredondado, -a [axedō'dadu, a] *adj* round, rounded

arredondar [axedō'da*] *vt* to round (off); (*conta*) to round up

arredores [axe'dɔriʃ] *mpl* suburbs; (*cercanias*) outskirts

arrefecer [axefe'se*] *vt* to cool; (*febre*) to lower; (*desanimar*) to discourage ♦ *vi* to cool (off); to get discouraged

ar-refrigerado [-xefriʒe'radu] *m* air conditioning

arregaçar [axega'sa*] *vt* to roll up

arregalado, -a [axega'ladu, a] *adj* (*olhos*) wide

arregalar [axega'la*] *vt*: ~ **os olhos** to stare in amazement

arrematar [axema'ta*] *vt* (*dizer concluindo*) to conclude; (*comprar*) to buy by auction; (*vender*) to sell by auction; (*COSTURA*) to finish off

arremessar [axeme'sa*] *vt* to throw, hurl; **arremesso** [axe'mesu] *m* throw

arremeter [axeme'te*] *vi* to lunge; ~ **contra** (*acometer*) to attack, assail

arrendamento [axēda'mētu] *m* (*ação*) leasing; (*contrato*) lease

arrendar [axē'da*] *vt* to lease

arrendatário, -a [axēda'tarju, a] *m/f* tenant

arrepender-se [axepē'dexsi] *vr* to repent; (*mudar de opinião*) to change one's mind; ~ **de** to regret, be sorry for; **arrependido, -a** [axepē'dʒidu, a] *adj* (*pessoa*) sorry; **arrependimento** [axepēdʒi'mētu] *m* regret; (*REL, de crime*) repentance

arrepiar [axe'pja*] *vt* (*amedrontar*) to horrify; (*cabelo*) to cause to stand on end; **arrepiar-se** *vr* to shiver; (*cabelo*) to stand on end; (**ser**) **de ~ os cabelos** (to be) hair-raising

arrepio [axe'piu] *m* shiver; (*de frio*) chill; **isso me dá ~s** it gives me the creeps

arriar [a'xja*] *vt* to lower; (*depor*) to lay down ♦ *vi* to drop; (*vergar*) to sag; (*desistir*) to give up; (*fig*) to collapse

arriscado, -a [axiʃ'kadu, a] *adj* risky; (*audacioso*) daring

arriscar [axiʃ'ka*] *vt* to risk; (*pôr em perigo*) to endanger, jeopardize; **arriscar-se** *vr* to take a risk; **~-se a fazer** to risk doing

arroba [a'xoba] *f* (*símbolo*) @, 'at' sign

arrogante [axo'gãtʃi] *adj* arrogant

arroio [a'xɔju] *m* stream

arrojado, -a [axo'ʒadu, a] *adj* (*design*) bold; (*temerário*) rash; (*ousado*) daring

arrolar [axo'la*] *vt* to list

arrombar [axō'ba*] *vt* (*porta*) to break down; (*cofre*) to crack

arrotar [axo'ta*] *vi* to belch ♦ *vt* (*alardear*) to boast of

arroz [a'xoʒ] *m* rice; ~ **doce** rice pudding

arruinar [axwi'na*] *vt* to ruin; (*destruir*) to destroy; **arruinar-se** *vr* to be ruined; (*perder a saúde*) to ruin one's health

arrumação [axuma'sãw] f arrangement; (*de um quarto etc*) tidying up; (*de malas*) packing

arrumadeira [axuma'dejra] f cleaning lady; (*num hotel*) chambermaid

arrumar [axu'ma*] vt to put in order, arrange; (*quarto etc*) to tidy up; (*malas*) to pack; (*emprego*) to get; (*vestir*) to dress up; (*desculpa*) to make up, find; (*vida*) to sort out; **arrumar-se** vr (*aprontar-se*) to get dressed, get ready; (*na vida*) to sort o.s. out; (*virar-se*) to manage

arte ['axtʃi] f art; (*habilidade*) skill; (*ofício*) trade, craft

artefato [axtʃi'fatu] (PT **-act-**) m (manufactured) article

artéria [ax'tɛrja] f (ANAT) artery

artesão, -sã [axte'zãw, zã] (*pl* **~s**, **~s**) m/f artisan, craftsman/woman

ártico, -a ['axtʃiku, a] adj Arctic ♦ m: **o A~** the Arctic

artificial [axtʃifi'sjaw] (*pl* **-ais**) adj artificial

artifício [axtʃi'fisju] m stratagem, trick

artigo [ax'tʃigu] m article; (COM) item; **~s** mpl (*produtos*) goods

artilharia [axtʃiʎa'ria] f artillery

artista [ax'tʃista] m/f artist; **artístico, -a** [ax'tʃistʃiku, a] adj artistic

artrite [ax'tritʃi] f (MED) arthritis

árvore ['axvori] f tree; (TEC) shaft; **~ de Natal** Christmas tree

as [aʃ] *art def* V **a**

ás [ajʃ] m ace

às [ajʃ] = **a** + **as**

asa ['aza] f wing; (*de xícara etc*) handle

ascendência [asẽ'dẽsja] f (*antepassados*) ancestry; (*domínio*) ascendancy, sway; **ascendente** [asẽ'dẽtʃi] adj rising, upward

ascender [asẽ'de*] vi to rise, ascend

ascensão [asẽ'sãw] (*pl* **-ões**) f ascent; (REL): **dia de A~** Ascension Day

asco ['aʃku] m loathing, revulsion; **dar ~ a** to revolt, disgust

asfalto [aʃ'fawtu] m asphalt

asfixia [aʃfik'sia] f asphyxia, suffocation

Ásia ['azja] f: **a ~** Asia

asiático, -a [a'zjatʃiku, a] adj, m/f Asian

asilo [a'zilu] m (*refúgio*) refuge; (*estabelecimento*) home; **~ político** political asylum

asma ['aʒma] f asthma

asneira [aʒ'nejra] f (*tolice*) stupidity; (*ato, dito*) stupid thing

asno ['aʒnu] m donkey; (*fig*) ass

aspas ['aʃpaʃ] fpl inverted commas

aspecto [aʃ'pɛktu] m aspect; (*aparência*) look, appearance; (*característica*) feature; (*ponto de vista*) point of view

aspereza [aʃpe'reza] f roughness; (*severidade*) harshness; (*rudeza*) rudeness

áspero, -a ['aʃperu, a] adj rough; (*severo*) harsh; (*rude*) rude

aspiração [aʃpira'sãw] (*pl* **-ões**) f aspiration; (*inalação*) inhalation

aspirador [aʃpira'do*] m (*de pó*) vacuum cleaner; **passar o ~ (em)** to vacuum

aspirante [aʃpi'rãtʃi] adj aspiring ♦ m/f candidate

aspirar [aʃpi'ra*] vt to breathe in; (*bombear*) to suck up ♦ vi to breathe; (*soprar*) to blow; (*desejar*): **~ a algo** to aspire to sth

aspirina [aʃpi'rina] f aspirin

asqueroso, -a [aʃke'rozu, ɔza] adj disgusting, revolting

assado, -a [a'sadu, a] adj roasted; (CULIN) roast ♦ m roast; **carne assada**

roast beef

assaltante [asaw'tãtʃi] m/f assailant; (de banco) robber; (de casa) burglar; (na rua) mugger

assaltar [asaw'ta*] vt to attack; (casa) to break into; (banco) to rob; (pessoa na rua) to mug; **assalto** [a'sawtu] m attack; raid, robbery; burglary, break-in; mugging; (BOXE) round

assar [a'sa*] vt to roast; (na grelha) to grill

assassinar [asasi'na*] vt to murder, kill; (POL) to assassinate; **assassinato** [asasi'natu] m murder, killing; assassination; **assassino, -a** [asa'sinu, a] m/f murderer; assassin

assaz [a'saʒ] adv (suficientemente) sufficiently; (muito) rather

assediar [ase'dʒja*] vt (sitiar) to besiege; (importunar) to pester; **assédio** [a'sedʒu] m siege; (insistência) insistence

assegurar [asegu'ra*] vt to secure; (garantir) to ensure; (afirmar) to assure; **assegurar-se** vr: **~-se de** to make sure of

asseio [a'seju] m cleanliness

assembléia [asẽ'blɛja] f assembly; (reunião) meeting; **~ geral (ordinária)** annual general meeting

assentar [asẽ'ta*] vt (fazer sentar) to seat; (colocar) to place; (estabelecer) to establish; (decidir) to decide upon ♦ vi (pó etc) to settle; **assentar-se** vr to sit down; **~ em ou a** (roupa) to suit

assentir [asẽ'tʃi*] vi: **~ (em)** to agree (to)

assento [a'sẽtu] m seat; (base) base

assíduo, -a [a'sidwu, a] adj (aluno) who attends regularly; (diligente) assiduous; (constante) constant; **ser ~ num lugar** to be a regular visitor to a place

assim [a'sĩ] adv (deste modo) like this, in this way, thus; (portanto) therefore; (igualmente) likewise; **~ ~** so-so; **~ mesmo** in any case; **e ~ por diante** and so on; **~ como** as well as; **como ~?** how do you mean?; **~ que** (logo que) as soon as

assimilar [asimi'la*] vt to assimilate; (apreender) to take in; (assemelhar) to compare

assinante [asi'nãtʃi] m/f (de jornal etc) subscriber

assinar [asi'na*] vt to sign

assinatura [asina'tura] f (nome) signature; (de jornal etc) subscription; (TEATRO) season ticket

assinto etc [a'sĩtu] vb V assentir

assistência [asiʃ'tẽsja] f (presença) presence; (público) audience; (auxílio) aid; **~ social** social work

assistente [asiʃ'tẽtʃi] adj assistant ♦ m/f spectator, onlooker; (ajudante) assistant; **~ social** social worker

assistir [asiʃ'tʃi*] vt, vi: **~ (a)** (MED) to attend (to); **~ a** to assist; (TV, filme, jogo) to watch; (reunião) to attend

assoar [aso'a*] vt: **~ o nariz** to blow one's nose; **assoar-se** vr (PT) to blow one's nose

assobiar [aso'bja*] vi to whistle

assobio [aso'biu] m whistle

associação [asosja'sãw] (pl -ões) f association; (organização) society; (parceria) partnership

associado, -a [aso'sjadu, a] adj associate ♦ m/f associate, member; (COM) associate; (sócio) partner

associar [aso'sja*] vt to associate; **associar-se** vr: **~-se a** to associate with

assombração [asõbra'sãw] (pl -ões) f ghost

assombro [a'sõbru] m amazement,

astonishment; (*maravilha*) marvel;
assombroso, -a [asõˈbrozu, ɔza] *adj* astonishing, amazing

assoviar [asoˈvja*] *vt* = **assobiar**

assovio [asoˈviu] *m* = **assobio**

assumir [asuˈmi*] *vt* to assume, take on; (*reconhecer*) to accept

assunto [aˈsũtu] *m* subject, matter; (*enredo*) plot

assustador, a [asuʃtaˈdo*, a] *adj* (*alarmante*) startling; (*amedrontador*) frightening

assustar [asuʃˈta*] *vt* to frighten; (*alarmar*) to startle; **assustar-se** *vr* to be frightened

asteca [aʃˈtɛka] *adj, m/f* Aztec

astrologia [aʃtroloˈʒia] *f* astrology

astronauta [aʃtroˈnawta] *m/f* astronaut

astronave [aʃtroˈnavi] *f* spaceship

astronomia [aʃtronoˈmia] *f* astronomy

astúcia [aʃˈtusja] *f* cunning

ata [ˈata] *f* (*de reunião*) minutes *pl*

atacado [ataˈkadu] *m*: **por ~** wholesale

atacante [ataˈkãtʃi] *adj* attacking ♦ *m/f* attacker, assailant ♦ (*FUTEBOL*) forward

atacar [ataˈka*] *vt* to attack; (*problema etc*) to tackle

atado, -a [aˈtadu, a] *adj* (*desajeitado*) clumsy, awkward; (*perplexo*) puzzled

atalho [aˈtaʎu] *m* (*caminho*) short cut

ataque [aˈtaki] *m* attack; **~ aéreo** air raid

atar [aˈta*] *vt* to tie (up), fasten; **não ~ nem desatar** (*pessoa*) to waver; (*negócio*) to be in the air

atarefado, -a [atareˈfadu, a] *adj* busy

atarracado, -a [ataxaˈkadu, a] *adj* stocky

até [aˈte] *prep* (*PT: + a : lugar*) up to, as far as; (*tempo etc*) until, till ♦ *adv* (*tb: ~ mesmo*) even; **~ certo ponto** to a certain extent; **~ em cima** to the top; **~ já** see you soon; **~ logo** bye!; **~ onde** as far as; **~ que** until; **~ que enfim!** at last!

atear [ateˈa*] *vt* (*fogo*) to kindle; (*fig*) to incite, inflame; **atear-se** *vr* to blaze; (*paixões*) to flare up

atéia [aˈteja] *f de* ateu

atemorizar [atemoriˈza*] *vt* to frighten; (*intimidar*) to intimidate

Atenas [aˈtenaʃ] *n* Athens

atenção [atẽˈsãw] (*pl* -ões) *f* attention; (*cortesia*) courtesy; (*bondade*) kindness; **~!** be careful!; **chamar a ~** to attract attention; **atencioso, -a** [atẽˈsjozu, ɔza] *adj* considerate

atender [atẽˈde*] *vt*: **~ (a)** to attend to; (*receber*) to receive; (*deferir*) to grant; (*telefone etc*) to answer; (*paciente*) to see ♦ *vi* to answer; (*dar atenção*) to pay attention; **atendimento** [atẽdʒiˈmẽtu] *m* service; (*recepção*) reception; **horário de atendimento** opening hours; (*em consultório*) surgery (*BRIT*) *ou* office (*US*) hours

atentado [atẽˈtadu] *m* attack; (*crime*) crime; (*contra a vida de alguém*) attempt on sb's life

atento, -a [aˈtẽtu, a] *adj* attentive; **estar ~ a** to be aware *ou* mindful of

atenuante [ateˈnwãtʃi] *adj* extenuating ♦ *m* extenuating circumstance

atenuar [ateˈnwa*] *vt* to reduce, lessen

aterragem [ateˈxaʒẽj] (*PT*) (*pl* -ns) *f* (*AER*) landing

aterrar [ateˈxa*] (*PT*) *vi* (*AER*) to land

aterrissagem [atexiˈsaʒẽ] (*BR*) (*pl* -ns) *f* (*AER*) landing

aterrissar [atexi'sa*] (BR) vi (AER) to land

aterrorizante [atexori'zãtʃi] adj terrifying

aterrorizar [atexori'za*] vt to terrorize

atestado [ateʃ'tadu] m certificate; (prova) proof; (JUR) testimony

ateu, atéia [a'tew, a'teja] adj, m/f atheist

atiçar [atʃi'sa*] vt (fogo) to poke; (incitar) to incite; (provocar) to provoke; (sentimento) to induce

atinar [atʃi'na*] vt (acertar) to guess correctly ♦ vi: ~ com (solução) to find; ~ em to notice; ~ a fazer algo to succeed in doing sth

atingir [atʃĩ'ʒi*] vt to reach; (acertar) to hit; (afetar) to affect; (objetivo) to achieve; (compreender) to grasp

atirador, a [atʃira'do*, a] m/f marksman/woman; ~ de tocaia sniper

atirar [atʃi'ra*] vt to throw, fling ♦ vi (arma) to shoot; **atirar-se** vr: ~-se a to hurl o.s. at

atitude [atʃi'tudʒi] f attitude; (postura) posture

atividade [atʃivi'dadʒi] f activity

ativo, -a [a'tʃivu, a] adj active ♦ m (COM) assets pl

atlântico, -a [at'lãtʃiku, a] adj Atlantic ♦ m: **o (Oceano) A~** the Atlantic (Ocean)

atlas ['atlaʃ] m inv atlas

atleta [at'lɛta] m/f athlete; **atlético, -a** [at'lɛtʃiku, a] adj athletic; **atletismo** [atle'tʃiʒmu] m athletics sg

atmosfera [atmoʃ'fɛra] f atmosphere

ato ['atu] m act, action; (cerimônia) ceremony; (TEATRO) act; **em ~ contínuo** straight after; **no ~** on the

spot; **no mesmo ~** at the same time

à-toa adj (insignificante) insignificant; (simples) simple, easy ♦ adv V toa

atômico, -a [a'tomiku, a] adj atomic

atomizador [atomiza'do*] m atomizer

átomo ['atomu] m atom

atônito, -a [a'tonitu, a] adj astonished, amazed

ator [a'to*] m actor

atordoado, -a [atox'dwadu, a] adj dazed

atordoar [atox'dwa*] vt to daze, stun

atormentar [atoxmẽ'ta*] vt to torment

atração [atra'sãw] (pl -ões) f attraction

atracar [atra'ka*] vt, vi (NÁUT) to moor; **atracar-se** vr to grapple

atrações [atra'sõjʃ] fpl de **atração**

atractivo, -a [atra'tʃivu, a] (PT) adj = atrativo

atraente [atra'ẽtʃi] adj attractive

atraiçoar [atraj'swa*] vt to betray

atrair [atra'i*] vt to attract; (fascinar) to fascinate

atrapalhar [atrapa'ʎa*] vt to confuse; (perturbar) to disturb; (dificultar) to hinder ♦ vi to be a nuisance

atrás [a'trajʃ] adv behind; (no fundo) at the back ♦ prep: ~ de behind; (no tempo) after; **dois meses ~** two months ago

atrasado, -a [atra'zadu, a] adj late; (país etc) backward; (relógio etc) slow; (pagamento) overdue; **atrasados** [atra'zaduʃ] mpl (COM) arrears

atrasar [atra'za*] vt to delay; (progresso, desenvolvimento: progresso) to hold back; (relógio) to put back; (pagamento) to be late with ♦ vi (*relógio etc*) to be slow; (*avião, pessoa*) to be late; **atrasar-se** *vr* to be late; (*num trabalho*) to fall behind; (*num pagamento*) to get into arrears

atraso [a'trazu] *m* delay; (*de país etc*) backwardness; **~s** *mpl* (COM) arrears; **com 20 minutos de ~** 20 minutes late

atrativo, -a [atra'tʃivu, a] *adj* attractive ♦ *m* attraction; (*incentivo*) incentive; **~s** *mpl* (*encantos*) charms

através [atra'vɛʃ] *adv* across; **~ de** across; (*pelo centro de*) through

atravessar [atrave'sa*] *vt* to cross; (*pôr ao través*) to put ou lay across; (*traspassar*) to pass through

atrever-se [atre'vexsi] *vr*: **~ a** to dare to; **atrevido, -a** [atre'vidu, a] *adj* cheeky; (*corajoso*) bold; **atrevimento** [atrevi'mẽtu] *m* cheek; boldness

atribuir [atri'bwi*] *vt*: **~ algo a** to attribute sth to; (*prêmios, regalias*) to confer sth on

atributo [atri'butu] *m* attribute

átrio ['atrju] *m* hall; (*pátio*) courtyard

atrito [a'tritu] *m* (*fricção*) friction; (*desentendimento*) disagreement

atriz [a'triʒ] *f* actress

atropelamento [atropela'mẽtu] *m* (*de pedestre*) road accident

atropelar [atrope'la*] *vt* to knock down, run over; (*empurrar*) to jostle

atuação [atwa'sãw] (*pl* -ões) *f* acting; (*de ator etc*) performance

atual [a'twaw] (*pl* -ais) *adj* current; (*pessoa, carro*) modern; **atualidade** [atwali'dadʒi] *f* present (time); **atualidades** *fpl* (*notícias*) news *sg*; **atualizar** [atwali'za*] *vt* to update; **atualmente** [atwaw'mẽtʃi] *adv* at present, currently; (*hoje em dia*) nowadays

atuante [a'twãtʃi] *adj* active

atuar [a'twa*] *vi* to act; **~ para** to contribute to; **~ sobre** to influence

atum [a'tũ] (*pl* -ns) *m* tuna (fish)

aturdido, -a [atux'dʒidu, a] *adj* stunned; (*com barulho*) deafened; (*com confusão, movimento*) bewildered

aturdir [atux'dʒi*] *vt* to stun; (*suj: barulho*) to deafen; (: *confusão, movimento*) to bewilder

audácia [aw'dasja] *f* boldness; (*insolência*) insolence; **audacioso, -a** [awda'sjozu, ɔza] *adj* daring; insolent

audição [awdʒi'sãw] (*pl* -ões) *f* audition

audiência [aw'dʒjẽsja] *f* audience; (*de tribunal*) session, hearing

audiovisual [awdʒjovi'zwaw] (*pl* -ais) *adj* audiovisual

auditar [awdʒi'ta*] *vt* to audit

auditor, a [awdʒi'to*, a] *m/f* auditor; (*juiz*) judge; (*ouvinte*) listener

auditoria [awdʒito'ria] *f*: **fazer a ~** to audit

auditório [awdʒi'tɔrju] *m* audience; (*recinto*) auditorium

auge ['awʒi] *m* height, peak

aula ['awla] *f* (PT: *sala*) classroom; (*lição*) lesson, class; **dar ~** to teach

aumentar [awmẽ'ta*] *vt* to increase; (*salários, preços*): **salários** to raise; (*sala, casa*) to expand, extend; (*suj: lente*) to magnify; (*acrescentar*) to add ♦ *vi* to increase; (*preço, salário: preço*) to rise, go up

aumento [aw'mẽtu] *m* increase; rise; (*ampliação*) enlargement; (*crescimento*) growth

aurora [aw'rɔra] *f* dawn

ausência [aw'zẽsja] *f* absence

ausentar-se [awzẽ'taxsi] *vr* (*ir-se*) to go away; (*afastar-se*) to stay away

ausente [aw'zɛtʃi] *adj* absent

austeridade [awʃteri'dadʒi] *f* austerity

austral [awʃ'traw] (*pl* -**ais**) *adj* southern

Austrália [awʃ'tralja] *f*: **a ~** Australia; **australiano, -a** [awʃtra-'ljanu, a] *adj, m/f* Australian

Áustria ['awʃtrja] *f*: **a ~** Austria; **austríaco, -a** [awʃ'triaku, a] *adj, m/f* Austrian

autêntico, -a [aw'tẽtʃiku, a] *adj* authentic; (*pessoa*) genuine; (*verdadeiro*) true, real

auto ['awtu] *m* car; **~s** *mpl* (*JUR: processo*) legal proceedings; (*documentos*) legal papers

autobiografia [awtobjogra'fia] *f* autobiography

autobronzeador [awtobrõzja'do*] *adj* self-tanning

autocarro [awto'kaxu] (*PT*) *m* bus

autodefesa [awtode'feza] *f* self-defence (*BRIT*), self-defense (*US*)

autodidata [awtodʒi'data] *adj* self-taught

autodisciplina [awtodʒisi'plina] *f* self-discipline

autódromo [aw'tɔdromu] *m* race track

auto-escola *f* driving school

auto-estrada *f* motorway (*BRIT*), expressway (*US*)

autografar [awtogra'fa*] *vt* to autograph

autógrafo [aw'tɔgrafu] *m* autograph

automático, -a [awto'matʃiku, a] *adj* automatic

automobilismo [awtomobi'liʒmu] *m* motoring; (*ESPORTE*) motor car racing

automóvel [awto'mɔvew] (*pl* -**eis**) *m* motor car (*BRIT*), automobile (*US*)

autonomia [awtono'mia] *f* autonomy

autópsia [aw'tɔpsja] *f* post-mortem, autopsy

autor, a [aw'to*, a] *m/f* author; (*de um crime*) perpetrator; (*JUR*) plaintiff

autoral [awto'raw] (*pl* -**ais**) *adj*: **direitos autorais** copyright *sg*

autoridade [awtori'dadʒi] *f* authority

autorização [awtoriza'sãw] (*pl* -**ões**) *f* permission, authorization; **dar ~ a alguém para** to authorize sb to

autorizar [awtori'za*] *vt* to authorize

auto-serviço *m* self-service

auto-suficiente *adj* self-sufficient

auxiliar [awsi'lja*] *adj* auxiliary ♦ *m/f* assistant ♦ *vt* to help; **auxílio** [aw'silju] *m* help, assistance

Av *abr* (= *avenida*) Ave

aval [a'vaw] (*pl* -**ais**) *m* guarantee

avalanche [ava'lãʃa] *f* avalanche

avaliação [avalja'sãw] (*pl* -**ões**) *f* valuation; (*apreciação*) assessment

avaliar [ava'lja*] *vt* to value; (*apreciar*) to assess

avançado, -a [avã'sadu, a] *adj* advanced; (*idéias, pessoa*) progressive

avançar [avã'sa*] *vt* to move forward ♦ *vi* to advance; **avanço** [a'vãsu] *m* advancement; (*progresso*) progress

avarento, -a [ava'rẽtu, a] *adj* mean ♦ *m/f* miser

avaria [ava'ria] *f* (*TEC*) breakdown; **avariado, -a** [ava'rjadu, a] *adj* (*máquina*) out of order; (*carro*) broken down; **avariar** [ava'rja*] *vt* to damage ♦ *vi* to suffer damage; (*TEC*) to break down

ave [a'vi] *f* bird

aveia [a'veja] *f* oats *pl*

avelã [ave'lã] *f* hazelnut

avenida [ave'nida] f avenue

avental [avẽ'taw] (pl -ais) m apron; (vestido) pinafore dress (BRIT), jumper (US)

aventura [avẽ'tura] f adventure; **aventurar** [avẽtu'ra*] vt to risk, venture

averiguação [averigwa'sãw] (pl -ões) f investigation, inquiry; (verificação) verification

averiguar [averi'gwa*] vt to investigate; (verificar) to verify

avermelhado, -a [avexme'ʎadu, a] adj reddish

avesso, -a [a'vesu, a] adj (lado) opposite, reverse ♦ m wrong side, reverse; **ao ~** inside out; **às avessas** (inverso) upside down; (oposto) the wrong way round

avestruz [avef'truʒ] m ostrich

aviação [avja'sãw] f aviation, flying

aviador, a [avja'do*, a] m/f aviator, airman/woman

avião [a'vjãw] (pl -ões) m aeroplane; **~ a jato** jet

avidez [avi'deʒ] f greed; (desejo) eagerness; **ávido, -a** ['avidu, a] adj greedy; eager

aviões [a'vjõjʃ] mpl de **avião**

avisar [avi'za*] vt to warn; (informar) to tell, let know; **aviso** [a'vizu] m (comunicação) notice

avistar [avif'ta*] vt to catch sight of

avô, -avó [a'vo, a'vɔ] m/f grand-father/mother; **avós** mpl grand-parents

avulso, -a [a'vuwsu, a] adj separate, detached

axila [a'ksila] f armpit

azar [a'za*] m bad luck; **~!** too bad, bad luck!; **estar com ~, ter ~** to be unlucky; **azarento, -a** [aza'rẽtu, a] adj unlucky

azedar [aze'da*] vt to turn sour ♦ vi to turn sour; (leite) to go off;

azedo, -a [a'zedu, a] adj sour; off; (fig) grumpy

azeite [a'zejtʃi] m oil; (de oliva) olive oil

azeitona [azej'tɔna] f olive

azia [a'zia] f heartburn

azougue [a'zogi] m (QUÍM) mercury

azul [a'zuw] (pl -uis) adj blue

azulejo [azu'leʒu] m (glazed) tile

azul-marinho adj inv navy blue

azul-turquesa adj inv turquoise

B

baba ['baba] f dribble

babá [ba'ba] f nanny

babaca [ba'baka] (col) adj stupid ♦ m/f idiot

babado [ba'badu] m frill; (col) piece of gossip

babador [baba'do*] m bib

babar [ba'ba*] vi to dribble; **babar-se** vr to dribble

baby-sitter ['bejbisite*] (pl ~s) m/f baby-sitter

bacalhau [baka'ʎaw] m (dried) cod

bacana [ba'kana] (col) adj great

bacharel [baʃa'rɛw] (pl -éis) m graduate

bacia [ba'sia] f basin; (ANAT) pelvis

backup [ba'kapi] (~s) m (COMPUT) back-up; **tirar um ~ de** to back up

baço, -a ['basu, a] adj dull; (metal) tarnished ♦ m (ANAT) spleen

bactéria [bak'tɛrja] f germ, bacterium; **~s** bacteria pl

badalar [bada'la*] vt, vi to ring

baderna [ba'dɛxna] f commotion

bafo ['bafu] m (bad) breath

bagaço [ba'gasu] m (de frutos) pulp; (PT: cachaça) brandy; **estar/ficar um ~** (fig: pessoa) to be/get run down

bagageiro [baga'ʒejru] m (AUTO)

roofrack; (*PT*) porter

bagagem [ba'gaʒɛ] f luggage; (*fig*) baggage; **recebimento de ~** (*AER*) baggage reclaim

bagatela [baga'tɛla] f trinket; (*fig*) trifle

bago ['bagu] m (*fruto*) berry; (*uva*) grape; (*de chumbo*) pellet

bagulho [ba'guʎu] m (*objeto*) piece of junk

bagunça [ba'gũsa] f mess, shambles sg; **bagunçado, -a** [bagũ'sadu, a] adj in a mess; **bagunçar** [bagũ'sa*] vt to mess up; **bagunceiro, -a** [bagũ'sejru, a] adj messy

baía [ba'ia] f bay

bailado [baj'ladu] m dance; (*balé*) ballet

bailarino, -a [bajla'rinu, a] m/f ballet dancer

baile ['bajli] m dance; (*formal*) ball; **~ à fantasia** fancy-dress ball

bainha [ba'iɲa] f (*de arma*) sheath; (*de costura*) hem

bairro ['bajxu] m district

baixa ['bajʃa] f decrease; (*de preço: redução*) reduction; (*: queda*) fall; (*em vendas*) drop; (*em combate*) casualty; (*do serviço*) discharge

baixar [baj'ʃa*] vt to lower; (*ordem*) to issue; (*lei*) to pass; (*COMPUT*) to download ♦ vi to go down (*ou* come down); (*temperatura, preço*) to drop, fall

baixinho [baj'ʃiɲu] adv (*falar*) softly, quietly; (*em segredo*) secretly

baixo, -a ['bajʃu, a] adj low; (*pessoa*) short, small; (*rio*) shallow; (*linguagem*) common; (*olhos, cabeça*) lowered; (*atitude*) mean; (*metal*) base ♦ adv low; (*em posição baixa*) low down; (*falar*) softly ♦ m (*MÚS*) bass; **em ~** below; (*em casa*) downstairs; **em voz baixa** in a quiet voice; **para ~** down, downwards;

(*em casa*) downstairs; **por ~ de** under, underneath; **baixo-astral** (*col*) m: **estar num baixo-astral** to be on a downer

bala ['bala] f bullet; (*BR: doce*) sweet

balança [ba'lãsa] f scales pl; **B~** (*ASTROLOGIA*) Libra; **~ comercial** balance of trade; **~ de pagamentos** balance of payments

balançar [balã'sa*] vt to swing; (*pesar*) to weigh (up) ♦ vi to swing; (*carro, avião*) to shake; (*em cadeira*) to rock; **balançar-se** vr to swing; **balanço** [ba'lãsu] m (*movimento*) swaying; (*brinquedo*) swing; (*de carro, avião*) shaking; (*COM: registro*) balance (sheet); (*: verificação*) audit; **fazer um balanço de** (*fig*) to take stock of

balão [ba'lãw] (*pl* -ões) m balloon

balbuciar [bawbu'sja*] vt, vi to babble

balbúrdia [baw'buxdʒja] f uproar, bedlam

balcão [baw'kãw] (*pl* -ões) m balcony; (*de loja*) counter; (*TEATRO*) circle; **~ de informações** information desk; **balconista** [bawko'niʃta] m/f shop assistant

balde ['bawdʒi] m bucket, pail

balé [ba'lɛ] m ballet

baleia [ba'leja] f whale

baliza [ba'liza] f (*estaca*) post; (*bóia*) buoy; (*luminosa*) beacon; (*ESPORTE*) goal

balneário [baw'njarju] m bathing resort

balões [ba'lõjʃ] mpl de **balão**

baloiço [ba'lojsu] (*PT*) m (*de criança*) swing; (*ação*) swinging

balsa ['bawsa] f raft; (*barca*) ferry

bamba ['bãba] adj, m/f expert

bambo, -a ['bãbu, a] adj slack, loose

banana [ba'nana] f banana; **bananeira** [bana'nejra] f banana tree

banca ['bãka] f bench; (escritório) office; (em jogo) bank; ~ (de jornais) newsstand; **bancada** [bã'kada] f (banco, POL) bench; (de cozinha) worktop

bancar [bã'ka*] vt to finance ♦ vi (fingir): ~ que to pretend that; **bancário, -a** [bã'karju, a] adj bank atr ♦ m/f bank employee

bancarrota [bãka'xota] f bankruptcy; **ir à** ~ to go bankrupt

banco ['bãku] m (assento) bench; (COM) bank; ~ **de areia** sandbank; ~ **de dados** (COMPUT) database

banda ['bãda] f band; (lado) side; (cinto) sash; **de** ~ sideways; **pôr de** ~ to put aside; ~ **desenhada** (PT) cartoon

bandeira [bã'dejra] f flag; (estandarte) banner; **bandeirinha** [bãdej'riɲa] m (ESPORTE) linesman

bandeja [bã'deʒa] f tray

bandido [bã'dʒidu, a] m bandit

bando ['bãdu] m band; (grupo) group; (de malfeitores) gang; (de ovelhas) flock; (de gado) herd; (de livros etc) pile

banha ['baɲa] f fat; (de porco) lard

banhar [ba'ɲa*] vt to wet; (mergulhar) to dip; (lavar) to wash; **banhar-se** vr to bathe

banheira [ba'ɲejra] f bath

banheiro [ba'ɲejru] m bathroom

banho ['baɲu] m bath; (mergulho) dip; **tomar** ~ to have a bath; (de chuveiro) to have a shower; ~ **de chuveiro** shower; ~ **de sol** sunbathing

banir [ba'ni*] vt to banish

banqueiro, -a [bã'kejru, a] m/f banker

banquete [bã'ketʃi] m banquet

baptismo etc [ba'tʃiʒmu] (PT) = **batismo** etc

bar [ba*] m bar

baralho [ba'raʎu] m pack of cards

barata [ba'rata] f cockroach

barateiro, -a [bara'tejru, a] adj cheap

barato, -a [ba'ratu, a] adj cheap ♦ adv cheaply

barba ['baxba] f beard; **fazer a** ~ to shave

bárbaro, -a [baxbaru, a] adj barbaric; (dor, calor) terrible; (maravilhoso) great

barbeador [baxbja'do*] m razor; (tb: ~ **elétrico**) shaver

barbear [bax'bja*] vt to shave; **barbear-se** vr to shave; **barbearia** [baxbja'ria] f barber's (shop)

barbeiro [bax'bejru] m barber; (loja) barber's

barca ['baxka] f barge; (de travessia) ferry

barco ['baxku] m boat; ~ **a motor** motorboat; ~ **a remo** rowing boat; ~ **a vela** sailing boat

barganha [bax'gaɲa] f bargain; **barganhar** [baxga'ɲa*] vt, vi to negotiate

barman [bax'mã] (pl -men) m barman

barra ['baxa] f bar; (faixa) strip; (traço) stroke; (alavanca) lever

barraca [ba'xaka] f (tenda) tent; (de feira) stall; (de madeira) hut; (de praia) sunshade; **barracão** [baxa-'kãw] (pl -ões) m shed; **barraco** [ba'xaku] m shack, shanty

barragem [ba'xaʒẽ] (pl -ns) f dam; (impedimento) barrier

barranco [ba'xãku] m ravine, gully; (de rio) bank

barrar [ba'xa*] vt to bar

barreira [ba'xejra] f barrier; (cerca) fence; (ESPORTE) hurdle

barricada [baxi'kada] f barricade

barriga [ba'xiga] f belly; **estar de** ~ to be pregnant; ~ **da perna** calf

barrigudo, -a [baxiˈgudu, a] adj
paunchy, pot-bellied

barril [baˈxiw] (pl **-is**) m barrel, cask

barro [ˈbaxu] m clay; (lama) mud

barulhento, -a [baruˈʎẽtu, a] adj
noisy

barulho [baˈruʎu] m (ruído) noise;
(tumulto) din

base [ˈbazi] f base; (fig) basis; **sem ~**
groundless; **com ~ em** based on; **na
~ de** by means of

basear [baˈzja*] vt to base; **basear-
se** vr: **~-se em** to be based on

básico, -a [ˈbaziku, a] adj basic

basquete [baʃˈketʃi] m = **basquetebol**

basquetebol [baʃketeˈbɔw] m
basketball

basta [ˈbaʃta] m: **dar um ~ em** to
call a halt to

bastante [baʃˈtãtʃi] adj (suficiente)
enough; (muito) quite a lot (of)
♦ adv enough; a lot

bastão [baʃˈtãw] (pl **-ões**) m stick

bastar [baʃˈta*] vi to be enough, be
sufficient; **bastar-se** vr to be self-
sufficient; **basta!** (that's) enough!; **~
para** to be enough to

bastardo, -a [baʃˈtaxdu, a] adj,
m/f bastard

bastões [baʃˈtõjʃ] mpl de **bastão**

bata [ˈbata] f (de mulher) smock; (de
médico) overall

batalha [baˈtaʎa] f battle; **bata-
lhador, a** [bataʎaˈdo*, a] adj strug-
gling ♦ m/f fighter; **batalhão**
[bataˈʎãw] (pl **-ões**) m battalion;
batalhar [bataˈʎa*] vi to battle,
fight; (esforçar-se) to make an effort,
try hard ♦ vt (emprego) to go after

batata [baˈtata] f potato; **~ doce**
sweet potato; **~s fritas** chips pl
(BRIT), French fries pl (US); (de pacote)
crisps pl (BRIT), potato chips pl (US)

bate-boca [batʃi-] (pl **~s**) m row,

quarrel

batedeira [bateˈdejra] f beater; (de
manteiga) churn; **~ elétrica** mixer

batente [baˈtẽtʃi] m doorpost

bate-papo [ˈbatʃi-] (pl **~s**) (BR) m
chat

bater [baˈte*] vt to beat, strike; (pé)
to stamp; (foto) to take; (porta) to
slam; (asas) to flap; (recorde) to
break; (roupa) to wear all the time
♦ vi to slam; (sino) to ring; (janela)
to bang; (coração) to beat; (sol) to
beat down; **bater-se** vr: **~-se para
fazer/por** to fight to do/for; **~ (à
porta)** to knock (at the door); **~ à
maquina** to type; **~ em** to hit; **~
com o carro** to crash one's car; **~
com a cabeça** to bang one's head; **~
com o pé (em)** to kick

bateria [bateˈria] f battery; (MÚS)
drums pl; **~ de cozinha** kitchen
utensils pl; **baterista** [bateˈriʃta]
m/f drummer

batida [baˈtʃida] f beat; (da porta)
slam; (à porta) knock; (da polícia)
raid; (AUTO) crash; (bebida) cocktail
of cachaça, fruit and sugar

batido, -a [baˈtʃidu, a] adj beaten;
(roupa) worn ♦ m: **~ de leite** (PT)
milkshake

batina [baˈtʃina] f (REL) cassock

batismo [baˈtʃiʒmu] m baptism,
christening

batizar [batʃiˈza*] vt to baptize,
christen

batom [baˈtõ] (pl **-ns**) m lipstick

batucada [batuˈkada] f dance percussion group

batucar [batuˈka*] vt, vi to drum

baú [baˈu] m trunk

baunilha [bawˈniʎa] f vanilla

bazar [baˈza*] m bazaar; (loja) shop

BCE m (= Banco Central Europeu)
ECB

bêbado, -a [ˈbebadu, a] adj, m/f

drunk

bebê [be'be] m baby

bebedeira [bebe'dejra] f drunkenness; **tomar uma ~** to get drunk

bêbedo, -a ['bebedu, a] adj, m/f = bêbado

bebedouro [bebe'douru] m drinking fountain

beber [be'be*] vt to drink; (absorver) to soak up ♦ vi to drink; **bebida** [be'bida] f drink

beça ['besa] (col) f: **à ~** (com vb): **ele comeu a ~** he ate a lot; (com n): **ela tinha livros à ~** she had a lot of books

beco ['beku] m alley, lane; **~ sem saída** cul-de-sac

bege ['bɛʒi] adj inv beige

beija-flor [bejʒa-'flɔ*] (pl **~es**) m hummingbird

beijar [bej'ʒa*] vt to kiss; **beijar-se** vr to kiss (one another); **beijo** ['bejʒu] m kiss; **dar beijos em alguém** to kiss sb

beira ['bejra] f edge; (de rio) bank; (orla) border; **à ~ de** on the edge of; (ao lado de) beside, by; (fig) on the verge of; **~ do telhado** eaves pl; **beira-mar** f seaside

belas-artes fpl fine arts

beldade [bew'dadʒi] f beauty

beleza [be'leza] f beauty; **que ~!** how lovely!

belga ['bewga] adj, m/f Belgian

Bélgica ['bewʒika] f: **a ~** Belgium

beliche [be'liʃi] m bunk

beliscão [beliʃ'kãw] (pl **-ões**) m pinch; **beliscar** [beliʃ'ka*] vt to pinch, nip; (comida) to nibble

Belize [be'lizi] m Belize

belo, -a ['bɛlu, a] adj beautiful

PALAVRA CHAVE

bem [bẽj] adv **1** (de maneira satisfatória, correta etc) well; **trabalha/**

come **~** she works/eats well; **respondeu ~** he answered correctly; **me sinto/não me sinto ~** I feel fine/I don't feel very well; **tudo ~?** – **tudo ~** how's it going? – fine

2 (valor intensivo) very; **um quarto ~ quente** a nice warm room; **~ se vê que** ... it's clear that ...

3 (bastante) quite, fairly; **a casa é ~ grande** the house is quite big

4 (exatamente): **~ ali** right there; **não é ~ assim** it's not quite like that

5 (estar ~): **estou muito ~ aqui** I feel very happy here; **está ~! vou fazê-lo** oh all right, I'll do it!

6 (de bom grado): **eu ~ que iria mas** ... I'd gladly go but ...

7 (cheirar) good, nice

♦ m **1** (bem-estar) good; **estou dizendo isso para o seu ~** I'm telling you for your own good; **o ~ e o mal** good and evil

2 (posses): **bens** goods, property sg; **bens de consumo** consumer goods; **bens de família** family possessions; **bens móveis/imóveis** moveable property sg/real estate sg

♦ excl **1** (aprovação): **~!** OK!; **muito ~!** well done!

2 (desaprovação): **~ feito!** it serves you right!

♦ adj inv (tom depreciativo): **gente ~** posh people

♦ conj **1**: **nem ~** as soon as, no sooner than; **nem ~ ela chegou começou a dar ordens** as soon as she arrived she started to give orders, no sooner had she arrived than she started to give orders

2: **se ~ que** though; **gostaria de ir se ~ que não tenho dinheiro** I'd like to go even though I've got no money

3: **~ como** as well as; **o livro ~ a peça foram escritos por ele** the book as well as the play was written by him

bem-conceituado, -a [bẽjkõsej'twadu, a] adj highly regarded
bem-disposto, -a [bẽjdʒiʃ'poʃtu, 'pɔʃta] adj well, in good form
bem-estar m well-being
bem-me-quer (pl ~es) m daisy
bem-vindo, -a adj welcome
bênção ['bẽsãw] (pl ~s) f blessing
beneficência [benefi'sẽsja] f kindness; (caridade) charity
beneficiar [benefi'sja*] vt to benefit; (melhorar) to improve; **beneficiar-se** vr to benefit
benefício [bene'fisju] m benefit; (vantagem) profit; (favor) favour (BRIT), favor (US); **em ~ de** in aid of;
benéfico, -a [be'nɛfiku, a] adj beneficial; (generoso) generous
benévolo, -a [be'nɛvolu, a] adj benevolent, kind
benfeitor, a [bẽfej'to*, a] m/f benefactor/benefactress
bengala [bẽ'gala] f walking stick
benigno, -a [be'nignu, a] adj kind; (agradável) pleasant; (MED) benign
bens [bẽjʃ] mpl de **bem**
bento, -a ['bẽtu, a] pp de **benzer** ♦ adj blessed; (água) holy
benzer [bẽ'ze*] vt to bless; **benzer-se** vr to cross o.s.
berço ['bexsu] m cradle; (cama) cot; (origem) birthplace
Berlim [bex'lĩ] n Berlin
berma ['bexma] (PT) f hard shoulder (BRIT), berm (US)
berrar [be'xa*] vi to bellow; (criança) to bawl; **berreiro** [be'xejru] m: **abrir o berreiro** to burst out crying; **berro** ['bexu] m yell
besta ['beʃta] adj stupid; (convencido) full of oneself; **~ de carga** beast of burden; **besteira** [beʃ'tejra] f

foolishness; **dizer besteiras** to talk nonsense; **fazer uma besteira** to do something silly; **bestial** [beʃ'tʃjaw] (pl -ais) adj bestial; (repugnante) repulsive
best-seller ['beʃt'selε*] (pl ~s) m best seller
betão [be'tãw] (PT) m concrete
beterraba [bete'xaba] f beetroot
bexiga [be'ʃiga] f bladder
bezerro, -a [be'zexu, a] m/f calf
BI abr m (PT: bilhete de identidade) identity card; see boxed note

---

BI

All Portuguese citizens are required to carry an identity card, known as the **BI** or bilhete de identidade. The photocard, which gives the holder's name, date of birth, marital status, height and a fingerprint, can be used instead of a passport for travel within the European Union. Failure to produce a valid identity card when stopped by the police can result in a fine.

Bíblia ['biblja] f Bible
bibliografia [bibljogra'fia] f bibliography
biblioteca [bibljo'tεka] f library; (estante) bookcase; **bibliotecário, -a** [bibljote'karju, a] m/f librarian
bica ['bika] f tap; (PT) black coffee, expresso
bicha ['biʃa] f (lombriga) worm; (BR: col, pej: homossexual) queer; (PT: fila) queue
bicho ['biʃu] m animal; (inseto) insect, bug
bicicleta [bisi'klεta] f bicycle; (col) bike; **andar de ~** to cycle; **~ do exército** exercise bike
bico ['biku] m (de ave) beak; (ponta)

point; (*de chaleira*) spout; (*boca*) mouth; (*de pena*) nib; (*do peito*) nipple; (*de gás*) jet; (*col: emprego*) casual job; (*chupeta*) dummy; **calar o ~** to shut up

bidê [bi'de] *m* bidet

bife ['bifi] *m* (beef) steak; **~ a cavalo** steak with fried eggs; **~ à milanesa** beef escalope; **~ de panela** beef stew

bifurcação [bifuxka'sãw] (*pl* **-ões**) *f* fork

bifurcar-se [bifux'kaxsi] *vr* to fork, divide

bigode [bi'gɔdʒi] *m* moustache

bijuteria [biʒute'ria] *f* (costume) jewellery (BRIT) ou jewelry (US)

bilhão [bi'ʎãw] (*pl* **-ões**) *m* billion

bilhar [bi'ʎa*] *m* (*jogo*) billiards *sg*

bilhete [bi'ʎetʃi] *m* ticket; (*cartinha*) note; **~ de ida** single (BRIT) ou one-way ticket; **~ de ida e volta** return (BRIT) ou round-trip (US) ticket; **bilheteira** [biʎe'tejra] (PT) *f* = **~ria**; **bilheteiro, -a** [biʎe'tejru, a] *m/f* ticket seller; **bilheteria** [biʎete'ria] *f* ticket office

bilhões [bi'ʎõjʃ] *mpl de* bilhão

bilíngüe [bi'lĩgwi] *adj* bilingual

binóculo [bi'nɔkulu] *m* binoculars *pl*; (*para teatro*) opera glasses *pl*

biografia [bjɔgra'fia] *f* biography

biologia [bjolo'ʒia] *f* biology

biombo ['bjõbu] *m* screen

bip [bip] *n* pager, paging device

biquíni [bi'kini] *m* bikini

birita [bi'rita] (*col*) *f* drink

Birmânia [bix'manja] *f*: **a ~** Burma

biruta [bi'ruta] *adj* crazy ♦ *f* windsock

bis [biʃ] *excl* encore!

bisavô, -ó [biza'vo, ɔ] *m/f* great-grandfather/great-grandmother; **bisavós** [biza'vɔʃ] *mpl* great-grandparents

biscate [biʃ'katʃi] *m* odd job

biscoito [biʃ'kojtu] *m* biscuit (BRIT), cookie (US)

bispo ['biʃpu] *m* bishop

bissexto, -a [bi'seʃtu, a] *adj*: **ano ~** leap year

bit [bitʃi] *m* (COMPUT) bit

bizarro, -a [bi'zaxu, a] *adj* bizarre

blasfemar [blaʃfe'ma*] *vi* to blaspheme; **blasfêmia** [blaʃ'femja] *f* blasphemy; (*ultraje*) curse

blazer ['blejze*] (*pl* **~s**) *m* blazer

blecaute [ble'kawtʃi] *m* power cut

blindado, -a [blĩ'dadu, a] *adj* armoured (BRIT), armored (US)

blitz [blitʃ] *f* police raid; (*na estrada*) police road block

bloco ['blɔku] *m* block; (POL) bloc; (*de escrever*) writing pad; **~ de carnaval** carnival troupe

bloqueador [blokja'do*] *m*: **~ solar** sunblock

bloquear [blo'kja*] *vt* to blockade; (*obstruir*) to block; **bloqueio** [blo'keju] *m* blockade; blockage

blusa ['bluza] *f* (*de mulher*) blouse; (*de homem*) shirt; **~ de lã** jumper; **blusão** [blu'zãw] (*pl* **-ões**) *m* jacket

boa ['boa] *adj f de* bom ♦ *f* boa constrictor

boate ['bwatʃi] *f* nightclub

boato ['bwatu] *m* rumour (BRIT), rumor (US)

bobagem [bo'baʒẽ] (*pl* **-ns**) *f* silliness, nonsense; (*dito, ato*) silly thing

bobo, -a ['bobu, a] *adj* silly, daft ♦ *m/f* fool ♦ *m* (*de corte*) jester; **fazer-se de ~** to act the fool

bobó [bo'bɔ] *m* beans, palm oil and manioc

boca ['boka] *f* mouth; (*entrada*) entrance; (*de fogão*) ring; **de ~ aberta** agape; **bater ~** to argue

bocadinho [boka'dʒinu] *m*: **um ~** (*pouco tempo*) a little while; (*pouquinho*) a little bit

bocado [bo'kadu] *m* mouthful, bite; (*pedaço*) piece, bit; **um ~ de tempo** quite some time

boçal [bo'saw] (*pl* **-ais**) *adj* ignorant; (*grosseiro*) uncouth

bocejar [bose'ʒa*] *vi* to yawn; **bocejo** [bo'seʒu] *m* yawn

bochecha [bo'ʃeʃa] *f* cheek; **bo-checho** [bo'ʃeʃu] *m* mouthwash

boda ['boda] *f* wedding; **~s** *fpl* (*aniversário de casamento*) wedding anniversary *sg*

bode ['bɔdʒi] *m* goat; **~ expiatório** scapegoat

bofetada [bofe'tada] *f* slap

bofetão [bofe'tãw] (*pl* **-ões**) *m* punch

boi [boj] *m* ox

bóia ['bɔja] *f* buoy; (*col*) grub; (*de braço*) armband, water wing

boiar [bo'ja*] *vt*, *vi* to float

boi-bumbá [-bü'ba] *n* (*BR*) *see boxed note*

BOI-BUMBÁ

The **boi-bumbá**, or *bumba-meu-boi*, is a traditional folk dance from north-eastern Brazil, which brings together human, animal and mythological characters in a theatrical performance. The ox, which the dance is named after, is played by a dancer wearing an iron frame covered in pieces of colourful fabric. Eventually the beast is "killed" and its meat is symbolically shared out before it comes back to life in the finale.

boicotar [bojko'ta*] *vt* to boycott; **boicote** [boj'kɔtʃi] *m* boycott

bola ['bɔla] *f* ball; **dar ~ para** (*flertar*) to flirt with; **ela não dá a menor ~** (*para isso*) she couldn't care less (about it); **não ser certo da ~** (*col*)

not to be right in the head

bolacha [bo'laʃa] *f* biscuit (*BRIT*), cookie (*US*); (*col: bofetada*) wallop; (*para chope*) beermat

boleia [bo'leja] *f* driver's seat; **dar uma ~ a alguém** (*PT*) to give sb a lift

boletim [bole'tʃĩ] (*pl* **-ns**) *m* report; (*publicação*) newsletter; **~ meteorológico** weather forecast

bolha ['boʎa] *f* (*na pele*) blister; (*de ar, sabão*) bubble

boliche [bo'liʃi] *m* bowling, skittles *sg*

bolinho [bo'liɲu] *m*: **~ de carne** meat ball; **~ de arroz/bacalhau** rice/dry cod cake

Bolívia [bo'livja] *f*: **a ~** Bolivia

bolo ['bolu] *m* cake; (*monte: de gente*) bunch; (: *de papéis*) bundle; **dar o ~ em alguém** to stand sb up; **vai dar ~** (*col*) there's going to be trouble

bolor [bo'lo*] *m* mould (*BRIT*), mold (*US*); (*nas plantas*) mildew

bolota [bo'lɔta] *f* acorn

bolsa ['bowsa] *f* bag; (*COM: tb*: **~ de valores**) stock exchange; **~ (de estudos)** scholarship

bolso ['bowsu] *m* pocket; **de ~** pocket *atr*

PALAVRA CHAVE

bom, boa [bõ, 'boa] (*pl* **bons, boas**) *adj* **1** (*ótimo*) good; **é um livro ~** *ou* **um ~ livro** it's a good book; **a comida está boa** the food is delicious; **o tempo está ~** the weather's fine; **ele foi muito ~ comigo** he was very nice *ou* kind to me

2 (*apropriado*): **ser ~ para** to be good for; **acho ~ você não ir** I think it's better if you don't go

3 (*irônico*): **um ~ quarto de hora** a good quarter of an hour; **que ~ motorista você é!** a fine *ou* some driver you are!; **seria ~ que ...!** a fine thing it would be if ...!; **essa é boa!** what a cheek!

4 (*saudação*): **~ dia!** good morning!; **boa tarde!** good afternoon!; **boa noite!** good evening!; (*ao deitar-se*) good night!; **tudo ~?** how's it going?

5 (*outras frases*): **está ~?** OK?

♦ *excl*: **~! all right!; ~, ... right, ...**

bomba ['bõba] *f* bomb; (*TEC*) pump; (*fig*) bombshell; **~ atômica/time/smoke bomb**; **~ de gasolina** petrol (*BRIT*) ou gas (*US*) pump; **~ de incêndio** fire extinguisher

bombardear [bõbax'dʒja*] *vt* to bomb; (*fig*) to bombard; **bombardeio** [bõbax'deju] *m* bombing, bombardment

bombeiro [bõ'bejru] *m* fireman; (*BR*: *encanador*) plumber; **o corpo de ~s** fire brigade

bombom [bõ'bõ] (*pl* -**ns**) *m* chocolate

bondade [bõ'dadʒi] *f* goodness, kindness; **tenha a ~ de vir** would you please come

bonde ['bõdʒi] (*BR*) *m* tram

bondoso, -a [bõ'dozu, ɔza] *adj* kind, good

boné [bo'nɛ] *m* cap

boneca [bo'nɛka] *f* doll

boneco [bo'nɛku] *m* dummy

bonito, -a [bo'nitu, a] *adj* pretty; (*gesto, dia*) nice ♦ *m* (*peixe*) tuna (fish), tunny

bônus ['bonuʃ] *m inv* bonus

boquiaberto, -a [bokja'bextu, a] *adj* dumbfounded, astonished

borboleta [boxbo'leta] *f* butterfly; (*BR*: *roleta*) turnstile

borbotão [boxbo'tãw] (*pl* -**ões**) *m* gush, spurt; **sair aos borbotões** to

gush out

borbulhar [boxbu'ʎa*] *vi* to bubble

borda ['bɔxda] *f* edge; (*do rio*) bank; **à ~ de** on the edge of

bordado [box'dadu] *m* embroidery

bordar [box'da*] *vt* to embroider

bordo ['bɔxdu] *m* (*de navio*) side; **a ~** on board

borra ['bɔxa] *f* dregs *pl*

borracha [bo'xaʃa] *f* rubber; **borracheiro** [boxa'ʃejru] *m* tyre (*BRIT*) ou tire (*US*) specialist

borrão [bo'xãw] (*pl* -**ões**) *m* (*rascunho*) rough draft; (*mancha*) blot

borrar [bo'xa*] *vt* to blot; (*riscar*) to cross out

borrifar [boxi'fa*] *vt* to sprinkle; **borrifo** [bo'xifu] *m* spray

borrões [bo'xõjʃ] *mpl de* **borrão**

bosque ['bɔʃki] *m* wood, forest

bossa ['bɔsa] *f* charm; (*inchaço*) swelling; **~ nova** (*MÚS*) *see boxed note*

BOSSA NOVA

Bossa nova is a type of music invented by young, middle-class inhabitants of Rio de Janeiro at the end of the 1950s. It has an obvious jazz influence, an unusual, rhythmic beat and lyrics praising beauty and love. **Bossa nova** became known around the world through the work of the conductor and composer Antônio Carlos Jobim whose compositions, working with the poet Vinícius de Morais, include the famous song "The Girl from Ipanema".

---

bota ['bɔta] *f* boot; **~s de borracha** wellingtons

botânica [bo'tanika] *f* botany

botão [bo'tãw] (*pl* -**ões**) *m* button; (*flor*) bud

botar [bo'ta*] *vt* to put; (*roupa, sa-*

patos) to put on; (*mesa*) to set; (*defeito*) to find; (*ovos*) to lay

bote [ˈbɔtʃi] *m* boat; (*com arma*) thrust; (*salto*) spring

botequim [botʃiˈkĩ] (*pl* -**ns**) *m* bar

botija [boˈtʃiʒa] *f* (earthenware) jug

botões [boˈtõjʃ] *mpl de* **botão**

boxe [ˈbɔksi] *m* boxing

brabo, -a [ˈbrabu, a] *adj* fierce; (*zangado*) angry; (*ruim*) bad; (*calor*) unbearable

braçada [braˈsada] *f* armful; (NATAÇÃO) stroke

bracelete [braseˈletʃi] *m* bracelet

braço [ˈbrasu] *m* arm; **de ~s cruzados** with arms folded; (*fig*) without lifting a finger; **de ~ dado** arm-in-arm

bradar [braˈda*] *vt, vi* to shout, yell; **brado** [ˈbradu] *m* shout, yell

braguilha [braˈɡiʎa] *f* flies *pl*

branco, -a [ˈbrãku, a] *adj* white ♦ *m/f* white man/woman ♦ *m* (*espaço*) blank; **em ~** blank; **noite em ~** sleepless night; **brancura** [brãˈkura] *f* whiteness

brando, -a [ˈbrãdu, a] *adj* gentle; (*mole*) soft

brasa [ˈbraza] *f* hot coal; **em ~** red-hot; **pisar em ~** to be on tenterhooks

brasão [braˈzãw] (*pl* -**ões**) *m* coat of arms

braseiro [braˈzejru] *m* brazier

Brasil [braˈziw] *m*: **o ~** Brazil; **brasileiro, -a** [braziˈlejru, a] *adj, m/f* Brazilian

Brasília [braˈzilja] *n* Brasília

brasões [braˈzõjʃ] *mpl de* **brasão**

bravata [braˈvata] *f* bravado, boasting

bravio, -a [braˈviu, a] *adj* (*selvagem*) wild; (*feroz*) ferocious

bravo, -a [ˈbravu, a] *adj* brave; (*furioso*) angry; (*mar*) rough ♦ *m*

brave man; **~!** bravo!; **bravura** [braˈvura] *f* courage, bravery

brecar [breˈka*] *vt* (*carro*) to stop; (*reprimir*) to curb ♦ *vi* to brake

brecha [ˈbrɛʃa] *f* breach; (*abertura*) opening; (*dano*) damage; (*col*) chance

breu [brew] *m* tar, pitch

breve [ˈbrɛvi] *adj* short; (*conciso, rápido*) brief ♦ *adv* soon; **em ~** soon, shortly; **até ~** see you soon

bridge [ˈbridʒi] *m* bridge

briga [ˈbriga] *f* fight; (*verbal*) quarrel

brigada [briˈgada] *f* brigade

brigão, -ona [briˈɡãw, ɔna] (*pl* -**ões, ~s**) *adj* quarrelsome ♦ *m/f* troublemaker

brigar [briˈga*] *vi* to fight; (*altercar*) to quarrel

brigões [briˈɡõjʃ] *mpl de* **brigão**

brigona [briˈɡɔna] *f de* **brigão**

brilhante [briˈʎãtʃi] *adj* brilliant ♦ *m* diamond

brilhar [briˈʎa*] *vi* to shine

brilho [briˈʎu] *m* (*luz viva*) brilliance; (*esplendor*) splendour (BRIT), splendor (US); (*nos sapatos*) shine; (*de metais, olhos*) gleam

brincadeira [brĩkaˈdejra] *f* fun; (*gracejo*) joke; (*de criança*) game; **deixe de ~s!** stop fooling!; **de ~** for fun

brincalhão, -ona [brĩkaˈʎãw, ɔna] (*pl* -**ões, ~s**) *adj* playful ♦ *m/f* joker, teaser

brincar [brĩˈka*] *vi* to play; (*gracejar*) to joke; **estou brincando** I'm only kidding; **~ de soldados** to play (at) soldiers; **~ com alguém** to tease sb

brinco [ˈbrĩku] *m* (*jóia*) earring

brindar [brĩˈda*] *vt* to drink to; (*presentear*) to give a present to; **brinde** [ˈbrĩdʒi] *m* toast; free gift

brinquedo [brĩˈkedu] *m* toy

brio [ˈbriu] *m* self-respect, dignity

brisa ['briza] f breeze

britânico, -a [bri'taniku, a] adj British ♦ m/f Briton

broche ['brɔʃi] m brooch

brochura [bro'ʃura] f (livro) paperback; (folheto) brochure, pamphlet

brócolis ['brɔkoliʃ] mpl broccoli sg

bronca ['brɔka] (col) f telling off; **dar uma ~ em** to tell off; **levar uma ~** to get told off

bronco, -a ['brɔku, a] adj (rude) coarse; (burro) thick

bronquite [brõ'kitʃi] f bronchitis

bronze ['brõzi] m bronze; **bronzeado, -a** [brõ'zjadu, a] adj (cor) bronze; (pelo sol) suntanned ♦ m suntan; **bronzear** [brõ'zja*] vt to tan; **bronzear-se** vr to get a tan

brotar [bro'ta*] vt to produce ♦ vi (manar) to flow; (BOT) to sprout; (nascer) to spring up

broto ['brotu] m bud; (fig) youngster

broxa ['brɔʃa] f (large) paint brush

bruços ['brusuʃ]: **de ~** adv face down

bruma ['bruma] f mist, haze

brusco, -a ['bruʃku, a] adj brusque; (súbito) sudden

brutal [bru'taw] (pl -ais) adj brutal

bruto, -a ['brutu, a] adj brutish; (grosseiro) coarse; (móvel) heavy; (petróleo) crude; (peso, COM) gross ♦ m brute; **em ~** raw, unworked

bruxa ['bruʃa] f witch; **bruxaria** [bruʃa'ria] f witchcraft

Bruxelas [bru'ʃelaʃ] n Brussels

bruxo ['bruʃu] m wizard

budismo [bu'dʒiʒmu] m Buddhism

bufar [bu'fa*] vi to puff, pant; (com raiva) to snort; (reclamar) to moan, grumble

bufê [bu'fe] m sideboard; (comida) buffet

buffer ['bafe*] (pl ~s) m (COMPUT) buffer

bugiganga [buʒi'gãga] f trinket; **~s** fpl (coisas sem valor) knicknacks

bula ['bula] f (MED) directions pl for use

bule ['buli] m (de chá) teapot; (de café) coffeepot

Bulgária [buw'garja] f: **a ~** Bulgaria; **búlgaro, -a** ['buwgaru, a] adj, m/f Bulgarian ♦ m (LING) Bulgarian

bunda ['bũda] (col) f bottom, backside

buquê [bu'ke] m bouquet

buraco [bu'raku] m hole; (de agulha) eye; **ser um ~** to be tough; **~ da fechadura** keyhole

burguês, -guesa [bux'geʃ, 'geza] adj middle-class, bourgeois; **burguesia** [buxge'zia] f middle class, bourgeoisie

burocracia [burokra'sia] f bureaucracy

burro, -a ['buxu, a] adj stupid ♦ m/f (ZOOL) donkey; (pessoa) fool, idiot; **pra ~** (col) a lot; (com adj) really; **~ de carga** (fig) hard worker

busca ['buʃka] f search; **em ~ de** in search of; **dar ~ a** to search for

buscar [buʃ'ka*] vt to fetch; (procurar) to look ou search for; **ir ~** to fetch, go for; **mandar ~** to send for

bússola ['busola] f compass

busto ['buʃtu] m bust

buzina [bu'zina] f horn; **buzinar** [buzi'na*] vi to sound one's horn, toot the horn ♦ vt to hoot

búzio ['buzju] m conch

C

c/ abr = **com**

Ca abr (= companhia) Co

cá [ka] adv here; **de ~** on this side; **para ~** here, over here; **para lá e para ~** back and forth; **de lá para ~** since then

caatinga [ka'tʃĩga] (*BR*) f scrub(-land)

cabana [ka'bana] f hut

cabeça [ka'besa] f head; (*inteligência*) brains pl; (*de uma lista*) top ♦ m/f leader; **de ~** off the top of one's head; (*calcular*) in one's head; **de ~ para baixo** upside down; **por ~** per person, per head; **cabeçada** [kabe'sada] f (*pancada com cabeça*) butt; (*FUTEBOL*) header; (*asneira*) blunder; **cabeçalho** [kabe'saʎu] m (*de livro*) title page; (*de página, capítulo*) heading

cabeceira [kabe'sejra] f (*de cama*) head

cabeçudo, -a [kabe'sudu, a] adj big-headed; (*teimoso*) pigheaded

cabeleira [kabe'lejra] f head of hair; (*postiça*) wig; **cabeleireiro, -a** [kabelej'rejru, a] m/f hairdresser

cabelo [ka'belu] m hair; **cortar/ fazer o ~** to have one's hair cut/ done; **cabeludo, -a** [kabe'ludu, a] adj hairy

caber [ka'be*] vi: **~ (em)** to fit; (*ser compatível*) to be appropriate (in); **~ a** (*em partilha*) to fall to; **cabe a alguém fazer** it is up to sb to do; **não cabe aqui fazer comentários** this is not the time or place to comment

cabide [ka'bidʒi] m (*coat hanger*); (*móvel*) hat stand; (*fixo à parede*) coat rack

cabine [ka'bini] f cabin; (*em loja*) fitting room; **~ do piloto** (*AER*) cockpit; **~ telefônica** telephone box (*BRIT*) ou booth

cabo [ka'bu] m (*extremidade*) end; (*de faca, vassoura etc*) handle; (*corda*) rope; (*elétrico etc*) cable; (*GEO*) cape; (*MIL*) corporal; **ao ~ de** at the end of; **de ~ a rabo** from

beginning to end; **levar a ~** to carry out; **dar ~ de** to do away with

caboclo, -a [ka'boklu, a] (*BR*) m/f mestizo

cabra ['kabra] f goat

cabreiro, -a [ka'brejru, a] (*col*) adj suspicious

cabrito [ka'britu] m kid

caça ['kasa] f hunting; (*busca*) hunt; (*animal*) quarry, game ♦ m (*AER*) fighter (plane); **caçador, a** [kasa'do*, a] m/f hunter

cação [ka'sãw] (*pl -ões*) m shark

caçar [ka'sa*] vt to hunt; (*com espingarda*) to shoot; (*procurar*) to seek ♦ vi to hunt, go hunting

caçarola [kasa'rɔla] f (*sauce*)pan

cacau [ka'kaw] m cocoa; (*BOT*) cacao

cacetada [kase'tada] f blow (with a stick)

cachaça [ka'ʃasa] f (*white*) rum

cachaceiro, -a [kaʃa'sejru, a] adj drunk ♦ m/f drunkard

cachê [ka'ʃe] m fee

cachecol [kaʃe'kɔw] (*pl -óis*) m scarf

cachimbo [ka'ʃĩbu] m pipe

cacho ['kaʃu] m bunch; (*de cabelo*) curl; (: *longo*) ringlet

cachoeira [kaʃ'wejra] f waterfall

cachorra [ka'ʃoxa] f bitch; (*cadela*) (*female*) puppy

cachorrinho, -a [kaʃo'xiɲu, a] m/f puppy

cachorro [ka'ʃoxu] m dog; (*cãozinho*) puppy; **cachorro-quente** (*pl cachorros-quentes*) m hot dog

cacique [ka'siki] m (*Indian*) chief; (*mandachuva*) local boss

caco ['kaku] m bit, fragment; (*pessoa velha*) old relic

caçoar [ka'swa*] vt, vi to mock

cacoete [ka'kwetʃi] m twitch, tic

cacto ['kaktu] m cactus

cada ['kada] *adj inv* each; (*todo*) every; **~ um** each one; **~ semana** each week; **a ~ 3 horas** every 3 hours; **~ vez mais** more and more

cadastro [ka'daʃtru] *m* register; (*ato*) registration; (*de criminosos*) criminal record

cadáver [ka'dave*] *m* corpse, (dead) body

cadê [ka'de] (*col*) *adv*: **~ ...?** where's/where are ...?, what's happened to ...?

cadeado [ka'dʒjadu] *m* padlock

cadeia [ka'deja] *f* chain; (*prisão*) prison; (*rede*) network

cadeira [ka'dejra] *f* chair; (*disciplina*) subject; (TEATRO) stall; (*função*) post; **~s** *fpl* (ANAT) hips; **~ de balanço/rodas** rocking chair/wheelchair

cadela [ka'dela] *f* (*cão*) bitch

caderneta [kadex'neta] *f* notebook; **~ de poupança** savings account

caderno [ka'dexnu] *m* exercise book; (*de notas*) notebook; (*de jornal*) section

caducar [kadu'ka*] *vi* to lapse, expire; **caduco, -a** [ka'duku, a] *adj* invalid, expired; (*senil*) senile; (BOT) deciduous

cães [kãjʃ] *mpl de* **cão**

cafajeste [kafa'ʒeʃtʃi] (*col*) *adj* roguish; (*vulgar*) vulgar, coarse ♦ *m/f* rogue; rough customer

café [ka'fɛ] *m* coffee; (*estabelecimento*) café; **~ com leite** white coffee (BRIT), coffee with cream (US); **~ preto** black coffee; **da manhã** (BR) breakfast

cafeteira [kafe'tejra] *f* coffee pot; (*máquina*) percolator; **cafezal** [kafe'zaw] (*pl* **-ais**) *m* coffee plantation; **cafezinho** [kafe'ziɲu] *m* small

black coffee

cagada [ka'gada] (*col!*) *f* shit (!)

cágado ['kagadu] *m* turtle

cagar [ka'ga*] (*col!*) *vi* to (have a) shit (!)

cagüetar [kagwe'ta*] *vt* to inform on; **cagüete** [ka'gwetʃi] *m* informer

caiba *etc* ['kajba] *vb V* **caber**

cãibra ['kãjbra] *f* (MED) cramp

caída [ka'ida] *f* = **queda**

caído, -a [ka'idu, a] *adj* dejected; (*derrubado*) fallen; (*pendente*) droopy; **~ por** (*apaixonado*) in love with

câimbra ['kãjbra] *f* = **cãibra**

caipirinha [kajpi'riɲa] *f* cocktail of cachaça, lemon and sugar

cair [ka'i*] *vi* to fall; **~ bem/mal** (*roupa*) to fit well/badly; (*col*: *pessoa*) to look good/bad; **~ em si** to come to one's senses; **ao ~ da noite** at nightfall; **essa comida me caiu mal** that food did not agree with me

Cairo ['kajru] *m*: **o ~** Cairo

cais [kajʃ] *m* (NÁUT) quay; (PT: FERRO) platform

caixa ['kajʃa] *f* box; (*cofre*) safe; (*de uma loja*) cashdesk ♦ *m/f* (*pessoa*) cashier ♦ *m*: **~ automático** cash machine; **pequena ~** petty cash; **~ de correio** letter box; **~ econômica** savings bank; **~ de mudanças** (BR) **ou de velocidades** (PT) gearbox; **~ postal** P.O. box; **~ registradora** cash register; **caixa-forte** (*pl* **caixas-fortes**) *f* vault

caixão [kaj'ʃãw] (*pl* **-ões**) *m* (*ataúde*) coffin; (*caixa grande*) large box

caixeiro-viajante, caixeira-viajante (*pl* **caixeiros-viajantes, caixeiras-viajantes**) *m/f* commercial traveller (BRIT) ou traveler (US)

caixilho [kajˈʃiʎu] m (*moldura*) frame

caixões [kajˈʃõjʃ] mpl de **caixão**

caixote [kajˈʃɔtʃi] m packing case; ~ **do lixo** (*PT*) dustbin (*BRIT*), garbage can (*US*)

caju [kaˈʒu] m cashew fruit

cal [kaw] f lime; (*na água*) chalk; (*para caiar*) whitewash

calabouço [kalaˈbosu] m dungeon

calado, -a [kaˈladu, a] adj quiet

calafrio [kalaˈfriu] m shiver; **ter ~s** to shiver

calamidade [kalamiˈdadʒi] f calamity, disaster

calão [kaˈlãw] (*PT*) m: (*baixo*) ~ slang

calar [kaˈlaˈ*] vt to keep quiet about; (*impor silêncio a*) to silence ♦ vi to go quiet; (*manter-se calado*) to keep quiet; **calar-se** vr to go quiet; to keep quiet; **cala a boca!** shut up!

calça [ˈkawsa] f (*tb*: ~**s**) trousers pl (*BRIT*), pants pl (*US*)

calçada [kawˈsada] f (*BR*: *passeio*) pavement (*BRIT*), sidewalk (*US*); (*PT*: *rua*) roadway

calçadão [kawsaˈdãw] (*pl* -**ões**) m pedestrian precinct (*BRIT*)

calçado, -a [kawˈsadu, a] adj (*rua*) paved ♦ m shoe; ~**s** mpl (*para os pés*) footwear sg

calçadões [kawsaˈdõjʃ] mpl de **calçadão**

calçamento [kawsaˈmẽtu] m paving

calcanhar [kawkaˈɲaˈ*] m (*ANAT*) heel

calção [kawˈsãw] (*pl* -**ões**) m shorts pl; ~ **de banho** swimming trunks pl

calcar [kawˈkaˈ*] vt to tread on; (*espezinhar*) to trample (on)

calçar [kawˈsaˈ*] vt (*sapatos, luvas*) to put on; (*pavimentar*) to pave;

calçar-se vr to put on one's shoes; **ela calça (número) 28** she takes size 28 (in shoes)

calcário [kawˈkarju] m limestone

calcinha [kawˈsiɲa] f panties pl

calço [ˈkawsu] m wedge

calções [kawˈsõjʃ] mpl de **calção**

calculador [kawkulaˈdo*] m = **calculadora**

calculadora [kawkulaˈdora] f calculator

calcular [kawkuˈlaˈ*] vt to calculate; (*imaginar*) to imagine; ~ **que** to reckon that

cálculo [ˈkawkulu] m calculation; (*MAT*) calculus; (*MED*) stone

calda [ˈkawda] f (*de doce*) syrup; ~**s** fpl (*águas termais*) hot springs

caldeirada [kawdejˈrada] (*PT*) f (*guisado*) fish stew

caldo [ˈkawdu] m broth; (*de fruta*) juice; ~ **de carne/galinha** beef/chicken stock; ~ **verde** potato and cabbage broth

calendário [kalẽˈdarju] m calendar

calhar [kaˈʎaˈ*] vi: **calhou viajarmos no mesmo avião** we happened to travel on the same plane; **calhou que** it so happened that; ~ **a** (*cair bem*) to suit; **se** ~ (*PT*) perhaps, maybe

calibre [kaˈlibri] m calibre (*BRIT*), caliber (*US*)

cálice [ˈkalisi] m wine glass; (*REL*) chalice

calista [kaˈliʃta] m/f chiropodist (*BRIT*), podiatrist (*US*)

calma [ˈkawma] f calm

calmante [kawˈmãtʃi] adj soothing ♦ m (*MED*) tranquillizer

calmo, -a [ˈkawmu, a] adj calm

calo [ˈkalu] m callus; (*no pé*) corn

calor [kaˈlo*] m heat; (*agradável, fig*) warmth; **está** ou **faz** ~ it is hot; **estar com** ~ to be hot

calorento, -a [kalo'rẽtu, a] adj (pessoa) sensitive to heat; (lugar) hot

caloria [kalo'ria] f calorie

caloroso, -a [kalo'rozu, ɔza] adj warm; (entusiástico) enthusiastic

calouro, -a [ka'loru, a] m/f (EDUC) fresher (BRIT), freshman (US)

calúnia [ka'lunja] f slander

calvo, -a ['kawvu, a] adj bald

cama ['kama] f bed; ~ **de casal** double bed; ~ **de solteiro** single bed; **de** ~ (doente) ill (in bed)

camada [ka'mada] f layer; (de tinta) coat

câmara ['kamara] f chamber; (FOTO) camera; ~ **municipal** (BR) town council; (PT) town hall; ~ **digital** digital camera; **em** ~ **lenta** in slow motion

camarada [kama'rada] adj friendly, nice; (preço) good ♦ m/f comrade; (sujeito) guy/woman

câmara-de-ar (pl câmaras-de-ar) f inner tube

camarão [kama'rãw] (pl -ões) m shrimp; (graúdo) prawn

camarões [kama'rõjʃ] mpl de camarão

camarote [kama'rɔtʃi] m (NÁUT) cabin; (TEATRO) box

cambaleante [kãba'ljãtʃi] adj unsteady (on one's feet)

cambalear [kãba'lja*] vi to stagger, reel

cambalhota [kãba'ʎɔta] f somersault

câmbio ['kãbju] m (dinheiro etc) exchange; (preço de câmbio) rate of exchange; ~ **livre** free trade; ~ **paralelo** black market

cambista [kã'biʃta] m money changer

Camboja [kã'bɔja] m: **o** ~ Cambodia

camelo [ka'melu] m camel

camião [ka'mjãw] (pl -ões) (PT) m lorry (BRIT), truck (US)

caminhada [kami'nada] f walk

caminhão [kami'nãw] (pl -ões) (BR) m lorry (BRIT), truck (US)

caminhar [kami'na*] vi to walk; (processo) to get under way; (negócios) to progress

caminho [ka'minu] m way; (vereda) road, path; ~ **de ferro** (PT) railway (BRIT), railroad (US); **a** ~ on the way, en route; **cortar** ~ to take a short cut; **pôr-se a** ~ to set off

caminhões [kami'nõjʃ] mpl de caminhão

caminhoneiro, -a [kaminoˈnejru, a] m/f lorry driver (BRIT), truck driver (US)

camiões [ka'mjõjʃ] mpl de camião

camioneta [kamjo'neta] (PT) f (para passageiros) coach; (comercial) van

camionista [kamjo'niʃta] (PT) m/f lorry driver (BRIT), truck driver (US)

camisa [ka'miza] f shirt; ~ **de dormir** nightshirt; ~ **esporte/pólo/social** sports/polo/dress shirt; **mudar de** ~ (ESPORTE) to change sides; **camisa-de-força** (pl camisas-de-força) f straitjacket

camiseta [kami'zeta] (BR) f T-shirt; (interior) vest

camisinha [kami'ziɲa] (col) f condom

camisola [kami'zɔla] f (BR) nightdress; (PT: pulôver) sweater; ~ **interior** (PT) vest

campainha [kampa'iɲa] f bell

campanário [kãpa'narju] m church tower, steeple

campanha [kã'paɲa] f (MIL etc) campaign; (planície) plain

campeão, -peã [kã'pjãw, 'pjã] (pl -ões, ~s) m/f champion; **campeo-**

nato [kã'pjo'natu] *m* championship

campestre [kã'pɛʃtri] *adj* rural, rustic

camping ['kãpĩŋ] (*BR*) (*pl* ~s) *m* camping; (*lugar*) campsite

campismo [kã'piʒmu] *m* camping; **parque de ~** campsite

campista [kã'piʃta] *m/f* camper

campo [kãpu] *m* field; (*fora da cidade*) countryside; (*ESPORTE*) ground; (*acampamento*) camp; (*TÊNIS*) court

camponês, -esa [kãpo'neʃ, eza] *m/f* countryman/woman; (*agricultor*) farmer

campus ['kãpuʃ] *m inv* campus

camuflagem [kamu'flaʒẽ] *f* camouflage

camundongo [kamũ'dõgu] (*BR*) *m* mouse

camurça [ka'muxsa] *f* suede

cana ['kana] *f* cane; (*col*: *cadeia*) nick; (*de açúcar*) sugar cane

Canadá [kana'da] *m*: **o ~** Canada; **canadense** [kana'dẽsi] *adj*, *m/f* Canadian

canal [ka'naw] (*pl* -**ais**) *m* channel; (*de navegação*) canal; (*ANAT*) duct

canalha [ka'naʎa] *f* rabble, mob ♦ *m/f* wretch, scoundrel

canalização [kanaliza'sãw] *f* plumbing

canalizador, a [kanaliza'do*, a] (*PT*) *m/f* plumber

canário [ka'narju] *m* canary

canastra [ka'naʃtra] *f* (big) basket

canção [kã'sãw] (*pl* -**ões**) *f* song; **~ de ninar** lullaby

cancela [kã'sela] *f* gate

cancelamento [kãsela'mẽtu] *m* cancellation

cancelar [kãse'la*] *vt* to cancel; (*riscar*) to cross out

câncer ['kãse*] *m* cancer; **C~**

(*ASTROLOGIA*) Cancer

canções [kã'sõjʃ] *fpl de* **canção**

cancro ['kãkru] (*PT*) *m* cancer

candelabro [kãde'labru] *m* candlestick; (*lustre*) chandelier

candidato, -a [kãdʒi'datu, a] *m/f* candidate; (*a cargo*) applicant

cândido, -a ['kãdʒidu, a] *adj* naive; (*inocente*) innocent

candomblé [kãdõ'ble] *m see boxed note*

CANDOMBLÉ

Candomblé is Brazil's most influential Afro-Brazilian religion. Practised mainly in Bahia, it mixes catholicism and Yoruba tradition. According to **candomblé**, believers become possessed by spirits and thus become an instrument of communication between divine and mortal forces. **Candomblé** ceremonies are great spectacles of African rhythm and dance, and are held in *terreiros*.

---

caneca [ka'nɛka] *f* mug

canela [ka'nɛla] *f* cinnamon; (*ANAT*) shin

caneta [ka'neta] *f* pen; **~ esferográfica/pilot** ballpoint/felt-tip pen; **~ seletora** (*COMPUT*) light pen

cangaceiro [kãga'sejru] (*BR*) *m* bandit

canguru [kãgu'ru] *m* kangaroo

canhão [ka'ɲãw] (*pl* -**ões**) *m* cannon; (*GEO*) canyon

canhoto, -a [ka'ɲotu, a] *adj* left-handed ♦ *m/f* left-handed person ♦ *m* (*de cheque*) stub

canibal [kani'baw] (*pl* -**ais**) *m/f* cannibal

canil [ka'niw] (*pl* -**is**) *m* kennel

canivete [kani'vetʃi] *m* penknife

canja ['kãʒa] *f* chicken broth; (*col*)

canjica [kãˈʒika] f maize porridge
cano [ˈkanu] m pipe; *(tubo)* tube; *(de arma de fogo)* barrel; *(de bota)* top; **~ de esgoto** sewer
canoa [kaˈnoa] f canoe
cansaço [kãˈsasu] m tiredness
cansado, -a [kãˈsadu, a] adj tired
cansar [kãˈsa*] vt to tire; *(entediar)* to bore ♦ vi to get tired; **cansar-se** vr to get tired; **cansativo, -a** [kãsaˈtʃivu, a] adj tiring; *(tedioso)* tedious
cantar [kãˈta*] vt, vi to sing ♦ m song
cantarolar [kãtaroˈla*] vt to hum
canteiro [kãˈtejru] m stonemason; *(de flores)* flower bed
cantiga [kãˈtʃiga] f ballad; **~ de ninar** lullaby
cantil [kãˈtʃiw] *(pl* **-is)** m canteen
cantina [kãˈtʃina] f canteen
cantis [kãˈtʃiʃ] mpl de **cantil**
canto [ˈkãtu] m corner; *(lugar)* place; *(canção)* song
cantor, a [kãˈto*, a] m/f singer
cão [kãw] *(pl* **cães)** m dog
caolho, -a [kaˈoʎu, a] adj cross-eyed
caos [ˈkaoʃ] m chaos
capa [ˈkapa] f cape; *(cobertura)* cover; **livro de ~ dura/mole** hardback/paperback (book)
capacete [kapaˈsetʃi] m helmet
capacidade [kapasiˈdadʒi] f capacity; *(aptidão)* ability, competence
capaz [kaˈpaʒ] adj able, capable; **ser ~ de** to be able to *(ou* capable of); **sou ~ de …** *(talvez)* I might …; **é ~ de chover hoje** it might rain today
capela [kaˈpɛla] f chapel
capim [kaˈpĩ] m grass
capitães [kapiˈtãjʃ] mpl de **capitão**
capital [kapiˈtaw] *(pl* **-ais)** adj, m

capital ♦ f *(cidade)* capital; **~ (em) ações** *(COM)* share capital
capitalismo [kapitaˈliʒmu] m capitalism; **capitalista** [kapitaˈliʃta] m/f capitalist
capitalizar [kapitaliˈza*] vt to capitalize on; *(COM)* to capitalize
capitão [kapiˈtãw] *(pl* **-ães)** m captain
capítulo [kaˈpitulu] m chapter
capô [kaˈpo] m *(AUTO)* bonnet *(BRIT)*, hood *(US)*
capoeira [kaˈpwejra] f *(PT)* hencoop; *(dança)* see boxed note

---
CAPOEIRA

Capoeira is a fusion of martial arts and dance which originated among African slaves in colonial Brazil. It is danced in a circle to the sound of the *berimbau*, a percussion instrument of African origin. Opposed by the Brazilian authorities until the beginning of the twentieth century, today **capoeira** is regarded as a national sport.

---

capota [kaˈpɔta] f *(AUTO)* hood, top
capotar [kapoˈta*] vi to overturn
capricho [kaˈpriʃu] m whim, caprice; *(teimosia)* obstinacy; *(apuro)* care; **caprichoso, -a** [kapriˈʃozu, ɔza] adj capricious; *(com apuro)* meticulous
Capricórnio [kapriˈkɔxnju] m Capricorn
cápsula [ˈkapsula] f capsule
captar [kapˈta*] vt *(atrair)* to win; *(RÁDIO)* to pick up
captura [kapˈtura] f capture; **capturar** [kaptuˈra*] vt to capture
capuz [kaˈpuʒ] m hood
cáqui [ˈkaki] adj khaki
cara [ˈkara] f face; *(aspecto)* appearance ♦ m *(col)* guy; **~ ou coroa?**

heads or tails?; **de ~** straightaway; **dar de ~ com** to bump into; **ser a ~ de** (*col*) to be the spitting image of; **ter ~ de** to look (like)
caracol [kara'kɔw] (*pl* **-óis**) *m* snail; (*de cabelo*) curl; **escada em ~** spiral staircase
caracteres [karak'teriʃ] *mpl de* **caráter**
característica [karakte'riʃtʃika] *f* characteristic, feature
característico, -a [karakte-'riʃtʃiku, a] *adj* characteristic
cara-de-pau (*pl* **caras-de-pau**) *adj* brazen; **ele é ~** he's very forward
caramelo [kara'mɛlu] *m* caramel; (*bala*) toffee
caranguejo [karã'geʒu] *m* crab
caras-pintadas *fpl see boxed note*

CARAS-PINTADAS

In 1992, during popular demonstrations calling for the impeachment of the then president Fernando Collor de Mello, students known as **caras-pintadas**, because they had the Brazilian flag painted on their faces, went through the streets shouting "Collor, out!" and similar slogans.

---

caratê [kara'te] *m* karate
caráter [ka'rate*] (*pl* **caracteres**) *m* character
caravana [kara'vana] *f* caravan
carbonizar [kaxboni'za*] *vt* to carbonize; (*queimar*) to char
carbono [kax'bɔnu] *m* carbon
carburador [kaxbura'do*] *m* carburettor (*BRIT*), carburetor (*US*)
cárcere ['kaxseri] *m* prison; **carcereiro, -a** [kaxse'rejru, a] *m/f* jailer, warder
cardápio [kax'dapju] (*BR*) *m* menu
cardeal [kax'dʒjaw] (*pl* **-ais**) *adj, m*

cardinal
cardíaco, -a [kax'dʒiaku, a] *adj* cardiac; **ataque/parada ~** heart attack/cardiac arrest
cardigã [kaxdʒi'gã] *m* cardigan
careca [ka'rɛka] *adj* bald
carecer [kare'se*] *vi*: **~ de** to lack; (*precisar*) to need
carência [ka'rẽsja] *f* lack; (*necessidade*) need; (*privação*) deprivation; **carente** [ka'rẽtʃi] *adj* wanting; (*pessoa*) needy, deprived
careta [ka'reta] *adj* (*col*) straight, square ♦ *f* grimace; **fazer uma ~** to pull a face
carga ['kaxga] *f* load; (*de navio, avião*) cargo; (*ato de carregar*) loading; (*ELET*) charge; (*fig: peso*) burden; (*MIL*) attack, charge; **dar ~ em** (*COMPUT*) to boot (up)
cargo ['kaxgu] *m* responsibility; (*função*) post; **a ~ de** in charge of; **ter a ~** to be in charge of; **tomar a ~** to take charge of
Caribe [ka'ribi] *m*: **o ~** the Caribbean (Sea)
carícia [ka'risja] *f* caress
caridade [kari'dadʒi] *f* charity; **obra de ~** charity
cárie [ˈkari] *f* tooth decay
carimbar [karĩ'ba*] *vt* to stamp; (*no correio*) to postmark
carimbo [ka'rĩbu] *m* stamp; (*postal*) postmark
carinho [ka'riɲu] *m* affection, fondness; (*carícia*) caress; **fazer ~** to caress; **com ~** affectionately; (*com cuidado*) with care; **carinhoso, -a** [kari'ɲozu, ɔza] *adj* affectionate
carioca [ka'rjɔka] *adj* of Rio de Janeiro ♦ *m/f* native of Rio de Janeiro ♦ *m* (*PT: café*) type of weak coffee
carnal [kax'naw] (*pl* **-ais**) *adj* carnal; **primo ~** first cousin
carnaval [kaxna'vaw] (*pl* **-ais**) *m*

carnival; (*fig*) mess; *see boxed note*

CARNAVAL

In Brazil, **Carnaval** is the popular festival held each year in the four days before Lent. It is celebrated in very different ways in different parts of the country. In Rio de Janeiro, for example, the big attraction is the parades of the *escolas de samba*, in Salvador the *trios elétricos*, in Recife the *frevo* and, in Olinda, the giant figures, such as the *Homem da meia-noite* and *Mulher do meio-dia*. In Portugal, **Carnaval** is celebrated on Shrove Tuesday, with street parties and processions taking place throughout the country.

---

carne ['kaxni] *f* flesh; (*CULIN*) meat; **em ~ e osso** in the flesh
carnê [kax'ne] *m* (*para compras*) payment book
carneiro [kax'nejru] *m* sheep; (*macho*) ram; **perna/costeleta de ~** leg of lamb/lamb chop
carnificina [kaxnifi'sina] *f* slaughter
caro, -a ['karu, a] *adj* dear; **cobrar/ pagar ~** to charge a lot/pay dearly
carochinha [karo'ʃina] *f*: **conto** ou **história da ~** fairy tale ou story
caroço [ka'rosu] *m* (*de frutos*) stone; (*endurecimento*) lump
carona [ka'rɔna] *f* lift; **viajar de ~** to hitchhike; **pegar uma ~** to get a lift
carpete [kax'petʃi] *m* (fitted) carpet
carpinteiro [kaxpĩ'tejru] *m* carpenter
carrapato [kaxa'patu] *m* (*inseto*) tick
carrasco [ka'xaʃku] *m* executioner; (*fig*) tyrant
carregado, -a [kaxe'gadu, a] *adj*

loaded; (*semblante*) sullen; (*céu*) dark; (*ambiente*) tense
carregador [kaxega'do*] *m* porter
carregamento [kaxega'mẽtu] *m* (*ação*) loading; (*carga*) load, cargo
carregar [kaxe'ga*] *vt* to load; (*levar*) to carry; (*bateria*) to charge; (*PT: apertar*) to press; (*levar para longe*) to take away ♦ *vi*: **~ em** to overdo; (*pôr enfase*) to bring out
carreira [ka'xejra] *f* run, running; (*profissão*) career; (*TURFE*) race; (*NÁUT*) slipway; (*fileira*) row; **às ~s** in a hurry
carretel [kaxe'tɛw] (*pl* **-éis**) *m* spool, reel
carrinho [ka'xiɲu] *m* trolley; (*brinquedo*) toy car; **~ (de criança)** pram; **~ de mão** wheelbarrow
carro ['kaxo] *m* car; (*de bois*) cart; (*de mão*) barrow; (*de máquina de escrever*) carriage; **~ de corrida/passeio/esporte** racing/saloon/sports car; **~ de praça** cab; **~ de bombeiro** fire engine
carroça [ka'xɔsa] *f* cart, waggon
carroceria [kaxose'ria] *f* (*AUTO*) bodywork
carro-chefe (*pl* **carros-chefes**) *m* (*de desfile*) main float; (*fig*) flagship, centrepiece (*BRIT*), centerpiece (*US*)
carrossel [kaxo'sɛw] (*pl* **-éis**) *m* merry-go-round
carruagem [ka'xwaʒẽ] (*pl* **-ns**) *f* carriage, coach
carta ['kaxta] *f* letter; (*de jogar*) card; (*mapa*) chart; **~ aérea/registrada** airmail/registered letter; **~ de condução** (*PT*) driving licence (*BRIT*), driver's license (*US*); **dar as ~s** to deal; **carta-bomba** (*pl* **cartas-bomba**) *f* letter bomb
cartão [kax'tãw] (*pl* **-ões**) *m* card; (*PT: material*) cardboard; **~ de crédito** credit card; **cartão-postal**

(pl **cartões-postais**) m postcard

cartaz [kax'taʒ] m poster, bill (US); **(estar) em ~** (TEATRO, CINEMA) (to be) showing

carteira [kax'tejra] f desk; (para dinheiro) wallet; (de ações) portfolio; **~ de identidade** identity card; **~ de motorista** driving licence (BRIT), driver's license (US)

carteiro [kax'tejru] m postman (BRIT), mailman (US)

cartões [kax'tõjʃ] mpl de **cartão**

cartola [kax'tɔla] f top hat

cartolina [kaxto'lina] f card

cartório [kax'tɔrju] m registry office

cartucho [kax'tuʃu] m cartridge; (saco de papel) packet

cartum [kax'tũ] (pl -ns) m cartoon

carvalho [kax'vaʎu] m oak

carvão [kax'vãw] (pl -ões) m coal; (de madeira) charcoal

casa ['kaza] f house; (lar) home; (COM) firm; (MAT: decimal) place; **em/para ~** (at) home/home; **~ de saúde** hospital; **~ da moeda** mint; **~ de banho** (PT) bathroom; **~ e comida** board and lodging; **~ de cômodos** tenement; **~ popular** ≈ council house

casação [kaza'kãw] (pl -ões) m overcoat

casaco [ka'zaku] m coat; (paletó) jacket

casacões [kaza'kõjʃ] mpl de **casação**

casal [ka'zaw] (pl -ais) m couple

casamento [kaza'mẽtu] m marriage; (boda) wedding

casar [ka'za*] vt to marry; (combinar) to match (up); **casar-se** vr to get married; to combine well

casarão [kaza'rãw] (pl -ões) m mansion

casca ['kaʃka] f (de árvore) bark; (de banana) skin; (de ferida) scab; (de

laranja) peel; (de nozes, ovos) shell; (de milho etc) husk; (de pão) crust

cascata [kaʃ'kata] f waterfall

casco ['kaʃku] m skull; (de animal) hoof; (de navio) hull; (para bebidas) empty bottle; (de tartaruga) shell

casebre [ka'zɛbri] m hovel, shack

caseiro, -a [ka'zejru, a] adj homemade; (pessoa, vida) domestic ♦ m/f housekeeper

caso ['kazu] m case; (tb: ~ amoroso) affair; (estória) story ♦ conj in case, if; **no ~ de** in case (of); **em todo ~** in any case; **neste ~** in that case; **~ necessário** if necessary; **criar ~** to cause trouble; **não fazer ~ de** to ignore; **~ de emergência** emergency

caspa ['kaʃpa] f dandruff

casquinha [kaʃ'kiɲa] f (de sorvete) cone; (pele) skin

cassar [ka'sa*] vt (direitos, licença) to cancel, withhold; (políticos) to ban

cassete [ka'setʃi] m cassette

cassetete [kase'tetʃi] m truncheon (BRIT), nightstick (US)

cassino [ka'sinu] m casino

castanha [kaʃ'taɲa] f chestnut; **~ de caju** cashew nut; **castanha-do-pará** [-'pa'ra] (pl **castanhas-do-pará**) f Brazil nut

castanheiro [kaʃta'ɲejru] m chestnut tree

castanho, -a [kaʃ'taɲu, a] adj brown

castelo [kaʃ'telu] m castle

castiçal [kaʃtʃi'saw] (pl -ais) m candlestick

castiço, -a [kaʃ'tʃisu, a] adj pure

castidade [kaʃtʃi'dadʒi] f chastity

castigar [kaʃtʃi'ga*] vt to punish; **castigo** [kaʃ'tʃigu] m punishment; (fig: mortificação) pain

casto, -a ['kaʃtu, a] adj chaste

casual [ka'zwaw] (*pl* **-ais**) *adj* chance *atr*, accidental; (*fortuito*) fortuitous; **casualidade** [kazwali-'dadʒi] *f* chance; (*acidente*) accident

cata ['kata] *f*: à ~ **de** in search of

catalizador [kataliza'do*] *m* catalyst

catalogar [katalo'ga*] *vt* to catalogue (*BRIT*), catalog (*US*)

catálogo [ka'talogu] *m* catalogue (*BRIT*), catalog (*US*); ~ (**telefônico**) telephone directory

catapora [kata'pɔra] (*BR*) *f* chickenpox

catar [ka'ta*] *vt* to pick (up); (*procurar*) to look for, search for; (*recolher*) to collect, gather

catarata [kata'rata] *f* waterfall; (*MED*) cataract

catarro [ka'taxu] *m* catarrh

catástrofe [ka'taʃtrɔfi] *f* catastrophe

cata-vento *m* weathercock

catedral [kate'draw] (*pl* **-ais**) *f* cathedral

categoria [katego'ria] *f* category; (*social*) rank; (*qualidade*) quality; **de alta ~** first-rate

cativar [katʃi'va*] *vt* to enslave; (*fascinar*) to captivate; (*atrair*) to charm

cativeiro [katʃi'vejru] *m* captivity; (*escravidão*) slavery; (*cadeia*) prison

cativo, -a [ka'tʃivu, a] *m/f* slave; (*prisioneiro*) prisoner

católico, -a [ka'tɔliku, a] *adj, m/f* catholic

catorze [ka'tɔxzi] *num* fourteen

caução [kaw'sãw] (*pl* **-ões**) *f* security, guarantee; (*JUR*) bail; **sob ~** on bail

caule ['kauli] *m* stalk, stem

causa ['kawza] *f* cause; (*motivo*) motive, reason; (*JUR*) lawsuit, case; **por ~ de** because of; **causador, a** [kawza'do*, a] *adj* which caused ♦ *m*

cause; causar [kaw'za*] *vt* to cause, bring about

cautela [kaw'tela] *f* caution; (*senha*) ticket; ~ (**de penhor**) pawn ticket; **cauteloso, -a** [kawte'lozu, ɔza] *adj* cautious, wary

cavado, -a [ka'vadu, a] *adj* (*olhos*) sunken; (*roupa*) low-cut

cavala [ka'vala] *f* mackerel

cavalaria [kavala'ria] *f* cavalry

cavaleiro [kava'lejru] *m* rider, horseman; (*medieval*) knight

cavalete [kava'letʃi] *m* stand; (*FOTO*) tripod; (*de pintor*) easel; (*de mesa*) trestle

cavalgar [kavaw'ga*] *vt* to ride ♦ *vi*: ~ **em** to ride on; ~ (**sobre**) to jump over

cavalheiro, -a [kava'ʎejru, a] *adj* courteous, gallant ♦ *m* gentleman

cavalo [ka'valu] *m* horse; (*XADREZ*) knight; **a** ~ on horseback; **50 ~s (-vapor)** ou (**de força**) 50 horsepower; ~ **de corrida** racehorse

cavaquinho [kava'kiɲu] *m* small guitar

cavar [ka'va*] *vt* to dig; (*esforçar-se para obter*) to try to get ♦ *vi* to dig; (*fig*) to delve; (*animal*) to burrow

cave ['kavi] (*PT*) *f* wine-cellar

caveira [ka'vejra] *f* skull

cavidade [kavi'dadʒi] *f* cavity

caxumba [ka'ʃuba] *f* mumps *sg*

CD *abr m* CD

cê [se] (*col*) *pron* = **você**

cear [sja*] *vt* to have for supper ♦ *vi* to dine

cebola [se'bola] *f* onion; **cebolinha** [sebo'liɲa] *f* spring onion

ceder [se'de*] *vt* to give up; (*dar*) to hand over; (*emprestar*) to lend ♦ *vi* to give in, yield

cedilha [se'dʒiʎa] *f* cedilla

cedo ['sedu] *adv* early; (*em breve*) soon

cedro ['sedru] *m* cedar

cédula ['sedula] *f* banknote; (*eleitoral*) ballot paper

CEE *abr f* (= *Comunidade Econômica Européia*) EEC

cegar [se'ga*] *vt* to blind; (*ofuscar*) to dazzle ♦ *vi* to be dazzling

cego, -a ['sεgu, a] *adj* blind; (*total*) complete, total; (*tesoura*) blunt ♦ *m/f* blind man/woman; **às cegas** blindly

cegonha [se'gɔɲa] *f* stork

cegueira [se'gejra] *f* blindness

CEI *abr f* (= *Comunidade de Estados Independentes*) CIS

ceia ['seja] *f* supper

cela ['sεla] *f* cell

celebração [selebra'sãw] (*pl* -ões) *f* celebration

celebrar [sele'bra*] *vt* to celebrate; (*exaltar*) to praise; (*acordo*) to seal

célebre ['sεlebri] *adj* famous, well-known

celeiro [se'lejru] *m* granary; (*depósito*) barn

celeste [se'lεʃtʃi] *adj* celestial, heavenly

celibatário, -a [seliba'tarju, a] *adj* unmarried, single ♦ *m/f* bachelor/spinster

celofane [selo'fani] *m* cellophane; **papel ~** cling film

célula ['sεlula] *f* (*BIO, ELET*) cell; **celular** [selu'la*] *adj* cellular ♦ *n*: (*telefone*) **celular** mobile (phone)

cem [sẽ] *num* hundred

cemitério [semi'tεrju] *m* cemetery; graveyard

cena ['sεna] *f* scene; (*palco*) stage

cenário [se'narju] *m* scenery; (*CINEMA*) scenario; (*de um acontecimento*) setting

cenoura [se'nora] *f* carrot

censo ['sẽsu] *m* census

censor, a [sẽ'so*, a] *m/f* censor

censura [sẽ'sura] *f* censorship; (*reprovação*) censure, criticism; **censurar** [sẽsu'ra*] *vt* to censure; (*filme, livro etc*) to censor

centavo [sẽ'tavu] *m* cent; **estar sem um ~** to be penniless

centeio [sẽ'teju] *m* rye

centelha [sẽ'teʎa] *f* spark

centena [sẽ'tena] *f* hundred; **às ~s** in hundreds

centenário, -a [sẽte'narju, a] *m* centenary

centígrado [sẽ'tʃigradu] *m* centigrade

centímetro [sẽ'tʃimetru] *m* centimetre (*BRIT*), centimeter (*US*)

cento ['sẽtu] *m*: **~ e um** one hundred and one; **por ~** per cent

centopeia [sẽto'peja] *f* centipede

central [sẽ'traw] (*pl* -**ais**) *adj* central ♦ *f* (*de polícia etc*) head office; **~ elétrica** (electric) power station; **~ telefônica** telephone exchange; **centralizar** [sẽtrali'za*] *vt* to centralize

centrar [sẽ'tra*] *vt* to centre (*BRIT*), center (*US*)

centro ['sẽtru] *m* centre (*BRIT*), center (*US*); (*de uma cidade*) town centre; **centroavante** [sẽtroa'vãtʃi] (*FUTEBOL*) centre forward

CEP ['sεpi] (*BR*) *abr m* (= *Código de Endereçamento Postal*) postcode (*BRIT*), zip code (*US*)

céptico, -a *etc* ['septiku, a] (*PT*) = **cético** *etc*

cera ['sera] *f* wax

cerâmica [se'ramika] *f* pottery

cerca ['sexka] *f* fence ♦ *prep*: **~ de** (*aproximadamente*) around, about; **~ viva** hedge

cercado [sex'kadu] *m* enclosure; (*para animais*) pen; (*para crianças*) playpen

cercanias [sexka'niaʃ] *fpl* outskirts;

(*vizinhança*) neighbourhood *sg* (BRIT), neighborhood *sg* (US)

cercar [sex'ka*] *vt* to enclose; (*rodear*) to surround; (*assediar*) to besiege

cerco ['sexku] *m* siege; **pôr a ~** to besiege

cereal [se'rjaw] *m* (*pl* **-ais**) *m* cereal

cérebro ['serebru] *m* brain; (*fig*) brains *pl*

cereja [se'reʒa] *f* cherry

cerimônia [seri'monja] *f* ceremony

cerração [sexa'sãw] *f* fog

cerrado, -a [se'xadu, a] *adj* shut, closed; (*denso*) thick ♦ *m* scrub (land)

certeza [sex'teza] *f* certainty; **com ~** certainly, surely; (*provavelmente*) probably; **ter ~ de/de que** to be certain *ou* sure of/to be sure that

certidão [sextʃi'dãw] (*pl* **-ões**) *f* certificate

certificado [sextʃifi'kadu] *m* certificate

certificar [sextʃifi'ka*] *vt* to certify; (*assegurar*) to assure; **certificar-se** *vr*: **~-se de** to make sure of

certo, -a ['sextu, a] *adj* certain, sure; (*exato, direito*) right; (*um, algum*) a certain ♦ *adv* correctly; **na certa** certainly; **ao ~** for certain; **está ~** okay, all right

cerveja [sex'veʒa] *f* beer; **cervejaria** [sexveʒa'ria] *f* (*fábrica*) brewery; (*bar*) bar, pub

cervical [sexvi'kaw] (*pl* **-ais**) *adj* cervical

cessação [sesa'sãw] *f* halting, ceasing

cessão [se'sãw] (*pl* **-ões**) *f* surrender

cessar [se'sa*] *vi* to cease, stop; **sem ~** continually; **cessar-fogo** *m inv* cease-fire

cessões [se'sõjʃ] *fpl de* **cessão**

cesta ['seʃta] *f* basket

cesto ['seʃtu] *m* basket; (*com tampa*) hamper

cético, -a ['setʃiku, a] *m/f* sceptic (BRIT), skeptic (US)

cetim [se'tʃĩ] *m* satin

céu [sɛw] *m* sky; (REL) heaven; (*da boca*) roof

cevada [se'vada] *f* barley

CFC *abr m* (= clorofluorocarbono) CFC

chá [ʃa] *m* tea

chácara ['ʃakara] *f* farm; (*casa de campo*) country house

chacina [ʃa'sina] *f* slaughter; **chacinar** [ʃasi'na*] *vt* (*matar*) to slaughter

chacota [ʃa'kɔta] *f* mockery

chafariz [ʃafa'riʒ] *m* fountain

chalé [ʃa'lɛ] *m* chalet

chaleira [ʃa'lejra] *f* kettle; (*bajulador*) crawler, toady

chama ['ʃama] *f* flame

chamada [ʃa'mada] *f* call; (MIL) call; (EDUC) register; (*no jornal*) headline; **dar uma ~ em alguém** to tell sb off

chamar [ʃa'ma*] *vt* to call; (*convidar*) to invite; (*atenção*) to attract ♦ *vi* to call; (*telefone*) to ring; **chamar-se** *vr* to be called; **chamo-me João** my name is John; **~ alguém de idiota/Dudu** to call sb an idiot/Dudu; **mandar ~** to summon, send for

chamariz [ʃama'riʒ] *m* decoy

chamativo, -a [ʃama'tʃivu, a] *adj* showy, flashy

chaminé [ʃami'nɛ] *f* chimney; (*de navio*) funnel

champanha [ʃã'paɲa] *m ou f* champagne

champanhe [ʃã'paɲi] *m ou f* = champanha

champu [ʃã'pu] (PT) *m* shampoo

chance ['ʃãsi] *f* chance

chantagear [ʃãta'ʒja*] vt to black-mail

chantagem [ʃã'taʒẽ] f blackmail

chão [ʃãw] (pl **~s**) m ground; (terra) soil; (piso) floor

chapa [ʃapa] f (placa) plate; (eleitoral) list; **~ de matrícula** (PT: AUTO) number (BRIT) ou license (US) plate; **oi, meu ~!** hi, mate!

chapéu [ʃa'pew] m hat

charco [ʃaxku] m marsh, bog

charme [ʃaxmi] m charm; **fazer ~** to be nice, use one's charm; **charmoso, -a** [ʃax'mozu, ɔza] adj charming

charrete [ʃa'xetʃi] f cart

charuto [ʃa'rutu] m cigar

chassi [ʃa'si] m (AUTO, ELET) chassis

chata [ʃata] f barge; V tb **chato**

chateação [ʃatʃja'sãw] (pl **-ões**) f bother, upset; (maçada) bore

chatear [ʃa'tʃja*] vt to bother, upset; (importunar) to pester; (entediar) to bore; (irritar) to annoy ♦ vi to be upsetting; to be boring; to be annoying; **chatear-se** vr to get upset; to get bored; to get annoyed

chatice [ʃa'tʃisi] f nuisance

chato, -a [ʃatu, a] adj flat; (tedioso) boring; (irritante) annoying; (que fica mal) rude ♦ m/f bore; (quem irrita) pain

chauvinista [ʃawvi'niʃta] adj chauvinistic ♦ m/f chauvinist

chavão [ʃa'vãw] (pl **-ões**) m cliché

chave [ʃavi] f key; (ELET) switch; **~ de porcas** spanner; **~ inglesa** (monkey) wrench; **~ de fenda** screwdriver

chávena [ʃavena] (PT) f cup

checar [ʃe'ka*] vt to check

check-up [tʃe'kapi] (pl **~s**) m check-up

chefe [ʃefi] m/f head, chief; (patrão) boss; **~ de estação** station-

master; **chefia** [ʃe'fia] f leadership; (direção) management; (repartição) headquarters sg; **chefiar** [ʃe'fja*] vt to lead

chegada [ʃe'gada] f arrival

chegado, -a [ʃe'gadu, a] adj near; (íntimo) close

chegar [ʃe'ga*] vt to bring near ♦ vi to arrive; (ser suficiente) to be enough; **chegar-se** vr: **~-se a** to approach; **chega!** that's enough!; **~ a** (atingir) to reach; (conseguir) to manage to

cheio, -a [ʃeju, a] adj full; (repleto) full up; (col: farto) fed up

cheirar [ʃej'ra*] vt, vi to smell; **~ a** to smell of; **cheiro** [ʃejru] m smell; **ter cheiro de** to smell of; **cheiroso, -a** [ʃej'rozu, ɔza] adj: **ser ou estar cheiroso** to smell nice

cheque [ʃeki] m cheque (BRIT), check (US); **~ de viagem** traveller's cheque (BRIT), traveler's check (US)

chiar [ʃja*] vi to squeak; (porta) to creak; (vapor) to hiss; (col: reclamar) to grumble

chiclete [ʃi'kletʃi] m chewing gum

chicória [ʃi'kɔrja] f chicory

chicote [ʃi'kɔtʃi] m whip

chifre [ʃifri] m horn

Chile [ʃili] m: **o ~** Chile

chimarrão [ʃima'xãw] (pl **-ões**) m mate tea without sugar taken from a pipe-like cup

chimpanzé [ʃĩpã'ze] m chimpanzee

China [ʃina] f: **a ~** China

chinelo [ʃi'nɛlu] m slipper

chinês, -esa [ʃi'nef, eza] adj, m/f Chinese ♦ m (LING) Chinese

chip [ʃipi] m (COMPUT) chip

Chipre [ʃipri] f Cyprus

chique [ʃiki] adj stylish, chic

chocalho [ʃo'kaʎu] m (MÚS, brinquedo) rattle; (para animais) bell

chocante [ʃo'kãtʃi] *adj* shocking; (*col*) amazing

chocar [ʃo'ka*] *vt* to hatch, incubate; (*ofender*) to shock, offend ♦ *vi* to shock; **chocar-se** *vr* to crash, collide; to be shocked

chocho, -a ['ʃoʃu, a] *adj* hollow, empty; (*fraco*) weak; (*sem graça*) dull

chocolate [ʃoko'latʃi] *m* chocolate

chofer [ʃo'fe*] *m* driver

chope ['ʃopi] *m* draught beer

choque[1] ['ʃɔki] *m* shock; (*colisão*) collision; (*impacto*) impact; (*conflito*) clash

choque[2] *etc vb V* **chocar**

choramingar [ʃoramĩ'ga*] *vi* to whine, whimper

chorão, -rona [ʃo'rãw, rɔna] (*pl* -ões, ~s) *adj* tearful ♦ *m/f* crybaby ♦ *m* (*BOT*) weeping willow

chorar [ʃo'ra*] *vt, vi* to weep, cry

chorinho [ʃo'riɲu] *m* type of Brazilian music

choro ['ʃoru] *m* crying; (*MÚS*) type of Brazilian music

choupana [ʃo'pana] *f* shack, hut

chouriço [ʃo'risu] *m* (*BR*) black pudding; (*PT*) spicy sausage

chover [ʃo've*] *vi* to rain; ~ a cântaros to rain cats and dogs

chulé [ʃu'lɛ] *m* foot odour (*BRIT*) ou odor (*US*)

chulo, -a ['ʃulu, a] *adj* vulgar

chumaço [ʃu'masu] *m* (*de papel, notas*) wad

chumbo ['ʃũbu] *m* lead; (*de caça*) gunshot; (*de dente*) filling; **sem ~** (*gasolina*) unleaded

chupar [ʃu'pa*] *vt* to suck

chupeta [ʃu'peta] *f* dummy (*BRIT*), pacifier (*US*)

churrasco [ʃu'xaʃku] *m*, **churrasqueira** [ʃuxaʃ'kejra] ♦ *m* barbecue

churrasquinho [ʃuxaʃ'kiɲu] *m* kebab

chutar [ʃu'ta*] *vt* to kick; (*col: adivinhar*) to guess at; (: *dar o fora em*) to dump ♦ *vi* to kick, to guess; (: *mentir*) to lie

chute ['ʃutʃi] *m* kick; (*col: mentira*) fib; **dar o ~ em alguém** (*col*) to give sb the boot

chuteira [ʃu'tejra] *f* football boot

chuva ['ʃuva] *f* rain; **chuveiro** [ʃu'vejru] *m* shower

chuviscar [ʃuviʃ'ka*] *vi* to drizzle; **chuvisco** [ʃu'viʃku] *m* drizzle

chuvoso, -a [ʃu'vozu, ɔza] *adj* rainy

Cia. *abr* (= *companhia*) Co.

cibercafé [sibexka'fɛ] *m* cybercafé

ciberespaço [sibexiʃ'pasu] *m* cyberspace

cicatriz [sika'triʒ] *f* scar; **cicatrizar** [sikatri'za*] *vi* to heal; (*rosto*) to scar

cicerone [sise'rɔni] *m* tourist guide

ciclismo [si'kliʒmu] *m* cycling

ciclista [si'kliʃta] *m/f* cyclist

ciclo ['siklu] *m* cycle

ciclovia [siklɔ'via] *f* cycle lane ou path

cidadã [sida'dã] *f de* **cidadão**

cidadania [sidada'nia] *f* citizenship

cidadão, -cidadã [sida'dãw, sida'dã] (*pl* ~s, ~s) *m/f* citizen

cidade [si'dadʒi] *f* town; (*grande*) city

ciência ['sjẽsja] *f* science

ciente ['sjẽtʃi] *adj* aware

científico, -a [sjẽ'tʃifiku, a] *adj* scientific

cientista [sjẽ'tʃiʃta] *m/f* scientist

cifra ['sifra] *f* cipher; (*algarismo*) number, figure; (*total*) sum

cigano, -a [si'ganu, a] *adj*, *m/f* gypsy

cigarra [si'gaxa] *f* cicada; (*ELET*) buzzer

cigarrilha [siga'xiʎa] f cheroot

cigarro [si'gaxu] m cigarette

cilada [si'lada] f ambush; (armadilha) trap; (embuste) trick

cilindro [si'lĩdru] m cylinder; (rolo) roller

cima ['sima] f: **de ~ para baixo** from top to bottom; **para ~** up; **em ~ de** on, on top of; **de ~ de** over; **de ~** from above; **lá em ~** up there; (em casa) upstairs; **ainda por ~** on top of that

cimento [si'mẽtu] m cement; (fig) foundation

cimo ['simu] m top, summit

cinco ['sĩku] num five

cineasta [sine'aʃta] m/f film maker

cinema [si'nema] f cinema

Cingapura [sĩga'pura] f Singapore

cínico, -a ['siniku, a] adj cynical ♦ m/f cynic; **cinismo** [si'niʒmu] m cynicism

cinqüenta [sĩ'kwẽta] num fifty

cinta ['sĩta] f sash; (de mulher) girdle

cintilar [sĩtʃi'la*] vi to sparkle, glitter

cinto ['sĩtu] m belt; **~ de segurança** safety belt; (AUTO) seatbelt

cintura [sĩ'tura] f waist; (linha) waistline

cinza ['sĩza] adj inv grey (BRIT), gray (US) ♦ f ash, ashes pl

cinzeiro [sĩ'zejru] m ashtray

cinzento, -a [sĩ'zẽtu, a] adj grey (BRIT), gray (US)

cio [siu] m: **no ~** on heat, in season

cipreste [si'prɛʃtʃi] m cypress (tree)

cipriota [si'prjɔta] adj, m/f Cypriot

circo ['sixku] m circus

circuito [six'kwitu] m circuit

circulação [sixkula'sãw] f circulation

circular [sixku'la*] adj circular ♦ f (carta) circular ♦ vi to circulate; (girar, andar) to go round ♦ vt to cir-

culate; (estar em volta de) to surround; (percorrer em roda) to go round

círculo ['sixkulu] m circle

circundar [sixkũ'da*] vt to surround

circunferência [sixkũfe'rẽsja] f circumference

circunflexo [sixkũ'fleksu] m circumflex (accent)

circunstância [sixkũ'ʃtãsja] f circumstance; **~s atenuantes** mitigating circumstances

cirurgia [sirux'ʒia] f surgery; **~ plástica/estética** plastic/cosmetic surgery

cirurgião, -giã [sirux'ʒjãw, 'ʒjã] (pl -ões, ~s) m/f surgeon

cirúrgico, -a [si'ruxʒiku, a] adj surgical

cirurgiões [sirux'ʒjõjʃ] mpl de **cirurgião**

cisco ['siʃku] m speck

cismado, -a [siʒ'madu, a] adj with fixed ideas

cismar [siʒ'ma*] vi (pensar): **~ em** to brood over; (antipatizar): **~ com** to take a dislike to ♦ vt: **~ que** to be convinced that; **~ de** ou **em fazer** (meter na cabeça) to get into one's head to do; (insistir) to insist on doing

cisne ['siʒni] m swan

cisterna [siʃ'texna] f cistern, tank

citação [sita'sãw] (pl -ões) f quotation; (JUR) summons sg

citar [si'ta*] vt to quote; (JUR) to summon

ciúme ['sjumi] m jealousy; **ter ~s de** to be jealous of; **ciumento, -a** [sju'mẽtu, a] adj jealous

cívico, -a ['siviku, a] adj civic

civil [si'viw] (pl -is) adj civil ♦ m/f civilian; **civilidade** [sivili'dadʒi] f politeness

civilização [siviliza'sãw] (*pl* -ões) *f* civilization

civis [si'vif] *pl de* **civil**

clamar [kla'ma*] *vt* to clamour (*BRIT*) *ou* clamor (*US*) for ♦ *vi* to cry out, clamo(u)r

clamor [kla'mo*] *m* outcry, uproar

clandestino, -a [klādeʃ'tʃinu, a] *adj* clandestine; (*ilegal*) underground

clara ['klara] *f* egg white

clarabóia [klara'bɔja] *f* skylight

clarão [kla'rãw] (*pl* -ões) *m* (*cintilação*) flash; (*claridade*) gleam

clarear [kla'rja*] *vi* (*dia*) to dawn; (*tempo*) to clear up, brighten up ♦ *vt* to clarify

claridade [klari'dadʒi] *f* brightness

clarim [kla'rĩ] (*pl* -ns) *m* bugle

clarinete [klari'netʃi] *m* clarinet

clarins [kla'rĩʃ] *mpl de* **clarim**

claro, -a ['klaru, a] *adj* clear; (*luminoso*) bright; (*cor*) light; (*evidente*) clear, evident ♦ *m* (*na escrita*) space; (*clareira*) clearing ♦ *adv* clearly; ~! of course!; ~ que sim!/não! of course!/of course not!; às claras openly

classe ['klasi] *f* class

clássico, -a ['klasiku, a] *adj* classical; (*fig*) classic; (*habitual*) usual ♦ *m* classic

classificação [klasifika'sãw] (*pl* -ões) *f* classification; (*ESPORTE*) place, placing

classificado, -a [klasifi'kadu, a] *adj* (*em exame*) successful; (*anúncio*) classified; (*ESPORTE*) placed ♦ *m* classified ad

classificar [klasifi'ka*] *vt* to classify; **classificar-se** *vr*: ~-se de algo to call o.s. sth, describe o.s. as sth

claustro ['klawftru] *m* cloister

cláusula ['klawzula] *f* clause

clausura [klaw'zura] *f* enclosure

clavícula [kla'vikula] *f* collarbone

clemência [kle'mẽsja] *f* mercy

clero ['klɛru] *m* clergy

clicar [kli'ka*] *vi* (*COMPUT*) to click

clichê [kli'ʃe] *m* (*FOTO*) plate; (*chavão*) cliché

cliente ['kljẽtʃi] *m* client, customer; (*de médico*) patient; **clientela** [kljẽ'tela] *f* clientele; (*de loja*) customers *pl*

clima ['klima] *m* climate

clímax ['klimaks] *m inv* climax

clínica ['klinika] *f* clinic; V tb **clínico**

clínico, -a ['kliniku, a] *adj* clinical ♦ *m/f* doctor; ~ **geral** general practitioner, GP

clipe ['klipi] *m* clip; (*para papéis*) paper clip

clique ['kliki] *m* (*COMPUT*) click; **dar um ~ duplo em** to double-click on

cloro ['klɔru] *m* chlorine

close ['klɔzi] *m* close-up

clube ['klubi] *m* club

coadjuvante [koadʒu'vãtʃi] *adj* supporting ♦ *m/f* (*num crime*) accomplice; (*TEATRO, CINEMA*) co-star

coador [koa'do*] *m* strainer; (*de café*) filter bag; (*para legumes*) colander

coalhada [koa'ʎada] *f* curd

coalizão [koali'zãw] (*pl* -ões) *f* coalition

coar [ko'a*] *vt* (*líquido*) to strain

coberta [ko'bɛxta] *f* cover, covering; (*NÁUT*) deck

cobertor [kobex'to*] *m* blanket

cobertura [kobex'tura] *f* covering; (*telhado*) roof; (*apartamento*) penthouse; (*TV, RÁDIO, JORNALISMO*) coverage; (*SEGUROS*) cover

cobiça [ko'bisa] *f* greed

cobiçar [kobi'sa*] *vt* to covet

cobra ['kɔbra] *f* snake

cobrador, a [kobra'do*, a] *m/f* collector; (*em transporte*) conductor

cobrança [ko'brãsa] f collection; *(ato de cobrar)* charging

cobrar [ko'bra*] vt to collect; *(preço)* to charge

cobre ['kɔbri] m copper; **~s** mpl *(dinheiro)* money sg

cobrir [ko'bri*] vt to cover

cocada [ko'kada] f coconut sweet

cocaína [koka'ina] f cocaine

coçar [ko'sa*] vt to scratch ♦ vi to itch; **coçar-se** vr to scratch o.s.

cócegas ['kɔsegaʃ] fpl: **fazer ~ em** to tickle; **tenho ~ nos pés** my feet tickle; **sentir ~** to be ticklish

coceira [ko'sejra] f itch; *(qualidade)* itchiness

cochichar [koʃi'ʃa*] vi to whisper; **cochicho** [ko'ʃiʃu] m whispering

cochilar [koʃi'la*] vi to snooze, doze; **cochilo** [ko'ʃilu] m nap

coco ['koku] m coconut

cócoras ['kɔkoraʃ] fpl: **de ~** squatting; **ficar de ~** to squat (down)

código ['kɔdʒigu] m code; **~ de barras** bar code

coelho [ko'eʎu] m rabbit

coerente [koe'rẽtʃi] adj coherent; *(conseqüente)* consistent

cofre ['kɔfri] m safe; *(caixa)* strongbox; **os ~s públicos** public funds

cogitar [koʒi'ta*] vt, vi to contemplate

cogumelo [kogu'mɛlu] m mushroom; **~ venenoso** toadstool

coice ['kojsi] m kick; *(de arma)* recoil; **dar ~s em** to kick

coincidência [koĩsi'dẽsja] f coincidence

coincidir [koĩsi'dʒi*] vi to coincide; *(concordar)* to agree

coisa ['kojza] f thing; *(assunto)* matter; **~ de** about

coitado, -a [koj'tadu, a] adj poor, wretched

cola ['kɔla] f glue

colaborador, a [kolabora'do*, a] m/f collaborator; *(em jornal)* contributor

colaborar [kolabo'ra*] vi to collaborate; *(ajudar)* to help; *(escrever artigos etc)* to contribute

colante [ko'lãtʃi] adj *(roupa)* skintight

colapso [ko'lapsu] m collapse; **~ cardíaco** heart failure

colar [ko'la*] vt to stick, glue; *(BR: copiar)* to crib ♦ vi to stick; to cheat ♦ m necklace

colarinho [kola'riɲu] m collar

colarinho-branco *(pl* **colarinhos-brancos)** m white-collar worker

colcha ['kowʃa] f bedspread

colchão [kow'ʃãw] *(pl* **-ões)** m mattress

colchete [kow'ʃetʃi] m clasp, fastening; *(parênteses)* square bracket; **~ de gancho** hook and eye; **~ de pressão** press stud, popper

colchões [kow'ʃõjʃ] mpl de **colchão**

coleção [kole'sãw] *(PT* **-cç-)** *(pl* **~ões)** f collection, **colecionador, a** [kolesjona'do*, a] *(PT* **-cc-)** m/f collector; **colecionar** [kolesjo'na*] *(PT* **-cc-)** vt to collect

colectar etc [kolek'ta*] *(PT)* = **coletar** etc

colega [ko'lega] m/f colleague; *(de escola)* classmate

colegial [kole'ʒjaw] *(pl* **-ais)** m/f schoolboy/girl

colégio [ko'lɛʒu] m school

coleira [ko'lejra] f collar

cólera ['kɔlera] f anger ♦ m ou f *(MED)* cholera

colesterol [koleʃte'rɔw] m cholesterol

coleta [ko'leta] f collection; **coletar** [kole'ta*] vt to tax; *(arrecadar)* to collect

colete [ko'letʃi] m waistcoat *(BRIT)*

vest (US); ~ **salva-vidas** life jacket (BRIT), life preserver (US)

coletivo, -a [kole'tʃivu, a] adj collective; (transportes) public ♦ m bus

colheita [ko'ʎejta] f harvest

colher [ko'ʎe*] vt to gather, pick; (dados) to gather ♦ f spoon; ~ **de chá/sopa** teaspoon/tablespoon

colidir [koli'dʒi*] vi: ~ **com** to collide with, crash into

coligação [koliga'sãw] (pl -ões) f coalition

colina [ko'lina] f hill

colisão [koli'zãw] (pl -ões) f collision

collant [ko'lã] (pl ~s) m tights pl (BRIT), pantihose (US); (blusa) leotard

colmeia [kow'meja] f beehive

colo ['kɔlu] m neck; (regaço) lap

colocar [kolo'ka*] vt to put, place; (empregar) to find a job for, place; (COM) to market; (pneus, tapetes) to fit; (questão, idéia) to put forward; (COMPUT: dados) to key (in)

Colômbia [ko'lõbja] f: **a** ~ Colombia

colônia [ko'lonja] f colony; (perfume) cologne; **colonial** [kolo'njaw] (pl -ais) adj colonial

colonizador, a [koloniza'do*, a] m/f colonist, settler

colono [ko'lɔnu, a] m/f settler; (cultivador) tenant farmer

coloquial [kolo'kjaw] (pl -ais) adj colloquial

colóquio [ko'lɔkju] m conversation; (congresso) conference

colorido, -a [kolo'ridu, a] adj colourful (BRIT), colorful (US) ♦ m colouring (BRIT), coloring (US)

colorir [kolo'ri*] vt to colour (BRIT), color (US)

coluna [ko'luna] f column; (pilar) pillar; ~ **dorsal** ou **vertebral** spine; **colunável** [kolu'navew] (pl -eis)

adj famous ♦ m/f celebrity; **colunista** [kolu'niʃta] m/f columnist

com [kõ] prep with; ~ **cuidado** carefully; **estar** ~ **câncer** to have cancer; **estar** ~ **dinheiro** to have some money on one; **estar** ~ **fome** to be hungry

coma ['kɔma] f coma

comandante [komã'dãtʃi] m commander; (MIL) commandant; (NÁUT) captain

comandar [komã'da*] vt to command

comando [ko'mãdu] m command

combate [kõ'batʃi] m combat; **combater** [kõba'te*] vt to fight; (opor-se a) to oppose ♦ vi to fight; **combater-se** vr to fight

combinação [kõbina'sãw] (pl -ões) f combination; (QUÍM) compound; (acordo) arrangement; (plano) scheme; (roupa) slip

combinar [kõbi'na*] vt to combine; (jantar etc) to arrange; (fuga etc) to plan ♦ vi (roupas etc) to go together; **combinar-se** vr to combine; (pessoas) to get on well together; ~ **com** (harmonizar-se) to go with; ~ **de fazer** to arrange to do; **combinado!** agreed!

comboio [kõ'boju] m (PT) train; (de navios, carros) convoy

combustível [kõbuʃ'tʃivew] m fuel

começar [kome'sa*] vt, vi to begin, start; ~ **a fazer** to begin ou start to do

começo [ko'mesu] m beginning, start

comédia [ko'mɛdʒja] f comedy

comemorar [komemo'ra*] vt to commemorate

comentar [komẽ'ta*] vt to comment on; (maliciosamente) to make comments about

comentário [komẽ'tarju] m comment, remark; (*análise*) commentary

comer [ko'me*] vt to eat; (*DAMAS, XADREZ*) to take, capture ♦ vi to eat; **dar de ~ a** to feed

comercial [komex'sjaw] (pl -ais) adj commercial; (*relativo ao negócio*) business atr ♦ m commercial

comercializar [komexsjali'za*] vt to market

comerciante [komex'sjãtʃi] m/f trader

comércio [ko'mexsju] m commerce; (*tráfico*) trade; (*negócio*) business; (*lojas*) shops pl; **~ eletrônico** e-commerce

comes ['komiʃ] mpl: **~ e bebes** food and drink

comestíveis [komeʃ'tʃiveis] mpl foodstuffs, food sg

comestível [komeʃ'tʃivew] (pl -eis) adj edible

cometer [kome'te*] vt to commit

comichão [komi'ʃãw] f itch, itching

comício [ko'misju] m (*POL*) rally, meeting; (*assembléia*) assembly

cômico, -a [ko'miku, a] adj comic(al) ♦ m comedian; (*de teatro*) actor

comida [ko'mida] f (*alimento*) food; (*refeição*) meal

comigo [ko'migu] pron with me

comilão, -lona [komi'lãw, lɔna] (pl -ões, ~s) adj greedy ♦ m/f glutton

comiserar-se [komize'raxsi] vr: **~ se (de)** to sympathize (with)

comissão [komi'sãw] (pl -ões) f commission; (*comitê*) committee

comissário [komi'sarju] m commissioner; (*COM*) agent; **~ de bordo** (*AER*) steward; (*NÁUT*) purser

comissões [komi'sõjʃ] fpl de **comissão**

comitê [komi'te] m committee

PALAVRA CHAVE

---

como ['komu] adv 1 (*modo*) as; **ela fez ~ eu pedi** she did as I asked; **~ se** as if; **~ quiser** as you wish; **seja ~ for** be that as it may

2 (*assim ~*) like; **ela tem olhos azuis ~ o pai** she has blue eyes like her father's; **ela trabalha numa loja, ~ a mãe** she works in a shop, as does her mother

3 (*de que maneira*) how; **~!** pardon?; **~!** what!; **~ assim?** what do you mean?; **~ não!** of course!

♦ conj (*porque*) as, since; **como estava tarde ele dormiu aqui** since it was late he slept here

comoção [komo'sãw] (pl -ões) f distress; (*revolta*) commotion

cômoda ['komada] f chest of drawers (*BRIT*), bureau (*US*)

comodidade [komodʒi'dadʒi] f comfort; (*conveniência*) convenience

comodismo [komo'dʒiʒmu] m complacency

cômodo, -a ['komodu, a] adj comfortable; (*conveniente*) convenient ♦ m room

comovente [komo'vẽtʃi] adj moving, touching

comover [komo've*] vt to move ♦ vi to be moving; **comover-se** vr to be moved

compacto, -a [kõ'paktu, a] adj compact; (*espesso*) thick; (*sólido*) solid ♦ m (*disco*) single

compadecer-se [kõpade'sexsi] vr: **~-se de** to be sorry for, pity

compadre [kõ'padri] m (col: *companheiro*) buddy, pal

compaixão [kõpaj'ʃãw] m compassion; (*misericórdia*) mercy

companheirismo [kõpaɲej-'riʒmu] *m* companionship

companheiro, -a [kõpa'ɲejru, a] *m/f* companion; (*colega*) friend; (*col*) buddy, mate

companhia [kõpa'ɲia] *f* company

comparação [kõpara'sãw] (*pl* **-ões**) *f* comparison

comparar [kõpa'ra*] *vt* to compare; **~ a** to liken to; **~ com** to compare with

comparecer [kõpare'se*] *vi* to appear, make an appearance; **~ a uma reunião** to attend a meeting

comparsa [kõ'paxsa] *m/f* (TEATRO) extra; (*cúmplice*) accomplice

compartilhar [kõpaxtʃi'ʎa*] *vt* to share ♦ *vi*: **~ de** to share in, participate in

compartimento [kõpaxtʃi'mẽtu] *m* compartment; (*aposento*) room

compasso [kõ'pasu] *m* (*instrumento*) pair of compasses; (MÚS) time; (*ritmo*) beat

compatível [kõpa'tʃivew] (*pl* **-eis**) *adj* compatible

compatriota [kõpa'trjɔta] *m/f* fellow countryman/woman

compensação [kõpẽsa'sãw] (*pl* **-ões**) *f* compensation; **em ~** on the other hand

compensar [kõpẽ'sa*] *vt* to make up for, compensate for; (*equilibrar*) to offset; (*cheque*) to clear

competência [kõpe'tẽsja] *f* competence, ability; (*responsabilidade*) responsibility; **competente** [kõpe'tẽtʃi] *adj* competent; (*apropriado*) appropriate; (*responsável*) responsible

competição [kõpetʃi'sãw] (*pl* **-ões**) *f* competition

competidor, a [kõpetʃi'do*, a] *m/f* competitor

competir [kõpe'tʃi*] *vi* to compete;

~ a alguém to be sb's responsibility; (*caber*) to be up to sb

competitivo, -a [kõpetʃi'tʃivu, a] *adj* competitive

compito *etc* [kõ'pitu] *vb* V **competir**

complementar [kõplemẽ'ta*] *adj* complementary ♦ *vt* to supplement

complemento [kõple'mẽtu] *m* complement

completamente [kõpleta'mẽtʃi] *adv* completely, quite

completar [kõple'ta*] *vt* to complete; (*tanque, carro*) to fill up; **~ dez anos** to be ten

completo, -a [kõ'pletu, a] *adj* complete; (*cheio*) full (up); **por ~** completely

complexo, -a [kõ'pleksu, a] *adj* complex ♦ *m* complex

complicação [kõplika'sãw] (*pl* **-ões**) *f* complication

complicado, -a [kõpli'kadu, a] *adj* complicated

complicar [kõpli'ka*] *vt* to complicate

complô [kõ'plo] *m* plot, conspiracy

componente [kõpo'nẽtʃi] *adj, m* component

compor [kõ'po*] (*irreg: como* **pôr**) *vt* to compose; (*discurso, livro*) to write; (*arranjar*) to arrange ♦ *vi* to compose; **compor-se** *vr* (*controlar-se*) to compose o.s.; **~-se de** to consist of

comporta [kõ'pɔxta] *f* (*de canal*) lock

comportamento [kõpoxta'mẽtu] *m* behaviour (BRIT), behavior (US)

comportar-se [kõpox'taxsi] *vt, vr* to behave; **~ mal** to misbehave, behave badly

composição [kõpozi'sãw] (*pl* **-ões**) *f* composition; (TIP) typesetting

compositor, a [kõpozi'to*, a] *m/f*

composer; (*TIP*) typesetter

compota [kõˈpɔta] f fruit in syrup

compra [ˈkõpɾa] f purchase; **fazer ~s** to go shopping; **comprador, a** [kõpɾaˈdo*, a] m/f buyer, purchaser

comprar [kõˈpɾa*] vt to buy

compreender [kõpɾjenˈde*] vt to understand; (*constar de*) to be comprised of; consist of; (*abranger*) to cover

compreensão [kõpɾjěˈsãw] f understanding, comprehension; **compreensivo, -a** [kõpɾjěˈsivu, a] adj understanding

compressa [kõˈpɾesa] f compress

comprido, -a [kõˈpɾidu, a] adj long; (*alto*) tall; **ao ~** lengthways

comprimento [kõpɾiˈmẽtu] m length

comprimido [kõpɾiˈmidu] m pill, tablet

comprimir [kõpɾiˈmi*] vt to compress

comprometer [kõpɾomeˈte*] vt to compromise; (*envolver*) to involve; (*arriscar*) to jeopardize; (*empenhar*) to pledge; **comprometer-se** vr: **~-se a** to undertake to, promise to

compromisso [kõpɾoˈmisu] m promise; (*obrigação*) commitment; (*hora marcada*) appointment; (*acordo*) agreement

comprovante [kõpɾoˈvãtʃi] m receipt

comprovar [kõpɾoˈva*] vt to prove; (*confirmar*) to confirm

compulsão [kõpuwˈsãw] f (pl **-ões**) compulsion; **compulsivo, -a** [kõpuwˈsivu, a] adj compulsive; **compulsório, -a** [kõpuwˈsɔrju, a] adj compulsory

computação [kõputaˈsãw] f computer science, computing

computador [kõputaˈdo*] m computer

computar [kõpuˈta*] vt (*calcular*) to calculate; (*contar*) to count

comum [koˈmũ] (pl **-ns**) adj ordinary, common; (*habitual*) usual; **em ~** in common

comungar [komũˈga*] vi to take communion

comunhão [komuˈɲãw] (pl **-ões**) f (*ger, REL*) communion

comunicação [komunikaˈsãw] (pl **-ões**) f communication; (*mensagem*) message; (*acesso*) access

comunicado [komuniˈkadu] m notice

comunicar [komuniˈka*] vt, vi to communicate; **comunicar-se** vr to communicate; **~-se com** (*entrar em contato*) to get in touch with

comunidade [komuniˈdadʒi] f community; **C~ dos Estados Independentes** Commonwealth of Independent States

comunismo [komuˈniʒmu] m communism; **comunista** [komuˈniʃta] adj, m/f communist

comuns [koˈmũʃ] pl de **comum**

conceber [kõseˈbe*] vt, vi to conceive

conceder [kõseˈde*] vt to allow; (*outorgar*) to grant; (*dar*) to give ♦ vi: **~ em** to agree to

conceito [kõˈsejtu] m concept, idea; (*fama*) reputation; (*opinião*) opinion; **conceituado, -a** [kõsejˈtwadu, a] adj well thought of, highly regarded

concentração [kõsětɾaˈsãw] (pl **-ões**) f concentration

concepção [kõsepˈsãw] (pl **-ões**) f (*geração*) conception; (*noção*) idea, concept; (*opinião*) opinion

concerto [kõˈsextu] m concert

concessão [kõseˈsãw] (pl **-ões**) f concession; (*permissão*) permission

concha ['kõʃa] f shell; (*para líquidos*) ladle
conchavo [kõ'ʃavu] m conspiracy
conciliar [kõsi'lja*] vt to reconcile
concluir [kõ'klwi*] vt, vi to conclude
conclusão [kõklu'zãw] (*pl* -ões) f end; (*dedução*) conclusion
conclusões [kõklu'zõjʃ] fpl de **conclusão**
concordância [kõkox'dãsja] f agreement
concordar [kõkox'da*] vi, vt to agree
concorrência [kõko'xẽsja] f competition; (*a um cargo*) application
concorrente [kõko'xẽtʃi] m/f competitor; (*candidato*) candidate
concorrer [kõko'xe*] vi to compete; ~ a to apply for
concretizar [kõkretʃi'za*] vt to make real; **concretizar-se** (*sonho*) to come true; (*ambições*) to be realized
concreto, -a [kõ'krɛtu, a] adj concrete ♦ m concrete
concurso [kõ'kuxsu] m contest; (*exame*) competition
conde ['kõdʒi] m count
condenação [kõdena'sãw] (*pl* -ões) f (*JUR*) conviction
condenar [kõde'na*] vt to condemn; (*JUR: sentenciar*) to sentence; (: *declarar culpado*) to convict
condensar [kõdẽ'sa*] vt to condense; **condensar-se** vr to condense
condescendência [kõdesẽ'dẽsja] f acquiescence
condescender [kõdesẽ'de*] vi to acquiesce; ~ a ou em to condescend to, deign to
condessa [kõ'desa] f countess
condição [kõdʒi'sãw] (*pl* -ões) f condition; (*social*) status; (*quali-*

dade) capacity; **com a ~ de que** on condition that, provided that; **em condições de fazer** (*pessoa*) able to do; (*carro etc*) in condition to do
condimento [kõdʒi'mẽtu] m seasoning
condomínio [kõdo'minju] m condominium
condução [kõdu'sãw] f driving; (*transporte*) transport; (*ônibus*) bus
conduta [kõ'duta] f conduct, behaviour (*BRIT*), behavior (*US*)
condutor, a [kõdu'to*, a] m/f (*de veículo*) driver ♦ m (*ELET*) conductor
conduzir [kõdu'zi*] vt (*levar*) to lead; (*FÍS*) to conduct; **conduzir-se** vr to behave; **conduzir a** to lead to
cone ['kõni] m cone
conectar [konek'ta*] vt to connect
conexão [konek'sãw] (*pl* -ões) f connection
confecção [kõfek'sãw] (*pl* -ões) f making; (*de um boletim*) production; (*roupa*) ready-to-wear clothes pl; (*negócio*) business selling ready-to-wear clothes
confeccionar [kõfeksjo'na*] vt to make; (*fabricar*) to manufacture
confecções [kõfek'sõjʃ] fpl de **confecção**
confeitaria [kõfejta'ria] f patisserie
conferência [kõfe'rẽsja] f conference; (*discurso*) lecture
conferir [kõfe'ri*] vt to check; (*comparar*) to compare; (*outorgar*) to grant ♦ vi to tally
confessar [kõfe'sa*] vt, vi to confess; **confessar-se** vr to confess
confete [kõ'fɛtʃi] m confetti
confiança [kõ'fjãsa] f confidence; (*fé*) trust; **de ~** reliable; **ter ~ em alguém** to trust sb
confiante [kõ'fjãtʃi] adj: ~ (**em**) confident (of)
confiar [kõ'fja*] vt to entrust; (*se-*

gredo) to confide ♦ *vi*: **~ em** to trust; (*ter fé*) to have faith in

confiável [kõˈfjavew] (*pl* -**eis**) *adj* reliable

confidência [kõfiˈdẽsja] *f* secret; **em ~** in confidence; **confidencial** [kõfidẽˈsjaw] (*pl* -**ais**) *adj* confidential

confins [kõˈfĩʃ] *mpl* limits, boundaries

confirmação [kõfixmaˈsãw] (*pl* -**ões**) *f* confirmation

confirmar [kõfixˈma*] *vt* to confirm

confiro *etc* [kõˈfiru] *vb* V **conferir**

confiscar [kõfiʃˈka*] *vt* to confiscate

confissão [kõfiˈsãw] (*pl* -**ões**) *f* confession

conflito [kõˈflitu] *m* conflict

conformar [kõfoxˈma*] *vt* to form ♦ *vi*: **~ com** to conform to; **conformar-se** *vr*: **~-se com** to resign o.s. to; (*acomodar-se*) to conform to

conforme [kõˈfɔxmi] *prep* according to; (*dependendo de*) depending on ♦ *conj* (*logo que*) as soon as; (*como*) as, according to what; (*à medida que*) as; **você vai? – ~ ~** are you going? – it depends

conformidade [kõfoxmiˈdadʒi] *f* agreement; **em ~ com** in accordance with

confortar [kõfoxˈta*] *vt* to comfort, console

confortável [kõfoxˈtavew] (*pl* -**eis**) *adj* comfortable

conforto [kõˈfoxtu] *m* comfort

confrontar [kõfrõˈta*] *vt* to confront; (*comparar*) to compare

confronto [kõˈfrõtu] *m* confrontation; (*comparação*) comparison

confundir [kõfũˈdʒi*] *vt* to confuse; **confundir-se** *vr* to get mixed up

confusão [kõfuˈzãw] (*pl* -**ões**) *f* confusion; (*tumulto*) uproar; (*problemas*) trouble

confuso, -a [kõˈfuzu, a] *adj* confused; (*problema*) confusing

confusões [kõfuˈzõjʃ] *fpl de* **confusão**

congelador [kõʒelaˈdo*] *m* freezer, deep freeze

congelamento [kõʒelaˈmẽtu] *m* freezing; (ECON) freeze

congelar [kõʒeˈla*] *vt* to freeze; **congelar-se** *vr* to freeze

congestão [kõʒeʃˈtãw] *f* congestion; **congestionado, -a** [kõʒeʃtʃjoˈnadu, a] *adj* congested; (*olhos*) bloodshot; (*rosto*) flushed; **congestionamento** [kõʒeʃtʃjonaˈmẽtu] *m* congestion; **um congestionamento (de tráfego)** a traffic jam

congestionar [kõʒeʃtʃjoˈna*] *vt* to congest; **congestionar-se** *vr* (*rosto*) to go red

congressista [kõgreˈsiʃta] *m/f* congressman/woman

congresso [kõˈgresu] *m* congress, conference

conhaque [koˈnaki] *m* cognac, brandy

conhecedor, a [koɲeseˈdo*, a] *adj* knowing ♦ *m/f* connoisseur, expert

conhecer [koɲeˈse*] *vt* to know; (*travar conhecimento com*) to meet; (*descobrir*) to discover; **conhecer-se** *vr* to meet; (*ter conhecimento*) to know each other

conhecido, -a [koɲeˈsidu, a] *adj* known; (*célebre*) well-known ♦ *m/f* acquaintance

conhecimento [koɲesiˈmẽtu] *m* (*tb*: **~s**) knowledge; (*idéia*) idea; (*conhecido*) acquaintance; (COM) bill of lading; **levar ao ~ de alguém** to bring to sb's notice

conjugado [kōʒuˈgadu] m studio

cônjuge [ˈkōʒuʒi] m spouse

conjunção [kōʒūˈsãw] (pl -ões) f union; (LING) conjunction

conjuntivite [kōʒūtʃiˈvitʃi] f conjunctivitis

conjuntivo [kōʒūˈtʃivu] (PT) m (LING) subjunctive

conjunto, -a [kōˈʒūtu, a] adj joint ♦ m whole; (coleção) collection; (músicos) group; (roupa) outfit

conosco [koˈnoʃku] pron with us

conquista [kōˈkiʃta] f conquest; **conquistador, a** [kōkiʃtaˈdo*, a] adj conquering ♦ m/f conqueror

conquistar [kōkiʃˈta*] vt to conquer; (alcançar) to achieve; (ganhar) to win

consagrado, -a [kōsaˈgradu, a] adj established

consciência [kōˈsjēsja] f conscience; (percepção) awareness; (senso de responsabilidade) conscientiousness

consciente [kōsˈjētʃi] adj conscious

conseguinte [kōseˈgītʃi] adj: **por ~** consequently

conseguir [kōseˈgi*] vt to get, obtain; **~ fazer** to manage to do, succeed in doing

conselho [kōˈseáu] m piece of advice; (corporação) council; **~s** mpl (advertência) advice sg; **~ de guerra** court martial; **C~ de ministros** (POL) Cabinet

consentimento [kōsētʃiˈmētu] m consent

consentir [kōsēˈtʃi*] vt to allow, permit; (aprovar) to agree to ♦ vi: **~ em** to agree to

consequência [kōseˈkwēsja] f consequence; **por ~** consequently

consertar [kōsexˈta*] vt to mend, repair; (remediar) to put right; **con-**

serto [kōˈsextu] m repair

conserva [kōˈsexva] f pickle; **em ~** pickled

conservação [kōsexvaˈsãw] f conservation; (de vida, alimentos) preservation

conservador, a [kōsexvaˈdo*, a] adj conservative ♦ m/f (POL) conservative

conservante [kōsexˈvātʃi] m preservative

conservar [kōsexˈva*] vt to preserve, maintain; (reter, manter) to keep, retain; **conservar-se** vr to keep

conservatório [kōsexvaˈtɔrju] m conservatory

consideração [kōsideraˈsãw] (pl -ões) f consideration; (estima) respect, esteem; **levar em ~** to take into account

considerar [kōsideˈra*] vt to consider; (prezar) to respect ♦ vi to consider

considerável [kōsideˈravew] (pl -eis) adj considerable

consigo¹ [kōˈsigu] pron (m) with him; (f) with her; (pl) with them; (com você) with you

consigo² etc vb V **conseguir**

consinto etc [kōˈsītu] vb V **consentir**

consistente [kōsiˈtētʃi] adj solid; (espesso) thick

consistir [kōsiʃˈtʃi*] vi: **~ em** to be made up of, consist of

consoante [kōsoˈãtʃi] f consonant ♦ prep according to ♦ conj: **~ prometera** as he had promised

consolação [kōsolaˈsãw] (pl -ões) f consolation

consolar [kōsoˈla*] vt to console

consolidar [kōsoliˈda*] vt to consolidate; (fratura) to knit ♦ vi to become solid; to knit together

consolo [kõ'solu] m consolation

consome etc [kõ'somi] vb V consumir

consórcio [kõ'sɔɹsju] m (união) partnership; (COM) consortium

conspiração [kõʃpira'sãw] (pl -ões) f plot, conspiracy

conspirar [kõʃpi'ra*] vt, vi to plot

constante [kõʃ'tãtʃi] adj constant

constar [kõʃ'ta*] vi to be in; **ao que me consta** as far as I know

constatar [kõʃta'ta*] vt to establish; (notar) to notice; (evidenciar) to show up

consternado, -a [kõʃtex'nadu, a] adj depressed; (desolado) distressed

constipação [kõʃtʃipa'sãw] (pl -ões) f constipation; (PT) cold; **apanhar uma ~** (PT) to catch a cold

constipado, -a [kõʃtʃi'padu, a] adj: **estar ~** to be constipated; (PT) to have a cold

constituição [kõʃtʃitwi'sãw] (pl -ões) f constitution

constituinte [kõʃtʃi'twĩtʃi] m/f (deputado) member ♦ f (BR): **a C~** the Constituent Assembly; ≈ Parliament

constituir [kõʃtʃi'twi*] vt to constitute; (formar) to form; (estabelecer) to establish; (nomear) to appoint

constrangimento [kõʃtrãʒi'mẽtu] m constraint; embarrassment

construção [kõʃtru'sãw] (pl -ões) f building, construction

construir [kõʃ'trwi*] vt to build, construct

construtivo, -a [kõʃtru'tʃivu, a] adj constructive

construtor, a [kõʃtru'to*, a] m/f builder

cônsul ['kõsuw] (pl -es) m consul; **consulado** [kõsu'ladu] m consulate

consulta [kõ'suwta] f consultation;

livro de ~ reference book; **horário de ~** surgery hours pl (BRIT), office hours pl (US); **consultar** [kõsuw-'ta*] vt to consult; **consultor, a** [kõsuw'to*, a] m/f consultant

consultório [kõsuw'tɔrju] m surgery

consumidor, a [kõsumi'do*, a] adj consumer atr ♦ m/f consumer

consumir [kõsu'mi*] vt to consume; (gastar) to use up; **consumir-se** vr to waste away

consumo [kõ'sumu] m consumption; **artigos de ~** consumer goods

conta ['kõta] f count; (em restaurante) bill; (fatura) invoice; (bancária) account; (de colar) bead; **~s** fpl (COM) accounts; **levar** ou **ter em ~** to take into account; **tomar ~ de** to take care of; (dominar) to take hold of; **afinal de ~s** after all; **dar-se ~ de** to realize; (notar) to notice; **~ corrente** current account

contabilidade [kõtabili'dadʒi] f book-keeping, accountancy

contabilista [kõtabi'liʃta] (PT) m/f accountant

contabilizar [kõtabili'za*] vt to write up, book

contacto etc [kõ'tatu] (PT) = **contato** etc

contador, a [kõta'do*, a] m/f (COM) accountant ♦ m (TEC: medidor) meter

contagiante [kõta'ʒjãtʃi] adj (alegria) contagious

contagiar [kõta'ʒja*] vt to infect

contágio [kõ'taʒju] m infection

contagioso, -a [kõta'ʒjozu, ɔza] adj (doença) contagious

contaminar [kõtami'na*] vt to contaminate

contanto que [kõ'tãtu ki] conj provided that

conta-quilómetros (PT) m inv speedometer

contar [kõ'ta*] vt to count; (narrar) to tell; (pretender) to intend ♦ vi to count; ~ **com** to count on; (esperar) to expect; ~ **em fazer** to count on doing, expect to do

contatar [kõta'ta*] vt to contact; **contato** [kõ'tatu] m contact; **entrar em contato com** to get in touch with, contact

contemplar [kõtẽ'pla*] vt to contemplate; (olhar) to gaze at

contemplativo, -a [kõtẽpla'tʃivu, a] adj (pessoa) thoughtful

contemporâneo, -a [kõtẽpo-'ranju, a] adj, m/f contemporary

contentamento [kõtẽta'mẽtu] m (felicidade) happiness; (satisfação) contentment

contente [kõ'tẽtʃi] adj happy; (satisfeito) pleased, satisfied

contento [kõ'tẽtu] m: **a ~** satisfactorily

conter [kõ'te*] (irreg: como **ter**) vt to contain, hold; (refrear) to restrain, hold back; (gastos) to curb

contestação [kõtʃ ta'sãw] (pl -ões) f challenge; (negação) denial

contestar [kõtʃ ta'ta*] vt to dispute, contest; (impugnar) to challenge

conteúdo [kõte'udu] m contents pl; (de um texto) content

contexto [kõ'teʃtu] m context

contigo [kõ'tʃigu] pron with you

contíguo, -a [kõ'tʃigwu, a] adj: ~ **a** next to

continental [kõtʃinẽ'taw] (pl -**ais**) adj continental

continente [kõtʃi'nẽtʃi] m continent

contingência [kõtʃi'ʒẽsja] f contingency

continuação [kõtʃinwa'sãw] f continuation

continuar [kõtʃi'nwa*] vt, vi to continue; ~ **falando** ou **a falar** to go

on talking; **ela continua doente** she is still sick

continuidade [kõtʃinwi'dadʒi] f continuity

contínuo, -a [kõ'tʃinwu, a] adj (persistente) continual; (sem interrupção) continuous ♦ m office boy

conto ['kõtu] m story, tale; (PT: dinheiro) 1000 escudos

contorcer [kõtox'se*] vt to twist; **contorcer-se** vr to writhe

contornar [kõtox'na*] vt (rodear) to go round; (ladear) to skirt; (fig: problema) to get round

contorno [kõ'toxnu] m outline; (da terra) contour; (do rosto) profile

contra ['kõtra] prep against ♦ m: **os prós e os ~s** the pros and cons; **dar o ~ (a)** to be opposed (to)

contra-ataque m counterattack

contrabandear [kõtrabã'dʒja*] vt to smuggle; **contrabandista** [kõtrabã'dʒiʃta] m/f smuggler; **contrabando** [kõtra'bãdu] m smuggling; (artigos) contraband

contraceptivo, -a [kõtrasep'tʃivu, a] adj contraceptive ♦ m contraceptive

contracheque [kõtra'ʃeki] m pay slip (BRIT), check stub (US)

contradição [kõtradʒi'sãw] (pl -ões) f contradiction

contraditório, -a [kõtradʒi'tɔrju, a] adj contradictory

contradizer [kõtradʒi'ze*] (irreg: como **dizer**) vt to contradict

contragosto [kõtra'goʃtu] m: **a ~** against one's will, unwillingly

contrair [kõtra'i*] vt to contract; (hábito) to form

contramão [kõtra'mãw] adj one-way ♦ f: **na ~** the wrong way down a one-way street

contraproducente [kõtraprodu-'sẽtʃi] adj counterproductive ♦ f: **na ~**

contrariar [kõtraˈrja*] vt to contradict; (aborrecer) to annoy

contrário, -a [kõˈtrarju, a] adj (oposto) opposite; (pessoa) opposed; (desfavorável) unfavourable (BRIT), unfavorable (US), adverse ♦ m opposite; do ~ otherwise; pelo ou ao ~ on the contrary; ao ~ the other way round

contra-senso m nonsense

contrastar [kõtraʃˈta*] vt to contrast; **contraste** [kõˈtraʃtʃi] m contrast

contratação [kõtrataˈsãw] f (de pessoal) employment

contratar [kõtraˈta*] vt (serviços) to contract; (pessoa) to employ, take on

contratempo [kõtraˈtẽpu] m setback; (aborrecimento) upset; (dificuldade) difficulty

contrato [kõˈtratu] m contract; (acordo) agreement

contribuição [kõtribwiˈsãw] (pl -ões) f contribution; (Imposto) tax

contribuinte [kõtriˈbwĩtʃi] m/f contributor; (que paga impostos) taxpayer

contribuir [kõtriˈbwi*] vt to contribute ♦ vi to contribute; (pagar impostos) to pay taxes

controlar [kõtroˈla*] vt to control

controle [kõˈtrɔli] m control; ~ remoto remote control; ~ de crédito (COM) credit control; ~ de qualidade (COM) quality control

controvérsia [kõtroˈvɛrsja] f controversy; (discussão) debate; **controverso, -a** [kõtroˈvɛrsu, a] adj controversial

contudo [kõˈtudu] conj nevertheless, however

contumaz [kõtuˈmajʒ] adj obstinate, stubborn

contusão [kõtuˈzãw] (pl -ões) f bruise

convalescer [kõvaleˈse*] vi to convalesce

convenção [kõvẽˈsãw] (pl -ões) f convention; (acordo) agreement

convencer [kõvẽˈse*] vt to convince; (persuadir) to persuade; **convencer-se** vr: **~-se de** to be convinced about; **convencido, -a** [kõvẽˈsidu, a] adj convinced; (col: imodesto) conceited, smug

convencional [kõvẽsjoˈnaw] (pl -ais) adj conventional

convenções [kõvẽˈsõjʃ] fpl de **convenção**

conveniência [kõveˈnjẽsja] f convenience

conveniente [kõveˈnjẽtʃi] adj convenient, suitable; (vantajoso) advantageous

convênio [kõˈvenju] m (reunião) convention; (acordo) agreement

convento [kõˈvẽtu] m convent

conversa [kõˈvɛrsa] f conversation; **~-fiada** idle chat; (promessa falsa) hot air

conversão [kõvɛrˈsãw] (pl -ões) f conversion

conversar [kõvɛrˈsa*] vi to talk

conversões [kõvɛrˈsõjʃ] fpl de **conversão**

converter [kõvɛrˈte*] vt to convert

convés [kõˈvɛʃ] (pl -eses) m (NÁUT) deck

convexo, -a [kõˈvɛksu, a] adj convex

convicção [kõvikˈsãw] (pl -ões) f conviction

convidado, -a [kõviˈdadu, a] m/f guest

convidar [kõviˈda*] vt to invite

convincente [kõvĩˈsẽtʃi] adj convincing

convir [kõˈvi*] (irreg: como **vir**) vi to

suit, be convenient; (*ficar bem*) to
be appropriate; (*concordar*) to
agree; **convém fazer isso o mais
rápido possível** we must do this as
soon as possible

convite [kõ'vitʃi] *m* invitation

convivência [kõvi'vẽsja] *f* living
together; (*familiaridade*) familiarity,
intimacy

conviver [kõvi've*] *vi*: ~ **com** (*viver
em comum*) to live with; (*ter familiaridade*) to get on with; **convívio**
[kõ'vivju] *m* living together; (*familiaridade*) familiarity

convocar [kõvo'ka*] *vt* to summon,
call upon; (*reunião, eleições*) to call;
(*para o serviço militar*) to call up

convosco [kõ'voʃku] *adv* with you

convulsão [kõvuw'sãw] (*pl* -**ões**) *f*
convulsion

cooper ['kupe*] *m* jogging; **fazer ~**
to go jogging

cooperação [koopera'sãw] *f* co-
operation

cooperar [koope'ra*] *vi* to cooperate

cooperativa [koopera'tʃiva] *f*
(*COM*) cooperative

cooperativo, -a [koopera'tʃivu, a] *adj* cooperative

coordenada [kooxde'nada] *f* coordinate

coordenar [kooxde'na*] *vt* to coordinate

copa ['kɔpa] *f* (*de árvore*) top;
(*torneio*) cup; ~**s** *fpl* (*CARTAS*) hearts

cópia ['kɔpja] *f* copy; **tirar ~ de** to
copy; **copiadora** [kopja'dora] *f*
duplicating machine

copiar [ko'pja*] *vt* to copy

copo ['kɔpu] *m* glass

coque ['kɔki] *m* (*penteado*) bun

coqueiro [ko'kejru] *m* (*BOT*)
coconut palm

coquetel [koke'tɛw] (*pl* -**éis**) *m*

cocktail; (*festa*) cocktail party

cor¹ [kɔ*] *m*: **de ~** by heart

cor² [ko*] *f* colour (*BRIT*), color (*US*);
de ~ colo(u)red

coração [kora'sãw] (*pl* -**ões**) *m*
heart; **de bom ~** kind-hearted; **de
todo o ~** wholeheartedly

corado, -a [ko'radu, a] *adj* ruddy

coragem [ko'raʒẽ] *f* courage; (*atrevimento*) nerve

corais [ko'rajʃ] *mpl de* **coral**

corajoso, -a [kora'ʒozu, ɔza] *adj*
courageous

coral [ko'raw] (*pl* -**ais**) *m* (*MÚS*)
choir; (*ZOOL*) coral

corante [ko'rãtʃi] *adj, m* colouring
(*BRIT*), coloring (*US*)

corar [ko'ra*] *vt* (*roupa*) to bleach
(in the sun) ♦ *vi* to blush; (*tornar-se
branco*) to bleach

corcunda [kox'kũda] *adj* hunch-
backed ♦ *f* hump ♦ *m/f* (*pessoa*)
hunchback

corda ['kɔxda] *f* rope, line; (*MÚS*)
string; (*varal*) clothes line; (*de relógio*) spring; **dar ~ em** to wind up;
~**s vocais** vocal chords

cordão [kox'dãw] (*pl* -**ões**) *m*
string, twine; (*jóia*) chain; (*no carnaval*) group; (*ELET*) lead; (*fileira*)
row

cordeiro [kox'dejru] *m* lamb

cordel [kox'dɛw] (*pl* -**éis**) *m* (*PT*)
string; **literatura de ~** pamphlet literature

cor-de-rosa *adj inv* pink

cordial [kox'dʒjaw] (*pl* -**ais**) *adj* cordial ♦ *m* (*bebida*) cordial

cordões [kox'dõjʃ] *mpl de* **cordão**

coreano, -a [ko'rjanu, a] *adj*
Korean ♦ *m/f* Korean ♦ *m* (*LING*)
Korean

Coréia [ko'reja] *f*: **a ~** Korea

coreto [ko'retu] *m* bandstand

córner ['kɔxne*] *m* (*FUTEBOL*) corner

coro ['koru] m chorus; (conjunto de cantores) choir

coroa [ko'roa] f crown; (de flores) garland ♦ m/f (BR: col) old timer

coroar [koro'a*] vt to crown; (premiar) to reward

coronel [koro'nεw] (pl -éis) m colonel; (político) local political boss

corpo ['koxpu] m body; (aparência física) figure; (: de homem) build; (de vestido) bodice; (MIL) corps sg; **de e alma** (fig) wholeheartedly; **~ diplomático** diplomatic corps sg

corporal [koxpo'raw] (pl -ais) adj physical

corpulento, -a [koxpu'lẽtu, a] adj stout

correção [koxe'sãw] (PT -cç-) (pl -ões) f correction; (exatidão) correctness; **casa de ~** reformatory

corre-corre [kɔxi'kɔxi] (pl ~s) m rush

correcto, -a etc [ko'xektu, a] (PT) = **correto** etc

corredor, a [koxe'do*, a] m/f runner ♦ m corridor; (em avião etc) aisle; (cavalo) racehorse

correia [ko'xeja] f strap; (de máquina) belt; (para cachorro) leash

correio [ko'xeju] m mail, post; (local) post office; (carteiro) postman (BRIT), mailman (US); **~ aéreo** air mail; **~ eletrônico** e-mail, electronic mail; **~ de voz** voice mail; **pôr no ~** to post

corrente [ko'xẽtʃi] adj (atual) current; (águas) running; (comum) usual, common ♦ f current; (cadeia, jóia) chain; **~ de ar** draught (BRIT), draft (US); **correnteza** [koxẽ'teza] f (de ar) draught (BRIT), draft (US); (de rio) current

correr [ko'xe*] vt to run; (viajar por) to travel across ♦ vi to run; (em carro) to drive fast, speed; (o tempo)

to elapse; (boato) to go round; (atuar com rapidez) to rush; **corre-ria** [koxe'ria] f rush

correspondência [koxeʃpõ'dẽsja] f correspondence; **correspondente** [koxeʃpõ'dẽtʃi] adj corresponding ♦ m correspondent

corresponder [koxeʃpõ'de*] vi: **~ a** to correspond to; (ser igual) to match (up to); **corresponder-se** vr: **~-se com** to correspond with

correto, -a [ko'xεtu, a] adj correct; (conduta) right; (pessoa) straight, honest

corretor, a [koxe'to*, a] m/f broker; **~ de fundos** ou **de bolsa** stockbroker; **~ de imóveis** estate agent (BRIT), realtor (US)

corrida [ko'xida] f running; (certame) race; (de taxi) fare; **~ de cavalos** horse race

corrido, -a [ko'xidu, a] adj quick; (expulso) driven out ♦ adv quickly

corrigir [koxi'ʒi*] vt to correct

corrimão [koxi'mãw] (pl ~s) m handrail

corriqueiro, -a [koxi'kejru, a] adj common; (problema) trivial

corromper [koxõ'pe*] vt to corrupt; (subornar) to bribe; **corromper-se** vr to be corrupted

corrosão [koxo'zãw] f corrosion; (fig) erosion

corrosivo, -a [koxo'zivu, a] adj corrosive

corrupção [koxup'sãw] f corruption

corrupto, -a [ko'xuptu, a] adj corrupt

Córsega ['kɔxsega] f: **a ~** Corsica

cortada [kox'tada] f: **dar uma ~ em alguém** (fig) to cut sb short

cortante [kox'tãtʃi] adj cutting

cortar [kox'ta*] vt to cut; (eliminar) to cut out; (água, telefone etc) to cut off; (*efeito*) to stop ♦ *vi* to cut; (*encurtar caminho*) to take a short cut; **~ o cabelo** (*no cabeleireiro*) to have one's hair cut; **~ a palavra de alguém** to interrupt sb

corte¹ ['kɔxtʃi] *m* cut; (*de luz*) power cut; **sem ~** (*tesoura etc*) blunt; **~ de cabelo** haircut

corte² ['kɔxtʃi] *f* court; **~s** *fpl* (*PT*) parliament *sg*

cortejo [kox'teʒu] *m* procession

cortês [kox'teʃ] (*pl* **-eses**) *adj* polite

cortesia [koxte'zia] *f* politeness; (*de empresa*) free offer

cortiça [kox'tʃisa] *f* cork

cortiço [kox'tʃisu] *m* slum tenement

cortina [kox'tʃina] *f* curtain

coruja [ko'ruʒa] *f* owl

corvo ['koxvu] *m* crow

coser [ko'ze*] *vt, vi* to sew

cosmético, -a [koʒ'mɛtʃiku, a] *adj* cosmetic ♦ *m* cosmetic

cospe *etc* ['kɔʃpi] *vb V* **cuspir**

costa ['kɔʃta] *f* coast; **~s** *fpl* (*dorso*) back *sg*; **dar as ~s a** to turn one's back on

Costa Rica *f*: **a ~** Costa Rica

costela [koʃ'tɛla] *f* rib

costeleta [koʃte'leta] *f* chop, cutlet; **~s** *fpl* (*suíças*) side-whiskers

costumar [koʃtu'ma*] *vt* (*habituar*) to accustom ♦ *vi*: **ele costuma chegar às 6.00** he usually arrives at 6.00; **costumava dizer ...** he used to say ...

costume [koʃ'tumi] *m* custom, habit; (*traje*) costume; **~s** *mpl* (*comportamento*) behaviour *sg* (*BRIT*), behavior *sg* (*US*); (*conduta*) conduct *sg*; (*de um povo*) customs; **de ~** usual; **como de ~** as usual

costumeiro, -a [koʃtu'mejru, a] *adj* usual, habitual

costura [koʃ'tura] *f* sewing; (*sutura*)

seam; **costurar** [koʃtu'ra*] *vt, vi* to sew; **costureira** [koʃtu'rejra] *f* dressmaker

cota ['kɔta] *f* quota, share

cotação [kota'sãw] (*pl* **-ões**) *f* (*de preços*) list, quotation; (*BOLSA*) price; (*consideração*) esteem; **~ bancária** bank rate

cotado, -a [ko'tadu, a] *adj* (*COM*: *ação*) quoted; (*bem-conceituado*) well thought of; (*num concurso*) fancied

cotar [ko'ta*] *vt* (*ações*) to quote; **~ algo em** to value sth at

cotejar [kote'ʒa*] *vt* to compare

cotidiano, -a [kotʃi'dʒjanu, a] *adj* daily, everyday ♦ *m*: **o ~** daily life

cotonete [koto'netʃi] *m* cotton bud

cotovelada [kotove'lada] *f* shove; (*cutucada*) nudge

cotovelo [koto'velu] *m* (*ANAT*) elbow; (*curva*) bend; **falar pelos ~s** to talk non-stop

coube *etc* ['kobi] *vb V* **caber**

couro ['koru] *m* leather; (*de um animal*) hide

couve ['kovi] *f* spring greens *pl*; **couve-flor** (*pl* **couves-flores**) *f* cauliflower

couvert [ku'vex] *m* cover charge

cova ['kɔva] *f* pit; (*caverna*) cavern; (*sepultura*) grave

covarde [ko'vaxdʒi] *adj* cowardly ♦ *m/f* coward; **covardia** [kovax-'dʒia] *f* cowardice

covil [ko'viw] (*pl* **-is**) *m* den, lair

covinha [ko'viɲa] *f* dimple

covis [ko'viʃ] *mpl de* **covil**

coxa ['kɔʃa] *f* thigh

coxear [ko'ʃja*] *vi* to limp

coxia [ko'ʃia] *f* aisle, gangway

coxo, -a ['kɔʃu, a] *adj* lame

cozer [ko'ze*] *vt, vi* to cook

cozido [ko'zidu] *m* stew

cozinha [ko'ziɲa] f kitchen; (arte) cookery

cozinhar [kozi'ɲa*] vt, vi to cook

cozinheiro, -a [kozi'ɲejru, a] m/f cook

CP abr = **Caminhos de Ferro Portugueses**

CPF (BR) abr m (= Cadastro de Pessoa Física) identification number

CPLP abr f (= Comunidade de Países de Língua Portuguesa) see boxed note

---

CPLP

The **CPLP** or **Comunidade de Países de Língua Portuguesa** was set up in 1996 to establish economic and diplomatic links between all countries where the official language is Portuguese. The members are Brazil, Portugal, Angola, Mozambique, Guinea-Bissau, Cape Verde and São Tomé & Príncipe. Portuguese is spoken by around 170 million people around the world today.

---

crachá [kra'ʃa] m badge

crânio ['kraniu] m skull

craque ['kraki] m/f ace, expert

crasso, -a ['krasu, a] adj crass

cratera [kra'tɛra] f crater

cravar [kra'va*] vt (prego etc) to drive (in); (com os olhos) to stare at; **cravar-se** vr to penetrate

cravo ['kravu] m carnation; (MÚS) harpsichord; (especiaria) clove; (na pele) blackhead; (prego) nail

creche ['krɛʃi] f crèche

credenciais [kredẽ'sjajʃ] fpl credentials

creditar [kredʒi'ta*] vt to guarantee; (COM) to credit; **~ algo a alguém** to credit sb with sth; (garantir) to assure sb of sth

crédito ['krɛdʒitu] m credit; **digno de ~** reliable

credo ['krɛdu] m creed; **~!** heavens!

credor, a [kre'do*, a] adj worthy, deserving; (COM: saldo) credit atr ♦ m/f creditor

creme ['krɛmi] adj inv cream ♦ m cream; (CULIN: doce) custard; **~ dental** toothpaste; **cremoso, -a** [kre'mozu, ɔza] adj creamy

crença ['krẽsa] f belief

crente ['krẽtʃi] m/f believer

crepúsculo [kre'puʃkulu] m dusk, twilight

crer [kre*] vt, vi to believe; **crer-se** vr to believe o.s. to be; **~ em** to believe in; **creio que sim** I think so

crescente [kre'sẽtʃi] adj growing ♦ m crescent

crescer [kre'se*] vi to grow; **crescimento** [kresi'mẽtu] m growth

crespo, -a ['krespu, a] adj (cabelo) curly

cretinice [kretʃi'nisi] f stupidity; (ato, dito) stupid thing

cretino [kre'tʃinu] m cretin, imbecile

cria ['kria] f (animal: sg) baby animal; (: pl) young pl

criação [kria'sãw] (pl -ões) f creation; (de animais) raising, breeding; (educação) upbringing; (animais domésticos) livestock pl; **filho de ~** adopted child

criado, -a ['kriadu, a] m/f servant

criador, a [kria'do*, a] m/f creator; **~ de gado** cattle breeder

criança ['kriãsa] adj childish ♦ f child; **criançada** [kriã'sada] f: **a criançada** the kids

criar [kria*] vt to create; (crianças) to bring up; (animais) to raise; (amamentar) to suckle, nurse; (planta) to grow; **criar-se** vr: **~-se (com)** to grow up (with); **criar caso** to make trouble

criatura [kria'tura] f creature; (indi-

víduo) individual

crime ['krimi] *m* crime; **criminal** [krimi'naw] (*pl* -ais) *adj* criminal; **criminalidade** [kriminali'dadʒi] *f* crime; **criminoso, -a** [krimi'nozu, ɔza] *adj*, *m/f* criminal

crina ['krina] *f* mane

crioulo, -a ['krjolu, a] *adj* creole ♦ *m/f* creole; (*BR: negro*) Black (person)

crise ['krizi] *f* crisis; (*escassez*) shortage; (*MED*) attack, fit

crista ['kriʃta] *f* (*de serra, onda*) crest; (*de galo*) cock's comb

cristal [kriʃ'taw] (*pl* -ais) *m* crystal; (*vidro*) glass; **cristais** *mpl* (*copos*) glassware *sg*; **cristalino, -a** [kriʃta'linu, a] *adj* crystal-clear

cristão, -tã [kriʃ'tãw, 'tã] (*pl* ~s, ~s) *adj*, *m/f* Christian

cristianismo [kriʃtʃja'niʒmu] *m* Christianity

Cristo ['kriʃtu] *m* Christ

critério [kri'tɛrju] *m* criterion; (*juízo*) discretion, judgement; **criterioso, -a** [krite'rjozu, ɔza] *adj* thoughtful, careful

crítica ['kritʃika] *f* criticism; *V tb* crítico

criticar [kritʃi'ka*] *vt* to criticize; (*um livro*) to review

crítico, -a ['kritʃiku, a] *adj* critical ♦ *m/f* critic

crivar [kri'va*] *vt* (*com balas etc*) to riddle

crivo ['krivu] *m* sieve

crocante [kro'kãtʃi] *adj* crunchy

crônica ['kronika] *f* chronicle; (*coluna de jornal*) newspaper column; (*texto jornalístico*) feature; (*conto*) short story

crônico, -a ['kroniku, a] *adj* chronic

cronológico, -a [krono'lɔʒiku, a] *adj* chronological

cronômetro [kro'nometru] *m* stopwatch

croquete [kro'ketʃi] *m* croquette

cru, a [kru, 'krua] *adj* raw; (*não refinado*) crude

crucial [kru'sjaw] (*pl* -ais) *adj* crucial

crucificação [krusifika'sãw] (*pl* -ões) *f* crucifixion

crucificar [krusifi'ka*] *vt* to crucify

crucifixo [krusi'fiksu] *m* crucifix

cruel [kru'ɛw] (*pl* -éis) *adj* cruel; **crueldade** [kruew'dadʒi] *f* cruelty

cruz [kruʒ] *f* cross; **C~ Vermelha** Red Cross

cruzado, -a [kru'zadu, a] *adj* crossed ♦ *m* (*moeda*) cruzado

cruzamento [kruza'mẽtu] *m* crossroads

cruzar [kru'za*] *vt* to cross ♦ *vi* (*NÁUT*) to cruise; (*pessoas*) to pass each other by; ~ **com** to meet

cruzeiro [kru'zejru] *m* (*cruz*) (*monumental*) cross; (*moeda*) cruzeiro; (*viagem de navio*) cruise

cu [ku] (*col!*) *m* arse (!); **vai tomar no ~** fuck off (!)

Cuba ['kuba] *f* Cuba

cubo ['kubu] *m* cube; (*de roda*) hub

cubro *etc* ['kubru] *vb V* **cobrir**

cuca ['kuka] (*col*) *f* head; **fundir a ~** (*quebrar a cabeça*) to rack one's brain; (*baratinar*) to boggle the mind; (*perturbar*) to drive crazy

cuco ['kuku] *m* cuckoo

cueca ['kwɛka] *f* (*BR: tb:* ~s: *para homens*) underpants *pl*; ~s *fpl* (*PT*) underpants *pl*; (: *para mulheres*) panties *pl*

cuíca ['kwika] *f* kind of musical instrument

cuidado [kwi'dadu] *m* care; **aos ~s de** in the care of; **ter ~** to be careful; ~! watch out!, be careful!; **tomar ~ (de)** to be careful (of); **cuidadoso, -a** [kwida'dozu, ɔza] *adj* careful

cuidar [kwi'da*] *vi:* ~ **de** to take care of, look after; **cuidar-se** *vr* to look after o.s.

cujo, -a ['kuʒu, a] *pron (de quem)* whose; *(de que)* of which

culinária [kuli'narja] *f* cookery

culpa ['kuwpa] *f* fault; *(JUR)* guilt; **ter ~ de** to be to blame for; **por ~ de** because of; **culpado, -a** [kuw'padu, a] *adj* guilty ♦ *m/f* culprit; **culpar** [kuw'pa*] *vt* to blame; *(acusar)* to accuse; **culpar-se** *vr* to take the blame; **culpável** [kuw'pavew] *(pl* **-eis)** *adj* guilty

cultivar [kuwtʃi'va*] *vt* to cultivate; *(plantas)* to grow; **cultivo** [kuw'tʃivu] *m* cultivation

culto, -a ['kuwtu, a] *adj* cultured ♦ *m (homenagem)* worship; *(religião)* cult

cultura [kuw'tura] *f* culture; *(da terra)* cultivation; **cultural** [kuwtu-'raw] *(pl* **culturais)** *adj* cultural

cume ['kumi] *m* top, summit; *(fig)* climax

cúmplice ['kũplisi] *m/f* accomplice

cumprimentar [kũprimẽ'ta*] *vt* to greet; *(dar parabéns)* to congratulate

cumprimento [kũpri'mẽtu] *m* fulfilment; *(saudação)* greeting; *(elogio)* compliment; ~**s** *mpl (saudações)* best wishes; ~ **de uma lei/ordem** compliance with a law/an order

cumprir [kũ'pri*] *vt (desempenhar)* to carry out; *(promessa)* to keep; *(lei)* to obey; *(pena)* to serve ♦ *vi* to be necessary; ~ **a palavra** to keep one's word; **fazer** ~ to enforce

cúmulo ['kumulu] *m* height; **é o ~!** that's the limit!

cunha ['kuɲa] *f* wedge

cunhado, -a [ku'ɲadu, a] *m/f* brother-in-law/sister-in-law

cunho ['kuɲu] *m (marca)* hallmark; *(caráter)* nature

cupim [ku'pĩ] *(pl* **-ns)** *m* termite

cupins [ku'pĩʃ] *mpl de* **cupim**

cúpula ['kupula] *f* dome; *(de abajur)* shade; *(de partido etc)* leadership; **(reunião de)** ~ summit (meeting)

cura ['kura] *f* cure; *(tratamento)* treatment; *(de carnes etc)* curing, preservation ♦ *m* priest

curar [ku'ra*] *vt (doença, carne)* to cure; *(ferida)* to treat; **curar-se** *vr* to get well

curativo [kura'tʃivu] *m* dressing

curiosidade [kurjozi'dadʒi] *f* curiosity; *(objeto raro)* curio

curioso, -a [ku'rjozu, ɔza] *adj* curious ♦ *m/f* snooper, inquisitive person; ~**s** *mpl (espectadores)* onlookers

curral [ku'xaw] *(pl* **-ais)** *m* pen, enclosure

currículo [ku'xikulu] *m (curriculum)* curriculum vitae

cursar [kux'sa*] *vt (aulas, escola)* to attend; *(cursos)* to follow; **ele está cursando História** he's studying *ou* doing history

curso ['kuxsu] *m* course; *(direção)* direction; **em ~** *(ano etc)* current; *(processo)* in progress

cursor [kux'so*] *m (COMPUT)* cursor

curtição [kuxtʃi'sãw] *(col)* f fun

curtir [kux'tʃi*] *vt (couro)* to tan; *(tornar rijo)* to toughen up; *(padecer)* to suffer, endure; *(col)* to enjoy

curto, -a ['kuxtu, a] *adj* short ♦ *m (ELET)* short (circuit); **curto-circuito** *(pl* **curtos-circuitos)** *m* short circuit

curva ['kuxva] *f* curve; *(de estrada, rio)* bend; ~ **fechada** hairpin bend

curvo, -a [ˈkuxvu, a] *adj* curved; *(estrada)* winding

cuscuz [kuʃˈkuʒ] *m* couscous

cuspe [ˈkuʃpi] *m* spit, spittle

cuspir [kuʃˈpi*] *vt, vi* to spit

custa [ˈkuʃta] *f*: **à ~ de** at the expense of; **~s** *fpl (JUR)* costs

custar [kuʃˈta*] *vi* to cost; *(ser difícil)*: **~ a fazer** to have trouble doing; *(demorar)*: **~ a fazer** to take a long time to do; **~ caro** to be expensive

custo [ˈkuʃtu] *m* cost; **a ~** with difficulty; **a todo ~** at all costs

cutelo [kuˈtɛlu] *m* cleaver

cutícula [kuˈtʃikula] *f* cuticle

cutucar [kutuˈka*] *vt (com o dedo)* to prod, poke; *(com o cotovelo)* to nudge

D

D *abr* = **Dom; Dona;** (= *direito*) r; (= *deve*) d

d/ *abr* = **dia**

da [da] = **de + a**

dá [da] *vb V* **dar**

dactilografar *etc* [datilograˈfa*] *(PT)* = **datilografar** *etc*

dádiva [ˈdadʒiva] *f* donation; *(oferta)* gift

dado, -a [ˈdadu, a] *adj* given; *(sociável)* sociable ♦ *m (em jogo)* die; *(fato)* fact; **~s** *mpl* dice; *(fatos, COMPUT)* data *sg*; **~ que** supposing that; *(uma vez que)* given that

daí [daˈji] *adv* = **de + aí** *(desse lugar)* from there; *(desse momento)* from then; **~ a um mês** a month later

dali [daˈli] *adv* = **de + ali** *(desse lugar)* from there

daltônico, -a [dawˈtoniku, a] *adj* colour-blind *(BRIT)*, color-blind *(US)*

dama [ˈdama] *f* lady; *(XADREZ, CARTAS)*

queen; **~s** *fpl (jogo)* draughts *(BRIT)*, checkers *(US)*; **~ de honra** bridesmaid

damasco [daˈmaʃku] *m* apricot

danado, -a [daˈnadu, a] *adj* damned; *(zangado)* furious; *(menino)* mischievous

dança [ˈdãsa] *f* dance; **dançar** [dãˈsa*] *vi* to dance

danificar [danifiˈka*] *vt* to damage

dano [ˈdanu] *m (tb: ~s)* damage, harm; *(a uma pessoa)* injury

dantes [ˈdãtʃiʃ] *adv* before, formerly

daquele, -a [daˈkeli, a] = **de + aquele/a**

daqui [daˈki] *adv* = **de + aqui** *(deste lugar)* from here; **~ a pouco** soon, in a little while; **~ a uma semana** a week from now; **~ em diante** from now on

daquilo [daˈkilu] = **de + aquilo**

dar [da*] *vt* **1** *(ger)* to give; *(festa)* to hold; *(problemas)* to cause; **~ algo a alguém** to give sb sth, give sth to sb; **~ de beber a alguém** to give sb a drink; **~ aula de francês** to teach French

2 *(produzir: fruta etc)* to produce

3 *(notícias no jornal)* to publish

4 *(cartas)* to deal

5 (+ *n: perífrase de vb*): **me dá medo/pena** it frightens/upsets me ♦ *vi* **1**: **~ com** *(coisa)* to find; *(pessoa)* to meet

2: **~ em** *(bater)* to hit; *(resultar)* to lead to; *(lugar)* to come to

3: **dá no mesmo** it's all the same

4: **~ de si** *(sapatos etc)* to stretch, give

5: **~ para** *(impess: ser possível)*: **dá para trocar dinheiro aqui?** can I change money here?; **vai ~ para eu**

ir amanhã I'll be able to go tomorrow; **dá para você vir amanhã – não, amanhã não vai** ~ can you come tomorrow? – no, I can't

6: ~ **para** (ser suficiente): ~ **para/ para fazer** to be enough for/to do; **dá para todo mundo?** is there enough for everyone?; **dar-se** vr **1** (sair-se): ~**se bem/mal** to do well/ badly

2: ~**se** (com alguém) to be acquainted (with sb); ~**se bem (com alguém)** to get on well (with sb)

3: ~**se por vencido** to give up

das [daʃ] = **de** + **as**

data ['data] f date; (época) time; ~ **de validade** best before date; **datar** [da'ta*] vt to date ♦ vi: **datar de** to date from

datilografar [datʃilogra'fa*] vt to type; **datilografia** [datʃilogra'fia] f typing; **datilógrafo, -a** [datʃi-'lɔgrafu, a] m/f typist (BRIT), stenographer (US)

d.C. abr (= depois de Cristo) A.D.

DDD abr (= discagem direta à distância) STD (BRIT), direct dialling

DDI abr (= discagem direta internacional) IDD, international direct call

─── PALAVRA CHAVE ───

de [dʒi] (de + o(s)/a(s) = do(s)/da(s); + ele(s)/ela(s) = dele(s)/dela(s); + esse(s)/ a(s) = desse(s)/da(s); + isso = disso; + este(s)/a(s) = deste(s)/a(s); + isto = disto; + aquele(s)/a(s) = daquele(s)/ a(s); + aquilo = daquilo) prep **1** (posse) of; **a casa** ~ **João/da irmã** João's/my sister's house; **é dele** it's his; **um romance** ~ a novel by

2 (origem, distância, com números) from; **sou** ~ **São Paulo** I'm from São Paulo; ~ **8 a 20** from 8 to 20; **sair do**

cinema to leave the cinema; ~ **dois em dois** two by two, two at a time

3 (valor descritivo): **um copo** ~ **vinho** a glass of wine; **um homem** ~ **cabelo comprido** a man with long hair; **o infeliz do homem** (col) the poor man; **um bilhete** ~ **avião** an air ticket; **uma criança** ~ **três anos** a three-year-old (child); **uma máquina** ~ **costurar** a sewing machine; **aulas** ~ **inglês** English lessons; **feito** ~ **madeira** made of wood; **vestido** ~ **branco** dressed in white

4 (modo): ~ **trem/avião** by train/ plane; ~ **lado** sideways

5 (hora, tempo): **às 8 da manhã** at 8 o'clock in the morning; ~ **dia/noite** by day/night; ~ **hoje a oito dias** a week from now; ~ **dois em dois dias** every other day

6 (comparações): **mais/menos** ~ **cem pessoas** more/less than a hundred people; **é o mais caro da loja** it's the most expensive in the shop; **ela é mais bonita do que sua irmã** she's prettier than her sister; **gastei mais do que pretendia** I spent more than I intended

7 (causa): **estou morto** ~ **calor** I'm boiling hot; **ela morreu** ~ **câncer** she died of cancer

8 (adj + ~ + infin): **fácil** ~ **entender** easy to understand

dê etc [de] vb V **dar**

debaixo [de'bajʃu] adv below, underneath ♦ prep: ~ **de** under, beneath

debate [de'batʃi] m discussion, debate; (disputa) argument; **debater** [deba'te*] vt to debate, discuss; **debater-se** vr to struggle

débeis ['debejʃ] pl de **débil**

débil ['debiw] (pl -eis) adj weak, feeble ♦ m: ~ **mental** mentally handicapped person; **debilidade** [debili'dadʒi] f weakness; **debilidade mental** mental handicap; **debilitar** [debili'ta*] vt to weaken; **debilitar-se** vr to become weak, weaken; **debilóide** [debi'lɔjdʒi] (col) adj idiotic ♦ m/f idiot

debitar [debi'ta*] vt: ~ $40 à ou na conta de alguém to debit $40 to sb's account; **débito** ['dɛbitu] m debit

debochado, -a [debo'ʃadu, a] adj (pessoa) sardonic; (jeito, tom) mocking

década ['dɛkada] f decade

decadência [deka'dẽsja] f decadence

decair [deka'i*] vi to decline

decapitar [dekapi'ta*] vt to behead, decapitate

decente [de'sẽtʃi] adj decent; (apropriado) proper; (honrado) honourable (BRIT), honorable (US); (trabalho) neat; **decentemente** [desẽtʃi'mẽtʃi] adv decently; properly; hono(u)rably

decepção [desep'sãw] (pl -ões) f disappointment; **decepcionar** [desepsjo'na*] vt to disappoint; (desiludir) to disillusion; **decepcionar-se** vr to be disappointed; to be disillusioned

decidido, -a [desi'dʒidu, a] adj (pessoa) determined; (questão) resolved

decidir [desi'dʒi*] vt to decide; (solucionar) to resolve; **decidir-se** vr: ~-se a to make up one's mind to; ~-se por to decide on, go for

decifrar [desi'fra*] vt to decipher; (futuro) to foretell; (compreender) to understand

decimal [desi'maw] (pl -ais) adj, m decimal

décimo, -a ['dɛsimu, a] adj tenth ♦ m tenth

decisão [desi'zãw] (pl -ões) f decision; **decisivo, -a** [desi'zivu, a] adj (fator) decisive; (jogo) deciding

declaração [deklara'sãw] (pl -ões) f declaration; (depoimento) statement

declarado, -a [dekla'radu, a] adj (intenção) declared; (opinião) professed; (inimigo) sworn; (alcoólatra) self-confessed; (cristão etc) avowed

declarar [dekla'ra*] vt to declare; (confessar) to confess

declinar [dekli'na*] vt (ger) to decline ♦ vi (sol) to go down; (terreno) to slope down; **declínio** [de'klinju] m decline

declive [de'klivi] m slope, incline

decolagem [deko'laʒẽ] (pl -ns) f (AER) take-off

decolar [deko'la*] vi (AER) to take off

decompor [dekõ'po*] (irreg: como **pôr**) vt to analyse; (apodrecer) to rot; **decompor-se** vr to rot, decompose

decomposição [dekõpozi'sãw] (pl -ões) f decomposition; (análise) dissection

decoração [dekora'sãw] f decoration; (TEATRO) scenery

decorar [deko'ra*] vt to decorate; (aprender) to learn by heart; **decorativo, -a** [dekora'tʃivu, a] adj decorative

decoro [de'koru] m decency; (dignidade) decorum

decorrente [deko'xẽtʃi] adj: ~ de resulting from

decorrer [deko'xe*] vi (tempo) to pass; (acontecer) to take place, happen ♦ m: no ~ de in the course of; ~ de to result from

decrescer [dekre'se*] vi to decrease, diminish

decretar [dekre'ta*] vt to decree, order; **decreto** [de'krɛtu] m decree, order; **decreto-lei** (pl **decretos-leis**) m act, law

dedal [de'daw] (pl **-ais**) m thimble

dedetizar [dedetʃi'za*] vt to spray with insecticide

dedicação [dedʒika'sãw] f dedication; (devotamento) devotion

dedicar [dedʒi'ka*] vt to dedicate; (tempo, atenção) to devote; **dedicar-se** vr: **~-se a** to devote o.s. to; **dedicatória** [dedʒika'tɔrja] f (de obra) dedication

dedo ['dedu] m finger; (do pé) toe; **~ anular/indicador/mínimo** ou **mindinho** ring/index/little finger; **~ polegar** thumb

dedução [dedu'sãw] (pl **-ões**) f deduction

deduzir [dedu'zi*] vt to deduct; (concluir) to deduce, infer

defasagem [defa'zaʒẽ] (pl **-ns**) f discrepancy

defeito [de'fejtu] m defect, flaw; **pôr ~s em** to find fault with; **com ~** broken, out of order; **para ninguém botar ~** (col) perfect; **defeituoso, -a** [defej'twozu, ɔza] adj defective, faulty

defender [defẽ'de*] vt to defend; **defender-se** vr to stand up for o.s.; (numa língua) to get by

defensiva [defẽ'siva] f: **estar** ou **ficar na ~** to be on the defensive

defensor, a [defẽ'so*, a] m/f defender; (JUR) defending counsel

defesa [de'feza] f defence (BRIT), defense (US); (JUR) counsel for the defence ♦ m (FUTEBOL) back

deficiente [defi'sjētʃi] adj (imperfeito) defective; (carente): **~ (em)** deficient (in)

déficit ['dɛfisitʃi] (pl **-s**) m deficit

definição [defini'sãw] (pl **-ões**) f definition

definir [defi'ni*] vt to define; **definir-se** vr to make a decision; (explicar-se) to make one's position clear; **~-se a favor de/contra algo** to come out in favo(u)r of/against sth

definitivamente [definitʃiva'metʃi] adv definitively; (permanentemente) for good; (sem dúvida) definitely

definitivo, -a [defini'tʃivu, a] adj final, definitive; (permanente) permanent; (resposta, data) definite

deformação [defoxma'sãw] (pl **-ões**) f loss of shape; (de corpo) deformation; (de imagem, pensamento) distortion

deformar [defox'ma*] vt to put out of shape; (corpo) to deform; (imagem, pensamento) to distort; **deformar-se** vr to lose shape; to be deformed; to become distorted

defronte [de'frõtʃi] adv opposite ♦ prep: **~ de** opposite

defumar [defu'ma*] vt (presunto) to smoke; (perfumar) to perfume

defunto, -a [de'fũtu, a] adj dead ♦ m/f dead person

degelar [deʒe'la*] vt to thaw; (geladeira) to defrost ♦ vi to thaw out; to defrost

degenerar [deʒene'ra*] vi: **~ (em)** to degenerate (into)

degolar [dego'la*] vt to decapitate

degradar [degra'da*] vt to degrade, debase; **degradar-se** vr to demean o.s.

degrau [de'graw] m step; (de escada de mão) rung

degustação [deguʃta'sãw] (pl **-ões**) f tasting, sampling; (saborear) savouring (BRIT), savoring (US)

degustar [deguʃ'ta*] vt (provar) to

taste; (*saborear*) to savour (BRIT), savor (US)
dei *etc* [dej] *vb* V **dar**
deitada [dej'tada] (*col*) *f*: **dar uma ~** to have a lie-down
deitado, -a [dej'tadu, a] *adj* (*estendido*) lying down; (*na cama*) in bed
deitar [dej'ta*] *vt* to lay down; (*na cama*) to put to bed; (*colocar*) to put, place; (*lançar*) to cast; (PT: *líquido*) to pour; **deitar-se** *vr* to lie down; to go to bed; **~ sangue** (PT) to bleed; **~ abaixo** to knock down, flatten; **~ a fazer algo** to start doing sth; **~ uma carta** (PT) to post a letter; **~ fora** to throw away ou out; **~ e rolar** (*col*) to do as one likes
deixa ['dejʃa] *f* clue, hint; (TEATRO) cue; (*chance*) chance
deixar [dej'ʃa*] *vt* to leave; (*abandonar*) to abandon; (*permitir*) to allow ♦ *vi*: **~ de** (*parar*) to stop; (*não fazer*) to fail to; **não posso ~ de ir** I must go; **~ cair** to drop; **~ alguém louco** to drive sb crazy ou mad; **~ alguém cansado/nervoso** *etc* to make sb tired/nervous *etc*; **deixa disso!** (*col*) come off it!; **deixa para lá!** (*col*) forget it!
dela ['dɛla] = **de + ela**
delatar [dela'ta*] *vt* (*pessoa*) to inform on; (*abusos*) to reveal; (à *polícia*) to report; **delator, a** [dela'to*, a] *m/f* informer
dele ['deli] = **de + ele**
delegacia [delega'sia] *f* office; **~ de polícia** police station
delegado, -a [dele'gadu, a] *m/f* delegate, representative; **~ de polícia** police chief
delegar [dele'ga*] *vt* to delegate
deleitar [delej'ta*] *vt* to delight; **deleitar-se** *vr*: **~-se com** to delight in
delgado, -a [dew'gadu, a] *adj* thin;

(*esbelto*) slim; (*fino*) fine
deliberação [delibera'sãw] (*pl* **-ões**) *f* deliberation; (*decisão*) decision
deliberar [delibe'ra*] *vt* to decide, resolve ♦ *vi* to deliberate
delicadeza [delika'deza] *f* delicacy; (*cortesia*) kindness
delicado, -a [deli'kadu, a] *adj* delicate; (*frágil*) fragile; (*cortês*) polite; (*sensível*) sensitive
delícia [de'lisja] *f* delight; (*prazer*) pleasure; **que ~!** how lovely!; **deliciar** [deli'sja*] *vt* to delight; **deliciar-se** *vr*: **deliciar-se com algo** to take delight in sth
delicioso, -a [deli'sjozu, ɔza] *adj* lovely; (*comida, bebida*) delicious
delinear [deli'nja*] *vt* to outline
delinqüente [delĩ'kwẽtʃi] *adj, m/f* delinquent, criminal
delirante [deli'rãtʃi] *adj* delirious; (*show, atuação*) thrilling
delirar [deli'ra*] *vi* (*com febre*) to be delirious; (*de ódio, prazer*) to go mad, go wild
delírio [de'lirju] *m* (MED) delirium; (*êxtase*) ecstasy; (*excitação*) excitement
delito [de'litu] *m* (*crime*) crime; (*falta*) offence (BRIT), offense (US)
demais [dʒi'majʃ] *adv* (*em demasia*) too much; (*muitíssimo*) a lot, very much ♦ *pron*: **os/as ~** the rest (of them); **já é ~!** this is too much!; **é bom ~** it's really good; **foi ~** (*col*: *bacana*) it was great
demanda [de'mãda] *f* lawsuit; (*disputa*) claim; (*requisição*) request; (ECON) demand; **em ~ de** in search of; **demandar** [demã'da*] *vt* (JUR) to sue; (*exigir, reclamar*) to demand
demasia [dema'zia] *f* excess, surplus; (*imoderação*) lack of moderation; **em ~** (*dinheiro, comida etc*) too

much; (*cartas, problemas etc*) too many

demasiadamente [demazjada-ˈmẽtʃi] *adv* too much; (*com adj*) too

demasiado, -a [demaˈzjadu, a] *adj* too much; (*pl*) too many ♦ *adv* too much; (*com adj*) too

demente [deˈmẽtʃi] *adj* insane, demented

demissão [demiˈsãw] (*pl* -ões) *f* dismissal; **pedir ~** to resign

demitir [demiˈtʃi*] *vt* to dismiss; (*col*) to sack, fire; **demitir-se** *vr* to resign

democracia [demokraˈsia] *f* democracy

democrático, -a [demoˈkratʃiku, a] *adj* democratic

demolir [demoˈli*] *vt* to demolish, knock down; (*fig*) to destroy

demônio [deˈmonju] *m* devil, demon; (*col: criança*) brat

demonstração [demõʃtraˈsãw] (*pl* -ões) *f* demonstration; (*de amizade*) show, display; (*prova*) proof

demonstrar [demõʃˈtra*] *vt* to demonstrate; (*provar*) to prove; (*amizade etc*) to show

demora [deˈmɔra] *f* delay; (*parada*) stop; **sem ~** at once, without delay; **qual é a ~ disso?** how long will this take?; **demorado, -a** [demoˈradu, a] *adj* slow; **demorar** [demoˈra*] *vt* to delay, slow down ♦ *vi* (*permanecer*) to stay; (*tardar a vir*) to be late; (*conserto*) to take (a long) time; **demorar-se** *vr* to stay for a long time, linger; **demorar a chegar** to be a long time coming; **vai demorar muito?** will it take long?; **não vou demorar** I won't be long

dendê [dẽˈde] *m* (*CULIN: óleo*) palm oil; (*BOT*) oil palm

dengoso, -a [dẽˈgozu, ɔza] *adj* coy; (*criança: choramingueiro*): **ser ~** to

be a crybaby

dengue [ˈdẽgi] *m* (*MED*) dengue

denominar [denomiˈna*] *vt*: **~ algo/alguém ...** to call sth/sb ...; **denominar-se** *vr* to be called; (*a si mesmo*) to call o.s.

denotar [denoˈta*] *vt* (*indicar*) to show, indicate; (*significar*) to signify

densidade [dẽsiˈdadʒi] *f* density; **disco de ~ simples/dupla** (*COMPUT*) single-/double-density disk

denso, -a [ˈdẽsu, a] *adj* dense; (*espesso*) thick; (*compacto*) compact

dentada [dẽˈtada] *f* bite

dentadura [dẽtaˈdura] *f* teeth *pl*, set of teeth; (*artificial*) dentures *pl*

dente [ˈdẽtʃi] *m* tooth; (*de animal*) fang; (*de elefante*) tusk; (*de alho*) clove; **falar entre os ~s** to mutter, mumble; **~ de leite/do siso** milk/wisdom tooth; **~ postiços** false teeth

dentista [dẽˈtʃiʃta] *m/f* dentist

dentre [ˈdẽtri] *prep* (from) among

dentro [ˈdẽtru] *adv* inside ♦ *prep*: **~ de** inside; (*tempo*) (with)in; **~ em pouco** *ou* **em breve** soon, before long; **de ~ para fora** inside out; **dar uma ~** (*col*) to get it right; **aí ~** in there; **por ~** on the inside; **estar por ~** (*col: fig*) to be in the know

denúncia [deˈnũsja] *f* denunciation; (*acusação*) accusation; (*de roubo*) report; **denunciar** [denũˈsja*] *vt* (*acusar*) to denounce; (*delatar*) to inform on; (*revelar*) to reveal

deparar [depaˈra*] *vt* to reveal; (*fazer aparecer*) to present ♦ *vi*: **~ com** to come across, meet; **deparar-se** *vr*: **~-se com** to come across, meet

departamento [depaxtaˈmẽtu] *m* department

dependência [depẽˈdẽsja] *f* dependence; (*edificação*) annexe

(*BRIT*), annex (*US*); (*colonial*) dependency; (*cômodo*) room

dependente [depẽ'dẽtʃi] m/f dependant

depender [depẽ'de*] vi: ~ **de** to depend on

depilar [depi'la*] vt (*pernas*) to wax; **depilatório** [depila'tɔrju] m hair-remover

deplorável [deplo'ravew] (*pl -eis*) adj deplorable; (*lamentável*) regrettable

depoimento [depoj'mẽtu] m testimony, evidence; (*na polícia*) statement

depois [de'pojʃ] adv afterwards ♦ prep: ~ **de** after; ~ **de comer** after eating; ~ **que** after

depor [de'po*] (*irreg: como pôr*) vt (*pôr*) to place; (*indicar*) to indicate; (*rei*) to depose; (*governo*) to overthrow ♦ vi (*JUR*) to testify, give evidence; (*na polícia*) to give a statement

depositar [depozi'ta*] vt to deposit; (*voto*) to cast; (*colocar*) to place

depósito [de'pɔzitu] m deposit; (*armazém*) warehouse, depot; (*de lixo*) dump; (*reservatório*) tank; ~ **de bagagens** left-luggage office (*BRIT*), checkroom (*US*)

depreciação [depresja'sãw] f depreciation

depreciar [depre'sja*] vt (*desvalorizar*) to devalue; (*COM*) to write down; (*menosprezar*) to belittle; **depreciar-se** vr to depreciate, lose value

depredar [depre'da*] vt to wreck

depressa [dʒi'prɛsa] adv fast, quickly; **vamos ~** let's get a move on!

depressão [depre'sãw] (*pl -ões*) f depression

deprimente [depri'mẽtʃi] adj depressing

deprimido, -a [depri'midu, a] adj depressed

deprimir [depri'mi*] vt to depress; **deprimir-se** vr to get depressed

deputado, -a [depu'tadu, a] m/f deputy; (*agente*) agent (*POL*) = Member of Parliament (*BRIT*), ≈ Representative (*US*)

der etc [de*] vb V **dar**

deriva [de'riva] f drift; **ir à ~** to drift; **ficar à ~** to be adrift

derivar [deri'va*] vt to divert; (*LING*) to derive ♦ vi to drift; **derivar-se** vr to be derived; (*ir à deriva*) to drift; (*provir*): ~(**-se**) (**de**) to derive ou be derived (from)

derradeiro, -a [dexa'dejru, a] adj last, final

derramamento [dexama'mẽtu] m spilling; (*de sangue, lágrimas*) shedding

derramar [dexa'ma*] vt to spill; (*entornar*) to pour; (*sangue, lágrimas*) to shed; **derramar-se** vr to pour out

derrame [de'xami] m haemorrhage (*BRIT*), hemorrhage (*US*)

derrapar [dexa'pa*] vi to skid

derreter [dexe'te*] vt to melt; **derreter-se** vr to melt; (*coisa congelada*) to thaw; (*enternecer-se*) to be touched

derrota [de'xɔta] f defeat, rout; (*NÁUT*) route; **derrotar** [dexo'ta*] vt (*vencer*) to defeat; (*em jogo*) to beat

derrubar [dexu'ba*] vt to knock down; (*governo*) to bring down; (*suj: doença*) to lay low; (*col: prejudicar*) to put down

desabafar [dʒizaba'fa*] vt (*sentimentos*) to give vent to ♦ vi: ~ (**com**) to unburden o.s. (to); **desabafar-se** vr: ~**-se** (**com**) to unburden o.s.

(to); **desabafo** [dʒiza'bafu] *m* confession

desabamento [dʒizaba'mẽtu] *m* collapse

desabar [dʒiza'ba*] *vi* (*edifício, ponte*) to collapse; (*chuva*) to pour down; (*tempestade*) to break

desabitado, -a [dʒizabi'tadu, a] *adj* uninhabited

desabotoar [dʒizabo'twa*] *vt* to unbutton

desabrigado, -a [dʒizabri'gadu, a] *adj* (*sem casa*) homeless; (*exposto*) exposed

desabrochar [dʒizabro'ʃa*] *vi* (*flores, fig*) to blossom

desacatar [dʒizaka'ta*] *vt* (*desrespeitar*) to have *ou* show no respect for; (*afrontar*) to defy; (*desprezar*) to scorn; **desacato** [dʒiza'katu] *m* disrespect; (*desprezo*) disregard

desacompanhado, -a [dʒiza-kõpa'ɲadu, a] *adj* on one's own, alone

desaconselhar [dʒizakõse'ʎa*] *vt*: ~ **algo (a alguém)** to advise (sb) against sth

desacordado, -a [dʒizakox'dadu, a] *adj* unconscious

desacordo [dʒiza'koxdu] *m* disagreement; (*desarmonia*) discord

desacostumado, -a [dʒizakoʃtu-'madu, a] *adj*: ~ **(a)** unaccustomed (to)

desacreditar [dʒizakredʒi'ta*] *vt* to discredit; **desacreditar-se** *vr* to lose one's reputation

desafiador, a [dʒizafja'do*, a] *adj* challenging; (*pessoa*) defiant ♦ *m/f* challenger

desafiar [dʒiza'fja*] *vt* to challenge; (*afrontar*) to defy

desafinado, -a [dʒizafi'nadu, a] *adj* out of tune

desafio [dʒiza'fiu] *m* challenge; (*PT: ESPORTE*) match, game

desaforado, -a [dʒizafo'radu, a] *adj* rude, insolent

desaforo [dʒiza'foru] *m* insolence, abuse

desafortunado, -a [dʒizafoxtu-'nadu, a] *adj* unfortunate, unlucky

desagradar [dʒizagra'da*] *vt* to displease ♦ *vi*: ~ **a alguém** to displease sb; **desagradável** [dʒiza-gra'davew] (*pl* -**eis**) *adj* unpleasant; **desagrado** [dʒiza'gradu] *m* displeasure

desaguar [dʒiza'gwa*] *vt* to drain ♦ *vi*: ~ **(em)** to flow *ou* empty (into)

desajeitado, -a [dʒizaʒej'tadu, a] *adj* clumsy, awkward

desalentado, -a [dʒizalẽ'tadu, a] *adj* disheartened

desalentar [dʒizalẽ'ta*] *vt* to discourage; (*deprimir*) to depress; **desalento** [dʒiza'lẽtu] *m* discouragement

desalinhado, -a [dʒizali'ɲadu, a] *adj* untidy

desalinho [dʒiza'liɲu] *m* untidiness

desalmado, -a [dʒizaw'madu, a] *adj* cruel, inhuman

desalojar [dʒizalo'ʒa*] *vt* (*expulsar*) to oust; **desalojar-se** *vr* to move out

desamarrar [dʒizama'xa*] *vt* to untie ♦ *vi* (*NÁUT*) to cast off

desamor [dʒiza'mo*] *m* dislike

desamparado, -a [dʒizãpa'radu, a] *adj* abandoned; (*sem apoio*) helpless

desanimação [dʒizanima'sãw] *f* dejection

desanimado, -a [dʒizani'madu, a] *adj* (*pessoa*) fed up, dispirited; (*festa*) dull; **ser** ~ (*pessoa*) to be apathetic

desanimar [dʒizani'ma*] *vt* to dishearten; (*desencorajar*) to ~ **(de fazer)** to discourage (from doing) ♦ *vi* to lose heart; to be discouraging; ~ **de**

fazer algo to lose the will to do sth; (*desistir*) to give up doing sth

desanuviar [dʒizanu'vja*] *vt* (*céu*) to clear; **desanuviar-se** *vr* to clear; (*fig*) to stop; **desanuviar alguém** to put sb's mind at rest

desaparafusar [dʒizaparafu'za*] *vt* to unscrew

desaparecer [dʒizapare'se*] *vi* to disappear, vanish; **desaparecido, -a** [dʒizapare'sidu, a] *adj* lost, missing ♦ *m/f* missing person; **desaparecimento** [dʒizaparesi'mẽtu] *m* disappearance; (*falecimento*) death

desapego [dʒiza'pegu] *m* indifference, detachment

desapercebido, -a [dʒizapexse'bidu, a] *adj* unnoticed

desapertar [dʒizapex'ta*] *vt* to loosen; (*livrar*) to free

desapontamento [dʒizapõta'mẽtu] *m* disappointment

desapontar [dʒizapõ'ta*] *vt* to disappoint

desapropriar [dʒizapro'prja*] *vt* (*bens*) to expropriate; (*pessoa*) to dispossess

desaprovar [dʒizapro'va*] *vt* to disapprove of; (*censurar*) to censure

desarmamento [dʒizaxma'mẽtu] *m* disarmament

desarmar [dʒizax'ma*] *vt* to disarm; (*desmontar*) to dismantle; (*bomba*) to defuse

desarmonia [dʒizaxmo'nia] *f* discord

desarranjo [dʒiza'xãʒu] *m* disorder; (*enguiço*) breakdown; (*diarréia*) diarrhoea (*BRIT*), diarrhea (*US*)

desarrumado, -a [dʒizaxu'madu, a] *adj* untidy, messy

desarrumar [dʒizaxu'ma*] *vt* to mess up; (*mala*) to unpack

desassossego [dʒizaso'segu] *m*

(*inquietação*) disquiet; (*perturbação*) restlessness

desastrado, -a [dʒizaʃ'tradu, a] *adj* clumsy

desastre [dʒi'zaʃtri] *m* disaster; (*acidente*) accident; (*de avião*) crash

desatar [dʒiza'ta*] *vt* (*nó*) to undo, untie ♦ *vi*: ~ **a fazer** to begin to do; ~ **a chorar** to burst into tears; ~ **a rir** to burst out laughing

desatento, -a [dʒiza'tẽtu, a] *adj* inattentive

desatinado, -a [dʒizatʃi'nadu, a] *adj* crazy, wild ♦ *m/f* lunatic

desatino [dʒiza'tʃinu] *m* madness; (*ato*) folly

desativar [dʒizatʃi'va*] *vt* (*firma*, *usina*) to shut down; (*veículos*) to withdraw from service; (*bomba*) to deactivate, defuse

desatualizado, -a [dʒizatwali'zadu, a] *adj* out of date; (*pessoa*) out of touch

desavença [dʒiza'vẽsa] *f* (*briga*) quarrel; (*discórdia*) disagreement; **em ~** at loggerheads

desavergonhado, -a [dʒiza-vexgo'ɲadu, a] *adj* shameless

desavisado, -a [dʒizavi'zadu, a] *adj* careless

desbastar [dʒiʒbaʃ'ta*] *vt* (*cabelo*, *plantas*) to thin (out); (*vegetação*) to trim

desbocado, -a [dʒiʒbo'kadu, a] *adj* foul-mouthed

desbotar [dʒiʒbo'ta*] *vt* to discolour (*BRIT*), discolor (*US*) ♦ *vi* to fade

desbragadamente [dʒiʒbragada-'mẽtʃi] *adv* (*beber*) to excess; (*mentir*) blatantly

desbravar [dʒiʒbra'va*] *vt* (*terras desconhecidas*) to explore

descabelar [dʒiʃkabe'la*] *vt*: ~ **alguém** to mess up sb's hair; **descabelar-se** *vr* to get one's hair messed up

descabido, -a [dʒiʃka'bidu, a] adj improper; (inoportuno) inappropriate

descafeinado [dʒiʃkafej'nadu] adj decaffeinated ♦ n decaff

descalçar [dʒiʃkaw'sa*] vt (sapatos) to take off; **descalçar-se** vr to take off one's shoes

descalço, -a [dʒiʃ'kawsu, a] adj barefoot

descansado, -a [dʒiʃkã'sadu, a] adj calm, quiet; (vagaroso) slow; **fique ~** don't worry; **pode ficar ~ que** ... you can rest assured that ...

descansar [dʒiʃkã'sa*] vt to rest; (apoiar) to lean ♦ vi to rest; to lean; **descanso** [dʒiʃ'kãsu] m rest; (folga) break; (para prato) mat

descarado, -a [dʒiʃka'radu, a] adj cheeky, impudent

descaramento [dʒiʃkara'mẽtu] m cheek, impudence

descarga [dʒiʃ'kaxga] f unloading; (MIL) volley; (ELET) discharge; (de vaso sanitário): **dar a ~** to flush the toilet

descarregamento [dʒiʃkaxega'mẽtu] m (de carga) unloading; (ELET) discharge

descarregar [dʒiʃkaxe'ga*] vt (carga) to unload; (ELET) to discharge; (aliviar) to relieve; (raiva) to vent, give vent to; (arma) to fire ♦ vi to unload; (bateria) to run out; **~ a raiva em alguém** to take it out on sb

descartar [dʒiʃkax'ta*] vt to discard; **descartar-se** vr: **~-se de** to get rid of; **descartável** [dʒiʃkax'tavew] (pl -eis) disposable

descascar [dʒiʃkaʃ'ka*] vt (fruta) to peel; (ervilhas) to shell ♦ vi (depois do sol) to peel; (cobra) to shed its skin

descaso [dʒiʃ'kazu] m disregard

descendência [desẽ'dẽsja] f descendants pl, offspring pl

descendente [desẽ'dẽtʃi] adj descending, going down ♦ m/f descendant

descer [de'se*] vt (escada) to go (ou come) down; (bagagem) to take down ♦ vi (saltar) to get off; (baixar) to go (ou come) down; **descida** [de'sida] f descent; (declive) slope; (abaixamento) fall, drop

desclassificar [dʒiʃklasifi'ka*] vt to disqualify; (desacreditar) to discredit

descoberta [dʒiʃko'bexta] f discovery; (invenção) invention

descoberto, -a [dʒiʃko'bextu, a] pp de **descobrir** ♦ adj bare, naked; (exposto) exposed ♦ m overdraft; **a ~** openly; **conta a ~** overdrawn account; **pôr ou sacar a ~** (conta) to overdraw

descobridor, a [dʒiʃkobri'do*, a] m/f discoverer; (explorador) explorer

descobrimento [dʒiʃkobri'mẽtu] m discovery; **D~s** mpl: **os D~s** the Discoveries; see boxed note

---

DESCOBRIMENTOS

Portugal enjoyed a period of unrivalled overseas expansion during the 15th century, mainly due to the seafaring expertise of Henry the Navigator. He organized and financed several voyages to Africa, which eventually led to the rounding of the Cape of Good Hope in 1488 by Bartolomeu Dias. In 1497, Vasco da Gama became the first European to travel by sea to India, where he established a lucrative spice trade, and a few years later, in 1500, Pedro Álvares Cabral reached Brazil, which he claimed for Portugal. Brazil remained under Portuguese rule until 1822.

---

descobrir [dʒiʃko'bri*] vt to discover; (tirar a cobertura de) to uncover; (panela) to take the lid off;

(*averiguar*) to find out; (*enigma*) to solve

descolar [dʒiʃko'la*] *vt* to unstick ♦ *vi*: **a criança não descola da mãe** the child won't leave his (*ou* her) mother's side

descolorante [dʒiʃkolo'rãtʃi] *m* bleach

descolorir [dʒiʃkolo'ri*] *vt* to discolour (*BRIT*), discolor (*US*); (*cabelo*) to bleach ♦ *vi* to fade

descompostura [dʒiʃkõpoʃ'tura] *f* (*repreensão*) dressing-down; (*insulto*) abuse; **passar uma ~ em alguém** to give sb a dressing-down; to hurl abuse at sb

descomunal [dʒiʃkomu'naw] (*pl* **-ais**) *adj* extraordinary; (*colossal*) huge, enormous

desconcentrar [dʒiʃkõsẽ'tra*] *vt* to distract; **desconcentrar-se** *vr* to lose one's concentration

desconexo, -a [dʒiʃko'neksu, a] *adj* (*desunido*) disconnected, unrelated; (*incoerente*) incoherent

desconfiado, -a [dʒiʃko'fjadu, a] *adj* suspicious, distrustful ♦ *m/f* suspicious person

desconfiança [dʒiʃkõ'fjãsa] *f* suspicion, distrust

desconfiar [dʒiʃkõ'fja*] *vi* to be suspicious; **~ de alguém** (*não ter confiança em*) to distrust sb; (*suspeitar*) to suspect sb; **~ que ...** to have the feeling that ...

desconfortável [dʒiʃkõfoʃ'tavew] (*pl* **-eis**) *adj* uncomfortable

desconforto [dʒiʃkõ'foxtu] *m* discomfort

descongelar [dʒiʃkõʒe'la*] *vt* to thaw out; **descongelar-se** *vr* to melt

desconhecer [dʒiʃkoɲe'se*] *vt* (*ignorar*) not to know; (*não reconhecer*) not to recognize; (*um benefício*)

not to acknowledge; (*não admitir*) not to accept; **desconhecido, -a** [dʒiʃkoɲe'sidu, a] *adj* unknown ♦ *m/f* stranger; **desconhecimento** [dʒiʃkoɲesi'mẽtu] *m* ignorance

desconsolado, -a [dʒiʃkõso'ladu, a] *adj* miserable, disconsolate

descontar [dʒiʃkõ'ta*] *vt* to deduct; (*não levar em conta*) to discount; (*não fazer caso de*) to make light of

descontentamento [dʒiʃkõtẽta'mẽtu] *m* discontent; (*desprazer*) displeasure

descontente [dʒiʃkõ'tẽtʃi] *adj* discontented, dissatisfied

desconto [dʒiʃ'kõtu] *m* discount; **com ~** at a discount; **dar um ~ (para)** (*fig*) to make allowances (for)

descontraído, -a [dʒiʃkõtra'idu, a] *adj* casual, relaxed

descontrair [dʒiʃkõtra'i*] *vt* to relax; **descontrair-se** *vr* to relax

descontrolar-se [dʒiʃkõtro'laxsi] *vr* (*situação*) to get out of control; (*pessoa*) to lose one's self-control

desconversar [dʒiʃkõvex'sa*] *vi* to change the subject

descortesia [dʒiʃkoxte'zia] *f* rudeness, impoliteness

descoser [dʒiʃko'ze*] *vt* (*descosturar*) to unstitch; (*rasgar*) to rip apart; **descoser-se** *vr* to come apart at the seams

descrença [dʒiʃ'krẽsa] *f* disbelief, incredulity

descrente [dʒiʃ'krẽtʃi] *adj* sceptical (*BRIT*), skeptical (*US*) ♦ *m/f* sceptic (*BRIT*), skeptic (*US*)

descrever [dʒiʃkre've*] *vt* to describe

descrição [dʒiʃkri'sãw] (*pl* **-ões**) *f* description; **descritivo, -a** [dʒiʃkri'tʃivu, a] *adj* descriptive

descrito, -a [dʒiʃˈkritu, a] *pp de* **descrever**

descubro *etc* [dʒiʃˈkubru] *vb V* **descobrir**

descuidado, -a [dʒiʃkwiˈdadu, a] *adj* careless

descuidar [dʒiʃkwiˈda*] *vt* to neglect ♦ *vi*: **~ de** to neglect, disregard; **descuido** [dʒiʃˈkwidu] *m* carelessness; *(negligência)* neglect; *(erro)* oversight, slip; **por descuido** inadvertently

desculpa [dʒiʃˈkuwpa] *f* excuse; *(perdão)* pardon; **pedir ~s a alguém por** *ou* **de algo** to apologise to sb for sth; **desculpar** [dʒiʃkuwˈpa*] *vt* to excuse; *(perdoar)* to pardon, forgive; **desculpar-se** *vr* to apologize; **desculpar algo a alguém** to forgive sb for sth; **desculpe!** (I'm) sorry, I beg your pardon; **desculpável** [dʒiʃkuwˈpavew] *(pl* -**eis**) *adj* forgivable

PALAVRA CHAVE

desde [ˈdeʒdʒi] *prep* **1** *(lugar)*: **~ até ...** from ... to ...; **andamos ~ a praia até o restaurante** we walked from the beach to the restaurant

2 *(tempo:* + *adv, n)*: **~ então** from then on, ever since; **~ já** *(de agora)* from now on; *(imediatamente)* at once, right now; **~ o casamento** since the wedding

3 *(tempo:* + *vb)* since; for; **conhecemo-nos ~ 1978/há 20 anos** we've known each other since 1978/for 20 years; **não o vejo ~ 1983** I haven't seen him since 1983

4 *(variedade)*: **~ os mais baratos até os mais luxuosos** from the cheapest to the most luxurious ♦ *conj*: **~ que** since; **~ que comecei a trabalhar não o vi mais** I haven't

seen him since I started work; **não saiu de casa ~ que chegou** he hasn't been out since he arrived

desdém [deʒˈdẽ] *m* scorn, disdain

desdenhar [deʒdeˈɲa*] *vt* to scorn, disdain

desdizer [dʒiʒdʒiˈze*] *(irreg: como dizer)* *vt* to contradict; **desdizer-se** *vr* to go back on one's word

desdobrar [dʒiʒdoˈbra*] *vt (abrir)* to unfold; *(esforços)* to increase, redouble; *(tropas)* to deploy; *(bandeira)* to unfurl; *(dividir em grupos)* to split up; **desdobrar-se** *vr* to unfold; *(empenhar-se)* to work hard, make a big effort

desejar [deseˈʒa*] *vt* to want, desire

desejo [deˈzeʒu] *m* wish, desire; **desejoso, -a** [dezeˈʒozu, ɔza] *adj*: **desejoso de algo** wishing for sth; **desejoso de fazer** keen to do

desembaraçar [dʒizẽbaraˈsa*] *vt (livrar)* to free; *(cabelo)* to untangle; **desembaraçar-se** *vr (desinibir-se)* to lose one's inhibitions; **~-se de** to get rid of

desembaraço [dʒizẽbaˈrasu] *m* liveliness; *(facilidade)* ease; *(confiança)* self-assurance

desembarcar [dʒizẽbaxˈka*] *vt (carga)* to unload; *(passageiros)* to let off ♦ *vi* to disembark; **desembarque** [dʒizẽˈbaxki] *m* landing, disembarkation; **"desembarque"** *(no aeroporto)* "arrivals"

desembolsar [dʒizẽbowˈsa*] *vt* to spend

desembrulhar [dʒizẽbruˈʎa*] *vt* to unwrap

desempacotar [dʒizẽpakoˈta*] *vt* to unpack

desempatar [dʒizẽpaˈta*] *vt* to decide ♦ *vi* to decide the match *(ou* race *etc)*; **desempate** [dʒizẽˈpatʃi] m: **partida de desempate** (jogo) play-off, decider

desempenhar [dʒizẽpe'na*] vt (cumprir) to carry out, fulfil (BRIT), fulfill (US); (papel) to play; **desempenho** [dʒize'peɲu] m performance; (de obrigações etc) fulfilment (BRIT), fulfillment (US)

desempregado, -a [dʒizẽpre-'gadu, a] adj unemployed ♦ m/f unemployed person

desempregar-se [dʒizẽpre'gaxsi] vr to lose one's job

desemprego [dʒize'pregu] m unemployment

desencadear [dʒizẽka'dʒja*] vt to unleash; (despertar) to provoke, trigger off ♦ vi (chuva) to pour; **desencadear-se** vr to break loose; (tempestade) to break

desencaixar [dʒizẽkaj'ʃa*] vt to put out of joint; (deslocar) to dislodge; **desencaixar-se** vr to become dislodged

desencaixotar [dʒizẽkajʃo'ta*] vt to unpack

desencarregar-se [dʒizẽkaxe-'gaxsi] vr (de obrigação) to discharge o.s.

desencontrar-se [dʒizẽkõ'traxsi] vr (não se encontrar) to miss each other; (perder-se um do outro: perder-se) to lose each other; **~ de** to miss; to get separated from

desencorajar [dʒizẽkora'ʒa*] vt to discourage

desencostar [dʒizẽkoʃ'ta*] vt to move away; **desencostar-se** vr: **desencostar-se de** to move away from

desenfreado, -a [dʒizẽ'frjadu, a] adj wild

desenganado, -a [dʒizẽga'nadu, a] adj incurable; (desiludido) disillusioned

desenganar [dʒizẽga'na*] vt: **~ alguém** to disillusion sb; (de falsas crenças) to open sb's eyes; (doente) to give up hope of curing; **desenganar-se** vr to become disillusioned; (sair de erro) to realize the truth; **desengano** [dʒizẽ'ganu] m disillusionment; (desapontamento) disappointment

desengonçado, -a [dʒizẽgõ'sadu, a] adj (mal-seguro) rickety; (pessoa) ungainly

desenhar [deze'ɲa*] vt to draw; (TEC) to design; **desenhar-se** vr (destacar-se) to stand out; (figurar-se) to take shape; **desenhista** [deze'niʃta] m/f (TEC) designer

desenho [de'zeɲu] m drawing; (modelo) design; (esboço) sketch; (plano) plan; **~ animado** cartoon

desenlace [dʒizẽ'lasi] m outcome

desenrolar [dʒizẽxo'la*] vt to unroll; (narrativa) to develop; **desenrolar-se** vr to unfold

desentender [dʒizẽtẽ'de*] vt to misunderstand; **desentender-se** vr: **~-se com** to have a disagreement with; **desentendido, -a** [dʒizẽtẽ'dʒidu, a] adj: **fazer-se de desentendido** to pretend not to understand; **desentendimento** [dʒizẽtẽdʒi'mẽtu] m misunderstanding

desenterrar [dʒizẽte'xa*] vt (cadáver) to exhume; (tesouro) to dig up; (descobrir) to bring to light

desentupir [dʒizẽtu'pi*] vt to unblock

desenvoltura [dʒizẽvow'tura] f self-confidence

desenvolver [dʒizẽvow've*] vt to develop; **desenvolver-se** vr to develop; **desenvolvimento** [dʒizẽvowvi'mẽtu] m development; (crescimento) growth; **país em**

desenvolvimento developing country

desequilibrado, -a [dʒizekili'bradu, a] *adj* unbalanced

deserção [dezex'sãw] *f* desertion

desertar [desex'ta*] *vt* to desert, abandon ♦ *vi* to desert; **deserto, -a** [de'zextu, a] *adj* deserted ♦ *m* desert; **desertor, a** [dezex'to*, a] *m/f* deserter

desesperado, -a [dʒizeʃpe'radu, a] *adj* desperate; (*furioso*) furious

desesperador, a [dʒizeʃpera'do*, a] *adj* desperate; (*enfurecedor*) maddening

desesperança [dʒizeʃpe'rãsa] *f* despair

desesperar [dʒizeʃpe'ra*] *vt* to drive to despair; (*enfurecer*) to infuriate; **desesperar-se** *vr* to despair; (*enfurecer-se*) to become infuriated; **desespero** [dʒizeʃ'peru] *m* despair, desperation; (*raiva*) fury

desestimular [dʒizeʃtʃimu'la*] *vt* to discourage

desfalcar [dʒiʃfaw'ka*] *vt* (*dinheiro*) to embezzle; (*reduzir*): ~ (**de**) to reduce (by); **a jogo está desfalcado** the game is incomplete

desfalecer [dʒiʃfale'se*] *vt* (*enfraquecer*) to weaken ♦ *vi* (*enfraquecer*) to weaken; (*desmaiar*) to faint

desfalque [dʒiʃ'fawki] *m* (*de dinheiro*) embezzlement; (*diminuição*) reduction

desfavorável [dʒiʃfavo'ravew] (*pl* -eis) *adj* unfavourable (*BRIT*), unfavorable (*US*)

desfazer [dʒiʃfa'ze*] (*irreg: como fazer*) *vt* (*costura*) to undo; (*dúvidas*) to dispel; (*agravo*) to redress; (*grupo*) to break up; (*contrato*) to dissolve; (*noivado*) to break off ♦ *vi*: ~ **de alguém** to belittle sb; **desfazer-se** *vr* to vanish; (*tecido*)

to come to pieces; (*grupo*) to break up; (*vaso*) to break; **~-se de** (*livrar-se*) to get rid of; **~-se em lágrimas/gentilezas** to burst into tears/go out of one's way to please

desfecho [dʒiʃ'feʃu] *m* ending, outcome

desfeito, -a [dʒiʃ'fejtu, a] *adj* undone; (*cama*) unmade; (*contrato*) broken

desfigurar [dʒiʃfigu'ra*] *vt* (*pessoa, cidade*) to disfigure; (*texto*) to mutilate; **desfigurar-se** *vr* to be disfigured

desfilar [dʒiʃfi'la*] *vi* to parade; **desfile** [dʒiʃ'fili] *m* parade, procession

desforra [dʒiʃ'fɔxa] *f* revenge; (*reparação*) redress; **tirar ~** to get even

desfrutar [dʒiʃfru'ta*] *vt* to enjoy ♦ *vi*: ~ **de** to enjoy

desgarrado, -a [dʒiʒga'xadu, a] *adj* stray; (*navio*) off course

desgastante [dʒiʒgaʃ'tãtʃi] *adj* (*fig*) stressful

desgastar [dʒiʒgaʃ'ta*] *vt* to wear away, erode; (*pessoa*) to wear out, get down; **desgastar-se** *vr* to be worn away; (*pessoa*) to get worn out; **desgaste** [dʒiʒ'gaʃtʃi] *m* wear and tear; (*mental*) stress

desgosto [dʒiʒ'goʃtu] *m* displeasure; (*pesar*) sorrow, unhappiness

desgraça [dʒiʒ'grasa] *f* misfortune; (*miséria*) misery; (*desfavor*) disgrace; **desgraçado, -a** [dʒiʒgra'sadu, a] *adj* poor ♦ *m/f* wretch; **estou com uma gripe desgraçada** (*col*) I've got a hell of a cold

desgrudar [dʒiʒgru'da*] *vt* to unstick ♦ *vi*: ~ **de** to tear o.s. away from; ~ **algo de algo** to take sth off sth

desidratar [dʒizidra'ta*] *vt* to

dehydrate

design [dʒiˈzãjn] m design

designar [dezigˈnaˈ] vt to designate; (nomear) to name, appoint; (dia, data) to fix

desigual [deziˈgwaw] (pl -ais) adj unequal; (terreno) uneven; **desigualdade** [dʒizigwawˈdadʒi] f inequality

desiludir [dʒiziluˈdʒiˈ] vt to disillusion; (causar decepção a) to disappoint; **desiludir-se** vr to lose one's illusions

desimpedido, -a [dʒizĩpeˈdʒidu, a] adj free

desinfetante [dʒizĩfeˈtãtʃi] (PT -ct-) adj, m disinfectant

desinfetar [dʒizĩfeˈtaˈ] (PT -ct-) vt to disinfect

desintegração [dʒizĩtegraˈsãw] f disintegration, break-up

desintegrar [dʒizĩteˈgraˈ] vt to separate; **desintegrar-se** vr to disintegrate, fall to pieces

desinteressado, -a [dʒizĩtereˈsadu, a] adj disinterested

desinteresse [dʒizĩteˈresi] m lack of interest

desistir [deziʃˈtʃiˈ] vi to give up; **~ de fumar** to stop smoking; **ele ia, mas no final desistiu** he was going, but in the end he gave up the idea ou he decided not to

desjejum [dʒiʒeˈʒũ] m breakfast

deslavado, -a [dʒiʒlaˈvadu, a] adj (pessoa, atitude) shameless; (mentira) blatant

desleal [dʒiʒleˈaw] (pl -ais) adj disloyal

desleixado, -a [dʒiʒlejˈʃadu, a] adj sloppy

desleixo [dʒiʒˈlejʃu] m sloppiness

desligado, -a [dʒiʒliˈgadu, a] adj (eletricidade) off; (pessoa) absentminded; **estar ~** to be miles away

desligar [dʒiʒliˈgaˈ] vt (TEC) to disconnect; (luz, TV, motor) to switch off; (telefone) to hang up; **desligar-se** vr: **~-se de algo** (afastar-se) to leave sth; (problemas etc) to turn one's back on sth; **não desligue** (TEL) hold the line

deslizar [dʒiʒliˈzaˈ] vi to slide; (por acidente) to slip; (passar de leve) to glide; **deslize** [dʒiʒˈlizi] m lapse; (escorregadela) slip

deslocado, -a [dʒiʒloˈkadu, a] adj (membro) dislocated; (desambientado) out of place

deslocar [dʒiʒloˈkaˈ] vt to move; (articulação) to dislocate; (funcionário) to transfer; **deslocar-se** vr to move; to be dislocated

deslumbramento [dʒiʒlũbraˈmẽtu] m dazzle; (fascinação) fascination

deslumbrante [dʒiʒlũˈbrãtʃi] adj dazzling; (casa, festa) amazing

deslumbrar [dʒiʒlũˈbraˈ] vt to dazzle; (maravilhar) to amaze; (fascinar) to fascinate ♦ vi to be dazzling; to be amazing; **deslumbrar-se** vr: **~-se com** to be fascinated by

desmaiado, -a [dʒiʒmaˈjadu, a] adj unconscious; (cor) pale

desmaiar [dʒiʒmaˈjaˈ] vi to faint; **desmaio** [dʒiʒˈmaju] m faint

desmancha-prazeres [dʒiʒˈmãnʃa-] m/f inv kill-joy, spoilsport

desmanchar [dʒiʒmãnˈʃaˈ] vt (costura) to undo; (contrato) to break; (noivado) to break off; (penteado) to mess up; **desmanchar-se** vr (costura) to come undone

desmarcar [dʒiʒmaxˈkaˈ] vt (compromisso) to cancel

desmascarar [dʒiʒmaʃkaˈraˈ] vt to unmask

desmazelado, -a [dʒiʒmazeˈladu, a] adj slovenly, untidy

desmedido, -a [dʒiʒme'dʒidu, a] adj excessive

desmentido [dʒiʒmē'tʃidu] m (negação) denial; (contradição) contradiction

desmentir [dʒiʒmē'tʃi*] vt (contradizer) to contradict; (negar) to deny

desmiolado, -a [dʒiʒmjo'ladu, a] adj brainless; (esquecido) forgetful

desmontar [dʒiʒmõ'ta*] vt (máquina) to take to pieces ♦ vi (do cavalo) to dismount, get down

desmoronamento [dʒiʒmorona-'mẽtu] m collapse

desmoronar [dʒiʒmoro'na*] vt to knock down ♦ vi to collapse

desnatado, -a [dʒiʒna'tadu, a] adj (leite) skimmed

desnaturado, -a [dʒiʒnatu'radu, a] adj inhumane ♦ m/f monster

desnecessário, -a [dʒiʒnese-'sarju, a] adj unnecessary

desnutrição [dʒiʒnutri'sãw] f malnutrition

desobedecer [dʒizobede'se*] vt to disobey; **desobediência** [dʒizobe-'dʒjēsja] f disobedience; **desobediente** [dʒizobe'dʒjētʃi] adj disobedient

desobstruir [dʒizobiʃ'trwi*] vt to unblock

desocupado, -a [dʒizoku'padu, a] adj (casa) empty, vacant; (disponível) free; (sem trabalho) unemployed

desocupar [dʒizoku'pa*] vt (casa) to vacate; (liberar) to free

desodorante [dʒizodo'rātʃi] (BR) -dorizante] m deodorant

desolação [dezola'sãw] f (consternação) grief; (de um lugar) desolation; **desolado, -a** [dezo'ladu, a] adj distressed; desolate

desonesto, -a [dezo'nɛʃtu, a] adj dishonest

desonra [dʒi'zõxa] f dishonour (BRIT), dishonor (US); (descrédito) disgrace; **desonrar** [dʒizõ'xa*] vt (infamar) to disgrace; (mulher) to seduce; **desonrar-se** vr to disgrace o.s.

desordem [dʒi'zoxdē] f disorder, confusion; **em ~** (casa) untidy

desorganizar [dʒizoxgani'za*] vt to disorganize; (dissolver) to break up; **desorganizar-se** vr to become disorganized; to break up

desorientação [dʒizorjēta'sãw] f bewilderment, confusion

desorientar [dʒizorjē'ta*] vt (desnortear) to throw off course; (perturbar) to confuse; (desvairar) to unhinge; **desorientar-se** vr to lose one's way; to get confused; to go mad

desovar [dʒizo'va*] vt to lay; (peixe) to spawn

despachado, -a [dʒiʃpa'ʃadu, a] adj (pessoa) efficient

despachar [dʒiʃpa'ʃa*] vt to dispatch, send off; (atender, resolver) to deal with; (despedir) to sack; **despachar-se** vr to hurry (up); **despacho** [dʒiʃ'paʃu] m dispatch; (de negócios) handling; (nota em requerimento) ruling; (reunião) consultation; (macumba) witchcraft

despeço etc [dʒiʃ'pesu] vb V despedir

despedaçar [dʒiʃpeda'sa*] vt (quebrar) to smash; (rasgar) to tear apart; **despedaçar-se** vr to smash; to tear

despedida [dʒiʃpe'dʒida] f farewell; (de trabalhador) dismissal

despedir [dʒiʃpe'dʒi*] vt (de emprego) to dismiss, sack; **despedir-se** vr: **~-se (de)** to say goodbye (to)

despeitado, -a [dʒiʃpej'tadu, a] *adj* spiteful; *(ressentido)* resentful

despeito [dʒiʃ'pejtu] *m* spite; **a ~ de** in spite of, despite

despejar [dʒiʃpe'ʒa*] *vt (água)* to pour; *(esvaziar)* to empty; *(inquilino)* to evict; **despejo** [dʒiʃ'peʒu] *m* eviction; **quarto de despejo** junk room

despencar [dʒiʃpẽ'ka*] *vi* to fall down, tumble down

despensa [dʒiʃ'pẽsa] *f* larder

despentear [dʒiʃpẽ'tʃa*] *vt (cabelo: sem querer)* to mess up; *(: de propósito)* to let down; **despentear-se** *vr* to mess one's hair up, to let one's hair down

despercebido, -a [dʒiʃpexse'bidu, a] *adj* unnoticed

desperdiçar [dʒiʃpexdʒi'sa*] *vt* to waste; *(dinheiro)* to squander; **desperdício** [dʒiʃpex'dʒisju] *m* waste

despertador [dʒiʃpexta'do*] *m (tb: relógio ~)* alarm clock

despertar [dʒiʃpex'ta*] *vt* to wake; *(suspeitas, interesse)* to arouse; *(reminiscências)* to revive; *(apetite)* to whet ♦ *vi* to wake up ♦ *m* awakening; **desperto, -a** [dʒiʃ'pextu, a] *adj* awake

despesa [dʒiʃ'peza] *f* expense; **~s** *fpl (de uma empresa)* expenses, costs; **~s gerais** *(COM)* overheads

despido, -a [dʒiʃ'pidu, a] *adj* naked, bare; *(livre)* free

despir [dʒiʃ'pi*] *vt (roupa)* to take off; *(pessoa)* to undress; *(despojar)* to strip; **despir-se** *vr* to undress

despojar [dʒiʃpo'ʒa*] *vt (casas)* to loot, sack; *(pessoas)* to rob

despontar [dʒiʃpõ'ta*] *vi* to emerge; *(sol)* to come out; (: *ao amanhecer)* to come up; **ao ~ do dia** at daybreak

desporto [dʒiʃ'poxtu] *(esp PT)* m sport

desprender [dʒiʃprẽ'de*] *vt* to loosen; *(desatar)* to unfasten; *(emitir)* to emit; **desprender-se** *vr (botão)* to come off; *(cheiro)* to be given off

despreocupado, -a [dʒiʃpreoku'pado, a] *adj* carefree, unconcerned

desprezar [dʒiʃpre'za*] *vt* to despise, disdain; *(não dar importância a)* to disregard, ignore; **desprezível** [dʒiʃpre'zivew] *(pl -eis)* *adj* despicable; **desprezo** [dʒiʃ'prezu] *m* scorn, contempt; **dar ao desprezo** to ignore

desproporcional [dʒiʃpropoxsjo-'naw] *adj* disproportionate

despropósito [dʒiʃpro'pɔzitu] *m* nonsense

desprovido, -a [dʒiʃpro'vidu, a] *adj* deprived; **~ de** without

desqualificar [dʒiʃkwalifi'ka*] *vt (ESPORTE etc)* to disqualify; *(tornar indigno)* to disgrace, lower

desregrado, -a [dʒiʒxe'gradu, a] *adj* disorderly, unruly; *(devasso)* immoderate

desrespeito [dʒiʒxeʃ'pejtu] *m* disrespect

desse *etc* ['desi] *vb V* **dar**

desse, -a ['desi, a] = **de + esse/a**

destacar [dʒiʃta'ka*] *vt (MIL)* to detail; *(separar)* to detach; *(enfatizar)* to emphasize ♦ *vi* to stand out; **destacar-se** *vr* to stand out; *(pessoa)* to be outstanding

destampar [dʒiʃtã'pa*] *vt* to take the lid off

destapar [dʒiʃta'pa*] *vt* to uncover

destaque [dʒiʃ'taki] *m* distinction; *(pessoa, coisa)* highlight

deste, -a ['deʃtʃi, a] = **de + este, -a**

destemido, -a [deʃte'midu, a] *adj* fearless, intrepid

destilar [deʃtʃi'la*] *vt* to distil *(BRIT)*,

distill (US)

destinação [deʃtʃinaˈsãw] (pl -ões) f destination

destinar [deʃtʃiˈna*] vt to destine; (dinheiro): ~ (para) to set aside (for); **destinar-se** vr: ~se a to be intended for; (carta) to be addressed to

destinatário, -a [deʃtʃinaˈtarju, a] m/f addressee

destino [deʃˈtʃinu] m destiny, fate; (lugar) destination; **com ~ a** bound for

destituir [deʃtʃiˈtwi*] vt to dismiss; ~ **de** (privar de) to deprive of

destrancar [dʒiʃtrãˈka*] vt to unlock

destratar [dʒiʃtraˈta*] vt to abuse, insult

destreza [deʃˈtreza] f skill; (agilidade) dexterity

destro, -a [ˈdɛʃtru, a] adj skilful (BRIT), skillful (US); (ágil) agile; (não canhoto) right-handed

destrocar [dʒiʃtroˈka*] vt to give back, return

destroçar [dʒiʃtroˈsa*] vt to destroy; (quebrar) to smash, break; **destroços** [dʒiʃˈtrɔsuʃ] mpl wreckage sg

destruição [dʒiʃtrwiˈsãw] f destruction

destruir [dʒiʃˈtrwi*] vt to destroy

desvairado, -a [dʒiʒvajˈradu, a] adj (louco) crazy, demented; (desorientado) bewildered

desvalorizar [dʒiʒvaloriˈza*] vt to devalue

desvantagem [dʒiʒvãˈtaʒẽ] (pl -ns) f disadvantage

desvão [dʒiʒˈvãw] (pl -s) m loft

desventura [dʒiʒveˈtura] f misfortune; (infelicidade) unhappiness

desviar [dʒiʒˈvja*] vt to divert; (golpe) to deflect; (dinheiro) to embezzle; **desviar-se** vr to turn away; ~se de to avoid; ~ os olhos to look away

desvio [dʒiʒˈviu] m diversion, detour; (curva) bend; (fig) deviation; (de dinheiro) embezzlement

detalhadamente [detaʎada-ˈmẽtʃi] adv in detail

detalhado, -a [detaˈʎadu, a] adj detailed

detalhar [detaˈʎa*] vt to (give in) detail

detalhe [deˈtaʎi] m detail

detectar [detekˈta*] vt to detect

detective [detekˈtivə] (PT) m/f = detetive

detector [detekˈto*] m detector

detenção [detẽˈsãw] (pl -ões) f detention

deter [deˈte*] (irreg: como ter) vt to stop; (prender) to arrest; (manter preso) to detain; (reter) to keep; (conter: riso) to contain; **deter-se** vr to stop; (ficar) to stay; (conter-se) to restrain o.s.

detergente [detexˈʒẽtʃi] m detergent

deteriorar [deterjoˈra*] vt to spoil, damage; **deteriorar-se** vr to deteriorate; (relações) to worsen

determinação [detexminaˈsãw] f determination; (decisão) decision; (ordem) order

determinado, -a [detexmiˈnadu, a] adj determined; (certo) certain, given

determinar [detexmiˈna*] vt to determine; (decretar) to order; (resolver) to decide (on); (causar) to cause

detestar [deteʃˈta*] vt to hate

detestável [deteʃˈtavew] (pl -eis) adj horrible, hateful

detetive [deteˈtʃivi] m/f detective

detido, -a [de'tʃidu, a] adj (*preso*) under arrest; (*minucioso*) thorough ♦ m/f person under arrest, prisoner

detonação [detona'sãw] (pl **-ões**) f explosion

detonar [deto'na*] vt, vi to detonate

detrás [de'trajʃ] adv behind ♦ prep: **~ de** behind

detrimento [detri'mẽtu] m: **em ~ de** to the detriment of

detrito [de'tritu] m debris sg; (*de comida*) remains pl; (*resíduo*) dregs pl

deturpação [detuxpa'sãw] f corruption; (*de palavras*) distortion

deturpar [detux'pa*] vt to corrupt; (*desfigurar*) to disfigure; (*palavras*) to twist

deu [dew] vb V **dar**

deus, a [dewʃ, dewsa] m/f god/goddess; **D~ me livre!** God forbid!; **graças a D~** thank goodness; **meu D~!** good Lord!

devagar [dʒiva'ga*] adv slowly

devaneio [deva'neju] m daydream

devassa [de'vasa] f investigation, inquiry

devassidão [devasi'dãw] f debauchery

devasso, -a [de'vasu, a] adj dissolute

devastar [devaʃ'ta*] vt to devastate; (*arruinar*) to ruin

deve [ˈdɛvi] m debit

devedor, a [deve'do*, a] adj (*pessoa*) in debt ♦ m/f debtor

dever [de've*] m duty ♦ vt to owe ♦ vi (*suposição*): **deve (de) estar doente** he must be ill; (*obrigação*): **devo partir às oito** I must go at eight; **você devia ir ao médico** you should go to the doctor; **que devo fazer?** what shall I do?

devidamente [devida'mẽtʃi] adv

properly; (*preencher formulário etc*) duly

devido, -a [de'vidu, a] adj (*maneira*) proper; (*respeito*) due; **~ a** due to, owing to; **no ~ tempo** in due course

devoção [devo'sãw] f devotion

devolução [devolu'sãw] f devolution; (*restituição*) return; (*reembolso*) refund; **~ de impostos** tax rebate

devolver [devow've*] vt to give back, return; (COM) to refund

devorar [devo'ra*] vt to devour; (*destruir*) to destroy

devotar [devo'ta*] vt to devote

dez [dɛʒ] num ten

dezanove [deza'nɔvə] (PT) num = **dezenove**

dezasseis [deza'sejʃ] (PT) num = **dezesseis**

dezassete [deza'seta] (PT) num = **dezessete**

dezembro [de'zẽbru] (PT **D~**) m December

dezena [de'zena] f: **uma ~ de ...** ten ...

dezenove [deze'nɔvi] num nineteen

dezesseis [deze'sejʃ] num sixteen

dezessete [dezi'setʃi] num seventeen

dezoito [dʒi'zojtu] num eighteen

dia [ˈdʒia] m day; (*claridade*) daylight; **~ a ~** day by day; **~ santo** holy day; **~ útil** weekday; **estar ou andar em ~ (com)** to be up to date (with); **de ~** in the daytime, by day; **mais ~ menos ~** sooner or later; **~ sim, ~ não** every other day; **no ~ seguinte** the next day; **bom ~** good morning; **dia-a-dia** m daily life, everyday life

diabete(s) [dʒia'bɛtʃi(ʃ)] f diabetes sg; **diabético, -a** [dʒia'bɛtʃiku, a] *adj, m/f* diabetic

diabo ['dʒjabu] *m* devil; **que ~!** (col) damn it!

diabrura [dʒja'brura] *f* prank; **~s** *fpl* (travessura) mischief *sg*

diafragma [dʒja'fragma] *m* diaphragm

diagnóstico [dʒjag'nɔʃtʃiku] *m* diagnosis

diagonal [dʒjago'naw] (*pl* -ais), *f* diagonal

diagrama [dʒja'grama] *m* diagram

dialeto [dʒja'letu] (*PT* -ect-) *m* dialect

dialogar [dʒjalo'ga*] *vi*: **~** (com alguém) to talk (to sb); (*POL*) to have ou hold talks (with sb)

diálogo [dʒi'alogu] *m* dialogue; (conversa) talk, conversation

diamante [dʒja'mãtʃi] *m* diamond

diâmetro [dʒi'ametru] *m* diameter

diante ['dʒjãtʃi] *prep*: **~ de** before; (na frente de) in front of; (problemas etc) in the face of; **e assim por ~** and so on; **para ~** forward

dianteira [dʒjã'tejra] *f* front, vanguard; **tomar a ~** to get ahead

dianteiro, -a [dʒjã'tejru, a] *adj* front

diapositivo [dʒjapozi'tʃivu] *m* (*FOTO*) slide

diária ['dʒjarja] *f* (de hotel) daily rate

diário, -a ['dʒjarju, a] *adj* daily ♦ *m* diary; (jornal) daily (newspaper); **~ de bordo** (*AER*) logbook

diarréia [dʒja'xeja] *f* diarrhoea (*BRIT*), diarrhea (*US*)

dica ['dʒika] (col) *f* hint

dicionário [dʒisjo'narju] *m* dictionary

dieta ['dʒjeta] *f* diet; **fazer ~** to be on a diet; (começar) to go on a diet

diferença [dʒife'rẽsa] *f* difference; **ela tem uma ~ comigo** she's got

something against me

diferenciar [dʒiferẽ'sja*] *vt* to differentiate

diferente [dʒife'rẽtʃi] *adj* different; **estar ~ com alguém** to be at odds with sb

difícil [dʒi'fisiw] (*pl* -eis) *adj* difficult; (improvável) unlikely; **o ~ é ...** the difficult thing is ...; **acho ~ ela aceitar nossa proposta** I think it's unlikely she will accept our proposal; **dificilmente** [dʒifisiw'mẽtʃi] *adv* with difficulty; (mal) hardly; (raramente) hardly ever

dificuldade [dʒifikuw'dadʒi] *f* difficulty; (aperto) em **~s** in trouble

dificultar [dʒifikuw'ta*] *vt* to make difficult; (complicar) to complicate

difundir [dʒifũ'dʒi*] *vt* to diffuse; (boato, rumor) to spread

digerir [dʒiʒe'ri*] *vt, vi* to digest

digestão [dʒiʒeʃ'tãw] *f* digestion

digital [dʒiʒi'taw] (*pl* -ais) *adj*: **impressão ~** fingerprint

digitar [dʒiʒi'ta*] *vt* (*COMPUT*: dados) to key (in)

dígito [dʒiʒitu] *m* digit

dignidade [dʒigni'dadʒi] *f* dignity

digno, -a [dʒignu, a] *adj* (merecedor) worthy; (nobre) dignified

digo ['dʒigu] *vb vb* dizer

dilatar [dʒila'ta*] *vt* to dilate, expand; (prolongar) to prolong; (retardar) to delay

dilema [dʒi'lema] *m* dilemma

diluir [dʒi'lwi*] *vt* to dilute

dilúvio [dʒi'luvju] *m* flood

dimensão [dʒimẽ'sãw] (*pl* -ões) *f* dimension; **dimensões** *fpl* (medidas) measurements

diminuição [dʒiminwi'sãw] *f* reduction

diminuir [dʒimi'nwi*] *vt* to reduce; (som) to turn down; (interesse) to lessen ♦ *vi* to lessen, diminish;

(*preço*) to go down; (*dor*) to wear off; (*barulho*) to die down

diminutivo, -a [dʒiminu'tʃivu, a] *adj* diminutive ♦ *m* (*LING*) diminutive

Dinamarca [dʒina'maxka] *f* Denmark; **dinamarquês, -quesa** [dʒinamax'keʃ, 'keza] *adj* Danish ♦ *m/f* Dane ♦ *m* (*LING*) Danish

dinâmico, -a [dʒi'namiku, a] *adj* dynamic

dínamo ['dʒinamu] *m* dynamo

dinheirão [dʒiɲej'rãw] *m*: **um ~** loads *pl* of money

dinheiro [dʒi'ɲejru] *m* money; **~ à vista** cash for paying in cash; **~ em caixa** money in the till; **~ em espécie** cash

dinossauro [dʒino'sawru] *m* dinosaur

diploma [dʒip'lɔma] *m* diploma

diplomacia [dʒiploma'sia] *f* diplomacy; (*fig*) tact

diplomata [dʒiplo'mata] *m/f* diplomat; **diplomático, -a** [dʒiplo'matʃiku, a] *adj* diplomatic

dique ['dʒiki] *m* dam; (*GEO*) dyke

direção [dʒire'sãw] (*PT* -cç-; *pl* -ões) *f* direction; (*endereço*) address; (*AUTO*) steering; (*administração*) management; (*comando*) leadership; (*diretoria*) board of directors; **em ~ a** towards

directo, -a *etc* [dʒi'rɛktu, a] (*PT*) = **direto** *etc*

direi *etc* [dʒi'rej] *vb V* **dizer**

direita [dʒi'rejta] *f* (*mão*) right hand; (*lado*) right-hand side; (*POL*) right wing; **à ~** on the right

direito, -a [dʒi'rejtu, a] *adj* (*lado*) right-hand; (*mão*) right; (*honesto*) honest; (*devido*) proper; (*justo*) right, just ♦ *m* right; (*JUR*) law ♦ *adv* straight; (*bem*) right; **de maneira certa**) properly; **~s** *mpl* (*humanos*) rights; (*alfandegários*)

duty *sg*

direto, -a [dʒi'rɛtu, a] *adj* direct ♦ *adv* straight; **transmissão direta** (*TV*) live broadcast

diretor, a [dʒire'to*, a] *adj* directing, guiding ♦ *m/f* director; (*de jornal*) editor; (*de escola*) head teacher; **diretoria** [dʒireto'ria] *f* (*COM*) management

dirigente [dʒiri'ʒẽtʃi] *m/f* (*de país, partido*) leader; (*diretor*) director; (*gerente*) manager

dirigir [dʒiri'ʒi*] *vt* to direct; (*COM*) to manage; (*veículo*) to drive ♦ *vi* to drive; **dirigir-se** *vr*: **~-se a** (*falar com*) to speak to; (*ir, recorrer*) to go to; (*esforços*) to be directed towards

discagem [dʒiʃ'kaʒẽ] *f* (*TEL*) dialling

discar [dʒiʃ'ka*] *vt* to dial

disciplina [dʒisi'plina] *f* discipline; **disciplinar** [dʒisipli'na*] *vt* to discipline

discípulo, -a [dʒi'sipulu, a] *m/f* disciple; (*aluno*) pupil

disc-jóquei [dʒiʃk-] *m/f* disc jockey, DJ

disco ['dʒiʃku] *m* disc; (*COMPUT*) disk; (*MÚS*) record; (*de telefone*) dial; **~ laser** (*máquina*) compact disc player, CD player; (*disco*) compact disc, CD; **~ flexível/rígido** (*COMPUT*) floppy/hard disk; **~ do sistema** system disk; **~ voador** flying saucer

discordar [dʒiʃkox'da*] *vi*: **~ de alguém em algo** to disagree with sb on sth

discórdia [dʒiʃ'kɔxdʒia] *f* discord, strife

discoteca [dʒiʃko'tɛka] *f* discotheque, disco

discrepância [dʒiʃkre'pãsja] *f* discrepancy; (*desacordo*) disagreement; **discrepante** [dʒiʃkre'pãtʃi] *adj* conflicting

discreto, -a [dʒiʃ'krɛtu, a] adj discreet; (modesto) modest; (prudente) shrewd; (roupa) plain; **discrição** [dʒiʃkri'sãw] f discretion

discriminação [dʒiʃkrimina'sãw] f discrimination

discriminar [dʒiʃkrimi'na*] vt to distinguish ♦ vi: ~ **entre** to discriminate between

discurso [dʒiʃ'kuxsu] m speech

discussão [dʒiʃku'sãw] (pl -ões) f discussion; (contenda) argument

discutir [dʒiʃku'tʃi*] vt to discuss ♦ vi: ~ (sobre algo) to talk (about sth); (contender) to argue (about sth)

disenteria [dʒizẽte'ria] f dysentery

disfarçar [dʒiʃfax'sa*] vt to pretend; **disfarçar-se** vr: ~se em ou de algo to disguise o.s. as sth; **disfarce** [dʒiʃ'faxsi] m disguise; (máscara) mask

dislexia [dʒiʒlek'sja] f dyslexia

disparar [dʒiʃpa'ra*] vt to shoot, fire ♦ vi to fire; (arma) to go off; (correr) to shoot off, bolt

disparatado, -a [dʒiʃpara'tadu, a] adj silly, absurd

disparate [dʒiʃpa'ratʃi] m nonsense, rubbish

disparidade [dʒiʃpari'dadʒi] f disparity

dispensar [dʒiʃpẽ'sa*] vt to excuse; (prescindir de) to do without; (conferir) to grant; **dispensável** [dʒiʃpẽ'savew] (pl -eis) adj expendable

dispersar [dʒiʃpex'sa*] vt, vi to disperse; **disperso, -a** [dʒiʃ'pɛxsu, a] adj scattered

displicência [dʒiʃpli'sẽsja] (BR) f negligence, carelessness; **displicente** [dʒiʃpli'sẽtʃi] adj careless

dispo etc ['dʒiʃpu] vb V **despir**

disponível [dʒiʃpo'nivew] (pl -eis)

adj available

dispor [dʒiʃ'po*] (irreg: como **pôr**) vt to arrange ♦ vi: ~ **de** to have the use of; (ter) to have, own; (pessoas) to have at one's disposal; **dispor-se** vr: ~**se a** (estar pronto a) to be prepared to, be willing to; (decidir) to decide to; ~ **sobre** to talk about; **disponha!** feel free!

disposição [dʒiʃpozi'sãw] (pl -ões) f arrangement; (humor) disposition; (inclinação) inclination; **à sua ~** at your disposal

dispositivo [dʒiʃpozi'tʃivu] m gadget, device; (determinação de lei) provision

disposto, -a [dʒiʃ'poʃtu, 'poʃta] adj: **estar ~ a** to be willing to; **estar bem ~** to look well

disputa [dʒiʃ'puta] f dispute, argument; (competição) contest; **disputar** [dʒiʃpu'ta*] vt to dispute; (concorrer a) to compete for; (lutar por) to fight over ♦ vi to quarrel, argue; to compete; **disputar uma corrida** to run a race

disquete [dʒiʃ'kɛtʃi] m (COMPUT) floppy disk, diskette

disse etc ['dʒisi] vb V **dizer**

disseminar [dʒisemi'na*] vt to disseminate; (espalhar) to spread

dissertar [dʒisex'ta*] vi to speak

dissidência [dʒisi'dẽsja] f (cisão) difference of opinion

disso ['dʒisu] = de + isso

dissolução [dʒisolu'sãw] f (libertinagem) debauchery; (de casamento) dissolution

dissolver [dʒisow've*] vt to dissolve; (dispersar) to disperse; (motim) to break up

dissuadir [dʒiswa'dʒi*] vt to dissuade; ~ **alguém de fazer algo** to talk sb out of doing sth, dissuade sb from doing sth

distância [dʒiʃ'tãsja] f distance; **a 3 quilómetros de ~** 3 kilometres (BRIT) ou kilometers (US) away

distanciar [dʒiʃtã'sja*] vt to distance, set apart; (colocar por intervalos) to space out; **distanciar-se** vr to move away; (fig) to distance o.s.

distante [dʒiʃ'tãtʃi] adj distant

distender [dʒiʃtē'de*] vt to expand; (estirar) to stretch; (dilatar) to distend; (músculo) to pull; **distender-se** vr to expand; to distend

distinção [dʒiʃtʃĩ'sãw] (pl -ões) f distinction; **fazer ~** to make a distinction

distinguir [dʒiʃtʃĩ'gi*] vt to distinguish; (avistar, ouvir) to make out; **distinguir-se** vr to stand out

distintivo, -a [dʒiʃtʃĩ'tʃivu, a] adj distinctive ♦ m (insígnia) badge; (emblema) emblem

distinto, -a [dʒiʃ'tʃĩtu, a] adj different; (eminente) distinguished; (claro) distinct; (refinado) refined

disto ['dʒiʃtu] = de + isto

distorcer [dʒiʃtox'se*] vt to distort

distração (PT -cç-; pl -ões) f (ulheamento) absent-mindedness; (divertimento) pastime; (descuido) oversight

distraído, -a [dʒiʃtra'idu, a] adj absent-minded; (não atento) inattentive

distrair [dʒiʃtra'i*] vt to distract; (divertir) to amuse

distribuição [dʒiʃtribwi'sãw] f distribution; (de cartas) delivery

distribuidor, a [dʒiʃtribwi'do*, a] m/f distributor ♦ m (AUTO) distributor ♦ f (COM) distribution company, distributor

distribuir [dʒiʃtribwi'*] vt to distribute; (repartir) to share out; (cartas) to deliver

distrito [dʒiʃ'tritu] m district; (dele-

gacia) police station; **~ eleitoral** constituency; **~ federal** federal area

distúrbio [dʒiʃ'tuxbju] m disturbance

ditado [dʒi'tadu] m dictation; (provérbio) saying

ditador [dʒita'do*] m dictator; **ditadura** [dʒita'dura] f dictatorship

ditar [dʒi'ta*] vt to dictate; (impor) to impose

dito, -a ['dʒitu, a] pp de **dizer**; **~ e feito** no sooner said than done

DIU abr m (= dispositivo intra-uterino) IUD

diurno, -a ['dʒiuxnu, a] adj daytime atr

divã [dʒi'vã] m couch, divan

divergir [dʒivex'ʒi*] vi to diverge; (discordar): **~ (de alguém)** to disagree (with sb)

diversão [dʒivex'sãw] (pl -ões) f amusement; (passatempo) pastime

diverso, -a [dʒi'vexsu, a] adj different; **~s** various, several

diversões [divex'sõjʃ] fpl de **diversão**

diversos [dʒi'vcxsuʃ] mpl (COM) sundries

divertido, -a [dʒivex'tʃidu, a] adj amusing, funny

divertimento [dʒivextʃi'mẽtu] m amusement, entertainment

divertir [dʒivex'tʃi*] vt to amuse, entertain; **divertir-se** vr to enjoy o.s., have a good time

dívida ['dʒivida] f debt; **contrair ~s** tò run into debt; **~ externa** foreign debt

dividir [dʒivi'dʒi*] vt to divide; (despesas, lucro, comida etc) to share; (separar) to separate ♦ vi (MAT) to divide; **dividir-se** vr to divide, split up

divindade [dʒivĩ'dadʒi] f divinity

divino, -a [dʒi'vinu, a] adj divine

♦ *m* Holy Ghost

divirjo *etc* [dʒi'vixʒu] *vb V* **divergir**

divisa [dʒi'viza] *f* emblem; (*frase*) slogan; (*fronteira*) border; (MIL) stripe; **~s** *fpl* (*câmbio*) foreign exchange *sg*

divisão [dʒivi'zãw] (*pl* **-ões**) *f* division; (*discórdia*) split; (*partilha*) sharing

divisões [dʒivi'zõjʃ] *fpl de* **divisão**

divisória [dʒivi'zɔrja] *f* partition

divorciado, -a [dʒivox'sjadu, a] *adj* divorced ♦ *m/f* divorcé(e)

divorciar [dʒivox'sja*] *vt* to divorce; **divorciar-se** *vr* to get divorced; **divórcio** [dʒi'vɔxsju] *m* divorce

divulgar [dʒivuw'ga*] *vt* (*notícias*) to spread; (*segredo*) to divulge; (*produto*) to market; (*livro*) to publish; **divulgar-se** *vr* to leak out

dizer [dʒi'ze*] *vt* to say ♦ *m* saying; **dizer-se** *vr* to claim to be; **diz-se** *ou* **dizem que** ... it is said that ...; **~ algo a alguém** to tell sb sth; (*falar*) to say sth to sb; **~ a alguém que** ... to tell sb that ...; **o que você diz da minha sugestão?** what do you think of my suggestion?; **querer ~** to mean; **quer ~** that is to say; **digo** (*ou seja*) I mean; **não diga!** you don't say!; **por assim ~** so to speak; **até ~ chega** as much as possible

do [du] = **de** + **o**

doação [doa'sãw] (*pl* **-ões**) *f* donation

doador, a [doa'do*, a] *m/f* donor

doar [do'a*] *vt* to donate, give

dobra ['dɔbra] *f* fold; (*prega*) pleat; (*de calças*) turn-up

dobradiça [dobra'dʒisa] *f* hinge

dobradinha [dobra'dʒiɲa] *f* (CULIN) tripe stew

dobrar [do'bra*] *vt* to double;

(*papel*) to fold; (*joelho*) to bend; (*esquina*) to turn, go round; (*fazer ceder*): **~ alguém** to talk sb round ♦ *vi* to double; (*sino*) to toll; (*vergar*) to bend; **dobrar-se** *vr* to double (up)

dobro ['dobru] *m* double

doce ['dosi] *adj* sweet; (*terno*) gentle ♦ *m* sweet

dóceis ['dɔsejʃ] *adj pl de* **dócil**

dócil ['dɔsiw] (*pl* **-eis**) *adj* docile

documentação [dokumẽta'sãw] *f* documentation; (*documentos*) papers *pl*

documentário, -a [dokumẽ'tarju, a] *adj* documentary ♦ *m* documentary

documento [doku'mẽtu] *m* document

doçura [do'sura] *f* sweetness; (*brandura*) gentleness

doença [do'ẽsa] *f* illness

doente [do'ẽtʃi] *adj* ill, sick ♦ *m/f* sick person; (*cliente*) patient

doentio, -a [doẽ'tʃiu, a] *adj* (*pessoa*) sickly; (*clima*) unhealthy; (*curiosidade*) morbid

doer [do'e*] *vi* to hurt, ache; **~ a alguém** (*pesar*) to grieve sb

doido, -a ['dojdu, a] *adj* mad, crazy ♦ *m/f* madman/woman

doído, -a [do'idu, a] *adj* painful; (*moralmente*) hurt; (*que causa dor*) painful

dois, duas [dojʃ, 'duaʃ] *num* two; **conversa a ~** tête-à-tête

dólar ['dɔla*] *m* dollar; **~ oficial/paralelo** dollar at the official/black-market rate; **~-turismo** dollar at the special tourist rate; **doleiro, -a** [do'lejru, a] *m/f* (black market) dollar dealer

dolorido, -a [dolo'ridu, a] *adj* painful, sore

doloroso, -a [dolo'rozu, ɔza] *adj*

painful

dom [dõ] m gift; (aptidão) knack

domar [do'ma*] vt to tame

doméstica [do'mɛʃtʃika] f maid

domesticado, -a [domeʃtʃi'kadu, a] adj domesticated; (manso) tame

domesticar [domeʃtʃi'ka*] vt to domesticate; (povo) to tame

doméstico, -a [do'mɛʃtʃiku, a] adj domestic; (vida) home atr

domicílio [domi'silju] m home, residence; **"entregamos a ~"** "we deliver"

dominador, a [domina'do*, a] adj (pessoa) domineering; (olhar) imposing ♦ m/f ruler

dominante [domi'nãtʃi] adj dominant; (predominante) predominant

dominar [domi'na*] vt to dominate; (reprimir) to overcome ♦ vi to dominate; **dominar-se** vr to control o.s.

domingo [do'mĩgu] m Sunday

domínio [do'minju] m home, (dominação) control; (território) domain; (esfera) sphere; **~ próprio** self-control

dona [ˈdɔna] f owner; (col: mulher) lady; **~ de casa** housewife; **D~ Lígia** Lígia; **D~ Luísa Souza** Mrs Luísa Souza

donde [ˈdõda] (PT) adv from where; (daí) thus

dono [ˈdonu] m owner

dopar [do'pa*] vt to drug

dor [do*] f ache; (aguda) pain; (fig) grief, sorrow; **~ de cabeça/dentes/ estômago** headache/toothache/ stomachache

dormente [dox'mẽtʃi] adj numb ♦ m (FERRO) sleeper

dormir [dox'mi*] vi to sleep; **~ fora** to spend the night away

dormitório [doxmi'tɔrju] m bed-

room; (coletivo) dormitory

dorso [ˈdoxsu] m back

dos [duʃ] = **de** + **os**

dosagem [do'zaʒẽ] m dosage

dose [ˈdɔzi] f dose

dossiê [do'sje] m dossier, file

dotado, -a [do'tadu, a] adj gifted; **~ de** endowed with

dotar [do'ta*] vt to endow

dou [do] vb V **dar**

dourado, -a [do'radu, a] adj golden; (com camada de ouro) gilt ♦ m gilt

doutor, a [do'to*, a] m/f doctor; **D~** (forma de tratamento) Sir; **D~ Eduardo Souza** Mr Eduardo Souza

doutrina [do'trina] f doctrine

doze [ˈdozi] num twelve

Dr(a). abr (= Doutor(a)) Dr.

dragão [dra'gãw] (pl -ões) m dragon

dragões [dra'gõjʃ] mpl de **dragão**

drama [ˈdrama] m drama; **dramático, -a** [dra'matʃiku, a] adj dramatic; **dramatizar** [dramatʃi'za*] vt, vi to dramatize

drástico, -a [ˈdraʃtʃiku, a] adj drastic

dreno [ˈdrɛnu] m drain

driblar [dri'bla*] vt, vi (FUTEBOL) to dribble

drinque [ˈdrĩki] m drink

droga [ˈdrɔga] f drug; (fig) rubbish; **drogado, -a** [dro'gadu, a] m/f drug addict; **drogar** [dro'ga*] vt to drug; **drogar-se** vr to take drugs

drogaria [droga'ria] f chemist's shop (BRIT), drugstore (US)

DTP abr m (= desktop publishing) DTP

duas [ˈduaʃ] f de **dois**

dublê [du'ble] m/f double

ducha [ˈduʃa] f shower

dueto [ˈdwetu] m duet

duna [ˈduna] f dune

dupla ['dupla] f pair; (ESPORTE): ~ **masculina/feminina/mista** men's/women's/mixed doubles

duplicar [dupli'ka*] vt to duplicate ♦ vi to double; **duplicata** [dupli-'kata] f duplicate; (título) trade note, bill

duplo, -a ['duplu, a] adj double ♦ m double

duque ['duki] m duke

duração [dura'sãw] f duration; **de pouca ~** short-lived

duradouro, -a [dura'doru, a] adj lasting

durante [du'rãtʃi] prep during; ~ **uma hora** for an hour

durar [du'ra*] vi to last

durável [du'ravew] (pl -eis) adj lasting

durex [du'reks] ® adj: **fita ~** adhesive tape, sellotape ® (BRIT), scotchtape ® (US)

durmo etc ['duxmu] vb V **dormir**

duro, -a ['duru, a] adj hard; (severo) harsh; (resistente, fig) tough; **estar ~** (col) to be broke

dúvida ['duvida] f doubt; **sem ~** undoubtedly, without a doubt; **duvidar** [duvi'da*] vt to doubt ♦ vi to have one's doubts; **duvidar de alguém/algo** to doubt sb/sth; **duvidar que ...** to doubt that ...; **duvido!** I doubt it!; **duvidoso, -a** [duvi'dozu, ɔza] adj doubtful; (suspeito) dubious

duzentos, -as [du'zẽtuʃ, aʃ] num two hundred

dúzia ['duzja] f dozen; **meia ~** half a dozen

DVD abr m (= disco digital versátil) DVD

dz. abr = **dúzia**

E

e [i] conj and; ~ **a bagagem?** what about the luggage?

é [ɛ] vb V **ser**

ébano ['ɛbanu] m ebony

eclipse [e'klipsi] m eclipse

eco ['ɛku] m echo; **ter ~** to catch on; **ecoar** [e'kwa*] vt to echo ♦ vi (ressoar) to echo

ecologia [ekolo'ʒia] f ecology

economia [ekono'mia] f economy; (ciência) economics sg; ~**s** fpl (poupanças) savings; **fazer ~ (de)** to economize (with)

econômico, -a [eko'nomiku, a] adj economical; (pessoa) thrifty; (COM) economic

economizar [ekonomi'za*] vt (gastar com economia) to economize on; (poupar) to save (up) ♦ vi to economize; to save up

écran [e'krã] (PT) m screen

ECU abr m ECU

edição [edʒi'sãw] (pl -ões) f publication; (conjunto de exemplares) edition; (TV, CINEMA) editing

edifício [edʒi'fisju] m building; ~ **garagem** multistorey car park (BRIT), multistory parking lot (US)

Edimburgo [edʒi'buxgu] n Edinburgh

editar [edʒi'ta*] vt to publish; (COMPUT etc) to edit

editor, a [edʒi'to*, a] adj publishing atr ♦ m/f publisher; (redator) editor ♦ f publishing company; **casa ~a** publishing house; **editoração** [edʒitora'sãw] f: **editoração eletrônica** desktop publishing; **editorial** [edʒitor'jaw] (pl -ais) adj publishing atr ♦ m editorial

edredão [edre'dãw] (pl -ões) (PT) m = **edredom**

edredom [edre'dõ] (pl -ns) m eiderdown

educação [eduka'sãw] f education; (*criação*) upbringing; (*de animais*) training; (*maneiras*) good manners pl; **educacional** [edukasjo'naw] (*pl* **-ais**) *adj* education *atr*

educar [edu'ka*] *vt* to educate; (*criar*) to bring up; (*animal*) to train

efectivo, -a *etc* [efek'tivu, a] (*PT*) *adj* = efetivo *etc*

efectuar [efek'twa*] (*PT*) *vt* = efetuar

efeito [e'fejtu] *m* effect; **fazer ~** to work; **levar a ~** to put into effect; **com ~** indeed

efeminado [efemi'nadu] *adj* effeminate

efervescente [efexve'sẽtʃi] *adj* fizzy

efetivamente [efetʃiva'mẽtʃi] *adv* effectively; (*realmente*) really, in fact

efetivo, -a [efe'tʃivu, a] *adj* effective; (*real*) actual, real; (*cargo, funcionário*) permanent

efetuar [efe'twa*] *vt* to carry out; (*soma*) to do, perform

eficácia [efi'kasja] f (*de pessoa*) efficiency; (*de tratamento*) effectiveness

eficaz [efi'kaʒ] *adj* (*pessoa*) efficient; (*tratamento*) effective

eficiência [efi'sjẽsja] f efficiency; **eficiente** [efi'sjẽtʃi] *adj* efficient

egípcio, -a [e'ʒipsju, a] *adj*, *m/f* Egyptian

Egito [e'ʒitu] (*PT* **-pt-**) *m*: **o ~** Egypt

egoísmo [ego'iʒmu] *m* selfishness, egoism; **egoísta** [ego'ista] *adj* selfish, egoistic ♦ *m/f* egoist

égua ['εgwa] f mare

ei [ej] *excl* hey!

ei-lo *etc* = eis + o

eis [ejʃ] *adv* (*sg*) here is; (*pl*) here are; **~ aí** there is; there are

eixo ['ejʃu] *m* (*de rodas*) axle; (*MAT*)

axis; (*de máquina*) shaft; **~ de transmissão** drive shaft

ejacular [eʒaku'la*] *vt* (*sêmen*) to ejaculate; (*líquido*) to spurt ♦ *vi* to ejaculate

ela ['εla] *pron* (*pessoa*) she; (*coisa*) it; (*com prep*) her; it; **~s** *fpl* they; (*com prep*) them; **~s por ~s** (*col*) tit for tat

elaboração [elabora'sãw] (*pl* **-ões**) f (*de uma teoria*) working out; (*preparo*) preparation

elaborar [elabo'ra*] *vt* to prepare; (*fazer*) to make; (*teoria*) to work out

elástico, -a [e'laʃtʃiku, a] *adj* elastic; (*flexível*) flexible; (*colchão*) springy ♦ *m* elastic band

ele ['eli] *pron* he; (*coisa*) it; (*com prep*) him; it; **~s** *mpl* they; (*com prep*) them

electri... *etc* [elektri] (*PT*) = **eletri...** *etc*

eléctrico, -a [e'lεktriku, a] (*PT*) *adj* = elétrico ♦ *m* tram (*BRIT*), streetcar (*US*)

electro... *etc* [elεktru] (*PT*) = **eletro...** *etc*

eléctrodo [e'lεktrodu] (*PT*) *m* = eletrodo

elefante, -ta [ele'fãtʃi, ta] *m/f* elephant

elegante [ele'gãtʃi] *adj* elegant; (*da moda*) fashionable

eleger [ele'ʒe*] *vt* to elect; (*escolher*) to choose

eleição [elej'sãw] (*pl* **-ões**) f election; (*escolha*) choice

eleito, -a [e'lejtu, a] *pp* de eleger ♦ *adj* elected; chosen

eleitor, a [elej'to*, a] *m/f* voter

elejo *etc* [e'lej'ʒu] *vb* V eleger

elementar [elemẽ'ta*] *adj* elementary; (*fundamental*) basic, fundamental

elemento [ele'mẽtu] *m* element;

(*parte*) component; (*recurso*) means; (*informação*) grounds pl; ~s mpl (*rudimentos*) rudiments

elenco [e'lẽku] m list; (*de atores*) cast

eletricidade [eletrisi'dadʒi] f electricity

eletricista [eletri'siʃta] m/f electrician

elétrico, -a [e'lɛtriku, a] adj electric; (*fig: agitado*) worked up

eletrificar [eletrifi'ka*] vt to electrify

eletrizar [eletri'za*] vt to electrify; (*fig*) to thrill

eletro... [e'lɛtru] prefixo electro...; **eletrocutar** [eletroku'ta*] vt to electrocute; **eletrodo** [e'lɛtrodu] m electrode; **eletrodomésticos** [eletrodo'mɛʃtʃikuʃ] (BR) mpl (electrical) household appliances

eletrônica [ele'tronika] f electronics sg

eletrônico, -a [ele'troniku, a] adj electronic

elevação [eleva'sãw] (pl -ões) f (ARQ) elevation; (*aumento*) rise; (*ato*) raising; (*altura*) height; (*promoção*) promotion; (*ponto elevado*) bump

elevador [eleva'do*] m lift (BRIT), elevator (US)

elevar [ele'va*] vt to lift up; (*voz, preço*) to raise; (*exaltar*) to exalt; (*promover*) to promote; **elevar-se** vr to rise

eliminar [elimi'na*] vt to remove; (*suprimir*) to delete; (*possibilidade*) to rule out; (MED, banir) to expel; (ESPORTE) to eliminate; **eliminatória** [elimina'tɔrja] f (ESPORTE) heat, preliminary round; (*exame*) test

elite [e'litʃi] f elite

elogiar [elo'ʒja*] vt to praise; **elogio** [elo'ʒiu] m praise; (*cumprimento*) compliment

El Salvador [ew-] n El Salvador

┌─PALAVRA CHAVE─┐

em [ẽ] (em + o(s)/a(s) = no(s)/na(s); + ele(s)/a(s) = nele(s)/a(s); + esse(s)/a(s) = nesse(s)/a(s); + isso = nisso; + este(s)/a(s) = neste(s)/a(s); + isto = nisto; + aquele(s)/a(s) = naquele(s)/a(s); + aquilo = naquilo) prep 1 (*posição*) in; (: *sobre*) on; **está na gaveta/no bolso** it's in the drawer/pocket; **está na mesa/no chão** it's on the table/floor

2 (*lugar*) in; (: *casa, escritório etc*) at; (: *andar, meio de transporte*) on; **no Brasil/em São Paulo** in Brazil/São Paulo; **~ casa/no dentista** at home/the dentist; **no avião** on the plane; **no quinto andar** on the fifth floor

3 (*ação*) into; **ela entrou na sala de aula** she went into the classroom; **colocar algo no bolso** to put sth into one's bag

4 (*tempo*) in, on; **~ 1962/3 semanas** in 1962/3 weeks; **no inverno** in the winter; **~ janeiro, no mês de janeiro** in January; **nessa ocasião/altura** on that occasion/at that time; **~ breve** soon

5 (*diferença*) **reduzir/aumentar ~ um 20%** to reduce/increase by 20%

6 (*modo*) **escrito ~ inglês** written in English

7 (*após vb que indica gastar etc*) on; **a metade do seu salário vai ~ comida** he spends half his salary on food

8 (*tema, ocupação*) **especialista no assunto** expert on the subject; **ele trabalha na construção civil** he works in the building industry

emagrecer [imagre'se*] vt to make thin ♦ vi to grow thin; (*mediante regime*) to slim; **emagrecimento**

[imaɾɛʃi'mẽtu] *m* (*mediante regime*) slimming

emaranhado, -a [imaɾaˈɲadu, a] *adj* tangled ♦ *m* tangle

embaixada [ẽbajˈʃada] *f* embassy

embaixador, a [ẽbajʃaˈdo*, a] *m/f* ambassador

embaixatriz [ẽbajʃaˈtriʒ] *f* ambassador; (*mulher de embaixador*) ambassador's wife

embaixo [ẽˈbajʃu] *adv* below, underneath ♦ *prep*: **~ de** under, underneath; **(lá) ~** (*em andar inferior*) downstairs

embalagem [ẽbaˈlaʒẽ] *f* packing; (*de produto: caixa etc*) packaging

embalar [ẽbaˈla*] *vt* to pack; (*balançar*) to rock

embaraçar [ẽbáraˈsa*] *vt* to hinder; (*complicar*) to complicate; (*encabular*) to embarrass; (*confundir*) to confuse; (*obstruir*) to block; **embaraçar-se** *vr* to become embarrassed

embaraço [ẽbaˈrasu] *m* hindrance; (*cábula*) embarrassment; **embaraçoso, -a** [ẽbaraˈsozu, ɔza] *adj* embarrassing

embarcação [ẽbaxkaˈsãw] (*pl* -ões) *f* vessel

embarcar [ẽbaxˈka*] *vt* to embark, put on board; (*mercadorias*) to ship, stow ♦ *vi* to go on board, embark

embarque [ẽˈbaxki] *m* (*de pessoas*) boarding, embarkation; (*de mercadorias*) shipment

embebedar [ẽbebeˈda*] *vt* to make drunk ♦ *vi*: **o vinho embebeda** wine makes you drunk; **embebedar-se** *vr* to get drunk

embelezar [ẽbeleˈza*] *vt* to make beautiful; (*casa*) to brighten up; **embelezar-se** *vr* to make o.s. beautiful

emblema [ẽˈblema] *m* emblem; (*na roupa*) badge

êmbolo [ˈẽbolu] *m* piston

embolsar [ẽbowˈsa*] *vt* to pocket; (*herança*) to come into; (*indenizar*) to refund

embora [ẽˈbɔra] *conj* though, although ♦ *excl* even so; **ir(-se) ~** to go away

emboscada [ẽboʃˈkada] *f* ambush

embriagar [ẽbrjaˈga*] *vt* to make drunk, intoxicate; **embriagar-se** *vr* to get drunk; **embriaguez** [ẽbrjaˈgeʒ] *f* drunkenness; (*fig*) rapture

embrião [ẽˈbrjãw] (*pl* -ões) *m* embryo

embromar [ẽbroˈma*] *vt* (*adiar*) to put off; (*enganar*) to cheat ♦ *vi* (*prometer e não cumprir*) to make empty promises, be all talk (and no action); (*protelar*) to stall; (*falar em rodeios*) to beat about the bush

embrulhar [ẽbruˈʎa*] *vt* (*pacote*) to wrap; (*enrolar*) to roll up; (*confundir*) to muddle up; (*enganar*) to cheat; (*estômago*) to upset; **embrulhar-se** *vr* to get into a muddle

embrulho [ẽˈbruʎu] *m* package, parcel; (*confusão*) mix-up

emburrar [ẽbuˈxa*] *vi* to sulk

embutido, -a [ẽbuˈtʃidu, a] *adj* (*armário*) built-in, fitted

emenda [ẽˈmẽda] *f* correction; (*de lei*) amendment; (*de uma pessoa*) improvement; (*ligação*) join; (*sambladura*) joint; (*costura*) seam

emendar [emẽˈda*] *vt* to correct; (*reparar*) to mend; (*injustiças*) to make amends for; (*lei*) to amend; (*ajuntar*) to put together; **emendar-se** *vr* to mend one's ways

ementa [eˈmẽta] (*PT*) *f* menu

emergência [imexˈʒẽsja] *f* emergence; (*crise*) emergency

emigrado 426 **empregado**

emigrado, -a [emi'gradu, a] *adj* emigrant

emigrante [emi'grãtʃi] *m/f* emigrant

emigrar [emi'gra*] *vi* to emigrate; (*aves*) to migrate

eminência [emi'nẽsja] *f* eminence; (*altura*) height; **eminente** [emi'nẽtʃi] *adj* eminent, distinguished; (GEO) high

emissão [emi'sãw] (*pl* -**ões**) *f* emission; (RÁDIO) broadcast; (*de moeda, ações*) issue

emissário, -a [emi'sarju, a] *m/f* emissary ♦ *m* outlet

emissões [emi'sõjʃ] *fpl de* **emissão**

emissor, a [emi'so*, a] *adj* (*de moeda-papel*) issuing ♦ *m* (RÁDIO) transmitter ♦ *f* (*estação*) broadcasting station; (*empresa*) broadcasting company

emitir [emi'tʃi*] *vt* (*som*) to give out; (*cheiro*) to give off; (*moeda, ações*) to issue; (RÁDIO) to broadcast; (*opinião*) to express ♦ *vi* (*emitir moeda*) to print money

emoção [emo'sãw] (*pl* -**ões**) *f* emotion; (*excitação*) excitement; **emocional** [imosjo'naw] (*pl* -**ais**) *adj* emotional; **emocionante** [imosjo'nãtʃi] *adj* moving, exciting; **emocionar** [imosjo'na*] *vt* to move; (*perturbar*) to upset; (*excitar*) to excite, thrill ♦ *vi* to be exciting; (*comover*) to be moving; **emocionar-se** *vr* to get emotional

emotivo, -a [emo'tʃivu, a] *adj* emotional

empacotar [empako'ta*] *vt* to pack, wrap up

empada [ẽ'pada] *f* pie

empadão [ẽpa'dãw] (*pl* -**ões**) *m* pie

empalidecer [ẽpalide'se*] *vi* to turn pale

empanturrar [ẽpãtu'xa*] *vt*: ~

alguém de algo to stuff sb full of sth

empatar [ẽpa'ta*] *vt* to hinder; (*dinheiro*) to tie up; (*no jogo*) to draw; (*tempo*) to take up ♦ *vi* (*no jogo*): ~ (**com**) to draw (with); **empate** [ẽ'patʃi] *m* draw; tie; (XADREZ) stalemate; (*em negociações*) deadlock

empecilho [ẽpe'siʎu] *m* obstacle; (*col*) snag

empenhar [ẽpe'ɲa*] *vt* (*objeto*) to pawn; (*palavra*) to pledge; (*empregar*) to exert; (*compelir*) to oblige; **empenhar-se** *vr*: ~**se em fazer** to strive to do, do one's utmost to do; **empenho** [ẽ'peɲu] *m* pawning; pledge; (*insistência*): **empenho (em)** commitment (to)

empilhar [ẽpi'ʎa*] *vt* to pile up

empinado, -a [ẽpi'nadu, a] *adj* upright; (*cavalo*) rearing; (*colina*) steep

empinar [ẽpi'na*] *vt* to raise, uplift

empobrecer [ẽpobre'se*] *vt* to impoverish ♦ *vi* to become poor; **empobrecimento** [ẽpobresi'mẽtu] *m* impoverishment

empolgação [ẽpowga'sãw] *f* excitement; (*entusiasmo*) enthusiasm

empolgante [ẽpow'gãtʃi] *adj* exciting

empolgar [ẽpow'ga*] *vt* to stimulate, fill with enthusiasm; (*prender a atenção de*): ~ **alguém** to keep sb riveted

empossar [ẽpo'sa*] *vt* to appoint

empreendedor, a [ẽprjẽde'do*, a] *adj* enterprising ♦ *m/f* entrepreneur

empreender [ẽprjẽ'de*] *vt* to undertake; **empreendimento** [ẽprjẽdʒi'mẽtu] *m* undertaking

empregada [ẽpre'gada] *f* (BR: *doméstica*) maid; (PT: *de restaurante*) waitress; V tb **empregado**

empregado, -a [ẽpre'gadu, a] *m/f*

employee; (*em escritório*) clerk ♦ *m* (*PT: de restaurante*) waiter

empregador, a [ẽpregaˈdo*, a] *m/f* employer

empregar [ẽpreˈga*] *vt* (*pessoa*) to employ; (*coisa*) to use; **empregar-se** *vr* to get a job

emprego [ẽˈpregu] *m* job; (*uso*) use

empreiteiro [ẽprejˈtejru] *m* contractor

empresa [ẽˈpreza] *f* undertaking; (*COM*) enterprise, firm; **empresário, -a** [ẽpreˈzarju, a] *m/f* businessman/woman; (*de cantor, boxeador etc*) manager

emprestado, -a [ẽpreʃˈtadu, a] *adj* on loan; **pedir ~** to borrow; **tomar algo ~** to borrow sth

emprestar [ẽpreʃˈta*] *vt* to lend; **empréstimo** [ẽˈpreʃtʃimu] *m* loan

empunhar [ẽpuˈɲa*] *vt* to grasp, seize

empurrão [ẽpuˈxãw] (*pl* -ões) *m* push, shove; **aos empurrões** jostling

empurrar [ẽpuˈxa*] *vt* to push

empurrões [ẽpuˈxõjʃ] *mpl* de empurrão

emudecer [emudeˈse*] *vt* to silence ♦ *vi* to fall silent, go quiet

enamorado, -a [enamoˈradu, a] *adj* enchanted; (*apaixonado*) in love

encabulado, -a [ẽkabuˈladu, a] *adj* shy

encadernação [ẽkadexnaˈsãw] (*pl* -ões) *f* (*de livro*) binding

encadernado, -a [ẽkadexˈnadu, a] *adj* bound; (*de capa dura*) hardback

encadernar [ẽkadexˈna*] *vt* to bind

encaixar [ẽkajˈʃa*] *vt* (*colocar*) to fit in; (*inserir*) to insert ♦ *vi* to fit; **encaixe** [ẽˈkajʃi] *m* (*ato*) fitting; (*ranhura*) groove; (*buraco*) socket

encalço [ẽˈkawsu] *m* pursuit; **ir no ~**

de to pursue

encalhar [ẽkaˈʎa*] *vi* (*embarcação*) to run aground; (*fig: processo*) to grind to a halt; (*: mercadoria*) to be returned, not to sell; (*col: ficar solteiro*) to be left on the shelf

encaminhar [ẽkamiˈɲa*] *vt* to direct; (*no bom caminho*) to put on the right path; (*processo*) to set in motion; **encaminhar-se** *vr*: **~se para/a** to set out for/to

encanar [ẽkaˈna*] *vt* to channel

encantado, -a [ẽkãˈtadu, a] *adj* delighted; (*castelo etc*) enchanted; (*fascinado*) **~ (por)** smitten (with)

encantador, a [ẽkãtaˈdo*, a] *adj* delightful, charming

encantamento [ẽkãtaˈmẽtu] *m* (*magia*) spell; (*fascinação*) charm

encantar [ẽkãˈta*] *vt* to bewitch; to charm; (*deliciar*) to delight

encanto [ẽˈkãtu] *m* delight; charm

encarar [ẽkaˈra*] *vt* to face; (*olhar*) to look at; (*considerar*) to consider

encargo [ẽˈkaxgu] *m* responsibility; (*ocupação*) job, assignment; (*fardo*) burden

encarnação [ẽkaxnaˈsãw] (*pl* -ões) *f* incarnation

encarnado, -a [ẽkaxˈnadu, a] *adj* red, scarlet

encarnar [ẽkaxˈna*] *vt* to embody, personify; (*TEATRO*) to play

encarregado, -a [ẽkaxeˈgadu, a] *adj*: **~ de** in charge of ♦ *m/f* person in charge ♦ *m* (*de operários*) foreman

encarregar [ẽkaxeˈga*] *vt*: **~ alguém de algo** to put sb in charge of sth; **encarregar-se** *vr*: **~se de fazer** to undertake to do

encenação [ẽsenaˈsãw] (*pl* -ões) *f* (*de peça*) staging, putting on; (*produção*) production; (*fingimento*) playacting; (*atitude fingida*) put-on

encerar 428 enevoado

encerar [ēse'ra*] vt to wax

encerramento [ēsexa'mētu] m close, end

encerrar [ēse'xa*] vt to shut in, lock up; (conter) to contain; (concluir) to close

encharcar [ēʃax'ka*] vt to flood; (ensopar) to soak, drench; **encharcar-se** vr to get soaked ou drenched

enchente [ē'ʃētʃi] f flood

encher [ē'ʃe*] vt to fill (up); (balão) to blow up; (tempo) to fill, take up ♦ vi (col) to be annoying; **encher-se** vr to fill up; **~-se (de)** (col) to get fed up (with); **enchimento** [ēʃi'mētu] m filling

enciclopédia [ēsiklo'pɛdʒja] f encyclopedia, encyclopaedia (BRIT)

encoberto, -a [ēko'bɛxtu, a] pp de **encobrir** ♦ adj concealed; (tempo) overcast

encobrir [ēko'bri*] vt to conceal, hide

encolher [ēko'ʎe*] vt (pernas) to draw up; (os ombros) to shrug; (roupa) to shrink ♦ vi to shrink; **encolher-se** vr (de frio) to huddle

encomenda [ēko'mēda] f order; feito de ~ made to order, custommade; **encomendar** [ēkomē'da*] vt: **encomendar algo a alguém** to order sth from sb

encontrar [ēkō'tra*] vt to find; (pessoa) to meet; (inesperadamente) to come across; (dar com) to bump into ♦ vi: **~ com** to bump into; **encontrar-se** vr (achar-se) to be; (ter encontro): **~-se (com alguém)** to meet (sb)

encontro [ē'kōtru] m (de pessoas) meeting; (MIL) encounter; **~ marcado** appointment; **ir/vir ao ~ de** to go/come and meet

encorajar [ēkora'ʒa*] vt to

encourage

encosta [ē'kɔʃta] f slope

encostar [ēkoʃ'ta*] vt (cabeça) to put down; (carro) to park; (pôr de lado) to put to one side; (pôr junto) to put side by side; (porta) to leave ajar ♦ vi to pull in; **encostar-se** vr: **~-se em** to lean against; (deitar-se) to lie down on; **~ em** to lean against; **~ a mão em** (bater) to hit

encosto [ē'koʃtu] m (arrimo) support; (de cadeira) back

encrencar [ēkrē'ka*] (col) vt (situação) to complicate; (pessoa) to get into trouble ♦ vi to get complicated; (carro) to break down; **encrencar-se** vr to get complicated; to get into trouble

encruzilhada [ēkruzi'ʎada] f crossroads sg

encurtar [ēkux'ta*] vt to shorten

endereçar [ēdere'sa*] vt (carta) to address; (encaminhar) to direct

endereço [ēde'resu] m address

endiabrado, -a [ēdʒja'bradu, a] adj devilish; (travesso) mischievous

endinheirado, -a [ēdʒiɲej'radu, a] adj rich, wealthy

endireitar [ēdʒirej'ta*] vt (objeto) to straighten; (fig: retificar) to put right; **endireitar-se** vr to straighten up

endividar-se [ēdʒivi'daxsi] vr to run into debt

endossar [ēdo'sa*] vt to endorse

endurecer [ēdure'se*] vt, vi to harden

energia [enex'ʒia] f energy, drive; (TEC) power, energy; **enérgico, -a** [e'nexʒiku, a] adj energetic, vigorous

enervante [enex'vātʃi] adj annoying

enevoado, -a [ene'vwadu, a] adj misty, hazy

enfado [ẽ'fadu] *m* annoyance;
  enfadonho, -a [ẽfa'doɲu, a] *adj*
  tiresome; (*aborrecido*) boring
enfarte [ẽ'faxtʃi] *m* (MED) coronary
ênfase ['ẽfazi] *f* emphasis, stress
enfastiado, -a [ẽfaʃ'tʃjadu, a] *adj*
  bored
enfático, -a [ẽ'fatʃiku, a] *adj*
  emphatic
enfatizar [ẽfatʃi'za*] *vt* to emphasize
enfeitar [ẽfej'ta*] *vt* to decorate;
  enfeitar-se *vr* to dress up; **enfeite**
  [ẽ'fejtʃi] *m* decoration
enfeitiçar [ẽfejtʃi'sa*] *vt* to bewitch, cast a spell on
enfermaria [ẽfexma'ria] *f* ward
enfermeiro, -a [ẽfex'mejru, a] *m/f*
  nurse
enfermidade [ẽfexmi'dadʒi] *f* illness
enfermo, -a [ẽ'fexmu, a] *adj* ill, sick
  ♦ *m/f* sick person, patient
enferrujar [ẽfexu'ʒa*] *vt* to rust,
  corrode ♦ *vi* to go rusty
enfiar [ẽ'fja*] *vt* (*meter*) to put;
  (*agulha*) to thread; (*vestir*) to slip
  on; **enfiar-se** *vr*: ~-se em to slip
  into
enfim [ẽ'fĩ] *adv* finally, at last; (*em
  suma*) in short; **até que ~!** at last!
enfoque [ẽ'fɔki] *m* approach
enforcar [ẽfox'ka*] *vt* to hang; (*trabalho, aulas*) to skip; **enforcar-se**
  vr to hang o.s.
enfraquecer [ẽfrake'se*] *vt* to
  weaken ♦ *vi* to grow weak
enfrentar [ẽfrẽ'ta*] *vt* to face; (*confrontar*) to confront; (*problemas*) to
  face up to
enfurecer [ẽfure'se*] *vt* to infuriate;
  enfurecer-se *vr* to get furious
enganado, -a [ẽga'nadu, a] *adj*
  mistaken; (*traído*) deceived
enganar [ẽga'na*] *vt* to deceive;

(*desonrar*) to seduce; (*cônjuge*) to
  be unfaithful to; (*fome*) to stave off;
  enganar-se *vr* to be wrong, be
  mistaken; (*iludir-se*) to deceive o.s.
engano [ẽ'gãnu] *m* mistake; (*ilusão*)
  deception; (*logro*) trick; **é ~** (TEL)
  I've (*ou* you've) got the wrong
  number
engarrafamento [ẽgaxafa'mẽtu]
  m bottling; (*de trânsito*) traffic jam
engarrafar [ẽgaxa'fa*] *vt* to bottle;
  (*trânsito*) to block
engasgar [ẽgaʒ'ga*] *vt* to choke ♦ *vi*
  to choke; (*máquina*) to splutter;
  engasgar-se *vr* to choke
engatinhar [ẽgatʃi'ɲa*] *vi* to crawl
engenharia [ẽʒeɲa'ria] *f* engineering; **engenheiro, -a** [ẽʒe'ɲejru, a]
  m/f engineer
engenhoso, -a [ẽʒe'ɲozu, ɔza] *adj*
  clever, ingenious
engessar [ẽʒe'sa*] *vt* (*perna*) to put
  in plaster; (*parede*) to plaster
englobar [ẽglo'ba*] *vt* to include
engodo [ẽ'godu] *m* bait
engolir [ẽgo'li*] *vt* to swallow
engordar [ẽgox'da*] *vt* to fatten ♦ *vi*
  to put on weight
engraçado, -a [ẽgra'sadu, a] *adj*
  funny, amusing
engradado [ẽgra'dadu] *m* crate
engraxador [ẽgraʃa'do*] (PT) *m*
  shoe shiner
engraxar [ẽgra'ʃa*] *vt* to polish
engrenagem [ẽgre'naʒẽ] (*pl* -ns) *f*
  (AUTO) gear
engrenar [ẽgre'na*] *vt* to put into
  gear; (*fig: conversa*) to strike up ♦ *vi*:
  ~ com alguém to get on with sb
engrossar [ẽgro'sa*] *vt* (*sopa*) to
  thicken; (*aumentar*) to swell; (*voz*)
  to raise ♦ *vi* to thicken; to swell; to
  rise; (*col: pessoa, conversa*) to turn
  nasty
enguia [ẽ'gia] *f* eel

enguiçar [ẽgi'sa*] vi (máquina) to break down ♦ vt to cause to break down; **enguiço** [ẽ'gisu] m snag; (desarranjo) breakdown

enigma [e'nigima] m enigma; (mistério) mystery

enjeitado, -a [ẽʒej'tadu, a] m/f foundling, waif

enjoado, -a [ẽ'ʒwadu, a] adj sick; (enfastiado) bored; (entadonho) boring; (mal-humorado) in a bad mood

enjoar [ẽ'ʒwa*] vt to make sick; to bore ♦ vi (pessoa) to be sick; (remédio, comida) to cause nausea; **enjoar-se** vr: **~-se de** to get sick of

enjôo [ẽ'ʒou] m sickness; (em carro) travel sickness; (em navio) seasickness; boredom

enlatado, -a [ẽla'tadu, a] adj tinned (BRIT), canned ♦ m (pej: filme) foreign import; **~s** mpl (comida) tinned (BRIT) ou canned foods

enlouquecer [ẽloke'se*] vt to drive mad ♦ vi to go mad

enlutado, -a [ẽlu'tadu, a] adj in mourning

enojar [eno'ʒa*] vt to disgust, sicken

enorme [e'nɔxmi] adj enormous, huge; **enormidade** [enoxmi'dadʒi] f enormity; **uma enormidade (de)** (col) a hell of a lot (of)

enquanto [ẽ'kwãtu] conj while; (considerado como) as; **~ isso** meanwhile; **por ~** for the time being; **~ ele não vem** until he comes; **~ que** whereas

enquête [ẽ'ketʒi] f survey

enraivecer [ẽxajve'se*] vt to enrage

enredo [ẽ'xedu] m (de uma obra) plot; (intriga) intrigue

enriquecer [ẽxike'se*] vt to make rich; (fig) to enrich ♦ vi to get rich; **enriquecer-se** vr to get rich

enrolar [ẽxo'la*] vt to roll up; (agasalhar) to wrap up; (col: enganar) to con ♦ vi (col) to waffle; **enrolar-se** vr to roll up; to wrap up; (col: confundir-se) to get mixed ou muddled up

enroscar [ẽxoʃ'ka*] vt (torcer) to twist, wind (round); **enroscar-se** vr to coil up

enrugar [ẽxu'ga*] vt (pele) to wrinkle; (testa) to furrow; (tecido) to crease ♦ vi (pele, mãos) to go wrinkly; (pessoa) to get wrinkles

ensaiar [ẽsa'ja*] vt to test, try out; (treinar) to practise (BRIT), practice (US); (TEATRO) to rehearse

ensaio [ẽ'saju] m test; (tentativa) attempt; (treino) practice; (TEATRO) rehearsal; (literário) essay

ensangüentar [ẽsãgwẽ'ta*] vt to stain with blood

enseada [ẽ'sjada] f inlet, cove; (baía) bay

ensejo [ẽ'seʒu] m chance, opportunity

ensinamento [ẽsina'mẽtu] m teaching; (exemplo) lesson

ensinar [ẽsi'na*] vt, vi to teach

ensino [ẽ'sinu] m teaching, tuition; (educação) education

ensolarado, -a [ẽsola'radu, a] adj sunny

ensopado, -a [ẽso'padu, a] adj soaked ♦ m stew

ensurdecer [ẽsuxde'se*] vt to deafen ♦ vi to go deaf

entalar [ẽta'la*] vt to wedge, jam; (encher): **ela me entalou de comida** she stuffed me full of food

entalhar [ẽta'ʎa*] vt to carve; **entalhe** [ẽ'taʎi] m groove, notch

entanto [ẽ'tãtu]: **no ~** adv yet, however

então [ẽ'tãw] adv then; **até ~** up to that time; **desde ~** ever since; **e ~?**

well then?; **para ~** so that; **pois ~** in that case; **~, você vai ou não?** so, are you going or not?

entardecer [ẽtaxde'se*] vi to get late ♦ m sunset

ente ['ẽtʃi] m being

enteado, -a [ẽ'tʃjadu, a] m/f step-son/stepdaughter

entediar [ẽte'dʒja*] vt to bore; **entediar-se** vr to get bored

entender [ẽtẽ'de*] vt to under-stand; (pensar) to think; (ouvir) to hear; **entender-se** vr to under-stand one another; **dar a ~** to imply; **no meu ~** in my opinion; **~ de música** to know about music; **~ de fazer** to decide to do; **~se por** to be meant by; **~se com alguém** to get along with sb; (dialogar) to sort things out with sb

entendido, -a [ẽtẽ'dʒidu, a] adj (col) gay; (conhecedor): **~ em** good at ♦ m/f expert; (col) homosexual, gay; **bem ~** that is

entendimento [ẽtẽdʒi'mẽtu] m understanding; (opinião) opinion; (combinação) agreement

enterrar [ẽte'xa*] vt to bury; (faca) to plunge; (lever à ruina) to ruin; (assunto) to close

enterro [ẽ'texu] m burial; (funeral) funeral

entidade [ẽtʃi'dadʒi] f (ser) being; (corporação) body; (coisa que existe) entity

entornar [ẽtox'na*] vt to spill; (fig: copo) to drink ♦ vi to drink a lot

entorpecente [ẽtoxpe'sẽtʃi] m narcotic

entorpecimento [ẽtoxpesi'mẽtu] m numbness; (torpor) lethargy

entorse [ẽ'tɔxsi] f sprain

entortar [ẽtox'ta*] vt (curvar) to bend; (empenar) to warp; **~ os olhos** to squint

entrada [ẽ'trada] f (ato) entrance; (lugar) entrance; (TEC) inlet; (de casa) doorway; (começo) begin-ning; (bilhete) ticket; (CULIN) starter, entrée; (COMPUT) input; (pagamento inicial) down payment; (corredor de casa) hall; **~s** fpl (no cabelo) reced-ing hairline sg; **~ gratuita** admission free; **"~ proibida"** "no entry", "no admittance"; **meia ~** half-price tick-et

entra-e-sai [ẽtrai'saj] m comings and goings pl

entranhado, -a [ẽtra'ɲadu, a] adj deep-rooted

entranhas [ẽ'traɲaʃ] fpl bowels, entrails; (sentimentos) feelings; (cen-tro) heart sg

entrar [ẽ'tra*] vi to go (ou come) in, enter; **~ com** (COMPUT: dados etc) to enter; **eu entrei com £10** I con-tributed £10; **~ de férias/licença** to start one's holiday (BRIT) ou vacation (US)/leave; **~ em** to go (ou come) into, enter; (assunto) to start onto; (comida, bebida) to start in on

entrave [ẽ'travi] m (fig) impedi-ment

entre ['ẽtri] prep (dois) between; (mais de dois) among(st); **~ si** amongst themselves

entreaberto, -a [ẽtrja'bɛxtu, a] adj half-open; (porta) ajar

entrega [ẽ'trega] f (de mercadorias) delivery; (a alguém) handing over; (rendição) surrender; **~ rápida** spe-cial delivery

entregar [ẽtre'ga*] vt to hand over; (mercadorias) to deliver; (confiar) to entrust; (devolver) to return; **entregar-se** vr (render-se) to give o.s. up; (dedicar-se) to devote o.s.

entregue [ẽ'tregi] pp de **entregar**

entrelinha [ẽtre'liɲa] f line space; **ler nas ~s** to read between the lines

entreolhar-se [ẽtrio'ʎaxsɪ] *vr* to exchange glances

entretanto [ẽtri'tãtu] *conj* however

entretenimento [ẽtriteni'mẽtu] *m* entertainment; (*distração*) pastime

entreter [ẽtri'te*] (*irreg: como ter*) *vt* to entertain, amuse; (*ocupar*) to occupy; (*manter*) to keep up; (*esperanças*) to cherish; **entreter-se** *vr* to amuse o.s.; to occupy o.s.

entrevista [ẽtre'viʃta] *f* interview; **~ coletiva (à imprensa)** press conference; **entrevistar** [ẽtreviʃ'ta*] *vt* to interview; **entrevistar-se** *vr* to have an interview

entristecer [ẽtriʃte'se*] *vt* to sadden, grieve ♦ *vi* to feel sad; **entristecer-se** *vr* to feel sad

entroncamento [ẽtrõka'mẽtu] *m* junction

entrudo [ẽ'trudu] (*PT*) *m* carnival; (*REL*) Shrovetide

entulhar [ẽtu'ʎa*] *vt* to cram full; (*suj: multidão*) to pack

entupido, -a [ẽtu'pidu, a] *adj* blocked; **estar ~** (*col: congestionado*) to have a blocked-up nose; (*de comida*) to be fit to burst, be full up

entupimento [ẽtupi'mẽtu] *m* blockage

entupir [ẽtu'pi*] *vt* to block, clog; **entupir-se** *vr* to become blocked; (*de comida*) to stuff o.s.

entusiasmar [ẽtuzjaʒ'ma*] *vt* to fill with enthusiasm; (*animar*) to excite; **entusiasmar-se** *vr* to get excited

entusiasmo [ẽtu'zjaʒmu] *m* enthusiasm; (*júbilo*) excitement

entusiasta [ẽtu'zjaʃta] *adj* enthusiastic ♦ *m/f* enthusiast

enumerar [enume'ra*] *vt* to enumerate; (*com números*) to number

envelhecer [ẽveʎe'se*] *vt* to age ♦ *vi* to grow old, age

envelope [ẽve'lɔpi] *m* envelope

envenenamento [ẽvenena'mẽtu] *m* poisoning; **~ do sangue** blood poisoning

envenenar [ẽvene'na*] *vt* to poison; (*fig*) to corrupt; (: *declaração, palavras*) to distort, twist; (*tornar amargo*) to sour ♦ *vi* to be poisonous; **envenenar-se** *vr* to poison o.s.

envergonhado, -a [ẽvexgo'ɲadu, a] *adj* ashamed; (*tímido*) shy

envergonhar [ẽvexgo'ɲa*] *vt* to shame; (*degradar*) to disgrace; **envergonhar-se** *vr* to be ashamed

enviado, -a [ẽ'vjadu, a] *m/f* envoy, messenger

enviar [ẽ'vja*] *vt* to send

envio [ẽ'viu] *m* sending; (*expedição*) dispatch; (*remessa*) remittance; (*de mercadorias*) consignment

enviuvar [ẽvju'va*] *vi* to be widowed

envolto, -a [ẽ'vowtu, a] *pp de* **envolver**

envolver [ẽvow've*] *vt* to wrap (up); (*cobrir*) to cover; (*comprometer, acarretar*) to involve; (*nos braços*) to embrace; **envolver-se** *vr* (*intrometer-se*) to become involved; (*cobrir-se*) to wrap o.s. up; **envolvimento** [ẽvowvi'mẽtu] *m* involvement

enxada [ẽ'ʃada] *f* hoe

enxaguar [ẽʃa'gwa*] *vt* to rinse

enxame [ẽ'ʃami] *m* swarm

enxaqueca [ẽʃa'keka] *f* migraine

enxergar [ẽʃex'ga*] *vt* (*avistar*) to catch sight of; (*divisar*) to make out; (*notar*) to observe, see

enxofre [ẽ'ʃofri] *m* sulphur (*BRIT*), sulfur (*US*)

enxotar [ẽʃo'ta*] *vt* to drive out

enxoval [ẽʃo'vaw] (*pl* **-ais**) *m* (*de noiva*) trousseau; (*de recém-nascido*) layette

enxugar [ẽʃu'ga*] vt to dry; (fig: texto) to tidy up

enxurrada [ẽʃu'xada] f (de água) torrent; (fig) spate

enxuto, -a [ẽ'ʃutu, a] adj dry; (corpo) shapely; (bonito) good-looking

épico, -a ['ɛpiku, a] adj epic ♦ m epic poet

epidemia [epide'mia] f epidemic

epilepsia [epile'psia] f epilepsy

episódio [epi'zɔdʒu] m episode

época ['ɛpoka] f time, period; (da história) age, epoch; **naquela ~** at that time; **fazer ~** to be epoch-making

equação [ekwa'sãw] (pl -ões) f equation

equador [ekwa'do*] m equator; **o E~** Ecuador

equilibrar [ekili'bra*] vt to balance; **equilibrar-se** vr to balance; **equilíbrio** [eki'librju] m balance

equipa [e'kipa] (PT) f team

equipamento [ekipa'mẽtu] m equipment, kit

equipar [eki'pa*] vt: **~ (com)** (navio) to fit out (with); (prover) to equip (with)

equipe [e'kipi] (BR) f team

equitação [ekita'sãw] f (ato) riding; (arte) horsemanship

equivalente [ekiva'lẽtʃi] adj, m equivalent

equivaler [ekiva'le*] vi: **~ a** to be the same as, equal

equivocado, -a [ekivo'kadu, a] adj mistaken, wrong

equivocar-se [ekivo'kaxsi] vr to make a mistake, be wrong

equívoco, -a [e'kivoku, a] adj ambiguous ♦ m (engano) mistake

era¹ ['ɛra] f era, age

era² etc vb V **ser**

erário [e'rarju] m exchequer

erecto, -a [e'rɛktu, a] (PT) adj = ereto

ereto, -a [e'rɛtu, a] adj upright, erect

erguer [ex'ge*] vt to raise, lift; (edificar) to build, erect; **erguer-se** vr to rise; (pessoa) to stand up

eriçar [eri'sa*] vt: **~ o cabelo de alguém** to make sb's hair stand on end; **eriçar-se** vr to bristle; (cabelos) to stand on end

erigir [eri'ʒi*] vt to erect

erosão [ero'zãw] f erosion

erótico, -a [e'rɔtʃiku, a] adj erotic

errado, -a [e'xadu, a] adj wrong; **dar ~** to go wrong

errar [e'xa*] vt (alvo) to miss; (conta) to get wrong ♦ vi to wander, roam; (enganar-se) to be wrong, make a mistake; **~ o caminho** to lose one's way

erro ['exu] m mistake; **salvo ~** unless I am mistaken; **~ de imprensa** misprint

errôneo, -a [e'xonju, a] adj wrong, mistaken; (falso) false, untrue

erudito, -a [eru'dʒitu, a] adj learned, scholarly ♦ m scholar

erva ['ɛxva] f herb; (col: dinheiro) dosh; (: maconha) dope; **~ daninha** weed

erva-mate (pl ervas-mates) f mate

ervilha [ex'viʎa] f pea

esbanjar [iʒbã'ʒa*] vt to squander, waste

esbarrar [iʒba'xa*] vi: **~ em** to bump into; (obstáculo, problema) to come up against

esbelto, -a [iʒ'bɛwtu, a] adj slim, slender

esboçar [iʒbo'sa*] vt to sketch; (delinear) to outline; (traçar) to draw up; **esboço** [iʒ'bosu] m sketch; (primeira versão) draft; (fig: resumo) outline

esbofetear [iʒbofe'tʃjaˌ*] *vt* to slap, hit

esburacar [iʒbura'kaˌ*] *vt* to make holes (*ou* a hole) in

esc (*PT*) *abr* = **escudo**

escabroso, -a [iʃka'brozu, ɔza] *adj* (*difícil*) tough; (*indecoroso*) indecent

escada [iʃ'kada] *f* (*dentro da casa*) staircase, stairs *pl*; (*fora da casa*) steps *pl*; (*de mão*) ladder; ~ **de incêndio** fire escape; ~ **rolante** escalator; **escadaria** [iʃkada'ria] *f* staircase

escala [iʃ'kala] *f* scale; (*NÁUT*) port of call; (*parada*) stop; **fazer** ~ **em** to call at; **sem** ~ non-stop·

escalada [iʃka'lada] *f* (*de guerra*) escalation

escalão [eʃka'lãw] (*pl* -**ões**) *m* step; (*MIL*) echelon

escalar [iʃka'laˌ*] *vt* (*montanha*) to climb; (*muro*) to scale; (*designar*) to select

escaldar [iʃkaw'daˌ*] *vt* to scald; **escaldar-se** *vr* to scald o.s.

escalões [eʃka'lõjʃ] *mpl de* **escalão**

escama [iʃ'kama] *f* (*de peixe*) scale; (*de pele*) flake

escancarado, -a [iʃkãka'radu, a] *adj* wide open

escandalizar [iʃkãdali'zaˌ*] *vt* to shock; **escandalizar-se** *vr* to be shocked; (*ofender-se*) to be offended

escândalo [iʃ'kãdalu] *m* scandal; (*indignação*) outrage; **fazer** *ou* **dar um** ~ to make a scene; **escandaloso, -a** [iʃkãda'lozu, ɔza] *adj* shocking, scandalous

Escandinávia [iʃkãdʒi'navja] *f*: **a** ~ Scandinavia; **escandinavo, -a** [iʃkãdʒi'navu, a] *adj, m/f* Scandinavian

escangalhar [iʃkãga'ʎaˌ*] *vt* to break, smash (up); (*a própria saúde*)

to ruin; **escangalhar-se** *vr*: ~-**se de rir** to split one's sides laughing

escapar [iʃka'paˌ*] *vi*: ~ **a** *ou* **de** to escape from; (*fugir*) to run away from; **escapar-se** *vr* to run away, flee; **deixar** ~ (*uma oportunidade*) to miss; (*palavras*) to blurt out; ~ **de boa** (*col*) to have a close shave

escapatória [iʃkapa'tɔrja] *f* way out; (*desculpa*) excuse

escape [iʃ'kapi] *m* (*de gás*) leak; (*AUTO*) exhaust

escapulir [iʃkapu'liˌ*] *vi*: ~ **(de)** to get away (from); (*suj: coisa*) to slip (from)

escárnio [iʃ'kaxnju] *m* mockery; (*desprezo*) derision

escarrar [iʃka'xaˌ*] *vt* to spit, cough up ♦ *vi* to spit

escarro [iʃ'kaxu] *m* phlegm, spit

escassear [iʃka'sjaˌ*] *vt* to skimp on ♦ *vi* to become scarce

escassez [iʃka'seʒ] *f* (*falta*) shortage

escasso, -a [iʃ'kasu, a] *adj* scarce

escavar [iʃka'vaˌ*] *vt* to excavate

esclarecer [iʃklare'seˌ*] *vt* (*situação*) to explain; (*mistério*) to clear up, explain; **esclarecer-se** *vr*: ~-**se (sobre algo)** to find out (about sth); **esclarecimento** [iʃklaresi'mẽtu] *m* explanation; (*informação*) information

escoadouro [iʃkoa'doru] *m* drain; (*cano*) drainpipe

escocês, -esa [iʃko'seʃ, seza] *adj* Scottish, Scots ♦ *m/f* Scot, Scotsman/woman

Escócia [iʃ'kɔsja] *f* Scotland

escola [iʃ'kɔla] *f* school; ~ **naval** naval college; ~ **primária** primary (*BRIT*) *ou* elementary (*US*) school; ~ **secundária** secondary (*BRIT*) *ou* high (*US*) school; ~ **particular/pública** private/state (*BRIT*) *ou* public (*US*) school; **~ de samba** see boxed note; **~ superior** college

---

ESCOLAS DE SAMBA

Escolas de samba are musical and recreational associations made up, among others, of samba dancers, percussionists and carnival dancers. Although they exist throughout Brazil, the most famous schools are in Rio de Janeiro. The schools in Rio rehearse all year long for the **carnaval**, where they appear for two days in the *Sambódromo*, the samba parade, and compete for the samba school championship. Characterised by their extravagance, the biggest schools have up to 4,000 members and are one of Brazil's major tourist attractions.

---

escolar [iʃkoˈla*] *adj* school *atr* ♦ *m/f* schoolboy/girl

escolha [iʃˈkoʎa] *f* choice

escolher [iʃkoˈʎe*] *vt* to choose, select

escolho [iʃˈkoʎu] *m* (*recife*) reef; (*rocha*) rock

escolta [iʃˈkɔwta] *f* escort; **escoltar** [iʃkowˈta*] *vt* to escort

escombros [iʃˈkõbruʃ] *mpl* ruins, debris *sg*

esconde-esconde [iʃkõdʒiʃ-ˈkõdʒi] *m* hide-and-seek

esconder [iʃkõˈde*] *vt* to hide, conceal; **esconder-se** *vr* to hide

esconderijo [iʃkõdeˈriʒu] *m* hiding place; (*de bandidos*) hideout

escondidas [iʃkõˈdʒidaʃ] *fpl*: **às ~** secretly

escopo [iʃˈkopu] *m* aim, purpose

escorar [iʃkoˈra*] *vt* to prop (up); (*amparar*) to support; (*esperar de*

espreita) to lie in wait for ♦ *vi* to lie in wait; **escorar-se** *vr*: **~-se em** (*fundamentar-se*) to go by; (*amparar-se*) to lean on

escore [iʃˈkɔri] *m* score

escoriação [iʃkorjaˈsãw] (*pl* -**ões**) *f* abrasion, scratch

escorpião [iʃkoxpiˈãw] (*pl* -**ões**) *m* scorpion; **E~** (*ASTROLOGIA*) Scorpio

escorrega [iʃkoˈxega] *m* slide; **escorregadela** [iʃkoxegaˈdela] *f* slip; **escorregadiço, -a** [iʃkoxegaˈdʒi(s)u, a] *adj* slippery; **escorregão** [iʃkoxeˈgãw] (*pl* -**ões**) *m* slip; (*fig*) slip(-up); **escorregar** [iʃkoxeˈga*] *vi* to slip; (*errar*) to slip up

escorrer [iʃkoˈxe*] *vt* to drain (off); (*verter*) to pour out ♦ *vi* (*pingar*) to drip; (*correr em fio*) to trickle

escoteiro [iʃkoˈtejru] *m* scout

escova [iʃˈkova] *f* brush; (*penteado*) blow-dry; **~ de dentes** toothbrush; **escovar** [iʃkoˈva*] *vt* to brush

escravatura [iʃkravaˈtura] *f* (*tráfico*) slave trade; (*escravidão*) slavery

escravidão [iʃkraviˈdãw] *f* slavery

escravizar [iʃkraviˈza*] *vt* to enslave; (*cativar*) to captivate

escravo, -a [iʃˈkravu, a] *adj* captive ♦ *m/f* slave

escrever [iʃkreˈve*] *vt, vi* to write; **escrever-se** *vr* to write to each other; **~ à máquina** to type

escrita [eʃˈkrita] *f* writing; (*letra*) handwriting

escrito, -a [eʃˈkritu, a] *pp de* **escrever** ♦ *adj* written ♦ *m* piece of writing; **~ à mão** handwritten; **dar por ~** to put in writing

escritor, a [iʃkriˈto*, a] *m/f* writer; (*autor*) author

escritório [iʃkriˈtɔrju] *m* office; (*em casa*) study

escritura [iʃkri'tura] f (JUR) deed; (na compra de imóveis) = exchange of contracts; **as Sagradas E~s** the Scriptures

escrivã [iʃkri'vã] f de **escrivão**

escrivaninha [iʃkriva'niɲa] f writing desk

escrivão, -vã [iʃkri'vãw, vã] (pl -ões, ~s) m/f registrar, recorder

escrúpulo [iʃ'krupulu] m scruple; (cuidado) care; **sem ~** unscrupulous; **escrupuloso, -a** [iʃkrupu'lozu, ɔza] adj scrupulous; careful

escudo [iʃ'kudu] m shield; (moeda) escudo

esculhambado, -a [iʃkuʎã'badu, a] (col!) adj shabby, slovenly; (estragado) knackered

esculhambar [iʃkuʎã'ba*] (col!) vt to mess up, fuck up (!) **~ alguém** (criticar) to give sb stick; (descompor) to give sb a bollocking (!)

esculpir [iʃkuw'pi*] vt to carve, sculpt; (gravar) to engrave

escultor, a [iʃkuw'to*, a] m/f sculptor

escultura [iʃkuw'tura] f sculpture

escuras [iʃ'kuraʃ] fpl: **às ~ in the** dark

escurecer [iʃkure'se*] vt to darken ♦ vi to get dark; **ao ~** at dusk

escuridão [iʃkuri'dãw] f (trevas) dark

escuro, -a [iʃ'kuru, a] adj dark; (dia) overcast; (pessoa) swarthy; (negócios) shady ♦ m darkness

escusar [iʃku'za*] vt to excuse, forgive; (justificar) to justify; (dispensar) to exempt; (não precisar de) not to need; **escusar-se** vr to apologize; **~-se de fazer** to refuse to do

escuta [iʃ'kuta] f listening; **à ~** listening out; **ficar na ~** to stand by

escutar [iʃku'ta*] vt to listen to;

(sem prestar atenção) to hear ♦ vi to listen; to hear

esfacelar [iʃfase'la*] vt to destroy

esfaquear [iʃfaki'a*] vt to stab

esfarrapado, -a [iʃfaxa'padu, a] adj ragged, tattered

esfera [iʃ'fera] f sphere; (globo) globe; (TIP, COMPUT) golfball

esfolar [iʃfo'la*] vt to skin; (arranhar) to graze; (cobrar demais a) to overcharge, fleece

esfomeado, -a [iʃfo'mjadu, a] adj famished, starving

esforçado, -a [iʃfox'sadu, a] adj committed, dedicated

esforçar-se [iʃfox'saxsi] vr: **~ para** to try hard to, strive to

esforço [iʃ'foxsu] m effort

esfregar [iʃfre'ga*] vt to rub; (com água) to scrub

esfriar [iʃ'frja*] vt to cool, chill ♦ vi to get cold; (fig) to cool off

esganar [iʃga'na*] vt to strangle, choke

esgotado, -a [iʃgo'tadu, a] adj exhausted; (consumido) used up; (livros) out of print; (ingressos) sold out

esgotamento [iʒgota'mẽtu] m exhaustion

esgotar [iʒgo'ta*] vt to drain, empty; (recursos) to use up; (pessoa, assunto) to exhaust; **esgotarse** vr to become exhausted; (mercadorias, edição) to be sold out; (recursos) to run out

esgoto [iʒ'gotu] m drain; (público) sewer

esgrima [iʒ'grima] f (esporte) fencing

esgueirar-se [iʒgei'raxsi] vr to slip away, sneak off

esguelha [iʒ'geʎa] f slant; **olhar alguém de ~** to look at sb out of the corner of one's eye

esguio, -a [eʒ'giu, a] adj slender

esmaecer [iʒmaje'se*] vi to fade

esmagador, a [iʒmagado*, a] adj crushing; (provas) irrefutable; (maioria) overwhelming

esmagar [iʒma'ga*] vt to crush

esmalte [iʒ'mawtʃi] m enamel; (de unhas) nail polish

esmeralda [iʒme'rawda] f emerald

esmerar-se [iʒme'raxsi] vr: ~ em fazer algo to take great care in doing sth

esmigalhar [iʒmiga'ʎa*] vt to crumble; (despedaçar) to shatter; (esmagar) to crush; **esmigalhar-se** vr to crumble; to smash, shatter

esmo ['eʒmu] m: a ~ at random; falar a ~ to prattle

esmola [iʒ'mɔla] f alms pl; pedir ~s to beg

esmurrar [iʒmu'xa*] vt to punch

esnobe [iʒ'nɔbi] adj snobbish ♦ m/f snob

espacial [iʃpa'sjaw] (pl -ais) adj space atr; nave ~ spaceship

espaço [iʃ'pasu] m space; (tempo) period; ~ para 3 pessoas room for 3 people; a ~s from time to time; **espaçoso, -a** [iʃpa'sozu, ɔza] adj spacious, roomy

espada [iʃ'pada] f sword; ~s fpl (CARTAS) spades

espadarte [iʃpa'daxtʃi] m swordfish

espairecer [iʃpajre'se*] vt to amuse, entertain ♦ vi to relax; **espairecer-se** vr to relax

espaldar [iʃpaw'da*] m (chair) back

espalhafato [iʃpaʎa'fatu] m din, commotion

espalhar [iʃpa'ʎa*] vt to scatter; (boato, medo) to spread; (luz) to shed; **espalhar-se** vr to spread; (refestelar-se) to lounge

espanador [iʃpana'do*] m duster

espancar [iʃpã'ka*] vt to beat up

Espanha [iʃ'paɲa] f: a ~ Spain; **espanhol, a** [iʃpa'ɲow, ola] (pl -óis, ~s) adj Spanish ♦ m/f Spaniard ♦ m (LING) Spanish; os espanhóis mpl the Spanish

espantado, -a [iʃpã'tadu, a] adj astonished, amazed; (assustado) frightened

espantalho [iʃpã'taʎu] m scarecrow

espantar [iʃpã'ta*] vt to frighten; (admirar) to amaze, astonish; (afugentar) to frighten away ♦ vi to be amazing; **espantar-se** vr to be astonished ou amazed; to be frightened

espanto [iʃ'pãtu] m fright, fear; (admiração) astonishment, amazement; **espantoso, -a** [iʃpã'tozu, ɔza] adj amazing

esparadrapo [iʃpara'drapu] m (sticking) plaster (BRIT), bandaid ® (US)

esparramar [iʃpaxa'ma*] vt to splash; (espalhar) to scatter

esparso, -a [iʃ'paxsu, a] adj scattered; (solto) loose

espasmo [iʃ'paʒmu] m spasm, convulsion

espatifar [iʃpatʃi'fa*] vt to smash; **espatifar-se** vr to smash; (avião) to crash

especial [iʃpe'sjaw] (pl -ais) adj special; em ~ especially; **especialidade** [iʃpesjali'dadʒi] f speciality (BRIT), specialty (US); (ramo de atividades) specialization; **especialista** [iʃpesja'liʃta] m/f specialist; (perito) expert; **especializar-se** [iʃpesjali'zaxsi] vr: **especializar-se (em)** to specialize (in)

espécie [iʃ'pɛsi] f (BIO) species; (tipo) sort, kind; causar ~ to be surprising; pagar em ~ to pay in cash

especificar [iʃpesifi'ka*] vt to

specify; **específico, -a** [iʃpe'sifiku, a] *adj* specific

espécime [iʃ'pɛsimi] *m* specimen

espécimen [iʃ'pɛsimẽ] (*pl* **~s**) *m* = espécime

espectáculo *etc* [iʃpek'takulu] (*PT*) *m* = espetáculo *etc*

espectador, a [iʃpekta'do*, a] *m/f* onlooker; (*TV*) viewer; (*ESPORTE*) spectator; (*TEATRO*) member of the audience; **~es** *mpl* (*TV*, *TEATRO*) audience *sg*

especular [iʃpeku'la*] *vi*: **~ (sobre)** to speculate (on)

espelho [iʃ'peʎu] *m* mirror; (*fig*) model; **~ retrovisor** (*AUTO*) rearview mirror

espera [iʃ'pɛra] *f* (*demora*) wait; (*expectativa*) expectation; **à ~ de** waiting for; **à minha ~** waiting for me

esperança [iʃpe'rãsa] *f* hope; (*expectativa*) expectation; **dar ~s a alguém** to raise sb's hopes; **esperançoso, -a** [iʃperã'sozu, ɔza] *adj* hopeful

esperar [iʃpe'ra*] *vt* to wait for; (*contar com: bebê*) to expect; (*desejar*) to hope for ♦ *vi* to wait; to expect

esperma [iʃ'pɛrma] *f* sperm

espertalhão, -lhona [iʃpexta-'ʎãw, ʎɔna] (*pl* **-ões**, **~s**) *adj* crafty, shrewd

esperteza [iʃpex'teza] *f* cleverness; (*astúcia*) cunning

esperto, -a [iʃ'pɛxtu, a] *adj* clever; (*espertalhão*) crafty

espesso, -a [iʃ'pesu, a] *adj* thick; **espessura** [iʃpe'sura] *f* thickness

espetacular [iʃpetaku'la*] *adj* spectacular

espetáculo [iʃpe'takulu] *m* (*TEATRO*) show; (*vista*) sight; (*cena ridícula*) spectacle; **dar ~** to make a spectacle

of o.s.

espetar [iʃpe'ta*] *vt* (*carne*) to put on a spit; (*cravar*) to stick; **espetar-se** *vr* to prick o.s.; **~ algo em algo** to pin sth to sth

espeto [iʃ'petu] *m* spit; (*pau*) pointed stick; **ser um ~** (*ser difícil*) to be awkward

espevitado, -a [iʃpevi'tadu, a] *adj* (*fig: vivo*) lively

espiã [iʃ'pjã] *f de* espião

espiada [iʃ'pjada] *f*: **dar uma ~** to have a look

espião, -piã [iʃ'pjãw, 'pjã] (*pl* -ões, **~s**) *m/f* spy

espiar [iʃ'pja*] *vt* to spy on; (*uma ocasião*) to watch out for; (*olhar*) to watch ♦ *vi* to spy; (*olhar*) to peer

espiga [iʃ'piga] *f* (*de milho*) ear

espinafre [iʃpi'nafri] *m* spinach

espingarda [iʃpĩ'gaxda] *f* shotgun, rifle

espinha [iʃ'piɲa] *f* (*de peixe*) bone; (*na pele*) spot, pimple; (*coluna vertebral*) spine

espinho [iʃ'piɲu] *m* thorn; (*de animal*) spine; (*fig: dificuldade*) snag; **espinhoso, -a** [iʃpi'nozu, ɔza] *adj* (*planta*) prickly, thorny; (*fig: difícil*) difficult; (: *problema*) thorny

espiões [iʃ'pjõjʃ] *mpl de* espião

espionagem [iʃpio'naʒẽ] *f* spying, espionage

espionar [iʃpjo'na*] *vt* to spy on ♦ *vi* to spy, snoop

espírito [iʃ'piritu] *m* spirit; (*pensamento*) mind; **~ esportivo** sense of humo(u)r; **E~ Santo** Holy Spirit

espiritual [iʃpiri'twaw] (*pl* **-ais**) *adj* spiritual

espirituoso, -a [iʃpiri'twozu, ɔza] *adj* witty

espirrar [iʃpi'xa*] *vi* to sneeze; (*jorrar*) to spurt out ♦ *vt* (*água*) to spurt; **espirro** [iʃ'pixu] *m* sneeze

esplêndido, -a [iʃˈplẽdʒidu, a] *adj* splendid

esplendor [iʃplẽˈdo*] *m* splendour (*BRIT*), splendor (*US*)

esponja [iʃˈpõʒa] *f* sponge

espontâneo, -a [iʃpõˈtanju, a] *adj* spontaneous; (*pessoa*) straightforward

esporádico, -a [iʃpoˈradʒiku, a] *adj* sporadic

esporte [iʃˈpɔxtʃi] (*BR*) *m* sport; **esportista** [iʃpoxˈtʃiʃta] *adj* sporting ♦ *m/f* sportsman/woman; **esportivo, -a** [iʃpoxˈtʃivu, a] *adj* sporting

esposa [iʃˈpoza] *f* wife

esposo [iʃˈpozu] *m* husband

espreguiçadeira [iʃpregisaˈdejra] *f* deck chair; (*com lugar para as pernas*) lounger

espreguiçar-se [iʃpregiˈsaxsi] *vr* to stretch

espreita [iʃˈprejta] *f*: **ficar à ~** to keep watch

espreitar [iʃprejˈta*] *vt* to spy on; (*observar*) to observe, watch

espremer [iʃpreˈme*] *vt* (*fruta*) to squeeze; (*roupa molhada*) to wring out; (*pessoas*) to squash; **espremer-se** *vr* (*multidão*) to be squashed together; (*uma pessoa*) to squash up

espuma [iʃˈpuma] *f* foam; (*de cerveja*) froth, head; (*de sabão*) lather; (*de ondas*) surf; **~ de borracha** foam rubber; **espumante** [iʃpuˈmãtʃi] *adj* frothy, foamy; (*vinho*) sparkling

esq. *abr* (= *esquerdo/a*)l

esquadra [iʃˈkwadra] *f* (*NÁUT*) fleet; (*PT*: *da polícia*) police station

esquadrão [iʃkwaˈdrãw] (*pl* -ões) *m* squadron

esquadrilha [iʃkwaˈdriʎa] *f* squadron

esquadrões [iʃkwaˈdrõjʃ] *mpl de* esquadrão

esquálido, -a [iʃˈkwalidu, a] *adj* squalid, filthy

esquartejar [iʃkwaxteˈʒa*] *vt* to quarter

esquecer [iʃkeˈse*] *vt, vi* to forget; **esquecer-se** *vr*: **~-se de** to forget; **esquecido, -a** [iʃkeˈsidu, a] *adj* forgotten; (*pessoa*) forgetful

esqueleto [iʃkeˈletu] *m* skeleton; (*arcabouço*) framework

esquema [iʃˈkema] *m* outline; (*plano*) scheme; (*diagrama*) diagram, plan

esquentar [iʃkẽˈta*] *vt* to heat (up), warm (up); (*fig: irritar*) to annoy ♦ *vi* to warm up; (*casaco*) to be warm; **esquentar-se** *vr* to get annoyed

esquerda [iʃˈkexda] *f* (*tb: POL*) left; **à ~** on the left

esquerdista [iʃkexˈdʒiʃta] *adj* leftwing ♦ *m/f* left-winger

esquerdo, -a [iʃˈkexdu, a] *adj* left

esqui [iʃˈki] *m* (*patim*) ski; (*esporte*) skiing; **~ aquático** water skiing; **fazer ~** to go skiing; **esquiar** [iʃˈkja*] *vi* to ski

esquilo [iʃˈkilu] *m* squirrel

esquina [iʃˈkina] *f* corner

esquisito, -a [iʃkiˈzitu, a] *adj* strange, odd

esquivar-se [iʃkiˈvaxsi] *vr*: **~ de** to escape from, get away from; (*deveres*) to get out of

esquivo, -a [iʃˈkivu, a] *adj* aloof, standoffish

essa [ˈesa] *pron*: **~ é/foi boa** that is/was a good one; **~ não, sem ~** come off it!; **vamos nessa** let's go!; **ainda mais ~!** that's all I need!; **corta ~!** cut it out!; **por ~s e outras** for these and other reasons; **~ de fazer ...** this business of doing ...

esse [ˈesi] *adj* (*sg*) that; (*pl*) those; (*BR*: *este*: *sg*) this; (: *pl*) these ♦ *pron* (sg) that one; (pl) those; (BR: este: sg) this one; (: pl) these

essência [e'sẽʒa] f essence; **essencial** [esẽ'sjaw] (pl -ais) adj essential; (principal) main ♦ m: **o essencial** the main thing

esta ['eʃta] f de **este**

estabelecer [iʃtabele'se*] vt to establish; (fundar) to set up

estabelecimento [iʃtabelesi'mẽtu] m establishment; (casa comercial) business

estábulo [iʃ'tabulu] m cow-shed

estaca [iʃ'taka] f post, stake; (de barraca) peg

estação [iʃta'sãw] (pl -ões) f station; (do ano) season; **~ de águas** spa; **~ balneária** seaside resort; **~ emissora** broadcasting station

estacionamento [iʃtasjona'mẽtu] m (ato) parking; (lugar) car park (BRIT), parking lot (US)

estacionar [iʃtasjo'na*] vt to park ♦ vi to park; (não mover) to remain stationary

estacionário, -a [iʃtasjo'narju, a] adj (veículo) stationary; (COM) slack

estações [iʃta'sõjʃ] fpl de **estação**

estada [iʃ'tada] f stay

estadia [iʃta'dʒia] f = **estada**

estádio [iʃ'tadʒiu] m stadium

estadista [iʃta'dʒiʃta] m/f statesman/woman

estado [iʃ'tadu] m state; **E~s Unidos (da América)** United States (of America); **~ civil** marital status; **~ de espírito** state of mind; **~ maior** staff; **estadual** [iʃta'dwaw] (pl -ais) adj state atr

estafa [iʃ'tafa] f fatigue; (esgotamento) nervous exhaustion

estagiário, -a [iʃta'ʒjarju, a] m/f probationer, trainee; (professor) student teacher; (médico) junior doctor

estágio [iʃ'taʒu] m (aprendizado) traineeship; (fase) stage

estagnado, -a [iʃtag'nadu, a] adj stagnant

estalar [iʃta'la*] vt to break; (os dedos) to snap ♦ vi to split, crack; (crepitar) to crackle

estalido [iʃta'lidu] m pop

estalo [iʃ'talu] m (do chicote) crack; (dos dedos) snap; (dos lábios) smack; (de foguete) bang; **~ de trovão** thunderclap; **de ~** suddenly

estampa [iʃ'tãpa] f (figura impressa) print; (ilustração) picture

estampado, -a [iʃtã'padu, a] adj printed ♦ m (tecido) print; (num tecido) pattern

estampar [iʃtã'pa*] vt to print; (marcar) to stamp

estancar [iʃtã'ka*] vt to staunch; (fazer cessar) to stop; **estancar-se** vr to stop

estância [iʃ'tãsja] f ranch, farm

estandarte [iʃtã'daxtʃi] m standard, banner

estanho [iʃ'taɲu] m (metal) tin

estante [iʃ'tãtʃi] f bookcase; (suporte) stand

PALAVRA CHAVE

estar [iʃ'ta*] vi 1 (lugar) to be; (em casa) to be in; (no telefone): **a Lúcia está? – não, ela não está** is Lúcia there? – no, she's not here

2 (estado) to be; **~ doente** to be ill; **~ bem** (de saúde) to be well; (financeiramente) to be well off; **~ calor/frio** to be hot/cold; **~ com fome/sede/medo** to be hungry/thirsty/afraid

3 (ação contínua): **~ fazendo** (BR) ou **a fazer** (PT) to be doing

4 (+ pp: = adj): **~ sentado/cansado** to be sitting down/tired

5 (+ pp: uso passivo): **está condenado à morte** he's been condemned

to death; **o livro está emprestado**
the book's been borrowed
6: ~ **de**: ~ **de férias/licença** to be on
holiday (BRIT) ou vacation (US)/leave;
ela estava de chapéu she had a hat
on, she was wearing a hat
7: ~ **para**: ~ **para fazer** to be about
to do; **ele está para chegar a qualquer momento** he'll be here any
minute; **não** ~ **para conversas** not
to be in the mood for talking
8: ~ **por fazer** to be still to be done
9: ~ **sem**: ~ **sem dinheiro** to have
no money; ~ **sem dormir** not to
have slept; **estou sem dormir há
três dias** I haven't slept for three
days; **está sem terminar** it isn't finished yet
10 (frases): **está bem, tá (bem)** (col)
OK; ~ **bem com** to be on good
terms with

estardalhaço [iʃtaxdaˈʎasu] m
fuss; (ostentação) ostentation

estas [ˈɛʃtaʃ] fpl de **este**

estatal [iʃtaˈtaw] ʹ (pl -ais) adj
nationalized, state-owned ♦ f state-
owned company

estático, -a [iʃˈtatʃiku, a] adj static

estatística [iʃtaˈtʃiʃtʃika] f statistic;
(ciência) statistics sg

estatizar [iʃtatʃiˈza*] vt to nationalize

estátua [iʃˈtatwa] f statue

estatura [iʃtaˈtura] f stature

estatuto [iʃtaˈtutu] m statute; (de
cidade) bye-law; (de associação) rule

estável [iʃˈtavew] (pl -eis) adj stable

este [ˈɛʃtʃi] m east ♦ adj inv (região)
eastern; (rumo, direção) easterly

este, -ta [ˈɛʃtʃi, ˈɛʃta] adj (sg) this;
(pl) these ♦ pron this one; (pl)
these; (a quem/que se referiu por último) the latter; **esta noite** (noite passada) last night; (noite de hoje)

tonight

esteira [iʃˈtejra] f mat; (de navio)
wake; (rumo) path

esteja etc [iʃˈteʒa] vb SV **estar**

estelionato [iʃteljoˈnatu] m fraud

estender [iʃtẽˈde*] vt to extend;
(mapa) to spread out; (pernas) to
stretch; (massa) to roll out; (conversa) to draw out; (corda) to pull
tight; (roupa molhada) to hang out;
estender-se vr to lie down; (fila,
terreno) to stretch, extend; ~ **a mão**
to hold out one's hand; **~-se sobre
algo** to dwell on sth, expand on sth

estéreis [iʃˈtɛrejʃ] adj pl de **estéril**

estereo... [iʃterju] prefixo stereo...;
estereofônico, -a [iʃterjoˈfoniku,
a] adj stereo(phonic); **estereótipo**
[iʃteˈrjɔtʃipu] m stereotype

estéril [iʃˈtɛriw] (pl -eis) adj sterile;
(terra) infertile; (fig) futile; **esterilizar** [iʃteriliˈza*] vt to sterilize

estético, -a [iʃˈtɛtʃiku, a] adj aesthetic (BRIT), esthetic (US)

esteve [iʃˈtevi] vb V **estar**

estibordo [iʃtʃiˈbɔxdu] m starboard

esticar [iʃtʃiˈka*] vt to stretch;
esticar-se vr to stretch out

estigma [iʃˈtʃigima] m mark, scar;
(fig) stigma

estilhaçar [iʃtʃiʎaˈsa*] vt to splinter; (despedaçar) to shatter;
estilhaçar-se vr to shatter; **esti-
lhaço** [iʃtʃiˈʎasu] m fragment; (de
pedra) chip; (de madeira, metal)
splinter

estilo [iʃˈtʃilu] m style; (TEC) stylus; ~
de vida way of life

estima [iʃˈtʃima] f esteem; (afeto)
affection; **ter ~ a** to have a high
regard for

estimação [iʃtʃimaˈsãw] f: ... **de ~**
favourite (BRIT) ..., favorite (US) ...

estimado, -a [iʃtʃiˈmadu, a] adj
respected; (em cartas): **E~ Senhor**

Dear Sir

estimar [iʃtʃi'ma*] vt to appreciate; (avaliar) to value; (ter estima a) to have a high regard for; (calcular aproximadamente) to estimate

estimativa [iʃtʃima'tʃiva] f estimate

estimulante [iʃtʃimu'lãtʃi] adj stimulating ♦ m stimulant

estimular [iʃtʃimu'la*] vt to stimulate; (incentivar) to encourage; **estímulo** [iʃ'tʃimulu] m stimulus; (ânimo) encouragement

estipular [iʃtʃipu'la*] vt to stipulate

estirar [iʃtʃi'ra*] vt to stretch (out); **estirar-se** vr to stretch

estive etc [iʃ'tʃivi] vb V estar

estocada [iʃto'kada] f stab, thrust

estocar [iʃto'ka*] vt to stock

estofo [iʃ'tofu] m (tecido) material; (para acolchoar) padding, stuffing

estojo [iʃ'toʒu] m case; ~ **de ferramentas** tool kit; ~ **de unhas** manicure set

estômago [iʃ'tomagu] m stomach; **ter ~ para (fazer)** algo to be up to (doing) sth

estontear [iʃtõ'tʃja*] vt to stun, daze

estoque [iʃ'tɔki] m (COM) stock

estorvo [iʃ'toxvu] m hindrance, obstacle; (amolação) bother, nuisance

estourado, -a [iʃto'radu, a] adj (temperamental) explosive; (col: cansado) shattered, worn out

estourar [iʃto'ra*] vi to explode; (pneu) to burst; (escândalo) to blow up; (guerra) to break out; (BR: chegar) to turn up, arrive; ~ **(com alguém)** (zangar-se) to blow up (at sb)

estouro [iʃ'toru] m explosion; **dar o ~** (fig: zangar-se) to blow up, blow one's top

estrábico, -a [iʃ'trabiku, a] adj cross-eyed

estraçalhar [iʃtrasa'ʎa*] vt (livro, objeto) to pull to pieces; (pessoa) to tear to pieces

estrada [iʃ'trada] f road; ~ **de ferro** (BR) railway (BRIT), railroad (US); ~ **principal** main road (BRIT), state highway (US)

estrado [iʃ'tradu] m (tablado) platform; (de cama) base

estragado, -a [iʃtra'gadu, a] adj ruined; (fruta) rotten; (muito mimado) spoiled, spoilt (BRIT)

estraga-prazeres [iʃtraga-] m/f inv spoilsport

estragar [iʃtra'ga*] vt to spoil; (arruinar) to ruin, wreck; (desperdiçar) to waste; (saúde) to damage; (mimar) to spoil; **estrago** [iʃ'tragu] m destruction; waste; damage; **os estragos da guerra** the ravages of war

estrangeiro, -a [iʃtrã'ʒejru, a] adj foreign ♦ m/f foreigner; **no** ~ abroad

estrangular [iʃtrãgu'la*] vt to strangle

estranhar [iʃtra'ɲa*] vt to be surprised at; (achar estranho): ~ **algo** to find sth strange; **estranhei o clima** the climate did not agree with me; **não é de se** ~ it's not surprising

estranho, -a [iʃ'traɲu, a] adj strange, odd; (influências) outside ♦ m/f (desconhecido) stranger; (de fora) outsider

estratégia [iʃtra'teʒa] f strategy

estrear [iʃ'trja*] vt (vestido) to wear for the first time; (peça de teatro) to perform for the first time; (veículo) to use for the first time; (filme) to show for the first time, première; (iniciar): ~ **uma carreira** to embark on ou begin a career ♦ vi (ator, *jogador*) to make one's first appearance; (*filme*, *peça*) to open

estrebaria [iʃtreba'ria] *f* stable

estréia [iʃ'treja] *f* (*de artista*) debut; (*de uma peça*) first night; (*de um filme*) opening

estreitar [iʃtrej'ta*] (*roupa*) to take in; (*abraçar*) to hug; (*laços de amizade*) to strengthen ♦ *vi* (*estrada*) to narrow

estreito, -a [iʃ'trejtu, a] *adj* narrow; (*saia*) straight; (*vínculo, relação*) close; (*medida*) strict ♦ *m* strait

estrela [iʃ'trela] *f* star; ~ **cadente** falling star; **estrelado, -a** [iʃtre-'ladu, a] *adj* (*céu*) starry; (*ovo*) fried

estremecer [iʃtreme'se*] *vt* to shake; (*amizade*) to strain; (*fazer tremer*): ~ **alguém** to make sb shudder ♦ *vi* to shake; (*tremer*) to tremble; (*horrorizar-se*) to shudder; (*amizade*) to be strained

estremecimento [iʃtremesi-'mētu] *m* shaking, trembling; (*tremor*) tremor; (*numa amizade*) tension

estresse [iʃ'tresi] *m* stress

estribeira [iʃtri'bejra] *f*: **perder as ~s** (*col*) to fly off the handle, lose one's temper

estribo [iʃ'tribu] *m* (*de cavalo*) stirrup; (*degrau*) step; (*fig*: *apoio*) support

estridente [iʃtri'dētʃi] *adj* shrill, piercing

estrofe [iʃ'trɔfi] *f* stanza

estrondo [iʃ'trõdu] *m* (*de trovão*) rumble; (*de armas*) din

estrutura [iʃtru'tura] *f* structure; (*armação*) framework; (*de edifício*) fabric

estudante [iʃtu'dãtʃi] *m/f* student; **estudantil** [iʃtudã'tʃiw] (*pl* -**is**) *adj* student *atr*

estudar [iʃtu'da*] *vt, vi* to study

estúdio [iʃ'tudʒu] *m* studio

estudioso, -a [iʃtu'dʒozu, ɔza] *adj* studious ♦ *m/f* student

estudo [iʃ'tudu] *m* study

estufa [iʃ'tufa] *f* (*fogão*) stove; (*de plantas*) greenhouse; (*de fogão*) plate warmer; **efeito** ~ greenhouse effect

estufado [iʃtu'fadu] (*PT*) *m* stew

estupefato, -a [iʃtupe'fatu, a] (*PT* -**ct**-) *adj* dumbfounded

estupendo, -a [iʃtu'pēdu, a] *adj* wonderful, terrific

estupidez [iʃtupi'deʒ] *f* stupidity; (*ato, dito*) stupid thing; (*grosseria*) rudeness

estúpido, -a [iʃ'tupidu, a] *adj* stupid; (*grosseiro*) rude, churlish ♦ *m/f* idiot; oaf

estuprar [iʃtu'pra*] *vt* to rape; **estupro** [iʃ'tupru] *m* rape

esvaziar [iʒva'zja*] *vt* to empty; **esvaziar-se** *vr* to empty

etapa [e'tapa] *f* stage

etc. *abr* (= *et cetera*) etc.

eternidade [etexni'dadʒi] *f* eternity

eterno, -a [e'texnu, a] *adj* eternal

ética ['ɛtʃika] *f* ethics *pl*

ético, -a [ə'tʃiku, a] *adj* ethical

Etiópia [e'tʃjɔpia] *f*: **a ~** Ethiopia

etiqueta [etʃi'keta] *f* etiquette; (*rótulo, em roupa*) label; (*que se amarra*) tag

étnico, -a ['ɛtʃniku, a] *adj* ethnic

etos [e'tuʃ] *m inv* ethos

eu [ew] *pron* I ♦ *m* self; **sou ~** it's me

EUA *abr mpl* (= *Estados Unidos da América*) USA

eucaristia [ewkariʃ'tʃia] *f* Holy Communion

euro ['ewru] *m* (*moeda*) euro

Europa [ew'rɔpa] *f*: **a ~** Europe; **europeu, -péia** [ewro'peu, 'peja] *adj, m/f* European

evacuar [eva'kwa*] *vt* to evacuate;

(*sair de*) to leave; (*MED*) to discharge ♦ *vi* to defecate

evadir [eva'dʒi*] *vt* to evade; **evadir-se** *vr* to escape

evangelho [evã'ʒeʎu] *m* gospel

evaporar [evapo'ra*] *vt*, *vi* to evaporate; **evaporar-se** *vr* to evaporate; (*desaparecer*) to vanish

evasão [eva'zãw] (*pl* -**ões**) *f* escape, flight; (*fig*) evasion

evasiva [eva'ziva] *f* excuse

evasivo, -a [eva'zivu, a] *adj* evasive

evasões [eva'zõjʃ] *fpl de* **evasão**

evento [e'vẽtu] *m* event; (*eventualidade*) eventuality

eventual [evẽ'tuaw] (*pl* -**ais**) *adj* fortuitous, accidental; **eventualidade** [evẽtwali'dadʒi] *f* eventuality

evidência [evi'dẽsja] *f* evidence, proof; **evidenciar** [evidẽ'sja*] *vt* to prove; (*mostrar*) to show; **evidenciar-se** *vr* to be evident, be obvious

evidente [evi'dẽtʃi] *adj* obvious, evident

evitar [evi'ta*] *vt* to avoid; ~ **de fazer algo** to avoid doing sth

evocar [evo'ka*] *vt* to evoke; (*espíritos*) to invoke

evolução [evolu'sãw] (*pl* -**ões**) *f* development; (*MIL*) manoeuvre (*BRIT*), maneuver (*US*); (*movimento*) movement; (*BIO*) evolution

evoluir [evo'lwi*] *vi* to evolve; ~ **para** to evolve into

ex- [ef-, eʒ-] *prefixo* ex-, former

Ex.ª *abr* = **Excelência**

exacto, -a [e'zatu, a] *etc* (*PT*) = **exato** *etc*

exagerar [ezaʒe'ra*] *vt* to exaggerate ♦ *vi* to exaggerate; (*agir com exagero*) to overdo it; **exagero** [eza'ʒeru] *m* exaggeration

exalar [eza'la*] *vt* (*odor*) to give off

exaltado, -a [ezaw'tadu, a] *adj* fanatical; (*apaixonado*) overexcited

exaltar [ezaw'ta*] *vt* (*elevar: pessoa, virtude*) to exalt; (*louvar*) to praise; (*excitar*) to excite; (*irritar*) to annoy; **exaltar-se** *vr* (*irritar-se*) to get worked up; (*arrebatar-se*) to get carried away

exame [e'zami] *m* (*EDUC*) examination, exam; (*MED etc*) examination; **fazer um** ~ (*EDUC*) to take an exam; (*MED*) to have an examination

examinar [ezami'na*] *vt* to examine

exasperar [ezaʃpe'ra*] *vt* to exasperate; **exasperar-se** *vr* to get exasperated

exatidão [ezatʃi'dãw] *f* accuracy; (*perfeição*) correctness

exato, -a [e'zatu, a] *adj* right, correct; (*preciso*) exact; ~! exactly!

exaustão [ezawʃ'tãw] *f* exhaustion; **exausto, -a** [e'zawʃtu, a] *adj* exhausted

exaustor [ezawʃ'to*] *m* extractor fan

exceção [ese'sãw] (*pl* -**ões**) *f* exception; **com** ~ **de** with the exception of; **abrir** ~ to make an exception

excedente [ese'dẽtʃi] *adj* excess; (*COM*) surplus ♦ *m* (*COM*) surplus

exceder [ese'de*] *vt* to exceed; (*superar*) to surpass; **exceder-se** *vr* (*cometer excessos*) to go too far; (*cansar-se*) to overdo things

excelência [ese'lẽsja] *f* excellence; **por** ~ par excellence; **Vossa E**~ Your Excellency; **excelente** [ese'lẽtʃi] *adj* excellent

excêntrico, -a [e'sẽtriku, a] *adj*, *m/f* eccentric

excepção [ese'sãw] (*PT*) *f* = **exceção**

excepcional [esepsjo'naw] (*pl* -**ais**) *adj* exceptional; (*especial*) special; (*MED*) handicapped

excepto etc [e'sɛtu] (PT) = **exceto** etc

excessivo, -a [ese'sivu, a] adj excessive

excesso [e'sɛsu] m excess; (COM) surplus

exceto [e'sɛtu] prep except (for), apart from

excitação [esita'sãw] f excitement

excitado, -a [esi'tadu, a] adj excited; (estimulado) aroused

excitante [esi'tãtʃi] adj exciting

excitar [esi'ta*] vt to excite; (estimular) to arouse; **excitar-se** vr to get excited

exclamação [iʃklama'sãw] (pl -ões) f exclamation

exclamar [iʃkla'ma*] vi to exclaim

excluir [iʃ'klwi*] vt to exclude, leave out; (eliminar) to rule out; (ser incompatível com) to preclude; **exclusão** [iʃklu'zãw] f exclusion; **exclusivo, -a** [iʃklu'zivu, a] adj exclusive

excursão [iʃkux'sãw] (pl -ões) f outing, excursion; **~ a pé** hike; **excursionista** [iʃkuxsjo'niʃta] m/f tourist; (para o dia) day-tripper; (a pé) hiker

execução [izeku'sãw] (pl -ões) f execution; (de música) performance

executar [izeku'ta*] vt to execute; (MÚS) to perform; (plano) to carry out; (papel teatral) to play

executivo, -a [izeku'tʃivu, a] adj, m/f executive

exemplar [ezẽ'pla*] adj exemplary ♦ m model, example; (BIO) specimen; (livro) copy; (peça) piece

exemplo [e'zẽplu] m example; **por ~** for example

exercer [ezex'se*] vt to exercise; (influência, pressão) to exert; (função) to perform; (profissão) to practise (BRIT), practice (US); (obri-

gações) to carry out

exercício [ezex'sisju] m exercise; (de medicina) practice; (MIL) drill; (COM) financial year

exercitar [izexsi'ta*] vt (profissão) to practise (BRIT), practice (US); (direitos, músculos) to exercise; (adestrar) to train

exército [e'zɛxsitu] m army

exibição [ezibi'sãw] (pl -ões) f show, display; (de filme) showing

exibir [ezi'bi*] vt to show, display; (alardear) to show off; (filme) to show, screen; **exibir-se** vr to show off; (indecentemente) to expose o.s.

exigência [ezi'ʒẽsja] f demand; (o necessário) requirement; **exigente** [ezi'ʒẽtʃi] adj demanding

exigir [ezi'ʒi*] vt to demand

exíguo, -a [e'zigwu, a] adj (diminuto) small; (escasso) scanty

exilado, -a [ezi'ladu, a] m/f exile

exilar [ezi'la*] vt to exile; **exilar-se** vr to go into exile; **exílio** [e'zilju] m exile; (forçado) deportation

existência [eziʃ'tẽsja] f existence; (vida) life

existir [eziʃ'tʃi*] vi to exist; **existe/existem ... (há)** there is/are ...

êxito ['ezitu] m result; (sucesso) success; (música, filme) hit; **ter ~ (em)** to succeed (in), be successful (in)

Exmo(s)/a(s) abr (= Excelentíssimo(s)/a(s)) Dear

êxodo ['ɛzodu] m exodus

exorcista [ezox'siʃta] m/f exorcist

exótico, -a [e'zɔtʃiku, a] adj exotic

expandir [iʃpã'dʒi*] vt to expand; (espalhar) to spread; **expandir-se** vr to expand; **~-se com alguém** to be frank with sb

expansão [iʃpã'sãw] f expansion, spread; (de alegria) effusiveness

expansivo, -a [iʃpã'sivu, a] adj

(*pessoa*) outgoing

expeça *etc* [iʃˈpɛsa] *vb V* **expedir**

expectativa [iʃpektaˈtʃiva] *f* expectation

expedição [iʃpedʒiˈsãw] (*pl* -**ões**) *f* (*viagem*) expedition; (*de mercadorias*) despatch; (*por navio*) shipment; (*de passaporte etc*) issue

expediente [iʃpeˈdʒjẽtʃi] *m* means; (*serviço*) working day; (*correspondência*) correspondence ♦ *adj* expedient; **~ bancário** banking hours *pl*; **~ do escritório** office hours *pl*

expedir [iʃpeˈdʒiʀ] *vt* to send, despatch; (*bilhete, passaporte, decreto*) to issue

expelir [iʃpeˈliʀ] *vt* to expel; (*sangue*) to spit

experiência [iʃpeˈrjẽsja] *f* experience; (*prova*) experiment, test; **em ~ on trial** '

experiente [iʃpeˈrjẽtʃi] *adj* experienced

experimentar [iʃperimẽˈtaʀ] *vt* (*comida*) to taste; (*vestido*) to try on; (*pôr à prova*) to try out, test; (*conhecer pela experiência*) to experience; (*sofrer*) to suffer, undergo; **experimento** [iʃperiˈmẽtu] *m* experiment

expilo *etc* [iʃˈpilu] *vb V* **expelir**

expirar [iʃpiˈraʀ] *vt* to exhale, breathe out ♦ *vi* to die; (*terminar*) to end

explicação [iʃplikaˈsãw] (*pl* -**ões**) *f* explanation

explicar [iʃpliˈkaʀ] *vt*, *vi* to explain; **explicar-se** *vr* to explain o.s.

explícito, -a [iʃˈplisitu, a] *adj* explicit, clear

explodir [iʃploˈdʒiʀ] *vt*, *vi* to explode

exploração [iʃploraˈsãw] *f* exploration; (*abuso*) exploitation; (*de uma mina*) working

explorador, a [iʃploraˈdo*, a] *m/f* explorer; (*de outros*) exploiter

explorar [iʃploˈraʀ] *vt* (*região*) to explore; (*mina*) to work, run; (*ferida*) to probe; (*trabalhadores etc*) to exploit

explosão [iʃploˈzãw] (*pl* -**ões**) *f* explosion; (*fig*) outburst; **explosivo, -a** [iʃploˈzivu, a] *adj* explosive; (*pessoa*) hot-headed ♦ *m* explosive

expor [iʃˈpo*] (*irreg*: *como* **pôr**) *vt* to expose; (*a vida*) to risk; (*teoria*) to explain; (*revelar*) to reveal; (*mercadorias*) to display; (*quadros*) to exhibit; **expor-se** *vr* to expose o.s.

exportação [iʃpoxtaˈsãw] *f* (*ato*) export(ing); (*mercadorias*) exports *pl*

exportador, a [iʃpoxtaˈdo*, a] *adj* exporting ♦ *m/f* exporter

exportar [iʃpoxˈtaʀ] *vt* to export

exposição [iʃposiˈsãw] (*pl* -**ões**) *f* exhibition; (*explicação*) explanation; (*declaração*) statement; (*narração*) account; (*FOTO*) exposure

exposto, -a [iʃˈpoʃtu, ˈpɔʃta] *adj* (*lugar*) exposed; (*quadro, mercadoria*) on show *ou* display ♦ *m*: **o acima** = the above

expressão [iʃpreˈsãw] (*pl* -**ões**) *f* expression

expressar [iʃpreˈsa*] *vt* to express; **expressivo, -a** [iʃpreˈsivu, a] *adj* expressive; (*pessoa*) demonstrative

expresso, -a [iʃˈpresu, a] *pp de* **exprimir** ♦ *adj* definite, clear; (*trem, ordem, carta*) express ♦ *m* express

expressões [iʃpreˈsõjʃ] *fpl de* **expressão**

exprimir [iʃpriˈmi*] *vt* to express

expulsão [iʃpulˈsãw] (*pl* -**ões**) *f* expulsion; (*ESPORTE*) sending off

expulsar [iʃpuwˈsa*] *vt* to expel; (*de uma festa, clube etc*) to throw out; (*inimigo*) to drive out; (*estrangeiro*) to expel, deport; (*jogador*) to send off

expulso, -a [iʃˈpuwsu, a] *pp de* expulsar

expulsões [iʃpulˈsõiʃ] *fpl de* expulsão

êxtase [ˈeʃtazi] *m* ecstasy

extensão [iʃtēˈsãw] (*pl* -**ões**) *f* (*ger*, *TEL*) extension; (*de uma empresa*) expansion; (*terreno*) expanse; (*tempo*) length, duration; (*de conhecimentos*) extent

extenso, -a [iʃˈtēsu, a] *adj* extensive; (*comprido*) long; (*artigo*) full, comprehensive; **por ~** in full

extenuante [iʃteˈnwātʃi] *adj* exhausting; (*debilitante*) debilitating

exterior [iʃteˈrjoʀ] *adj* (*de fora*) outside, exterior; (*aparência*) outward; (*comércio*) foreign ♦ *m* (*da casa*) outside; (*aspecto*) outward appearance; **do ~** (*do estrangeiro*) from abroad; **no ~** abroad

exterminar [iʃtexmiˈnaʀ] *vt* (*inimigo*) to wipe out, exterminate; (*acabar com*) to do away with

externo, -a [iʃˈtexnu, a] *adj* external; (*aparente*) outward; **aluno ~** day pupil

extinguir [iʃtʃĩˈgiʀ] *vt* (*fogo*) to put out, extinguish; (*um povo*) to wipe out; **extinguir-se** *vr* (*fogo, luz*) to go out; (*BIO*) to become extinct

extinto, -a [iʃˈtʃĩtu, a] *adj* (*fogo*) extinguished; (*língua, pessoa*) dead; (*animal, vulcão*) extinct; (*associação etc*) defunct; **extintor** [iʃtʃĩˈtoʀ] *m* (fire) extinguisher

extorquir [iʃtoxˈkiʀ] *vt* to extort

extorsão [iʃtoxˈsãw] *f* extortion

extra [ˈɛʃtra] *adj* extra ♦ *m/f* extra person; (*TEATRO*) extra

extração [iʃtraˈsãw] (*PT* -**cç**-) (*pl* -ões) *f* extraction; (*de loteria*) draw

extracto [iʃˈtratu] (*PT*) *m* = **extrato**

extrair [iʃtraˈjiʀ] *vt* to extract, take out

extraordinário, -a [iʃtraoxdʒiˈnarju, a] *adj* extraordinary; (*despesa*) extra; (*reunião*) special

extrato [iʃˈtratu] *m* extract; (*resumo*) summary; **~ (bancário)** (bank) statement

extravagância [iʃtravaˈgãsja] *f* extravagance; **extravagante** [iʃtravaˈgãtʃi] *adj* extravagant; (*roupa*) outlandish; (*conduta*) wild

extravasar [iʃtravaˈzaʀ] *vi* to overflow

extraviado, -a [iʃtraˈvjadu, a] *adj* lost, missing

extraviar [iʃtraˈvjaʀ] *vt* to mislay; (*pessoa*) to lead astray; (*dinheiro*) to embezzle; **extraviar-se** *vr* to get lost; **extravio** [iʃtraˈviu] *m* loss; embezzlement; (*fig*) deviation

extremado, -a [iʃtreˈmadu, a] *adj* extreme

extremidade [iʃtremiˈdadʒi] *f* extremity; (*do dedo*) tip; (*ponta*) end; (*beira*) edge

extremo, -a [iʃˈtrɛmu, a] *adj* extreme ♦ *m* extreme; **ao ~** extremely

extrovertido, -a [eʃtrovexˈtʃidu, a] *adj* extrovert, outgoing ♦ *m/f* extrovert

exultante [ezuwˈtãtʃi] *adj* jubilant, exultant

F

fã [fã] (*col*) *m/f* fan

fábrica [ˈfabrika] *f* factory; **~ de cerveja** brewery; **a preço de ~** wholesale

fabricação [fabrikaˈsãw] *f* manufacture; **~ em série** mass production

fabricar [fabri'ka*] *vt* to manufacture, make

fábula ['fabula] *f* fable; (*conto*) tale

fabuloso, -a [fabu'lozu, ɔza] *adj* fabulous

faca ['faka] *f* knife; **facada** [fa'kada] *f* stab, cut

façanha [fa'saɲa] *f* exploit, deed

facção [fak'sãw] (*pl* **-ões**) *f* faction

face ['fasi] *f* face; (*bochecha*) cheek; **em ~ de** in view of; **fazer ~ a** to face up to; **disquete de ~ simples/dupla** (*COMPUT*) single-/double-sided disk

fáceis ['fasejʃ] *adj pl de* **fácil**

faceta [fa'seta] *f* facet

fachada [fa'ʃada] *f* façade, front

fácil ['fasiw] (*pl* **-eis**) *adj* easy; (*temperamento, pessoa*) easy-going ♦ *adv* easily; **facilidade** [fasili'dadʒi] *f* ease; (*jeito*) facility; **facilidades** *fpl* (*recursos*) facilities; **ter facilidade para algo** to have a talent for sth

facilitar [fasili'ta*] *vt* to facilitate, make easy; (*fornecer*): **~ algo a alguém** to provide sb with sth

faço *etc* ['fasu] *vb V* **fazer**

fac-símile [fak'simili] (*pl* **~s**) *m* (*cópia*) facsimile; (*carta*) fax; (*máquina*) fax (machine); **enviar por ~** to fax

facto ['faktu] (*PT*) *m* = **fato**

factor [fak'to*] (*PT*) *m* = **fator**

factual [fak'twaw] (*pl* **-ais**) *adj* factual

factura *etc* [fak'tura] (*PT*) = **fatura** *etc*

faculdade [fakuw'dadʒi] *f* (*ger*, *EDUC*) faculty; (*poder*) power

facultativo, -a [fakuwta'tʃivu, a] *adj* optional ♦ *m* doctor

fadado, -a [fa'dadu, a] *adj* destined

fadiga [fa'dʒiga] *f* fatigue

fadista [fa'dʒiʃta] *m/f* fado singer ♦ *m* (*PT*) ruffian

fado ['fadu] *m* fate; (*canção*) fado;

see boxed note

FADO

The best-known musical form in Portugal is the melancholic *fado*, which is traditionally sung by a soloist (known as a *fadista*) accompanied by the Portuguese *guitarra*. There are two main types of *fado*: Coimbra *fado* is traditionally sung by men, and is considered to be more cerebral than the *fado* from Lisbon, which is sung by both men and women. The theme is nearly always one of deep nostalgia known as *saudade*, and the harsh reality of life.

---

faia ['faja] *f* beech (tree)

faisão [faj'zãw] (*-ies, pl* **-ães**) *m* pheasant

faísca [fa'iʃka] *f* spark; (*brilho*) flash

faisões [faj'zõjʃ] *mpl de* **faisão**

faixa ['fajʃa] *f* (*cinto, JUDÔ*) belt; (*tira*) strip; (*área*) zone; (*AUTO: pista*) lane; (*BR: para pedestres*) zebra crossing (*BRIT*), crosswalk (*US*); (*MED*) bandage; (*num disco*) track

fala ['fala] *f* speech; **chamar às ~s** to call to account; **sem ~** speechless

falante [fa'lãtʃi] *adj* talkative

falar [fa'la*] *vt* (*língua*) to speak; (*besteira etc*) to talk; (*dizer*) to say; (*verdade, mentira*) to tell ♦ *vi* to speak; **~ algo a alguém** to tell sb sth; **~ de** *ou* **em algo** to talk about sth; **~ com alguém** to talk to sb; **por ~ em** speaking of; **sem ~ em** not to mention; **falou!, 'tá falado!** (*col*) OK!

falcão [faw'kãw] (*pl* **-ões**) *m* falcon

falecer [fale'se*] *vi* to die; **falecimento** [falesi'mẽtu] *m* death

falência [fa'lẽsja] *f* bankruptcy; **abrir ~** to declare o.s. bankrupt; **ir à**

~ to go bankrupt; **levar à ~** to bankrupt

falésia [fa'lɛzja] f cliff

falha ['faʎa] f fault; (lacuna) omission; (de caráter) flaw

falhar [fa'ʎa*] vi to fail; (não acertar) to miss; (errar) to be wrong

falho, -a ['faʎu, a] adj faulty; (deficiente) wanting

falido, -a [fa'lidu, a] adj, m/f bankrupt

falir [fa'li*] vi to fail; (COM) to go bankrupt

falsário, -a [faw'sarju, a] m/f forger

falsidade [fawsi'dadʒi] f falsehood; (fingimento) pretence (BRIT), pretense (US)

falsificar [fawsifi'ka*] vt (forjar) to forge; (falsear) to falsify; (adulterar) to adulterate; (desvirtuar) to misrepresent

falso, -a ['fawsu, a] adj false; (fraudulento) dishonest; (errôneo) wrong; (jóia, moeda, quadro) fake; **pisar em ~** to blunder

falta ['fawta] f (carência) lack; (ausência) absence; (defeito, culpa) fault; (FUTEBOL) foul; **por ou na ~ de** for lack of; **sem ~** without fail; **fazer ~** to be lacking, be needed; **sentir ~ de alguém/algo** to miss sb/sth; **ter ~ de** to lack, be in need of

faltar [faw'ta*] vi to be lacking, be wanting; (pessoa) to be absent; (falhar) to fail; **~ ao trabalho** to be absent from work; **~ à palavra** to break one's word; **falta pouco para ... it won't be long until ...**

fama ['fama] f (renome) fame; (reputação) reputation

família [fa'milja] f family

familiar [fami'lja*] adj (da família) family atr; (conhecido) familiar ♦ m/f relation, relative; **familiaridade** [familjari'dadʒi] f familiarity; (sem-

cerimônia) informality

faminto, -a [fa'mĩtu, a] adj hungry; (fig): **~ de** eager for

famoso, -a [fa'mozu, ɔza] adj famous

fanático, -a [fa'natʃiku, a] adj fanatical ♦ m/f fanatic

fantasia [fãta'zia] f fantasy; (imaginação) imagination; (capricho) fancy; (traje) fancy dress

fantasiar [fãta'zja*] vt to imagine ♦ vi to daydream; **fantasiar-se** vr to dress up (in fancy dress)

fantasma [fã'taʒma] m ghost; (alucinação) illusion

fantástico, -a [fã'taʃtʃiku, a] adj fantastic; (ilusório) imaginary; (incrível) unbelievable

fantoche [fã'toʃi] m puppet

farda ['faxda] f uniform

fardo ['faxdu] m bundle; (carga) load; (fig) burden

farei etc [fa'rej] vb V **fazer**

farinha [fa'riɲa] f: **~ (de mesa)** (manioc) flour; **~ de rosca** breadcrumbs pl; **~ de trigo** plain flour

farmacêutico, -a [faxma-'sewtʃiku, a] adj pharmaceutical ♦ m/f pharmacist, chemist (BRIT)

farmácia [fax'masja] f pharmacy, chemist's (shop) (BRIT)

faro ['faru] m sense of smell; (fig) flair

farofa [fa'rɔfa] f (CULIN) side dish based on manioc flour

farol [fa'rɔw] m (pl -óis) m lighthouse; (AUTO) headlight; **com ~ alto** (AUTO) on full (BRIT) ou high (US) beam; **com ~ baixo** dipped headlights pl (BRIT), dimmed beam (US)

farra ['faxa] f binge, spree

farrapo [fa'xapu] m rag

farsa ['faxsa] f farce; **farsante** [fax'sãtʃi] m/f joker

fartar [fax'ta*] vt to satiate; (encher)

to fill up; **fartar-se** vr to gorge o.s.

farto, -a [ˈfaxtu, a] adj full, satiated; (abundante) plentiful; (aborrecido) fed up

fartura [faxˈtura] f abundance

fascinante [fasiˈnãtʃi] adj fascinating

fascinar [fasiˈna*] vt to fascinate; (encantar) to charm; **fascínio** [faˈsinju] m fascination

fascismo [faˈsiʒmu] m fascism

fase [ˈfazi] f phase

fatal [faˈtaw] (pl -ais) adj (mortal) fatal; (inevitável) inevitable; **fatalidade** [fataliˈdadʒi] f fate; (desgraça) disaster

fatia [faˈtʃia] f slice

fatigante [fatʃiˈgãtʃi] adj tiring; (aborrecido) tiresome

fatigar [fatʃiˈga*] vt to tire; (aborrecer) to bore; **fatigar-se** vr to get tired

Fátima [ˈfatima] n Fatima; see boxed note

FÁTIMA

Fátima, situated in central Portugal, is known worldwide as a site of pilgrimage for Catholics. It is said that, in 1917, the Virgin Mary appeared six times to three shepherd children (os três pastorinhos). Millions of pilgrims visit Fátima every year.

---

fato [ˈfatu] m fact; (acontecimento) event; (PT: traje) suit; **~ de banho** (PT) swimming costume (BRIT), bathing suit (US); **de ~** in fact, really

fator [faˈto*] m factor

fatura [faˈtura] f bill, invoice; **faturar** [fatuˈra*] vt to invoice; (dinheiro) to make ♦ vi (col: ganhar dinheiro) to rake it in

fava [ˈfava] f broad bean; **mandar**

alguém às **~s** to send sb packing

favela [faˈvɛla] f slum

favor [faˈvo*] m favour (BRIT), favor (US); **a ~ de** in favo(u)r of; **por ~** please; **faça** ou **faz o ~ de ...** would you be so good as to ..., kindly ...;
favorável [favoˈravew] (pl -eis) adj: **favorável (a)** favo(u)rable (to);
favorecer [favoreˈse*] vt to favo(u)r; (beneficiar) to benefit; (suj: vestido) to suit; (: retrato) to flatter;
favorito [favoˈritu, a] adj, m/f favo(u)rite

fax [faks] m (carta) fax; (máquina) fax (machine); **enviar por ~** to fax

faxina [faˈʃina] f: **fazer ~** to clean up; **faxineiro, -a** [faʃiˈnejru, a] m/f cleaner

fazenda [faˈzẽda] f farm; (de café) plantation; (de gado) ranch; (pano) cloth, fabric; (ECON) treasury; **fazendeiro** [fazẽˈdejru] m farmer; (de café) plantation-owner; (de gado) rancher, ranch-owner

---

PALAVRA CHAVE

fazer [faˈze*] vt **1** (fabricar, produzir) to make; (construir) to build; (pergunta) to ask; (poema, música) to write; **~ um filme/ruído** to make a film/noise

2 (executar) to do; **o que você está fazendo?** what are you doing?; **~ a comida** to do the cooking; **~ o papel de** (TEATRO) to play

3 (estudos, alguns esportes) to do; **~ medicina/direito** to do ou study medicine/law; **~ ioga/ginástica** to do yoga/keep-fit

4 (transformar, tornar): **sair o fará sentir melhor** going out will make him feel better; **sua partida fará o trabalho mais difícil** his departure will make work more difficult

5 (como sustituto de vb): **ele bebeu**

fé

451

feminino

e eu fiz o mesmo he drank and I did likewise
6: ~ **anos**: ele faz anos hoje it's his birthday today; **fiz 30 anos ontem** I was 30 yesterday
♦ vi **1** (*portar-se*) to act, behave; ~ **bem/mal** to do the right/wrong thing; **não fiz por mal** I didn't mean it; **faz como quem não sabe** act as if you don't know anything
2: ~ **com que alguém faça algo** to make sb do sth
♦ vb impess **1**: **faz calor/frio** it's hot/cold
2 (*tempo*): **faz um ano** a year ago; **faz dois anos que ele se formou** it's two years since he graduated; **faz três meses que ele está aqui** he's been here for three months
3: **não faz mal** never mind; **tanto faz** it's all the same; **fazer-se** vr **1**: ~**-se de desentendido** to pretend not to understand
2: **faz-se com ovos e leite** it's made with eggs and milk; **isso não se faz** that's not done

fé [fε] f faith; (*crença*) belief; (*confiança*) trust; **de boa/má** ~ in good/bad faith
febre ['fεbri] f fever; (*fig*) excitement; ~ **do feno** hay fever; **febril** [fe'briw] (*pl* -**is**) adj feverish
fechado, -a [fe'ʃadu, a] adj shut, closed; (*pessoa*) reserved; (*sinal*) red; (*luz, torneira*) off; (*tempo*) overcast; (*cara*) stern
fechadura [feʃa'dura] f lock
fechar [fe'ʃa*] vt to close, shut; (*concluir*) to finish, conclude; (*luz, torneira*) to turn off; (*rua*) to close off; (*ferida*) to close up; (*bar, loja*) to close down ♦ vi to close (up); shut; to close down; (*tempo*) to cloud over; **fechar-se** vr to close, shut;

(*pessoa*) to withdraw; ~ **à chave** to lock
fecho ['feʃu] m fastening; (*trinco*) latch; (*término*) close; ~ **ecler** zip fastener (*BRIT*), zipper (*US*)
fécula ['fεkula] f starch
feder [fe'de*] vi to stink
federação [federa'sãw] (*pl* -**ões**) f federation
federal [fede'raw] (*pl* -**ais**) adj federal; (*col*: *grande*) huge
fedor [fe'do*] m stench
feijão [fej'ʒãw] (*pl* -**ões**) m bean(s) (*pl*); (*preto*) black bean(s) (*pl*); **feijoada** [fej'ʒwada] f (*CULIN*) meat, rice and black beans
feio, -a ['feju, a] adj ugly; (*situação*) grim; (*atitude*) bad; (*tempo*) horrible ♦ adv (*perder*) badly
feira ['fejra] f fair; (*mercado*) market
feiticeira [fejtʃi'sejra] f witch
feiticeiro, -a [fejtʃi'sejru, a] adj bewitching, enchanting ♦ m wizard
feitiço [fej'tʃisu] m charm, spell
feitio [fej'tʃiu] m shape, pattern; (*caráter*) nature, manner; (*TEC*) workmanship
feito, -a ['fejtu, a] pp de **fazer** ♦ adj finished, ready ♦ m act, deed; (*façanha*) feat ♦ conj like; ~ **a mão** hand-made; **homem** ~ grown man
feiúra [fe'jura] f ugliness
felicidade [felisi'dadʒi] f happiness; (*sorte*) good luck; (*êxito*) success; ~**s** fpl (*congratulações*) congratulations
felicitações [felisita'sõjʃ] fpl congratulations, best wishes
feliz [fe'liʒ] adj happy; (*afortunado*) lucky; **felizmente** [feliʒ'mẽtʃi] adv fortunately
feltro ['fewtru] m felt
fêmea ['femja] f female
feminino, -a [femi'ninu, a] adj feminine; (*sexo*) female; (*equipe,*

feminista

fevereiro

roupa) women's ♦ m (LING) feminine

feminista [femi'nifta] adj, m/f feminist

fenda ['fẽda] f slit, crack; (GEO) fissure

feno ['fenu] m hay

fenomenal [fenome'naw] (pl -ais) adj phenomenal; (espantoso) amazing; (pessoa) brilliant

fenômeno [fe'nomenu] m phenomenon

fera ['fɛra] f wild animal

feriado [fe'rjadu] m holiday (BRIT), vacation (US)

férias ['fɛrjaʃ] fpl holidays, vacation sg; **de ~** on holiday; **tirar ~** to have ou take a holiday

ferida [fe'rida] f wound, injury; V tb ferido

ferido, -a [fe'ridu, a] adj injured; (em batalha) wounded; (magoado) hurt ♦ m/f casualty

ferimento [feri'mẽtu] m injury; (em batalha) wound

ferir [fe'ri*] vt to injure; (tb fig) to hurt; (em batalha) to wound; (ofender) to offend

fermentar [fexmẽ'ta*] vi to ferment

fermento [fex'mẽtu] m yeast; **~ em pó** baking powder

feroz [fe'rɔʒ] adj fierce, ferocious; (cruel) cruel

ferradura [fexa'dura] f horseshoe

ferragem [fe'xaʒẽ] (pl -ns) f (peças) hardware; (guarnição) metalwork; **loja de ferragens** ironmonger's (BRIT), hardware store

ferramenta [fexa'mẽta] f tool; (caixa de ~s) tool kit; **~ de busca** (COMPUT) search engine

ferrão [fe'xãw] (pl -ões) m goad; (de inseto) sting

ferreiro [fe'xejru] m blacksmith

ferrenho, -a [fe'xeɲu, a] adj (von-

tade) iron

ferro ['fɛxu] m iron; **~s** mpl (algemas) shackles, chains; **~ batido** wrought iron; **~ de passar** iron; **~ fundido** cast iron; **~ ondulado** corrugated iron

ferrões [fe'xõjʃ] mpl de ferrão

ferrolho [fe'xoʎu] m (trinco) bolt

ferrovia [fexo'via] f railway (BRIT), railroad (US); **ferroviário, -a** [fexo'vjarju, a] adj railway atr (BRIT), railroad atr (US) ♦ m/f railway ou railroad worker

ferrugem [fe'xuʒẽ] f rust

fértil ['fɛxtʃiw] (pl -eis) adj fertile; **fertilizante** [fextʃili'zãtʃi] m fertilizer; **fertilizar** [fextʃili'za*] vt to fertilize

ferver [fex've*] vt, vi to boil; **~ de raiva/indignação** to seethe with rage/indignation; **~ em fogo baixo** (CULIN) to simmer

fervilhar [fexvi'ʎa*] vi to simmer; (com atividade) to hum; (pulular): **~ de** to swarm with

fervor [fex'vo*] m fervour (BRIT), fervor (US)

festa ['fɛʃta] f (reunião) party; (conjunto de ceremônias) festival; **~s** fpl (carícia) embrace sg; **boas ~s** Merry Christmas and a Happy New Year; **dia de ~** public holiday

festejar [feʃte'ʒa*] vt to celebrate; (acolher) to welcome, greet; **festejo** [feʃ'teʒu] m festivity; (ato) celebration

festival [feʃtʃi'vaw] (pl -ais) m festival

festividade [feʃtʃivi'dadʒi] f festivity

festivo, -a [feʃ'tʃivu, a] adj festive

fetiche [fe'tʃiʃi] m fetish

feto ['fɛtu] m (MED) foetus (BRIT), fetus (US)

fevereiro [feve'rejru] (PT F-) m

February

fez [feʒ] *vb V* fazer

fezes ['fɛziʃ] *fpl* faeces (BRIT), feces (US)

fiado, -a ['fjadu, a] *adv*: **comprar/vender ~** to buy/sell on credit

fiador, a [fja'do*, a] *m/f* (JUR) guarantor; (COM) backer

fiambre ['fjãbri] *f* cold meat; (*presunto*) ham

fiança ['fjãsa] *f* guarantee; (JUR) bail; **prestar ~ por** to stand bail for; **sob ~** on bail

fiar ['fja*] *vt* (*algodão etc*) to spin; (*confiar*) to entrust; (*vender a crédito*) to sell on credit; **fiar-se** *vr*: **~-se em** to trust

fibra ['fibra] *f* fibre (BRIT), fiber (US)

─────────────────────
PALAVRA CHAVE
─────────────────────

ficar [fi'ka*] *vi* **1** (*permanecer*) to stay; (*sobrar*) to be left; **~ perguntando/olhando** etc to keep asking/looking etc; **~ por fazer** to have still to be done; **~ para trás** to be left behind

2 (*tornar-se*) to become: **~ cego/surdo/louco** to go blind/deaf/mad; **fiquei contente ao saber da notícia** I was happy when I heard the news; **~ com raiva/medo** to get angry/frightened; **~ de bem/mal com alguém** (*col*) to make up/fall out with sb

3 (*posição*) to be: **a casa fica ao lado da igreja** the house is next to the church; **~ sentado/deitado** to be sitting down/lying down

4 (*tempo: durar*): **ele ficou duas horas para resolver** he took two hours to decide; (: *ser adiado*): **a reunião ficou para amanhã** the meeting was postponed until the following day

5: **~ bem** (*comportamento*): **sua ati-**

tude não ficou bem his (*ou her etc*) behaviour was inappropriate; (*cor*): **você fica bem em azul** blue suits you, you look good in blue; (*roupa*): **~ bem para** to suit

6: **~ bom** (*de saúde*) to be cured; (*trabalho, foto etc*) to turn out well

7: **~ de fazer algo** (*combinar*) to arrange to do sth; (*prometer*) to promise to do sth

8: **~ de pé** to stand up

ficção [fik'sãw] *f* fiction

ficha ['fiʃa] *f* (tb: **~ de telefone**) token; (tb: **~ de jogo**) chip; (*de fichário*) (index) card; (POLÍCIA) record; (PT: ELET) plug; (*em loja, lanchonete*) ticket

fichário [fi'ʃarju] *m* filing cabinet; (*caixa*) card index; (*caderno*) file

ficheiro [fi'ʃejru] (PT) *m* = **fichário**

fictício, -a [fik'tʃisju, a] *adj* fictitious

fidelidade [fideli'dadʒi] *f* fidelity, loyalty; (*exatidão*) accuracy

fiel [fjew] (*pl* -**éis**) *adj* (*leal*) faithful, loyal; (*acurado*) accurate; (*que não falha*) reliable

figa ['figa] *f* talisman; **fazer uma ~** to make a *figa* ≈ cross one's fingers; **de uma ~** (*col*) damned

fígado ['figadu] *m* liver

figo ['figu] *m* fig; **figueira** [fi'gejra] *f* fig tree

figura [fi'gura] *f* figure; (*forma*) form, shape; (LING) figure of speech; (*aspecto*) appearance

figurino [figu'rinu] *m* model; (*revista*) fashion magazine

fila ['fila] *f* row, line; (BR: *fileira de pessoas*) queue (BRIT), line (US); (*num teatro, cinema*) row; **em ~** in a row; **fazer ~** to form a line, queue; **indiana** single file

filé [fi'lɛ] *m* (*bife*) steak; (*peixe*) fillet

fileira [fi'lejru] f row, line; **~s** fpl (serviço militar) military service sg

filho, -a ['fiʎu, a] m/f son/daughter; **~s** mpl children; (de animais) young

filhote [fi'ʎɔtʃi] m (de leão, urso etc) cub; (cachorro) pup(py)

filial [fi'ljaw] (pl **-ais**) f (sucursal) branch

Filipinas [fili'pinaʃ] fpl: **as ~** the Philippines

filmadora [fiwma'dora] f camcorder

filmar [fiw'ma*] vt, vi to film

filme ['fiwmi] m film (BRIT), movie (US)

filosofia [filozo'fia] f philosophy; **filósofo, -a** [fi'lɔzofu, a] m/f philosopher

filtrar [fiw'tra*] vt to filter; **filtrar-se** vr to filter; (infiltrar-se) to infiltrate

filtro ['fiwtru] m (TEC) filter

fim [fĩ] (pl **-ns**) m (motivo) aim, purpose; (de história, filme) ending; **a ~ de** in order to; **no ~ das contas** after all; **por ~** finally; **sem ~** endless; **levar ao ~** to carry through; **pôr ou dar ~ a** to put an end to; **ter ~** to come to an end; **~ de semana** weekend

finado, -a [fi'nadu, a] m/f deceased; **dia dos F~s** day of the dead; see boxed note

---

DIA DOS FINADOS

The **dia dos Finados**, 2 November, a holiday throughout Brazil, is dedicated to remembering the dead. On this day, people usually gather in cemeteries to remember their family dead, and also to worship at the graves of popular figures from Brazilian culture and society, such as singers, actors and other personalities. It is popularly believed that these people can work miracles.

---

final [fi'naw] (pl **-ais**) adj final, last ♦ m end; (MÚS) finale ♦ f (ESPORTE) final; **finalista** [fina'liʃta] m/f finalist; **finalizar** [finali'za*] vt to finish, conclude

finanças [fi'nãsaʃ] fpl finance sg; **financeiro, -a** [finã'sejru, a] adj financial ♦ m/f financier; **financiar** [finã'sja*] vt to finance

fingimento [fĩʒi'mẽtu] m pretence (BRIT), pretense (US)

fingir [fĩ'ʒi*] vt to feign ♦ vi to pretend; **fingir-se** vr: **~-se de** to pretend to be

finito, -a [fi'nitu, a] adj finite

finlandês, -esa [fĩlã'deʃ, eza] adj Finnish ♦ m/f Finn ♦ m (LING) Finnish

Finlândia [fĩ'lãdʒia] f: **a ~** Finland

fino, -a ['finu, a] adj fine; (delgado) slender; (educado) polite; (som, voz) shrill; (elegante) refined ♦ adv: **falar ~** to talk in a high voice

fins [fĩʃ] mpl de **fim**

fio ['fiu] m thread; (BOT) fibre (BRIT), fiber (US); (ELET) wire; (TEL) line; (de líquido) trickle; (gume) edge; (encadeamento) series; **horas/dias a ~** hours/days on end

firma ['fixma] f signature; (COM) firm, company

firmar [fix'ma*] vt to secure, make firm; (assinar) to sign; (estabelecer) to establish; (basear) to base ♦ vi (tempo) to settle; **firmar-se** vr: **~-se em** (basear-se) to rest on, be based on

firme ['fixmi] adj firm; (estável) stable; (sólido) solid; (tempo) settled ♦ adv firmly; **firmeza** [fix'meza] f firmness; stability; solidity

fiscal [fiʃ'kaw] (pl **-ais**) m/f supervisor; (aduaneiro) customs officer; (de impostos) tax inspector; **fiscalizar** [fiʃkali'za*] vt to supervise; (examinar) to inspect, check

fisco ['fiʃku] *m*: **o ~** the Inland Revenue (*BRIT*), ≈ the Internal Revenue Service (*US*)

física ['fizika] *f* physics *sg*; *V tb* **físico**

físico, -a ['fiziku, a] *adj* physical ♦ *m/f* (*cientista*) physicist ♦ *m* (*corpo*) physique

fisionomia [fizjono'mia] *f* (*rosto*) face; (*ar*) expression, look; (*aspecto de algo*) appearance

fissura [fi'sura] *f* crack

fita ['fita] *f* tape; (*tira*) strip, band; (*filme*) film; (*para máquina de escrever*) ribbon; **~ durex** ® adhesive tape, sellotape ® (*BRIT*), scotchtape ® (*US*); **~ métrica** tape measure

fitar [fi'ta*] *vt* to stare at, gaze at

fivela [fi'vɛla] *f* buckle

fixar [fik'sa*] *vt* to fix; (*colar, prender*) to stick; (*data, prazo, regras*) to set; (*atenção*) to concentrate; **fixar-se** *vr*: **~-se em** (*assunto*) to concentrate on; (*detalhe*) to fix on; (*apegar-se a*) to be attached to; **~ os olhos em** to stare at; **~ residência** to set up house

fixo, -a ['fiksu, a] *adj* fixed; (*firme*) firm; (*permanente*) permanent; (*cor*) fast

fiz *etc* [fiʒ] *vb V* **fazer**

flagelado, -a [flaʒe'ladu, a] *m/f*: **os ~s** the afflicted, the victims

flagrante [fla'grãtʃi] *adj* flagrant; **apanhar em ~** (*delito*) to catch redhanded *ou* in the act

flagrar [fla'gra*] *vt* to catch

flanela [fla'nɛla] *f* flannel

flash [flaʃ] *m* (*FOTO*) flash

flauta ['flawta] *f* flute

flecha ['flɛʃa] *f* arrow

fleu(g)ma ['flewma] *f* phlegm

flexível [flek'sivew] (*pl* **-eis**) *adj* flexible

floco ['flɔku] *m* flake; **~ de milho** cornflake; **~ de neve** snowflake

flor [flo*] *f* flower; (*o melhor*): **a ~ de** the cream of, the pick of; **em ~** in bloom; **à ~ de** on the surface of

florescente [flore'sẽtʃi] *adj* (*BOT*) in flower; (*próspero*) flourishing

florescer [flore'se*] *vi* (*BOT*) to flower; (*prosperar*) to flourish

floresta [flo'rɛʃta] *f* forest; **~ tropical** rainforest; **florestal** [floreʃ'taw] (*pl* **florestais**) *adj* forest *atr*

florido, -a [flo'ridu, a] *adj* (*jardim*) in flower

fluente [flu'ẽtʃi] *adj* fluent

fluido, -a ['flwidu, a] *adj* fluid ♦ *m* fluid

fluir [flwi'*] *vi* to flow

fluminense [flumi'nẽsi] *adj* from the state of Rio de Janeiro ♦ *m/f* native *ou* inhabitant of the state of Rio de Janeiro

flutuar [flu'twa*] *vi* to float; (*bandeira*) to flutter; (*fig: vacilar*) to waver

fluvial [flu'vjaw] (*pl* **-ais**) *adj* river *atr*

fluxo ['fluksu] *m* (*corrente*) flow; (*ELET*) flux; **~ de caixa** (*COM*) cash flow

fobia [fo'bia] *f* phobia

foca ['fɔka] *f* seal

focinho [fo'siɲu] *m* snout; (*col: cara*) face, mug (*col*)

foco ['fɔku] *m* focus; (*MED, fig*) seat, centre (*BRIT*), center (*US*); **fora de ~ em/fora de ~** out of focus, in/out of focus

fofo, -a ['fofu, a] *adj* soft; (*col: pessoa*) cute

fofoca [fo'fɔka] *f* piece of gossip; **~s** *fpl* (*mexericos*) gossip *sg*; **fofocar** [fofo'ka*] *vi* to gossip

fogão [fo'gãw] (*pl* **-ões**) *m* stove, cooker

fogareiro [foga'rejru] *m* stove

foge *etc* ['fɔʒi] *vb V* fugir

fogo ['fogu] *m* fire; (*fig*) ardour (*BRIT*), ardor (*US*); **você tem ~?** have you got a light?; **~s de artifício** fireworks; **pôr ~ a** to set fire to

fogões [fo'gõjʃ] *mpl de* fogão

fogueira [fo'gejra] *f* bonfire

foguete [fo'getʃi] *m* rocket

foi [foj] *vb V* ir; ser

folclore [fowk'lɔri] *m* folklore

folclórico, -a [fowk'lɔriku, a] *adj* (*música etc*) folk; (*comida, roupa*) ethnic

fôlego ['folegu] *m* breath; (*folga*) breathing space; **perder o ~** to get out of breath

folga ['fɔwga] *f* rest, break; (*espaço livre*) clearance; (*ócio*) inactivity; (*col: atrevimento*) cheek; **dia de ~** day off; **folgado, -a** [fow'gadu, a] *adj* (*roupa*) loose; (*vida*) leisurely; (*col: atrevido*) cheeky; **folgar** [fow'ga*] *vt* to loosen ♦ *vi* (*descansar*) to rest; (*divertir-se*) to have fun

folha ['foʎa] *f* leaf; (*de papel, de metal*) sheet; (*página*) page; (*de faca*) blade; (*jornal*) paper; **novo em ~** brand new; **~ de estanho** tinfoil (*BRIT*), aluminum foil (*US*)

folhagem [fo'ʎaʒẽ] *f* foliage

folheto [fo'ʎetu] *m* booklet, pamphlet

fome ['fɔmi] *f* hunger; (*escassez*) famine; (*fig: avidez*) longing; **passar ~** to go hungry; **estar com** *ou* **ter ~** to be hungry

fomentar [fomẽ'ta*] *vt* to instigate, incite; **fomento** [fo'mẽtu] *m* (*estímulo*) incitement

fone ['fɔni] *m* telephone; phone; (*peça do telefone*) receiver

fonte ['fõtʃi] *f* (*nascente*) spring; (*chafariz*) fountain; (*origem*) source; (*ANAT*) temple

for *etc* [fo*] *vb V* ir; ser

fora¹ ['fɔra] *adv* out, outside ♦ *prep* (*além de*) apart from ♦ *m*: **dar o ~** (*bateria, radio*) to give out; (*pessoa*) to leave, be off; **dar um ~** (*pessoa*) to slip up; **dar um ~ em/levar um ~** (*namorado*) to chuck ou dump/be given the boot; (*esnobar*) to snub sb/get the brush-off; **~ de** outside; **~ de si** beside o.s.; **estar ~** (*viajando*) to be away; **estar ~ (de casa)** (*de casa*) to be out; **lá ~** outside; (*no exterior*) abroad; **jantar ~** to eat out; **com os braços de ~** with bare arms; **ser de ~** to be from out of town; **ficar de ~** not to join in; **lá para ~** outside; **ir para ~** (*viajar*) to go out of town; **com a cabeça para ~ da janela** with one's head sticking out of the window; **costurar/cozinhar para ~** to do sewing/cooking for other people; **por ~** on the outside; **cobrar ~** (*BRIT*) to charge extra, extra; **~ de dúvida** beyond doubt; **~ de propósito** irrelevant

fora² *etc vb V* ir; ser

foragido, -a [fora'ʒidu, a] *adj, m/f* (*fugitivo*) fugitive

forasteiro, -a [foraʃ'tejru, a] *m/f* outsider, stranger; (*de outro país*) foreigner

forca ['foxka] *f* gallows *sg*

força ['foxsa] *f* strength; (*TEC, ELET*) power; (*esforço*) effort; (*coerção*) force; **à ~** by force; **à ~ de** by dint of; **com ~** hard; **por ~** of necessity; **fazer ~** to try (hard); **~ de trabalho** workforce

forçado, -a [fox'sadu, a] *adj* forced; (*afetado*) false

forçar [fox'sa*] *vt* to force; (*olhos, voz*) to strain

forma ['fɔxma] *f* form; (*de um objeto*) shape; (*físico*) figure; (*maneira*) way; (*MED*) fitness; **desta ~** in this way; **de qualquer ~** anyway; **manter a ~** to keep fit

fôrma ['fɔxma] f (CULIN) cake tin; (molde) mould (BRIT), mold (US)

formação [foxma'sãw] (pl -ões) f formation; (antecedentes) background; (caráter) make-up; (profissional) training

formado, -a [fox'madu, a] adj (modelado): **ser ~ de** to consist of ♦ m/f graduate

formal [fox'maw] (pl -ais) adj formal; **formalidade** [foxmali'dadʒi] f formality

formar [fox'ma*] vt to form; (constituir) to constitute, make up; (educar) to train; **formar-se** vr to form; (EDUC) to graduate

formatar [foxma'ta*] vt (COMPUT) to format

formidável [foxmi'davew] (pl -eis) adj tremendous, great

formiga [fox'miga] f ant

formigar [foxmi'ga*] vi to abound; (sentir comichão) to itch

formoso, -a [fox'mozu, ɔza] adj beautiful; (esplêndido) superb

fórmula ['fɔxmula] f formula

formular [foxmu'la*] vt to formulate; (queixas) to voice

formulário [foxmu'larju] m form; **~s** mpl: **~s contínuos** (COMPUT) continuous stationery f

fornecedor, a [foxnese'do*, a] m/f supplier ♦ f (empresa) supplier

fornecer [foxne'se*] vt to supply, provide; **fornecimento** [foxnesi-'mẽtu] m supply

forno ['foxnu] m (CULIN) oven; (TEC) furnace; (para cerâmica) kiln; **alto ~** blast furnace

foro ['foru] m forum; (JUR) Court of Justice; **~s** mpl (privilégios) privileges

forro ['foxu] m covering; lining

fortalecer [foxtale'se*] vt to strengthen

fortaleza [foxta'leza] f fortress; (força) strength; (moral) fortitude

forte ['fɔxtʃi] adj strong; (pancada) hard; (chuva) heavy; (tocar) loud; (dor) sharp ♦ adv strongly; (tocar) loud(ly) ♦ m fort; (talento) strength; **ser ~ em algo** (versado) to be good at sth ou strong in sth

fortuito, -a [fox'twitu, a] adj accidental

fortuna [fox'tuna] f fortune, (good) luck; (riqueza) fortune, wealth

fosco, -a ['foʃku, a] adj dull; (opaco) opaque

fósforo ['fɔʃforu] m match

fossa ['fɔsa] f pit

fosse etc ['fɔsi] vb V ir; ser

fóssil ['fɔsiw] (pl -eis) m fossil

fosso ['fosu] m trench, ditch

foto ['fɔtu] f photo

fotocópia [foto'kɔpja] f photocopy; **fotocopiadora** [fotokoja-'dora] f photocopier; **fotocopiar** [fotoko'pja*] vt to photocopy

fotografar [fotogra'fa*] vt to photograph

fotografia [fotogra'fia] f photography; (uma ~) photograph

fotógrafo, -a [fo'tɔgrafu, a] m/f photographer

foz [fɔʒ] f mouth of river

fração [fra'sãw] (pl -ões) f fraction

fracassar [fraka'sa*] vi to fail; **fracasso** [fra'kasu] m failure

fracção [fra'sãw] (PT) f = **fração**

fraco, -a ['fraku, a] adj weak; (sol, som) faint

fractura etc [fra'tura] (PT) f = **fratura** etc

frade ['fradʒi] m (REL) friar; (: monge) monk

frágil ['fraʒiw] (pl -eis) adj (débil) fragile; (COM) breakable; (pessoa) frail; (saúde) delicate, poor

fragmento [fragˈmẽtu] m fragment

fragrância [fraˈgrãsja] f fragrance, perfume

fralda [ˈfrawda] f (da camisa) shirt tail; (para bebê) nappy (BRIT), diaper (US); (de montanha) foot

framboesa [frãˈbeza] f raspberry

França [ˈfrãsa] f France

francamente [frãkaˈmẽtʃi] adv (abertamente) frankly; (realmente) really

francês, -esa [frãˈseʃ, eza] adj French ♦ m/f Frenchman/woman ♦ m (LING) French

franco, -a [ˈfrãku, a] adj frank; (isento de pagamento) free; (óbvio) clear ♦ m franc; **entrada franca** free admission

frango [ˈfrãgu] m chicken

franja [ˈfrãʒa] f fringe (BRIT), bangs pl (US)

franqueza [frãˈkeza] f frankness

franquia [frãˈkia] f (COM) franchise; (isenção) exemption

franzino, -a [frãˈzinu, a] adj skinny

fraqueza [fraˈkeza] f weakness

frasco [ˈfraʃku] m bottle

frase [ˈfrazi] f sentence; ~ **feita** set phrase

fratura [fraˈtura] f fracture, break; **fraturar** [fratuˈra*] vt to fracture

fraude [ˈfrawdʒi] f fraud

freada [freˈada] (BR) f: **dar uma** ~ to slam on the brakes

frear [freˈa*] (BR) vt to curb, restrain; (veículo) to stop ♦ vi (veículo) to brake

freezer [ˈfrize*] m freezer

freguês, -guesa [freˈgeʃ, ˈgeza] m/f customer; (PT) parishioner

freguesia [fregeˈzia] f customers pl; parish

freio [ˈfreju] m (BR: de veículo) brake; (de cavalo) bridle; (bocado do ~) bit;

~ **de mão** handbrake

freira [ˈfrejra] f nun

frenesi [freneˈzi] m frenzy; **frenético, -a** [freˈnɛtʃiku, a] adj frantic, frenzied

frente [ˈfrẽtʃi] f front; (rosto) face; (fachada) façade; ~ **a** ~ face to face; **de** ~ **para** facing; **em** ~ **de** in front of; (de fronte a) opposite; **para a** ~ ahead, forward; **porta da** ~ front door; **seguir em** ~ to go straight on; **na minha** (ou sua etc) ~ in front of me (ou you etc); **sair da** ~ to get out of the way; **pra** ~ (col) fashionable, trendy

frequência [freˈkwẽsja] f frequency; **com** ~ often, frequently

frequentar [frekwẽˈta*] vt to frequent

frequente [freˈkwẽtʃi] adj frequent

fresco, -a [ˈfreʃku, a] adj fresh; (vento, tempo) cool; (col: efeminado) camp; (: afetado) pretentious; (: cheio de luxo) fussy ♦ m (ar) fresh air

frescobol [freʃkoˈbɔw] m (kind of) racketball (played mainly on the beach)

frescura [freʃˈkura] f freshness; (frialdade) coolness; (col: luxo) fussiness; (: afetação) pretentiousness

frete [ˈfrɛtʃi] m (carregamento) freight, cargo; (tarifa) freightage

frevo [ˈfrevu] m improvised Carnival dance

fria [ˈfria] f: **dar uma** ~ **em** alguém to give sb the cold shoulder; **estar/entrar numa** ~ (col) to be in/get into a mess

fricção [frikˈsãw] f friction; (ato) rubbing; (MED) massage; **friccionar** [friksjoˈna*] vt to rub

frieza [friˈeza] f coldness; (indiferença) coolness

frigideira [friʒiˈdejra] f frying pan

frigorífico [frigoˈrifiku] m refrigerator; (*congelador*) freezer

frio, -a ['friu, a] *adj* cold ♦ *m* cold; **~s** *mpl* (*CULIN*) cold meats; **estou com ~** I'm cold; **faz** ou **está ~** it's cold

frisar [fri'za*] *vt* (*encrespar*) to curl; (*salientar*) to emphasize

fritar [fri'ta*] *vt* to fry

fritas ['fritas] *fpl* chips (*BRIT*), French fries (*US*)

frito, -a ['fritu, a] *adj* fried; (*col*): **estar ~** to be done for

frívolo, -a ['frivolu, a] *adj* frivolous

fronha ['froɲa] *f* pillowcase

fronteira [frõ'tejra] *f* frontier, border

frota ['frɔta] *f* fleet

frouxo, -a ['froʃu, a] *adj* loose; (*corda*, fig: *pessoa*) slack; (*fraco*) weak; (*col: condescendente*) soft

frustrar [fruʃ'tra*] *vt* to frustrate

fruta ['fruta] *f* fruit; **frutífero, -a** [fru'tʃiferu, a] *adj* (*proveitoso*) fruitful; (*árvore*) fruit-bearing

fruto ['frutu] *m* (*BOT*) fruit; (*resultado*) result, product; **dar ~** (fig) to bear fruit

fubá [fu'ba] *m* corn meal

fuga ['fuga] *f* flight, escape; (*de gás etc*) leak

fugir [fu'ʒi*] *vi* to flee, escape; (*prisioneiro*) to escape

fugitivo, -a [fuʒi'tʃivu, a] *adj*, *m/f* fugitive

fui [fuj] *vb* V **ir; ser**

fulano, -a [fu'lanu, a] *m/f* so-and-so

fuligem [fu'liʒẽ] *f* soot

fulminante [fuwmi'nãtʃi] *adj* devastating; (*palavras*) scathing

fulo, -a ['fulu, a] *adj*: **estar** ou **ficar ~ de raiva** to be furious

fumaça [fu'masa] (*BR*) *f* (*de fogo*) smoke; (*de gás*) fumes *pl*

fumador, a [fuma'do*, a] (*PT*) *m/f* smoker

fumante [fu'mãtʃi] *m/f* smoker

fumar [fu'ma*] *vt*, *vi* to smoke

fumo ['fumu] *m* (*PT*: *de fogo*) smoke; (: *de gás*) fumes *pl*; (*BR*: *tabaco*) tobacco; (*fumar*) smoking

função [fũ'sãw] *f* function; (*ofício*) duty; (*papel*) role; (*espetáculo*) performance

funcionalismo [fũsjona'liʒmu] *m*: **~ público** civil service

funcionamento [fũsjona'mẽtu] *m* functioning, working; **pôr em ~** to set going, start

funcionar [fũsjo'na*] *vi* to function; (*máquina*) to work, run; (*dar bom resultado*) to work

funcionário, -a [fũsjo'narju, a] *m/f* official; **~ (público)** civil servant

funções [fũ'sõjʃ] *fpl de* **função**

fundação [fũda'sãw] (*pl* **-ões**) *f* foundation

fundamental [fũdamẽ'taw] (*pl* **-ais**) *adj* fundamental, basic

fundamento [fũda'mẽtu] *m* (fig) foundation, basis; (*motivo*) motive

fundar [fũ'da*] *vt* to establish, found; (*basear*) to base; **fundar-se** *vr*: **~-se em** to be based on

fundir [fũ'dʒi*] *vt* to fuse; (*metal*) to smelt, melt down; (*COM: empresas*) to merge; (*em molde*) to cast; **fundir-se** *vr* to melt; (*juntar-se*) to merge

fundo, -a ['fũdu, a] *adj* deep; (*fig*) profound ♦ *m* (*do mar, jardim*) bottom; (*profundidade*) depth; (*base*) basis; (*da loja, casa, do papel*) back; (*de quadro*) background; (*de dinheiro*) fund ♦ *adv* deeply; **~s** *mpl* (*COM*) funds; (*da casa etc*) back *sg*; **a ~** thoroughly; **no ~** at the bottom; (*da casa etc*) at the back; (fig) basically

fúnebre ['funebri] *adj* funeral *atr*, funereal; (fig) gloomy

funeral [fune'raw] (*pl* **-ais**) *m* funeral

funil [fu'niw] (*pl* **-is**) *m* funnel

furacão [fura'kãw] (*pl* **-ões**) *m*

hurricane

furado, -a [fuˈradu, a] *adj* perforated; (*pneu*) flat; (*orelha*) pierced

furão, -rona [fuˈrãw, ˈrɔna] (*pl* **-ões, ~s**) *m* ferret ♦ *m/f* (*col*) go-getter ♦ *adj* (*col*) hard-working, dynamic

furar [fuˈra*] *vt* to perforate; (*orelha*) to pierce; (*penetrar*) to penetrate; (*frustrar*) to foil; (*fila*) to jump ♦ *vi* (*col: programa*) to fall through

fúria [ˈfurja] *f* fury, rage; **furioso, -a** [fuˈrjozu, ɔza] *adj* furious

furo [ˈfuru] *m* hole; (*num pneu*) puncture

furões [fuˈrõjʃ] *mpl de* **furão**

furona [fuˈrɔna] *f de* **furão**

furor [fuˈro*] *m* fury, rage; **fazer ~** to be all the rage

furtar [fuxˈta*] *vt, vi* to steal; **furtar-se vr: ~-se a** to avoid

furtivo, -a [fuxˈtʃivu, a] *adj* furtive, stealthy

furto [ˈfuxtu] *m* theft

fusão [fuˈzãw] (*pl* **-ões**) *f* fusion; (*COM*) merger; (*derretimento*) melting; (*união*) union

fusível [fuˈzivew] (*pl* **-eis**) *m* fuse

fuso [ˈfuzu] *m* (*TEC*) spindle; **~ horário** time zone

fusões [fuˈzõjʃ] *fpl de* **fusão**

futebol [futʃiˈbɔw] *m* football; **~ de salão** five-a-side football

futevôlei [futʃiˈvolej] *m see boxed note*

FUTEVÔLEI

Futevôlei is a type of volleyball in which the ball is allowed to touch only the feet, legs, trunk and head of the players. It is very popular on the beaches of Rio de Janeiro, where tournaments take place during the summer, in which many famous footballers take part.

---

fútil [ˈfutʃiw] (*pl* **-eis**) *adj* (*pessoa*) shallow; (*insignificante*) trivial

futilidade [futʃiliˈdadʒi] *f* (*de pessoa*) shallowness; (*insignificância*) triviality; (*coisa*) trivial thing

futuro, -a [fuˈturu, a] *adj* future ♦ *m* future; **no ~** in the future

fuzil [fuˈziw] (*pl* **-is**) *m* rifle; **fuzilar** [fuziˈla*] *vt* to shoot

fuzis [fuˈziʃ] *mpl de* **fuzil**

G

g. *abr* (= *grama*) gr.

G7 *abr* (= *Grupo dos Sete*) G7

gabar [gaˈba*] *vt* to praise; **gabar-se vr: ~-se de** to boast about

gabinete [gabiˈnetʃi] *m* (*COM*) office; (*escritório*) study; (*POL*) cabinet

gado [ˈgadu] *m* livestock; (*bovino*) cattle; **~ leiteiro** dairy cattle; **~ suíno** pigs *pl*

gafanhoto [gafaˈɲotu] *m* grasshopper

gafe [ˈgafi] *f* gaffe, faux pas

gagueira [gaˈgejra] *f* stutter

gaguejar [gageˈʒa*] *vi* to stammer, stutter

gaiato, -a [gaˈjatu, a] *adj* funny

gaiola [gaˈjɔla] *f* cage; (*cadeia*) jail ♦ *m* (*barco*) riverboat

gaita [ˈgajta] *f* harmonica; **~ de foles** bagpipes *pl*

gaivota [gajˈvɔta] *f* seagull

gajo [ˈgaʒu] *m* (*PT: col*) *m* guy, fellow

gala [ˈgala] *f*: **traje de ~** evening dress; **festa de ~** gala

galão [gaˈlãw] (*pl* **-ões**) *m* (*MIL*) stripe; (*medida*) gallon; (*PT: café*) white coffee; (*passamanaria*) braid

Galápagos [gaˈlapaguʃ]: **(as) Ilhas ~** *fpl* (the) Galapagos Islands

galáxia [gaˈlaksja] *m* galaxy

galera [ga'lɛra] f (NÁUT) galley; (col: pessoas, público) crowd

galeria [gale'ria] f gallery; (TEATRO) circle

Gales ['galiʃ] m: **País de ~** Wales

galho ['gaʎu] m (de árvore) branch

galinha [ga'liɲa] f hen; (CULIN) chicken; **galinheiro** [gali'ɲejru] m hen-house

galo ['galu] m cock, rooster; (inchação) bump; **missa do ~** midnight mass

galões [ga'lõjʃ] mpl de **galão**

galopar [galo'pa*] vi to gallop; **galope** [ga'lɔpi] m gallop

gama ['gama] f (MÚS) scale; (fig) range; (ZOOL) doe

gambá [gã'ba] m (ZOOL) opossum

Gana ['gana] m Ghana

gana ['gana] f craving, desire; (ódio) hate; **ter ~s de (fazer) algo** to feel like (doing) sth; **ter ~ de alguém** to hate sb

ganância [ga'nãsja] f greed; **ganancioso, -a** [ganã'sjozu, ɔza] adj greedy

gancho ['gãʃu] m hook; (de calça) crotch

gangue ['gãgi] (col) f gang

ganhador, a [gaɲa'do*, a] adj winning ♦ m/f winner

ganha-pão ['gaɲa-] (pl -ães) m living, livelihood

ganhar [ga'ɲa*] vt to win; (salário) to earn; (adquirir) to get; (lugar) to reach; (lucrar) to gain ♦ vi to win; **~ de alguém** (num jogo) to beat sb; **ganho, -a** ['gaɲu, a] pp de **ganhar** ♦ m profit, gain; **ganhos** mpl (ao jogo) winnings

ganso, -a ['gãsu, a] m/f gander/goose

garagem [ga'raʒẽ] (pl -ns) f garage

garanhão [gara'ɲãw] (pl -ões) m stallion

garantia [garã'tʃia] f guarantee; (de dívida) surety

garantir [garã'tʃi*] vt to guarantee; **garantir-se** vr: **~se** to contra algo to defend o.s. against sth; **~ que ...** to maintain that ...

garçom [gax'sõ] (BR) (pl -ns) m waiter

garçonete [gaxso'netʃi] (BR) f waitress

garçons [gax'sõʃ] mpl de **garçom**

garfo ['gaxfu] m fork

gargalhada [gaxga'ʎada] f burst of laughter; **rir às ~s** to roar with laughter; **dar ou soltar uma ~** to burst out laughing

gargalo [gax'galu] m (tb fig) bottleneck

garganta [gax'gãta] f throat; (GEO) gorge, ravine

gargarejo [gaxga'reʒu] m (ato) gargling; (líquido) gargle

gari ['gari] m/f (na rua) roadsweeper (BRIT), streetsweeper (US); (lixeiro) dustman (BRIT), garbage man (US)

garoa [ga'roa] f drizzle; **garoar** [ga'rwa*] vi to drizzle

garotada [garo'tada] f: **a ~** the kids pl

garoto, -a [ga'rotu, a] m/f boy/girl; (namorado) boyfriend/girlfriend ♦ m (PT: café) coffee with milk

garoupa [ga'ropa] f (peixe) grouper

garra ['gaxa] f claw; (de ave) talon; (fig: entusiasmo) enthusiasm, drive; **~s** fpl (fig) clutches

garrafa [ga'xafa] f bottle

garupa [ga'rupa] f (de cavalo) hindquarters pl; (de moto) back seat; **andar na ~** (de moto) to ride pillion

gás [gajʃ] m gas; **gases** mpl (do intestino) wind sg; **~ natural** natural gas

gasóleo [ga'zɔlju] m diesel oil

gasolina [gazo'lina] f petrol (BRIT), gas(oline) (US)

gasosa [ga'zɔza] f fizzy drink

gasoso, -a [ga'zozu, ɔza] adj (água) sparkling; (bebida) fizzy

gastador, -deira [gaʃta'do*, 'dejra] adj, m/f spendthrift

gastar [gaʃ'ta*] vt to spend; (gasolina, eletricidade) to use; (roupa, sapato) to wear out; (salto, piso etc) to wear down; (saúde) to damage; (desperdiçar) to waste ♦ vi to spend; to wear out; to wear down; **gastar-se** vr to wear out; to wear down

gasto, -a [gaʃtu, a] pp de **gastar** ♦ adj spent; (frase) trite; (sapato etc, fig: pessoa) worn out; (salto, piso) worn down ♦ m (despesa) expense; **~s** mpl (COM) expenses, expenditure sg

gata [gata] f (she-)cat

gatilho [ga'tʃiλu] m trigger

gato [gatu] m cat; **~ montês** wild cat

gatuno, -a [ga'tunu, a] adj thieving ♦ m/f thief

gaveta [ga'veta] f drawer

gaze [gazi] f gauze

geada ['ʒjada] f frost

geladeira [ʒela'dejra] (BR) f refrigerator, icebox (US)

gelado, -a [ʒe'ladu, a] adj frozen ♦ m (PT: sorvete) ice cream

gelar [ʒe'la*] vt to freeze; (vinho etc) to chill ♦ vi to freeze

gelatina [ʒela'tʃina] f gelatine; (sobremesa) jelly (BRIT), jello (US)

geléia [ʒe'lɛja] f jam

gélido, -a ['ʒɛlidu, a] adj chill, icy

gelo ['ʒelu] adj inv light grey (BRIT) ou gray (US) ♦ m ice; (cor) light grey (BRIT) ou gray (US)

gema ['ʒema] f yolk; (pedra preciosa) gem

gêmeo, -a ['ʒemju, a] adj, m/f twin;

G~s mpl (ASTROLOGIA) Gemini sg

gemer [ʒe'me*] vi (de dor) to groan, moan; (lamentar-se) to wail; (animal) to whine; (vento) to howl; **gemido** [ʒe'midu] m groan, moan; wail; whine

gene ['ʒeni] m gene

Genebra [ʒe'nɛbra] n Geneva

general [ʒene'raw] (pl -ais) m general

generalizar [ʒenerali'za*] vt to propagate ♦ vi to generalize; **generalizar-se** vr to become general, spread

gênero ['ʒeneru] m type, kind; (BIO) genus; (LING) gender; **~s** mpl (produtos) goods; **~s alimentícios** foodstuffs; **~ humano** humankind, human race

generosidade [ʒenerozi'dadʒi] f generosity

generoso, -a [ʒene'rozu, ɔza] adj generous

genética [ʒe'nɛtʃika] f genetics sg

gengibre [ʒe'ʒibri] m ginger

gengiva [ʒe'ʒiva] f (ANAT) gum

genial [ʒe'njaw] (pl -ais) adj inspired, brilliant; (col) terrific, fantastic

gênio ['ʒenju] m (temperamento) nature; (irascibilidade) temper; (talento, pessoa) genius; **de bom/mau ~** good-natured/bad-tempered

genital [ʒeni'taw] (pl -ais) adj: **órgãos genitais** genitals pl

genro ['ʒexu] m son-in-law

gente ['ʒetʃi] f people pl; (col) folks pl, family; (: alguém): **tem ~ batendo à porta** there's somebody knocking at the door; **a ~** (: nós: suj) we; (: objeto) us; **a casa da ~** our house; **toda a ~** everybody; **~ grande** grown-ups pl

gentil [ʒe'tʃiw] (pl -is) adj kind; **gentileza** [ʒetʃi'leza] f kindness;

por gentileza if you please; **tenha a gentileza de fazer ...?** would you be so kind as to do ...?

genuíno, -a [ʒe'nwinu, a] adj genuine

geografia [ʒeogra'fia] f geography

geometria [ʒeome'tria] f geometry

geração [ʒera'sãw] (pl -ões) f generation

gerador, a [ʒera'do*, a] m/f (produtor) creator ♦ m (TEC) generator

geral [ʒe'raw] (pl -ais) adj general ♦ f (TEATRO) gallery; **em ~** in general, generally; **de um modo ~** on the whole; **geralmente** [ʒeraw'mẽtʃi] adv generally, usually

gerânio [ʒe'ranju] m geranium

gerar [ʒe'ra*] vt to produce; (eletricidade) to generate

gerência [ʒe'rẽsja] f management; **gerenciar** [ʒerẽ'sja*] vt, vi to manage

gerente [ʒe'rẽtʃi] adj managing ♦ m/f manager

gerir [ʒe'ri*] vt to manage, run

germe [ʒɛxmi] m (embrião) embryo; (micróbio) germ

gesso [ʒesu] m plaster (of Paris)

gestante [ʒeʃ'tãtʃi] f pregnant woman

gesticular [ʒeʃtʃiku'la*] vi to make gestures, gesture

gesto [ʒɛʃtu] m gesture

Gibraltar [ʒibraw'ta*] f Gibraltar

gigante, -ta [ʒi'gãtʃi, a] adj gigantic, huge ♦ m giant; **gigantesco, -a** [ʒigã'teʃku, a] adj gigantic

gim [ʒĩ] (pl -ns) m gin

ginásio [ʒi'nazju] m gymnasium; (escola) secondary (BRIT) ou high (US) school

ginástica [ʒi'naʃtʃika] f gymnastics sg; (para fortalecer o corpo) keep-fit

ginecologia [ʒinekolo'ʒia] f gynaecology (BRIT), gynecology (US)

ginecologista [ʒinekolo'ʒiʃta] m/f gynaecologist (BRIT), gynecologist (US)

ginjinha [ʒĩ'ʒiɲa] (PT) f cherry brandy

gira-discos ['ʒira-] (PT) m inv record-player

girafa [ʒi'rafa] f giraffe

girar [ʒi'ra*] vt to turn, rotate; (como pião) to spin ♦ vi to go round; to spin; (vaguear) to wander

girassol [ʒira'sɔw] (pl -óis) m sunflower

giratório, -a [ʒira'tɔrju, a] adj revolving

gíria ['ʒirja] f (calão) slang; (jargão) jargon

giro¹ ['ʒiru] m turn; **dar um ~** to go for a wander; (em veículo) to go for a spin; **que ~!** (PT) terrific!

giro² etc vb V gerir

giz [ʒiʒ] m chalk

glacê [gla'se] m icing

glacial [gla'sjaw] (pl -ais) adj icy

glamouroso, -a [glamu'rozu, ɔza] adj glamorous

glândula ['glãdula] f gland

global [glo'baw] (pl -ais) adj global; (total) overall; **quantia ~** lump sum

globo ['globu] m globe; **~ ocular** eyeball

glória ['glɔrja] f glory; **glorificar** [glorifi'ka*] vt to glorify; **glorioso, -a** [glo'rjozu, ɔza] adj glorious

glossário [glo'sarju] m glossary

gnomo ['gnomu] m gnome

Goa ['goa] n Goa

goiaba [go'jaba] f guava; **goiabada** [goja'bada] f guava jelly

gol [gɔw] (pl ~s) m goal

gola ['gɔla] f collar

gole ['gɔli] m gulp, swallow; (pequeno) sip; **tomar um ~ de** to sip

goleiro [go'lejru] (BR) m goalkeeper

golfe ['gowfi] m golf; **campo de ~**

golf course

golfinho [gow'fiɲu] m (ZOOL) dolphin

golfo ['gowfu] m gulf

golinho [go'liɲu] m sip; **beber algo aos ~s** to sip sth

golo ['golu] (PT) m = **gol**

golpe ['gɔwpi] m (tb fig) blow; (de mão) smack; (de punho) punch; (manobra) ploy; (de vento) gust; **de um só ~** at a stroke; **dar um ~ em alguém** to hit sb; (fig: trapacear) to trick sb; **~ de (estado)** coup (d'état); **~ de mestre** masterstroke; **golpear** [gow'pja*] vt to hit; (com navalha) to stab; (com o punho) to punch

goma ['goma] f gum, glue; (de roupa) starch; **~ de mascar** chewing gum

gomo ['gomu] m (de laranja) slice

gordo, -a ['goxdu, a] adj fat; (gorduroso) greasy; (carne) fatty; (fig: quantia) considerable, ample ♦ m/f fat man/woman

gordura [gox'dura] f fat; (derretida) grease; (obesidade) fatness; **gorduroso, -a** [goxdu'rozu, ɔza] adj (pele) greasy; (comida) fatty

gorila [go'rila] m gorilla

gorjeta [gox'ʒeta] f tip, gratuity

gorro ['goxu] m cap; (de lã) hat

gosma ['gɔʒma] f spittle; (fig) slime

gostar [goʃ'ta*] vi: **~ de** to like; (férias, viagem etc) to enjoy; **gostar-se** vr to like each other; **~ mais de ...** to prefer ..., like ... better

gosto ['goʃtu] m taste; (prazer) pleasure; **a seu ~** to your liking; **com ~** willingly; (vestir-se) tastefully; (comer) heartily; **de bom/mau ~** in good/bad taste; **ter ~ de** to taste of ; **gostoso, -a** [goʃ'tozu, ɔza] adj tasty; (agradável) pleasant; (cheiro)

lovely; (risada) good; (col: pessoa) gorgeous

gota ['gota] f drop; (de suor) bead; (MED) gout; **~ a ~** drop by drop

goteira [go'tejra] f (cano) gutter; (buraco) leak

gourmet [gux'me] (pl **~s**) m/f gourmet

governador, a [govexnado*, a] m/f governor

governamental [govexnamẽ'taw] (pl **-ais**) adj government atr

governanta [govex'nãta] f (de casa) housekeeper; (de criança) governess

governante [govex'nãtʃi] adj ruling ♦ m/f ruler ♦ f governess

governar [govex'na*] vt to govern, rule; (barco) to steer

governo [go'vexnu] m government; (controle) control

gozação [goza'sãw] (pl **-ões**) f enjoyment; (zombaria) teasing; (uma ~) joke

gozado, -a [go'zadu, a] adj funny; (estranho) strange, odd

gozar [go'za*] vt to enjoy; (col: rir de) to make fun of ♦ vi to enjoy o.s.; **~ de** to enjoy; to make fun of; **gozo** ['gozu] m (prazer) pleasure; (uso) enjoyment, use; (orgasmo) orgasm

Grã-Bretanha [grã-bre'taɲa] f Great Britain

graça ['grasa] f (REL) grace; (charme) charm; (gracejo) joke; (JUR) pardon; **de ~** (grátis) for nothing; (sem motivo) for no reason; **sem ~** dull, boring; **fazer ou ter ~** to be funny; **ficar sem ~** to be embarrassed; **~s a** thanks to

gracejar [grase'ʒa*] vi to joke; **gracejo** [gra'seʒu] m joke

gracioso, -a [gra'sjozu, ɔza] adj (pessoa) charming; (gestos) gracious

grade ['gradʒi] f (no chão) grating; (grelha) grill; (na janela) bars pl; (col: cadeia) nick, clink

gradear [gra'dʒja*] vt (janela) to put bars up at; (jardim) to fence off

graduação [gradwa'sãw] (pl -ões) f (classificação) grading; (EDUC) graduation; (MIL) rank

gradual [gra'dwaw] (pl -ais) adj gradual

graduar [gra'dwa*] vt (classificar) to grade; (luz, fogo) to regulate; **graduar-se** vr to graduate

gráfica ['grafika] f graphics sg; V tb gráfico

gráfico, -a ['grafiku, a] adj graphic ♦ m/f printer ♦ m (MAT) graph; (diagrama) diagram, chart; **~s** mpl (COMPUT) graphics; **~ de barras** bar chart

grã-fino, -a [grã'finu, a] (col) adj posh ♦ m/f nob, toff

grama ['grama] m gramme ♦ f (BR: capim) grass

gramado [gra'madu] (BR) m lawn; (FUTEBOL) pitch

gramática [gra'matʃika] f grammar; **gramatical** [gramatʃi'kaw] (pl -ais) adj grammatical

grampeador [grãpja'do*] m stapler

grampear [grã'pja*] vt to staple

grampo ['grãpu] m staple; (no cabelo) hairgrip; (de carpinteiro) clamp; (de chapéu) hatpin

granada [gra'nada] f (MIL) shell; **~ de mão** hand grenade

grande ['grãdʒi] adj big, large; (alto) tall; (notável, intenso) great; (longo) long; (adulto) grown-up; **mulher ~** big woman; **~ mulher** great woman; **grandeza** [grã'deza] f size; (fig) greatness; (ostentação) grandeur

grandioso, -a [grã'dʒjozu, ɔza] adj

magnificent, grand

granito [gra'nitu] m granite

granizo [gra'nizu] m hailstone; **chover ~** to hail; **chuva de ~** hailstorm

granulado, -a [granu'ladu, a] adj grainy; (açúcar) granulated

grão ['grãw] (pl ~s) m grain; (semente) seed; (de café) bean; **grão-de-bico** (pl grãos-de-bico) m chickpea

gratidão [gratʃi'dãw] f gratitude

gratificação [gratʃifika'sãw] (pl -ões) f gratuity, tip; (bônus) bonus; (recompensa) reward

gratificar [gratʃifi'ka*] vt to tip; (dar bônus a) to give a bonus to; (recompensar) to reward

grátis ['gratʃiʃ] adj free

grato, -a ['gratu, a] adj grateful; (agradável) pleasant

gratuito, -a [gra'twitu, a] adj (grátis) free; (infundado) gratuitous

grau [graw] m degree; (nível) level; (EDUC) class; **em alto ~** to a high degree; **ensino de primeiro/segundo ~** primary (BRIT) ou elementary (US)/secondary education

gravação [grava'sãw] f (em madeira) carving; (em disco, fita) recording

gravador [grava'do*] m tape recorder

gravar [gra'va*] vt to carve; (metal, pedra) to engrave; (na memória) to fix; (disco, fita) to record

gravata [gra'vata] f tie; **~ borboleta** bow tie

grave ['gravi] adj serious; (tom) deep; **gravemente** [grave'mẽtʃi] adv (doente, ferido) seriously

grávida ['gravida] adj pregnant

gravidade [gravi'dadʒi] f gravity

gravidez [gravi'deʒ] f pregnancy

gravura [gra'vura] f (em madeira)

engraving; (*estampa*) print

graxa ['graʃa] f (*para sapatos*) polish; (*lubrificante*) grease

Grécia ['grɛsja] f: a ~ Greece; **grego, -a** ['gregu, a] adj, m/f Greek ♦ m (LING) Greek

grelha ['grɛʎa] f grill; (*de fornalha*) grate; **bife na ~** grilled steak; **grelhado** [gre'ʎadu] m (*prato*) grill

grêmio ['gremju] m (*associação*) guild; (*clube*) club

grená [gre'na] adj, m dark red

greve ['grɛvi] f strike; **fazer ~** to go on strike; **~ branca** go-slow; **grevista** [gre'viʃta] m/f striker

grilo ['grilu] m cricket; (AUTO) squeak; (*col: de pessoa*) hang-up; **qual é o ~?** what's the matter?; **não tem ~!** (*col*) (there's) no problem!

gringo, -a ['grĩgu, a] (*col: pej*) m/f foreigner

gripado, -a [gri'padu, a] adj: **estar/ ficar ~** to have/get a cold

gripe ['gripi] f flu, influenza

grisalho, -a [gri'zaʎu, a] adj (*cabelo*) grey (BRIT), gray (US)

gritante [gri'tãtʃi] adj (*hipocrisia*) glaring; (*desigualdade*) gross; (*mentira*) blatant; (*cor*) loud, garish

gritar [gri'ta*] vt to shout, yell ♦ vi to shout; (*de dor, medo*) to scream; **~ com alguém** to shout at sb; **gritaria** [grita'ria] f shouting, din; **grito** ['gritu] m shout; (*de medo*) scream; (*de dor*) cry; (*de animal*) call; **dar um grito** to cry out; **falar aos gritos** to shout

Groenlândia [grwẽ'lãdʒja] f: a ~ Greenland

grosseiro, -a [gro'sejru, a] adj rude; (*piada*) crude; (*modos, tecido*) coarse; **grosseria** [grose'ria] f rudeness; (*ato*): **fazer uma grosseria** to be rude; (*dito*): **dizer uma grosseria** to be rude, say something rude

grosso, -a ['grosu, 'grɔsa] adj thick; (*áspero*) rough; (*voz*) deep; (*col: pessoa, piada*) rude ♦ m: **o ~ de** the bulk of; **grossura** [gro'sura] f thickness

grotesco, -a [gro'teʃku, a] adj grotesque

grudar [gru'da*] vt to glue, stick ♦ vi to stick

grude ['grudʒi] f glue; **grudento, -a** [gru'dẽtu, a] adj sticky

grunhir [gru'ni*] vi (*porco*) to grunt; (*tigre*) to growl; (*resmungar*) to grumble

grupo ['grupu] m group

gruta ['gruta] f grotto

guarda ['gwaxda] m/f policeman/ woman ♦ f (*vigilância*) guarding; (*de objeto*) safekeeping ♦ m (MIL) guard; **estar de ~** to be on guard; **pôr-se em ~** to be on one's guard; **a G~ Civil** the Civil Guard; **guarda-chuva** (*pl* **guarda-chuvas**) m umbrella; **guarda-costas** m inv (NÁUT) coastguard boat; (*capanga*) bodyguard; **guardados** [gwax'daduʃ] mpl keepsakes, valuables; **guarda-louça** (*pl* **guarda-louças**) m sideboard; **guardanapo** [gwaxda'napu] m napkin; **guarda-noturno** (*pl* **guardas-noturnos**) m night watchman; **guardar** [gwax'da*] vt to put away; (*zelar por*) to guard; (*lembrança, segredo*) to keep; **guardar-se** vr (*defender-se*) to protect o.s.; **guardar-se de** (*acautelar-se*) to guard against; **guarda-redes** (PT) m inv goalkeeper; **guarda-roupa** (*pl* **guarda-roupas**) m wardrobe; **guarda-sol** (*pl* **guarda-sóis**) m sunshade, parasol

guardião, -diã [gwax'dʒjãw, 'dʒjã] (*pl* **-ães** ou **-ões, -s**) m/f guardian

guarnição [gwaxni'sãw] (*pl* **-ões**) f (MIL) garrison; (NÁUT) crew; (CULIN) garnish

Guatemala [gwate'mala] *f:* **a ~** Guatemala

gude ['gudʒi] *m:* **bola de ~** marble; (*jogo*) marbles *pl*

guerra ['gɛxa] *f* war; **em ~** at war; **fazer ~** to wage war; **~ civil** civil war; **~ mundial** world war; **guerreiro, -a** [ge'xejru, a] *adj* (*espírito*) fighting; (*belicoso*) warlike ♦ *m* warrior

guerrilha [ge'xiʎa] *f* (*luta*) guerrilla warfare; (*tropa*) guerrilla band; **guerrilheiro, -a** [gexi'ʎejru, a] *m/f* guerrilla

guia ['gia] *f* guidance; (*COM*) permit, bill of lading; (*formulário*) advice slip ♦ *m* (*livro*) guide(book) ♦ *m/f* (*pessoa*) guide

Guiana ['gjana] *f:* **a ~** Guyana

guiar [gja*] *vt* to guide; (*AUTO*) to drive ♦ *vi* to drive; **guiar-se** *vr:* **~-se por** to go by

guichê [gi'ʃe] *m* ticket window; (*em banco, repartição*) window, counter

guinada [gi'nada] *f:* **dar uma ~** (*com o carro*) to swerve

guincho ['gĩʃu] *m* (*de animal, rodas*) squeal; (*de pessoa*) shriek

guindaste [gĩ'daʃtʃi] *m* hoist, crane

guisado [gi'zadu] *m* stew

guitarra [gi'taxa] *f* (electric) guitar

gula ['gula] *f* gluttony, greed

guloseima [gulo'zejma] *f* delicacy, titbit

guloso, -a [gu'lozu, ɔza] *adj* greedy

H

há [a] *vb V* **haver**

hábil ['abiw] (*pl* **-eis**) *adj* competent, capable; (*astucioso, esperto*) clever; (*sutil*) diplomatic; **em tempo ~** in reasonable time; **habilidade**

[abili'dadʒi] *f* skill, ability; (*astúcia, esperteza*) shrewdness; (*tato*) discretion; **habilidoso, -a** [abili'dozu, ɔza] *adj* skilled, clever

habilitação [abilita'sãw] (*pl* **-ões**) *f* competence; (*ato*) qualification; **habilitações** *fpl* (*conhecimentos*) qualifications

habilitar [abili'ta*] *vt* to enable; (*dar direito a*) to qualify, entitle; (*preparar*) to prepare

habitação [abita'sãw] (*pl* **-ões**) *f* dwelling, residence; (*alojamento*) housing

habitante [abi'tãtʃi] *m/f* inhabitant

habitar [abi'ta*] *vt* to live in; (*povoar*) to inhabit ♦ *vi* to live

hábito ['abitu] *m* habit; (*social*) custom; (*REL: traje*) habit

habituado, -a [abi'twadu, a] *adj:* **~ a (fazer) algo** used to (doing) sth

habitual [abi'twaw] (*pl* **-ais**) *adj* usual

habituar [abi'twa*] *vt:* **~ alguém a** to get sb used to, accustom sb to; **habituar-se** *vr:* **~-se a** to get used to

hacker ['ake*] (*pl* **~s**) *m* (*COMPUT*) hacker

Haia ['aja] *n* The Hague

haja *etc* ['aʒa] *vb V* **haver**

hálito ['alitu] *m* breath

hall [xɔw] (*pl* **~s**) *m* hall; (*de teatro, hotel*) foyer; **~ de entrada** entrance hall

hambúrguer [ã'buxge*] *m* hamburger

hão [ãw] *vb V* **haver**

hardware ['xadwe*] *m* '(*COMPUT*) hardware

harmonia [axmo'nia] *f* harmony

harmonioso, -a [axmo'njozu, ɔza] *adj* harmonious

harmonizar

468

hipermercado

harmonizar [axmoni'za*] vt (MÚS) to harmonize; (conciliar): ~ algo (com algo) to reconcile sth (with sth); **harmonizar-se** vr: ~(-se) (idéias etc) to coincide; (pessoas) to be in agreement

harpa ['axpa] f harp

Havaí [ava'i] m: o ~ Hawaii

PALAVRA CHAVE
---

haver [a've*] vb aux **1** (ter) to have; **ele havia saído/comido** he had left/eaten

2: ~ **de**: **quem ~ia de dizer que ...?** who would have thought that ...?

♦ vb impess **1** (existência): **há** (sg) there is; (pl) there are; **o que é que há?** what's the matter?; **o que é que houve?** what happened?, what was that?; **não há de quê** don't mention it, you're welcome; **haja o que houver** come what may

2 (tempo): **há séculos/cinco dias que não o vejo** I haven't seen him for ages/five days; **há um ano que ela chegou** it's a year since she arrived; **há cinco dias (atrás)** five days ago

♦ haver-se vr: ~-se com alguém to sort things out with sb

♦ m (COM) credit; ~es mpl (pertences) property sg, possessions; (riqueza) wealth sg

haxixe [a'ʃiʃi] m hashish

hebraico, -a [e'brajku, a] adj Hebrew ♦ m (LING) Hebrew

Hébridas ['ebrida] fpl: as (ilhas) ~ the Hebrides

hediondo, -a [e'dʒjõdu, a] adj vile, revolting; (crime) heinous

hei [ej] vb V haver

hélice ['elisi] f propeller

helicóptero [eli'kɔpteru] m helicopter

hematoma [ema'tɔma] m bruise

hemorragia [emoxa'ʒia] f haemorrhage (BRIT), hemorrhage (US); ~ **nasal** nosebleed

hemorróidas [emo'xɔjdaʃ] fpl haemorrhoids (BRIT), hemorrhoids (US), piles

hepatite [epa'tʃitʃi] f hepatitis

hera ['era] f ivy

herança [e'rãsa] f inheritance; (fig) heritage

herdar [ex'da*] vt: ~ algo (de) to inherit sth (from); ~ a to bequeath to

herdeiro, -a [ex'dejru, a] m/f heir(ess)

herói [e'rɔj] m hero

heroína [ero'ina] f heroine; (droga) heroin

hesitação [ezita'sãw] f (pl -ões) hesitation

hesitante [ezi'tãtʃi] adj hesitant

hesitar [ezi'ta*] vi to hesitate

heterossexual [eterosek'swaw] (pl -ais) adj, m/f heterosexual

híbrido, -a ['ibridu, a] adj hybrid

hidratante [idra'tãtʃi] adj moisturizer

hidráulico, -a [i'drawliku, a] adj hydraulic

hidrelétrico, -a [idre'letriku, a] (PT -ct-) adj hydroelectric

hidro... [idru] prefixo hydro..., water... atr

hidrogênio [idro'ʒenju] m hydrogen

hierarquia [jerax'kia] f hierarchy

hífen ['ifẽ] (pl ~s) m hyphen

higiene [i'ʒjeni] f hygiene; **higiênico, -a** [i'ʒjeniku, a] adj hygienic; (pessoa) clean; **papel higiênico** toilet paper

hindu [ĩ'du] adj, m/f Hindu

hino ['inu] m hymn; ~ **nacional** national anthem

hipermercado [ipexmex'kadu] m

hypermarket

hipertensão [ipextẽ'sãw] f high blood pressure

hipismo [i'piʒmu] m (turfe) horse racing; (equitação) (horse) riding

hipnotizar [ipnotʃi'za*] vt to hypnotize

hipocrisia [ipokri'sia] f hypocrisy; **hipócrita** [i'pɔkrita] adj hypocritical ♦ m/f hypocrite

hipódromo [i'pɔdromu] m racecourse

hipopótamo [ipo'pɔtamu] m hippopotamus

hipoteca [ipo'teka] f mortgage; **hipotecar** [ipote'ka*] vt to mortgage

hipótese [i'pɔtezi] f hypothesis; na ~ de in the event of; em ~ alguma under no circumstances; na melhor/pior das ~s at best/worst

hispânico, -a [iʃ'paniku, a] adj Hispanic

histeria [iʃte'ria] f hysteria; **histérico, -a** [iʃ'teriku, a] adj hysterical

história [iʃ'tɔrja] f history; (conto) story; ~s fpl (chateação) bother sg, fuss sg; isso é outra ~ that's a different matter; que ~ é essa? what's going on?; **historiador, a** [iʃtorja'do*, a] m/f historian; **histórico, -a** [iʃ'tɔriku, a] adj historical; (fig: notável) historic ♦ m history

hobby ['xɔbi] (pl -bies) m hobby

hoje ['oʒi] adv today; (tb: ~ em dia) now(adays); ~ à noite tonight

Holanda [o'lãda] f: a ~ Holland; **holandês, -esa** [olã'deʃ, eza] adj Dutch ♦ m/f Dutchman/woman ♦ m (LING) Dutch

holocausto [olo'kawʃtu] m holocaust

holofote [olo'fɔtʃi] m searchlight; (em campo de futebol etc) floodlight

homem ['omẽ] (pl -ns) m man; (a humanidade) mankind; ~ de empresa ou negócios businessman; ~ de estado statesman

homenagear [omena'ʒja*] vt (pessoa) to pay tribute to, honour (BRIT), honor (US)

homenagem [ome'naʒẽ] f tribute; (REL) homage; **prestar ~ a alguém** to pay tribute to sb

homens ['omẽʃ] mpl de homem

homeopático, -a [omjo'patʃiku] adj homoeopathic

homicida [omi'sida] adj homicidal ♦ m/f murderer; **homicídio** [omi'sidʒju] m murder; **homicídio involuntário** manslaughter

homologar [omolo'ga*] vt to ratify

homólogo, -a [o'mɔlogu, a] adj homologous; (fig) equivalent ♦ m/f opposite number

homossexual [omosek'swal] (pl -ais) adj, m/f homosexual

Honduras [õ'duraʃ] f Honduras

honestidade [oneʃtʃi'dadʒi] f honesty; (decência) decency; (justeza) fairness

honesto, -a [o'neʃtu, a] adj honest; (decente) decent; (justo) fair, just

honorário, -a [ono'rarju, a] adj honorary; **honorários** [ono'rarjuʃ] mpl fees

honra ['õxa] f honour (BRIT), honor (US); **em ~ de** in hono(u)r of

honrado, -a [õ'xadu, a] adj honest; (respeitado) honourable (BRIT), honorable (US)

honrar [õ'xa*] vt to honour (BRIT), honor (US)

honroso, -a [õ'xozu, ɔza] adj hono(u)rable

hóquei ['ɔkej] m hockey; ~ sobre gelo ice hockey

hora ['ɔra] f (60 minutos) hour; (momento) time; a que ~s? (at

what time?; **que ~s são?** what time
is it?; **são duas ~s** it's two o'clock;
você tem as ~s? have you got the
time?; **fazer ~** to kill time; **de ~ em
~** every hour; **na ~** on the spot;
chegar na ~ to be on time; **de última ~ ♦** adj last-minute ♦ adv at the
last minute; **meia ~** half an hour; **~s
extras** overtime sg; **horário, -a**
[oˈrarju, a] adj: **100 km horários**
100 km an hour ♦ m timetable;
(hora) time; **horário de expediente**
working hours pl; (de um escritório)
office hours pl

horizontal [orizõˈtaw] (pl -ais) adj
horizontal

horizonte [oriˈzõtʃi] m horizon

horóscopo [oˈrɔʃkopu] m horoscope

horrendo, -a [oˈxẽdu, a] adj horrendous, frightful

horripilante [oxipiˈlãtʃi] adj horri-
fying, hair-raising

horrível [oˈxivew] (pl -eis) adj
awful, horrible

horror [oˈxo*] m horror; **que ~!** how
awful!; **ter ~ a algo** to hate sth; **horrorizar** [oxoriˈza*] vt to horrify,
frighten; **horroroso, -a** [oxoˈrozu,
ɔza] adj horrible, ghastly

horta [ˈɔxta] f vegetable garden

hortaliças [oxtaˈlisaʃ] fpl vegetables

hortelã [oxteˈlã] f mint; **~ pimenta**
peppermint

horticultor, a [oxtʃikuwˈto*, a]
m/f market gardener (BRIT), truck
farmer (US)

hortifrutigranjeiros [oxtʃifrutʃi-
grãˈʒejruʃ] mpl fruit and vegetables

horto [ˈɔxtu] m market garden
(BRIT), truck farm (US)

hospedagem [oʃpeˈdaʒẽ] f guest
house

hospedar [oʃpeˈda*] vt to put up;
hospedar-se vr to stay, lodge;

hospedaria [oʃpedaˈria] f guest
house

hóspede [ˈɔʃpedʒi] m (amigo)
guest; (estranho) lodger

hospedeira [oʃpeˈdejra] f landlady;
(PT: de bordo) stewardess, air hostess (BRIT)

hospício [oʃˈpisju] m mental hospital

hospital [oʃpiˈtaw] (pl -ais) m hospital

hospitalidade [oʃpitaliˈdadʒi] f
hospitality

hostil [oʃˈtʃiw] (pl -is) adj hostile;
hostilizar [oʃtʃiliˈza*] vt to antagonize; (MIL) to wage war on

hotel [oˈtew] (pl -éis) m hotel; **hote-
leiro, -a** [oteˈlejru, a] m/f hotelier

houve etc [ˈovi] vb V **haver**

humanidade [umaniˈdadʒi] f (os
homens) man(kind); (compaixão)
humanity

humanitário, -a [umaniˈtarju, a]
adj humane

humano, -a [uˈmanu, a] adj human; (bondoso) humane

humidade [umiˈdadə] (PT) f dampness; (clima) humidity

húmido, -a [ˈumidu, a] (PT) adj wet,
moist; (roupa) damp; (clima) humid

humildade [umiwˈdadʒi] f humil-
ity; (pobreza) poverty

humilde [uˈmiwdʒi] adj humble;
(pobre) poor

humilhar [umiˈʎa*] vt to humiliate

humor [uˈmo*] m mood, temper;
(graça) humour (BRIT), humor (US);
de bom/mau ~ in a good/bad
mood; **humorista** [umoˈriʃta] m/f
comedian; **humorístico, -a** [umo-
ˈriʃtʃiku, a] adj humorous

húngaro, -a [ˈũgaru, a] adj, m/f
Hungarian

Hungria [ũˈgria] f: **a ~** Hungary

hurra [ˈuxa] m cheer ♦ excl hurrah!

I

ia etc ['ia] vb V **ir**

iate ['jatʃi] m yacht; **~ clube** yacht club

ibérico, -a [i'bɛriku, a] adj, m/f Iberian

ibero-americano, -a [iberu-] adj, m/f Ibero-American

ICM (BR) abr m (= Imposto sobre Circulação de Mercadorias) = VAT

ícone ['ikoni] m (GER, COMPUT) icon

icterícia [ikte'risja] f jaundice

ida ['ida] f going, departure; **~ e volta** round trip, return; **a (viagem de)~** the outward journey; **na ~** on the way there

idade [i'dadʒi] f age; **ter cinco anos de ~** to be five (years old); **de meia ~** middle-aged; **qual é a ~ dele?** how old is he?; **na minha ~** at my age; **ser menor/maior de ~** to be under/of age; **pessoa de ~** elderly person; **I~ Média** Middle Ages pl

ideal [ide'jaw] (pl **-ais**) m, adj ideal;
idealista [idea'liʃta] adj idealistic ♦ m/f idealist

idéia [i'dɛja] f idea; (mente) mind;
mudar de ~ to change one's mind;
não ter a mínima ~ to have no idea;
não faço ~ I can't imagine; **estar com ~ de fazer** to plan to do

idem ['idẽj] pron ditto

idêntico, -a [i'dẽtʃiku, a] adj identical

identidade [idẽtʃi'dadʒi] f identity

identificação [idẽtʃifika'sãw] f identification

identificar [idẽtʃifi'ka*] vt to identify; **identificar-se** vr: **~-se com** to identify with

idioma [i'dʒɔma] m language

idiota [i'dʒɔta] adj idiotic ♦ m/f idiot

ido, -a ['idu, a] adj past

idolatrar [idola'tra*] vt to idolize

ídolo ['idolu] m idol

idoso, -a [i'dozu, ɔza] adj elderly, old

ignição [igni'sãw] (pl **-ões**) f ignition

ignorado, -a [igno'radu, a] adj unknown

ignorância [igno'rãsja] f ignorance; **ignorante** [igno'rãtʃi] adj ignorant, uneducated ♦ m/f ignoramus

ignorar [igno'ra*] vt not to know; (não dar atenção a) to ignore

igreja [i'grɛʒa] f church

igual [i'gwaw] (pl **-ais**) adj equal; (superfície) even ♦ m/f equal

igualar [igwa'la*] vt to equal; (fazer igual) to make equal; (nivelar) to level ♦ vi: **~ a ou com** to be equal to, be the same as; (ficar no mesmo nível) to be level with; **igualar-se** vr: **~-se a alguém** to be sb's equal

igualdade [igwaw'dadʒi] f equality; (uniformidade) uniformity

igualmente [igwaw'mẽtʃi] adv equally; (também) likewise, also; **~!** (saudação) the same to you!

ilegal [ile'gaw] (pl **-ais**) adj illegal

ilegítimo, -a [ile'ʒitʃimu, a] adj illegitimate; (ilegal) unlawful

ilegível [ile'ʒivew] (pl **-eis**) adj illegible

ileso, -a [i'lɛzu, a] adj unhurt

iletrado, -a [ile'tradu, a] adj illiterate

ilha ['iʎa] f island; **ilhéu, ilhoa** [i'ʎɛw, i'ʎoa] m/f islander

ilícito, -a [i'lisitu, a] adj illicit

ilimitado, -a [ilimi'tadu, a] adj unlimited

iludir [ilu'dʒi*] vt to delude; (enganar) to deceive; (a lei) to evade

iluminação [ilumina'sãw] (pl **-ões**) f lighting; (fig) enlightenment

iluminar [ilumiˈna*] vt to light up; (estádio etc) to floodlight; (fig) to enlighten

ilusão [iluˈzãw] (pl -ões) f illusion; (quimera) delusion; **ilusório, -a** [iluˈzɔrju, a] adj deceptive

ilustração [iluʃtraˈsãw] (pl -ões) f illustration

ilustrado, -a [iluʃˈtradu, a] adj illustrated; (erudito) learned

ilustrar [iluʃˈtra*] vt to illustrate; (instruir) to instruct

ilustre [iˈluʃtri] adj illustrious; **um ~ desconhecido** a complete stranger

ímã [ˈimã] m magnet

imagem [iˈmaʒẽ] (pl -ns) f image; (semelhança) likeness; (TV) picture; **imagens** fpl (LITERATURA) imagery sg

imaginação [imaʒinaˈsãw] (pl -ões) f imagination

imaginar [imaʒiˈna*] vt to imagine; (supor) to suppose; **imaginar-se** vr to imagine o.s.; **imagine só!** just imagine!; **imaginário, -a** [imaʒiˈnarju, a] adj imaginary

imaturo, -a [iˈmaturu, a] adj immature

imbatível [ĩbaˈtʃivew] (pl -eis) adj invincible

imbecil [ĩbeˈsiw] (pl -is) adj stupid ♦ m/f imbecile; **imbecilidade** [ĩbesiliˈdadʒi] f stupidity

imediações [imedʒaˈsõjʃ] fpl vicinity sg, neighbourhood sg (BRIT), neighborhood sg (US)

imediatamente [imedʒataˈmẽtʃi] adv immediately, right away

imediato, -a [imeˈdʒatu, a] adj immediate; (seguinte) next; **~ a** next to; **de ~** straight away

imenso, -a [iˈmẽsu, a] adj immense, huge; (ódio, amor) great

imigração [imigraˈsãw] (pl -ões) f immigration

imigrante [imiˈgrãtʃi] adj, m/f immigrant

iminente [imiˈnẽtʃi] adj imminent

imitação [imitaˈsãw] (pl -ões) f imitation

imitar [imiˈta*] vt to imitate; (assinatura) to copy

imobiliária [imobiˈljarja] f estate agent's (BRIT), real estate broker's (US)

imobiliário, -a [imobiˈljarju, a] adj property atr

imobilizar [imobiliˈza*] vt to immobilize; (fig) to bring to a standstill

imoral [imoˈraw] (pl -ais) adj immoral

imortal [imoxˈtaw] (pl -ais) adj immortal

imóvel [iˈmɔvew] (pl -eis) adj motionless, still; (não movediço) immovable ♦ m property; (edifício) building; **imóveis** mpl (propriedade) real estate sg, property sg

impaciência [ĩpaˈsjẽsja] f impatience; **impacientar-se** [ĩpasjẽˈtaxsi] vr to lose one's patience; **impaciente** [ĩpaˈsjẽtʃi] adj impatient

impacto [ĩˈpaktu] (PT -cte) m impact

ímpar [ˈĩpa*] adj (número) odd; (sem igual) unique, unequalled

imparcial [ĩpaxˈsjaw] (pl -ais) adj fair, impartial

impecável [ĩpeˈkavew] (pl -eis) adj perfect, impeccable

impeço etc [ĩˈpesu] vb V impedir

impedido, -a [ĩpeˈdʒidu, a] adj (FUTEBOL) offside; (PT: TEL) engaged (BRIT), busy (US)

impedimento [ĩpedʒiˈmẽtu] m impediment

impedir [ĩpeˈdʒi*] vt to obstruct; (estrada, tráfego) to block; (movimento, progresso) to impede; **~ alguém de fazer algo** to prevent sb from doing sth; (*proibir*) tu forbid sb to do sth; **~ (que aconteça)** algo to prevent sth (happening)

impenetrável [ĩpene'travew] (*pl -eis*) *adj* impenetrable

impensado, -a [ĩpē'sadu, a] *adj* thoughtless; (*não calculado*) unpremeditated; (*imprevisto*) unforeseen

impensável [ĩpē'savew] (*pl -eis*) *adj* unthinkable

imperador [ĩpera'do*] *m* emperor

imperativo, -a [ĩpera'tʃivu, a] *adj* imperative ♦ *m* imperative

imperatriz [ĩpera'triʒ] *f* empress

imperdoável [ĩpex'dwavew] (*pl -eis*) *adj* unforgivable, inexcusable

imperfeito, -a [ĩpex'fejtu, a] *adj* imperfect ♦ *m* (*LING*) imperfect (tense)

imperial [ĩpe'rjaw] (*pl -ais*) *adj* imperial

imperícia [ĩpe'risja] *f* inability; (*inexperiência*) inexperience

império [ĩ'perju] *m* empire

impermeável [ĩpex'mjavew] (*pl -eis*) *adj*: **~ a** (*tb fig*) impervious to; (*à água*) waterproof ♦ *m* raincoat

impertinente [ĩpextʃi'nētʃi] *adj* irrelevant; (*insolente*) impertinent

impessoal [ĩpe'swaw] (*pl -ais*) *adj* impersonal

ímpeto ['ĩpetu] *m* (*TEC*) impetus; (*movimento súbito*) start; (*de cólera*) fit; (*de emoção*) surge; (*de chamas*) fury; **agir com ~** to act on impulse; **levantar-se num ~** to get up with a start

impetuoso, -a [ĩpe'twozu, ɔza] *adj* (*pessoa*) headstrong, impetuous; (*ato*) rash, hasty

impiedoso, -a [ĩpje'dozu, ɔza] *adj* merciless, cruel

implacável [ĩpla'kavew] (*pl -eis*)

adj relentless; (*pessoa*) unforgiving

implantação [ĩplãta'sãw] (*pl -ões*) *f* introduction; (*MED*) implant

implementar [ĩplemē'ta*] *vt* to implement

implicar [ĩpli'ka*] *vt* (*envolver*) to implicate; (*pressupor*) to imply ♦ *vi*: **~ com alguém** (*chatear*) to tease sb, pick on sb; **implicar-se** *vr* to get involved; **~ (em)** algo to involve sth

implícito, -a [ĩ'plisitu, a] *adj* implicit

implorar [ĩplo'ra*] *vt*: **~ (algo a alguém)** to beg ou implore (sb for sth)

imponente [ĩpo'nētʃi] *adj* impressive, imposing

impopular [ĩpopu'la*] *adj* unpopular; **impopularidade** [ĩpopulari'dadʒi] *f* unpopularity

impor [ĩ'po*] (*irreg: como* **pôr**) *vt* to impose; (*respeito*) to command; **impor-se** *vr* to assert o.s.; **~ algo a alguém** to impose sth on sb

importação [ĩpoxta'sãw] (*pl -ões*) *f* (*ato*) importing; (*mercadoria*) import

importador, a [ĩpoxta'do*, a] *adj* import *atr* ♦ *m/f* importer

importância [ĩpox'tãsja] *f* importance; (*de dinheiro*) sum, amount; **não tem ~** it doesn't matter, never mind; **ter ~** to be important; **sem ~** unimportant; **importante** [ĩpox'tãtʃi] *adj* important ♦ *m*: **o (mais) importante** the (most) important thing

importar [ĩpox'ta*] *vt* (*COM*) to import; (*trazer*) to bring in; (*causar*: *prejuízos etc*) to cause; (*implicar*) to imply ♦ *vi* to matter, be important; **importar-se** *vr*: **~-se com algo** to mind sth; **não me importo** I don't care

importunar [ĩpoxtu'na*] *vt* to

bother, annoy

importuno, -a [ĩpox'tunu, a] adj annoying; (inoportuno) inopportune ♦ m/f nuisance

imposição [ĩpozi'sãw] (pl -ões) f imposition

impossibilitado, -a [ĩposibili'tadu, a] adj: ~ **de fazer** unable to do

impossibilitar [ĩposibili'ta*] vt: ~ **algo** to make sth impossible; ~ **alguém de fazer**, ~ **a alguém fazer** to prevent sb doing; ~ **algo a alguém**, ~ **alguém para algo** to make sth impossible for sb

impossível [ĩpo'sivew] (pl -eis) adj impossible; (insuportável: pessoa) insufferable; (incrível) incredible

imposto, -a [ĩ'poʃtu] m tax; **antes/depois de ~s** before/after tax; ~ **de renda** (BR) income tax; ~ **predial** rates pl; **I~ sobre Circulação de Mercadorias (e Serviços)** (BR), ~ **sobre valor acrescentado** (PT) value added tax (BRIT), sales tax (US)

impotente [ĩpo'tẽtʃi] adj powerless; (MED) impotent

impraticável [ĩpratʃi'kavew] (pl -eis) adj impracticable; (rua, rio etc) impassable

impreciso, -a [ĩpre'sizu, a] adj vague; (falto de rigor) inaccurate

imprensa [ĩ'prẽsa] f printing; (máquina, jornais) press

imprescindível [ĩpreʃsĩ'dʒivew] (pl -eis) adj essential, indispensable

impressão [ĩpre'sãw] (pl -ões) f impression; (de livros) printing; (marca) imprint; **causar boa ~** to make a good impression; **ficar com/ter a ~ (de) que** to get/have the impression that

impressionante [ĩpresjo'nãtʃi] adj impressive

impressionar [ĩpresjo'na*] vt to af-

fect ♦ vi to be impressive; (pessoa) to make an impression; **impressionar-se** vr: **~-se (com algo)** to be moved (by sth)

impresso, -a [ĩ'presu, a] pp de **imprimir** ♦ adj printed ♦ m (para preencher) form; (folheto) leaflet; **~s** mpl (formulário) printed matter sg

impressões [ĩpre'sõjʃ] fpl de **impressão**

impressora [ĩpre'sora] f printing machine; (COMPUT) printer; ~ **matricial/a laser** dot-matrix/laser printer

imprestável [ĩpreʃ'tavew] (pl -eis) adj (inútil) useless; (pessoa) unhelpful

imprevisível [ĩprevi'zivew] (pl -eis) adj unforeseeable

imprevisto, -a [ĩpre'viʃtu, a] adj unexpected, unforeseen ♦ m: **um ~** something unexpected

imprimir [ĩpri'mi*] vt to print; (marca) to stamp; (infundir) to instil (BRIT), instill (US); (COMPUT) to print out

impróprio, -a [ĩ'prɔprju, a] adj inappropriate; (indecente) improper

improvável [ĩpro'vavew] (pl -eis) adj unlikely

improvisar [ĩprovi'za*] vt, vi to improvise; (TEATRO) to ad-lib

improviso [ĩpro'vizu]: **de ~** adv (de repente) suddenly; (sem preparação) without preparation

imprudente [ĩpru'dẽtʃi] adj (irrefletido) rash; (motorista) careless

impulsivo, -a [ĩpuw'sivu, a] adj impulsive

impulso [ĩ'puwsu] m impulse; (fig: estímulo) urge

impune [ĩ'puni] adj unpunished; **impunidade** [ĩpuni'dadʒi] f impunity

imundície [imũ'dʒisji] f filth; **imundo, -a** [i'mũdu, a] adj filthy;

(*obsceno*) dirty

imune [i'muni] *adj*: ~ **a** immune to;
imunidade [imuni'dadʒi] *f* immunity

inábil [i'nabiw] (*pl* -**eis**) *adj* incapable; (*desajeitado*) clumsy

inabitado, -a [inabi'tadu, a] *adj* uninhabited

inacabado, -a [inaka'badu, a] *adj* unfinished

inacreditável [inakredʒi'tavew] (*pl* -**eis**) *adj* unbelievable, incredible

inactivo, -a *etc* [ina'tivu, a] (*PT*) = **inativo/a** *etc*

inadequado, -a [inade'kwadu, a] *adj* inadequate; (*impróprio*) unsuitable

inadiável [ina'dʒjavew] (*pl* -**eis**) *adj* pressing

inadimplência [inadʒĩ'plẽsja] *f* (*JUR*) breach of contract, default

inanimado, -a [inani'madu, a] *adj* inanimate

inaptidão [inaptʃi'dãw] (*pl* -**ões**) *f* inability

inatingível [inatʃĩ'ʒivew] (*pl* -**eis**) *adj* unattainable

inativo, -a [ina'tʃivu, a] *adj* inactive; (*aposentado, reformado*) retired

inato, -a [i'natu, a] *adj* innate, inborn

inauguração [inawgura'sãw] (*pl* -**ões**) *f* inauguration; (*de exposição*) opening; **inaugural** [inawgu'raw] (*pl* -**ais**) *adj* inaugural; **inaugurar** [inawgu'ra*] *vt* to inaugurate; (*exposição*) to open

incansável [ĩkã'savew] (*pl* -**eis**) *adj* tireless, untiring

incapacidade [ĩkapasi'dadʒi] *f* incapacity; (*incompetência*) incompetence

incapacitado, -a [ĩkapasi'tadu, a] *adj* (*inválido*) disabled, handicapped ♦ *m/f* handicapped person; **estar ~**

de fazer to be unable to do

incapaz [ĩka'pajʒ] *adj, m/f* incompetent; ~ **de fazer** incapable of doing; ~ **para** unfit for

incendiar [ĩsẽ'dʒja*] *vt* to set fire to; (*fig*) to inflame; **incendiar-se** *vr* to catch fire

incêndio [ĩ'sẽdʒju] *m* fire; ~ **criminoso** *ou* **premeditado** arson

incenso [ĩ'sẽsu] *m* incense

incentivar [ĩsẽtʃi'va*] *vt* to stimulate, encourage

incentivo [ĩsẽ'tʃivu] *m* incentive; ~ **fiscal** tax incentive

incerteza [ĩsex'teza] *f* uncertainty

incerto, -a [ĩ'sextu, a] *adj* uncertain

incessante [ĩse'sãtʃi] *adj* incessant

incesto [ĩ'seʃtu] *m* incest

inchado, -a [ĩ'ʃadu, a] *adj* swollen; (*fig*) conceited

inchar [ĩ'ʃa*] *vt, vi* to swell

incidência [ĩsi'dẽsja] *f* incidence, occurrence

incidente [ĩsi'dẽtʃi] *m* incident

incisivo, -a [ĩsi'zivu, a] *adj* cutting, sharp; (*fig*) incisive

incitar [ĩsi'ta*] *vt* to incite; (*pessoa, animal*) to drive on

inclinação [ĩklina'sãw] (*pl* -**ões**) *f* inclination; ~ **da cabeça** nod

inclinado, -a [ĩkli'nadu, a] *adj* (*terreno*) sloping; (*corpo, torre*) leaning

inclinar [ĩkli'na*] *vt* to tilt; (*cabeça*) to nod ♦ *vi* to slope; (*objeto*) to tilt; **inclinar-se** *vr* to tilt; (*dobrar o corpo*) to bow, stoop; **~-se sobre algo** to lean over sth

incluir [ĩ'klwi*] *vt* to include; (*em carta*) to enclose; **incluir-se** *vr* to be included

inclusão [ĩklu'zãw] *f* inclusion; **inclusive** [ĩklu'zivi] *prep* including ♦ *adv* inclusive; (*até mesmo*) even

incoerente [ĩkoe'rẽtʃi] *adj* incoherent; (*contraditório*) inconsistent

incógnita [ĩˈkɔgnita] f (MAT) unknown; (fato incógnito) mystery; **incógnito, -a** [ĩˈkɔgnitu, a] adj unknown ♦ adv incognito (US)

incolor [ĩkoˈlo*] adj colourless (BRIT), colorless (US)

incomodar [ĩkomoˈda*] vt to bother, trouble; (aborrecer) to annoy ♦ vi to be bothersome; **incomodar-se** vr to bother, put o.s. out; **~-se com algo** to be bothered by sth, mind sth; **não se incomode!** don't worry!

incômodo, -a [ĩˈkomodu, a] adj uncomfortable; (incomodativo) troublesome; (inoportuno) inconvenient ♦ m (molestia) trouble, bother; (menstruação) period

incompetente [ĩkõpeˈtẽtʃi] adj, m/f incompetent

incompleto, -a [ĩkõˈpletu, a] adj incomplete

incompreendido, -a [ĩkõprjẽˈdʒidu, a] adj misunderstood

incomum [ĩkoˈmũ] adj uncommon

incomunicável [ĩkomuniˈkavew] (pl -eis) adj cut off; (privado de comunicação, fig) incommunicado; (preso) in solitary confinement

inconformado, -a [ĩkõfoxˈmadu, a] adj bitter; **~ com** unreconciled to

inconfundível [ĩkõfũˈdʒivew] (pl -eis) adj unmistakeable

inconsciência [ĩkõˈsjẽsja] f (MED) unconsciousness; (irreflexão) thoughtlessness

inconsciente [ĩkõˈsjẽtʃi] adj unconscious ♦ m unconscious

inconseqüente [ĩkõseˈkwẽtʃi] adj inconsistent; (contraditório) illogical; (irresponsável) irresponsible

inconsistente [ĩkõsiˈtẽtʃi] adj inconsistent; (sem solidez) runny

inconstante [ĩkõˈtãtʃi] adj fickle; (tempo) changeable

incontável [ĩkõˈtavew] (pl -eis) adj countless

incontestável [ĩkõteʃˈtavew] (pl -eis) adj undeniable

incontrolável [ĩkõtroˈlavew] (pl -eis) adj uncontrollable

inconveniência [ĩkõveˈnjẽsja] f inconvenience; (impropriedade) inappropriateness

inconveniente [ĩkõveˈnjẽtʃi] adj inconvenient; (inoportuno) awkward; (grosseiro) rude; (importuno) annoying ♦ m disadvantage; (obstáculo) difficulty, problem

incorporar [ĩkoxpoˈra*] vt to incorporate; (juntar) to add; (COM) to merge; **incorporar-se** vr: **~-se a** ou **em** to join

incorreto, -a [ĩkoˈxetu, a] (PT -ect-) adj incorrect; (desonesto) dishonest

incrédulo, -a [ĩˈkredulu, a] adj incredulous; (cético) sceptical (BRIT), skeptical (US) ♦ m/f sceptic (BRIT), skeptic (US)

incrível [ĩˈkrivew] (pl -eis) adj incredible

incumbência [ĩkũˈbẽsja] f task, duty

incumbir [ĩkũˈbi*] vt: **~ alguém de algo** ou **algo a alguém** to put sb in charge of sth ♦ vi: **~ a alguém** to be sb's duty; **incumbir-se** vr: **~-se de** to undertake, take charge of

indagação [ĩdagaˈsãw] (pl -ões) f investigation; (pergunta) inquiry, question

indagar [ĩdaˈga*] vt to investigate ♦ vi to inquire; **indagar-se** vr: **~-se a si mesmo** to ask o.s.; **~ algo de alguém** to ask sb about sth

indecente [ĩdeˈsẽtʃi] adj indecent, improper; (obsceno) rude, vulgar

indeciso, -a [ĩdeˈsizu, a] adj undecided; (indistinto) vague; (hesitante) hesitant, indecisive

indecoroso, -a [ĩdekoˈrozu, ɔza] adj indecent, improper

indefeso, -a [ĩde'fɛzu, a] adj unde-
fended; (*população*) defenceless
(*BRIT*), defenseless (*US*)

indefinido, -a [ĩdefi'nidu, a] adj
indefinite; (*vago*) vague, undefined;
por tempo ~ indefinitely

indefiro etc [ĩde'firu] vb V **indeferir**

indelicado, -a [ĩdeli'kadu, a] adj
impolite, rude

indenização [indeniza'sãw] (*PT*
-mn-) (*pl* -ões) f compensation;
(*COM*) indemnity

indenizar [ĩdeni'za*] (*PT* -mn-) vt: ~
alguém por ou **de algo** (*compensar*)
to compensate sb for sth; (*por gastos*) to reimburse sb for sth

independência [ĩdepẽ'dẽsja] f independence; **independente**
[ĩdepẽ'dẽtʃi] adj independent

indesejável [ĩdeze'ʒavew] (*pl* -eis)
adj undesirable

indevido, -a [ĩde'vidu, a] adj
(*imerecido*) unjust; (*impróprio*) inappropriate

Índia ['ĩdʒa] f: **a ~** India; **as ~s
Ocidentais** the West Indies; **india-
no, -a** [ĩ'dʒjanu, a] adj, m/f Indian

indicação [indʒika'sãw] (*pl* -ões) f
indication; (*de termômetro*) reading;
(*para um cargo, prêmio*) nomination; (*recomendação*) recommendation; (*de um caminho*) directions *pl*

indicado, -a [ĩdʒi'kadu, a] adj
appropriate

indicador, a [ĩdʒika'do*, a] adj: ~
de indicative of ♦ m indicator; (*TEC*)
gauge; (*dedo*) index finger; (*ponteiro*) pointer

indicar [ĩdʒi'ka*] vt to indicate;
(*apontar*) to point to; (*temperatura*)
to register; (*recomendar*) to recommend; (*para um cargo*) to nominate; (*determinar*) to determine;
~ o caminho a alguém to give sb

directions

indicativo, -a [ĩdʒika'tʃivu, a] adj
(*tb: LING*) indicative

índice ['ĩdʒisi] m (*de livro*) index;
(*taxa*) rate

indício [ĩ'dʒisju] m (*sinal*) sign;
(*vestígio*) trace; (*JUR*) clue

indiferença [ĩdʒife'rẽsa] f indifference; **indiferente** [ĩdʒife'rẽtʃi] adj
indifferent; **isso me é indiferente**
it's all the same to me

indígena [ĩ'dʒiʒena] adj, m/f native; (*índio: da América*) Indian

indigência [ĩdʒi'ʒẽsja] f poverty;
(*fig*) lack, need

indigestão [ĩdʒiʒeʃ'tãw] f indigestion

indigesto, -a [ĩdʒi'ʒɛʃtu, a] adj
indigestible

indignação [ĩdʒigna'sãw] f indig-
nation; **indignado, -a** [ĩdʒig'nadu,
a] adj indignant

indignar [ĩdʒig'na*] vt to anger,
incense; **indignar-se** vr to get
angry

indigno, -a [ĩ'dʒignu, a] adj unworthy; (*desprezível*) disgraceful, despicable

índio, -a ['ĩdʒju, a] adj, m/f (*da
América*) Indian; **o Oceano Í~** the
Indian Ocean

indireto, -a [ĩdʒi'rɛtu, a] (*PT* -ct-)
adj indirect

indiscreto, -a [ĩdʒiʃ'krɛtu, a] adj
indiscreet

indiscriminado, -a [ĩdʒiʃkrimi-
'nadu, a] adj indiscriminate

indiscutível [ĩdʒiʃku'tʃivew] (*pl
-eis*) adj indisputable

indispensável [ĩdʒiʃpẽ'savew] (*pl
-eis*) adj essential, vital ♦ m: **o ~** the
essentials *pl*

indispor [ĩdʒiʃ'po*] (*irreg: como
pôr*) vt (*de saúde*) to make ill; (*aborrecer*) to upset; **indisposto, -a**

indistinto

indistinto 478 **infelicidade**

[ĩdʒiˈpoʃtu, ˈpɔʃta] *adj* unwell,
poorly; upset

indistinto, -a [ĩdʒiʃˈtʃĩtu, a] *adj*
indistinct

individual [ĩdʒiviˈdwaw] (*pl* **-ais**)
adj individual

indivíduo [ĩdʒiˈvidwu] *m* individual; (*col: sujeito*) guy

indócil [ĩˈdɔsiw] (*pl* **-eis**) *adj* unruly,
wayward; (*impaciente*) restless

índole [ˈĩdoli] *f* (*temperamento*)
nature; (*tipo*) sort, type

indolor [ĩdoˈloˀ] *adj* painless

indomável [ĩdoˈmavew] (*pl* **-eis**)
adj (*animal*) untameable; (*coragem*)
indomitable

Indonésia [ĩdoˈnɛzja] *f*: **a ~** Indonesia

indulgente [ĩduwˈʒẽtʃi] *adj* indulgent; (*atitude*) lenient

indústria [ĩˈduʃtrja] *f* industry;
industrial [ĩduʃˈtrjaw] (*pl* **-ais**) *adj*
industrial ♦ *m/f* industrialist; **industrializar** [ĩduʃtrjaliˈzaˀ] *vt* (*país*) to
industrialize; (*aproveitar*) to process

induzir [ĩduˈziˀ] *vt* to induce; (*persuadir*) to persuade

inédito, -a [iˈnɛdʒitu, a] *adj* (*livro*)
unpublished; (*incomum*) unheard-of, rare

ineficaz [inefiˈkajʒ] *adj* (*remédio*,
medida) ineffective; (*empregado*,
máquina) inefficient

ineficiente [inefiˈsjẽtʃi] *adj* inefficient

inegável [ineˈgavew] (*pl* **-eis**) *adj*
undeniable

inelutável [ineluˈtavew] (*pl* **-eis**)
adj inescapable

inepto, -a [iˈnɛptu, a] *adj* inept,
incompetent

inequívoco, -a [ineˈkivoku, a]
adj (*evidente*) clear; (*inconfundível*)
unmistakable

inércia [iˈnɛxsja] *f* lethargy; (*Fís*)
inertia

inerente [ineˈrẽtʃi] *adj*: **~ a** inherent in *ou* to

inerte [iˈnɛxtʃi] *adj* lethargic; (*Fís*)
inert

inescrupuloso, -a [ineʃkrupuˈlozu, ɔza] *adj* unscrupulous

inesgotável [ineʒgoˈtavew] (*pl*
-eis) *adj* inexhaustible; (*superabundante*) boundless

inesperado, -a [ineʃpeˈradu, a] *adj*
unexpected, unforeseen ♦ *m*: **o ~**
the unexpected

inesquecível [ineʃkeˈsivew] (*pl*
-eis) *adj* unforgettable

inestimável [ineʃtʃiˈmavew] (*pl*
-eis) *adj* invaluable

inevitável [ineviˈtavew] (*pl* **-eis**)
adj inevitable

inexato, -a [ineˈzatu, a] (*PT* **-ct-**) *adj*
inaccurate

inexistência [ineziʃˈtẽsja] *f* lack

inexistente [ineziʃˈtẽtʃi] *adj* nonexistent

inexperiência [ineʃpeˈrjẽsja] *f* inexperience; **inexperiente** [ineʃpeˈrjẽtʃi] *adj* inexperienced; (*ingênuo*)
naive

inexpressivo, -a [ineʃpreˈsivu, a]
adj expressionless

infalível [ĩfaˈlivew] (*pl* **-eis**) *adj* infallible; (*sucesso*) guaranteed

infância [ĩˈfãsja] *f* childhood

infantil [ĩfãˈtʃiw] (*pl* **-is**) *adj* (*ingênuo*) childlike; (*pueril*) childish;
(*para crianças*) children's

infarto [ĩˈfaxtu] *m* heart attack

infecção [ĩfɛkˈsãw] (*pl* **-ões**) *f* infection; **infeccionar** [ĩfɛksjoˈnaˀ] *vt*
(*ferida*) to infect; **infeccioso, -a**
[ĩfɛkˈsjozu, ɔza] *adj* infectious

infectar [ĩfɛkˈtaˀ] (*PT*) *vt* = **infetar**

infelicidade [ĩfelisiˈdadʒi] *f* unhappiness; (*desgraça*) misfortune

infeliz [ĩfe'liʒ] adj unhappy; (infausto) unlucky; (ação, medida) unfortunate; (sugestão, idéia) inappropriate ♦ m/f unhappy person; **infelizmente** [ĩfeliʒ'mẽtʃi] adv unfortunately

inferior [ĩfe'rjo*] adj: ~ (a) (em valor, qualidade) inferior (to); (mais baixo) lower (than) ♦ m/f inferior, subordinate; **inferioridade** [ĩferjori'dadʒi] f inferiority

infernal [ĩfex'naw] (pl -ais) adj infernal

inferno [ĩ'fɛxnu] m hell; vá pro ~! (col) piss off!

infetar [ĩfe'ta*] vt to infect

infiel [ĩ'fjew] (pl -éis) adj disloyal; (marido, mulher) unfaithful; (texto) inaccurate ♦ m/f (REL) non-believer

ínfimo, -a ['ĩfimu, a] adj lowest; (qualidade) poorest

infindável [ĩfĩ'davew] (pl -eis) adj unending, constant

infinidade [ĩfini'dadʒi] f infinity; uma ~ de countless

infinitivo [ĩfini'tʃivu] m (LING) infinitive

infinito, -a [ĩfi'nitu, a] adj infinite ♦ m infinity

inflação [ĩfla'sãw] f inflation; **inflacionário, -a** [ĩflasjo'narju, a] adj inflationary

inflamação [ĩflama'sãw] (pl -ões) f inflammation; **inflamado, -a** [ĩfla'madu, a] adj (MED) inflamed; (discurso) heated

inflamar [ĩfla'ma*] vt (madeira, pólvora) to set fire to; (MED, fig) to inflame; **inflamar-se** vr to catch fire; (fig) to get worked up; **~-se de algo** to be consumed with sth

inflamável [ĩfla'mavew] (pl -eis) adj inflammable

inflar [ĩ'fla*] vt to inflate, blow up; **inflar-se** vr to swell (up)

inflexível [ĩflek'sivew] (pl -eis) adj stiff, rigid; (fig) unyielding

influência [ĩ'flwẽsja] f influence; **sob a ~ de** under the influence of; **influenciar** [ĩflwẽ'sja*] vt to influence ♦ vi: **influenciar em algo** to influence sth, have an influence on sth; **influenciar-se** vr: **influenciar-se por** to be influenced by; **influente** [ĩ'flwẽtʃi] adj influential; **influir** [ĩ'flwi*] vi to matter, be important; **influir em** ou **sobre** to influence, have an influence on

informação [ĩfoxma'sãw] (pl -ões) f (piece of) information; (notícia) news sg; **informações** fpl (detalhes) information sg; **Informações** (TEL) directory enquiries (BRIT), information (US); **pedir informações sobre** to ask about, inquire about

informal [ĩfox'maw] (pl -ais) adj informal; **informalidade** [ĩfoxmali'dadʒi] f informality

informante [ĩfox'mãtʃi] m informant; (JUR) informer

informar [ĩfox'ma*] vt: ~ **alguém (de/sobre algo)** to inform sb (of/about sth) ♦ vi to inform, be informative; **informar-se** vr: **~-se de** to find out about, inquire about; **~ de** to report on

informática [ĩfox'matʃika] f computer science; (ramo) computing, computers pl

informativo, -a [ĩfoxma'tʃivu, a] adj informative

informatizar [ĩfoxmatʃi'za*] vt to computerize

infortúnio [ĩfox'tunju] m misfortune

infração [ĩfra'sãw] (PT -cç-; pl -ões) f breach, infringement; (ESPORTE) foul

infractor, a [ĩfra'to*, a] (PT) m/f = infrator, a

infrator, a [ĩfra'to*, a] m/f offender

infringir [ĩfrĩˈʒi*] vt to infringe, contravene

infrutífero, -a [ĩfruˈtʃiferu, a] adj fruitless

infundado, -a [ĩfũˈdadu, a] adj groundless, unfounded

ingênuo, -a [ĩˈʒenwu, a] adj ingenuous, naïve; (comentário) harmless ♦ m/f naïve person

ingerir [ĩʒeˈri*] vt to ingest; (engolir) to swallow

Inglaterra [ĩglaˈtexa] f: a ~ England; **inglês, -esa** [ĩˈgleʃ, eza] adj English ♦ m/f Englishman/woman ♦ m (LING) English; **os ingleses** mpl the English

ingrato, -a [ĩˈgratu, a] adj ungrateful

ingrediente [ĩgreˈdʒjẽtʃi] m ingredient

íngreme [ĩˈgremi] adj steep

ingressar [ĩgreˈsa*] vi: ~ em to enter, go into; (um clube) to join

ingresso [ĩˈgresu] m (entrada) entry; (admissão) admission; (bilhete) ticket

inibição [inibiˈsãw] (pl -ões) f inhibition

inibido, -a [iniˈbidu, a] adj inhibited

inibir [iniˈbi*] vt to inhibit

iniciação [inisjaˈsãw] (pl -ões) f initiation

inicial [iniˈsjaw] (pl -ais) adj, f initial

iniciar [iniˈsja*] vt, vi (começar) to begin, start; ~ **alguém em algo** (arte, seita) to initiate sb into sth

iniciativa [inisjaˈtʃiva] f initiative; a ~ **privada** (ECON) private enterprise

início [iˈnisju] m beginning, start; **no ~** at the start

inimigo, -a [iniˈmigu, a] adj, m/f enemy

inimizade [inimiˈzadʒi] f enmity, hatred

ininterrupto, -a [inĩteˈxuptu, a] adj continuous; (esforço) unstinting; (vôo) non-stop; (serviço) 24-hour

injeção [inʒeˈsãw] (PT -cç-; pl -ões) f injection

injetar [inʒeˈta*] (PT -ct-) vt to inject

injúria [ĩˈʒurja] f insult

injustiça [ĩʒuʃˈtʃisa] f injustice

injusto, -a [ĩˈʒuʃtu, a] adj unfair, unjust

inocência [inoˈsẽsja] f innocence

inocentar [inosẽˈta*] vt: ~ **alguém (de algo)** to clear sb (of sth)

inocente [inoˈsẽtʃi] adj innocent ♦ m/f innocent man/woman

inócuo, -a [iˈnɔkwu, a] adj harmless

inofensivo, -a [inofẽˈsivu, a] adj harmless, inoffensive

inoportuno, -a [inopoxˈtunu, a] adj inconvenient, inopportune

inovação [inovaˈsãw] (pl -ões) f innovation

inoxidável [inoksiˈdavew] (pl -eis) adj: **aço** ~ stainless steel

INPS (BR) abr m (= Instituto Nacional de Previdência Social) ≈ DSS (BRIT), ≈ Welfare Dept (US)

inquérito [ĩˈkeritu] m inquiry; (JUR) inquest

inquietação [ĩkjetaˈsãw] f anxiety, uneasiness; (agitação) restlessness

inquietante [ĩkjeˈtãtʃi] adj worrying, disturbing

inquietar [ĩkjeˈta*] vt to worry, disturb; **inquietar-se** vr to worry, bother; **inquieto, -a** [ĩˈkjetu, a] adj anxious, worried; (agitado) restless

inquilino, -a [ĩkiˈlinu, a] m/f tenant

insalubre [ĩsaˈlubri] adj unhealthy

insanidade [ĩsaniˈdadʒi] f madness, insanity; **insano, -a** [ĩˈsanu, a] adj insane

insatisfação [ĩsatʃiʃfaˈsãw] f dissatisfaction

insatisfatório, -a [ĩsatʃisfa'tɔrju, a] *adj* unsatisfactory

insatisfeito, -a [ĩsatʃis'fejtu, a] *adj* dissatisfied, unhappy

inscrever [ĩʃkre've*] *vt* to inscribe; (*aluno*) to enrol (BRIT), enroll (US); (*em registro*) to register

inscrição [ĩʃkri'sãw] (*pl* -ões) *f* inscription

inscrito, -a [ĩʃ'kritu, a] *pp* de **inscrever**

insecto etc [ĩ'sɛtu] (PT) = **inseto** etc

insegurança [ĩsegu'rãsa] *f* insecurity; **inseguro, -a** [ĩse'guru, a] *adj* insecure

insensatez [ĩsẽsa'teʒ] *f* folly, madness; **insensato, -a** [ĩsẽ'satu, a] *adj* unreasonable, foolish

insensível [ĩsẽ'sivew] (*pl* -eis) *adj* insensitive; (*dormente*) numb

inserir [ĩse'ri*] *vt* to insert, put in; (COMPUT: *dados*) to enter

inseticida [ĩsetʃi'sida] *m* insecticide

inseto [ĩ'sɛtu] *m* insect

insignificante [ĩsiɡnifi'kãtʃi] *f* insignificant

insinuar [ĩsi'nwa*] *vt* to insinuate, imply

insípido, -a [ĩ'sipidu, a] *adj* insipid

insiro etc [ĩ'siru] *vb* V **inserir**

insistência [ĩsis'tẽsja] *f*: ~ (**em**) insistence (on); (*obstinação*) persistence (in); **insistente** [ĩsis'tẽtʃi] *adj* (*pessoa*) insistent; (*apelo*) urgent

insistir [ĩsis'tʃi*] *vi*: ~ (**em**) to insist (on); (*perseverar*) to persist (in); ~ (**em**) **que** to insist that

insolação [ĩsola'sãw] *f* sunstroke; **pegar uma** ~ to get sunstroke

insolente [ĩso'lẽtʃi] *adj* insolent

insólito, -a [ĩ'sɔlitu, a] *adj* unusual

insônia [ĩ'sonja] *f* insomnia

insosso, -a [ĩ'sosu, a] *adj* unsalted; (*sem sabor*) tasteless; (*pessoa*) uninteresting, dull

inspeção [ĩʃpe'sãw] (PT -cç-; *pl* -ões) *f* inspection, check; **inspecionar** [ĩʃpesjo'na*] (PT -cc-) *vt* to inspect

inspetor, a [ĩʃpe'to*, a] (PT -ct-) *m/f* inspector

inspiração [ĩʃpira'sãw] (*pl* -ões) *f* inspiration

inspirador, a [ĩʃpira'do*, a] *adj* inspiring

inspirar [ĩʃpi'ra*] *vt* to inspire; (MED) to inhale; **inspirar-se** *vr* to be inspired

instalação [ĩʃtala'sãw] (*pl* -ões) *f* installation; ~ **elétrica** (*de casa*) wiring

instalar [ĩʃta'la*] *vt* to install; (*estabelecer*) to set up; **instalar-se** *vr* (*numa cadeira*) to settle down

instantâneo, -a [ĩʃtã'tanju, a] *adj* instant, instantaneous ♦ *m* (FOTO) snap

instante [ĩʃ'tãtʃi] *adj* urgent ♦ *m* moment; **num** ~ in an instant, quickly; **só um** ~! just a moment!

instável [ĩʃ'tavew] (*pl* -eis) *adj* unstable; (*tempo*) unsettled

instintivo, -a [ĩʃtʃĩ'tʃivu, a] *adj* instinctive

instinto [ĩʃ'tʃĩtu] *m* instinct; **por** ~ instinctively

instituição [ĩʃtʃitwi'sãw] (*pl* -ões) *f* institution

instituto [ĩʃtʃi'tutu] *m* (*escola*) institute; (*instituição*) institution; ~ **de beleza** beauty salon

instrução [ĩʃtru'sãw] (PT -cç-; *pl* -ões) *f* education; (*erudição*) learning; (*diretriz*) instruction; (MIL) training; **instruções** *fpl* (*para o uso*) instructions (for use)

instrutor, a [ĩʃtru'to*, a] (PT) *m/f*

= **instrutor, a**

instruído, -a [ĩʃ'trwidu, a] adj educated

instruir [ĩʃ'trwi*] vt to instruct; (MIL) to train; **instruir-se** vr: **~-se em algo** to learn sth; **~ alguém de** ou **sobre algo** to inform sb about sth

instrumento [ĩʃtru'mẽtu] m instrument; (ferramenta) implement; (JUR) deed, document; **~ de cordas/percussão/sopro** stringed/percussion/wind instrument; **~ de trabalho** tool

instrutivo, -a [ĩʃtru'tʃivu, a] adj instructive

instrutor, a [ĩʃtru'to*, a] m/f instructor; (ESPORTE) coach

insubordinação [ĩsuboxdʒina'sãw] f rebellion; (MIL) insubordination

insubstituível [ĩsubʃtʃi'twivew] (pl **-eis**) adj irreplaceable

insuficiência [ĩsufi'sjẽsja] f inadequacy; (carência) shortage; (MED) deficiency; **~ cardíaca** heart failure; **insuficiente** [ĩsufi'sjẽtʃi] adj insufficient; (EDUC: nota) = fail; (pessoa) incompetent

insulina [ĩsu'lina] f insulin

insultar [ĩsuw'ta*] vt to insult; **insulto** [ĩ'suwtu] m insult

insuperável [ĩsupe'ravew] (pl **-eis**) adj (dificuldade) insuperable; (qualidade) unsurpassable

insuportável [ĩsupox'tavew] (pl **-eis**) adj unbearable

insurgir-se [ĩsux'ʒixsi] vr to rebel, revolt

insurreição [ĩsuxej'sãw] (pl **-ões**) f rebellion, insurrection

intato, -a [ĩ'tatu, a] (PT **-act-**) adj intact

íntegra [ĩ'tegra] f: **na ~** in full

integral [ĩte'graw] (pl **-ais**) adj

whole ♦ f (MAT) integral; **pão ~** wholemeal (BRIT) ou wholewheat (US) bread; **integralmente** [ĩtegraw'mẽtʃi] adv in full, fully

integrar [ĩte'gra*] vt to unite, combine; (completar) to form, make up; (MAT, raças) to integrate; **integrar-se** vr to become complete; **~-se em** ou **a algo** to join sth; (adaptar-se) to integrate into sth

integridade [ĩtegri'dadʒi] f entirety; (fig: de pessoa) integrity

íntegro, -a [ĩ'tegru, a] adj entire; (honesto) upright, honest

inteiramente [ĩtejra'mẽtʃi] adv completely

inteirar [ĩtej'ra*] vt (completar) to complete; **inteirar-se** vr: **~-se de** to find out about; **~ alguém de** to inform sb of

inteiro, -a [ĩ'tejru, a] adj whole, entire; (ileso) unharmed; (não quebrado) undamaged

intelecto [ĩte'lektu] m intellect; **intelectual** [ĩtelek'twaw] (pl **-ais**) adj, m/f intellectual

inteligência [ĩteli'ʒẽsja] f intelligence; **inteligente** [ĩteli'ʒẽtʃi] adj intelligent, clever

inteligível [ĩteli'ʒivew] (pl **-eis**) adj intelligible

intenção [ĩtẽ'sãw] (pl **-ões**) f intention; **segundas intenções** ulterior motives; **ter a ~ de** to intend to; **intencionado, -a** [ĩtẽsjo'nadu, a] adj: **bem intencionado** well-meaning; **mal intencionado** spiteful; **intencional** [ĩtẽsjo'naw] (pl **-ais**) adj intentional, deliberate; **intencionar** [ĩtẽsjo'na*] vt to intend

intensificar [ĩtẽsifi'ka*] vt to intensify; **intensificar-se** vr to intensify

intensivo, -a [ĩtẽ'sivu, a] adj intensive

intenso, -a [ĩ'tẽsu, a] *adj* intense; (*emoção*) deep; (*impressão*) vivid; (*vida social*) full

interação [ĩtera'sãw] (*PT* **-cç-**) *f* interaction

interativo, -a [ĩtera'tʃivu, a] (*PT* **-ct-**) *adj* (*COMPUT*) interactive

intercâmbio [ĩtex'kãbju] *m* exchange

interdição [ĩtexdʒi'sãw] (*pl* **-ões**) *f* (*de estrada, porta*) closure; (*JUR*) injunction

interditar [ĩtexdʒi'ta*] *vt* (*importação etc*) to ban; (*estrada, praia*) to close off; (*cinema etc*) to close down

interessado, -a [ĩtere'sadu, a] *adj* interested; (*amizade*) self-seeking

interessante [ĩtere'sãtʃi] *adj* interesting

interessar [ĩtere'sa*] *vt* to interest ♦ *vi* to be interesting; **interessar-se** *vr*: **~-se em** *ou* **por** to take an interest in, be interested in; **a quem possa ~** to whom it may concern

interesse [ĩte'resi] *m* interest; (*próprio*) self-interest; (*proveito*) advantage; **no ~ de** for the sake of; **por ~** (*próprio*) for one's own ends; **interesseiro, -a** [ĩtere'sejru, a] *adj* self-seeking

interface [ĩtex'fasi] *f* (*COMPUT*) interface

interferência [ĩtexfe'rẽsja] *f* interference

interferir [ĩtexfe'ri*] *vi*: **~ em** to interfere in

interfone [ĩtex'fɔni] *m* intercom

interior [ĩte'rjo*] *adj* inner, inside; (*COM*) domestic, internal ♦ *m* inside, interior; (*do país*): **no ~** inland; **Ministério do I~** ≈ Home Office (*BRIT*), ≈ Department of the Interior (*US*)

interjeição [ĩtexʒej'sãw] (*pl* **-ões**) *f* interjection

interlocutor, a [ĩtexloku'to*, a]

m/f speaker; **meu ~** the person I was speaking to

intermediário, -a [ĩtexme-'dʒjarju, a] *adj* intermediary ♦ *m/f* (*COM*) middleman; (*mediador*) intermediary, mediator

intermédio [ĩtex'mɛdʒu] *m*: **por ~ de** through

interminável [ĩtexmi'navew] (*pl* **-eis**) *adj* endless

internação [ĩtexna'sãw] (*pl* **-ões**) *f* (*de doente*) admission

internacional [ĩtexnasjo'naw] (*pl* **-ais**) *adj* international

internações [ĩtexna'sõjʃ] *fpl de* **internação**

internar [ĩtex'na*] *vt* (*aluno*) to put into boarding school; (*doente*) to take into hospital; (*MIL, POL*) to intern

internauta [ĩtex'nawta] *m/f* Internet user

Internet [ĩtex'netʃi] *f*: **a ~** the Internet

interno, -a [ĩ'texnu, a] *adj* internal; (*POL*) domestic ♦ *m/f* (*tb*: **aluno ~**) boarder; (*MED*: *estudante*) houseman (*BRIT*), intern (*US*); **de uso ~** (*MED*) for internal use

interpretação [ĩtexpreta'sãw] (*pl* **-ões**) *f* interpretation; (*TEATRO*) performance

interpretar [ĩtexpre'ta*] *vt* to interpret; (*um papel*) to play; **intérprete** [ĩ'texpretʃi] *m/f* interpreter; (*TEATRO*) performer, artist

interrogação [ĩtexoga'sãw] (*pl* **-ões**) *f* interrogation; **ponto de ~** question mark

interrogar [ĩtexo'ga*] *vt* to question, interrogate; (*JUR*) to cross-examine

interromper [ĩtexõ'pe*] *vt* to interrupt; (*parar*) to stop; (*ELET*) to cut off

interrupção [ĩtexup'sãw] (*pl* -ões) *f* interruption; (*intervalo*) break

interruptor [ĩtexup'to*] *m* (*ELET*) switch

interseção [ĩtexse'sãw] (*PT* -cç-; *pl* -ões) *f* intersection

interurbano, -a [ĩterux'banu, a] *adj* (*TEL*) long-distance ♦ *m* long-distance *ou* trunk call

intervalo [ĩtex'valu] *m* interval; (*descanso*) break; **a ~s** every now and then

intervenção [ĩtexvẽ'sãw] (*pl* -ões) *f* intervention; **~ cirúrgica** (*MED*) operation

intervir [ĩtex'vi*] (*irreg: como* vir) *vi* to intervene; (*sobrevir*) to come up

intestino [ĩtes'tʃinu] *m* intestine

intimação [ĩtʃima'sãw] (*pl* -ões) *f* (*ordem*) order; (*JUR*) summons

intimar [ĩtʃi'ma*] *vt* (*JUR*) to summon; **~ alguém a fazer** *ou* **a alguém que faça** to order sb to do

intimidade [ĩtʃimi'dadʒi] *f* intimacy; (*vida privada*) private life; (*familiaridade*) familiarity; **ter ~ com alguém** to be close to sb

íntimo, -a [ĩ'tʃimu, a] *adj* intimate; (*sentimentos*) innermost; (*amigo*) close; (*vida*) private ♦ *m/f* close friend; **no ~** at heart

intolerante [ĩtole'rãtʃi] *adj* intolerant

intolerável [ĩtole'ravew] (*pl* -eis) *adj* intolerable, unbearable

intoxicação [ĩtoksika'sãw] *f* poisoning; **~ alimentar** food poisoning

intoxicar [ĩtoksi'ka*] *vt* to poison

intranet [ĩtra'netʃi] *f* intranet

intransigente [ĩtrãsi'ʒẽtʃi] *adj* uncompromising; (*fig: rígido*) strict

intransitável [ĩtrãsi'tavew] (*pl* -eis) *adj* impassable

intransitivo, -a [ĩtrãsi'tʃivu, a] *adj* intransitive

intransponível [ĩtrãʃpo'nivew] (*pl* -eis) *adj* (*rio*) impossible to cross; (*problema*) insurmountable

intratável [ĩtra'tavew] (*pl* -eis) *adj* (*pessoa*) contrary, awkward; (*doença*) untreatable; (*problema*) insurmountable

intriga [ĩ'triga] *f* intrigue; (*enredo*) plot; (*fofoca*) piece of gossip; **~s** (*fofocas*) gossip *sg*; **~ amorosa** (*PT*) love affair; **intrigante** [ĩtri'gãtʃi] *m/f* troublemaker ♦ *adj* intriguing; **intrigar** [ĩtri'ga*] *vt* to intrigue ♦ *vi* to be intriguing

introdução [ĩtrodu'sãw] (*pl* -ões) *f* introduction

introduzir [ĩtrodu'zi*] *vt* to introduce

intrometer-se [ĩtrome'texsi] *vr* to interfere, meddle; **intrometido, -a** [ĩtrome'tʃidu, a] *adj* interfering; (*col*) nosey ♦ *m/f* busybody

introvertido, -a [ĩtrovex'tʃidu, a] *adj* introverted ♦ *m/f* introvert

intruso, -a [ĩ'truzu, a] *m/f* intruder

intuição [ĩtwi'sãw] (*pl* -ões) *f* intuition

intuito [ĩ'tuito] *m* intention, aim

inumano, -a [inu'manu, a] *adj* inhuman

inúmero, -a [i'numeru, a] *adj* countless, innumerable

inundação [inũda'sãw] (*pl* -ões) *f* (*enchente*) flood; (*ato*) flooding

inundar [inũ'da*] *vt* to flood; (*fig*) to inundate ♦ *vi* to flood

inusitado, -a [inuzi'tadu, a] *adj* unusual

inútil [i'nutʃiw] (*pl* -eis) *adj* useless; (*esforço*) futile; (*desnecessário*) pointless; **inutilizar** [inutʃili'za*] *vt* to make useless, render useless; (*incapacitar*) to put out of action; (*danificar*) to ruin; (*esforços*) to thwart; **inutilmente** [inutʃiw-

'mētʃi] *adv* in vain

invadir [ĩva'dʒi*] *vt* to invade; (*suj:
água*) to overrun; (: *sentimento*) to
overcome

inválido, -a [ĩ'validu, a] *adj, m/f*
invalid

invariável [ĩva'rjavew] (*pl* -eis) *adj*
invariable

invasão [ĩva'zãw] (*pl* -ões) *f* inva-
sion

invasor, a [ĩva'zo*, a] *adj* invading
♦ *m/f* invader

inveja [ĩ'veʒa] *f* envy; **invejar**
[ĩve'ʒa*] *vt* to envy; (*cobiçar*) to
covet ♦ *vi* to be envious; **invejoso,
-a** [ĩve'ʒozu, ɔza] *adj* envious

invenção [ĩvē'sãw] (*pl* -ões) *f* invention

inventar [ĩvē'ta*] *vt* to invent

inventivo, -a [ĩvē'tʃivu, a] *adj*
inventive

inventor, a [ĩvē'to*, a] *m/f* inventor

inverno [ĩ'vɛxnu] *m* winter

inverossímil [ĩvero'simiw] (*PT*
-osí-) (*pl* -eis) *adj* unlikely, improbable; (*inacreditável*) implausible

inverso, -a [ĩ'vɛxsu, a] *adj* inverse;
(*oposto*) opposite; (*ordem*) reverse
♦ *m* opposite, reverse; **ao ~ de** contrary to

inverter [ĩvex'te*] *vt* to alter;
(*ordem*) to invert, reverse; (*colocar
às avessas*) to turn upside down,
invert

invés [ĩ'vɛʃ] *m*: **ao ~ de** instead of

investigação [ĩveʃtʃiga'sãw] (*pl*
-ões) *f* investigation; (*pesquisa*)
research

investigar [ĩveʃtʃi'ga*] *vt* to investigate; (*examinar*) to examine

investimento [ĩveʃtʃi'mẽtu] *m* investment

investir [ĩveʃ'tʃi*] *vt* (*dinheiro*) to
invest

inviável [ĩ'vjavew] (*pl* -eis) *adj*

impracticable

invicto, -a [ĩ'viktu, a] *adj* uncon-
quered

invisível [ĩvi'zivew] (*pl* -eis) *adj*
invisible

invisto *etc* [ĩ'viʃtu] *vb* V **investir**

invocar [ĩvo'ka*] *vt* to invoke

invólucro [ĩ'volukru] *m* (*cobertura*)
covering; (*envoltório*) wrapping;
(*caixa*) box

involuntário, -a [ĩvolũ'tarju, a]
adj involuntary; (*ofensa*) unintentional

iodo [i'jodu] *m* iodine

ioga [i'jɔga] *f* yoga

iogurte [jo'guxtʃi] *m* yogurt

IR (*BR*) *abr m* = **Imposto de Renda**

PALAVRA CHAVE

ir [i*] *vi* **1** to go; (*a pé*) to walk; (*a
cavalo*) to ride; (*viajar*) to travel; **~
caminhando** to walk; **fui de trem** I
went *ou* travelled by train; **vamos!,
vamos nessa!** (*col*), **vamos embora!** let's go!; **já vou!** I'm coming!; **~
atrás de alguém** (*seguir*) to follow
sb; (*confiar*) to take sb's word for
it

2 (*progredir: pessoa, coisa*) to go; **o
trabalho vai muito bem** work is
going very well; **como vão as
coisas?** how are things going?; **vou
muito bem** I'm very well; (*na escola
etc*) I'm getting on very well

♦ *vb aux* **1** (+ *infin*): **vou fazer** I will
do, I am going to do

2 (+ *gerúndio*): **~ fazendo** to keep
on doing

♦ *ir-se vr* to go away, leave

---

ira [i'ra] *f* anger, rage

Irã [i'rã] *m*: **o ~** Iran

irado, -a [i'radu, a] *adj* angry, irate

iraniano, -a [ira'njanu, a] *adj, m/f*
Iranian

Irão [i'rãw] (*PT*) *m* = Irã

Iraque [i'raki] *m*: **o** ~ Iraq; **ira-quiano, -a** [ira'kjanu, a] *adj, m/f* Iraqi

ir-e-vir (*pl* ires-e-vires) *m* comings and goings *pl*

Irlanda [ix'lãda] *f*: **a** ~ Ireland; **a ~ do Norte** Northern Ireland; **irlandês, -esa** [ixlã'deʃ, eza] *adj* Irish ♦ *m/f* Irishman/woman ♦ *m* (*LING*) Irish

irmã [ix'mã] *f* sister; ~ **de criação** adoptive sister; ~ **gêmea** twin sister

irmão [ix'mãw] (*pl* ~s) *m* brother; (*fig: similar*) twin; (*col: companheiro*) mate; ~ **de criação** adoptive brother; ~ **gêmeo** twin brother

ironia [iro'nia] *f* irony

irra! ['ixa] (*PT*) *excl* damn!

irracional [ixasjo'naw] (*pl* -ais) *adj* irrational

irreal [ixe'aw] (*pl* -ais) *adj* unreal

irregular [ixegu'la*] *adj* irregular; (*vida*) unconventional; (*feições*) unusual; (*aluno, gênio*) erratic

irrelevante [ixele'vãtʃi] *adj* irrelevant

irremediável [ixeme'dʒjavew] (*pl* -eis) *adj* irremediable; (*sem remédio*) incurable

irrequieto, -a [ixe'kjetu, a] *adj* restless

irresistível [ixeziʃ'tʃivew] (*pl* -eis) *adj* irresistible

irresponsável [ixeʃpõ'savew] (*pl* -eis) *adj* irresponsible

irrigar [ixi'ga*] *vt* to irrigate

irritação [ixita'sãw] (*pl* -ões) *f* irritation

irritadiço, -a [ixita'dʒisu, a] *adj* irritable

irritante [ixi'tãtʃi] *adj* irritating, annoying

irritar [ixi'ta*] *vt* to irritate; **irritar-se** *vr* to get angry, get annoyed

irromper [ixõ'pe*] *vi* (*entrar subitamente*): ~ **(em)** to burst in(to)

isca ['iʃka] *f* (*PESCA*) bait; (*fig*) lure, bait

isenção [izẽ'sãw] (*pl* -ões) *f* exemption

isentar [izẽ'ta*] *vt* to exempt; (*livrar*) to free

Islã [iʒ'lã] *m* Islam

Islândia [iʒ'lãdʒa] *f*: **a** ~ Iceland

isolado, -a [izo'ladu, a] *adj* isolated; (*solitário*) lonely

isolamento [izola'mẽtu] *m* isolation; (*ELET*) insulation

isolar [izo'la*] *vt* to isolate; (*ELET*) to insulate

isqueiro [iʃ'kejru] *m* (cigarette) lighter

Israel [iʒxa'ɛw] *m* Israel; **israelense** [iʒxae'lẽsi] *adj, m/f* Israeli

isso ['isu] *pron* that; (*col: isto*) this; ~ **mesmo** exactly; **por ~** therefore, so; **por ~ mesmo** for that very reason; **só ~?** is that all?

isto ['iʃtu] *pron* this; ~ **é** that is, namely

Itália [i'talja] *f*: **a** ~ Italy; **italiano, -a** [ita'ljanu, a] *adj, m/f* Italian ♦ *m* (*LING*) Italian

Itamarati [itamara'tʃi] *m*: **o** ~ the Brazilian Foreign Ministry; *see boxed note*

ITAMARATI

The Palace of Itamarati was built in 1855 in Rio de Janeiro. It became the seat of government when Brazil became a republic in 1889, and was later the Foreign Ministry. It ceased to be this when the Brazilian capital was transferred to Brasília, but **Itamarati** is still used to refer to the Foreign Ministry.

---

item ['itẽ] (*pl* -ns) *m* item

itinerário [itʃine'rarju] m itinerary; (caminho) route

lugoslávia [jugoʒ'lavja] f: a ~ Yugoslavia; **iugoslavo, -a** [jugoʒ'lavu, a] adj, m/f Yugoslav(ian)

J

já [ʒa] adv already; (em perguntas) yet; (agora) now; (imediatamente) right away; (agora mesmo) right now ♦ conj on the other hand; **até ~** bye; **desde ~** from now on; **~ não** no longer; **~ que** as, since; **~ se vê** of course; **~ vou** I'm coming; **~ até** even; **~, ~** right away

jabuti [ʒabu'tʃi] m giant tortoise

jabuticaba [ʒabutʃi'kaba] f jaboticaba (type of berry)

jaca [ʒaka] f jack fruit

jacaré [ʒaka're] (BR) m alligator

jacto [ʒaktu] (PT) m = **jato**

jaguar [ʒa'gwa*] m jaguar

jaguatirica [ʒagwatʃi'rika] f leopard cat

Jamaica [ʒa'majka] f: **a ~** Jamaica

jamais [ʒa'majʃ] adv never; (com palavra negativa) ever

janeiro [ʒa'nejru] (PT J-) m January

janela [ʒa'nɛla] f window

jangada [ʒã'gada] f raft

jantar [ʒã'ta*] m dinner ♦ vt to have for dinner ♦ vi to have dinner

Japão [ʒa'pãw] m: **o ~** Japan; **japonês, -esa** [ʒapo'neʃ, eza] adj, m/f Japanese ♦ m (LING) Japanese

jararaca [ʒara'raka] f jararaca (snake)

jardim [ʒax'dʒĩ] (pl **-ns**) m garden; **~ zoológico** zoo; **jardim-de-infância** (pl **jardins-de-infância**) m kindergarten; **jardinagem** [ʒaxdʒi'naʒē] f gardening

jardineira [ʒaxdʒi'nejra] f (caixa)

trough; (calça) dungarees pl; V tb **jardineiro**

jardineiro, -a [ʒaxdʒi'nejru, a] m/f gardener

jardins [ʒax'dʒĩʃ] mpl de **jardim**

jargão [ʒax'gãw] m jargon

jarra [ʒaxa] f pot

jarro [ʒaxu] m jug

jasmim [ʒaʒ'mĩ] m jasmine

jato [ʒatu] m jet; (de luz) flash; (de ar) blast; **a ~** at top speed

jaula [ʒawla] f cage

javali [ʒava'li] m wild boar

jazigo [ʒa'zigu] m grave; (monumento) tomb

jazz [dʒɛz] m jazz

jeito [ʒejtu] m (maneira) way; (aspecto) appearance; (habilidade) skill, knack; (modos pessoais) manner; **ter ~ de** to look like; **não ter ~** (pessoa) to be awkward; (situação) to be hopeless; **dar um ~ em** (pé) to twist; (quarto, casa, papéis) to tidy up; (consertar) to fix; **dar um ~** to find a way; **o ~ é ...** the thing to do is ...; **é o ~** it's the best way; **ao ~ de** in the style of; **com ~** tactfully; **daquele ~** (fam) in that way; (em desordem, mal) anyhow; **de qualquer ~** anyway; **de ~ nenhum!** no way!

jejuar [ʒe'ʒwa*] vi to fast

jejum [ʒe'ʒũ] (pl **-ns**) m fast; **em ~** fasting

Jesus [ʒe'zuʃ] m Jesus ♦ excl heavens!

jibóia [ʒi'bɔja] f boa (constrictor)

jiló [ʒi'lɔ] m kind of vegetable

jingle [ʒi'dʒigew] m jingle

joalheria [ʒoaʎe'ria] f jeweller's (shop) (BRIT), jewelry store (US)

joaninha [ʒwa'niɲa] f ladybird (BRIT), ladybug (US)

joelho [ʒo'eʎu] m knee; **de ~s** kneeling; **ficar de ~s** to kneel down

jogada [ʒo'gada] f move; (lanço)

throw; (negócio) scheme, move
jogador, a [ʒoga'do*, a] m/f player;
(de jogo de azar) gambler
jogar [ʒo'ga*] vt to play; (em jogo de
azar) to gamble; (atirar) to throw;
(indiretas) to drop ♦ vi to play; to
gamble; (barco) to pitch; ~ **fora** to
throw away
jogging ['ʒɔgĩ] m jogging; (roupa)
track suit; **fazer ~** to go jogging,
jog
jogo ['ʒogu] m game; (jogar) play;
(de azar) gambling; (conjunto) set;
(artimanha) trick; **J~s Olímpicos**
Olympic Games
jóia ['ʒɔja] f jewel
Jordânia [ʒox'danja] f: **a ~** Jordan;
Jordão [ʒox'dãw] m: **o (rio) Jordão**
the Jordan (River)
jornada [ʒox'nada] f journey; ~ **de
trabalho** working day
jornal [ʒox'naw] (pl -ais) m newspaper; (TV, RÁDIO) news sg; **jor-
naleiro, -a** [ʒoxna'lejru, a] m/f
newsagent (BRIT), newsdealer (US)
jornalismo [ʒoxna'liʒmu] m journalism; **jornalista** [ʃoxna'liʃta] m/f
journalist
jovem ['ʒɔvẽ] (pl -ns) adj young
♦ m/f young person
jovial [ʒo'vjaw] (pl -ais) adj jovial,
cheerful
Jr abr = **Júnior**
judaico, -a [ʒu'dajku, a] adj Jewish
judeu, judia [ʒu'dew, ʒu'dʒia] adj
Jewish ♦ m/f Jew
judiação [ʒudʒja'sãw] f ill-treatment
judiar [ʒu'dʒja*] vi: ~ **de** to ill-treat
judicial [ʒudʒi'sjaw] (pl -ais) adj
judicial
judiciário, -a [ʒudʒi'sjarju, a] adj
judicial; **o (poder) ~** the judiciary
judô [ʒu'do] m judo
juiz, -íza [ʒwiʒ, 'iza] m/f judge; (em
jogos) referee; ~ **de paz** justice of

the peace; **juizado** [ʒwi'zado] m
court
juízo ['ʒwizu] m judgement; (parecer) opinion; (siso) common sense;
(foro) court; **perder o ~** to lose one's
mind; **não ter ~** to be foolish;
tomar ou **criar ~** to come to one's
senses; **chamar/levar a ~** to sum-
mon/take to court; ~! behave yourself!
julgamento [ʒuwga'mẽtu] m
judgement; (audiência) trial; (sentença) sentence
julgar [ʒuw'ga*] vt to judge; (achar)
to think; (JUR: sentenciar) to sentence; **julgar-se** vr: ~-se **algo** to
consider o.s. sth, think of o.s. as sth
julho ['ʒuʎu] (PT J-) m July
jumento, -a [ʒu'mẽtu, a] m/f donkey
junção [ʒũ'sãw] (pl -ões) f (ato)
joining; (junta) join
junco ['ʒũku] m reed, rush
junções [ʒũ'sõjʃ] fpl de **junção**
junho ['ʒuɲu] (PT J-) m June
júnior ['ʒunjo*] (pl **juniores**) adj
younger, junior ♦ m/f (ESPORTE)
junior; **Eduardo Autran J~** Eduardo
Autran Junior
junta ['ʒũta] f board, committee;
(POL) junta; (articulação, juntura)
joint
juntar [ʒũ'ta*] vt to join; (reunir) to
bring together; (aglomerar) to gather together; (recolher) to collect up;
(acrescentar) to add; (dinheiro) to
save up ♦ vi to gather; **juntar-se** vr
to gather; (associar-se) to join up;
~-se **a alguém** to join sb
junto, -a ['ʒũtu, a] adj joined;
(chegado) near; **ir ~s** to go together; ~ **a/de** near/next to; **segue ~**
(COM) please find enclosed
jura ['ʒura] f vow
jurado, -a [ʒu'radu, a] adj sworn

489

♦ *m/f* juror

juramento [ʒuraˈmẽtu] *m* oath

jurar [ʒuˈra*] *vt, vi* to swear; **jura?** really?

júri [ˈʒuri] *m* jury

jurídico, -a [ʒuˈridʒiku, a] *adj* legal

juros [ˈʒuruʃ] *mpl* (ECON) interest *sg*; **~ simples/compostos** simple/compound interest

justamente [ʒuʃtaˈmẽtʃi] *adv* fairly, justly; (*precisamente*) exactly

justiça [ʒuʃˈtʃisa] *f* justice; (*poder judiciário*) judiciary; (*eqüidade*) fairness; (*tribunal*) court; **com ~** justly, fairly; **ir à ~** to go to court; **justiceiro, -a** [ʒuʃtʃiˈsejru, a] *adj* righteous; (*inflexível*) inflexible

justificação [ʒuʃtʃifikaˈsãw] (*pl* **-ões**) *f* justification

justificar [ʒuʃtʃifiˈka*] *vt* to justify

justo, -a [ˈʒuʃtu, a] *adj* just, fair; (*legítimo*: *queixa*) legitimate, justified; (*exato*) exact; (*apertado*) tight ♦ *adv* just

juvenil [ʒuveˈniw] (*pl* **-is**) *adj* youthful; (*roupa*) young; (*livro*) for young people; (ESPORTE: *equipe, campeonato*) youth *atr*, junior

juventude [ʒuvẽˈtudʒi] *f* youth; (*jovialidade*) youthfulness; (*jovens*) young people *pl*, youth

K

kg *abr* (= *quilograma*) kg

kit [ˈkitʃi] (*pl* **~s**) *m* kit

kitchenette [kitʃeˈnetʃi] *f* studio flat

km *abr* (= *quilômetro*) km

km/h *abr* (= *quilômetros por hora*) km/h

L

-la [la] *pron* her; (*você*) you; (*coisa*) it

lá [la] *adv* there ♦ *m* (MÚS) A; **~ fora** outside; **~ em baixo** down there; **por ~** (*direção*) that way; (*situação*) over there; **até ~** (*no espaço*) there; (*no tempo*) until then

lã [lã] *f* wool

labia [ˈlabja] *f* (*astúcia*) cunning; **ter ~** to have the gift of the gab

lábio [ˈlabju] *m* lip

labirinto [labiˈritu] *m* labyrinth, maze

laboratório [laboraˈtɔrju] *m* laboratory

laca [ˈlaka] *f* lacquer

laçar [laˈsa*] *vt* to bind, tie

laço [ˈlasu] *m* bow; (*de gravata*) knot; (*armadilha*) snare; (*fig*) bond, tie; **dar um ~** to tie a bow

lacrar [laˈkra*] *vt* to seal (with wax); **lacre** [ˈlakri] *m* sealing wax

lacuna [laˈkuna] *f* gap; (*omissão*) omission; (*espaço em branco*) blank

ladeira [laˈdejra] *f* slope

lado [ˈladu] *m* side; (MIL) flank; (*rumo*) direction; **ao ~** (*perto*) close by; **a casa ao ~** the house next door; **ao ~ de** beside; **deixar de ~** to set aside; (*fig*) to leave out; **de um ~ para outro** back and forth

ladra [ˈladra] *f* thief, robber; (*picareta*) crook

ladrão, -ona [laˈdrãw, ɔna] (*pl* **-ões, ~s**) *adj* thieving ♦ *m/f* thief, robber; (*picareta*) crook

ladrilho [laˈdriʎu] *m* tile; (*chão*) tiled floor, tiles *pl*

ladrões [laˈdrõjʃ] *mpl de* **ladrão**

lagarta [laˈgaxta] *f* caterpillar

lagartixa [lagaxˈtʃiʃa] *f* gecko

lagarto [laˈgaxtu] *m* lizard

lago [ˈlagu] *m* lake; (*de jardim*) pond

lagoa [la'goa] *f* pool, pond; (*lago*) lake

lagosta [la'goʃta] *f* lobster

lagostim [lagoʃ'tʃĩ] (*pl* **-ns**) *m* crayfish

lágrima ['lagrima] *f* tear

laje [ʼlaʒi] *f* paving stone, flagstone

lama [ʼlama] *f* mud

lamaçal [lama'saw] (*pl* **-ais**) *m* quagmire; (*pântano*) bog, marsh

lamber [lã'be*] *vt* to lick; **lambida** [lã'bida] *f*: **dar uma lambida em algo** to lick sth

lambuzar [lãbu'za*] *vt* to smear

lamentar [lamẽ'ta*] *vt* to lament; (*sentir*) to regret; **lamentar-se** *vr*: **~-se (de algo)** to lament (sth); **~ (que)** to be sorry (that); **lamentável** [lamẽ'tavew] (*pl* **-eis**) *adj* regrettable; (*deplorável*) deplorable;

lamento [la'mẽtu] *m* lament; (*gemido*) moan

lâmina [ʼlamina] *f* (*chapa*) sheet; (*placa*) plate; (*de faca*) blade; (*de persiana*) slat

lâmpada [ʼlãpada] *f* lamp; (*tb*: **~ elétrica**) light bulb; **~ de mesa** table lamp

lança [ʼlãsa] *f* lance, spear

lançamento [lãsa'mẽtu] *m* throwing; (*de navio, produto, campanha*) launch; (*de disco, filme*) release; (*COM: em livro*) entry

lançar [lã'sa*] *vt* to throw; (*navio, produto, campanha*) to launch; (*disco, filme*) to release; (*COM: em livro*) to enter; (*em leilão*) to bid

lance [ʼlãsi] *m* (*arremesso*) throw; (*incidente*) incident; (*história*) story; (*situação*) position; (*fato*) fact; (*ESPORTE: jogada*) shot; (*em leilão*) bid; (*de escada*) flight; (*de casas*) row; (*episódio*) moment; (*de muro, estrada*) stretch

lancha [ʼlãʃa] *f* launch; **~ torpedeira** torpedo boat

lanchar [lã'ʃa*] *vi* to have a snack ♦ *vt* to have as a snack; **lanche** [ʼlãʃi] *m* snack

lanchonete [lãʃo'netʃi] (*BR*) *f* snack bar

lânguido, -a [ʼlãgidu, a] *adj* languid, listless

lanterna [lã'tɛxna] *f* lantern; (*portátil*) torch (*BRIT*), flashlight (*US*)

lápide [ʼlapidʒi] *f* (*tumular*) tombstone; (*comemorativa*) memorial stone

lápis [ʼlapiʃ] *m inv* pencil; **~ de cor** coloured (*BRIT*) *ou* colored (*US*) pencil, crayon; **~ de olho** eyebrow pencil; **lapiseira** [lapi'zejra] *f* propelling (*BRIT*) *ou* mechanical (*US*) pencil; (*caixa*) pencil case

Lapônia [la'ponja] *f*: **a ~** Lapland

lapso [ʼlapsu] *m* lapse; (*de tempo*) interval; (*erro*) slip

lar [la*] *m* home

laranja [la'rãʒa] *adj inv* orange ♦ *f* orange ♦ *m* (*cor*) orange; **laranjada** [larã'ʒada] *f* orangeade; **laranjeira** [larã'ʒejra] *f* orange tree

lareira [la'rejra] *f* hearth, fireside

larga [ʼlaxga] *f*: **à ~** lavishly; **dar ~s a** to give free rein to; **viver à ~** to lead a lavish life

largada [lax'gada] *f* start; **dar a ~** to start; (*fig*) to make a start

largar [lax'ga*] *vt* to let go of, release; (*deixar*) to leave; (*deixar cair*) to drop; (*risada*) to let out; (*velas*) to unfurl; (*piada*) to tell; (*pôr em liberdade*) to let go ♦ *vi* (*NÁUT*) to set sail; **largar-se** *vr* (*desprender-se*) to free o.s.; (*ir-se*) to go off; (*pôr-se*) to proceed

largo, -a [ʼlaxgu, a] *adj* wide, broad; (*amplo*) extensive; (*roupa*) loose, baggy; (*conversa*) long ♦ *m* (*praça*) square; (*alto-mar*) open sea; **ao ~** at a distance, far off; **passar de ~**

sobre um assunto to gloss over a subject; **passar ao ~ de algo** (fig) to sidestep sth; **largura** [laˈɡura] f width, breadth

laringite [lariˈʒitʃi] f laryngitis

lasanha [laˈzaɲa] f lasagna

lasca [ˈlaʃka] f (de madeira, metal) splinter; (de pedra) chip; (fatia) slice

laser [ˈlejzeʳ] m laser; **raio ~** laser beam

lástima [ˈlaʃtʃima] f pity, compassion; (infortúnio) misfortune; **é uma ~ (que)** it's a shame (that); **lastimar** [laʃtʃiˈmaˣ] vt to lament; **lastimar-se** vr to complain, be sorry for o.s

lata [ˈlata] f tin (BRIT), can; (material) tin-plate; ~ **de lixo** rubbish bin (BRIT), garbage can (US); ~ **velha** (col: carro) old banger (BRIT) ou clunker (US)

latão [laˈtāw] m brass

lataria [lataˈria] f (AUTO) bodywork; (enlatados) canned food

latejar [lateˈʒaˣ] vi to throb

latente [laˈtētʃi] adj latent

lateral [lateˈraw] (pl -ais) adj side, lateral ♦ f (FUTEBOL) sideline ♦ m (FUTEBOL) throw-in

latido [laˈtʃidu] m bark(ing), yelp(ing)

latifundiário, -a [latʃifūˈdʒjarju, a] m/f landowner

latifúndio [latʃiˈfūdʒju] m large estate

latim [laˈtʃĩ] m (LING) Latin; **gastar o seu ~** to waste one's breath

latino, -a [laˈtʃinu, a] adj Latin; **latino-americano, -a** adj, m/f Latin-American

latir [laˈtʃiˣ] vi to bark, yelp

latitude [latʃiˈtudʒi] f latitude; (largura) breadth; (fig) scope

latrocínio [latroˈsinju] m armed robbery

laudo [ˈlawdu] m (JUR) decision; (resultados) findings pl; (peça escrita) report

lava [ˈlava] f lava

lavabo [laˈvabu] m toilet

lavadeira [lavaˈdejra] f washerwoman

lavadora [lavaˈdora] f washing machine

lavagem [laˈvaʒē] f washing; ~ **a seco** dry cleaning; ~ **cerebral** brainwashing

lavanda [laˈvāda] f (BOT) lavender; (colônia) lavender water; (para lavar os dedos) fingerbowl

lavar [laˈvaˣ] vt to wash; (culpa) to wash away; ~ **a seco** to dry clean

lavatório [lavaˈtɔrju] m washbasin; (aposento) toilet

lavoura [laˈvora] f tilling; (agricultura) farming; (terreno) plantation

lavrador, a [lavraˈdoˣ, a] m/f farmhand

laxativo, -a [laʃaˈtʃivu, a] adj laxative ♦ m laxative

lazer [laˈzeˣ] m leisure

leal [leˈaw] (pl -ais) adj loyal; **lealdade** [leawˈdadʒi] f loyalty

leão [leˈãw] (pl -ões) m lion; **L~** (ASTROLOGIA) Leo

lebre [ˈlɛbri] f hare

lecionar [lesjoˈnaˣ] (PT -cc-) vt, vi to teach

lectivo, -a [lɛkˈtʃivu, a] (PT) adj = letivo

legal [leˈɡaw] (pl -ais) adj legal, lawful; (col) fine; (: pessoa) nice ♦ adv (col) well; **(tá) ~!** OK!; **legalidade** [legaliˈdadʒi] f legality, lawfulness; **legalizar** [legaliˈzaˣ] vt to legalize; (documento) to·authenticate

legendário, -a [leʒēˈdarju, a] adj legendary

legislação [leʒiʒlaˈsãw] f legislation

legislar [leʒiʒˈlaˣ] vi to legislate ♦ vt

to pass

legislativo, -a [leʒiʒla'tʃivu, a] *adj* legislative ♦ *m* legislature

legitimar [leʒitʃi'ma*] *vt* to legitimize; (*justificar*) to legitimate

legítimo, -a [le'ʒitʃimu, a] *adj* legitimate; (*justo*) rightful; (*autêntico*) genuine; **legítima defesa** self-defence (*BRIT*), self-defense (*US*)

legume [le'gumi] *m* vegetable

lei [lej] *f* law; (*regra*) rule; (*metal*) standard

leigo, -a [lejgu, a] *adj* (*REL*) lay, secular ♦ *m* layman; **ser ~ em algo** (*fig*) to be no expert at sth, be unversed in sth

leilão [lej'lãw] (*pl -ões*) *m* auction; **vender em ~** to sell by auction, auction off; **leiloar** [lej'lwa*] *vt* to auction

leio *etc* ['leju] *vb* V **ler**

leitão, -toa [lej'tãw, 'toa] (*pl -ões, ~s*) *m/f* sucking (*BRIT*) *ou* suckling (*US*) pig

leite ['lejtʃi] *m* milk; **~ em pó** powdered milk; **~ desnatado** *ou* **magro** skimmed milk; **~ de magnésia** milk of magnesia; **~ semidesnatado** semi-skimmed milk; **leiteira** [lej'tejra] *f* (*para ferver*) milk pan; (*para servir*) milk jug; **leiteiro, -a** [lej'tejru, a] *adj* (*vaca, gado*) dairy ♦ *m/f* milkman/woman

leito ['lejtu] *m* bed

leitões [lej'tõjʃ] *mpl de* **leitão**

leitor, a [lej'to*, a] *m/f* reader; (*professor*) lector

leitura [lej'tura] *f* reading; (*livro etc*) reading matter

lema ['lema] *m* motto; (*POL*) slogan

lembrança [lẽ'brãsa] *f* recollection, memory; (*presente*) souvenir; **~s** *fpl* (*recomendações*) **~s a sua mãe!** regards to your mother!

lembrar [lẽ'bra*] *vt, vi* to remem-

ber; **lembrar-se** *vr*: **~(-se) de** to remember; **~(-se) (de) que** to remember that; **~ algo a alguém, ~ alguém de algo** to remind sb of sth; **~ alguém de que, ~ a alguém que** to remind sb that; **ele lembra meu irmão** he reminds me of my brother, he is like my brother; **lembrete** [lẽ'bretʃi] *m* reminder

leme ['lemi] *m* rudder; (*NÁUT*) helm; (*fig*) control

lenço ['lẽsu] *m* handkerchief; (*de pescoço*) scarf; (*de cabeça*) headscarf; **~ de papel** tissue

lençol [lẽ'sɔw] (*pl -óis*) *m* sheet; **estar em maus lençóis** to be in a fix

lenda ['lẽda] *f* legend; (*fig: mentira*) lie; **lendário, -a** [lẽ'darju, a] *adj* legendary

lenha ['leɲa] *f* firewood

lente ['lẽtʃi] *f* lens *sg*; **~ de aumento** magnifying glass; **~s de contato** contact lenses

lentidão [lẽtʃi'dãw] *f* slowness

lento, -a ['lẽtu, a] *adj* slow

leoa [le'oa] *f* lioness

leões [le'õjʃ] *mpl de* **leão**

leopardo [ljo'paxdu] *m* leopard

lepra ['lepra] *f* leprosy

leque ['lɛki] *m* fan; (*fig*) array

ler [le*] *vt, vi* to read

lesão [le'zãw] (*pl -ões*) *f* harm, injury; (*JUR*) violation; (*MED*) lesion; **~ corporal** (*JUR*) bodily harm

lesar [le'za*] *vt* to harm, damage; (*direitos*) to violate

lésbica ['lɛʒbika] *f* lesbian

lesma ['leʒma] *f* slug; (*fig: pessoa*) slowcoach

lesões [le'zõjʃ] *fpl de* **lesão**

lesse *etc* ['lɛsi] *vb* V **ler**

leste ['lɛʃtʃi] *m* east

letal [le'taw] (*pl -ais*) *adj* lethal

letargia [letax'ʒia] *f* lethargy

letivo, -a [le'tʃivu, a] *adj* school *atr*;

ano ~ academic year

letra ['letra] *f* letter; *(caligrafia)* handwriting; *(de canção)* lyrics *pl*; **L~s** *fpl (curso)* language and literature; **à ~** literally; **ao pé da ~** literally, word for word; **~ de câmbio** *(COM)* bill of exchange; **~ de imprensa** print; **letrado, -a** [le'tradu, a] *adj* learned, erudite ♦ *m/f* scholar; **letreiro** [le'trejru] *m* sign, notice; *(inscrição)* inscription; *(CINEMA)* subtitle

leu *etc* [lew] *vb V* **ler**

léu [lew] *m*: **ao ~** *(à toa)* aimlessly; *(à mostra)* uncovered

leucemia [lewse'mia] *f* leukaemia *(BRIT)*, leukemia *(US)*

levado, -a [le'vadu, a] *adj* mischievous; *(criança)* naughty

levantador, a [levãta'do*, a] *adj* lifting ♦ *m/f*: **~ de pesos** weightlifter

levantamento [levãta'mẽtu] *m* lifting, raising; *(revolta)* uprising, rebellion; *(arrolamento)* survey

levantar [levã'ta*] *vt* to lift, raise; *(voz, capital)* to raise; *(apanhar)* to pick up; *(suscitar)* to arouse; *(ambiente)* to brighten up ♦ *vi* to stand up; *(da cama)* to get up; *(dar vida)* to brighten; **levantar-se** *vr* to stand up; *(da cama)* to get up; *(rebelar-se)* to rebel

levar [le'va*] *vt* to take; *(portar)* to carry; *(tempo)* to pass, spend; *(roupa)* to wear; *(lidar com)* to handle; *(induzir)* to lead; *(filme)* to show; *(peça teatral)* to do, put on; *(vida)* to lead ♦ *vi* to get a beating; **~ a** to lead to; **~ a mal** to take amiss

leve ['lɛvi] *adj* light; *(insignificante)* slight; **de ~** lightly, softly

leviandade [levjã'dadʒi] *f* frivolity

leviano, -a [le'vjanu, a] *adj* frivolous

lha(s) [ʎa(ʃ)] *pron* = **lhe** + **a(s)**

lhe [ʎi] *pron (a ele)* to him; *(a ela)* to her; *(a você)* to you

lhes [ʎiʃ] *pron pl (a eles/elas)* to them; *(a vocês)* to you

lho(s) [ʎu(ʃ)] = **lhe** + **o(s)**

li *etc* [li] *vb V* **ler**

Líbano ['libanu] *m*: **o ~** (the) Lebanon

libélula [li'bɛlula] *f* dragonfly

liberação [libera'sãw] *f* liberation

liberal [libe'raw] *(pl -ais)* adj, *m/f* liberal

liberar [libe'ra*] *vt* to release; *(libertar)* to free

liberdade [libex'dadʒi] *f* freedom; **~s** *fpl (direitos)* liberties; **pôr alguém em ~** to set sb free; **~ condicional** probation; **~ de palavra** freedom of speech; **~ sob palavra** parole

libertação [libexta'sãw] *f* release

libertar [libex'ta*] *vt* to free, release

libertino, -a [libex'tʃinu, a] *adj* loose-living ♦ *m/f* libertine

liberto, -a [li'bextu, a] *pp de* **libertar**

Líbia ['libja] *f*: **a ~** Libya

libidinoso, -a [libidʒi'nozu, ɔza] *adj* lecherous, lustful

líbio, -a [li'libju, a] *adj*, *m/f* Libyan

libra ['libra] *f* pound; **L~** *(ASTROLOGIA)* Libra

lição [li'sãw] *(pl -ões)* f lesson

licença [li'sẽsa] *f* licence *(BRIT)*, license *(US)*; *(permissão)* permission; *(do trabalho, MIL)* leave; **com ~** excuse me; **estar de ~** to be on leave; **dá ~?** may I?

licenciado, -a [lisẽ'sjadu, a] *m/f* graduate

licenciar [lisẽ'sja*] *vt* to license; **licenciar-se** *vr (EDUC)* to graduate; *(ficar de licença)* to take leave; **licenciatura** [lisẽsja'tura] *f (título)* degree; *(curso)* degree course

liceu [li'sew] *(PT)* m secondary *(BRIT)* ou high *(US)* school

lições [li'sõjʃ] *fpl de* **lição**

licor [li'ko*] *m* liqueur

lidar [li'da*] *vi:* ~ **com** (*ocupar-se*) to deal with; (*combater*) to struggle against; ~ **em algo** to work in sth

líder ['lide*] *m/f* leader; **liderança** [lide'rãsa] *f* leadership; (*ESPORTE*) lead; **liderar** [lide'ra*] *vt* to lead

liga ['liga] *f* league; (*de meias*) suspender (*BRIT*), garter (*US*); (*metal*) alloy

ligação [liga'sãw] (*pl* -**ões**) *f* connection; (*fig: de amizade*) bond; (*TEL*) call; (*relação amorosa*) liaison; **fazer uma ~ para alguém** to call sb; **não consigo completar a ~** (*TEL*) I can't get through; **caiu a ~** (*TEL*) I (ou he *etc*) was cut off

ligado, -a [li'gadu, a] *adj* (*TEC*) connected; (*luz, rádio etc*) on; (*metal*) alloy

ligadura [liga'dura] *f* bandage

ligamento [liga'mẽtu] *m* ligament

ligar [li'ga*] *vt* to tie, bind; (*unir*) to join, connect; (*luz, TV*) to switch on; (*afetivamente*) to bind together; (*carro*) to start (up) ♦ *vi* (*telefonar*) to ring; **ligar-se** *vr* to join; ~**se com alguém** to join with sb; ~**se a algo** to be connected with sth; ~ **para alguém** to ring sb up; ~ **para** *ou* **a algo** (*dar atenção*) to take notice of sth; (*dar importância*) to care about sth; **eu nem ligo** it doesn't bother me; **não ligo a mínima (para)** I couldn't care less (about)

ligeiro, -a [li'ʒejru, a] *adj* light; (*ferimento*) slight; (*referência*) passing; (*conhecimentos*) scant; (*rápido*) quick, swift; (*ágil*) nimble ♦ *adv* swiftly, nimbly

lilás [li'laʃ] *adj, m* lilac

lima ['lima] *f* (*laranja*) type of (*very sweet*) orange; (*ferramenta*) file; ~ **de unhas** nailfile

limão [li'mãw] (*pl* -**ões**) *m* lime; **limão(-galego)** (*pl* **limões(-galegos)**) *m* lemon

limiar [li'mja*] *m* threshold

limitação [limita'sãw] (*pl* -**ões**) *f* limitation, restriction

limitar [limi'ta*] *vt* to limit, restrict; **limitar-se** *vr:* ~**se a** to limit o.s. to; ~**se com** to border on; **limite** [li'mitʃi] *m* limit, boundary; (*fig*) limit; **passar dos limites** to go too far

limo ['limu] *m* (*BOT*) water weed; (*lodo*) slime

limoeiro [li'mwejru] *m* lemon tree

limões [li'mõjʃ] *mpl de* **limão**

limonada [limo'nada] *f* lemonade (*BRIT*), lemon soda (*US*)

limpar [lĩ'pa*] *vt* to clean; (*lágrimas, suor*) to wipe away; (*polir*) to shine, polish; (*fig*) to clean up; (*roubar*) to rob

limpeza [lĩ'peza] *f* cleanliness; (*esmero*) neatness; (*ato*) cleaning; ~ **pública** rubbish (*BRIT*) *ou* garbage (*US*) collection, sanitation

limpo, -a [lĩpu, a] *pp de* **limpar** ♦ *adj* clean; (*céu, consciência*) clear; (*COM*) net; (*fig*) pure; (*col: pronto*) ready; **passar a** ~ to make a fair copy; **tirar a** ~ to find out the truth about, clear up; **estar** ~ **com alguém** (*col*) to be in with sb

linchar [lĩ'ʃa*] *vt* to lynch

lindo, -a [li'ĩdu, a] *adj* lovely

lingerie [lĩʒe'ri] *m* lingerie

língua [lĩgwa] *f* tongue; (*linguagem*) language; **botar a ~ para fora** to stick out one's tongue; **dar com a ~ nos dentes** to let the cat out of the bag; **estar na ponta da ~** to be on the tip of one's tongue

linguado [lĩ'gwadu] *m* (*peixe*) sole

linguagem [lĩ'gwaʒẽ] (*pl* -**ns**) *f* (*tb: COMPUT*) language; (*falada*) speech;

~ **de máquina** (*COMPUT*) machine language

linguarudo, -a [lĩgwa'rudu, a] *adj* gossiping ♦ *m/f* gossip

lingüiça [lĩ'gwisa] *f* sausage

linha ['liɲa] *f* line; (*para costura*) thread; (*barbante*) string, cord; ~**s** *fpl* (*carta*) letter *sg*; **em** ~ in line, in a row; (*COMPUT*) on line; **fora de** ~ (*COMPUT*) off line; **manter/perder a** ~ to keep/lose one's cool; **o telefone não deu** ~ the line was dead; **aérea** airline; ~ **de mira** sights *pl*; ~ **de montagem** assembly line; ~ **férrea** railway (*BRIT*), railroad (*US*)

linho ['liɲu] *m* linen; (*planta*) flax

liquidação [likida'sãw] (*pl* -**ões**) *f* liquidation; (*em loja*) (clearance) sale; (*de conta*) settlement; **em** ~ on sale

liquidar [liki'da*] *vt* to liquidate; (*conta*) to settle; (*mercadoria*) to sell off; (*assunto*) to lay to rest ♦ *vi* (*loja*) to have a sale; **liquidar-se** *vr* (*destruir-se*) to be destroyed; ~ (**com**) **alguém** (*fig: arrasar*) to destroy sb; (*: matar*) to do away with sb

liqüidificador [likwidʒifika'do*] *m* liquidizer

líquido, -a ['likidu, a] *adj* liquid, fluid; (*COM*) net ♦ *m* liquid

lira ['lira] *f* lyre; (*moeda*) lira

lírico, -a ['liriku, a] *adj* lyric(al)

lírio ['lirju] *m* lily

Lisboa [liʒ'boa] *n* Lisbon; **lisboeta** [liʒ'bweta] *adj* Lisbon *atr* ♦ *m/f* inhabitant *ou* native of Lisbon

liso, -a ['lizu, a] *adj* smooth; (*tecido*) plain; (*cabelo*) straight; (*col: sem dinheiro*) broke

lisonjear [lizõ'ʒja*] *vt* to flatter

lista ['liʃta] *f* list; (*listra*) stripe; (*PT: menu*) menu; ~ **negra** blacklist; ~ **telefônica** telephone directory; **listar** [liʃ'ta*] *vt* (*COMPUT*) to list

listra ['liʃtra] *f* stripe; **listrado, -a** [liʃ'tradu, a] *adj* striped

literal [lite'raw] (*pl* -**ais**) *adj* literal

literário, -a [lite'rarju, a] *adj* literary

literatura [litera'tura] *f* literature; ~ **de cordel** *see boxed note*

LITERATURA DE CORDEL

Literatura de cordel is a type of literature typical of the north-east of Brazil, and published in the form of cheaply printed booklets. Their authors hang these booklets from wires attached to walls in the street so that people can look at them. While they do this, the authors sing their stories aloud. **Literatura de cordel** deals both with local events and people, and with everyday public life, almost always in an irreverent manner.

---

litoral [lito'raw] (*pl* -**ais**) *adj* coastal ♦ *m* coast, seaboard

litro ['litru] *m* litre (*BRIT*), liter (*US*)

livrar [li'vra*] *vt* to release, liberate; (*salvar*) to save; **livrar-se** *vr* to escape; ~**-se** to get rid of; (*compromisso*) to get out of; **Deus me livre!** Heaven forbid!

livraria [livra'ria] *f* bookshop (*BRIT*), bookstore (*US*)

livre ['livri] *adj* free; (*lugar*) unoccupied; (*desimpedido*) clear, open; ~ **de impostos** tax-free; **livre-arbítrio** *m* free will

livro ['livru] *m* book; ~ **brochado** paperback; ~ **de bolso** pocket-sized book; ~ **de cheques** cheque book (*BRIT*), check book (*US*); ~ **de consulta** reference book; ~ **encadernado** *ou* **de capa dura** hardback

lixa ['liʃa] *f* sandpaper; (*de unhas*) nailfile; (*peixe*) dogfish; **lixar** [li'ʃa*] *vt* to sand

lixeira [li'ʃejra] *f* dustbin (BRIT), garbage can (US)

lixeiro [li'ʃejru] *m* dustman (BRIT), garbage man (US)

lixo ['liʃu] *m* rubbish, garbage (US); **ser um ~** (col) to be rubbish; **~ atômico** nuclear waste

-lo [lu] *pron* him; (você) you; (coisa) it

lobo ['lobu] *m* wolf

locação [loka'sãw] *f* (pl -ões) *f* lease; (de vídeo etc) rental

locador, a [loka'do*, a] *m/f* (de casa) landlord; (de carro, filme) rental agent ♦ *f* rental company; **~a de vídeo** video rental shop

local [lo'kaw] (pl -ais) *adj* local ♦ *m* site, place ♦ *f* (notícia) story; **localidade** [lokali'dadʒi] *f* (lugar) locality; (povoação) town; **localização** [lokaliza'sãw] (pl -ões) *f* location; **localizar** [lokali'za*] *vt* to locate; (situar) to place; **localizar-se** *vr* to be located; (orientar-se) to get one's bearings

loção [lo'sãw] (pl -ões) *f* lotion; **~ após-barba** aftershave (lotion)

locatário, a [loka'tarju, a] *m/f* (de casa) tenant; (de carro, filme) hirer

loções [lo'sõjʃ] *fpl* de **loção**

locomotiva [lokomo'tʃiva] *f* railway (BRIT) ou railroad (US) engine, locomotive

locomover-se [lokomo'vexsi] *vr* to move around

locutor, a [loku'to*, a] *m/f* (TV, RÁDIO) announcer

lodo ['lodu] *m* (lama) mud; (limo) slime

lógica ['lɔʒika] *f* logic; **lógico, -a** ['lɔʒiku, a] *adj* logical; **(é) lógico!** of course!

logo ['lɔgu] *adv* (imediatamente) right away, at once; (em breve) soon; (justamente) just, right; (mais

tarde) later; **~, ~** straightaway, without delay; **~ mais** later; **~ no começo** right at the start; **~ que, tão ~** as soon as; **até ~!** bye!; **~ antes/depois** just before/shortly afterwards; **~ de saída** ou **de cara** straightaway, from far away

logotipo [logo'tʃipu] *m* logo

lograr [lo'gra*] *vt* (alcançar) to achieve; (obter) to get, obtain; (enganar) to cheat; **~ fazer** to manage to do

loiro, -a ['lojru, a] *adj* = **louro/a**

loja ['lɔʒa] *f* shop; **lojista** [lo'ʒiʃta] *m/f* shopkeeper

lombo ['lõbu] *m* back; (carne) loin

lona ['lɔna] *f* canvas

Londres ['lõdriʃ] *n* London; **londrino, -a** [lõ'drinu, a] *adj* London *atr* ♦ *m/f* Londoner

longa-metragem (pl **longas-metragens**) *m*: **(filme de) ~** feature (film)

longe ['lõʒi] *adv* far, far away ♦ *adj* distant; **ao ~** in the distance; **de ~** from far away; (sem dúvida) by a long way; **~ de** a long way ou far from; **~ disso** far from it; **ir ~ demais** (fig) to go too far

longínquo, -a [lõ'ʒĩkwu, a] *adj* distant, remote

longitude [lõʒi'tudʒi] *f* (GEO) longitude

longo, -a ['lõgu, a] *adj* long ♦ *m* (vestido) long dress, evening dress; **ao ~ de** along, alongside

lotação [lota'sãw] *f* capacity; (de funcionários) complement; (BR: ônibus) bus; **~ completa** ou **esgotada** (TEATRO) sold out

lotado, -a [lo'tadu, a] *adj* (TEATRO) full; (ônibus) full up; (bar, praia) packed, crowded

lotar [lo'ta*] *vt* to fill, pack; (funcionário) to place ♦ *vi* to fill up

lote ['lɔtʃi] m portion, share; (em leilão) lot; (terreno) plot; (de ações) parcel, batch

loteria [lote'ria] f lottery; **~ esportiva** football pools pl (BRIT), lottery (US)

louça ['losa] f china; (conjunto) crockery; (tb: **~ sanitária**) bathroom suite; **de ~** china atr; **~ de barro** earthenware; **~ de jantar** dinner service; **lavar a ~** to do the washing up (BRIT) ou the dishes

louco, -a ['loku, a] adj crazy, mad; (sucesso) runaway; (frio) freezing ♦ m/f lunatic; **~ varrido** raving mad; **~ de fome/raiva** ravenous/hopping mad; **~ por** crazy about; **deixar alguém ~** to drive sb crazy; **loucura** [lo'kura] f madness; (ato) crazy thing; **ser loucura (fazer)** to be crazy (to do); **ser uma loucura** to be crazy; (col: ser muito bom) to be fantastic

louro, -a ['loru, a] adj blond, fair ♦ m laurel; (CULIN) bay leaf; (papagaio) parrot; **~s** mpl (fig) laurels

louva-a-deus ['lova-] m inv praying mantis

louvar [lo'va*] vt to praise ♦ vi: **~ a** to praise; **louvável** [lo'vavew] (pl -eis) adj praiseworthy

louvor [lo'vo*] m praise

LP abr m LP

Ltda. abr (= Limitada) Ltd (BRIT), Inc. (US)

lua ['lua] f moon; **estar** ou **viver no mundo da ~** to have one's head in the clouds; **estar de ~** (col) to be in a mood; **ser de ~** (col) to be moody; **~ cheia/nova** full/new moon; **lua-de-mel** f honeymoon

luar ['lwa*] m moonlight

lubrificante [lubrifi'kãtʃi] m lubricant

lubrificar [lubrifi'ka*] vt to lubricate

lúcido, -a ['lusidu, a] adj lucid

lúcio ['lusju] m (peixe) pike

lucrar [lu'kra*] vt (tirar proveito) to profit from ou by; (dinheiro) to make; (gozar) to enjoy ♦ vi to make a profit; **~ com** ou **em** to profit by

lucrativo, -a [lukra'tʃivu, a] adj lucrative, profitable

lucro ['lukru] m gain; (COM) profit; **~s e perdas** (COM) profit and loss

lugar [lu'ga*] m place; (espaço) space, room; (para sentar) seat; (emprego) job; (ocasião) opportunity; **em ~ de** instead of; **dar ~ a** (causar) to give rise to; **~ comum** commonplace; **em primeiro ~** in the first place; **em algum/nenhum/todo ~** somewhere/nowhere/everywhere; **em outro ~** somewhere else, elsewhere; **ter ~** (acontecer) to take place; **~ de nascimento** place of birth; **lugarejo** [luga'reʒu] m village

lula ['lula] f squid

lume ['lumi] m fire; (luz) light

luminária [lumi'narja] f lamp; **~s** fpl (iluminações) illuminations

luminosidade [luminozi'dadʒi] f brightness

luminoso, -a [lumi'nozu, ɔza] adj luminous; (fig: raciocínio) clear; (: idéia, talento) brilliant; (letreiro) illuminated

lunar [lu'na*] adj lunar ♦ m (na pele) mole

lunático, -a [lu'natʃiku, a] adj mad

lusitano, -a [luzi'tanu, a] adj Portuguese, Lusitanian

luso, -a ['luzu, a] adj Portuguese; **luso-brasileiro, -a** (pl lusos-brasileiros, -as) adj Luso-Brazilian

lustre ['luʃtri] m gloss, sheen; (fig) lustre (BRIT), luster (US); (luminária) chandelier

luta ['luta] f fight, struggle; **~ de boxe** boxing; **~ livre** wrestling;
lutador, a [luta'do*, a] m/f fighter; (atleta) wrestler; **lutar** [lu'ta*] vi to fight, struggle; (luta livre) to wrestle ♦ vt (caratê, judô) to do; **lutar contra/por algo** to fight against/for sth; **lutar para fazer algo** to fight ou struggle to do sth; **lutar com** (dificuldades) to struggle against; (competir) to fight with
luto ['lutu] m mourning; (tristeza) grief; **de ~** in mourning; **pôr ~** to go into mourning
luva ['luva] f glove; **~s** fpl (pagamento) payment sg; (ao locador) fee sg
Luxemburgo [luʒe'buxgu] m: **o ~** Luxembourg
luxo ['luʃu] m luxury; **de ~** luxury atr; **dar-se ao ~ de** to allow o.s. to; **luxuoso, -a** [lu'ʃwozu, ɔza] adj luxurious
luxúria [lu'ʃurja] f lust
luz [luʒ] f light; (eletricidade) electricity; **à ~ de** by the light of; (fig) in the light of; **a meia ~** with subdued lighting; **dar à ~ (um filho)** to give birth (to a son); **deu-me uma ~** I had an idea

M

ma [ma] pron = **me** + **a**
má [ma] f de **mau**
maca ['maka] f stretcher
maçã [ma'sã] f apple; **~ do rosto** cheekbone
macabro, -a [ma'kabru, a] adj macabre
macacão [maka'kãw] (pl **-ões**) m (de trabalhador) overalls pl (BRIT), coveralls pl (US); (da moda) jumpsuit

macaco, -a [ma'kaku, a] m/f monkey ♦ m (MECÂNICA) jack; (fato) **~** (PT) overalls pl (BRIT), coveralls pl (US); **~ velho** (fig) old hand
macacões [maka'kõjʃ] mpl de **macacão**
maçador, a [masa'do*, a] (PT) adj boring
maçaneta [masa'neta] f knob
maçante [ma'sãtʃi] (BR) adj boring
macarrão [maka'xãw] m pasta; (em forma de canudo) spaghetti; **macarronada** [makaxo'nada] f pasta with cheese and tomato sauce
Macau [ma'kaw] n Macao
macete [ma'setʃi] m mallet
machado [ma'ʃadu] m axe (BRIT), ax (US)
machista [ma'ʃiʃta] adj chauvinistic, macho ♦ m male chauvinist
macho ['maʃu] adj male; (fig) virile, manly; (valentão) tough ♦ m male; (TEC) tap
machucado, -a [maʃu'kadu, a] adj hurt; (pé, braço) bad ♦ m injury; (área machucada) sore patch
machucar [maʃu'ka*] vt to hurt; (produzir contusão) to bruise ♦ vi to hurt; **machucar-se** vr to hurt o.s.
maciço, -a [ma'sisu, a] adj solid; (espesso) thick; (quantidade) massive
macieira [ma'sjejra] f apple tree
macio, -a [ma'siu, a] adj soft; (liso) smooth
maço ['masu] m (de folhas, notas) bundle; (de cigarros) packet
maçom [ma'sõ] (pl **-ns**) m (free)mason
maconha [ma'kɔɲa] f dope; **cigarro de ~** joint
maçons [ma'sõʃ] mpl de **maçom**
má-criação (pl **-ões**) f rudeness; (ato, dito) rude thing

mácula 499 mais

mácula [ma'kula] f stain, blemish

macumba [ma'kũba] f ≈ voodoo; (*despacho*) macumba offering; **macumbeiro, -a** [makũ'bejru, a] adj ≈ voodoo atr ♦ m/f follower of macumba

madama [ma'dama] f = madame

madame [ma'dami] f (*senhora*) lady; (col: *dona-de-casa*) lady of the house

Madeira [ma'dejra] f: **a ~** Madeira

madeira [ma'dejra] f wood ♦ m Madeira (wine); **de ~** wooden; **bater na ~** (*fig*) to touch (*BRIT*) ou knock on (*US*) wood; **~ compensada** plywood

madeirense [madej'rẽsi] adj, m/f Madeiran

madeixa [ma'dejʃa] f (*de cabelo*) lock

madrasta [ma'draʃta] f stepmother

madrepérola [madre'pɛrola] f mother of pearl

Madri [ma'dri] n Madrid

Madrid [ma'drid] (*PT*) n Madrid

madrinha [ma'driɲa] f godmother

madrugada [madru'gada] f (*early*) morning; (*alvorada*) dawn, daybreak

madrugar [madru'ga*] vi to get up early; (*aparecer cedo*) to be early

maduro, -a [ma'duro, a] adj ripe; (*fig*) mature; (: *prudente*) prudent

mãe [mãj] f mother; **~ adotiva** ou **de criação** adoptive mother

maestro, -trina [ma'ɛʃtru, 'trina] m/f conductor

má-fé f malicious intent

magia [ma'ʒia] f magic

mágica [ˈmaʒika] f magic; (*truque*) magic trick; V tb **mágico**

mágico, -a [ˈmaʒiku, a] adj magic ♦ m/f magician

magistério [maʒiʃˈtɛrju] m (*ensino*) teaching; (*profissão*) teaching pro-

fession; (*professorado*) teachers pl

magnata [magˈnata] m magnate, tycoon

magnético, -a [magˈnɛtʃiku, a] adj magnetic

magnífico, -a [magˈnifiku, a] adj splendid, magnificent

magnitude [magniˈtudʒi] f magnitude

mago [ˈmagu] m magician; **os reis ~s** the Three Wise Men, the Three Kings

mágoa [ˈmagwa] f (*tristeza*) sorrow, grief; (*fig*: *desagrado*) hurt

magoado, -a [maˈgwadu, a] adj hurt

magoar [maˈgwa*] vt, vi to hurt; **magoar-se** vr: **~-se com algo** to be hurt by sth

magro, -a [ˈmagru, a] adj (*pessoa*) slim; (*carne*) lean; (*fig*: *parco*) meagre (*BRIT*), meager (*US*); (*leite*) skimmed

maio [ˈmaju] (*PT* M-) m May

maiô [maˈjo] (*BR*) m swimsuit

maionese [majoˈnezi] f mayonnaise

maior [maˈjɔ*] adj (*compar*: *de tamanho*) bigger; (: *de importância*) greater; (*superl*: *de tamanho*) biggest; (: *de importância*) greatest ♦ m/f adult; **~ de idade** of age, adult; **~ de 21 anos** over 21; **maioria** [majoˈria] f majority; **a maioria de** most of; **maioridade** [majoriˈdadʒi] f adulthood

---

PALAVRA CHAVE

mais [majʃ] adv 1 (*compar*): **~ magro/inteligente (do que)** thinner/more intelligent (than); **ele trabalha ~ (do que eu)** he works more (than me)

2 (*superl*): **o ~ ...** the most ...; **o ~ magro/inteligente** the thinnest/

most intelligent

3 (*negativo*): **ele não trabalha ~ aqui** he doesn't work here any more; **nunca ~** never again

4 (+ *adj*: *valor intensivo*): **que livro ~ chato!** what a boring book!

5: **por ~ que** however much; **por ~ que se esforce** ... no matter how hard you try ...; **por ~ que eu quisesse** ... much as I should like to ...

6: **a ~**: **temos um a ~** we've got one extra

7 (*tempo*): **~ cedo ou ~ tarde** sooner or later; **a ~ tempo** sooner; **logo ~** later on; **no ~ tardar** at the latest

8 (*frases*): **~ ou menos** more or less; **~ uma vez** once more; **cada vez ~** more and more; **sem ~ nem menos** out of the blue

♦ *adj* **1** (*compar*): **~ (do que)** more (than); **ele tem ~ dinheiro (do que o irmão)** he's got more money (than his brother)

2 (*superl*): **ele é quem tem ~ dinheiro** he's got most money

3 (+ *números*): **ela tem ~ de dez bolsas** she's got more than ten bags

4 (*negativo*): **não tenho ~ dinheiro** I haven't got any more money

5 (*adicional*) else; **~ alguma coisa?** anything else?; **nada/ninguém ~** nothing/no-one else

♦ *prep*: **2 ~ 2 são 4** 2 and 2 are 4; **2 ~ 2** 2 and 2 ou plus 2 are 4

♦ *m*: **o ~** the rest

maisena [maj'zena] *f* cornflower
maiúscula [ma'juʃkula] *f* capital letter
majestade [maʒeʃ'tadʒi] *f* majesty
majestoso, -a [maʒeʃ'tozu, ɔza] *adj* majestic
major [ma'ʒɔ*] *m* (*MIL*) major

majoritário, -a [maʒori'tarju, a] *adj* majority *atr*

mal [maw] (*pl* **~es**) *m* harm; (*MED*) illness ♦ *adv* badly; (*quase não*) hardly ♦ *conj* hardly; **~ desliguei o fone, a campainha tocou** I had hardly put the phone down when the doorbell rang; **falar ~ de alguém** to speak ill of sb, run sb down; **não faz ~** never mind; **estar ~ (doente)** to be ill; **passar ~** to be sick; **estar de ~ com alguém** not to be speaking to sb

mal- [mal-] *prefixo* badly

mala ['mala] *f* suitcase; (*BR*: *AUTO*) boot, trunk (*US*); **~s** *fpl* (*bagagem*) luggage *sg*; **fazer as ~s** to pack

malabarismo [malaba'riʒmu] *m* juggling; **malabarista** [malab-'riʃta] *m/f* juggler

mal-acabado, -a *adj* badly finished; (*pessoa*) deformed

malagueta [mala'geta] *f* chilli (*BRIT*) ou chili (*US*) pepper

Malaísia [mala'izja] *f*: **a ~** Malaysia

malandragem [malã'draʒẽ] *f* (*patifaria*) double-dealing; (*preguiça*) idleness; (*esperteza*) cunning

malandro, -a [ma'lãdru, a] *adj* double-dealing; (*preguiçoso*) idle; (*esperto*) wily, cunning ♦ *m/f* crook; idler, layabout; streetwise person

malária [ma'larja] *f* malaria

mal-arrumado, -a [-axu'madu, a] *adj* untidy

malcomportado, -a [mawkõpox-'tadu, a] *adj* badly behaved

malcriado, -a [maw'krjadu, a] *adj* rude ♦ *m/f* slob

maldade [maw'dadʒi] *f* cruelty; (*malícia*) malice

maldição [mawdʒi'sãw] (*pl* **-ões**) *f* curse

maldito, -a [maw'dʒitu, a]

damned

maldizer [mawdʒiˈze*] (*irreg: como* **dizer**) vt to curse

maldoso, -a [mawˈdozu, ɔza] adj wicked; (*malicioso*) malicious

maledicência [maledʒiˈsɛsja] f slander

mal-educado, -a adj rude ♦ m/f slob

malefício [maleˈfisju] m harm;
maléfico, -a [maˈlefiku, a] adj (*pessoa*) malicious; (*prejudicial: efeito*) harmful, injurious

mal-entendido, -a adj misunderstood ♦ m misunderstanding

mal-estar m indisposition; (*embaraço*) uneasiness

malfeito, -a [mawˈfejtu, a] adj (*roupa*) poorly made; (*corpo*) misshapen

malfeitor, a [mawfejˈto*, a] m/f wrong-doer

malha [ˈmaʎa] f (*de rede*) mesh; (*tecido*) jersey; (*suéter*) sweater; (*de ginástica*) leotard; **fazer** ~ (*PT*) to knit; **artigos de** ~ knitwear

malhar [maˈʎa*] vt (*bater*) to beat; (*cereais*) to thresh; (*col: criticar*) to knock, run down

mal-humorado, -a [-umoˈradu, a] adj grumpy, sullen

malícia [maˈlisja] f malice; (*astúcia*) slyness; (*esperteza*) cleverness;
malicioso, -a [maliˈsjozu, ɔza] adj malicious; sly; clever; (*mente suja*) dirty-minded

maligno, -a [maˈlignu, a] adj evil, malicious; (*danoso*) harmful; (*MED*) malignant

malograr [maloˈgra*] vt (*planos*) to upset; (*frustrar*) to thwart, frustrate ♦ vi (*planos*) to fall through; (*fracassar*) to fail; **malograr-se** vr to fall through; to fail

mal-passado, -a adj underdone;

(*bife*) rare

malsucedido, -a [mawsuseˈdʒido, a] adj unsuccessful

Malta [ˈmawta] f Malta

malta [ˈmawta] (*PT*) f gang, mob

maltrapilho, -a [mawtraˈpiʎu, a] adj in rags, ragged ♦ m/f ragamuffin

maltratar [mawtraˈta*] vt to illtreat; (*com palavras*) to abuse; (*estragar*) to ruin, damage

maluco, -a [maˈluku, a] adj crazy, daft ♦ m/f madman/woman

malvadeza [mawvaˈdeza] f wickedness; (*ato*) wicked thing

malvado, -a [mawˈvadu, a] adj wicked

Malvinas [mawˈvinaʃ] fpl: **as (ilhas)** ~ the Falklands, the Falkland Islands

mama [ˈmama] f breast

mamadeira [mamaˈdejra] (*BR*) f feeding bottle

mamãe [maˈmãj] f mum, mummy

mamão [maˈmãw] (*pl* **-ões**) m papaya

mamar [maˈma*] vt to suck; (*dinheiro*) to extort ♦ vi to be breastfed; **dar de** ~ **a um bebê** to (breast)feed a baby

mamífero [maˈmiferu] m mammal

mamilo [maˈmilu] m nipple

mamões [maˈmõjʃ] mpl de **mamão**

manada [maˈnada] f herd, drove

mancada [mãˈkada] f (*erro*) mistake; (*gafe*) blunder; **dar uma** ~ to blunder

mancar [mãˈka*] vi to cripple ♦ vi to limp; **mancar-se** vr (*col*) to get the message, take the hint

Mancha [ˈmãʃa] f: **o canal da** ~ the English Channel

mancha [ˈmãʃa] f stain; (*na pele*) mark, spot; **sem** ~**s** (*reputação*) spotless; **manchado, -a** [mãˈʃadu, a] adj soiled; (*malhado*) mottled,

manchete 502 manso

spotted; **manchar** [mãˈʃaʳ] vt to stain, mark; (reputação) to soil
manchete [mãˈʃetʃi] f headline
manco, -a [ˈmãku, a] adj crippled, lame ♦ m/f cripple
mandado [mãˈdadu] m order; (JUR) writ; (: tb: ~ **de segurança**) injunction; ~ **de prisão/busca** warrant for sb's arrest/search warrant; ~ **de segurança** injunction
mandão, -dona [mãˈdãw, ˈdɔna] (pl -ões, ~s) adj bossy, domineering
mandar [mãˈdaʳ] vt (ordenar) to order; (enviar) to send ♦ vi to be in charge; **mandar-se** vr (col: partir) to make tracks, get going; (fugir) to take off; ~ **buscar** ou **chamar** to send for; ~ **fazer um vestido** to have a dress made; ~ **que alguém faça**, ~ **alguém fazer** to tell sb to do; **o que é que você manda?** (col) what can I do for you?; ~ **em alguém** to boss sb around
mandato [mãˈdatu] m mandate; (ordem) order; (POL) term of office
mandioca [mãˈdʒjɔka] f cassava, manioc
mandões [mãˈdõjʃ] mpl de **mandão**
mandona [mãˈdɔna] f de **mandão**
maneira [maˈnejra] f (modo) way; (estilo) style, manner; ~s fpl (modas) manners; à ~ de like; de ~ que so that; de ~ alguma ou nenhuma not at all; desta ~ in this way; de qualquer ~ anyway; não houve ~ de convencê-lo it was impossible to convince him
maneiro, -a [maˈnejru, a] adj (ferramenta) easy to use; (roupa) attractive; (trabalho) easy; (pessoa) capable; (col: bacana) great, brilliant
manejar [maneˈʒaʳ] vt (instrumento) to handle; (máquina) to work; **manejo** [maˈneʒu] m handling
manequim [maneˈkĩ] (pl -ns) m (boneco) dummy ♦ m/f model
mangá [mãˈga] f sleeve; (fruta) mango; **em ~s de camisa** in (one's) shirt sleeves
mangueira [mãˈgejra] f hose(pipe); (árvore) mango tree
manha [ˈmaɲa] f guile, craftiness; (destreza) skill; (ardil) trick; (birra) tantrum; **fazer** ~ to have a tantrum
manhã [maˈɲã] f morning; **de** ou **pela** ~ in the morning; **amanhã/hoje de** ~ tomorrow/this morning
manhoso, -a [maˈɲozu, ɔza] adj crafty, sly
mania [maˈnia] f (MED) mania; (obsessão) craze; **estar com** ~ **de** ... to have a thing about ...; **maníaco, -a** [maˈniaku, a] adj manic ♦ m/f maniac
manicômio [maniˈkomju] m asylum, mental hospital
manifestação [manifeʃtaˈsãw] (pl -ões) f show, display; (expressão) expression, declaration; (política) demonstration
manifestar [manifeʃˈtaʳ] vt to show, display; (declarar) to express, declare
manifesto, -a [maniˈfeʃtu, a] adj obvious, clear ♦ m manifesto
manipulação [manipulaˈsãw] f handling; (fig) manipulation
manipular [manipuˈlaʳ] vt to manipulate; (manejar) to handle
manivela [maniˈvɛla] f crank
manjericão [mãʒeriˈkãw] m basil
manobra [maˈnɔbra] f manoeuvre (BRIT), maneuver (US); (de mecanismo) operation; (de trens) shunting; **manobrar** [manoˈbraʳ] vt to manoeuvre ou maneuver; (mecanismo) to operate, work; (governar) to take charge of; (manipular) to manipulate ♦ vi to manoeuvre ou maneuver
manso, -a [ˈmãsu, a] adj gentle;

(*mar*) calm; (*animal*) tame

manta ['mãta] *f* blanket; (*xale*) shawl; (*agasalho*) cloak

manteiga [mã'tejga] *f* butter; **~ de cacau** cocoa butter

manter [mã'te*] (*irreg: como* **ter**) *vt* to maintain; (*num lugar*) to keep; (*uma família*) to support; (*a palavra*) to keep; (*princípios*) to abide by; **manter-se** *vr* to support o.s.; (*permanecer*) to remain; **mantimento** [mãtʃi'mẽtu] *m* maintenance; **mantimentos** *mpl* (*alimentos*) provisions

manual [ma'nwaw] (*pl* **-ais**) *adj* manual ♦ *m* handbook, manual

manufatura [manufa'tura] (*PT* **-ct-**) *f* manufacture; **manufaturar** [manufatu'ra*] (*PT* **-ct-**) *vt* to manufacture

manusear [manu'zja*] *vt* to handle; (*livro*) to leaf through

manutenção [manutẽ'sãw] *f* maintenance; (*da casa*) upkeep

mão [mãw] (*pl* **~s**) *f* hand; (*de animal*) paw; (*de pintura*) coat; (*de direção*) flow of traffic; **à ~** by hand; (*perto*) at hand; **de segunda ~** second-hand; **em ~** by hand; **dar a ~ a alguém** to hold sb's hand; (*cumprimentar*) to shake hands with sb; **dar uma ~ a alguém** to give sb a hand, help sb out; **~ única/dupla** one-way/two-way traffic; **rua de duas ~s** two-way street; **mão-de-obra** *f* (*trabalhadores*) labour (*BRIT*), labor (*US*); (*coisa difícil*) tricky thing

mapa ['mapa] *m* map; (*gráfico*) chart

maquiagem [ma'kjaʒẽ] *f* = **maquilagem**

maquiar [ma'kja*] *vt* to make up; **maquiar-se** *vr* to make o.s. up, put on one's make-up

maquilagem [maki'laʒẽ] (*PT* **-lha-**)

f make-up; (*ato*) making up

máquina ['makina] *f* machine; (*de trem*) engine; (*fig*) machinery; **~ de calcular/costura/escrever** calculator/sewing machine/typewriter; **~ fotográfica** camera; **~ de filmar** camera; (*de vídeo*) camcorder; **~ de lavar (roupa)/pratos** washing machine/dishwasher; **escrito à ~** typewritten

maquinar [maki'na*] *vt* to plot ♦ *vi* to conspire

maquinista [maki'niʃta] *m* (*FERRO*) engine driver; (*NÁUT*) engineer

mar [ma*] *m* sea; **por ~** by sea; **fazer-se ao ~** to set sail; **pleno ~, ~ alto** high sea; **o ~ Morto/Negro/Vermelho** the Dead/Black/Red Sea

maracujá [maraku'ʒa] *m* passion fruit; **pé de ~** passion flower

maratona [mara'tona] *f* marathon

maravilha [mara'viʎa] *f* marvel, wonder; **maravilhoso, -a** [maravi-'ʎozu, ɔza] *adj* marvellous (*BRIT*), marvelous (*US*)

marca ['maxka] *f* mark; (*COM*) make, brand; (*carimbo*) stamp; **~ de fábrica** trademark; **~ registrada** registered trademark

marcação [maxka'sãw] (*pl* **-ões**) *f* marking; (*em jogo*) scoring; (*de instrumento*) reading; (*TEATRO*) action; (*PT: TEL*) dialling

marcador [maxka'do*] *m* marker; (*de livro*) bookmark; (*ESPORTE: quadro*) scoreboard; (: *jogador*) scorer

marcapasso [maxka'pasu] *m* (*MED*) pacemaker

marcar [max'ka*] *vt* to mark; (*hora, data*) to fix, set; (*PT: TEL*) to dial; (*gol, ponto*) to score ♦ *vi* to make one's mark; **~ uma consulta, ~ hora** to make an appointment; **~ um encontro com alguém** to arrange to meet sb

marcha ['maxʃa] f march; (de acontecimentos) course; (passo) pace; (AUTO) gear; (progresso) progress; ~ à ré (BR), ~ atrás (PT) reverse (gear); pôr-se em ~ to set off

marchar [max'ʃa*] vi to go; (andar a pé) to walk; (MIL) to march

marco ['maxku] m landmark; (de janela) frame; (fig) frontier; (moeda) mark

março ['maxsu] (PT M-) m March

maré [ma'rɛ] f tide

marechal [mare'ʃaw] (pl -ais) m marshal

maremoto [mare'mɔtu] m tidal wave

marfim [max'fī] m ivory

margarida [maxga'rida] f daisy; (COMPUT) daisy wheel

margarina [maxga'rina] f margarine

margem ['maxʒē] (pl -ns) f (borda) edge; (de rio) bank; (litoral) shore; (de impresso) margin; (fig: tempo) time; (: lugar) space; à ~ de alongside

marginal [maxʒi'naw] (pl -ais) adj marginal ♦ m/f delinquent

marido [ma'ridu] m husband

marimbondo [marī'bōdu] m hornet

marinha [ma'riɲa] f (tb: ~ de guerra) navy; ~ mercante merchant navy; marinheiro [mari'ɲejru] m seaman, sailor

marinho, -a [ma'riɲu, a] adj sea atr, marine

mariposa [mari'poza] f moth

marítimo, -a [ma'ritʃimu, a] adj sea atr

marketing ['maxketʃīŋ] m marketing

marmelada [maxme'lada] f quince jam

marmelo [max'melu] m quince

marmita [max'mita] f (vasilha) pot

mármore ['maxmori] m marble

marquês, -quesa [max'keʃ, 'keza] m/f marquis/marchioness

marquise [max'kizi] f awning, canopy

Marrocos [ma'xɔkuʃ] m: o ~ Morocco

marrom [ma'xō] (pl -ns) adj, m brown

martelar [maxte'la*] vt to hammer; (amolar) to bother ♦ vi to hammer; (insistir): ~ (em algo) to keep ou harp on (about sth); **martelo** [max'telu] m hammer

mártir ['maxtʃi*] m/f martyr; **martírio** [max'tʃirju] m martyrdom; (fig) torment

marxista [max'ksiʃta] adj, m/f Marxist

mas [ma(j)ʃ] conj but ♦ pron = **me** + **as**

mascar [maʃ'ka*] vt to chew

máscara ['maʃkara] f mask; (para limpeza de pele) face pack; **sob a ~ de** under the guise of; **mascarar** [maʃka'ra*] vt to mask; (disfarçar) to disguise; (encobrir) to cover up

mascote [maʃ'kɔtʃi] f mascot

masculino, -a [maʃku'linu, a] adj masculine; (BIO) male

massa ['masa] f (FÍS, fig) mass; (de tomate) paste; (CULIN: de pão) dough; (: macarrão etc) pasta

massacrar [masa'kra*] vt to massacre; **massacre** [ma'sakri] f massacre

massagear [masa'ʒja*] vt to massage; **massagem** [ma'saʒē] (pl -ns) f massage

mastigar [maʃtʃi'ga*] vt to chew

mastro ['maʃtru] m (NÁUT) mast; (para bandeira) flagpole

masturbar-se [maʃtux'baxsi*] vr to masturbate

mata ['mata] f forest, wood

matadouro [mataˈdoru] *m* slaughter-house

matança [maˈtãsa] *f* massacre; (*de reses*) slaughter(ing)

matar [maˈta*] *vt* to kill; (*sede*) to quench; (*fome*) to satisfy; (*aula*) to skip; (*trabalho: não aparecer*) to skive off; (: *fazer rápido*) to dash off; (*adivinhar*) to guess ♦ *vi* to kill; **matar-se** *vr* to kill o.s.; (*esfalfar-se*) to wear o.s. out; **um calor/uma dor de ~** stifling heat/excruciating pain

mate [ˈmatʃi] *adj* matt ♦ *m* (*chá*) maté tea; (*xeque-~*) checkmate

matemática [mateˈmatʃika] *f* mathematics *sg*, maths *sg* (*BRIT*), math (*US*); **matemático, -a** [mateˈmatʃiku, a] *adj* mathematical ♦ *m/f* mathematician

matéria [maˈterja] *f* matter; (*TEC*) material; (*EDUC: assunto*) subject; (*tema*) topic; (*jornalística*) story, article; **em ~ de** on the subject of

material [mateˈrjaw] (*pl* -**ais**) *adj* material; (*físico*) physical ♦ *m* material; (*TEC*) equipment; **materialista** [materjaˈliʃta] *adj* materialist; **materializar** [materjaliˈza*] *vt* to materialize; **materializar-se** *vr* to materialize

matéria-prima (*pl* **matérias-primas**) *f* raw material

maternal [matexˈnaw] (*pl* -**ais**) *adj* motherly, maternal; **escola ~** nursery (school); **maternidade** [matexniˈdadʒi] *f* motherhood, maternity; (*hospital*) maternity hospital

materno, -a [maˈtexnu, a] *adj* motherly, maternal; (*língua*) native

matinê [matʃiˈne] *f* matinée

matiz [maˈtʃiʒ] *m* (*de cor*) shade

mato [ˈmatu] *m* scrubland, bush; (*plantas agrestes*) scrub; (*o campo*) country

matraca [maˈtraka] *f* rattle

matrícula [maˈtrikula] *f* (*lista*) register; (*inscrição*) registration; (*pagamento*) enrolment (*BRIT*) ou enrollment (*US*) fee; (*PT: AUTO*) registration number (*BRIT*), license number (*US*); **fazer a ~** to enrol (*BRIT*), enroll (*US*)

matrimonial [matrimoˈnjaw] (*pl* -**ais**) *adj* marriage *atr*, matrimonial

matrimônio [matriˈmonju] *m* marriage

matriz [maˈtriʒ] *f* (*MED*) womb; (*fonte*) source; (*molde*) mould (*BRIT*), mold (*US*); (*COM*) head office

maturidade [maturiˈdadʒi] *f* maturity

mau, má [maw, ma] *adj* bad; (*malvado*) evil, wicked ♦ *m* bad; (*REL*) evil; **os ~s** *mpl* (*pessoas*) the baddies (*num filme*) the baddies

maus-tratos *mpl* ill-treatment *sg*

maxila [makˈsila] *f* jawbone

maxilar [maksiˈla*] *m* jawbone

máxima [ˈmasima] *f* maxim

máximo, -a [ˈmasimu, a] *adj* (*maior que todos*) greatest; (*o maior possível*) maximum ♦ *m* maximum; (*cúmulo*) peak; (*temperature*) high; **no ~** at most; **ao ~** to the utmost

MCE *abr m* = Mercado Comum Europeu

me [mi] *pron* (*direto*) me; (*indireto*) (to) me; (*reflexivo*) (to) myself

meado [ˈmjadu] *m* middle; **em ~s ou no(s) ~(s) de julho** in mid-July

Meca [ˈmeka] *n* Mecca

mecânica [meˈkanika] *f* (*ciência*) mechanics *sg*; (*mecanismo*) mechanism; *V tb* mecânico

mecânico, -a [meˈkaniku, a] *adj* mechanical ♦ *m/f* mechanic

mecanismo [mekaˈniʒmu] *m* mechanism

meço *etc* [ˈmesu] *vb* V **medir**

medalha [me'daʎa] f medal; **medalhão** [meda'ʎãw] (pl -ões) m medallion

média ['mɛdʒja] f average; (café) coffee with milk; **em ~** on average

mediano, -a [me'dʒjanu, a] adj medium; (médio) average; (mediocre) mediocre

mediante [me'dʒjãtʃi] prep by (means of), through; (a troco de) in return for

medicação [medʒika'sãw] (pl -ões) f treatment; (medicamentos) medication

medicamento [medʒika'mẽtu] m medicine

medicina [medʒi'sina] f medicine

médico, -a [medʒiku, a] adj medical ♦ m/f doctor; **receita médica** prescription

medida [me'dʒida] f measure; (providência) step; (medição) measurement; (moderação) prudence; **à ~ que** while, as; **na ~ em que** in so far as; **feito sob ~** made to measure; **ir além da ~** to go too far; **tirar as ~s de alguém** to take sb's measurements; **tomar ~s** to take steps; **tomar as ~s de** to measure

medieval [medʒje'vaw] (pl -ais) adj medieval

médio, -a ['mɛdʒju, a] adj (dedo, classe) middle; (tamanho, estatura) medium; (mediano) average; **ensino ~** secondary education

medíocre [me'dʒiokri] adj mediocre

medir [me'dʒi*] vt to measure; (atos, palavras) to weigh; (avaliar: consequências, distâncias) to weigh up ♦ vi to measure; **quanto você mede?** – **meço 1,60 m** how tall are you? – I'm 1.60 m (tall)

meditar [medʒi'ta*] vi to meditate; **~ sobre algo** to ponder (on) sth

mediterrâneo, -a [medʒite'xanju, a] adj Mediterranean ♦ m: **o M~** the Mediterranean

medo ['medu] m fear; **com ~** afraid; **meter ~ em alguém** to frighten sb; **ter ~ de** to be afraid of

medonho, -a [me'doɲu, a] adj terrible, awful

medroso, -a [me'drozu, ɔza] adj (com medo) frightened; (tímido) timid

megabyte [mega'bajtʃi] m megabyte

meia ['meja] f stocking; (curta) sock; (meia-entrada) half-price ticket ♦ num six; **meia-idade** f middle age; **pessoa de meia-idade** middle-aged person; **meia-noite** f midnight

meigo, -a ['mejgu, a] adj sweet

meio, -a ['meju, a] adj half ♦ adv a bit, rather ♦ m middle; (social, profissional) milieu; (tb: ~ ambiente) environment; (maneira) way; (recursos: tb: ~s) means pl; **~ quilo** half a kilo; **um mês e ~** one and a half months; **cortar ao ~** to cut in half; **dividir algo ~ a ~** to divide sth in half ou fifty-fifty; **em ~ a** amid; **no ~ (de)** in the middle (of); **~s de comunicação (de massa)** (mass) media pl; **por ~ de** through; **meio-dia** m midday, noon; **meio-fio** m kerb (BRIT), curb (US); **meio-termo** (pl meios-termos) m (fig) compromise

mel [mɛw] m honey

melaço [me'lasu] m treacle (BRIT), molasses pl (US)

melancia [melã'sia] f watermelon

melancolia [melãko'lia] f melancholy, sadness; **melancólico, -a** [melã'kɔliku, a] adj melancholy, sad

melão [me'lãw] (pl -ões) m melon

melhor [me'ʎɔ*] adj, adv (compar)

better; (*superl*) best; ~ **que nunca**
better than ever; **quanto mais** ~ the
more the better; **seria** ~ **começar-**
mos we had better begin; **tanto** ~
so much the better; **ou** ~ ... (*ou*
antes) or rather ...; **melhora**
[me'ʎɔɾa] f improvement; **melho-**
ras! get well soon!; **melhorar**
[meʎo'ra*] vt to improve, make better; (*doente*) to cure ♦ vi to improve,
get better

melindroso, -a [meli'drozu, ɔza]
adj sensitive, touchy; (*problema,*
situação) tricky; (*operação*) delicate
melodia [melo'dʒia] f melody;
(*composição*) tune
melodrama [melo'drama] m melodrama
melões [me'lõjʃ] mpl de **melão**
melro ['mɛwxu] m blackbird
membro ['mẽbru] m member;
(*ANAT*: braço, perna) limb
memória [me'mɔrja] f memory; **~s**
fpl (*de autor*) memoirs; **de** ~ by
heart
memorizar [memori'za*] vt to
memorize
mencionar [mẽsjo'na*] vt to mention
mendigar [mẽdʒi'ga*] vt to beg
for ♦ vi to beg; **mendigo, -a**
[mẽ'dʒigu, a] m/f beggar
menina [me'nina] f: ~ **do olho**
pupil; **ser a** ~ **dos olhos de alguém**
(*fig*) to be the apple of sb's eye; *V tb*
menino
meninada [meni'nada] f kids *pl*
menino, -a [me'ninu, a] m/f boy/
girl
menopausa [meno'pawza] f menopause
menor [me'nɔ*] *adj* (*mais pequeno*:
compar) smaller; (: *superl*) smallest;
(*mais jovem*: *compar*) younger; (: *su-*
perl) youngest; (*o mínimo*) least,

slightest; (*tb*: ~ **de idade**) under age
♦ m/f juvenile, young person; (*JUR*)
minor; **não tenho a** ~ **idéia** I
haven't the slightest idea

PALAVRA CHAVE

menos ['menuʃ] *adj* **1** (*compar*): ~
(do que) (*quantidade*) less (than);
(*número*) fewer (than); **com** ~ **entu-**
siasmo with less enthusiasm; ~
gente fewer people
2 (*superl*) least; **é o que tem** ~ **culpa**
he is the least to blame
♦ *adv* **1** (*compar*): ~ **(do que)** less
(than); **gostei** ~ **do que do outro** I
liked it less than the other one
2 (*superl*): **é o** ~ **inteligente da**
classe he is the least bright in his
class; **de todas elas é a que** ~ **me**
agrada out of all of them she's the
one I like least; **pelo** ~ at the (very)
least
3 (*frases*): **temos sete a** ~ we are
seven short; **não é para** ~ it's no
wonder; **isso é o de** ~ that's nothing
♦ *prep* (*exceção*) except; (*números*)
minus; **todos** ~ **eu** everyone except
(for) me; **5** ~ **2** 5 minus 2
♦ *conj*: **a** ~ **que** unless; **a** ~ **que ele**
venha amanhã unless he comes
tomorrow
♦ *m*: **o** ~ the least

menosprezar [menuʃpre'za*] vt
(*subestimar*) to underrate; (*des-*
prezar) to despise, scorn
mensageiro, -a [mẽsa'ʒejru, a]
m/f messenger
mensagem [mẽ'saʒẽ] (*pl* **-ns**) f
message
mensal [mẽ'saw] (*pl* **-ais**) *adj*
monthly; **ele ganha £1000 mensais**
he earns £1000 a month; **mensa-**
lidade [mẽsali'dadʒi] f monthly

payment; **mensalmente** [mɛsaw-
'mɛtʃi] adv monthly

menstruação [mɛ̃trwa'sãw] f period; (MED) menstruation

menta ['mɛ̃ta] f mint

mental [mɛ̃'taw] (pl -ais) adj mental; **mentalidade** [mɛ̃tali'dadʒi] f
mentality

mente ['mɛ̃tʃi] f mind; **de boa ~**
willingly; **ter em ~** to bear in mind

mentir [mɛ̃'tʃi*] vi to lie

mentira [mɛ̃'tʃira] f lie; (ato) lying;
parece ~ que it seems incredible
that; **de ~** not for real; **!** (acusação)
that's a lie!, you're lying!; (de surpresa) you don't say!, no!; **mentiroso, -a** [mɛ̃tʃi'rozu, ɔza] adj
lying ♦ m/f liar

menu [me'nu] m (tb: COMPUT) menu

mercado [mex'kadu] m market;
M~ Comum Common Market; **~
negro ou paralelo** black market

mercadoria [mexkado'ria] f commodity; **~s** fpl (produtos) goods

mercearia [mexsja'ria] f grocer's
(shop) (BRIT), grocery store

mercúrio [mex'kurju] m mercury

merda ['mexda] (col!) f shit (!)
♦ m/f (pessoa) jerk; **a ~ do carro**
the bloody (BRIT) ou goddamn (US!) car

merecer [mere'se*] vt to deserve;
(consideração) to merit; (valer) to be
worth ♦ vi to be worthy; **merecido, -a** [mere'sidu, a] adj deserved;
(castigo, prêmio) just

merenda [me'rẽda] f packed lunch

merengue [me'rẽgi] m meringue

mergulhador, a [mexguʎa'do*, a]
m/f diver

mergulhar [mexgu'ʎa*] vi to dive;
(penetrar) to plunge ♦ vt: **~ algo em
algo** (num líquido) to dip sth into
sth; (na terra etc) to plunge sth
into sth; **mergulho** [mex'guʎu] m
dip(ping), immersion; (em natação)

dive; **dar um mergulho** (na praia)
to go for a dip

mérito ['mɛritu] m merit

mero, -a ['mɛru, a] adj mere

mês [meʃ] m month

mesa ['meza] f table; (de trabalho)
desk; (comitê) board; (numa reunião) panel; **pôr/tirar a ~** to lay/
clear the table; **à ~** at the table; **~ de
toalete** dressing table; **~ telefônica**
switchboard

mesada [me'zada] f monthly allowance; (de criança) pocket money

mesa-de-cabeceira (pl **mesas-
de-cabeceira**) f bedside table

mesmo, -a ['meʒmu, a] adj same;
(enfático) very ♦ adv (exatamente)
right; (até) even; (realmente) really
♦ m/f: **o, a mesma** the same
(one); **o ~ (a mesma coisa)** the same
(thing); **este ~ homem** this very
man; **ele ~ o fez** he did it himself;
dá no ~ ou na mesma it's all the
same; **aqui/agora/hoje ~** right
here/right now/this very day; **~ que**
even if; **é ~** it's true; **é ~?** really?; **(é)
isso ~!** exactly!; **por isso ~** that's
why; **nem ~** not even; **só ~** only;
por si ~ by oneself

mesquinho, -a [meʃ'kiɲu, a] adj
mean

mesquita [meʃ'kita] f mosque

mestiço, -a [meʃ'tʃisu, a] adj half-
caste, of mixed race; (animal) crossbred ♦ m/f half-caste; crossbred

mestre, -a ['mɛʃtri, a] adj (chave,
viga) master; (linha, estrada) main
♦ m/f master/mistress; (professor)
teacher; **obra mestra** masterpiece

meta ['mɛta] f (em corrida) finishing
post; (gol) goal; (objetivo) aim

metade [me'tadʒi] f half; (meio)
middle

metáfora [me'tafora] f metaphor

metal [me'taw] (pl -ais) m metal

metais *mpl* (MÚS) brass *sg*; **metáli-co, -a** [me'taliku, a] *adj* metallic; (*de metal*) metal *atr*

metalúrgico, -a [meta'luxʒiku, a] *m/f* metalworker

meteorologia [meteorolo'ʒia] *f* meteorology; **meteorologista** [meteorolo'ʒiʃta] *m/f* meteorologist; (TV, RÁDIO) weather forecaster

meter [me'te*] *vt* (*colocar*) to put; (*envolver*) to involve; (*introduzir*) to introduce; **meter-se** (*esconder-se*) to hide; ~**se a fazer algo** to decide to have a go at sth; ~**se com** (*provocar*) to pick a quarrel with; (*associar-se*) to get involved with; ~**se em** to get involved in; (*intrometer-se*) to interfere in

meticuloso, -a [metʃiku'lozu, ɔza] *adj* meticulous

metido, -a [me'tʃidu, a] *adj* (*envolvido*) involved; (*intrometido*) med-dling; ~ **(a besta)** snobbish

metódico, -a [me'tɔdʒiku, a] *adj* methodical

método ['metodu] *m* method

metralhadora [metraʎa'dora] *f* sub-machine gun

métrico, -a ['metriku, a] *adj* metric

metro ['metru] *m* metre (BRIT), meter (US); (PT) = **metrô**

metrô [me'tro] (BR) *m* underground (BRIT), subway (US)

metrópole [me'trɔpoli] *f* metropolis; (*capital*) capital

meu, minha [mew, 'miɲa] *adj* my ♦ *pron* mine; **os** ~**s** *mpl* (*minha família*) my family ou folks (col); **um amigo** ~ a friend of mine

mexer [me'ʃe*] *vt* to move; (*cabeça: dizendo sim*) to nod; (: *dizendo não*) to shake; (*misturar*) to stir; (*ovos*) to scramble ♦ *vi* to move; **mexer-se** *vr* to move; (*apressar-se*) to get a move on; ~ **em algo** to touch sth;

mexa-se! get going!, move your-self!

mexerico [meʃe'riku] *m* piece of gossip; ~**s** *mpl* (*fofocas*) gossip *sg*

México ['mɛʃiku] *m*: **o** ~ Mexico

mexido, -a [me'ʃidu, a] *adj* (*papéis*) mixed up; (*ovos*) scrambled

mexilhão [meʃi'ʎãw] (*pl* -ões) *m* mussel

mi [mi] *m* (MÚS) E

miar [mja*] *vi* to miaow; (*vento*) to whistle

miau [mjaw] *m* miaow

micro... [mikru] *prefixo* micro...;

micro(computador) [mikro(kõputa'do*)] *m* micro(computer);

microfone [mikro'fɔni] *m* microphone; **microondas** [mikro'õdaʒ] *m inv* (tb: **forno de microondas**) microwave (oven); **microprocessador** [mikroprosesa'do*] *m* microprocessor; **microscópio** [mikro'ʃkɔpju] *m* microscope

mídia ['midʒja] *f* media *pl*

migalha [mi'gaʎa] *f* crumb; ~**s** *fpl* (*restos, sobras*) scraps

migrar [mi'gra*] *vi* to migrate

mijar [mi'ʒa*] (*col*) *vi* to pee; **mijar-se** *vr* to wet o.s

mil [miw] *num* thousand; **dois** ~ two thousand

milagre [mi'lagri] *m* miracle; **por** ~ miraculously; **milagroso, -a** [mila-'grozu, ɔza] *adj* miraculous

milhão [mi'ʎãw] (*pl* -ões) *m* million; **um** ~ **de vezes** hundreds of times

milhar [mi'ʎa*] *m* thousand; **turis-tas aos** ~**es** tourists in their thousands

milho ['miʎu] *m* maize (BRIT), corn (US)

milhões [mi'ʎõjʃ] *mpl* de **milhão**

miligrama [mili'grama] *m* milli-gram(me)

milionário, -a [miljo'narju, a] *m/f* millionaire

militante [mili'tãtʃi] *adj* militant ♦ *m/f* activist; (*extremista*) militant

militar [mili'ta*] *adj* military ♦ *m* soldier ♦ *vi* to fight; **~ em** (MIL: *regimento*) to serve in; (POL: *partido*) to belong to, to be active in; (*profissão*) to work in

mim [mĩ] *pron* me; (*reflexivo*) myself; **de ~ para ~** to myself

mimar [mi'ma*] *vt* to pamper, spoil

mímica ['mimika] *f* mime

mimo ['mimu] *m* gift; (*pessoa, coisa encantadora*) delight; (*carinho*) tenderness; (*gentileza*) kindness; **cheio de ~s** (*criança*) spoiled, spoilt (BRIT)

mimoso, -a [mi'mozu, ɔza] *adj* (*delicado*) delicate; (*carinhoso*) tender, loving; (*encantador*) delightful

mina ['mina] *f* mine

mindinho [mĩ'dʒiɲu] *m* (*tb*: **dedo ~**) little finger

mineiro, -a [mi'nejru, a] *adj* mining *atr* ♦ *m/f* miner

mineral [mine'raw] (*pl* **-ais**) *adj, m* mineral

minério [mi'nɛrju] *m* ore

míngua ['mĩgwa] *f* lack; **à ~ de** for want of; **viver à ~** to live in poverty; **minguado, -a** [mĩ'gwadu, a] *adj* scant; (*criança*) stunted; **minguado de algo** short of sth

minguar [mĩ'gwa*] *vi* (*diminuir*) to decrease, dwindle; (*faltar*) to run short

minha ['miɲa] *f de* **meu**

minhoca [mi'nɔka] *f* (earth)worm

mini... [mini] *prefixo* mini...

miniatura [minja'tura] *adj, f* miniature

MiniDisc [mini'dʒiʃki] ® *m* MiniDisc ®

mínima ['minima] *f* (*temperatura*) low; (MÚS) minim

mínimo, -a ['minimu, a] *adj* minimum ♦ *m* minimum; (*tb*: **dedo ~**) little finger; **não dou ou ligo a mínima para isso** I couldn't care less about it; **a mínima importância/idéia** the slightest importance/idea; **no ~** at least

minissaia [mini'saja] *f* miniskirt

ministério [minif'tɛrju] *m* ministry; **~ da Fazenda** ≈ Treasury (BRIT), ≈ Treasury Department (US); **M~ das Relações Exteriores** ≈ Foreign Office (BRIT), ≈ State Department (US)

ministro, -a [mi'niʃtru, a] *m/f* minister

minoria [mino'ria] *f* minority

minto *etc* ['mĩtu] *vb* V **mentir**

minucioso, -a [minu'sjozu, ɔza] *adj* (*indivíduo, busca*) thorough; (*explicação*) detailed

minúsculo, -a [mi'nuʃkulu, a] *adj* minute, tiny; **letra minúscula** lower case

minuta [mi'nuta] *f* rough draft

minuto [mi'nutu] *m* minute

miolo ['mjolu] *m* inside; (*polpa*) pulp; (*de maçã*) core; **~s** *mpl* (*cérebro, inteligência*) brains

míope ['miopi] *adj* short-sighted

mira ['mira] *f* (*de fuzil*) sight; (*pontaria*) aim; (*fig*) aim, purpose; **à ~ de** on the lookout for; **ter em ~** to have one's eye on

miragem [mi'raʒẽ] (*pl* **-ns**) *f* mirage

miscelânea [mise'lanja] *f* miscellany; (*confusão*) muddle

miserável [mize'ravew] (*pl* **-eis**) *adj* (*digno de compaixão*) wretched; (*pobre*) impoverished; (*avaro*) stingy, mean; (*insignificante*) paltry; (*lugar*) squalid; (*infame*) despicable ♦ *m* wretch; (*coitado*) poor thing; (*pessoa infame*) rotter

miséria [mi'zɛrja] f misery; (*pobreza*) poverty; (*avareza*) stinginess

misericórdia [mizeri'kɔxdʒja] f (*compaixão*) pity, compassion; (*graça*) mercy

missa ['misa] f (REL) mass

missão [mi'sãw] (pl -ões) f mission; (*dever*) duty

míssil ['misiw] (pl -eis) m missile

missionário, -a [misjo'narju, a] m/f missionary

missões [mi'sõjʃ] fpl de **missão**

mistério [miʃ'tɛrju] m mystery; **misterioso, -a** [miʃte'rjozu, ɔza] adj mysterious

mistificar [miʃtʃifi'ka*] vt, vi to fool

misto, -a ['miʃtu, ·a] adj mixed; (*confuso*) mixed up ♦ m mixture; **misto-quente** (pl **mistos-quentes**) m toasted cheese and ham sandwich

mistura [miʃ'tura] f mixture; (*ato*) mixing; **misturar** [miʃtu'ra*] vt to mix; (*confundir*) to mix up; **misturar-se** vr: **~-se com** to mingle with

mitigar [mitʃi'ga*] vt (*raiva*) to temper; (*dor*) to relieve; (*sede*) to lessen

mito ['mitu] m myth

miudezas [mju'dezaʃ] fpl minutiae; (*bugigangas*) odds and ends; (*objetos pequenos*) trinkets

miúdo, -a ['mjudu, a] adj tiny, minute ♦ m/f (PT: *criança*) youngster, kid; **~s** mpl (*dinheiro*) change sg; (*de aves*) giblets; **dinheiro ~** small change

mm abr (= *milímetro*) mm

mo [mu] pron = **me** + **o**

moa etc ['moa] vb V **moer**

móbil ['mɔbiw] (pl -eis) adj = **móvel**

móbile ['mɔbili] m mobile

mobília [mo'bilja] f furniture; **mobiliar** [mobi'lja*] (BR) vt to furnish; **mobiliário** [mobi'ljarju] m furnishings pl

moça ['mosa] f girl, young woman

Moçambique [mosã'biki] m Mozambique

moção [mo'sãw] (pl -ões) f motion

mochila [mo'ʃila] f rucksack

mocidade [mosi'dadʒi] f youth; (*os moços*) young people pl

moço, -a ['mosu, a] adj young ♦ m young man, lad

moções [mo'sõjʃ] fpl de **moção**

moda ['mɔda] f fashion; **estar na ~** to be in fashion, be all the rage; **fora da ~** old-fashioned; **sair da** ou **cair de ~** to go out of fashion

modalidade [modali'dadʒi] f kind; (*ESPORTE*) event

modelo [mo'delu] m model; (*criação de estilista*) design

moderado, -a [mode'radu, a] adj moderate; (*clima*) mild

moderar [mode'ra*] vt to moderate; (*violência*) to control, restrain; (*velocidade*) to reduce; (*voz*) to lower; (*gastos*) to cut down

modernizar [modexni'za*] vt to modernize; **modernizar-se** vr to modernize

moderno, -a [mo'dɛxnu, a] adj modern; (*atual*) present-day

modéstia [mo'deʃtʃja] f modesty

modesto, -a [mo'deʃtu, a] adj modest; (*simples*) simple, plain; (*vida*) frugal

módico, -a ['mɔdʒiku, a] adj moderate; (*preço*) reasonable; (*bens*) scant

modificar [modʒifi'ka*] vt to modify, alter

modista [mo'dʒiʃta] f dressmaker

modo ['mɔdu] m (*maneira*) way, manner; (*método*) way; (*MÚS*) mode; **~s** mpl (*comportamento*) manners; **de (tal) ~ que** so (that); **de ~ nenhum** in no way; **de qualquer ~**

anyway, anyhow; **~ de emprego** instructions *pl* for use

módulo [ˈmɔdulu] *m* module

moeda [ˈmwɛda] *f* (*uma ~*) coin; (*dinheiro*) currency; **uma ~ de 10p** a 10p piece; **~ corrente** currency; **Casa da M~** ≈ the Mint (*BRIT*), ≈ the (*US*) Mint

moedor [moeˈdo*] *m* (*de café*) grinder; (*de carne*) mincer

moer [mwe*] *vt* (*café*) to grind; (*cana*) to crush

mofado, -a [moˈfadu, a] *adj* mouldy (*BRIT*), moldy (*US*)

mofo [ˈmofu] *m* (*BOT*) mo(u)ld; **cheiro de ~** musty smell

mogno [ˈmɔgnu] *m* mahogany

mói *etc* [mɔj] *vb V* **moer**

moía *etc* [moˈia] *vb V* **moer**

moído, -a [moˈidu, a] *adj* (*café*) ground; (*carne*) minced; (*cansado*) tired out; (*corpo*) aching

moinho [moˈiɲu] *m* mill; (*de café*) grinder; **~ de vento** windmill

mola [ˈmɔla] *f* (*TEC*) spring; (*fig*) motive, motivation

moldar [mowˈda*] *vt* to mould (*BRIT*), mold (*US*); (*metal*) to cast; **molde** [ˈmɔwdʒi] *m* mo(u)ld; (*de papel*) pattern; (*fig*) model; **molde de vestido** dress pattern

moldura [mowˈdura] *f* (*de pintura*) frame

mole [ˈmɔli] *adj* soft; (*sem vigor*) listless; (*carnes*) flabby; (*col: fácil*) easy; (*lento*) slow; (*preguiçoso*) sluggish ♦ *adv* (*lentamente*) slowly

moleque [moˈlɛki] *m* (*de rua*) urchin; (*menino*) youngster; (*pessoa sem palavra*) unreliable person; (*canalha*) scoundrel ♦ *adj* (*levado*) mischievous; (*brincalhão*) funny

molestar [moleʃˈta*] *vt* to upset; (*enfadar*) to annoy; (*importunar*) to bother

moléstia [moˈlɛʃtʃa] *f* illness

moleza [moˈleza] *f* softness; (*falta de energia*) listlessness; (*falta de força*) weakness; **ser (uma) ~** (*col*) to be easy; **na ~** without exerting oneself

molhado, -a [moˈʎadu, a] *adj* wet, damp

molhar [moˈʎa*] *vt* to wet; (*de leve*) to moisten, dampen; (*mergulhar*) to dip; **molhar-se** *vr* to get wet

molho¹ [ˈmɔʎu] *m* (*de chaves*) bunch; (*de trigo*) sheaf

molho² [ˈmoʎu] *m* (*CULIN*) sauce; (: *de salada*) dressing; (: *de carne*) gravy; **pôr de ~** to soak; **estar/ deixar de ~** (*roupa etc*) to be/leave to soak

momentâneo, -a [momẽˈtanju, a] *adj* momentary

momento [moˈmẽtu] *m* moment; (*TEC*) momentum; **a todo ~** constantly; **de um ~ para outro** suddenly; **no ~ em que** just as

Mônaco [ˈmonaku] *m* Monaco

monarquia [monaxˈkia] *f* monarchy

monitor [moniˈto*] *m* monitor

monopólio [monoˈpɔlju] *m* monopoly; **monopolizar** [monopoliˈza*] *vt* to monopolize

monotonia [monotoˈnia] *f* monotony; **monótono, -a** [moˈnɔtonu, a] *adj* monotonous

monstro, -a [ˈmõʃtru, a] *adj inv* giant ♦ *m* (*tb fig*) monster; **monstruoso, -a** [mõʃtruˈozu, ɔza] *adj* monstrous; (*enorme*) gigantic, huge

montagem [mõˈtaʒẽ] (*pl* **-ns**) *f* assembly; (*ARQ*) erection; (*CINEMA*) editing; (*TEATRO*) production

montanha [mõˈtaɲa] *f* mountain; **montanha-russa** *f* roller coaster

montante [mõˈtãtʃi] *m* amount, sum; **a ~** (*nadar*) upstream

montar [mõ'ta*] *vt* (*cavalo*) to mount, get on; (*colocar em*) to put on; (*cavalgar*) to ride; (*peças*) to assemble, put together; (*loja, máquina*) to set up; (*casa*) to put up; (*peça teatral*) to put on ♦ *vi* to ride; **~ a** ou **em** (*animal*) to get on; (*cavalgar*) to ride; (*despesa*) to come to

monte ['mõtʃi] *m* hill; (*pilha*) heap, pile; **um ~ de** (*muitos*) a lot of, lots of; **gente aos ~s** loads of people

montra ['mõtra] (*PT*) *f* shop window

monumental [monumẽ'taw] (*pl* **-ais**) *adj* monumental; (*fig*) magnificent, splendid

monumento [monu'mẽtu] *m* monument

moqueca [mo'kɛka] *f* fish or seafood simmered in coconut cream and palm oil; **~ de camarão** prawn *moqueca*

morada [mo'rada] *f* home, residence; (*PT*: *endereço*) address; **moradia** [mora'dʒia] *f* home, dwelling; **morador, a** [mora'do*, a] *m/f* resident; (*de casa alugada*) tenant

moral [mo'raw] (*pl* **-ais**) *adj* moral ♦ *f* (*ética*) ethics *pl*; (*conclusão*) moral ♦ *m* (*de pessoa*) sense of morality; (*ânimo*) morale; **moralidade** [morali'dadʒi] *f* morality

morango [mo'rãgu] *m* strawberry

morar [mo'ra*] *vi* to live, reside

mórbido, -a ['mɔxbidu, a] *adj* morbid

morcego [mox'segu] *m* (*BIO*) bat

mordaça [mox'dasa] *f* (*de animal*) muzzle; (*fig*) gag

mordaz [mox'daʒ] *adj* scathing

morder [mox'de*] *vt* to bite; (*corroer*) to corrode; **mordida** [mox-'dʒida] *f* bite

mordomia [moxdo'mia] *f* (*de executivos*) perk; (*col*: *regalia*) luxury, comfort

mordomo [mox'dɔmu] *m* butler

moreno, -a [mo'renu, a] *adj* dark(-skinned); (*de cabelos*) dark(-haired); (*de tomar sol*) brown ♦ *m/f* dark person

mormaço [mox'masu] *m* sultry weather

morno, -a ['moxnu, 'mɔxna] *adj* lukewarm, tepid

morrer [mox'xe*] *vi* to die; (*luz, cor*) to fade; (*fogo*) to die down; (*AUTO*) to stall

morro ['moxu] *m* hill; (*favela*) slum

mortadela [moxta'dɛla] *f* salami

mortal [mox'taw] (*pl* **-ais**) *adj* mortal; (*letal, insuportável*) deadly ♦ *m* mortal

mortalidade [moxtali'dadʒi] *f* mortality

morte ['mɔxtʃi] *f* death

mortífero, -a [mox'tʃiferu, a] *adj* deadly, lethal

morto, -a ['moxtu, 'mɔxta] *pp de* **matar** ♦ *pp de* **morrer** ♦ *adj* dead; (*cor*) dull; (*exausto*) exhausted; (*inexpressivo*) lifeless ♦ *m/f* dead man/woman; **estar/ser ~** to be dead/killed; **estar ~ de inveja** to be green with envy; **estar ~ de vontade de** to be dying to

mos [muʃ] *pron* = **me** + **os**

mosca ['mɔʃka] *f* fly; **estar às ~s** (*bar etc*) to be deserted

Moscou [moʃ'ku] (*BR*) *n* Moscow

Moscovo [moʃ'kovu] (*PT*) *n* Moscow

mosquito [moʃ'kitu] *m* mosquito

mostarda [moʃ'taxda] *f* mustard

mosteiro [moʃ'tejru] *m* monastery; (*de monjas*) convent

mostrador [moʃtra'do*] *m* (*de relógio*) face, dial

mostrar [moʃ'tra*] *vt* to show; (*mercadorias*) to display; (*provar*) to demonstrate, prove; **mostrar-se** vr to show o.s. to be; (exibir-se) to show off

motel [mo'tɛw] (pl **-éis**) m motel

motivar [motʃi'va*] vt (causar) to cause, bring about; (estimular) to motivate; **motivo** [mo'tʃivu] m (causa): **motivo (de ou para)** cause (of), reason (for); (fim) motive; (ARTE, MÚS) motif; **por motivo de** because of, owing to

moto ['mɔtu] f motorbike ♦ m (lema) motto

motocicleta [motosi'klɛta] f motorcycle, motorbike

motociclista [motosi'kliʃta] m/f motorcyclist

motociclo [moto'siklu] (PT) m = **motocicleta**

motor, motriz [mo'to*, mo'triʒ] adj: **força motriz** driving force ♦ m motor; (de carro, avião) engine; ~ **diesel/de explosão** diesel/internal combustion engine

motorista [moto'riʃta] m/f driver

móvel ['mɔvew] (pl **-eis**) adj movable ♦ m piece of furniture; **móveis** mpl (mobília) furniture sg

mover [mo've*] vt to move; (cabeça) to shake; (mecanismo) to drive; (campanha) to start (up); **mover-se** vr to move

movimentado, -a [movimē'tadu, a] adj (rua, lugar) busy; (pessoa) active; (show, música) up-tempo

movimentar [movimē'ta*] vt to move; (animar) to liven up

movimento [movi'mētu] m movement; (TEC) motion; (na rua) activity, bustle; **de muito** ~ busy

muamba ['mwãba] (col) f (contrabando) contraband; (objetos roubados) loot

muçulmano, -a [musuw'manu, a] adj, m/f Moslem

muda ['muda] f (planta) seedling; (vestuário) outfit; ~ **de roupa** change of clothes

mudança [mu'dãsa] f change; (de casa) move; (AUTO) gear

mudar [mu'da*] vt to change; (deslocar) to move ♦ vi to change; (ave) to moult (BRIT), molt (US); **mudar-se** vr (de casa) to move (away); ~ **de roupa/de assunto** to change clothes/the subject; ~ **de casa** to move (house); ~ **de idéia** to change one's mind

mudez [mu'deʒ] f muteness; (silêncio) silence

mudo, -a ['mudu, a] adj dumb; (calado, CINEMA) silent; (telefone) dead ♦ m/f mute

_____ PALAVRA CHAVE _____

muito, -a ['mũjtu, a] adj (quantidade) a lot of; (: em frase negativa ou interrogativa) much; (número) lots of, a lot of; many; ~ **esforço** a lot of effort; **faz** ~ **calor** it's very hot; ~ **tempo** a long time; **muitas amigas** lots ou a lot of friends; **muitas vezes** often

♦ pron a lot; (em frase negativa ou interrogativa: sg) much; (: pl) many; **tenho** ~ **que fazer** I've got a lot to do; ~**s dizem que** ... a lot of people say that ...

♦ adv 1 a lot; (+ adj) very; (+ comparar): ~ **melhor** much ou far ou a lot better; **gosto** ~ **disto** I like it a lot; **sinto** ~ I'm very sorry; ~ **interessante** very interesting

2 (resposta) very; **está cansado?** – ~ are you tired? – very

3 (tempo): ~ **depois** long after; **há** ~ a long time ago; **não demorou** ~ it didn't take long

mula ['mula] f mule

mulato, -a [ɪnuˈlatu, a] *adj, m/f* mulatto

muleta [muˈleta] *f* crutch; *(fig)* support

mulher [muˈʎe*] *f* woman; *(esposa)* wife

multa [ˈmuwta] *f* fine; **levar uma ~** to be fined; **multar** [muwˈta*] *vt* to fine; **multar alguém em $1000** to fine sb $1000

multi... [muwtʃi] *prefixo* multi...

multidão [muwtʃiˈdãw] *(pl* -ões) *f* crowd; **uma ~ de** *(muitos)* lots of

multimídia [muwtʃiˈmidʒja] *adj* multimedia

multinacional [muwtʃinasjoˈnaw] *(pl* -ais) *adj, f* multinational

multiplicar [muwtʃipliˈka*] *vt* to multiply; *(aumentar)* to increase

múltiplo, -a [ˈmuwtʃiplu, a] *adj* multiple ♦ *m* multiple

múmia [ˈmumja] *f* mummy

mundial [mũˈdʒjaw] *(pl* -ais) *adj* worldwide; *(guerra, recorde)* world *atr* ♦ *m* world championship

mundo [ˈmũdu] *m* world; **todo o ~** everybody; **um ~ de** lots of, a great many

munição [muniˈsãw] *(pl* -ões) *f (de armas)* ammunition; *(chumbo)* shot; *(MIL)* munitions *pl*, supplies *pl*

municipal [munisiˈpaw] *(pl* -ais) *adj* municipal

município [muniˈsipju] *m* local authority; *(cidade)* town; *(condado)* county

munições [muniˈsõjʃ] *fpl de* munição

munir [muˈni*] *vt*: **~ de** to provide with, supply with; **munir-se** *vr*: **~-se de** *(provisões)* to equip o.s. with

muralha [muˈraʎa] *f (de fortaleza)* rampart; *(muro)* wall

murchar [muxˈʃa*] *vt (BOT)* to wither; *(sentimentos)* to dull; *(pessoa)* to

sadden ♦ *vi* to wither, wilt; *(fig)* to fade

murmurar [muxmuˈra*] *vi* to murmur, whisper; *(queixar-se)* to mutter, grumble; *(água)* to ripple; *(folhagem)* to rustle ♦ *vt* to murmur;

murmúrio [muxˈmurju] *m* murmuring, whispering; grumbling; rippling; rustling

muro [ˈmuru] *m* wall

murro [ˈmuxu] *m* punch; **dar um ~ em alguém** to punch sb

musa [ˈmuza] *f* muse

musculação [muʃkulaˈsãw] *f* body-building

músculo [ˈmuʃkulu] *m* muscle; **musculoso, -a** [muʃkuˈlozu, ɔza] *adj* muscular

museu [muˈzew] *m* museum; *(de pintura)* gallery

musgo [ˈmuʒgu] *m* moss

música [ˈmuzika] *f* music; *(canção)* song; **músico, -a** [ˈmuziku, a] *adj* musical ♦ *m/f* musician

mutilar [mutʃiˈla*] *vt* to mutilate; *(pessoa)* to maim; *(texto)* to cut

mútuo, -a [ˈmutwu, a] *adj* mutual

N

N *abr* (= *norte*) N

na [na] = **em + a**

-na [na] *pron* her; *(coisa)* it

nabo [ˈnabu] *m* turnip

nação [naˈsãw] *(pl* -ões) *f* nation

nacional [nasjoˈnaw] *(pl* -ais) *adj* national; *(carro, vinho etc)* domestic, home-produced; **nacionalidade** [nasjonaliˈdadʒi] *f* nationality; **nacionalismo** [nasjonaˈliʒmu] *m* nationalism; **nacionalista** [nasjonaˈliʃta] *adj, m/f* nationalist

nações [naˈsõjʃ] *fpl de* nação

nada [ˈnada] *pron* nothing ♦ *adv* at

all; **antes de mais** ~ first of all; **não é ~ difícil** it's not at all hard, it's not hard at all; ~ **mais** nothing else; ~ **de novo** nothing new; **obrigado – de** ~ thank you – not at all *ou* don't mention it

nadador, a [nada'do*, a] *m/f* swimmer

nadar [na'da*] *vi* to swim

nádegas ['nadegaʃ] *fpl* buttocks

nado ['nadu] *m*: **atravessar a** ~ to swim across; ~ **borboleta/de costas/de peito** butterfly (stroke)/backstroke/breaststroke

naipe ['najpi] *m* (*cartas*) suit

namorado, -a [namo'radu, a] *m/f* boyfriend/girlfriend

namorar [namo'ra*] *vt* (*ser namorado de*) to be going out with

namoro [na'moru] *m* relationship

não [nãw] *adv* not; (*resposta*) no ♦ *m* no; ~ **sei** I don't know; ~ **muito** not much; ~ **só ... mas também** not only ... but also; **agora** ~ not now; ~ **tem de quê** don't mention it; ~ **é?** isn't it?, won't you? (*etc, segundo o verbo precedente*); **eles são brasileiros, ~ é?** they're Brazilian, aren't they?

não– [nãw–] *prefixo* non-

naquele(s), -a(s) [na'keli(ʃ), na'kela(ʃ)] = **em** + **aquele(s), a(s)**

naquilo [na'kilu] = **em** + **aquilo**

narcótico, -a [nax'kɔtʃiku, a] *adj* narcotic ♦ *m* narcotic

narina [na'rina] *f* nostril

nariz [na'riʒ] *m* nose

narração [naxa'sãw] (*pl* -ões) *f* narration; (*relato*) account

narrar [na'xa*] *vt* to narrate

narrativa [naxa'tʃiva] *f* narrative; (*história*) story

nas [naʃ] = **em** + **as**

-nas [naʃ] *pron* them

nascença [na'sẽsa] *f* birth; **de** ~ by

birth; **ele é surdo de** ~ he was born deaf

nascente [na'sẽtʃi] *m*: **o** ~ the East, the Orient ♦ *f* (*fonte*) spring

nascer [na'se*] *vi* to be born; (*plantas*) to sprout; (*o sol*) to rise; (*ave*) to hatch; (*fig: ter origem*) to come into being ♦ *m*: ~ **do sol** sunrise; **ele nasceu para médico** *etc* he's a born doctor *etc*; **nascimento** [nasi'mẽtu] *m* birth; (*fig*) origin; (*estirpe*) descent

nata ['nata] *f* cream

natação [nata'sãw] *f* swimming

natais [na'tajʃ] *adj pl de* **natal**

Natal [na'taw] *m* Christmas; **Feliz** ~! Merry Christmas!

natal [na'taw] (*pl* -ais) *adj* (*relativo ao nascimento*) natal; (*país*) native; **cidade** ~ home town

natalino, -a [nata'linu, a] *adj* Christmas *atr*

nativo, -a [na'tʃivu, a] *adj, m/f* native

natural [natu'raw] (*pl* -ais) *adj* natural; (*nativo*) native ♦ *m/f* native; **ão** ~ (*CULIN*) fresh, uncooked; **naturalidade** [naturali'dadʒi] *f* naturalness; **de naturalidade paulista** *etc* born in São Paulo *etc*; **naturalizar** [naturali'za*] *vt* to naturalize; **naturalizar-se** *vr* to become naturalized; **naturalmente** [naturaw'mẽtʃi] *adv* naturally; **naturalmente!** of course!

natureza [natu'reza] *f* nature; (*espécie*) kind, type

nau [naw] *f* (*literário*) ship

naufrágio [naw'fraʒu] *m* shipwreck; **náufrago, -a** ['nawfragu, a] *m/f* castaway

náusea ['nawzea] *f* nausea; **dar ~s a alguém** to make sb feel sick; **sentir ~s** to feel sick

náutico, -a ['nawtʃiku, a] *adj*

nautical
naval [na'vaw] (*pl* **-ais**) *adj* naval;
construção ~ shipbuilding
navalha [na'vaʎa] *f* (*de barba*)
razor; (*faca*) knife
nave ['navi] *f* (*de igreja*) nave
navegação [navega'sãw] *f* navigation, sailing; **~ aérea** air traffic;
companhia de ~ shipping line
navegar [nave'ga*] *vt* to navigate;
(*mares*) to sail ♦ *vi* to sail; (*dirigir o
rumo*) to navigate
navio [na'viu] *m* ship; **~ aeródro-
mo/cargueiro/petroleiro** aircraft
carrier/cargo ship/oil tanker; **~ de
guerra** (*BR*) battleship
nazi [na'zi] (*PT*) *adj, m/f* = **nazista**
nazista [na'ziʃta] *adj, m/f* Nazi
NB *abr* (= *note bem*) NB
neblina [ne'blina] *f* fog, mist
nebuloso, -a [nebu'lozu, ɔza] *adj*
foggy, misty; (*céu*) cloudy; (*fig*)
vague
necessário, -a [nese'sarju, a] *adj*
necessary ♦ *m*: **o ~** the necessities *pl*
necessidade [nesesi'dadʒi] *f* need,
necessity; (*o que se necessita*) need;
(*pobreza*) poverty, need; **ter ~ de** to
need; **em caso de ~** if need be
necessitado, -a [nesesi'tadu, a]
adj needy, poor; **~ de** in need of
necessitar [nesesi'ta*] *vt* to need,
require ♦ *vi*: **~ de** to need
neerlandês, -esa [neexlã'deʃ, eza]
adj Dutch ♦ *m/f* Dutchman/woman
Neerlândia [neex'lãdʒa] *f* the
Netherlands *pl*
negar [ne'ga*] *vt* to deny; (*recusar*)
to refuse; **negar-se** *vr*: **~-se a** to
refuse to
negativa [nega'tʃiva] *f* negative;
(*recusa*) denial
negativo, -a [nega'tʃivu, a] *adj*
negative ♦ *m* (*TEC*, *FOTO*) negative
♦ *excl* (*col*) nope!

negligência [negli'ʒẽsja] *f* negligence, carelessness; **negligente**
[negli'ʒẽtʃi] *adj* negligent, careless
negociação [negosja'sãw] (*pl*
-ões) *f* negotiation
negociante [negosja'tʃi] *m/f*
businessman/woman
negociar [nego'sja*] *vt* to negotiate; (*COM*) to trade ♦ *vi*: **~ (com)** to
trade ou deal (in); to negotiate
(with)
negócio [ne'gɔsju] *m* (*COM*) business; (*transação*) deal; (*questão*)
matter; (*col*: *troço*) thing; (*assunto*) affair, business; **homem de ~s**
businessman; **a ~s** on business;
fechar um ~ to make a deal
negro, -a ['negru, a] *adj* black;
(*raça*) Black; (*fig*: *lúgubre*) black,
gloomy ♦ *m/f* Black man/woman
nele(s), -a(s) ['neli(ʃ), 'nɛla(ʃ)] =
em + ele(s), ela(s)
nem [nẽj] *conj* nor, neither; **~
(sequer)** not even; **~ que** even if; **~
bem** hardly; **~ um só** not a single
one; **~ estuda ~ trabalha** he neither
studies nor works; **~ eu** nor me;
sem ~ without even; **~ todos** not
all; **~ tanto** not so much; **~ sempre**
not always
nenê [ne'ne] *m/f* baby
neném [ne'nẽj] (*pl* **-ns**) *m/f* = **nenê**
nenhum, a [ne'nũ, 'numa] *adj* no,
not any ♦ *pron* (*nem um só*) none,
not one; (*de dois*) neither; **~ lugar**
nowhere
neozelandês, -esa [neozelã'deʃ,
deza] *adj* New Zealand *atr* ♦ *m/f*
New Zealander
nervo ['nexvu] *m* (*ANAT*) nerve; (*fig*)
energy, strength; (*em carne*) sinew;
nervosismo [nexvo'ziʒmu] *m* (*ner-
vosidade*) nervousness; (*irritabili-
dade*) irritability; **nervoso, -a** [nex
'vozu, ɔza] *adj* nervous; (*irritável*)

touchy, on edge; (*exaltado*) worked up; **ele me deixa nervoso** he gets on my nerves

nesse(s), -a(s) ['nesi(ʃ), 'nɛsa(ʃ)] = em + esse(s), -a(s)

neste(s), -a(s) ['neʃti(ʃ), 'nɛʃta(ʃ)] = em + este(s), -a(s)

neto, -a ['nɛtu, a] *m/f* grandson/daughter; **~s** *mpl* grandchildren

neurose [new'rɔzi] *f* neurosis

neurótico, -a [new'rɔtʃiku, a] *adj, m/f* neurotic

neutralizar [newtrali'za*] *vt* to neutralize; (*anular*) to counteract

neutro, -a ['newtru, a] *adj* (LING) neuter; (*imparcial*) neutral

nevar [ne'va*] *vi* to snow; **nevasca** [ne'vaʃka] *f* snowstorm; **neve** ['nɛvi] *f* snow

névoa ['nevoa] *f* fog; **nevoeiro** [nevo'ejru] *m* thick fog

nexo ['nɛksu] *m* connection, link; **sem ~** disconnected, incoherent

Nicarágua [nika'ragwa] *f*: **a ~** Nicaragua

nicotina [niko'tʃina] *f* nicotine

Nigéria [ni'ʒɛrja] *f*: **a ~** Nigeria

Nilo ['nilu] *m*: **o ~** the Nile

ninguém [nĩ'gẽj] *pron* nobody, no-one

ninho ['niɲu] *m* nest; (*toca*) lair; (*lar*) home

nisso ['nisu] = em + isso

nisto ['niʃtu] = em + isto

nitidez [nitʃi'deʒ] *f* (*clareza*) clarity; (*brilho*) brightness; (*imagem*) sharpness

nítido, -a ['nitʃidu, a] *adj* clear, distinct; (*brilhante*) bright; (*imagem*) sharp, clear

nível ['nivew] (*pl* -eis) *m* level; (*fig*: *padrão*) standard; (: *ponto*) point, pitch; **~ de vida** standard of living

no [nu] = em + o

-no [nu] *pron* him; (*coisa*) it

n° *abr* (= *número*) no

nó [nɔ] *m* knot; (*de uma questão*) crux; **~s dos dedos** knuckles; **dar um ~** to tie a knot

nobre ['nɔbri] *adj, m/f* noble; **horário ~** prime time; **nobreza** [no'breza] *f* nobility

noção [no'sãw] (*pl* -ões) *f* notion, idea; **noções** *fpl* (*rudimentos*) rudiments, basics; **~ vaga** inkling; **não ter a menor ~ de algo** not to have the slightest idea about sth

nocaute [no'kawtʃi] *m* knockout ♦ *adv*: **pôr alguém ~** to knock sb out

nocivo, -a [no'sivu, a] *adj* harmful

noções [no'sõjʃ] *fpl* de **noção**

nocturno, -a [no'tuxnu, a] (*PT*) *adj* = **noturno**

nódoa ['nɔdwa] *f* spot; (*mancha*) stain

nogueira [no'gejra] *f* (*árvore*) walnut tree; (*madeira*) walnut

noite ['nojtʃi] *f* night; **à ~** at night, in the evening; **boa ~** good evening; (*despedida*) good night; **da ~ para o dia** overnight; **tarde da ~** late at night

noivado [noj'vadu] *m* engagement

noivo, -a ['nojvu, a] *m/f* (*prometido*) fiancé(e); (*no casamento*) bridegroom/bride; **os ~s** (*prometidos*) the engaged couple; (*no casamento*) the bride and groom; (*recém-casados*) the newlyweds

nojento, -a [no'ʒẽtu, a] *adj* disgusting

nojo ['noʒu] *m* nausea; (*repulsão*) disgust, loathing; **ela é um ~** she's horrible; **este trabalho está um ~** this work is messy

no-la(s) = nos + a(s)

no-lo(s) = nos + o(s)

nome ['nɔmi] *m* name; (*fama*) fame; **de ~** by name; **escritor de ~** famous writer; **um restaurante de ~** a restaurant with a good reputation; **em ~ de** in the name of; **~ de batismo** Christian name

nomeação [nomja'sãw] (*pl* **-ões**) *f* nomination; (*para um cargo*) appointment

nomear [no'mja*] *vt* to nominate; (*conferir um cargo a*) to appoint; (*dar nome a*) to name

nominal [nomi'naw] (*pl* **-ais**) *adj* nominal

nono, -a ['nonu, a] *num* ninth

nora ['nɔra] *f* daughter-in-law

nordeste [nox'dɛ∫ti] *m, adj* northeast

norma ['nɔxma] *f* standard, norm; (*regra*) rule; **como ~** as a rule

normal [nox'maw] (*pl* **-ais**) *adj* normal; (*habitual*) usual; **normalizar** [noxmali'za*] *vt* to bring back to normal; **normalizar-se** *vr* to return to normal

noroeste [nor'wɛ∫ti] *adj* northwest, northwestern ♦ *m* northwest

norte ['nɔxt∫i] *adj* northern, north; (*vento, direção*) northerly ♦ *m* north; **norte-americano, -a** *adj, m/f* (North) American

Noruega [nor'wega] *f* Norway; **norueguês, -esa** [norwe'ge∫, geza] *adj, m/f* Norwegian ♦ *m* (*LING*) Norwegian

nos [nuʃ] = **em + os** *pron* (*direto*) us; (*indireto*) us, to us, for us; (*reflexivo*) (to) ourselves; (*recíproco*) (to) each other

-nos [nuʃ] *pron* them

nós [nɔʃ] *pron* we; (*depois de prep*) us; **~ mesmos** we ourselves

nosso, -a ['nɔsu, a] *adj* our ♦ *pron* ours; **um amigo ~** a friend of ours; **Nossa Senhora** (*REL*) Our Lady

nostalgia [no∫taw'ʒia] *f* nostalgia; (*saudades da pátria etc*) homesick-

ness; **nostálgico, -a** [no∫'tawʒiku, a] *adj* nostalgic; homesick

nota ['nɔta] *f* note; (*EDUC*) mark; (*conta*) bill; (*cédula*) banknote; **~ de venda** sales receipt; **~ fiscal** receipt

notar [no'ta*] *vt* to notice, note; **notar-se** *vr* to be obvious; **fazer ~** to call attention to; **notável** [no'tavew] (*pl* **-eis**) *adj* notable, remarkable

notícia [no't∫isja] *f* (*uma ~*) piece of news; (*TV etc*) news item; **~s** *fpl* (*informações*) news *sg*; **pedir ~s de** to inquire about; **ter ~s de** to hear from; **noticiário** [not∫i'sjarju] *m* (*de jornal*) news section; (*CINEMA*) newsreel; (*TV, RÁDIO*) news bulletin

notoriedade [notorje'dadʒi] *f* renown, fame

notório, -a [no'tɔrju, a] *adj* well-known

noturno, -a [no'tuxnu, a] *adj* nocturnal, nightly; (*trabalho*) night *atr* ♦ *m* (*trem*) night train

nova ['nɔva] *f* piece of news; **~s** *fpl* (*novidades*) news *sg*

novamente [nova'mẽt∫i] *adv* again

novato, -a [no'vatu, a] *adj* inexperienced, raw ♦ *m/f* beginner, novice; (*EDUC*) fresher

nove ['nɔvi] *num* nine

novela [no'vɛla] *f* short novel, novella; (*RÁDIO, TV*) soap opera

novelo [no'velu] *m* ball of thread

novembro [no'vẽbru] (*PT* **N-**) *m* November

noventa [no'vẽta] *num* ninety

novidade [novi'dadʒi] *f* novelty; (*notícia*) piece of news; **~s** *fpl* (*notícias*) news *sg*

novilho, -a [no'viʎu, a] *m/f* young bull/heifer

novo, -a ['novu, 'nɔva] *adj* new; (*jovem*) young; (*adicional*) further;

de ~ again

noz [nɔʒ] *f* nut; *(da nogueira)* walnut; **~ moscada** nutmeg

nu, a [nu, 'nua] *adj* naked; *(arvore, sala, parede)* bare ♦ *m* nude

nublado, a [nu'bladu, a] *adj* cloudy, overcast

nuca ['nuka] *f* nape (of the neck)

nuclear [nu'klja*] *adj* nuclear

núcleo ['nuklju] *m* nucleus *sg*; *(centro)* centre (BRIT), center (US)

nudez [nu'deʒ] *f* nakedness, nudity; *(de paredes etc)* bareness

nudista [nu'dʒista] *adj*, *m/f* nudist

nulo, -a ['nulu, a] *adj* (JUR) null, void; *(nenhum)* non-existent; *(sem valor)* worthless; *(esforço)* vain, useless

num [nũ] = em + um

numa(s) ['numa(ʃ)] = em + uma(s)

numeral [nume'raw] *(pl* **-ais)** *m* numeral

numerar [nume'ra*] *vt* to number

numérico, -a [nu'mɛriku, a] *adj* numerical

número ['numeru] *m* number; *(de jornal)* issue; *(TEATRO etc)* act; *(de sapatos, roupa)* size; **sem ~** countless; **~ de matrícula** registration (BRIT) ou license plate (US) number

numeroso, -a [nume'rozu, ɔza] *adj* numerous

nunca ['nũka] *adv* never; **~ mais** never again; **quase ~** hardly ever; **mais que ~** more than ever

nuns [nũʃ] = em + uns

núpcias ['nupsjaʃ] *fpl* nuptials, wedding *sg*

nutrição [nutri'sãw] *f* nutrition

nutritivo, -a [nutri'tʃivu, a] *adj* nourishing

nuvem ['nuvẽj] *(pl* **-ns)** *f* cloud; *(de insetos)* swarm

O

o, a [u, a] *art def* **1** the; **o livro/a mesa/os estudantes** the book/table/students

2 *(com n abstrato: não se traduz)*: **o amor/a juventude** love/youth

3 *(posse: traduz-se muitos vezes por adj possessivo)*: **quebrar o braço** to break one's arm; **ele levantou a mão** he put his hand up; **ela colocou o chapéu** she put her hat on

4 *(valor descritivo)*: **ter a boca grande/os olhos azuis** to have a big mouth/blue eyes

♦ *pron demostrativo*: **meu livro e o seu** my book and yours; **as de Pedro são melhores** Pedro's are better; **não a(s) branca(s) mas a(s) cinza(s)** not the white one(s) but the grey one(s)

♦ *pron relativo*: **o que** *etc* **1** *(indef)*: **o(s) que quiser(em) pode(m) sair** anyone who wants to can leave; **leve o que mais gustar** take the one you like best

2 *(def)*: **o que comprei ontem** the one I bought yesterday; **os que sairam** those who left

3: **o que** what; **o que eu acho/mais gosto** what I think/like most

♦ *pron pessoal* **1** *(pessoa: m)*: him; *(: f)* her; *(: pl)* them; **não posso vê-lo(s)** I can't see him/them; **vemo-la todas as semanas** we see her every week

2 *(animal, coisa: sg)* it; *(: pl)* them; **não posso vê-lo(s)** I can't see it/them; **acharam-nos na praia** they found us on the beach

obedecer [obede'se*] *vi*: **~ a** to obey; **obediência** [obe'dʒẽsja] *f* obedience; **obediente** [obe'dʒẽtʃi] *adj* obedient

óbito ['ɔbitu] *m* death; **atestado de ~** death certificate

objeção [obʒe'sãw] (*PT* -cç-; *pl* -ões) *f* objection; **fazer** *ou* **pôr objeções a** to object to

objetivo, -a [obʒe'tʃivu, a] (*PT* -ct-) *adj* objective ♦ *m* objective

objeto [ob'ʒetu] (*PT* -ct-) *m* object

oblíquo, -a [o'blikwu, a] *adj* oblique; (*olhar*) sidelong

obra ['ɔbra] *f* work; (*ARQ*) building, construction; (*TEATRO*) play; **em ~s** under repair; **ser ~ de alguém/algo** to be the work of sb/the result of sth; **~ de arte** work of art; **~s públicas** public works; **obra-prima** (*pl* **obras-primas**) *f* masterpiece

obrigação [obriga'sãw] (*pl* -ões) *f* obligation; (*COM*) bond

obrigado, -a [obri'gadu, a] *adj* obliged, compelled ♦ *excl* thank you; (*recusa*) no, thank you

obrigar [obri'ga*] *vt* to oblige, compel; **obrigar-se** *vr*: **~-se a fazer algo** to undertake to do sth; **obrigatório, -a** [obriga'tɔrju, a] *adj* compulsory, obligatory

obsceno, -a [obi'senu, a] *adj* obscene

obscurecer [obiʃkure'se*] *vt* to darken; (*entendimento, verdade etc*) to obscure ♦ *vi* to get dark

obscuro, -a [obi'ʃkuru, a] *adj* dark; (*fig*) obscure

observação [obisexva'sãw] (*pl* -ões) *f* observation; (*comentário*) remark, comment; (*de leis, regras*) observance

observador, a [obisexva'do*, a] *m/f* observer

observar [obisex'va*] *vt* to observe; (*notar*) to notice; **~ algo a alguém** to point sth out to sb

observatório [obisexva'tɔrju] *m* observatory

obsessão [obise'sãw] (*pl* -ões) *f* obsession; **obsessivo, -a** [obise-'sivu, a] *adj* obsessive

obsoleto, -a [obiso'letu, a] *adj* obsolete

obstáculo [obi'ʃtakulu] *m* obstacle; (*dificuldade*) hindrance, drawback

obstinado, -a [obiʃtʃi'nadu, a] *adj* obstinate, stubborn

obstrução [obiʃtru'sãw] (*pl* -ões) *f* obstruction; **obstruir** [obiʃtrwi*] *vt* to obstruct; (*impedir*) to impede

obter [obi'te*] (*irreg: como* **ter**) *vt* to obtain, get; (*alcançar*) to gain

obturação [obitura'sãw] (*pl* -ões) *f* (*de dente*) filling

obtuso, -a [obi'tuzu, a] *adj* (*ger*) obtuse; (*fig: pessoa*) thick

óbvio, -a ['ɔbvju, a] *adj* obvious; **(é) ~!** of course!

ocasião [oka'zjãw] (*pl* -ões) *f* opportunity, chance; (*momento, tempo*) occasion; **ocasionar** [okazjo'na*] *vt* to cause, bring about

oceano [o'sjanu] *m* ocean

ocidental [osidẽ'taw] (*pl* -ais) *adj* western ♦ *m/f* westerner

ocidente [osi'dẽtʃi] *m* west

ócio ['ɔsju] *m* (*lazer*) leisure; (*inação*) idleness; **ocioso, -a** [o'sjozu, ɔza] *adj* idle; (*vaga*) unfilled

oco, -a ['oku, a] *adj* hollow, empty

ocorrência [oko'xẽsja] *f* incident, event; (*circunstância*) circumstance

ocorrer [oko'xe*] *vi* to happen, occur; (*vir ao pensamento*) to come to mind; **~ a alguém** to happen to sb; to occur to sb

oculista [oku'liʃta] *m/f* optician

óculo ['ɔkulu] *m* spyglass; **~s** *mpl* (*para ver melhor*) glasses, spectacles; **~s de proteção** goggles

ocultar [okuw'ta*] vt to hide, conceal; **oculto, -a** [o'kuwtu, a] adj hidden; (desconhecido) unknown; (secreto) secret; (sobrenatural) occult

ocupação [okupa'sãw] (pl -ões) f occupation

ocupado, -a [oku'padu, a] adj (pessoa) busy; (lugar) taken, occupied; (BR: telefone) engaged (BRIT), busy (US); **sinal de ~** (BR: TEL) engaged tone (BRIT), busy signal (US)

ocupar [oku'pa*] vt to occupy; (tempo) to take up; (pessoa) to keep busy; **ocupar-se** vr: **~-se com** ou **de** ou **em algo** (dedicar-se a) to deal with sth; (cuidar de) to look after sth; (passar seu tempo com) to occupy o.s. with sth

odiar [o'dʒja*] vt to hate; **ódio** ['odʒju] m hate, hatred; **odioso, -a** [o'dʒjozu, ɔza] adj hateful

odor [o'do*] m smell

oeste ['wɛʃtʃi] m west ♦ adj inv (região) western; (direção, vento) westerly

ofegante [ofe'gãtʃi] adj breathless, panting

ofender [ofẽ'de*] vt to offend; **ofender-se** vr: **~-se (com)** to take offence (BRIT) ou offense (US) (at)

ofensa [o'fẽsa] f insult; (à lei, moral) offence (BRIT), offense (US); **ofensiva** [ofẽ'siva] f offensive; **ofensivo, -a** [ofẽ'sivu, a] adj offensive

oferecer [ofere'se*] vt to offer; (dar) to give; (jantar) to give; (propor) to propose; (dedicar) to dedicate; **oferecer-se** vr (pessoa) to offer o.s., volunteer; (oportunidade) to present itself, arise; **~-se para fazer** to offer to do; **oferecimento** [oferesi'mẽtu] m offer; **oferta** [o'fɛxta] f offer; (dádiva) gift; (COM)

bid; (em loja) special offer

oficial [ofi'sjaw] (pl -ais) adj official ♦ m/f official; (MIL) officer; **~ de justiça** bailiff

oficina [ofi'sina] f workshop; **~ mecânica** garage

ofício [o'fisju] m profession, trade; (REL) service; (carta) official letter; (função) function; (encargo) job, task

oitavo, -a [oj'tavu, a] num eighth

oitenta [oj'tẽta] num eighty

oito ['ojtu] num eight

olá [o'la] excl hello!

olaria [ola'ria] f (fábrica: de louças de barro) pottery; (: de tijolos) brickworks sg

óleo ['ɔlju] m (lubricante) oil; **~ diesel/de bronzear** diesel/suntan oil; **oleoso, -a** [o'ljozu, ɔza] adj oily; (gorduroso) greasy

olfato [ow'fatu] m sense of smell

olhada [o'ʎada] f glance, look; **dar uma ~** to have a look

olhadela [oʎa'dɛla] f peep

olhar [o'ʎa*] vt to look at; (observar) to watch; (ponderar) to consider; (cuidar de) to look after ♦ vi to look ♦ m look; **olhar-se** vr to look at o.s.; (duas pessoas) to look at each other; **~ fixamente** to stare at; **~ para** to look at; **~ por** to look after; **~ fixo** stare

olho ['oʎu] m (ANAT, de agulha) eye; (vista) eyesight; **~ nele!** watch him!; **~ vivo!** keep your eyes open!; **a ~** (medir, calcular etc) by eye; **~ mágico** (na porta) peephole; **~ roxo** black eye; **num abrir e fechar de ~s** in a flash

olimpíada [olĩ'piada] f: **as O~s** the Olympics

oliveira [oli'vejra] f olive tree

ombro ['õbru] m shoulder; **encolher os ~s, dar de ~s** to shrug one's shoulders

omeleta [ome'leta] (PT) f = **omelete**

omelete [ome'letʃi] (BR) f omelette (BRIT), omelet (US)

omissão [omi'sãw] (pl **-ões**) f omission; (negligência) negligence

omitir [omi'tʃi*] vt to omit

omoplata [omo'plata] f shoulder blade

onça ['õsa] f ounce; (animal) jaguar

onda ['õda] f wave; (moda) fashion; ~ **curta/média/longa** short/medium/long wave; ~ **de calor** heat wave

onde ['õdʒi] adv where ♦ conj where, in which; **de ~ você é?** where are you from?; **por ~** through which; **por ~?** which way?; ~ **quer que** wherever

ondulado, -a [õdu'ladu, a] adj wavy

ônibus ['onibuʃ] (BR) m inv bus; **ponto de ~** bus-stop

ontem ['õtẽ] adv yesterday; ~ **à noite** last night

ONU ['onu] abr f (= Organização das Nações Unidas) UNO

ônus ['onuʃ] m inv onus; (obrigação) obligation; (COM) charge; (encargo desagradável) burden

onze ['õzi] num eleven

opaco, -a [o'paku, a] adj opaque; (obscuro) dark

opção [op'sãw] (pl **-ões**) f option, choice; (preferência) first claim, right

OPEP [o'pɛpi] abr f (= Organização dos Países Exportadores de Petróleo) OPEC

ópera ['ɔpera] f opera

operação [opera'sãw] (pl **-ões**) f operation; (COM) transaction

operador, a [opera'do*, a] m/f operator; (cirurgião) surgeon; (num cinema) projectionist

operar [ope'ra*] vt to operate; (produzir) to effect, bring about; (MED) to operate on ♦ vi to operate; (agir) to act, function; (suceder) to take place; (MED) to have an operation

operar-se vr to have an operation

operário, -a [ope'rarju, a] adj working ♦ m/f worker; **classe operária** working class

opinar [opi'na*] vt to think ♦ vi to give one's opinion

opinião [opi'njãw] (pl **-ões**) f opinion; **mudar de ~** to change one's mind

oponente [opo'nẽtʃi] adj opposing ♦ m/f opponent

opor [o'po*] (irreg: como **pôr**) vt to oppose; (resistência) to put up, offer; (objeção, dificuldade) to raise; **opor-se** vr: **~-se a** to object to; (resistir) to oppose

oportunidade [opoxtuni'dadʒi] f opportunity

oportunista [opoxtu'niʃta] adj, m/f opportunist

oportuno, -a [opox'tunu, a] adj (momento) opportune, right; (oferta de ajuda) well-timed; (conveniente) convenient, suitable

oposição [opozi'sãw] (pl **-ões**) f opposition; **em ~ a** against; **fazer ~ a** to oppose

oposto, -a [o'poʃtu, 'pɔʃta] adj opposite; (em frente) facing; (opiniões) opposing ♦ m opposite

opressão [opre'sãw] (pl **-ões**) f oppression; **opressivo, -a** [opre-'sivu, a] adj oppressive

oprimir [opri'mi*] vt to oppress; (comprimir) to press

optar [op'ta*] vi to choose; ~ **por** to opt for; ~ **por fazer** to opt to do

óptico, -a etc ['ɔtiku, a] (PT) = **ótico** etc

óptimo, -a etc ['ɔtimu, a] (PT) adj = **ótimo** etc

ora ['ɔra] *adv* now ♦ *conj* well; **por** ~ for the time being; ~ ..., ~ ... one moment ..., the next ...; ~ **bem** now then

oração [ora'sãw] (*pl* -**ões**) *f* prayer; (*discurso*) speech; (LING) clause

oral [o'raw] (*pl* -**ais**) *adj* oral ♦ *f* oral (exam)

orar [o'ra*] *vi* (REL) to pray

órbita ['ɔxbita] *f* orbit; (*do olho*) socket

Órcades ['ɔxkadʒiʃ] *fpl*: **as** ~ **the** Orkneys

orçamento [oxsa'mẽtu] *m* (*do estado etc*) budget; (*avaliação*) estimate

orçar [ox'sa*] *vt* to value, estimate ♦ *vi*: ~ **em** (*gastos etc*) to be valued at, be put at

ordem ['ɔxdẽ] (*pl* -**ns**) *f* order; **até nova** ~ until further notice; **de primeira** ~ first-rate; **estar em** ~ to be tidy; **por** ~ in order, in turn; ~ **do dia** agenda; ~ **pública** public order, law and order

ordenado, -a [oxde'nadu, a] *adj* (*posto em ordem*) in order; (*metódico*) orderly ♦ *m* salary, wages *f*

ordens ['ɔxdẽʃ] *fpl de* **ordem**

ordinário, -a [oxdʒi'narju, a] *adj* ordinary; (*comum*) usual; (*mediocre*) mediocre; (*grosseiro*) coarse, vulgar; (*de má qualidade*) inferior; **de** ~ usually

orelha [o'reʎa] *f* ear; (*aba*) flap

órfã ['ɔxfã] *f de* **órfão**

órfão, -fã ['ɔxfãw, fã] (*pl* ~**s**) *adj*, *m/f* orphan

orgânico, -a [ox'ganiku, a] *adj* organic

organismo [oxga'niʒmu] *m* organism; (*entidade*) organization

organização [oxganiza'sãw] (*pl* -**ões**) *f* organization; **organizar** [oxgani'za*] *vt* to organize

órgão ['ɔxgãw] (*pl* ~**s**) *m* organ; (*governamental etc*) institution,

body

orgasmo [ox'gaʒmu] *m* orgasm

orgia [ox'ʒia] *f* orgy

orgulho [ox'guʎu] *m* pride; (*arrogância*) arrogance; **orgulhoso, -a** [oxgu'ʎozu, ɔza] *adj* proud; haughty

orientação [orjẽta'sãw] *f* direction; (*posição*) position; ~ **educacional** training, guidance

oriental [orjẽ'taw] (*pl* -**ais**) *adj* eastern; (*do Extremo Oriente*) oriental

orientar [orjẽ'ta*] *vt* to orientate; (*indicar o rumo*) to direct; (*aconselhar*) to guide; **orientar-se** *vr* to get one's bearings; ~**-se por algo** to follow sth

oriente [o'rjẽtʃi] *m*: **o O**~ the East; **Extremo O**~ Far East; **O**~ **Médio** Middle East

origem [o'riʒẽ] (*pl* -**ns**) *f* origin; (*ascendência*) lineage, descent; **lugar de** ~ birthplace

original [oriʒi'naw] (*pl* -**ais**) *adj* original; (*estranho*) strange, odd ♦ *m* original; **originalidade** [oriʒinali'dadʒi] *f* originality; (*excentricidade*) eccentricity

originar [oriʒi'na*] *vt* to give rise to, start; **originar-se** *vr* to arise; ~**-se de** to originate from

oriundo, -a [o'rjũdu, a] *adj*: ~ **de** arising from; (*natural*) native of

orla ['ɔxla] *f*: ~ **marítima** seafront

ornamento [oxna'mẽtu] *m* adornment, decoration

orquestra [ox'keʃtra] (PT -**esta**) *f* orchestra

orquídea [ox'kidʒa] *f* orchid

ortodoxo, -a [oxto'dɔksu, a] *adj* orthodox

ortografia [oxtogra'fia] *f* spelling

orvalho [ox'vaʎu] *m* dew

os [uʃ] *art def* V **o**

osso ['osu] *m* bone

ostensivo, -a [oʃtẽ'sivu, a] adj ostensible

ostentar [oʃtẽ'ta*] vt to show; (alardear) to show off, flaunt

ostra ['oʃtra] f oyster

OTAN ['otã] abr f (= Organização do Tratado do Atlântico Norte) NATO

ótica ['ɔtʃika] f optics sg; (loja) optician's; (fig: ponto de vista) viewpoint; V tb **ótico**

ótico, -a ['ɔtʃiku, a] adj optical ♦ m/f optician

otimista [otʃi'miʃta] adj optimistic ♦ m/f optimist

ótimo, -a ['ɔtʃimu, a] adj excellent, splendid ♦ excl great!, super!

ou [o] conj or; ~ **este** ~ **aquele** either this one or that one; ~ **seja** in other words

ouço etc ['osu] vb V **ouvir**

ouriço [o'risu] m (europeu) hedgehog; (casca) shell

ouro ['oru] m gold; ~s mpl (CARTAS) diamonds

ousadia [oza'dʒia] f daring; **ousado, -a** [o'zadu, a] adj daring, bold

ousar [o'za*] vt, vi to dare

outono [o'tɔnu] m autumn

PALAVRA CHAVE

---

outro, -a ['otru, a] adj **1** (distinto: sg) another; (: pl) other; **outra coisa** something else; **de ~ modo, de outra maneira** otherwise; **no ~ dia** the next day; **ela está outra** (mudada) she's changed

2 (adicional): **traga-me ~ café, por favor** can I have another coffee, please?; **outra vez** again

♦ pron **1 o** ~ the other one; **(os) ~s** (the) others; **de ~** somebody else's

2 (recíproco): **odeiam-se uns aos ~s** they hate one another ou each other

3: ~ **tanto** the same again; **comer** ~

---

tanto to eat the same ou as much again; **ele recebeu uma dezena de telegramas e outras tantas chamadas** he got about ten telegrams and as many calls

outubro [o'tubru] (PT **O-**) m October

ouvido [o'vidu] m (ANAT) ear; (sentido) hearing; **de ~** by ear; **dar ~s a** to listen to

ouvinte [o'vĩtʃi] m/f listener; (estudante) auditor

ouvir [o'vi*] vt to hear; (com atenção) to listen to; (missa) to attend ♦ vi to hear; to listen; ~ **dizer que ...** to hear that ...; ~ **falar de** to hear of

ova ['ɔva] f roe

oval [o'vaw] (pl **-ais**) adj, f oval

ovário [o'varju] m ovary

ovelha [o'veʎa] f sheep

óvni ['ɔvni] m UFO

ovo ['ovu] m egg; ~s **de granja** free-range eggs; ~ **pochê** (BR) ou **escalfado** (PT) poached egg; ~ **estrelado** ou **frito** fried egg; ~s **mexidos** scrambled eggs; ~ **quente/cozido duro** hard-boiled/soft-boiled egg

oxidar [oksi'da*] vt to rust; **oxidar-se** vr to rust, go rusty

oxigenado, -a [oksiʒe'nadu, a] adj (cabelo) bleached; **água oxigenada** peroxide

oxigênio [oksi'ʒenju] m oxygen

ozônio [o'zonju] m ozone; **camada de ~** ozone layer

P

P. abr (= Praça) Sq.

p.a. abr (= por ano) p.a.

pá [pa] f shovel; (de remo, hélice) blade ♦ m (PT) pal, mate; ~ **de lixo** dustpan

paca ['paka] f (ZOOL) paca

pacato, -a [pa'katu, a] adj (pessoa) quiet; (lugar) peaceful

paciência [pa'sjēsja] f patience; **paciente** [pa'sjētʃi] adj, m/f patient

pacífico, -a [pa'sifiku, a] adj (pessoa) peace-loving; (aceito sem discussão) undisputed; (sossegado) peaceful; **o (Oceano) P~** the Pacific (Ocean)

pacote [pa'kɔtʃi] m packet; (embrulho) parcel; (ECON, COMPUT, TURISMO) package

pacto ['paktu] m pact; (ajuste) agreement

padaria [pada'ria] f bakery, baker's (shop)

padeiro [pa'dejru] m baker

padiola [pa'dʒjɔla] f stretcher

padrão [pa'drãw] (pl **-ões**) m standard; (medida) gauge; (desenho) pattern; (fig: modelo) model; **~ de vida** standard of living

padrasto [pa'draʃtu] m stepfather

padre ['padri] m priest

padrinho [pa'driɲu] m godfather; (de noivo) best man; (patrono) sponsor

padroeiro, -a [pa'drwejru, a] m/f patron; (santo) patron saint

padrões [pa'drõjʃ] mpl de **padrão**

pães [pãjʃ] mpl de **pão**

pagã [pa'gã] f de **pagão**

pagador, a [paga'do*, a] adj paying ♦ m/f payer; (de salário) pay clerk; (de banco) teller

pagamento [paga'mētu] m payment; **~ a prazo** ou **em prestações** payment in instal(l)ments; **~ à vista** cash payment; **~ contra entrega** (COM) COD, cash on delivery

pagão, -gã [pa'gãw, gã] (pl **~s**, **~s**) adj, m/f pagan

pagar [pa'ga*] vt to pay; (compras, pecados) to pay for; (o que devia) to

pay back; (retribuir) to repay ♦ vi to pay; **~ por algo** (tb fig) to pay for sth; **~ a prestações** to pay in instal(l)ments; **~ de contado** (PT) to pay cash

página ['paʒina] f page

pago, -a ['pagu, a] pp de **pagar** ♦ adj paid; (fig) even ♦ m pay

pai [paj] m father; **~s** mpl parents

painel [paj'nɛw] (pl **-éis**) m panel; (quadro) picture; (AUTO) dashboard; (de avião) instrument panel

país [pa'jiʃ] m country; (região) land; **~ natal** native land

paisagem [paj'zaʒē] (pl **-ns**) f scenery, landscape

paisano, -a [paj'zanu, a] adj civilian ♦ m/f (não militar) civilian; (compatriota) fellow countryman

Países Baixos mpl: **os ~** the Netherlands

paixão [paj'ʃãw] (pl **-ões**) f passion

palácio [pa'lasju] m palace; **~ da justiça** courthouse; **o Planalto** see boxed note

---

PALÁCIO DO PLANALTO

Palácio do Planalto is the seat of the Brazilian government, in Brasília. The name comes from the fact that the Brazilian capital is situated on a plateau. It has come to be a byword for central government.

---

paladar [pala'da*] m taste; (ANAT) palate

palafita [pala'fita] f (estacaria) stilts pl; (habitação) stilt house

palavra [pa'lavra] f word; (fala) speech; (promessa) promise; (direito de falar) right to speak; **dar a ~ a alguém** to give sb the chance to speak; **ter ~** (pessoa) to be reliable; **~s cruzadas** crossword (puzzle) sg;

palavrão [pala'vrãw] (pl -ões) m swearword

palco ['palku] m (TEATRO) stage; (fig: local) scene

Palestina [paleʃ'tʃina] f: **a ~** Palestine; **palestino, -a** [paleʃ'tʃinu, a] adj, m/f Palestinian

palestra [pa'lɛʃtra] f chat, talk; (conferência) lecture

paletó [pale'tɔ] m jacket

palha ['paʎa] f straw

palhaço [pa'ʎasu] m clown

pálido, -a ['palidu, a] adj pale

palito [pa'litu] m stick; (para os dentes) toothpick

palma ['pawma] f (folha) palm leaf; (da mão) palm; **bater ~s** to clap; **palmada** [paw'mada] f slap

palmeira [paw'mejra] f palm tree

palmo ['pawmu] m span; **~ a ~** inch by inch

palpável [paw'pavew] (pl -eis) adj tangible; (fig) obvious

pálpebra ['pawpebra] f eyelid

palpitação [pawpita'sãw] (pl -ões) f beating, throbbing; **palpitações** fpl (batimentos cardíacos) palpitations

palpitante [pawpi'tãtʃi] adj beating, throbbing; (fig: emocionante) thrilling; (: de interesse atual) sensational

palpitar [pawpi'ta*] vi (coração) to beat

palpite [paw'pitʃi] m (intuição) hunch; (JOGO, TURFE) tip; (opinião) opinion

pampa ['pãpa] f pampas

Panamá [pana'ma] m: **o ~** Panama, the Panama Canal

pancada [pã'kada] f (no corpo) blow, hit; (choque) knock; (de relógio) stroke; **dar ~ em alguém** to hit sb; **pancadaria** [pãkada'ria] f (surra) beating; (tumulto) fight

pandeiro [pã'dejru] m tambourine

pane ['pani] f breakdown

panela [pa'nɛla] f (de barro) pot; (de metal) pan; (de cozinhar) saucepan; (no dente) hole; **~ de pressão** pressure cooker

panfleto [pã'fletu] m pamphlet

pânico ['paniku] m panic; **entrar em ~** to panic

pano ['panu] m cloth; (TEATRO) curtain; (vela) sheet, sail; **~ de pratos** tea-towel; **~ de pó** duster; **~ de fundo** (tb fig) backdrop

panorama [pano'rama] m view

panqueca [pã'kɛka] f pancake

pantanal [pãta'naw] (pl -ais) m swampland

pântano ['pãtanu] m marsh, swamp

pantera [pã'tɛra] f panther

pão [pãw] (pl pães) m bread; **o P~ de Açúcar** (no Rio) Sugarloaf Mountain; **~ torrado** toast; **pão-duro** (pl pães-duros) (col) adj mean, stingy ♦ m/f miser; **pãozinho** [pãw'ziɲu] m roll

papa ['papa] m Pope; (mingau) porridge

papagaio [papa'gaju] m parrot; (pipa) kite

papai [pa'paj] m dad, daddy; **P~ Noel** Santa Claus, Father Christmas

papel [pa'pɛw] (pl -éis) m paper; (TEATRO, função) role; **~ de embrulho/de escrever/de alumínio** wrapping paper/writing paper/tinfoil; **~ higiênico/usado** toilet/waste paper; **~ de parede/de seda/transparente** wallpaper/tissue paper/tracing paper; **papelada** [pape'lada] f pile of papers; (burocracia) paperwork, red tape; **papelão** [pape'lãw] m cardboard; (fig) fiasco; **papelaria** [papela'ria] f stationer's (shop); **papel-carbono** m carbon paper

papo ['papu] (col) m (conversa) chat; **bater** ou **levar um ~** (col) to have a chat; **ficar de ~ para o ar** (fig) to laze around

paquerar [pake'ra*] (col) vi to flirt ♦ vt to chat up

paquistanês, -esa [pakifta'neʃ, eza] adj, m/f Pakistani

Paquistão [pakiʃ'tãw] m: **o ~** Pakistan

par [pa*] adj (igual) equal; (número) even ♦ m pair; (casal) couple; (pessoa na dança) partner; **~ a ~** side by side, level; **sem ~** incomparable

para ['para] prep for; (direção) to, towards; **~ que** so that, in order that; **~ quê?** what for?, why?; **ir ~ casa** to go home; **~ com** (atitude) towards; **de lá ~ cá** since then; **~ a semana** next week; **estar ~** to be about to; **é ~ nós ficarmos aqui?** should we stay here?

parabéns [para'bẽjʃ] mpl congratulations; (no aniversário) happy birthday; **dar ~ a** to congratulate

pára-brisa ['para-] (pl ~s) m windscreen (BRIT), windshield (US)

pára-choque ['para-] (pl ~s) m (AUTO) bumper

parada [pa'rada] f stop; (COM) stoppage; (militar, colegial) parade

parado, -a [pa'radu, a] adj (imóvel) standing still; (sem vida) lifeless; (carro) stationary; (máquina) out of action; (olhar) fixed; (trabalhador, fábrica) idle

paradoxo [para'dɔksu] m paradox

parafuso [para'fuzu] m screw

paragem [pa'raʒẽ] (pl -ns) f stop; **paragens** fpl (lugares) places, parts; **~ de eléctrico** (PT) tram (BRIT) ou streetcar (US) stop

parágrafo [pa'ragrafu] m paragraph

Paraguai [para'gwaj] m: **o ~** Paraguay; **paraguaio, -a** [para'gwaju, a] adj, m/f Paraguayan

paraíso [para'izu] m paradise

pára-lama ['para-] (pl ~s) m wing (BRIT), fender (US); (de bicicleta) mudguard

paralelepípedo [paralele'pipedu] m paving stone

paralelo, -a [para'lɛlu, a] adj parallel

paralisar [parali'za*] vt to paralyse; (trabalho) to bring to a standstill; **paralisar-se** vr to become paralysed; (fig) to come to a standstill; **paralisia** [parali'zia] f paralysis

paranóico, -a [para'nɔjku, a] adj, m/f paranoid

parapeito [para'pejtu] m wall, parapet; (da janela) windowsill

pára-quedas ['para-] m inv parachute; **pára-quedista** [parake'dʒiʃta] m/f parachutist ♦ m (MIL) paratrooper

parar [pa'ra*] vi to stop; (ficar) to stay ♦ vt to stop; **fazer ~** (deter) to stop; **~ na cadeia** to end up in jail; **~ de fazer** to stop doing

pára-raios ['para-] m inv lightning conductor

parasita [para'zita] m parasite

parceiro, -a [pax'sejru, a] adj matching ♦ m/f partner

parcela [pax'sɛla] f piece, bit; (de pagamento) instalment (BRIT), installment (US); (de terra) plot; (de eleitorado etc) section; (MAT) item

parceria [paxse'ria] f partnership

parcial [pax'sjaw] (pl -ais) adj partial; (feito por partes) in parts; (pessoa) bias(s)ed; (POL) partisan; **parcialidade** [paxsjali'dadʒi] f bias, partiality

pardal [pax'daw] (pl **-ais**) m sparrow

pardieiro [pax'dʒjejru] m ruin, heap

pardo, -a ['paxdu, a] adj (cinzento) grey (BRIT), gray (US); (castanho) brown; (mulato) mulatto

parecer [pare'se*] m, vi (ter a aparência de) to look, seem; **parecer-se** vr: **~-se com alguém** to look like sb; **~ (com)** (ter semelhança com) to look (like); **ao que parece** apparently; **parece-me que** I think that, it seems to me that; **que lhe parece?** what do you think?; **parece que** it looks as if

parecido, -a [pare'sidu, a] adj alike, similar; **~ com** like

parede [pa'redʒi] f wall

parente, -a [pa'rētʃi] m/f relative, relation; **parentesco** [parē'teʃku] m relationship; (fig) connection

parêntese [pa'rētezi] m parenthesis; (na escrita) bracket; (fig: digressão) digression

páreo ['parju] m race; (fig) competition

parir [pa'ri*] vt to give birth to ♦ vi to give birth; (mulher) to have a baby

Paris [pa'riʃ] n Paris; **parisiense** [pari'zjēsi] adj, m/f Parisian

parlamentar [paxlamē'ta*] adj parliamentary ♦ m/f member of parliament

parlamento [paxla'mētu] m parliament

paróquia [pa'rɔkja] f (REL) parish

parque ['paxki] m park; **~ industrial/infantil** industrial estate/children's playground; **~ nacional** national park

parte ['paxtʃi] f part; (quinhão) share; (lado) side; (ponto) point; (JUR) party; (papel) role; **a maior ~ de** most of; **à ~** aside; (separado)

separate; (separadamente) separately; (além de) apart from; **da ~ de alguém** on sb's part; **em alguma/qualquer ~** somewhere/anywhere; **em ~ alguma** nowhere; **por toda (a) ~** everywhere; **pôr de ~** to set aside; **tomar ~ em** to take part in; **dar ~ de alguém à polícia** to report sb to the police

participação [paxtʃisipa'sāw] f participation; (COM) stake, share; (comunicação) announcement, notification

participar [paxtʃisi'pa*] vt to announce, notify of ♦ vi: **~ de** ou **em** to participate in, take part in; (compartilhar) to share in

particípio [paxtʃi'sipju] m participle

particular [paxtʃiku'la*] adj particular, special; (privativo, pessoal) private ♦ m particular; (indivíduo) individual; **~es** mpl (pormenores) details; **em ~** in private; **particularmente** [paxtʃikulax'mētʃi] adv privately; (especialmente) particularly

partida [pax'tʃida] f (saída) departure; (ESPORTE) game, match

partidário, -a [paxtʃi'darju, a] adj supporting ♦ m/f supporter, follower

partido [pax'tʃidu] m (POL) party; **tirar ~ de** to profit from; **tomar o ~ de** to side with

partilhar [paxtʃi'ʎa*] vt to share; (distribuir) to share out

partir [pax'tʃi*] vt to break; (dividir) to divide, split ♦ vi (pôr-se a caminho) to set off, set out; (ir-se embora) to leave, depart; **partir-se** vr to break; **a ~ de** (starting) from

parto ['paxtu] m (child)birth; **estar em trabalho de ~** to be in labour (BRIT) ou labor (US)

Páscoa ['paʃkwa] f Easter; (dos judeus) Passover

pasmo, -a ['paʒmu, a] adj astonished ♦ m amazement

passa ['pasa] f raisin

passadeira [pasa'dejra] f (tapete) stair carpet; (mulher) ironing lady; (PT: para peões) zebra crossing (BRIT), crosswalk (US)

passado, -a [pa'sadu, a] adj past; (antiquado) old-fashioned; (fruta) bad; (peixe) off ♦ m past; **o ano ~** last year; **bem/mal passado** (carne) well done/rare

passageiro, -a [pasa'ʒejru, a] adj passing ♦ m/f passenger

passagem [pasa'ʒẽ] (pl **-ns**) f passage; (preço de condução) fare; (bilhete) ticket; **~ de ida e volta** return ticket, round trip ticket (US); **~ de nível** (BRIT) grade (US) crossing; **~ de pedestres** pedestrian crossing (BRIT), crosswalk (US); **~ subterrânea** underpass, subway (BRIT)

passaporte [pasa'pɔxtʃi] m passport

passar [pa'sa*] vt to pass; (exceder) to go beyond, exceed; (o ferro) to iron; (o tempo) to spend; (a outra pessoa) to pass on; (pomada) to put on ♦ vi to pass; (na rua) to go past; (tempo) to go by; (dor) to wear off; (terminar) to be over; **passar-se** (acontecer) to go on, happen; ~ **bem** (de saúde) to be well; **passava das dez horas** it was past ten o' clock; ~ **alguém para trás** to con sb; (cônjuge) to cheat on sb; ~ **por algo** (sofrer) to go through sth; (transitar: estrada) to go along sth; (ser considerado como) to be thought of as sth; ~ **sem** to do without

passarela [pasa'rɛla] f footbridge

pássaro ['pasaru] m bird

passatempo [pasa'tẽpu] m pastime

passe ['pasi] m pass

passear [pa'sja*] vt to take for a walk ♦ vi (a pé) to go for a walk; (sair) to go out; ~ **a cavalo** (ou de carro) to go for a ride; **passeata** [pa'sjata] f (marcha coletiva) protest march; **passeio** [pa'seju] m walk; (de carro) drive, ride; (excursão) outing; (calçada) pavement (BRIT), sidewalk (US); **dar um passeio** to go for a walk; (de carro) to go for a drive ou ride

passível [pa'sivew] (pl **-eis**) adj: ~ **de** (dor etc) susceptible to; (pena, multa) subject to

passivo, -a [pa'sivu, a] adj passive ♦ m (COM) liabilities pl

passo ['pasu] m step; (medida) pace; (modo de andar) walk; (ruído dos passos) footstep; (sinal de pé) footprint; **ao ~ que** while; **ceder o ~** a to give way to

pasta ['paʃta] f paste; (de couro) briefcase; (de cartolina) folder; (de ministro) portfolio; ~ **dentífrica** ou **de dentes** toothpaste

pastar [paʃ'ta*] vt to graze on ♦ vi to graze

pastel [paʃ'tɛw] (pl **-éis**) adj inv (cor) pastel ♦ m samosa

pastelão [paʃte'lãw] m slapstick

pastelaria [paʃtela'ria] f cake shop; (comida) pastry

pasteurizado, -a [paʃtewri'zadu, a] adj pasteurized

pastilha [paʃ'tʃiʎa] f (MED) tablet; (doce) pastille; (COMPUT) chip

pastor, a [paʃ'to*, a] m/f shepherd(ess) ♦ m (REL) clergyman, pastor

pata ['pata] f (pé de animal) foot, paw; (ave) duck; (col: pé) foot

patamar [pata'ma*] m (de escada)

landing; (fig) level
patente [pa'tẽtʃi] adj obvious, evident ♦ f (COM) patent
paternal [patex'naw] (pl -ais) adj paternal, fatherly; **paternidade** [patexni'dadʒi] f paternity; **paterno, -a** [pa'texnu, a] adj paternal, fatherly; **casa paterna** family home
pateta [pa'teta] adj stupid, daft ♦ m/f idiot
patético, -a [pa'tɛtʃiku, a] adj pathetic, moving
patife [pa'tʃifi] m scoundrel, rogue
patim [pa'tʃĩ] (pl -ns) m skate; **patins em linha** Rollerblades ®; **patins de roda** roller skates; **patinar** [patʃi'na*] vi to skate; (AUTO: derrapar) to skid
patins [pa'tʃĩʃ] mpl de **patim**
pátio [ˈpatʃju] m (de uma casa) patio, backyard; (espaço cercado de edifícios) courtyard; (tb: ~ de recreio) playground; (MIL) parade ground
pato [ˈpatu] m duck; (macho) drake
patologia [patolo'ʒia] f pathology; **patológico, -a** [pato'lɔʒiku, a] adj pathological
patrão [pa'trãw] (pl -ões) m (COM) boss; (dono de casa) master; (proprietário) landlord; (NÁUT) skipper
pátria [ˈpatrja] f homeland
patrimônio [patri'monju] m (herança) inheritance; (fig) heritage; (bens) property
patriota [pa'trjɔta] m/f patriot
patrocinador, a [patrosina'do*, a] m/f sponsor, backer
patrocinar [patrosi'na*] vt to sponsor; (proteger) to support; **patrocínio** [patro'sinju] m sponsorship, backing; support
patrões [pa'trõjʃ] mpl de **patrão**
patrulha [pa'truʎa] f patrol; **patrulhar** [patru'ʎa*] vt, vi to patrol

pau [paw] m (madeira) wood; (vara) stick; ~s mpl (CARTAS) clubs; ~ a ~ neck and neck; ~ de bandeira flagpole
pausa [ˈpawza] f pause; (intervalo) break; (descanso) rest
pauta [ˈpawta] f (linha) (guide)line; (ordem do dia) agenda; (indicações) guidelines pl; sem ~ (papel) plain; em ~ on the agenda
pavão, -voa [pa'vãw, 'voa] (pl -ões, ~s) m/f peacock/peahen
pavilhão [pavi'ʎãw] (pl -ões) m tent; (de madeira) hut; (no jardim) summerhouse; (em exposição) pavilion; (bandeira) flag
pavimento [pavi'mẽtu] m (chão, andar) floor; (da rua) road surface
pavões [pa'võjʃ] mpl de **pavão**
pavor [pa'vo*] m dread, terror; ter ~ de to be terrified of; **pavoroso, -a** [pavo'rozu, ɔza] adj dreadful, terrible
paz [pajʒ] f peace; fazer as ~es to make up, be friends again
PC abr m = personal computer
Pça. abr (= Praça) Sq.
pé [pɛ] m foot; (da mesa) leg; (fig: base) footing; (de milho, café) plant; ir a ~ to walk, go on foot; ao ~ de near, by; ao ~ da letra literally; estar de ~ (festa etc) to be on; em ou de ~ standing (up); dar no ~ (col) to run away, take off; não ter ~ nem cabeça (fig) to make no sense
peão [pjãw] (PT: pl -ões) m pedestrian
peça [ˈpesa] f piece; (AUTO) part; (aposento) room; (TEATRO) play; ~ de reposição spare part; ~ de roupa garment
pecado [pe'kadu] m sin
pecar [pe'ka*] vi to sin; ~ por excesso de zelo to be over-zealous

pechincha [pe'ʃĩʃa] f (*vantagem*) godsend; (*coisa barata*) bargain; **pechinchar** [peʃĩ'ʃa*] vi to bargain, haggle

peço *etc* ['pɛsu] *vb* V **pedir**

peculiar [peku'lja*] *adj* special, peculiar; (*particular*) particular; **peculiaridade** [pekuljari'dadʒi] f peculiarity

pedaço [pe'dasu] *m* piece; (*fig: trecho*) bit; **aos ~s** in pieces

pedágio [pe'daʒju] (BR) *m* (*pagamento*) toll

pedal [pe'daw] (*pl* **-ais**) *m* pedal; **pedalar** [peda'la*] *vt*, *vi* to pedal

pedante [pe'dãtʃi] *adj* pretentious ♦ *m/f* pseud

pedestre [pe'dɛʃtri] (BR) *m* pedestrian

pedicuro, -a [pedʒi'kuru, a] *m/f* chiropodist (BRIT), podiatrist (US)

pedido [pe'dʒidu] *m* request; (COM) order; **~ de demissão** resignation; **~ de desculpa** apology

pedinte [pe'dʒĩtʃi] *m/f* beggar

pedir [pe'dʒi*] *vt* to ask for; (COM, *comida*) to order; (*exigir*) to demand ♦ *vi* to ask; (*num restaurante*) to order; **~ algo a alguém** to ask sb for sth; **~ a alguém que faça, ~ para alguém fazer** to ask sb to do

pedra ['pɛdra] f stone; (*rochedo*) rock; (*de granizo*) hailstone; (*de açúcar*) lump; (*quadro-negro*) slate; **~ de gelo** ice cube; **pedreiro** [pe'drejru] *m* stonemason

pegada [pe'gada] f (*de pé*) footprint; (FUTEBOL) save

pegado, -a [pe'gadu, a] *adj* stuck; (*unido*) together

pegajoso, -a [pega'ʒozu, ɔza] *adj* sticky

pegar [pe'ga*] *vt* to catch; (*selos*) to stick (on); (*segurar*) to take hold of; (*hábito, mania*) to get into; (*com-*

preender) to take in; (*trabalho*) to take on; (*estação de rádio*) to pick up, get ♦ *vi* to stick; (*planta*) to take; (*moda*) to catch on; (*doença*) to be catching; (*motor*) to start; **~ em** (*segurar*) to grab, pick up; **ir ~** (*buscar*) to go and get; **~ um emprego** to get a job; **~ fogo a algo** to set fire to sth; **~ no sono** to fall asleep

pego, -a ['pɛgu, a] *pp de* **pegar**

peito ['pejtu] *m* (ANAT) chest; (*de ave, mulher*) breast; (*fig*) courage

peitoril [pejto'riw] (*pl* **-is**) *m* windowsill

peixada [pej'ʃada] f fish cooked in a seafood sauce

peixaria [pejʃa'ria] f fish shop, fishmonger's (BRIT)

peixe ['pejʃi] *m* fish; **P~s** *mpl* (ASTROLOGIA) Pisces *sg*

pela ['pɛla] = **por + a**

pelada [pe'lada] f football game; *see boxed note*

PELADA

Pelada is an improvised, generally short, game of football, which in the past was played with a ball made out of socks, or an inflatable rubber ball. It is still played today on any piece of open land, or even in the street.

---

pelado, -a [pe'ladu, a] *adj* (*sem pele*) skinned; (*sem pêlo, cabelo*) shorn; (*nu*) naked, in the nude; (*sem dinheiro*) broke

pelar [pe'la*] *vt* (*tirar a pele*) to skin; (*tirar o pêlo*) to shear

pelas ['pɛlaʃ] = **por + as**

pele ['pɛli] f skin; (*couro*) leather; (*como agasalho*) fur; (*de animal*) hide

película [pe'likula] f film

pelo ['pɛlu] = **por + o**

pêlo ['pelu] *m* hair; (*de animal*) fur,

coat; **nu em ~** stark naked
pelos ['pelu∫] = **por** + **os**
peludo, -a [pe'ludu, a] adj hairy;
(animal) furry
pena ['pena] f feather; (de caneta)
nib; (escrita) writing; (JUR) penalty,
punishment; (sofrimento) suffering;
(piedade) pity; **que ~!** what a
shame!; **dar ~** to be upsetting; **ter ~
de** to feel sorry for; **~ capital** capital
punishment
penal [pe'naw] (pl -ais) adj penal;
penalidade [penali'dadʒi] f (JUR)
penalty; (castigo) punishment; **penalizar** [penali'za*] vt to trouble;
(castigar) to penalize
pênalti ['penawt∫i] m (FUTEBOL)
penalty (kick)
penar [pe'na*] vt to grieve ♦ vi to
suffer
pendência [pē'dēsja] f dispute,
quarrel
pendente [pē'dēt∫i] adj hanging;
(por decidir) pending; (inclinado)
sloping; (dependent): **~ (de)** dependent (on) ♦ m pendant
pêndulo ['pēdulu] m pendulum
pendurar [pēdu'ra*] vt to hang
penedo [pe'nedu] m rock, boulder
peneira [pe'nejra] f sieve; **peneirar**
[penej'ra*] vt to sift, sieve ♦ vi
(chover) to drizzle
penetrante [pene'trãt∫i] adj (olhar)
searching; (ferida) deep; (frio) bit-
ing; (som, análise) penetrating,
piercing; (dor, arma) sharp; (inteligência, idéias) incisive
penetrar [pene'tra*] vt to get into,
penetrate; (compreender) to understand ♦ vi: **~ em** ou **por** ou **entre** to
penetrate; **~ em** (segredo) to find
out
penhasco [pe'na∫ku] m cliff, crag
penhorar [peɲo'ra*] vt (dar em penhor) to pledge, pawn

penicilina [penisi'lina] f penicillin
península [pe'nīsula] f peninsula
pênis ['peni∫] m inv penis
penitência [peni'tēsja] f penitence;
(expiação) penance; **penitenciária**
[penitē'sjarja] f prison
penoso, -a [pe'nozu, ɔza] adj (assunto, tratamento) painful; (trabalho) hard
pensamento [pēsa'mētu] m
thought; (mente) mind; (opinião)
way of thinking; (idéia) idea
pensão [pē'sãw] (pl -ões) f (tb: casa de ~) boarding house; (comida)
board; **~ completa** full board; **~ de
aposentadoria** (retirement) pension
pensar [pē'sa*] vi to think; (imaginar) to imagine; **~ em** to think of
ou about; **~ fazer** to intend to do;
pensativo, -a [pēsa't∫ivu, a] adj
thoughtful, pensive
pensionista [pēsjo'ni∫ta] m/f pensioner
pensões [pē'sõj∫] fpl de **pensão**
pente ['pēt∫i] m comb; **penteado,
-a** [pē't∫jadu, a] adj (cabelo) in
place; (pessoa) smart ♦ m hairdo,
hairstyle; **pentear** [pē't∫ja*] vt to
comb; (arranjar o cabelo) to do,
style; **pentear-se** vr to comb one's
hair; to do one's hair
penúltimo, -a [pe'nuwt∫imu, a]
adj last but one, penultimate
penumbra [pe'nũbra] f twilight,
dusk; (sombra) shadow; (meia-luz)
half-light
penúria [pe'nurja] f poverty
peões [pjõj∫] mpl de **peão**
pepino [pe'pinu] m cucumber
pequeno, -a [pe'kenu, a] adj small;
(mesquinho) petty ♦ m boy
pequerrucho [peke'xu∫u] m thimble
Pequim [pe'kĩ] n Peking, Beijing

pêra ['pera] f pear

perambular [perãbu'la*] vi to wander

perante [pe'rãtʃi] prep before, in the presence of

per capita [pex'kapita] adv, adj per capita

perceber [pexse'be*] vt to realize; (por meio dos sentidos) to perceive; (compreender) to understand; (ver) to see; (ouvir) to hear; (ver ao longe) to make out; (dinheiro: receber) to receive

percentagem [pexsẽ'taʒẽ] f percentage

percepção [pexsep'sãw] f perception; **perceptível** [pexsep'tʃivew] (pl -eis) adj perceptible, noticeable; (som) audible

percevejo [pexse'veʒu] m (inseto) bug; (prego) drawing pin (BRIT), thumbtack (US)

perco etc ['pexku] vb V perder

percorrer [pexko'xe*] vt (viajar por) to travel (across ou over); (passar por) to go through, traverse; (investigar) to search through

percurso [pex'kuxsu] m (espaço percorrido) distance (covered); (trajeto) route; (viagem) journey

percussão [pexku'sãw] f (MÚS) percussion

perda ['pexda] f loss; (desperdício) waste; **~s e danos** damages, losses

perdão [pex'dãw] m pardon, forgiveness; **~!** sorry!, I beg your pardon!

perder [pex'de*] vt to lose; (tempo) to waste; (trem, show, oportunidade) to miss ♦ vi to lose; **perder-se** vr to get lost; (arruinar-se) to be ruined; (desaparecer) to disappear; **~-se de alguém** to lose sb

perdição [pexdʒi'sãw] f perdition, ruin; (desonra) depravity

perdido, -a [pex'dʒidu, a] adj lost; **~s e achados** lost and found, lost property

perdiz [pex'dʒiʒ] f partridge

perdoar [pex'dwa*] vt to forgive

perdurar [pexdu'ra*] vi to last a long time; (continuar a existir) to still exist

perecível [pere'sivew] (pl -eis) adj perishable

peregrinação [peregrina'sãw] (pl -ões) f (viagem) travels pl; (REL) pilgrimage

peregrino, -a [pere'grinu, a] m/f pilgrim

peremptório, -a [perẽp'tɔrju, a] adj final; (decisivo) decisive

perene [pe'reni] adj everlasting; (BOT) perennial

perfeição [pexfej'sãw] f perfection

perfeitamente [pexfejta'mẽtʃi] adv perfectly ♦ excl exactly!

perfeito, -a [pex'fejtu, a] adj perfect ♦ m (LING) perfect

perfil [pex'fiw] (pl -is) m profile; (silhueta) silhouette, outline; (ARQ) (cross) section

perfume [pex'fumi] m perfume, scent

perfurar [pexfu'ra*] vt (o chão) to drill a hole in; (papel) to punch (a hole in)

pergunta [pex'gũta] f question; **fazer uma ~ a alguém** to ask sb a question; **perguntar** [pexgũ'ta*] vt to ask; (interrogar) to question ♦ vi: **perguntar por alguém** to ask after sb; **perguntar-se** vr to wonder; **perguntar algo a alguém** to ask sb sth

perícia [pe'risja] f expertise; (destreza) skill; (exame) investigation

periferia [perife'ria] f periphery; (da cidade) outskirts pl

perigo [pe'rigu] m danger; **peri-**

goso, -a [peri'gozu, ɔza] adj dàngerous; (arriscado) risky

periódico, -a [pe'rjɔdʒiku, a] adj periodic ♦ m (revista) magazine, periodical; (jornal) (news)paper

período [pe'riodu] m period; (estação) season

peripécia [peri'pɛsja] f (aventura) adventure; (incidente) turn of events

periquito [peri'kitu] m parakeet

perito, -a [pe'ritu, a] adj expert ♦ m/f expert; (quem faz perícia) investigator

permanecer [pexmane'se*] vi to remain; (num lugar) to stay; (continuar a ser) to remain, keep; ~ **parado** to keep still

permanência [pexma'nẽsja] f permanence; (estada) stay; **permanente** [pexma'nẽtʃi] adj (dor) constant; (cor) fast; (residência, pregas) permanent ♦ m (cartão) pass ♦ f perm

permissão [pexmi'sãw] f permission, consent; **permissivo, -a** [pexmi'sivu, a] adj permissive

permitir [pexmi'tʃi*] vt to allow, permit

perna ['pɛxna] f leg; ~**s tortas** bow legs

pernil [pex'niw] (pl -**is**) m (de animal) haunch; (CULIN) leg

pernilongo [pexni'lõgu] m mosquito

pernis [pex'nif] mpl de **pernil**

pernoitar [pexnoj'ta*] vi to spend the night

pérola ['pɛrola] f pearl

perpendicular [pexpẽdʒiku'la*] adj, f perpendicular

perpetuar [pexpe'twa*] vt to perpetuate; **perpétuo, -a** [pex'pɛtwu, a] adj perpetual

perplexo, -a [pex'plɛksu, a] adj bewildered, puzzled; (indeciso) un-

certain; **ficar ~** to be taken aback

persa ['pɛxsa] adj, m/f Persian

perseguição [pexsegi'sãw] f pursuit; (REL, POL) persecution

perseguir [pexse'gi*] vt to pursue; (correr atrás) to chase (after); (REL, POL) to persecute; (importunar) to harass, pester

perseverante [pexseve'rãtʃi] adj persistent

perseverar [pexseve'ra*] vi: ~ **(em)** to persevere (in), persist (in)

Pérsia ['pɛxsja] f: **a ~** Persia

persiana [pex'sjana] f blind

Pérsico, -a ['pɛxsiku, a] adj: **o golfo ~** the Persian Gulf

persigo etc [pex'sigu] vb V **perseguir**

persistente [pexsif'tẽtʃi] adj persistent

persistir [pexsif'tʃi*] vi: ~ **(em)** to persist (in)

personagem [pexso'naʒẽ] (pl -**ns**) m/f famous person, celebrity; (num livro, filme) character

personalidade [pexsonali'dadʒi] f personality

perspectiva [pexfpek'tʃiva] f perspective; (panorama) view; (probabilidade) prospect

perspicácia [pexfpi'kasja] f insight, perceptiveness; **perspicaz** [pexfpi'kajʃ] adj observant; (sagaz) shrewd

persuadir [pexswa'dʒi*] vt to persuade; **persuadir-se** vr to convince o.s.; **persuasão** [pexswa'zãw] f persuasion; **persuasivo, -a** [pexswa'zivu, a] adj persuasive

pertencente [pextẽ'sẽtʃi] adj: ~ **a** pertaining to

pertencer [pextẽ'se*] vi: ~ **a** to belong to; (referir-se) to concern

pertences [pex'tẽsif] mpl (de uma pessoa) belongings

pertinência [pextʃi'nẽsja] f relevance; **pertinente** [pextʃi'nẽtʃi] adj relevant; (apropriado) appropriate

perto, -a ['pextu, a] adj nearby ♦ adv near; **~ de** near to; (em comparação com) next to; **de ~** closely; (ver) close up; (conhecer) very well

perturbar [pextux'ba*] vt to disturb; (abalar) to upset, trouble; (atrapalhar) to put off; (andamento, trânsito) to disrupt; (envergonhar) to embarrass; (alterar) to alter

Peru [pe'ru] m: **o ~** Peru

peru, a [pe'ru, a] m/f turkey

peruca [pe'ruka] f wig

perverso, -a [pex'vexsu, a] adj perverse; (malvado) wicked

perverter [pexvex'te*] vt to corrupt, pervert; **pervertido, -a** [pexvex'tʃidu, a] adj perverted ♦ m/f pervert

pesadelo [peza'delu] m nightmare

pesado, -a [pe'zadu, a] adj heavy; (ambiente) tense; (trabalho) hard; (estilo) dull, boring; (andar) slow; (piada) coarse; (comida) stodgy; (tempo) sultry ♦ adv heavily

pêsames ['pezamiʃ] mpl condolences, sympathy sg

pesar [pe'za*] vt to weigh; (fig) to weigh up ♦ vi to weigh; (ser pesado) to be heavy; (influir) to carry weight; (causar mágoa): **~ a** to hurt, grieve ♦ m grief; **~ sobre** (recair) to fall upon

pesaroso, -a [peza'rozu, ɔza] adj sorrowful, sad; (arrependido) regretful, sorry

pesca ['peʃka] f fishing; (os peixes) catch; **ir à ~** to go fishing

pescada [peʃ'kada] f whiting

pescado [peʃ'kadu] m fish

pescador, a [peʃka'do*, a] m/f fisherman/woman; **~ à linha** angler

pescar [peʃ'ka*] vt (peixe) to catch; (tentar apanhar) to fish for; (retirar da água) to fish out ♦ vi to fish

pescoço [peʃ'kosu] m neck

peso ['pezu] m weight; (fig: ônus) burden; (importância) importance; **~ bruto/líquido** gross/net weight

pesquisa [peʃ'kiza] f inquiry, investigation; (científica, de mercado) research; **pesquisar** [peʃki'za*] vt, vi to investigate; to research

pêssego ['pesegu] m peach

pessimista [pesi'miʃta] adj pessimistic ♦ m/f pessimist

péssimo, -a ['pɛsimu, a] adj very bad, awful

pessoa [pe'soa] f person; **~s** fpl (gente) people; **pessoal** [pe'swaw] (pl **-is**) adj personal ♦ m personnel pl, staff pl; (col) people pl, folks pl

pestana [peʃ'tana] f eyelash

peste ['pɛʃtʃi] f epidemic; (bubônica) plague; (fig) pest, nuisance

pétala ['pɛtala] f petal

petição [petʃi'sãw] (pl **-ões**) f request; (documento) petition

petisco [pe'tʃiʃku] m savoury (BRIT), savory (US), titbit (BRIT), tidbit (US)

petróleo [pe'trɔlju] m oil, petroleum; **~ bruto** crude oil

petulância [petu'lãsja] f impudence; **petulante** [petu'lãtʃi] adj impudent

peúga ['pjuga] (PT) f sock

pevide [pe'vidʒi] (PT) f (de melão) seed; (de maçã) pip

p. ex. abr (= por exemplo) e.g.

pia ['pia] f wash basin; (da cozinha) sink; **~ batismal** font

piada ['pjada] f joke

pianista [pja'niʃta] m/f pianist

piano ['pjanu] m piano

piar [pja*] vi (pinto) to cheep; (coruja) to hoot

picada [pi'kada] f (de agulha etc) prick; (de abelha) sting; (de mosquito, cobra) bite; (de avião) dive; (de navalha) stab; (atalho) path, trail

picante [pi'kātʃi] adj (tempero) hot

pica-pau ['pika-] (pl **~s**) m woodpecker

picar [pi'ka*] vt to prick; (suj: abelha) to sting; (: mosquito) to bite; (: pássaro) to peck; (um animal) to goad; (carne) to mince; (papel) to shred; (fruta) to chop up ♦ vi (comichar) to prickle

picareta [pika'reta] f pickaxe (BRIT), pickax (US) ♦ m/f crook

pico ['piku] m (cume) peak; (ponta aguda) sharp point; (PT: um pouco) a bit; **mil e ~** just over a thousand

picolé [piko'lε] m lolly

picotar [piko'ta*] vt to perforate; (bilhete) to punch

piedade [pje'dadʒi] f piety; (compaixão) pity; **ter ~ de** to have pity on; **piedoso, -a** [pje'dozu, ɔza] adj pious; (compassivo) merciful

pifar [pi'fa*] (col) vi (carro) to break down; (rádio etc) to go wrong; (plano, programa) to fall through

pijama [pi'ʒama] m ou f pyjamas pl (BRIT), pajamas pl (US)

pilantra [pi'lātra] (col) m/f crook

pilar [pi'la*] vt to pound, crush ♦ m pillar

pilha ['piʎa] f (ELET) battery; (monte) pile, heap

pilhagem [pi'ʎaʒē] f (ato) pillage; (objetos) plunder, booty

pilhar [pi'ʎa] vt to plunder, pillage; (roubar) to rob; (surpreender) to catch

pilotar [pilo'ta*] vt (avião) to fly

piloto [pi'lotu] m (tb: motorista) (racing) driver; (bico de gás) pilot light ♦ adj inv (usina, plano) pilot; (peça) sample atr

pílula ['pilula] f pill; **a ~ (anticoncepcional)** the pill

pimenta [pi'mēta] f (CULIN) pepper; **~ de Caiena** cayenne pepper; **pimenta-do-reino** f black pepper; **pimenta-malagueta** (pl **pimentas-malagueta**) f chilli (BRIT) ou chili (US) pepper; **pimentão** [pimē'tāw] (pl **-ões**) m (BOT) pepper

pinça ['pīsa] f (de sobrancelhas) tweezers pl; (de casa) tongs pl; (MED) callipers pl (BRIT), calipers pl (US)

pincel [pī'sew] (pl **-éis**) m brush; (para pintar) paintbrush; **pincelar** [pīse'la*] vt to paint

pinga ['pīga] f (cachaça) rum; (PT: trago) drink

pingar [pī'ga*] vi to drip

pingo ['pīgu] m (gota) drop

pingue-pongue [pīgi-'põʒi] ® m ping-pong ®

pingüim [pī'gwĩ] (pl **-ns**) m penguin

pinheiro [pi'nejru] m pine (tree)

pinho ['pinu] m pine

pino ['pinu] m (peça) pin; (AUTO: na porta) lock; **a ~** upright

pinta ['pīta] f (mancha) spot

pintar [pī'ta*] vt to paint; (cabelo) to dye; (rosto) to make up; (descrever) to describe; (imaginar) to picture ♦ vi to paint; **pintar-se** vr to make o.s. up

pintarroxo [pīta'xoʃu] m (BR) linnet; (PT) robin

pinto ['pĩtu] m chick; (col!) prick (!)

pintor, a [pĩ'to*, a] m/f painter

pintura [pĩ'tura] f painting; (maquiagem) make-up

piolho ['pjoʎu] m louse

pioneiro, a [pjo'nejru, a] m/f pioneer

pior ['pjɔ*] adj, adv (compar) worse; (superl) worst ♦ m: **o ~** worst of all;

piorar [pjo'ra*] vt to make worse, worsen ♦ vi to get worse

pipa ['pipa] f barrel, cask; (de papel) kite

pipi [pi'pi] (col) m pee; **fazer ~** to have a pee

pipoca [pi'pɔka] f popcorn

pipocar [pipo'ka*] vi to go pop, pop

pique etc vb V **picar**

piquenique [piki'niki] m picnic

pirâmide [pi'ramidʒi] f pyramid

piranha [pi'raɲa] f piranha (fish)

pirata [pi'rata] m pirate

pires ['piris] m inv saucer

Pireneus [piri'newʃ] mpl: **os ~ the** Pyrenees

pirulito [piru'litu] (BR) m lollipop

pisar [pi'za*] vt to tread on; (esmagar, subjugar) to crush ♦ vi to step, tread

pisca-pisca [piʃka-'piʃka] (pl ~s) m (AUTO) indicator

piscar [piʃ'ka*] vt to blink; (dar sinal) to wink; (estrelas) to twinkle ♦ m: **num ~ de olhos** in a flash

piscina [pi'sina] f swimming pool

piso ['pizu] m floor

pisotear [pizo'tʃja*] vt to trample (on)

pista ['piʃta] f (vestígio) trace; (indicação) clue; (de corridas) track; (AVIAT) runway; (de estrada) lane; (de dança) (dance) floor

pistola [piʃ'tɔla] f pistol

pitada [pi'tada] f (porção) pinch

pivete [pi'vetʃi] m child thief

pivô [pi'vo] m pivot; (fig) central figure, prime mover

pizza ['pitsa] f pizza

placa ['plaka] f plate; (AUTO) number plate (BRIT), license plate (US); (comemorativa) plaque; (na pele) blotch; **~ de sinalização** roadsign

placar [pla'ka*] m scoreboard

plácido, -a ['plasidu, a] adj calm; (manso) placid

plágio ['plaʒu] m plagiarism

planalto [pla'nawtu] m tableland, plateau

planar [pla'na*] vi to glide

planear [pla'nja*] (PT) vt = **planejar**

planejamento [planeʒa'mẽtu] m planning; **~ familiar** family planning

planejar [plane'ʒa*] (BR) vt to plan; (edifício) to design

planeta [pla'neta] m planet

planície [pla'nisi] f plain

plano, -a ['planu, a] adj flat, level; (liso) smooth ♦ m plan; **em primeiro/em último ~** in the foreground/background; **P~ Real** see boxed note

---

PLANO REAL

The **Plano Real**, launched in 1994, was a plan for the economic stabilization of Brazil. In an attempt to contain inflation without resorting to measures such as a price and wage freeze, the government changed the Brazilian currency from the *cruzeiro* to the *real*. In addition, it speeded up the privatization of state-owned companies, reduced public spending and raised interest rates to rein in consumer demand.

---

planta ['plãta] f plant; (de pé) sole; (ARQ) plan

plantação [plãta'sãw] f (ato) planting; (terreno) planted land; (plantio) crops pl

plantão [plã'tãw] (pl -ões) m duty; (noturno) night duty; (plantonista) person on duty; (MIL: serviço) sentry duty; (: pessoa) sentry; **estar de ~ to** be on duty

plantar [plã'ta*] vt to plant; (estaca) to drive in; (estabelecer) to set up

plantões [plã'tõjʃ] mpl de **plantão**

plástico, -a ['plaʃtʃiku, a] adj plastic ♦ m plastic

plataforma [plata'fɔxma] f platform; ~ de exploração de petróleo oil rig; ~ de lançamento launch pad

platéia [pla'teja] f (TEATRO etc) stalls pl (BRIT), orchestra (US); (espectadores) audience

platina [pla'tʃina] f platinum

platinados [platʃi'naduʃ] mpl (AUTO) points

plausível [plaw'zivew] (pl -eis) adj credible, plausible

playground [plej'grãwdʒi] (pl ~s) m (children's) playground

plenamente [plena'mẽtʃi] adv fully, completely

pleno, -a ['plenu, a] adj full; (completo) complete; em ~ dia in broad daylight; em ~ inverno in the middle ou depths of winter

plural [plu'raw] (pl -ais) adj, m plural

pneu ['pnew] m tyre (BRIT), tire (US)

pneumonia [pnewmo'nia] f pneumonia

pó [pɔ] m powder; (sujeira) dust; sabão em ~ soap powder; tirar o ~ (de algo) to dust (sth)

pobre ['pɔbri] adj poor ♦ m/f poor person; **pobreza** [po'breza] f poverty

poça ['posa] f puddle, pool

poção [po'sãw] (pl -ões) f potion

poço ['posu] m well; (de mina, elevador) shaft

poções [po'sõjʃ] fpl de **poção**

pôde etc ['podʒi] vb V **poder**

pó-de-arroz m face powder

poder [po'de*] vi 1 (capacidade) can, be able to; não posso fazê-lo I can't do it, I'm unable to do it

2 (ter o direito de) can, may, be allowed to; posso fumar aqui? can I smoke here?; pode entrar? (posso?) can I come in?

3 (possibilidade) may, might, could; pode ser maybe; pode ser que it may be that; ele ~á vir amanhã he might come tomorrow

4: não ~ com: não posso com ele I cannot cope with him

5 (col: indignação): pudera! no wonder!; como é que pode? you're joking!

♦ m power; (autoridade) authority; ~ aquisitivo purchasing power; estar no ~ to be in power; em ~ de alguém in sb's hands

poderoso, -a [pode'rozu, ɔza] adj mighty, powerful

podre ['podri] adj rotten; **podridão** [podri'dãw] f decay, rottenness; (fig) corruption

põe etc [põj] vb V **pôr**

poeira ['pwejra] f dust; ~ radioativa fall-out; **poeirento, -a** [pwej'rẽtu, a] adj dusty

poema ['pwema] m poem

poesia [poe'zia] f poetry; (poema) poem

poeta ['pweta] m poet; **poético, -a** ['pwetʃiku, a] adj poetic; **poetisa** [pwe'tʃiza] f (woman) poet

pois [pojʃ] adv (portanto) so; (PT: assentimento) yes ♦ conj as, since; (mas) but; ~ bem well then; ~ é that's right; ~ não! (BR) of course!; ~ não? (BR: numa loja) what can I do for you?; (PT) isn't it?, aren't you?, didn't they? etc; ~ sim! certainly not!; ~ **(então)** then

polaco, -a [po'laku, a] *adj* Polish
♦ *m/f* Pole ♦ *m* (LING) Polish

polar [po'la*] *adj* polar

polegada [pole'gada] *f* inch

polegar [pole'ga*] *m* (*tb*: **dedo ~**)
thumb

polêmica [po'lemika] *f* controversy; **polêmico, -a** [po'lemiku, a] *adj*
controversial

pólen ['pɔlẽ] *m* pollen

polícia [po'lisja] *f* police, police
force ♦ *m/f* policeman/woman;
policial [poli'sjaw] (*pl* **-ais**) *adj*
police *atr* ♦ *m/f* (BR) policeman/
woman; **novela** *ou* **romance policial** detective novel; **policiar**
[poli'sja*] *vt* to police; (*instintos,
modos*) to control, keep in check

polidez [poli'deʒ] *f* good manners
pl, politeness

polido, -a [po'lidu, a] *adj* polished,
shiny; (*cortês*) well-mannered, polite

pólio ['pɔlju] *f* polio

polir [po'li*] *vt* to polish

política [po'litʃika] *f* politics *sg*;
(*programa*) policy; **político, -a**
[po'litʃiku, a] *adj* political ♦ *m/f*
politician

pólo ['pɔlu] *m* pole; (ESPORTE) polo;
P~ **Norte/Sul** North/South Pole

polonês, -esa [polo'neʃ, eza] *adj*
Polish ♦ *m/f* Pole ♦ *m* (LING) Polish

Polônia [po'lonja] *f*: **a ~** Poland

polpa ['powpa] *f* pulp

poltrona [pow'trona] *f* armchair

poluição [polwi'sãw] *f* pollution;
poluir [po'lwi*] *vt* to pollute

polvo ['powvu] *m* octopus

pólvora ['pɔwvora] *f* gunpowder

pomada [po'mada] *f* ointment

pomar [po'ma*] *m* orchard

pomba ['põba] *f* dove

pombo ['põbu] *m* pigeon

pompa ['põpa] *f* pomp

pomposo, -a [põ'pozu, ɔza] *adj*
pompous

ponderação [põdera'sãw] *f* consideration, meditation; (*prudência*)
prudence

ponderado, -a [põde'radu, a] *adj*
prudent

ponderar [põde'ra*] *vt* to consider,
weigh up ♦ *vi* to meditate, muse

ponho *etc* ['poɲu] *vb* V **pôr**

ponta ['põta] *f* tip; (*de faca*) point;
(*de sapato*) toe; (*extremidade*) end;
(FUTEBOL: *posição*) wing; (: *jogador*)
winger; **uma ~ de** (*um pouco*) a
touch of; ~ **do dedo** fingertip

pontada [põ'tada] *f* (*dor*) twinge

pontapé [põta'pɛ] *m* kick; **dar ~s
em alguém** to kick sb

pontaria [põta'ria] *f* aim; **fazer ~** to
take aim

ponte ['põtʃi] *f* bridge; ~ **aérea** air
shuttle, airlift; ~ **de safena** (heart)
bypass operation

ponteiro [põ'tejru] *m* (*indicador*)
pointer; (*de relógio*) hand

pontiagudo, -a [põtʃja'gudu, a]
adj sharp, pointed

ponto ['põtu] *m* point; (MED, COSTURA,
TRICÔ) stitch; (*pequeno sinal, do i*)
dot; (*na pontuação*) full stop (BRIT),
period (US); (*na pele*) spot; (*de
ônibus*) stop; (*de táxi*) rank (BRIT),
stand (US); (*matéria escolar*) subject;
estar a ~ de fazer to be on the
point of doing; **às cinco em ~ at**
five o'clock on the dot; **dois ~s**
colon *sg*; ~ **de admiração** (PT)
exclamation mark; ~ **de exclamação/interrogação** exclamation/
question mark; ~ **de vista** point of
view, viewpoint; **ponto-e-vírgula**
(*pl* **ponto-e-vírgulas**) *m* semicolon

pontuação [põtwa'sãw] *f* punctuation

pontual 541 **porém**

pontual [põ'twaw] (*pl* -ais) *adj*
punctual
pontudo, -a [põ'tudu, a] *adj* pointed
popa ['popa] *f* stern
população [popula'sãw] (*pl* -ões) *f*
population
popular [popu'la*] *adj* popular;
popularidade [populari'dadʒi] *f*
popularity
pôquer ['poke*] *m* poker

PALAVRA CHAVE

por [po*] (*por + o(s), a(s) = pelo(s),
pela(s)*) *prep* **1** (*objetivo*) for; **lutar
pela pátria** to fight for one's country
2 (+ *infin*): **está ~ acontecer** it is
about to happen, it is yet to happen; **está ~ fazer** it is still to be
done
3 (*causa*) out of, because of; **~ falta
de fundos** through lack of funds; **~
hábito/natureza** out of habit/by
nature; **faço isso ~ ela** I do it for
her; **~ isso** therefore, for that
reason; **a razão pela
qual ...** the reason why ...; **pelo
amor de Deus!** for Heaven's sake!
4 (*tempo*): **pela manhã** in the morning; **~ volta das duas horas** at
about two o'clock; **ele vai ficar ~
uma semana** he's staying for a
week
5 (*lugar*): **~ aqui** this way; **viemos
pelo parque** we came through the
park; **passar ~ São Paulo** to pass
through São Paulo; **~ fora/dentro**
outside/inside
6 (*troca, preço*) for; **trocar o velho
pelo novo** to change old for new;
comprei o livro ~ dez libras I
bought the book for ten pounds
7 (*valor proporcional*): **~ cento** per
cent; **~ hora/dia/semana/mês/ano**
hourly/daily/weekly/monthly/year-
ly; **~ cabeça** a ou per head; **~ mais**

difícil *etc* **que seja** however difficult
etc it is
8 (*modo, meio*) by; **~ correio/avião**
by post/air; **~ si** by o.s.; **~ escrito** in
writing; **entrar pela entrada principal** to go in through the main
entrance
9: **~ que** (*por causa*) because (*PT*),
why (*BR*); **~ quê?** why?
10: **~ mim tudo bem** as far as I'm
concerned, that's OK

PALAVRA CHAVE

pôr [po*] *vt* **1** (*colocar*) to put;
(*roupas*) to put on; (*objeções, dúvidas*) to raise; (*ovos, mesa*) to lay;
(*defeito*) to find; **pôe mais forte** turn
it up; **você põe açúcar?** do you take
sugar?; **~ de lado** to set aside
2 (+ *adj*) to make; **você está me
pondo nervoso** you're making me
nervous
♦ **pôr-se** *vr* **1** (*sol*) to set
2 (*colocar-se*): **~-se de pé** to stand
up; **ponha-se no meu lugar** put
yourself in my position
3: **~-se a** to start to; **ela pôs-se a
chorar** she started crying
♦ *m*: **o ~ do sol** sunset

porão [po'rãw] (*pl* -ões) *m* (*de casa*)
basement; (: *armazém*) cellar
porca ['pɔxka] *f* (*animal*) sow
porção [pox'sãw] (*pl* -ões) *f* portion, piece; **uma ~ de** a lot of
porcaria [pɔxka'ria] *f* filth; (*dito sujo*) obscenity; (*coisa ruim*) piece of junk
porcelana [poxse'lana] *f* porcelain
porcentagem [poxsẽ'taʒẽ] (*pl* -ns)
f percentage
porco, -a ['poxku, 'pɔxka] *adj* filthy
♦ *m* (*animal*) pig; (*carne*) pork
porções [pox'sõjʃ] *fpl de* **porção**
porém [po'rẽ] *conj* however

pormenor [poxme'no*] *m* detail

pornografia [poxnogra'fia] *f* pornography

poro ['pɔru] *m* pore

porões [po'rõjs] *mpl de* **porão**

porque ['poxke] *conj* because; (*interrogativo:* PT) why

porquê [pox'ke] *adv* why ♦ *m* reason, motive; **~?** (PT) why?

porrete [po'xetʃi] *m* club

porta ['pɔxta] *f* door; (*de um jardim*) gate

portador, a [poxta'do*, a], *m/f* bearer

portagem [pox'taʒẽ] (PT) (*pl* -ns) *f* toll

portal [pox'taw] (*pl* -ais) *m* doorway

porta-luvas *m inv* (AUTO) glove compartment

porta-malas *m inv* (AUTO) boot (BRIT), trunk (US)

porta-níqueis *m inv* purse

portanto [pox'tãtu] *conj* so, therefore

portão [pox'tãw] (*pl* -ões) *m* gate

portar [pox'ta*] *vt* to carry; **portar-se** *vr* to behave

portaria [poxta'ria] *f* (*de um edifício*) entrance hall; (*recepção*) reception desk; (*do governo*) edict, decree

portátil [pox'tatʃiw] (*pl* -eis) *adj* portable

porta-voz (*pl* ~es) *m/f* (*pessoa*) spokesman/woman

porte ['pɔxtʃi] *m* transport; (*custo*) freight charge, carriage; **~ pago** post paid; **de grande ~** far-reaching, important

porteiro, -a [pox'tejru, a] *m/f* caretaker; **~ eletrônico** entryphone

pórtico ['pɔxtʃiku] *m* porch, portico

porto ['pɔxtu] *m* (*do mar*) port, harbour (BRIT), harbor (US); (*vinho*) port;

o P~ Oporto

portões [pox'tõjs] *mpl de* **portão**

Portugal [poxtu'gaw] *m* Portugal;
português, -guesa [portu'geʃ, 'geza] *adj* Portuguese ♦ *m/f* Portuguese *inv* ♦ *m* (LING) Portuguese

porventura [poxvẽ'tura] *adj* by chance; **se ~ você ...** if you happen to ...

pôs [poʃ] *vb V* **pôr**

posar [po'za*] *vi* (FOTO): **~ (para)** to pose (for)

posição [pozi'sãw] (*pl* -ões) *f* position; (*social*) standing, status; **posicionar** [pozisjo'na*] *vt* to position

positivo, -a [pozi'tʃivu, a] *adj* positive

possante [po'sãtʃi] *adj* powerful, strong; (*carro*) flashy

posse ['pɔsi] *f* possession, ownership; **~s** *fpl* (*pertences*) possessions, belongings; **tomar ~ de** to take possession of

possessão [poxvẽ'sãw] *f* possession;
possessivo, -a [pose'sivu, a] *adj* possessive

possibilidade [posibili'dadʒi] *f* possibility; **~s** *fpl* (*recursos*) means

possibilitar [posibili'ta*] *vt* to make possible, permit

possível [po'sivew] (*pl* -eis) *adj* possible; **fazer todo o ~** to do one's best

posso *etc* ['pɔsu] *vb V* **poder**

possuidor, a [poswi'do*, a], *m/f* owner

possuir [po'swi*] *vt* (*casa, livro etc*) to own; (*dinheiro, talento*) to possess

postal [poʃ'taw] (*pl* -ais) *adj* postal ♦ *m* postcard

poste ['pɔʃtʃi] *m* pole, post

posterior [poʃte'rjo*] *adj* (*mais tarde*) subsequent, later; (*traseiro*) rear, back; **posteriormente** [poʃterjoxˈmẽtʃi] adv later, subsequently

postiço, -a [poʃˈtʃisu, a] adj false, artificial

posto, -a [ˈpoʃtu, ˈpɔʃta] pp de **pôr** ♦ m post, position; (emprego) job; ~ **de gasolina** service ou petrol station; ~ **que** although; ~ **de saúde** health centre ou center

póstumo, -a [ˈpɔʃtumu, a] adj posthumous

postura [poʃˈtura] f posture; (aspecto físico) appearance

potável [poˈtavew] (pl -eis) adj drinkable; **água** ~ drinking water

pote [ˈpɔtʃi] m jug, pitcher; (de geléia) jar; (de creme) pot; **chover a** ~**s** (PT) to rain cats and dogs

potência [poˈtẽsja] f power

potencial [potẽˈsjaw] (pl -ais) adj, m potential

potente [poˈtẽtʃi] adj powerful, potent

PALAVRA CHAVE
---

pouco, -a [ˈpoku, a] adj **1** (sg) little, not much; ~ **tempo** little ou not much time; **de** ~ **interesse** of little interest, not very interesting; **pouca coisa** not much

2 (pl) few, not many; **uns** ~**s** a few, some; **poucas vezes** rarely; **poucas crianças comem o que devem** few children eat what they should

♦ adv **1** little, not much; **custa** ~ it doesn't cost much; **dentro em** ~, **daqui a** ~ shortly; ~ **antes** shortly before

2 (+ adj: = negativo): **ela é** ~ **inteligente/simpática** she's not very bright/friendly

3: **por** ~ **eu não morri** I almost died

4: ~ **a** ~ little by little

5: **aos** ~**s** gradually

♦ m: **um** ~ a little, a bit; **nem um** ~ not at all

poupador, a [popaˈdo*, a] adj thrifty

poupança [poˈpãsa] f thrift; (economias) savings pl; (tb: **caderneta de** ~) savings bank

poupar [poˈpa*] vt to save; (vida) to spare

pouquinho [poˈkiɲu] m: **um** ~ **(de)** a little

pousada [poˈzada] f (hospedagem) lodging; (hospedaria) inn

pousar [poˈza*] vt to place; (mão) to rest ♦ vi (avião, pássaro) to land; (pernoitar) to spend the night

povo [ˈpovu] m people; (raça) people pl, race; (plebe) common people pl; (multidão) crowd

povoação [povwaˈsãw] (pl -ões) f (aldeia) village, settlement; (habitantes) population

povoado [poˈvwadu] m village

povoar [poˈvwa*] vt (de habitantes) to people, populate; (de animais etc) to stock

pra [pra] (col) prep = **para a**

praça [ˈprasa] f (largo) square; (mercado) marketplace; (soldado) soldier; ~ **de touros** bullring

praga [ˈpraga] f nuisance; (maldição) curse; (desgraça) misfortune; (erva daninha) weed

pragmático, -a [pragˈmatʃiku, a] adj pragmatic

praia [ˈpraja] f beach

prancha [ˈprãʃa] f plank; (de surfe) board

prata [ˈprata] f silver; (col: cruzeiro) ≈ quid (BRIT), ≈ buck (US)

prateado, -a [praˈtʃjadu, a] adj silver-plated; (brilhante) silvery; (cor) silver ♦ m (cor) silver; (de um objeto) silver-plating; **papel** ~ silver paper

prateleira 544 **prédio**

prateleira [prate'lejra] f shelf
prática ['pratʃika] f practice; (experiência) experience, know-how; (costume) habit, custom; V tb **prático**
praticante [pratʃi'kãtʃi] adj practising (BRIT), practicing (US) ♦ m/f apprentice; (de esporte) practitioner
praticar [pratʃi'ka*] vt to practise (BRIT), practice (US); (roubo, operação) to carry out; **prático, -a** ['pratʃiku, a] adj practical ♦ m/f expert
prato ['pratu] m plate; (comida) dish; (de uma refeição) course; (de toca-discos) turntable; **~s** mpl (MÚS) cymbals
praxe ['praksi] f custom, usage; **de ~** usually; **ser de ~** to be the norm; **código da ~** see boxed note

---
PRAXE

Student life in Portugal follows the traditions set out in a written set of rules known as the *código da praxe*. It begins in freshers' week, where freshers are jeered at by their seniors, and are subjected to a number of humiliating practical jokes, such as having their hair cut against their will and being made to walk around town in fancy dress.

---

prazer [pra'ze*] m pleasure; **muito ~ em conhecê-lo** pleased to meet you
prazo ['prazu] m term, period; (vencimento) expiry date, time limit; **a curto/médio/longo ~** in the short/medium/long term; **comprar a ~** to buy on hire purchase (BRIT) ou on the installment plan (US)
precário, -a [pre'karju, a] adj precarious; (escasso) failing
precaução [prekaw'sãw] f (pl -ões) f precaution

precaver-se [preka'vexsi] vr: **~ (contra ou de)** to be on one's guard (against); **precavido, -a** [preka-'vidu, a] adj cautious
prece ['presi] f prayer; (súplica) entreaty
precedente [prese'dẽtʃi] adj preceding ♦ m precedent
preceder [prese'de*] vt, vi to precede; **~ a algo** to precede sth; (ter primazia) to take precedence over sth
precioso, -a [pre'sjozu, ɔza] adj precious
precipício [presi'pisju] m precipice; (fig) abyss
precipitação [presipita'sãw] f haste; (imprudência) rashness
precipitado, -a [presipi'tadu, a] adj hasty; (imprudente) rash
precisamente [presiza'mẽtʃi] adv precisely
precisar [presi'za*] vt to need; (especificar) to specify; **precisar-se** vr: **"precisa-se"** "needed"; **~ de** to need; (uso impess) **não precisa você se preocupar** you needn't worry
preciso, -a [pre'sizu, a] adj precise, accurate; (necessário) necessary; (claro) concise; **é ~ você ir** you must go
preço ['presu] m price; (custo) cost; (valor) value; **a ~ de banana** (BR) ou **de chuva** (PT) dirt cheap
precoce [pre'kɔsi] adj precocious; (antecipado) early
preconceito [prekõ'sejtu] m prejudice
precursor, a [prekux'so*, a] m/f precursor, forerunner; (mensageiro) herald
predador [preda'do*] m predator
predileto, -a [predʒi'letu, a] (PT -ct-) adj favourite (BRIT), favorite (US)
prédio ['predʒju] m building; **~ de**

apartamentos block of flats (BRIT), apartment house (US)

predispor [predʒiʃ'po*] (irreg: como pôr) vt: ~ **alguém contra** to prejudice sb against; **predispor-se** vr: ~-**se a/para** to get o.s. in the mood to/for

predominar [predomi'na*] vi to predominate, prevail

preencher [preẽ'ʃe*] vt (formulário) to fill in (BRIT) ou out, complete; (requisitos) to fulfil (BRIT), fulfill (US), meet, to fill

prefácio [pre'fasju] m preface

prefeito, -a [pre'fejtu, a] m/f mayor; **prefeitura** [prefej'tura] f town hall

preferência [prefe'rẽsja] f preference; (AUTO) priority; **de** ~ preferably; **preferencial** [preferẽ'sjaw] (pl -**ais**) adj (rua) main ♦ f main road (with priority)

preferido, -a [prefe'ridu, a] adj favourite (BRIT), favorite (US)

preferir [prefe'ri*] vt to prefer

prefiro etc [pre'firu] vb V **preferir**

prefixo [pre'fiksu] m (LING) prefix; (TEL) code

prega ['prega] f pleat, fold

pregar¹ [pre'ga*] vt, vi to preach

pregar² [pre'ga*] vt (com prego) to nail; (fixar) to pin, fasten; (cosendo) to sew on; ~ **uma peça** to play a trick; ~ **um susto em alguém** to give sb a fright

prego ['pregu] m nail; (col: casa de penhor) pawn shop

preguiça [pre'gisa] f laziness; (animal) sloth; **estar com** ~ to feel lazy; **preguiçoso, -a** [pregi'sozu, ɔza] adj lazy

pré-histórico, -a [pre-] adj prehistoric

preia-mar (PT) f high tide

prejudicar [preʒudʒi'ka*] vt to

damage; (atrapalhar) to hinder; **prejudicial** [preʒudʒi'sjaw] (pl -**ais**) adj damaging; (à saúde) harmful

prejuízo [pre'ʒwizu] m damage, harm; (em dinheiro) loss; **em** ~ **de** to the detriment of

prematuro, -a [prema'turu, a] adj premature

premiado, -a [pre'mjadu, a] adj prize-winning; (bilhete) winning ♦ m/f prize-winner

premiar [pre'mja*] vt to award a prize to; (recompensar) to reward

prêmio ['premju] m prize; (recompensa) reward; (SEGUROS) premium

prenda ['prẽda] f gift, present; (em jogo) forfeit; ~**s domésticas** housework sg

prendedor [prẽde'do*] m fastener; (de cabelo, gravata) clip; ~ **de roupa** clothes peg; ~ **de papéis** paper clip

prender [prẽ'de*] vt to fasten, fix; (roupa) to pin; (cabelo) to put back; (capturar) to arrest; (atar, ligar) to tie; (atenção) to catch; (afetivamente) to tie, bind; (reter: doença, compromisso) to keep; (movimentos) to restrict; **prender-se** vr to get caught, stick; ~-**se a alguém** (por amizade) to be attached to sb

preocupação [preokupa'sãw] (pl -**ões**) f preoccupation; (inquietação) worry, concern

preocupar [preoku'pa*] vt to preoccupy; (inquietar) to worry; **preocupar-se** vr: ~-**se com** to worry about, be worried about

preparação [prepara'sãw] (pl -**ões**) f preparation

preparar [prepa'ra*] vt to prepare; **preparar-se** vr to get ready; **preparativos** [prepara'tʃivuʃ] mpl preparations, arrangements

preponderante [prepõde'rãtʃi] adj

predominant

preposição [prepozi'sãw] (*pl* -**ões**) *f* preposition

prepotente [prepo'tẽtʃi] *adj* predominant; (*despótico*) despotic; (*atitude*) overbearing

presa ['preza] *f* (*na guerra*) spoils *pl*; (*vítima*) prey; (*dente de animal*) fang

prescrever [preʃkre've*] *vt* to prescribe; (*prazo*) to set

presença [pre'zẽsa] *f* presence; (*frequência*) attendance; **ter boa ~** to be presentable; **presenciar** [prezẽ'sja*] *vt* to be present at; (*testemunhar*) to witness

presente [pre'zẽtʃi] *adj* present; (*fig: interessado*) attentive; (: *evidente*) clear, obvious ♦ *m* present *f* (*COM: carta*) **a ~** this letter; **os ~s** those present; **presentear** [prezẽ'tʃja*] *vt*: **presentear alguém (com algo)** to give sb (sth as) a present

preservação [prezexva'sãw] *f* preservation

preservar [prezex'va*] *vt* to preserve, protect; **preservativo** [prezexva'tʃivu] *m* preservative, (*anticoncepcional*) condom

presidente, -a [prezi'dẽtʃi, ta] *m/f* president

presidiário, -a [prezi'dʒjarju, a] *m/f* convict

presídio [pre'zidʒju] *m* prison

presidir [prezi'dʒi*] *vt*, *vi*: **~ (a)** to preside over; (*reunião*) to chair; (*suj: leis, critérios*) to govern

presilha [pre'ziʎa] *f* fastener; (*para o cabelo*) slide

preso, -a ['prezu, a] *adj* imprisoned; (*capturado*) under arrest; (*atado*) tied ♦ *m/f* prisoner; **estar ~ a alguém** to be attached to sb

pressa ['prɛsa] *f* haste, hurry; (*rapi-*

dez) speed; (*urgência*) urgency; **às ~s** hurriedly; **estar com ~** to be in a hurry; **ter ~ de** *ou* **em fazer** to be in a hurry to do

presságio [pre'saʒu] *m* omen, sign; (*pressentimento*) premonition

pressão [pre'sãw] (*pl* -**ões**) *f* pressure; **(colchete de) ~** press stud, popper

pressentimento [presẽtʃi'mẽtu] *m* premonition

pressentir [presẽ'tʃi*] *vt* to foresee; (*suspeitar*) to sense

pressionar [presjo'na*] *vt* (*botão*) to press; (*coagir*) to pressure ♦ *vi* to press, put on pressure

pressões [pre'sõjʃ] *fpl de* **pressão**

pressupor [presu'po*] (*irreg: como* **pôr**) *vt* to presuppose

prestação [preʃta'sãw] (*pl* -**ões**) *f* instalment (*BRIT*), installment (*US*); (*por uma casa*) repayment

prestar [preʃ'ta*] *vt* (*cuidados*) to give; (*favores, serviços*) to do; (*contas*) to render; (*informações*) to supply; (*uma qualidade a algo*) to lend ♦ *vi*: **~ a alguém para algo** to be of use to sb for sth; **prestar-se** *vr*: **~-se a** to be suitable for; (*admitir*) to lend o.s. to; (*dispor-se*) to be willing to; **~ atenção** to pay attention

prestativo, -a [preʃta'tʃivu, a] *adj* helpful, obliging

prestes ['prɛʃtʃiʃ] *adj inv* ready; (*a ponto de*): **~ a partir** about to leave

prestígio [preʃ'tʃiʒu] *m* prestige

presunção [prezũ'sãw] (*pl* -**ões**) *f* presumption; (*vaidade*) conceit, self-importance; **presunçoso, -a** [prezũ'sozu, ɔza] *adj* vain, self-important

presunto [pre'zũtu] *m* ham

pretendente [pretẽ'dẽtʃi] *m/f* claimant; (*candidato*) candidate, applicant ♦ *m* suitor

pretender [pretẽ'de*] vt to claim; (cargo, emprego) to go for; ~ fazer to intend to do

pretensão [pretẽ'sãw] (pl -ões) f claim; (vaidade) pretension; (propósito) aim; (aspiração) aspiration; **pretensioso, -a** [pretẽ'sjozu, ɔza] adj pretentious

pretérito [pre'tɛritu] m (LING) preterite

pretexto [pre'teʃtu] m pretext

preto, -a ['pretu, a] adj black ♦ m/f Black (man/woman)

prevalecer [prevale'se*] vi to prevail; **prevalecer-se** vr: ~-se de (aproveitar-se) to take advantage of

prevenção [prevẽ'sãw] (pl -ões) f prevention; (preconceito) prejudice; (cautela) caution; **estar de ~ com ou contra alguém** to be bias(s)ed against sb

prevenido, -a [preve'nidu, a] adj cautious, wary

prevenir [preve'ni*] vt to prevent; (avisar) to warn; (preparar) to prepare

prever [pre've*] (irreg: como **ver**) vt to predict, foresee; (pressupor) to presuppose

previdência [previ'dēsja] f foresight; (precaução) precaution

previdente [previ'dētʃi] adj: **ser ~** to show foresight

prévio, -a ['prɛvju, a] adj prior; (preliminar) preliminary

previsão [previ'zãw] (pl -ões) f foresight; (prognóstico) prediction, forecast; ~ **do tempo** weather forecast

previsível [previ'zivew] (pl -eis) adj predictable

previsões [previ'zõjʃ] fpl de **previsão**

prezado, -a [pre'zadu, a] adj esteemed; (numa carta) dear

prezar [pre'za*] vt (amigos) to value highly; (autoridade) to respect; (gostar de) to appreciate

primário, -a [pri'marju, a] adj primary; (elementar) basic, rudimentary; (primitivo) primitive ♦ m (curso) elementary education

primavera [prima'vɛra] f spring; (planta) primrose

primeira [pri'mejra] f (AUTO) first (gear)

primeiro, -a [pri'mejru, a] adj, adv first; **de primeira** first-class

primitivo, -a [primi'tʃivu, a] adj primitive; (original) original

primo, -a ['primu, a] m/f cousin; ~ **irmão** first cousin

princesa [prĩ'seza] f princess

principal [prĩsi'paw] (pl -ais) adj principal; (entrada, razão, rua) main ♦ m head, principal; (essencial, de dívida) principal

príncipe ['prĩsipi] m prince

principiante [prĩsi'pjãtʃi] m/f beginner

principiar [prĩsi'pja*] vt, vi to begin

princípio [prĩ'sipju] m beginning, start; (origem) origin; (legal, moral) principle; ~**s** mpl (de matéria) rudiments

prioridade [prjori'dadʒi] f priority

prisão [pri'zãw] (pl -ões) f imprisonment; (cadeia) prison, jail; (detenção) arrest; ~ **de ventre** constipation; **prisioneiro, -a** [prizjo'nejru, a] m/f prisoner

privação [priva'sãw] (pl -ões) f deprivation; **privações** fpl (penúria) hardship sg

privacidade [privasi'dadʒi] f privacy

privações [priva'sõjʃ] fpl de **privação**

privada [pri'vada] f toilet

privado, -a [pri'vadu, a] *adj* private; (*carente*) deprived

privar [pri'va*] *vt* to deprive

privativo, -a [priva't∫ivu, a] *adj* (*particular*) private; ~ **de** peculiar to

privilegiado, -a [privile'ʒjadu, a] *adj* privileged; (*excepcional*) unique, exceptional

privilegiar [privile'ʒja*] *vt* to privilege; (*favorecer*) to favour (*BRIT*), favor (*US*)

privilégio [privi'lεʒu] *m* privilege

pró [prɔ] *adv* for, in favour (*BRIT*) ou favor (*US*) ♦ *m* advantage; **os ~s e os contras** the pros and cons; **em ~ de** in favo(u)r of

pró- [prɔ] *prefixo* pro-

proa ['proa] *f* prow, bow

probabilidade [probabili'dadʒi] *f* probability; **~s** *fpl* (*chances*) odds

problema [prob'lema] *m* problem

procedência [prose'dẽsja] *f* origin, source; (*lugar de saída*) point of departure

proceder [prose'de*] *vi* to proceed; (*comportar-se*) to behave; (*agir*) to act ♦ *m* conduct; **procedimento** [prosedʒi'mẽtu] *m* conduct, behaviour (*BRIT*), behavior (*US*); (*processo*) procedure; (*JUR*) proceedings *pl*

processamento [prosesa'mẽtu] *m* processing; (*JUR*) prosecution; (*verificação*) verification; **~ de texto** word processing

processar [prose'sa*] *vt* (*JUR*) to take proceedings against, prosecute; (*requerimentos*, *COMPUT*) to process

processo [pro'sesu] *m* process; (*procedimento*) procedure; (*JUR*) lawsuit, legal proceedings *pl*; (: *autos*) record; (*conjunto de documentos*) documents *pl*

procissão [prosi'sãw] (*pl* -**ões**) *f* procession

proclamação [proklama'sãw] *f* proclamation; **P~ da República** (*BR*) see boxed note

PROCLAMAÇÃO DA REPÚBLICA

Commemorated on 15 November, which is a public holiday in Brazil, the proclamation of the republic in 1889 was a military coup, led by Marshal Deodoro da Fonseca. It brought down the empire which had been established after independence, and installed a federal republic in Brazil.

proclamar [prokla'ma*] *vt* to proclaim

procura [pro'kura] *f* search; (*COM*) demand

procuração [prokura'sãw] *f*: **por ~** by proxy

procurador, a [prokura'do*, a] *m/f* attorney; **P~ Geral da República** Attorney General

procurar [proku'ra*] *vt* to look for, seek; (*emprego*) to apply for; (*ir visitar*) to call on; (*contatar*) to get in touch with; **~ fazer** to try to do

prodígio [pro'dʒiʒu] *m* prodigy

produção [produ'sãw] (*pl* -**ões**) *f* production; (*volume de produção*) output; (*produto*) product; **~ em massa**, **~ em série** mass production

produtivo, -a [produ't∫ivu, a] *adj* productive; (*rendoso*) profitable

produto [pro'dutu] *m* product; (*renda*) proceeds *pl*, profit

produtor, a [produ'to*, a] *adj* producing ♦ *m/f* producer

produzir [produ'zi*] *vt* to produce; (*ocasionar*) to cause, bring about; (*render*) to bring in

proeminente [proemi'nẽt∫i] *adj* prominent

proeza [pro'eza] f achievement, feat

profanar [profa'na*] vt to desecrate, profane; **profano, -a** [pro'fanu, a] adj profane ♦ m/f layman/woman

profecia [profe'sia] f prophecy

professor, a [profe'so*, a] m/f teacher; (universitário) lecturer

profeta, -isa [pro'feta, profe'tʃiza] m/f prophet; **profetizar** [profetʃi'za*] vt, vi to prophesy, predict

profissão [profi'sãw] (pl -ões) f profession; **profissional** [profisjo'naw] (pl -ais) adj, m/f professional; **profissionalizante** [profisjonali'zatʃi] adj (ensino) vocational

profundidade [profũdʒi'dadʒi] f depth

profundo, -a [pro'fũdu, a] adj deep; (fig) profound

profusão [profu'zãw] f profusion, abundance

prognóstico [prog'nɔʃtʃiku] m prediction, forecast

programa [pro'grama] m programme (BRIT), program (US); (COMPUT) program; (plano) plan; (diversão) thing to do; (de um curso) syllabus; **programação** [programa'sãw] f planning; (TV, RÁDIO, COMPUT) programming; **programador, a** [programa'do*, a] m/f programmer; **programar** [progra'ma*] vt to plan; (COMPUT) to program

progredir [progre'dʒi*] vi to progress; (avançar) to move forward; (infecção) to progress

progressista [progre'siʃta] adj, m/f progressive

progressivo, -a [progre'sivu, a] adj progressive; (gradual) gradual

progresso [pro'gresu] m progress

progrido etc [pro'gridu] vb V **progredir**

proibição [proibi'sãw] (pl -ões) f prohibition, ban

proibir [proi'bi*] vt to prohibit; (livro, espetáculo) to ban; "**é proibido fumar**" "no smoking"; ~ **alguém de fazer**, ~ **que alguém faça** to forbid sb to do

projeção [proʒe'sãw] (PT -cç-; pl -ões) f projection

projetar [proʒe'ta*] (PT -ct-) vt to project

projétil [pro'ʒɛtʃiw] (PT -ct-; pl -eis) m projectile, missile

projeto [pro'ʒetu] (PT -ct-) m project; (plano, ARQ) plan; (TEC) design; ~ **de lei** bill

projetor [proʒe'to*] (PT -ct-) m (CINEMA) projector

proliferar [prolife'ra*] vi to proliferate

prolongação [prolõga'sãw] f extension

prolongado, -a [prolõ'gadu, a] adj prolonged; (alongado) extended

prolongar [prolõ'ga*] vt to extend, lengthen; (decisão etc) to postpone; (vida) to prolong; **prolongar-se** vr to extend; (durar) to last

promessa [pro'mɛsa] f promise

prometer [prome'te*] vt, vi to promise

promíscuo, -a [pro'miʃkwu, a] adj disorderly, mixed up; (comportamento sexual) promiscuous

promissor, a [promi'so*, a] adj promising

promoção [promo'sãw] (pl -ões) f promotion; **fazer ~ de alguém/algo** to promote sb/sth

promotor, a [promo'to*, a] m/f promoter; (JUR) prosecutor

promover [promo've*] vt to promote; (causar) to cause, bring about

pronome [pro'nɔmi] m pronoun

pronto, -a [prõtu, a] adj ready;

(*rápido*) quick, speedy; (*imediato*) prompt ♦ *adv* promptly; **de ~** promptly; **estar ~ a ...** to be prepared *ou* willing to ...; **pronto-socorro** (*pl* **prontos-socorros**) (*PT*) *m* towtruck

pronúncia [proˈnũsjɐ] *f* pronunciation; (*JUR*) indictment

pronunciar [pronũˈsjaʳ] *vt* to pronounce; (*discurso*) to make, deliver; (*JUR: réu*) to indict; (: *sentença*) to pass

propaganda [propaˈɡãdɐ] *f* (*POL*) propaganda; (*COM*) advertising; (: *uma ~*) advert, advertisement; **fazer ~ de** to advertise

propagar [propaˈɡaʳ] *vt* to propagate; (*fig: difundir*) to disseminate

propensão [propẽˈsãw] (*pl* **-ões**) *f* inclination, tendency; **propenso, -a** [proˈpẽsu, a] *adj*: **propenso a** inclined to; **ser propenso a** to be inclined to, have a tendency to

propina [proˈpinɐ] *f* (*gorjeta*) tip; (*PT*: *cota*) fee

propor [proˈpoʳ] (*irreg: como* **pôr**) *vt* to propose; (*oferecer*) to offer; (*um problema*) to pose; **propor-se** *vr*: **~-se (a) fazer** (*pretender*) to intend to do; (*visar*) to aim to do; (*dispor-se*) to decide to do; (*oferecer-se*) to offer to do

proporção [propoxˈsãw] (*pl* **-ões**) *f* proportion; **proporções** *fpl* (*dimensões*) dimensions; **proporcional** [propoxsjoˈnaw] (*pl* **-ais**) *adj* proportional; **proporcionar** [propoxsjoˈnaʳ] *vt* to provide, give; (*adaptar*) to adjust, adapt

proposição [propoziˈsãw] (*pl* **-ões**) *f* proposition, proposal

proposital [propoziˈtaw] (*pl* **-ais**) *adj* intentional

propósito [proˈpɔzitu] *m* (*intenção*) purpose; (*objetivo*) aim; **a ~ by the**

way; **a ~ de** with regard to; **de ~ on** purpose

proposta [proˈpɔʃtɐ] *f* proposal; (*oferecimento*) offer

propriamente [proprjaˈmẽtʃi] *adv* properly, exactly; **~ falando** *ou* **dito** strictly speaking

propriedade [proprjeˈdadʒi] *f* property; (*direito de proprietário*) ownership; (*o que é apropriado*) propriety

proprietário, -a [proprjeˈtarju, a] *m/f* owner, proprietor

próprio, -a [ˈprɔprju, a] *adj* own, of one's own; (*mesmo*) very, selfsame; (*hora, momento*) opportune, right; (*nome*) proper; (*característico*) characteristic; (*sentido*) proper, true; (*depois de pronome*) -self; **~ (para)** suitable (for); **eu ~** I myself; **por si ~** of one's own accord; **ele é o ~ inglês** he's a typical Englishman; **é o ~** it's him himself

prorrogação [proxoɡaˈsãw] (*pl* **-ões**) *f* extension

prosa [ˈprɔza] *f* prose; (*conversa*) chatter; (*fanfarrice*) boasting, bragging ♦ *adj* full of oneself

prospecto [proʃˈpɛktu] *m* leaflet; (*em forma de livro*) brochure

prosperar [proʃpeˈraʳ] *vi* to prosper, thrive; **prosperidade** [proʃperiˈdadʒi] *f* prosperity; (*bom êxito*) success; **próspero, -a** [ˈprɔʃperu, a] *adj* prosperous; (*bem sucedido*) successful; (*favorável*) favourable (*BRIT*), favorable (*US*)

prosseguir [proseˈɡiʳ] *vt*, *vi* to continue; **~ em** to continue to

prostíbulo [proʃˈtʃibulu] *m* brothel

prostituta [proʃtʃiˈtuta] *f* prostitute

prostrado, -a [proʃˈtradu, a] *adj* prostrate

protagonista [protaɡoˈniʃta] *m/f* protagonist

proteção [prote'sãw] (*PT* -**cç**-) *f* protection

protector, a [protek'to*, a] (*PT*) = protetor, a

proteger [prote'ʒe*] *vt* to protect; **protegido, -a** [prote'ʒidu, a] *m/f* protégé(e)

proteína [prote'ina] *f* protein

protejo *etc* [pro'teʒu] *vb V* **proteger**

protestante [protef'tãtʃi] *adj, m/f* Protestant

protestar [protef'ta*] *vt, vi* to protest; **protesto** [pro'teftu] *m* protest

protetor, a [prote'to*, a] *adj* protective ♦ *m/f* protector; ~ **solar** sunscreen; ~ **de tela** (*COMPUT*) screensaver

protuberância [protube'rãsja] *f* bump; **protuberante** [protube-'rãtʃi] *adj* sticking out

prova ['prɔva] *f* proof; (*TEC: teste*) test, trial; (*EDUC: exame*) examination; (*sinal*) sign; (*de comida, bebida*) taste; (*de roupa*) fitting; (*ESPORTE*) competition; (*TIP*) proof; ~**(s)** *f(pl)* (*JUR*) evidence *sg*; **à** ~ **de bala/fogo/água** bulletproof/fireproof/waterproof; **pôr à** ~ to put to the test

provar [pro'va*] *vt* to prove; (*comida*) to taste, try; (*roupa*) to try on ♦ *vi* to try

provável [pro'vavew] (*pl* -**eis**) *adj* probable, likely

provedor, a [prove'do*, a] *m/f* supplier; ~ **de acesso à Internet** Internet service provider

proveito [pro'vejtu] *m* advantage; (*ganho*) profit; **em** ~ **de** for the benefit of; **fazer** ~ **de** to make use of; **proveitoso, -a** [provej'tozu, ɔza] *adj* profitable, advantageous; (*útil*) useful

proveniente [prove'njẽtʃi] *adj*: **proveniente de** originating from;

(*que resulta de*) arising from

prover [pro've*] (*irreg: como* **ver**) *vt* to provide, supply; (*vaga*) to fill ♦ *vi*: ~ **a** to take care of, see to

provérbio [pro'vexbju] *m* proverb

providência [provi'dẽsja] *f* providence; ~**s** *fpl* (*medidas*) measures, steps; **providencial** [providẽ'sjaw] (*pl* -**ais**) *adj* opportune; **providenciar** [providẽ'sja*] *vt* to provide; (*tomar providências*) to arrange ♦ *vi* to make arrangements, take steps; **providenciar para que** to see to it that

província [pro'vĩsja] *f* province; **provinciano, -a** [provĩ'sjanu, a] *adj* provincial

provisório, -a [provi'zɔrju, a] *adj* provisional, temporary

provocador, a [provoka'do*, a] *adj* provocative

provocante [provo'kãtʃi] *adj* provocative

provocar [provo'ka*] *vt* to provoke; (*ocasionar*) to cause; (*atrair*) to tempt, attract; (*estimular*) to rouse, stimulate

próximo, -a ['prɔsimu, a] *adj* (*no espaço*) near, close; (*no tempo*) close; (*seguinte*) next; (*amigo, parente*) close; (*vizinho*) neighbouring (*BRIT*), neighboring (*US*) ♦ *adv* near ♦ *m* fellow man; ~ **a** *ou* **de** near, close to; **até a próxima!** see you again soon!

prudência [pru'dẽsja] *f* care, prudence; **prudente** [pru'dẽtʃi] *adj* prudent

prurido [pru'ridu] *m* itch

psicanálise [psika'nalizi] *f* psychoanalysis

psicologia [psikolo'ʒia] *f* psychology; **psicológico, -a** [psiko-'lɔʒiku, a] *adj* psychological; **psicólogo, -a** [psi'kɔlogu, a] *m/f* psychologist

psique ['psiki] f psyche

psiquiatra [psi'kjatra] m/f psychiatrist

psiquiatria [psikja'tria] f psychiatry

psíquico, -a ['psikiku, a] adj psychological

puberdade [pubex'dadʒi] f puberty

publicação [publika'sãw] f publication

publicar [publi'ka*] vt to publish; (divulgar) to divulge; (proclamar) to announce

publicidade [publisi'dadʒi] f publicity; (COM) advertising; **publicitário, -a** [publisi'tarju, a] adj publicity atr; advertising atr

público, -a ['publiku, a] adj public ♦ m public; (CINEMA, TEATRO etc) audience

pude etc ['pudʒi] vb V **poder**

pudera etc [pu'dera] vb V **poder**

pudim [pu'dʒĩ] (pl -ns) m pudding

pudor [pu'do*] m bashfulness, modesty; (moral) decency

pular [pu'la*] vi to jump; (no Carnaval) to celebrate ♦ vt to jump (over); (páginas, trechos) to skip; ~ **Carnaval** to celebrate Carnival; ~ **corda** to skip

pulga ['puwga] f flea

pulmão [puw'mãw] (pl -ões) m lung

pulo¹ ['pulu] m jump; **dar um ~ em** to stop off at

pulo² etc vb V **polir**

pulôver [pu'love*] (BR) m pullover

pulsação [puwsa'sãw] f pulsation, beating; (MED) pulse

pulseira [puw'sejra] f bracelet; (de sapato) strap

pulso ['puwsu] m (ANAT) wrist; (MED) pulse; (fig) vigour (BRIT), vigor (US), energy

punha etc ['puɲa] vb V **pôr**

punhado [pu'ɲadu] m handful

punhal [pu'ɲaw] (pl -ais) m dagger

punho ['puɲu] m fist; (de manga) cuff; (de espada) hilt

punição [puni'sãw] (pl -ões) f punishment

punir [pu'ni*] vt to punish

pupila [pu'pila] f (ANAT) pupil

purê [pu're] m purée; ~ **de batatas** mashed potatoes

pureza [pu'reza] f purity

purificar [purifi'ka*] vt to purify

puritano, -a [puri'tanu, a] adj puritanical; (seita) puritan ♦ m/f puritan

puro, -a ['puru, a] adj pure; (uísque etc) neat; (verdade) plain; (intenções) honourable (BRIT), honorable (US); (estilo) clear

pus¹ [puʃ] m pus

pus² etc [puʃ] vb V **pôr**

puser etc [pu'ze*] vb V **pôr**

puta ['puta] (col!) f whore; V tb **puto**

puto, -a ['putu, a] (col!) m/f (sem-vergonha) bastard ♦ adj (zangado) furious; (incrível): **um ~ ...** a hell of a ...; **o ~ de ...** the bloody ...

pútrido, -a ['putridu, a] adj putrid, rotten

puxador [puʃa'do*] m handle, knob

puxão [pu'ʃãw] (pl -ões) m tug, jerk

puxar [pu'ʃa*] vt to pull; (sacar) to pull out; (assunto) to bring up; (conversa) to strike up; (briga) to pick ♦ vi: ~ **de uma perna** to limp; ~ **a** to take after

puxões [pu'ʃõjʃ] mpl de **puxão**

Q

QG abr m (= Quartel-General) HQ

QI abr m (= Quociente de Inteligência) IQ

quadra ['kwadra] f (quarteirão) block; (de tênis etc) court; (período) time, period

quadrado, -a [kwa'dradu, a] adj

square ♦ m square ♦ m/f (col) square

quadril [kwa'driw] (pl **-is**) m hip

quadrinho [kwa'driɲu] m: **história em ~s** (BR) cartoon, comic strip

quadris [kwa'driʃ] mpl de **quadril**

quadro ['kwadru] m painting; (gravura, foto) picture; (lista) list; (tabela) chart, table; (TEC: painel) panel; (pessoal) staff; (time) team; (TEATRO, fig) scene; **quadro-negro** (pl **quadros-negros**) m blackboard

quadruplicar [kwadrupli'ka*] vt, vi to quadruple

qual [kwaw] (pl **-ais**) pron which ♦ conj as, like ♦ excl what!; **o ~** which; (pessoa: suj) who; (: objeto) whom; **seja ~ for** whatever ou whichever it may be; **cada ~** each one

qualidade [kwali'dadʒi] f quality

qualificação [kwalifika'sãw] (pl **-ões**) f qualification

qualificado, -a [kwalifi'kadu, a] adj qualified

qualificar [kwalifi'ka*] vt to qualify; (avaliar) to evaluate; **qualificar-se** vr to qualify; **~ de** ou **como** to classify as

qualquer [kwaw'ke*] (pl **quaisquer**) adj, pron any; **~ pessoa** anyone, anybody; **~ um dos dois** either; **~ que seja** whichever it may be; **a ~ momento** at any moment

quando ['kwãdu] adv when ♦ conj when; (interrogativo) when?; (ao passo que) whilst; **~ muito** at most

quantia [kwã'tʃia] f sum, amount

quantidade [kwãtʃi'dadʒi] f quantity, amount

quanto, -a ['kwãtu, a] adj **1** (interrogativo: sg) how much?; (: pl) how many?; **~ tempo?** how long?

2 (o (que for) necessário) all that, as much as; **daremos ~s exemplares ele precisar** we'll give him as many copies as ou all the copies he needs

3: tanto/tantos ... ~ as much/many ... as

♦ pron **1** how much?; how many?; **~ custa?** how much?; **a ~ está o jogo?** what's the score?

2: tudo ~ everything that, as much as

3: tanto/tantos ~ ... as much/as many as ...

4: um tanto ~ somewhat, rather

♦ adv **1: ~ a** as regards; **~ a mim** for me

2: ~ antes as soon as possible

3: ~ mais (principalmente) especially; (muito menos) let alone; **~ mais cedo melhor** the sooner the better

4: tanto ~ possível as much as possible; **tão ... ~ ...** as ... as ...

♦ conj: **~ mais trabalha, mais ele ganha** the more he works, the more he earns; **~ mais, (tanto) melhor** the more, the better

quarenta [kwa'rẽta] num forty

quarentena [kwarẽ'tena] f quarantine

quaresma [kwa'reʒma] f Lent

quarta ['kwaxta] f (tb: **~-feira**) Wednesday; (parte) quarter; (AUTO) fourth (gear); **quarta-feira** (pl **quartas-feiras**) f Wednesday; **quarta-feira de cinzas** Ash Wednesday

quarteirão [kwaxtej'rãw] (pl **-ões**) m (de casas) block

quartel [kwax'tew] (pl **-éis**) m barracks sg; **quartel-general** m head-

quarters pl
quarteto [kwax'tetu] m quartet(te)
quarto, -a ['kwaxtu, a] num fourth
♦ m quarter; (aposento) room; ~
de banho/dormir bathroom/bedroom; **três ~s de hora** three quarters of an hour
quase ['kwazi] adv almost, nearly; ~
nunca hardly ever
quatorze [kwa'toxzi] num fourteen
quatro ['kwatru] num four

┌─ PALAVRA CHAVE ─┐

que [ki] conj 1 (com oração subordinada: muitas vezes não se traduz) that; **ele disse ~ viria** he said (that) he would come; **não há nada ~ fazer** there's nothing to be done; **espero ~ sim/não** I hope so/not; **dizer ~ sim/não** to say yes/no
2 (consecutivo: muitas vezes não se traduz): **é tão pesado ~ não consigo levantá-lo** it's so heavy (that) I can't lift it
3 (comparações): (**do**) ~ than; V tb **mais; menos; mesmo**
♦ pron 1 (coisa) which, that; (+ prep) which; **o chapéu ~ você comprou** the hat (that ou which) you bought
2 (pessoa: suj) who, that; (: complemento) whom, that; **o amigo ~ me levou ao museu** the friend who took me to the museum; **a moça ~ eu convidei** the girl (that ou whom) I invited
3 (interrogativo) what?; **o ~ você disse?** what did you say?
4 (exclamação) what!; ~ **pena!** what a pity!; ~ **lindo!** how lovely!

quê [ke] m (col) something ♦ pron what; ~! what!; **não tem de** ~ don't mention it; **para ~?** what for?; **por ~?** why?
quebra ['kɛbra] f break, rupture; (falência) bankruptcy; (de energia elétrica) cut; **de** ~ in addition; **quebra-cabeça** (pl quebra-cabeças) m puzzle, problem; (jogo) jigsaw puzzle
quebrado, -a [ke'bradu, a] adj broken; (cansado) exhausted; (falido) bankrupt; (carro, máquina) broken down; (telefone) out of order
quebra-nozes m inv nutcrackers pl (BRIT), nutcracker (US)
quebrar [ke'bra*] vt to break ♦ vi to break; (carro) to break down; (COM) to go bankrupt; (ficar sem dinheiro) to go broke
queda ['kɛda] f fall; (fig) downfall; **ter ~ para algo** to have a bent for sth; ~ **de barreira** landslide; **queda-d'água** (pl quedas-d'água) f waterfall
queijo ['kejʒu] m cheese
queimado, -a [kej'madu, a] adj burnt; (de sol: machucado) sunburnt; (: bronzeado) brown, tanned; (plantas, folhas) dried up
queimadura [kejma'dura] f burn; (de sol) sunburn
queimar [kej'ma*] vt to burn; (roupa) to scorch; (com líquido) to scald; (bronzear a pele) to tan; (planta, folha) to wither ♦ vi to burn; **queimar-se** vr (pessoa) to burn o.s.; (de sol) to tan
queima-roupa f: **à** ~ point-blank, at point-blank range
queira etc ['kejra] vb V **querer**
queixa ['kejʃa] f complaint; (lamentação) lament; **fazer ~ de alguém** to complain about sb
queixar-se [kej'ʃaxsi] vr to complain; ~ **de** to complain about; (dores etc) to complain of
queixo ['kejʃu] m chin; (maxilar) jaw; **bater o** ~ to shiver
quem [kẽj] pron who; (como objeto)

who(m); **de ~ é isto?** whose is this?; **~ diria!** who would have thought (it)!; **~ sabe** (*talvez*) perhaps

Quênia [ˈkẹnja] *m*: **o ~** Kenya

quente [ˈkẽtʃi] *adj* hot; (*roupa*) warm

quer [kɛ*] *vb V* **querer ♦** *conj*: **~ ... ~ ...** whether ... or ...; **~ chova ~ não** whether it rains or not; **onde/quando/quem ~ que** wherever/whenever/whoever; **o que ~ que seja** whatever it is

---
PALAVRA CHAVE
---

querer [ke're*] *vt* 1 (*desejar*) to want; **quero mais dinheiro** I want more money; **queria um chá** I'd like a cup of tea; **quero ajudar/que vá** I want to help/you to go; **você vai ~ sair amanhã?** do you want to go out tomorrow?; **eu vou ~ uma cerveja** (*num bar etc*) I'd like a beer; **por/sem ~** intentionally/unintentionally; **como queira** as you wish

2 (*perguntas para pedir algo*): **você quer fechar a janela?** will you shut the window?; **quer me dar uma mão?** can you give me a hand?

3 (*amar*) to love

4 (*convite*): **quer entrar/sentar** do come in/sit down

5: **~ dizer** (*significar*) to mean; (*pretender dizer*) to mean to say; **quero dizer** I mean; **quer** (*com outras palavras*) in other words

♦ *vi*: **~ bem a** to be fond of

♦ querer-se *vr* to love one another

♦ *m* (*vontade*) wish; (*afeto*) affection

querido, -a [ke'ridu, a] *adj* dear **♦** *m/f* darling; **Q~ João** Dear John

querosene [kero'zεni] *m* kerosene

questão [keʃ'tãw] (*pl* **-ões**) *f* question, inquiry; (*problema*) matter, question; (*JUR*) case; (*contenda*) dis-

pute, quarrel; **fazer ~ (de)** to insist (on); **em ~** in question; **há ~ de um ano** about a year ago; **questionar** [keʃtʃjo'na*] *vi* to question **♦** *vt* to question, call into question; **questionário** [keʃtʃjo'narju] *m* questionnaire; **questionável** [keʃtʃjo-'navɛw] (*pl* **-eis**) *adj* questionable

quicar [ki'ka*] *vt*, *vi* to bounce

quieto, -a [ˈkjεtu, a] *adj* quiet; (*imóvel*) still; **quietude** [kje'tudʒi] *f* calm, tranquillity

quilate [kiˈlatʃi] *m* carat

quilo [ˈkilu] *m* kilo; **quilobyte** [kilo'bajtʃi] *m* kilobyte; **quilograma** [kilo'grama] *m* kilogram; **quilometragem** [kilome'traʒẽ] *f* number of kilometres *ou* kilometers travelled, = mileage; **quilômetro** [ki'lometru] *m* kilometre (*BRIT*), kilometer (*US*)

quilowatt [kilo'watʃi] *m* kilowatt

química [ˈkimika] *f* chemistry

químico, -a [ˈkimiku, a] *adj* chemical **♦** *m/f* chemist

quina [ˈkina] *f* corner; (*de mesa etc*) edge; **de ~** edgeways (*BRIT*), edgewise (*US*)

quindim [kĩˈdʒĩ] *m* sweet made of egg yolks, coconut and sugar

quinhão [ki'ɲãw] (*pl* **-ões**) *m* share, portion

quinhentos, -as [ki'ɲẽtuʃ, aʃ] *num* five hundred

quinhões [ki'ɲõjʃ] *mpl de* **quinhão**

quinquilharias [kĩkiʎa'riaʃ] *fpl* odds and ends; (*miudezas*) knickknacks, trinkets

quinta [ˈkĩta] *f* (*tb*: **~-feira**) Thursday; (*propriedade*) estate; (*PT*) farm; **quinta-feira** [ˈkĩta'fejra] (*pl* **quintas-feiras**) *f* Thursday

quintal [kĩˈtaw] (*pl* **-ais**) *m* back yard

quinteto [kĩ'tetu] *m* quintet(te)

quinto, -a [ˈkĩtu, a] *num* fifth

quinze ['kĩzɪ] *num* fifteen; **duas e ~** a quarter past (BRIT) ou after (US) two; **~ para as sete** a quarter to (BRIT) ou of (US) seven

quinzena [kĩ'zena] *f* two weeks, fortnight (BRIT); **quinzenal** [kĩze-'naw] (*pl* **~is**) *adj* fortnightly; **quinzenalmente** [kĩzenaw'mẽtʃi] *adv* fortnightly

quiosque ['kjɔʃkɪ] *m* kiosk

quis *etc* [kiʒ] *vb V* **querer**

quiser *etc* [ki'zɛ*] *vb V* **querer**

quisto ['kiʃtu] *m* cyst

quitanda [ki'tãda] *f* grocer's (shop) (BRIT), grocery store (US)

quitar [ki'ta*] *vt* (*dívida: pagar*) to pay off; (: *perdoar*) to cancel; (*devedor*) to release

quite ['kitʃi] *adj* (*livre*) free; (*com um credor*) squared up; (*igualado*) even; **estar ~ (com alguém)** to be quits (with sb)

quitute [ki'tutʃi] *m* titbit (BRIT), tidbit (US)

quota ['kwɔta] *f* quota; (*porção*) share, portion

quotidiano, -a [kwɔtʃi'dʒjanu, a] *adj* everyday

R

R *abr* (= *rua*) St

R$ *abr* = **real**

rã ['xã] *f* frog

rabanete [xaba'netʃi] *m* radish

rabiscar [xabiʃ'ka*] *vt* to scribble; (*papel*) to scribble on ♦ *vi* to scribble; (*desenhar*) to doodle; **rabisco** [xa'biʃku] *m* scribble

rabo ['xabu] *m* tail

rabugento, -a [xabu'ʒẽtu, a] *adj* grumpy

raça ['xasa] *f* breed; (*grupo étnico*) race; **cão/cavalo de ~** pedigree dog/thoroughbred horse

racha ['xaʃa] *f* (*fenda*) split; (*greta*) crack; **rachadura** [xaʃa'dura] *f* crack; **rachar** [xa'ʃa*] *vt* to crack; (*objeto, despesas*) to split; (*lenha*) to chop ♦ *vi* to split; (*cristal*) to crack; **rachar-se** *vr* to split; to crack

racial [xa'sjaw] (*pl* **-ais**) *adj* racial

raciocínio [xasjo'sinju] *m* reasoning

racional [xasjo'naw] (*pl* **-ais**) *adj* rational; **racionalizar** [xasjonali-'za*] *vt* to rationalize

racionamento [xasjona'mẽtu] *m* rationing

racismo [xa'siʒmu] *m* racism; **racista** [xa'siʃta] *adj, m/f* racist

radar [xa'da*] *m* radar

radiação [xadʒja'sãw] *f* radiation

radiador [xadʒja'do*] *m* radiator

radiante [xa'dʒjãtʃi] *adj* radiant

radical [xadʒi'kaw] (*pl* **-ais**) *adj* radical

radicar-se [xadʒi'kaxsi] *vr* to take root; (*fixar residência*) to settle

rádio ['xadʒju] *m* radio; **radioativo, -a** [xadʒjua-'tʃivu, a] (*PT* **-act-**) *adj* radioactive; **radiodifusão** [xadʒjodʒifu'zãw] *f* broadcasting; **radiografar** [xadʒjogra'fa*] *vt* to X-ray; **radiografia** [xadʒjogra'fia] *f* X-ray

raia ['xaja] *f* (*risca*) line; (*fronteira*) boundary; (*limite*) limit; (*de corrida*) lane; (*peixe*) ray

raiar [xa'ja*] *vi* to shine

rainha [xa'iɲa] *f* queen

raio ['xaju] *m* (*de sol*) ray; (*de luz*) beam; (*de roda*) spoke; (*relâmpago*) flash of lightning; (*alcance*) range; (*MAT*) radius; **~s X** X-rays

raiva ['xajva] *f* rage, fury; (*MED*) rabies *sg*; **estar/ficar com ~** to be/get angry (with); **ter ~ de** to hate; **raivoso, -a** [xaj'vozu, ɔza] *adj* furious

raiz [xa'iʒ] f root; (origem) origin, source; ~ **quadrada** square root

rajada [xa'ʒada] f (vento) gust

ralado, -a [xa'ladu, a] adj grated; **ralador** [xala'do*] m grater

ralar [xa'la*] vt to grate

ralhar [xa'ʎa*] vi to scold; ~ **com alguém** to tell sb off

rali [xa'li] m rally

ralo, -a [xalu, a] adj (cabelo) thinning; (tecido) flimsy; (vegetação) sparse; (sopa) thin, watery; (café) weak ♦ m (de água) rose, nozzle; (de pia, banheiro) drain

rama ['xama] f branches pl, foliage; **pela ~** superficially; **ramagem** [xa'maʒẽ] f branches pl, foliage; **ramal** [xa'maw] (pl **~is**) m (FERRO) branch line; (TEL) extension; (AUTO) side road

ramificar-se [xamifi'kaxsi] vr to branch out

ramo ['xamu] m branch; (profissão, negócios) line; (de flores) bunch; **Domingo de R~s** Palm Sunday

rampa ['xãpa] f ramp; (ladeira) slope

rancor [xã'ko*] m bitterness; (ódio) hatred; **rancoroso, -a** [xãko'rozu, ɔza] adj bitter, resentful; hateful

rançoso, -a [xã'sozu, ɔza] adj rancid; (cheiro) musty

ranger [xã'ʒe*] vi to creak ♦ vt: ~ **os dentes** to grind one's teeth

ranhura [xa'ɲura] f groove; (para moeda) slot

rapar [xa'pa*] vt to scrape; (a barba) to shave; (o cabelo) to crop

rapariga [xapa'riga] f girl

rapaz [xa'pajʒ] m boy; (col) lad

rapidez [xapi'deʒ] f speed

rápido, -a ['xapidu, a] adj fast, quick ♦ adv fast, quickly ♦ m (trem) express

rapina [xa'pina] f robbery; **ave de ~** bird of prey

raptar [xap'ta*] vt to kidnap; **rapto** ['xaptu] m kidnapping; **raptor** [xap'to*] m kidnapper

raquete [xa'ketʃi] f racquet

raquítico, -a [xa'kitʃiku, a] adj (franzino) puny; (vegetação) sparse

raramente [xara'mẽtʃi] adv rarely, seldom

rarefeito, -a [xare'fejtu, a] adj rarefied; (multidão, população) sparse

raro, -a ['xaru, a] adj rare ♦ adv rarely, seldom

rascunho [xaʃ'kuɲu] m draft, rough copy

rasgado, -a [xaʒ'gadu, a] adj (roupa) torn, ripped

rasgão [xaʒ'gãw] (pl **-ões**) m tear, rip

rasgar [xaʒ'ga*] vt to tear, rip; (destruir) to tear up, rip up; **rasgar-se** vr to split; **rasgo** ['xaʒgu] m tear, rip

rasgões [xaʒ'gõjʃ] mpl de **rasgão**

raso, -a ['xazu, a] adj (liso) flat, level; (não fundo) shallow; (baixo) low; **soldado ~** private

raspa ['xaʃpa] f (de madeira) shaving; (de metal) filing

raspão [xaʃ'pãw] (pl **-ões**) m scratch, graze

raspar [xaʃ'pa*] vt to scrape; (alisar) to file; (tocar de raspão) to graze; (arranhar) to scratch; (pêlos, cabeça) to shave; (apagar) to rub out ♦ vi: ~ **em** to scrape

raspões [xaʃ'põjʃ] mpl de **raspão**

rasteira [xaʃ'tejra] f: **dar uma ~ em alguém** to trip sb up

rasteiro, -a [xaʃ'tejru, a] adj crawling; (planta) creeping

rastejar [xaʃte'ʒa*] vi to crawl; (furtivamente) to creep; (fig: rebaixar-se) to grovel ♦ vt (fugitivo etc) to track

rasto ['xaʃtu] m (pegada) track; (de

veículo) trail; (*fig*) sign, trace; **andar de ~s** to crawl

rastro ['xaʃtru] *m* = rasto

rata ['xata] *f* rat; (*pequena*) mouse

ratificar [xatʃifi'ka*] *vt* to ratify

rato ['xatu] *m* rat; (*pequeno*) mouse; **~ de hotel/praia** hotel/beach thief;

ratoeira [xa'twejra] *f* rat trap; mousetrap

ravina [xa'vina] *f* ravine

razão [xa'zãw] (*pl* **-ões**) *f* reason; (*argumento*) reasoning; (*MAT*) ratio ♦ *m* (*COM*) ledger; **à ~ de** at the rate of; **em ~ de** on account of; **dar ~ a alguém** to support sb; **ter/não ter ~** to be right/wrong; **razoável** [xa'zwavew] (*pl* **-eis**) *adj* reasonable

r/c (*PT*) *abr* = **rés-do-chão**

RDSI *abr* f (= *Rede Digital de Serviços Integrados*) ISDN

ré [xɛ] *f* (*AUTO*) reverse (gear); **dar (marcha à) ~** to reverse, back up; V *tb* **réu**

reabastecer [xeabaʃte'se*] *vt* (*avião*) to refuel; (*carro*) to fill up; **reabastecer-se** *vr*: **~-se de** to replenish one's supply of

reação [xea'sãw] (*PT* **-çç-**; *pl* **-ões**) *f* reaction

reagir [xea'ʒi*] *vi* to react; (*doente, time perdedor*) to fight back; **~ a** (*resistir*) to resist; (*protestar*) to rebel against

reais [xe'ajʃ] *adj pl de* **real**

reaja *etc* [xe'aʒa] *vb* V **reagir**; **reaver**

reajuste [xea'ʒuʃtʃi] *m* adjustment

real [xe'aw] (*pl* **-ais**) *adj* real; (*relativo à realeza*) royal ♦ *m* (*moeda*) real

realçar [xeaw'sa*] *vt* to highlight;

realce [xe'awsi] *m* emphasis; (*mais brilho*) highlight; **dar realce a** to enhance

realeza [xea'leza] *f* royalty

realidade [xeali'dadʒi] *f* reality; **na ~** actually, in fact

realista [xea'liʃta] *adj* realistic ♦ *m/f* realist

realização [xealiza'sãw] *f* realization (*BRIT*), fulfillment (*US*), fulfilment (*BRIT*), fulfillment (*US*); (*de projeto*) execution, carrying out

realizador, a [xealiza'do*, a] *adj* enterprising

realizar [xeali'za*] *vt* to achieve; (*projeto*) to carry out; (*ambições, sonho*) to fulfil (*BRIT*), fulfill (*US*), realize; (*negócios*) to transact; (*perceber*) to realize; **realizar-se** *vr* to take place; (*ambições*) to be realized; (*sonhos*) to come true

realmente [xeaw'mẽtʃi] *adv* really; (*de fato*) actually

reanimar [xeani'ma*] *vt* to revive; (*encorajar*) to encourage; **reanimar-se** *vr* to cheer up

reatar [xea'ta*] *vt* to resume, take up again

reaver [xea've*] *vt* to recover, get back

rebaixar [xebaj'ʃa*] *vt* to lower; (*mercadorias*) to lower the price of; (*humilhar*) to put down, humiliate ♦ *vi* to drop; **rebaixar-se** *vr* to demean o.s

rebanho [xe'baɲu] *m* (*de carneiros, fig*) flock; (*de gado, elefantes*) herd

rebelar-se [xebe'laxsi] *vr* to rebel; **rebelde** [xe'bɛwdʒi] *adj* rebellious; (*indisciplinado*) unruly, wild ♦ *m/f* rebel; **rebeldia** [xebew'dʒia] *f* rebelliousness; (*fig*: *obstinação*) stubbornness; (: *oposição*) defiance

rebelião [xebe'ljãw] (*pl* **-ões**) *f* rebellion

rebentar [xebẽ'ta*] *vi* (*guerra*) to break out; (*louça*) to smash; (*corda*) to snap; (*represa*) to burst; (*ondas*) to break ♦ *vt* to smash; to snap; (*porta*) to break down

rebocador [xeboka'do*] *m* tug(boat)

rebocar [xebo'ka*] *vt* (*paredes*)

plaster; (veículo) to tow

rebolar [xebo'la*] vt to swing ♦ vi to sway

reboque¹ [xe'bɔki] m tow; (veículo: tb: carro ~) trailer; (cabo) towrope; (BR: de socorro) towtruck; **a ~ on** ou in (US) tow

reboque² etc vb V **rebocar**

rebuçado [xebu'sadu] (PT) m sweet, candy (US)

recado [xe'kadu] m message; **deixar ~** to leave a message

recaída [xeka'ida] f relapse

recair [xeka'i*] vi (doente) to relapse

recalcar [xekaw'ka*] vt to repress

recalque etc [xe'kawki] vb V **recalcar**

recanto [xe'kãtu] m corner, nook

recapitular [xekapitu'la*] vt to sum up, recapitulate; (fatos) to review; (matéria escolar) to revise

recatado, -a [xeka'tadu, a] adj (modesto) modest; (reservado) reserved

recauchutado, -a [xekawʃu'tadu, a] adj: **pneu ~** (AUTO) retread, remould (BRIT)

recear [xe'sja*] vt to fear ♦ vi: **~ por** to fear for; **~ fazer/que** to be afraid to do/that

receber [xese'be*] vt to receive; (ganhar) to earn, get; (hóspedes) to take in; (convidados) to entertain; (acolher bem) to welcome ♦ vi (~ convidados) to entertain; **recebimento** [xesebi'mẽtu] (BR) m receipt; (de uma carta) receipt; **acusar o recebimento de** to acknowledge receipt of

receio [xe'seju] m fear; **ter ~ de que** to fear that

receita [xe'sejta] f income; (do Estado) revenue; (MED) prescription; (CULIN) recipe; **R~ Federal** ≈ Inland Revenue (BRIT), ≈ IRS (US); **receitar** [xesej'ta*] vt to prescribe

recém [xe'sẽ] adv recently, newly; **recém-casado, -a** adj: **os recém-casados** the newlyweds; **recém-chegado, -a** m/f newcomer; **recém-nascido, -a** m/f newborn child

recente [xe'sẽtʃi] adj recent; (novo) new ♦ adv recently; **recentemente** [xesẽtʃi'mẽtʃi] adv recently

receoso, -a [xe'sjozu, ɔza] adj frightened, fearful; **estar ~ de (fazer)** to be afraid of (doing)

recepção [xesep'sãw] (pl -ões) f reception; (PT: de uma carta) receipt; **acusar a ~ de** (PT) to acknowledge receipt of; **recepcionista** [xesepsjo'niʃta] m/f receptionist

receptivo, -a [xesep'tʃivu, a] adj receptive; (acolhedor) welcoming

receptor [xesep'to*] m receiver

recessão [xese'sãw] (pl -ões) f recession

recesso [xe'sesu] m recess

recessões [xese'sõjʃ] fpl de **recessão**

recheado, -a [xe'ʃjadu, a] adj (ave, carne) stuffed; (empada, bolo) filled; (cheio) full, crammed

rechear [xe'ʃja*] vt to fill; (ave, carne) to stuff; **recheio** [xe'ʃeju] m stuffing; (de empada, de bolo) filling; (o conteúdo) contents pl

rechonchudo, -a [xeʃõ'ʃudu, a] adj chubby, plump

recibo [xe'sibu] m receipt

reciclar [xesi'kla*] vt to recycle

recinto [xe'sĩtu] m enclosure; (lugar) area

recipiente [xesi'pjẽtʃi] m container, receptacle

recíproco, -a [xe'siproku, a] adj reciprocal

recitar [xesi'ta*] vt to recite

reclamação [xeklama'sãw] (pl

-ões) f complaint

reclamar [xekla'ma*] vt to demand; (herança) to claim ♦ vi to complain

reclinar [xekli'na*] vt to rest, lean; **reclinar-se** vr to lie back; (deitarse) to lie down

recobrar [xeko'bra*] vt to recover, get back; **recobrar-se** vr to recover

recolher [xeko'ʎe*] vt to collect; (coisas dispersas) to pick up; (gado, roupa do varal) to bring in; (juntar) to gather together; **recolhido**, -a [xeko'ʎidu, a] adj secluded; (pessoa) withdrawn; **recolhimento** [xekoʎi'mẽtu] m retirement; (arrecadação) collection; (ato de levar) taking

recomeçar [xekome'sa*] vt, vi to restart

recomendação [xekomẽda'sãw] (pl **-ões)** f recommendation; **recomendações** fpl (cumprimentos) regards

recomendar [xekomẽ'da*] vt to recommend; **recomendável** [xekomẽ'davew] (pl **-eis)** adj advisable

recompensa [xekõ'pẽsa] f reward; **recompensar** [xekõpẽ'sa*] vt to reward

recompor [xekõ'po*] (irreg: como **pôr**) vt to reorganize; (restabelecer) to restore

reconciliar [xekõsi'lja*] vt to reconcile

reconhecer [xekoɲe'se*] vt to recognize; (MIL) to reconnoitre (BRIT), reconnoiter (US); **reconhecido**, -a [xekoɲe'sidu, a] adj recognized; (agradecido) grateful, thankful; **reconhecimento** [xekoɲesi'mẽtu] m recognition; (admissão) admission; (gratidão) gratitude; (MIL) reconnaissance; **reconhecí-**

vel [xekoɲe'sivew] (pl **-eis)** adj recognizable

reconstruir [xekõʃ'trwi*] vt to rebuild

recordação [xekoxda'sãw] (pl **-ões)** f (reminiscência) memory; (objeto) memento

recordar [xekox'da*] vt to remember; (parecer) to look like; (recapitular) to revise; **recordar-se** vr: ~se **de** to remember; ~ **algo a alguém** to remind sb of sth

recorde [xe'kɔxdʒi] adj inv record atr ♦ m record

recorrer [xeko'xe*] vi: ~ **a** to turn to; (valer-se de) to resort to

recortar [xekox'ta*] vt to cut out; **recorte** [xe'kɔxtʃi] m (ato) cutting out; (de jornal) cutting, clipping

recreação [xekrja'sãw] f recreation

recreativo, -a [xekrja'tʃivu, a] adj recreational

recreio [xe'kreju] m recreation

recriminar [xekrimi'na*] vt to reproach, reprove

recrutamento [xekruta'mẽtu] m recruitment

recrutar [xekru'ta*] vt to recruit

rectângulo [xek'tãgulu] (PT) = **retângulo**

recto, -a etc ['xɛktu, a] (PT) = **reto** etc

recuar [xe'kwa*] vt to move back ♦ vi to move back; (exército) to retreat

recuperação [xekupera'sãw] f recovery

recuperar [xekupe'ra*] vt to recover; (tempo perdido) to make up for; (reabilitar) to rehabilitate; **recuperar-se** vr to recover

recurso [xe'kuxsu] m resource; (JUR) appeal; ~s mpl (financeiros) resources

recusa [xe'kuza] f refusal; (negação)

denial; **recusar** [xeku'za*] *vt* to refuse; to deny; **recusar-se** *vr*: **recusar-se a** to refuse to

redação [xeda'sãw] (*PT* -**cç**-; *pl* -**ões**) *f* (*ato*) writing; (*EDUC*) composition, essay; (*redatores*) editorial staff

redator, a [xeda'to*, a] (*PT* -**act**-) *m/f* journalist; (*editor*) editor; (*quem redige*) writer

rede ['xedʒi] *f* net; (*de dormir*) hammock; (*cilada*) trap; (*FERRO, TEC, ELG*) network; **a R~** (*a Internet*) the Net

rédea ['xedʒja] *f* rein

redentor, a [xedẽ'to*, a] *adj* redeeming

redigir [xedʒi'ʒi*] *vt, vi* to write

redobrar [xedo'bra*] *vt* (*aumentar*) to increase; (*esforços*) to redouble

redondamente [xedõda'mẽtʃi] *adv* (*completamente*) completely

redondezas [xedõ'dezaʃ] *fpl* surroundings

redondo, -a [xe'dõdu, a] *adj* round

redor [xe'do*] *m*: **ao** *ou* **em ~ (de)** around, round about

redução [xedu'sãw] (*pl* -**ões**) *f* reduction

redundância [xedũ'dãsja] *f* redundancy; **redundante** [xedũ'dãtʃi] *adj* redundant

reduzido, -a [xedu'zidu, a] *adj* reduced; (*limitado*) limited; (*pequeno*) small

reduzir [xedu'zi*] *vt* to reduce; **reduzir-se** *vr*: **~-se a** to be reduced to; (*fig: resumir-se em*) to come down to

reembolsar [xeẽbow'sa*] *vt* to recover; (*restituir*) to reimburse; (*depósito*) to refund; **reembolso** [xeẽ'bowsu] *m* (*de depósito*) refund; (*de despesa*) reimbursement

reencontro [xeẽ'kõtru] *m* reunion

refazer [xefa'ze*] (*irreg: como* **fazer**) *vt* to redo; (*consertar*) to repair;

refazer-se *vr* (*MED etc*) to recover

refeição [xefej'sãw] (*pl* -**ões**) *f* meal; **refeitório** [xefej'tɔrju] *m* refectory

refém [xe'fẽ] (*pl* -**ns**) *m* hostage

referência [xefe'rẽsja] *f* reference; **~s** *fpl* (*informações para emprego*) references; **fazer ~ a** to make reference to, refer to

referente [xefe'rẽtʃi] *adj*: **~ a** concerning, regarding

referir [xefe'ri*] *vt* to relate, tell; **referir-se** *vr*: **~-se a** to refer to

REFESA *f* (= *Rede Ferroviária SA*) ≈ BR

refinamento [xefina'mẽtu] *m* refinement

refinaria [xefina'ria] *f* refinery

refiro *etc* [xe'firu] *vb V* **referir**

refletir [xefle'tʃi*] (*PT* -**ct**-) *vt* to reflect ♦ *vi*: **~ em** *ou* **sobre** to consider, think about

reflexão [xeflek'sãw] (*pl* -**ões**) *f* reflection

reflexo, -a [xe'fleksu, a] *adj* (*luz*) reflected; (*ação*) reflex ♦ *m* reflection; (*ANAT*) reflex; (*no cabelo*) highlight

reflexões [xeflek'sõjʃ] *fpl* de **reflexão**

reflito *etc* [xe'flitu] *vb V* **refletir**

reforçado, -a [xefox'sadu, a] *adj* reinforced; (*pessoa*) strong; (*café da manhã, jantar*) hearty

reforçar [xefox'sa*] *vt* to reinforce; (*revigorar*) to invigorate; **reforço** [xe'foxsu] *m* reinforcement

reforma [xe'fɔxma] *f* reform; (*ARQ*) renovation; **reformado, -a** [xefox'madu, a] *adj* reformed; renovated; (*MIL*) retired; **reformar** [xefox'ma*] *vt* to reform; to renovate; **reformar-se** *vr* to reform

refractário, -a [xefra'tarju, a] (*PT*) *adj* = **refratário/a**

refrão [xe'frãw] (*pl* -**ãos** *ou* -**ães**) *m* chorus, refrain; (*provérbio*) saying

refratário, -a [xefra'tarju, a] *adj* (*TEC*) heat-resistant; (*CULIN*) oven-proof

refrear [xefre'a*] *vt* (*cavalo*) to rein in; (*inimigo*) to contain, check; (*paixões, raiva*) to control; **refrear-se** *vr* to restrain o.s

refrescante [xefreʃ'kãtʃi] *adj* refreshing

refrescar [xefreʃ'ka*] *vt* (*ar, ambiente*) to cool; (*pessoa*) to refresh ♦ *vi* to cool down

refresco [xe'freʃku] *m* cool fruit drink, squash; ~**s** *mpl* (*refrigerantes*) refreshments

refrigerador [xefriʒera'do*] *m* refrigerator, fridge (*BRIT*)

refrigerante [xefriʒe'rãtʃi] *m* soft drink

refugiado, -a [xefu'ʒjadu, a] *adj, m/f* refugee

refugiar-se [xefu'ʒjaxsi] *vr* to take refuge; **refúgio** [xe'fuʒju] *m* refuge

refugo [xe'fugu] *m* rubbish, garbage (*US*); (*mercadoria*) reject

refutar [xefu'ta*] *vt* to refute

rega ['xɛga] (*PT*) *f* irrigation

regador [xega'do*] *m* watering can

regalia [xega'lia] *f* privilege

regar [xe'ga*] *vt* (*plantas, jardim*) to water; (*umedecer*) to sprinkle

regatear [xega'tʃja*] *vt* (*o preço*) to haggle over, bargain for ♦ *vi* to haggle

regenerar [xeʒene'ra*] *vt* to regenerate

reger [xe'ʒe*] *vt* to govern; (*orquestra*) to conduct; (*empresa*) to run ♦ *vi* to rule; (*maestro*) to conduct

região [xe'ʒjãw] (*pl* -**ões**) *f* region, area

regime [xe'ʒimi] *m* (*POL*) regime;

(*dieta*) diet; (*maneira*) way; **estar de** ~ to be on a diet

regimento [xeʒi'mẽtu] *m* regiment

regiões [xe'ʒjõjʃ] *fpl de* **região**

regional [xeʒjo'naw] (*pl* -**ais**) *adj* regional

registrar [xeʒiʃ'tra*] (*PT* -**ista**-) *vt* to register; (*anotar*) to record

registro [xe'ʒiʃtru] (*PT* -**to**) *m* registration; (*anotação*) recording; (*livro, LING*) register; (*histórico*) record; ~ **civil** registry office

regra ['xɛgra] *f* rule; ~**s** *fpl* (*MED*) periods

regressar [xegre'sa*] *vi* to come (*ou* go) back, return; **regressivo, -a** [xegre'sivu, a] *adj* regressive; **contagem regressiva** countdown; **regresso** [xe'grɛsu] *m* return

régua ['xɛgwa] *f* rule; ~ **de calcular** slide rule

regulador [xegula'do*] *m* regulator

regulamento [xegula'mẽtu] *m* rules *pl*, regulations *pl*

regular [xegu'la*] *adj* regular; (*estatura*) average, medium; (*tamanho*) normal; (*razoável*) not bad ♦ *vt* to regulate; (*reger*) to govern; (*máquina*) to adjust; (*carro, motor*) to tune ♦ *vi* to work, function; **regularidade** [xegulari'dadʒi] *f* regularity

rei [xej] *m* king; **Dia de R~s** Epiphany; **R~ Momo** carnival king

reinado [xej'nadu] *m* reign

reinar [xej'na*] *vi* to reign

reino ['xejnu] *m* kingdom; (*fig*) realm; **o R~ Unido** the United Kingdom

reivindicação [xejvĩdʒika'sãw] (*pl* -**ões**) *f* claim, demand

reivindicar [xejvĩdʒi'ka*] *vt* to claim; (*aumento salarial, direitos*) to demand

rejeição [xeʒej'sãw] (pl -ões) f rejection

rejeitar [xeʒej'ta*] vt to reject; (recusar) to refuse

rejo etc ['xeʒu] vb V **reger**

rejuvenescer [xeʒuvene'se*] vt to rejuvenate

relação [xela'sãw] (pl -ões) f relation; (conexão) connection; (relacionamento) relationship; (MAT) ratio; (lista) list; **com** ou **em ~** a regarding, with reference to; **relações públicas** public relations; **relacionamento** [xelasjona'mẽtu] m relationship; **relacionar** [xelasjo'na*] vt to make a list of; (ligar): **relacionar algo com algo** to connect sth with sth, relate sth to sth; **relacionar-se** vr to be connected ou related

relâmpago [xe'lãpagu] m flash of lightning; **~s** mpl (clarões) lightning sg

relance [xe'lãsi] m glance; **olhar de ~** to glance at

relapso, -a [xe'lapsu, a] adj (negligente) negligent

relatar [xela'ta*] vt to give an account of

relativo, -a [xela'tʃivu, a] adj relative

relato [xe'latu] m account

relatório [xela'tɔrju] m report

relaxado, -a [xela'ʃadu, a] adj relaxed; (desleixado) slovenly, sloppy; (relapso) negligent

relaxante [xela'ʃãtʃi] adj relaxing

relaxar [xela'ʃa*] vt, vi to relax

relegar [xele'ga*] vt to relegate

relembrar [xelẽ'bra*] vt to recall

relevante [xele'vãtʃi] adj relevant

relevo [xe'levu] m relief

religião [xeli'ʒjãw] (pl -ões) f religion; **religioso, -a** [xeli'ʒozu, ɔza] adj religious ♦ m/f religious person; (frade/freira) monk/nun

relíquia [xe'likja] f relic; **~ de família** family heirloom

relógio [xe'lɔʒu] m clock; (de gás) meter; **~ (de sol)** (wrist)watch; **~ de sol** sundial

relutante [xelu'tãtʃi] adj reluctant

relva ['xɛwva] f grass; (terreno gramado) lawn

relvado [xew'vadu] (PT) m lawn

remar [xe'ma*] vt, vi to row

rematar [xema'ta*] vt to finish off; **remate** [xe'matʃi] m (fim) end; (acabamento) finishing touch

remediar [xeme'dʒja*] vt to put right, remedy

remédio [xe'mɛdʒju] m (medicamento) medicine; (recurso, solução) remedy; (JUR) recourse; **não tem ~** there's no way

remendar [xemẽ'da*] vt to mend; (com pano) to patch; **remendo** [xe'mẽdu] m repair; patch

remessa [xe'mɛsa] f shipment; (de dinheiro) remittance

remetente [xeme'tẽtʃi] m/f sender

remeter [xeme'te*] vt to send, dispatch; (dinheiro) to remit

remexer [xeme'ʃe*] vt (papéis) to shuffle; (sacudir: braços) to wave; (folhas) to shake; (revolver: areia, lama) to stir up ♦ vi: **~ em** to rummage through

reminiscência [xemini'sẽsja] f reminiscence

remo ['xemu] m oar; (ESPORTE) rowing

remoção [xemo'sãw] f removal

remorso [xe'mɔxsu] m remorse

remoto, -a [xe'mɔtu, a] adj remote

remover [xemo've*] vt to move; (transferir) to transfer; (demitir) to dismiss; (retirar, afastar) to remove; (terra) to churn up

renal [xe'naw] (pl -ais) adj renal, kidney atr

Renascença [xena'sẽsa] f: a ~ the Renaissance

renascer [xena'se*] vi to be reborn; (fig) to revive

renascimento [xenasi'mẽtu] m rebirth; (fig) revival; **o R~** the Renaissance

renda ['xẽda] f income; (nacional) revenue; (de aplicação, locação) yield; (tecido) lace

render [xẽ'de*] vt (lucro, dinheiro) to bring in, yield; (preço) to fetch; (homenagem) to pay; (graças) to give; (serviços) to render; (armas) to surrender; (guarda) to relieve; (causar) to bring ♦ vi (dar lucro) to pay; **render-se** vr to surrender; **rendição** [xẽdʒi'sãw] f surrender

rendimento [xẽdʒi'mẽtu] m income; (lucro) profit; (juro) yield, interest

renegar [xene'ga*] vt (crença) to renounce; (detestar) to hate; (trair) to betray; (negar) to deny; (desprezar) to reject

renomado, -a [xeno'madu, a] adj renowned

renome [xe'nɔmi] m renown

renovação [xenova'sãw] (pl -ões) f renewal; (ARQ) renovation

renovar [xeno'va*] vt to renew; (ARQ) to renovate

rentabilidade [xẽtabili'dadʒi] f profitability

rentável [xẽ'tavew] (pl -eis) adj profitable

renúncia [xe'nũsja] f resignation

renunciar [xenũ'sja*] vt to give up, renounce ♦ vi to resign; (abandonar): ~ **a algo** to give sth up

reouve etc [xe'ovi] vb V **reaver**

reouver etc [xeo've*] vb V **reaver**

reparação [xepara'sãw] (pl -ões) f mending, repairing; (de mal, erros) remedying; (fig) amends pl,

reparation

reparar [xepa'ra*] vt to repair; (forças) to restore; (mal, erros) to remedy; (prejuizo, danos, ofensa) to make amends for; (notar) to notice ♦ vi: ~ **em** to notice; **reparo** [xe'paru] m repair; (crítica) criticism; (observação) observation

repartição [xepaxtʃi'sãw] (pl -ões) f distribution

repartir [xepax'tʃi*] vt (distribuir) to distribute; (dividir entre vários) to share out; (dividir em várias porções) to divide up

repelente [xepe'lẽtʃi] adj, m repellent

repelir [xepe'li*] vt to repel

repente [xe'pẽtʃi] m outburst; **de ~** suddenly; (col: talvez) maybe

repentino, -a [xepẽ'tʃinu, a] adj sudden

repercussão [xepexku'sãw] (pl -ões) f repercussion

repercutir [xepexku'tʃi*] vt to echo ♦ vi to reverberate, echo; (fig): ~ **(em)** to have repercussions (on)

repertório [xepex'tɔrju] m list; (coleção) collection; (MÚS) repertoire

repetidamente [xepetʃida'mẽtʃi] adv repeatedly

repetido, -a [xepe'tʃidu, a] adj: repetidas vezes repeatedly, again and again

repetir [xepe'tʃi*] vt to repeat ♦ vi (ao comer) to have seconds; **repetir-se** vr to happen again; (pessoa) to repeat o.s.; **repetitivo, -a** [xepetʃi'tʃivu, a] adj repetitive

repilo etc [xe'pilu] vb V **repelir**

repito etc [xe'pitu] vb V **repetir**

repleto, -a [xe'pletu, a] adj replete, full up

réplica ['xeplika] f replica; (contestação) reply, retort

replicar [xepli'ka*] vt to answer,

reply to ♦ *vi* to reply, answer back

repolho [xe'poʎu] *m* cabbage

repor [xe'po*] (*irreg: como* **pôr**) *vt* to put back, replace; (*restituir*) to return; **repor-se** *vr* to recover

reportagem [xepox'taʒē] (*pl* **-ns**) *f* reporting; (*notícia*) report

repórter [xe'pɔxte*] *m/f* reporter

repousar [xepo'za*] *vi* to rest; **repouso** [xe'pozu] *m* rest

repreender [xeprjē'de*] *vt* to reprimand; **repreensão** [xeprjē'sãw] (*pl* **-ões**) *f* reprimand

represália [xepre'zalja] *f* reprisal

representação [xeprezēta'sãw] (*pl* **-ões**) *f* representation; (*TEATRO*) performance; **representante** [xeprezē'tātʃi] *m/f* representative

representar [xeprezē'ta*] *vt* to represent; (*TEATRO: papel*) to play; (*: peça*) to put on ♦ *vi* to act; **representativo, -a** [xeprezēta'tʃivu, a] *adj* representative

repressão [xepre'sãw] (*pl* **-ões**) *f* repression

reprimir [xepri'mi*] *vt* to repress

reprodução [xeprodu'sãw] (*pl* **-ões**) *f* reproduction

reproduzir [xeprodu'zi*] *vt* to reproduce; (*repetir*) to repeat; **reproduzir-se** *vr* to breed

reprovar [xepro'va*] *vt* to disapprove of; (*aluno*) to fail

réptil [ˈxɛptʃiw] (*pl* **-eis**) *m* reptile

república [xe'publika] *f* republic; **republicano, -a** [xepubli'kanu, a] *adj, m/f* republican

repudiar [xepu'dʒja*] *vt* to repudiate; **repúdio** [xe'pudʒju] *m* repudiation

repugnância [xepug'nāsja] *f* repugnance; **repugnante** [xepug'nātʃi] *adj* repugnant

repulsa [xe'puwsa] *f* (*ato*) rejection; (*sentimento*) repugnance; (*física*)

repulsion; **repulsivo, -a** [xepuw-'sivu, a] *adj* repulsive

reputação [xeputa'sãw] (*pl* **-ões**) *f* reputation

requeijão [xekej'ʒãw] *m* cheese spread

requerer [xeke're*] *vt* (*emprego*) to apply for; (*pedir*) to request; (*exigir*) to require; **requerimento** [xekeri-'mētu] *m* application; request; (*petição*) petition

requintado, -a [xekī'tadu, a] *adj* refined, elegant

requinte [xe'kītʃi] *m* refinement, elegance; (*cúmulo*) height

requisito [xeki'zitu] *m* requirement

rés-do-chão [xɛʒ-] (*PT*) *m inv* ground floor (*BRIT*), first floor (*US*)

reserva [xe'zɛxva] *f* reserve; (*para hotel, fig*) reservation ♦ *m/f* (*ESPORTE*) reserve

reservado, -a [xezex'vadu, a] *adj* reserved

reservar [xezex'va*] *vt* to reserve; (*guardar de reserva*) to keep; (*forças*) to conserve; **reservar-se** *vr* to save o.s

reservatório [xezexva'tɔrju] *m* reservoir

resfriado, -a [xeʃ'frjadu, a] (*BR*) *adj*: **estar/ficar ~** to have a cold/catch (a) cold ♦ *m* cold, chill

resgatar [xeʒga'ta*] *vt* (*salvar*) to rescue; (*prisioneiro*) to ransom; (*retomar*) to get back, recover; **resgate** [xeʒ'gatʃi] *m* rescue; ransom; recovery

residência [xezi'dēsja] *f* residence; **residencial** [xezidē'sjaw] (*pl* **-ais**) *adj* residential; (*computador, telefone etc*) home *atr*; **residente** [xezi'dētʃi] *adj, m/f* resident

residir [xezi'dʒi*] *vi* to live, reside

resíduo [xe'zidwu] *m* residue

resignação [xezigna'sãw] (*pl* **-ões**)

f resignation

resignar-se [xezig'naxsi] vr: ~ **com** to resign o.s. to

resina [xe'zina] f resin

resistente [xezif'tẽtfi] adj resistant; (material, objeto) hard-wearing, strong

resistir [xezif'tfi*] vi to hold; (pessoa) to hold out; ~ **a** to resist; (sobreviver) to survive

resmungar [xeʒmũ'ga*] vt, vi to mutter, mumble

resolução [xezolu'sãw] (pl -ões) f resolution; (de um problema) solution; **resoluto, -a** [xezo'lutu, a] adj decisive

resolver [xezow've*] vt to sort out; (problema) to solve; (questão) to resolve; (decidir) to decide; **resolver-se** vr: ~**se (a fazer)** to make up one's mind (to do), decide (to do)

respectivo, -a [xefpek'tfivu, a] adj respective

respeitar [xefpej'ta*] vt to respect; **respeitável** [xefpej'tavew] (pl -eis) adj respectable; (considerável) considerable

respeito [xef'pejtu] m: ~ **a** (ou **por**) respect (for); ~**s** mpl (cumprimentos) regards; **a** ~ **de, com** ~ **a** as to, as regards; (sobre) about; **dizer** ~ **a** to concern; **em** ~ **a** with respect to

respiração [xefpira'sãw] f breathing

respirar [xefpi'ra*] vt, vi to breathe

respiro [xef'piru] m breath

resplandecente [xefplãde'sẽtfi] adj resplendent

responder [xefpõ'de*] vt to answer ♦ vi to answer; (ser respondão) to answer back; ~ **por** to be responsible for, answer for

responsabilidade [xefpõsabili'dadʒi] f responsibility

responsabilizar [xefpõsabili'za*] vt: ~ **alguém (por algo)** to hold sb responsible (for sth); **responsabilizar-se** vr: ~**se por** to take responsibility for

responsável [xefpõ'savew] (pl -eis) adj: ~ **(por)** responsible (for); ~ **a** answerable to, accountable to

resposta [xef'pɔfta] f answer, reply

resquício [xef'kisju] m (vestígio) trace

ressabiado, -a [xesa'bjadu, a] adj wary; (ressentido) resentful

ressaca [xe'saka] f undertow; (mar bravo) rough sea; (fig: de quem bebeu) hangover

ressaltar [xesaw'ta*] vt to emphasize ♦ vi to stand out

ressalva [xe'sawva] f safeguard

ressentido, -a [xesẽ'tfidu, a] adj resentful

ressentimento [xesẽtfi'mẽtu] m resentment

ressentir-se [xesẽ'tfixsi] vr: ~ **de** (ofender-se) to resent; (magoar-se) to be hurt by; (sofrer) to suffer from, feel the effects of

ressurgimento [xesuxʒi'mẽtu] m resurgence, revival

ressurreição [xesuxej'sãw] (pl -ões) f resurrection

ressuscitar [xesusi'ta*] vt, vi to revive

restabelecer [xeftabele'se*] vt to re-establish, restore; **restabelecer-se** vr to recover, recuperate; **restabelecimento** [xeftabelesi'mẽtu] m re-establishment; restoration; recovery

restante [xef'tãtfi] adj remaining ♦ m rest

restar [xef'ta*] vi to remain, be left

restauração [xeftawra'sãw] (pl -ões) f restoration; (de costumes, usos) revival

restaurante [xeʃtaw'rãtʃi] m restaurant

restaurar [xeʃtaw'ra*] vt to restore

restituição [xeʃtʃitwi'sãw] (pl -ões) f restitution, return; (de dinheiro) repayment

restituir [xeʃtʃi'twi*] vt to return; (dinheiro) to repay; (forças, saúde) to restore; (usos) to revive; (reempossar) to reinstate

resto ['xɛʃtu] m rest; (MAT) remainder; ~s mpl (sobras) remains; (de comida) scraps

restrição [xeʃtri'sãw] (pl -ões) f restriction

restringir [xeʃtrĩ'ʒi*] vt to restrict

resultado [xezuw'tadu] m result

resultante [xezuw'tãtʃi] adj resultant; ~ de resulting from

resultar [xezuw'ta*] vi: ~ (de/em) to result (from/in) ♦ vi (vir a ser) to turn out to be

resumir [xezu'mi*] vt to summarize; (livro) to abridge; (reduzir) to reduce; (conter em resumo) to sum up; **resumo** [xe'zumu] m summary, résumé; **em resumo** in short, briefly

retaguarda [xeta'gwaxda] f rearguard; (posição) rear

retaliação [xetalja'sãw] (pl -ões) f retaliation

retângulo [xe'tãgulu] m rectangle

retardar [xetax'da*] vt to hold up, delay; (adiar) to postpone

reter [xe'te*] (irreg: como **ter**) vt (guardar, manter) to keep; (deter) to stop; (segurar) to hold; (ladrão, suspeito) to detain; (na memória) to retain; (lágrimas, impulsos) to hold back; (impedir de sair) to keep back

reticente [xetʃi'sẽtʃi] adj reticent

retificar [xetʃifi'ka*] vt to rectify

retirada [xetʃi'rada] f (MIL) retreat; (salário, saque) withdrawal

retirar [xetʃi'ra*] vt to withdraw; (afastar) to take away, remove; (retirar-se) vr to withdraw; (de uma festa etc) to leave; (MIL) to retreat

reto, -a ['xɛtu, a] adj straight; (fig: justo) fair; (: honesto) honest, upright ♦ m (ANAT) rectum

retorcer [xetox'se*] vt to twist; **retorcer-se** vr to wriggle, writhe

retornar [xetox'na*] vi to return, go back; **retorno** [xe'toxnu] m return; **dar retorno** to do a U-turn; **retorno (do carro)** (COMPUT) (carriage) return

retraído, -a [xetra'idu, a] adj (tímido) reserved, timid

retrair [xetra'i*] vt to withdraw; (contrair) to contract; (pessoa) to make reserved

retrato [xe'tratu] m portrait; (FOTO) photo; (fig: efígie) likeness; (: representação) portrayal; **~ falado** identikit ® picture

retribuir [xetri'bwi*] vt to reward, recompense; (pagar) to remunerate; (hospitalidade, favor, sentimento, visita) to return

retroceder [xetrose'de*] vi to retreat, fall back; **retrocesso** [xetro'sesu] m retreat; (ao passado) return

retrógrado, -a [xe'trɔgradu, a] adj retrograde; (reacionário) reactionary

retrospecto [xetro'ʃpektu] m: **em ~** in retrospect

retrovisor [xetrovi'zo*] adj, m: **(espelho) ~** (rear-view) mirror

réu, -ré [xɛw, xɛ] m/f defendant; (culpado) culprit, criminal

reumatismo [xewma'tʃiʒmu] m rheumatism

reunião [xeu'njãw] (pl -ões) f meeting; (ato, reencontro) reunion; (festa) get-together, party; **~ de cúpula** summit (meeting)

reunir [xeu'ni*] vt (pessoas) to

bring together; (*partes*) to join, unite; (*qualidades*) to combine; **reunir-se** *vr* to meet; **~-se a** to join

revanche [xe'vãʃi] *f* revenge

reveillon [xeve'jõ] *m* New Year's Eve

revelação [xevela'sãw] (*pl* -ões) *f* revelation

revelar [xeve'la*] *vt* to reveal; (*FOTO*) to develop; **revelar-se** *vr* to turn out to be

revelia [xeve'lia] *f* default; **à ~** by default; **à ~ de** without the knowledge *ou* consent of

revendedor, a [xevẽde'do*, a] *m/f* dealer

rever [xe've*] (*irreg: como* **ver**) *vt* to see again; (*examinar*) to check; (*revisar*) to revise

reverência [xeve'rẽsja] *f* reverence, respect; (*ato*) bow; (: *de mulher*) curtsey; **fazer uma ~** to bow, to curtsey

reverenciar [xeverẽ'sja*] *vt* to revere

reverso [xe'vexsu] *m* reverse

reverter [xevex'te*] *vt* to revert

revés [xe'vɛʃ] *m* reverse; (*infortúnio*) setback, mishap; **ao ~** (*roupa*) inside out; **de ~** (*olhar*) askance

revestir [xeveʃ'tʃi*] *vt* (*paredes etc*) to cover; (*interior de uma caixa etc*) to line

revezar [xeve'za*] *vt, vi* to alternate; **revezar-se** *vr* to take turns, alternate

revidar [xevi'da*] *vt* (*soco, insulto*) to return; (*retrucar*) to answer; (*crítica*) to rise to, respond to ♦ *vi* to hit back; (*retrucar*) to respond

revirar [xevi'ra*] *vt* to turn round; (*gaveta*) to turn out, go through

revisão [xevi'zãw] (*pl* -ões) *f* revision; (*de máquina*) overhaul; (*de carro*) service; (*JUR*) appeal

revisar [xevi'za*] *vt* to revise

revisões [xevi'zõjʃ] *fpl de* **revisão**

revista [xe'viʃta] *f* (*busca*) search; (*MIL, exame*) inspection; (*publicação*) magazine; (: *profissional, erudita*) journal; (*TEATRO*) revue

revistar [xeviʃ'ta*] *vt* to search; (*tropa*) to review; (*examinar*) to examine

revisto *etc* [xe'viʃtu] *vb V* **revestir**

revogar [xevo'ga*] *vt* to revoke

revolta [xe'vɔwta] *f* revolt; (*fig: indignação*) disgust; **R~ da Vacina** *see boxed note*

REVOLTA DA VACINA

This was a popular movement of opposition to the government, which took place in Rio de Janeiro in 1904 following the passing of a law which made vaccination against smallpox compulsory. It was the culmination of general dissatisfaction with health reforms undertaken at that time by the scientist Osvaldo Cruz, and the relocation programme of the prefect Pereira Passos, as a result of which part of the population of Rio had been moved from the slums and shanty towns of the central region to suburbs much further out.

---

revoltado, -a [xevow'tadu, a] *adj* in revolt; (*indignado*) disgusted; (*amargo*) bitter

revoltante [xevow'tãtʃi] *adj* disgusting, revolting

revoltar [xevow'ta*] *vt* to disgust; **revoltar-se** *vr* to rebel, revolt; (*indignar-se*) to be disgusted

revolto, -a [xe'vowtu, a] *pp de* **revolver** ♦ *adj* (*década*) turbulent; (*mundo*) troubled; (*cabelo*) untidy, unkempt; (*mar*) rough; (*desarruma-do*) untidy

revolução [xevolu'sãw] (*pl* **-ões**) *f* revolution; **revolucionar** [xevo-lùsjo'na*] *vt* to revolutionize; **revolucionário, -a** [xevolusjo'narju, a] *adj, m/f* revolutionary

revolver [xevow've*] *vi* to revolve, rotate

revólver [xe'vɔwve*] *m* revolver

reza ['xeza] *f* prayer; **rezar** [xe'za*] *vi* to pray

riacho ['xjaʃu] *m* brook, stream

ribeiro [xi'bejru] *m* brook, stream

rico, -a ['xiku, a] *adj* rich; (*PT: lindo*) beautiful; (:: *excelente*) splendid ♦ *m/f* rich man/woman

ridicularizar [xidʒikulari'za*] *vt* to ridicule

ridículo, -a [xi'dʒikulu, a] *adj* ridiculous

rifa ['xifa] *f* raffle

rifle ['xifli] *m* rifle

rigidez [xiʒi'deʒ] *f* rigidity, stiffness; (*austeridade*) severity, strictness

rígido, -a ['xiʒidu, a] *adj* rigid, stiff; (*fig*) strict

rigor [xi'go*] *m* rigidity; (*meticulosidade*) rigour (*BRIT*), rigor (*US*); (*severidade*) harshness, severity; (*exatidão*) precision; **ser de ~** to be essential *ou* obligatory; **rigoroso, -a** [xigo-'rozu, ɔza] *adj* rigorous; (*severo*) strict; (*exigente*) demanding; (*minucioso*) precise, accurate; (*inverno*) hard, harsh

rijo, -a ['xiʒu, a] *adj* tough, hard; (*severo*) harsh, severe

rim [xĩ] (*pl* **-ns**) *m* kidney; **rins** *mpl* (*parte inferior das costas*) small *sg* of the back

rima ['xima] *f* rhyme; (*poema*) verse, poem; **rimar** [xi'ma*] *vt, vi* to rhyme

rímel ['ximew] ® (*pl* **-eis**) *m* mascara

ringue ['xĩgi] *m* ring

rins [xĩʃ] *mpl* de **rim**

Rio ['xiu] *m*: **o ~ (de Janeiro)** Rio de Janeiro)

rio ['xiu] *m* river

riqueza [xi'keza] *f* wealth, riches *pl*; (*qualidade*) richness

rir [xi*] *vi* to laugh; **~ de** to laugh at

risada [xi'zada] *f* laughter

risca ['xiʃka] *f* stroke; (*listra*) stripe; (*no cabelo*) parting

riscar [xiʃ'ka*] *vt* (*marcar*) to mark; (*apagar*) to cross out; (*desenhar*) to outline

risco ['xiʃku] *m* (*marca*) mark, scratch; (*traço*) stroke; (*desenho*) drawing, sketch; (*perigo*) risk; **correr o ~ de** to run the risk of

riso ['xizu] *m* laughter; **risonho, -a** [xi'zoɲu, a] *adj* smiling; (*contente*) cheerful

ríspido, -a ['xiʃpidu, a] *adj* brusque; (*áspero*) harsh

ritmo ['xitʃmu] *m* rhythm

rito ['xitu] *m* rite

ritual [xi'twaw] (*pl* **-ais**) *adj, m* ritual

rival [xi'vaw] (*pl* **-ais**) *adj, m/f* rival; **rivalidade** [xivali'dadʒi] *f* rivalry; **rivalizar** [xivali'za*] *vt* to rival ♦ *vi*: **rivalizar com** to compete with, vie with

roa *etc* ['xoa] *vb* V **roer**

robô [xo'bo] *m* robot

robusto, -a [xo'buʃtu, a] *adj* strong, robust

roça ['xɔsa] *f* plantation; (*no mato*) clearing; (*campo*) country

rocha ['xɔʃa] *f* rock; (*penedo*) crag

rochedo [xo'ʃedu] *m* crag, cliff

rock-and-roll [-â'xɔw] *m* rock and roll

roda ['xɔda] *f* wheel; (*círculo*) circle; **~ dentada** cog(wheel); **em** *ou* **à ~**

de round, around

rodada [xo'dada] f (de bebidas, ESPORTE) round

rodar [xo'da*] vt to turn, spin; (viajar por) to tour, travel round; (quilômetros) to do; (filme) to make; (imprimir) to print; (COMPUT: programa) to run ♦ vi to turn round; (AUTO) to drive around; ~ **por** (a pé) to wander around; (de carro) to drive around

rodeio [xo'deju] m (em discurso) circumlocution; (subterfúgio) subterfuge; (de gado) round-up; fazer ~s to beat about the bush; sem ~s plainly, frankly

rodela [xo'dɛla] f (pedaço) slice

rodízio [xo'dʒizju] m rota; em ~ on a rota basis

rodopiar [xodo'pja*] vi to whirl around, swirl

rodovia [xodo'via] f highway, ≈ motorway (BRIT), ≈ interstate (US)

rodoviária [xodo'vjarja] f (tb: estação ~) bus station; V tb rodoviário

rodoviário, -a [xodo'vjarju, a] adj road atr; (polícia) traffic atr

roer [xwe*] vt to gnaw, nibble; (enferrujar) to corrode; (afligir) to eat away

rogar [xo'ga*] vi to ask, request; ~ a alguém que faça (algo) to beg sb to do (sth)

rói [xɔj] vb V roer

roía etc [xo'ia] vb V roer

rolar [xo'la*] vt, vi to roll

roleta [xo'leta] f roulette; (borboleta) turnstile

rolha [xoʎa] f cork

roliço, -a [xo'lisu, a] adj (pessoa) plump, chubby; (objeto) round, cylindrical

rolo ['xolu] m (de papel etc) roll; (para nivelar o solo, para pintura)

roller; (para cabelo) curler; (col: briga) brawl, fight; **cortina de ~** roller blind; **~ compressor** steamroller

Roma ['xoma] n Rome

romã [xo'mã] f pomegranate

romance [xo'mãsi] m novel; (caso amoroso) romance; **~ policial** detective story

romano, -a [xo'manu, a] adj, m/f Roman

romântico, -a [xo'mãtʃiku, a] adj romantic

rombo ['xõbu] m (buraco) hole; (fig: desfalque) embezzlement; (: prejuízo) loss, shortfall

Romênia [xo'menja] f: **a ~** Romania; **romeno, -a** [xo'menu, a] adj, m/f Rumanian ♦ m (LING) Rumanian

romper [xõ'pe*] vt to break; (rasgar) to tear; (relações) to break off ♦ vi (sol) to appear, emerge; (: surgir) to break through; (ano, dia) to start, begin; **~ em pranto** ou **lágrimas** to burst into tears; **rompimento** [xõpi'mẽtu] m breakage; (fenda) break; (de relações) breaking off

roncar [xõ'ka*] vi to snore; **ronco** ['xõku] m snore

ronda ['xõda] f patrol, beat; fazer a ~ **de** to go the rounds of, patrol; **rondar** [xõ'da*] vt to patrol; (espreitar) to prowl ♦ vi to prowl, lurk; (fazer a ronda) to patrol; **a inflação ronda os 30% ao mês** inflation is in the region of 30% a month

rosa ['xɔza] adj inv pink ♦ f rose; **rosado, -a** [xo'zadu, a] adj rosy, pink

rosário [xo'zarju] m rosary

rosbife [xoʒ'bifi] m roast beef

rosca ['xoʃka] f spiral, coil; (de parafuso) thread; (pão) ring-shaped *loaf*

roseira [xo'zejra] f rosebush

rosnar [xoʒ'na*] vi (cão) to growl, snarl; (murmurar) to mutter, mumble

rosto ['xoʃtu] m face

rota ['xɔta] f route, course

rotativo, -a [xota'tʃivu, a] adj rotary

roteiro [xo'tejru] m itinerary; (ordem) schedule; (guia) guidebook; (de filme) script

rotina [xo'tʃina] f routine; **rotineiro, -a** [xotʃi'nejru, a] adj routine

roto, -a ['xotu, a] adj broken; (rasgado) torn

rotular [xotu'la*] vt to label; **rótulo** ['xɔtulu] m label

roubar [xo'ba*] vt to steal; (loja, casa, pessoa) to rob ♦ vi to steal; (em jogo, no preço) to cheat; ~ algo a alguém to steal sth from sb; **roubo** ['xobu] m theft, robbery

rouco, -a ['roku, a] adj hoarse

round ['xãwdʒi] (pl ~s) m (BOXE) round

roupa ['xopa] f clothes pl, clothing; ~ de baixo underwear; ~ de cama bedclothes pl, bed linen

roupão [xo'pãw] (pl -ões) m dressing gown

rouxinol [xoʃi'nɔw] (pl -óis) m nightingale

roxo, -a ['xoʃu, a] adj purple, violet

royalty ['xɔjawtʃi] (pl -ies) m royalty

rua ['xua] f street; ~ principal main street; ~ sem saída no through road, cul-de-sac

rubéola [xu'bɛola] f (MED) German measles sg

rubi [xu'bi] m ruby

rubor [xu'bo*] m blush; (fig) shyness, bashfulness; **ruborizar-se**

rubrica [xu'brika] f (signed) initials pl

rubro, -a ['xubru, a] adj (faces) rosy, ruddy

ruço, -a ['xusu, a] adj grey (BRIT), gray (US), dun; (desbotado) faded

rude [xudʒi] adj (ingênuo) simple; (grosseiro) rude; **rudeza** [xu'deza] f simplicity; rudeness

rudimento [xudʒi'mẽtu] m rudiment

ruela ['xwɛla] f lane, alley

ruga ['xuga] f (na pele) wrinkle; (na roupa) crease

ruge ['xuʒi] m rouge

rugido [xu'ʒidu] m roar

rugir [xu'ʒi*] vi to roar

ruído ['xwidu] m noise; **ruidoso, -a** [xwi'dozu, ɔza] adj noisy

ruim [xu'ĩ] (pl -ns) adj bad; (defeituoso) defective

ruína [xu'ina] f ruin; (decadência) downfall

ruins [xu'ĩʃ] pl de ruim

ruir ['xwi*] vi to collapse, go to ruin

ruivo, -a ['xwivu, a] adj red-haired ♦ m/f redhead

rum [xũ] m rum

rumo ['xumu] m course, bearing; (fig) course; ~ a bound for; **sem ~** adrift

rumor [xu'mo*] m noise; (notícia) rumour (BRIT), rumor (US); report

ruptura [xup'tura] f break, rupture

rural [xu'raw] (pl -ais) adj rural

rush [xʌʃ] m rush; **(a hora do)** ~ rush hour

Rússia ['xusja] f: a ~ Russia; **russo, -a** ['xusu, a] adj, m/f Russian ♦ m (LING) Russian

rústico, -a ['xuʃtʃiku, a] adj rustic; (pessoa) simple; (utensílio, objeto) crude

S

S. abr (= Santo, -a ou São) St

SA abr (= Sociedade Anônima) Ltd (BRIT), Inc. (US)

sã [sã] f de **são**

Saara [sa'ara] m: o ~ the Sahara

sábado ['sabadu] m Saturday

sabão [sa'bãw] m (pl -ões) m soap

sabedoria [sabedo'ria] f wisdom; (erudição) learning

saber [sa'be*] vt, vi to know; (descobrir) to find out ♦ m knowledge; a ~ namely; ~ **fazer** to know how to do, be able to do; **que eu saiba** as far as I know

sabiá [sa'bja] m/f thrush

sabido, -a [sa'bidu, a] adj knowledgeable; (esperto) shrewd

sábio, -a ['sabju, a] adj wise; (erudito) learned ♦ m/f wise person; (erudito) scholar

sabões [sa'bõjʃ] mpl de **sabão**

sabonete [sabo'netʃi] m toilet soap

sabor [sa'bo*] m taste, flavour (BRIT), flavor (US); **saborear** [sabo'rja*] vt to taste, savour (BRIT), savor (US); **saboroso, -a** [sabo'rozu, ɔza] adj tasty, delicious

sabotagem [sabo'taʒẽ] f sabotage

sabotar [sabo'ta*] vt to sabotage

saca ['saka] f sack

sacar [sa'ka*] vt to take out; (dinheiro) to withdraw; (arma, cheque) to draw; (ESPORTE) to serve; (col: entender) to understand ♦ vi (col: entender) to understand; ~ **sobre um devedor** to borrow money from sb

saca-rolhas m inv corkscrew

sacerdote [sasex'dɔtʃi] m priest

saciar [sa'sja*] vt (fome, curiosidade) to satisfy; (sede) to quench

saco ['saku] m bag; (enseada) inlet;

~ **de café** coffee filter; ~ **de dormir** sleeping bag

sacode etc [sa'kɔdʒi] vb V **sacudir**

sacola [sa'kɔla] f bag

sacramento [sakra'mẽtu] m sacramento

sacrificar [sakrifi'ka*] vt to sacrifice; **sacrifício** [sakri'fisju] m sacrifice

sacrilégio [sakri'lɛʒju] m sacrilege

sacro, -a ['sakru, a] adj sacred

sacudida [saku'dʒida] f shake

sacudir [saku'dʒi*] vt to shake; **sacudir-se** vr to shake

sádico, -a ['sadʒiku, a] adj sadistic

sadio, -a [sa'dʒiu, a] adj healthy

safado, -a [sa'fadu, a] adj shameless; (imoral) dirty; (travesso) mischievous ♦ m rogue

safira [sa'fira] f sapphire

safra ['safra] f harvest

Sagitário [saʒi'tarju] m Sagittarius

sagrado, -a [sa'gradu, a] adj sacred, holy

saia ['saja] f skirt

saiba etc ['sajba] vb V **saber**

saída [sa'ida] f exit, way out; (partida) departure; (ato: de pessoa) going out; (fig: solução) way out; (COMPUT: de programa) exit; (: de dados) output; ~ **de emergência** emergency exit

sair [sa'i*] vi to go (ou come) out; (partir) to leave; (realizar-se) to turn out; (COMPUT) to exit; **sair-se** vr: ~**-se bem/mal de** to be successful/ unsuccessful in

sal [saw] m (pl **sais**) m salt; **sem** ~ (comida) salt-free; (pessoa) lacklustre (BRIT), lackluster (US)

sala ['sala] f room; (num edifício público) hall; (classe, turma) class; ~ (de aula) classroom; ~ **de espera/ (de estar)/de jantar** waiting/living/ dining room; ~ **de operação** (MED) operating theatre (BRIT) ou theater (US)

salada [sa'lada] f salad; (fig) confusion, jumble

sala-e-quarto (pl ~s ou **salas-e-quarto**) m two-room flat (BRIT) ou apartment (US)

salão [sa'lãw] (pl -ões) m large room, hall; (exposição) show; ~ de beleza beauty salon

salário [sa'larju] m wages pl, salary

saldo ['sawdu] m balance; (sobra) surplus

saleiro [sa'lejru] m salt cellar

salgadinho [sawga'dʒiɲu] m savoury (BRIT), savory (US), snack

salgado, -a [saw'gadu, a] adj salty, salted

salgar [saw'ga*] vt to salt

salgueiro [saw'gejru] m willow; ~ chorão weeping willow

salientar [saljẽ'ta*] vt to point out; (acentuar) to stress, emphasize; **saliente** [sa'ljẽtʃi] adj prominent; (evidente) clear, conspicuous; (importante) outstanding; (assanhado) forward

saliva [sa'liva] f saliva

salmão [saw'mãw] (pl -ões) m salmon

salmoura [saw'mora] f brine

salões [sa'lõjʃ] mpl de **salão**

salsa ['sawsa] f parsley

salsicha [saw'siʃa] f sausage; **salsichão** [sawsi'ʃãw] (pl -ões) m sausage

saltar [saw'ta*] vt to jump (over), leap (over); (omitir) to skip ♦ vi to jump, leap; (sangue) to spurt out; (de ônibus, cavalo): ~ de to get off

salto ['sawtu] m jump, leap; (de calçado) heel; ~ de vara/em altura/em distância pole vault/high jump/long jump

salubre [sa'lubri] adj healthy, salubrious

salvação [sawva'sãw] f salvation

salvador [sawva'do*] m saviour (BRIT), savior (US)

salvamento [sawva'mẽtu] m rescue; (de naufrágio) salvage

salvar [saw'va*] vt to save; (resgatar) to rescue; (objetos, de ruína) to salvage; (honra) to defend; **salvar-se** vr to escape

salva-vidas m inv (bóia) lifebuoy ♦ m/f inv (pessoa) lifeguard; **barco ~** lifeboat

salvo, -a ['sawvu, a] adj safe ♦ prep except, save; **a ~** in safety

samba ['sãba] m samba; see boxed note

SAMBA

The greatest form of musical expression of the Brazilian people, the **samba** is a type of music and dance of African origin. It embraces a number of rhythmic styles, such as *samba de breque*, *samba-enredo*, *samba-canção* and *pagode*, among others. Officially, the first samba, entitled *Pelo telefone*, was written in Rio in 1917.

---

sanar [sa'na*] vt to cure; (remediar) to remedy

sanção [sã'sãw] (pl -ões) f sanction; **sancionar** [sãsjo'na*] vt to sanction

sandália [sã'dalja] f sandal

sandes ['sãdʒ] (PT) f inv sandwich

sanduíche [sãd'wiʃi] (BR) m sandwich

saneamento [sanja'mẽtu] m sanitation

sanear [sa'nja*] vt to clean up

sangrar [sã'gra*] vt, vi to bleed; **sangrento, -a** [sã'grẽtu, a] adj bloody; (CULIN: carne) rare

sangue ['sãgi] m blood

sanguessuga [sãgi'suga] f leech

sanguinário, -a [sãgi'narju, a] adj bloodthirsty

sanguíneo, -a [sã'ginju, a] adj: **grupo ~** blood group; **pressão sanguínea** blood pressure; **vaso ~** blood vessel

sanidade [sani'dadʒi] f (saúde) health; (mental) sanity

sanita [sa'nita] (PT) f toilet, lavatory

sanitário, -a [sani'tarju, a] adj sanitary; **vaso ~** toilet, lavatory (bowl); **sanitários** [sani'tarjuʃ] mpl toilets

santidade [sãtʃi'dadʒi] f holiness, sanctity

santo, -a [ˈsãtu, a] adj holy ♦ m/f saint

santuário [sã'twarju] m shrine, sanctuary

São [sãw] m Saint

são, sã [sãw, sã] (pl ~s, ~s) adj healthy; (conselho) sound; (mentalmente) sane; **~ e salvo** safe and sound

São Paulo [-'pawlu] n São Paulo

sapataria [sapata'ria] f shoe shop

sapateiro [sapa'tejru] m shoemaker; (vendedor) shoe salesman; (que conserta) shoe repairer; (loja) shoe repairer's

sapatilha [sapa'tʃiʎa] f (de balé) shoe; (sapato) pump; (de atleta) running shoe

sapato [sa'patu] m shoe

sapo [ˈsapu] m toad

saque¹ [ˈsaki] m (de dinheiro) withdrawal; (COM) draft, bill; (ESPORTE) serve; (pilhagem) plunder, pillage; **~ a descoberto** (COM) overdraft

saque² etc vb V **sacar**

saquear [sa'kja*] vt to pillage, plunder

sarampo [sa'rãpu] m measles sg

sarar [sa'ra*] vt to cure; (ferida) to heal ♦ vi to recover

sarcasmo [sax'kaʒmu] m sarcasm

sarda [ˈsaxda] f freckle

Sardenha [sax'deɲa] f: **a ~** Sardinia

sardinha [sax'dʒiɲa] f sardine

sargento [sax'ʒẽtu] m sergeant

sarjeta [sax'ʒeta] f gutter

Satã [sa'tã] m Satan

Satanás [sata'naʃ] m Satan

satélite [sa'tɛlitʃi] m satellite

sátira [ˈsatʃira] f satire

satisfação [satʃiʃfa'sãw] (pl -ões) f satisfaction; (recompensa) reparation; **satisfatório, -a** [satʃiʃfa'tɔrju, a] adj satisfactory

satisfazer [satʃiʃfa'ze*] (irreg: como **fazer**) vt to satisfy ♦ vi to be satisfactory; **satisfazer-se** vr to be satisfied; (saciar-se) to fill o.s. up; **~ a** to satisfy; **satisfeito, -a** [satʃiʃ'fejtu, a] adj satisfied; (saciado) full; **dar-se por satisfeito com algo** to be content with sth

saudação [sawda'sãw] (pl -ões) f greeting

saudade [saw'dadʒi] f longing, yearning; (lembrança nostálgica) nostalgia; **deixar ~s** to be greatly missed; **ter ~(s) de** (desejar) to long for; (sentir falta de) to miss; **~(s) de casa, ~(s) da pátria** homesickness sg

saudar [saw'da*] vt to greet; (dar as boas vindas) to welcome; (aclamar) to acclaim

saudável [saw'davew] (pl -eis) adj healthy; (moralmente) wholesome

saúde [sa'udʒi] f health; (brinde) toast; **~!** (brindando) cheers!; (quando se espirra) bless you!; **beber à ~ de** to drink to, toast; **estar bem/mal de ~** to be well/ill

saudosismo [sawdo'ziʒmu] m nostalgia

saudoso, -a [saw'dozu, ɔza] adj (nostálgico) nostalgic; (da família ou *terra natal*) homesick; (*de uma pessoa*) longing; (*que causa saudades*) much-missed

sauna ['sawna] *f* sauna

saxofone [sakso'fɔni] *m* saxophone

sazonal [sazo'naw] (*pl* **-ais**) *adj* seasonal

scanner ['skane*] *m* scanner

┌─────────────────────┐
│ *PALAVRA CHAVE* │
└─────────────────────┘

se [si] *pron* **1** (*reflexivo: impess*) oneself; (: *m*) himself; (: *f*) herself; (: *coisa*) itself; (: *você*) yourself; (: *pl*) themselves; (: *vocês*) yourselves; **ela está ~ vestindo** she's getting dressed; (*usos léxicos del pron*) *V o vb em questão p. ex.* **arrepender-se**

2 (*uso recíproco*) each other, one another; **olharam-~** they looked at each other

3 (*impess*): **come-~ bem aqui** you can eat well here; **sabe-~ que ... it** is known that ...; **vende(m)-~ jornais naquela loja** they sell newspapers in that shop

♦ *conj* **if**; (*em pergunta indireta*) whether; **~ bem que** even though

sê [se] *vb V* **ser**

sebe ['sɛbi] (*PT*) *f* fence; **~ viva** hedge

sebo ['sebu] *m* tallow; **seboso, -a** [se'bozu, ɔza] *adj* greasy; (*sujo*) dirty

seca ['sɛka] *f* drought

secador [seka'do*] *m*: **~ de cabelo/roupa** hairdryer/clothes horse

seção [se'sãw] (*pl* **-ões**) *f* section; (*em loja, repartição*) department

secar [se'ka*] *vt* to dry; (*planta*) to parch ♦ *vi* to dry; to wither; (*fonte*) to dry up

secção [sek'sãw] (*PT*) = **seção**

seco, -a ['seku, a] *adj* dry; (*ríspido*) curt, brusque; (*magro*) thin; (*pessoa: frio*) cold; (: *sério*) serious

seções [se'sõjʃ] *fpl de* **seção**

secretaria [sekreta'ria] *f* general office; (*de secretário*) secretary's office; (*ministério*) ministry

secretária [sekre'tarja] *f* writing desk; **~ eletrônica** (*telephone*) answering machine; *V tb* **secretário**

secretário, -a [sekre'tarju, a] *m/f* secretary; **S~ de Estado de ...** Secretary of State for ...

secreto, -a [se'krɛtu, a] *adj* secret

sector [sek'to*] (*PT*) *m* = **setor**

século ['sɛkulu] *m* century; (*época*) age

secundário, -a [sekũ'darju, a] *adj* secondary

seda ['seda] *f* silk

sedativo [seda'tʃivu] *m* sedative

sede[1] ['sɛdʒi] *f* (*de empresa, instituição*) headquarters *sg*; (*de governo*) seat; (*REL*) see, diocese

sede[2] ['sedʒi] *f* thirst; **estar com** *ou* **ter ~** to be thirsty; **sedento, -a** [se'dẽtu, a] *adj* thirsty

sediar [se'dʒja*] *vt* to base

sedimento [sedʒi'mẽtu] *m* sediment

sedução [sedu'sãw] (*pl* **-ões**) *f* seduction

sedutor, -a [sedu'to*, a] *adj* seductive; (*oferta etc*) tempting

seduzir [sedu'zi*] *vt* to seduce; (*fascinar*) to fascinate

segmento [seg'mẽtu] *m* segment

segredo [se'gredu] *m* secret; (*sigilo*) secrecy; (*de fechadura*) combination

segregar [segre'ga*] *vt* to segregate

seguidamente [segida'mẽtʃi] *adv* (*sem parar*) continuously; (*logo depois*) soon afterwards

seguido, -a [se'gidu, a] *adj* following; (*contínuo*) continuous, consecutive; **~ de** *ou* **por** followed by; **três dias ~s** three days running; **horas seguidas** for hours on end;

em seguida next; (*logo depois*) soon afterwards; (*imediatamente*) immediately, right away

seguimento [segi'mẽtu] *m* continuation; **dar ~ a** to proceed with; **em ~ de** after

seguinte [se'gĩtʃi] *adj* following, next; **eu lhe disse o ~** this is what I said to him

seguir [se'gi*] *vt* to follow; (*continuar*) to continue ♦ *vi* to follow; to continue, carry on; (*ir*) to go; **seguir-se** *vr*: **~-se (a)** to follow; **logo a ~** next; **seguir-se (de)** to result (from)

segunda [se'gũda] *f* (*tb*: **~-feira**) Monday; (*AUTO*) second (gear); **de ~** second-rate; **segunda-feira** (*pl* **segundas-feiras**) *f* Monday

segundo, -a [se'gũdu, a] *adj* second ♦ *prep* according to ♦ *conj* as, from what ♦ *adv* secondly ♦ *m* second; **de segunda mão** secondhand; **de segunda (classe)** secondclass; **ele disse according to what he said; ~ dizem** apparently; **~ me consta** as far as I know; **segundas intenções** ulterior motives

seguramente [segura'mẽtʃi] *adv* certainly; (*muito provavelmente*) surely

segurança [segu'rãsa] *f* security; (*ausência de perigo*) safety; (*confiança*) confidence ♦ *m/f* security guard; **com ~** assuredly

segurar [segu'ra*] *vt* to hold; (*amparar*) to hold up; (*COM*: *bens*) to insure ♦ *vi*: **~ em** to hold; **segurar-se** *vr*: **~-se em** to hold on to

seguro, -a [se'guru, a] *adj* safe; (*livre de risco, firme*) secure; (*certo*) certain, assured; (*confiável*) reliable; (*de si mesmo*) confident; (*tempo*) settled ♦ *adv* confidently ♦ *m* (*COM*) insurance; **estar ~ de/de que** to be

sure of/that; **fazer ~** to take out an insurance policy; **~ contra acidentes/incêndio** accident/fire insurance; **seguro-saúde** (*pl* **seguros-saúde**) *m* health insurance

sei [sej] *vb V* **saber**

seio ['seju] *m* breast, bosom; (*âmago*) heart; **~ paranasal** sinus

seis [sejʃ] *num* six

seita ['sejta] *f* sect

seixo ['sejʃu] *m* pebble

seja *etc* ['seʒa] *vb V* **ser**

sela ['sɛla] *f* saddle

selar [se'la*] *vt* (*carta*) to stamp; (*documento oficial, pacto*) to seal; (*cavalo*) to saddle

seleção [sele'sãw] (*PT* **-cç-**) (*pl* **-ões**) *f* selection; (*ESPORTE*) team

selecionar [selesjo'na*] (*PT* **-cc-**) *vt* to select

seleções [sele'sõjʃ] *fpl de* **seleção**

seleto, -a [se'lɛtu, a] (*PT* **-ct-**) *adj* select

selim [se'lĩ] (*pl* **-ns**) *m* saddle

selo ['selu] *m* stamp; (*carimbo, sinete*) seal

selva ['sewva] *f* jungle

selvagem [sew'vaʒẽ] (*pl* **-ns**) *adj* wild; (*feroz*) fierce; (*povo*) savage; **selvageria** [sewvaʒe'ria] *f* savagery

sem [sẽ] *prep* without ♦ *conj*: **~ que eu peça** without my asking; **estar/ficar ~ dinheiro/gasolina** to have no/have run out of money/petrol

semáforo [se'maforu] *m* (*AUTO*) traffic lights *pl*; (*FERRO*) signal

semana [se'mana] *f* week; **semanal** [sema'naw] (*pl* **~is**) *adj* weekly; **semanário** [sema'narju] *m* weekly (publication)

semear [se'mja*] *vt* to sow

semelhança [seme'ʎãsa] *f* similarity, resemblance; **semelhante** [seme'ʎãtʃi] *adj* similar; (*tal*) such ♦ *m* fellow creature

sêmen 577 sentir

sêmen ['semẽ] m semen

semente [se'mẽtʃi] f seed

semestral [semeʃ'traw] (pl -ais) adj half-yearly, bi-annual

semestre [se'mεʃtri] m six months; (EDUC) semester

semi... [semi] prefixo semi..., half...; **semicírculo** [semi'sixkulu] m semicircle; **semifinal** [semi'finaw] (pl **semifinais**) f semi-final

seminário [semi'narju] m seminar; (REL) seminary

sem-número m: **um ~ de coisas** loads of things

sempre ['sẽpri] adv always; **você vai?** (PT) are you still going?; **~ que** whenever; **como ~** as usual; **a comida/hora** etc **de ~** the usual food/ time etc

sem-terra m/f inv landless labourer (BRIT) ou laborer (US)

sem-teto m/f inv: **os ~** the homeless

sem-vergonha adj inv shameless ♦ m/f inv (pessoa) rogue

senado [se'nadu] m senate; **senador, a** [sena'do*, a] m/f senator

senão [se'nãw] (pl **-ões**) conj otherwise; (mas sim) but, but rather ♦ prep except ♦ m flaw, defect

senha ['seɲa] f sign; (palavra de passe) password; (de caixa automático) PIN number; (recibo) receipt; (passe) pass

senhor, a [se'ɲo*, a] m (homem) man; (formal) gentleman; (homem idoso) elderly man; (REL) lord; (dono) owner; (tratamento) Mr(.); (tratamento respeitoso) sir ♦ f (mulher) lady; (esposa) wife; (mulher idosa) elderly lady; (dona) owner; (tratamento) Mrs(.), Ms(.); (tratamento respeitoso) madam; **o ~**, **a ~a** (você) you; **nossa ~a!** (col) gosh!; **sim, ~(a)!** yes indeed!

senhorita [seɲo'rita] f young lady; (tratamento) Miss, Ms(.); **a ~** (você) you

senil [se'niw] (pl **-is**) adj senile

senões [se'nõjʃ] mpl de **senão**

sensação [sẽsa'sãw] (pl **-ões**) f sensation; sensacional [sẽsasjo'naw] (pl **-ais**) adj sensational

sensato, -a [sẽ'satu, a] adj sensible

sensível [sẽ'sivew] (pl **-eis**) adj sensitive; (visível) noticeable; (considerável) considerable; (dolorido) tender

senso ['sẽsu] m sense; (juízo) judgement

sensual [sẽ'swaw] (pl **-ais**) adj sensual

sentado, -a [sẽ'tadu, a] adj sitting

sentar [sẽ'ta*] vt to seat ♦ vi to sit; **sentar-se** vr to sit down

sentença [sẽ'tẽsa] f (JUR) sentence; **sentenciar** [sẽtẽ'sja*] vt (julgar) to pass judgement on; (condenar por sentença) to sentence

sentido, -a [sẽ'tʃidu, a] adj (magoado) hurt; (choro, queixa) heartfelt ♦ m sense; (direção) direction; (atenção) attention; (aspecto) respect; **~!** (MIL) attention!; **em certo ~** in a sense; **(não) ter ~** (not) to be acceptable; **"~ único"** (PT: sinal) "one-way"

sentimental [sẽtʃimẽ'taw] (pl **-ais**) adj sentimental; **vida ~** love life

sentimento [sẽtʃi'mẽtu] m feeling; (senso) sense; **~s** mpl (pêsames) condolences

sentinela [sẽtʃi'nεla] f sentry, guard

sentir [sẽ'tʃi*] vt to feel; (perceber, pressentir) to sense; (ser afetado por) to be affected by; (magoar-se) to be upset by ♦ vi to feel; (sofrer) to suffer; **sentir-se** vr to feel; (julgar-se) to consider o.s. (to be); **~ (a) falta**

de to miss; **~ cheiro/gosto (de)** to
smell/taste; **~ vontade de** to feel
like; **sinto muito** I am very sorry
separação [separa'sãw] (*pl* **-ões**) *f*
separation
separado, -a [sepa'radu, a] *adj*
separate; **em ~** separately, apart
separar [sepa'ra*] *vt* to separate;
(*dividir*) to divide; (*pôr de lado*) to
put aside; **separar-se** *vr* to separate; to be divided
sepultamento [sepuwta'mẽtu] *m*
burial
sepultar [sepuw'ta*] *vt* to bury;
sepultura [sepuw'tura] *f* grave,
tomb
seqüência [se'kwẽsja] *f* sequence
sequer [se'kɛ*] *adv* at least; **(nem) ~**
not even
seqüestrador, a [sekwjeʃtra'do*, a]
m/f kidnapper; (*de avião etc*) hijacker
seqüestrar [sekwjeʃ'tra*] *vt* (*bens*)
to seize, confiscate; (*raptar*) to
kidnap; (*avião etc*) to hijack;
seqüestro [se'kwjeʃtru] *m* seizure;
abduction, kidnapping; hijack

PALAVRA CHAVE

ser [se*] *vi* **1** (*descrição*) to be; **ela é
médica/muito alta** she's a doctor/
very tall; **é Ana** (*TEL*) Ana speaking
ou here; **ela é de uma bondade
incrível** she's incredibly kind; **ele
está** *é* **zangado** he's really angry; **~
de mentir/briga** to be the sort to
lie/fight
2 (*horas, datas, números*): **é uma
hora** it's one o'clock; **são seis e
meia** it's half past six; **é dia 1º de
junho** it's the first of June; **somos/
são seis** there are six of us/them
3 (*origem, material*): **~ de** to be ou
come from; (*feito de*) to be made
of; (*pertencer*) to belong to; **sua**

família é da Bahia his (*ou her etc*)
family is from Bahia; **a mesa é de
mármore** the table is made of marble; **é de Pedro** it's Pedro's, it
belongs to Pedro
4 (*em orações passivas*): **já foi
descoberto** it had already been discovered
5 (*locuções com subjun*): **ou seja**
that is to say; **seja quem for** whoever it may be; **se eu fosse você** if I
were you; **se não fosse você**, ... if it
hadn't been for you, ...
6 (*locuções*): **a não ~** except; **a não
~ que** unless; **é** (*resposta afirmativa*)
yes; ..., **não é?**..., isn't it?, ..., don't
you? *etc*; **ah, é?** really?; **que foi?** (*o
que aconteceu?*) what happened?;
(*qual é o problema?*) what's the
problem?; **~á que** ...? I wonder if
...?

♦ *m* being; **~es** *mpl* (*criaturas*) creatures

sereia [se'reja] *f* mermaid
sereno, -a [se'rɛnu, a] *adj* calm;
(*tempo*) fine, clear
série ['sɛri] *f* series; (*seqüência*)
sequence, succession; (*EDUC*) grade;
(*categoria*) category; **fora de ~** out
of order; (*fig*) extraordinary
seriedade [serje'dadʒi] *f* seriousness; (*honestidade*) honesty
seringa [se'rĩga] *f* syringe
sério, -a ['sɛrju, a] *adj* serious; (*honesto*) honest, decent; (*responsável*)
responsible; (*confiável*) reliable;
(*roupa*) sober ♦ *adv* seriously; **a ~**
seriously; **~?** really?
sermão [ser'mãw] (*pl* **-ões**) *m* sermon; (*fig*) telling-off
serpente [sex'pẽtʃi] *f* snake
serpentina [sexpẽ'tʃina] *f* streamer
serra ['sɛxa] *f* (*montanhas*) mountain range; (*TEC*) saw

serralheiro, -a [sexa'ʎejru, a] m/f locksmith

serrano, -a [se'xanu, a] adj highland atr ♦ m/f highlander

serrar [se'xa*] vt to saw

sertanejo, -a [sexta'neʒu, a] adj rustic, country ♦ m/f inhabitant of the sertão

sertão [sex'tãw] (pl -ões) m backwoods pl, bush (country)

servente [sex'vẽtʃi] m/f servant; (operário) labourer (BRIT), laborer (US)

serviçal [sexvi'saw] (pl -ais) adj obliging, helpful ♦ m/f servant; (trabalhador) wage earner

serviço [sex'visu] m service; (de chá etc) set; **estar de ~** to be on duty; **prestar ~** to help

servidor, a [sexvi'do*, a] m/f servant; (funcionário) employee; ~ **público** civil servant

servil [sex'viw] (pl -is) adj servile

servir [sex'vi*] vt to serve ♦ vi to serve; (ser útil) to be useful; (ajudar) to help; (roupa: caber) to fit; **servir-se** vr: **~-se (de)** (comida, café) to help o.s. (to); (meios): **~-se de** to use, make use of; **~ de** (prover) to supply with, provide with; **você está servido?** (num bar) are you all right for a drink?; **~ de algo** to serve as sth; **qualquer ônibus serve** any bus will do

servis [sex'viʃ] adj pl de servil

sessão [se'sãw] (pl -ões) f (do parlamento etc) session; (reunião) meeting; (de cinema) showing

sessenta [se'sẽta] num sixty

sessões [se'sõjʃ] fpl de sessão

sesta [ˈsɛʃta] f siesta, nap

seta [ˈseta] f arrow

sete [ˈsɛtʃi] num seven

setembro [se'tẽbru] (PT S-) m September; **7 de setembro** see

boxed note

setenta [se'tẽta] num seventy

sétimo, -a [ˈsɛtʃimu, a] num seventh

setor [se'to*] m sector

seu, sua [sew, ˈsua] adj (dele) his; (dela) her; (de coisa) its; (deles, delas) their; (de você, vocês) your ♦ pron: **(o) ~, (a) sua** his; hers; its; theirs; yours ♦ m (senhor) Mr(.)

severidade [severi'dadʒi] f severity

severo, -a [se'vɛru, a] adj severe

sexo [ˈsɛksu] m sex

sexta [ˈseʃta] f (tb: **~-feira**) Friday; **sexta-feira** (pl **sextas-feiras**) f Friday; **Sexta-feira Santa** Good Friday

sexto, -a [ˈseʃtu, a] num sixth

sexual [se'kswaw] (pl -ais) adj sexual; (vida, ato) sex atr

sexy [ˈsɛksi] (pl ~s) adj sexy

s.f.f. (PT) abr = **se faz favor**

short [ˈʃɔxtʃi] m (pair of) shorts pl

si [si] pron oneself; (ele) himself; (ela) herself; (coisa) itself; (PT: você) yourself, you; (: vocês) yourselves; (eles, elas) themselves

SIDA [ˈsida] (PT) abr f (= síndrome de deficiência imunológica adquirida) **a ~** AIDS

siderúrgica [side'ruxʒika] f steel industry

sigilo [si'ʒilu] m secrecy

sigla ['sigla] f acronym; (abreviação) abbreviation

significado [signifi'kadu] m meaning

significar [signifi'ka*] vt to mean, signify; **significativo, -a** [signifika'tʃivu, a] adj significant

signo ['signu] m sign

sigo etc ['sigu] vb V **seguir**

sílaba ['silaba] f syllable

silenciar [silẽ'sja*] vt to silence

silêncio [si'lẽsju] m silence, quiet; **silencioso, -a** [silẽ'sjozu, ɔza] adj silent, quiet ♦ m (AUTO) silencer (BRIT), muffler (US)

silhueta [si'ʎweta] f silhouette

silvestre [siw'vɛʃtri] adj wild

sim [sĩ] adv yes; **creio que ~** I think so

símbolo ['sĩbolu] m symbol

simetria [sime'tria] f symmetry

similar [simi'la*] adj similar

simpatia [sĩpa'tʃia] f liking; (afeto) affection; (afinidade, solidariedade) sympathy; **~s** fpl (inclinações) sympathies; **simpático, -a** [sĩ'patʃiku, a] adj (pessoa, decoração etc) nice; (lugar) pleasant, nice; (amável) kind; **simpatizante** [sĩpatʃi'zãtʃi] adj sympathetic ♦ m/f sympathizer; **simpatizar** [sĩpatʃi'za*] vi: **simpatizar com** (pessoa) to like; (causa) to sympathize with

simples ['sĩpliʃ] adj inv simple; (único) single; (fácil) easy; (mero) mere; (ingênuo) naïve ♦ adv simply; **simplicidade** [sĩplisi'dadʒi] f simplicity; **simplificar** [sĩplifi'ka*] vt to simplify

simular [simu'la*] vt to simulate

simultaneamente [simuwtanja'mẽtʃi] adv simultaneously

simultâneo, -a [simuw'tanju, a] adj simultaneous

sinagoga [sina'gɔga] f synagogue

sinal [si'naw] (pl -ais) m sign; (gesto, TEL) signal; (na pele) mole; (: de nascença) birthmark; (depósito) deposit; (tb: **~ de tráfego, ~ luminoso**) traffic light; **por ~** (por falar nisso) by the way; (aliás) as a matter of fact; **~ de chamada** (TEL) ringing tone; **~ de discar** (BR) ou **de marcar** (PT) dialling tone (BRIT), dial tone (US); **~ de ocupado** (BR) ou **de impedido** (PT) engaged tone (BRIT), busy signal (US); **sinalização** [sinaliza'sãw] f (ato) signalling; (para motoristas) traffic signs pl

sinceridade [sĩseri'dadʒi] f sincerity

sincero, -a [sĩ'seru, a] adj sincere

sindicalista [sĩdʒika'liʃta] m/f trade unionist

sindicato [sĩdʒi'katu] m trade union; (financeiro) syndicate

síndrome ['sĩdromi] f syndrome; **~ de Down** Down's syndrome

sinfonia [sĩfo'nia] f symphony

singular [sĩgu'la*] adj singular; (extraordinário) exceptional; (bizarro) odd, peculiar

sino ['sinu] m bell

sintaxe [sĩ'tasi] f syntax

síntese ['sĩtezi] f synthesis; **sintético, -a** [sĩ'tetʃiku, a] adj synthetic; **sintetizar** [sĩtetʃi'za*] vt to synthesize

sinto etc ['sĩtu] vb V **sentir**

sintoma [sĩ'tɔma] m symptom

sinuca [si'nuka] f snooker

sinuoso, -a [si'nwozu, ɔza] adj (caminho) winding; (linha) wavy

siri [si'ri] m crab

Síria ['sirja] f: **a ~** Syria; **sírio, -a** ['sirju, a] adj, m/f Syrian

sirvo etc ['sixvu] vb V **servir**

sistema [siʃ'tɛma] *m* system; (*método*) method

site ['sajtʃi] *m* (*na Internet*) website

sitiar [si'tʃja*] *vt* to besiege

sítio ['sitʃju] *m* (MIL) siege; (*propriedade rural*) small farm; (PT: *lugar*) place

situação [sitwa'sãw] (*pl* -ões) *f* situation; (*posição*) position

situado, -a [si'twadu, a] *adj* situated

situar [si'twa*] *vt* to place, put; (*edifício*) to situate, locate; **situar-se** *vr* to position o.s.; (*estar situado*) to be situated

slogan [iʃ'lɔgã] (*pl* ~s) *m* slogan

SME *abr m* (= *Sistema Monetário Europeu*) ERM

smoking [iʒ'mɔkiʃ] (*pl* ~s) *m* dinner jacket (BRIT), tuxedo (US)

só [sɔ] *adj* alone; (*único*) single; (*solitária*) solitary ♦ *adv* only; **a ~s** alone

soar [swa*] *vi* to sound ♦ *vt* (*horas*) to strike; (*instrumento*) to play; **~ a** to sound like; **~ bem/mal** (*fig*) to go down well/badly

sob [sob] *prep* under; (*juramento*) on oath; **~ medida** (*roupa*) made to measure

sobe *etc* ['sɔbi] *vb V* **subir**

soberano, -a [sobe'ranu, a] *adj* sovereign; (*fig: supremo*) supreme ♦ *m/f* sovereign

sobra ['sɔbra] *f* surplus, remnant; **~s** *fpl* (*restos*) remains; (*de tecido*) remnants; (*de comida*) leftovers; **ter algo de ~** to have sth extra; (*tempo, comida, motivos*) to have plenty of sth; **ficar de ~** to be left over

sobrado [so'bradu] *m* (*andar*) floor; (*casa*) house (*of two or more storeys*)

sobrancelha [sobrã'seʎa] *f* eyebrow

sobrar [so'bra*] *vi* to be left; (*dúvidas*) to remain

sobre ['sobri] *prep* on; (*por cima de*) over; (*acima de*) above; (*a respeito de*) about

sobrecarregar [sobrikaxe'ga*] *vt* to overload

sobremesa [sobri'meza] *f* dessert

sobrenatural [sobrinatu'raw] (*pl* -ais) *adj* supernatural

sobrenome [sobri'nɔmi] (BR) *m* surname, family name

sobrepor [sobri'po*] (*irreg: como* **pôr**) *vt*: **~ algo a algo** to put sth on top of sth

sobressair [sobrisa'i*] *vi* to stand out; **sobressair-se** *vr* to stand out

sobressalente [sobrisa'lẽtʃi] *adj*, *m* spare

sobressalto [sobri'sawtu] *m* start; (*temor*) trepidation; **de ~** suddenly

sobretaxa [sobri'taʃa] *f* surcharge

sobretudo [sobri'tudu] *m* overcoat ♦ *adv* above all, especially

sobrevivência [sobrivi'vẽsja] *f* survival; **sobrevivente** [sobrivi'vẽtʃi] *adj* surviving ♦ *m/f* survivor

sobreviver [sobrivi've*] *vi*: **~ (a)** to survive

sobrinho, -a [so'briɲu, a] *m/f* nephew/niece

sóbrio, -a ['sɔbrju, a] *adj* sober; (*moderado*) moderate, restrained

socar [so'ka*] *vt* to hit, strike; (*calcar*) to crush, pound; (*massa de pão*) to knead

social [so'sjaw] (*pl* -ais) *adj* social; **socialista** [sosja'liʃta] *adj*, *m/f* socialist

sociedade [sosje'dadʒi] *f* society; (COM: *empresa*) company; (*associação*) association; **~ anônima** limited company (BRIT), incorporated company (US)

sócio, -a ['sɔsju, a] *m/f* (COM) partner; (de clube) member

soco ['soku] m punch; **dar um ~ em** to punch

socorrer [soko'xe*] vt to help, assist; (salvar) to rescue; **socorrer-se** vr: **~-se de** to resort to, have recourse to; **socorro** [so'koxu] m help, assistance; (reboque) breakdown (BRIT) ou tow (US) truck; **socorro!** help!; **primeiros socorros** first aid sg

soda ['sɔda] f soda (water)

sofá [so'fa] m sofa, settee; **sofá-cama** (pl **sofás-camas**) m sofa-bed

sofisticado, -a [sofiʃtʃi'kadu, a] adj sophisticated; (afetado) pretentious

sofrer [so'fre*] vt to suffer; (acidente) to have; (agüentar) to bear, put up with; (experimentar) to undergo ♦ vi to suffer; **sofrido, -a** [so'fridu, a] adj long-suffering; **sofrimento** [sofri'mẽtu] m suffering

software [sof'twe*] m (COMPUT) software

sogro, -a ['sogru, 'sɔgra] m/f father-in-law/mother-in-law

sóis [sɔjʃ] mpl de **sol**

soja ['sɔʒa] f soya (BRIT), soy (US)

sol [sɔw] (pl **sóis**) m sun; (luz) sunshine, sunlight; **fazer ~** to be sunny; **tomar ~** to sunbathe

sola ['sɔla] f sole

solar [so'la*] adj solar; **energia/painel ~** solar energy/panel

soldado [sow'dadu] m soldier

soldar [sow'da*] vt to weld

soleira [so'lejra] f doorstep

solene [so'lɛni] adj solemn; **solenidade** [soleni'dadʒi] f solemnity; (cerimônia) ceremony

soletrar [sole'tra*] vt to spell

solicitar [solisi'ta*] vt to ask for; (emprego etc) to apply for; (ami-

zade, atenção) to seek; **~ algo a alguém** to ask sb for sth

solícito, -a [so'lisitu, a] adj helpful

solidão [soli'dãw] f solitude; (sensação) loneliness

solidariedade [solidarje'dadʒi] f solidarity

solidário, -a [soli'darju, a] adj: **ser ~ a ou com** (pessoa) to stand by; (causa) to be sympathetic to, sympathize with

sólido, -a ['sɔlidu, a] adj solid

solitário, -a [soli'tarju, a] adj lonely; (isolado) solitary ♦ m hermit

solo ['sɔlu] m ground, earth; (MÚS) solo

soltar [sow'ta*] vt to set free; (desatar) to loosen; (largar) to let go of; (emitir) to emit; (grito) to let out; (cabelo) to let down; (freio) to release; **soltar-se** vr to come loose; (desinibir-se) to let o.s. go

solteirão, -ona [sowtej'rãw, rɔna] (pl **-ões**, **~s**) adj unmarried, single ♦ m/f confirmed bachelor/spinster

solteiro, -a [sow'tejru, a] adj unmarried, single ♦ m/f bachelor/single woman

solteirões [sowtej'rõjʃ] mpl de **solteirão**

solteirona [sowtej'rɔna] f de **solteirão**

solto, -a ['sowtu, a] pp de **soltar** ♦ adj loose; (livre) free; (sozinho) alone

solução [solu'sãw] (pl **-ões**) f solution

soluçar [solu'sa*] vi (chorar) to sob; (MED) to hiccup

solucionar [solusjo'na*] vt to solve; (decidir) to resolve

soluço [so'lusu] m sob; (MED) hiccup

soluções [solu'sõjʃ] fpl de **solução**

som [sõ] (pl **-ns**) m sound; **~ cd**

compact disc player

soma ['sɔma] f sum; **somar** [so'ma*] vt (adicionar) to add (up); (chegar a) to add up to, amount to ♦ vi to add up

sombra ['sõbra] f shadow; (proteção) shade; (clandestinidade) trace, sign

sombrinha [sõ'briɲa] f parasol, sunshade

sombrio, -a [sõ'briu, a] adj shady, dark; (triste) gloomy

some etc [sɔmi] vb V **sumir**

somente [sɔ'mẽtʃi] adv only

somos ['sõmoʃ] vb V **ser**

sonâmbulo, -a [so'nãbulu, a] m/f sleepwalker

sondar [sõ'da*] vt to probe; (opinião etc) to sound out

soneca [so'nɛka] f nap, snooze

sonegar [sone'ga*] vt (dinheiro, valores) to conceal, withhold; (furtar) to steal, pilfer; (impostos) to dodge, evade; (informações, dados) to withhold

soneto [so'netu] m sonnet

sonhador, -a [soɲa'do*, a] adj dreamy ♦ m/f dreamer

sonhar [so'ɲa*] vt, vi to dream; ~ **com** to dream about; **sonho** ['sɔɲu] m dream; (CULIN) doughnut

sono ['sɔnu] m sleep; **estar com** ou **ter ~** to be sleepy

sonolento, -a [sono'lẽtu, a] adj sleepy, drowsy

sonoro, -a [so'nɔru, a] adj resonant

sons [sõʃ] mpl de **som**

sonso, -a ['sõsu, a] adj sly, artful

sopa ['sopa] f soup

soporífero [sopo'riferu], **soporífico** [sopo'rifiku] m sleeping drug

soprar [so'pra*] vt to blow; (balão) to blow up; (vela) to blow out; (dizer em voz baixa) to whisper ♦ vi to blow; **sopro** ['sopru] m blow, puff; (de vento) gust

sórdido, -a ['sɔxdʒidu, a] adj sordid; (imundo) squalid

soro ['soru] m (MED) serum

sorridente [soxi'dẽtʃi] adj smiling

sorrir [so'xi*] vi to smile; **sorriso** [so'xizu] m smile

sorte ['sɔxtʃi] f luck; (casualidade) chance; (destino) fate, destiny; (condição) lot; (espécie) sort, kind; **de ~ que** so that; **dar ~** (trazer sorte) to bring good luck; (ter sorte) to be lucky; **estar com** ou **ter ~** to be lucky

sortear [sox'tʃja*] vt to draw lots for; (rifar) to raffle; (MIL) to draft; **sorteio** [sox'teju] m draw; raffle; draft

sortido, -a [sox'tʃidu, a] adj (abastecido) supplied, stocked; (variado) assorted; (loja) well-stocked

sortudo, -a [sox'tudu, a] (col) adj lucky

sorvete [sox'vetʃi] (BR) m ice cream

SOS abr SOS

sossegado, -a [sose'gadu, a] adj peaceful, calm

sossegar [sose'ga*] vt to calm, quieten ♦ vi to quieten down

sossego [so'segu] m peace (and quiet)

sótão ['sɔtãw] (pl ~s) m attic, loft

sotaque [so'taki] m accent

sotavento [sota'vẽtu] m (NÁUT) lee

soterrar [sote'xa*] vt to bury

sou [so] vb V **ser**

soube etc ['sobi] vb V **saber**

soutien [su'tʃjã] (PT) m = **sutiã**

sova ['sɔva] f beating, thrashing

sovaco [so'vaku] m armpit

soviético, -a [so'vjetʃiku, a] adj, m/f Soviet

sovina [so'vina] adj mean, stingy ♦ m/f miser

sozinho, -a [sɔ'ziɲu, a] adj (all)

alone, by oneself; (*por si mesmo*) by oneself

squash [iʃ'kweʃ] *m* squash

Sr. *abr* (= *senhor*) Mr(.)

Sr.ª *abr* (= *senhora*) Mrs(.)

Sr.ta *abr* (= *senhorita*) Miss

status [iʃ'tatus] *m* status

sua ['sua] *f de* seu

suar [swa*] *vt, vi* to sweat

suástica ['swaʃtʃika] *f* swastika

suave ['swavi] *adj* gentle; (*música, voz*) soft; (*sabor, vinho*) smooth; (*cheiro*) delicate; (*dor*) mild; (*trabalho*) light; **suavidade** [suavi'dadʒi] *f* gentleness; softness

subalterno, -a [subaw'texnu, a] *adj, m/f* subordinate

subconsciente [subkõ'sjẽtʃi] *adj, m* subconscious

subdesenvolvido, -a [subdʒizẽvow'vidu, a] *adj* underdeveloped

subentender [subẽtẽ'de*] *vt* to understand, assume; **subentendido, -a** [subẽtẽ'dʒidu, a] *adj* implied ♦ *m* implication

subestimar [subeʃtʃi'ma*] *vt* to underestimate

subida [su'bida] *f* ascent, climb; (*ladeira*) slope; (*de preços*) rise

subir [su'bi*] *vi* to go up; (*preço, de posto etc*) to rise ♦ *vt* to raise; (*ladeira, escada, rio*) to climb, go up; ~ **em** to climb, go up; (*cadeira, palanque*) to climb onto, get up onto; (*ônibus*) to get on

súbito, -a ['subitu, a] *adj* sudden ♦ *adv* (*tb*: **de ~**) suddenly

subjetivo, -a [subʒe'tʃivu, a] (*PT* -ct-) *adj* subjective

subjuntivo, -a [subʒũ'tʃivu, a] *adj* subjunctive ♦ *m* subjunctive

sublime [su'blimi] *adj* sublime

sublinhar [subli'ɲa*] *vt* to underline; (*destacar*) to emphasize, stress

sublocar [sublo'ka*] *vt, vi* to sublet

submarino, -a [subma'rinu, a] *adj* underwater ♦ *m* submarine

submergir [submex'ʒi*] *vt* to submerge; **submergir-se** *vr* to submerge

submeter [subme'te*] *vt* to subdue; (*plano*) to submit; (*sujeitar*): ~ **a** to subject to; **submeter-se** *vr*: ~**-se a** to submit to; (*operação*) to undergo

submirjo *etc* [sub'mixʒu] *vb V* **submergir**

submisso, -a [sub'misu, a] *adj* submissive

subnutrição [subnutri'sãw] *f* malnutrition

subornar [subox'na*] *vt* to bribe; **suborno** [su'boxnu] *m* bribery

subseqüente [subse'kwẽtʃi] *adj* subsequent

subserviente [subsex'vjẽtʃi] *adj* obsequious, servile

subsidiária [subsi'dʒjarja] *f* (*COM*) subsidiary (company)

subsidiário, -a [subsi'dʒjarju, a] *adj* subsidiary

subsídio [sub'sidʒu] *m* subsidy; (*ajuda*) aid

subsistência [subsiʃ'tẽsja] *f* subsistence

subsistir [subsiʃ'tʃi*] *vi* to exist; (*viver*) to subsist

subsolo [sub'sɔlu] *m* (*de prédio*) basement

substância [sub'ʃtãsja] *f* substance; **substancial** [subʃtã'sjaw] (*pl* -ais) *adj* substantial

substantivo [subʃtã'tʃivu] *m* noun

substituir [subʃtʃi'twi*] *vt* to substitute; **substituto, -a** [subʃti'tutu, a] *adj, m/f* substitute

subterrâneo, -a [subite'xanju, a] *adj* subterranean, underground

subtil *etc* [sub'tiw] (*PT*) = **sutil** *etc*

subtrair [subtra'i*] vt to steal; (deduzir) to subtract ♦ vi to subtract

subumano, -a [subu'manu, a] adj subhuman; (desumano) inhuman

suburbano, -a [subux'banu, a] adj suburban

subúrbio [su'buxbju] m suburb

subvenção [subvẽ'sãw] (pl -ões) f subsidy, grant

subversivo, -a [subvex'sivu, a] adj, m/f subversive

sucata [su'kata] f scrap metal

sucção [suk'sãw] f suction

suceder [suse'de*] vi to happen ♦ vi to succeed; ~ a (num cargo) to succeed; (seguir) to follow

sucessão [suse'sãw] (pl -ões) f succession; **sucessivo, -a** [suse'sivu, a] adj successive

sucesso [su'sɛsu] m success; (música, filme) hit; **fazer** ou **ter ~** to be successful

sucinto, -a [su'sĩtu, a] adj succinct

suco ['suku] (BR) m juice

suculento, -a [suku'lẽtu, a] adj succulent

sucumbir [sukũ'bi*] vi to succumb; (morrer) to die, perish

sucursal [sukux'saw] (pl -ais) f (COM) branch

Sudão [su'dãw] m: o ~ (the) Sudan

sudeste [su'dɛʃtʃi] m south-east

súdito ['sudʒitu] m (de rei etc) subject

sudoeste [sud'wɛʃtʃi] m south-west

Suécia ['swɛsja] f: a ~ Sweden; **sueco, -a** ['swɛku, a] adj Swedish ♦ m/f Swede ♦ m (LING) Swedish

suéter ['swete*] (BR) m ou f sweater

suficiente [sufi'sjẽtʃi] adj sufficient, enough

sufixo [su'fiksu] m suffix

sufocante [sufo'kãtʃi] adj suffocating; (calor) sweltering, oppressive

sufocar [sufo'ka*] vt, vi to suffocate

sugar [su'ga*] vt to suck

sugerir [suʒe'ri*] vt to suggest

sugestão [suʒeʃ'tãw] (pl -ões) f suggestion; **dar uma ~** to make a suggestion; **sugestivo, -a** [suʒeʃ-'tʃivu, a] adj suggestive

sugiro etc [su'ʒiru] vb V **sugerir**

Suíça ['swisa] f: a ~ Switzerland

suíças ['swisaʃ] fpl sideburns; V tb **suíço**

suicida [swi'sida] adj suicidal ♦ m/f suicidal person; (morto) suicide; **suicidar-se** [swisi'daxsi] vr to commit suicide; **suicídio** [swi-'sidʒju] m suicide

suíço, -a ['swisu, a] adj, m/f Swiss

suíte ['switʃi] f (MÚS, em hotel) suite

sujar [su'ʒa*] vt to dirty ♦ vi to make a mess; **sujar-se** vr to get dirty

sujeira [su'ʒejra] f dirt; (estado) dirtiness; (col) dirty trick

sujeito, -a [su'ʒejtu, a] adj: ~ a subject to ♦ m (LING) subject ♦ m/f man/ woman

sujo, -a ['suʒu, a] adj dirty; (fig: desonesto) dishonest ♦ m dirt

sul [suw] adj inv south, southern ♦ m: o ~ the south; **sul-africano, -a** adj, m/f South African; **sul-americano, -a** adj, m/f South American

sulco [suw'ku] m furrow

suma ['suma] f: **em ~** in short

sumário, -a [su'marju, a] adj (breve) brief, concise; (JUR) summary; (biquíni) skimpy ♦ m summary

sumiço [su'misu] m disappearance

sumir [su'mi*] vi to disappear, vanish

sumo, -a ['sumu, a] adj (importância) extreme; (qualidade) supreme ♦ m (PT) juice

sunga ['sũga] f swimming trunks pl

suor [swɔ*] m sweat

super- [supe*-] prefixo super-

superado, -a [supe'radu, a] adj

(idéias) outmoded

superar [supe'ra*] *vt (rival)* to surpass; *(inimigo, dificuldade)* to overcome; *(expectativa)* to exceed

superficial [supexfi'sjaw] *(pl* **-ais)** *adj* superficial

superfície [supex'fisi] *f* surface; *(extensão)* area; *(fig: aparência)* appearance

supérfluo, -a [su'pexflwu, a] *adj* superfluous

superior [supe'rjo*] *adj* superior; *(mais elevado)* higher; *(quantidade)* greater; *(mais acima)* upper ♦ *m* superior; **superioridade** [superjori'dadʒi] *f* superiority

superlotado, -a [supexlo'tadu, a] *adj* crowded; *(excessivamente cheio)* overcrowded

supermercado [supexmex'kadu] *m* supermarket

superpotência [supexpo'tẽsja] *f* superpower

superstição [supexʃtʃi'sãw] *(pl* **-ões)** *f* superstition; **supersticioso, -a** [supexʃtʃi'sjozu, ɔza] *adj* superstitious

supervisão [supexvi'zãw] *f* supervision; **supervisionar** [supexvizjo'na*] *vt* to supervise; **supervisor, a** [supexvi'zo*, a] *m/f* supervisor

suplementar [suplemẽ'ta*] *adj* supplementary ♦ *vt* to supplement

suplemento [suple'mẽtu] *m* supplement

súplica ['suplika] *f* supplication, plea; **suplicar** [supli'ka*] *vt, vi* to plead, beg

suplício [su'plisju] *m* torture

supor [su'po*] *(irreg: como pôr) vt* to suppose; *(julgar)* to think

suportar [supox'ta*] *vt* to hold up, support; *(tolerar)* to bear, tolerate; **suportável** [supox'tavew] *(pl* **-eis)** *adj* bearable; **suporte** [su'pɔxtʃi] *m*

support

suposto, -a [su'poʃtu, 'pɔʃta] *adj* supposed ♦ *m* assumption, supposition

supremo, -a [su'premu, a] *adj* supreme

suprimir [supri'mi*] *vt* to suppress

surdez [sux'deʒ] *f*: **aparelho para a ~** hearing aid

surdo, -a [su'xdu, a] *adj* deaf; *(som)* muffled, dull ♦ *m/f* deaf person; **surdo-mudo, surda-muda** *adj* deaf and dumb ♦ *m/f* deaf-mute

surfe ['suxfi] *m* surfing

surgir [sux'ʒi*] *vi* to appear; *(problema, oportunidade)* to arise

surjo *etc* ['suxʒu] *vb* V **surgir**

surpreendente [suxprjẽ'dẽtʃi] *adj* surprising

surpreender [suxprjẽ'de*] *vt* to surprise; **surpreender-se** *vr*: **~-se (de)** to be surprised (at); **surpresa** [sux'preza] *f* surprise; **surpreso, -a** [sux'prezu, a] *pp de* **surpreender** ♦ *adj* surprised

surra ['suxa] *f (ger, ESPORTE)*: **dar uma ~ em** to thrash; **levar uma ~ (de)** to get thrashed (by); **surrar** [su'xa*] *vt* to beat, thrash

surtir [sux'tʃi*] *vt* to produce, bring about

surto ['suxtu] *m* outbreak

suscetível [suse'tʃivew] *(pl* **-eis)** *adj* susceptible; **~ de** liable to

suspeita [suʃ'pejta] *f* suspicion; **suspeitar** [suʃpej'ta*] *vt* to suspect ♦ *vi*: **suspeitar de algo** to suspect sth; **suspeito, -a** [suʃ'pejtu, a] *adj, m/f* suspect

suspender [suʃpẽ'de*] *vt (levantar)* to lift; *(pendurar)* to hang; *(trabalho, funcionário etc)* to suspend; *(encomenda)* to cancel; *(sessão)* to adjourn, defer; *(viagem)* to put off; **suspensão** [suʃpẽ'sãw] *(pl* **-ões)** *f* (*ger*, *AUTO*) suspension; (*de trabalho*, *pagamento*) stoppage; (*de viagem*, *sessão*) deferment; (*de encomenda*) cancellation; **suspense** [suʃ'pɛsi] *m* suspense; **filme de suspense** thriller; **suspenso, -a** [suʃ'pẽsu, a] *pp de* **suspender**

suspensórios [suʃpẽ'sɔrjuʃ] *mpl* braces (*BRIT*), suspenders (*US*)

suspirar [suʃpi'ra*] *vi* to sigh; **suspiro** [suʃ'piru] *m* sigh; (*doce*) meringue

sussurrar [susu'xa*] *vt, vi* to whisper; **sussurro** [su'suxu] *m* whisper

sustentar [suʃtẽ'ta*] *vt* to sustain; (*prédio*) to hold up; (*padrão*) to maintain; (*financeiramente*, *acusação*) to support; **sustentável** [suʃtẽ'tavew]. (*pl* -**eis**) *adj* sustainable; **sustento** [suʃ'tẽtu] *m* sustenance; (*subsistência*) livelihood; (*amparo*) support

susto ['suʃtu] *m* fright, scare

sutiã [su'tʃiã] *m* bra(ssiere)

sutil [su'tʃiw] (*pl* -**is**) *adj* subtle; **sutileza** [sutʃi'leza] *f* subtlety

T

ta [ta] = **te** + **a**

tabacaria [tabaka'ria] *f* tobacconist's (shop)

tabaco [ta'baku] *m* tobacco

tabela [ta'bela] *f* table, chart; (*lista*) list; **por ~** indirectly

taberna [ta'bɛxna] *f* tavern, bar

tablete [ta'blɛtʃi] *m* (*de chocolate*) bar

tabu [ta'bu] *adj, m* taboo

tábua ['tabwa] *f* plank, board; (*MAT*) table; **~ de passar roupa** ironing board

tabuleiro [tabu'lejru] *m* tray; (*XADREZ*) board

tabuleta [tabu'leta] *f* (*letreiro*) sign, signboard

taça ['tasa] *f* cup

tacha ['taʃa] *f* tack

tachinha [ta'ʃiŋa] *f* drawing pin (*BRIT*), thumb tack (*US*)

tácito, -a ['tasitu, a] *adj* tacit

taco ['taku] *m* (*BILHAR*) cue; (*GOLFE*) club

táctico, -a *etc* ['tatiku, a] (*PT*) = **tático** *etc*

tacto ['tatu] (*PT*) *m* = **tato**

tagarela [taga'rela] *adj* talkative
♦ *m/f* chatterbox; **tagarelar** [tagare'la*] *vi* to chatter

Tailândia [tai'lãdʒja] *f*: **a ~** Thailand

tal [taw] (*pl* **tais**) *adj* such; **~ e coisa** this and that; **um ~ de Sr. X** a certain Mr. X; **que ~?** what do you think?; (*PT*) how are things?; **que ~ um cafezinho?** what about a coffee?; **que ~ nós irmos ao cinema?** what about (us) going to the cinema?; **~ pai, ~ filho** like father, like son; **~ como** such as; (*da maneira que*) just as; **~ qual** just like; **o ~ professor** that teacher; **a ~ ponto** to such an extent; **de ~ maneira** in such a way; **e ~ e** and so on; **o ~, a ~** (*col*) the greatest; **o Pedro de ~** Peter what's-his-name; **na rua ~** in such and such a street; **foi um ~ de gente ligar lá para casa** there were people ringing home non-stop

tala ['tala] *f* (*MED*) splint

talão [ta'lãw] (*pl* -**ões**) *m* (*de recibo*) stub; **~ de cheques** cheque book (*BRIT*), check book (*US*)

talco ['tawku] *m* talcum powder; **pó de ~** (*PT*) talcum powder

talento [ta'lẽtu] *m* talent; (*aptidão*) ability

talha ['taʎa] *f* carving; (*vaso*) pitcher; (*NÁUT*) tackle

talher [ta'ʎɛ*] m set of cutlery; **~es** mpl cutlery sg

talho ['taʎu] m (corte) cutting, slicing; (PT: açougue) butcher's (shop)

talo ['talu] m stalk, stem

talões [ta'lõjʃ] mpl de **talão**

talvez [taw'veʒ] adv perhaps, maybe

tamanco [ta'mãku] m clog, wooden shoe

tamanduá [tamã'dwa] m anteater

tamanho, -a [ta'maɲu, a] adj such (a) great ♦ m size

tâmara ['tamara] f date

também [tã'bẽj] adv also, too, as well; (além disso) besides; **~ não** not ... either, nor

tambor [tã'bo*] m drum

tamborim [tãbo'rĩ] (pl **-ns**) m tambourine

Tâmisa ['tamiza] m: **o ~** the Thames

tampa ['tãpa] f lid; (de garrafa) cap

tampão [tã'pãw] (pl **-ões**) m tampon; (de olho) (eye) patch

tampar [tã'pa*] vt (lata, garrafa) to put the lid on; (cobrir) to cover

tampinha [tã'piɲa] f lid, top

tampo ['tãpu] m lid

tampões [tã'põjʃ] mpl de **tampão**

tampouco [tã'poku] adv nor, neither

tangente [tã'ʒẽtʃi] f tangent

tangerina [tãʒe'rina] f tangerine

tanque ['tãki] m tank; (de lavar roupa) sink

tanto, -a ['tãtu, a] adj, pron (sg) so much; (: + interrogativa/negativa) as much; (pl) so many; (: + interrogativa/negativa) as many ♦ adv so much; **~ ... como** ... both ... and ...; **~ ... quanto** ... as much ... as ...; **~ tempo** so long; **quarenta e tantos anos** forty-odd years; **~ faz** it's all the same to me, I don't mind; **um ~ (quanto)** (como adv) rather, some-

what; **~ (assim) que** so much so that

tão [tãw] adv so; **~ rico quanto** as rich as; **tão-só** adv only

tapa ['tapa] m ou f slap

tapar [ta'pa*] vt to cover; (garrafa) to cork; (caixa) to put the lid on; (orifício) to block up; (encobrir) to block out

tapear [ta'pja*] vt, vi to cheat

tapeçaria [tapesa'ria] f tapestry

tapete [ta'petʃi] m carpet, rug

tardar [tax'da*] vi to delay; (chegar tarde) to be late ♦ vt to delay; **sem mais ~** without delay; **~ a** ou **em fazer** to take a long time to do; **o mais ~** at the latest

tarde [ta'txdʒi] f afternoon ♦ adv late; **mais cedo ou mais ~** sooner or later; **antes ~ do que nunca** better late than never; **boa ~!** good afternoon!; **à ou de ~** in the afternoon

tardio, -a [tax'dʒiu, a] adj late

tarefa [ta'refa] f task, job; (faina) chore

tarifa [ta'rifa] f tariff; (para transportes) fare; (lista de preços) price list; **~ alfandegária** customs duty

tartaruga [taxta'ruga] f turtle

tasca ['taʃka] (PT) f cheap eating place

tática ['tatʃika] f tactics pl

tático, -a ['tatʃiku, a] adj tactical

tato ['tatu] m touch; (fig: diplomacia) tact

tatu [ta'tu] m armadillo

tatuagem [ta'twaʒẽ] (pl **-ns**) f tattoo

taxa ['taʃa] f (imposto) tax; (preço) fee; (índice) rate; **~ de câmbio** exchange/interest rate; **taxação** [taʃa'sãw] f taxation; **taxar** [ta'ʃa*] vt (fixar o preço de) to fix the price of; (lançar impostos sobre) to tax

táxi ['taksi] m taxi

tchau [tʃaw] *excl* bye!

tcheco, -a [ˈtʃɛku, a] *adj, m/f* Czech

Tcheco-Eslováquia [tʃekuiʒloˈvakja] *f* = **Tchecoslováquia**

Tchecoslováquia [tʃekoʒloˈvakja] *f*: **a ~** Czechoslovakia

te [tʃi] *pron* you; *(para você)* (to) you

té [tɛ] *prep abr de* **até**

tear [tʃjaˈ*] *m* loom

teatral [tʃjaˈtraw] *(pl* -**ais**) *adj* theatrical; *(grupo)* theatre *atr (BRIT)*, theater *atr (US)*; *(obra, arte)* dramatic

teatro [ˈtʃjatru] *m* theatre *(BRIT)*, theater *(US)*; *(obras)* plays *pl*, dramatic works *pl*; *(gênero, curso)* drama; **peça de ~** play

tecer [teˈse*] *vt, vi* to weave; **tecido** [teˈsidu] *m* cloth, material; *(ANAT)* tissue

tecla [ˈtɛkla] *f* key; **teclado** [tekˈladu] *m* keyboard

técnica [ˈtɛknika] *f* technique; *V tb* **técnico**

técnico, -a [ˈtɛkniku, a] *adj* technical ♦ *m/f* technician; *(especialista)* expert

tecnologia [teknoloˈʒia] *f* technology; **tecnológico, -a** [teknoˈlɔʒiku, a] *adj* technological

tecto [ˈtɛktu] *(PT)* *m* = **teto**

tédio [ˈtɛdʒju] *m* tedium, boredom; **tedioso, -a** [teˈdʒjozu, ɔza] *adj* tedious, boring

teia [ˈteja] *f* web; **~ de aranha** cobweb

teimar [tejˈma*] *vi* to insist, keep on; **~ em** to insist on

teimosia [tejmoˈzia] *f* stubbornness; **~ em fazer** insistence on doing

teimoso, -a [tejˈmozu, ɔza] *adj* obstinate; *(criança)* wilful *(BRIT)*, willful *(US)*

Tejo [ˈteʒu] *m*: **o (rio) ~** the (River) Tagus

tela [ˈtɛla] *f* fabric, material; *(de pintar)* canvas; *(CINEMA, TV)* screen

tele... [ˈtɛle] *prefixo* tele...; **telecomunicações** [telekomunikaˈsõjʃ] *fpl* telecommunications; **teleconferência** [telekõfeˈrẽsja] *f* teleconference

teleférico [teleˈfɛriku] *m* cable car

telefonar [telefoˈna*] *vi*: **~ para alguém** to (tele)phone sb

telefone [teleˈfɔni] *m* phone, telephone; *(número)* (tele)phone number; *(telefonema)* phone call; **~ celular** cellphone, mobile phone; **~ de carro** carphone; **telefonema** [telefoˈnɛma] *m* phone call; **dar um telefonema** to make a phone call; **telefónico, -a** [teleˈfoniku, a] *adj* telephone *atr*; **telefonista** [telefoˈniʃta] *m/f* telephonist; *(na companhia telefónica)* operator

telégrafo [teˈlɛgrafu] *m* telegraph

telegrama [teleˈgrama] *m* telegram, cable; **passar um ~** to send a telegram

tele...: telejornal [teleʒoxˈnaw] *(pl* -**jornais**) *m* television news *sg*; **telenovela** [telenoˈvɛla] *f (TV)* soap opera; **telescópio** [teleˈskɔpju] *m* telescope; **telespectador, a** [teleʃpektaˈdo*, a] *m/f* viewer

teletrabalho [teletraˈbaʎu] *m* teleworking

televendas [teleˈvẽdaʃ] *fpl* telesales

televisão [televiˈzãw] *f* television; **~ por assinatura** pay television; **~ a cabo** cable television; **~ a cores** colo(u)r television; **~ digital** digital television; **~ via satélite** satellite television; **aparelho de ~** television set; **televisionar** [televizjoˈna*] *vt* to televise; **televisivo, -a** [televiˈzivu, a] *adj* television *atr*

televisor [televi'zo*] m (aparelho) television (set), TV (set)

telex [te'lɛks] m telex; **enviar por ~** to telex

telha ['teʎa] f tile; (col: cabeça) head; **ter uma ~ de menos** to have a screw loose

telhado [te'ʎadu] m roof

tema ['tema] m theme; (assunto) subject; **temática** [te'matʃika] f theme

temer [te'me*] vt to fear, be afraid of ♦ vi to be afraid

temeroso, -a [teme'rozu, ɔza] adj fearful, afraid; (pavoroso) dreadful

temido, -a [te'midu, a] adj fearsome, frightening

temível [te'mivew] (pl -eis) adj = **temido**

temor [te'mo*] m fear

temperado, -a [tẽpe'radu, a] adj (clima) temperate; (comida) seasoned

temperamento [tẽpera'mẽtu] m temperament, nature

temperar [tẽpe'ra*] vt to season

temperatura [tẽpera'tura] f temperature

tempero [tẽ'peru] m seasoning, flavouring (BRIT), flavoring (US)

tempestade [tẽpeʃ'tadʒi] f storm; **tempestuoso, -a** [tẽpeʃ'twozu, ɔza] adj stormy

templo ['tẽplu] m temple; (igreja) church

tempo ['tẽpu] m time; (meteorológico) weather; (LING) tense; **o ~ todo** the whole time; **a ~** on time; **ao mesmo ~** at the same time; **a um ~** at once; **com ~** in good time; **de ~ em ~** from time to time; **nesse meio ~** in the meantime; **quanto ~?** how long?; **mais ~** longer; **há ~s** for ages; (atrás) ages ago; **~ livre** spare time; **primeiro/segundo ~** (ESPORTE)

first/second half

temporada [tẽpo'rada] f season; (tempo) spell

temporal [tẽpo'raw] (pl -ais) m storm, gale

temporário, -a [tẽpo'rarju, a] adj temporary, provisional

tenacidade [tenasi'dadʒi] f tenacity

tenaz [te'najz] adj tenacious

tencionar [tẽsjo'na*] vt to intend, plan

tenda ['tẽda] f tent

tendão [tẽ'dãw] (pl -ões) m tendon

tendência [tẽ'dẽsja] f tendency; (da moda etc) trend; **a ~ de** ou **a fazer** the tendency to do; **tendencioso, -a** [tẽdẽ'sjozu, ɔza] adj tendentious, bias(s)ed

tendões [tẽ'dõjʃ] mpl de **tendão**

tenebroso, -a [tene'brozu, ɔza] adj dark, gloomy; (fig) horrible

tenho etc ['tẽɲu] vb V **ter**

tênis ['teniʃ] m inv tennis; (sapatos) training shoes pl; (um sapato) training shoe; **~ de mesa** table tennis; **tenista** [te'niʃta] m/f tennis player

tenor [te'no*] m (MÚS) tenor

tenro, -a ['tẽxu, a] adj tender; (macio) soft; (delicado) delicate; (novo) young

tensão [tẽ'sãw] f tension; (pressão) pressure, strain; (rigidez) tightness; (ELET: voltagem) voltage

tenso, -a ['tẽsu, a] adj tense; (sob pressão) under stress, strained

tentação [tẽta'sãw] f temptation

tentáculo [tẽ'takulu] m tentacle

tentador, -a [tẽta'do*, a] adj tempting

tentar [tẽ'ta*] vt to try; (seduzir) to tempt ♦ vi to try; **tentativa** [tẽta'tʃiva] f attempt; **tentativa de homicídio/suicídio/roubo** attempted murder/suicide/robbery; **por**

tentativas by trial and error

tênue ['tenwi] *adj* tenuous; (*fino*) thin; (*delicado*) delicate; (*luz, voz*) faint; (*pequeníssimo*) minute

teor [te'o*] *m* (*conteúdo*) tenor; (*sentido*) meaning, drift

teoria [teo'ria] *f* theory; **teoricamente** [teorika'mɛtʃi] *adv* theoretically, in theory; **teórico, -a** [te-'ɔriku, a] *adj* theoretical ♦ *m/f* theoretician

tépido, -a ['tɛpidu, a] *adj* tepid

PALAVRA CHAVE

---

ter [te*] *vt* 1 (*possuir, ger*) to have; (*na mão*) to hold; **você tem uma caneta?** have you got a pen?; **ela vai ~ neném** she is going to have a baby

2 (*idade, medidas, estado*) to be; **ela tem 7 anos** she's 7 (years old); **a mesa tem 1 metro de comprimento** the table is 1 metre long; **~ fome/sorte** to be hungry/lucky; **~ frio/calor** to be cold/hot

3 (*conter*) to hold, contain; **a caixa tem um quilo de chocolates** the box holds one kilo of chocolates

4: **~ que** *ou* **de fazer** to have to do

5: **~ a ver com** to have to do with

6: **ir ~ com** to (go and) meet

♦ *vb impess* 1: **tem** (*sg*) there is; (*pl*) there are; **tem 3 dias que não saio de casa** I haven't been out for 3 days

2: **não tem de quê** don't mention it

---

terapeuta [tera'pewta] *m/f* therapist

terapia [tera'pia] *f* therapy

terça ['tɛxsa] *f* (*tb:* **~-feira**) Tuesday; **terça-feira** (*pl* **terças-feiras**) *f* Tuesday; **terça-feira gorda** Shrove Tuesday

terceiro, -a [tex'sejru, a] *num* third; **~s** *mpl* (*os outros*) outsiders

terço ['texsu] *m* third (part)

termas ['tɛxmaʃ] *fpl* bathhouse *sg*

térmico, -a ['tɛxmiku, a] *adj* thermal; **garrafa térmica** (Thermos ®) flask

terminal [texmi'naw] (*pl* **-ais**) *adj* terminal ♦ *m* (*de rede, ELET, COMPUT*) terminal ♦ *f* terminal; **~ (de vídeo)** monitor, visual display unit

terminar [texmi'na*] *vt* to finish ♦ *vi* (*pessoa*) to finish; (*coisa*) to end; **~ de fazer** to finish doing; (*ter feito há pouco*) to have just done; **~ por fazer algo** to end up doing sth

término ['texminu] *m* end, termination

termo ['texmu] *m* term; (*fim*) end, termination; (*limite*) limit, boundary; (*prazo*) period; (*PT:* **garrafa**) (Thermos ®) flask; **meio ~** compromise; **em ~s (de)** in terms (of)

termômetro [tex'mometru] *m* thermometer

terno, -a ['tɛxnu, a] *adj* gentle, tender ♦ *m* (*BR:* *roupa*) suit; **ternura** [tex'nura] *f* gentleness, tenderness

terra ['tɛxa] *f* earth, world; (*AGR, propriedade*) land; (*pátria*) country; (*chão*) ground; (*GEO*) soil; (*pó*) dirt

terraço [te'xasu] *m* terrace

terramoto [texa'mɔtu] (*PT*) *m* = **terremoto**

terreiro [te'xejru] *m* yard, square

terremoto [texe'mɔtu] *m* earthquake

terreno, -a [te'xɛnu, a] *adj* ground, land; (*porção de terra*) plot of land ♦ *m* (*GEO*) earthly

térreo, -a ['tɛxju, a] *adj:* **andar ~** (*BR*) ground floor (*BRIT*), first floor (*US*)

terrestre [te'xɛʃtri] *adj* land *atr*

terrina [te'xina] *f* tureen

território [texi'tɔrju] *m* territory

terrível [te'xivew] (*pl* **-eis**) *adj* terrible, dreadful

terror [te'xo*] *m* terror, dread; **terrorista** [texo'rifta] *adj, m/f* terrorist

tese ['tɛzi] *f* proposition, theory; (*EDUC*) thesis; **em ~** in theory

teso, -a ['tezu, a] *adj* (*cabo*) taut; (*rígido*) stiff

tesoura [te'zora] *f* scissors *pl*; **uma ~** a pair of scissors

tesouraria [tezora'ria] *f* treasury

tesouro [te'zoru] *m* treasure; (*erário*) treasury, exchequer; (*livro*) thesaurus

testa ['tɛfta] *f* brow, forehead

testamento [tefta'mẽtu] *m* will, testament; (*REL*): **Velho/Novo T~** Old/New Testament

testar [tef'ta*] *vt* to test; (*deixar em testamento*) to bequeath

teste ['tɛfti] *m* test

testemunha [tefte'muɲa] *f* witness; **testemunhar** [teftemu'ɲa*] *vi* to testify ♦ *vt* to give evidence about; (*presenciar*) to witness; (*confirmar*) to demonstrate; **testemunho** [tefte'muɲu] *m* evidence

testículo [tef'tʃikulu] *m* testicle

teta ['tɛta] *f* teat, nipple

tétano ['tɛtanu] *m* tetanus

teto ['tɛtu] *m* ceiling; (*telhado*) roof; (*habitação*) home

teu, tua [tew, 'tua] *adj your* ♦ *pron* yours

teve ['tevi] *vb V* ter

têxtil ['tejftʃiw] (*pl* **-eis**) *m* textile

texto ['teftu] *m* text

textura [tef'tura] *f* texture·

thriller ['srila*] (*pl* **-s**) *m* thriller

ti [tʃi] *pron you*

tia ['tʃia] *f* aunt

Tibete [tʃi'betʃi] *m*: **o ~** Tibet

tido, -a ['tʃidu, a] *pp de* ter ♦ *adj*: **~ como** *ou* **por** considered to be

tigela [tʃi'ʒɛla] *f* bowl

tigre ['tʃigri] *m* tiger

tijolo [tʃi'ʒolu] *m* brick

til [tʃiw] (*pl* **tis**) *m* tilde

timbre ['tʃibri] *m* insignia, emblem; (*selo*) stamp; (*MÚS*) tone, timbre; (*de voz*) tone; (*em papel de carta*) heading

time ['tʃimi] (*BR*) *m* team; **de segundo ~** (*fig*) second-rate

tímido, -a ['tʃimidu, a] *adj* shy, timid

tímpano ['tʃipanu] *m* eardrum; (*MÚS*) kettledrum

tina ['tʃina] *f* vat

tingir [tʃi'ʒi*] *vt* to dye; (*fig*) to tinge

tinha *etc* ['tʃiɲa] *vb V* ter

tinjo *etc* ['tʃiʒu] *vb V* tingir

tinta ['tʃita] *f* (*de pintar*) paint; (*de escrever*) ink; (*para tingir*) dye; (*fig: vestígio*) shade, tinge

tinto, -a ['tʃitu, a] *adj* dyed; (*fig*) stained; **vinho ~** red wine

tintura [tʃi'tura] *f* dye; (*ato*) dyeing; (*fig*) tinge, hint

tinturaria [tʃitura'ria] *f* drycleaner's

tio ['tʃiu] *m* uncle

típico, -a ['tʃipiku, a] *adj* typical

tipo ['tʃipu] *m* type; (*de imprensa*) print; (*de impressora*) typeface; (*col: sujeito*) guy, chap; (*pessoa*) person

tipografia [tʃipogra'fia] *f* printing; (*estabelecimento*) printer's

tíquete [tʃi'ketʃi] *m* ticket

tira ['tʃira] *f* strip ♦ *m* (*BR: col*) cop

tira-gosto (*pl* **~s**) *m* snack, savoury (*BRIT*); **tirano, -a** [tʃi'ranu, a] *adj* tyrannical ♦ *m/f* tyrant

tirar [tʃi'ra*] *vt* to take away; (*de dentro*) to take out; (*de cima*) to take off; (*roupa, sapatos*) to take off; (*arrancar*) to pull out; (*férias*) to take, have; (*boas notas*) to get; (*salário*) to earn; (*curso*) to do, take;

(mancha) to remove; *(foto, cópia)* to take; *(mesa)* to clear; **~ algo a alguém** to take sth from sb

tiritar [tʃiri'ta*] *vi* to shiver

tiro ['tʃiru] *m* shot; *(ato de disparar)* shooting; **~ ao alvo** target practice; **trocar ~s** to fire at one another

tiroteio [tʃiro'teju] *m* shooting, exchange of shots

tis [tʃiʃ] *mpl de* **til**

titular [tʃitu'la*] *adj* titular ♦ *m/f* holder

título ['tʃitulu] *m* title; *(COM)* bond; *(universitário)* degree; **~ de propriedade** title deed

tive *etc* ['tʃivi] *vb V* **ter**

to [tu] = **te + o**

toa ['toa] *f* towrope; **à ~** at random; *(sem motivo)* for no reason; *(inutilmente)* in vain, for nothing

toalete [twa'letʃi] *m (banheiro)* toilet; *(traje)* outfit ♦ *f*: **fazer a ~** to have a wash

toalha [to'aʎa] *f* towel

toca ['tɔka] *f* burrow, hole

toca-discos *(BR) m inv* record-player

toca-fitas *m inv* cassette player

tocaia [to'kaja] *f* ambush

tocante [to'kãtʃi] *adj* moving, touching; **no ~ a** regarding, concerning

tocar [to'ka*] *vt* to touch; *(MÚS)* to play ♦ *vi* to touch; to play; *(campainha, sino, telefone)* to ring; **tocar-se** *vr* to touch (each other); **~ a** *(dizer respeito a)* to concern, affect; **~ em** to touch; *(assunto)* to touch upon; **~ para alguém** *(telefonar)* to ring sb (up), call sb (up); **pelo que me toca** as far as I am concerned

tocha ['tɔʃa] *f* torch

todavia [toda'via] *adv* yet, still, however

todo, -a ['todu, 'tɔda] *adj* **1** *(com artigo sg)* all; **toda a carne** all the meat; **toda a noite** all night, the whole night; **~ o Brasil** the whole of Brazil; **a toda (velocidade)** at full speed; **~ o mundo** *(BR)*, **toda a gente** *(PT)* everybody, everyone; **em toda (a) parte** everywhere

2 *(com artigo pl)* all; (: *cada*) every; **~s os livros** all the books; **~s os dias/todas as noites** every day/night; **~s os que querem sair** all those who want to leave; **~s nós** all of us

♦ *adv*: **ao ~** altogether; *(no total)* in all; **de ~** completely

♦ *pron*: **~s** *mpl* everybody, everyone; **~** *sg* everything

todo-poderoso, -a *adj* all-powerful ♦ *m*: **o T~** the Almighty

toicinho [toj'siɲu] *m* bacon fat

toldo ['towdu] *m* awning, sun blind

tolerância [tole'rãsja] *f* tolerance; **tolerante** [tole'rãtʃi] *adj* tolerant

tolerar [tole'ra*] *vt* to tolerate; **tolerável** [tole'ravew] *(pl* **-eis***)* adj* tolerable, bearable; *(satisfatório)* passable; *(falta)* excusable

tolice [to'lisi] *f* stupidity, foolishness; *(ato, dito)* stupid thing

tolo, -a ['tolu, a] *adj* foolish, silly, stupid ♦ *m/f* fool

tom [tõ] *m (pl* **-ns***) m* tone; *(MÚS: altura)* pitch; (: *escala)* key; *(cor)* shade

tomada [to'mada] *f* capture; *(ELET)* socket

tomar [to'ma*] *vt* to take; *(capturar)* to capture, seize; *(decisão)* to make; *(bebida)* to drink; **~ café** *(de manhã)* to have breakfast

tomara [to'mara] *excl* **~!** only!

que venha hoje I hope he comes today

tomate [to'matʃi] m tomato

tombadilho [tõba'dʒiʎu] m deck

tombar [tõ'ba*] vi to fall down, tumble down ♦ vt to knock down, knock over; **tombo** ['tõbu] m tumble, fall

tomilho [to'miʎu] m thyme

tona ['tɔna] f surface; **vir à ~** to come to the surface; (fig) to emerge; **trazer à ~** to bring up; (recordações) to bring back

tonalidade [tonali'dadʒi] f (de cor) shade; (MÚS: tom) key

tonelada [tone'lada] f ton

tônica ['tɔnika] f (água) tonic (water); (fig) keynote

tônico ['tɔniku] m tonic; **acento ~** stress

tons [tõʃ] mpl de **tom**

tonteira [tõ'tejra] f dizziness

tonto, -a ['tõtu, a] adj stupid, silly; (zonzo) dizzy, lightheaded; (atarantado) flustered

topar [to'pa*] vt to agree to ♦ vi: **~ com** to come across; **topar-se** vr (duas pessoas) to run into one another; **~ em** (tropeçar) to stub one's toe on; (esbarrar) to run into; (tocar) to touch

tópico, -a ['tɔpiku, a] adj topical ♦ m topic

topless [tɔp'lɛs] adj inv topless

topo ['topu] m top; (extremidade) end, extremity

toque¹ ['tɔki] m touch; (de instrumento musical) playing; (de campainha) ring; (retoque) finishing touch

toque² etc vb V **tocar**

Tóquio ['tɔkju] n Tokyo

tora ['tɔra] f (pedaço) piece; (de madeira) log; (sesta) nap

toranja [to'rãʒa] f grapefruit

torção [tox'sãw] (pl -ões) m twist; (MED) sprain

torcedor, a [toxse'do*], a] m/f supporter, fan

torcer [tox'se*] vt to twist; (MED) to sprain; (desvirtuar) to distort, misconstrue; (roupa: espremer) to wring; (: na máquina) to spin; (vergar) to bend ♦ vi: **~ por** (time) to support; **torcer-se** vr to squirm, writhe

torcicolo [toxsi'kɔlu] m stiff neck

torcida [tox'sida] f (pavio) wick; (ESPORTE: ato de torcer) cheering; (: torcedores) supporters pl

torções [tox'sõjʃ] mpl de **torção**

tormenta [tox'mẽta] f storm

tormento [tox'mẽtu] m torment; (angústia) anguish

tornar [tox'na*] vi to return, go back ♦ vt: **~ algo em algo** to make sth into sth; **tornar-se** vr to become: **~ a fazer algo** to do sth again

torneio [tox'neju] m tournament

torneira [tox'nejra] f tap (BRIT), faucet (US)

torno ['toxnu] m lathe; (CERÂMICA) wheel; **em ~ de** (ao redor de) around; (sobre) about

tornozelo [toxno'zelu] m ankle

torpe ['tɔxpi] adj vile

torrada [to'xada] f toast; **uma ~** a piece of toast; **torradeira** [toxa-'dejra] f toaster

torrão [to'xãw] (pl -ões) m turf, sod; (terra) soil, land; (de açúcar) lump

torrar [to'xa*] vt to toast; (café) to roast

torre ['toxi] f tower; (XADREZ) castle, rook; (ELET) pylon; **~ de controle** (AER) control tower

tórrido, -a ['tɔxidu, a] adj torrid

torrões [to'xõjʃ] mpl de **torrão**

torso ['toxsu] m torso

torta ['tɔxta] f pie, tart

torto, -a ['toxtu, 'tɔxta] adj twisted, crooked; **a ~ e a direito** indiscriminately

tortuoso, -a [tox'twozu, ɔza] adj winding

tortura [tox'tura] f torture; (fig) anguish; **torturar** [toxtu'ra*] vt to torture; to torment

tos [tuʃ] = **te + os**

tosco, -a ['toʃku, a] adj rough, unpolished; (grosseiro) coarse, crude

tosse ['tɔsi] f cough; **~ de cachorro** whooping cough; **tossir** [to'si*] vi to cough

tosta ['tɔʃta] (PT) f toast; **~ mista** toasted cheese and ham sandwich

tostão [toʃ'tãw] m cash

tostar [toʃ'ta*] vt to toast; (pele, pessoa) to tan; **tostar-se** vr to get tanned

total [to'taw] (pl **-ais**) adj, m total

totalitário, -a [totali'tarju, a] adj totalitarian

totalmente [totaw'mẽtʃi] adv totally

touca ['toka] f bonnet; **~ de banho** bathing cap

toupeira [to'pejra] f mole; (fig) numbskull, idiot

tourada [to'rada] f bullfight; **toureiro** [to'rejru] m bullfighter

touro ['toru] m bull; **T~** (ASTROLOGIA) Taurus

tóxico, -a ['tɔksiku, a] adj toxic ♦ m poison; (droga) drug; **toxicômano, -a** [toksi'komanu, a] m/f drug addict

TPM abr f (= tensão pré-menstrual) PMT

trabalhadeira [trabaʎa'dejra] f: **ela é ~** she's a hard worker

trabalhador, a [trabaʎa'do*, a] adj hard-working, industrious; (POL: classe) working ♦ m/f worker

trabalhar [traba'ʎa*] vi to work ♦ vt (terra) to till; (madeira, metal) to work; (texto) to work on; **~ com** (comerciar) to deal in; **~ de** ou **como** to work as; **trabalhista** [traba'ʎiʃta] adj labour atr (BRIT), labor atr (US); **trabalho** [tra'baʎu] m work; (emprego, tarefa) job; (ECON) labo(u)r; **trabalho braçal** manual work; **trabalho doméstico** housework; **trabalhoso, -a** [traba-'ʎozu, ɔza] adj laborious, arduous

traça ['trasa] f moth

traçado [tra'sadu] m sketch, plan

tração [tra'sãw] f traction

traçar [tra'sa*] vt to draw; (determinar) to set out, outline; (planos) to draw up; (escrever) to compose

tracção [tra'sãw] (PT) f = **tração**

traço ['trasu] m line, dash; (vestígio) trace, vestige; (aspecto) feature, trait; **~s** mpl (do rosto) features; **~ (de união)** hyphen; (entre frases) dash

tractor [tra'to*] (PT) m = **trator**

tradição [tradʒi'sãw] (pl **-ões**) f tradition; **tradicional** [tradʒisjo'naw] (pl **-ais**) adj traditional

tradução [tradu'sãw] (pl **-ões**) f translation

tradutor, a [tradu'to*, a] m/f translator

traduzir [tradu'zi*] vt to translate

trafegar [trafe'ga*] vi to move, go

tráfego ['trafegu] m traffic

traficante [trafi'kãtʃi] m/f trafficker, dealer

traficar [trafi'ka*] vi: **~ (com)** to deal (in)

tráfico ['trafiku] m traffic

tragar [tra'ga*] vt to swallow; (fumaça) to inhale; (suportar) to tolerate ♦ *vi* to inhale

tragédia [tra'ʒedʒja] *f* tragedy; **trágico, -a** ['traʒiku, a] *adj* tragic

trago¹ ['tragu] *m* mouthful

trago² *etc vb* V **trazer**

traição [traj'sãw] (*pl* -ões) *f* treason, treachery; (*deslealdade*) disloyalty; (*infidelidade*) infidelity; **traiçoeiro, -a** [traj'swejru, a] *adj* treacherous; disloyal

traidor, a [traj'do*, a] *m/f* traitor

trailer ['trejla*] (*pl* ~s) *m* trailer; (*tipo casa*) caravan (BRIT), trailer (US)

traineira [traj'nejra] *f* trawler

trair [tra'i*] *vt* to betray; (*mulher, marido*) to be unfaithful to; (*esperanças*) not to live up to; **trair-se** *vr* to give o.s. away

trajar [tra'ʒa*] *vt* to wear

traje ['traʒi] *m* dress, clothes *pl*; ~ de banho swimsuit

trajeto [tra'ʒetu] (*PT* -ct-) *m* course, path

trajetória [traʒe'tɔrja] (*PT* -ct-) *f* trajectory, path; (*fig*) course

tralha ['traʎa] *f* fishing net

trama ['trama] *f* (*tecido*) weft (BRIT), woof (US); (*enredo, conspiração*) plot

tramar [tra'ma*] *vt* (*tecer*) to weave; (*maquinar*) to plot ♦ *vi*: ~ **contra** to conspire against

trâmites ['tramitʃiʃ] *mpl* procedure *sg*, channels

trampolim [trãpo'lĩ] (*pl* -ns) *m* trampoline; (*de piscina*) diving board; (*fig*) springboard

tranca ['trãka] *f* (*de porta*) bolt; (*de carro*) lock

trança ['trãsa] *f* (*cabelo*) plait; (*galão*) braid

trancar [trã'ka*] *vt* to lock

tranquilidade [trãkwili'dadʒi] *f* tranquillity; (*paz*) peace

tranquilizante [trãkwili'zãtʃi] (*MED*) *m* tranquillizer

tranquilizar [trãkwili'za*] *vt* to calm, quieten; (*despreocupar*): ~ **alguém** to reassure sb, put sb's mind at rest; **tranquilizar-se** *vr* to calm down

tranquilo, -a [trã'kwilu, a] *adj* peaceful; (*mar, pessoa*) calm; (*criança*) quiet; (*consciência*) clear; (*seguro*) sure, certain

transação [trãza'sãw] (*PT* -cç-) (*pl* -ões) *f* transaction

transbordar [trãʒbox'da*] *vi* to overflow

transbordo [trãʒ'boxdu] *m* (*de viajantes*) change, transfer

transe ['trãzi] *m* ordeal; (*lance*) plight; (*hipnótico*) trance

transeunte [trã'zjũtʃi] *m/f* passer-by

transferência [trãʃfe'rẽsja] *f* transfer

transferir [trãʃfe'ri*] *vt* to transfer; (*adiar*) to postpone

transformação [trãʃfoxma'sãw] (*pl* -ões) *f* transformation

transformador [trãʃfoxma'do*] (*ELET*) *m* transformer

transformar [trãʃfox'ma*] *vt* to transform; **transformar-se** *vr* to turn

transfusão [trãʃfu'zãw] (*pl* -ões) *f* transfusion

transição [trãzi'sãw] (*pl* -ões) *f* transition

transistor [trãziʃ'to*] *m* transistor

transitar [trãzi'ta*] *vi*: ~ **por** to move through; (*rua*) to go along

transitivo, -a [trãzi'tʃivu, a] *adj* (*LING*) transitive

trânsito ['trãzitu] *m* transit, passage; (*na rua: veículos*) traffic; (*: pessoas*) flow; **transitório, -a** [trãzi'tɔrju, a] *adj* transitory; (*período*) transitional

transmissão [trãʒmi'sãw] (*pl* -ões-)

f transmission; (*transferência*) transfer; ~ **ao vivo** live broadcast

transmissor [trãʒmi'so*] *m* transmitter

transmitir [trãʒmi'tʃi*] *vt* to transmit; (RÁDIO, TV) to broadcast; (*transferir*) to transfer; (*recado, notícia*) to pass on

transparência [trãʃpa'rẽsja] *f* transparency; (*de água*) clarity; **transparente** [trãʃpa'rẽtʃi] *adj* transparent; (*roupa*) see-through; (*água*) clear

transpirar [trãʃpi'ra*] *vi* to perspire; (*divulgar-se*) to become known; (*verdade*) to come out ♦ *vt* to exude

transplante [trãʃ'plãtʃi] *m* transplant

transportar [trãʃpox'ta*] *vt* to transport; (*levar*) to carry; (*enlevar*) to entrance, enrapture

transporte [trãʃ'pɔxtʃi] *m* transport; (COM) haulage

transtorno [trãʃ'toxnu] *m* upset, disruption

trapaça [tra'pasa] *f* swindle, fraud; **trapacear** [trapa'sja*] *vt, vi* to swindle; **trapaceiro, -a** [trapa-'sejru, a] *adj* crooked, cheating ♦ *m/f* swindler, cheat

trapalhão, -lhona [trapa'ʎãw, 'ʎona] (*pl* **-ões, ~s**) *m/f* bungler, blunderer

trapo ['trapu] *m* rag

traquéia [tra'kɛja] *f* windpipe

trarei *etc* [tra'rej] *vb* V **trazer**

trás [trajʃ] *prep, adv*: **para ~** backwards; **por ~** behind; **de ~** from behind

traseira [tra'zejra] *f* rear; (ANAT) bottom

traseiro, -a [tra'zejru, a] *adj* back, rear ♦ *m* (ANAT) bottom

traste ['trajtʃi] *m* thing; (*coisa sem valor*) piece of junk

tratado [tra'tadu] *m* treaty

tratamento [trata'mẽtu] *m* treatment

tratar [tra'ta*] *vt* to treat; (*tema*) to deal with; (*combinar*) to agree ♦ *vi*: ~ **com** to deal with; (*combinar*) to agree with; ~ **de** to deal with; **de que se trata?** what is it about?

trato ['tratu] *m* treatment; (*contrato*) agreement, contract; ~**s** *mpl* (*relações*) dealings

trator [tra'to*] *m* tractor

trauma ['trawma] *m* trauma

travão [tra'vãw] (PT: *pl* **-ões**) *m* brake

travar [tra'va*] *vt* (*roda*) to lock; (*iniciar*) to engage in; (*conversa*) to strike up; (*luta*) to wage; (*carro*) to stop; (*passagem*) to block; (*movimentos*) to hinder ♦ *vi* (PT) to brake

trave ['travi] *f* beam; (ESPORTE) crossbar

através [tra'vɛʃ] *m* slant, incline; **de ~** across, sideways

travessa [tra'vɛsa] *f* crossbeam, crossbar; (*rua*) lane, alley; (*prato*) dish; (*para o cabelo*) comb, slide

travessão [trave'sãw] (*pl* **-ões**) *m* (*de balança*) arm, beam; (*pontuação*) dash

travesseiro [trave'sejru] *m* pillow

travessia [trave'sia] *f* (*viagem*) journey, crossing

travesso, -a [tra'vesu, a] *adj* mischievous, naughty

travessões [trave'sõjʃ] *mpl de* **travessão**

travessura [trave'sura] *f* mischief, prank

travões [tra'võjʃ] *mpl de* **travão**

trazer [tra'ze*] *vt* to bring

trecho ['treʃu] *m* passage; (*de rua, caminho*) stretch; (*espaço*) space

trégua ['trɛgwa] *f* truce; (*descanso*) respite

treinador, a [trejna'do*, a] m/f
trainer

treinamento [trejna'mẽtu] m training

treinar [trej'na*] vt to train;
treinar-se vr to train; **treino**
['trejnu] m training

trejeito [tre'ʒejtu] m gesture; (careta) grimace, face

trela ['trela] f lead, leash

trem [trẽj] (pl **-ns**) m train; **~ de
aterrissagem** (avião) landing gear

tremendo, -a [tre'mẽdu, a] adj
tremendous; (terrível) terrible, awful

tremer [tre'me*] vi to shudder,
quake; (terra) to shake; (de frio,
medo) to shiver

tremor [tre'mo*] m tremor; **~ de
terra** (earth) tremor

trêmulo, -a ['tremulu, a] adj shaky,
trembling

trenó [tre'nɔ] m sledge, sleigh (BRIT),
sled (US)

trens [trẽjʃ] mpl de **trem**

trepadeira [trepa'dejra] f (BOT)
creeper

trepar [tre'pa*] vt to climb ♦ vi: **~
em** to climb

trepidar [trepi'da*] vi to tremble,
shake

três [treʃ] num three

trevas ['trevaʃ] fpl darkness sg

trevo ['trevu] m clover; (de vias)
intersection

treze ['trezi] num thirteen

triângulo ['trjãgulu] m triangle

tribal [tri'baw] (pl **-ais**) adj tribal

tribo ['tribu] f tribe

tribuna [tri'buna] f platform, ros-
trum; (REL) pulpit

tribunal [tribu'naw] (pl **-ais**) m
court; (comissão) tribunal

tributar [tribu'ta*] vt to tax; (pagar)
to pay

tributo [tri'butu] m tribute; (impos-

to) tax

triço [tri'ko] m knitting; **tricotar**
[triko'ta*] vt, vi to knit

trigo ['trigu] m wheat

trilha ['triʎa] f (caminho) path;
(rasto) track, trail; **~ sonora** soundtrack

trilhão [tri'ʎãw] (pl **-ões**) m billion
(BRIT), trillion (US)

trilho [tri'ʎu] m (BR: FERRO) rail; (vereda) path, track

trilhões [tri'ʎõjʃ] mpl de **trilhão**

trimestral [trimeʃ'traw] (pl **-ais**)
adj quarterly; **trimestralmente**
[trimeʃtraw'mẽtʃi] adv quarterly

trimestre [tri'meʃtri] m (EDUC) term;
(COM) quarter

trincar [trĩ'ka*] vt to crunch;
(morder) to bite; (dentes) to grit ♦ vi
to crunch

trinco ['trĩku] m latch

trinta ['trĩta] num thirty

trio ['triu] m trio; **~ elétrico** music
float; see boxed note

> ### TRIO ELÉTRICO
>
> **Trios elétricos** are lorries, carrying
> floats equipped for sound and/or
> live music, which parade through
> the streets during carnaval, espe-
> cially in Bahia. Bands and popular
> performers on the floats draw
> crowds by giving frenzied per-
> formances of various types of
> music.

tripa ['tripa] f gut, intestine; **~s** fpl
(intestinos) bowels; (vísceras) guts;
(CULIN) tripe sg

tripé [tri'pɛ] m tripod

triplicar [tripli'ka*] vt, vi to treble;
triplicar-se vr to treble

tripulação [tripula'sãw] (pl **-ões**) f
crew

tripulante [tripu'lãtʃi] m/f crew

member

triste ['triʃtʃi] *adj* sad; (*lugar*) depressing; **tristeza** [triʃ'teza] *f* sadness; gloominess

triturar [tritu'ra*] *vt* to grind

triunfar [trjũ'fa*] *vi* to triumph; **triunfo** [tri'ũfu] *m* triumph

trivial [tri'vjaw] (*pl* -**ais**) *adj* common(place), ordinary; (*insignificante*) trivial

triz [triʒ] *m*: **por um ~** by a hair's breadth

troca ['trɔka] *f* exchange, swap

trocadilho [troka'dʒiʎu] *m* pun, play on words

trocado [tro'kadu] *m*: ~(**s**) (small) change

trocador, a [troka'do*, a] *m/f* (*em ônibus*) conductor

trocar [tro'ka*] *vt* to exchange, swap; (*mudar*) to change; (*inverter*) to change ou swap round; (*confundir*) to mix up; **trocar-se** *vr* to change; ~ **dinheiro** to change money

troco ['trɔku] *m* (*dinheiro*) change; (*revide*) retort, rejoinder

troféu [tro'fɛw] *m* trophy

tromba ['trõba] *f* (*do elefante*) trunk; (*de outro animal*) snout

trombeta [trõ'beta] *f* trumpet

trombone [trõ'bɔni] *m* trombone

trombose [trõ'bɔzi] *f* thrombosis

tronco ['trõku] *m* trunk; (*ramo*) branch; (*de corpo*) torso, trunk

trono ['trɔnu] *m* throne

tropa ['trɔpa] *f* troop; (*exército*) army; **ir para a ~** (*PT*) to join the army

tropeçar [trope'sa*] *vi* to stumble, trip; (*fig*) to blunder

tropical [tropi'kaw] (*pl* -**ais**) *adj* tropical

trópico ['trɔpiku] *m* tropic

trotar [tro'ta*] *vi* to trot; **trote** ['trɔtʃi] *m* trot; (*por telefone etc*) hoax call

trouxe *etc* ['trosi] *vb V* **trazer**

trovão [tro'vãw] (*pl* -**ões**) *m* clap of thunder; (*trovoada*) thunder; **trovejar** [trove'ʒa*] *vi* to thunder; **trovoada** [tro'vwada] *f* thunderstorm

trunfo ['trũfu] *m* trump (card)

truque ['truki] *m* trick; (*publicitário*) gimmick

truta ['truta] *f* trout

tu [tu] (*PT*) *pron* you

tua ['tua] *f de* **teu**

tuba ['tuba] *f* tuba

tubarão [tuba'rãw] (*pl* -**ões**) *m* shark

tuberculose [tubexku'lɔzi] *f* tuberculosis

tubo ['tubu] *m* tube, pipe; ~ **de ensaio** test tube

tucano [tu'kanu] *m* toucan

tudo ['tudu] *pron* everything; ~ **quanto** everything that; **antes de** ~ first of all; **acima de** ~ above all

tufão [tu'fãw] (*pl* -**ões**) *m* typhoon

tulipa [tu'lipa] *f* tulip

tumba ['tũba] *f* tomb; (*lápide*) tombstone

tumor [tu'mo*] *m* tumour (*BRIT*), tumor (*US*)

túmulo ['tumulu] *m* tomb; (*sepultura*) burial

tumulto [tu'muwtu] *m* uproar, trouble; (*grande movimento*) bustle; (*balbúrdia*) hubbub; (*motim*) riot; **tumultuado, -a** [tumuw'twadu, a] *adj* riotous, heated; **tumultuar** [tumuw'twa*] *vt* to disrupt; (*amotinar*) to rouse, incite

túnel ['tunew] (*pl* -**eis**) *m* tunnel

túnica ['tunika] *f* tunic

Tunísia [tu'nizja] *f*: **a ~** Tunisia

tupi [tu'pi] *m* Tupi (tribe); (*LING*) Tupi

◆ *m/f* Tupi Indian
tupi-guarani [-gwara'ni] *m* (*LING*)
see boxed note

TUPI-GUARANI

This is an important branch of
indigenous languages from the
tropical region of South America.
It takes in thirty indigenous peoples and includes Tupi, Guarani,
and other languages. Before
Brazil was discovered by the
Portuguese, it had 1,300 indigenous languages, 87% of which
are now extinct due to the exter-
mination of indigenous peoples
and the loss of territory.

---

tupiniquim [tupini'kĩ] (*pej*) (*pl*
-ns) *adj* Brazilian (Indian)
turbilhão [tuxbi'ʎãw] (*pl* -ões) *m* (*de*
vento) whirlwind; (*de água*) whirlpool
turbulência [tuxbu'lẽsja] *f* turbulence; **turbulento, -a** [tuxbu'lẽtu,
a] *adj* turbulent
turco, -a ['tuxku, a] *adj* Turkish
◆ *m/f* Turk ◆ *m* (*LING*) Turkish
turismo [tu'riʒmu] *m* tourism; **turista** [tu'riʃta] *m/f* tourist ◆ *adj*
(*classe*) tourist *atr*
turma ['tuxma] *f* group; (*EDUC*) class
turno ['tuxnu] *m* shift; (*vez*) turn;
(*ESPORTE, de eleição*) round; **por ~s**
alternately, by turns, in turn
turquesa [tux'keza] *adj inv* turquoise
Turquia [tux'kia] *f*: **a ~** Turkey
tusso *etc* ['tusu] *vb V* **tossir**
tutela [tu'tɛla] *f* protection; (*JUR*)
guardianship
tutor, a [tu'to*, a] *m/f* guardian
tutu [tu'tu] *m* (*CULIN*) beans, bacon
and manioc flour
TV [te've] *abr f* (= *televisão*) TV

UE *abr f* (= *União Européia*) EU
UEM *abr f* (= *União Econômica e
Monetária*) EMU
Uganda [u'gãda] *m* Uganda
uísque ['wiʃki] *m* whisky (*BRIT*),
whiskey (*US*)
uivar [wi'va*] *vi* to howl; (*berrar*) to
yell; **uivo** [i'wivu] *m* howl; (*fig*)
yell
úlcera ['uwsera] *f* ulcer
ultimamente [uwtʃima'mẽtʃi] *adv*
lately
ultimato [uwtʃi'matu] *m* ultimatum
último, -a ['uwtʃimu, a] *adj* last;
(*mais recente*) latest; (*qualidade*)
lowest; (*fig*) final; **por ~** finally; **nos
~s anos** in recent years; **a última**
(*notícia*) the latest (news)
ultra- [uwtra-] *prefixo*
ultrajar [uwtra'ʒa*] *vt* to outrage;
(*insultar*) to insult, offend; **ultraje**
[uw'traʒi] *m* outrage; (*insulto*) insult, offence (*BRIT*), offense (*US*)
ultramar [uwtra'ma*] *m* overseas
ultrapassado, -a [uwtrapa'sadu,
a] *adj* (*idéias etc*) outmoded
ultrapassar [uwtrapa'sa*] *vt* (*atravessar*) to cross, go beyond; (*ir além
de*) to exceed; (*transgredir*) to
overstep; (*AUTO*) to overtake (*BRIT*),
pass (*US*); (*ser superior a*) to surpass
◆ *vi* (*AUTO*) to overtake (*BRIT*), pass
(*US*)
ultra-som *m* ultrasound
ultravioleta [uwtravjo'leta] *adj*
ultraviolet

PALAVRA CHAVE

um, uma [ũ, 'uma] (*pl* **uns, umas**)
num one; **~ e outro** both; **~ a ~** one
by one; **à ~a** (*hora*) at one (o'clock)
◆ *adj*: **uns cinco** about five; **uns
poucos** a few

♦ *art indef* **1** (*sg*) a; (: *antes de vogal ou 'h' mudo*) an; (*pl*) some; **ela é de ~a beleza incrível** she's incredibly beautiful
2 (*dando ênfase*): **estou com ~a fome!** I'm so hungry!
3: **~ ao outro** one another; (*entre dois*) each other

umbigo [u'bigu] *m* navel

umbilical [ũbili'kaw] (*pl -ais*) *adj*: **cordão ~** umbilical cord

umedecer [umede'se*] *vt* to moisten, wet; **umedecer-se** *vr* to get wet

umidade [umi'dadʒi] *f* dampness; (*clima*) humidity

úmido, -a ['umidu, a] *adj* wet, moist; (*roupa*) damp; (*clima*) humid

unânime [u'nanimi] *adj* unanimous

unha ['uɲa] *f* nail; (*garra*) claw; **unhada** [u'ɲada] *f* scratch

união [u'njãw] (*pl -ões*) *f* union; (*ato*) joining; (*unidade, solidariedade*) unity; (*casamento*) marriage; (*TEC*) joint; **a U~ Européia** the European Union

unicamente [unika'mẽtʃi] *adv* only

único, -a ['uniku, a] *adj* only; (*sem igual*) unique; (*um só*) single

unidade [uni'dadʒi] *f* unity; (*TEC, COM*) unit; **~ central de processamento** (*COMPUT*) central processing unit; **~ de disco** (*COMPUT*) disk drive

unido, -a [u'nidu, a] *adj* joined, linked; (*fig*) united

unificar [unifi'ka*] *vt* to unite; **unificar-se** *vr* to join together

uniforme [uni'fɔxmi] *adj* uniform; (*semelhante*) alike, similar; (*superfície*) even ♦ *m* uniform; **uniformizado, -a** [unifoxmi'zadu, a] *adj*

uniform, standardized; (*vestido de uniforme*) in uniform; **uniformizar** [unifoxmi'za*] *vt* to standardize

uniões [u'njõjʃ] *fpl de* **união**

unir [u'ni*] *vt* to join together; (*ligar*) to link; (*pessoas, fig*) to unite; (*misturar*) to mix together; **unir-se** *vr* to come together; (*povos etc*) to unite

uníssono [u'nisonu] *m*: **em ~** in unison

universal [univex'saw] (*pl -ais*) *adj* universal; (*mundial*) worldwide

universidade [univexsi'dadʒi] *f* university; **universitário, -a** [univexsi'tarju, a] *adj* university *atr* ♦ *m/f* (*professor*) lecturer; (*aluno*) university student

universo [uni'vɛxsu] *m* universe; (*mundo*) world

uns [ũʃ] *mpl de* **um**

untar [ũ'ta*] *vt* (*esfregar*) to rub; (*com óleo, manteiga*) to grease

urbanismo [uxba'niʒmu] *m* town planning

urbano, -a [ux'banu, a] *adj* (*da cidade*) urban; (*fig*) urbane

urgência [ux'ʒẽsja] *f* urgency; **com toda ~** as quickly as possible; **urgente** [ux'ʒẽtʃi] *adj* urgent

urina [u'rina] *f* urine; **urinar** [uri'na*] *vi* to urinate ♦ *vt* (*sangue*) to pass; (*cama*) to wet; **urinar-se** *vr* to wet o.s.; **urinol** [uri'nɔw] (*pl -óis*) *m* chamber pot

urna ['uxna] *f* urn; **~ eleitoral** ballot box

urrar [u'xa*] *vt, vi* to roar; (*de dor*) to yell

urso, -a ['uxsu, a] *m/f* bear

URSS *abr f* (= *União das Repúblicas Socialistas Soviéticas*): **a ~** the USSR

urtiga [ux'tʃiga] *f* nettle

Uruguai [uru'gwaj] *m*: **o ~** Uruguay

urze ['uxzi] *m* heather

usado, -a [u'zadu, a] *adj* used; (*comum*) common; (*roupa*) worn; (*gasto*) worn out; (*de segunda mão*) second-hand

usar [u'za*] *vt* (*servir-se de*) to use; (*vestir*) to wear; (*gastar com o uso*) to wear out; (*barba, cabelo curto*) to have, wear ♦ *vi*: **~ de** to use; **modo de ~** directions *pl*

usina [u'zina] *f* (*fábrica*) factory; (*de energia*) plant

uso ['uzu] *m* use; (*utilização*) usage; (*prática*) practice

usual [u'zwaw] (*pl* **-ais**) *adj* usual; (*comum*) common

usuário, -a [u'zwarju, a] *m/f* user

usufruir [uzu'frwi*] *vt* to enjoy ♦ *vi*: **~ de** to enjoy

úteis ['utejʃ] *pl de* **útil**

utensílio [ute'silju] *m* utensil

útero ['uteru] *m* womb, uterus

útil ['utʃiw] (*pl* **-eis**) *adj* useful; (*vantajoso*) profitable, worthwhile; **utilidade** [utʃili'dadʒi] *f* usefulness; **utilização** [utʃiliza'sãw] *f* use; **utilizar** [utʃili'za*] *vt* to use; **utilizar-se** *vr*: **utilizar-se de** to make use of

uva ['uva] *f* grape

V

v *abr* (= *volt*) v

vá *etc* [va] *vb V* **ir**

vã [vã] *f de* **vão**

vaca ['vaka] *f* cow; **carne de ~** beef

vacilar [vasi'la*] *vi* to hesitate; (*balançar*) to sway; (*cambalear*) to stagger; (*luz*) to flicker; (*col*) to slip up

vacina [va'sina] *f* vaccine; **vacinar** [vasi'na*] *vt* to vaccinate

vácuo ['vakwu] *m* vacuum; (*fig*) void; (*espaço*) space

vadiar [va'dʒja*] *vi* to lounge about; (*não trabalhar*) to idle about; (*pe-*

rambular) to wander

vadio, -a [va'dʒiu, a] *adj* (*ocioso*) idle, lazy; (*vagabundo*) vagrant ♦ *m/f* idler; vagabond, vagrant

vaga ['vaga] *f* wave; (*em hotel, trabalho*) vacancy

vagabundo, -a [vaga'bũdu, a] *adj* vagrant; (*vadio*) lazy, idle; (*de má qualidade*) shoddy ♦ *m/f* tramp

vagão [va'gãw] (*pl* **-ões**) *m* (*de passageiros*) carriage; (*de cargas*) wagon; **vagão-leito** (*pl* **vagões-leitos**) (*PT*) *m* sleeping car; **vagão-restaurante** (*pl* **vagões-restaurantes**) *m* buffet car

vagar [va'ga*] *vi* to wander about; (*barco*) to drift; (*ficar vago*) to be vacant

vagaroso, -a [vaga'rozu, ɔza] *adj* slow

vagina [va'ʒina] *f* vagina

vago, -a ['vagu, a] *adj* vague; (*desocupado*) vacant, free

vagões [va'gõjʃ] *mpl de* **vagão**

vai *etc* [vaj] *vb V* **ir**

vaia ['vaja] *f* booing; **vaiar** [va'ja*] *vt, vi* to boo, hiss

vaidade [vaj'dadʒi] *f* vanity; (*futilidade*) futility

vaidoso, -a [vaj'dozu, ɔza] *adj* vain

vaivém [vaj'vẽj] *m* to-ing and fro-ing

vala ['vala] *f* ditch

vale ['vali] *m* valley; (*escrito*) voucher; **~ postal** postal order

valente [va'lẽtʃi] *adj* brave; **valentia** [valẽ'tʃia] *f* courage, bravery; (*proeza*) feat

valer [va'le*] *vi* to be worth; (*ser válido*) to be valid; (*ter influência*) to carry weight; (*servir*) to serve; (*ser proveitoso*) to be useful; **valer-se** *vr*: **~-se de** to use, make use of; **~ a pena** to be worthwhile; **~ por** (*equivaler*) to be worth the same as;

para ~ (*muito*) very much, a lot; (*realmente*) for real, properly; **vale dizer** in other words; **mais vale ... (do que ...)** it would be better to ... (than ...)

valeta [va'leta] *f* gutter

valha *etc* ['vaʎa] *vb V* **valer**

validade [vali'dadʒi] *f* validity

validar [vali'da*] *vt* to validate; **válido, -a** ['validu, a] *adj* valid

valioso, -a [va'ljozu, ɔza] *adj* valuable

valise [va'lizi] *f* case, grip

valor [va'lo*] *m* value; (*mérito*) merit; (*coragem*) courage; (*preço*) price; (*importância*) importance; **~es** *mpl* (*morais*) values; (*num exame*) marks; (*COM*) securities; **dar ~ a** to value; **valorizar** [valori'za*] *vt* to value

valsa ['vawsa] *f* waltz

válvula ['vawvula] *f* valve

vampiro, -a [vã'piru, a] *m/f* vampire

vandalismo [vãda'liʒmu] *m* vandalism

vândalo, -a ['vãdalu, a] *m/f* vandal

vangloriar-se [vãglo'rjaxsi] *vr*: **~ de** to boast of *ou* about

vanguarda [vã'gwaxda] *f* vanguard; (*arte*) avant-garde

vantagem [vã'taʒẽ] (*pl* **-ns**) *f* advantage; (*ganho*) profit, benefit; **tirar ~ de** to take advantage of; **vantajoso, -a** [vãta'ʒozu, ɔza] *adj* advantageous; (*lucrativo*) profitable; (*proveitoso*) beneficial

vão¹, vã [vãw, vã] (*pl* **~s, ~s**) *adj* vain; (*fútil*) futile ♦ *m* (*intervalo*) space; (*de porta etc*) opening

vão² *vb V* **ir**

vapor [va'po*] *m* steam; (*navio*) steamer; (*de gas*) vapour (*BRIT*), vapor (*US*); **vaporizador** [vaporiza'do*] *m* (*de perfume*) spray

vaqueiro [va'kejru] *m* cowboy

vara ['vara] *f* stick; (*TEC*) rod; (*JUR*) jurisdiction; (*de porcos*) herd; **salto de ~** pole vault; **~ de condão** magic wand

varal [va'raw] (*pl* **-ais**) *m* clothes line

varanda [va'rãda] *f* verandah; (*balcão*) balcony

varar [va'ra*] *vt* to pierce; (*passar*) to cross

varejista [vare'ʒiʃta] (*BR*) *m/f* retailer ♦ *adj* (*mercado*) retail

varejo [va'reʒu] (*BR*) *m* (*COM*) retail trade; **a ~** retail

variação [varja'sãw] (*pl* **-ões**) *f* variation

variado, -a [va'rjadu, a] *adj* varied; (*sortido*) assorted

variar [va'rja*] *vt, vi* to vary; **variável** [va'rjavew] (*pl* **-eis**) *adj* variable; (*tempo, humor*) changeable

varicela [vari'sɛla] *f* chickenpox

variedade [varje'dadʒi] *f* variety

varinha [va'riɲa] *f* wand; **~ de condão** magic wand

vário, -a ['varju, a] *adj* (*diverso*) varied; (*pl*) various, several; (*COM*) sundry

varíola [va'riola] *f* smallpox

varizes [va'riʒiʃ] *fpl* varicose veins

varrer [va'xe*] *vt* to sweep; (*fig*) to sweep away

vascular [vaʃku'ʎa*] *vt* (*pesquisar*) to research; (*remexer*) to rummage through

vaselina [vaze'lina] ® *f* vaseline ®

vasilha [va'ziʎa] *f* (*para líquidos*) jug; (*para alimentos*) dish; (*barril*) barrel

vaso ['vazu] *m* pot; (*para flores*) vase

vassoura [va'sora] *f* broom

vasto, -a ['vaʃtu, a] *adj* vast

vatapá [vata'pa] *m* fish or chicken with coconut milk, shrimps, peanuts, palm oil and spices

Vaticano [vatʃiˈkanu] m: **o ~** the Vatican

vazamento [vazaˈmẽtu] m leak

vazão [vaˈzãw] (pl **-ões**) f flow; (venda) sale; **dar ~ a** (expressar) to give vent to; (atender) to deal with; (resolver) to attend to

vazar [vaˈza*] vt to empty; (derramar) to spill; (verter) to pour out ♦ vi to leak

vazio, -a [vaˈziu, a] adj empty; (pessoa) empty-headed, frivolous; (cidade) deserted ♦ m emptiness; (deixado por alguém/algo) void

vazões [vaˈzõjʃ] fpl de **vazão**

vê etc [ve] vb V **ver**

veado [ˈvjadua] m deer; **carne de ~** venison

vedado, -a [veˈdadu, a] adj (proibido) forbidden; (fechado) enclosed

vedar [veˈda*] vt to ban, prohibit; (buraco) to stop up; (entrada, passagem) to block; (terreno) to close off

veemente [vjeˈmẽtʃi] adj vehement

vegetação [veʒetaˈsãw] f vegetation

vegetal [veʒeˈtaw] (pl **-ais**) adj vegetable atr; (reino, vida) plant atr ♦ m vegetable

vegetalista [veʒetaˈliʃta] adj, m/f vegan

vegetariano, -a [veʒetaˈrjanu, a] adj, m/f vegetarian

veia [ˈveja] f vein

veículo [veˈikulu] m vehicle; (fig: meio) means sg

veio [ˈveju] vb V **vir** ♦ m (de rocha) vein; (na mina) seam; (de madeira) grain

vejo etc [ˈveʒu] vb V **ver**

vela [ˈvɛla] f candle; (AUTO) spark plug; (NÁUT) sail; **barco à ~** sailing boat

velar [veˈla*] vt to veil; (ocultar) to hide; (vigiar) to keep watch over; (um doente) to sit up with ♦ vi (não dormir) to stay up; (vigiar) to keep watch; **~ por** to look after

veleiro [veˈlejru] m sailing boat (BRIT), sailboat (US)

velejar [veleˈʒa*] vi to sail

velhaco, -a [veˈʎaku, a] adj crooked ♦ m/f crook

velhice [veˈʎisi] f old age

velho, -a [ˈvɛʎu, a] adj old ♦ m/f old man/woman

velocidade [velosiˈdadʒi] f speed, velocity; (PT: AUTO) gear

velório [veˈlɔrju] m wake

veloz [veˈlɔʒ] adj fast

vem [vẽj] vb V **vir**

vêm [vẽj] vb V **vir**

vencedor, a [vẽseˈdo*, a] adj winning ♦ m/f winner

vencer [vẽˈse*] vt (num jogo) to beat; (competição) to win; (inimigo) to defeat; (exceder) to surpass; (obstáculos) to overcome; (percorrer) to pass ♦ vi (num jogo) to win; **vencido, -a** [vẽˈsidu, a] adj: **dar-se por vencido** to give in; **vencimento** [vẽsiˈmẽtu] m (COM) expiry; (data) expiry date; (salário) salary; (de gêneros alimentícios etc) sell-by date; **vencimentos** mpl (ganhos) earnings

venda [ˈvẽda] f sale; (pano) blindfold; (mercearia) general store; **à ~** on sale, for sale

vendaval [vẽdaˈvaw] (pl **-ais**) m gale

vendedor, a [vẽdeˈdo*, a] m/f seller; (em loja) sales assistant; **~ ambulante** street vendor

vender [vẽˈde*] vt, vi to sell; **~ por atacado/a varejo** to sell wholesale/retail

veneno [veˈnɛnu] m poison; **vene-**

noso, -a [vene'nozu, ɔza] *adj* poisonous

venerar [vene'ra*] *vt* to revere; (REL) to worship

venéreo, -a [ve'nerju, a] *adj*: **doença venérea** venereal disease

Venezuela [vene'zwɛla] *f*: **a ~** Venezuela

venha *etc* [ˈveɲa] *vb* V **vir**

ventania [vẽtaˈnia] *f* gale

ventar [vẽ'ta*] *vi*: **está ventando** it is windy

ventilação [vẽtʃilaˈsãw] *f* ventilation

ventilador [vẽtʃilaˈdo*] *m* ventilator; (elétrico) fan

ventilar [vẽtʃi'la*] *vt* to ventilate; (roupa, sala) to air

vento [ˈvẽtu] *m* wind; (brisa) breeze; **ventoinha** [vẽ'twiɲa] *f* weathercock, weather vane; (PT: AUTO) fan

ventre [ˈvẽtri] *m* belly

ver [ve*] *vt* to see; (olhar para, examinar) to look at; (televisão) to watch ♦ *vi* to see ♦ *m*: **a meu ~** in my opinion; **vai ~ que** ... maybe ...; **não tem nada a ~ (com)** it has nothing to do (with)

veracidade [verasiˈdadʒi] *f* truthfulness

veraneio [veraˈneju] *m* summer holidays *pl* (BRIT) ou vacation (US)

verão [veˈrãw] (*pl* -ões) *m* summer

verba [ˈvɛxba] *f* allowance; **~(s)** *f(pl)* (recursos) funds *pl*

verbal [vex'baw] (*pl* -ais) *adj* verbal

verbete [vex'betʃi] *m* (num dicionário) entry

verbo [ˈvɛxbu] *m* verb

verdade [vex'dadʒi] *f* truth; **de ~** (falar) truthfully; (ameaçar etc) really; **na ~** in fact; **para falar a ~** to tell the truth; **verdadeiro, -a** [vexdaˈdejru, a] *adj* true; (genuíno) real; (pessoa) truthful

verde [ˈvexdʒi] *adj* green; (fruta) unripe ♦ *m* green; (plantas etc) greenery

verdura [vex'dura] *f* (hortaliça) greens *pl*; (BOT) greenery; (cor verde) greenness

verdureiro, -a [vexduˈrejru, a] *m/f* greengrocer (BRIT), produce dealer (US)

vereador, a [verjaˈdo*, a] *m/f* councillor (BRIT), councilor (US)

veredicto [vereˈdʒiktu] *m* verdict

verga [ˈvexga] *f* (vara) stick; (de metal) rod

vergonha [vex'goɲa] *f* shame; (timidez) embarrassment; (humilhação) humiliation; (ato indecoroso) indecency; (brio) self-respect; **ter vergonha** to be ashamed; (tímido) to be shy; **vergonhoso, -a** [vexgoˈɲozu, ɔza] *adj* shameful; (indecoroso) disgraceful

verídico, -a [veˈridʒiku, a] *adj* true, truthful

verificar [verifiˈka*] *vt* to check; (confirmar) to verify

verme [ˈvɛxmi] *m* worm

vermelho, -a [vex'meʎu, a] *adj* red ♦ *m* red

vermute [vex'mutʃi] *m* vermouth

verniz [vex'niʒ] *m* varnish; (couro) patent leather

verões [veˈrõjʃ] *mpl de* **verão**

verossímil [veroˈsimiw] (*PT* -osí-) (*pl* -eis) *adj* likely, probable; (crível) credible

verruga [ve'xuga] *f* wart

versão [vex'sãw] (*pl* -ões) *f* version; (tradução) translation

versátil [vex'satʃiw] (*pl* -eis) *adj* versatile

verso [ˈvɛxsu] *m* verse; (linha) line of poetry

versões [vex'sõjʃ] *fpl de* **versão**

verter [vex'te*] *vt* to pour; (por

acaso) to spill; (*traduzir*) to translate; (*lágrimas, sangue*) to shed ♦ *vi*: **~ de** to spring from; **~ em** (*rio*) to flow into

vertical [vextʃi'kaw] (*pl* **-ais**) *adj* vertical; (*de pé*) upright, standing ♦ *f* vertical

vertigem [vex'tʃiʒẽ] *f* (*medo de altura*) vertigo; (*tonteira*) dizziness; **vertiginoso, -a** [vextʃiʒi'nozu, ɔza] *adj* dizzy, giddy; (*velocidade*) frenetic

vesgo, -a ['veʒgu, a] *adj* cross-eyed

vesícula [ve'zikula] *f*: **~ (biliar)** gall bladder

vespa ['veʃpa] *f* wasp

véspera ['veʃpera] *f*: **a ~ de** the day before; **a ~ de Natal** Christmas Eve

vestiário [veʃ'tʃjarju] *m* (*em casa, teatro*) cloakroom; (*ESPORTE*) changing room; (*de ator*) dressing room

vestíbulo [veʃ'tʃibulu] *m* hall (way), vestibule; (*TEATRO*) foyer

vestido, -a [veʃ'tʃidu, a] *adj*: **~ de branco** *etc* dressed in white *etc* ♦ *m* dress

vestígio [veʃ'tʃiʒju] *m* (*rastro*) track; (*fig*) sign, trace

vestimenta [veʃtʃi'mẽta] *f* garment

vestir [veʃ'tʃi*] *vt* (*uma criança*) to dress; (*pôr sobre si*) to put on; (*trajar*) to wear; (*comprar, dar roupa para*) to clothe; (*fazer roupa para*) to make clothes for; **vestir-se** *vr* to get dressed

vestuário [veʃ'twarju] *m* clothing

vetar [ve'ta*] *vt* to veto

veterano, -a [vete'ranu, a] *adj, m/f* veteran

veterinário, -a [veteri'narju, a] *m/f* vet(erinary surgeon)

veto ['vɛtu] *m* veto

véu [vɛw] *m* veil

vexame [ve'ʃami] *f* shame, dis-

grace; (*tormento*) affliction; (*humilhação*) humiliation; (*afronta*) insult

vez [veʒ] *f* time; (*turno*) turn; **uma ~** once; **algumas ~es, às ~es** sometimes; **~ por outra** sometimes; **cada ~ (que)** every time; **de ~ em quando** from time to time; **em ~ de** instead of; **uma ~ que** since; **3 ~es 6** 3 times 6; **de uma ~ por todas** once and for all; **muitas ~es** many times; (*frequentemente*) often; **toda ~ que** every time; **um de cada ~** one at a time; **uma ~ ou outra** once in a while

via¹ ['via] *f* road, route; (*meio*) way; (*documento*) copy; (*conduto*) channel ♦ *prep* via, by way of; **em ~ de** about to; **por ~ terrestre/marítima** by land/sea

via² *etc vb V* ver

viaduto [vja'dutu] *m* viaduct

viagem ['vjaʒẽ] (*pl* **-ns**) *f* journey, trip; (*o viajar*) travel; (*NÁUT*) voyage; **viagens** *fpl* (*jornadas*) travels; **~ de ida e volta** return trip, round trip

viajante [vja'ʒãtʃi] *adj* travelling (*BRIT*), traveling (*US*) ♦ *m* traveller (*BRIT*), traveler (*US*)

viajar [vja'ʒa*] *vi* to travel

viável ['vjavew] (*pl* **-eis**) *adj* feasible, viable

víbora ['vibora] *f* viper

vibração [vibra'sãw] (*pl* **-ões**) *f* vibration; (*fig*) thrill

vibrante [vi'brãtʃi] *adj* vibrant; (*discurso*) stirring

vibrar [vi'bra*] *vt* to brandish; (*fazer estremecer*) to vibrate; (*cordas*) to strike ♦ *vi* to vibrate; (*som*) to echo

vice ['visi] *m/f* deputy

vice- [visi-] *prefixo* vice-; **vice-presidente, -a** *m/f* vice president; **vice-versa** [-'vɛxsa] *adv* vice-versa

viciado, -a [vi'sjadu, a] *adj* addicted; (*ar*) foul ♦ *m/f* addict; **~ em algo** addicted to sth

viciar [vi'sja*] *vt* (*falsificar*) to falsify; **viciar-se** *vr*: **~-se em algo** to become addicted to sth

vício ['visju] *m* vice; (*defeito*) failing; (*costume*) bad habit; (*em entorpecentes*) addiction

viço ['visu] *m* vigour (*BRIT*), vigor (*US*); (*da pele*) freshness

vida ['vida] *f* life; (*duração*) lifetime; (*fig*) vitality; **com ~** alive; **ganhar a ~** to earn one's living; **modo de ~** way of life; **dar a ~ por algo/por fazer algo** to give one's right arm for sth/ to do sth; **estar bem de ~** to be well off

vide ['vidʒi] *vt* see; **~ verso** see over

videira [vi'dejra] *f* grapevine

vidente [vi'dẽtʃi] *m/f* clairvoyant

vídeo ['vidʒju] *m* video; **videocassete** [vidʒjuka'setʃi] *m* video cassette *ou* tape; (*aparelho*) video (recorder); **videoteipe** [vidʒju-'tejpi] *m* video tape

vidraça [vi'drasa] *f* window pane

vidrado, -a [vi'dradu, a] *adj* glazed; (*porta*) glass *atr*; (*olhos*) glassy

vidro ['vidru] *m* glass; (*frasco*) bottle; **fibra de ~** fibreglass (*BRIT*), fiberglass (*US*); **~ de aumento** magnifying glass

vier *etc* ['vje*] *vb* V **vir**

viés [vje'ʃ] *m* slant; **ao** *ou* **de ~** diagonally

vieste V ['vjeʃtʃi] *vb* V **vir**

Vietnã [vjet'nã] *m*: **o ~** Vietnam; **vietnamita** [vjetna'mita] *adj*, *m/f* Vietnamese

viga ['viga] *f* beam; (*de ferro*) girder

viger [vi'ʒe*] *vi* to be in force

vigia [vi'ʒia] *f* watching; (*NÁUT*) watch; porthole ♦ *m* night watchman; **vigiar** [vi'ʒja*] *vt* to watch; (*ocultamente*) to spy on; (*presos, fronteira*)

guard ♦ *vi* to be on the lookout

vigilância [viʒi'lãsja] *f* vigilance; **vigilante** [viʒi'lãtʃi] *adj* vigilant; (*atento*) alert

vigor [vi'go*] *m* energy, vigour (*BRIT*), vigor (*US*); **em ~** in force; **entrar/pôr em ~** to take effect/put into effect; **vigoroso, -a** [vigo-'rozu, ɔza] *adj* vigorous

vil [viw] (*pl* **vis**) *adj* vile

vila ['vila] *f* town; (*casa*) villa

vilão, -lã [vi'lãw, 'lã] (*pl* **~s, ~s**) *m/f* villain

vilarejo [vila'reʒu] *m* village

vim [vĩ] *vb* V **vir**

vime ['vimi] *m* wicker

vinagre [vi'nagri] *m* vinegar

vinco ['vĩku] *m* crease; (*sulco*) furrow; (*no rosto*) line

vincular [vĩku'la*] *vt* to link, tie; **vínculo** ['vĩkulu] *m* bond, tie; (*relação*) link

vinda ['vĩda] *f* arrival; (*regresso*) return; **dar as boas ~s a** to welcome

vingança [vĩ'gãsa] *f* vengeance, revenge; **vingar** [vĩ'ga*] *vt* to avenge; **vingar-se** *vr*: **vingar-se de** to take revenge on; **vingativo, -a** [vĩga'tʃivu, a] *adj* vindictive

vinha¹ ['viɲa] *f* vineyard; (*planta*) vine

vinha² *etc* *vb* V **vir**

vinho ['viɲu] *m* wine; **~ branco/rosado/tinto** white/rosé/red wine; **~ seco/doce** dry/sweet wine; **~ do Porto** port

vinte ['vĩtʃi] *num* twenty

viola ['vjɔla] *f* viola

violação [vjola'sãw] (*pl* **-ões**) *f* violation; **~ de domicílio** housebreaking

violão [vjo'lãw] (*pl* **-ões**) *m* guitar

violar [vjo'la*] *vt* to violate; (*a lei*) to break

violência [vjo'lẽsja] *f* violence; **vio-**

lentar [vjolẽ'ta*] *vt* to force; (*mulher*) to rape; **violento, -a** [vjo'lẽtu, a] *adj* violent

violeta [vjo'leta] *f* violet

violino [vjo'linu] *m* violin

violões [vjo'lõjʃ] *mpl de* **violão**

violoncelo [vjolõ'sɛlu] *m* cello

vir¹ [vi*] *vi* to come; ~ **a ser** to turn out to be; **a semana que vem** next week

vir² *etc vb* V **ver**

vira-lata [vira-] (*pl* ~s) *m* (*cão*) mongrel

virar [vi'ra*] *vt* to turn; (*página, disco, barco*) to turn over; (*copo*) to empty; (*transformar em*) to become ♦ *vi* to turn; (*barco*) to capsize; (*mudar*) to change; **virar-se** *vr* to turn; (*voltar-se*) to turn round; (*defender-se*) to fend for o.s

virgem ['vixʒẽ] (*pl* -ns) *adj* virgin; **V~** (ASTROLOGIA) Virgo

vírgula ['vixgula] *f* comma; (*decimal*) point

viril [vi'riw] (*pl* -is) *adj* virile

virilha [vi'riʎa] *f* groin

viris [vi'riʃ] *adj pl de* **viril**

virtual [vix'twaw] (*pl* -ais) *adj* virtual; (*potencial*) potential

virtude [vix'tudʒi] *f* virtue; **em ~ de** owing to, because of; **virtuoso, -a** [vix'twozu, ɔza] *adj* virtuous

virulento, -a [viru'lẽtu, a] *adj* virulent

vírus ['viruʃ] *m inv* virus

vis [viʃ] *adj pl de* **vil**

visão [vi'zãw] (*pl* -ões) *f* vision; (ANAT) eyesight; (*vista*) sight; (*maneira de perceber*) view

visar [vi'za*] *vt* (*alvo*) to aim at; (*ter em vista*) to have in view; (*ter como objetivo*) to aim for

vísceras ['viseraʃ] *fpl* innards, bowels

viseira [vi'zejra] *f* visor

visita [vi'zita] *f* visit, call; (*pessoa*) visitor; **fazer uma ~ a** to visit; **visitante** [vizi'tãtʃi] *adj* visiting ♦ *m/f* visitor; **visitar** [vizi'ta*] *vt* to visit

visível [vi'zivew] (*pl* -eis) *adj* visible

vislumbrar [viʒlũ'bra*] *vt* to glimpse, catch a glimpse of; **vislumbre** [viʒ'lũbri] *m* glimpse

visões [vi'zõjʃ] *fpl de* **visão**

visor [vi'zo*] *m* (FOTO) viewfinder

visse *etc* [visi] *vb* V **ver**

vista ['viʃta] *f* sight; (MED) eyesight; (*panorama*) view; **à** ou **em ~ de** in view of; **dar na ~** to attract attention; **dar uma ~ de olhos em** to glance at; **fazer ~ grossa (a)** to turn a blind eye (to); **ter em ~** to have in mind; **à ~** visible, showing; (COM) in cash; **até a ~!** see you!

visto, -a ['viʃtu, a] *pp de* **ver** ♦ *adj* seen ♦ *m* (*em passaporte*) visa; (*em documento*) stamp; **pelo ~** by the looks of things

visto *etc vb* V **vestir**

vistoria [viʃto'ria] *f* inspection

vistoso, -a [viʃ'tozu, ɔza] *adj* eye-catching

visual [vi'zwaw] (*pl* -ais) *adj* visual; **visualizar** [vizwali'za*] *vt* to visualize

vital [vi'taw] (*pl* -ais) *adj* vital; **vitalício, -a** [vita'lisju, a] *adj* for life

vitamina [vita'mina] *f* vitamin; (*para beber*) fruit crush

vitela [vi'tɛla] *f* calf; (*carne*) veal

vítima ['vitʃima] *f* victim

vitória [vi'tɔrja] *f* victory; **vitorioso, -a** [vito'rjozu, ɔza] *adj* victorious

vitrina [vi'trina] *f* = **vitrine**

vitrine [vi'trini] *f* shop window; (*armário*) display case

viúvo, -a ['vjuvu, a] *m/f* widower/widow

viva ['viva] *m* cheer; **~!** hurray!

vivaz [vi'vajʒ] *adj* lively

viveiro [vi'vejru] *m* nursery

vivência [vi'vẽsja] *f* existence; *(experiência)* experience

vivenda [vi'vẽda] *f (casa)* residence

viver [vi've'] *vt, vi* to live ♦ *m* life; **~ de** to live on

víveres ['viverɛʃ] *mpl* provisions

vívido, -a ['vividu, a] *adj* vivid

vivo, -a ['vivu, a] *adj* living; *(esperto)* clever; *(cor)* bright; *(criança, debate)* lively ♦ *m*: **os ~s** the living

vizinhança [vizi'ñãsa] *f* neighbourhood *(BRIT)*, neighborhood *(US)*

vizinho, -a [vi'ziñu, a] *adj* neighbouring *(BRIT)*, neighboring *(US)*; *(perto)* nearby ♦ *m/f* neighbour *(BRIT)*, neighbor *(US)*

voar [vo'a'] *vi* to fly; *(explodir)* to blow up, explode

vocabulário [vokabu'larju] *m* vocabulary

vocábulo [vo'kabulu] *m* word

vocação [voka'sãw] *(pl -ões)* *f* vocation; *(inclinação)* calling

vocacional [vokasjo'naw] *(pl -ais)* *adj* vocational, *(orientação)* careers *atr*

vocal [vo'kaw] *(pl -ais)* *adj* vocal

você [vo'se(ʃ)] *pron (pl)* you

vodca ['vɔdʒka] *f* vodka

vogal [vo'gaw] *(pl -ais)* *f (LING)* vowel

vol. *abr (= volume)* vol.

volante [vo'lãtʃi] *m* steering wheel

vôlei ['volej] *m* volleyball

voleibol [volej'bow] *m* = **vôlei**

volt ['vɔwtʃi] *(pl -s)* *m* volt

volta ['vɔwta] *f* turn; *(regresso)* return; *(curva)* bend, curve; *(circuito)* lap; *(resposta)* retort; **dar uma ~ (a pé)** to go for a walk; *(de carro)* to go for a drive; **estar de ~** to be back; **na ~ do correio** by return (post); **por ~ de** about, around; **à**

ou **em ~ de** around; **na ~** *(no caminho de ~)* on the way back

voltagem [vowl'taʒẽ] *f* voltage

voltar [vow'ta'] *vt* to turn ♦ *vi* to return, go *(ou* come) back; **voltar-se** *vr* to turn round; **~ a fazer** to do again; **~ a si** to come to; **~-se para** to turn to; **~-se contra** to turn against

volume [vo'lumi] *m* volume; *(pacote)* package; **volumoso, -a** [volu'mozu, ɔza] *adj* bulky, big

voluntário, -a [volũ'tarju, a] *adj* voluntary ♦ *m/f* volunteer

volúpia [vo'lupja] *f* pleasure, ecstasy

volúvel [vo'luvew] *(pl -eis)* *adj* fickle

vomitar [vomi'ta'] *vt, vi* to vomit; **vômito** ['vomitu] *m (ato)* vomiting; *(efeito)* vomit

vontade [võ'tadʒi] *f* will; *(desejo)* wish; **com ~** *(com prazer)* with pleasure; *(com gana)* with gusto; **estar com** *ou* **ter ~ de fazer** to feel like doing

vôo ['vou] *(PT* **voo)** *m* flight; **levantar ~** to take off; **~ livre** *(ESPORTE)* hang-gliding

voraz [vo'rajʒ] *adj* voracious

vos [vuʃ] *pron* you; *(indireto)* to you

vós [vɔʃ] *pron* you

vosso, -a ['vɔsu, a] *adj* your ♦ *pron*: **(o) ~** yours

votação [vota'sãw] *(pl -ões)* *f* vote, ballot; *(ato)* voting

votar [vo'ta'] *vt (eleger)* to vote for; *(aprovar)* to pass; *(submeter a votação)* to vote on ♦ *vi* to vote; **voto** ['vɔtu] *m (em eleição)* vote; *(promessa)* vow; **votos** *mpl (desejos)* wishes

vou [vou] *vb V* **ir**

vovó [vo'vɔ] *f* grandma

vovô [vo'vo] *m* grandad

voz [vɔʒ] *f* voice; *(clamor)* cry; a

meia ~ in a whisper; **de viva** ~ orally; **ter** ~ **ativa** to have a say; **em** ~ **alta/baixa** aloud/in a low voice; ~ **de comando** command

vulcão [vuwˈkãw] (*pl* ~**s** *ou* ~**ões**) *m* volcano

vulgar [vuwˈga*] *adj* common; (*pej*: *pessoa etc*) vulgar; **vulgaridade** [vuwgariˈdadʒi] *f* commonness; vulgarity

vulgo [ˈvuwgu] *m* common people *pl* ♦ *adv* commonly known as

vulnerável [vuwneˈravew] (*pl* -**eis**) *adj* vulnerable

vulto [ˈvuwtu] *m* figure; (*volume*) mass; (*fig*) importance; (*pessoa importante*) important person

W

walkie-talkie [wɔkiˈtɔki] (*pl* ~**s**) *m* walkie-talkie

watt [ˈwɔtʃi] (*pl* ~**s**) *m* watt

X

xadrez [ʃaˈdreʒ] *m* chess; (*tabuleiro*) chessboard; (*tecido*) checked cloth

xampu [ʃãˈpu] *m* shampoo

xarope [ʃaˈrɔpi] *m* syrup; (*para a tosse*) cough syrup

xeque [ˈʃɛki] *m* (*soberano*) sheikh; **pôr em** ~ (*fig*) to call into question; **xeque-mate** (*pl* **xeques-mate**) *m* checkmate

xerife [ʃeˈrifi] *m* sheriff

xerocar [ʃeroˈka*] *vt* to photocopy, Xerox ®

xerox [ʃeˈrɔks] ® *m* (*copia*) photocopy; (*máquina*) photocopier

xícara [ˈʃikara] (*BR*) *f* cup

xingar [ʃĩˈga*] *vt* to swear at ♦ *vi* to swear

Xingu [ʃĩˈgu] *m*: **Parque Indígena do** ~ *see boxed note*

XINGU

The Xingu National Park was created in 1961 by the federal government and directed by the brothers Orlando and Cláudio Vilasboas, who were known internationally for their efforts to preserve Brazil's indigenous people. Situated in the north of the state of Mato Grosso, it aims to preserve indigenous culture. It brings together sixteen communities, a total of two thousand Indians.

Z

zagueiro [zaˈgejru] *m* (*FUTEBOL*) fullback

Zâmbia [ˈzãbja] *f* Zambia

zangado, -a [zãˈgadu, a] *adj* angry; annoyed; (*irritadiço*) bad-tempered

zangar [zãˈga*] *vt* to annoy, irritate ♦ *vi* to get angry; **zangar-se** *vr* (*aborrecer-se*) to get annoyed; ~**se com** to get cross with

zarpar [zaxˈpa*] *vi* (*navio*) to set sail; (*ir-se*) to set off; (*fugir*) to run away

zebra [ˈzebra] *f* zebra

zelador, a [zelaˈdo*, a] *m/f* caretaker

zelar [zeˈla*] *vt, vi*: ~ (**por**) to look after

zelo [ˈzelu] *m* devotion, zeal; **zeloso, -a** [zeˈlozu, ɔza] *adj* zealous; (*diligente*) hard-working

zerar [zeˈra*] *vt* (*conta, inflação*) to reduce to zero; (*déficit*) to pay off, wipe out

zero [ˈzɛru] *m* zero; (*ESPORTE*) nil; **zero-quilômetro** *adj inv* brand new

ziguezague [zigi'zagi] *m* zigzag

Zimbábue [zī'babwi] *m*: **o ~** Zimbabwe

zinco ['zīku] *m* zinc

-zinho, -a [-'ziɲu, a] *sufixo* little; **florzinha** little flower

zíper ['zipe*] *m* zip (*BRIT*), zipper (*US*)

zodíaco [zo'dʒiaku] *m* zodiac

zoeira ['zwejra] *f* din

zombar [zõ'ba*] *vi* to mock; **~ de** to make fun of; **zombaria** [zõba'ria] *f* mockery, ridicule

zona ['zɔna] *f* area; (*de cidade*) district; (*GEO*) zone; (*col: local de* meretrício) red-light district; (: *confusão*) mess; (: *tumulto*) free-for-all; **~ eleitoral** electoral district, constituency

zonzo, -a ['zõzu, a] *adj* dizzy

zôo ['zou] *m* zoo

zoológico, -a [zo'lɔʒiku, a] *adj* zoological; **jardim ~** zoo

zumbido [zũ'bidu] *m* buzz(ing); (*de tráfego*) hum

zumbir [zũ'bi*] *vi* to buzz; (*ouvido*) to ring ♦ *m* buzzing; ringing

zunzum [zũ'zũ] *m* buzz(ing)

zurrar [zu'xa*] *vi* to bray

PORTUGUESE VERB FORMS

1 Gerund. **2** Imperative. **3** Present. **4** Imperfect. **5** Preterite. **6** Future. **7** Present subjunctive. **8** Imperfect subjunctive. **9** Future subjunctive. **10** Past participle. **11** Pluperfect. **12** Personal infinitive.

etc indicates that the irregular root is used for all persons of the tense, e.g. **ouvir 7** ouça ouça, ouças, ouça, ouçamos, ouçais, ouçam.

abrir 10 aberto

acudir 2 acode **3** acudo, acodes, acode, acodem

aderir 3 adiro **7** adira

advertir 3 advirto **7** advirta *etc*

agir 3 ajo **7** aja *etc*

agradecer 3 agradeço **7** agradeça *etc*

agredir 2 agride **3** agrido, agrides, agride, agridem **7** agrida *etc*

AMAR 1 amando **2** ama, amai **3** amo, amas, ama, amamos, amais, amam **4** amava, amavas, amava, amávamos, amavéis, amavam **5** amei, amaste, amou, amamos (PT: amámos), amastes, amaram **6** amarei, amarás, amará, amaremos, amareis, amarão **7** ame, ames, ame, amemos, ameis, amem **8** amasse, amasses, amasse, amássemos, amásseis, amassem **9** amar, amares, amar, ámarmos, amardes, amarem **10** amado **11** amara, amáras, amara, amáramos, amáreis, amaram **12** amar, amares, amar, amarmos, amardes, amarem

ansiar 2 anseia **3** anseio, anseias, anseia, anseiam **7** anseie *etc*

apreçar 7 aprece *etc*

arrancar 7 arranque *etc*

arruinar 2 arruína **3** arruíno, arruínas, arruína, arruínam **7** arruíne, arruínes, arruíne, arruínem

aspergir 3 aspirjo **7** aspirja *etc*

atribuir 3 atribuo, atribuis, atribui, atribuímos, atribuís, atribuem

averiguar 7 averigúe, averigúes, averigúe, averigúem

boiar 2 bóia **3** bóio, bóias, bóia, bóiam **7** bóie, bóies, bóie, bóiem

bulir 2 bole **3** bulo, boles, bole, bolem

caber 2 caibo **3** coube *etc* **7** caiba **8** coubesse *etc* **9** couber *etc*

cair 2 cai **3** caio, cais, cai, caímos, caís, caem **4** caía *etc* **5** caí, caíste **7** caia *etc* **8** caísse *etc*

cobrir 3 cubro **7** cubra *etc* **10** coberto

colorir 3 coluro **7** colura *etc*

compelir 3 compilo **7** compila *etc*

crer 2 crê **3** creio, crês, crê, cremos, credes, crêem **5** cri, creste, creu, cremos, crestes, creram **7** creia *etc*

cuspir 2 cospe **3** cuspo, cospes, cospe, cospem

dar 2 dá **3** dou, dás, dá, damos, dais, dão **5** dei, deste, deu, demos, destes, deram **7** dê, dês,

dê, demos, deis, dêem
8 desse etc 9 der etc 11 dera etc

deduzir 2 deduz **3** deduzo,
deduzes, deduz

denegrir 2 denigre **3** denigro,
denigres, denigre, denigrem
7 denigre etc

despir 3 dispo **7** dispa etc

dizer 2 diz (dize) **3** digo, dizes,
diz, dizemos, dizeis, dizem
5 disse etc **6** direi etc **7** diga etc
8 dissesse etc **9** disser etc **10** dito

doer 2 dói dôe (BR), doo (PT),
dóis, dói

dormir 3 durmo **7** durma etc

escrever 10 escrito

ESTAR 3 está **3** estou, estás,
está, estamos, estais, estão
4 estava etc **5** estive, estiveste,
esteve, estivemos, estivestes,
estiveram **7** esteja etc **8** estivesse
etc **9** estiver etc **11** estivera etc

extorquir 3 extorco **7** extorca etc

FAZER 3 faço **5** fiz, fizeste, fez,
fizemos, fizestes, fizeram **6** farei
etc **7** faça etc **8** fizesse etc **9** fizer
etc **10** feito **11** fizera etc

ferir 3 firo **7** fira etc

fluir 3 fluo, fluis, flui, fluímos,
fluís, fluem

fugir 2 foge **3** fujo, foges, foge,
fogem **7** fuja etc

ganhar 10 ganho

gastar 10 gasto

gerir 3 giro **7** gira etc

haver 2 há **3** hei, hás, há,
havemos, haveis, hão **4** havia etc
5 houve, houveste, houve,
houvemos, houvestes,
houveram **7** haja etc **8** houvesse
etc **9** houver etc **11** houvera etc

ir 1 indo **2** vai **3** vou, vais, vai,
vamos, ides, vão **4** ia etc **5** fui,
foste, foi, fomos, fostes, foram

7 vá, vás, vá, vamos, vades, vão
8 fosse, fosses, fosse, fôssemos,
fôsseis, fossem **9** for etc **10** ido
11 fora etc

ler 2 lê **3** leio, lês, lê, lemos,
ledes, lêem **5** li, leste, leu,
lemos, lestes, leram **7** leia etc

medir 3 meço, **7** meça etc

mentir 3 minto **7** minta etc

ouvir 3 ouço **7** ouça etc

pagar 10 pago

parar 2 pára **3** paro, paras, pára

parir 3 pairo **7** paira etc

pecar 7 peque etc

pedir 3 peço **7** peça etc

perder 3 perco **7** perca etc

poder 3 posso **5** pude, pudeste,
pôde, pudemos, pudestes,
puderam **7** possa etc **8** pudesse
etc **9** puder etc **11** pudera etc

polir 3 pule **3** pulo, pules, pule,
pulem **7** pula etc

pôr 1 pondo **2** põe **3** ponho,
pões, põe, pomos, pondes,
põem **4** punha etc **5** pus,
puseste, pôs, pusemos,
pusestes, puseram **6** porei etc
7 ponha etc **8** pusesse etc
9 puser etc **10** posto
11 pusera etc

preferir 3 prefiro **7** prefire etc

pervenir 2 previne **3** previno,
prevines, previne, previnem
7 previna etc

prover 2 provê **3** provejo,
provês, provê, provemos,
provedes, provêem **5** provi,
proveste, proveu, provemos,
provestes, proveram **7** proveja
etc **8** provesse etc **9** prover etc

querer 3 quero, queres, quer
5 quis, quiseste, quis, quisemos,
quisestes, quiseram **7** queira etc
8 quisesse etc **9** quiser etc

614

11 quisera *etc*
refletir 3 reflito 7 reflita *etc*
repetir 3 repito 7 repita *etc*
requerer 3 requeiro, requeres, requer 7 requeira *etc*
reunir 2 reúne 3 reúno, reúnes, reúne, reúnem 7 reúna *etc*
rir 2 ri 3 rio, ris, ri, rimos, rides, ridem 5 ri, riste, riu, rimos, ristes, riram 7 ria *etc*
saber 3 sei, sabes, sabe, sabemos, sabeis, sabem 5 soube, soubeste, soube, soubemos, soubestes, souberam 7 saiba *etc* 8 soubesse *etc* 9 souber *etc* 11 soubera *etc*
seguir 3 sigo 7 siga *etc*
sentir 3 sinto 7 sinta *etc*
ser 2 sê 3 sou, és, é, somos, sois, são 4 era *etc* 5 fui, foste, foi, fomos, fostes, foram 7 seja *etc* 8 fosse *etc* 9 for *etc* 11 fora *etc*
servir 3 sirvo 7 sirva *etc*
subir 2 sobe 3 subo, sobes, sobe, sobem
suster 2 sustém 3 sustenho, sustens, sustém, sustendes, sustêm 5 susteve, sustiveste, susteve, sustivemos, sustivestes, sustiveram 7 sustenha *etc*
ter 2 tem 3 tenho, tens, tem, temos, tendes, têm 4 tinha *etc* 5 tive, tiveste, teve, tivemos, tivestes, tiveram 6 terei *etc* 7 tenha *etc* 8 tivesse *etc* 9 tiver *etc* 11 tivera *etc*
torcer 3 torço 7 torça *etc*
tossir 3 tusso 7 tussa *etc*
trair 2 trai 3 traio, trais, trai, traímos, trais, traem 7 traia *etc*
trazer 2 (traze) traz 3 trago, trazes, traz, 5 trouxe, trouxeste, trouxe, trouxemos, trouxestes, trouxeram 6 trarei *etc* 7 traga *etc*

8 trouxesse *etc* 9 trouxer *etc* 11 trouxera *etc*
UNIR 1 unindo 2 une, uni 3 uno, unes, une, unimos, unis, unem 4 unia, unias, uníamos, uníeis, uniam 5 uni, uniste, uniu, unimos, unistes, uniram 6 unirei, unirás, unirá, uniremos, unireis, unirão 7 una, unas, una, unamos, unais, unam 8 unisse, unisses, unisse, uníssemos, unísseis, unissem 9 unir, unires, unir, unirmos, unirdes, unirem 10 unido 11 unira, uniras, unira, uníramos, uníreis, uniram 12 unir, unires, unir, unirmos, unirdes, unirem
valer 3 valho 7 valha *etc*
ver 2 vê 3 vejo, vês, vê, vemos, vedes, vêem 4 via *etc* 5 vi, viste, viu, vimos, vistes, viram 7 veja *etc* 8 visse *etc* 9 vir *etc* 10 visto 11 vira
vir 1 vindo, 2 vem 3 venho, vens, vem, vimos, vindes, vêm 4 vinha *etc* 5 vim, vieste, veio, viemos, viestes, vieram 7 venha *etc* 8 viesse *etc* 9 vier *etc* 10 vindo 11 viera *etc*
VIVER 1 vivendo 2 vive, vivei 3 vivo, vives, vive, vivemos, viveis, vivem 4 vivia, vivias, vivia, vivíamos, vivíeis, viviam 5 vivi, viveste, viveu, vivemos, vivestes, viveram 6 viverei, viverás, viverá, viveremos, vivereis, viverão 7 viva, vivas, viva, vivamos, vivais, vivam 8 vivesse, vivesses, vivesse, vivêssemos, vivêsseis, vivessem 9 viver, viveres, viver, vivermos, viverdes, viverem 10 vivido 11 vivera, viveras, vivera, vivêramos, vivêreis, viveram 12 viver, viveres, viver, vivermos, viverdes, viverem

VERBOS IRREGULARES EM INGLÊS

present	pt	pp	present	pt	pp
arise	arose	arisen	fall	fell	fallen
awake	awoke	awoken	feed	fed	fed
be	was, were	been	feel	felt	felt
(am, is,			fight	fought	fought
are;			find	found	found
being)			fling	flung	flung
bear	bore	born(e)	fly	flew	flown
beat	beat	beaten	forbid	forbad(e)	forbidden
begin	began	begun	forecast	forecast	forecast
bend	bent	bent	forget	forgot	forgotten
bet	bet,	bet,	forgive	forgave	forgiven
	betted	betted	freeze	froze	frozen
bid (at	bid	bid	get	got	got,
auction)					(US) gotten
bind	bound	bound	give	gave	given
bite	bit	bitten	go (goes)	went	gone
bleed	bled	bled	grind	ground	ground
blow	blew	blown	grow	grew	grown
break	broke	broken	hang	hung	hung
breed	bred	bred	hang	hanged	hanged
bring	brought	brought	(execute)		
build	built	built	have	had	had
burn	burnt,	burnt,	hear	heard	heard
	burned	burned	hide	hid	hidden
burst	burst	burst	hit	hit	hit
buy	bought	bought	hold	held	held
can	could	(been able)	hurt	hurt	hurt
cast	cast	cast	keep	kept	kept
catch	caught	caught	kneel	knelt,	knelt,
choose	chose	chosen		kneeled	kneeled
cling	clung	clung	know	knew	known
come	came	come	lay	laid	laid
cost	cost	cost	lead	led	led
creep	crept	crept	lean	leant,	leant,
cut	cut	cut		leaned	leaned
deal	dealt	dealt	leap	leapt,	leapt,
dig	dug	dug		leaped	leaped
do (does)	did	done	learn	learnt,	learnt,
draw	drew	drawn		learned	learned
dream	dreamed,	dreamed,	leave	left	left
	dreamt	dreamt	lend	lent	lent
drink	drank	drunk	let	let	let
drive	drove	driven	lie (lying)	lay	lain
eat	ate	eaten			

616

present	pt	pp	present	pt	pp
light	lit, lighted	lit, lighted	sow	sowed	sown, sowed
lose	lost	lost	speak	spoke	spoken
make	made	made	speed	sped, speeded	sped, speeded
may	might	–			
mean	meant	meant	spell	spelt, spelled	spelt, spelled
meet	met	met			
mistake	mistook	mistaken	spend	spent	spent
mow	mowed	mown, mowed	spill	spilt, spilled	spilt, spilled
			spin	spun	spun
must	(had to)	(had to)	spit	spat	spat
pay	paid	paid	spoil	spoiled, spoilt	spoiled, spoilt
put	put	put			
quit	quit, quitted	quit, quitted	spread	spread	spread
			spring	sprang	sprung
read	read	read	stand	stood	stood
rid	rid	rid	steal	stole	stolen
ride	rode	ridden	stick	stuck	stuck
ring	rang	rung	sting	stung	stung
rise	rose	risen	stink	stank	stunk
run	ran	run	stride	strode	stridden
saw	sawed	sawed, sawn	strike	struck	struck
say	said	said			
see	saw	seen	swear	swore	sworn
sell	sold	sold	sweep	swept	swept
send	sent	sent	swell	swelled	swollen, swelled
set	set	set			
sew	sewed	sewn	swim	swam	swum
shake	shook	shaken	swing	swung	swung
shear	sheared	shorn, sheared	take	took	taken
			teach	taught	taught
shed	shed	shed	tear	tore	torn
shine	shone	shone	tell	told	told
shoot	shot	shot	think	thought	thought
show	showed	shown	throw	threw	thrown
shrink	shrank	shrunk	thrust	thrust	thrust
shut	shut	shut	tread	trod	trodden
sing	sang	sung	wake	woke, waked	woken, waked
sink	sank	sunk			
sit	sat	sat	wear	wore	worn
sleep	slept	slept	weave	wove	woven
slide	slid	slid	weep	wept	wept
sling	slung	slung	win	won	won
slit	slit	slit	wind	wound	wound
smell	smelt, smelled	smelt, smelled	wring	wrung	wrung
			write	wrote	written

DATAS

DATES

▶ Dias da semana

▶ Days of the week

segunda(-feira)	Monday
terça(-feira)	Tuesday
quarta(-feira)	Wednesday
quinta(-feira)	Thursday
sexta(-feira)	Friday
sábado	Saturday
domingo	Sunday

▶ Meses

▶ Months

janeiro	January
fevereiro	February
março	March
abril	April
maio	May
junho	June
julho	July
agosto	August
setembro	September
outubro	October
novembro	November
dezembro	December

Note that the days of the week and the months start with a capital letter in Portugal and a small letter in Brazil.

▶ Vocabulário útil

▶ Useful vocabulary

Que dia é hoje?	What day is it today?
Hoje é dia 28.	Today is the 28th.
Quando?	When?
hoje	today
amanhã	tomorrow
ontem	yesterday
hoje de manhã/à tarde	this morning/afternoon
em duas semanas	in two weeks *ou* a fortnight
daqui a uma semana	in a week's time
o mês passado/que vem	last/next month

▶ **Que horas são?**   ▶ **What time is it?**

É meio-dia/meia-noite.

It's midday/midnight.

É uma e quinze.
É uma e um quarto (*PT*).

It's one fifteen.

Faltam dez para as duas.
São duas menos dez (*PT*).

It's ten to two.

São três e meia.

It's half past three.

Faltam vinte para as oito.
São oito menos vinte (*PT*).

It's twenty to eight.

São nove (horas) da
manhã/da noite.

It's nine o'clock in the
morning/at night.

NÚMEROS		NUMBERS

▶ Números cardinais		▶ Cardinal numbers
um (uma)	1	one
dois (duas)	2	two
três	3	three
quatro	4	four
cinco	5	five
seis	6	six
sete	7	seven
oito	8	eight
nove	9	nine
dez	10	ten
onze	11	eleven
doze	12	twelve
treze	13	thirteen
catorze	14	fourteen
quinze	15	fifteen
dezesseis (BR), dezasseis (PT)	16	sixteen
dezessete (BR), dezassete (PT)	17	seventeen
dezoito	18	eighteen
dezenove (BR), dezanove (PT)	19	nineteen
vinte	20	twenty
vinte e um (uma)	21	twenty-one
trinta	30	thirty
quarenta	40	forty
cinqüenta (BR), cinquenta (PT)	50	fifty
sessenta	60	sixty
setenta	70	seventy
oitenta	80	eighty
noventa	90	ninety

cem	100	a hundred
cento e um (uma)	101	a hundred and one
duzentos(-as)	200	two hundred
trezentos(-as)	300	three hundred
quinhentos(-as)	500	five hundred
mil	1.000/1,000	a thousand
um milhão	1.000.000/1,000,000	a million

▶ Frações etc   ▶ Fractions etc

zero vírgula cinco	0,5/0.5	zero point five
três vírgula quatro	3,4/3.4	three point four
dez por cento	10%	ten per cent
cem por cento	100%	a hundred per cent

▶ Números ordinais   ▶ Ordinal numbers

primeiro	1º/1st	first
segundo	2º/2nd	second
terceiro	3º/3rd	third
quarto	4º/4th	fourth
quinto	5º/5th	fifth
sexto	6º/6th	sixth
sétimo	7º/7th	seventh
oitavo	8º/8th	eighth
nono	9º/9th	ninth
décimo	10º/10th	tenth
décimo primeiro	11º/11th	eleventh
vigésimo	20º/20th	twentieth
trigésimo	30º/30th	thirtieth
quadragésimo	40º/40th	fortieth
qüinquagésimo (BR), quinquagésimo (PT)	50º/50th	fiftieth
centésimo	100º/100th	hundredth
centésimo primeiro	101º/101st	hundred-and-first
milésimo	1000º/1000th	thousandth

FRASES ÚTEIS

USEFUL PHRASES

▶ **Saudações**

▶ **Greetings**

Oi! *(BR)*, Olá! *(PT)*
Hello!

Adeus!
Goodbye!

Tchau!
Bye!

Bom dia.
Good morning.

Boa tarde.
Good afternoon.

Boa noite. *(para saudar)*
Good evening.

(para despedir-se)
Good night.

Bem-vindo!
Welcome!

Como está?
How are you?

Bem, obrigado.
I'm fine, thank you.

Prazer em conhecê-lo.
Pleased to meet you.

Tudo bem?
How's life?

Até amanhã!
See you tomorrow!

Até logo!
See you later!

Boa sorte!
Good luck!

Felicidades!
Congratulations!

Divirta-se!
Have fun!

Saúde! *(brinde)*
Cheers!

Saúde! *(ao espirrar)* *(BR)*,
Bless you!

Santinho! *(PT)*

Cuide-se!
Take care!

Bom apetite!
Enjoy your meal!

Parabéns!
Happy Birthday!

Feliz Natal!
Merry Christmas!

Feliz Ano Novo!
Happy New Year!

▶ **Ao telefone**

▶ **On the telephone**

Alô? *(BR)*, Estou? *(PT)*
Hello?

Quem fala?
Who's speaking?

Aqui fala a Laura.
It's Laura speaking.

Posso falar com ...?
Could I speak to ..., please?

O meu (número de) telefone
My phone number is ...

é ...

Está ocupado.
It's engaged.

Ninguém atende.
There's no reply.

Fala português/inglês?

Não desligue, por favor.
Eu gostaria de falar com o ramal 3395.
Quer deixar recado?

Pode dizer que eu liguei?
Volto a ligar mais tarde.
Acho que você ligou para o número errado.

Do you speak Portuguese/ English?
Please hold the line.
Could you put me through to extension 3395?
Would you like to leave a message?
Could you tell him that I called?
I'll call back later.
I'm afraid you have the wrong number.

▶ Cartas

Exmo(-a). Senhor(a)
  Atenciosamente

Caro Sr. Fontes
  Atenciosamente
  Cordialmente
  Cumprimentos

Cara Carlota
  Um abraço
  Um beijo

Envio anexo ...
Obrigado(-a) pela sua carta.

▶ Letter Writing

Dear Sir/Madam
  Yours faithfully

Dear Mr. Fontes
  Yours sincerely
  Best wishes
  Kind regards

Dear Carlota
  All the best
  With love from ...

Please find enclosed ...
Thank you for your letter.

▶ Correio eletrônico

Você tem e-mail/correio eletrônico?
Qual é o seu endereço de e-mail/correio eletrônico?
Meu endereço de e-mail/ correio eletrônico é ...
emma@coolmail.com
= "emma arroba coolmail ponto com"
Mandarei os detalhes para você por e-mail/correio eletrônico.

▶ E-mail

Do you have e-mail?

What's your e-mail address?

My e-mail address is ...

emma@coolmail.com
= "emma at coolmail dot com"
I'll e-mail you the details.